# DICTIONARY

## OF

# SCIENCE

## AND

# TECHNOLOGY

# DICTIONARY

# OF

# SCIENCE

# AND

# TECHNOLOGY

Simon Collin

BLOOMSBURY

# A BLOOMSBURY REFERENCE BOOK

First edition published 2003

Bloomsbury Publishing Plc
38 Soho Square
London W1D 3HB

© Bloomsbury Publishing 2003

**British Library Cataloguing-in-Publication Data**

A catalogue record for this book is available from the British Library

ISBN 0-7475-6620-8

Text computer typeset by Bloomsbury Publishing
Printed in Italy by Legoprint

## PREFACE

This dictionary provides a wide range of vocabulary drawn from across the fields of science and technology, and also includes many general terms frequently used in scientific documents and reports.

The words are explained in language that is as simple as possible and examples are given in many cases to show how the word is used in context, making the dictionary accessible to users at all levels. In some cases, additional information about a word is added in a Note, or a wider context is offered in a Comment.

I am grateful to the following people for their valuable comments and advice on the text: Lesley Brown, Judith Cheney, Clare Conboy, Rich Cutler, Lynn Davy, Susan Jellis, Geoffrey Priddle and Charlotte Regan.

Thanks are also due to Katy McAdam, Sarah Lusznat, Daisy Jackson, Emma Djonokusumo, Joel Adams, Ruth Hillmore, Irene Lakhani and Sandra Anderson for the excellent presentation of the text.

# SUBJECT LABELS USED IN THE
## DICTIONARY OF SCIENCE AND TECHNOLOGY

| | | | |
|---|---|---|---|
| ACOUSTICS | Acoustics | INSECTS | Insects |
| AEROSP | Aerospace | LOGIC | Logic |
| AGRIC | Agriculture | MANUF | Manufacturing |
| ANAT | Anatomy | MARINE BIOL | Marine biology |
| ANTHROP | Anthropology | MATHS | Mathematics |
| ARCHAEOL | Archaeology | MEASURE | Measurements |
| ASTRON | Astronomy | MECH ENG | Mechanical engineering |
| AUTOMOT | Automotive | MED | Medicine |
| AVIAT | Aviation | MEDIA | Media |
| BIOCHEM | Biochemistry | METALL | Metallurgy |
| BIOL | Biology | METEOROL | Meteorology |
| BIOTECH | Biotechnology | MICROBIOL | Microbiology |
| BIRDS | Birds | MINERALS | Minerals |
| BOT | Botany | NAUT | Nautical |
| CHEM | Chemistry | NAVIG | Navigation |
| CHEM ELEM | Chemical elements | OCEANOG | Oceanography |
| COMPUT | Computing | ONLINE | Online |
| CONSTR | Construction | OPHTHALMOL | Ophthalmology |
| CRYSTALS | Crystals | OPTICS | Optics |
| DENT | Dentistry | PALAEONT | Palaeontology |
| EARTH SCI | Earth science | PHARM | Pharmacology |
| ECOL | Ecology | PHOTOGRAPHY | Photography |
| ELEC | Electricity | PHYS | Physics |
| ELEC ENG | Electrical engineering | PHYSIOL | Physiology |
| ELECTRONICS | Electronics | PLANTS | Plants |
| ENG | Engineering | PRINTING | Printing |
| ENVIRON | Environment | PSYCHIAT | Psychiatry |
| FISH | Fish | PSYCHOL | Psychology |
| FISHERIES | Fisheries | SCI | Science |
| FOOD | Food | SOC SCI | Social sciences |
| FOOD INDUST | Food industry | STATS | Statistics |
| FORESTRY | Forestry | TECH | Technology |
| FUNGI | Fungi | TELECOM | Telecommunications |
| GENETICS | Genetics | TEXTILES | Textiles |
| GEOG | Geography | TIME | Time |
| GEOL | Geology | TRANSP | Transport |
| HEALTH | Health | TREES | Trees |
| IMMUNOL | Immunology | VET | Veterinary medicine |
| INDUST | Industry | ZOOL | Zoology |

# A

**A¹** *symbol* **1.** MATHS the hexadecimal equivalent of the decimal number 10 **2.** MEASURE ampere

**A²** *noun* ASTRON a class of stars with a surface temperature of 7500–10 000° C, and strong spectral lines due to hydrogen. Examples include Sirius, Deneb, Vega and other bright stars. (NOTE: A stars tend to be white or bluish in colour. Apparent in the spectra of A stars are ionised metals like magnesium and calcium.)

**A:** *noun* COMPUT (*in some operating systems*) the first disk drive on the system ○ *To see what is stored on your floppy disk, use the DOS command 'DIR A'.*

**ab-** *prefix* away from

**abandon** *verb* COMPUT to clear a document, file or work from the computer's memory without saving it to disk or tape ○ *Once you have abandoned your spreadsheet, you cannot retrieve it again.*

**abate** *verb* to become less strong or intense ○ *The wind has abated.*

**abatement** *noun* a reduction in strength or intensity

**abbreviate** *verb* to shorten a word or a text

**abbreviated address** *noun* COMPUT a username that has fewer characters than the full name, making it easier to remember or type in

**abbreviation** *noun* the short form of a word

**abdomen** *noun* ANAT **1.** (*in a vertebrate*) a space in front of the body below the diaphragm and above the pelvis, containing the stomach, intestines, liver and other vital organs **2.** (*in an arthropod*) the rear section of the body

**abdominal aorta** *noun* ANAT the part of the aorta between the diaphragm and

the point where it divides into the iliac arteries

**abducent nerve** *noun* ANAT the sixth cranial nerve which controls the muscle which makes the eyeball turn

**abduct** *verb* PHYSIOL to pull away from the centre line of the body. Opposite **adduct**

**abend** *noun* COMPUT an unexpected stoppage of a program that is being run, due to a fault, error or power failure ○ *An interrupt from a faulty printer caused an abend.* Full form **abnormal end**

**aberrant** *adjective* not usual or typical

**aberration** *noun* **1.** something which is not usual or typical **2.** a distortion of a television picture caused by a corrupt signal or incorrect adjustment **3.** ASTRON the difference between the observed and the calculated position of an astronomical body, caused by the time taken for light or other radiation to travel from it to the observer **4.** OPTICS the imperfect formation of an image by a telescope or other optical instrument

COMMENT: Varieties of optical aberration include chromatic aberration, the differential focusing of light of different wavelengths, and spherical aberration, the imperfect focusing of light because of the use of a spherical rather than a parabolic lens or mirror surface.

**abiogenesis** *noun* BIOL the theory that life can arise from nonliving materials

**abiotic** *adjective* BIOL not relating to living organisms

**ablation** *noun* **1.** MED the removal of a layer of tissue by surgery **2.** COMPUT a method of writing data to an optical storage device, by which a laser burns a hole or pit representing digital bits of data into the surface of the device **3.** GEOL the removal of snow or ice from the surface of a glacier by melting or by the action of the wind

**ablation zone** *noun* GEOL a section of a glacier from which it loses snow or ice by ablation

**abnormal** *adjective* not usual or typical ○ *abnormal error* ○ *It's abnormal for two consecutive disk drives to break down.*

**abnormal end** *noun* COMPUT full form of **abend**

**abnormality** *noun* a form or action which is not usual or typical

**abnormally** *adverb* not as usual ○ *The signal is abnormally weak.* ○ *The error rate is abnormally high.*

**abnormal weather conditions** *plural noun* METEOROL unusual or unfavourable weather conditions

**abort** *verb* **1.** to end something before it is finished ○ *Weather conditions forced them to abort the test flight.* **2.** MED to end a pregnancy in order not to have a child **3.** BIOL to give birth before the usual end of a pregnancy (*technical*) Also called **miscarry 4.** COMPUT to end a process when a malfunction occurs by switching the computer off manually or by an internal feature ○ *The program was aborted by pressing the red button.*

**abortion** *noun* MED a situation where an unborn baby leaves the uterus before the end of pregnancy, especially during the first 28 weeks of pregnancy when it is not likely to survive birth (*technical*) □ **to have an abortion** to have an operation to end a pregnancy in order not to have a child

**abort sequence** *noun* COMPUT a unique sequence of bits that indicates that the transmission will be abnormally terminated. ♦ **reset**

**ABO system** *noun* MED a system of classifying blood groups

**above** *preposition, adverb* higher or more than ○ *2000 metres above sea level* ○ *The temperature was above 40° C for several weeks.* ○ *The occurrence of matching pairs was 70% or above.* ○ *All the results are above average.*

**ABR** *abbreviation* COMPUT available bit rate

**abrasion** *noun* **1.** MED a condition where the surface of the skin has been rubbed off by a rough surface and

bleeds **2.** EARTH SCI the wearing away of rock

**ABS** *noun* COMPUT a programming instruction that returns the magnitude of a number without the number's sign ○ *The command ABS(-13) will return the answer 13.* Full form **absolute function**

**abscess** *noun* MED a painful swollen area where pus forms, often accompanied by high temperature

**abscisic acid** *noun* BIOCHEM a plant hormone which is involved in seed formation and in the closure of leaf pores during drought (NOTE: It was originally thought to promote leaf fall, but its importance in this is now doubtful.)

**abscission** *noun* BOT the shedding of a leaf or fruit due to the formation of a layer of cells between the leaf or fruit and the rest of the plant (NOTE: It occurs in autumn, or at any time of the year in diseased parts of a plant.)

**absence** *noun* the fact of not being present □ **in the absence of** because something is not present ○ *in the absence of any other symptoms*

**absent** *adjective* not present ○ *Normal symptoms of malaria are absent in this form of the disease.*

**absolute** *adjective* **1.** very great ○ *absolute confidence in the results* **2.** complete or total ○ *No absolute correlation with climate change has yet been established.* ■ *noun* an unchanging principle

**absolute address** *noun* COMPUT **1.** a computer storage address that directly, without any modification, accesses a location or device ○ *Program execution is slightly faster if you code only with absolute addresses.* Compare **indexed address.** Also called **actual address, machine address 2.** a computer storage address that can only access one location

**absolute alcohol** *noun* CHEM alcohol which contains no water

**absolute assembler** *noun* COMPUT a type of assembly language program designed to produce code which uses only absolute addresses and values

**absolute code** *noun* COMPUT a binary code which directly operates the central processing unit, using only absolute addresses and values. ♦ **object code** (NOTE: This is the final form of a program after a compiler or assembler pass.)

**absolute coordinate** noun MATHS one of the coordinates that describe the distance of a point from the intersection of axes. Compare **relative coordinate**

**absolute function** noun COMPUT full form of **ABS**

**absolute humidity** noun PHYS the mass of water vapour in a given quantity of air

**absolute loader** noun COMPUT a program that loads a section of code into the main memory. Compare **bootstrap loader**

**absolute magnitude** noun ASTRON the magnitude of a star or other astronomical object, seen from a distance of 10 **parsecs**

COMMENT: The apparent magnitude of astronomical objects seen from the Earth depends upon their intrinsic brightness and also upon how far away they are, so that the Moon can outshine everything else in the night sky by being the nearest astronomical object. Comparing astronomical objects as they would appear from a uniform distance removes this effect.

**absolute pressure** noun PHYS (of a gas) a unit of force per unit of area without comparison to other pressure ○ *Aircraft show absolute pressure in inches of mercury on the inlet manifold pressure gauge.*

**absolute temperature** noun PHYS the temperature derived from the laws of thermodynamics rather than based on the properties of substances. Also called **thermodynamic temperature** (NOTE: Its unit is the kelvin.)

**absolute time** noun COMPUT the length of time that an audio disc has been playing

**absolute value** noun MATHS a size or value of a number regardless of its sign, e.g. the absolute value of −64.32 is 64.32

**absolute zero** noun PHYS the lowest temperature possible, 0 K or −273.15° C (NOTE: Absolute zero is the condition of having no thermal energy at all and is theoretically impossible, although scientists have managed to cool some materials to very near it.)

**absorb** verb 1. to take something in ○ *The atmosphere absorbs radio waves.* ○ *Warm air absorbs moisture more easily than cold air.* ○ *Our bodies absorb oxygen.* ○ *Salt absorbs moisture in the air.* 2. □ **to absorb information** to take in and understand information ○ *There wasn't enough time to absorb the details of the report before the meeting.*

**absorbent** adjective able to absorb ■ noun a substance or part of an organism such as a root tip which can take up something such as moisture or nutrients

**absorptance** noun PHYS a measure of how completely an object or substance absorbs radiant energy (NOTE: It equals the ratio of the energy absorbed to the total energy falling on the object.)

**absorption** noun 1. the act of taking something in ○ *There is absorption of energy by the tyre when the aircraft lands.* 2. PHYSIOL the taking into the body of substances such as proteins or fats which have been digested from food and enter the bloodstream from the stomach and intestines 3. CHEM the take up by one type of substance by another, e.g. of a liquid by a solid or a gas by a liquid 4. COMPUT the power loss of a signal when travelling through a medium, due to its absorptance

**absorption filter** noun PHYS a filter that blocks specific colours of light

**absorption line** noun ASTRON a dark line seen in a stellar spectrum, caused by radiation passing through a cool medium on its journey to the observer (NOTE: Absorption lines give information about cool matter such as interstellar gas clouds, planetary atmospheres and stellar atmospheres.)

**absorption plant** noun INDUST a part of a petroleum processing plant, where oil is extracted from natural gas

**absorption rate** noun PHYS the rate at which a liquid is absorbed by a solid

**absorption spectrum** noun PHYS the pattern of dark bands seen when electromagnetic radiation passes through an absorbing medium and is observed with a spectroscope (NOTE: It results from some frequencies of the radiation being absorbed more completely than others. Different substances absorb at different frequencies and hence produce characteristic absorption spectra that can be used to identify them.)

**absorptive capacity** *noun* BIOL the ability of a substance or part of an organism to take up something such as moisture or nutrients

**absorptivity** *noun* PHYS same as **absorptance**

**abstract** *noun* a short summary of a document ○ *It's quicker to search through the abstracts than the full text.*

**abstract data type** *noun* COMPUT a general data type that can store any kind of information ○ *The stack is a structure of abstract data types which can store any type of data from an integer to an address.*

**abstraction** *noun* ENVIRON the removal of water from a river or other source for industrial or agricultural use

**abundance** *noun* **1.** a large amount or number of something ○ *The area supports an abundance of wildlife.* **2.** ASTRON the relative amount of a particular type of star, galaxy, atom or other item in an overall population

COMMENT: Elemental abundances, the amounts of different atomic species in substances or objects such as meteorites or Moon rock, yield information about the early history of the solar system. The abundances of different types and ages of stars in the galaxy tell us about the evolution of both stars and galaxies. Stellar abundances are the proportions of different atoms in different types of star, and provide information about their ages and development. In the Sun, every million hydrogen atoms is accompanied by 63,000 atoms of helium, the next most abundant type.

**abundant** *adjective* occurring or available in large quantities ○ *a region of abundant rainfall* ○ *The ocean has an abundant supply of krill.*

**abyss** *noun* EARTH SCI a very deep part of the sea

**abyssal** *adjective* EARTH SCI referring to the deepest part of the sea

**abyssal plain** *noun* EARTH SCI a flat part of the seabed at the deepest level, approximately 4000 m below sea level

**abyssal zone** *noun* EARTH SCI a deep and dark part of the sea below the euphotic zone, at its deepest about 4000 m deep, where light cannot reach and plant and animal life is rare (NOTE: The deepest part of the sea is the **hadal** zone)

**abyssobenthic** *adjective* MARINE BIOL referring to an organism living on the floor of the deepest part of a sea or lake

**abyssopelagic** *adjective* MARINE BIOL referring to an organism living in the deepest part of a sea or lake, at depths greater than 3000 m

**Ac** *symbol* CHEM ELEM actinium

**AC¹** *noun* ELEC electric current whose value varies with time in a regular, sinusoidal way, changing the direction of flow each half cycle. Full form **alternating current**

**AC²** *abbreviation* METEOROL altocumulus

**acaricide** *noun* BIOL a poison used to kill mites and ticks

**acarid** *noun* BIOL a mite or tick, a small insect which feeds on plants or animals by piercing the outer skin and sucking juices

**Acarida** *noun* ZOOL the order of animals including mites and ticks

**Acarina** *noun* ZOOL same as **Acarida**

**ACC** *noun* COMPUT the most important internal CPU storage register, containing the result of an operation or the data word which is to be processed. Full form **accumulator**

**accelerate** *verb* to increase in speed ○ *After start-up, the engine accelerates up to idling speed.* ○ *The aircraft accelerated down the runway and took off.* Opposite **decelerate**

**accelerated graphics port** *noun* COMPUT an interface in a computer between a graphics controller and the motherboard that transfers data very quickly, providing high-performance three-dimensional graphics and video processing capabilities. Abbreviation **AGP** (NOTE: This port does not replace a PCI bus but works with it.)

**acceleration** *noun* **1.** the act of accelerating ○ *Acceleration can be felt as the aircraft begins its take-off run.* □ **acceleration due to gravity** acceleration of an object due to the gravitational attraction of the Earth, with a standard value of 9.80665 ms⁻². Symbol **g** **2.** PHYS the rate of change of velocity. Opposite **deceleration 3.** an outward force caused by change in direction without changing speed ○ *Acceleration forces can be felt during aerobatic manoeuvres.*

COMMENT: The SI units of acceleration are ms$^{-2}$ metres per second per second. The formula to calculate acceleration is a = (v – u)/t where a = acceleration, v = final velocity, u = starting velocity and t = time taken.

**acceleration time** *noun* COMPUT **1.** the time taken for a disk drive to spin a disk at the correct speed, from rest ○ *Allow for acceleration time in the access time.* **2.** the total time between an access instruction being issued to a peripheral and the data being transferred

**accelerator** *noun* **1.** ENG a machine which changes the velocity of an object and so increases its kinetic energy **2.** CHEM a substance which changes the speed at which a chemical reaction takes place

**accelerator board**, **accelerator card** *noun* COMPUT a circuit board which carries a faster or more advanced version of the same processor that runs a computer, enabling the computer to run faster

**accelerator key** *noun* COMPUT a combination of keys which, when pressed together, carry out a function that would otherwise have to be selected from a menu using a mouse. For example, instead of selecting the File menu then the Save option, using the accelerator keys Alt and S does the same thing.

**accentuate** *verb* to make something stronger ○ *Moving accentuated the pain.*

**accept** *verb* **1.** to take or receive something which is offered **2.** to be able to take or receive something ○ *Some units accept electrical inputs from the autopilot.* **3.** □ **to accept responsibility** to be willing to be answerable for something ○ *The department accepted responsibility for the incident.* **4.** COMPUT to establish a session or connection with another device

**acceptable** *adjective* allowable or approved of, although it may not be perfect ○ *The error rate was very low and is acceptable.* ○ *There must be a continuous flow of clean oil at an acceptable temperature.* □ **acceptable limits** generally agreed standards or restrictions within a range of maximum and minimum figures

**acceptable daily intake** *noun* BIOL the quantity of a substance such as a nutrient, vitamin, additive or pollutant which a person or animal can safely consume in a lifetime. Abbreviation **ADI**

**acceptable use policy** *noun* COMPUT a set of rules which describe what a user can write or do on the Internet without offending other users. Abbreviation **AUP**

**acceptance** *noun* **1.** a willingness to believe something ○ *There is a growing acceptance that safety is the main priority.* **2.** a willingness to do or use something ○ *acceptance of new technology* **3.** the action of accepting something

**acceptance angle** *noun* OPTICS the angle of total field of view of a lens or fibre optic

**acceptance sampling** *noun* INDUST the testing of a small random part of a batch to see if the whole batch is up to standard

**access** COMPUT *noun* the right or opportunity to use a computer and read or alter files stored in it (NOTE: This is usually controlled by a security device such as a password.) □ **to bar someone access to a system** to prevent a person from using a system ○ *Temporary staff are barred access to the system.* □ **to have access to something** to be able to get, examine or reach something ○ *to have access to a file of data* ■ *verb* to call up data which is stored in a computer ○ *She accessed the employee's file to check the date of birth.*

**access arm** *noun* COMPUT a mechanical device in a disk drive, used to position the read/write head over the correct track on a disk ○ *The access arm moves to the parking region during transport.*

**access barred** *adjective* COMPUT unable to be accessed without special permission

**access code** *noun* COMPUT a series of characters or symbols which must be entered to identify a user before access to a computer is permitted. ♦ **password**

**access control** *noun* COMPUT a security device such as a password which only allows selected users to use a computer system or read files

**access control list** *noun* COMPUT a security system which has usernames and passwords checked by the operating system to find out if a specific user is allowed access to a resource or feature of a network or shared computer. Abbreviation **ACL**

**access head** *noun* COMPUT a part of a disk drive which moves to the correct part of the disk's surface and reads information stored on the disk

**accessibility** *noun* the ease with which something can be reached or found ○ *Accessibility of components and equipment during servicing enables work to be done more quickly.*

**accessible** *adjective* easy to reach or find ○ *Instruments which need resetting in flight must be accessible to the crew.* ○ *Details of customers are easily accessible from the main computer files.*

**accession number** *noun* COMPUT a number in a record that shows in which order each record was entered

**access level** *noun* COMPUT a predefined access category for users of a computer or system. The lowest access level might allow the user to only view data, while the highest access level allows a user to do anything.

**access line** *noun* COMPUT a permanently connected communications line between a terminal and a computer

**access log** *noun* COMPUT a file on a website server computer that contains a record of every visitor to the website, showing when a person visited and which pages were viewed ○ *The access log is invaluable – we produce graphs of the pages that are most popular using an access log analyser program.* ○ *He analysed the access log to see if their competitor had visited their website.*

**access method** *noun* COMPUT 1. the means used for the internal transfer of data between a computer's memory and display or peripheral devices (NOTE: Differences in the methods used are often the cause of compatibility problems.) 2. a set of rules that allows a device to send data onto a network (NOTE: Token passing and CSMA/CD are two methods commonly used in a local area network.)

**access name** *noun* COMPUT a unique name that identifies an object in a database

**accessor** *noun* COMPUT a person who accesses data

**accessory** *noun* a system or piece of equipment of secondary importance ○ *a camera with several accessories* ○ *The special offer includes a range of accessories including a mouse and modem.* ■

*adjective* of secondary importance ○ *There are many accessory systems which need engine power to operate them, e.g. pumps, generators and magnetos.*

**accessory nerve** *noun* ANAT the eleventh cranial nerve, which supplies the muscles in the neck and shoulders

**access path** *noun* COMPUT a description of the location of a stored file within a directory structure of a disk

**access period** *noun* COMPUT a period of time during which a user can access data

**access permission** *noun* COMPUT a description of all the access rights for a particular user

**access point** *noun* COMPUT a test point on a circuit board or in software, allowing an engineer to check signals or data

**access provider** *noun* COMPUT ◊ Internet service provider

**access rights** *plural noun* COMPUT permission for a specific user to access a particular file or data object

**access time** *noun* COMPUT 1. the total time which a storage device takes between the data being requested and returned ○ *The access time of this dynamic RAM chip is around 200 nS – we have faster versions if your system clock is running faster.* 2. the length of time required to find a file or program, either in the main memory or a secondary memory source 3. the time taken to find and retrieve a particular piece of data from memory or a hard disk

**accident** *noun* an unfortunate or harmful event ○ *Accidents must be reported.* ○ *The lab assistant was injured in the accident.* □ **by accident** without being planned

**accidental** *adjective* 1. not deliberate or intentional ○ *Always keep backup copies in case of accidental damage to the master file.* 2. referring to an accident ○ *We were told of his accidental death.*

**accident prevention** *noun* the establishing of procedures to stop accidents happening

**acclimatisation**, **acclimatization**, **acclimation** *noun* BIOL the process of adapting to a different environment (NOTE: This process is known as **acclimatisation** if the changes occur naturally and **acclimation** if they are produced in laboratory conditions.)

**acclimatise, acclimatize** *verb* BIOL **1.** to make an organism become used to a different environment, usually a change in climate **2.** to become used to a different sort of environment

COMMENT: When an organism such as a plant or animal is acclimatising, it is adapting physically to different environmental conditions, such as changes in food supply, temperature or altitude.

**accommodation** *noun* PHYSIOL the ability of the lens of the eye to focus on objects at different distances, using the ciliary muscle

**accommodation reflex** *noun* PHYSIOL a reaction of the pupil when the eye focuses on an object which is close

**accomplishment** *noun* PHYS work done ○ *Power is measured by units of accomplishment correlated with time.*

**accordance** *noun* □ **in accordance with** following something such as rules, instructions or laws ○ *Fuels must be used in accordance with instructions.*

**accordingly** *adverb* as needed ○ *Check for increasing manifold pressure and reduce power accordingly.*

**according to** *preposition* **1.** in relation to ○ *The force exerted will vary according to a number of factors.* **2.** as written or said by somebody else ○ *According to the co-pilot, engine vibration was detected in engine number one.* □ **according to instructions** exactly as said in the instructions □ **according to requirements** as required

**account** *noun* **1.** a spoken or written report about something ○ *We gave a brief account of our experimental procedures.* **2.** COMPUT a record of a user's name, password and rights to access a network or online system ○ *If you are a new user, you will have to ask the supervisor to create an account for you.* □ **to take something into account** to consider something carefully ○ *When planning a flight, wind speed and direction must be taken into account.*

**account for** *verb* **1.** to constitute something ○ *Kevlar and carbon fibre account for a large percentage of the materials used in modern aircraft.* **2.** to provide the main reason for something ○ *High humidity accounted for the difference between the two results.* **3.** COMPUT to keep track of how much time

and resources each user of a network or online system uses

**account name** *noun* COMPUT the unique name of a user on a network or online system ○ *John Smith's account name is JSMITH.*

**accrete** *verb* to increase in amount by slow external addition ○ *Ice accretes on the rotor.*

**accretion** *noun* **1.** the growth of inorganic objects by the attachment of material to their surface **2.** BIOL the growth of a substance around an object ○ *an accretion of calcium round the joint* **3.** EARTH SCI an accumulation of sediments **4.** ASTRON the accumulation of a number of objects to form a single larger one (NOTE: It is thought that the planets, including the Earth, were built up by the accretion of **planetesimals** which formed a cloud around the Sun almost five billion years ago.)

**accumulate** *verb* **1.** to collect and increase ○ *Cold air flows downwards and accumulates over low ground.* ○ *Large quantities of fat accumulated in the arteries.* ○ *Sediment and debris accumulate at the bottom of a lake.* **2.** to gather several things together over a period of time ○ *We have gradually accumulated a large databank of names and addresses.*

**accumulated temperature** *noun* AGRIC the number of hours during which the temperature is above a particular point, taken as the minimum temperature necessary for growing a specific crop (NOTE: In the UK, this is usually taken to be the number of hours above 6° C.)

**accumulation** *noun* the act of becoming greater in size or quantity over a period of time ○ *the risk of accumulation of toxins in the food chain*

**accumulation zone** *noun* GEOL a section of a glacier's movement downstream during which it increases in mass

**accumulative** *adjective* produced by accumulation ○ *The accumulative effect of these toxins is considerable.*

**accumulator** *noun* **1.** INDUST a device for storing energy ○ *An accumulator is fitted to store hydraulic fluid.* ○ *This rechargeable electric cell is an accumulator.* **2.** COMPUT the most important internal storage register in a CPU, containing the result of an operation or the data word which is to be processed

○ *Store the two bytes of data in registers A and B and execute the add instruction – the answer will be in the accumulator.* Abbreviation **ACC**

**accumulator register** *noun* COMPUT same as **accumulator**

**accuracy** *noun* **1.** the state of being correct □ **to check for accuracy** to make certain that information or results are correct **2.** precision ○ *The accuracy of modern navigational equipment is much greater than older systems.* **3.** COMPUT the total number of bits used to define a number in a computer (NOTE: The more bits that are allocated the more accurate the definition of the number is.)

**accurate** *adjective* **1.** correct ○ *Skill in accurate flying can only be achieved by practice.* ○ *The printed bar code has to be accurate to within a thousandth of a micron.* ○ *The results of the lab tests should help the consultant make an accurate diagnosis.* **2.** precise ○ *This watch is very accurate.*

**accurately** *adverb* with no errors ○ *The OCR had difficulty in reading the new font accurately.* ○ *The mistake occurred because the data had not been accurately keyed.*

**acellular** *adjective* referring to an organism that is not made up of separate cells

**acentric** *adjective* GENETICS referring to a chromosome that lacks the structure at which the two arms of a chromosome join (**centromere**)

**Acer** *noun* TREES the genus of trees including maples and sycamores

**acetaldehyde** *noun* CHEM a colourless volatile liquid with an unpleasant smell. Formula: $CH_3CHO$.

**acetamide** *noun* CHEM a white crystalline solid with moisture-absorbing properties, used in the manufacture of organic chemicals. Formula: $CH_3CONH_2$.

**acetate** *noun* CHEM a salt or ester of acetic acid

**acetic** *adjective* CHEM containing a product of vinegar or acetic acid

**acetic acid** *noun* CHEM a colourless hygroscopic acid with a sharp smell that is the main component of vinegar. Formula: $CH_3COOH$.

**acetone** *noun* CHEM a colourless liquid that has a sweetish smell and is flammable, used as a solvent and in the manufacture of organic chemicals. It is formed in the body after vomiting or as a result of diabetes. Formula: $CH_3COCH_3$.

**acetylcholine** *noun* BIOCHEM a substance that is released from the ends of some nerve fibres to transmit impulses to other nerve cells or to muscles. Formula: $C_7H_{17}NO_3$.

**acetyle chloride** *noun* CHEM a colourless liquid with a strong unpleasant smell, used to introduce the organic group $CH_3$- into compounds

**acetylene** *noun* CHEM a colourless hydrocarbon gas that is highly flammable, used in welding and the manufacture of organic chemicals. Formula: $C_2H_2$.

**acetylide** *noun* CHEM a potentially explosive compound of acetylene containing a metal ion

**acetylsalicylic acid** *noun* PHARM the chemical name for the drug aspirin

**achene** *noun* BOT a dry single-seeded fruit that does not split open (NOTE: Achenes are produced by plants such as dandelions and sunflowers.)

**achieve** *verb* to succeed in doing or having something ○ *In order to achieve an acceptable result the experiment must be replicated.*

**achievement** *noun* the successful completion of something demanding ○ *For trainee pilots, the first solo flight is a great achievement.*

**achromatic** *adjective* OPTICS referring to an optical device that has been corrected for chromatic aberration

**achromatic colour** *noun* OPTICS colour within the range between black and white displayed by a graphics adapter, or a shade of grey

**achromatic lens** *noun* OPTICS a lens in which two or more lenses with different properties are combined to prevent distortion

**ACIA** *noun* COMPUT a circuit that allows a computer to transmit and receive serial data using asynchronous access. Full form **asynchronous communications interface adapter**

**acid** *noun* CHEM **1.** a chemical compound containing hydrogen which dissolves in water and forms hydrogen, or reacts with an alkali to form a salt and water, and turns litmus paper red **2.** any bitter juice

**acid deposition** *noun* ENVIRON same as **acid rain**

**acidic** *adjective* CHEM referring to acids ○ *has acidic properties*

**acidic rock** *noun* EARTH SCI a rock which contain a high proportion of silica

**acidic solution** *noun* CHEM a solution with a pH of less than 7 (NOTE: It is usually a solution which has water as the solvent.)

**acidic water** *noun* CHEM water which contains acid

**acidification** *noun* CHEM the process of becoming acid or of making a substance more acid ○ *Acidification of the soil leads to the destruction of some living organisms.*

**acidify** *verb* CHEM to make a substance more acid, or to become more acid ○ *Fallout acidifies lakes.* ○ *Fallout causes lakes to acidify.*

**acidity** *noun* **1.** CHEM the proportion of acid in a substance ○ *The alkaline solution may help to reduce acidity.* **2.** MED a form of indigestion where the patient has a burning feeling in the stomach caused by too much acid forming there

COMMENT: Acidity and alkalinity are measured according to the pH scale. pH7 is neutral; numbers above pH7 show alkalinity, while pH6 and below are acid.

**acid-neutralising capacity** *noun* CHEM the ability of water to neutralise acids. Abbreviation **ANC** (NOTE: It is shown by the amount of bicarbonate it contains.)

**acidosis** *noun* MED an unusually high proportion of acid waste products such as urea in the blood, sometimes caused by a metabolic dysfunction

**acid precipitation** *noun* ENVIRON same as **acid rain**

**acid-proof** *adjective* CHEM able to resist the harmful effects of an acid

**acid rain** *noun* ENVIRON precipitation such as rain or snow which contains a higher level of acid than normal

COMMENT: Acid rain is mainly caused by sulphur dioxide, nitrogen oxide and other pollutants being released into the atmosphere when fossil fuels such as oil or coal containing sulphur are burnt. Carbon combines with sulphur trioxide from sulphur-rich fuel to form particles of an acid substance. The effects of acid rain are primarily felt by wildlife. The water in lakes becomes very clear as fish and microscopic animal life are killed. It is believed that it is acid rain that kills trees, especially conifers, making them gradually lose their leaves and die. Acid rain can damage surfaces such as stone buildings when it falls on them.

**acid soot** *noun* ENVIRON acid carbon particles which fall from smoke from chimneys

**ACK** *noun* COMPUT a signal that is sent from a receiver to indicate that a transmitted message has been received and that it is ready for the next one ○ *The printer generates an ACK signal when it has received data.* Full form **acknowledge**

**Ackerman's function** *noun* COMPUT a recursive function used to test the ability of a compiler to cope with recursion

**acknowledge** COMPUT *noun* a signal that is sent from a receiver to indicate that a transmitted message has been received and that it is ready for the next one ■ *verb* **1.** to tell the person who sent something that it has been received **2.** to send a signal from a receiver to show that a transmitted message has been received

**acknowledge character** *noun* COMPUT a special code sent by a receiver to indicate to the transmitter that a message has been correctly received

**ACL** *abbreviation* COMPUT access control list

**acorn** *noun* BOT the fruit of an oak tree

**acoustic** *adjective* referring to sound

**acoustic feedback** *adjective* ACOUSTICS ◊ **feedback**

**acoustician** *noun* ACOUSTICS a person who specialises in the study of sound

**acoustic nerve** *noun* ANAT the eighth cranial nerve, which governs hearing and balance

**acoustics** *noun* ACOUSTICS the study of sound, especially noise levels in buildings

**ACPI** *noun* COMPUT a part of the Microsoft Windows 98 software system that allows the operating system to automatically configure compatible hardware. Full form **advanced configuration and power interface**

**acqua regia** *noun* CHEM a solution that can dissolve metals, made up of one part nitric acid and three parts hydrochloric acid

**acquired** *adjective* **1.** BIOL not inherited but developed in response to the environment **2.** COMPUT accepting, capturing or collecting information

**acquired character** *noun* BIOL a character which develops in response to the environment

**acquired immunity** *noun* MED immunity which is not inherited but has developed in response to infection or inoculation

**ACR** *abbreviation* audio cassette recorder

**acre** *noun* AGRIC, MEASURE a unit of measurement of land area, equal to 4840 square yards or 0.4047 hectares

**acreage** *noun* AGRIC the area of a piece of land measured in acres

**acrid** *adjective* having a strong bitter smell or taste

**acro-** *prefix* referring to a point or tip

**acrocentric** *adjective* GENETICS referring to a chromosome that has arms of unequal length, because the structure at which the two arms join (**centromere**) is located near one end

**acrolein** *noun* CHEM a poisonous strong-smelling liquid used in the production of resins and medicines

**acronym** *noun* a word which is made up of the initial letters of several words and is pronounced as a word ○ *NASA is the acronym for National Aeronautics and Space Administration.*

**acrosome** *noun* BIOL a sac or cap at the front of a sperm cell that releases enzymes to digest the egg coats enabling the sperm to penetrate the egg

**acrylic acid** *noun* CHEM a colourless acid with corrosive properties, used in the manufacture of acrylate resin. Formula: $CH_2CHCO_2H$.

**acrylic fibre** *noun* CHEM a synthetic textile fibre made from acrylonitrile

**acrylonitrile** *noun* CHEM a colourless toxic liquid which is moderately volatile, used in the manufacture of acrylic fibre, resin, rubber and thermoplastics. Formula: $CH_2CHCN$.

**ACS** *noun* COMPUT a server that sends data in one direction, one character at a time. Full form **asynchronous communication server**

**act** *verb* **1.** to behave in a particular way ○ *The crew must act with authority.* **2.** to take on a role ○ *Mountain ranges act as a barrier.* ○ *The governor spill valve also acts as a safety relief valve.* **3.** to produce an effect ○ *Gravity acts vertically downwards.*

**ACTH** *noun* BIOCHEM a hormone which stimulates the adrenal glands to produce steroid hormones. Full form **adrenocorticotrophic hormone**

**actin** *noun* BIOCHEM a protein which, with myosin, forms the contractile tissue of muscle

**actinic radiation** *noun* PHYS a type of radiation which can cause a chemical reaction

**actinide** *noun* CHEM ELEM one of the radioactive elements which are in the same category as uranium in the periodic table and have atomic numbers from 89 to 104

COMMENT: Actinides are waste products from nuclear fission. They pose problems for disposal as some of them have very long half-lives. They can be reduced to more disposable forms by burning in fast reactors.

**actinium** *noun* CHEM ELEM a natural radioactive element, produced by the decay of uranium-235 (NOTE: The chemical symbol is **Ac**; the atomic number is **89** and the atomic weight is **226**.)

**actinomycete** *noun* MICROBIOL a bacterium shaped like a rod or filament. Order: Actinomycetales. (NOTE: Some actinomycetes cause diseases while some are sources of antibiotics .)

**action** *noun* **1.** something done or to be done ○ *Appropriate action should be taken to avoid contamination.* **2.** the effect that something has ○ *worn away by the action of rain* ○ *the action of the drug on the nervous system* **3.** COMPUT something that happens when the user does something, e.g. presses a special key that moves the cursor to the action bar at the top of the screen

**action bar** *noun* COMPUT the top line of the screen that displays the menu names

**action code** *noun* COMPUT a single letter associated with a specific menu option to speed up selection so that when the letter is pressed the menu option is selected

**action-object** *noun* COMPUT an object to which a user specifies that an action should be applied

**action potential** *noun* PHYSIOL a transitory alteration in electrical potential occurring between the inside and the outside of a nerve or muscle fibre, caused by transmission of a nerve impulse

**activate** *verb* **1.** to start a process or to make something start working ○ *Pressing CR activates the printer.* **2.** COMPUT (*in an authoring tool or programming language*) to make a button or menu option or field on a screen layout available to a user ○ *If the button or field is not activated, it is normally displayed greyed out and does not respond if a user selects it.*

**activated carbon, activated charcoal** *noun* CHEM a form of carbon to which gases can stick, used in filters or added to water as it is being treated before domestic consumption

**activated sludge** *noun* ENVIRON solid sewage containing active microorganisms and air, mixed with untreated sewage to speed up the purification process

**activation** *noun* the act of making something start to work

**activation energy** *noun* CHEM the amount of energy required to start a chemical reaction by breaking a chemical bond

**activator** *noun* CHEM a substance which activates a process ○ *a compost activator*

**active** *adjective* **1.** doing something, usually energetically, or being alert ○ *Kiwis are only active after dark.* ○ *Mental exercises keep the mind active and alert.* **2.** in action or in use □ **the system is active** the system is on and working **3.** not passive □ **in a secondary radar system, the target is active** in a secondary radar system the target transmits a signal **4.** COMPUT busy, working or being used **5.** MED (*of disease*) not dormant ○ *after two years of active rheumatoid disease*

**active application** *noun* COMPUT an application currently being used by a user

**active Cb cloud** *noun* METEOROL a cumulonimbus cloud that is developing

**active file** *noun* COMPUT a computer file which is being worked on

**active galactic nucleus** *noun* ASTRON a zone in the central region of some galaxies where a mass of up to 100 million times that of the Sun is concentrated, emitting large and variable amounts of radiation. Abbreviation **AGN**

**active high** *noun* ELECTRONICS an electronic signal which is valid when it is high or logical one

**active ingredient** *noun* BIOL the main medicinal ingredient of an ointment or lotion as opposed to the base. Abbreviation **AI**

**active line** *noun* COMPUT a line in a communications link or port which is being used to transfer data or carry control signals

**active link** *noun* COMPUT the link currently being used to transfer information

**active low** *noun* ELECTRONICS an electronic signal which is valid when it is low or logical zero

**active margin** *noun* EARTH SCI an area at the edge of a continental mass where volcanic activity is frequent

**active mass** *noun* CHEM a concentration of a substance which is part of a chemical reaction

**active matrix display** *noun* COMPUT a type of colour display used in laptop computers (NOTE: normally called TFT display)

**active organic matter** *noun* BIOCHEM organic matter in the process of being broken down by bacteria. Abbreviation **AOM**

**active principle** *noun* PHARM the main medicinal ingredient of a drug which makes it have the required effect on a patient

**Active Server Page** *noun* COMPUT a webpage that is created only when accessed by a visitor, allowing the website to display up-to-date information or information from a database ○ *The database search results page is implemented as an Active Server Page.* Abbreviation **ASP**

**active site** *noun* BIOCHEM the region of an enzyme molecule where a substance (**substrate**) is bound and acted upon by the enzyme

**active star** *noun* COMPUT a network consisting of a central point with nodes branching out, in which one central computer controls and routes all messages between devices

**active storage** *noun* COMPUT a fast-access RAM whose locations can be directly and immediately addressed by the central processing unit, used as main storage

**Active Streaming Format** *noun* COMPUT a multimedia delivery format developed by Microsoft for delivery over the Internet and used in its NetShow product. Abbreviation **ASF**

**active transport** *noun* BIOCHEM a transfer of substances across a cell membrane for which energy is required

**active video signal** *noun* COMPUT the part of a video signal which contains the picture information

**active volcano** *noun* EARTH SCI a volcano which is erupting, or likely to erupt

**active window** *noun* COMPUT **1.** an area of display screen in which a user is currently working. ♦ **window 2.** the window that is currently the focus of cursor movements and screen displays

**ActiveX** *noun* COMPUT a programming language and program definition used to create small applications designed to enhance the functionality of a webpage

COMMENT: ActiveX applications, called applets, are often used to add database or multimedia effects to a website that cannot be supported with basic HTML commands. When a user visits the webpage that uses the ActiveX applet, the program is automatically downloaded by the user's browser and run on the user's computer.

**activity** *noun* **1.** the actions that living beings undertake ○ *research activities* ○ *The hillside showed signs of human activity.* **2.** the effect that something has **3.** an action or movement ○ *volcanic activity* **4.** COMPUT being active or busy

**activity loading** *noun* COMPUT a method of organising disk contents so that the most frequently accessed files or programs can be loaded quickly

**activity ratio** *noun* COMPUT the number of files currently in use compared to the total number stored

**act on, act upon** *verb* **1.** (*of force*) to produce an effect on something ○ *Bending and twisting forces act on a propeller.* ○ *The antibiotic acted quickly on the infection.* **2. act upon** to do something as the result of something which has been said ○ *He acted upon your suggestion.*

**actual** *adjective* real rather than expected or guessed ○ *What are the actual figures for the number of students this year?*

**actual address** *noun* COMPUT same as **absolute address**

**actual code** *noun* COMPUT a binary code which directly operates the central processing unit, using only absolute addresses and values (NOTE: This is the final form of a program after a compiler or assembler pass.)

**actual instruction** *noun* COMPUT the instruction executed as a result of the modification of an original instruction

**actually** *adverb* in fact ○ *The design is such that, although the aircraft loses altitude rapidly, it does not actually stall.*

**actuate** *verb* **1.** to switch on or put into operation a system or a piece of equipment ○ *A lever actuates the fire deluge system.* ○ *The fore and aft movement of the control column actuates the elevators.* **2.** to put a procedure into action ○ *Receipt of the distress signal will actuate the emergency procedures.*

**actuation** *noun* the act of causing a device or part to move

**actuator** *noun* **1.** ENG a device which changes electrical or hydraulic energy into mechanical motion (NOTE: The actuator is sensitive to engine rpm. Actuators are classified as either linear or rotary.) **2.** COMPUT a mechanical device which can be controlled by an external signal, e.g. the read/write head in a disk drive

**ACU** *noun* COMPUT a device which allows a computer to call stations or dial telephone numbers automatically. Full form **automatic calling unit**

**acuity** *noun* **1.** PHYSIOL the ability of the eye to define shades and shapes of an object **2.** BIOL the ability of the ear to detect frequency or volume changes

**acute** *adjective* BIOL **1.** referring to a disease which comes on rapidly and can be dangerous ○ *She had an acute attack of shingles.* **2.** referring to a pain which is sharp and intense ○ *acute chest pains* ▶ compare **chronic**

**acute toxicity** *noun* MED the concentration of a toxic substance which makes people seriously ill or can cause death

**acyclic** *adjective* BOT referring to flowers whose parts are arranged in a spiral, not a whorl

**acyl group** *noun* CHEM a group of compounds with the basic chemical structure RCO-

**A/D** *abbreviation* COMPUT analog to digital

**ADA** *noun* COMPUT a high-level programming language that is used mainly in military, industrial and scientific fields

**adapt** *verb* **1.** to change to suit new conditions ○ *The animals have gradually adapted to the change in climate.* ○ *People adapt to the reduced amounts of oxygen available at high altitudes.* **2.** to change or modify something for special use ○ *The engine can be adapted for use in single-engine aircraft.*

**adaptability** *noun* BIOL the ability of an organism to change to fit a new situation

**adaptation** *noun* **1.** the act of changing or modifying something for special use ○ *Doppler VOR is an adaptation of VOR to reduce errors caused by location.* Also called **adaption 2.** the adjustment to new conditions ○ *Adaptation to time changes when travelling west to east takes time.* Also called **adaption 3.** BIOL a change in an organism so that it is better able to survive or reproduce, thereby contributing to its fitness

**adapter, adaptor** *noun* COMPUT a device that allows two or more incompatible devices to be connected together ○ *The cable adapter allows attachment of the scanner to the SCSI interface.* ○ *The cable to connect the scanner to the adapter is included in the package.*

**adapter plug** *noun* COMPUT a plug which allows devices with different types of plug to be fitted into the same socket

**adaption** *noun* same as **adaptation**

**adaptive channel allocation** *noun* COMPUT the provision of communications channels according to demand rather than as a fixed allocation

**adaptive compression** *noun* COMPUT a data compression system that continuously monitors the data it is compressing and adjusts its own algorithm to provide the most efficient compression

**adaptive differential pulse code modulation** *noun* COMPUT a CCITT standard that defines a method of converting a voice or analog signal into a compressed digital signal. Abbreviation **ADPCM**

**adaptive optics** *noun* ASTRON an optical system capable of adjusting to compensate for atmospheric distortion (NOTE: Adaptive optics was advanced during the 1980s and 1990s because of spending by the US on the Strategic Defense Initiative, which called for methods of firing laser beams accurately through the atmosphere. The method is now entering wider use with big ground-based telescopes such as the Keck telescope in Hawaii, from which images matching in quality those from the Hubble Space Telescope have been obtained.)

**adaptive packet assembly** *noun* COMPUT a method used by the MNP error-correcting protocol to adjust the size of data packets according to the quality of the telephone line. The better the line is, the bigger the packet size can be.

**adaptive radiation** *noun* BIOL the development of a species from a single ancestor in such a way that different forms evolve to fit different environmental conditions

**adaptive routing** *noun* COMPUT the ability of a system to change its communications routes according to various events or situations such as line failure (NOTE: The messages are normally sent along the most cost-effective path unless there is a problem with that route, in which case they are automatically rerouted.)

**adaptor** *noun* COMPUT another spelling of **adapter**

**ADC** *noun* COMPUT an electronic device that converts an analog input signal to a digital form that can be processed by a computer. Full form **analog to digital converter**

**add** *verb* **1.** MATHS to make a total from something ○ *Add the two numbers together to find the sum.* ○ *In the spreadsheet each column should be added to make a subtotal.* **2.** to put together two or more things to make a larger group or a group with different properties ○ *A substance is added to the fuel to clean fuel injectors.* ○ *The software house has added a new management package to its range of products.* ○ *Adding or deleting material from the text is easy using function keys.*

**addend** *noun* MATHS a number added to the augend in an addition

**adder** *noun* COMPUT a device or routine that provides the sum of two or more digital or analog inputs □ **full adder, three input adder** a binary addition circuit which can produce the sum of two inputs, and can also accept a carry input, producing a carry output if necessary □ **half adder** a binary addition circuit which can produce the sum of two inputs and a carry output if necessary, but will not accept a carry input □ **two input adder** a binary addition circuit which can produce the sum of two inputs and a carry output if necessary, but will not accept a carry input

COMMENT: A parallel adder takes one clock cycle to add two words, while a serial adder takes a time equal to the number of bits in a word to add.

**adder-subtractor** *noun* COMPUT a device that can either add or subtract

**add file** *noun* COMPUT a special file in which new records are stored prior to updating the main database

**addict** *noun* MED a person who is addicted to a harmful drug

**addicted** *adjective* BIOL physiologically or psychologically dependent on a harmful drug

**addictive** *adjective* BIOL referring to a drug which people can become addicted to ○ *Heroin is addictive.*

**add-in** COMPUT *adjective* added to a computer program or piece of equipment ○ *an add-in processor card.* ○ *Processing is much faster with add-in cards.* ■ *noun* a computer program or piece of equipment which is added to another

**addition** *noun* **1.** MATHS a mathematical operation which combines numbers ○ *The addition sign is +.* ○ *Addition is normally taught before subtraction, multiplication and division.* **2.** CHEM ◊ **addition reaction** ○ *With the addition of methanol, the turbine inlet temperature is restored.* **3.** □ **in addition** also □ **in addition to** as well as

**additional** *adjective* extra ○ *Can we link three additional workstations to the network?*

**addition reaction** *noun* CHEM a chemical reaction in which two substances combine to form a third substance with no by-products or other substances being formed. Compare **substitution reaction** (NOTE: usually refers to reactions in organic chemistry)

**addition record** *noun* COMPUT a record with changes used to update a master record or file

**addition sign** *noun* MATHS a sign (+) used to show that numbers are added. Also called **plus sign**

**addition time** *noun* COMPUT the time an adder takes to carry out an add operation

**addition without carry** *noun* COMPUT an addition operation without any carry bits or words

**additive** *noun* **1.** FOOD INDUST a chemical which is added to food to improve its appearance or to prevent it from going bad ○ *The tin of beans contains a number of additives.* ○ *These animal foodstuffs are free from all additives.* **2.** CHEM a chemical which is added to something to improve it ○ *A new fuel additive made from plants could help reduce energy costs.*

COMMENT: Colour additives are added to food to improve its appearance. Some are natural organic substances like saffron, carrot juice or caramel, but others are synthetic. Other substances added to food to prevent decay or to keep the food in the right form are emulsifiers, which bind different foods together as mixtures, and stabilisers, which can keep a sauce semiliquid and prevent it from separating into solids and liquids. The European Union allows some additives to be added to food and these are given E numbers.

**add-on** COMPUT *noun* a piece of software or hardware that is added to a computer system to improve its performance ○ *The add-on will boost the computer's storage capabilities.* ○ *The new add-on board allows colour graphics to be displayed.* ■ *adjective* added to a computer system to improve its performance ▶ opposite (all senses) **built-in**

**add register** *noun* COMPUT a register which is an adder

**address** COMPUT *noun* **1.** a number allowing a central processing unit in a computer system to reference a physical location in a storage medium ○ *Each separate memory word has its own unique address.* **2.** a unique number that identifies a device on a network ○ *This is the address at which the data starts.* ■ *verb* to put the location data onto an address bus to identify which word in memory or storage device is to be accessed ○ *A larger address word increases the amount of memory a computer can address.*

**addressable** *adjective* COMPUT able to be addressed ○ *With the new operating system, all of the 5 MB of installed RAM is addressable.*

**addressable cursor** *noun* COMPUT a cursor which can be programmed to be placed in a specific position

**addressable point** *noun* COMPUT in a graphics system, any point or pixel that can be directly addressed

**address base** *noun* COMPUT a part of an address that defines the origin to which the logical address is added

**address book** *noun* COMPUT **1.** a list of node addresses **2.** a list of the network addresses of other users to which electronic mail can be sent

**address bus** *noun* COMPUT a physical connection that carries the address data in parallel form from the central processing unit to external devices

**address code** *noun* COMPUT a special code that identifies the part of a document that is an address

**address format** *noun* COMPUT a set of rules defining the way the operands, data and addresses are arranged in an instruction

**addressing** *noun* COMPUT the process of accessing a location in memory

**addressing mode** *noun* COMPUT the way in which a location is addressed, e.g. sequential, indexed or direct

**address mapping** *noun* COMPUT a virtual address translated to an absolute address

**address mask** *noun* COMPUT a pattern of binary data bits that is used to block out parts of an address data word. It is usually used to separate the network and subnet parts of an address within a long Internet or IP address. ○ *The address mask '111000' will block off the last three bits of any address data.*

**address modification** *noun* COMPUT the changing of the address field, so that it can refer to a different location

**address register** *noun* COMPUT a register in a computer that is able to store all the bits that make up an address which can then be processed as a single unit (NOTE: In small micros, the address register is usually made up of two data bytes.)

**address resolution** *noun* COMPUT the conversion of an Internet address into the correct physical network address that corresponds to the distant computer or resource

**address resolution protocol** *noun* COMPUT a protocol used within the TCP/IP standard that is used to determine whether the source and destination address in a packet are in the data-link control (DLC) or Internet protocol (IP) format. Once the format of the address is known, the packet can be correctly routed over a network. Abbreviation **ARP**

**address space** *noun* COMPUT the total number of possible locations that can be directly addressed by the program or CPU

**address track** *noun* COMPUT a track on a magnetic disk containing the addresses of files, etc., stored on other tracks

**address word** *noun* COMPUT a computer word, usually made up, in a small micro, of two data words that contain the address data

**add time** *noun* MATHS a period of time taken to perform one addition operation either of a central processing unit or adder

**adduct** *verb* PHYSIOL to pull towards the centre line of the body ■ *noun* CHEM a chemical compound formed in an addition reaction between at least two different compounds or elements

**adenine** *noun* BIOCHEM one of the four basic components of DNA

**adenosine** *noun* BIOCHEM a compound, consisting of the base adenine and the sugar ribose, found in DNA, RNA and energy-carrying molecules such as ATP

**adenosine diphosphate** *noun* BIOCHEM full form of **ADP**

**adenosine monophosphate** *noun* BIOCHEM full form of **AMP**

**adenosine triphosphate** *noun* BIOCHEM full form of **ATP**

**adenovirus** *noun* MICROBIOL a virus that causes infections of the nose and throat in humans

**adequate** *adjective* sufficient ○ *The compressor must provide an adequate airflow through the engine.* ○ *The brain must have an adequate supply of blood.* ○ *Does the children's diet provide them with an adequate quantity of iron?*

**ADH** *abbreviation* BIOCHEM antidiuretic hormone

**adhere** *verb* to attach firmly ○ *Clear ice adheres strongly to airframes.*

**adhesion** *noun* PHYS an intermolecular attraction between dissimilar materials that are touching each other, causing them to stick together

**adhesive** *noun* a glue ○ *A 'superglue' is an all-purpose adhesive.* ■ *adjective* having the sticking quality of glue ○ *adhesive tape* ○ *Adhesive bonding of aluminium parts is widely employed.*

**ADI** *abbreviation* BIOL acceptable daily intake

**adiabatic** *adjective* PHYS referring to a change in temperature in a mass of air as a result of compression or expansion caused by an increase or decrease in atmospheric pressure without loss or gain of heat to or from its surroundings. Also called **inversion**

COMMENT: A parcel of rising air expands, because the surrounding pressure falls. Also its temperature falls because no heat can enter or leave it. If a parcel of air descends, the opposite happens and the air temperature rises.

**adiabatically** *adverb* PHYS without losing or gaining heat ○ *The air mass rises adiabatically through the atmosphere.*

**adiabatic heating** *noun* PHYS the heating of descending air caused by an increase in atmospheric pressure without heat transfer, as when a bicycle pump is used

**adiabatic lapse rate** *noun* METEOROL the rate at which air temperature decreases as it rises above the Earth's surface. ▷ **lapse rate**

**adipic acid** *noun* CHEM a crystalline white solid used in nylon manufacture. Formula: $C_6H_{10}O_4$.

**adipo-** *prefix* BIOCHEM fat

**adipose** *adjective* BIOCHEM containing or made of fat

**adipose tissue** *noun* a tissue where the cells contain fat which replaces the normal fibrous tissue when too much food is eaten

**aditus** *noun* ANAT an opening or entrance to a passage

**adjacent** *adjective* next to or near to ○ *They work in adjacent laboratories.*

**adjunct register** *noun* COMPUT a 32-bit register in which the top 16 bits are used for control information and only the bottom 16 bits are available for use by a program

**adjust** *verb* to change something to fit new conditions or so that it works better ○ *You can adjust the brightness and contrast by turning a knob.*

**adjustable** *adjective* designed to be adjusted ○ *An adjustable stop on the throttle control ensures a positive idling speed.*

**adjustment** *noun* 1. a change to improve the setting or position of something ○ *Maximum system pressure is often controlled by adjustment of the main engine-driven pump.* ○ *The brightness needs adjustment.* ○ *The joystick needs adjustment as it sometimes gets stuck.* 2. BIOL a process of physical change in response to external environmental changes

**adjuvant** *noun* PHARM an agent added to a drug to improve its effectiveness

**administrator** *noun* COMPUT 1. a person who manages an organisation, institution or business 2. a person who is responsible for looking after a network including installing, configuring and maintaining it

**admit** *verb* to allow someone or something to enter ○ *Cold air can be admitted through adjustable louvres or shutters.*

**admittance** *noun* PHYS a measure of how easily an electrical current can flow through a medium (NOTE: It is the reciprocal of impedance.)

**adnexa** *plural noun* ANAT structures attached to an organ

**adobe** *noun* **1.** EARTH SCI a fine clay from which bricks can be made **2.** bricks made from fine clay, dried in the sun

**adopt** *verb* to choose to use or have something as standard equipment or as a procedure ○ *We need to adopt a new strategy.* ○ *The organisation has adopted strict energy-saving measures.*

**adoption** *noun* the act or an instance of using something as standard equipment or as a procedure ○ *In spite of the adoption of the axial flow type compressor, some engines retain the centrifugal type.*

**ADP** *noun* **1.** COMPUT data processing done by a computer. Full form **automatic data processing 2.** BIOCHEM a compound involved in chemical reactions that release large amounts of energy in the tissues of living organisms. Full form **adenosine diphosphate**

**ADPCM** *abbreviation* COMPUT adaptive differential pulse code modulation

**adrenal** *adjective* ANAT situated near a kidney

**adrenal gland** *noun* ANAT one of two endocrine glands at the top of the kidneys which produce adrenaline and other hormones

**adrenaline** *noun* BIOCHEM a hormone secreted by the medulla of the adrenal glands which has an effect similar to stimulation of the sympathetic nervous system (NOTE: The US term is **epinephrine**.)

COMMENT: Adrenaline is produced when a person experiences surprise, shock, fear or excitement. It speeds up the heartbeat and raises blood pressure. It is administered as an emergency treatment for acute anaphylaxis and in cardiopulmonary resuscitation.

**adrenergic** *adjective* BIOL referring to neurons or receptors stimulated by adrenaline

COMMENT: Three types of adrenergic receptor act in different ways when stimulated by adrenaline. Alpha receptors constrict the bronchi, beta 1 receptors speed up the heartbeat and beta 2 receptors dilate the bronchi.

**adrenoceptor** *noun* ANAT a cell or neuron which is stimulated by adrenaline

**adrenocorticotrophic hormone** *noun* BIOCHEM full form of **ACTH**

**adrenoreceptor** *noun* ANAT same as **adrenoceptor**

**ADSL** *noun* COMPUT a high-speed transmission standard that uses the same wires as a normal telephone service, but is much faster and provides a user with an always-on connection to the Internet so there is no need to dial an access number and no delay. Full form **asymmetric digital subscriber line** (NOTE: Data is usually transferred from the Internet to the user's computer at 2 Mbps but transferred from the user's computer to the Internet at a slower rate of 256 Kbps.)

**adsorb** *verb* CHEM (*of a solid*) to bond with a gas or vapour which touches its surface

**adsorbable** *adjective* CHEM referring to a solid that is able to bond with a gas or vapour which touches its surface

**adsorbate** *noun* CHEM a substance that is adsorbed

**adsorbent** CHEM *adjective* capable of adsorption ■ *noun* a solid which is able to bond with a gas or vapour which touches its surface

**adsorption** *noun* CHEM the bonding of a solid with a gas or vapour which touches its surface

**adult** BIOL *adjective* having reached maturity ■ *noun* an organism which has reached maturity

**advance** *noun* **1.** an instance of new development and progress ○ *advances in gene therapy* **2.** □ **in advance of** before ■ *verb* to move or be moved forwards □ **to advance the ignition** to adjust the timing of the ignition in an engine so that the spark occurs earlier

**advanced** *adjective* **1.** modern and sophisticated ○ *advanced techniques* **2.** more complicated or more difficult to learn ○ *advanced mathematics* **3.** having developed further ○ *the advanced stages of a disease* **4.** moved forwards □ **the throttle lever is advanced** the throttle lever is physically moved forwards

**advanced gas-cooled reactor** *noun* INDUST a type of nuclear reactor, in which carbon dioxide is used as the coolant and is passed into water tanks to create the steam which will drive the turbines. Abbreviation **AGR**

**advanced program to program communication** *noun* COMPUT a set of protocols developed by IBM that allows peer-to-peer communication between workstations connected to an SNA network. Abbreviation **APPC**

**Advanced Research Projects Agency Network** *noun* COMPUT an original network of interconnected computers, linked by leased lines, that formed the first prototype for the current Internet and was developed by the US Department of Defense (Defense Advanced Research Projects Agency). Abbreviation **ARPANET**

**advanced run-length limited** *noun* COMPUT a method of storing data onto a hard disk that is faster and more efficient than RLL. Abbreviation **ARLL**

**advanced technology attachment packet interface** *noun* COMPUT a standard interface that is used for CD-ROMs. Abbreviation **ATAPI**

**advantage** *noun* a good or beneficial factor ○ *The multi-wheel combination has the advantage of smaller and lighter undercarriage structures.* □ **to take advantage of** to get the most benefit from a situation. Opposite **disadvantage**

**advantageous** *adjective* providing an advantage

**advect** *verb* METEOROL (*of air*) to move in a horizontal direction due to convection ○ *Dispersal of hill fog takes place when surface heating lifts the cloud base or drier air is advected.*

**advection** *noun* METEOROL a movement of air in a horizontal direction. Compare **convection**

**advection fog** *noun* a fog which forms when warmer moist air moves over a colder surface, either land or sea

**advent** *noun* the arrival of something new ○ *With the advent of satellite navigation systems, pilots of light aircraft have a more accurate means of knowing their position.*

**adventitious** *adjective* **1.** BIOL on the outside or in an unusual place **2.** BOT referring to a root which develops from a plant's stem and not from another root

**adverse** *adjective* **1.** bad or poor ○ *Adverse weather conditions delayed planting.* **2.** harmful or unfavourable ○ *The treatment had an adverse effect on his dermatitis.* ○ *She had an adverse reaction to penicillin.* **3.** moving in the opposite direction ○ *adverse winds*

**adverse yaw** *noun* AEROSP a sideways turn caused by aileron drag, in the opposite direction to the direction of the intended turn

**advice** *noun* a suggestion about what should be done ○ *The doctor's advice was to stay in bed.* ○ *He took my advice and went home.* (NOTE: no plural: **some advice** or **a piece of advice**)

**advisability** *noun* the degree to which a particular action is a good idea or not

**advisable** *adjective* to be recommended ○ *Where possible, it is advisable to closely check the condition of the tyres.*

**advise** *verb* **1.** to inform someone **2.** to recommend something □ **to advise against something** to recommend that something should not be done

**advisory** *adjective* giving advice and information

**advisory board, advisory committee** *noun* a group of specialists who can give advice

**advisory lock** *noun* COMPUT a lock placed on a region of a file by one process to prevent any other process accessing the same data

**advisory system** *noun* COMPUT an expert system that provides advice to a user

**aeolian deposits** *plural noun* EARTH SCI sediments which are blown by the wind. ♦ **loess**

**aer-** *prefix* CHEM air

**aerate** *verb* **1.** to put a gas, especially carbon dioxide or air, into a liquid so that bubbles are formed ○ *aerated water* ♦ **de-aerate 2.** CHEM to allow air to enter a substance, especially soil ○ *Worms are useful because they aerate the soil.*

**aeration** *noun* CHEM **1.** the process of putting a gas, especially carbon dioxide or air, into a liquid ○ *The purpose of the booster pump is to prevent fuel aeration.* **2.** the process of putting air into a substance ○ *aeration of the soil*

COMMENT: The process of aeration of soil is mainly brought about by the movement of water into and out of the soil. Rainwater drives out the air and then, as the water drains away or is used by plants, fresh air is drawn into the soil to fill the spaces. The aeration process is also assisted by changes in temperature, good drainage, cultivation and open soil structure. Sandy soils are usually well aerated; clay soils are poorly aerated.

**aerator** *noun* CHEM a device to put a gas, especially carbon dioxide or air, into a liquid. ♦ **de-aerator**

**aerial** *adjective* **1.** referring to the air **2.** AEROSP referring to an aircraft in the air ■ *noun* a device to send or receive radio or TV signals (NOTE: The US term for this meaning is **antenna**.)

**aerial perspective** *noun* COMPUT a view of a three-dimensional landscape as if the viewer is above the scene

**aerial photography** *noun* AEROSP photography done from an aircraft in the air

**aerial root** *noun* BOT a root of some plants, which hangs in the air or clings to other plants and takes up moisture from the air

**aero-** *prefix* AEROSP **1.** air ○ *aerodynamic* **2.** aircraft ○ *aero-engine*

**aerobe** *noun* MICROBIOL a living thing, particularly a microorganism, that needs oxygen for metabolism

**aerobic** *adjective* BIOCHEM needing oxygen for its existence or for a biochemical reaction to occur. Opposite **anaerobic**

**aerobic digester** *noun* BIOCHEM a digester which operates in the presence of oxygen

**aerobic digestion** *noun* BIOCHEM the processing of waste, especially organic waste such as manure, in the presence of oxygen

**aerobic respiration** *noun* BIOCHEM a process where the oxygen which is breathed in is used to conserve energy as ATP

**aerobiosis** *noun* BIOCHEM a biological activity which occurs in the presence of oxygen

**aerodynamic** *adjective* **1.** referring to the way in which objects are affected when they move through the atmosphere **2.** referring to a smooth rounded shape which moves easily through the air

**aerodynamic braking** *noun* AEROSP the braking effect of drag

**aerodynamic design** *noun* ENG a design of an aircraft or vehicle which moves easily through the air because of its shape

**aerodynamic forces** *plural noun* PHYS forces of the air which act on aircraft in flight

**aerodynamics** *noun* the science of dynamics and interaction of moving objects with the atmosphere (NOTE: takes a singular verb)

**aero-engine** *noun* AEROSP an engine used in aircraft ○ *Most piston aero-engines are cooled by air.*

**aerofoil** *noun* AEROSP a surface which is shaped to produce more lift than drag when moved through the air ○ *Wings, ailerons, elevators, fins and propellers are all examples of aerofoils.* (NOTE: The US term is **airfoil**.)

**aerogenerator** *noun* INDUST a windmill with fast-moving sails used to generate mechanical power or electricity

**aeronautical** *adjective* AEROSP referring to aeronautics

**aeronautical engineering** *noun* AEROSP the science or study of the design of aircraft

**aeronautics** *noun* **1.** AEROSP the science of aircraft design, construction, operation or navigation **2.** NAVIG the theory and practice of aircraft navigation (NOTE: takes a singular verb)

**aeroplane** *noun* a power-driven, heavier-than-air craft with fixed wings (NOTE: Many people use the words **aeroplane** and **aircraft** synonymously. However, aeroplanes, hot-air balloons, helicopters, airships and gliders are all **aircraft**. The US term is is **airplane**.)

**aeroplane performance** *noun* AEROSP a description in figures regarding the speed of the aircraft, rate of climb, length of take-off run, etc.

**aeroshell** *noun* AEROSP the outer casing of a planetary landing spacecraft, designed to protect it from frictional heat generated when it passes through an atmosphere

**aerosol** *noun* **1.** a quantity of tiny particles of liquid suspended in a gas under pressure, sprayed from a container **2.** a can of liquid with a propellant gas under pressure, which is used to spray the liquid in the form of tiny drops **3.** a quantity of tiny particles of liquid or powder which stay suspended in the atmosphere

COMMENT: Aerosols in the atmosphere may be formed of liquid, as in the case of mist, or of solid particles, as in the case of dust storms. Aerosols in the atmosphere are the form in which pollutants such as smoke are dispersed. Commercial aerosols use CFCs as propellants, but these are believed to be responsible for the destruction of ozone in the upper atmosphere and are gradually being replaced by less destructive propellants.

**aerosol propellant** *noun* a gas used in an aerosol can to make the spray of liquid come out

**aestivation** *noun* ZOOL dormancy in some animals such as lungfish during the summer or periods of drought

**aetiological agent** *noun* BIOL an agent which causes a disease

**aetiology** *noun* BIOL the causes of a disease, or the study of those causes

**affect** *verb* to have an influence on or change something ○ *Humidity and air density are factors which affect the output of the engine.* ○ *Wind direction and speed only affect the movement of the aircraft over the ground.* Compare **effect**

**afferent** *adjective* BIOL conducting liquid or electrical impulses towards the inside

**afferent nerve** *noun* ANAT same as **sensory nerve**

**affinity** *noun* CHEM an attraction between two substances

**affirmative acknowledgment** *noun* TELECOM a signal from a receiver indicating that it has accepted a message and is ready for the next one

**affluent** *adjective* **1.** wealthy **2.** EARTH SCI referring to water which is flowing freely ■ *noun* EARTH SCI a stream which flows into a larger river

**afforest** *verb* AGRIC to plant an area with trees

**afforestation** *noun* **1.** AGRIC the growing of trees as a crop ○ *There is likely to be an increase in afforestation of upland areas if the scheme is introduced.* **2.** EARTH SCI the planting of trees on land previously used for other purposes

**aflatoxin** *noun* FOOD INDUST a toxin produced by the fungus *Aspergillus flavus*, which grows on seeds and nuts and affects stored grain

**AFLP** *abbreviation* BIOTECH amplified fragment length polymorphism

**AFP** *noun* COMPUT a protocol used to communicate between workstations and

servers in a network of Apple Macintosh computers. Full form **Appletalk filing protocol**

**afrormosia** *noun* TREES a hardwood tree from West Africa, now becoming scarce

**after-** *prefix* coming later

**aftercare** *noun* ENVIRON arrangements for preventing future pollution from an environmentally sensitive activity that has ceased

**aftereffects** *plural noun* BIOL changes which appear only some time after the cause ○ *The operation had some unpleasant aftereffects.*

**afterglow** COMPUT ◊ **persistence**

**aftershock** *noun* EARTH SCI a weaker shock which follows the main shock of an earthquake

**Ag** *symbol* CHEM ELEM silver

**agamospermy** *noun* BOT same as **apomixis**

**agar, agar agar** *noun* BIOL a culture medium based on an extract of seaweed used for growing microorganisms in laboratories

**agbiotech** *noun* BIOTECH the biotechnology applied to agriculture

**AGC** *noun* ELECTRONICS an electronic circuit that adjusts the level of an incoming signal so that it is suitable for the next part of the circuit. Full form **automatic gain control**

**age** *noun* the number of years during which a person or thing has existed ○ *The size varies according to age.* ■ *verb* to grow old

**age group** *noun* all people of a particular age

**agency** *noun* the act of causing something to happen ○ *The disease develops through the agency of bacteria present in the bloodstream.*

**Agenda 21** *noun* ENVIRON a global environmental programme and statement of principles concerning sustainable development, agreed in 1992 at the Earth Summit in Rio de Janeiro, Brazil

**agent** *noun* **1.** CHEM a chemical substance which causes a change ○ *an anti-icing agent* **2.** COMPUT a program or piece of software that runs on a workstation in a network, sending performance and statistical information about the workstation to a central network management console **3.** COMPUT a series of commands or actions that are carried out automatically on a particular file or data **4.** BIOL a substance or organism which causes a disease or condition ○ *They identified the disease agent.*

**Agent Orange** *noun* CHEM an extremely poisonous herbicide used as a defoliant (NOTE: It was used by US forces in the Vietnam War.)

**age-specific rate** *noun* MED the number of live births per 1000 women of a particular age group per year

**agglomerate** *noun* EARTH SCI a rock made up of fragments of lava fused by heat

**agglutinate** *verb* BIOL to form into groups or clusters

**agglutination** *noun* BIOL the action of the grouping together of cells, e.g. bacterial cells in the presence of serum or blood cells when blood of different types is mixed

**agglutination test** *noun* **1.** MICROBIOL a test used to identify bacteria **2.** MED a test used to identify if a woman is pregnant

**agglutinin** *noun* BIOCHEM a factor in a serum which makes cells group together

**agglutinogen** *noun* BIOCHEM a factor in red blood cells which reacts with a specific agglutinin in serum

**aggravate** *verb* to make something worse ○ *The treatment seems to aggravate the disease.* ○ *The effects of acid rain on the soil have been aggravated by chemical runoff.*

**aggregate** *noun* **1.** the total obtained by adding ○ *The aggregate of the capacity of all the fuel tanks is 50 gallons.* **2.** COMPUT a collection of data objects **3.** INDUST crushed stones used to make concrete or road surfaces **4.** EARTH SCI a mass of soil and rock particles stuck together ■ *verb* to make up a whole or total ○ *Ice crystals aggregate to form snowflakes.* ■ to come together to form a mass

**aggregate bandwidth** *noun* the total bandwidth of a channel carrying a multiplexed data stream

**aggregate function** *noun* COMPUT a mathematical database function performed on a selected field in every record in a selected database

**aggregate line speed** *noun* COMPUT the maximum speed at which

data can be transmitted through a particular channel

**aggregate operator** *noun* COMPUT a command in a database management program that starts an aggregate function

**aggregation** *noun* ECOL a dispersal of plants or animals, where the individuals remain quite close together

**AGN** *abbreviation* ASTRON active galactic nucleus

**agnathan** *noun* MARINE BIOL a sea vertebrate that has no jaw nor the two pairs of fins or legs that are characteristic of vertebrates such as lampreys and hagfish. Subphylum: Agnatha. (NOTE: Modern examples have eel-shaped bodies and slimy scaleless skin, but many extinct agnathans were covered with bony plates and scales.)

**agonist** *noun* BIOCHEM a substance such as a hormone, neurotransmitter or drug that binds to a cell's receptors to trigger a response

**AGP** *abbreviation* COMPUT accelerated graphics port (NOTE: This port does not replace a PCI bus but works with it.)

**AGR** *abbreviation* INDUST advanced gas-cooled reactor

**agree** *verb* **1.** to have the same idea or opinion about something **2.** to come to an understanding

**agreed** *adjective* generally accepted ○ *The millibar is an agreed unit of pressure.*

**agreement** *noun* the act or fact of having the same idea or opinion as somebody

**agri-, agro-** *prefix* AGRIC referring to agriculture or to the cultivation of land

**agribusiness** *noun* AGRIC the business of farming and making products and equipment used by farmers

COMMENT: The term is used to refer to large-scale farming businesses run along the lines of a conventional company, often involving the growing, processing, packaging and sale of farm products.

**agricultural** *adjective* AGRIC referring to farming

**agricultural engineer** *noun* AGRIC **1.** a person trained in applying the principles of science to farming **2.** a person who designs, manufactures or repairs farm machinery and equipment

**agricultural engineering** *noun* AGRIC the applying of the principles of science to farming

**agriculturalist** *noun* AGRIC a person trained in applying the principles of science to farming

**agricultural policy** *noun* AGRIC a government's way of dealing with all matters concerning agriculture

**agricultural waste** *noun* AGRIC waste matter produced on a farm, e.g. manure from animals

**agriculture** *noun* AGRIC the cultivation of land, including horticulture, fruit growing, crop and seed growing, dairy farming and livestock breeding

**agro-** *prefix* AGRIC referring to agriculture or to the cultivation of land

**agrochemical industry** *noun* AGRIC the branch of industry which produces pesticides and fertilisers used on farms

**agrochemicals** *plural noun* AGRIC pesticides and fertilisers developed artificially for agricultural use

**agroclimatology** *noun* AGRIC the study of climate and its effect on agriculture

**agroecology** *noun* AGRIC, ECOL the ecology of a crop-producing area

**agroecosystem** *noun* AGRIC a community of organisms in a crop-producing area

**agroforestry** *noun* AGRIC the growing of farm crops and trees together as a farming unit

**agroindustry** *noun* AGRIC an industry dealing with the supply, processing and distribution of farm products

**agronomist** *noun* AGRIC a person who studies the cultivation of crops

**agronomy** *noun* AGRIC the scientific study of the cultivation of crops

COMMENT: The use of land to raise crops for food first started about 10,000 years ago. All plants grown for food have been developed over many centuries from wild plants, which have been progressively bred to give the best yields in different types of environment. Genes from wild plants tend to be more hardy and resistant to disease and are used in breeding new cultivated varieties.

**AH** *abbreviation* MEASURE ampere-hour

**ahead** *adverb* in front

**ahead of** *preposition* **1.** in front of ○ *Air ahead of a cold front is warmer than air behind a cold front.* **2.** at an earlier time than ○ *Paris is one hour ahead of London* ○ *The report was published ahead of schedule.* **3.** before ○ *We need to have the data ahead of next week's meeting.*

**AI**[1] *noun* COMPUT the design and development of computer programs that attempt to imitate human intelligence and decision-making functions, providing basic reasoning and other human characteristics. Full form **artificial intelligence**

**AI**[2] *abbreviation* **1.** BIOL active ingredient **2.** AEROSP attitude indicator **3.** AGRIC artificial insemination

**aid** *noun* **1.** help given to someone **2.** something which helps someone do something ○ *The computer is a great aid to rapid processing of large amounts of information.* ○ *Crop sprayers are useful aids in combating insect-borne disease.* **3.** help in the form of people, food, medicines, equipment, etc., given to a developing country ○ *food aid to the disaster area* ○ *The country spends 7% of its gross national product on aid to Third World countries.* **4.** a machine, tool or drug which helps someone do something ■ *verb* to help or give support to someone or something ○ *They were aided in their research by the detailed records kept by observers.* ○ *Changing to lead-free petrol will aid the fight against air pollution.*

**AIDS** *noun* MED a disease of the immune system caused by the HIV virus, characterised by increased susceptibility to infections and cancers. Full form **Acquired Immune Deficiency Syndrome** (NOTE: It is transmitted through blood or bodily secretions such as semen.)

**aileron** *noun* AEROSP a horizontal control surface hinged to an aircraft wing which provides movement such as banking or turning around the longitudinal axis of the aeroplane ○ *By rotating the yoke the ailerons are moved and the aircraft rolls into a turn.* (NOTE: The word comes from the French 'aile', meaning 'wing'.)

**ailment** *noun* MED an illness, though not generally a very serious one ○

*Chickenpox is one of the common childhood ailments.*

**aim** *noun* a goal or objective ■ *verb* **1.** to point something such as a weapon or a remark at someone or something **2.** to intend or to try to do something

**aiming symbol, aiming field** *noun* COMPUT a symbol displayed on screen which defines the area in which a light pen can be detected

**air** *noun* a mixture of gases forming the Earth's atmosphere, which cannot be seen, but which exists all around us and which is breathed ○ *The air in the mountains felt cold.*

COMMENT: The composition of air in the lower atmosphere is: nitrogen (78%), oxygen (21%), argon (less than 1%) and trace quantities of carbon dioxide, helium, hydrogen, krypton, neon, ozone and xenon. Air pollution can be caused by human action such as industrial processes or smoking tobacco, but also by natural disasters such as volcanic eruptions and forest fires.

**air bladder** *noun* MARINE BIOL an air-filled sac that helps the fronds of a seaweed to float in the water

**airborne** *adjective* **1.** (*of aircraft*) lifted and kept in the air by aerodynamic forces ○ *Shortly after the aircraft becomes airborne, the undercarriage is retracted.* **2.** METEOROL carried by the air ○ *There is a high risk of airborne pollution near the factory.*

**airborne combustion product** *noun* INDUST a gas, vapour or solid produced by burning and transported through the air

**airborne lead** *noun* ENVIRON particles of lead carried in the air, causing pollution

**airborne pollutant** *noun* ENVIRON a substance which is released into the air and is carried along by it, causing pollution

**airbrush** *noun* COMPUT a painting tool that creates a diffuse pattern of dots ○ *We used the airbrush tool to create the cloud effects in this image.*

**air cleaner** *noun* ENG a filter which removes unwanted substances from the air

**air conditioner** *noun* ENG a device which controls the temperature, ventilation and humidity in a building or vehicle

**air conditioning** *noun* ENG a system which controls the temperature, ventilation and humidity in a building or vehicle

**air conduction** *noun* PHYSIOL the conduction of sounds through the channel from the outside to the inner ear

**air-cooled** *adjective* ENG cooled by means of a flow of air, not water

**air-cooling** *noun* ENG the cooling of something by means of a current of air

**aircraft** *noun* AEROSP a vehicle that flies ○ *Aeroplanes, gliders, balloons, airships and helicopters are all aircraft.* ♦ **aeroplane** (NOTE: The plural is **aircraft.**)

**air current** *noun* PHYS a flow of air

**air density** *noun* PHYS the density of the atmosphere

**air filter** *noun* a device to remove solid particles from the air in engine and ventilation systems

**airflow** *noun* **1.** AEROSP a movement of air over an aircraft caused by the movement of the aircraft through the air **2.** ENG a current of air flowing through or past an object or body ○ *The compressor must provide an adequate airflow through the engine.*

**airfoil** *noun US* AEROSP US spelling of **aerofoil**

**airframe** *noun* AEROSP an aircraft body without engines, instruments, etc ○ *The airframe has to be built to very specific requirements.*

**air frost** *noun* METEOROL the condition where the air temperature above ground level is below 0° C

**air gap** *noun* a narrow gap between a recording or playback head and the magnetic medium

**air gap type spark plug** *noun* AUTOMOT a spark plug with a gap between the electrodes across which the spark jumps

**air gas** *noun* INDUST a mixture of carbon monoxide and nitrogen made by passing air over hot coke and used as a fuel

**airglow** *noun* ASTRON a faint glow in the night sky caused by fluorescence of air molecules in the upper atmosphere

COMMENT: The airglow can exist at 600 km or more above the Earth's surface. The air at this height glows as the result of interaction with solar radiation, especially when ultraviolet radiation from the Sun forms nitrogen oxides with the emission of visible light. Although interesting in its own right, the airglow can hamper other astronomical observations.

**air intake** *noun* AEROSP the front part of a jet engine where air enters

**air mass** *noun* METEOROL a very large mass of air in the atmosphere in which the temperature is almost constant, divided from another mass by a weather front

**air passage** *noun* ANAT a set of tubes, formed of the nose, pharynx, larynx, trachea and bronchi, which takes air to the lungs

**airplane** *noun US* AEROSP US spelling of **aeroplane**

**air pollutant** *noun* ENVIRON a substance such as gas or smoke which contaminates the air around or the atmosphere

**air pollution** *noun* the contamination of the air by substances such as gas or smoke. Also called **atmospheric pollution**

**air pressure** *noun* METEOROL the normal pressure of the air on the surface of the Earth

**air purification** *noun* ENG the removal of unwanted substances from the air

**air quality** *noun* ENVIRON the state of the air around in terms of degree of pollution

**air quality index** *noun* ENVIRON a numerical scale that indicates how polluted the air is in a specific place

**air quality standards** *plural noun* ENVIRON legal limits on specific pollutants in the air around

**air sac** *noun* ANAT same as **alveolus**

**airship** *noun* AEROSP a powered, gas-filled balloon which can be steered

**airspace** *noun* AEROSP a part of the atmosphere in which aircraft fly which is subject to the laws of a particular country or controlling authority ○ *Civilian airspace over Europe has become very crowded.*

**airspeed** *noun* AEROSP the speed of an aircraft relative to the air around it ○ *Maintain a constant airspeed on final approach.*

**airspeed indicator** *noun* AEROSP the primary cockpit or flight deck instrument which shows the pilot the speed of the aircraft in relation to the air around it ○ *Airspeed is shown in knots on the airspeed indicator.* Abbreviation **ASI**

**airstream** *noun* AEROSP a flow of air in a particular direction

COMMENT: Unlike airflow, airstream does not refer to the movement of air around an airframe and its aerodynamic effect.

**air stripping** *noun* ENVIRON a technique for removing pollutants from water in which water is split into minute particles

**airtight** *adjective* ENG not leaking air

**air-to-ground visibility** *noun* AEROSP the degree to which an object can be seen easily on the ground from the air ○ *Glare caused by reflection of sunlight from the top of a layer of fog or haze can seriously reduce air-to-ground visibility.*

**airway** *noun* ANAT a passage in the body through which air passes, especially the trachea

**Airy disc** *noun* PHYS a small disc of light produced by a lens or mirror forming an image of a point source of light such as a star. It is caused by diffraction spreading the light out.

**akinetic** *adjective* BIOL without movement

**Al** *symbol* CHEM ELEM aluminium

**alabaster** *noun* MINERALS a hard white semitranslucent variety of calcite

**alanine** *noun* BIOCHEM an amino acid in protein

**alarm** *noun* a ringing of a bell or another sound which warns of a danger ○ *All staff must leave the building if the alarm sounds.* ○ *An alarm rings when the printer has run out of paper.*

**albedo** *noun* PHYS, ASTRON a measurement of the ability of a surface to reflect light, shown as the proportion of solar energy which strikes the Earth and is reflected back by a particular surface

COMMENT: Albedo is highest on light shiny surfaces such as snow. It is lowest on dark uneven surfaces, e.g. masses of leaves, which absorb solar energy. Among the Earth's near neighbours, albedos range from Mercury's 6% to Venus's 76%, while the Earth's is 36%. Earth and Venus have high albedos because of their cloud-filled atmospheres.

**albinism** *noun* BIOL an inherited lack of pigmentation in an organism (NOTE: A person with albinism has unusually white skin and hair.)

**albino** *noun* BIOL an organism which is deficient in the colouring pigment melanin and has little or no pigmentation in skin, hair or eyes

**albumen** *noun* BIOL the white of an egg, containing albumin

**albumin** *noun* BIOL a common protein, soluble in water and found in plant and animal tissue and digested in the intestine

**albumose** *noun* BIOL an intermediate product in the digestion of protein

**alcohol** *noun* **1.** FOOD INDUST, CHEM a colourless liquid which is formed by the action of yeast on sugar solutions. It is a component of drinks such as wine and whisky and is also an ingredient of organic chemicals and medicines. Formula: $C_2H_5OH$. **2.** CHEM an organic compound containing the -OH group

**aldehyde** *noun* CHEM one of the main groups of organic compound hydrocarbons with the general formula RCHO, where R is an alkyl group

**aldol** *noun* CHEM a thick oily liquid used in the vulcanisation of rubber, solvent and perfumes

**aldose** *noun* BIOCHEM a sugar (**monosaccharide**) containing an aldehyde group

**aldosterone** *noun* BIOCHEM a hormone secreted by the adrenal gland which regulates the balance of sodium and potassium in the body and the amount of body fluid

**aldrin** *noun* AGRIC an organochlorine insecticide, used to control cabbage root fly, wireworms and leatherjackets (NOTE: There is an agreement to restrict the use of this insecticide.)

**alert** *noun* COMPUT a warning message sent from software to warn a person or application that an error or problem has occurred

**alert box** *noun* COMPUT a warning panel displayed on screen to warn a user about something ○ *The alert box warned me that I was about to delete all my files.*

**aleurone** *noun* BOT a protein found in the outer skin of seeds

**alfalfa** *noun* PLANTS same as **lucerne**

**alga** *noun* BIOL a tiny single-celled or multi-celled organism living in water or in moist conditions, which contains chlorophyll but has no stems, roots or leaves (NOTE: The plural is **algae**.)

COMMENT: Algae were formerly regarded as plants because they contain chlorophyll, but are now classified separately. Seaweeds are forms of algae. Algae grow rapidly in water which is rich in phosphates. When the phosphate level increases, for example when fertiliser runoff enters the water, the algae multiply to form huge floating mats called blooms, blocking out the light and inhibiting the growth of other organisms. When the algae die, they combine with all the oxygen in the water so that other organisms suffocate.

**algal** *adjective* BIOL referring to algae ○ *Algal populations increase rapidly when phosphates are present.*

**algal bloom** *noun* BIOL a mass of algae which develops rapidly in a lake as a result of eutrophication

**algal control** *noun* ENVIRON prevention of the growth of algae

**algebra** *noun* MATHS the use of letters in mathematical operations to represent unknown numbers or a range of possible numbers

**algebraic language** *noun* COMPUT a context-free language

**-algia** *suffix* BIOL pain

**algicide** *noun* ENVIRON a substance used to kill algae

**ALGOL** *noun* COMPUT a high-level programming language using algorithmic methods for mathematical and technical applications. Full form **algorithmic language**

**algorithm** *noun* MATHS a set of rules used to define or perform a specific task or to solve a specific problem

**algorithmic** *adjective* MATHS expressed using algorithms

**algorithmic language** *noun* COMPUT a computer language designed to process and express algorithms, e.g. ALGOL

**alias** *noun* COMPUT a representative name given to a file, port, device, spreadsheet cell or range of cells ○ *The operating system uses the alias COM1 to represent the serial port address 3FCh.*

**alicyclic** *adjective* CHEM referring to organic compounds with carbon atoms joined in a string or ring

**alien** *adjective* **1.** COMPUT different or not fitting the usual system **2.** BIOL not native to an area, but introduced by people ○ *A fifth of the area of the national park is under alien conifers.* ○ *Alien species, introduced by settlers as domestic animals, have brought about the extinction of some endemic species.* ■ *noun* BIOL an alien organism or species

**alight** *adjective* burning ○ *The forest fire was still alight after two days.*

**align** *verb* **1.** to position something along an axis or line **2.** to add spaces between words in a line to make sure that the line of text fills the whole line and that the column or page has straight sides **3.** to set something in a correct position in relation to something else ○ *Aligned white marks on the wheel and tyre indicate that there is no creep.*

**aligner** *noun* COMPUT a device used to make sure that the paper is straight in a printer

**alignment** *noun* **1.** the positioning of something along an axis or line **2.** the setting of something in a correct position in relation to something else □ **to check the alignment of something** to make sure something is in the correct position □ **in alignment** correctly aligned

**alignment pin** *noun* ENG a peg that fits in a hole to ensure that two devices are correctly positioned in relation to each other

**alimentary canal** *noun* ANAT a tube in the body going from the mouth to the anus, including the throat, stomach and intestines, through which food passes and is digested

**alimentation** *noun* BIOL feeding

**aliphatic** *adjective* CHEM referring to organic compounds that have carbon atoms joined in a string (**open chain**)

**aliphatic hydrocarbon** *noun* CHEM a hydrocarbon compound that does not contain benzene. Compare **aromatic compound**

**alive** *adjective* not dead ○ *The patient was still alive but in a coma.*

**alkali** *noun* CHEM a substance which reacts with an acid to form a salt and water. It may be either a soluble base or a solution of a base that has a pH value

of more than 7. (NOTE: The plural is **alkalis**; an alternative US plural is **alkalies**.)

**alkali metal** *noun* CHEM ELEM an element in group 1 of the periodic table, all of which are silver-coloured, soft and react with water (NOTE: The metals are lithium, sodium, potassium, rubidium, caesium and francium.)

**alkaline** *adjective* CHEM containing more alkali than acid and having a pH value of more than 7

**alkaline-earth metal** *noun* CHEM ELEM a metallic element in group 2 of the periodic table, with a valency of two (NOTE: The metals are beryllium, magnesium, calcium, strontium, barium and radium.)

**alkalinity** *noun* CHEM the amount of alkali in something such as soil, water or a body ○ *Hyperventilation causes fluctuating carbon dioxide levels in the blood, resulting in an increase of blood alkalinity.*

COMMENT: Alkalinity and acidity are measured according to the pH scale. pH7 is neutral, and pH8 and upwards are alkaline. Alkaline solutions are used to counteract the effects of acid poisoning and also of bee stings. If a strong alkali such as ammonia is swallowed, the patient should drink water and an acid such as orange juice.

**alkaloid** *adjective* BIOL similar to an alkali ■ *noun* BIOCHEM one of many poisonous substances found in plants which use them as a defence against herbivores (NOTE: Many alkaloids such as atropine, morphine or quinine are also useful as medicines.)

**alkalosis** *noun* MED an unusually high alkalinity in the blood or other body fluids

**alkane** *noun* CHEM a hydrocarbon containing carbon-to-carbon or carbon-to-hydrogen single bonds only, belonging to a series with the general chemical formula $C_nH_{2n+2}$

**alkene** *noun* CHEM a hydrocarbon containing one carbon-to-carbon double bond, belonging to a series with the general chemical formula $C_nH_{2n}$

**alkyl benzenesulfonate, alkyl benzenesulphonate** *noun* CHEM a surface-acting agent used in detergents, which is not biodegradable and creates large amounts of foam in sewers and rivers

**alkyl group** *noun* CHEM a group created by removing a hydrogen atom from an aliphatic hydrocarbon such as an alkane

**alkyl halide** *noun* CHEM an organic compound created by replacing one or more hydrogen atoms in an alkane with halogen atoms

**alkyne** *noun* CHEM an open-chain hydrocarbon in which there is one carbon-to-carbon triple bond, belonging to a series whose members all have the same general chemical formula. Formula: $C_nH_{2n-2}$.

**allantois** *noun* ANAT a sac found in the embryos of mammals, birds and reptiles (NOTE: In mammals, it combines with the chorion to form the placenta and umbilical cord.)

**allele** *noun* GENETICS one of two or more alternative forms of a gene, situated in the same area (**locus**) on paired chromosomes and controlling the inheritance of the same characteristic

**allelomorph** *noun* GENETICS same as **allele**

**allelopathy** *noun* ECOL the release by one plant of a chemical substance that restricts the germination or growth of another plant

**allergen** *noun* MED a substance which produces hypersensitivity

COMMENT: Allergens are usually proteins, and include foods, dust and hair of animals, as well as pollen from flowers. Allergic reaction to serum is known as anaphylaxis. Treatment of allergies depends on correctly identifying the allergen to which the patient is sensitive. This is done by patch tests in which drops of different allergens are placed on scratches in the skin. Food allergens discovered in this way can be avoided, but other allergens (such as dust and pollen) can hardly be avoided and have to be treated by a course of desensitising injections.

**allergenic** *adjective* MED producing an allergy ○ *the allergenic properties of fungal spores*

**allergenic agent** *noun* MED a substance which produces an allergy

**allergic** *adjective* MED affected by an allergy ○ *She is allergic to cats.* ○ *I'm allergic to penicillin.*

**allergic agent** *noun* MED same as **allergenic agent**

**allergic reaction** *noun* MED an effect such as a skin rash or sneezing produced by a substance to which a person has an allergy ○ *He showed an allergic reaction to chocolate.*

**allergy** *noun* MED a sensitivity to substances such as pollen or dust, which cause a physical reaction ○ *She has an allergy to household dust.* ○ *He has a penicillin allergy.*

**alleviate** *verb* to reduce or lessen the harmful effect of something ○ *Anti-icing additives are available to alleviate the problem of icing up.*

**alleviation** *noun* a reduction or lessening of the harmful effect of something ○ *Deep regular breathing may provide some alleviation from stress.*

**allo-** *prefix* different

**allocate** *verb* **1.** to provide something for a particular purpose ○ *Research grants are allocated to both large and small projects.* **2.** COMPUT to divide a period of time or a piece of work in various ways and share it out between users ○ *The operating system allocated most of main memory to the spreadsheet program.*

**allocation** *noun* **1.** the provision of something for a particular purpose ○ *the allocation of assignments to students.* **2.** COMPUT the dividing of memory, disk space, printer use, program or operating system time or a device in various ways

**allogamy** *noun* BOT fertilisation by pollen from different flowers or from flowers of genetically different plants of the same species

COMMENT: Some fruit trees are self-fertile, that is, they fertilise themselves with their own pollen. Others need pollinators that are usually different cultivars of the same species.

**allogenic succession** *noun* ECOL the establishment of different communities in a particular area as a result of external environmental factors such as climatic change

**allograft** *noun* MED a graft of tissue from one individual to another of the same species

**allopatric** *adjective* ECOL referring to plants of the same species which grow in different parts of the world and so do not cross-breed

**allophone** *noun* ACOUSTICS the smallest unit of sound from which speech can be formed. ♦ **phoneme**

**allotrope** *noun* CHEM one of many forms in which a chemical element can occur, each with differing physical properties (NOTE: For example, diamonds, graphite and coal are allotropes of carbon.)

**allotropy** *noun* CHEM the existence of different structural forms of an element

**allow** *verb* to enable, permit or authorise something ○ *An engine should be run at low rpm after flight to allow engine components to cool.* ○ *We will allow more time for the report to be presented.* □ **to allow for** to make something available or take something into consideration ○ *The schedule does not allow for delays.*

**allowable** *adjective* permitted ○ *maximum allowable tyre pressure*

**allowance** *noun* **1.** a consideration for possibilities or changing circumstances □ **to make allowances for** to take something into account **2.** something which is allowed

**alloy** *noun* a metal such as brass made from a compound of two or more metallic elements

COMMENT: Many metals have practical disadvantages in the pure state and alloys have been developed to make the best use of their advantages.

**all-terrain vehicle** *noun* AUTOMOT a vehicle which can be driven over all types of land surface

**alluvial** *adjective* EARTH SCI referring to alluvium

**alluvial deposits** *plural noun* EARTH SCI deposits of silt on the bed of a river or lake

**alluvial fan** *noun* EARTH SCI a fan-shaped deposit of sediment built up by a river where the slope of the bed becomes less sharp

**alluvial flat** *noun* EARTH SCI a flat area along a river where silt is deposited when the river floods

**alluvial mining** *noun* MIN EXTRACT the extraction of minerals from alluvial deposits, e.g. panning for gold

**alluvial plain** *noun* EARTH SCI same as **alluvial flat**

**alluvial silt** *noun* EARTH SCI same as **alluvium**

**alluvial soils** *plural noun* EARTH SCI same as **alluvial deposits**

**alluvial terrace** *noun* EARTH SCI a flat plain left when a river cuts more deeply into the bottom of a valley

**alluvium** *noun* EARTH SCI silt deposited by rivers or by a lake

**allyl group** *noun* CHEM a group of unsaturated hydrocarbons with the general formula $CH_2{=}CHCH_2{-}$

**aloft** *adjective* up in the air ○ *A pressure gradient occurs aloft from land to sea.*

**alpha** *noun* **1.** COMPUT the first working attempt of a computer product ○ *The new software is still in an alpha product stage.* **2.** COMPUT data that defines the properties of a pixel or part of an image **3.** the first letter of the Greek alphabet

**alphabet** *noun* COMPUT the 26 letters used to make words

**alpha beta technique** *noun* COMPUT a technique used in artificial intelligence for solving game and strategy problems

**alphabetically** *adverb* in alphabetical order ○ *The files are arranged alphabetically under the customer's name.*

**alphabetical order** *noun* COMPUT the arrangement of words or records such as files and index cards in the order of the letters of the alphabet

**alphabetic character set** *noun* COMPUT the set of characters, both capitals and small letters, which make up the alphabet

**alphabetise, alphabetize** *verb* to put items into alphabetical order ○ *Enter the bibliographical information and then alphabetise it on author's name.*

**alpha blending** *noun* COMPUT control over the transparency of a graphical object, normally used to display complex graphical objects such as glass and water

**alpha cell** *noun* ANAT one of the types of cells in glands such as the pancreas which have more than one type of cell

**alpha decay** *noun* PHYS radioactive disintegration of a substance due to the emission of alpha particles

**alpha diversity** *noun* ECOL the number of species occurring in a small area

**alphageometric** *adjective* COMPUT referring to a set of codes that instruct a teletext terminal to display various graphics patterns or characters

**alphameric** *adjective US* COMPUT same as **alphanumeric**

**alphamosaic** *adjective* COMPUT referring to a character set used in teletext to provide alphanumeric and graphics characters

**alphanumeric** *adjective* COMPUT **1.** using both letters and numbers **2.** referring to data that includes letters and numbers

**alphanumeric string** *noun* COMPUT a series of alphanumeric characters that are manipulated and treated as a single unit

**alpha particle** *noun* PHYS a nucleus of the same composition as a helium atom with two protons and two neutrons (NOTE: It is emitted by the nuclei of some radioactive elements such as radon, and when emitted will pass through gas but not through solids.)

**alpha-particle sensitivity** *noun* COMPUT a problem experienced by some electronic memory devices that will lose data stored in them when exposed to alpha radiation

**alpha radiation** *noun* PHYS radiation by alpha particles from radioactive nuclei

**alpha ray** *noun* PHYS a stream of alpha particles

**alphasort** *verb* COMPUT to sort information into alphabetical order

**alpha waste** *noun* PHYS radioactive waste emitting alpha particles

**Alphonsine Tables** *plural noun* ASTRON a book of tables of astronomical data, mainly planetary positions, published at Toledo, Spain, in 1273 and used throughout the Middle Ages in Europe

**alpine** *adjective* EARTH SCI referring to the Alps, or to other high mountains

**alpine pasture** *noun* AGRIC the grass fields in high mountains which are used by cattle farmers in the summer

**alpine plant** *noun* BOT a plant which grows on or comes originally from high mountains ○ *Alpine vegetation grows above the tree line.*

**alt** *noun* COMPUT a type of newsgroup on the Internet that contains discussions about alternative subjects

COMMENT: Alt newsgroups are not official newsgroups and are not supported or monitored by any company. Some online service providers do not allow their subscribers to view all the newsgroups because they may contain offensive and pornographic material.

**alter** *verb* to modify something and make it different ○ *The rudder linkage was altered to comply with certification requirements.* □ **to alter course** to change to a different route

**alterable** *adjective* COMPUT which can be altered

**alteration** *noun* **1.** a modification ○ *It was discovered that alterations had been made to the log book.* ○ *As a result of the accident, alterations were made to the design of the system.* **2.** the making of a modification

**alternate** COMPUT *verb* to change from one state to another and back, over and over again ■ *adjective* **1.** changing from one to another **2.** every other ○ *A, c, e and g are alternate letters as are b, d, f and h*

**alternately** *adverb* COMPUT so as to change from one to the other

**alternate mode** *noun* COMPUT an application for multi-user use, where two operators can access and share a single file at the same time

**alternate route** *noun* COMPUT a backup path in a communications system, used in case of a fault or breakdown

**alternating current** *noun* ELEC electric current whose value varies with time in a regular sinusoidal way, changing the direction of flow each half cycle. Abbreviation **AC**

COMMENT: The mains electricity supply uses alternating current to minimise transmission power loss, with a frequency of 50Hz in the UK and 60Hz in the US

**alternation** *noun* COMPUT a logical function that produces a true output if any input is true

**alternative** *noun* something which can be done instead of something else ○ *What is the alternative to re-keying all the data?* □ **we have no alternative** there is nothing else we can do ■ *adjective* **1.** COMPUT other or which can take the place of something **2.** different or not following the usual way ○ *searching for alternative sources of energy*

**alternative denial** *noun* COMPUT a logical function whose output is false if all inputs are true and true if any input is false

**alternative energy** *noun* INDUST the energy produced by tidal power, wind power, solar power etc rather than by fossil fuels or nuclear power

**alternative medicine** *noun* MED the treating of diseases and disorders with procedures and remedies, e.g. herbal medicines or acupuncture, which are not usually used by traditionally trained doctors

**alternative technology** *noun* INDUST the use of methods of producing energy which cause less pollution than fossil fuels and nuclear power, e.g. wind power, tidal power or solar power

**alternator** *noun* ELEC a device for producing alternating current electricity that can be driven by a motor, or by water or wind power

**alti-** *prefix* height

**altimeter** *noun* AEROSP a pressure or radio instrument for measuring vertical distance or altitude

**altimeter display** *noun* AEROSP an analogue or digital appearance of altitude information

**altimeter reading** *noun* AEROSP the altitude indicated by an altimeter

**altimeter setting** *noun* AEROSP an adjustment of the sub-scale of an altimeter to adjust the base level of the altimeter to seal level or another level

**Alt key** *noun* COMPUT a special key on the keyboard of a PC used to activate special functions in an application ○ *Press Alt and P at the same time to print your document.*

COMMENT: The Alt key has become the standard method of activating a menu bar in any software running on a PC. For example, Alt-F normally displays the File menu of a program, Alt-X normally exits the program.

**alto-** *prefix* moderate or high altitude

**altocumulus** *noun* METEOROL a layer of small white cumulus clouds at moderate altitude above 3000 m, usually meaning fair weather. Compare **stratocumulus**

**altostratus** *noun* METEOROL a high thin uniform cloud above 3000 m, usually seen as a front is approaching

**altruism** *noun* the behaviour by an animal that lessens its chances of survival or of producing offspring, but increases those chances for another individual of the same species

**ALU** *abbreviation* COMPUT arithmetic logic unit

**alum** *noun* CHEM a naturally occurring potassium aluminium sulfate used as a mordant in dyeing. Formula: $K_2SO_4.Al_2(SO_4)_3.24H_2O$.

**alumina** *noun* CHEM a white aluminium oxide used in catalysts, abrasives and the manufacture of artificial rubies and sapphires. Formula: $Al_2O_3$. (NOTE: It is extracted from corundum and bauxite.)

**aluminate** *noun* CHEM a salt of aluminium and a metal oxide

**aluminium** *noun* CHEM ELEM a metallic element extracted from the ore bauxite (NOTE: The chemical symbol is **Al**; the atomic number is **13** and the atomic weight is **26.98**.)

**aluminium chloride** *noun* CHEM a white crystalline material used in medicines, cosmetics, pigments and antiperspirants. Formula: $AlCl_3$ or $Al_2Cl_6$.

**aluminium hydroxide** *noun* CHEM a chemical substance used as an antacid to treat indigestion. Formula: $Al(OH)_3$.

**aluminium oxide** *noun* CHEM same as **alumina**

**aluminium sulfate, aluminium sulphate** *noun* CHEM a white crystalline material used in paper manufacture, textiles and water purification. Formula: $Al_2(SO_4)_3$.

**aluminous cement** *noun* **high-alumina cement, aluminous cement** INDUST cement made of bauxite and limestone, used because it resists heat

**alveoli** *plural noun* ANAT plural of **alveolus**

**alveolus** *noun* ANAT a thin-walled air sac that occurs in large numbers in each lung and allows oxygen to enter and carbon dioxide to leave the blood

**always on** *adjective* COMPUT referring to a feature of high-speed broadband communications devices in which the computer appears to be permanently connected to the net and you do not need to dial up a special number (NOTE: It is characteristic of cable modems and ADSL which link a computer to the Internet.)

**Am** *symbol* CHEM ELEM americium

**AM** *abbreviation* ELEC amplitude modulation

**amber** *noun* BIOL a yellow translucent fossil conifer resin, sometimes containing fossilised insects

**ambi-** *prefix* BIOL both

**ambient** *adjective* **1.** referring to normal background conditions **2.** referring to normal surrounding atmospheric conditions

**ambient noise** *noun* PHYS normal background noise that is present all the time, normally given a reference pressure level of 0.00002 pascal

**ambient quality standards** *plural noun* ENVIRON levels of acceptable clean air which a national body tries to enforce

**ambient temperature** *noun* ECOL the temperature of the air in which an organism lives

**ambiguity** *noun* something heard or seen which can be understood in more than one way, resulting in possible confusion

**ambiguity error** *noun* an error due to incorrect selection of ambiguous data

**ambiguous** *adjective* referring to ambiguity (NOTE: For example, the term 'current flow' is ambiguous because it can be understood in two ways: 'electrical flow' or 'flow at the present time')

**ameba** *noun* MICROBIOL another spelling of **amoeba**

**amelioration** *noun* an improvement, or the process of improving

**amend** *verb* to update or correct a document or procedure

**amendment** *noun* a change, updating, improvement or correction to a document or procedure, etc.

**amendment record** *noun* COMPUT a record containing new information used to update a master record or file

**amenity** *noun* ENVIRON **1.** the pleasantness of your surroundings **2.** something which makes your surroundings more pleasant, e.g. a park, swimming pool or sports centre

**amenity society** *noun* ENVIRON a group of people dedicated to the protection and improvement of their local surroundings

**American National Standards Institute** *noun* COMPUT an organisation which specifies computer and software standards including those that define network standards and high-level programming languages. Abbreviation **ANSI**

**American Standard Code for Information Interchange** *noun* COMPUT a code which represents alphanumeric characters as binary codes. Abbreviation **ASCII**

**americium** *noun* CHEM ELEM an artificial radioactive element (NOTE: The chemical symbol is **Am**; the atomic number is **95** and the atomic weight is **243**.)

**amide group** *noun* CHEM a group of organic compounds in which one of the hydrogen atoms of an ammonia structure $NH_3$ is replaced by an acyl group -RCO

**amine** *noun* CHEM any organic derivative of ammonia in which one or more hydrogen atoms is replaced with an alkyl group

**amino acid** *noun* BIOCHEM a chemical compound which is broken down from proteins in the digestive system and then used by the body to form its own protein ○ *Proteins are first broken down into amino acids.*

COMMENT: Amino acids all contain carbon, hydrogen, nitrogen and oxygen, as well as other elements. Some amino acids are produced in the body itself, but others have to be absorbed from food. The eight essential amino acids are: isoleucine, leucine, lysine, methionine, phenylalanine, threonine, tryptophan and valine.

**amino group** *noun* CHEM a group of compounds with the basic chemical structure $-NH_2$

**amitosis** *noun* BIOL multiplication of a cell by splitting the nucleus

**ammeter** *noun* ELEC an instrument for measuring current flowing in a circuit

**ammonia** *noun* CHEM a gas with an unpleasant smell that is easily soluble in water. Formula: $NH_3$.

**ammonia-soda process** *noun* CHEM ◊ **Solvay process**

**ammonia water** *noun* CHEM a solution of ammonia in water. Formula: NH₄OH.

**ammonification** *noun* CHEM the treatment or impregnation of something with ammonia

**ammonium** *noun* CHEM an ion formed from ammonia

**ammonium carbonate** *noun* CHEM a white crystalline material which is a component of smelling salts and baking powder. Formula: $(NH_4)_2CO_3$.

**ammonium chloride** *noun* CHEM a white crystalline material used in cough medicines, soldering flux and batteries. Formula: $NH_4Cl$.

**ammonium fixation** *noun* CHEM the absorption of ammonium ions by the soil

**ammonium ion** *noun* CHEM a positively charged ion formed from a reaction of ammonia with a hydrogen ion. Formula: $NH_4^+$.

**ammonium nitrate** *noun* CHEM a popular fertiliser used as top dressing (NOTE: It is available in a special prilled or granular form, and can be used both as a straight fertiliser and in compounds.)

**ammonium phosphate** *noun* AGRIC a fertiliser which can be used straight, but is more often used in compounds (NOTE: Applications may increase the acidity of the soil.)

**ammonium sulfate, ammonium sulphate** *noun* CHEM a colourless crystalline solid that is soluble in water, used as a fertiliser. Formula: $(NH_4)_2SO_4$. Also called **sulfate of ammonia**

**amniocentesis** *noun* MED a test to determine the health, sex, or genetic constitution of a foetus performed by removing a sample of amniotic fluid through a needle inserted into the mother's womb

**amnion** *noun* BIOL the inner of two membranes that enclose an embryo and surrounding fluid of a bird, reptile or mammal

**amniote** *noun* ZOOL a vertebrate that develops from an embryo that is contained within an amnion, e.g. a bird, reptile or mammal

**amniotic fluid** *noun* ANAT the fluid that surrounds and protects a foetus (NOTE: It flows out through the vagina before a baby is born.)

**amoeba** *noun* MICROBIOL a single-celled organism found in water, wet soil, or as a parasite of other organisms. Genus: *Amoeba*. (NOTE: An amoeba consists of a shapeless protoplasmic mass enclosed by a flexible membrane and forms temporary projections (**pseudopodia**) in order to move. Plural is **amoebae**.)

**amoebiasis** *noun* MED an infection caused by an amoeba, which can result in amoebic dysentery in the large intestine **intestinal amoebiasis** and can sometimes infect the lungs **pulmonary amoebiasis**

**amoebic** *adjective* MICROBIOL referring to an amoeba

**amoebic dysentery** *noun* MED a mainly tropical form of dysentery caused by *Entamoeba histolytica* which enters the body through contaminated water or unwashed food

**amoebicide** *noun* CHEM a substance which kills amoebae

**amoebocyte** *noun* BIOL a cell that resembles an amoeba, especially in the way it moves and engulfs particles

**amorphous** *adjective* with no regular shape

**amount** *noun* a quantity of something ○ *What is the largest amount of data which can be processed in one hour?*

**amount to** *verb* **1.** to make a total ○ *The total keyboarded characters amount to ten million.* ○ *Rainfall in some areas only amounts to a few millimetres per annum.* **2.** to be equivalent to something ○ *The government's attitude amounts to a dismissal of the acid rain problem.*

**amp** *noun* MEASURE same as **ampere** (NOTE: usually used with figures: **a 13-amp fuse**)

**AMP** *noun* BIOCHEM a compound involved in chemical reactions that release large amounts of energy in the tissues of living organisms. Full form **adenosine monophosphate**

**amperage** *noun* EDUC the strength of an electric current expressed in amperes ○ *Measuring the amperage of a motor can give a rough estimate of the load on the motor.*

**ampere** *noun* ELEC, MEASURE in the SI system, the basic unit of electric current equal to a current between two parallel conductors in a vacuum that produces a force equal to $2 \times 10^{-7}$ newtons per metre ○ *Current flow is measured in amperes.*

**ampere-hour** *noun* MEASURE a measurement of electric current over time. Abbreviation **AH**

**ampersand** *noun* COMPUT printing sign (&) which represents 'and'

**amphetamine** *noun* PHARM a drug that stimulates the central nervous system, formerly used to treat depression and as an appetite suppressant

**Amphibia** *plural noun* ZOOL a class of egg-laying animals which live partly in water and partly on land and whose larvae live in water (NOTE: Amphibia include frogs, toads and newts.)

**amphibian** ZOOL *adjective* referring to an organism which lives both in water and on land ■ *noun* an animal which lives both in water and on land, e.g. a frog

**amphibious** *adjective* ZOOL referring to an animal which lives both in water and on land ■ *noun* a vehicle which can travel both on water and on land

**amphoteric** *adjective* CHEM able to react as an acid in the presence of a strong base or as a base in the presence of a strong acid

**amp-hour** *noun* ELEC, MEASURE same as **ampere-hour**

**ample** *adjective* plenty of ○ *During the course you will have ample opportunity or time to demonstrate your skill.*

**amplicon** *noun* GENETICS a fragment of nucleic acid that is the product of artificial large-scale reproduction of genetic material

**amplification** *noun* ACOUSTICS the output-to-input signal strength ratio ○ *Increase the amplification of the input signal.* ○ *The amplification is so high, the signal is distorting.*

**amplified fragment length polymorphism** *noun* BIOTECH a rapid method that uses the polymerase chain reaction technique to detect variations in DNA sequences between individuals. Abbreviation **AFLP**

**amplifier** *noun* ELEC an electronic circuit that increases the power of a signal

**amplify** *verb* ELEC to increase the strength of an electrical signal ○ *An electric current is amplified and then transmitted.* (NOTE: **amplifying – amplifies – amplified**)

**amplitude** *noun* PHYS a range of variation of the strength or size of a signal or quantity such as the height of a wave, the magnitude of a variable star, or any other measured amount

**amplitude modulation** *noun* ELEC a method of carrying data by varying the size of a carrier signal, which is of fixed frequency, according to the data

**ampoule, ampule** *noun* BIOL a small glass container, closed at the neck, used to contain sterile drugs for use in injections

**AMU** *abbreviation* PHYS, MEASURE atomic mass unit

**amyl-** *prefix* BIOCHEM starch

**amylase** *noun* BIOCHEM an enzyme which converts starch into maltose

**amyl group** *noun* CHEM a group of monovalent alkyls with the general formula $C_5H_{11}$-. Also called **pentyl group**

**amylopsin** *noun* BIOCHEM an enzyme which converts starch into maltose

**amylose** *noun* BIOCHEM a carbohydrate of starch

**an-, ana-** *prefix* without or lacking

**anabatic wind** *noun* METEOROL a stream of wind currents which are caused by solar heating of the land and rise up south-facing mountainsides. Compare **katabatic wind**

**anabolic** *adjective* BIOCHEM referring to a substance which synthesises protein

**anabolic steroid** *noun* BIOCHEM a steroid hormone which promotes tissue growth

**anabolism** *noun* BIOCHEM the process of building up complex chemical substances on the basis of simpler ones

**anadromous** *adjective* MARINE BIOL referring to a species of fish which hatches in fresh water and becomes adult in salt water. Compare **catadromous**

**anadromy** *noun* MARINE BIOL a form of migration of fish such as salmon which are hatched in fresh water, migrate to the sea and then return to fresh water to spawn. Compare **catadromy**

**anaemia** *noun* MED a condition where the level of red blood cells is less than normal or where the haemoglobin is reduced, making it more difficult for the blood to carry oxygen (NOTE: the US spelling is **anemia**.)

**anaemic** *adjective* MED affected by anaemia (NOTE: The US spelling is **anemic**.)

**anaerobe** *noun* MICROBIOL a microorganism which lives without oxygen, e.g. the tetanus bacillus

**anaerobic** *adjective* BIOCHEM not needing oxygen for existence. Opposite **aerobic**

**anaerobic decomposition** *noun* BIOCHEM the breakdown of organic material by microorganisms without the presence of oxygen

**anaerobic digester** *noun* ENVIRON a digester which operates without oxygen ○ *Anaerobic digesters can be used to convert cattle manure into gas.*

COMMENT: Anaerobic digesters for pig, cattle and poultry waste feed the waste into a tank where it breaks down biologically without the presence of oxygen to give off large amounts of methane. This gas is then used to generate electricity. The remaining slurry can be applied directly to the land.

**anaerobic digestion** *noun* BIOCHEM the breakdown of organic material without the presence of oxygen, a process which permanently removes the unpleasant smell of many organic wastes so that they can be used on agricultural land

**anaerobic respiration** *noun* BIOCHEM the series of biochemical processes which lead to the formation of ATP without oxygen

**anaerobiosis** *noun* BIOCHEM a biological activity which occurs without the presence of oxygen

**anaesthesia** *noun* **1.** BIOL the loss of the feeling of pain **2.** MED the inducing of loss of the feeling of pain using anaesthetics (NOTE: the US spelling is **anesthesia**.)

**anaesthetic** *adjective* BIOL producing a loss of feeling ■ *noun* MED a substance given to a patient to suppress feeling before an operation (NOTE: The US spelling is **anesthetic**.)

**anaesthetic induction** *noun* MED the process of inducing anaesthesia in a patient

**anaesthetic risk** *noun* MED the risk that an anaesthetic may cause serious unwanted side effects

**analgesia** *noun* MED a reduction of the feeling of pain without loss of consciousness

**analgesic** *adjective* BIOL referring to analgesia ■ *noun* PHARM a painkilling drug which produces analgesia and reduces pyrexia

COMMENT: There are two types of analgesic: non-opioid, e.g. paracetamol and aspirin (acetylsalicylic acid), and opioid e.g. codeine phosphate. Opioid analgesics are used for severe pain relief in terminal care, as cough suppressants and to reduce gut motility in cases of diarrhoea. Analgesics are commonly used as local anaesthetics, e.g. in dentistry.

**analog** *noun* TECH a representation and measurement of numerical data by continuously variable physical quantities such as the size of electrical voltages. Compare **digital**

**analog computer** *noun* COMPUT a computer which processes data in analog form rather than digital form

**analog data** *noun* COMPUT data that is represented as a continuously variable signal (NOTE: Speech is a form of analog data.)

**analog display** *noun* COMPUT a screen that can display an infinite range of colours or shades of grey (NOTE: VGA monitors are a form of analog display. Digital displays can only display a finite range of colours.)

**analog gate** *noun* COMPUT a logic gate whose output is proportional to an input signal

**analog input card** *noun* COMPUT a card containing all the circuitry on one PCB required for amplifying and converting analog input signals to a digital form

**analogous** *adjective* similar ○ *Isobars are analogous to contour lines.*

**analog signal** *noun* COMPUT a continuously varying signal

**analog to digital** *noun* COMPUT the process of changing from an analog form to a digitally coded form. Abbreviation **A to D, A/D**

**analogue** *adjective* **1.** TECH another spelling of **analog 2.** ELEC □ **analogue display** a traditional hands and face display on a clock. Compare

**analyse** *verb* **1.** to examine something in detail ○ *We'll need to analyse the effect of the new reporting procedures.* **2.**

to separate a substance into its parts ○ *The laboratory is analysing the soil samples.* ○ *When the water sample was analysed it was found to contain traces of bacteria.*

**analyser** *noun* a machine which analyses blood or tissue samples automatically

**analysis** *noun* **1.** the process of examining something in detail **2.** the process of breaking down a substance into its parts in order to study them closely ○ *Samples of material were removed for analysis.*

**analyst** *noun* **1.** a person who examines samples of substances to find out what they are made of ○ *a health and safety analyst* **2.** a person who carries out a study of a problem

**analytical engine** *noun* COMPUT a mechanical calculating machine developed by Charles Babbage in 1833 which is generally considered the first general-purpose digital computer

**analyze** *verb* US spelling of **analyse**

**analyzer** *noun* US spelling of **analyser**

**anamorphic** *adjective* OPTICS referring to an image that has unequal vertical and horizontal scaling, making it appear squashed or taller than the original

**anaphase** *noun* BIOL a stage in cell division, after the metaphase and before the telophase

**anastomosis** *noun* BIOL a connection made between two vessels or two tubes, either naturally or by surgery

**anatomical** *adjective* ANAT referring to anatomy ○ *the anatomical features of a foetus*

**anatomy** *noun* **1.** ANAT the inner structure of the body of an animal or plant ○ *human anatomy* **2.** BIOL the scientific study of the structure of the body ○ *a degree in anatomy* **3.** the description of the structure and shape of a particular part ○ *the anatomy of a bone or leaf*

**ANC** *abbreviation* CHEM acid-neutralising capacity

**ancestral file** *noun* COMPUT a hierarchical system of backing up files as in son to father to grandfather file, where the son is the current working file

**anchor cell** *noun* COMPUT a cell in a spreadsheet program that defines the start of a range of cells

**ancient woodland** *noun* BOT a wooded area which has been covered with trees for many hundreds of years

**ancillary equipment** *noun* COMPUT equipment which is used to make a task easier, but which is not absolutely necessary

**AND circuit, AND element** *noun* MATHS ▸ **AND gate**

**AND element** *noun* COMPUT same as **AND gate**

**AND function** *noun* MATHS a logical function whose output is true if both its inputs are true

COMMENT: If both inputs are 1, results of the AND will be 1. If one of the input digits is 0, then AND will produce a 0.

**AND gate** *noun* ELECTRONICS an electronic gate that performs a logical AND function on electrical signals. Also called **AND circuit, AND element**

**androecium** *noun* BOT the male parts of a flower, consisting of the stamens

**androgen** *noun* BIOCHEM a male sex hormone that promotes the development of male secondary sexual characteristics (NOTE: Testosterone is an androgen.)

**anechoic** *adjective* ACOUSTICS not having or producing echoes

**anechoic chamber** *noun* ACOUSTICS a completely quiet room in which sound or radio waves do not reflect off the walls

**anemia** *noun* MED US spelling of **anaemia**

**anemic** *adjective* MED US spelling of **anaemic**

**anemograph** *noun* an instrument which maintains a continuous recording of wind direction and speed on a graph ○ *The anemograph gives a continuous recording of wind velocity which is displayed on a chart and reveals the pattern of gusts, squalls and lulls.*

**anemometer** *noun* METEOROL an instrument, usually attached to a building, which provides wind-speed information

COMMENT: An anemometer is formed of four cups at the ends of the arms of a crosspiece, which is mounted horizontally on a pivot and turns round as the wind blows. It can be linked to an anemograph, which records the wind speed on a roll of paper.

**anergy** noun **1.** BIOL the state of being weak or lacking energy **2.** PHYSIOL a lack of immunity

**aneroid barometer** noun METEOROL a barometer with a vacuum to which a diaphragm is attached, which moves as the atmospheric pressure changes

**aneroid capsule** noun METEOROL a thin flexible cylindrical box, usually made of metal, which has most of the air removed from it and which expands and contracts with changes in atmospheric pressure ○ *A decrease in atmospheric pressure will allow the aneroid capsule to expand.*

**aneroid switch** noun ENG a switch operated by an aneroid capsule

**anesthesia** noun BIOL, MED US spelling of **anaesthesia**

**anesthetic** adjective, noun BIOL, MED US spelling of **anaesthetic**

**aneuploid** adjective GENETICS referring to a cell or organism with fewer or more chromosomes than usual for its type

**aneurine** noun BIOL same as **thiamine**

**angiosperm** noun BOT a plant in which the sex organs are carried within the flowers and the seeds are enclosed in a fruit. Compare **gymnosperm**

**angle** noun MATHS the difference in direction between two lines or surfaces measured in degrees

**angle of incidence** noun PHYS, MATHS the angle that a ray or other beam makes with the normal or line perpendicular to a surface which is strikes

**angle of reflection** noun PHYS, MATHS the angle of a reflected ray or other beam with the normal line perpendicular to a surface from which it is reflected

**angle of refraction** noun PHYS, MATHS the angle of a refracted or absorbed ray or other beam with the normal line perpendicular to a surface which it has refracted

**angstrom** noun MEASURE, PHYS a unit of measurement used especially for wavelengths of light and equal to one ten billionth of a metre (NOTE: The angstrom is not an SI unit and is falling out of official scientific favour.)

**angular** adjective referring to an angle, or forming an angle ○ *The angular difference between the direction of magnetic north and compass north is called variation.*

**angular measure** noun MATHS the measurement of angles, commonly by dividing a complete circle into 360 degrees, with each degree divided into 60 minutes and each minute into 60 seconds

**angular momentum** noun PHYS a momentum a body possesses as the result of circular or other angular motion (NOTE: In astronomy it is usually encountered when considering objects in orbit.)

**angular velocity** noun PHYS the velocity of a body in its orbit, or other angular motion, measured either in distance per unit time (kilometres per second) or angle per unit time (degrees per second)

**anhydride** noun CHEM a compound formed by the removal of water from another compound

**anhydrite** noun MINERALS a colourless or lightly tinted anhydrous calcium sulfate mineral used in the manufacture of cement and fertilisers

**anhydrous** adjective CHEM referring to a compound or crystal that contains no water

**anhydrous alcohol** noun CHEM same as **absolute alcohol**

**aniline** noun CHEM a colourless oily liquid that is poisonous and is aromatic in structure. Formula: $C_6H_5NH_2$. (NOTE: It is used in the manufacture of dyes, resin, pharmaceuticals and explosives.)

**animal** ZOOL adjective referring to organisms which can feel sensations and move voluntarily ■ noun an organism which can feel sensations and move voluntarily

**animal ecology** noun ECOL the study of the relationship between animals and their environment

**animal husbandry** noun AGRIC the process of breeding and looking after farm animals

**animated GIF** noun COMPUT a simple animation effect created by saving several small graphic images within one file so that they can be repeatedly displayed in sequence giving an impression of animation (NOTE: It is often used to create animated buttons or other effects on a webpage.)

**animation** *noun* COMPUT the creation of the illusion of movement by displaying a series of slightly different images on screen (NOTE: The images are displayed very rapidly to give the effect of smooth movement.)

**anion** *noun* CHEM an ion with a negative electric charge

**anisotropic** *adjective* CHEM referring to something with physical properties which are different according to direction, e.g. non-symmetrical crystals with different dimensions or refractive indices along each of two or more axes

**ankylose** *verb* PHYSIOL (*of bones*) to fuse together

**anneal** *verb* INDUST to heat something and allow it to cool slowly in order to strengthen it ○ *Sheet and plate magnesium are annealed at the rolling mill.*

**annelid** *noun* ZOOL an invertebrate organism with a flat segmented body. Phylum: Anelida. (NOTE: Earthworms and leeches are annelids.)

**annihilation** *noun* PHYS the process in which a particle reacts with its antiparticle, destroying both and releasing energy in the form of radiation or other particles

**annual** *adjective* **1.** happening or done once a year **2.** over a period of one year ○ *Overload operations should not exceed 5% of annual departures.* ■ *noun* a plant whose life cycle of germination, flowering and fruiting takes place within the period of a year

**annual inspection** *noun* a yearly inspection

**annual ring** *noun* BOT a ring of new wood formed each year in the trunk of a tree and which can easily be seen when the tree is cut down

COMMENT: As a tree grows, the wood formed in the spring has more open cells than that formed in later summer. The difference in texture forms the visible rings. In tropical countries, trees grow all the year round and so do not form rings.

**annular** *adjective* shaped like a ring ○ *Annular inner and outer air casings form a tunnel around the spine of the engine.*

**annulus** *noun* a ring, or a structure shaped like a ring

**annunciation** *noun* an announcement or indication on an annunciator

**annunciator, annunciator panel** *noun* ELEC a device which gives off a sound or light as a warning or to indicate if something is active

**anode** *noun* a positive electrical terminal of a device. Opposite **cathode**

**anodise** *verb* CHEM to coat or cover something by using electrolysis ○ *Anti-corrosion treatment includes chromic acid anodising of aluminium parts.*

**anomalistic year** *noun* TIME a year measured by the time the Earth takes to revisit the apses of its orbit, and equal to 365.26 days

**anomalous** *adjective* referring to something departing from the expected order or range ○ *an anomalous instrument reading* ○ *an anomalous result*

**anomaly** *noun* something which departs from the expected order or range ○ *Any anomalies in the localiser will be detected during calibration.*

**anonymous FTP** *noun* COMPUT a method commonly used on the Internet that allows a user to connect to a remote computer using the FTP protocol and log in as a guest to download publicly accessible files (NOTE: If you are using the FTP protocol to connect to a remote computer and you are asked for a log-in name and password, you can normally gain access to the remote computer's public areas by entering 'anonymous' as the log-in user name and your full email address as the password.)

**Anopheles** *noun* BIOL a mosquito which carries the malaria parasite

**anorthosite** *noun* GEOL a coarse-grained igneous rock formed at great depth that is widespread in the highlands of the Moon and is also found on Earth

**anoxia** *noun* PHYSIOL a complete lack of oxygen ○ *The investigation established that the cause of death was anoxia.*

**anoxic** *adjective* CHEM referring to water which lacks oxygen

**anoxybiosis** *noun* BIOL a biological activity occurring where there is a lack of oxygen

**ANSI** *abbreviation* COMPUT American National Standards Institute

**ANSI C** *noun* COMPUT a standard version of the C programming language

**ANSI driver** *noun* COMPUT a small resident software program that interprets ANSI screen control codes and controls the screen appropriately

**ANSI escape sequence** *noun* COMPUT a sequence of ANSI screen control characters that controls the colours and attributes of text on screen (NOTE: The sequence must begin with the ASCII character Esc (ASCII 27) and the character [ (ASCII 91).)

**answer** *noun* a reply or solution to a question ■ *verb* **1.** to reply or provide the solution to a question **2.** COMPUT to reply to a signal and set up a communications link ○ *The first modem originates the call and the second answers it.*

**antacid** *noun* BIOL a medicine or other substance which stops too much acid forming or alters the amount of acid in the stomach

**antagonist** *noun* **1.** ANAT a muscle which opposes another muscle in a movement **2.** a substance **3.** PHYSIOL a substance which acts through specific receptors to block the action of another substance, but which has no observable physiological effect itself ○ *Atropine is a cholinergic antagonist and blocks the effects of acetylcholine.*

**Antarctic** *adjective* GEOG referring to the Antarctic ■ *noun* EARTH SCI a continent at the South Pole, largely covered with snow and ice

**Antarctica** *noun* GEOG an area of land around the South Pole

**Antarctic air** *noun* METEOROL a mass of cold air which is permanently over the Antarctic region

**Antarctic Circle** *noun* GEOG a parallel running round the Earth at latitude 66°32′S, to the south of which lies the Antarctic region

**ante-** *prefix* BIOL before

**antenna** *noun* **1.** *US* ZOOL one of a pair of long thin sensors on the heads of insects, crustaceans and some other arthropods **2.** TELECOM a radio or television aerial ○ *Long-range radars require a large antenna.* ○ *Possibly the largest single antenna is the huge dish at Arecibo in Puerto Rico.* (NOTE: The plural is **antennas** or **antennae**; **aerial** is preferred in UK English.)

**anterior** *adjective* BIOL situated in front □ **anterior aspect** viewed from the front ○ *the anterior aspect of part of the body* Opposite **posterior**

**anther** *noun* BOT a part of a stamen which produces pollen

**antheridium** *noun* BOT the male sex organ in algae, fungi, ferns and mosses

**anthocyanin** *noun* BIOCHEM a water-soluble plant pigment responsible for blue, violet and red colours

**anthracene** *noun* CHEM a crystalline material with an aromatic structure used in the manufacture of dyes and other organic chemicals. Formula: $C_{14}H_{10}$.

**anthracite** *noun* INDUST a type of shiny hard black coal which burns well and does not produce much smoke

**anthracosis** *noun* MED a disease of the lungs, caused by inhaling coal dust

**anthropic principle** *noun* ASTRON the idea that the universe is in its present form to allow life capable of observing it to evolve (NOTE: The principle is the opposite of the commonsense view that life arises as a result of the structure of the universe. It is controversial because it involves a cause, life, coming after the effect, the universe. Some cosmologists claim that it is wrong, unnecessary or unscientific. Others look at the coincidences which are necessary for intelligent life)

**anthropogenic** *adjective* ENVIRON caused by or resulting from human activities

**anthropomorphic software** *noun* COMPUT software that appears to react to what a user says

**anti-** *prefix* against or opposing

**anti-aliasing** *noun* COMPUT **1.** a method of reducing the effects of jagged edges in graphics by using shades of grey to blend in along edges **2.** the adding of sound signals between the sound samples to create a smoother sound

**antibacterial** *adjective* BIOL preventing or reducing the growth of bacteria

**antibacterial activity** *noun* BIOL an effective action against bacteria

**antibiotic** *adjective* BIOL preventing or reducing the growth of bacteria and fungi ■ *noun* PHARM a drug such as penicillin which was originally developed from fungi and which stops the spread of bacteria or fungi ○ *He was given a course of antibiotics.*

COMMENT: Penicillin is one of the commonest antibiotics, together with streptomycin, tetracycline and erythromycin. Although antibiotics are widely and successfully used, new forms of bacteria have developed which are resistant to them. They have no effectiveness against viruses.

**antibody** *noun* BIOCHEM a protein which is produced in the body in response to foreign substances such as bacteria or viruses ○ *Tests showed that he was antibody-positive.*

**anticaking additive, anticaking agent** *noun* FOOD INDUST an additive added to food to prevent it becoming solid (NOTE: Anticaking additives have the E numbers E530 – 578.)

**anticipate** *verb* to realise what may happen and do what is necessary in readiness

**anticipation** *noun* the process of realising what may happen and doing what is necessary in readiness

**anticline** *noun* GEOL (*in rock formations*) a fold where the newest layers of rock are on the surface. Compare **syncline**

**anticlockwise** *adjective, adverb* referring to a circular movement in the direction opposite to that in which the hands of a clock move ○ *Turn the nut anticlockwise to loosen it.* Opposite **clockwise**

**anticoagulant** *noun* PHARM a natural or synthetic agent that prevents the formation of blood clots

**anticodon** *noun* GENETICS (*in transfer RNA*) a set of three consecutive nucleotides in transfer RNA involved in the formation of a protein

**anticoincidence circuit, anticoincidence function** *noun* COMPUT a logical function whose output is true if either of two inputs is true, and false if both inputs are the same

**anti-corrosion** *adjective* METALL protecting against corrosion, especially rust ○ *an anti-corrosion treatment*

**anticyclone** *noun* METEOROL an area of high atmospheric pressure, usually associated with fine dry weather in summer and fog in winter (NOTE: Winds circulate round an anticyclone clockwise in the northern hemisphere and

anticlockwise in the southern hemisphere.)

**anticyclonic** *adjective* **1.** METEOROL referring to anticyclones **2.** EARTH SCI referring to the opposite direction to the rotation of the Earth

**anticyclonically** *adverb* METEOROL in the opposite direction to the rotation of the Earth

**anticyclonic gloom** *noun* METEOROL a period of grey weather during the daytime, when low stratocumulus clouds form at the approach of an anticyclone

**antidiuretic hormone** *noun* BIOCHEM same as **vasopressin**. abbreviation **ADH**

**antidote** *noun* PHARM a substance which counteracts the effect of a poison ○ *There is no satisfactory antidote to cyanide.*

**antifoam, anti-foaming agent** *noun* INDUST a chemical substance added to a detergent or to sewage to prevent foam from forming

**antifouling, antifouling paint** *noun* a special pesticide painted onto the bottom of a ship to prevent organisms growing on the hull (NOTE: It may be toxic enough to pollute sea water.)

**antifungal** *adjective* INDUST referring to a substance which kills or controls fungi

**antigen** *noun* BIOL a substance such as a virus or germ in the body which makes the body produce antibodies to attack it

**antigravity** *noun* PHYS a theoretical gravitational force in which mass repels rather than attracts other mass and radiation (NOTE: Although never observed, antigravity has a role in modern physics and cosmology, where whole 'antigravity universes' are postulated. On a smaller scale, some astronomical objects including Kerr black holes seem able to drive light away from them.)

**antihistamine** *noun* PHARM a drug used to control the effects of an allergy which releases histamine

**anti-icing** *adjective* preventing icing ○ *an anti-icing additive* ○ *anti-icing fluid*

**antilogarithm** *noun* MATHS a number whose logarithm is the given number (NOTE: For logarithm$_a$b = c, then antilogarithm$_a$c = b.)

**antimalarial** *adjective, noun* PHARM used to treat malaria

**antimatter** *noun* PHYS matter of the opposite charge, magnetic spin or other characteristic to the equivalent particles making up the bulk of the mass of the present universe (NOTE: Examples of antimatter include positrons, identical to electrons except for having a positive rather than negative electrical charge, and antiprotons, which are identical to protons except for having a negative rather than positive electrical charge. Little is known about why there is so little antimatter in the universe we see around us, but when matter and antimatter meet they annihilate each other with a release of energy.)

**antimony** *noun* CHEM ELEM a crystalline silvery-white element that is toxic and occurs in metallic and nonmetallic forms. It is used in alloys and semiconductors and found in ores, e.g. stibnite. (NOTE: The chemical symbol is **Sb**; the atomic number is **51** and the atomic weight is **121.75**.)

**antioncogene** *noun* GENETICS a recessive gene which is thought to suppress the growth of a cancer by limiting cell multiplication

**antioxidant** *noun* INDUST a substance which prevents oxidation, used to prevent materials such as rubber from deteriorating and added to processed food to prevent oil going bad (NOTE: In the EU, antioxidant food additives have numbers E300–321.)

**antiparticle** *noun* PHYS an elementary particle with the same mass as a corresponding particle but with opposite values for other properties (NOTE: When an antiparticle and its particle interact, mutual annihilation occurs.)

**antipodes** *plural noun* GEOG two points on opposite sides of the Earth

**antipollution** *adjective* ENVIRON intended to reduce or stop environmental pollution

**antiseptic** *adjective* BIOL preventing or reducing the growth of harmful microorganisms ○ *She gargled with an antiseptic mouthwash.* ■ *noun* PHARM a substance which prevents germs growing or spreading ○ *The nurse painted the wound with antiseptic.*

**antiserum** *noun* PHARM a serum taken from an animal which has developed antibodies to bacteria and is used to give temporary immunity to a disease (NOTE: The plural is **antisera**.)

**antistatic mat** *noun* COMPUT a special rubberised mat which dissipates static electricity charge through an electrical earth connection (NOTE: An operator touches the mat before handling sensitive electronic components which could be damaged by static electricity.)

**antitoxic serum** *noun* PHARM same as **antiserum**

**antitoxin** *noun* BIOL an antibody produced by the body to counteract a poison in the body

**antivenin, antivenene, antivenom** *noun* PHARM a serum which is used to counteract the poison from snake or insect bites

**anti-virus software** *noun* COMPUT software which removes a virus from a file

**antrum** *noun* ANAT a cavity inside the body, especially one in bone

**anus** *noun* ANAT the opening in the alimentary canal through which faeces are expelled

**anvil** *noun* a metal block which ends in a point, has a rounded bottom and a flat top, and on which metal objects such as horseshoes are made ○ *A cumulonimbus cloud has a characteristic anvil shape.*

**anvil cloud** *noun* METEOROL a cloud formation, in a dark cumulonimbus thundercloud, which has the shape of an anvil

**AOM** *abbreviation* ENVIRON active organic matter

**AONB** *abbreviation* ENVIRON Area of Outstanding Natural Beauty

**aorta** *noun* ANAT a large artery which takes blood away from the left side of the heart and carries it to other arteries

COMMENT: The aorta is a blood vessel which carries all arterial blood from the heart. It is about 45 cm long. It leaves the left ventricle, rises, at which point the carotid arteries branch off, then goes downwards through the abdomen and divides into the two iliac arteries.

**aortic** *adjective* ANAT referring to the aorta

**aortic valve** *noun* ANAT a valve with three flaps at the opening into the aorta

**apart** *adverb* away from one another

**apatite** *noun* MINERALS a glassy calcium phosphate mineral used in fertilisers and as a source of phosphorus

**aperture** *noun* **1.** PHOTOGRAPHY a lens diaphragm that allows the amount of light that reaches film to be regulated **2.** PHYS an opening in a device that allows a specific amount of light or a signal to pass through it

**aperture card** *noun* PHOTOGRAPHY a method of storing microfilmed information with a card surround, which can contain punched information

**aperture mask** *noun* PHYS a mask in colour monitors, used to keep separate the red, green and blue beams

**aperture synthesis** *noun* PHYS a process used mainly in radio astronomy whereby signals received by more than one telescope are combined mathematically to give the effect of using a single much larger one

**aphelion** *noun* ASTRON in the orbit of a planet, comet, or other astronomical object, the point that is farthest from the Sun

**aphid** *noun* BIOL a small insect such as blackfly or greenfly which sucks sap from plants and can multiply very rapidly ○ *The aphid population showed a 19% increase.*

COMMENT: Cereal aphids are various species of greenfly. Winged females feed on cereal crops in May and June. The grain aphid causes empty or small grain by puncturing the grain as it develops, letting the grain contents seep out. Aphids can carry virus diseases from infected plants to healthy plants.

**Aphis** *noun* ZOOL the genus of insects which comprises aphids

**aphotic zone** *noun* OCEANOG a region in a sea or lake below about 1500 m, so deep that sunlight cannot penetrate it

**API** *abbreviation* COMPUT application programming interface ○ *If I follow the published API for this system, my program will work properly.*

**apical meristem** *noun* BOT the actively dividing tissue at the tip of a shoot or root that produces the new tissue for growth

**API scale** *noun* MEASURE a scale of gravity or density of crude oil on which the heaviest oils have the lowest numbers

**APL** *noun* COMPUT a high-level programming language used in scientific and mathematical work. Full form **A programming language**

**APM** *noun* COMPUT a specification which allows an operating system such as earlier versions of Windows to control the power management features of a computer (NOTE: This standard has been replaced by the ACPI standard in Windows 98 and Windows NT 5.0.)

**apoenzyme** *noun* BIOCHEM the protein part of an enzyme that only becomes catalytically active after it combines with a nonprotein-supporting molecule (**coenzyme**)

**apogee** *noun* ASTRON the point in a satellite's orbit where it is most distant from the Earth (NOTE: For orbits around other objects, the terms aphelion, for the Sun, and apluna, for the Moon, are used.)

**apolipoprotein E** *noun* BIOCHEM a compound found in three forms which transports lipids within the cell and across cell membranes (NOTE: The genes for two of the forms are linked with an increased risk of Alzheimer's disease.)

**apomixis** *noun* BIOL a form of asexual reproduction in which embryos are formed from unfertilised eggs

**aponeurosis** *noun* ANAT a band of tissue which attaches muscles to each other

**aposematic coloration** *noun* ZOOL the natural brightly coloured markings on an animal warning predators that it is poisonous

**apparatus** *noun* equipment used in a laboratory or hospital ○ *The hospital has installed new apparatus in the physiotherapy department.* ○ *The blood sample was tested in a special piece of apparatus.* (NOTE: no plural: **a piece of apparatus; some new apparatus**)

**apparent** *adjective* **1.** clearly understood because of what our understanding or senses tell us ○ *It became apparent that carbon monoxide was entering the cabin.* **2.** appearing to be ○ *an apparent failure of the system*

**apparent magnitude** *noun* ASTRON the brightness of an object in the sky as seen from the Earth. Compare **absolute magnitude**

**APPC** *abbreviation* COMPUT advanced program to program communications

**appear** *verb* **1.** to be seen or to come into view ○ *The results will appear on the monitor.* **2.** to seem to be ○ *Although air may appear to be still, it is, in fact, moving.*

**appearance** *noun* **1.** an instance of being seen or coming into view ○ *the sudden appearance of a new variant of the disease* **2.** the way something looks ○ *had the appearance of fine hairs*

**append** *verb* COMPUT to add a file or data to an existing file or record ○ *If you enter the DOS command COPY A+B, the file B will be appended to the end of file A.*

**appendage** *noun* ANAT a body part or organ that projects from the main body, e.g. a tail, wing or fin

**appendicular skeleton** *noun* ANAT the part of the skeleton consisting of the pelvic girdle, pectoral girdle and the bones of the arms and legs

**appendix** *noun* a section at the back of a book, containing additional information ○ *For further details see the appendix.* ○ *A complete list is printed in the appendix.* (NOTE: The plural is **appendices**.)

**applet** *noun* COMPUT **1.** a small utility used to configure a computer ○ *There are applets to help format your disk and configure your keyboard.* **2.** a small application designed to enhance the functionality of a webpage, e.g. adding multimedia effects (NOTE: Applet originally referred to the icons in the Control Panel window within Microsoft Windows.)

**Appleton layer** *noun* METEOROL same as **F region**

**appliance** *noun* INDUST a device or instrument, especially an electrical one used in the home, e.g. a vacuum cleaner, washing machine or iron

**appliance computer** *noun* COMPUT a ready-to-run computer system that can be bought in a shop, taken home and used immediately for a particular purpose

**applicable** *adjective* **1.** relevant ○ *Rule 24 is not applicable in this case* **2.** suitable, necessary or appropriate ○ *Emergency systems are checked when applicable.*

**application** *noun* **1.** a formal request **2.** the act of putting a substance on a surface ○ *the application of a coat of paint* **3.** the act or instance of using an existing ability ○ *an application for reward funds* ○ *an application for an account on the university network* ○ *When an accident occurs, the application of knowledge and skills is important.* **4.** COMPUT a task which a computer performs or a problem which a computer solves

**application file** *noun* COMPUT a binary file stored on disk that contains the machine code instructions of a program

**application icon** *noun* COMPUT a small graphical symbol that represents an application program in a graphical user interface

**application layer** *noun* COMPUT the seventh and top layer in an ISO/OSI network, which allows a user to request functions such as transfer files, send mail and use resources (NOTE: The other layers are not normally accessed by users.)

**application-orientated language** *noun* COMPUT a programming language that provides functions which allow the user to solve specific application problems

**application program** *noun* COMPUT ♦ **application software**

**application programming interface** *noun* COMPUT a set of standard program functions and commands that allow any programmer to interface a program with another application ○ *If I follow the published API for this system, my program will work properly.* Abbreviation **API**

**application service provider** *noun* COMPUT a specialist company that installs, configures and manages software on its own server and then allows any business to use the software via the Internet or a private network (NOTE: The user does not realise that the software is located on a distant server, and the business does not need to buy or support the software, which is usually rented.)

**application software** *noun* COMPUT a program which is used by a user to make the computer do what is required, designed to allow a particular task to be performed ○ *The multi-window editor is* *used to create and edit applications programs.*

**application-specific integrated circuits** *plural noun* COMPUT specially designed ICs for one particular function or to special specifications. Abbreviation **ASIC**

**applicator** *noun* an instrument for applying a substance

**apply** *verb* **1.** to make a formal request for something ○ *You can apply for a research grant.* **2.** to put something on a surface ○ *to apply a coat of paint* ○ *Apply a plaster to the skin.* **3.** to use existing knowledge or skills ○ *Apply the same method as in the example.* **4.** (*of rules, regulations, orders, instructions, etc.*) to be relevant ○ *The rules which apply to the measurement of wind velocities on isobaric charts apply equally to contour charts.* (NOTE: **applying – applies – applied**)

**APPN** *noun* COMPUT an extension to the IBM SNA protocol which allows workstations to share information on a peer-to-peer basis without the need for a central mainframe. Full form **advanced peer-to-peer networking** (NOTE: It is often used to route information around a network and dynamically adjust the route if part of the network is damaged.)

**appreciable** *adjective* **1.** possible to measure ○ *Appreciable weakening may be permitted without risk of failure.* **2.** significantly large ○ *The shortfall is appreciable.*

**appreciate** *verb* **1.** to recognise the importance or significance of something ○ *The map reader is in a position to appreciate the relative values of the features seen on the ground.* **2.** to be thankful or grateful for something ○ *The students appreciated the extra help given by their instructor.* **3.** to increase in value ○ *The value of the building has appreciated by 100% in 10 years.*

**approach** *noun* **1.** a path towards something ○ *The approach to the site was blocked by an overturned lorry.* **2.** a way of achieving or doing something or dealing with a problem ○ *a radical approach to the problem of desertification* □ **to take a different approach to a situation** to deal with or manage a situation in a different way ■ *verb* to move nearer in place or time to something ○

*The aircraft is approaching a danger area.*

**appropriate** *adjective* suitable or necessary

**appropriate action** *noun* a suitable action demanded by the situation ○ *If you feel that safety standards are not being met, you will have to take appropriate action.*

**appropriately** *adverb* as appropriate or as needed

**appropriate technology** *noun* ENVIRON a technology that is suited to the local environment, usually involving skills or materials that are available locally ○ *Biomethanation is an appropriate technology for use in rural areas.*

**approval** *noun* agreement that something can be done ○ *The procedure needs official approval.*

**approve** *verb* to allow or give permission for something ○ *The air traffic controller approved the emergency landing.*

**approve of** *verb* to believe something to be right or good

**approx** *abbreviation* approximate *or* approximately

**approximate** *adjective* not exact □ **an approximate distance of 60 nm** about 60 nautical miles ■ *verb* to be close to ○ *The number of people working in the building approximates 2000.* (NOTE: can be shortened to: **approx**)

**approximately** *adverb* not exactly ○ *Approximately 2000 people work in the building.* (NOTE: can be shortened to: **approx**)

**approximating** *adjective* close by or similar to ○ *results approximating to the norm*

**approximation** *noun* a calculation which is not exact ○ *Can you give me an approximation of keyboarding time?* ○ *The final figure is only an approximation.*

**approximation error** *noun* an error caused by rounding off a real number

**appulse** *noun* ASTRON a close approach of two astronomical objects as seen from the Earth (NOTE: Their true distances apart in space may be very large even when they are almost aligned from the point of view of a terrestrial observer.)

**A programming language** *noun* COMPUT full form of **APL**

**apse** *noun* ASTRON a line joining the two foci of an ellipse such as the orbit of a planet or satellite and the nearest and farthest points of the ellipse itself

**APT** *noun* COMPUT a programming language used to control numerically controlled machines. Full form **automatically programmed tools**

**aquaculture, aquafarming** *noun* FISHERY the breeding and keeping of fish, shellfish or plants for food in special ponds

**aquaplaning** *noun* the act of sliding in an uncontrolled way over a thin layer of water on a road or runway

**aquarium** *noun* BIOL a container with water and a display of fish and other animals or plants that live in water

**aquatic** *adjective* referring to water

**aquatic animal** *noun* ZOOL an animal which lives in water

**aquatic ecosystem** *noun* ECOL an ecosystem such as a river, pond, lake or ocean that is based on water

**aqueous** *adjective* PHYS referring to a solution made with water

**aqueous humour** *noun* ANAT the clear watery fluid that circulates between the cornea and the lens of the eye

**aquiclude** *noun* GEOL a body of rock or soil, e.g. clay, through which water passes very slowly

**aquiculture** *noun* FISHERIES same as **aquaculture**

**aquifer** *noun* GEOL a body of porous rock or soil through which water passes and in which water gathers to supply wells

**Ar** *symbol* CHEM ELEM argon

**Arabic numeral, Arabic figure** *noun* COMPUT, MATHS a number such as 1, 2, 3 or 4, as opposed to the Roman numerals I, II, III or IV ○ *The page numbers are written in Arabic numerals.*

**arable** *adjective* AGRIC referring to land on which crops are grown

**arable farming** *noun* AGRIC the growing of crops, as opposed to dairy farming, cattle farming, etc.

**arable soil** *noun* AGRIC soil which is able to be used for the cultivation of crops

**arachidonic acid** *noun* BIOCHEM an essential fatty acid

**arachnid** *noun* ZOOL an animal with four pairs of legs and a body with two segments. Class: Arachnida. (NOTE: Spiders, scorpions and mites are arachnids.)

**arachnoid membrane** *noun* ANAT the middle of the three membranes that surround the brain and spinal cord of the vertebrate central nervous system

**aragonite** *noun* MINERALS a colourless, blue to violet, or yellow form of calcium carbonate

**arbitrary** *adjective* decided by chance rather than by careful logical thought ○ *an arbitrary unit of measurement*

**arbitration software** *noun* software that is responsible for allocating resources to devices, often used to manage the way Plug and Play adapters use other resources in a computer

**arboreal** *adjective* BOT referring to trees

**arboreal animal** *noun* ZOOL an animal which lives in trees

**arboretum** *noun* BOT a collection of trees from different parts of the world, grown for scientific study

**arboricide** *noun* AGRIC a chemical substance such as 2,4,5-T which kills trees

**arboriculture** *noun* FORESTRY the study of the cultivation of trees

**arborist** *noun* FORESTRY a person who studies the cultivation of trees

**arbovirus** *noun* MED a virus transmitted by blood-sucking insects

**arc** *noun* MATHS a part of the circumference of a circle, or the shape of this ○ *A nautical mile is the length of an arc on the Earth's surface subtended by an angle of one minute at the centre of the Earth.* ■ *verb* (*of a spark, especially one produced by an electric current*) to jump across a gap ○ *The spark arcs from one electrode to another.* ○ *The condenser prevents spark plugs from arcing.*

**Archie** *noun* COMPUT a system of servers on the Internet that catalogues the public files that are available

**archipelago** *noun* GEOG a group of islands

**architecture** *noun* COMPUT the layout and interconnection of a computer's internal hardware and the logical relationships between CPU, memory and I/O devices

**archival quality** *noun* COMPUT the length of time that a copy can be stored before it becomes illegible

**archive** COMPUT *noun* a store of data kept over a long period, usually in compressed form ■ *verb* to put data in storage

**archive attribute, archive bit** *noun* COMPUT a liquid that changes between two forms with different optical properties such as colour depending on variations in temperature or applied voltage (NOTE: It is used in visual display units.)

**archive file** *noun* COMPUT a file containing data which is out of date but which is kept for future reference

**archive flag** *noun* COMPUT same as **archive attribute**

**arc lamp** *noun* ELEC an intensely bright light produced by passing current through a gap between two electrodes used, e.g., in floodlights, spotlights on film sets and specialised laboratory lamps

**ARCNET, ARCnet** *noun* COMPUT a network hardware and cable standard developed by Datapoint Corporation. Full form **attached resource computer network** (NOTE: It is a token bus network that transmits data at between 2.5 and 4 Mbps. New versions of ARCnet transfer data at 20 and 100 Mbps over fibre-optic cable. ARCNET uses a single token that moves from one workstation to the next carrying data and uses a star-wired cable topology.)

**Arctic** GEOG *adjective* referring to the area around the North Pole ■ *noun* an area of the Earth's surface around the North Pole, north of the Arctic Circle

**arctic air** *noun* METEOROL a mass of cold air which forms over the Arctic region and then moves south

**Arctic Circle** *noun* GEOG a parallel running round the Earth at latitude 66°32 N to the north of which lies the Arctic region

**Arctogea** *noun* EARTH SCI one of the main biogeographical regions of the Earth, comprising the Palaearctic, Nearctic, Oriental and Ethiopian regions

**arcuate artery** *noun* ANAT a curved artery in the foot or kidney

**area** *noun* **1.** the measurement of the space taken up by something, calculated by multiplying the length by the width ○ *The area of this office is 3400 square feet.* ○ *We are looking for an area of about 100 square metres.* **2.** COMPUT a section of memory or code that is reserved for a specific purpose **3.** EARTH SCI a region of land ○ *The whole area has been contaminated by waste from the power station.*

**area fill** *noun* an instruction to fill an area of a screen or an enclosed pattern with a colour or pattern

**area graph** *noun* MATHS a line graph in which the area below the line is filled with a pattern or colour

**Area of Outstanding Natural Beauty** *noun* ENVIRON a region in England and Wales which is not a National Park but which is considered sufficiently attractive to be preserved from overdevelopment. Abbreviation **AONB**

**area search** *noun* COMPUT a search for specific data within a specific section of memory or files

**Arecibo** *noun* ASTRON the site on Puerto Rico of the world's largest single dish radio telescope, 305 m in diameter, made by excavating an existing crater

**arete** *noun* EARTH SCI a sharp ridge between two valleys

**arg** *abbreviation* COMPUT argument

**arginine** *noun* BIOCHEM an essential amino acid and a constituent of proteins. Formula: $C_6H_{14}N_4O_2$.

**argon** *noun* CHEM ELEM an inert gas, which occurs in air and of which isotopes form in the cooling systems of reactors. It is used in electric light bulbs. (NOTE: The chemical symbol is **Ar**; the atomic number is **18** and the atomic weight is **39.95**.)

**argument** *noun* **1.** COMPUT a discussion of something without agreeing ○ *They got into an argument over the documents.* **2.** a reason or a set of reasons used to persuade somebody to accept a point of view ○ *The main argument against the plan is cost.* **3.** COMPUT a variable acted upon by an operator or function ○ *If you enter the words 'MULTIPLY A, B', the processor will recognise the operator, MULTIPLY, and use* *it with the two arguments, A and B.* Compare **operand**

**argument separator** *noun* COMPUT a punctuation mark or symbol which separates several arguments on one line ○ *The command 'MULTIPLY A, B' uses a comma as the argument separator.*

**arid** *adjective* EARTH SCI referring to soil which is very dry or an area of land which has very little rain

**aridity** *noun* EARTH SCI the state of being extremely dry

**arid zone** *noun* EARTH SCI an area in the tropics between about 15° and 30° north and south which is very dry and covered with deserts

**arise** *verb* to occur or come to notice ○ *New ideas have started to arise.* (NOTE: **arising – arose – arisen**)

**Aristotle** *noun* SCI a Greek philosopher who lived from 384–322 BC whose Earth-centred astronomy dominated the science for 18 centuries (NOTE: The system he set out allowed only for uniform circular motions to preserve the perfection of the heavens, calling for more and more complex models of the universe, especially the orbits of the Sun, Moon and planets about the Earth. His work in animal classification was also notable.)

**arithmetic** *adjective* MATHS referring to mathematical functions such as addition, subtraction, division and multiplication

**arithmetic instruction** *noun* COMPUT a program instruction in which the operator defines the arithmetic operation to be carried out

**arithmetic logic unit** *noun* COMPUT a hardware section of a central processing unit that performs all the mathematical and logical functions. Abbreviation **ALU**

**arithmetic mean** *noun* MATHS the average of a set of numbers (NOTE: It is calculated by adding all the numbers together and then dividing the total by the number in the set.)

**arithmetic operator** *noun* MATHS a symbol which indicates an arithmetic function, e.g. + for addition or x for multiplication

**arithmetic register** *noun* COMPUT a memory location which stores operands

**arithmetic shift** *noun* COMPUT a word or data moved one bit to the left or

right inside a register, losing the bit shifted off the end

**-arium** *suffix* a display, usually involving water

**ARLL** *abbreviation* COMPUT advanced run-length limited

**arm** *noun* **1.** a lever or projection **2.** a horizontal distance from a reference point to the centre of gravity ○ *The principle of the arm is used in weight and balance calculations for an aircraft.* **3.** ANAT the part of the body which goes from the shoulder to the hand, formed of the upper arm, the elbow and the forearm ○ *She broke her arm skiing* ○ *Lift your arms up above your head.* ■ *verb* COMPUT **1.** to prepare a device or machine or routine for action or inputs **2.** to define which interrupt lines are active

**armature** *noun* ELEC an assembly of rotating coils in an electric motor or dynamo (NOTE: Secondary windings are wound over the primary windings and the whole assembly is known as an armature.)

**armed interrupt** *noun* COMPUT an interrupt line which has been made active using an interrupt mask

**aromatic** *adjective* having a pleasant smell ■ *noun* CHEM a substance, plant or chemical which has a pleasant smell

**aromatic compound** *noun* CHEM a compound such as benzene, with a ring of carbon atoms with single and double bonds

**aromatic hydrocarbon** *noun* CHEM ◊ **aromatic compound**

**ARP** *abbreviation* COMPUT address resolution protocol

**ARPANET** *abbreviation* COMPUT Advanced Research Projects Agency Network

**ARQ** *abbreviation* COMPUT automatic repeat request

**arrange** *verb* **1.** to plan and prepare something ○ *to arrange a meeting* **2.** to put something in a special position ○ *A series of dipoles is arranged in a circle.*

**arrangement** *noun* **1.** a plan to do something **2.** the position of a number of different parts ○ *The diagram shows a simple arrangement of pistons, cylinders and pipes.*

**array** *noun* **1.** TELECOM a set of aerials in a specific arrangement **2.** COMPUT an ordered structure containing individually accessible elements referenced by numbers, used to store tables or sets of related data

**array dimension** *noun* COMPUT a number of elements in an array, given as rows and columns

**array processor** *noun* COMPUT a computer that can act upon several arrays of data simultaneously, for very fast mathematical applications ○ *The array processor allows the array that contains the screen image to be rotated with one simple command.*

**arrest** *verb* to stop something or prevent something from happening □ **to arrest the spread of a fire** to stop the fire spreading ■ *noun* a sudden stoppage

**arrester** *noun* a device or substance which prevents or stops something from happening

**arrow** *noun* a printed sign which points to something

**arrow keys** *noun* COMPUT one of a set of four keys on a keyboard which move the cursor or pointer around the screen, controlling movement up, down, left and right

**arrow pointer** *noun* COMPUT a small arrow on-screen which can be moved using a mouse

**arroyo** *noun* EARTH SCI a gully with a stream at the bottom, found in desert regions of the US. Compare **wadi**

**arsenate** *noun* CHEM an arsenic acid salt

**arsenic** *noun* CHEM ELEM a grey semimetallic chemical element that forms poisonous compounds such as arsenic trioxide, which was formerly used in some medicines (NOTE: The chemical symbol is **As**; the atomic number is **33** and the atomic weight is **74.92**.)

**arsenic acid** *noun* CHEM a white poisonous crystalline solid containing arsenic, used in pigment and insecticide manufacture. Formula: $H_3AsO_4$.

**arsenical** *noun* CHEM a drug or insecticide which is one of the group of poisonous oxides of arsenic

**arsenic oxide** *noun* CHEM a toxic colourless compound with three solid forms, obtained by burning arsenic in air or as a by-product of smelting. It is used in glass-making. Formula: $As_2O_3$.

**arsenide** *noun* CHEM a compound of arsenic and a metallic element

**arsine** *noun* CHEM a colourless and highly toxic gas that smells of garlic, used in the manufacture of organic chemicals, semiconductors and chemical weapons. Formula: $AsH_3$.

**artefact** *noun* ENVIRON a human-made object

**arterio-** *prefix* ANAT referring to arteries

**arteriole** *noun* ANAT a very small artery

**artery** *noun* ANAT a blood vessel taking blood from the heart to the tissues of the body

COMMENT: In most arteries the blood has been oxygenated in the lungs and is bright red. In the pulmonary artery, the blood is deoxygenated and so is darker. The arterial system begins with the aorta which leaves the heart and from which all the arteries branch.

**artesian well** *noun* ENG a well which has been bored into a confined aquifer, the hydrostatic pressure usually being strong enough to force the water to the surface

**arthropod** *noun* ZOOL an invertebrate with jointed limbs, a segmented body, and a chitin exoskeleton. Phylum: Arthropoda. (NOTE: Insects, arachnids, centipedes and crustaceans are arthropods.)

**article** *noun* COMPUT a single message in a newsgroup

**articulation** *noun* ANAT a joint or series of joints

**artifact** *noun* **1.** COMPUT a very small error in a video signal **2.** COMPUT a very small error in a digital version of an analog signal **3.** ENVIRON another spelling of **artefact**

**artificial** *adjective* made by humans and not existing naturally

**artificial community** *noun* BOT a plant community kept by people, as in a garden

**artificial fertiliser** *noun* AGRIC a fertiliser manufactured from chemicals

**artificial horizon** *noun* AEROSP the horizon line on the attitude indicator

**artificial insemination** *noun* AGRIC a method of breeding livestock by injecting sperm from specially selected males into the female. Abbreviation **AI**

**artificial intelligence** *noun* COMPUT the design of computer programs and systems that attempt to imitate human intelligence and decision-making functions, providing basic reasoning and human characteristics. Abbreviation **AI**

**artificial light** *noun* a light produced by electricity, gas, etc.

**artificial manure** *noun* AGRIC a manufactured chemical substance used to increase the nutrient level of the soil

**artificial rain** *noun* rain which is made by scattering crystals of salt and other substances into clouds

**artificial selection** *noun* AGRIC the selection by people of individual animals or plants from which to breed further generations because the animals or plants have useful characteristics

**artiodactyl** *noun* ZOOL a herbivorous hoofed animal that walks on its toes of which there are an even number on each foot. Order: Artiodactyla. (NOTE: Cows, camels, pigs or deer are artiodactyls.)

**artwork** *noun* COMPUT graphical work or images

**aryl group** *noun* CHEM a compound formed by removing one hydrogen atom from an aromatic compound

**As** *symbol* CHEM ELEM arsenic

**asbestos** *noun* INDUST a fibrous mineral substance, used as a shield against fire and as an insulating material in many industrial and construction processes

COMMENT: Asbestos was formerly widely used in cement and cladding and other types of fireproof construction materials. It is now recognised that asbestos dust can cause many lung diseases, leading in some cases to forms of cancer, with the result that constructions containing asbestos are being demolished or rebuilt with alternative materials. Blue asbestos is extremely toxic and is banned in many countries; white and brown asbestos can be safely used in some forms.

**asbestos cement** *noun* INDUST a mixture of asbestos and cement, used to make pipes, tiles and other small items used in construction

**asbestos fibre** *noun* INDUST threads of asbestos which can be woven into rope or tape, etc.

**asbestosis** *noun* MED a disease of the lungs caused by inhaling asbestos dust

**ascend** *verb* to move slowly upwards ○ *Hot air ascends.* □ **in ascending or-**

**der** in order of number or rank with the smallest or less important at the bottom and the largest or more important at the top

**ascender** *noun* COMPUT a part of a character that rises above the main line of printed characters, as the 'tail' of 'b' or 'd'

**ascending aorta** *noun* ANAT the first section of the aorta as it leaves the heart and rises

**ascent** *noun* a slow upwards movement ○ *the forced ascent of air over high ground* ○ *In a stable atmosphere where the ascent of air is forced, precipitation is mostly light and occasionally moderate.* Opposite **descent**

**ascertain** *verb* to make sure about something ○ *Control surfaces should be moved by hand to ascertain that they have full and free movement.*

**ASCII** *abbreviation* COMPUT American Standard Code for Information Interchange

**ASCII character** *noun* COMPUT a character which is in the ASCII list of codes

**ASCIIZ string** *noun* COMPUT a sequence of ASCII characters followed by the ASCII code zero which indicates the end of the sequence

**ascorbic acid** *noun* CHEM vitamin C
COMMENT: Ascorbic acid is found in fresh fruit, especially oranges and lemons, and in vegetables. Lack of vitamin C can cause anaemia and scurvy.

**-ase** *suffix* BIOL an enzyme

**asepsis** *noun* MED, MICROBIOL a state of having no infection

**aseptic** *adjective* MED, MICROBIOL referring to asepsis ○ *It is important that aseptic techniques should be used in microbiological experiments.*

**aseptic surgery** *noun* MED surgery using sterilised equipment, rather than relying on killing germs with antiseptic drugs

**asexual** *adjective* BIOL not involving sexual reproduction

**asexual reproduction** *noun* BIOL reproduction by taking cuttings of plants or by cloning

**ASF** *abbreviation* COMPUT Active Streaming Format

**ash** *noun* **1.** TREES a European hardwood tree. Genus: *Fraxinus*. **2.** CHEM a grey or black powder formed of minerals left after an organic substance has been burnt

**ASI** *abbreviation* AEROSP airspeed indicator

**ASIC** *abbreviation* COMPUT application-specific integrated circuits

**ASP** *abbreviation* COMPUT **1.** Active Server Page **2.** application service provider

**asparagine** *noun* BIOCHEM an amino acid found in protein

**aspartic acid** *noun* BIOL an amino acid found in sugar

**aspect** *noun* **1.** a part of a problem or subject ○ *Vertical motion is an important aspect of meteorology.* **2.** a view of something from a particular position

**aspect ratio** *noun* COMPUT a ratio of the width to the height of pixel shapes

**aspen** *noun* TREES a hardwood tree with leaves that tremble in the wind. Genus: *Populus*.

**as per** *preposition* according to □ **as per sample** as shown in the sample □ **as per specification** according to the details given in the specification

**asphalt** *noun* INDUST a black substance formed from bitumen

COMMENT: Asphalt is found naturally in tar sands, but is also manufactured as a by-product of petroleum distillation. It is used, when melted, to paint on roofs to make them waterproof or to mix with aggregate to make hard road surfaces.

**aspirin** *noun* BIOL **1.** a common pain-killing drug **2.** a tablet of this drug

**ASR** *noun* COMPUT a device or terminal that can transmit and receive information

COMMENT: An ASR terminal can input information via a keyboard or via a tape cassette or paper tape. It can receive information and store it in internal memory or on tape.

**assay** *noun* CHEM an act of testing of a substance

**assemble** *verb* **1.** to put a number of parts together to form something ○ *Parts are made in different countries but the aeroplane is assembled in France.* **2.** COMPUT to make a whole from various smaller parts ○ *The parts for the disk drive are made in Japan and assembled in France.* **3.** COMPUT to translate assembly code into machine

code ○ *There is a short wait during which the program is assembled into object code.* ○ *Syntax errors were spotted while the source program was being assembled.* **4.** COMPUT to insert specific library routines, macros or parameters into a program

**assembler, assembler program** *noun* COMPUT a program which converts a program written in assembly language into machine code

**assembly** *noun* **1.** the process of putting an item together from various parts ○ *There are no assembly instructions to show you how to put the computer together.* **2.** COMPUT the process of converting a program into machine code

**assembly code** *noun* COMPUT a set of mnemonics which are used to represent machine code instructions in an assembler

**assembly language** *noun* COMPUT a programming language used to code information which will then be converted to machine code

**assembly language program** *noun* COMPUT a number of assembly code instructions which perform a task

**assembly program** *noun* COMPUT same as **macro assembler**

**assertion** *noun* **1.** COMPUT (*in a computer program*) a series of instructions that define a fact or rule **2.** a fact that is true or defined as being true

**assess** *verb* to consider something carefully to make a judgment about it

**assessment** *noun* **1.** careful consideration of something to make a judgment about it **2.** a judgment based on evidence

**asset** *noun* COMPUT a separate data element such as a video, audio or image which is used in a multimedia application

**assign** *verb* **1.** to set something apart beforehand or allocate something for a specific purpose **2.** to give someone or a machine something to do ○ *He was assigned the job of checking the sales figures.* ○ *Two PCs have been assigned to outputting the labels.* **3.** COMPUT to set a variable equal to a string of characters or numbers **4.** COMPUT to keep part of a computer system for use while a program is running

**assigned number** *noun* COMPUT a document which contains a list of unique numbers that are each assigned to an Internet or network manufacturer's device, protocol or other resource (NOTE: Manufacturers apply for a unique ID number from the IANA organisation.)

**assimilate** verb BIOCHEM to take into the body's tissues substances which have been absorbed into the blood from digested food

**assimilation** noun BIOCHEM the action of assimilating food substances

**associate** verb to be linked to or accompanied by something else ○ Turbulence is often associated with strong winds.

**association** noun 1. a group of people with similar interests 2. a link between two things ○ They were looking for an association between specific brain chemicals and the disease. 3. BOT a group of plants living together in a large area, forming a stable community

**associative memory** noun COMPUT a method of data retrieval which uses part of the data rather than an address to locate the data

**associative processor** noun COMPUT a processor that uses associative memory

**associative storage** noun COMPUT same as **associative memory**

**assumption** noun an understanding about something which is not based on facts or proof

**astatine** noun CHEM ELEM a natural radioactive element (NOTE: The chemical symbol is **At**; the atomic number is **85** and the atomic weight is **210**.)

**aster** noun BIOL a structure shaped like a star, seen around a centrosome during cell division

**asterisk** noun COMPUT 1. a graphical symbol ( * ) used in programming as a sign for multiplication 2. a graphical symbol used in many operating systems to mean 'any character'

**asteroid** noun ASTRON a body found in the solar system, intermediate in size between a planet and a meteorite

COMMENT: The largest asteroids are hundreds of kilometres across and the smallest only hundreds of metres. They mostly orbit just inside the orbit of Jupiter. Asteroids are material from the earliest days of the solar system, so information about them is of great astronomical value.

**asteroid belt** noun ASTRON the region between the orbits of Mars and Jupiter where most asteroids are concentrated

**asthenosphere** noun EARTH SCI part of the interior of the Earth, formed of molten matter below the lithosphere

**astigmatism** noun OPTICS, OPHTHALMOL a defect in a lens or mirror that prevents light rays from meeting at a single point (NOTE: It results in the formation of an imperfect image. Astigmatism in the eye is very common and can be overcome by wearing glasses.)

**astrology** noun ASTRON an ancient but still popular system of attempting to predict the future from astronomical events (NOTE: It separated from scientific astronomy in the 17th century as knowledge of the solar system grew, weakening the argument that the positions of the planets in the sky could affect people's lives.)

**astrometrical** adjective ASTRON referring to astrometry

**astrometry** noun ASTRON a branch of astronomy involving precise measurements of the positions of objects in the sky, with the use of meridian telescopes, which can now record hundreds of observations per night onto computer disks (NOTE: The **European Space Agency's Hipparcos telescope** was the first to be launched to perform astrometrical observations above the turbulence of the Earth's atmosphere.)

**astronaut** noun ASTRON a human traveller in space

**astronomical unit** noun ASTRON a measure of distance used in solar system studies, equal to the average distance of the Earth from the Sun, 149.6 million km. Abbreviation **AU**

**astronomy** noun ASTRON the study of natural objects in space, including Earth (NOTE: Modern astronomy is related closely to other sciences, especially physics, and has many subdivisions, notably **cosmology** and **astrophysics**)

**astrophysicist** noun ASTRON a scientist who specialises in astrophysics

**astrophysics** noun ASTRON a branch of astronomy which examines astronomical phenomena in terms of the laws and principles of physics

**asulam** *noun* AGRIC a powerful herbicide, used to remove tenacious plants such as bracken

**asymmetric, asymmetrical** *adjective* not identical or equal on each side of an imaginary central dividing line

**asymmetric compression** *noun* COMPUT a method of reducing the space taken by data which requires a lot of processing time and power to compress an image or video sequence but is very quick to decompress (NOTE: It is usually used when creating video sequences for distribution.)

**asymmetric digital subscriber line** *noun* COMPUT a high-speed transmission standard that uses the same wires as a normal telephone service, but is much faster and provides a user with an always-on connection to the Internet so there is no need to dial an access number and no delay (NOTE: Data is usually transferred from the Internet to the user's computer at 2 Mbps but transferred from the user's computer to the Internet at a slower rate of 256 Kbps.)

**async** *adjective* COMPUT same as **asynchronous** (*informal*)

**asynchronous** *adjective* COMPUT referring to serial data or equipment which does not depend on being synchronised with another piece of equipment

**asynchronous transfer mode** *noun* COMPUT 1. a method of transferring data very rapidly, at up to 155 Mbps, across a network using fixed-length data cells 53 octets long 2. a CCITT and ANSI standard defining cell relay transmission ► abbreviation **ATM**

**At** *symbol* CHEM ELEM astatine

**ATAPI** *abbreviation* COMPUT advanced technology attachment packet interface

**atavism** *noun* GENETICS the reappearance of a genetically controlled feature in an organism after it has been absent for several generations, usually as a result of an accidental recombination of genes

**at hazard** *adverb* at risk, in danger

**Atlantic Ocean** *noun* GEOG an ocean to the north of the Antarctic, south of the Arctic, west of Europe and Africa and east of North and South America

**atlas** *noun* 1. GEOG a book of maps and other geographical information 2. a book of diagrams, charts and other information about a single subject such as anatomy

**ATM** *abbreviation* COMPUT asynchronous transfer mode

**atmosphere** *noun* 1. METEOROL a mass of gases surrounding the Earth or any astronomical object such as a planet or star 2. PHYS, MEASURE a unit of measurement of pressure, equal to 101 325 pascals or equal to a height of 760 mm of mercury

COMMENT: Earth's atmosphere extends to a height of several thousand kilometres, but is concentrated in the 20km immediately above the planet's surface. Its pressure decreases with height. The atmosphere is divided into the troposphere, stratosphere, mesosphere and thermosphere. Around the Earth, the main gases found in the atmosphere are: nitrogen and oxygen, less than 1% carbon dioxide and argon, plus traces of hydrogen, helium, krypton, neon, ozone and xenon.

**atmospheric** *adjective* METEOROL referring to the atmosphere

**atmospheric attenuation** *noun* ELEC the weakening of a radio signal as it passes through the air

**atmospheric contamination** *noun* ENVIRON pollution of the air with harmful substances

**atmospheric lifetime** *noun* ENVIRON ◊ **lifetime**

**atmospheric nitrogen** *noun* CHEM nitrogen as found in the atmosphere

**atmospheric pollutant** ENVIRON same as **air pollutant**

**atmospheric pollution** ENVIRON same as **air pollution**

**atmospheric pressure** *noun* METEOROL the normal pressure of the air on the surface of the Earth

**atmospheric pressure zones** *plural noun* METEOROL a band of a specific atmospheric pressure around the Earth

**atmospheric refraction** *noun* PHYS a change in direction of waves as a result of variations in temperature, pressure and humidity, particularly at lower altitudes

**A to D** *abbreviation* COMPUT analog to digital

**atoll** *noun* EARTH SCI an island in warm seas, made of coral and shaped like a ring

**atom** *noun* **1.** CHEM a fundamental unit of a chemical element and the smallest part of an element that can exist independently **2.** COMPUT a value or string that cannot be reduced to a simpler form

COMMENT: An atom of any chemical element consists of a positively charged nucleus surrounded by negatively charged electrons in a particular orbit, the orbit being defined by the energy levels. The mass of an atom is mostly defined by the nucleus, which is composed of positively charged protons and neutrally charged neutrons. Hydrogen is the only atom with just a proton in its nucleus.

**atomic** *adjective* **1.** PHYS referring to atoms **2.** COMPUT referring to an operation that returns data to its original state if it is stopped during processing

**atomic bomb** *noun* ◊ **atomic weapon**

**atomic energy** *noun* INDUST energy created during a nuclear reaction, either fission or fusion, which, in a nuclear reactor, produces heat warming water and forming steam which runs a turbine to generate electricity

COMMENT: Atomic energy is produced from the fission of atoms of uranium-235. One of the problems associated with the production of atomic energy is the radioactive waste produced by nuclear reactors. This takes various forms: it can be a gas such as krypton or xenon, spent fuel rods or water from cooling processes.

**atomic fission** *noun* PHYS the splitting of the nucleus of an atom such as uranium-235 into several small nuclei which then release energy and neutrons. Also called **nuclear fission**

**atomic fusion** *noun* PHYS the joining together of several nuclei to form a single large nucleus, creating energy, as in a hydrogen bomb

**atomicity** *noun* CHEM the number of atoms found in a molecule of a chemical element, e.g. the atomicity of ozone ($O_3$) is 3

**atomic mass** *noun* CHEM the mass of an atom measured in atomic mass units

**atomic mass unit** *noun* PHYS, MEASURE a unit of measurement of mass, used to express the weight of an atom or molecule and equal to one twelfth of the

mass of an atom of carbon-12. Abbreviation **AMU**. Symbol **u**

**atomic number** *noun* CHEM a number of positive electric charges round the nucleus of an atom, equal to the number of protons in the atom (NOTE: Atomic number is used to give an element a place in the periodic table.)

**atomic orbital** *noun* PHYS the space around a nucleus in which there is a high probability of finding an electron orbiting the nucleus. ◊ **orbital**

**atomic pile** *noun* INDUST a nuclear reactor

**atomic power** *noun* INDUST the power generated by a nuclear reactor, or electricity generated by a nuclear power station

**atomic-powered** *adjective* INDUST operated by nuclear power

**atomic power station** *noun* INDUST a power station in which nuclear reactions are used to provide energy to run turbines that generate electricity

**atomic waste** *noun* ENVIRON radioactive waste from a nuclear reactor, including spent fuel rods and coolant

**atomic weapon** *noun* ENVIRON a bomb or missile whose destructive power is produced by nuclear fission or fusion

**atomic weight** *noun* MEASURE ◊ **relative atomic mass**

**atomise** *verb* to reduce liquids to a fine spray ○ *The fuel must be atomised or vaporised to combine with the air to permit combustion.*

**atomiser** *noun* INDUST an instrument that sprays liquid in the form of very small drops like mist. Also called **nebuliser**

**atomize** *verb* another spelling of **atomise**

**atomizer** *noun* another spelling of **atomiser**

**atopy** *noun* MED a hereditary allergic reaction

**ATP** *abbreviation* BIOCHEM adenosine triphosphate

**atrazine** *noun* AGRIC a residual herbicide which acts on the soil

**atresia** *noun* MED an unusual closing or absence of a tube in the body

**atrium** *noun* **1.** ANAT one of the two upper chambers in the heart. Compare

**ventricle 2.** BIOL a cavity in the ear behind the eardrum (NOTE: The plural is **atria**.)

COMMENT: The two atria in the heart both receive blood from veins. The right atrium receives venous blood from the superior and inferior vena cavae and the left atrium receives oxygenated blood from the pulmonary veins.

**atrophy** *noun* MED the shrinking of a body part or organ because of disease, damage or lack of use

**atropine** *noun* PHARM an alkaloid that affects heart rate, found in deadly nightshade

**attach** *verb* **1.** to join, fix or connect one thing to another **2.** COMPUT to make a connection or link ○ *I issued the command to attach to the local server.* **3.** COMPUT to connect a node or login to a server on a network

**attached processor** *noun* COMPUT a microprocessor that performs specific functions under the control of a central processor

**attachment** *noun* **1.** the joining, fixing or connecting of one thing to another ○ *The attachment of a wing improved the grip and handling of the car.* **2.** an accessory which can be attached ○ *The video camera is sold with a number of attachments including a carrying strap and a battery pack.* **3.** COMPUT a device which is attached to a machine for a special purpose ○ *There is a special single sheet feed attachment.* **4.** COMPUT a named file which is transferred together with an electronic mail message ○ *There is an attachment with my last mail message – it contains the sales report.*

**attack** *noun* ACOUSTICS the shape of the start of a sound signal over time. ▸ **sustain, decay**

**attain** *verb* to reach or achieve something, often with difficulty ○ *In order to attain a fuller understanding of gas turbines, it is essential to know something about basic gas laws.*

**attempt** *noun* a try ○ *Any attempt to increase range by applying more power is of little or no benefit.* ■ *verb* to try to do something

**attend** *verb* **1.** COMPUT to be present at an event ○ *attend a seminar* **2.** to exist or happen in connection with something else (*formal*) ○ *Serious consequences may attend this decision.*

**attendant** *adjective* accompanying something else ○ *Fuel spillage and attendant fire risk must be minimised.* ■ *noun* a person whose job is to look after a public place, or to look after and help other people

**attend to** *verb* **1.** to deal with something or someone ○ *We need to attend to the feedback first of all.* **2.** to pay attention to something (*formal*) ○ *Please attend to this safety advice immediately.*

**attention** *noun* special care or treatment ○ *This routine requires the attention of the processor every minute.*

**attenuate** *verb* (*of a radio signal*) to lose power or strength ○ *A wave attenuates or loses strength as range increases.*

**attenuation** *noun* (*of radio signal*) a reduction or loss of signal strength, the difference between transmitted and received power measured in decibels ○ *If the cable is too long, the signal attenuation will start to cause data errors.* ○ *Atmospheric attenuation is negligible until the upper end of the UHF band when it increases rapidly to limit the highest usable frequency to about 10 GHz.* Opposite **gain**

**attenuative** *adjective* weakening a radio signal ○ *rain has an attenuative effect*

**attitude** *noun* **1.** a way of thinking, feeling or behaving about something **2.** AEROSP the position of the aircraft in the air in relation to the horizon ○ *Angle of attack will vary with changes in engine speed and aircraft attitude.*

**attitude indicator** *noun* AEROSP a flight instrument which gives the pilot pitch and bank information ○ *In light aircraft, the attitude indicator is situated on the instrument panel, directly in front of the pilot.* Abbreviation **AI**

COMMENT: The attitude indicator is sometimes referred to as the artificial horizon. In instrument flight training, the attitude indicator is the primary reference instrument.

**atto-** *prefix* MEASURE one quintillionth, $10^{-18}$. Symbol **a**

**attract** *verb* to cause something to draw near ○ *If two magnets, with unlike poles are brought together, they will attract each other.* ○ *The solid attracts the gas to its surface.*

**attractant** *noun* CHEM a chemical that attracts an organism

COMMENT: Artificially produced attractants can be used to attract insects, which can then be killed.

**attraction** *noun* the act or an instance of being drawn near to something ○ *The strength of the magnetic force will depend, amongst other things, on the magnitude of attraction at the magnetic source.*

**attribute** *noun* **1.** a characteristic or quality **2.** COMPUT a field entry in a file ○ *This attribute controls the colour of the screen.* **3.** COMPUT a piece of information concerning the display or presentation of information

**attrition** *noun* the wearing away of something, as may be caused by friction ○ *Examination showed attrition of two extensor tendons.*

**Au** *symbol* CHEM ELEM gold

**AU** *symbol* ASTRON astronomical unit

**audibility threshold** *noun* the level of sound which a person can just hear. Also called **hearing threshold**

**audible** *adjective* able to be heard ○ *The fire detection system should contain an audible warning device.*

**audible indication** *noun* a sound such as a warning bleep

**audio** *adjective, noun* PHYS referring to sound or to things that can be heard

**audio-, audi-** *prefix* hearing or sound

**audio board** *noun* ◊ **sound card**

**audio cassette recorder** *noun* ELECTRONICS a machine to transfer audio signals onto magnetic tape. Abbreviation **ACR**

**audio file** *noun* a digital sound sample stored on disk

**audiogram** *noun* BIOL a graph drawn by an audiometer

**audiometer** *noun* BIOL an instrument for testing hearing or for testing the range of sounds that the human ear can detect

**audio range** *noun* ACOUSTICS the frequency range between 50 and 20 000 Hz that can be detected by a human ear

**audio response unit** *noun* a speech synthesiser that allows a computer to give verbal responses to requests

**audit** *noun* **1.** a check on figures, scientific data or procedures **2.** COMPUT an act of noting tasks carried out by a computer ■ *verb* COMPUT to examine the state of a system and check that it is still secure or working properly

**auditory** *adjective* BIOL relating to the ears or to the hearing process

**auditory acuity** *noun* BIOL the ability to hear sounds clearly

**auditory nerve** *noun* ANAT a nerve that transmits impulses concerned with hearing and balance from the inner ear to the brain

**augend** *noun* MATHS (*in an addition*) the number to which another number is added to produce the sum

**Auger effect** *noun* PHYS the emission of an electron from an excited positive ion to produce an ion with a double charge

**augment** *verb* to increase

**augmented addressing** *noun* MATHS the production of a usable address word from two shorter words

**augmenter** *noun* MATHS a value added to another

**AUP** *abbreviation* COMPUT acceptable use policy

**aural** *adjective* BIOL referring to hearing ○ *The aural and visual alerts will continue until the operator takes action to cancel them.*

**aureole** *noun* **1.** METEOROL a glow visible round the Sun, when seen through thin mist **2.** ANAT the dark area around a nipple

**auricle** *noun* **1.** ANAT the outer ear. Also called **pinna 2.** ANAT an atrium of the heart **3.** ANAT an ear-shaped part in each upper chamber of the heart **4.** BOT a part of a grass plant found at the base of a leaf

**auriferous** *adjective* METALL referring to a deposit which bears gold

**Aurora Australis** *noun* METEOROL a spectacular illumination of the southern sky caused by ionised particles striking the atmosphere. Also called **Southern Lights**

**Aurora Borealis** *noun* METEOROL same as **Northern Lights**

**Australasian Region** *noun* EARTH SCI Notogea, one of the distinct biogeographical regions into which the Earth is divided, covering Australia,

New Zealand and most of the islands in the Pacific Ocean

**Australia Telescope** *noun* ASTRON the southern hemisphere's largest radio telescope, with six dishes over a 6 km area, situated in New South Wales

**autecology** *noun* ECOL the study of an individual species in its environment. Compare **synecology**

**authentic** *adjective* COMPUT real or genuine

**authenticate** *verb* COMPUT to confirm that something is real or genuine

**author** COMPUT *noun* a person who wrote a program ■ *verb* to create a multimedia application by combining sound, video and images

**authorisation** *noun* 1. the permission or power to do something 2. the giving of permission to access a system

**authorisation code** *noun* COMPUT a code used to restrict access to a computer system to authorised users only

**authorise** *verb* 1. to give permission for something to be done ○ *to authorise the purchase of a new computer system* 2. to give someone the authority to do something ○ *The lab was authorised to conduct the tests.*

**authorised** *adjective* permitted

**authorised user** *noun* COMPUT a person who is allowed to access a computer system

**authority** *noun* 1. the power to act 2. an official body that controls an area or region ○ *You will have to apply to the local planning authority.*

**author level** *noun* COMPUT a mode of an authoring software package that is used by the author to design the application

**auto** *adjective* working without the user needing to act

**auto-** *prefix* 1. automatic or automated 2. self

**autocatalysis** *noun* CHEM the catalytic acceleration of a chemical reaction by a product of the same reaction

**autoclave** *noun* CHEM a strong steel vessel in which pressure can be raised artificially, used for steam sterilisation and chemical reactions at high temperature

**autoecology** *noun* ECOL same as **autecology**

**autogamy** *noun* 1. BOT pollination with pollen from the same flower 2. ZOOL the division of a protozoon's nucleus into two parts which reunite

**autogenic succession** *noun* ECOL the establishment of different communities in a particular area as a result of biological changes, including colonisation and changes to the environment

**autoimmune** *adjective* BIOL referring to an immune reaction to antigens in a person's own tissue

**autolysis** *noun* BIOL the action of cells destroying themselves with their own enzymes

**automate** *verb* to make a device or procedure automatic

**automated system** *noun* a system that has been made less dependent on direct human control or management

**automatic** *adjective* 1. done without needing to think ○ *In the early stages of training, student pilots have to think about the use of the flying controls but after a while these actions become automatic.* 2. working by itself without the need of an operator ○ *The normal activation method of the sprinkler system is automatic.*

**automatically** *adverb* COMPUT without a person giving instructions ○ *The compiler automatically corrected the syntax errors.* ○ *An SBC automatically limits the movement of the machine.* ○ *The program is run automatically when the computer is switched on.* ♦ **APT**

**automatic gain control** *noun* ELECTRONICS an electronic circuit that adjusts the level of an incoming signal so that it is suitable for the next part of the circuit. Abbreviation **AGC**

**automatic hyphenation** *noun* COMPUT a feature of a software program that looks up in an electronic dictionary how to split and hyphenate words correctly

**automatic power off** *noun* COMPUT the process of equipment switching itself off if it has not been used for a time

**automatic repeat request** *noun* COMPUT an error correction system used in some modems that asks for data to be re-transmitted if there are errors. Abbreviation **ARQ**

**automation** *noun* an automatic operation or control of a piece of equipment, process or system ○ *Automation of* *throttle control has removed the need for pilots to monitor airspeed so closely.*

**autonomic** *adjective* governing itself independently

**autonomic nervous system** *noun* ANAT the nervous system formed of ganglia linked to the spinal column, which regulates the automatic functioning of the main organs of the body such as the heart and lungs

**autoradiography** *noun* BIOL, MED the technique of placing a sample or specimen in contact with a photographic plate prior to developing a photograph that reveals the distribution of radioactivity in it

**auto repeat** *noun* COMPUT a facility where a character is automatically repeated if the key is kept pressed down

**auto save** *noun* COMPUT a feature of some application programs such as word-processor or database software that automatically saves the file being used every few minutes in case of a power failure or system crash

**auto scan** *noun* COMPUT the ability of a monitor to maintain the same rectangular image size when changing from one resolution to another

**autosome** *noun* GENETICS a chromosome that does not determine sex

**autotroph, autotrophic organism** *noun* BIOL an organism such as a green plant or bacterium which manufactures its own organic constituents from inorganic materials. Compare **heterotroph, chemotroph**

**autumn** *noun* a season of the year, following summer and before winter, when days become shorter and the weather progressively colder

**autumnal** *adjective* referring to the autumn

**autumnal equinox** *noun* ASTRON one of the two occasions in the year when the Sun crosses the celestial equator and night and day are each 12 hours long, occurring around 22 September

**AUX** *noun* COMPUT a serial communications port under the DOS operating system. Full form **AUXILIARY**

**auxiliary** *adjective* referring to a secondary system that is used when necessary

**auxiliary equipment** *noun* backup or secondary equipment in case of a breakdown

**auxiliary gearbox** *noun* ENG a gear-box that allows main engine power to be used for secondary systems

**auxiliary memory** *noun* COMPUT same as **auxiliary storage**

**auxiliary processor** *noun* COMPUT an extra, specialised processor, such as an array or numerical processor that can work with a main processor to increase execution speed

**auxiliary storage, auxiliary store** *noun* COMPUT a data storage medium such as a magnetic tape or floppy disk that is not the main high-speed computer storage ○ *Disk drives and magnetic tape provide auxiliary storage on this machine.* Also called **auxiliary memory**

**auxin** *noun* BOT a plant hormone that encourages tissue growth

COMMENT: Some herbicides act as synthetic auxins by upsetting the balance of plant growth.

**availability** *noun* the fact of being available

**available** *adjective* able to be had or used ○ *available in all branches* ○ *item no longer available* ○ *items available to order only*

**available bit rate** *noun* COMPUT a service provided by an ATM network that tries to provide the bandwidth requested by a customer but cannot guarantee to do so. Abbreviation **ABR**

**available list** *noun* COMPUT a list of unallocated memory and resources in a computer system

**available point** *noun* COMPUT the smallest single unit or point of a display whose colour and brightness can be controlled

**available power** *noun* COMPUT, ENG the maximum electrical or processing power that a system can deliver

**available time** *noun* the time during which a system may be used

**avalanche** *noun* **1.** EARTH SCI a large mass of snow that becomes detached and falls down the side of a mountain **2.** a large mass of rock or mud that falls down a mountainside in heavy rain **3.** COMPUT a series of actions beginning with one which starts a number of others

○ *There was an avalanche of errors after I pressed the wrong key.*

**avalanche wind** *noun* EARTH SCI a very strong wind caused by an avalanche

**avatar** *noun* COMPUT **1.** the graphic image that is used to represent a real person in a cyberspace or three-dimensional system, e.g. in an adventure game **2.** the name for the superuser account on a UNIX system ▶ also called **root**

**average** *adjective* typical or usual ○ *of average ability* ○ *below average performance* ■ *noun* MATHS a number calculated by adding together several figures and dividing by the number of figures added ○ *the average for the last three months* ○ *sales average* Also called **arithmetic mean** ■ *adjective* MATHS referring to an average ■ *verb* MATHS to produce as an average figure

**avert** *verb* to avoid something ○ *To avert a collision, he changed direction.*

**Aves** *noun* ZOOL the class that comprises birds

COMMENT: Birds are closely related to reptiles and have scales on their legs. Their forelimbs have developed into wings.

**avicide** *noun* ZOOL a substance that kills birds

**avifauna** *noun* ZOOL all the birds that live naturally in a specific area (NOTE: The plural is **avifauna** or **avifaunas**.)

**avionics** *noun* AEROSP the electronic communication, navigation and flight-control equipment of an aircraft

**Avogadro's constant** *noun* PHYS same as **Avogadro's number**

**Avogadro's law** *noun* PHYS the physical principle that equal volumes of different gases at the same temperature and pressure contain the same number of molecules

**Avogadro's number** *noun* PHYS the number of atoms or molecules contained in one mole of a substance (NOTE: Its value is $6.022 \times 10^{23}$)

**avoid** *verb* **1.** to prevent something from happening ○ *He just managed to avoid an accident.* **2.** to keep away from or not do something ○ *Avoid entering this area when the red light is on.* ○ *Avoid alcohol with this medication.*

**aware** *adjective* knowing and conscious of something

**awareness** *noun* the state of being aware

**axenic** *adjective* MICROBIOL referring to a culture of an organism that is free from contamination by other organisms

**axial** *adjective* referring to an axis

**axial-flow turbine** *noun* ENG a turbine with blades like those on a ship's propeller, rotating horizontally

**axial skeleton** *noun* ANAT the main part of the skeleton, formed of the spine, skull, ribs and breastbone

**axil** *noun* BOT the angle between a leaf or branch and the stem from which it grows

**axillary artery** *noun* ANAT an artery leading from the subclavian artery in the armpit

**axis** *noun* **1.** an imaginary line around which a body rotates ○ *The Earth rotates around its own axis.* ○ *An aircraft moves around three axes – vertical, longitudinal and lateral.* **2.** ANAT an imaginary line through the centre of a plant or animal **3.** ANAT a central vessel which divides into other vessels **4.** MATHS the horizontal or vertical scale on a graph ○ *The plot shows the effect of airspeed on lift, with airspeed shown on the horizontal axis and lift on the vertical axis.* (NOTE: The plural is **axes**.)

**axle** *noun* ENG a shaft on which a wheel is mounted ○ *Unequal tyre pressures, where two wheels are mounted on the same axle, will result in one tyre carrying a greater share of the load than the other.*

**axon** *noun* ANAT a nerve fibre that sends impulses from one neuron to another, linking with the dendrites of the other neuron

**axon covering** *noun* ANAT a myelin sheath that covers a nerve

**azeotrope** *noun* CHEM a mixture of liquids with a different boiling point from that of any of its components, retaining its composition as a vapour

**azerty keyboard** *noun* COMPUT a keyboard on which the keys are arranged with the first line beginning AZERTY. Compare **QWERTY keyboard** (NOTE: It is used mainly in Europe.)

**azimuth** *noun* **1.** the position of an object in the horizontal plane, usually measured in degrees clockwise from the north **2.** COMPUT the angle of a tape head to a reference such as a tape plane

**azine** *noun* CHEM an organic compound with a ring containing a total of six carbon and nitrogen atoms per molecule

**azobacter** *noun* MICROBIOL a nitrogen-fixing bacterium belonging to a group found in soil

**azo dye** *noun* CHEM an organic dye containing an azo group, usually orange, yellow or brown (NOTE: They may be added to food to give it colour.)

**azygos vein** *noun* ANAT a vein that brings blood back into the vena cava from the abdomen

# B

**b** *abbreviation* COMPUT bit ■ *symbol* MEASURE, PHYS barn

**B** *abbreviation* COMPUT byte ■ *symbol* **1.** CHEM ELEM boron **2.** COMPUT the hexadecimal equivalent of the decimal number 11

**Ba** *symbol* CHEM ELEM barium

**Babbage, Charles (1792–1871)** COMPUT British inventor of the first automatic calculator and inventor of the forerunner of digital computers

**babbitt metal** *noun* METALL a soft alloy containing a high proportion of tin, along with copper and antimony, often containing lead, used in the manufacture of antifriction bearings

**babble** *noun* ACOUSTICS crosstalk or noise from other sources which interferes with a signal

**BAC** *abbreviation* BIOTECH bacterial artificial chromosome

**bacillary** *adjective* BIOL referring to a bacillus

**bacillary dysentery** *noun* MED dysentery caused by the bacillus *Shigella* in contaminated food

**bacillus** *noun* BIOL a bacterium shaped like a rod (NOTE: The plural is **bacilli**.)

**back** *noun* **1.** ANAT the part of the body from the neck downwards to the waist, which is made up of the spine and the bones attached to it ○ *She strained her back working in the garden.* Also called **dorsum** (NOTE: For other terms referring to the back, see words beginning with **dors-**.) **2.** the opposite side to the front ○ *There is a wide range of connectors at the back of the main unit.* ■ *verb* **1.** to help a person or enterprise **2.** METEOROL (*of wind*) to change direction, anticlockwise in the northern hemisphere and clockwise in the southern hemisphere. Opposite **veer**

**backbone** *noun* **1.** ANAT a series of bones, the vertebrae, linked together to form a flexible column running from the pelvis to the skull **2.** COMPUT a high-speed high-capacity connection path that links smaller sub-networks, normally used to connect servers on a network ○ *We have linked the servers in each office using a high-speed backbone.* (NOTE: Smaller workgroups or networks are connected to the backbone as segments or ribs.)

**backcross** GENETICS *verb* to cross an organism, especially a hybrid, with one of its parents or an individual genetically identical to that parent ■ *noun* a hybrid obtained by backcrossing

**backdoor** *noun* COMPUT an unauthorised route into a computer system that bypasses the main security or password protection scheme

**backdrop** *noun* COMPUT a static background image in front of which are displayed actors or scenes

**back-end processor** *noun* COMPUT a special-purpose auxiliary processor

**background** *noun* **1.** a person's past work or experience ○ *His background is in the computer industry.* ○ *The company is looking for someone with a background of success in the electronics industry.* ○ *Do you know anything about his background?* **2.** COMPUT a part of a picture which is behind the main object of interest ○ *The new graphics processor chip can handle background, foreground and sprite movement independently.* **3.** COMPUT a system in a computer where low-priority work can be done in the intervals when very important work is not being done ■ *adjective* referring to conditions which are always present in the environment, but are less obvious or less important than others ○ *processing in the background*

**background carboxyhaemoglobin level** *noun* PHYSIOL the

concentration of carboxyhaemoglobin in the blood of a person living a normal existence without exposure to particularly high levels of carbon dioxide

**background colour** noun COMPUT the colour of a computer screen display ○ *White background colour with black characters is less stressful for the eyes than other colour combinations.* (NOTE: Characters and graphics are normally displayed in a different foreground colour.)

**background concentration** noun **1.** ENVIRON same as **background pollution 2.** PHYS same as **background radiation**

**background level** noun PHYS, GEOL the general level of something such as noise or pollution which is always there

**background noise** noun **1.** a general level of noise which is always there in the environment ○ *The other machines around this device will produce a lot of background noise.* **2.** (*in an electronic instrument*) noise which is present along with the required signal ○ *The modem is sensitive to background noise.*

**background pollution** noun the general level of air pollution in an area, disregarding any specifically local factors, e.g. the presence of a coal-fired power station

**background printing** noun COMPUT the process of printing from a computer while it is processing another task ○ *Background printing can be carried out while another document is being edited.*

**background radiation** noun PHYS, GEOL radiation from natural sources like rocks, the soil or the atmosphere, and not from a single artificial source

COMMENT: Background radiation can depend on the geological structure of the area. Places above granite are particularly subject to high levels of radiation. Other sources of background radiation are: cosmic rays from outer space, radiation from waste products of nuclear power plants which has escaped into the environment and radiation from TV and computer screens.

**background task** noun COMPUT a process executed at any time by a computer system, not normally noticed by the user

**backing store, backing storage, backing memory** noun COMPUT a permanent storage medium onto which data can be recorded before being processed by the computer or after processing for later retrieval ○ *By adding another disk drive, I will increase the backing store capabilities.* ○ *Paper tape is one of the slowest access backing stores.*

**backlight** noun COMPUT a light that provides illumination from behind

**backlit display** noun COMPUT a liquid crystal display unit that has a backlight fitted to improve the contrast of the display

**backlog** noun COMPUT a quantity of work or tasks that have yet to be processed ○ *The programmers can't deal with the backlog of programming work.*

**back mutation** noun GENETICS the changing back of a mutated gene to its original form

**backout** verb COMPUT to restore a file to its original condition before any changes were made

**back panel** noun COMPUT a panel at the rear of a computer which normally holds the connectors to peripherals such as keyboard, printer, video display unit and mouse

**backplane** noun COMPUT the part of the body of a computer which holds the circuit boards, buses and expansion connectors (NOTE: The backplane does not provide any processing functions.)

**backscatter** EARTH SCI noun the sending back of radiation ○ *Backscatter contributes to an increase in albedo.* ■ verb to send back radiation ○ *A proportion of incoming solar radiation is backscattered by air in the atmosphere.*

**backshore** noun EARTH SCI the part of a beach between the foreshore and where permanent vegetation grows

**backslash** noun COMPUT the printed or keyboard symbol \ (NOTE: It is ASCII character 92, the sign used in MS-DOS to represent the root directory of a disk or to separate subdirectories in a path.)

**backspace** noun COMPUT a movement of the cursor to the preceding character, or a key that effects this

**backspace character** noun COMPUT a code that causes a backspace action in a display device. Abbreviation **BS**

**backswamp** *noun* EARTH SCI a marshy area in a flood plain

**backtrack** *verb* COMPUT to carry out list processing in reverse, starting with the goal and working towards the proofs

**back up** COMPUT *verb* **1.** to support or help something or someone ○ *He brought along a file of documents to back up his claim.* ○ *The printout backed up his argument for a new system.* **2.** to make a copy of a file, data or a disk ○ *The company accounts were backed up on disk as a protection against fire damage.* ○ *The program enables users to back up hard disk files with a single command.* ■ *noun* a copy of a file or set of data kept for security against errors in the original or master copy

**backup** *noun* a system, instrument, computer disk or other resource to be used if the first one fails ○ *The backup failed as well.* ○ *Backup generators are driven by the engine.* ■ *adjective* COMPUT to be used if the first one fails

**backup copy** *noun* COMPUT a copy of a computer disk to be kept in case the original disk is damaged ○ *The most recent backup copy is kept in the safe.*

**Backus-Naur-Form** *noun* COMPUT a system of writing and expressing the syntax of a programming language. Abbreviation **BNF**

**backward** *adjective* directed towards the back ○ *a backward movement*

**backward channel** *noun* TELECOM a channel from the receiver to transmitter allowing the receiver to send control and handshaking signals

**backward error correction** *noun* TELECOM a correction of errors which are detected by the receiver and a signal sent to the transmitter to request re-transmission of the data

**backwards** *adverb* towards the back ○ *move backwards* (NOTE: The US term is **backward**.)

**backwards compatible** *noun* COMPUT **1.** working with all the old adapter cards designed for earlier versions of the computer **2.** providing the same functions as the previous version and able to read the files created in the previous version

**backwash** *noun* EARTH SCI the flow of seawater down a beach. Compare **swash**

**backwater** *noun* EARTH SCI **1.** stagnant water connected to a river or stream **2.** water behind a dam or tide

**bacteria** plural of **bacterium**

**bacteria bed** *noun* INDUST a filter bed of rough stone, forming the last stage in the treatment of sewage

**bacterial** *adjective* MICROBIOL referring to or caused by bacteria ○ *Children with sickle-cell anaemia are susceptible to bacterial infection.*

**bacterial artificial chromosome** *noun* BIOTECH a sequence of DNA taken from an organism and inserted in a bacterium

**bacterial contamination** *noun* MICROBIOL the pollution of something such as water or food by bacteria

**bacterial decay** *noun* MICROBIOL decay caused by the action of bacteria

**bacterial strain** *noun* MICROBIOL a distinct type of bacterium

**bactericidal** *adjective* MICROBIOL destroying bacteria

**bactericide** *noun* MICROBIOL a substance that destroys bacteria

**bacteriological warfare** *noun* ENVIRON war where one side tries to kill or affect the people of the enemy side by infecting them with bacteria

**bacteriology** *noun* MICROBIOL the scientific study of bacteria

**bacteriophage** *noun* MICROBIOL a virus that affects bacteria

**bacteriostat** *noun* MICROBIOL a substance that inhibits the growth and activity of bacteria but does not kill them

**bacterium** *noun* MICROBIOL a submicroscopic organism, belonging to a large group, some of which help in the decomposition of organic matter, some of which are permanently in the intestines of animals and can break down food tissue and some of which cause disease

COMMENT: Bacteria can be shaped like rods (bacilli), like balls (cocci) or have a spiral form (such as spirochaetes). Bacteria, especially bacilli and spirochaetes, can move and reproduce very rapidly.

**bad sector** *noun* COMPUT a disk sector that has been wrongly formatted or that contains an error or fault and is unable to be correctly written to or read from ○ *You will probably receive error messages when you copy files that are stored on bad sectors on a disk.*

**baffle** *noun* a metal plate for preventing the free movement of sound or liquids ○ *Integral fuel tanks can be strengthened by fitting baffle plates.* ○ *The baffle in the recording studio works as a sound absorber to remove unwanted echoes.*

**bag** *noun* COMPUT a number of elements in no particular order

**Baily's beads** *plural noun* ASTRON bright points of sunlight that briefly appear around the Moon immediately before and after a total eclipse of the Sun (NOTE: They are caused by sunlight shining through valleys on the Moon.)

**Bakelite** *trademark* INDUST a synthetic resin, particularly a phenol-formaldehyde resin

**balance** *noun* **1.** a state in which two sides are equal or in proportion ○ *The propelling nozzle size is extremely important and must be designed to obtain the correct balance of pressure, temperature and thrust.* **2.** a state on which weights or forces are evenly distributed **3.** a state in which proportions of substances are correct, e.g. in the diet ○ *to maintain a healthy balance of vitamins in the diet* **4.** a state of staying upright and not falling ○ *He stood on top of the fence and kept his balance.* **5.** COMPUT the placing of text and graphics on a page in an attractive way ○ *The DTP package allows the user to see whether the overall page balance is correct.* **6.** a device for weighing, made with springs or weights ○ *He weighed the powder in a spring balance.* ■ *verb* **1.** to plan something so that two parts are equal or in proportion **2.** to provide an opposite and equal weight, force or importance to something else ○ *The pressure exerted by the weight of the atmosphere above the level of the bowl balances a column of mercury in the tube.* **3.** to stay steady, especially when resting on the centre of gravity

**balanced circuit** *noun* ELECTRONICS an electronic circuit that presents a correct load to a communications line (NOTE: The correct load is usually equal to the impedance of a element.)

**balanced diet** *noun* BIOL a diet which provides all the nutrients needed in the correct proportions

**balanced error** *noun* STATS the equal probability that any error could occur out of a number of possible errors

**balanced line** *noun* TELECOM a communications line that is terminated at each end with a balanced circuit, preventing signal reflections

**balanced routing** *noun* COMPUT a method of using all possible routes through a network equally

**balance of nature** *noun* ECOL a situation where relative numbers of different organisms living in the same ecosystem remain more or less constant □ **to disturb the balance of nature** to make a change to the environment which has the effect of putting some organisms at a disadvantage against others

**baleen** *noun* MARINE BIOL a series of plates like a comb, which hang down from the upper jaw of some whales and act like a sieve

**baleen whale** *noun* MARINE BIOL a whale that has two breathing holes and feeds with the help of baleen. Suborder: Mysticeti.

COMMENT: Baleen whales are the larger of the two groups of whales (the others being the toothed whales or Odontoceti). They live on plankton and other tiny marine animals. They eat by sucking in a huge quantity of water and then forcing it out with their tongues through the baleen, which catches the plankton.

**ball** *noun* **1.** BIOL a round object **2.** ANAT the soft part of the hand below the thumb **3.** ANAT the soft part of the foot below the big toe

**ball and socket joint** *noun* ANAT a joint where the round end of a long bone is attached to a cup-shaped hollow in another bone in such a way that the long bone can move in almost any direction

**ballast** *noun* ENG material such as stones carried in the hull of a ship to make it heavier and so less likely to roll

**balloon** *noun* a large bag inflatable with hot air or gas to provide lift, but without power ○ *Meteorologists send balloons into the upper atmosphere to collect useful information.*

**Balmer series** *noun* ASTRON a series of spectral lines characterising hydrogen and seen in visible light (NOTE: The Balmer series is easily observable in the spectra of the Sun and other stars and is caused by the movement of electrons to and from the energy level possible in hydrogen above the normal ground state.)

**balun** *noun* ELEC ENG a transformer that matches two circuits that have different impedances ○ *We have used a balun to connect the coaxial cable to the twisted-pair circuit.*

**band** *noun* 1. a strip ○ *A jet stream is a narrow band of high-altitude strong winds.* 2. ELEC a range of numbers or frequencies between two limits within a radio system 3. COMPUT a group of tracks on a magnetic disk 4. EARTH SCI a layer of rock

**banded** *adjective* GEOL referring to rock arranged in layers

**bandpass filter** *noun* ELEC ENG an electronic filter that allows a range of frequencies to pass, but reduces in power all frequencies outside the specified range

**band printer** *noun* COMPUT a printer in which the characters are located along a movable steel belt

**band sprayer** *noun* AGRIC a crop sprayer that applies chemicals in narrow strips, mostly used with precision seeders

**bandwidth** *noun* 1. ELEC ENG a range of frequencies 2. ELEC a measure of the amount of data that can be transmitted along a cable or channel or other medium ○ *This fibre-optic cable has a greater bandwidth than the old copper cable and so it can carry data at higher speeds.* 3. COMPUT a measure of the range of frequencies that a monitor or CRT will accept and display (NOTE: High-resolution monitors display more pixels per area so need high-speed data input and so a higher bandwidth.)

**bandwidth on demand** *noun* ON-LINE a system used with a switching service such as ISDN in a wide area network that allows users to send as much information as they want by automatically allocating extra channels to cope with higher bandwidth requirements (NOTE: The network will adjust to transmit the required amount of information.)

**bank** *noun* 1. a collection of similar devices ○ *A bank of minicomputers processes all the raw data.* 2. MED a place where blood or organs from donors can be stored until needed 3. ENVIRON a place where waste materials can be collected for recycling 4. a piece of land at the side of water such as a river or lake 5. a long heap of sand or snow such as a

sandbank in shallow water, in either a river or the sea, or a snowbank along the side of a road 6. AVIAT a rotating or rolling movement of an aircraft around its longitudinal axis to a particular angle ○ *An attitude indicator gives the pilot pitch and bank information.* ■ *verb* AVIAT (*of aircraft*) to rotate or roll around its longitudinal axis to a particular angle ○ *Stresses are increased when the aircraft banks, turns or pulls out of a dive.*

COMMENT: Memory banks are used to expand the main memory of a computer by having a number of memory chips arranged into banks. Each bank operates over the same address range but is selected independently by a special code.

**bank switching** *noun* COMPUT the selection of a particular memory bank from a group

**banner ad, banner advertisement** *noun* COMPUT an image that carries an advertising slogan, logo or message and is displayed on a webpage

**bar** *noun* 1. ENG a long straight solid piece of material, usually metal ○ *The part is made from a solid bar of aluminium.* 2. METEOROL a unit of atmospheric pressure, equal to 1000 millibars or 105 Pa 3. COMPUT a thick line or block of colour 4. a long bank of sand submerged at high tide at the entrance to a harbour, river or bay ■ *verb* to stop someone from doing something □ **to bar entry to a file** to stop someone accessing a file

**barbiturate** *noun* PHARM a sedative drug

**bar chart** *noun* MATHS a graph on which values are represented as vertical or horizontal bars of different heights or lengths

**bar code** *noun* COMPUT data represented as a series of printed stripes of varying widths (NOTE: Bar codes are widely used on goods in supermarkets and in automated data systems such as those in lending libraries.)

**bar-code reader** *noun* COMPUT an optical device that reads data from a bar code

**bare board** *noun* COMPUT a circuit board with no components on it (NOTE: It usually refers to a memory expansion board that does not yet have any memory chips mounted on it.)

**barium** *noun* CHEM ELEM a chemical element that forms poisonous compounds (NOTE: The chemical symbol is **Ba**; the atomic number is **56** and the atomic weight is **137.34**.)

**barium concrete** *noun* CHEM a concrete with barium added to it, used to absorb radiation

**barium meal** *noun* MED a liquid solution containing barium sulfate which a patient drinks so that an X-ray can be taken of his or her alimentary tract

**barium sulfate, barium sulphate** *noun* CHEM a white insoluble odourless powder which is opaque to X-rays and used in X-ray photography. Formula: $BaSO_4$.

**bark** *noun* **1.** BOT the hard outer layer of a tree, formed of dead tissue **2.** ZOOL the cry of an animal of the dog family, e.g. a wolf or fox

**barley** *noun* PLANTS a common cereal crop. Latin name: *Hordeum sativum*.

COMMENT: Barley is widely grown in northern temperate countries, with the largest production in Germany and France. It is an important arable crop in the UK The grain is mainly used for livestock feeding and for malting for use in producing alcoholic drinks such as beer and whisky. It is rarely used for making flour.

**barn** *noun* MEASURE, PHYS a unit of area used to measure nuclear cross-sections, equal to $10^{-28}m^2$. Symbol **b**

**baro-** *prefix* METEOROL referring to weight or pressure

**barograph** *noun* METEOROL an instrument that records changes in atmospheric pressure, made by attaching a pen to a barometer and recording fluctuations in pressure on a roll of paper

**barometer** *noun* METEOROL an instrument which measures changes in atmospheric pressure and is used to forecast changes in the weather

**barometric** *adjective* METEOROL referring to a barometer

**barometrically** *adverb* METEOROL by use of a barometer

**barometric corrections** *plural noun* METEOROL corrections made to the reading on a mercury thermometer to allow for altitude and outside temperature

**barometric pressure** *noun* METEOROL atmospheric pressure indicated by a barometer

**barometric tendency** *noun* METEOROL the amount of decrease in atmospheric pressure with increase in altitude

**barrage** *noun* CIV ENG a construction to prevent or regulate the flow of tides, used either to prevent flooding, as in the Thames Barrage, or to harness tidal power

COMMENT: The advantages of building barrages to harness tidal power are that they are economical to run and use no fuel. They do pose particular environmental problems, as do all dams, in that they may change the ecosystem of the surrounding countryside. A barrage would have an effect on the estuary marshlands, on the river behind it, and possibly on the movement of coastal silt by the tides.

**Barr body** *noun* GENETICS an inactive X chromosome present in the cells of women and female animals (NOTE: It is used in a test to determine sex.)

**barred spiral galaxy** *noun* ASTRON a galaxy in which the stars appear as a spiral with a bright bar across the centre

**barrel** *noun* **1.** ELEC ENG a conducting post in a terminal **2.** INDUST a large cylindrical container for liquids such as beer, wine and oil **3.** MEASURE, INDUST the amount of a liquid contained in a standard barrel of 42 US gallons, used as a measure of the quantity of crude oil produced and equal to 159 litres or 35 imperial gallons

**barren** *adjective* **1.** ECOL unable to support plant or animal life ○ *a barren desert* **2.** BIOL unable to reproduce

**barrier** *noun* a wall or other structure that prevents something going through

**barrier beach, barrier island** *noun* EARTH SCI a bank of sand or a strip of land lying along the shore and separated from it by a lagoon

**barrier reef** *noun* a long coral reef lying along the shore and enclosing a lagoon

**baryon** *noun* PHYS a subatomic particle belonging to a group that undergoes strong interactions, has a mass greater than or equal to that of the proton, and consists of three quarks

**basal** *adjective* **1.** affecting a foundation or basis **2.** basic or fundamental

**basal area** *noun* BOT the area of woodland actually covered by the trunks of trees

**basal ganglia** *plural noun* ANAT the masses of grey matter at the base of each cerebral hemisphere which receive impulses from the thalamus and influence the motor output from the frontal cortex

**basal metabolic rate** *noun* BIOL the amount of energy used by a body in exchanging oxygen and carbon dioxide when at rest. Abbreviation **BMR** (NOTE: It is a measure of the energy needed to keep the body functioning and the temperature normal.)

**basalt** *noun* GEOL a fine dark volcanic rock

**basaltic** *adjective* GEOL referring to or containing basalt ○ *Most volcanic lava is basaltic.*

**base** *noun* **1.** the original, lowest or first position **2.** the main ingredient of something such as a paint or an ointment **3.** CHEM a substance that reacts with an acid to form a salt **4.** COMPUT a collection of files used as a reference **5.** MATHS a number that is taken as the basis of a system of calculation, representing the number of units in the system **6.** COMPUT (*in object-oriented programming*) a class from which other classes can be derived by inheritance ■ *verb* **1.** to start to calculate from a position ○ *We based our calculations on the basic keyboarding rate.* **2.** to develop something from something else ○ *The operation of the auxiliary power unit is based on the gas turbine engine.* ○ *The principle of vapour cycle cooling is based upon the ability of a refrigerant to absorb heat.*

**base 10** *noun* MATHS a decimal number system using the ten digits 0 – 9

**base 16** *noun* MATHS a hexadecimal number system using the ten digits 0 – 9 and six letters A – F

**base 2** *noun* MATHS a binary number system using the two digits 0 and 1

**base 8** *noun* MATHS an octal number system using the eight digits 0 – 7

**base address** *noun* COMPUT an initial address in a program used as a reference for others

**baseband** *noun* **1.** TELECOM the frequency range of a signal before it is processed or transmitted **2.** COMPUT digital signals transmitted without modulation **3.** COMPUT information modulated with a single carrier frequency

**baseband modem** *noun* TELECOM a communications circuit that transmits an unmodulated baseband signal over a short distance ○ *Do not use a baseband modem with a normal phone line.*

**baseband signalling** *noun* TELECOM the transmitting of data as varying voltage levels across a link

**base font** *noun* COMPUT the default font and point size used by a word-processing program

**base hardware** *noun* COMPUT the minimum hardware that a particular software package needs in order to run

**base level** *noun* **1.** the lowest level of something, from which other levels are calculated **2.** GEOL the depth below which erosion would be unable to occur

**baseline** *noun* **1.** ASTRON (*In interferometry*) the distance between the farthest-separated points at which data are collected **2.** COMPUT a line which defines the size and layout of a page in an application **3.** COMPUT the horizontal line along which characters are printed or displayed

**baseline conditions** *plural noun* ENVIRON (*in economic analyses*) the basic health, environmental and economic conditions that exist before any policy intervention

**baseline emission** *noun* ENVIRON emission of greenhouse gases that would occur without policy intervention

**base memory** *noun* COMPUT the first 640 kb of random access memory fitted to a PC

**basement** *noun* GEOL the lowest level of rocks, which have been covered by sediment

**basement membrane** *noun* ANAT a membrane at the base of an epithelium

**base metal** *noun* CHEM a common metal such as copper, lead or tin

**base pair** *noun* GENETICS a set of two bases such as adenine–thymine or cytosine–guanine on separate strands of DNA, held together by hydrogen bonds. Abbreviation **bp**

**base register** *noun* COMPUT a register in a CPU, but not usually in small computers, that contains the address of the start of a program

**base unit** *noun* MEASURE one of the seven SI units on which other units are based (NOTE: The SI base units are: ampere, candela, kelvin, kilogram, metre, mole and second.)

**basic** *adjective* **1.** from which everything else comes ○ *This chapter provides a basic understanding from which the study of meteorology can develop.* ○ *Everyone should know basic maths.* ○ *The basic architecture is the same for all computer models in this range.* **2.** CHEM referring to a chemical substance which reacts with an acid to form a salt

**BASIC** *noun* COMPUT a high-level programming language for developing programs in a conversational way, providing an easy introduction to computer programming. Full form **beginner's all-purpose symbolic instruction code**

**basic encoding rule** *noun* COMPUT a standard method of encoding data that is stored in the ASN language. Abbreviation **BER** (NOTE: It is often used in libraries and other Internet data sites.)

**basic input/output operating system** *noun* COMPUT a set of system routines that interface between high-level program instructions and the system peripherals to control the input and output to various standard devices such as the screen, keyboard and disk drives. Abbreviation **BIOS**

**basic law** *noun* a fundamental rule

**basic principle** *noun* a central or fundamental idea or theory

**basic rock** *noun* GEOL a rock such as basalt which contains little silica

**basic salt** *noun* CHEM a chemical compound formed when an acid reacts with a base

**basic slag** *noun* AGRIC calcium phosphate, produced as waste from blast furnaces and used as a fertiliser because of its phosphate content

**basic solution** *noun* CHEM a water solution with a pH greater than 7

**basilar artery** *noun* ANAT an artery that lies at the base of the brain

**basilic vein** *noun* ANAT a large vein running along the inside of the arm

**basin** *noun* EARTH SCI a large low-lying area of land, drained by a large river system or surrounding an ocean ○ *Thousands of tributaries drain into the Amazon basin.* ○ *A ring of vol-* canoes lies around the edge of the Pacific basin.

**basis** *noun* the central and most important part of something from which everything else is derived ○ *The basis of air navigation is the triangle of velocities.* (NOTE: The plural is **bases**.)

**bass** *noun* ACOUSTICS the lower end of the range of audible frequencies that make up a sound

**bastnaesite, bastnasite** *noun* MINERALS a rare mineral containing lanthanum and cerium

**batch** COMPUT *noun* **1.** a group of items which are made at one time ○ *The last batch of disk drives is faulty.* **2.** a group of documents which are processed at the same time ○ *today's batch of orders* **3.** a group of tasks or amount of data to be processed as a single unit ○ *We deal with the orders in batches of fifty.* ■ *verb* **1.** to put data or tasks together in groups **2.** to put items together in groups

**batch file** *noun* COMPUT a file stored on disk that contains a sequence of system commands ○ *This batch file is used to save time and effort when carrying out a routine task.* (NOTE: When the batch file is run, the commands are executed, saving a user typing them in.)

**batch number** *noun* COMPUT a reference number attached to a batch

**batch processing** *noun* COMPUT a system of data processing where information is collected into batches before being processed by the computer in one machine run. Compare **immediate processing**

COMMENT: Batch processing is the opposite to interactive processing (where the user gives instructions and receives an immediate response).

**batch total** *noun* COMPUT the sum of a number of batches of data, used for error checking, validation or to provide useful information

**Batesian mimicry** *noun* ZOOL a form of mimicry where one species mimics another which is poisonous, so as to avoid being eaten

**bathy-** *prefix* OCEANOG referring to the part of the seabed between 1000 and 3000 m deep

**bathyal zone** *noun* OCEANOG a region of the ocean extending from the edge of the continental shelf, which slopes down sharply into deeper water, to a depth of about 4000 m

**bathylimnetic** *adjective* GEOG referring to the deepest part of a lake

**BATNEEC** *noun* ENVIRON a principle applied to the control of emissions into the air, land and water from polluting processes, in order to minimise pollution without the use of advanced technology or expensive methods

**battery** *noun* ELEC a chemical device which produces electrical current

**battery-backed** *adjective* COMPUT with a battery backup ○ *The RAM disk card has the option to be battery-backed.* ○ *Battery-backed CMOS memory replaces a disk drive in this portable.*

**battery backup** *noun* COMPUT the use of a battery to provide power to a volatile device such as a RAM chip to retain data after a computer has been switched off

**battery capacity** *noun* ELEC the amount of electrical energy a battery can store and deliver, expressed in ampere hours

**battery charger** *noun* ELEC a device for charging a battery by converting mains voltage AC to a DC voltage suitable for the battery

**battery charging** *noun* ELEC the replenishing of the charge stored in a rechargeable battery

**battery discharge** *noun* ELEC a loss or release of electrical supply from a battery

**battery meter** *noun* ELEC a device that indicates how much life or working time is left in a battery

**battery-operated** *adjective* ELEC powered or run by an electric battery

**baud** *noun* COMPUT a measure of the number of signal changes transmitted per second

**Baudot code** *noun* COMPUT a five-bit character transmission code, used mainly in teleprinters

**baud rate** *noun* COMPUT the rate of transmission of signal charge, per second ○ *The baud rate of the binary signal was 300 bits per second.* ○ *A modem with auto-baud scanner can automatically sense at which baud rate it should operate.*

COMMENT: Baud rate is often considered to be the same as bits per second, but in fact it depends on the protocol used and the error checking. 300 baud is roughly equivalent to 30 characters per second using standard error checking.

**bauxite** *noun* CHEM a mineral that contains aluminium ore

**bay** *noun* **1.** EARTH SCI a wide curved coastline, partly enclosing an area of sea **2.** ENG a space or area in a structure where equipment can be fitted or located

**bay bar, bay barrier** *noun* EARTH SCI a bank of sand or strip of land lying along the coastline of a bay

**bayonet fitting** *noun* ELEC a type of attachment with two side pins, found on some light bulbs

**B box** *noun* COMPUT altrnative for **base register**

**bcc** *abbreviation* COMPUT blind carbon copy

**BCC** *abbreviation* COMPUT block character check

**BCD** *abbreviation* COMPUT binary coded decimal ○ *The BCD representation of decimal 8 is 1000.*

**BCH code** *abbreviation* COMPUT Bose-Chandhuri-Hocquenghem code

**BCNF** *abbreviation* COMPUT Boyce-Codd normal form

**BCPL** *noun* COMPUT a high-level programming language

**Be** *symbol* CHEM ELEM beryllium

**beach** *noun* EARTH SCI an area of sand or small stones by the side of the sea, a lake or a river

**beach sediment** *noun* GEOL stone, sand, mud and shells deposited on a beach by the sea, by a river or by erosion of the cliffs

**beacon** *noun* **1.** AEROSP a light or radio signal for navigational purposes **2.** COMPUT a signal transmitted repeatedly by a device that is malfunctioning on a network

**beacon frame** *noun* COMPUT a special frame within the FDDI protocol that is sent after a network break has occurred. ♦ **FDDI**

**bead** *noun* COMPUT a small section of a program that is used for a single task

**beam** *noun* **1.** ENG a long thick solid bar used as a support ○ *A beam is de-*

*signed with a breaking load of 12 tons but when a three-ton load is applied repeatedly, the beam may fail.* **2.** PHYS a narrow shaft of light or radiation ○ *A beam of laser light is used in this printer to produce high-resolution graphics.*

**beam deflection** *noun* ELEC ENG the moving of the electron beam in a CRT across the screen

**beam sharpening** *noun* ELEC ENG the making of a radio or light beam narrower ○ *Any system employing beam sharpening is vulnerable to side lobe generation at the transmitter.*

**bear** *verb* **1.** to carry or to hold ○ *The undercarriage has to bear the weight of the aircraft on the ground.* □ **this bears no relation to that** this is not connected with that **2.** to tolerate something ○ *I can't bear such a long delay.* **3.** to give birth to offspring ○ *to bear a child*

**bearing** *noun* **1.** NAVIG an angle, measured in a clockwise direction, of a distant point relative to a reference ○ *To plot a position line from the non-directional radio beacon, it is first necessary to convert the relative bearing to a true bearing and then calculate the reciprocal.* **2.** ENG a device containing steel balls or needles which allows free rotation of one component around another

**Beaufort scale** *noun* METEOROL a scale rising from 0 to 12 used to refer to the strength of wind ○ *The meteorological office has issued a warning of force 12 winds.*

COMMENT: The Beaufort scale was devised in the 18th century by a British admiral. The descriptions of the winds and their speeds in knots are: 0, calm (0 knots); 1, light air (2 knots); 2, light breeze (5 knots); 3, gentle breeze (9 knots); 4, moderate breeze (13 knots); 5, fresh breeze (19 knots); 6, strong breeze (24 knots); 7, near gale (30 knots); 8, gale (37 knots); 9, strong gale (44 knots); 10, storm (52 knots); 11, violent storm (60 knots); 12, hurricane (above 60 knots).

**becquerel** *noun* PHYS, MEASURE the SI unit of measurement of radiation, 1 becquerel being the amount of radioactivity in a substance where one nucleus decays per second. Symbol **Bq.** ♦ **rad** (NOTE: now used in place of the **curie**)

**bed** *noun* **1.** EARTH SCI the bottom of a river, lake or the sea ○ *a fish which feeds on the seabed* ○ *The river bed is*

choked with weeds. **2.** GEOL a layer of sediment in rock ○ *The cliffs show clearly several beds of sandstone.*

**bedding** *noun* GEOL sediment in different layers

**bedrock** *noun* GEOL the rock which is found under a layer of ore or coal

**beech** *noun* TREES a common temperate hardwood tree. Genus: *Fagus.*

**beep** *noun* an audible warning noise ○ *The printer will make a beep when it runs out of paper.* ■ *verb* to make a beep ○ *The computer beeped when the wrong key was hit.*

**beetle** *noun* INSECTS an insect with hard covers on the wings. Order: Coleoptera.

**beginning of file** *noun* COMPUT a character or symbol that shows the start of a valid section of data. Abbreviation **bof**

**behaviour** *noun* BIOL the way in which a living organism responds to a stimulus

**behavioural** *adjective* BIOL referring to behaviour

**behavioural ecology** *noun* ECOL the study of the patterns of behaviour in animals

**behavioural scientist** *noun* BIOL a person who specialises in the study of behaviour

**behaviourism** *noun* PSYCHOL a psychological theory that only the subject's behaviour should be studied to discover his or her motivation or problems

**behaviourist** *noun* PSYCHIAT a psychologist who follows behaviourism

**bel** *noun* ACOUSTICS, MEASURE a unit of relative loudness equal to 10 decibels

**bell character** *noun* COMPUT a control code that causes a machine to produce an audible signal (NOTE: It is equivalent to ASCII code 7.)

**below** *preposition* **1.** lower in position than ○ *below sea level* ○ *the beach below the cliffs* **2.** less in number or quantity than ○ *below freezing point* **3.** EARTH SCI downstream from ○ *the Thames below London*

**below freezing point** *adjective, adverb* PHYS less than or lower than freezing point

**belt** *noun* **1.** a long, relatively narrow area ○ *a belt of trees* **2.** ENG a loop of strong material connecting two pulleys or wheels, one driving the other

**belt-driven** *adjective* ENG moved by a belt linked to another wheel which, in turn, is moved by a motor or an engine ○ *Generators are belt-driven or shaft-driven.*

**benchmark** *noun* **1.** a point in an index which is important, and can be used to compare with other figures **2.** COMPUT a program used to test the performance of software or hardware or a system ○ *The magazine gave the new program's benchmark test results.*

**bend** *noun* a curve ■ *verb* to curve from a straight shape

**bend downwards** *verb* to curve down from a horizontal position

**bending load** *noun* ENG a load causing bending of a structure

**bend upwards** *verb* to curve up from a horizontal position ○ *The wings support the weight of the aircraft and they bend upwards in flight.*

**benign** *adjective* MED not cancerous and unlikely to cause a medical problem

**benthic** *adjective* EARTH SCI on or living on the bottom of the sea or of a lake

**benthic fauna** *noun* MARINE BIOL organisms living on the bottom of the sea or of a lake

**benthos** *noun* MARINE BIOL a collection of organisms living on the bottom of the sea or of a lake

**benzene** *noun* CHEM a simple aromatic hydrocarbon produced from coal tar and very carcinogenic. Formula: $C_6H_6$.

**benzene hexachloride** *noun* CHEM a white or yellow powder used as an insecticide as a dust or spray against pea and bean weevil, and as a seed dressing against wireworm. Formula: $C_6H_6Cl_6$.

**benzene ring** *noun* CHEM the molecular structure of benzene and its derivatives with six carbon atoms bonded in a hexagon by alternating single and double bonds

**benzoic acid** *noun* CHEM the simplest aromatic carboxylic acid, a white crystalline solid found in some natural resins. Formula: $C_6H_5COOH$. (NOTE: It is used as a food preservative and in pharmaceuticals and cosmetics manufacture.)

**benzpyrene** *noun* CHEM an inflammable carcinogenic substance found in coal tar, produced in the exhaust fumes from petrol engines, from coal- and oil-burning appliances and from smoking tobacco

**BER** *abbreviation* COMPUT **1.** basic encoding rule **2.** bit error rate

**bergschrund** *noun* EARTH SCI a deep wide crevasse found between a cirque glacier and its back wall

**berkelium** *noun* CHEM ELEM a synthetic radioactive element in the actinide series of the periodic table produced by bombardment of americium-241 with helium ions (NOTE: The chemical symbol is **Bk**; the atomic number is **97** and the atomic weight is **247**.)

**berry** *noun* BOT a small fleshy seed-bearing fruit, e.g. a tomato or a gooseberry

**beryl** *noun* MINERALS a hard crystalline mineral composed of beryllium aluminium silicate and used as a gemstone (NOTE: It occurs in white, yellow, pink, green or blue forms.)

**beryllium** *noun* CHEM ELEM a metallic element used in making various alloys (NOTE: The chemical symbol is **Be**; the atomic number is **4** and the atomic weight is **9.01**.)

**bespoke software** *noun* COMPUT software that has been written especially for a customer's particular requirements

**Bessemer converter** *noun* METALL a type of furnace in which air is blown through molten metal

**Bessemer process** *noun* INDUST a method of making steel

COMMENT: The Bessemer process involves heating molten metal and blowing air into it at the same time in a Bessemer converter. The process is used to remove phosphorus and carbon from pig iron. The air forms iron oxide, which removes impurities from the molten metal, including carbon monoxide which burns off. Finally, manganese is added to the metal to remove the iron oxide.

**best-before date** *noun* FOOD INDUST a date stamped on foodstuffs sold in supermarkets, which is the last date when the food is guaranteed to be in good condition. Compare **sell-by date**

**best fit** *noun* **1.** the nearest match to a requirement **2.** COMPUT a function that selects the smallest free space in main memory for a requested virtual page

**beta** *noun* **1.** COMPUT the second working attempt of a computer product **2.** the second letter of the Greek alphabet

**beta blocker** *noun* PHARM a drug that controls heart rate, used in the treatment of high blood pressure and stress

**beta cell** *noun* ANAT a cell that produces insulin

**beta decay** *noun* PHYS the radioactive decay of an atomic nucleus during which a beta particle is emitted

**beta diversity** *noun* ECOL the number of species in a wide region

**beta particle** *noun* PHYS an electron given off in radioactive decay or otherwise found outside an atom (NOTE: Beta particles are among the commonest components of radiation. They will pass through thin substances such as metal and can harm living tissue.)

**beta radiation** *noun* CHEM radiation formed of beta particles

**beta test** *noun* COMPUT a second stage of tests performed on new software just before it is due to be released ○ *The application has passed the alpha tests and is just entering the beta test phase.*

**beta version** *noun* COMPUT a version of a software application that is almost ready to be released

**Betz limit** *noun* INDUST the maximum power that can be produced by a wind turbine

**beware** *verb* to watch out for something unwanted, unpleasant or dangerous ○ *Beware of inferior reproductions.*

**beyond** *preposition* farther away than ○ *The radio horizon extends beyond the visible horizon.*

**bezel** *noun* COMPUT the front cover of a computer's casing or disk drive unit

**Bézier curve** *noun* COMPUT a geometric curve whose overall shape is defined by two midpoints, called control handles

COMMENT: Bézier curves are a feature of many high-end design software packages. They allow a designer to create smooth curves by defining a number of points. The Postscript page description language uses Bézier curves to define the shapes of characters during printing.

**BGP** *noun* COMPUT a protocol that allows routers to share routing informa-

tion to allow each router to calculate the most efficient path for information (NOTE: This protocol is most often used between routers installed at Internet service providers.)

**Bh** *symbol* CHEM ELEM bohrium

**BHC** *abbreviation* CHEM benzene hexachloride

**Bi** *symbol* CHEM ELEM bismuth

**bi-** *prefix* two or twice

**bias** *noun* **1.** ELEC an electrical reference level **2.** MATHS a deviation of statistical results from a reference level

**biased** *adjective* having a bias

**biased data** *plural noun* data or records that point to one conclusion

**biased exponent** *noun* MATHS the value of the exponent in a floating point number

**bicarbonate** *noun* CHEM an acid salt of carbonic acid

**biceps** *noun* ANAT a muscle with two attachment points at one end, especially a large muscle **biceps brachii** in the upper arm

**biconcave** *adjective* OPTICS referring to a lens which is concave on both sides

**biconvex** *adjective* OPTICS referring to a lens which is convex on both sides

**bicuspid** *adjective* BIOL with two points or cusps ○ *bicuspid teeth* ■ *noun* DENT a tooth with two cusps or points, especially a human premolar

**bicuspid valve** *noun* ANAT a valve in the heart which allows blood to flow from the left atrium to the left ventricle but not in the opposite direction

**bid** *verb* COMPUT (*of a computer*) to gain control of a network in order to transmit data ○ *The terminal had to bid three times before there was a gap in transmissions on the network.*

**bi-directional** *adjective* COMPUT referring to an operation or process that can occur in forward and reverse directions ○ *bi-directional file transfer*

**bi-directional bus** *noun* COMPUT data or control lines that can carry signals travelling in two directions

**bi-directional printer** *noun* COMPUT a printer which is able to print characters from left to right and from right to left as the head is moving forwards or backwards across the paper speeding up the printing operation

**biennial** BOT *adjective* happening every two years ■ *noun* a plant that completes its life cycle over a period of two years

**bifurcation** *noun* **1.** BIOL a place where something divides into two parts **2.** COMPUT a system where there are only two possible results ○ *The result of a binary multiplication is a bifurcation: the result is either 1 or 0.*

**big bang** *noun* ASTRON the event which according to most modern cosmogony began the universe

COMMENT: The big bang is assumed to have happened some 18 billion years ago. At that time, it seems, all the matter now distributed throughout the universe was in a single compact mass. Since then it has formed into galaxies, stars, planets and other objects, expanding constantly.

**big crunch** *noun* ASTRON the possible end of the universe, according to the theory that states that if the universe is dense enough, it will eventually finish expanding and contract again under its own mass, collapsing back into a single small volume in a reverse action replay of the big bang

**big game** *plural noun* ZOOL large wild animals. e.g. elephants and tigers, hunted and killed for sport, especially formerly.

**bight** *noun* EARTH SCI a wide curve in a shoreline

**bilateral symmetry** *noun* the characteristic of being able to be divided by an imaginary plane into equivalent right and left halves

**bile** *noun* BIOL a thick bitter brownish yellow fluid produced by the liver and used to digest fatty substances

**bile duct** *noun* ANAT a tube along which bile flows from the liver and, when present, the gall bladder to the small intestine (NOTE: The common bile duct is formed by the merging of hepatic and cystic ducts.)

**bile salts** *plural noun* BIOCHEM alkaline salts in the bile

**bilharziasis** *noun* MED same as **schistosomiasis**

**bilinear filtering** *noun* COMPUT a method of removing unwanted image defects by looking at the four adjacent pixels that surround each pixel to check that there is no sudden change in colour

**bilirubin** *noun* PHYSIOL a reddish-yellow bile pigment formed by the breakdown of haemoglobin in the liver (NOTE: Excess bilirubin in the blood causes jaundice.)

**billion** *noun* **1.** MATHS a number equal to one thousand million (NOTE: In the US it has always meant one thousand million, but in the UK it formerly meant one million million, and it is still sometimes used with this meaning. With figures it is usually written **bn: 5 bn.**) **2.** a number equal to one million million (*dated*)

**BIM** *noun* COMPUT a character indicating the start of a data stream stored on a disk drive or tape. Full form **beginning of information mark**

**bimetallic** *adjective* CHEM made of two metals

**bimetallic strip** *noun* ELEC ENG a strip of two separate metals with different rates of expansion, joined together side by side so that when the strip is heated it bends and makes or breaks electrical contact ○ *Circuit breakers use a bimetallic strip as the sensing element.*

**binary** *adjective* **1.** COMPUT referring to a number notation system, base 2, which uses only the digits 0 and 1 **2.** made of two parts **3.** CHEM referring to a compound or alloy containing two different elements ■ *noun* **1.** COMPUT same as **binary digit 2.** ASTRON same as **binary star**

**binary adder** *noun* COMPUT a device that provides the sum of two or more binary digits

**binary arithmetic** *noun* MATHS rules and functions governing arithmetic operations in base 2

**binary bit** *noun* COMPUT same as **binary digit**

**binary cell** *noun* COMPUT a storage element for one bit

**binary chop** *noun* COMPUT same as **binary search**

**binary code** *noun* COMPUT a pattern of binary digits that represents various symbols or elements

**binary coded decimal** *noun* COMPUT full form of **BCD**

**binary digit** *noun* COMPUT the smallest single unit in binary notation, either a 0 or a 1

**binary file** *noun* COMPUT a file that contains data rather than alphanumeric characters ○ *The program instructions are stored in the binary file.* ○ *Your letter is a text file, not a binary file.* (NOTE: A binary file can include any character code and cannot always be displayed or edited.)

**binary fission** *noun* BIOL a common method of asexual reproduction by which one cell divides into two similar or identical cells

**binary half adder** *noun* COMPUT a binary adder that can produce the sum of two inputs, producing a carry output if necessary, but cannot accept a carry input

**binary large object** *noun* COMPUT a field in a database record that can contain a large quantity of binary data, normally a bitmap image. Abbreviation **blob**

**binary number** *noun* COMPUT same as **binary digit**

**binary operation** *noun* COMPUT **1.** an operation on two operands **2.** an operation on an operand in binary form

**binary search** *noun* COMPUT a fast search method for use on ordered lists of data (NOTE: The search key is compared with the data in the middle of the list and one half is discarded, and this is repeated with the remaining half until only the required data item is left.)

**binary star** *noun* ASTRON a star system with two members (NOTE: Most stars are binary stars. The different types include eclipsing, spectroscopic, visual and astrometric binaries according to the methods needed to separate them observationally.)

**binary system** *noun* MATHS a system that operates with binary digits

**binary-to-decimal conversion** *noun* MATHS the process of converting a binary digit into its equivalent decimal value

**binaural** *adjective* BIOL referring to or using both ears

**binaural sound** *noun* ACOUSTICS a method of recording sound so that it gives the impression of stereophony when played back

**bind** *verb* **1.** COMPUT to link and convert one or more object code programs into a form that can be executed **2.** MANUF to glue or attach sheets of paper

along their spine to form a book **3.** CHEM to form a chemical bond

**binder** *noun* COMPUT a program that converts object code into a form that can be executed

**binding agent** *noun* CHEM a substance that causes two or more other substances to stick together or combine

**binding energy** *noun* PHYS the energy required to separate a system into its individual components

**binding target** *noun* ENVIRON an environmental standard that must be met in the future

**BinHex** *noun* COMPUT a method of encoding binary data into ASCII characters (NOTE: Software programs and data files are stored as binary data using all eight bits of information within one byte of storage space, whereas ASCII characters can be stored in just the first seven of the eight bits of storage space within one byte.)

**binocular vision** *noun* BIOL the ability to see with both eyes at the same time (NOTE: It gives a stereoscopic effect and allows a person to judge distances.)

**binomial classification** *noun* BIOL the scientific system of naming organisms devised by the Swedish scientist Carolus Linnaeus (1707–78)

COMMENT: The Linnaean system of binomial classification gives each organism a name made up of two Latin words. The first is a generic name referring to the genus to which the organism belongs, and the second is a specific name referring to the particular species. Organisms are usually identified by using both their generic and specific names, e.g. *Homo sapiens* (human), *Felis catus* (domestic cat) and *Sequoia sempervirens* (redwood). A third name can be added to give a subspecies. The generic name is written or printed with a capital letter and the specific name with a lowercase letter. Both names are usually given in italics or are underlined if written or typed.

**binomial nomenclature** *noun* BIOL the naming of every type of organism with a unique two-word Latin or Latinised scientific name, the first word denoting the genus and the second the species

**bio-** *prefix* referring to living organisms

**bioaccumulation** *noun* ENVIRON the accumulation of substances such as toxic chemicals up the food chain

**bioaeration** *noun* INDUST the treatment of sewage by pumping activated sludge into it

**bioassay** *noun* BIOCHEM a test of a substance by examining the effect it has on living organisms

**bioaugmentation** *noun* ENVIRON the addition of microorganisms to human or industrial waste to reinforce natural biological processes

**biocenosis** *noun* BIOL US spelling of **biocoenosis**

**biochemical** *adjective* BIOCHEM referring to biochemistry

**biochemical oxygen demand** *noun* ENVIRON abbreviation **BOD**. ◊ **biological oxygen demand**

**biochemist** *noun* BIOCHEM a scientist who specialises in biochemistry

**biochemistry** *noun* BIOCHEM the chemistry of living tissues

**biocide** *noun* BIOL a substance that kills living organisms ○ *Biocides used in agriculture run off into lakes and rivers.* ○ *The biological effect of biocides in surface waters can be very severe.*

**bioclimatology** *noun* ECOL the study of the effect that the climate has on living organisms

**biocoenosis** *noun* **1.** ECOL a varied community of organisms living in the same small area, e.g. in the bark of a tree **2.** the relationship between the organisms in such a community

**biocontrol** *noun* AGRIC same as **biological control**

**bioconversion** *noun* INDUST the changing of organic waste into a source of energy, e.g. the production of methane gas from the decomposition of organic matter

**biodegradability** *noun* ENVIRON the degree to which a material such as packaging can be decomposed by natural processes

**biodegradable** *adjective* ENVIRON easily decomposed by organisms such as bacteria or by natural processes such as the effect of sunlight or the sea ○ *Organochlorines are not biodegradable and enter the food chain easily.*

**biodegradation** *noun* BIOCHEM the breaking down of a substance by natural processes, e.g. the breakdown of activated sludge by bacteria

**biodegrade** *verb* ENVIRON to decay as the result of natural processes

**biodetergent** *noun* INDUST a detergent with added enzymes, which makes the washing process more effective

**biodiesel** *noun* INDUST a substitute for diesel fuel made wholly or partly from organic products, especially oils extracted from plants

**biodiversity** *noun* BIOL the presence of a large number of species

**biodiversity prospecting** *noun* ENVIRON the process of searching among wild organisms for new species or genetic characteristics that may have potential commercial value

**biodynamics** *noun* BIOL the study of living organisms and the production of energy

**bioecology** *noun* ENVIRON the study of the relationships among organisms and between them and their physical environment, with particular emphasis on the effect of humans on the environment

**bioenergetics** *noun* BIOL same as **biodynamics**

**bioengineering** *noun* **1.** BIOL the science of manipulating and combining different genetic material to produce living organisms with particular characteristics **2.** INDUST the use of biochemical processes on an industrial scale to produce drugs and foodstuffs or to recycle waste

**bioerosion** *noun* BIOL erosion or decay due to living things

**biofeedback** *noun* MED the control of the autonomic nervous system by the patient's conscious thoughts as a response to the results of tests or scans

**biofilter** *noun* ENVIRON a filter system that uses microorganisms to convert the organic compounds of a pollutant to carbon dioxide, water and salts

**biofuel** *noun* INDUST a fuel from organic domestic waste and other sources that does not use up fossil fuels ○ *Coppice wood can be grown as biofuel.*

**biogas** *noun* INDUST a mixture of methane and carbon dioxide produced from fermenting waste such as animal refuse ○ *Farm biogas systems may be* *uneconomic unless there is a constant demand for heat.* ○ *The use of biogas systems in rural areas of developing countries is increasing.*

**biogenesis** *noun* BIOL the theory that living things can only be produced from other living things and cannot be spontaneously generated

**biogeochemical** *adjective* BIOL referring to biogeochemistry

**biogeochemical cycle** *noun* BIOL a process in which nutrients from living organisms are transferred into the physical environment and back to the organisms (NOTE: This process is essential for organic life to continue.)

**biogeochemistry** *noun* BIOCHEM the study of living organisms and their relationship to the chemical components of the Earth such as its soil, rocks and minerals

**biogeographer** *noun* ECOL a scientist who studies regions with distinct fauna and flora

**biogeographical region** *noun* ECOL a large region of the Earth with distinct fauna and flora

**biogeography** *noun* ECOL the study of the relationship between organisms and the geography of the particular region where they exist, including how they originally came to the region

**biogeosphere** *noun* EARTH SCI the top layer of the Earth's crust, which contains living organisms

**biohydrology** *noun* ECOL the study of the interactions between the water cycle and plants and animals

**bioinsecticide** *noun* AGRIC an insecticide developed from natural toxins

**biolistics** *noun* BIOTECH a method of genetic modification involving the shooting of small particles of gold coated with DNA or messenger RNA directly into cells or tissues at high velocity

**biological** *adjective* referring to biology

**biological association** *noun* ECOL a group of associated organisms

**biological clock** *noun* PHYSIOL the circadian rhythm of daily activities and bodily processes such as eating, defecating and sleeping, frequently controlled by hormones

**biological control** *noun* AGRIC the control of pests by using predators and natural processes to remove them

COMMENT: Biological control of insects involves using bacteria, viruses, parasites and predators to destroy the insects. Plants can be controlled by herbivorous animals such as cattle.

**biological desert** *noun* ENVIRON an area where there is no life (NOTE: Heavy pollution can turn the bottom of a lake into a biological desert.)

**biological detergent** *noun* ENVIRON a detergent with added enzymes, which makes the washing process more effective

**biological diversity** *noun* BIOL same as **biodiversity**

**Biological Diversity Convention** *noun* ENVIRON one of two binding treaties agreed at the Earth Summit, in Rio de Janeiro in June 1992, requiring states to take steps to preserve ecologically valuable areas and species

**biological half-life** *noun* ENVIRON the time taken for half of an amount of radioactive material to be eliminated naturally from a living organism

**biological indicator** *noun* ENVIRON an organism that is known to respond to specific changes in the environment

**biologically decomposable** *adjective* BIOL same as **biodegradable**

**biological magnification** *noun* ENVIRON same as **bioaccumulation**

**biological monitoring** *noun* ENVIRON the process of checking the changes that take place in a habitat over time

**biological oceanography** *noun* MARINE BIOL the study of marine plants and animals and the way they interact with marine environments. Compare **marine biology**

**biological oxygen demand** *noun* ENVIRON the amount of pollution in water, shown as the amount of oxygen needed to oxidise the polluting substances. Abbreviation **BOD**

COMMENT: Diluted sewage passed into rivers contains dissolved oxygen, which is absorbed by bacteria as they oxidise the pollutants in the sewage. The oxygen is replaced by oxygen from the air. Diluted sewage should not absorb more than 20 ppm of dissolved oxygen.

**biological pesticide** *noun* AGRIC same as **biopesticide**

**biological treatment** *noun* INDUST the processing of sewage by using bacteria to break up the organic matter

**biological weathering** *noun* GEOL the process of change in the state of soil or rock through actions such as burrowing or root growth undertaken by living organisms

**biologist** *noun* BIOL a scientist who specialises in biology

**biology** *noun* BIOL the study of living organisms

**bioluminescence** *noun* PHYSIOL the production of light by organisms (NOTE: Bioluminescence is found in many deep-sea animals, fireflies and some bacteria and fungi.)

**biomagnification** *noun* ENVIRON same as **bioaccumulation**

**biomass** *noun* **1.** ECOL the sum of all living organisms in a given area or at a given trophic level, usually expressed in terms of living or dry mass **2.** INDUST organic matter used to produce energy

COMMENT: The burning of biomass for domestic heating may be a way of disposing of refuse, but it carries the risk of adding to air pollution.

**biomass energy** *noun* INDUST energy produced by burning renewable materials such as wood

**biomass fuel** *noun* INDUST same as **biofuel**

**biomaterial** *noun* ENVIRON a biodegradable material of plant origin

**biome** *noun* ECOL a large ecological region characterised by its vegetation and climate and all the living organisms in it

COMMENT: The ten principal biomes are: mountains, polar regions, tropical rainforest, grasslands, deserts, temperate forests, monsoon forests, deciduous forests, coniferous forests and evergreen shrub forests.

**biometeorology** *noun* ECOL the scientific study of the weather and its effect on organisms

**biomethanation** *noun* INDUST a system of producing biogas for use as fuel or light

**biomonitoring** *noun* ENVIRON the measurement and tracking of a chemical substance in an organism or in biologi-

cal material such as blood or urine, in order to monitor exposure to pollution, chemicals or other hazards

**bion** *noun* BIOL a single living organism in an ecosystem

**biopesticide** *noun* AGRIC a pesticide made from biological sources such as viruses or toxins that occur naturally

COMMENT: Biopesticides have the advantage that they do not harm the environment as they are easily inactivated and broken down by sunlight. This is, however, a practical disadvantage for a farmer who uses them, since they may not be as efficient in controlling pests as artificial chemical pesticides, which are persistent but difficult to control.

**biophyte** *noun* BOT a plant such as a sundew that obtains nutrients from the decomposing bodies of insects, which it traps and kills

**bioprocess** *noun* BIOTECH a method used to produce commercially useful biological material

**bioreactor** *noun* BIOTECH a large tank used for growing microorganisms in industrial production

**bioremediation** *noun* ENVIRON the use of living organisms such as bacteria to remove environmental pollutants from soil, water or gases ○ *Bioremediation is used in the clean-up of oil spills.*

**biorhythm** *noun* PHYSIOL a change that takes place within living organisms on a cyclical basis, e.g. sleeping, waking, or the reproductive cycle. ♦ **biological clock** (NOTE: It is believed by some people that behaviour, mood and sense of wellbeing are affected by biorhythms.)

**BIOS** *abbreviation* COMPUT basic input/output operating system

**biosensor** *noun* BIOTECH an apparatus in which a biological agent such as an enzyme is used to detect, measure or analyse specific chemicals (NOTE: Biosensors are increasingly used in tests to diagnose medical conditions such as high blood pressure.)

**biosphere** *noun* ECOL the part of the Earth and its atmosphere where organisms live (NOTE: It includes parts of the lithosphere, the hydrosphere and the atmosphere.)

**biosphere reserve** *noun* ENVIRON an environmentally sensitive area with protected status managed primarily to preserve natural ecological conditions (NOTE: Biosphere reserves may be open to tourists.)

**biospheric cycle** *noun* ENVIRON a natural cyclical process that supports life on Earth (NOTE: The oxygen cycle, carbon cycle, nitrogen cycle and water cycle are all biospheric cycles.)

**biostimulation** *noun* ENVIRON the addition of nutrients to polluted waste or ground in order to enhance the remedial activity of microorganisms

**biosynthesis** *noun* BIOCHEM the production of chemical compounds by a living organism

**biota** *noun* ECOL the flora and fauna of a region

**biotechnology** *noun* the use of technology to manipulate and combine different genetic materials to produce organisms with particular characteristics

COMMENT: Biotechnology offers the potential to increase farm production and food processing efficiency, to lower food costs, to enhance food quality and safety and to increase international competitiveness.

**biotic** *adjective* ECOL referring to the living constituents of an environment

**biotic barrier** *noun* ECOL a set of conditions which prevent members of a species moving to other regions

**biotic carrier potential** *noun* ECOL an assessment of the maximum increase in the number of individuals in a species, disregarding the effects of competition and natural selection

**biotic climax** *noun* ECOL a stable biotic community

**biotic community** *noun* ECOL a community of organisms in a specific area

**biotic factor** *noun* ECOL an organism in the context of an environment

**biotic index** *noun* ENVIRON a scale for showing the quality of an environment by indicating the types of organisms present in it

**biotic potential** *noun* ECOL same as **biotic carrier potential**

**biotic pyramid** *noun* ECOL a graphical representation of the structure of an ecosystem in terms of which organism eats which (NOTE: The base is composed of producer organisms, usually plants, then herbivores, then carnivores. It may be measured in terms of number, biomass or energy.)

**biotic succession** *noun* ECOL the sequence of changes that takes place in the composition of a group of organisms under the influence of their changing environment

**biotin** *noun* BIOL a B group vitamin found in egg yolks, liver and yeast

**biotope** *noun* ECOL a small area with uniform biological conditions such as climate, soil or altitude

**biotron** *noun* SCI a facility in which temperature and other environmental conditions can be controlled

**biotype** *noun* ECOL a group of similar individuals within a species

**biphenyl** *noun* CHEM a white or colourless crystalline substance, used as a fungicide, in the production of dyes and as a preservative applied to the skins of citrus fruit. Formula: $C_6H_5C_6H_5$. (NOTE: The preservative has E number E230.)

**bipolar** *adjective* COMPUT with two levels

**bipolar disorder** *noun* PSYCHIAT a psychiatric disorder in which the patient experiences extreme mood swings

**bipolar junction transistor** *noun* ELEC a transistor constructed of three layers of alternating types of doped semiconductor (p-n-p or n-p-n). Abbreviation **BJT**

COMMENT: Each layer has a terminal labelled emitter, base and collector. Usually the base signal controls the current flow between the emitter and collector.

**bipolar neuron** *noun* ANAT a neuron with two processes found in the retina

**bipolar signal** *noun* COMPUT the use of positive and negative voltage levels to represent the binary digits

**bipolar transistor** *noun* COMPUT same as **bipolar junction transistor**

**biquinary code** *noun* COMPUT a code in which decimal digits are represented as two digits added together (NOTE: Decimal digits less than 5 are represented as 0 + the digit; decimal digits greater than 4 are represented as 5 + the digit minus 5.)

**birch** *noun* TREES a common hardwood tree found in northern temperate zones. Latin name: *Betula pendula*.

**bird** *noun* BIOL an animal that lays eggs and has wings

COMMENT: All birds are members of the class Aves. They have feathers and the forelimbs have developed into wings, though not all birds are now able to fly. Birds are closely related to reptiles, and have scales on their legs. Some birds, for example rooks, pigeons and pheasants, can cause very serious damage to crops: various controls can be used such as shooting, scarecrows and destruction of nests. Birds also destroy many pests, for example wireworms, leatherjackets and caterpillars. Some birds such as chickens are farmed for food.

**bird of passage** *noun* ZOOL a bird that migrates from one area to another, stopping for a short time before moving on

**bird of prey** *noun* BIRDS a carnivorous bird

**bird sanctuary** *noun* BIRDS a place where birds can breed and live in a protected environment

**birth** *noun* BIOL the event of being born ○ *Birth and death are natural processes.* ○ *The cow gave birth to twin calves.*

**birth control** *noun* HEALTH the restriction of the number of children born by using contraception

**birth defect** *noun* BIOL a malformation that exists in a person's or animal's body from birth

**birthrate** *noun* BIOL the number of births per year, shown per thousand of the population ○ *a birth rate of 15 per thousand* ○ *There has been a severe decline in the birth rate.*

**bisexual** *adjective* BIOL with both male and female characteristics in the same individual

**bismuth** *noun* CHEM ELEM a chemical element, used to form alloys with a low melting point (NOTE: The chemical symbol is **Bi**; the atomic number is **83** and the atomic weight is **208.98**.)

**bistable** *adjective* ELEC (*of a device or circuit*) having two possible states, on and off

**bistable circuit** *noun* ELEC a circuit which can be switched between two states

**bisulfate, bisulphate** *noun* CHEM same as **hydrogen sulfate**

**bit** *noun* COMPUT **1.** the smallest single unit in binary notation, either a 0 or a 1 **2.** the smallest unit of data that a system can handle

**bit addressing** *noun* COMPUT the selecting of a register and examining one bit within it

**bit blit, bitblit** *verb* COMPUT to move a block of bits from one memory location to another

**bit depth** *noun* COMPUT a number of bits used to represent the number of colours that can be displayed on a screen or printer at one time ○ *The bit depth of each pixel is represented by a number of bits associated with the pixel that describe the number of colours that can be displayed.* ○ *A bit depth of four provides 16 colours, a bit depth of eight provides 256 colours.*

**bit error rate** *noun* COMPUT the ratio of the number of bits received to the number of errors in a transmission. Abbreviation **BER**

**bit handling** *noun* COMPUT the commands and processes that allow bit manipulation or changing

**bit-map, bitmap** *verb* COMPUT to define events or data by using an array of single bits (NOTE: This can be an image or graphics or a table of devices in use.)

**bit-mapped font** *noun* COMPUT a font whose characters are made up of patterns of pixels. Compare **vector font**

**bit-mapped graphic** *noun* COMPUT an image whose individual pixels can be controlled by changing the value of their stored bits

**bit position** *noun* COMPUT the place of a bit of data in a computer word

**bit rate** *noun* COMPUT a measure of the number of bits transmitted per second. Abbreviation **bps**

**bit-slice architecture** *noun* COMPUT the construction of a large word size computer by joining a number of smaller word size blocks ○ *The bit-slice design uses four four-bit word processors to make a sixteen-bit processor.*

**bits per inch** *noun* COMPUT a number of bits that can be recorded per inch of recording medium. Abbreviation **BPI**

**bits per pixel** *noun* COMPUT a number of bits assigned to store the colour of each pixel. Abbreviation **BPP** (NOTE: One bit provides black or white, four bits gives 16 colour combinations, eight bits gives 256 colour combinations.)

**bits per second** *noun* COMPUT a measure of the number of binary digits transmitted every second. Abbreviation **bps**

**bitumen** *noun* CHEM a solid hydrocarbon, contained in coal. Also called **tar**

**bituminous coal** *noun* INDUST coal containing a high percentage of tar

**bituminous sand, bituminous shale** *noun* GEOL same as **oil sand**

**bivalent** *adjective* **1.** GENETICS relating to structurally identical chromosomes that come together as a pair during the initial stage of meiosis **2.** CHEM having a valency of two

**biz** *noun* COMPUT a type of newsgroup that contains business discussions and opportunities (NOTE: Only the biz newsgroups are supposed to discuss commercial matters. Other related newsgroups are for technical or academic discussion.)

**BJT** *abbreviation* ELEC bipolar junction transistor

**black** *adjective* **1.** COMPUT with no colour **2.** PHYS having no colour or appearing very dark owing to the absorption of all or nearly all light ○ *Thick black smoke poured out of the factory chimneys.*

**black and white** *noun* COMPUT **1.** the use of shades of grey to represent colours on a monitor or display **2.** an image in which each pixel is either black or white with no shades of grey

**black bean** *noun* TREES a very hard tropical wood, resistant to termites

**black beetle** *noun* ZOOL a cockroach which is a common household pest in Asia. Latin name: *Blatta orientalis*.

**black body** *noun* ASTRON an object or body which follows perfectly the physical laws on how matter should emit and absorb radiation

**black carbon** *noun* ENVIRON carbon in the form of fine particles which rise in the smoke produced by the burning of fuels such as coal, wood or oil

**Black Death** *noun* MED a serious form of bubonic plague, which caused a pandemic during the Middle Ages

**black dwarf** *noun* ASTRON the final dark form of a white dwarf star, reached when all its heat has been radiated away

COMMENT: The black dwarf stage would take so long to reach that, even if the theory is correct, none may yet exist anywhere in the universe. But since every star weighing less than 1.4 times the Sun's mass is set to become one, there are going to be billions of them at some future point in the universe's development, unless they are all swept up by the contraction of an oscillatory universe. A black dwarf would contain no nuclear or other activity recognisable by outsiders and would be detectable mainly by its gravitation.

**black earth** *noun* GEOL a dark fertile soil, rich in organic matter, found in the temperate grass-covered plains of Russia and North and South America

**black frost** *noun* METEOROL a condition when the air is dry and the ground temperature is lower than the air temperature, but no white frost forms

**black hole** *noun* ASTRON a zone from which no radiation can normally escape, formed by the collapse of a star of just over two solar masses or more

COMMENT: The theoretical description of a black hole, where time slows to a halt and other bizarre physical effects occur, was drawn up in 1916, and since then further complications such as the addition of rotation and electrical charge have been made, as well as observational knowledge of objects like the Crab Nebula which seem to contain black holes. The cores of galaxies such as our own seem to contain massive black holes of millions of solar masses, which can be detected by measuring the orbital motion of stars near the centre of the galaxy. Their velocities betray the presence of an unusually large mass at the core of the galaxy.

**black ice** *noun* METEOROL ice which is clear, not white and opaque as frost, and which forms on the surface of roads

**blackout** *noun* ELEC a complete loss of electrical power. ♦ **brownout**

**black spot** *noun* BOT a fungal disease that attacks plants, causing black spots to appear on the leaves

**bladder** *noun* **1.** BOT an inflated modified leaf of some plant that traps insects **2.** MARINE BIOL same as **air bladder 3.** ANAT same as **urinary bladder**

**blade** *noun* **1.** a flattened part of a propeller or rotor. ♦ **aerofoil 2.** BOT a thin flat leaf such as a leaf of grass

**blade angle** *noun* AVIAT the angle between the axis of a blade and the axis of rotation ○ *With a variable pitch propeller, the blade angle may be changed in flight.*

**blade tip** *noun* AVIAT the end of a blade farthest from the centre of rotation

**blade twist** *noun* **1.** AVIAT the reduction in the blade angle of a propeller from root to tip **2.** the unwanted variation in the pitch of a propeller blade from root to tip caused by aerodynamic loads

**blank** *adjective* **1.** (*of paper*) with nothing written, printed or drawn on it ○ *a blank sheet of paper* **2.** COMPUT empty or with nothing written on it **3.** COMPUT an instruction in a program that is only there to satisfy language syntax or to make up a block length

**blanket** *noun* a thick covering ○ *A blanket of snow covered the fields.* ○ *The town was covered in a blanket of smog.* ■ *verb* to cover something thickly ○ *Thick fog blanketed the airport.*

**blanket bog** *noun* ECOL a wide area of marshy ground

**blank form** *noun* a form without the details filled in

**blanking interval** *noun* COMPUT a period during which a screen displays nothing, in between two images or during the picture beam flyback

**blank instruction** *noun* COMPUT a program instruction which does nothing

**blank string, empty string** *noun* COMPUT same as **null string**

**blast** *noun* PHYS the impact from an explosion ○ *Thousands of people would be killed by the blast.* ■ *verb* COMPUT **1.** to write data into a programmable ROM device **2.** to free sections of previously allocated memory or resources

**-blast** *suffix* BIOL a very early stage in the development of a cell

**blast effect** *noun* ENVIRON a result of the impact from an explosion, e.g. damage caused

**blast furnace** *noun* INDUST a heating device for producing iron or copper from ore (NOTE: The ore, coke and limestone are heated together, air is blown through the mixture and the mol-

ten metal is drawn off into moulds. The waste matter from this process is known as slag.)

**blasto-** *prefix* BIOL a germ cell

**blastocyst** *noun* BIOL a mammalian embryo as it is when it implants in the wall of the womb

**blastula** *noun* BIOL an embryo at an early stage of development, comprising a hollow ball of cells

**bleach** *verb* CHEM to make something whiter or lighter in colour, or to become whiter or lighter in colour

**bleaching** *noun* **1.** CHEM the removal of colour by the action of a chemical or of sunlight **2.** MARINE BIOL a process in which coral discolours or loses its symbiotic algae ○ *There have been several incidents of coral bleaching on reefs around Easter Island and northeastern Australia.*

**bleaching agent** *noun* CHEM something that removes colour, e.g. a chemical or the action of sunlight

**bleaching powder** *noun* CHEM a white powder prepared by the action of chlorine on calcium hydroxide and from which chlorine is liberated by the action of a dilute acid. Formula: $CaCl(OCl)$. (NOTE: It is used as a bleaching agent or disinfectant.)

**bleed** *verb* **1.** BIOL to exude blood or sap from a wound **2.** ENG to remove liquid or gas from a system ■ *noun* COMPUT **1.** a line of printing that runs off the edge of the paper **2.** a badly adjusted colour monitor in which colours of adjoining pixels blend

**bleed screw** *noun* ENG a small screw in the highest point of a hydraulic system to allow for the removal of air or vapour

**bleep** COMPUT *noun* an audible warning noise ○ *The printer will make a bleep when it runs out of paper.* ■ *verb* to make a bleep

**blight** *noun* BOT a disease of various plants, caused by different fungi, that rapidly destroys a plant or plant part

**blind** *adjective* **1.** BIOL unable to see **2.** COMPUT not responding to specific codes

**blind carbon copy** *noun* COMPUT a method of sending a message to several users without the knowledge of individual recipients. Compare **carbon copy**. Abbreviation **BCC**

**blind spot** *noun* **1.** ACOUSTICS a part of an auditorium where the performance cannot be heard clearly **2.** ANAT the area of the retina without rods or cones where the optic nerve enters

**blip** *noun* COMPUT a small mark on a tape or film counted to determine the position

**blit** *verb* COMPUT (*in computer graphics*) to process or move a block of bits from one memory location to another

**blitter** *noun* COMPUT an electronic component designed to blit ○ *The new blitter chip speeds up the graphics display.*

**blob** *abbreviation* COMPUT binary large object

**block** *noun* **1.** a large mass of something **2.** COMPUT a series of items grouped together **3.** COMPUT a number of stored records treated as a single unit **4.** a wide printed bar ■ *verb* **1.** to prevent a fluid or other substance from passing freely through a pipe, channel or filter ○ *At high altitude, any water condensing out of the fuel could freeze and block the filters.* **2.** to prevent a course of action ○ *The government blocked attempts to prevent the building of the new airport.*

**blockage** *noun* **1.** a collection of something blocking a pipe, channel or filter ○ *Ice crystals may form to cause a blockage of the fuel filter.* **2.** the state of being blocked ○ *The blockage was caused by ice.*

**block character check** *noun* COMPUT an error detection method for blocks of transmitted data. Abbreviation **BCC**

**block code** *noun* COMPUT an error detection and correction code for block data transmission

**block cursor** *noun* COMPUT a cursor in the shape of a solid rectangle that fills a character position

**block diagram** *noun* COMPUT a graphical representation of a system or program operation

**block gap** *noun* COMPUT a blank magnetic tape between the end of one block of data and the start of the next in backing store

**blocking factor** *noun* COMPUT a number of records in a block of data

**block transfer** *noun* COMPUT the process of moving large numbers of records around in memory

**blood** *noun* BIOL the red liquid that is pumped by the heart around an animal's body

COMMENT: Blood is formed of red and white corpuscles, platelets and plasma. It circulates round the body, going from the heart and lungs along arteries and returning to the heart through veins. As it moves round the body it takes oxygen to the tissues and removes waste material from them. Blood also carries hormones produced by glands to the various organs that need them.

**blood bank** *noun* HEALTH SERV a section of a hospital where blood given by donors is stored for use in transfusions

**blood cell** *noun* BIOL a red or white cell that is one of the components of blood

**blood chemistry** *noun* **1.** MED a record of the changes that take place in blood during disease and treatment **2.** BIOL substances that make up blood and can be analysed in blood tests, the results of which are useful in diagnosing disease

**blood corpuscle** *noun* BIOL same as **blood cell**

**blood count** *noun* **1.** MED a test to count the number of different blood cells in a quantity of blood **2.** BIOL the number of blood cells counted

**blood glucose level** *noun* BIOL the amount of glucose present in the blood ○ *The normal blood glucose level stays at about 60 to 100 mg of glucose per 100 ml of blood.*

**blood group** *noun* BIOL one of the different types of blood by which groups of people are identified

COMMENT: Blood is classified in various ways. The most common classifications are by the agglutinogens in red blood corpuscles (factors A and B) and by the Rhesus factor. Blood can therefore have either factor (Group A or Group B) or both factors (Group AB) or neither (Group O) and each of these groups can be Rhesus negative or positive.

**blood grouping** *noun* the classifying of people according to their blood groups

**blood pigment** *noun* BIOL same as **haemoglobin**

**blood plasma** *noun* BIOL a watery liquid which forms the greatest part of blood

**blood platelet** *noun* BIOL a small blood cell which releases thromboplastin and which multiplies rapidly after an injury to cause the blood to clot

**blood poisoning** *noun* MED a condition where bacteria are present in blood and cause illness

**blood pressure** *noun* BIOL the pressure at which the blood is pumped round the body by the heart

COMMENT: Blood pressure is measured using a sphygmomanometer, where a rubber tube is wrapped round the patient's arm and inflated. Two readings of blood pressure are taken: the systolic pressure, when the heart is contracting and so pumping out, and the diastolic pressure (which is always a lower figure) when the heart relaxes. Normal adult values are considered to be 160/95, unless the patient is diabetic or has heart disease, when lower target values are set.

**blood serum** *noun* BIOL a yellowish watery liquid that separates from blood when the blood clots

**bloodstream** *noun* BIOL blood as it passes round the body

**blood sugar level** *noun* BIOL same as **blood glucose level**

**blood test** *noun* BIOL a laboratory test to find the chemical composition of a patient's blood

**blood vessel** *noun* ANAT a tube that carries blood round the body. ♦ **artery, capillary, vein**

**bloom** BOT *noun* a flower ○ *The blooms on the orchids have been ruined by frost.* ■ *verb* to flower ○ *The plant blooms at night.* ○ *Some cacti only bloom once every seven years.*

**bloop** *verb* COMPUT to pass a magnet over a tape to erase signals which are not needed

**blow** *noun* a sudden movement of air or gas ○ *the blow of air through a Bessemer converter* ■ *verb* **1.** COMPUT to program a PROM device with data **2.** (*of air, wind*) to move ○ *The sea breeze may blow almost parallel to the coast.* **3.** ELEC (*of a fuse*) to break, as it should, when the circuit is overloaded (NOTE: **blowing – blew – blown**)

**blow-back** *noun* a sudden movement of fluid in the opposite direction to the general flow ○ *A sudden release of pressure may cause a blow-back.*

**blow-by** *noun* AUTOMOT unburnt fuel mixed with air and other gases produced by an internal combustion engine which escapes past the piston rings

COMMENT: In many parts of the world emission of gases from pistons is controlled by law, since these gases contribute significantly to atmospheric pollution.

**blower** *noun* a device for blowing air ○ *Air for combustion is obtained from a blower.*

**blue** *noun* the colour which is that of a clear unclouded sky in the daytime

**blue-green algae** *plural noun* BIOL same as **cyanobacterium** (*dated*)

**blue mud** *noun* OCEANOG a deposit found on the seabed in the Pacific Ocean and elsewhere, containing decaying organic matter and iron sulfide, the latter giving it its blue colour

**blueprint** *noun* a copy of an original set of specifications or a design in graphical form

**blue shift** *noun* PHYS a reduction in the wavelength of radiation caused by the observer and source approaching each other

COMMENT: This manifestation of the Doppler effect is seen far less often than the red shift in astronomy, since the latter is widely caused by the expansion of the universe. Blue and red shifts are used together in astronomy for measuring rotations of planets and stars, since blue shift is observed as an object emitting light moves closer to the observer, defined in the Doppler effect, and seen as higher frequency of the light wakes from the object.

**Bluetooth** *trademark* COMPUT a short-range radio communications system that is designed to provide a simple way for computer, Internet and input devices to communicate (NOTE: The technology was developed by a group of computer and telecoms companies that included Ericsson, IBM, Intel, Nokia and Toshiba.)

**blue vitriol** *noun* CHEM same as **copper sulfate**

**blur** OPTICS *noun* an image where the edges or colours are not clear ■ *verb* to make the edges or colours of an image fuzzy ○ *The image becomes blurred when you turn the focus knob.*

**blurred vision** *noun* BIOL a condition in which a person does not see objects clearly

**BMI** *abbreviation* MED body mass index

**BMP** *noun* COMPUT a three-letter extension to a filename that indicates that the file contains a bit-mapped graphics image ○ *This paint package lets you import BMP files.*

**BMR** *abbreviation* BIOL basal metabolic rate

**bn** *abbreviation* COMPUT billion

**BNC connector** *noun* COMPUT a cylindrical metal connector with a copper core that is at the end of coaxial cable and is used to connect cables together (NOTE: It attaches by pushing and twisting the outer cylinder onto two locking pins.)

**BNF** *abbreviation* COMPUT Backus-Naur-Form

**board** *noun* COMPUT a flat insulation material on which electronic components are mounted and connected

**BOD** *abbreviation* ENVIRON **1.** biochemical oxygen demand **2.** biological oxygen demand ○ *The main aim of sewage treatment is to reduce the BOD of the liquid.*

**body** *noun* **1.** ANAT the main part of a person, not including the head or arms and legs **2.** the whole physical bulk of a person ○ *The dead man's body was found several days later.* **3.** a mass or piece of material **4.** the main part of something **5.** (*in scientific description*) an object ○ *Acceleration is the rate of change of velocity of a body.*

**body cavity** *noun* ZOOL same as **coelom**

**body fat** *noun* BIOL tissue where the cells contain fat, which replaces the normal fibrous tissue when too much food is eaten

**body fluid** *noun* PHYSIOL a fluid or secretion of the body, e.g. blood, saliva, semen, vaginal secretions, milk, urine, sweat or tears

**body mass index** *noun* MED a figure obtained by dividing the weight in kilos of a person by the square of his or her height in metres. Abbreviation **BMI**

COMMENT: If a person is 1m 70 (i.e. 5' 7") and weighs 82kg (i.e. 180 pounds), his or her BMI is 28 (i.e. above normal).

**body of air** *noun* METEOROL a large quantity of air behaving in a characteristic way

**body of sternum** *noun* ANAT the main central part of the breastbone

**body of vertebra** *noun* ANAT the main part of a vertebra, which supports the weight of the body

**body of water** *noun* a separate and distinct mass of water

**bof, BOF** *abbreviation* COMPUT beginning of file

**bog** *noun* **1.** EARTH SCI soft wet land, usually with moss growing on it, which does not decompose, but forms a thick layer of acid peat ○ *Bog mosses live on nutrients which fall in rain.* **2.** an area of bog

**boggy** *adjective* EARTH SCI soft and wet like a bog

**bogland** *noun* EARTH SCI an area of bog

**bohrium** *noun* CHEM ELEM an artificially produced radioactive chemical element (NOTE: The chemical symbol is **Bh**; the atomic number is **107** and the atomic weight is **264**.)

**Bohr theory** *noun* PHYS a theory of atomic structure suggesting that electrons move around a nucleus in distinct orbits, with a jump between orbits accompanied by the absorption or emission of a photon (NOTE: It was the earliest important attempt to apply quantum theory to atomic structure.)

**boil** *verb* **1.** PHYS to heat a liquid until it reaches a temperature at which it changes into gas ○ *Boil the water before pouring it in.* **2.** to reach boiling point ○ *Water boils at 100° C.*

**boiler** *noun* **1.** ENG a container in which water is boiled to make steam to drive something such as a turbine **2.** a container in which water is heated for domestic use

**boilerplate** *noun* COMPUT a final document that has been put together using standard sections of text held in a word processor

**boiling point** *noun* PHYS the temperature at which a liquid changes into gas ○ *The boiling point of water is 100° C.*

**boiling water reactor** *noun* INDUST a nuclear reactor fuelled by uranium, in which light water is heated to form steam which drives the turbines. Abbreviation **BWR**

**boldface** *noun* a thicker and darker form of a typeface

**bole** *noun* BOT the base of a tree trunk

**bolt** *noun* ENG a metal rod, with a head, which screws into a nut ○ *Titanium is used for making bolts.* ○ *The two halves of the wheel are held by bolts.* ■ *verb* to attach something with a bolt ○ *Aircraft wheels are constructed in two halves which are bolted together.*

**bolt of lightning** *noun* a single electrical discharge of lightning

**Boltzmann constant** *noun* PHYS the ratio of the universal gas constant to Avogadro's number, $1.38 \times 10^{-23}$ joules per kelvin

**Boltzmann distribution** *noun* PHYS a law that describes the temperature of a material such as a gas cloud with the number of molecules within it at different possible energy levels

**bomb** COMPUT *noun* a routine in a program designed to crash the system or destroy data at a specific time ■ *verb* (*of software*) to fail (*informal*) ○ *The program bombed, and we lost all the data.* ○ *The system can bomb if you set up several desk accessories or memory-resident programs at the same time.*

**bond** CHEM *noun* the force which links atoms to form molecules. Also called **chemical bond** ■ *verb* 1. (*of two substances*) to link together ○ *Adsorption is the bonding of a gas to a solid surface.* 2. (*of atoms*) to form a chemical bond

**bond energy** *noun* CHEM the energy contained in a chemical bond between two atoms in a molecule and therefore required to break it

**bone** *noun* ANAT 1. one of the calcified pieces of connective tissue which make the skeleton ○ *He fell over and broke a bone in his ankle.* ○ *There are several small bones in the human ear.* 2. a hard substance which forms a bone

COMMENT: Bones are formed of a hard outer layer (compact bone) which is made up of a series of layers of tissue (Haversian systems) and a softer inner part (cancellous bone or spongy bone) which contains bone marrow.

**bone conduction** *noun* PHYSIOL the conduction of sound waves to the inner ear through the bones of the skull rather than through the air

**bone marrow** *noun* ANAT soft tissue inside bones

COMMENT: Two types of bone marrow are found. Red bone marrow and myeloid tissue are found in the cavities of vertebrae, the sternum and other flat bones, and form red blood cells. As a person gets older, fatty yellow bone marrow develops in the central cavity of long bones.

**bone marrow transplant** *noun* MED a transplant of bone marrow from a donor to a recipient (NOTE: For other terms referring to bone marrow, see words beginning with **myel-, myelo-**.)

**bonemeal** *noun* AGRIC a fertiliser made of ground bones or horns, reduced to a fine powder (NOTE: It is also given as a fine meal for growing animals, for the calcium, phosphorus and magnesium it contains.)

**bone structure** *noun* 1. ANAT a system of jointed bones forming the body 2. BIOL the arrangement of the various components of a bone

**book** *noun* COMPUT a multimedia title. The name comes from the fact that most multimedia titles are arranged as a series of different pages which together form a book. ♦ **ebook**

**bookmark** *noun* COMPUT 1. a code inserted at a particular point in a document that allows the user to move straight to that point at a later date 2. a website address stored in a web browser that allows the user to move straight to the website at a later date without re-typing the address

**Boolean algebra, Boolean logic** *noun* MATHS a set rules for defining, simplifying and manipulating logical functions, based on statements that are true or false

**Boolean operator** *noun* COMPUT a logical operator such as AND or OR

**Boolean value** *noun* COMPUT one of two values, either true or false

**boom** *noun* ACOUSTICS a sudden loud noise, especially one caused by an aircraft travelling at speeds greater than the speed of sound

COMMENT: Shock waves from a boom can cause objects to resonate so violently that they are damaged. Supersonic aircraft generally fly at speeds greater than the speed of sound only over the sea, to avoid noise nuisance and damage to property.

**boost** *verb* COMPUT to make something increase ○ *The extra hard disk will boost our storage capacity by 25 MB.* ○ *An oil pump boosts engine oil pressure.*

**booster** *noun* **1.** something which gives extra help or support **2.** a device which increases the force or amount of something

**booster pump** *noun* ENG a centrifugal pump often positioned at the lowest point of a liquid fuel tank to ensure positive pressure in the supply lines to the engine ○ *Fuel is fed through a filter and a booster pump.* ○ *The purpose of the booster pump is to prevent fuel aeration.*

**boot** *verb* COMPUT to execute a set of instructions automatically in order to reach a required state

**bootable** *adjective* COMPUT (*of a storage device*) holding the commands to boot up a computer and load the operating system (NOTE: The main hard disk is normally a bootable device as is the floppy disk drive.)

**boot disk** *noun* COMPUT a special disk which contains a bootstrap loader and the operating system software ○ *After you switch on the computer, insert the boot disk.*

**bootleg** *noun* COMPUT an illegal copy of recorded material

**boot partition** *noun* COMPUT (*on a hard disk with more than one partition*) the partition that contains the bootstrap loader and operating system

**bootstrap loader** *noun* COMPUT a set of instructions that are executed by the computer before a program is loaded, usually to load the operating system once the computer is switched on

**borane** *noun* CHEM a compound containing boron and hydrogen, used in rocket and jet fuels

**borax** *noun* CHEM a white crystalline salt that is an ore of boron, used as a cleaning agent, water softener, preservative and in glass and ceramics manufacture. Formula: $Na_2B_4O_7.10H_2O$. (NOTE: It occurs naturally as tincal.)

**bore** *noun* **1.** INDUST a measurement across the inside of a pipe or hole ○ *The central heating uses small-bore copper piping.* ○ *The well has a 2-metre bore.*

**2.** EARTH SCI a tidal wave which rushes up the estuary of a river at high tide ■ *verb* INDUST to make a round hole in the ground ○ *They have bored six test holes to try to find water.*

**boreal** *adjective* METEOROL referring to the climate in the northern hemisphere between 60° and 40° N with short hot summers and longer cold winters

**Borealis** METEOROL ◊ **Northern Lights**

**borehole** *noun* INDUST a hole bored in the ground ○ *The borehole is intended to test the geology of the site to see if it is suitable for burying nuclear waste.* ○ *Boreholes supply water of excellent quality.*

**boric acid** *noun* CHEM a soluble weak acidic white crystalline solid, used as a fire retardant and antiseptic and in the manufacture of heat-resistant glass and ceramics. Formula: $H_3BO_3$.

**-borne** *suffix* carried by

**boron** *noun* CHEM ELEM a chemical element from which control rods in reactors are made. Boron is also essential for healthy plant growth as a trace element in soils. (NOTE: The chemical symbol is **B**; the atomic number is **5** and the atomic weight is **10.81**.)

**borrow** *verb* MATHS (*in arithmetic processes such as subtraction*) to transfer a unit from a higher category to count in a lower one, compensating for it later (NOTE: To take 19 from 21 you have to borrow 1 from the tens and take 9 from 11 then compensate and take 2 from 2.)

**Bose-Chandhuri-Hocquenghem code** *noun* COMPUT an error correcting code for data storage and transmission. Abbreviation **BCH code**

**boson** *noun* PHYS a fundamental particle with zero or integral spin and no restriction on the number of identical particles that may be in the same state (NOTE: Photons and alpha particles are bosons.)

**botanical** *adjective* BOT referring to botany

**botanical garden** *noun* BOT a place where plants are grown for showing to the public and for scientific study

**botanical insecticide** *noun* AGRIC an insecticide made from a substance extracted from plants, e.g. pyrethrum, derived from chrysanthemums, and nicotine, derived from tobacco plants

**botanical specimen** *noun* BOT a plant collected for study

**botanist** *noun* BOT a scientist who studies plants

**botany** *noun* BOT the scientific study of plants

**bottled gas** *noun* INDUST a gas such as liquefied petroleum gas produced from refining crude oil and sold in pressurised metal containers for use as fuel, e.g for domestic heating or camp stoves.

**bottom** *noun* EARTH SCI **1.** the floor of a sea, lake or river **2.** a flat area along a river where silt is deposited when the river floods

**bottom feeder** *noun* MARINE BIOL an organism such as a fish which collects food on the bottom or in the deepest water of the sea, a lake or a river

**bottom up programming** *noun* COMPUT the process of combining low-level instructions to form a high-level instruction which can then be further combined

**bottom water** *noun* GEOG water in the deepest part of the sea, a lake or a river

**boulder** *noun* GEOL a large rounded piece of rock

**boulder clay** *noun* GEOL a clay soil mixed with rocks of different sizes, found in glacial deposits

**bounce** *noun* COMPUT a multiple key contact caused by a faulty switch

**boundary** *noun* a limit between two areas ○ *The boundary between two air masses is called the frontal surface.*

**boundary layer** *noun* **1.** METEOROL the altitude at which airflow is affected by the ground **2.** PHYS a layer of fluid next to the surface over which it is flowing and, because of friction, travelling more slowly than layers farther from the surface

**boundary protection** *noun* COMPUT the preventing of any computer program from writing into a reserved area of memory

**boundary register** *noun* COMPUT a computer register in a multi-user system that contains the addresses for the limits of one user's memory allocation

**bounding box** *noun* COMPUT a rectangle that determines the shape and position of an image that has been placed in a document or on screen

**bounds** *plural noun* COMPUT the limits or area in which someone can operate

**Bourdon gauge** *noun* ENG a pressure gauge consisting of a flattened curved tube that straightens under internal pressure

**Bovidae** *plural noun* ZOOL the largest class of even-toed ungulates, including cattle, antelopes, gazelles, sheep and goats

**bovine** *adjective* ZOOL referring to cattle

**bovine somatotrophin** BIOCHEM full form of **BST**

**bovine spongiform encephalopathy** full form of **BSE**

**Bowman's capsule** *noun* ANAT a cup-shaped extension of a kidney tubule into which waste and water are filtered from the blood to produce urine

**Boyce-Codd normal form** COMPUT ◊ **normal form**. Abbreviation **BCNF**

**Boyle's law** *noun* PHYS the principle that the volume of a confined gas at constant temperature is inversely related to its pressure

**BPI, bpi** *abbreviation* COMPUT bits per inch

**BPP** *abbreviation* COMPUT bits per pixel

**bps** *abbreviation* COMPUT bits per second ○ *Their transmission rate is 60 000 bps through a parallel connection.*

**Bq** *symbol* becquerel

**Br** *symbol* CHEM ELEM bromine

**brace** *verb* MECH ENG to strengthen a construction using cross-members and/or wires

**braces** *plural noun* COMPUT curly bracket characters, {}, used in some programming languages to enclose a routine

**brachial artery** *noun* ANAT an artery running down the arm from the axillary artery to the elbow, where it divides into the radial and ulnar arteries

**bracket** *noun* **1.** ENG a triangular or L-shaped metal support **2.** PHYS a range of frequencies within a band of radio frequencies **3.** a mark, ( or ), used to enclose text or numbers, usually in pairs

**bracket together** *verb* MATHS to print brackets round several items to show that they are treated in the same way and separated from the rest of the mathematical equation or text

**brackish** *adjective* GEOG referring to water which contains salt, though less than seawater, and is not good to drink

**bract** *noun* BOT a small green leaf at the base of a flower

**Bragg's law** *noun* PHYS an equation for predicting the angle at which X-rays reflected from a crystal will be most intense

**braiding** *noun* GEOG a phenomenon which occurs when a river becomes divided into several channels with small islands or bars between them

**brain** *noun* ANAT the cranial part of the central nervous system, situated inside the skull

COMMENT: The main part of the brain is the cerebrum, formed of two sections or hemispheres, which relate to thought and to sensations from either side of the body. At the back of the head and beneath the cerebrum is the cerebellum, which coordinates muscle reaction and balance. Also in the brain are the hypothalamus which governs body temperature, hunger, thirst and sexual urges, and the tiny pituitary gland, which produces hormones that regulate other glands.

**brain dead** *adjective* MED with the brain and central nervous system no longer working

**brain death** *noun* MED the time at which the brain and central nervous system stop working (NOTE: It is measured by strict medical and legal criteria as life support may be switched off and organs removed for transplantation once a person has been certified brain dead.)

**brain stem** *noun* ANAT the part of the brain that connects the cerebral hemispheres and the spinal cord (NOTE: It is composed of the midbrain, pons and medulla oblongata.)

**brake** *noun* ENG a device for stopping a vehicle or a machine ■ *verb* to slow down or to stop by pressing the brakes ○ *He had to brake hard after landing in order to turn off at the correct taxiway.* (NOTE: **braking – braked**; do not confuse with **break**)

**brake drum** *noun* MECH ENG the part of the brake mechanism attached to the wheel and against which the brake shoes rub, preventing the wheel from turning

**brake shoe** *noun* MECH ENG a long curved block that presses against a brake drum to slow or stop a wheel

**bran** *noun* FOOD INDUST an outside covering of wheat seed (NOTE: It is removed to make white flour, but is an important source of roughage, and used in muesli and other breakfast cereals.)

**branch** *noun* **1.** COMPUT a possible path or jump from one instruction to another **2.** a line linking one or more devices to the main network ○ *The faulty station is on this branch.* **3.** BOT a woody stem growing out from the main trunk of a tree **4.** EARTH SCI a smaller stream separating from but still forming part of a river ■ *verb* COMPUT to jump from one section of a program to another, often using a test or decision with two or more possible results that lead to two different points in the program

COMMENT: In BASIC, the instruction GOTO makes the system jump to the line indicated; this is an unconditional branch. The instruction IF...THEN is a conditional branch, because the jump will only take place if the condition is met.

**branch cable** *noun* ELEC ENG a cable that runs from a main cable to a node

**branched chain** *noun* CHEM a molecular structure that has side chains or branches attached to specific atoms of the original chain

**brand** *noun* COMPUT a make of product, which can be recognised by a name or by a design ○ *The number one brand of magnetic tape.* ○ *The company is developing a new brand of screen cleaner.*

**brass** *noun* METALL an alloy of copper and zinc

**breadboard** *noun* ELEC ENG a device that allows prototype electronic circuits to be constructed easily without permanent connections or soldering

**break** *noun* **1.** COMPUT the action of pressing a key to stop a program execution **2.** the key pressed to stop a program execution ■ *verb* **1.** to fail to carry out the duties of an agreement ○ *The company has broken the agreement.* **2.** COMPUT to decipher a difficult code ○ *He finally broke the cipher system.*

**breakbone fever** *noun* MED a tropical disease caused by an arbovirus, transmitted by mosquitoes (NOTE: The patient suffers a high fever, pains in the joints, headache and a rash.)

**break down** *verb* to stop working because of mechanical failure ○ *The modem has broken down.* ○ *What do you do when your line printer breaks down?*

**breakdown** *noun* **1.** a failure of a system or organisation **2.** the separation of a substance into its elements

**breakdown process** *noun* the action of separating into elements or of decomposing

**breaking load** *noun* MECH ENG a load capable of being supported before a structure breaks

**breakout box** *noun* COMPUT a device that displays the status of lines within an interface, cable or connector ○ *The serial interface doesn't seem to be working – use the breakout box to see which signals are present.*

**breakpoint** *noun* COMPUT a symbol inserted into a program which stops its execution at that point to allow registers, variables and memory locations to be examined (NOTE: It is used when debugging a program.)

**breakup** *noun* COMPUT the loss or distortion of a signal

**breakwater** *noun* ENG a strong wall or fence which is built from the shore into the sea in order to block the force of waves and so prevent erosion

**breastbone** *noun* ANAT same as **sternum**

**breath** *noun* BIOL the air which goes in and out of the body when you breathe ○ *He ran so fast he was out of breath.* ○ *Stop for a moment to get your breath back.* ○ *She took a deep breath and dived into the water.*

**breathe** *verb* BIOL to take air into the lungs and blow air out through the nose or mouth ○ *He could not breathe under water.* ○ *The patient has begun to breathe normally.*

COMMENT: Children breathe about 20 to 30 times per minute, men 16–18 per minute, and women slightly faster than men. The breathing rate increases if the person is taking exercise or has a fever. Some babies hold their breath and go blue in the face, especially when crying or during a temper tantrum.

**breathe in** *verb* BIOL to take air into your lungs ○ *He breathed in the smoke from the fire and it made him cough.*

**breathe out** *verb* BIOL to let the air out of your lungs ○ *The doctor told him to take a deep breath and breathe out slowly.*

**breather** *noun* MECH ENG a pipe connecting the crankshaft to the atmosphere to prevent build-up of crankcase pressure

**breathing** *noun* BIOL the process of taking air into the lungs and blowing it out again through the mouth or nose ○ *If breathing is difficult or has stopped, begin artificial ventilation immediately.* (NOTE: For other terms referring to breathing, see words beginning with **pneumo-**.)

**breccia** *noun* GEOL a type of rough rock made of sharp fragments of other rocks fused together

**breed** *noun* AGRIC a class of organisms of a specific species which have been developed by people over a period of time for desirable characteristics ○ *a hardy breed of sheep* ○ *Two new breeds of rice have been developed.* ■ *verb* **1.** BIOL (*of organisms*) to produce young ○ *Rabbits breed very rapidly.* **2.** BIOL to encourage something to develop ○ *Insanitary conditions help to breed disease.* **3.** AGRIC to produce an improved animal or plant by crossing two parent animals or plants showing the desired characteristics ○ *Farmers have bred new hardy forms of sheep.* □ **to breed true** to reproduce all the characteristics of the species in the next generation ○ $F_1$ *hybrids do not breed true.*

**breeder** *noun* AGRIC a person who breeds new forms of animals or plants ○ *a cat breeder* ○ *a cattle breeder* ○ *a rose breeder* ○ *a plant breeder*

**breeder reactor** *noun* PHYS a nuclear reactor which produces more fissile material than it consumes

COMMENT: Uranium-238 is a natural uranium isotope which can be used to produce the fissile plutonium-239. In a breeder reactor, uranium-238 is used as a blanket round the plutonium fuel, and when the plutonium is fissioned high-speed neutrons are produced which change on contact with the uranium-238 and eventually produce a slightly greater quantity of plutonium-239 than that originally used as fuel. The excess plutonium can be used as a fuel in another breeder reactor or in an ordinary burner reactor.

**breeding** noun AGRIC the crossing of different plants or animals to produce offspring with desirable characteristics

**breeding ground** noun ECOL an area where birds or animals come each year to breed

**breeding season** noun BIOL the time of year when organisms produce offspring

**breeze** noun **1.** METEOROL a light wind **2.** INDUST the solid waste of burnt coal or other material from a furnace

**breeze block** noun INDUST a large building brick made from breeze and cement

**Bremsstrahlung** noun PHYS radiation given out by fast-moving electrons or other particles encountering electromagnetic fields, observed especially in radio astronomy (NOTE: Bremsstrahlung energy is released because of severe deceleration of electrons in a magnetic field and is observable in cosmic radiation.)

**bridge** COMPUT verb to use bridgeware to help transfer programs, data files, etc., to another system ■ noun **1.** a device that connects two networks together and allow information to flow between them (NOTE: Bridges function at the data link layer of the OSI network model.) **2.** matching communications equipment that makes sure that power losses are kept to a minimum **3.** hardware or software that allows parts of an old system to be used on a new system ○ *A bridging product is available for companies with both generations of machines.*

**bridgeware** noun COMPUT the hardware or software used to make the transfer from one computer system to another easier by changing file format, translation etc.

**brief** adjective lasting only for a short time ■ noun a set of general instructions to enable somebody to perform his or her duties ○ *The inspector's brief is to find out as much as possible about the causes of accidents.* ■ verb to give basic information to somebody

**brightness** noun COMPUT the luminance of an object which can be seen on a screen ○ *A control knob allows you to adjust brightness and contrast.*

**brilliant** adjective COMPUT (*of light or colour*) very bright and shining

**bring up** verb COMPUT to start a computer system

**British Standards Institute** noun COMPUT an organisation that monitors design and safety standards in the UK. Abbreviation **BSI**

**British thermal unit** noun PHYS, MEASURE the amount of heat needed to raise the temperature of one pound of water by one degree Fahrenheit (NOTE: Its approximate SI equivalent is 1055 joules.)

**brittle** adjective breaking easily ○ *Absorption of oxygen and nitrogen from the air at temperatures above 1000° F makes titanium brittle.*

**broad** adjective wide ○ *Broad paths are left through the forest plantations to act as firebreaks.*

**broadband** noun COMPUT, TELECOM a transmission method that combines several channels of data onto a carrier signal and can carry the data over long distances. Compare **baseband**

COMMENT: The three most popular broadband communication devices are ISDN, cable modems and ADSL (part of the wider DSL standard). Each country has different prevalent standards and pricing models. For example, ISDN provides a digital link that can transfer data at the rate of 64 kbps. It dials an access number and provides a link when required. ADSL, in contrast, provides a direct connection that appears to be 'always on' using a network adapter to link the computer to the Internet provider. ADSL normally supports a transfer speed of up to 2 Mbps.

**broadcast** noun **1.** TELECOM data transmission to many receivers **2.** COMPUT a message or data sent to a group of users ■ verb ELEC, TELECOM, COMPUT to distribute information over a wide area or audience ○ *He broadcast the latest news over the WAN.*

**broadcast message** noun TELECOM a message sent to everyone on a network ○ *Five minutes before we shut down the LAN, we send a broadcast message to all users.*

**broadcast network** noun TELECOM a network for sending data to a number of receivers

**broadcast quality** *noun* TELECOM the quality of video image or signal that is used by professional television stations ○ *We can use your multimedia presentation as the advert on TV if it's of broadcast quality.*

**broadleaf, broadleaf tree** *noun* BOT a deciduous tree such as beech or oak which has wide leaves, as opposed to the needles on conifers

**broad-leaved** *adjective* BOT (*of a tree*) which has wide leaves rather than needles

**broad-leaved evergreen** *noun* BOT an evergreen tree with large leaves, e.g a rhododendron or tulip tree.

**broadly** *adverb* **1.** widely **2.** generally ○ *broadly speaking*

**broad-spectrum** *adjective* BIOCHEM referring to an antibiotic or pesticide which destroys or controls many types of organism

**broad-spectrum antibiotic** *noun* PHARM an antibiotic used to control many types of bacteria

**bromide** *noun* **1.** CHEM a salt of hydrobromic acid **2.** PHARM potassium bromide, formerly used as a sedative

**bromine** *noun* CHEM ELEM a chemical element used in various industrial processes and in antiknock additives for petrol (NOTE: The chemical symbol is **Br**; the atomic number is **35** and the atomic weight is **79.90**.)

**bromoform** *noun* CHEM same as **tribromomethane**

**bronchiole** *noun* ANAT a narrow tube branching from a main air tube or bronchus in a lung

**bronchus** *noun* ANAT a tube that conveys air from the windpipe to a lung

**brood** *noun* BIOL a group of offspring produced at the same time, especially a group of young birds ○ *The territory provides enough food for two adults and a brood of six or eight young.*

**brook** *noun* GEOG a little stream

**brouter** *noun* COMPUT a device that combines the functions of a router and bridge to connect networks together ○ *The brouter provides dynamic routing and can bridge two local area networks.*

**brown** *adjective* **1.** of a colour like the colour of earth or wood **2.** ENVIRON not produced from renewable sources

**brown algae** *plural noun* MARINE BIOL brown seaweed. Phylum: Phaeophyta.

**brown bread** *noun* FOOD INDUST bread made with flour which has not been bleached or refined (NOTE: Not all brown bread is made with wholemeal flour.)

**brown coal** *noun* INDUST a type of soft coal which is not as efficient a fuel as anthracite and produces smoke when it burns. Also called **lignite**

**brown dwarf** *noun* ASTRON an object intermediate in mass between a star and a planet, giving out some radiation but not massive enough to allow full-scale fusion

COMMENT: Thought to be common in areas of star formation, brown dwarfs have proved elusive to observe but one, Gliese 229b, was definitively seen in 1995, 19 light years from Earth in the constellation Lepus. Other candidates for brown dwarf status have since been claimed.

**brown earth** *noun* EARTH SCI good fertile soil, slightly acid and containing humus

**brown electricity** *noun* INDUST electricity produced from coal or gas, and not from wind power, tidal power, etc. ⭘ **green electricity**

**brown fat** *noun* BIOL animal fat which can easily be converted to energy, and is believed to offset the effects of ordinary white fat

**brown flour** *noun* FOOD INDUST wheat flour which contains some bran and has not been bleached

**brown fumes** *plural noun* ENVIRON fumes from tarry substances produced by coal burning at low temperatures

**Brownian movement** *noun* PHYS the random movement of microscopic particles floating in a liquid or gas (NOTE: It results from the particles colliding with the molecules that surround them.)

**brownout** *noun* COMPUT a power failure producing a low voltage level rather than no voltage. ⭘ **blackout**

**brown podzolic soil** *noun* GEOL brown earth from which humus particles have been leached by rain

**brown rice** *noun* FOOD INDUST a rice grain that has had the husk removed, but has not been milled and polished to remove the bran

**brown-ring test** *noun* CHEM a test used to detect nitrate in a sample (NOTE: The sample is mixed with ferrous sulfate, and sulfuric acid is added. If a brown line is visible where the mixture meets the acid, this indicates that the sample contains a nitrate.)

**brown smoke** *noun* ENVIRON smoke from tarry substances produced by coal burning at low temperatures

**browse** *verb* COMPUT **1.** to view data in a database or online system **2.** to search through and access database material without permission

**browser** *noun* COMPUT a software program that is used to navigate through webpages stored on the Internet

COMMENT: A browser program asks the Internet server (called the HTTP server) to send it a page of information. This page is stored in the HTML layout language which is decoded by the browser and displayed on screen. The browser displays any hotspots and will jump to another page if the user clicks on a hyperlink.

**browsing** *noun* COMPUT the process of moving through a multimedia title or a list of files or through sites on the Internet in no particular order (NOTE: The user controls which page to move to next and what to view.)

**Brucella** *noun* BIOL a type of rod-shaped bacterium

**brush** *noun* **1.** ELEC a small replaceable block of carbon which rubs against the surface of a commutator in a generator or electric motor ○ *At high altitude, the air becomes drier and this causes a greatly increased rate of wear on the brushes.* **2.** COMPUT a tool in paint package software which draws pixels on screen ○ *The paint package lets you vary the width of the brush in pixels and the colour it produces.* **3.** BOT same as **brushwood**

**brush killer** *noun* AGRIC a powerful herbicide which destroys the undergrowth

**brushwood** *noun* BOT undergrowth with twigs and small branches

**brute force method** *noun* COMPUT a problem-solving method which depends on computer power rather than elegant programming techniques

**bryophyte** *noun* BOT a nonflowering plant, frequently growing in damp places, with separate gamete- and spore-bearing forms, e.g. moss. Division: *Bryophyta*.

**BS** *abbreviation* COMPUT backspace

**BSE** *noun* VET a fatal brain disease of cattle. Also called **mad cow disease**. Full form **bovine spongiform encephalopathy**

**BSI** *abbreviation* British Standards Institute

**BST** *noun* BIOCHEM a growth hormone of cattle, sometimes added to feed to improve milk production. Full form **bovine somatotrophin**

**Btu, BTU, BThU** *abbreviation* PHYS, MEASURE British thermal unit

**bubble chamber** *noun* PHYS a chamber filled with a liquid in which the trail of a moving particle shows up as a line of bubbles

**bubble jet printer** *noun* COMPUT an inkjet printer which produces characters by sending a stream of tiny drops of ink onto the paper

**bubble memory** *noun* COMPUT a method of storing binary data using the magnetic properties of some materials, allowing very large amounts of data to be stored in primary memory

**bubble sort** *noun* COMPUT a sorting method which repeatedly exchanges various pairs of data items until they are in order

**bubonic plague** *noun* MED a fatal disease of the lymph system caused by *Pasteurella pestis* transmitted to humans by fleas from rats

**bucket** *noun* COMPUT a storage area containing data for an application

**buckle** *verb* PHYS to bend out of shape because of heat or force ○ *Overheating will make the battery plates buckle.*

**bud** *noun* BOT a young shoot on a plant, which will later become a leaf or flower

**budding** *noun* BOT a way of propagating plants in which a bud from one plant is grafted onto another plant

**buffer** *noun* **1.** COMPUT a circuit that isolates and protects a system from damaging inputs from driven circuits or peripherals **2.** COMPUT a temporary storage area for data waiting to be processed **3.** CHEM a substance that keeps a constant balance between acid and alkali **4.** CHEM a solution in which the pH is not changed by adding acid or alkali ■ *verb*

**1.** COMPUT to use a temporary storage area to hold data until the processor or device is ready to deal with it **2.** CHEM to prevent a solution from becoming acid or alkaline ○ *If a lake is well buffered, it will not have a low pH factor, even if acid rain falls into it.* ○ *Bicarbonate is the main buffering factor in fresh water.*

**buffer action** *noun* CHEM the process of keeping a balance between acid and alkali

**buffer land** *noun* ENVIRON land between a protected area, e.g. a nature reserve, and the surrounding countryside or town. Also called **buffer zone**

**buffer size** *noun* COMPUT the total number of characters that can be held in a buffer

**buffer zone** *noun* ENVIRON same as **buffer land**

**buffet** *noun* AEROSP the shaking of an aircraft caused by the breakdown of the airflow over the upper surface of the wing ○ *Large aircraft use a stick shaker to supplement the natural stall warning of buffet.* ■ *verb* (of water or wind) to push something around with great force ○ *The storm buffeted the coast.* ○ *The aircraft was buffeted by strong crosswinds as it made its final approach to land.*

COMMENT: Buffet is a warning to the pilot that the smooth airflow over the wing is breaking down and that corrective action should be taken to prevent a stall.

**buffet speed** *noun* AEROSP the speed at which buffet is first noticed

**bug** *noun* **1.** COMPUT an error in a computer program which makes it run incorrectly (*informal*) **2.** ZOOL a little insect (*informal*) **3.** ZOOL a winged insect belonging to the class Hemiptera

**buggy** *noun* a small computer-controlled vehicle

**build** *noun* COMPUT a particular version of a program ○ *This is the latest build of the new software.* ■ *verb* **1.** ENG to make a construction ○ *The developer is planning to build 2500 new houses on the greenfield site.* ○ *The female birds build nests of straw in holes in trees.* **2.** COMPUT to develop software

**building** *noun* **1.** ENVIRON a construction such as a house, shop or office **2.** EARTH SCI the process of constructing something

**building area** *noun* ENVIRON an area of land on which building may take place or is taking place. Also called **building zone**

**building block** *noun* COMPUT a self-contained unit that can be joined to others to form a system

**building zone** ENVIRON same as **building area**

**build up** *verb* to form by accumulation ○ *In these conditions, ice builds up on the leading edges.* ○ *The pesticide gradually built up in the food chain.*

**build-up** *noun* a gradual accumulation ○ *a build-up of DDT in the food chain* ○ *a build-up of static electricity*

**built environment** *noun* ENVIRON built-up areas seen as the environment in which humans live

**built-in** *adjective* COMPUT referring to a feature that is already included in a system ○ *The built-in adapter card makes it fully IBM compatible.* ○ *The computer has a built-in hard disk.* ○ *The printer has several built-in fonts.*

**built-up area** *noun* ENVIRON an area which is full of houses, shops, offices and other buildings, with very little open space

**bulb** *noun* **1.** ELEC a glass ball that produces light when electricity is supplied ○ *The bulb has an element that heats up and glows brightly when you switch on the electricity.* ○ *If a lamp does not work, the bulb may need replacing.* **2.** something shaped like a lamp bulb ○ *The most common type of hygrometer is the wet and dry bulb thermometer arrangement.* **3.** BOT a fleshy stem like an onion, formed of layers of tissue, which can be planted and which will produce flowers and seed

**bulk erase** *noun* COMPUT the erasing of a complete magnetic disk or tape in one action

**bulkhead** *noun* AEROSP a dividing partition across the structure of the fuselage separating one compartment from another for reasons of safety or strength ○ *A fireproof bulkhead is provided to separate the cool area of the engine from the hot area.*

**bulking agent** *noun* INDUST an additive which causes a substance to stick together in coagulated masses

**bulk storage medium** *noun* COMPUT a medium that is able to store large amounts of data in a convenient size and form ○ *Magnetic tape is a reliable bulk storage medium.*

**bulldozer** *noun* ENG a piece of earth-moving equipment, like a tractor with a blade in front, used for pushing soil or rocks and for levelling surfaces

**bullet** *noun* COMPUT a symbol, often a filled circle or square in front of a line of text, used to draw attention to a particular line in a list

**bund** *noun* ENG a soil wall built across a slope to retain water or to hold waste in a sloping landfill site

**bundle** *noun* 1. TELECOM a number of optic fibres gathered together 2. COMPUT a package containing a computer together with software or accessories offered at a special price ○ *The bundle now includes a PC with spreadsheet and database applications for just £999.* ■ *verb* COMPUT to market at a special price a package that contains a computer together with a range of software or accessories

**bundled software** *noun* COMPUT software included in the price of a computer system

**Bunsen burner** *noun* SCI a portable tube-shaped gas burner with an adjustable hole controlling air intake and flame characteristics, used in laboratories

**buoyancy** *noun* PHYS the ability to float on a liquid or air

**burette** *noun* MEASURE, CHEM a glass tube with a scale marked on the side and a stopcock at the bottom, used to release accurately measured quantities of liquid during chemical analysis

**burn** *noun* MED an injury to skin and tissue caused by light, heat, radiation, electricity or a chemical ■ *verb* 1. ENVIRON to destroy or damage something by fire ○ *Several hundred hectares of forest were burnt in the fire.* 2. to use fuel or food to produce energy ○ *Swimming will help you burn calories.*

**burner** *noun* INDUST a device for burning something such as fuel or waste

**burner reactor** *noun* INDUST a normal type of nuclear reactor in which fuel, e.g. uranium-239, is used to generate heat by fission

**burn in** *verb* COMPUT 1. to mark a monitor screen after displaying a high brightness image for too long 2. to write data into a PROM chip

**burn out** *noun* COMPUT excess heat or incorrect use that causes an electronic circuit or device to fail

**burn-up** *noun* INDUST the amount of fuel burnt in a nuclear reactor, shown as a proportion of the fuel originally used

**burst** *noun* 1. ELEC a short isolated sequence of transmitted signals 2. PHYS a minor explosion caused by increased pressure ○ *The risk of tyre burst through overheating is increased by hard application of the brakes.* 3. a very short period of activity followed by no activity ○ *a burst of energy* ○ *The ground installation transmits a code in two short bursts.* ■ *verb* to explode because of increased pressure or a puncture ○ *Metal debris on the runway may cause a tyre to burst.* (NOTE: **bursting – burst**)

**burst mode** *noun* ELEC the transfer of a batch of data across a bus with no interruptions

**bus** *noun* COMPUT 1. a communication link consisting of a set of leads or wires which connects different parts of a computer hardware system, and over which data is transmitted and received by various circuits in the system 2. a central source of information which supplies several devices

**bus arbitration** *noun* COMPUT a protocol and control of transmission over a bus that ensures fair usage by several users

**busbar** *noun* ELEC an electrical conductor used to carry a particular power supply to various pieces of equipment ○ *Complex busbars are thick metal strips or rods to which input and output connections are made.*

**bus clock** *noun* COMPUT the speed at which data is transferred along the main bus in a computer

**bus driver** *noun* COMPUT a high power transistor or amplifier that can provide enough power to transmit signals to a number of devices

**bus extender, bus extension card** *noun* COMPUT 1. a device that extends an 8-bit bus to accommodate 16-bit add-in cards 2. a special board used by repair engineers that moves an add-in board up to a position that is easier to work on

**bush** *noun* BOT **1.** a low shrub or small tree ○ *a coffee bush* **2.** (*in semi-arid regions*) wild land covered with bushes and small trees

**bush-fallow** *noun* AGRIC subsistence agriculture in which land is cultivated for a few years until its natural fertility is exhausted, then allowed to rest for a considerable period during which the natural vegetation regenerates itself, after which the land is cleared and cultivated again

**bus master** *noun* COMPUT a device that controls the bus while transmitting (NOTE: Bus master status can move between sending stations.)

**bus structure** *noun* COMPUT the way in which buses are organised, e.g. whether serial, parallel or bidirectional

**bus topology** *noun* COMPUT a network topology in which all devices are connected to a single cable which has terminators at each end ○ *Ethernet is a network that uses the bus topology.* ○ *Token ring uses a ring topology.*

**busy** *adjective* COMPUT **1.** occupied in doing something or in working ○ *When the busy line goes low, the printer will accept more data.* □ **the line is busy** the telephone line is being used **2.** an electrical signal indicating that a device is not ready to receive data

**butadiene** *noun* CHEM a colourless and flammable gas, used in synthetic rubber and in nylon and latex paint manufacture. Formula: $CH_2=CHCH=CH_2$. (NOTE: It is a product of petroleum.)

**butane** *noun* CHEM a colourless flammable gas with two different isomers, used as a fuel. Formula: $C_4H_{10}$. (NOTE: It is derived from natural gas and petroleum distillation, and is used as a bottled domestic fuel.)

**butanedioic acid** *noun* CHEM a crystalline carboxylic acid formed during the fermentation of sugar, occurring in some plants and in amber. Formula: $HOOC-(CH_2)_2COOH$. Also called **succinic acid**

**butanol** *noun* CHEM a colourless liquid with four different molecular structures (**isomers**), used as a solvent and in organic chemical manufacture. Formula: $C_4H_9OH$. Also called **butyl alcohol**

**button** *noun* COMPUT **1.** a switch that carries out an action ○ *Use the mouse to move the cursor to the icon and start the application by pressing the mouse button.* **2.** a square shape displayed on a screen that will carry out a particular action if selected with a pointer or keyboard ○ *There are two buttons at the bottom of the status window, select the left button to cancel the operation or the right to continue.*

**button bar** *noun* COMPUT a line of square shapes displayed on screen each of which start an action or program when selected

**butyl alcohol** *noun* CHEM same as **butanol**

**Buys Ballot's law** *noun* METEOROL a rule for identifying low pressure areas based on the Coriolis effect stating that in the northern hemisphere, if the wind is blowing from behind you, then the low pressure area is to the left, while in the southern hemisphere it is to your right

**buzz** ELEC *noun* a sound like a loud hum ■ *verb* to make a loud hum

**buzzer** *noun* ELEC an electrical device which makes a loud hum

**BWR** *abbreviation* INDUST boiling water reactor

**by-catch** *noun* FISHERY species such as dolphins, sharks and turtles caught during fishing but not required, so thrown back dead into the sea ○ *By-catch is a major environmental problem as it involves the uncontrolled destruction of populations.*

**bypass** *noun* an alternative route, pipe, or channel ○ *A turbine bypass in the form of an alternative exhaust duct is fitted with a valve.*

**by-pass** *noun* ENVIRON a road built around a town, to relieve traffic congestion ○ *Since the by-pass was built, traffic in the town has been reduced by half.* ■ *verb* to avoid something by going around it ○ *They by-passed the normal complaints procedure and went straight to the director of the chemical company.* ○ *The plans are to build a new main road, by-passing the town.*

**by-product** *noun* INDUST something additional produced during a process

**byte** *noun* COMPUT a group of bits or binary digits, usually eight, which a computer operates on as a single unit

**bytecode** *noun* COMPUT a form of Java instructions that can be executed in a Java Virtual Machine

# C

**C** *symbol* **1.** CHEM ELEM carbon **2.** MEASURE Celsius **3.** MEASURE centi- **4.** ELEC coulomb **5.** COMPUT the hexadecimal number equivalent to decimal 12 ■ *noun* COMPUT a high level programming language developed mainly for writing structured systems programs (NOTE: The C language was originally developed for and with the UNIX operating system.)

**C++** *noun* COMPUT a high-level programming language based on its predecessor, C, but providing object oriented programming functions

**Ca** *symbol* CHEM ELEM calcium

**cable** *noun* **1.** a thick metal wire **2.** ELEC a flexible conducting electrical or optical link ○ *The cable has the wrong connector for this printer.*

**cable connector** *noun* ELEC the connector at each end of a cable

**cable matcher** *noun* ELEC a device that change the impedance of a cable so that the cable can be used with a specific device

**cable modem** *noun* COMPUT a device that provides high-speed access to the Internet via the coaxial cable, used to distribute cable television signals

**cable plant** *noun* ELEC all the cables, connectors and patch panels within a building or office

**cable tester** *noun* ELEC a piece of test equipment used to find breaks, faults or cracks in cabling

**cache** COMPUT *noun* a section of high-speed memory which stores data that the computer can access quickly ■ *verb* to store data in a cache ○ *This central processing unit caches instructions, improving performance by 15 per cent.*

**cache hit** *noun* COMPUT a retrieval of data from cache memory rather than from the storage device, indicating that time was saved and the cache was useful

**cache memory** *noun* COMPUT same as **cache**

**CAD** *abbreviation* COMPUT computer-aided design *or* computer-assisted design

**caddy** *noun* COMPUT a plastic or metal case for a CD-ROM

**cadmium** *noun* CHEM ELEM a metallic element which is naturally present in soil and rock in association with zinc and is used for making rods for nuclear reactors (NOTE: The chemical symbol is **Cd**; the atomic number is **48** and the atomic weight is **112.40**.)

**cadmium sulfide, cadmium sulphide** *noun* CHEM an orange or yellow solid used as a colouring, e.g. in paints. Formula: CdS.

**caducous** *adjective* BIOL referring to a part of a plant or animal which becomes detached during the organism's life

**CAE** *abbreviation* COMPUT computer-aided engineering *or* computer-assisted engineering

**caesium** *noun* CHEM ELEM a metallic alkali element which is one of the main radioactive pollutants taken up by fish (NOTE: The chemical symbol is **Cs**; the atomic number is **55** and the atomic weight is **132.91**.)

**caesium clock** *noun* PHYS a very accurate clock in which caesium atoms are stimulated by an alternating magnetic field (NOTE: A precise time is determined when the frequencies of the atoms and the magnetic field are the same.)

**CAI** *abbreviation* COMPUT computer-aided instruction *or* computer-assisted instruction

**cal** *abbreviation* PHYS, MEASURE calorie

**CAL** *abbreviation* COMPUT **1.** computer-aided learning **2.** computer-assisted learning

**calc-** *prefix* calcium

**calcareous** *adjective* EARTH SCI referring to a soil which is chalky and contains calcium or a rock such as chalk or limestone which contains calcium

**calci-** same as **calc-**

**calcicole, calcicolous plant** *noun* BOT a plant which grows well on chalky or alkaline soils. Also called **calciphile**

**calciferol** *noun* BIOL vitamin $D_2$

**calcification** *noun* CHEM the process of hardening by forming deposits of calcium salts

**calcified** *adjective* BIOL made hard ○ *Bone is calcified connective tissue.*

**calcifuge** *noun* BOT a plant which prefers acid soils and cannot exist on chalky or alkali soils. Also called **calciphobe**

**calcimorphic soil** *noun* GEOL soil which is rich in lime

**calcin** *verb* CHEM to heat something at high temperature

**calcination** *noun* CHEM the heating of something at high temperature, e.g. in the production of metal oxides

**calciphile** *noun* BOT same as **calcicole**

**calciphobe** *noun* BOT same as **calcifuge**

**calcite** *noun* MINERALS a colourless or white crystalline form of calcium carbonate, used in cement, plaster, glass and paints. Formula: $CaCO_3$. (NOTE: It is the main constituent of limestone, marble and chalk.)

**calcitonin** *noun* BIOCHEM a hormone, produced chiefly by the thyroid gland in mammals, that promotes the deposition of calcium in bones

**calcium** *noun* CHEM ELEM a metallic chemical element which is naturally present in limestone and chalk and is essential to biological processes (NOTE: The chemical symbol is **Ca**; the atomic number is **20** and atomic weight is **40.08**.)

COMMENT: Calcium is essential for various bodily processes such as blood clotting and is a major component of bones and teeth. It is an important element in a balanced diet. Milk, cheese, eggs and certain vegetables are its main sources.

In birds, calcium is responsible for the formation of strong eggshells. Water which passes through limestone contains a high level of calcium and is called 'hard'.

**calcium bicarbonate** *noun* CHEM same as **calcium hydrogencarbonate**

**calcium carbide** *noun* CHEM a greyish-black solid that is white when pure, used for acetylene gas generation. Formula: $CaC_2$.

**calcium carbonate** *noun* CHEM a white insoluble solid formed from animal organisms that is naturally abundant and is used in the production of cement, antacids, paint and toothpaste. Formula: $CaCO_3$. (NOTE: It is found in chalk, limestone and marble.)

**calcium cycle** *noun* BIOL a cycle of events by which calcium in the soil is taken up into plants, passed to animals which eat the plants and then passed back to the soil again when the animals die and decompose

**calcium deficiency** *noun* BIOL a lack of calcium in an animal's bloodstream

**calcium hydrogencarbonate** *noun* CHEM a solid formed when calcium carbonate is dissolved in water containing carbon dioxide. Formula: $CaCO_3 + H_2O - Ca(HCO_3)_2$. Also called **calcium bicarbonate**

**calcium hydroxide** *noun* CHEM a white alkaline powder used in acid soil treatment, cement, plaster, and glass manufacture. Formula: $Ca(OH)_2$. Also called **slaked lime**

**calcium oxide** *noun* CHEM a chemical used in many industrial processes and also spread on soil to reduce acidity. Formula: $CaO$. Also called **quicklime**

**calcium sulfate, calcium sulphate** *noun* CHEM a white odourless powder used as a drying agent, a building material and in plaster of Paris. Formula: $CaSO_4$.

**calcium supplement** *noun* HEALTH an addition of calcium to the diet, or as injections, to improve the level of calcium in the bloodstream

**calculate** *verb* **1.** MATHS to find the answer to a problem using numbers ○ *The DP manager calculated the rate for keyboarding.* ○ *You need to calculate the remaining disk space.* **2.** to estimate something ○ *I calculate that we have six months' stock left.*

**calculated field** *noun* COMPUT a field within a database record that contains the results of calculations performed on other fields

**calculation** *noun* MATHS the answer to a mathematical problem

**calculator** *noun* an electronic machine which works out the answers to numerical problems ○ *My pocket calculator needs a new battery.* ○ *He worked out the discount on his calculator.*

**calculus** *noun* MATHS a branch of mathematics that deals with the behaviour of functions with continuous variables

**calibrate** *verb* **1.** to make a scale on a measuring instrument **2.** to check or change the scale or graduations on a measuring instrument to make it accurate ○ *The international standard atmosphere is used to calibrate pressure altimeters.* **3.** to measure the inside diameter of a tube or passage

**calibrated airspeed** *noun* AEROSP indicated airspeed corrected for instrumentation and installation errors. Abbreviation **CAS**

**calibration** *noun* **1.** the establishment or adjustment of a scale on a measuring instrument **2.** ELEC the comparison of a signal from an input with a known scale to provide a standardised reading

**calibre** *noun* an interior diameter of a tube, blood vessel, etc.

**californium** *noun* CHEM ELEM a synthetic radioactive metallic element in the actinide series of the periodic table (NOTE: The chemical symbol is **Cf**; the atomic number is **98** and the atomic weight is **251**. It is produced by bombardment of curium or americium with neutrons, and is used as a neutron source.)

**call** *verb* COMPUT to transfer control to a separate program or routine from a main program ○ *After an input is received, the first function is called.*

**callback** *noun* COMPUT a security system designed to reduce the risk of an unauthorised user connecting to a computer installed with dial-in networking (NOTE: Communications software and a modem are used to dial the remote computer and enter a name and password. The remote computer then hangs up the telephone line and calls back on a preset telephone number.)

**calling** *noun* COMPUT a signal to request attention, sent from a terminal or device to the main computer

**calling sequence** *noun* COMPUT a series of program commands required to direct execution to or back from a subroutine

**call instruction** *noun* COMPUT a programming instruction that directs control to a routine with control passed back once the routine has finished (NOTE: Before the call, the program counter contents are saved to show where to return to in the main program.)

**calm** *noun* METEOROL a period when there is no wind at all

**calomel** *noun* AGRIC a poisonous substance used to kill moss on lawns and to treat pinworms in the intestine. Formula: $Hg_2Cl_2$. Also called **mercurous chloride**

**calomel half cell** *noun* CHEM an electrode formed of mercury, mercury (I) chloride and potassium, providing a known potential and used as a reference point

**caloric** *adjective* PHYS referring to calories

**caloric energy** *noun* PHYS the amount of energy shown as a number of calories

**caloric requirement** *noun* BIOL the amount of energy, shown in calories, which an animal or a human being needs each day

**calorie** *noun* MEASURE, PHYS a unit of measurement of heat or energy. Symbol **cal** (NOTE: The **joule**, an SI measure, is now more usual (1 calorie = 4.186 joules).)

COMMENT: One calorie is the amount of heat needed to raise the temperature of one gram of water by one degree Celsius. The kilocalorie (shortened to 'Calorie') is also used as a measurement of the energy content of food and to show the caloric requirement or amount of energy needed by an average person. The average adult in an office job requires about 3,000 calories per day, supplied by carbohydrates and fats to give energy and proteins to replace tissue. More strenuous physical work needs more calories. If a person eats more than the number of calories needed by his energy output or for his growth, the extra calories are stored in the body as fat.

**Calorie** *noun* PHYS same as **kilocalorie**. Symbol **Cal, kcal**

**calorific** *adjective* PHYS, PHYSIOL referring to calories, especially in food

**calorific value** *noun* PHYSIOL same as **energy value** ○ *The tin of beans has 250 calories or has a calorific value of 250 calories.*

**calorimeter** *noun* PHYS a piece of equipment that measures the amount of heat given out or taken in during a process such as combustion or a change of state

**calyx** *noun* BOT a part of a flower shaped like a cup, made up of the green sepals which cover the flower when it is in bud (NOTE: The plural is **calyces**.)

**cam** *noun* MECH ENG an oval or egg-shaped wheel which, when rotating, converts circular motion into reciprocating motion ○ *In a piston engine, the shape of each cam is designed to give the correct amount of opening to the valve.*

**CAM** *abbreviation* COMPUT **1.** computer-aided manufacture **2.** computer-assisted manufacture **3.** content-addressable memory

**cambium** *noun* BOT in plant roots and stems, a cylindrical layer of cells that produces new sap-conducting tissues and increases girth

**Cambridge ring** *noun* COMPUT a local area networking standard used for connecting several devices and computers together in a ring with simple cable links

**camouflage** ZOOL *noun* the natural hiding of an animal's shape by colours or patterns ○ *The stripes on the zebra are a form of camouflage which makes the animal less easy to see in long grass.* ■ *verb* to hide the shape of an animal by using colours or patterns on the skin

**camphor** *noun* CHEM a white solid with a characteristic odour, used medicinally and in the manufacture of celluloid plastics and explosives

**camplate** *noun* MECH ENG a rotating or non-rotating plate with cams on it ○ *The fuel pump consists of a rotor assembly fitted with several plungers, the ends of which bear onto a non-rotating camplate.*

**camshaft** *noun* MECH ENG a rotating shaft-carrying cam, which opens and closes valves in a piston engine ○ *As the camshaft rotates, the cam will transmit a lifting force.*

**Canadian deuterium-uranium reactor** *noun* INDUST a nuclear reactor using uranium oxide as a fuel and heavy water containing deuterium as a moderator and coolant. Abbreviation **CANDU** (NOTE: There is a reactor of this type at Pickering, Ontario in Canada.)

**canal** *noun* ENG **1.** a waterway made by people for ships to travel along **2.** a waterway made by people to take water to irrigate land

**cancel** *verb* COMPUT to stop a process or instruction before it has been fully executed

**cancer** *noun* MED a malignant growth or tumour which develops in tissue and destroys it, which can spread by metastasis to other parts of the body and cannot be controlled by the body itself

COMMENT: Cancers can be divided into cancers of the skin (carcinomas) and cancers of connective tissue such as bone or muscle (sarcomas). Cancer can be caused by tobacco, radiation and many other factors. There is evidence that constant exposure to the Sun can cause cancer (melanoma) of fair skin and depletion of the ozone layer in the atmosphere may increase the incidence of skin cancer. Many cancers are curable by surgery, by chemotherapy or by radiation, especially if they are detected early.

**cancerous** *adjective* MED referring to cancer ○ *a cancerous growth*

**candela** *noun* PHYS, MEASURE an SI unit measuring the brightness of a light ○ *The red and green wing tip navigation lights must be at least 5 candela.* Symbol **cd**

**candle power** *noun* a former unit of brightness, replaced by the candela ○ *Estimation of visibility is achieved by noting the distances at which lights of a known candle power can be observed.*

**CANDU** *abbreviation* Canadian deuterium-uranium reactor

**canine** *adjective* ZOOL referring to dogs ■ *noun* DENT same as **canine tooth**

**canine tooth** *noun* DENT a pointed tooth, between the incisors and bicuspids of a mammal

**cankered** *adjective* BIOL (*of skin or plant tissue*) having lesions

**Cannizzaro reaction** *noun* CHEM an alkaline chemical reaction in which aldehydes are broken down into alcohols and acid salts

**canonical schema** *noun* COMPUT a model of a database that is independent of the hardware or software available

**canopy** *noun* BOT branches and leaves of trees which act as an umbrella over the ground beneath

**canopy cover** *noun* BOT the percentage of the surface of the ground which is covered by the leaves and branches of trees

**cantilever** *noun* MECH ENG a beam fixed and supported at one end only ○ *The wings are of cantilever design.*

**canyon** *noun* GEOG a deep valley with steep sides

**cap** *noun* **1.** a top or lid ○ *the exhaust valve cap* **2.** FUNGI the dome-shaped structure of some fungi which bears spores on its undersurface

**capability** *noun* the fact of being able to do something ○ *This scanner has the capability of working at 2400 dpi.*

**capability list** *noun* COMPUT a list of operations that can be carried out

**capable** *adjective* able to do something ○ *That is the highest speed that this printer is capable of.* ○ *The software is capable of far more complex functions.* ○ *The machine is capable of carrying out hundreds of tests an hour.*

**capacitance** *noun* ELEC the ability of a component to store electrical charge ○ *Capacitance is measured in farads and can either be a fixed amount or a variable amount.* ○ *If the supply frequency is low, the voltage has more time to build up a larger charge, or capacitance.*

**capacitative, capacititive** *adjective* ELEC having capacitance

**capacitor** *noun* ELEC an electronic component which can store charge

**capacitor storage** *noun* ELEC a device using the capacitative properties of a material to store data

**capacity** *noun* **1.** the ability to do something easily ○ *Energy is the capacity for performing work.* **2.** the amount of something which a container can hold ○ *Each cylinder has a capacity of 0.5 litres.* **3.** INDUST the amount which can be produced or the amount of work which can be done ○ *industrial* or *manufacturing* or *production capacity* □ **to work at full capacity** to do as much work as possible □ **to use up spare** *or* **excess capacity** to make use of time or space which is not fully used

**capillarity** *noun* PHYS same as **capillary action**

**capillary** *noun* **1.** ANAT a tiny blood vessel between the arterioles and the venules, which carries blood and nutrients into the tissues **2.** BIOL a tiny tube carrying a liquid in the body

**capillary action, capillary flow** *noun* PHYS a movement of a liquid upwards inside a narrow tube or upwards through the soil

COMMENT: Capillary flow has an important effect on water in soil, as it does not drain away. Water moves through the soil by capillary action, i.e. by the surface tension between the water and the walls of the fine tubes or capillaries. It is a very slow movement, and may not be fast enough to supply plant roots in a soil which is drying out.

**caprylic acid** *noun* CHEM same as **octanoic acid**

**capstan** *noun* COMPUT a spindle of a tape player or tape backup unit that keeps the tape pressed against the magnetic read/write head or pinch roller

**capsule** *noun* **1.** a small closed container **2.** ANAT a membrane round an organ, egg, etc. **3.** BOT a dry seed case which bursts open to allow the seeds to shoot out

**capture** *verb* COMPUT **1.** to take data into a computer system ○ *The software allows captured images to be edited.* ○ *Scanners usually capture images at a resolution of 300 dots per inch (dpi).* □ **to capture a printer port** to redirect data intended for a local printer port over a network to a shared printer □ **to capture a screen** to store the image that is currently displayed on the screen in a file **2.** (*in a Token-Ring network*) to remove a token from the network in order to transmit data across the network

**carapace** *noun* ZOOL a thick hard case or shell of bone or chitin covering part of the body, especially the back, of an animal such as a crab or turtle

**carbamide** *noun* CHEM same as **urea**

**carbanion** *noun* CHEM a negatively charged organic ion in which carbon has three covalent bonds

**carbene** *noun* CHEM a highly reactive, transient molecule in which a carbon atom has only three bonds

**carbide** *noun* CHEM a compound of carbon and another element, generally a metal

**carbohydrate** *noun* BIOL an organic compound which derives from sugar and which is the main ingredient of many types of food

COMMENT: Carbohydrates are compounds of carbon, hydrogen and oxygen. They are found in particular in sugar and starch from plants, and provide the body with energy. Plants build up valuable organic substances from simple materials. The most important part of this process, which is called photosynthesis, is the production of carbohydrates such as sugars, starches and cellulose by green plants which convert carbon dioxide and water using sunlight as energy. Carbohydrates form the largest part of the food of animals.

**carbolic acid** *noun* CHEM same as phenol

**carbon** *noun* CHEM ELEM a common non-metallic element that is an essential component of living matter and organic chemical compounds (NOTE: The chemical symbol is **C**; the atomic number is **6** and the atomic weight is **12.01**.)

**carbon-14 dating** *noun* TECH same as **carbon dating**

**carbonaceous** *adjective* CHEM referring to rock such as coal which is rich in hydrocarbons

**carbonate** *noun* CHEM a compound formed from a base and carbonic acid ■ *verb* INDUST to add carbon dioxide to a drink to make it fizzy

**carbonation** *noun* FOOD INDUST the adding of carbon dioxide to a drink to make it fizzy

**carbon black** *noun* CHEM a fine carbon powder derived from petroleum or natural gas and used as a pigment and in making rubber

**carbon brush** *noun* ELEC a small, replaceable, carbon block in an electric motor, generator or alternator which allows the passage of electric current

**carbon copy** *noun* COMPUT a feature of electronic mail software that allows you to send a copy of a message to another user. ◆ **blind carbon copy**. Abbreviation **cc**

**carbon cycle** *noun* **1.** BIOCHEM the circulation of carbon, by which carbon atoms from carbon dioxide are incorporated into organic compounds in plants during photosynthesis (NOTE: They are then oxidised into carbon dioxide again during respiration by the plants or by herbivores which eat them and by carnivores which eat the herbivores, thus releasing carbon to go round the cycle again.) **2.** PHYS (*in astrophysics*) the fusion of a hydrogen nucleus with a carbon nucleus at the start of a complex process whereby nitrogen and oxygen nuclei are also produced en route (NOTE: The final products are a helium nucleus and a carbon nucleus, so that the carbon is a catalyst in the reaction and is left over for recycling in another fusion.)

**carbon dating** *noun* TECH the process of finding out how old something is by analysing the amount of carbon dioxide in it which has decayed. Also called **carbon-14 dating**

**carbon deposit** *noun* a residue of burnt oil deposited in a combustion chamber in the course of the combustion process ○ *Carbon deposits on a spark-plug electrode may cause misfiring.*

**carbon dioxide** *noun* CHEM a colourless odourless non-flammable atmospheric gas largely responsible for the greenhouse effect. Formula: $CO_2$.

COMMENT: Carbon dioxide exists naturally in air and is produced by burning or by rotting organic matter. In animals, the body's metabolism makes the tissues burn carbon, which is then breathed out by the lungs as waste carbon dioxide. Carbon dioxide is removed from the atmosphere by plants when it is split by chlorophyll in photosynthesis to form carbon and oxygen. It is also dissolved from the atmosphere in seawater. The increasing release of carbon dioxide into the atmosphere, especially from burning fossil fuels, contributes to the greenhouse effect. Carbon dioxide is used in solid form as a means of keeping food cold. It is also used in fizzy drinks and has the E number 290. It is used as a coolant in some nuclear reactors. Carbon dioxide is found in the atmospheres of the Earth, Venus and Mars. On Earth it is produced mainly by volcanoes and was the atmosphere's dominant active component (nitrogen, the main component, is chemically inert) until photosynthesis began and oxygen was produced

**carbon disulfide, carbon disulphide** noun CHEM a colourless toxic flammable liquid containing impurities giving it a characteristic smell of rotten eggs. Formula: $CS_2$. (NOTE: It is used as a solvent for rubber vulcanisation, as a pesticide and in Cellophane and rayon manufacture.)

**carbon emissions** plural noun ENVIRON the carbon dioxide and carbon monoxide produced by motor vehicles and industrial processes and regarded as atmospheric pollutants

**carbon fibre** noun **1.** INDUST a thin strong strand of pure carbon which can be combined with other materials to make them stronger **2.** EARTH SCI a light and strong composite material containing strands of pure carbon

**carbonic acid** noun CHEM a weak acid formed in small quantities when carbon dioxide is dissolved in water. Formula: $H_2CO_3$.

**carbonisation** noun BIOCHEM the process by which fossil plants have become carbon

**carbonise** verb CHEM to cover or coat a surface with carbon

**carbonium ion** noun CHEM an organic ion containing a carbon atom bearing a positive charge

**carbon monoxide** noun CHEM a colourless, odourless and poisonous gas found in fumes from car engines, from burning gas and cigarette smoke. Formula: CO.

COMMENT: Carbon monoxide exists in tobacco smoke and in car exhaust fumes and is dangerous because it is easily absorbed into the blood and takes the place of the oxygen in the blood, combining with haemoglobin to form carboxyhaemoglobin, which has the effect of starving the tissues of oxygen. Carbon monoxide has no smell and people do not realise that they are being poisoned by it until they become unconscious, with a characteristic red colouring to the skin.

**carbon sequestration** noun the uptake and storage of carbon

**carbon sink** noun ECOL a part of the biosphere, e.g. a tropical forest, which absorbs carbon, as opposed to animals which are a carbon source, releasing it into the atmosphere in the form of carbon dioxide

**carbon tetrachloride** noun CHEM a dense nonflammable toxic liquid that is colourless with a sweetish smell. Formula: $CCl_4$. (NOTE: It is used as a solvent, refrigerant and dry-cleaning agent and in fire extinguishers.)

**carbonyl chloride** noun CHEM same as **phosgene**

**carbonyl group** noun CHEM a chemical group formed with a double-bond between carbon and oxygen atoms, C=O, occurring in aldehydes, carboxylic acids and ketones

**carborundum** noun CHEM a dark crystalline abrasive material composed of silicon carbide

**carboxyhaemoglobin** noun BIOCHEM a compound of carbon monoxide and haemoglobin formed when a person breathes in carbon monoxide from car fumes or from ordinary cigarette smoke

**carboxyl group** noun CHEM the acid group -COOH:

**carboxylic acid** noun CHEM an organic acid that contains the carboxyl group

**carburation** noun MECH ENG the process of mixing fuel with air in a carburettor ○ Carburation must ensure that rapid and complete burning will take place within the cylinder.

**carburettor** noun AUTOMOT a device for mixing air with fuel in the right quantities before combustion ○ Most carburettors are installed so that they are in a warm position.

**carcin-** prefix MED cancer

**carcinogen** noun MED a substance which produces cancer

COMMENT: Carcinogens are found in pesticides such as DDT, in asbestos, aromatic compounds such as benzene, and radioactive substances.

**carcinogenesis** noun MED the formation of cancer in tissue

**carcinogenic** adjective MED causing cancer

**carcinogenic agent** noun MED a substance which causes cancer

**card** *noun* COMPUT **1.** a small piece of stiff paper or plastic **2.** a sheet of insulating material on which electronic components can be mounted

**card edge connector** *noun* COMPUT a series of metal tracks ending at the edge and on the surface of a card, allowing it to be plugged into an edge connector to provide electrical contact for data transmission

**cardi-, cardio-** *prefix* ANAT the heart

**cardiac** *adjective* ANAT referring to the heart

**cardiac muscle** *noun* ANAT the muscle of the heart wall

**cardinal** *adjective* MATHS referring to a positive integer ○ *13, 19 and 27 are cardinal numbers, −2.3 and 7.45 are not.*

**cardinal points** *plural noun* GEOG the four points on the horizon, north, south, east and west, which are used to show direction

**cardiogram** *noun* MED a recording of heart movements

**cardioid microphone** *noun* ACOUSTICS a highly sensitive microphone which is used to pick up sound in a specific area

**cardioid response** *noun* ACOUSTICS a heart-shaped response curve of an antenna or microphone when a signal source is moved around it

**cardiovascular system** *noun* ANAT a system of organs and blood vessels, including the heart, arteries and veins, in which the blood circulates round the body

**caret** *noun* COMPUT a symbol ( ^ ) that is often used to represent the Control key

**carnallite** *noun* MINERALS a white or pale mineral containing hydrated magnesium and potassium chlorides, used as a source of potassium and in fertilisers

**carnassial** *noun* DENT one of the sharp molar and premolar teeth of a carnivore that are adapted for cutting flesh

**carnivore** *noun* ZOOL an animal which eats meat

**carnivorous** *adjective* BIOL which eats meat ○ *a carnivorous animal*

**carnivorous plant** *noun* BOT a plant which attracts insects, traps them and then digests their bodies

**Carnot cycle** *noun* MECH ENG a theoretical heat-engine cycle that is reversible and gives maximum efficiency

**carotene** *noun* BIOCHEM an orange or red plant pigment (NOTE: Some carotenes are converted to vitamin A by animals.)

**carotenoid** *noun* BIOCHEM an orange or red plant pigment belonging to a group that includes carotenes

**carotid artery** *noun* ANAT one of two main arteries that carry blood to the head and neck

**carotid body** *noun* ANAT a mass of cells and nerve fibres in each carotid artery in the neck that detects acidity and oxygen levels in the blood so that they can be regulated by the body

**carotid pulse** *noun* ANAT a pulse in the carotid artery at the side of the neck

**carpal** *adjective* ANAT relating to the bones of the wrist

**carpel** *noun* BIOL a female part of a plant, formed of an ovary and stigma

**carpus** *noun* ANAT a bone belonging to the set of eight that make up the wrist (NOTE: The plural is **carpi**.)

**carr** *noun* GEOG an area of wetland which supports some trees

**carrier** *noun* **1.** COMPUT a device which holds a section of microfilm **2.** PHYS same as **carrier signal 3.** MED a person who carries bacteria of a disease in his or her body and who can transmit the disease to others without showing any sign of it personally **4.** MED an insect which carries disease and infects humans **5.** MED a healthy person who carries a genetic variation that causes a hereditary disease, e.g. haemophilia

**carrier detect** *noun* COMPUT a signal generated by a modem to inform the local computer that it has detected a carrier signal from a remote modem. Abbreviation **CD**

**carrier frequency** *noun* COMPUT the frequency of a carrier signal before it is modulated

**carrier gas** *noun* INDUST a gas used in an aerosol can to make the spray come out. Also called **carrier solvent**

**carrier sense multiple access-collision detection** *noun* COMPUT a network communications protocol used on an Ethernet network that prevents two sources transmitting at the same time by waiting for a quiet moment, then attempting to transmit. Abbreviation **CSMA-CD**

**carrier signal** *noun* COMPUT a continuous high frequency waveform that can be modulated by a signal ○ *He's not using a modem – there's no carrier signal on the line.* Also called **carrier**

**carrier solvent** *noun* INDUST same as **carrier gas**

**carrier wave** *noun* TELECOM the continuous transmission of a wave of constant amplitude and frequency

**carry** *verb* COMPUT to move something from one place to another ○ *The fibre optic link carried all the data.* ○ *The information-carrying abilities of this link are very good.* ■ *noun* MATHS an extra digit due to an addition the result being greater than the number base used ○ *When 5 and 7 are added, there is an answer of 2 and a carry which is put in the next column, giving 12.*

**carry bit, carry flag** *noun* COMPUT a single data bit that is used to indicate that a carry has occurred during an add operation

**carrying capacity** *noun* ECOL the maximum number of individuals of a species that can be supported in a given area

**carry look ahead** *noun* COMPUT a high speed electronic device that can predict if a carry will be generated by a sum operation and add it in. Compare **ripple-through carry**

**cartesian coordinates** *plural noun* COMPUT a positional system that uses two axes at right angles to represent a point which is located with two numbers, giving a position on each

**cartesian structure** *noun* COMPUT a data structure whose size is fixed and the elements are in a linear order

**cartilage** *noun* ANAT thick connective tissue which lines the joints and acts as a cushion and which forms part of the structure of an organ

**cartilaginous fish** *noun* ZOOL a fish with a cartilage skeleton. Class: Chondrichthyes. (NOTE: Sharks, rays and catfish are cartilaginous fish.)

**cartridge** *noun* COMPUT a removable cassette, containing a disk, tape, program or data, usually stored in ROM

**CAS** *abbreviation* AEROSP calibrated airspeed

**cascade** *noun* **1.** EARTH SCI a small waterfall **2.** CHEM a system for purifying substances, where the substance passes through a series of identical processes, each stage increasing the level of purity ■ *verb* EARTH SCI (*of liquid*) to fall down like a waterfall

**cascade carry** *noun* COMPUT a carry generated in an adder from an input carry signal

**cascading menu** *noun* COMPUT a secondary menu that is displayed to the side of the main pull-down menu

**cascading style sheet** *noun* COMPUT a method of describing the font, spacing and colour of text within a webpage and storing this information in a style sheet that can be applied to any text within the page. Abbreviation **CSS**

**case** *noun* **1.** an outer covering ○ *Cooling air is directed through passages in the engine case to control engine case temperature.* **2.** an example, situation or circumstance ○ *Wind directions are measured from magnetic north in the case of landing and take-off.* **3.** MED a single occurrence of a disease ○ *There were two hundred cases of cholera in the recent outbreak.* **4.** MED a person who has a disease or who is undergoing treatment **5.** COMPUT a programming command that jumps to various points in a program depending on the result of a test

**case-hardened** *adjective* METALL referring to a metal which has been given a hard outside layer by heating with carbon

**case history** *noun* MED an account of what has happened to a patient undergoing treatment

**case sensitive** *adjective* (*of a command or operation*) only working when the characters are entered in either uppercase or lowercase letters ○ *The password is case sensitive.*

**case sensitive search** *noun* a search function that succeeds only if the search word and the characters in the search word are both uppercase or lowercase in the same sequence

**cash crop** *noun* AGRIC a crop which is grown to be sold rather than eaten by the person who grows it

**cassette** *noun* a sealed plastic container used to store and protect magnetic tape

COMMENT: Using cassette tape allows computer data to be stored for future retrieval. It is used instead of disk system on small computers or as a slow, serial access, high-capacity back-up medium for large systems.

**cast** *noun* COMPUT **1.** an instruction in a programming language that converts data from one type to another ○ *To convert the variable from an integer to a character type, use the cast command.* **2.** each individual part of a multimedia presentation or animation (NOTE: The members of a cast can be individual images, sound clips or text.)

**cast-based animation** *noun* COMPUT a type of animation in which everything is an object with defined movement, colour, shape, etc. (NOTE: A script controls the actions of each object.)

**caste** *noun* a position in a hierarchical society

**caste system** *noun* ZOOL a system where animals have different roles in a society (NOTE: In the case of bees, there are three different groups: the queen, the workers (sterile females) and the drones (males).)

**cast iron** *noun* CHEM a very hard alloy of iron, silicon and 1.7% to 4.5% carbon, which is smelted and poured into moulds to shape it

**CAT** *abbreviation* **1.** AEROSP clear air turbulence **2.** COMPUT computer-aided testing *or* computer-assisted testing **3.** COMPUT computer-aided training *or* computer-assisted training **4.** COMPUT computerised tomography

**catabolic** *adjective* CHEM referring to catabolism

**catabolism** *noun* CHEM the breaking down of complex chemicals into simple chemicals

**catadromous, katadromous** *adjective* MARINE BIOL referring to fish which live in fresh water and go into the sea to spawn. Compare **anadromous**

**catadromy** *noun* MARINE BIOL a migration of fish such as eels from fresh water to the sea for spawning. Compare **anadromy**

**catalogue** COMPUT *noun* a list of contents or items in order ■ *verb* to make a catalogue of items stored ○ *All the terminals were catalogued, with their location, call sign and attribute table.*

**catalyse** *verb* CHEM to act as a catalyst in helping to make a chemical process take place (NOTE: The US spelling is **catalyze**.)

**catalysis** *noun* CHEM a process in which a chemical reaction is helped by a substance, the catalyst, which does not change during the process

**catalyst** *noun* CHEM a substance which produces or helps a chemical reaction without itself changing ○ *An enzyme which acts as a catalyst in the digestive process.*

**catalytic** *adjective* CHEM referring to catalysis

**catalytic converter** *noun* INDUST a device attached to the exhaust pipe of a motor vehicle which reduces the emission of carbon monoxide. Also called **catalytic muffler**

COMMENT: A catalytic convertor is a box filled with a catalyst, for example platinum. Converters can only be used on motor vehicles burning unleaded petrol, as the lead compounds in leaded petrol rapidly coat the catalyst in the converter and prevent it from functioning.

**catalytic cracker** *noun* INDUST an oil-refinery device in which heat and a catalyst are used to break down large molecules in crude oil into smaller ones that are useful as fuel

**catalytic muffler** *noun* INDUST same as **catalytic converter**

**catalytic reaction** *noun* CHEM a chemical reaction which is caused by a catalyst which does not change during the reaction

**catastrophe** *noun* COMPUT a serious fault, error or breakdown of equipment, usually leading to serious damage and shutdown of a system

**catastrophe theory** *noun* ASTRON a theory of planetary formation involving collision or near-collision between the Sun and another passing star (NOTE: Such catastrophe theories now have few adherents. They should not be confused with a different catastrophe theory, related to concepts of chaos and non-linearity, which explains sudden events in geometrical terms.)

**catchment, catchment area** *noun* **1.** EARTH SCI an area of land which collects and drains the rainwater which falls on it, e.g. the area round a lake or the basin of a river. Also called **drainage area**,

**drainage basin 2.** ENVIRON an area around a school, hospital, shopping centre, etc., from which pupils, patients, customers, etc. come

**catchment basin** noun EARTH SCI same as **catchment**

**catecholamine** noun BIOCHEM a compound belonging to a class that act as neurotransmitters or hormones (NOTE: Adrenaline is a catecholamine.)

**categorise** verb to put items into groups, classes or categories ○ *Figure 2 categorises the types of wave by frequency band.*

**category** noun an official class or group

**Category 1** noun COMPUT a standard that defines an older-style unshielded twisted-pair cable that is formed by loosely twisting two insulated wires together to reduce noise and interference (NOTE: This type of cable is not suitable for data transmission.)

**Category 2** noun COMPUT (*in the EIA/TIA 568 specification*) a standard that defines a type of unshielded twisted-pair cable that can be used to transmit data at rates up to 4 MHz

**Category 3** noun COMPUT (*in the EIA/TIA 568 specification*) a standard that defines a type of unshielded twisted-pair cable that can be used to transmit data at rates of up to 10 MHz (NOTE: This type of cable is the minimum standard of cable required for a 10BaseT network. The standard suggests that the cable should have three twists per foot of cable.)

**Category 4** noun COMPUT (*in the EIA/TIA 568 specification*) a standard that defines a type of unshielded twisted-pair cable that is the minimum standard of cable required for data transmission rates up to 16 Mbit/second on a Token Ring network

**Category 5** noun COMPUT (*in the EIA/TIA 568 specification*) a standard that defines a type of cable that can carry data transmitted at up to 100 MHz and is suitable for FDDI over copper wire, 100BaseT or other high-speed networks

**category wiring** noun COMPUT (*in the EIA/TIA 568 specification*) one of five levels of standards that define the type of cable or wire used in a network

**catena** noun **1.** COMPUT a number of items in a chained list **2.** COMPUT a series of characters in a word **3.** EARTH SCI a diagram showing the differences in soil caused by drainage

**catenate** verb **1.** COMPUT to join together two or more sets of data **2.** CHEM to form a chain of atoms of the same element

**cathode** noun ELEC a negative electrical terminal of a device or battery. Compare **anode**

**cathode ray oscilloscope** noun PHYS an electrical instrument with a cathode ray tube that displays the shape or size of an electrical signal on the screen

**cathode ray tube** noun **1.** a device used for displaying characters, figures or graphical information, similar to a TV set. Abbreviation **CRT 2.** PHYS a sealed glass tube with one flat end coated on the inside with a luminescent compound and an electron gun at the other end (NOTE: The gun fires a stream of electrons that are visible as a dot on the screen. The dot can be moved around the screen by applying an electrical charge to two metal plates next to the electron gun that deflect the stream of electrons)

COMMENT: Cathode ray tubes are used in television sets, computer monitors and VDUs. A CRT consists of a vacuum tube, one end of which is flat and coated with phosphor, the other end containing an electron beam source. Characters or graphics are visible when the controllable electron beam strikes the phosphor causing it to glow.

**cathode ray tube storage** noun a cathode ray tube with a long persistence phosphor screen coating that retains an image for a long time

**cation** noun CHEM an ion with a positive electric charge

**cation exchange** noun CHEM an exchange which takes place when the ions of calcium, magnesium and other metals found in soil replace the hydrogen ions in acid

**catkin** noun BOT a long structure consisting of many flowers together on a thin stem, found on temperate trees such as hazel, birch and oak

**CAT scan** noun MED same as **CT scan**

**cattle** *plural noun* ZOOL domestic farm animals raised for their milk and meat. Class: Bovidae. ○ *herds of cattle* ○ *dairy cattle*

**caudal anaesthetic** *noun* BIOL an anaesthetic often used in childbirth, where the drug is injected into the base of the spine to remove feeling in the lower part of the trunk

**caudal vertebrae** *plural noun* ANAT the vertebrae nearest the base of the spinal column

**cause** *noun* the reason for something happening ○ *If the ammeter shows a high state of charge after start up, it is quite normal and no cause for alarm.* ■ *verb* to make something happen ○ *Air in the fuel line can cause an engine to flame-out or stop.* □ **to cause damage** to harm something ○ *The breakdown of the electricity supply caused damage estimated at £100 000.*

**caustic** *adjective* CHEM acid

**caustic lime** *noun* CHEM quicklime or calcium oxide. Formula: CaO.

**caustic potash** *noun* CHEM same as **potassium hydroxide**

**caustic soda** *noun* CHEM a compound of sodium and water used to make soap and to clear blocked drains. Formula: NaOH. Also called **sodium hydroxide**

**caution** *noun* **1.** careful consideration ○ *We advise caution in accepting the recommendation.* **2.** care in doing something ○ *exercise extreme caution* ○ *proceed with caution*

**CAV** *abbreviation* COMPUT constant angular velocity

**cave** *noun* EARTH SCI a large hole under the ground, usually in rock

**cavern** *noun* EARTH SCI a very large cave, formed by water which has dissolved limestone or other calcareous rock

**cavitation** *noun* the formation of vapour-filled cavities or holes in liquids and gases, caused by low pressure and high speed ○ *Most reservoirs are pressurised to provide a positive fluid pressure at the pump inlet and thus prevent cavitation and the formation of bubbles.*

**cavity** *noun* a hole inside a solid substance

**cavity wall** *noun* CONSTR a wall made of two ranges of bricks, with a space in between them, giving greater insulation

**CB** *abbreviation* METEOROL cumulonimbus

**CBR** *abbreviation* COMPUT constant bit rate

**cc** *abbreviation* **1.** COMPUT carbon copy **2.** BIOL cubic centimetre

**CCD** *abbreviation* COMPUT charge-coupled device

**CCD memory** *noun* COMPUT capacitors used with MOS transistors to store data, allowing either serial or random access

**CCITT** *noun* COMPUT an international committee that defines communications protocols and standards. Full form **Comité Consultatif International Téléphonique et Télégraphique**

**cd** *abbreviation* PHYS, MEASURE candela

**Cd** *symbol* CHEM ELEM cadmium

**CD** *abbreviation* carrier detect

**CD-audio, CD-DA** *noun* COMPUT a standard that defines how music can be stored in digital form as a series of numbers on a compact disc. Full form **compact disc-digital audio**

**CD-I, CD-i** *noun* COMPUT hardware and software standards that combine sound, data, video and text onto a compact disc and allow a user to interact with the software stored on a CD-ROM. Full form **compact disc-interactive** (NOTE: The standard defines encoding, compression and display functions.)

**CDM** *abbreviation* ENVIRON Clean Development Mechanism

**cDNA** *abbreviation* GENETICS complementary DNA

**CD-R** *noun* COMPUT the technology that allows a user to write data to and read from a compact disc ○ *A CD-R disc can be played in any standard CD-ROM drive but needs a special CD-R drive to write data to the disc.* Full form **recordable compact disc**

**CD-ROM** *noun* COMPUT a small plastic disc which is used as a high capacity ROM device. Full form **compact disc-ROM** (NOTE: Data is stored in binary form as holes etched on the surface which are then read by a laser.)

**CD-ROM drive** *noun* COMPUT a mechanical device that spins a compact disc and reads data stored on the surface of the disc using a tiny laser beam

**CD-ROM Extended Architecture** *noun* COMPUT an extended CD-ROM format that defines how audio, images and data are stored on a CD-ROM disc. Abbreviation **CD-ROM/XA**

**CD-ROM Extensions** *plural noun* COMPUT software required to allow an operating system, typically DOS, to access a CD-ROM drive

**CD-ROM mode 1** *noun* COMPUT a standard original method of storing data in the High Sierra file format

**CD-ROM mode 2** *noun* COMPUT a higher capacity storage format that stores data in the space used in mode 1 for error correction. Neither mode 1 nor mode 2 can play audio and simultaneously read data, hence the XA extension.

**CD-ROM re-writable** *noun* COMPUT a disc technology that can read a standard CD-ROM, write to a CD-R or write data many times to the same CD-R

**CD-ROM/XA** *abbreviation* COMPUT CD-ROM Extended Architecture

**cedar** *noun* TREES an American tree which has soft red wood which is resistant to water. Latin name: *Thuya plicata*. (NOTE: The wood is used mainly for outdoor construction work.)

**ceiling** *noun* an upper layer or level

**cel** *noun* COMPUT a single frame in an animation sequence

**-cele, -coele** *suffix* BIOL referring to a hollow

**celestial** *adjective* referring to the sky

**celestial body** *noun* ASTRON an astronomical object that is a permanent feature in the sky, e.g. a star or a planet

**celestial equator** *noun* ASTRON an imaginary line in the sky above the Earth's equator

**celestial navigation** *noun* NAVIG navigation by using the stars in the sky to establish location

**celestial sphere** *noun* ASTRON the region of space that seems to surround the Earth and in which astronomical objects are seen

**celi-** *prefix* BIOL a hollow, usually the abdomen

**cell** *noun* **1.** ELEC a system of positive and negative plates for storage of electricity that form a battery ○ *A battery is a device which converts chemical energy into electrical energy and is made up of a number of cells.* **2.** BIOL a tiny unit of matter which is the base of all plant and animal tissue **3.** COMPUT a single function or number in a spreadsheet program **4.** COMPUT a single memory location, capable of storing a data word, accessed by an individual address **5.** COMPUT a fixed-length packet of data, e.g. one in the ATM system containing 53-octets of data **6.** METEOROL the central part of a thunder cloud ○ *The life cycle of the thunderstorm cell ends when the downdraughts have spread throughout the cloud.*

COMMENT: A biological cell is a unit which can reproduce itself. It is made up of a jelly-like substance (cytoplasm) which surrounds a nucleus and contains many other small organelles which are different according to the type of cell. Cells reproduce by division (mitosis) and the chemical reactions that occur with them are the basis of metabolism. The process of division and reproduction of cells is how the human body is formed.

**cell body** *noun* BIOL a part of a nerve cell which surrounds the nucleus and from which the axon and dendrites begin

**cell division** *noun* BIOL the way in which a cell reproduces itself by dividing into new cells

COMMENT: There are two types of cell division. Mitosis leads to two new cells, each with a nucleus containing the same number of chromosomes as the original cell. Meiosis leads to four new cells, each with a nucleus containing half the number of chromosomes of the original cell, and is the means of producing gametes.

**cell membrane** *noun* BIOL a membrane enclosing the cytoplasm of a cell. Also called **plasma membrane**

**cellular** *adjective* **1.** BIOL referring to cells **2.** made of many similar parts connected together

**cellular plant** *noun* BOT a plant with no distinct stem, leaves, etc.

**cellular tissue** *noun* BIOL a form of connective tissue with large spaces within cells

**cellulose** *noun* **1.** BIOCHEM a carbohydrate which makes up a large percentage of plant matter, especially cell walls **2.** INDUST a chemical substance processed from wood, used for making paper, film and artificial fibres

COMMENT: Cellulose is not digestible, and is passed through the digestive system as roughage.

**cell wall** *noun* BIOL the outermost layer of a cell in plants and some fungi, algae and bacteria, which provides protection and support

**Celsius** *noun* MEASURE a scale of temperature where the freezing and boiling points of water are, respectively, 0° and 100°. Symbol **C**. Also called **centigrade** (NOTE: It is used in many countries, except in the US, where the Fahrenheit system is still preferred.)

COMMENT: To convert Celsius temperatures to Fahrenheit, multiply by 1.8 and add 32. So 20° C is equal to 68°F.

**cement** *noun* **1.** EARTH SCI material which binds things together, e.g. that which binds minerals together to form sedimentary rocks **2.** INDUST a powder which if mixed with water and then dried sets hard like stone

COMMENT: Various types of cement are used in construction. The commonest is made of burnt lime with clay and other mineral compounds. High-alumina cement is used in stressed concrete and is made from ground bauxite.

**cement kiln** *noun* INDUST a furnace where lime is burnt to make cement

**center** *noun* US spelling of **centre**

**centi-** *prefix* MEASURE one hundredth, $10^{-2}$. Symbol **c**

**centigrade** *noun* PHYS a scale of temperature where the freezing and boiling points of water are 0° and 100°

**centilitre** *noun* a unit of measurement of liquid equivalent to one hundredth of a litre. Symbol **cl**

**centimetre** *noun* a unit of measurement of length, equivalent to one hundredth of a metre. Symbol **cm**

**centimorgan** *noun* MEASURE, GENETICS a unit of measurement that indicates how close genes are to each other on the same chromosome

**central** *adjective* in the middle

**central heating** *noun* UTIL a system for heating a building where hot water or hot air is circulated round from a single source of heat, usually a boiler

**centralise, centralize** *verb* to put something into the centre or into the middle position ○ *The operating jack centralises the control surface after the turn.*

**centralised computer network** *noun* COMPUT a network with processing power provided by a central computer

**centralised data processing** *noun* COMPUT data processing facilities located in a centralised place that can be accessed by other users

**central memory** *noun* COMPUT an area of memory whose locations can be directly and immediately addressed by the CPU. Abbreviation **CM**

**central nervous system** *noun* ANAT the brain and spinal cord which link together all the nerves. Abbreviation **CNS**

**central processing unit** *noun* COMPUT a group of circuits which perform the basic functions of a computer, made up of three main parts: the control unit, the arithmetic and logic unit and the input/output unit. Abbreviation **CPU**

**centre** *noun* a point in the middle of something ○ *The centre of the hurricane passed over the city* ○ *A park is to be built in the centre of the town* (NOTE: The US spelling is **center**.) ■ *verb* **1.** to move something to a central position ○ *Centre the control column.* (NOTE: The US spelling is **center**.) **2.** COMPUT to align the read/write head correctly on a magnetic disk or tape (NOTE: The US spelling is **center**.) **3.** COMPUT to place a piece of text in the centre of the paper or display screen ○ *Which key do you press to centre the heading?* (NOTE: British English is **centred – centring**, but the US spelling is **centered – centering**.)

**centreline** *noun* AEROSP a painted or imaginary line running along the centre of a runway (NOTE: The US spelling is **centerline**.)

**centre of curvature** *noun* MATHS the central point of a circle whose radius is at right angles to a line tangent to any point on the concave side of a smooth curve

**centre of gravity** *noun* **1.** PHYS the point at which a body can be balanced ○ *Distribution of the tanks and the fuel in the tanks is vital in maintaining the aircraft centre of gravity and trim.* Abbreviation **CG 2.** the point through which the resultant force of gravity acts

**centre text** *noun* COMPUT an option in a wordprocessing or DTP package that changes the formatting of a line of text so that it is in the centre of the page or frame

**centrifugal** *adjective* going away from the centre

**centrifugal force** *noun* PHYS the force of acceleration away from the axis around which a body rotates

**centrifugal switch** *noun* ELEC a switch operated by centrifugal force

**centrifugation** *noun* the separating of the components of a liquid in a centrifuge. Also called **centrifuging**

**centrifuge** *noun* a device which uses centrifugal force to separate or remove liquids ■ *verb* to separate liquids by using centrifugal force ○ *The rotating vanes of the breather centrifuge the oil from the mist.*

**centrifuging** *noun* same as **centrifugation**

**centring** *noun* COMPUT the action of putting text in the centre of the screen ○ *Centring of headings is easily done, using this function key.* (NOTE: The US spelling is **centering**.)

**centriole** *noun* BIOL a small structure found in the cytoplasm of a cell, which forms asters during cell division

**centripetal** *adjective* going towards the centre

**centripetal force** *noun* PHYS, MATHS the force of acceleration towards the axis around which a body rotates

**centromere** *noun* GENETICS the point at which two strands (**chromatids**) of a chromosome join and at which the spindle fibres are attached during cell division

**Centronics interface** *noun* COMPUT a parallel printer interface devised by Centronics Inc

**centrosome** *noun* BIOL a region of cytoplasm in a cell, near the nucleus and containing the centrioles

**cephalopod** *noun* MARINE BIOL a marine invertebrate with a well-developed head and tentacles, e.g. an octopus, squid, or cuttlefish. Class: Cephalopoda.

**cephalothorax** *noun* ZOOL the fused head and thorax found in arachnids such as spiders and in many crustaceans

**cereal** *noun* BOT a specialised type of grass which is cultivated for its grains, especially to make flour for breadmaking or for animal feed

COMMENT: Cereals are all members of the Graminales family. Oats, wheat, barley, maize and rye are commonly grown in colder temperate areas, and rice, sorghum and millet in warmer regions. Cereal production has considerably expanded and improved with the introduction of better methods of sowing, combine harvesters, grain driers, bulk handling and chemical aids such as herbicides, fungicides, insecticides and growth regulators.

**cerebellum** *noun* ANAT the part of the brain, located beneath and behind the front part (**cerebrum**), which controls and coordinates muscular activity and maintains balance (NOTE: It typically consists of two interconnected hemispheres.)

**cerebral artery** *noun* ANAT one of the main arteries which take blood into the brain

**cerebral cortex** *noun* ANAT the much-folded outer layer of the front part of the brain (NOTE: Among its functions are the perception of sensations, learning, thought and memory.)

**cerebral hemisphere** *noun* ANAT one of the two halves of the front part of the brain (**cerebrum**)

**cerebrospinal fluid** *noun* ANAT the colourless fluid that fills the spaces around and within the brain and spinal cord to cushion against injury

**cerebrum** *noun* ANAT the main part of the brain

COMMENT: The cerebrum is the largest part of the brain, formed of two sections (the cerebral hemispheres) which run along the length of the head. The cerebrum controls the main mental processes, including the memory.

**Cerenkov counter** *noun* PHYS a device for measuring Cerenkov radiation emitted by a particle

**Cerenkov radiation** *noun* PHYS the light emitted by an electrically charged particle as it travels through a transparent medium at a speed greater than that of light in the same medium

**cerium** *noun* CHEM ELEM a soft grey metallic element, the most abundant of the rare-earth group, used in glassmaking, ceramics, cigarette-lighter flints (NOTE: The chemical symbol is

Ce; the atomic number is **58** and the atomic weight is **140.12**.)

**CERN** noun COMPUT a science and atomic research laboratory in Switzerland where the World Wide Web was originally invented

**certain** adjective **1.** specific ○ in certain areas ○ at certain times ○ under certain circumstances ○ with certain exceptions **2.** sure ○ There are certain to be horizontal differences in the mean temperature of a layer.

**certificate** noun COMPUT a unique set of numbers that identifies a person or company and is used to prove the person's identity over the Internet

COMMENT: A certificate is normally used to provide security over the Internet (for secure email or secure website transactions). A trusted company issues the certificate once it is satisfied that the person or company is legitimate, authentic and who they claim to be. The company can then use this certificate to prove its identity, create secure messages or set up a secure website to accept payments online.

**certificate authority** noun COMPUT an independent server or company on the Internet which supplies or validates a special digital certificate to prove that another company is genuine (NOTE: A certificate authority issues a special encrypted number that complies with the X.509 standard and is encrypted with a public-key encryption system.)

**certificate of approval** noun a document showing that an item has been approved officially

**certify** verb to authorise or permit the use of something

**cervical vertebra** noun ANAT a vertebra of the set found in the neck

**cervix** noun ANAT **1.** the narrow passage between the womb and the vagina **2.** a neck, or a narrow part like a neck

**Cetacea** noun ZOOL a large mammal such as a dolphin, porpoise or whale which lives in the sea. Order: Cetacea.

**CF** abbreviation COMPUT compact Flash

**CFC** abbreviation CHEM chlorofluorocarbon

**CFM** abbreviation CHEM chlorofluoromethane

**CG** abbreviation PHYS centre of gravity

**CGA** abbreviation COMPUT colour graphics adapter

**CGI** abbreviation COMPUT common gateway interface

**chain** noun **1.** COMPUT a series of files or data items linked sequentially **2.** COMPUT a series of instructions to be executed sequentially **3.** a number of metal rings attached together to make a line **4.** a number of components linked together, or a number of connected events ■ verb COMPUT to link files or data items in series by storing a pointer to the next file or item at each entry ○ More than 1000 articles or chapters can be chained together when printing.

**chained file** noun COMPUT a file in which an entry will contain data and an address to the next entry that has the same data content, allowing rapid retrieval of all identical data records. Also called **threaded file**

**chained list** noun COMPUT a list in which each element contains data and an address to the next element in the list

**chained record** noun COMPUT a data record in a chained file

**chaining** noun COMPUT the execution of a very large program by executing small segments of it at a time, allowing programs larger than memory capacity to be run

**chaining search** noun COMPUT the searching of a file of elements arranged as a chained list

**chain reaction** noun **1.** PHYS a nuclear reaction in which a neutron hits a nucleus, makes it split and so releases further neutrons **2.** CHEM a chemical reaction where each stage is started by a chemical substance which reacts with another, producing further substances which can continue to react

**chalk** noun EARTH SCI a fine white limestone rock formed of calcium carbonate

COMMENT: Chalk is found widely in many parts of northern Europe. Formed from animal organisms it is also used as an additive (E170) in white flour.

**chalky** adjective EARTH SCI referring to soil which is full of chalk

**chamber** noun a small enclosed compartment

**change** verb **1.** to make something different **2.** to use one thing instead of another ■ *noun* COMPUT same as **change record**

**change record** *noun* COMPUT a record containing new data which is to be used to update a master record

**channel** *noun* 1. ELEC a frequency range used for the transmission of radio signals ○ *The system operates on VHF communications between 118 and 135.95 MHz giving 360 channels at 50 kHz spacing.* 2. COMPUT a physical connection between two points that allows data to be transmitted, e.g. a link between a central processing unit and a peripheral 3. ENG a deep part of a harbour or sea passage where ships can pass, or a stretch of water between two seas 4. GEOG a bed of a river or stream ■ *verb* 1. to send signals or data via a particular path 2. to send water in a particular direction (NOTE: British English is **channelled – channelling**, but the US spelling is **channeled – channeling**.)

**channelise** *verb* ENG to straighten a stream which has many bends, in order to make the water flow faster

**channelling** *noun* COMPUT a protective pipe containing cables or wires

**chaos theory** *noun* PHYS a theory stating that when a system is sensitive to small differences in initial values, the future behaviour of that system may be unpredictable

**chapter** *noun* COMPUT a section of a main program that can be executed in its own right, without the rest of the main program being required

**char** *noun* COMPUT a data type which defines a variable as containing data that represents a character using the ASCII code

**character** *noun* 1. COMPUT a graphical symbol which appears as a printed or displayed mark, e.g. one of the letters of the alphabet, a number or a punctuation mark 2. PSYCHIAT the way in which a person thinks and behaves 3. ZOOL the way in which an animal or plant is different from others

**character-based** *adjective* COMPUT (*of a screen design*) drawn using ASCII characters rather than graphical windows

**characterise** *verb* to be a characteristic of something or someone ○ *Deserts are characterised by little rainfall, arid soil and very little vegetation.*

**characteristic** *noun* 1. a property or feature of something ○ *One of the characteristics of the octopus is that it can send out a cloud of ink when attacked.* 2. COMPUT the value of an exponent in a floating point number ○ *The floating point number $1.345 \times 10^3$ has a characteristic of 3.* ■ *adjective* typical ○ *This fault is characteristic of this make and model of personal computer.*

**characteristic species** *noun* ECOL a species typical of and only occurring in a certain region

**character key** *noun* COMPUT a word processor control used to process text one character at a time

**character matrix** *noun* COMPUT a pattern of dots that makes up a displayed character

**character mode** *noun* COMPUT a mode that can only display the characters defined in the built-in character set

**character printer** *noun* COMPUT a device that prints characters one at a time ○ *A daisy wheel printer is a character printer.*

**character recognition** *noun* COMPUT a system that optically reads written or printed characters into a computer, using various algorithms to ensure that characters are correctly recognised

**character rounding** *noun* COMPUT the process of making a displayed character more pleasant to look at, within the limits of pixel size, by making sharp corners and edges smooth

**character set** *noun* COMPUT a list of all the characters which can be displayed or printed

**characters per inch** *plural noun* COMPUT a number of printed characters which fit within the space of one inch ○ *You can select 10 or 12 characters per inch with the green button.* Abbreviation **cpi**

**characters per second** *plural noun* COMPUT the number of characters which are transmitted or printed per second. Abbreviation **cps**

**character string** *noun* COMPUT an amount of storage allocated for a series of alphanumeric characters

**character stuffing** *noun* COMPUT an addition of blank characters to a file to increase its length to a preset size

**charcoal** *noun* INDUST an impure form of carbon, formed when wood is burnt in the absence of oxygen

**charge** *noun* **1.** ELEC a quantity of electricity measured in coulombs **2.** PHYS the number of or excess of or lack of electrons in a material or component (NOTE: An electron possesses the smallest unit of negative charge (e) equal to 1.602102 x $10^{-19}$. A proton possesses the equivalent positive charge.) ■ *verb* ELEC to supply a device with an electric charge

**chargeable** *adjective* ELEC referring to a battery which can be charged

**charge-coupled device** *noun* ELEC an electronic device operated by charge, especially one which converts photons of light into a digital signal, converting an optical image into a digital image. Abbreviation **CCD**

**charge-coupled device memory** *noun* ELEC a set of capacitors used, with MOS transistors, to store data, allowing serial and random access

**Charles' law** *noun* CHEM a law describing the relationship between the volume of a gas and its temperature at constant pressure

**charm** *noun* PHYS a quantum characteristic of some elementary particles such as quarks

**chart** *noun* a diagram showing information as a series of lines or blocks ■ *verb* to make a chart of something

**chassis** *noun* COMPUT a metal frame that houses the circuit boards together with the wiring and sockets required in a computer system or other equipment

**cheapernet** *noun* COMPUT thin-wire ethernet (*informal*)

**check** *noun* **1.** COMPUT the act of making sure that something is correct **2.** COMPUT a short pause in a process **3.** US a tick used to mark or approve an item ■ *verb* COMPUT to examine to make sure that something is in good working order ○ *The separate parts of the system were all checked for faults before being packaged.* □ **to check something against something else** to compare two things to see if they correspond to each other in the expected way ○ *He checked the computer printout against the invoices.*

**check bit** *noun* COMPUT one bit of a binary word that is used to provide a parity check

**check box** *noun* COMPUT a small box displayed with a cross or tick inside it if the option has been selected, or empty if the option is not selected ○ *Select the option by moving the cursor to the check box and pressing the mouse button.*

**check digit, check number** *noun* COMPUT an additional digit inserted into transmitted text to monitor and correct errors

**check point** *noun* COMPUT a point in a program where data and program status can be recorded or displayed

**check register** *noun* COMPUT temporary storage for received data before it is checked against the same data received via another path or method

**checksum, check total** *noun* COMPUT a program which checks that data is correct, summing it and comparing the sum with a stored value ○ *The data must be corrupted if the checksum is different.*

**chela** *noun* ZOOL a grasping claw, e.g. one of the front claws of a crab or lobster (NOTE: The plural is **chelae**.)

**chelate** *noun* CHEM a chemical compound containing metallic and nonmetallic atoms ■ *adjective* ZOOL having or being shaped like the grasping claws (**chelae**) of crabs and lobsters

**chemical** CHEM *adjective* referring to chemistry ■ *noun* a substance formed of chemical elements or produced by a chemical process ○ *the widespread use of chemicals in agriculture* ○ *The machine analyses the chemicals found in the collected samples.*

**chemical agent** *noun* a substance which makes another substance react

**chemical bond** *noun* CHEM same as **bond**

**chemical change** *noun* CHEM a change in which a chemical reaction is produced and a new substance created

**chemical combination** *noun* CHEM the process by which chemicals combine to form compounds, governed by general principles including the laws of conservation of mass, constant proportions and multiple proportions

**chemical composition** *noun* the chemicals which make up a substance

**chemical compound** *noun* a substance formed from two or more chemical elements, in which the proportions of the elements are always the same

**chemical dating** *noun* ARCHAEOL the determining of the age of something by chemical analysis

**chemical element** *noun* a substance which exists independently and cannot be broken down into simpler substances

**chemical engineering** *noun* INDUST a branch of engineering which deals with the design, construction and operation of processes and equipment used in the production of industrial chemicals

**chemical equation** *noun* CHEM a representation, using chemical symbols, of the process involved in a chemical reaction

**chemical equilibrium** *noun* CHEM a chemical reaction which is in a balanced state, the reactants and products staying in the same ratio

**chemical fertiliser** *noun* AGRIC same as **artificial fertiliser**

**chemical mutagen** *noun* CHEM a chemical substance which causes mutation

**chemical name** *noun* the technical name for a substance ○ *Sodium hydroxide is the chemical name for caustic soda.*

**chemical oxygen demand** *noun* ECOL the amount of oxygen taken up by organic matter in water used as a measurement of the amount of organic matter in sewage. Abbreviation **COD**

**chemical plant** *noun* INDUST a factory where chemicals are produced

**chemical process** *noun* CHEM a reaction which happens when two or more chemicals come into contact

**chemical reaction** *noun* CHEM a process in which atoms or groups of atoms are redistributed, changing the molecular composition of the original substances

**chemical residue** *noun* CHEM waste left after a chemical process has taken place

**chemical symbol** *noun* CHEM a letter or letters used to indicate an element, used especially in formulae, etc. (NOTE: Examples are **C** for carbon and **Co** for cobalt.)

**chemical toilet** *noun* a toilet containing chemicals to neutralise the bodily waste

**chemical treatment** *noun* INDUST the processing of sewage by adding chemical substances to it

**chemical warfare** *noun* MIL war using chemical weapons

**chemical warhead** *noun* MIL the front part of a missile containing a poisonous chemical

**chemical weapon** *noun* MIL a missile or other weapon containing a poisonous chemical, e.g. a nerve gas or defoliant

**chemist** *noun* CHEM a scientist who specialises in the study of chemistry

**chemistry** *noun* CHEM **1.** the study of substances, elements and compounds and their reactions with each other **2.** chemical substances existing together ○ *Human action has radically altered the chemistry of the atmosphere.*

**chemistry of the blood** *noun* same as **blood chemistry**

**chemo-** *prefix* CHEM chemistry

**chemoautotrophic** *adjective* BIOL which oxidises nitrogen or other chemical elements to create a source of food. Compare **photoautotrophic**

**chemolithotrophic** *adjective* BIOL referring to organisms such as bacteria which obtain energy from inorganic substances

**chemo-organotrophic** *adjective* BIOL referring to an organism such as an animal which obtains its energy from organic sources

**chemoreceptor** *noun* BIOL a cell which responds to the presence of a chemical compound by activating a sensory nerve. ♦ **exteroceptor, interoceptor, receptor**

**chemosphere** *noun* EARTH SCI the zone in the Earth's atmosphere, above the upper part of the troposphere and within the stratosphere, where chemical changes take place under the influence of the Sun's radiation

**chemosterilant** *noun* CHEM a chemical substance which sterilises by killing microbes or bacteria

**chemosynthesis** *noun* CHEM the production by bacteria of organic material using chemical reactions

**chemotaxis** *noun* BIOL a movement of a cell which is attracted to or repelled by a chemical substance

**chemotroph** *noun* BIOL a producer which converts the energy found in inorganic chemical compounds into more complex energy, without using sunlight (NOTE: Algae and bacteria are chemotrophs.)

**chemotrophic** *adjective* BIOL obtaining energy from sources such as organic matter. Compare **phototrophic** (NOTE: Most animals are chemotropic.)

**chemotropism** *noun* BIOL the movement or growth of an organism in response to a chemical stimulus

**chernozem** *noun* EARTH SCI same as **black earth**

COMMENT: Chernozem is found in the temperate grass-covered plains of Russia and North and South America.

**chiasma** *noun* GENETICS the point at which two chromatids cross over each other, join and exchange genetic material during meiosis (NOTE: The plural is **chiasmata**.)

**child process, child program** *noun* COMPUT a routine or program called by another program which remains active while the second program runs (NOTE: The smaller window cannot be moved outside the boundary of the main window and is closed when the main window is closed.)

**child window** *noun* COMPUT a window within a main window

**Chile saltpetre** *noun* CHEM an impure form of sodium nitrate occurring naturally in large deposits in Chile and Peru. Formula: $NaNO_3$.

**chill** *noun* METEOROL coldness

**chimaera** *noun* GENETICS another spelling of **chimera**

**chimera** *noun* GENETICS an organism, especially a plant, with two genetically varying types of tissue due to grafting or mutation

**chimeric** *adjective* GENETICS composed of genetically different tissues, either naturally or as a result of a laboratory procedure

**chimney stack** *noun* INDUST same as **stack**

**china clay** *noun* INDUST a fine white clay used for making china and also for coating shiny paper. Also called **kaolin**

**chinook** *noun* METEOROL a warm wind that blows from the Rocky mountains down onto the Canadian plains in winter

**chip** *noun* COMPUT a device consisting of a small piece of a crystal of a semiconductor onto which are etched or manufactured a number of components such as transistors, resistors and capacitors, which together perform a function

**chip architecture** *noun* COMPUT the design and layout of components on a chip

**chip count** *noun* COMPUT the number of chips on a printed circuit board or in a device ○ *It's no good, the chip count is still too high.*

**chip select** *noun* COMPUT a single line on a chip that will enable it to function when a signal is present. Abbreviation **CS**

**chip set** *noun* COMPUT a group of chips which together will carry out a function

**chirality** *noun* CHEM the characteristic of existing in left-hand and right-hand forms, usually referring to optical compounds and optics

**chitin** *noun* CHEM a tough waterproof substance that forms part of the outer skeleton of insects and the cell walls of fungi

**chloral** *noun* CHEM a colourless oily liquid with a strong and unpleasant smell. Formula: $CCl_3CHO$.

**chloral hydrate** *noun* PHARM a white water-soluble crystalline solid, used as a sedative. Formula: $C_2H_3Cl_2O_2$.

**chloride** *noun* CHEM a salt of hydrochloric acid

**chlorinate** *verb* ENVIRON to treat something with chlorine, especially to sterilise drinking water or water in a swimming pool by adding chlorine

**chlorinated** *adjective* CHEM treated with chlorine

**chlorinated hydrocarbon insecticide** *noun* AGRIC a type of insecticide made synthetically as a compound of chlorine. Also called **organochlorine**

COMMENT: Chlorinated hydrocarbon insecticides include DDT, aldrin and lindane. These types of insecticide are very persistent, with a long half-life of up to 15 years, while organic phosphorous insecticides have a much shorter life.

Chlorinated hydrocarbon insecticides not only kill insects, but also enter the food chain and kill small animals and birds which feed on the insects.

**chlorination** *noun* CHEM sterilisation by adding chlorine

COMMENT: Chlorination is used to kill bacteria in drinking water, in swimming pools and sewage farms, and has many industrial applications such as sterilisation in food processing.

**chlorine** *noun* CHEM ELEM a powerful greenish chemical element, used to sterilise water and for bleaching (NOTE: The chemical symbol is **Cl**; the atomic number is **17** and the atomic weight is **35.45**.)

**chlorine demand** *noun* CHEM the amount of chlorine needed to kill bacteria in a given quantity of sewage

**chlorine monoxide** *noun* CHEM a substance which forms in the stratosphere and destroys ozone

**chlorite** *noun* MINERALS a soft black or green mineral found in metamorphic rocks

**chloro-, chlor-** *prefix* **1.** CHEM chlorine **2.** EARTH SCI green

**chlorofluorocarbon** *noun* CHEM a compound of fluorine and chlorine, used as a propellant in aerosol cans, in the manufacture of plastic foam boxes for takeaway food, as a refrigerant in refrigerators and air conditioners and as cleaners of circuit boards for computers. Abbreviation **CFC, CFM**

COMMENT: CFCs are classified by numbers: CFC-10 is used in aerosols; CFC-11 is used to make plastic foam; CFC-12 is a coolant for refrigerators; and CFC-13 is a cleaning substance used in the electronics industry. When CFCs are released into the atmosphere, they rise slowly, taking about seven years to reach the stratosphere. But once they are there, under the influence of the Sun's ultraviolet light they break down into chlorine atoms which destroy the ozone layer. This allows harmful solar UV radiation to pass through to the Earth's surface. Because it takes so long for the CFCs to reach the stratosphere, any reduction in their use on Earth does not have an immediate effect on the concentrations in the stratosphere. Replacements for CFCs are being developed, which should reduce the problem eventually. It is a pity that CFCs have this unfortunate effect on the ozone layer, since in other ways they are ideal gases, being stable and non-toxic.

**chlorofluoromethane** *noun* CHEM a gas that is a volatile organic compound, generated from landfill sites, petrol engine exhausts and other industrial processes. In the chemical industry, it is often manufactured from carbon tetrachloride. Formula: $CH_2CHO$. Abbreviation **CFM**

**chloroform** *noun* CHEM a colourless sweet-smelling toxic liquid with a low boiling temperature, which rapidly changes to a vapour, and causes drowsiness or unconsciousness if inhaled. Formula: $CHCl_3$. (NOTE: It is known to have damaged the ozone layer.)

**chloromethane** *noun* BIOCHEM a gas which is a compound of carbon and chlorine, formed by fungi as they rot wood (NOTE: It acts in a similar way to CFCs in depleting the ozone layer.)

**chlorophyll** *noun* BOT a green pigment in plants

COMMENT: Chlorophyll absorbs light energy from the Sun and supplies plants with the energy to enable them to carry out photosynthesis. It is also used as a colouring (E140) in processed food.

**Chlorophyta** *plural noun* BOT a large phylum of algae that processes chlorophyll

**chloroplast** *noun* BIOL a tiny sac within the cells of plants and algae which contains chlorophyll and other pigments and is the place where photosynthesis occurs (NOTE: The number of chloroplasts in a cell varies, but each consists of interconnected stacks of disc-shaped membranes in fluid, surrounded by a double membrane.)

**chloroplatinic acid** *noun* CHEM a compound formed by dissolving platinum in aqua regia. Formula: $H_2PtCl_6$. Also called **platinic chloride, hexahydrate acid**

**chloroprene** *noun* CHEM a colourless organic liquid used in neoprene manufacture. Formula: $CH_2CHCClCH_2$.

**chlorosis** *noun* BOT a reduction of chlorophyll in plants, making the leaves turn yellow

**choke** *noun* **1.** AUTOMOT a valve in a carburettor which controls the amount of air combining with fuel **2.** ELEC same as **inductor** ■ *verb* **1.** to become, or cause somebody to become, unable to breathe **2.** to block a tube, channel or opening, making a liquid unable to move ○ *The reservoirs became choked with rapidly growing weeds.*

**choke tube** *noun* AUTOMOT same as **venturi tube** ○ *Increase in rpm increases the speed of air passing through the choke tube or venturi.*

**cholesterol** *noun* BIOCHEM a fatty substance found in fats and oils and also produced by the liver and forming an essential part of all cells

COMMENT: Cholesterol is found in brain cells, the adrenal glands, liver and bile acids. Cholesterol is formed by the body, and high blood cholesterol levels are associated with diets rich in animal fat such as butter and fat meat. Excess cholesterol can be deposited in the walls of arteries, causing atherosclerosis.

**cholinergic** *adjective* PHARM producing, activated by, or having effects similar to those of acetylcholine

**chordate** *noun* ZOOL an animal that has a main dorsal nerve cord, a skeletal rod (**notocord**) and gill slits at some stage during its development. Phylum: Chordata. (NOTE: All vertebrates are chordates, as well as some primitive marine invertebrate animals.)

**chord keying** *noun* COMPUT the action of pressing two or more keys at the same time to perform a function

COMMENT: To access a second window, chord keying of Control and F2 may be necessary. Chord keying a shift and character delete keys at the same time will delete a line of text.

**chorion** *noun* ANAT the outer membrane surrounding the embryo of mammals, reptiles and birds (NOTE: In mammals it combines with the allantois to form the placenta.)

**chorionic gonadotrophin** *noun* BIOCHEM a hormone produced by the placenta in mammals that helps maintain a pregnancy

**choroid** *noun* ANAT (*in vertebrates*) a brownish membrane between the retina and the white of the eye that contains many blood vessels

**CHP plant** *abbreviation* PHYS combined heat and power plant

**Christmas disease** *noun* MED a type of haemophilia

**Christmas factor** *noun* MED a substance in plasma, the lack of which causes Christmas disease

**chrom-** *prefix* same as **chromo-**

**chroma** *noun* COMPUT a measure of colour hue and saturation

**chromatic** *adjective* referring to colours

**chromatic aberration** *noun* PHYS a defect in a lens that causes light of different colours to be refracted differently

**chromatid** *noun* GENETICS one of two parallel strands into which each chromosome divides during cell division, attached to each other by a centromere

**chromatin** *noun* GENETICS the material of which chromosomes are formed, consisting of proteins, DNA and small amounts of RNA

**chromatography** *noun* CHEM a scientific method for separating and analysing chemicals through a porous medium

**chromatolysis** *noun* GENETICS the breakdown of chromatin within a damaged cell nucleus

**chromatophore** *noun* **1.** BIOL a cell which contains pigment, e.g. a cell in the eyes, hair and skin, or a cell which enables an animal such as a chameleon to change colour **2.** BOT a cell in plants or algae which contains chlorophyll

**chrominance signal** *noun* COMPUT a section of a colour monitor signal containing colour hue and saturation information

**chromium** *noun* CHEM ELEM a metallic trace element, used to make alloys (NOTE: The chemical symbol is **Cr**; the atomic number is **24** and the atomic weight is **52.00**.)

**chromo-** *prefix* **1.** colour **2.** chromium

**chromomere** *noun* GENETICS a small dense granule of chromatin found at intervals along a chromosome during cell division

**chromonema** *noun* GENETICS the coiled central filament that forms the core of each strand (**chromatid**) of a chromosome

**chromophore** *noun* CHEM a structure that is part of a molecule and gives colour in dyes and other compounds

**chromosomal** *adjective* GENETICS referring to chromosomes

**chromosome** *noun* GENETICS the rod-shaped structure in the nucleus of a cell, formed of DNA which carries the genes

COMMENT: Each species has its own characteristic chromosomal make-up. Cattle have 60 chromosomes and wheat have 42. Human cells have 46 chromosomes, 23 inherited from each parent. Among these are the X and Y chromosomes, which are responsible for sexual differences. The female has one pair of X chromosomes and the male one X and one Y chromosome. Sperm carry either an X or a Y chromosome. If a sperm with a Y chromosome fertilises a female's ovum the resulting offspring will be a male (XY); otherwise it will be a female (XX).

**chromosome aberration** *noun* GENETICS an abnormality in the number, arrangement or other characteristic of chromosomes

**chromosome band** *noun* GENETICS a pattern produced in a chromosome by a stain, which makes it identifiable from other chromosomes

**chromosome map** *noun* GENETICS an illustration that shows the relative extent and position of each gene on a chromosome

**chromosome number** *noun* GENETICS the number of chromosomes present in each cell nucleus of a specific animal or plant

**chronic** *adjective* MED referring to a disease or condition which lasts for a long time ○ *The forest was suffering from chronic soil acidification.* Compare **acute**

**chronic toxicity** *noun* BIOL high exposure to harmful levels of a toxic substance over a period of time

**chronological order** *noun* an arrangement of records or files according to their dates

**chrysalis** *noun* ZOOL **1.** a stage in the development of a butterfly or moth when the pupa is protected in a hard case **2.** the hard case in which a pupa is protected

**chunk** *noun* COMPUT a basic part of a RIFF file that consists of an identifier and data

**chunk ID** *noun* COMPUT the identifier of a RIFF file chunk

**chute** *noun* **1.** ENG a sloping channel along which water, rubbish, etc. may pass **2.** EARTH SCI a waterfall

**chyle** *noun* PHYSIOL a fluid with a milky consistency containing lymph and emulsified fat that is formed in the small intestine during the digestion process

**chyme** *noun* PHYSIOL a thick fluid containing partially digested food and gastric secretions that is passed from the stomach to the small intestine

**Ci** *abbreviation* PHYS, MEASURE curie

**-cide** *suffix* killing

**CIF** *abbreviation* COMPUT common intermediate format

**cilia** plural of **cilium**

**ciliary** *adjective* BIOL referring to cilia

**ciliary body** *noun* ANAT a ring-shaped thickening at the front of the eye that connects the pigmented layer (**choroid**) to the iris diaphragm (NOTE: It contains the ciliary muscle, which changes the shape of the lens in focusing the eye.)

**ciliary feeder** *noun* ZOOL a mollusc which feeds by sucking water and the organisms it contains through cilia

**ciliary ganglion** *noun* ANAT a parasympathetic ganglion in the orbit of the eye, supplying the intrinsic eye muscles

**ciliated epithelium** *noun* BIOL a simple epithelium where the cells have tiny hairs or cilia

**cilium** *noun* BIOL one of many tiny projections resembling hairs which line cells in passages in the body and, by moving backwards and forwards, drive particles or fluid along the passage (NOTE: The plural is **cilia**.)

**CIM** *abbreviation* COMPUT **1.** computer input microfilm **2.** computer-integrated manufacturing

**cinders** *plural noun* **1.** CHEM a material left when the flames from a burning substance have gone out **2.** EARTH SCI the small pieces of lava and rock thrown up in a volcanic eruption

**cinematics** another spelling of **kinematics**

**cinnamic acid** *noun* CHEM a white odourless substance that is insoluble in water, used in perfumes. Formula: $C_6H_5CHCHCOOH$.

**cipher** *noun* COMPUT a system of transforming a message into an unreadable form with a secret code ○ *Always* *use a secure cipher when sending data over a telephone line.*

**ciphertext** *noun* COMPUT the data output from a cipher. Compare **plaintext**

**CIR** *abbreviation* COMPUT current instruction register

**circadian rhythm** *noun* BIOL a rhythm of daily activities and bodily processes such as eating, defecating and sleeping that is frequently controlled by hormones (NOTE: It repeats every twenty-four hours and is found both in plants and animals.)

**circle** *noun* **1.** MATHS a line forming a round shape **2.** a round shape formed by objects or people

**circuit** *noun* ELEC a connection between electronic components that perform a function

**circuit analyser** *noun* ELEC a device that measures voltage, current, impedance or signal in a circuit

**circuit board** *noun* ELEC an insulating board used to hold components which are then connected together electrically to form a circuit. Also called **circuit card**

**circuit breaker** *noun* ELEC an electrical device used to interrupt an electrical supply when there is too much current flow

**circuit capacity** *noun* ELEC the information-carrying capacity of a particular circuit

**circuit card** *noun* COMPUT same as **circuit board**

**circuit design** *noun* COMPUT a layout of components and interconnections in a circuit

**circuit diagram** *noun* ELEC a graphical description of a circuit ○ *The CAD program will plot the circuit diagram rapidly.*

**circuitry** *noun* ELEC a system of electrical circuits ○ *In an anti-skid braking system, circuitry is employed which can detect individual wheel deceleration.* ○ *The circuitry is still too complex.*

**circuit switching** *noun* ELEC a design of communication system in which a path from sender to receiver is created when required rather than using a permanent, fixed line (NOTE: The normal telephone system is an example of a circuit switching network.)

**circular** *adjective* shaped like a circle ○ *Anodes are circular plates with centre holes.*

**circular buffer** *noun* a computer-based queue that uses two markers, for the top and bottom of the line of stored items (NOTE: The markers move as items are read from or written to the stack.)

**circular file** *noun* COMPUT a data file that has no visible beginning or end and each item points to the location of the next item with the last item pointing back to the first

**circular list** *noun* COMPUT a list in which each element contains data and an address to the next element in the list with the last item pointing back to the first

**circular reference** *noun* COMPUT an error condition that occurs when two equations in two cells reference each other

**circular saw** *noun* INDUST a saw with a circular action which moves in a circle

**circular shift** *noun* COMPUT a rotation of bits in a word with the previous last bit inserted in the first bit position

**circulate** *verb* to move round in such a way as to arrive at the point of departure ○ *Water circulates via the radiator and pump through to the engine block itself.*

**circulation** *noun* **1.** the act of moving round in such a way as to arrive at the point of departure ○ *The general circulation is indicated by the arrows.* □ **circulation of carbon** the process by which carbon atoms from carbon dioxide are incorporated into organic compounds in plants during photosynthesis **2.** PHYSIOL same as **circulation of the blood**

**circulation of carbon** *noun* BOT the process by which carbon atoms from carbon dioxide are incorporated into organic compounds in plants during photosynthesis (NOTE: The carbon atoms are then oxidised into carbon dioxide again during respiration by the plants or by herbivores which eat them and by carnivores which eat the herbivores, so releasing carbon to go round the cycle again.)

**circulation of the blood** *noun* PHYSIOL the movement of blood around the body from the heart through the arteries to the capillaries and back to the heart through the veins ○ *She has poor circulation in her legs.* ○ *Rub your hands to get the circulation going.*

**circulatory** *adjective* ANAT referring to the circulation of the blood

**circulatory system** *noun* ANAT the system of arteries and veins which, together with the heart, make the blood circulate around the body

COMMENT: Blood circulates around the body, carrying oxygen from the lungs and nutrients from the liver through the arteries and capillaries to the tissues. The capillaries exchange the oxygen for waste matter such as carbon dioxide which is taken back to the lungs to be expelled. At the same time the blood obtains more oxygen in the lungs to be taken to the tissues. The circulation pattern is as follows: blood returns through the veins to the right atrium of the heart; from there it is pumped through the right ventricle into the pulmonary artery, and then into the lungs; from the lungs it returns through the pulmonary veins to the left atrium of the heart and is pumped from there through the left ventricle into the aorta and from the aorta into the other arteries.

**circum-** *prefix* around

**circumference** *noun* MATHS the distance around the edge of a circle

**circumflex nerve** *noun* ANAT a sensory and motor nerve in the upper arm

**circumpolar** *adjective* GEOG around the North or South Pole

**circumpolar vortex** *noun* METEOROL a circular movement of air around one of the Poles. Also called **polar vortex**

**cirque** *noun* EARTH SCI a scoop-shaped hollow formed in mountains or high plateaux by small, separate glaciers. Also called **corrie, cwm**

**cirrocumulus** *noun* METEOROL a form of high cloud, occurring above 5000 m, like altocumulus with little clouds

**cirrostratus** *noun* METEOROL a high layer of cloud

**cirrus** *noun* METEOROL a high cloud, occurring above 5000 m, forming a mass of separate clouds which look as if they are made of fibres, but which are formed of ice crystals

**CIS** *abbreviation* COMPUT contact image sensor

**CISC** *abbreviation* COMPUT complex instruction set computer

**cistron** *noun* GENETICS a section of DNA that contains the genetic code for a short chain of amino acids (**polypeptide**) and is the smallest functional unit carrying genetic information

**citric acid** *noun* CHEM an acid found in fruit such as oranges, lemons and grapefruit

**citric acid cycle** *noun* BIOCHEM same as **Krebs cycle**

**civil engineering** *noun* ENG the application of the principles of science to the design, construction and use of roads, bridges, dams, etc.

**cl** *abbreviation* MEASURE centilitre

**Cl** *symbol* CHEM ELEM chlorine

**clad** *verb* to protect something by covering it ○ *Alloys can be protected from corrosion by cladding the exposed surface with a thin layer of aluminium.*

**cladding** *noun* a protective material surrounding something

**cladistics** *noun* BIOL a system of classifying organisms in groups according to characteristics that they have inherited from a common ancestor

**clamper** *noun* ELEC a circuit which limits the level of a signal from a scanning head or other input device to a maximum before this is converted to a digital value

**clarification** *noun* INDUST the process of removing solid waste matter from sewage

**clarification basin** *noun* INDUST a tank in which solid waste matter is removed from sewage

**class** *noun* **1.** COMPUT the definition of what a particular software routine will do or what sort of data a variable can hold **2.** BIOL one of the divisions into which organisms are categorised ○ *Groups of families are classified into orders and groups of orders into classes.*

**classification** *noun* a system by which things are put into order so as to be able to refer to them again and identify them easily ○ *the Linnaean classification of plants and animals* ○ *the ABO classification of blood*

**classify** *verb* **1.** to allocate something to a category ○ *The area has been classified as an Area of Outstanding Natu-*

ral Beauty. ○ *The pollution records are classified under the name of the site which has been polluted.* **2.** to put things into order so as to be able to refer to them again and identify them easily ○ *Blood groups are classified according to the ABO system.* **3.** to make information secret ○ *The reports on the accident are classified and may not be consulted by the public.*

**class interval** *noun* COMPUT a range of values that can be contained in a class

**clathrate** *noun* CHEM a solid compound containing molecules of one component enclosed within the crystal structure of the other component ■ *adjective* BOT appearing or built like a lattice

**clavicle** *noun* **1.** ANAT a human collar bone **2.** ZOOL a bone or structure that is similar in function to the human clavicle or collar bone (NOTE: It can be reduced or absent in many mammals.)

**clay** *noun* EARTH SCI a type of heavy non-porous soil made of fine particles of silicate

**clayey** *adjective* EARTH SCI containing clay ○ *These plants do best in clayey soils.*

**clay land** *noun* EARTH SCI land where the soil has a lot of clay in it

**claypan** *noun* EARTH SCI a hollow on the surface of clay land where rain collects

**clean** *adjective* **1.** not dirty **2.** COMPUT with no errors or with no programs ○ *I'll have to start again – I just erased the only clean copy.* ■ *verb* to make something clean

**clean air** *noun* ENVIRON air which does not contain impurities

**clean copy** *noun* COMPUT a copy which is ready for keyboarding and does not have many changes on it

**Clean Development Mechanism** *noun* ENVIRON a scheme by which an industrialised country can receive credit for emission reductions in a developing country which result from projects financed by the industrialised country. Abbreviation **CDM**

**clean power station** *noun* INDUST a power station which gives off little pollution or radiation

**clean room** *noun* COMPUT an area where hard disks, wafers and chips are manufactured in a dust free environment

**cleanse** *verb* to make clean

**cleanser** *noun* a powder or liquid used for cleaning

**clean technology** *noun* INDUST an industrial process which causes little or no pollution

**clean up** *verb* ENVIRON to remove refuse, waste substances or pollutants from a place ○ *They are working to clean up the beaches after the oil spill.*

**clean-up** *noun* ENVIRON an act of removing refuse, waste substances or pollutants ○ *The local authorities have organised a large-scale clean-up of polluted beaches.*

**clean-up costs** *plural noun* ENVIRON the amount of money which has to be spent to remove pollutants, e.g. after an environmental disaster such as an oil spill

**clear** *adjective* **1.** easily understood ○ *There's no clear way of explaining the problem.* **2.** easily seen through ○ *Acid rain turns lakes crystal clear.* □ **clear of** free from something undesirable ○ *The area is now clear of pollution.* ■ *noun* METEOROL a clear sky ■ *verb* **1.** to remove something which is in the way in order to make space for something else ○ *They cleared hectares of jungle to make a new road to the capital.* ○ *We are clearing rainforest at a faster rate than before.* **2.** COMPUT to wipe out, erase or set to zero a computer file, variable or section of memory ○ *to clear an area of memory* ○ *to clear the data register* ○ *Type CLS to clear the screen.* ○ *All arrays are cleared each time the program is run.* **3.** COMPUT to release a communications link when transmissions have finished

**clear air** *noun* METEOROL an atmosphere with no mist or smoke

**clear air turbulence** *noun* AEROSP turbulence encountered in the atmosphere where no cloud is present ○ *Clear air turbulence can be particularly dangerous because it is often unexpected due to lack of visual warning.* Abbreviation **CAT**

**clearance** *noun* the act of removing something which is in the way in order to make space for something else

**clearcut** FORESTRY *noun* the cutting down of all the trees in an area ■ *verb* to clear an area of forest by cutting down all the trees

**clear to send** noun COMPUT an RS232C signal that a line or device is ready for data transmission. Abbreviation **CTS**

**cleavage** noun MINERALS the splitting of rocks or minerals along natural planes of weakness determined by their internal crystal structure (NOTE: The angle of cleavage is one of the features used to identify minerals.)

**click** COMPUT noun **1.** a sound of short duration, often used to indicate that a key has been pressed **2.** an act of pressing a key or button on a keyboard ○ *You move through text and graphics with a click of the button.* ■ verb to press and release a key or button on a keyboard or the mouse ○ *Use the mouse to enlarge a frame by clicking inside its border.*

**click through rate** noun COMPUT the number of times that visitors click on a displayed banner advertisement on a website, used as a method of charging the advertiser. Abbreviation **CTR**

**client** noun COMPUT a workstation, PC or terminal connected to a network that can send instructions to a server and display results

**client application** noun COMPUT an application that can accept linked or embedded objects from a server application or application that is used in a client-server system

**client-server architecture** noun COMPUT a distribution of processing power in which a central server computer carries out the main tasks in response to instructions from terminals or workstations

**client-server network** noun COMPUT a method of organising a network in which one central dedicated computer, the server, looks after tasks such as security, user accounts, printing and file sharing, while clients, i.e. the terminals or workstations connected to the server, run standard applications. Compare **peer-to-peer network**

**client side** adjective COMPUT referring to data or a program that runs on the client's computer rather than on a server (NOTE: A JavaScript program runs on the user's web browser and is a client side application, while a cookie is data stored on the user's hard disk.)

**cliff** noun EARTH SCI the steep side of an area of high ground, often by the sea

**climate** noun METEOROL the general weather patterns that a place has

COMMENT: Climate is influenced by many factors, in particular the latitude of the region, whether it is near the sea or far inland and the altitude.

**climate change** noun ENVIRON the long-term alteration in global weather patterns regarded as a potential consequence of atmospheric pollution

COMMENT: Sometimes climate change is used interchangeably with 'global warming', but scientists tend to use the term in the wider sense to include natural changes in the climate.

**climate feedback** noun METEOROL a process that is activated by the direct climate change caused by variations in the balance between incoming solar radiation and outgoing infra-red radiation (NOTE: Climate feedbacks may increase (positive feedback) or diminish (negative feedback) the magnitude of direct climate change.)

**climate lag** noun METEOROL a delay which occurs in climate change as a result of a factor that changes very slowly

**climate model** noun METEOROL a quantitative representation on a computer of the characteristics of the atmosphere, oceans, land surface and ice and the ways in which they interact

**climate modelling** noun METEOROL a simulation of the climate using computer-based models

**climatic** adjective METEOROL referring to climate

**climatic climax** noun METEOROL a stable state (**climax**) which is controlled by climatic factors

**climatic factor** noun ECOL a condition of climate which affects the organisms living in a specific area

**climatic zone** noun ECOL one of the eight areas of the Earth which have distinct climates

COMMENT: The climatic zones are: the two polar regions (the Arctic and Antarctic); the boreal in the northern hemisphere, south of the Arctic; two temperate zones, one in the northern hemisphere and one in the southern hemisphere; two subtropical zones, including the deserts; and the equatorial zone which has a damp tropical climate.

**climatological** adjective METEOROL referring to climatology ○ *Scientists* *have gathered climatological statistics from weather stations all round the world.*

**climatological data** *plural noun* METEOROL information and statistics about climate

**climatological station** *noun* METEOROL a scientific research centre where the climate is studied

**climatologist** *noun* METEOROL a scientist who specialises in the study of the climate

**climatology** *noun* METEOROL the scientific study of the climate

**climax** *noun* ECOL a final stable state in the development of an ecosystem

**climax community** *noun* BOT a plant community which has been stable for many years and which is unlikely to change unless the climate changes or there is human interference

**climb** *noun* (*of aircraft*) the action of increasing altitude by use of power ○ *Fine pitch enables full engine speed to be used during take-off and climb.* ■ *verb* (*of aircraft*) to increase altitude by use of power ○ *After take-off, the aircraft climbed to 5000 ft.*

**cline** *noun* BIOL the set of gradual changes which take place in a species according to geographical and climatic differences across the environment in which it lives

**clinical medicine** *noun* MED the study and treatment of patients in a hospital ward or in the doctor's surgery as opposed to the operating theatre or laboratory

**clinical pathology** *noun* MED the study of disease as applied to the treatment of patients

**clinker** *noun* INDUST the lumps of ash and hard residue from furnaces, used to make road surfaces or breeze blocks

**clinostat** *noun* BOT a slowly rotating platform on which a plant is placed so that it is exposed to a stimulus such as light equally on all sides

**clip** *verb* COMPUT to select an area of an image that is smaller than the original

**clip-art** *noun* COMPUT a set of pre-drawn images or drawings that a user can incorporate into a presentation or graphic ○ *We have used some clip-art to enhance our presentation.*

**clipboard** *noun* COMPUT a software utility that temporarily stores any type of data, e.g. a word or image ○ *Copy the text to the clipboard, then paste it back into a new document.*

**clisere** *noun* ECOL the succession of communities influenced by the climate of an area

**clitoris** *noun* ANAT a sensitive erectile female organ found at the front of the vulva in mammals, and also in some reptiles and birds (NOTE: In humans it lies immediately behind the junction of the labia minora.)

**CLNP** *abbreviation* COMPUT connectionless network protocol

**cloaca** *noun* ZOOL the terminal region of the gut with the intestinal, urinary and genital canals opening into it (NOTE: It is present in reptiles, amphibians, birds, many fishes, and in some invertebrates.)

**clock** *noun* 1. a device which shows the time 2. COMPUT a circuit which generates pulses used to synchronise equipment ■ *verb* COMPUT to synchronise signals or circuits with a clock pulse

**clock cycle** *noun* COMPUT the period of time between two consecutive clock pulses

**clock frequency** *noun* the frequency of the main clock that synchronises a computer system ○ *The main clock frequency is 10 MHz.*

**clock pulse** *noun* COMPUT a regular pulse used for timing or synchronising purposes

**clockwise** *adjective, adverb* describing a circular movement in the same direction as the hands of a clock, from left to right ○ *in a clockwise direction* Opposite **anticlockwise**

**clog** *verb* 1. to become blocked ○ *The drain clogs easily.* 2. to prevent movement of fluid through a pipe, channel or filter because of a build-up of solid matter ○ *Most filters allow unfiltered fluid to pass to the system when waste clogs the filter.*

**clone** *noun* 1. BIOL a group of cells derived from a single cell by asexual reproduction and therefore identical to the first cell 2. BIOL an organism produced asexually, e.g. by taking cuttings from a plant 3. COMPUT a computer or circuit that behaves in the same way as the original it was copied from ○ *They have* *copied our new personal computer and brought out a cheaper clone.* ○ *Higher performance clones are available for all the models in our range.* ■ *verb* BIOTECH to reproduce an individual organism by asexual means

**cloning** *noun* BIOL the reproduction of an individual organism by asexual means

**close** *verb* COMPUT to shut down access to a file or disk drive

**closed bus system** *noun* COMPUT a computer with no expansion bus that makes it very difficult for a user to upgrade

**closed chain** *noun* CHEM a number of molecules arranged in a ring

**closed loop** *noun* COMPUT a computer control operation in which data is fed back from the output of the controlled device to the controlling loop

**closed subroutine** *noun* COMPUT a number of computer instructions in a program that can be called at any time, with control being returned on completion to the next instruction in the main program

**Clostridium** *noun* BIOL a type of bacterium (NOTE: Species of Clostridium cause botulism, tetanus and gas gangrene, but also increase the nitrogen content of soil.)

**clot** PHYSIOL *verb* (*of blood*) to become thick and stop flowing, forming a scab if exposed to the air ■ *noun* a mass of thickened blood that forms over a wound or in a blood vessel

**clotting factor** *noun* MED one of a group of substances in the blood that are essential for normal clotting and scab formation over a wound

**cloud** *noun* METEOROL 1. a mass of water vapour or ice particles in the sky which can produce rain 2. a mass of particles suspended in the air ○ *Clouds of smoke poured out of the factory chimney.* ○ *The eruption sent a cloud of ash high into the atmosphere.* ○ *Dust clouds swept across the plains.* (NOTE: As a plural, **clouds** means several separate clouds; otherwise the singular **cloud** can be used to refer to a large continuous mass: **there is a mass of cloud over the southern part of the country.**)

COMMENT: Clouds are formed as humid air rises and then cools, causing the water

in it to condense. They are classified by meteorologists into ten categories: cirrus, cirrocumulus and cirrostratus (high clouds); altocumulus and altostratus (middle clouds); and stratocumulus, nimbostratus, cumulus, cumulonimbus and stratus (low clouds).

**cloudbank** *noun* METEOROL a mass of low clouds

**cloudbase** *noun* METEOROL the bottom part of a layer of cloud

**cloudburst** *noun* METEOROL a sudden rainstorm

**cloud ceiling** *noun* METEOROL the height of cloud cover

**cloud chamber** *noun* PHYS a piece of laboratory equipment in which clouds can be formed for the study of ionisation

**cloud cover** *noun* METEOROL the amount of sky which is covered by clouds

**cloud formation** *noun* METEOROL 1. the natural production and development of clouds 2. a pattern of clouds in the sky

**cloudlayer** *noun* METEOROL a mass of clouds at a specific height above the land

**cloudless** *adjective* METEOROL without clouds

**cloudy** *adjective* 1. METEOROL covered with clouds 2. not clear or transparent ○ *a cloudy liquid*

**clump** *noun* 1. BOT a group of trees or plants growing together ○ *a clump of bushes* 2. a group of items brought close together in a mass ○ *to form a clump* 3. a small mass of a substance ○ *a clump of soil* ■ *verb* PHYS to collect or stick together

**clumping** *noun* the formation of a mass of things in close association

**cluster** *noun* 1. a group of similar things that are close together 2. STATS a number of similar events happening at a similar time or in a similar place ○ *a cluster of leukaemia patients in the area of the nuclear power station* 3. COMPUT one or more sectors on a hard disk that are used to store a file or part of a file 4. COMPUT a number of terminals, stations, devices or memory locations grouped together in one place

**CLUT** *noun* COMPUT a table of numbers used in Windows and graphics programs to store the range of colours used in an image. Full form **colour look-up table**

**CLV** *abbreviation* COMPUT constant linear velocity

**cm** *abbreviation* MEASURE centimetre

**CM** *abbreviation* COMPUT central memory

**CMI** *abbreviation* COMPUT computer-managed instruction

**CMIP** *abbreviation* COMPUT common management information protocol

**CMIS** *noun* COMPUT a powerful network management system. Full form **common management information specification**

**CML** *abbreviation* COMPUT computer-managed learning

**CMOS** *abbreviation* COMPUT complementary metal oxide semiconductor

COMMENT: The final package uses very low power but is relatively slow and sensitive to static electricity as compared to TTL integrated circuits. The main use is in portable computers where battery power is being used.

**CMYK** *noun* COMPUT (*in graphics and DTP*) a method of describing a colour by its four component colours. Full form **cyan-magenta-yellow-black**

**CNC** *abbreviation* COMPUT computer numeric control

**cnidarian** *noun* ZOOL a marine invertebrate with tentacles surrounding its mouth, e.g. a sea anemone, coral and jellyfish. Phylum: Cnidaria.

**CNS** *abbreviation* ANAT central nervous system

**Co** *symbol* CHEM ELEM cobalt

**CO** *symbol* CHEM carbon monoxide

**co-** *prefix meaning* together

**CO₂**, **CO2** *symbol* CHEM carbon dioxide

**coagulant** *noun* BIOCHEM a substance which can make blood coagulate

**coagulate** *verb* BIOCHEM (*of a liquid*) to become semi-solid as suspended particles clump together ○ *Blood coagulates in contact with air.*

**coagulation** *noun* BIOCHEM (*of a liquid*) the process of becoming semi-solid

**coal** *noun* INDUST a solid black organic substance found in layers underground in most parts of the world, burnt to provide heat or power

COMMENT: Coal was formed many millions of years ago from organic refuse deposited in swamps. Decaying plants formed peat, which was pressed by other layers of deposits to form first lignite, or brown coal, and then coal itself. Coal is composed mainly of carbon and can be classified into various grades. Lignite is soft and not a very efficient fuel. Bituminous coals are harder and contain more carbon. Anthracite is the hardest coal, being almost pure carbon, and is the most efficient producer of heat. Coal is used commercially to fuel power stations, to burn to produce gas and to make coke, which burns at a higher temperature and is used in metal refining. It is also processed to make various forms of smokeless fuels used in domestic heating appliances. Coal affects the environment in two ways: (a) in the mining process, waste matter can create ugly slag heaps and can contaminate rivers, and old mines create subsidence as they fill in; (b) burning coal emits toxic smoke, especially sulphur oxides and fly ash, together with carcinogenic substances such as benzopyrene. These emissions cause smog at low levels and can rise into the atmosphere and contribute to the greenhouse effect.

**coal basin** *noun* EARTH SCI a part of the Earth's surface containing layers of coal

**coal deposit** *noun* EARTH SCI a layer of coal in the rocks beneath the Earth's surface

**coalesce** *verb* to join together to form a large mass or number ○ *The moisture in the air coalesces into large water droplets.*

**coalescence** *noun* the process of joining together to form a larger mass or number ○ *Coalescence of water vapour in the atmosphere forms larger droplets of water.*

**coal-fired power station** *noun* INDUST a power station which burns coal rather than gas or oil

**coal gas** *noun* INDUST a gas produced by processing coal, leaving coke as a residue

**coal gasification** *noun* INDUST the process of converting coal into gas to be used as fuel in gas-fired power stations

**coal grinding** *noun* INDUST the reduction of coal to fine particles in a crushing machine

**coal mine** *noun* INDUST a hole dug in the ground to extract coal

**coal seam** *noun* EARTH SCI a layer of coal in the rocks beneath the Earth's surface

**coal tar** *noun* INDUST one of several liquids with a strong distinctive smell formed by distillation of coal (NOTE: It is used in the pharmaceutical industry and as a wood preservative.)

**coarse** *adjective* **1.** referring to a particle or grain of sand which is larger than others ○ *Coarse sand fell to the bottom of the liquid as sediment, while the fine grains remained suspended.* **2.** rough

**coast** *noun* EARTH SCI the zone where the land meets the sea

**coastal** *adjective* EARTH SCI near the coast ○ *a plant found in coastal waters*

**coastal fishery** *noun* FISHERY an area of sea near the coast where fish are caught

**coastal fog** *noun* METEOROL a type of advection fog which forms along the coast

**coastal protection** *noun* ENVIRON the protecting of the coast from being eroded by the action of the sea

**coastal refraction** *noun* TELECOM a change in direction of sound waves when a signal crosses a coastline from sea to land

**coastline** *noun* EARTH SCI the outline of a coast

**coat** *noun* a thin covering of a substance such as paint ○ *The coats of paint on a large aircraft significantly increase its weight.* ■ *verb* to cover something with a thin layer of a substance such as paint ○ *Metals are coated for protection against corrosion.*

**coating** *noun* **1.** a thin layer of a substance ○ *There are two coatings on the inside of CRT screens.* **2.** the act of covering something with a thin layer of a substance

**co-axial cable, coax** *noun* ELEC a cable made up of a central core surrounded by an insulating layer then a second shielding conductor. Compare **twisted-pair cable**

COMMENT: Co-axial cable is used for high-frequency, low-loss applications including thin Ethernet network cabling.

**cobalt** *noun* CHEM ELEM a metallic element used to make alloys (NOTE: The chemical symbol is **Co**; the atomic number is **27** and the atomic weight is **58.93**.)

**cobalt-60** *noun* CHEM, MED a radioactive isotope used in radiotherapy to treat cancer

**cobble** *noun* ENG a large round stone used to make road surfaces

**COBOL** *abbreviation* COMPUT common business-oriented language

**coccus** *noun* MICROBIOL a bacterium shaped like a ball (NOTE: The plural is **cocci**.)

COMMENT: Cocci grow together in groups, either in clumps (staphylococci) or in long chains (streptococci).

**coccyx** *noun* ANAT a bone at the base of the spinal column in apes and humans

**cochlea** *noun* ANAT a part of the inner ear in mammals, birds and some reptiles which detects sounds of different pitch (NOTE: In mammals it is spirally coiled and contains numerous tiny hair cells which move in response to sound waves, causing nerve impulses to travel to the brain, which interprets them as sound.)

**cochlear nerve** *noun* ANAT a division of the auditory nerve

**cock** *noun* ENG a manually controlled valve or tap to control the flow of a liquid ○ *It is necessary to have a master cock for each engine.*

**coconut palm** *noun* TREES a palm tree with large hard-shelled edible nuts. Latin name: *Cocos nucifera.*

**cocoon** *noun* ZOOL a hollow silky structure made by many invertebrates to protect their eggs or developing pupae

**COD** *abbreviation* BIOCHEM chemical oxygen demand

**code** *noun* **1.** a system of numbers, letters or symbols used to represent language or other information **2.** GENETICS same as **genetic code 3.** COMPUT rules used to convert instructions or data from one form to another **4.** COMPUT a sequence of computer instructions ■ *verb* **1.** to convert instructions or data into another form **2.** COMPUT to write a program in a programming language **3.**

GENETICS (*of a codon or gene*) to provide the genetic information which causes a specific amino acid to be produced ○ *Genes are sections of DNA that code for a specific protein sequence.*

**CODEC** *noun* COMPUT a device which encodes a signal being sent or decodes a signal received, used in many advanced PABX systems. Full form **coder/decoder**

**code element** *noun* COMPUT the voltage or signal used to represent binary digits

**code group** *noun* COMPUT a special sequence of five code bits that represent an FDDI symbol

**codepage** *noun* COMPUT the definition of the character produced by each key on the keyboard

**coder** *noun* COMPUT a device which encodes a signal

**coding** *noun* COMPUT the act of putting a code on something

**codistillation** *noun* ENVIRON the process by which molecules of toxic substances can be evaporated into clouds over land and then fall back into the sea as rain

**cod liver oil** *noun* PHARM an oil from the liver of codfish (NOTE: It is rich in calories and in vitamins A and D and is often used as a diet supplement.)

**codominant** *adjective* **1.** ECOL (of a species) equally abundant in a community ○ *codominant genes* ○ *There are three codominant tree species in this forest.* **2.** GENETICS (of alleles of a gene) not being fully dominant over other alleles in a heterozygous individual

**codon** *noun* GENETICS a unit consisting of a set of three consecutive nucleotides in messenger RNA that specify a particular amino acid in protein synthesis

**coefficient** *noun* MATHS a mathematical quantity placed before and multiplying another (NOTE: In 4xy, 4 is the coefficient of x.)

**-coele** *suffix* BIOL another spelling of **-cele**

**coelenterate** *noun* ZOOL an organism which has a soft bag-like body and a gut with only one opening. Phylum: Coelenterata. (NOTE: Sea anemones, corals and jellyfish are all coelenterates.)

**coeliac** *adjective* ANAT referring to the abdomen

**coeliac disease** *noun* MED a disease of the small intestine resulting from an inability to digest wheat protein (NOTE: The protein gluten causes the body's own immune system to attack and damage the gut lining.)

**coeliac ganglion** *noun* ANAT a ganglion on each side of the origins of the diaphragm, connected with the coeliac plexus

**coelom** *noun* ANAT the body cavity in most many-celled animals including people

**coenocyte** *noun* BOT a mass of cytoplasm containing many nuclei within a common cell wall

**coenocytic** *adjective* BOT referring to a coenocyte (NOTE: The threads (**hyphae**) of many fungi and the bodies of some algae are coenocytic.)

**coenzyme** *noun* BIOCHEM a non-protein compound that combines with the protein part of an enzyme (**apoenzyme**) to make it active

**coffee** *noun* **1.** BOT a bush or small tree widely grown in the tropics for its seeds. Latin name: *Coffea arabica.* **2.** the drink prepared from the seeds of coffee bushes

**coffee plantation** *noun* AGRIC a plantation of coffee bushes

**cogeneration** *noun* INDUST the production of heat and power, as in a combined heat and power installation

**cohesion** *noun* PHYS the force of attraction between the molecules of a solid or liquid that holds them together

**coil** *noun* ELEC a device consisting of coiled wire for converting low voltage to high voltage ○ *A voltage coil is connected across the generator.*

**coincide** *verb* to happen at the same time and/or in the same place

**coincidence function, coincidence operation** MATHS same as **AND function**

**coincidence gate, coincidence circuit, coincidence element** *noun* ELECTRONICS same as **AND gate**

**coke** *noun* INDUST a fuel manufactured by heating coal to high temperatures without the presence of air

COMMENT: Coke is produced in coking ovens, where coal is heated to white heat without air. This removes most of the tar and the resulting fuel burns at a much higher temperature than coal and produces very little smoke or ash. It is used in blast furnaces.

**coke burner** *noun* INDUST a device in which coal is heated to produce coke

**col** *noun* **1.** EARTH SCI a high pass between two mountains **2.** METEOROL a low pressure area between two anticyclones

**cold** *adjective* COMPUT **1.** not hot ○ *The machines work badly in cold weather.* **2.** without being prepared ■ *noun* **1.** low temperature ○ *Sheep can withstand the cold.* **2.** MED a common infection in the nose

**cold-blooded** *adjective* ZOOL referring to an animal such as a reptile or fish which has cold blood. ◊ **poikilotherm**

COMMENT: The body temperature of cold-blooded animals changes with the outside temperature.

**cold boot** *noun* COMPUT same as **cold start**

**cold desert** *noun* EARTH SCI an area with little vegetation because of the cold temperatures

**cold front** *noun* METEOROL the edge of an advancing mass of cold air, associated with an area of low pressure, bringing clouds and rain as it meets the warmer air which it displaces

**cold hardening** *noun* BOT the process by which a conifer prepares for the winter by reducing the amount of water contained in its needles

**cold setting materials** *noun* INDUST materials which do not need heat to harden

**cold start** *noun* COMPUT the switching on of a computer or running of a program from its original start point

**cold trough** *noun* METEOROL a long area of low pressure with cold air in it, leading away from the centre of a depression

**coleopteran** *noun* INSECTS an insect such as a beetle with modified tough forewings that act as covers for the membranous hindwings. Order: Coleoptera.

**coleoptile** *noun* BOT a sheath which protects the stem tip (**plumule**) of a germinating grass seed as it grows to the surface

**coliform** *adjective* BIOL referring to bacteria which are similar in shape to *Escherichia coli*

**collagen** *noun* BIOL a fibrous protein forming connective bundles of connective tissue, bone and cartilage

**collagen disease** *noun* MED a disease that affects the connective tissue (NOTE: Collagen diseases include rheumatic fever and rheumatoid arthritis.)

**collagenous** *adjective* **1.** BIOL containing collagen **2.** MED referring to collagen disease

**collapse** *noun* a sudden and complete fall ■ *verb* to fall suddenly and completely ○ *The magnetic field will reach a maximum in one direction, collapse to zero and reach a maximum in the opposite direction.*

**collate** *verb* to compare and put items in order

**collateral circulation** *noun* MED the enlargement of some secondary blood vessels, as a response when the main vessels become slowly blocked

**collator** *noun* COMPUT a piece of software that collates data

**collect** *verb* to gather or gather something over a period of time ○ *Water collects in the hollows.* ○ *Any given object will usually collect ice more quickly at high speed.*

**collection** *noun* COMPUT **1.** the process of gathering together or of gathering something together **2.** a series of items brought together

**collector panel** *noun* INDUST same as **solar panel**

**collide** *verb* to hit or to crash into something ○ *Some particles will collide with each other.*

**collimator** *noun* OPTICS a lens or mirror used in an optical system to produce light in a parallel beam for further processing, e.g. in a spectrograph

**collision** *noun* **1.** a crash between two objects such as vehicles or molecules **2.** COMPUT an event that occurs when two electrical signals meet and interfere with each other over a network, normally causing an error

**colloid** *noun* PHYS a substance with very small particles that do not settle but remain in suspension in a liquid

**colloidal** *adjective* PHYS referring to a colloid

**colloidally dispersed particles** *plural noun* PHYS particles which remain in suspension in a liquid

**co-located** *adjective* having the same location

**co-location** *noun* COMPUT the putting of several computers used as Internet servers at a specialist site designed to support and maintain servers on behalf of their customers

**colon** *noun* PRINTING a printing sign, ( : ), which shows a break in a string of words or introduces an explanation

**colonial** *adjective* ECOL referring to a colony

**colonial animal** *noun* ZOOL an animal such as an ant which usually lives in colonies

**colonisation** *noun* ECOL the act of colonising a place ○ *Islands are particularly subject to colonisation by species of plants or animals introduced by people.*

**colonise** *verb* ECOL to begin to live in a place as a group ○ *Derelict city sites rapidly become colonised by plants.* ○ *Rats have colonised the river banks.*

**coloniser** *noun* ECOL an animal or plant which colonises an area

**colony** *noun* ECOL a group of animals, plants or microorganisms living together in a place ○ *a colony of ants*

**color** *noun* US spelling of **colour**

**coloration** *noun* ZOOL the colours or patterns of an animal ○ *protective coloration*

**colorimeter** *noun* OPTICS a device for measuring the concentration of a solution of a coloured substance by reference to standard solutions or standard colour slides

**colostrum** *noun* PHYSIOL a yellowish fluid that is rich in antibodies and minerals produced by a mother's breasts after giving birth and prior to the production of true milk (NOTE: It provides newborns with immunity to infections.)

**colour** *noun* the set of differing wavelengths of light that are reflected from objects and sensed by the eyes ○ *Flowers use colour to attract insects.* ■ *verb* to give colour to something ○ *The chemical coloured the water blue.*

**colour balance** *noun* OPTICS an adjustment of the red, green and blue primary colours to produce a pure white colour (NOTE: When configuring a colour monitor, a colour sensor is placed on the screen and the red, green and blue electron gun settings are adjusted to produce a pure white colour.)

**colour bit** *noun* COMPUT a data bit assigned to a pixel to describe its colour (NOTE: One bit provides two colours, two bits give four colours and eight bits allow 256 colour combinations.)

**colour cell** *noun* COMPUT the smallest area on a screen that can display colour information

**colour cycling** *noun* COMPUT the changing of the colours in a palette over a period of time, normally used to create a special effect or animation

**colour depth** *noun* COMPUT the number of different colours that can be displayed by any single pixel in a display (NOTE: It is determined by the number of colour bits in each pixel.)

**colour display** *noun* COMPUT a display device able to represent characters or graphics in colour

**colour graphics adapter** *noun* COMPUT a popular microcomputer colour display system. Abbreviation **CGA**

**colour index** *noun* ASTRON a quantitative measure of the colour of astronomical objects

COMMENT: Colour indices compare the brightness of an object through two or more filters at different wavelengths. B-V (blue minus visual, the straw colour which marks the peak acuity of the human eye) is the most commonly used colour index. The smaller the value of B-V, the bluer a star appears and the hotter it is.

**colouring** *noun* FOOD INDUST same as **food colouring**

COMMENT: Colouring additives have E numbers 100 to 180. Some are natural pigments, for example riboflavine (E101), carrot juice (E160) or chlorophyll (E140) and are safe. Others such as tartrazine (E102) and other azo dyes are suspected of being carcinogenic. Also suspect is caramel (E150), which is the most widely used colouring substance.

**colour key** *noun* OPTICS an image manipulation technique used to superimpose one image on another (NOTE: It is often used with two video sources to create special effects: one image is photographed against a coloured background and then superimposed with another image to produce a combined picture.)

**colourless** *adjective* with no colour ○ *Water is a colourless liquid.*

**colour palette** *noun* COMPUT the selection of colours that are currently being used in an image

**colour printer** *noun* COMPUT a printer that can produce hard copy in colour (NOTE: Colour printers include colour ink-jet, colour dot-matrix and thermal-transfer printers.)

**colour saturation** *noun* PHYS the purity of a colour signal

**colour separation** *noun* PRINTING the separating of a colour image into its constituent colours to produce printing plates (NOTE: Full colour printing needs four-colour separation to produce four printing plates for the cyan, magenta, yellow and black (CMYK) inks that together create a colour image.)

**colour standard** *noun* ELEC ENG one of three international standards used to describe how colour TV and video images are displayed and transmitted (NOTE: The three standards are NTSC, PAL and SECAM.)

**colour temperature** *noun* PHYS a shade of the colour white that would be seen if pure carbon were heated to a particular temperature in Kelvin (NOTE: The standard for many TV and video systems is a colour temperature of 6500 K, known as Illuminant D65.)

**column** *noun* **1.** a solid with a tall narrow shape ○ *Basalt rocks form columns in some parts of the world.* **2.** a body of fluid with a tall, narrow shape ○ *Torricelli first demonstrated that the atmosphere has weight by showing that it can support a column of liquid.* **3.** a vertical section of a table in a document ○ *Column four of the table shows the totals of the other three.*

**columnar** *adjective* in the form of a column ○ *Igneous rocks may have a columnar structure.*

**columnar graph** *noun* MATHS a graph on which values are shown as vertical or horizontal bars

**column chromatography** *noun* CHEM chromatography using a column of powder as the porous medium

**COM** *abbreviation* COMPUT **1.** common object model **2.** Component Object Model **3.** computer output on microfilm

**COMAL** *noun* COMPUT a structured programming language similar to BASIC. Full form **common algorithmic language**

**combat** *verb* to fight against something ○ *The medical team is combating an outbreak of diphtheria.* ○ *What can we do to combat the spread of the disease?*

**comb filter** *noun* ELEC an electronic device used to separate the luma (Y) and chroma (C) signals from a composite video signal

**combination** *noun* the act of bringing two or more things together or of coming together

**combinational** *adjective* combining a number of separate elements

**combinational circuit** *noun* ELECTRONICS an electronic circuit consisting of a number of connected components

**combinational logic** *noun* COMPUT a logic function made up of a number of separate logic gates

**combine** *verb* to bring two or more things together to make one or to come together to make one

**combined head** *noun* COMPUT a transducer that can read and write data from the surface of a magnetic storage medium, e.g. a floppy disk

**combined heat and power plant** *noun* INDUST a power station that produces both electricity and hot water for the local population. Abbreviation **CHP plant** (NOTE: Such a plant may operate on almost any fuel, including refuse.)

**combined station** *noun* COMPUT a high-level data link control station that processes commands and responses

**combined symbol matching** *noun* an efficient optical character recognition system. Abbreviation **CSM**

**combust** *verb* CHEM to burn something ○ *The region combusts 75% of its refuse for heat reclamation.*

**combustible** *adjective* burning easily ○ *made of combustible materials* ○ *Wood and paper are easily combustible.*

**combustion** *noun* PHYS the burning of a substance with oxygen

**combustion chamber** *noun* MECH ENG the part of the cylinder in a piston engine where the ignition of the fuel/air mixture takes place

**combustion residue** *noun* PHYS the material left after combustion has taken place

**comet** *noun* ASTRON an astronomical object that is a mass of ice and dust and has a long luminous tail produced by vaporisation when its orbit passes close to the Sun

**comma** *noun* a symbol (,) that is often used to separate data, variables or arguments

**comma-delimited** *adjective* COMPUT (*of a file*) in which each item or field of data is separated by a comma

**command** *noun* COMPUT **1.** an electrical signal that will start or stop a process **2.** a word or phrase that is recognised by a computer system and starts or terminates an action ○ *an interrupt command* ○ *The command to execute the program is RUN.*

**command-and-control regulations** *plural noun* ENVIRON rules that require polluters to meet specific emission-reduction targets, often using specific types of equipment

**command-driven program** *noun* COMPUT a program which requires the user to enter instructions at every stage

**command interpreter** *noun* COMPUT a program within an operating system which recognises a set of system commands and controls the processor, screen and storage devices accordingly ○ *When you type in the command 'DIR', the command interpreter asks the disk drive for a list of files and instructs the monitor to display the list.*

**command language** *noun* COMPUT a programming language made up of procedures for various tasks, which can be called up by a series of commands

**command line** *noun* COMPUT **1.** a program line that contains a command instruction **2.** a command prompt and system command

**command line operating system** *noun* COMPUT a type of computer system software which is controlled by a user typing in commands (NOTE: These systems are now largely replaced by systems which allow a user to control the system through images.)

**command register** *noun* COMPUT a register which stores the instruction to be carried out

**commence** *verb* to start doing something

**commensal** BIOL *noun* an organism which lives on another plant or animal but does not harm it or influence it in any way. ♦ **parasite, symbiont** ■ *adjective* referring to a commensal

**commensalism** *noun* BIOL the state of organisms existing together as commensals

**comment** *noun* **1.** an opinion expressed in speech or writing ○ *critical comments* ○ *Thank you for your helpful comments on my paper.* **2.** COMPUT a helpful note in a program to guide other programmers who might read it ○ *The lack of comments is annoying.* ○ *BASIC allows comments to be written after a REM instruction.*

**comminution** *noun* INDUST the crushing or grinding of rock, ore or sewage into small particles

**comminutor** *noun* INDUST a crushing machine that reduces particles to a smaller size

**committee** *noun* a group of people dealing with a particular subject or problem

**common** *adjective* **1.** occurring frequently ○ *a common spelling error* **2.** used or done by several people ○ *a common ethical stance* **3.** ordinary ○ *common household chemicals*

**common business-oriented language** *noun* COMPUT full form of **COBOL**

**common carotid artery** *noun* ANAT a main artery running up each side of the lower part of the neck

**common channel signalling** *noun* COMPUT the act of signalling via one channel used as a communications link to a number of devices or circuits

**common gateway interface** *noun* COMPUT a standard that defines how a webpage can call special scripts stored on an Internet server to carry out enhancing functions. Abbreviation **CGI**

**common iliac artery** *noun* ANAT one of two arteries which branch from the aorta in the abdomen (NOTE: In turn they divide into the internal iliac artery, leading to the pelvis, and the external iliac artery, leading to the leg.)

**common intermediate format** *noun* COMPUT a standard for video images that displays an image 352 pixels wide and 288 pixels high. Abbreviation **CIF**

**common management information protocol** *noun* COMPUT a protocol officially adopted by the International Standards Organisation and used to carry network management information across a network. Abbreviation **CMIP**

**common object model** *noun* COMPUT a standard defined by Microsoft to standardise the way an application can access an object. Abbreviation **COM** (NOTE: This is a rival standard to CORBA.)

**common object request broker architecture** *noun* COMPUT a standard defined by the Object Management Group to standardise the way an application can access an object. Abbreviation **CORBA** (NOTE: This is a rival standard to COM.)

**common salt** *noun* CHEM a white powder used to make food, especially meat, fish and vegetables, taste better. Also called **sodium chloride**

**comms** *plural noun* COMPUT same as **communications** (*informal*)

**communicate** *verb* to pass information

**communicating artery** *noun* ANAT one of two arteries which connect the blood supply from each side of the brain, forming part of the circle of Willis

**communication** *noun* COMPUT the passing of information

**communications** *plural noun* COMPUT the processes by which data is transmitted and received, by means of telephones, satellites, radio or any medium capable of carrying signals

**communications channel** *noun* COMPUT a physical link over which data can be transmitted

**communications port** *noun* COMPUT a socket or physical connection allowing one device to communicate with another

**communications protocol** *noun* COMPUT a set of parameters that define how the transfer of information will be controlled ○ *The communications protocol for most dial-up online services is*

*eight-bit words, no stop bit and even parity.*

**communications software** *noun* COMPUT software that allows a user to control a modem and use an online service

**community** *noun* **1.** a group of people who live and work in a district ○ *The health services serve the local community.* **2.** ECOL a group of different organisms which live together in an area, and which are usually dependent on each other for existence

**community architecture** *noun* ENVIRON a way of designing new housing projects or adapting old buildings, in which the people living in the area as well as specialists are involved in the planning

**community ecology** *noun* ECOL the study of the processes that determine the composition and structure of the mixture of different species found in a specific area

**community heating** *noun* ENG the heating of houses and shops in an area from a central source

**community medicine** *noun* MED the study of medical practice which examines groups of people and the health of the community, including housing, pollution and other environmental factors

**community physician** *noun* MED a doctor who specialises in community medicine

**community services** *plural noun* MED services which are available to the community

**community transport** *noun* ENVIRON a bus or rail service which is available to the community

**commutator** *noun* ELEC a device containing metal bars connected to the coils of a generator to produce electrical current ○ *As the power output required is DC not AC, a commutator is fixed at one end of the armature.*

**comp** *noun* COMPUT a type of newsgroup that provides discussion about computers and computer programming

**compact** *adjective* referring to something which does not take up much space ■ *verb* to reduce the space taken by something

**compact code** *noun* COMPUT a minimum number of program instructions required for a task

**compact disc** *noun* COMPUT a small plastic disc that contains audio signals in digital form etched onto the surface. Abbreviation **CD**

**compact Flash** *noun* COMPUT a tiny memory expansion device that uses Flash-ROM to store up to 512 Mb of data, often used in MP3 music players and digital cameras. Abbreviation **CF**

**compacting algorithm** *noun* COMPUT a formula for reducing the amount of space required by text

**companding** *noun* COMPUT a combination of two processes that reduce or compact data before transmission or storage then restore packed data to its original form. Full form **compressing and expanding**

**companion planting** *noun* BOT the use of companion plants

**companion plants** *plural noun* BOT plants which grow best in association with other plants

COMMENT: Beans and peas help root plants such as carrots and beetroot. Marigolds help reduce aphid infestation. Companion planting is often used by organic growers to reduce the need for pesticides.

**comparable** *adjective* able to be compared equally with something else ○ *Titanium is non-magnetic and has an electrical resistance comparable to that of stainless steel.*

**comparative risk analysis** *noun* a comparison of two types of risk

**comparator** *noun* COMPUT a logical device whose output is true if there is a difference between two inputs

**compare** *verb* to find the similarities and dissimilarities between two or more things ○ *When the chart is properly oriented, it is easier to compare the distance between landmarks on the ground to their corresponding distances on the chart.* ○ *An aneroid barometer is small compared with a mercury barometer.* (NOTE: **compare with** is usually used to express difference **compare to** to express similarity)

**comparison** *noun* the bringing out of differences and similarities between two or more things ○ *A table showing a comparison of fixed points on various*

temperature scales is given on page three.

**compartment** *noun* FORESTRY a section of a managed plantation of trees

**compass** *noun* NAVIG an instrument with a needle which always points to the magnetic north

**compass bearing** *noun* NAVIG the direction or position relative to a fixed point measured in degrees on a compass

**compass quadrant** *noun* NAVIG a quarter part of a circle centred on a navigational aid

**compatibility** *noun* COMPUT the ability of two hardware or software devices to function together

COMMENT: By conforming to the standards of another manufacturer or organisation, compatibility of hardware and software allows programs and hardware to be interchanged without modification.

**compatible** COMPUT *adjective* referring to two hardware or software devices that function correctly together ○ **is the hardware IBM-compatible?** will it work if used with an IBM computer? ■ *noun* a hardware or software device that functions correctly with other equipment ○ *This computer is much cheaper than the other compatibles.*

**compensate** *verb* to make up for the loss of something ○ *The fall in air temperature increases the air density and so compensates to some extent for the loss of the thrust due to atmospheric pressure.*

**compensation point** *noun* ECOL the point at which the rate of photosynthesis is the same as the rate of respiration (NOTE: It can be measured as the point at which carbon dioxide used by plants equals the oxygen they release.)

**competition** *noun* ECOL the struggle for limited resources such as food or light occurring between organisms of the same or different species

**competitive exclusion principle** *noun* ECOL a general rule that when two species compete for the same resources, one species ultimately loses (NOTE: The loser has to adapt its feeding habits or behaviour, migrate to another area, experience a decrease in population, or become extinct.)

**competitive release** noun ECOL the process by which a species may expand its niche if it has no competitors

**compilation** noun COMPUT the translation of an encoded source program into machine-readable code

**compilation error** noun COMPUT a syntax error found during program compilation, resulting in the job being aborted

**compile** verb COMPUT to convert a high-level language program into a machine code program that can be executed by itself

**compiler, compiler program** noun COMPUT a piece of software that converts an encoded program into a machine code program ○ *The new compiler has an in-built editor.*

**complement** MATHS noun 1. the inversion of a binary digit ○ *The complement is found by changing the 1s to 0s and 0s to 1s.* 2. the result obtained after subtracting a number from one less than the radix ■ verb to invert a binary digit

**complementary** adjective fitting in with and improving the performance of something

**complementary DNA** noun GENETICS single-stranded DNA made in a laboratory using the enzyme reverse transcriptase so that its base sequence is complementary to a messenger RNA template (NOTE: It may be used in gene cloning or as a gene probe.)

**complementary gene** noun GENETICS a gene that produces an observable effect in an organism only in association with another gene

**complementary metal oxide semiconductor** noun COMPUT an integrated circuit design and construction method using a pair of complementary transistors. Abbreviation **CMOS**

**complementary operation** noun MATHS a logical operation that results in the logical NOT of a function

**complementation** noun MATHS a number system used to represent positive and negative numbers

**complemented** adjective MATHS referring to a binary digit that has had a complement performed on it

**complete** adjective 1. finished or ready ○ *The spelling check is complete.* ○ *When this job is complete, the next in the queue is processed.* 2. requiring

nothing else in order to function ■ verb to finish something ○ *When you have completed the keyboarding, pass the text through the spelling checker.*

**complete operation** noun COMPUT an operation that retrieves the necessary operands from memory, performs the operation, returns the results and operands to memory and reads the next instruction to be processed

**completion** noun the finishing of a task

**complex** adjective COMPUT very complicated or difficult to understand ○ *The complex mathematical formula was difficult to solve.* ○ *The controller must work hard to operate this complex network.* ■ noun 1. CHEM a compound in which molecules or ions form coordinate bonds with a central metal atom 2. COMPUT a whole made up of many different parts

**complex instruction set computer** noun COMPUT a computer whose instruction set contains a number of long complicated instructions. Compare **reduced instruction set computer**. Abbreviation **CISC** (NOTE: These instructions make programming easier, but reduce execution speed.)

**complexity** noun the state of being complicated or difficult to understand ○ *Up-to-date design does not necessarily mean structural complexity.*

**complex number** noun MATHS a number written as $a + ib$, where $i$ is the square root of minus one (NOTE: Complex numbers may be either real or imaginary.)

**compliance** noun the act of obeying a regulation or conforming to a set of standards

**compliant** adjective conforming to a particular set of standards ○ *If you want to read PhotoCD compact discs in your computer you must be sure that the CD-ROM drive is PhotoCD or CD-ROM XA compliant.*

**complicate** verb to make something more difficult ○ *Map reading is often complicated by seasonal variations.*

**complicated** adjective not easy to understand or solve

**complicated concept** noun an idea or series of ideas or principles which are difficult to understand

**complicated problem** *noun* a problem which takes a long time and a lot of work to solve

**complication** *noun* a difficulty or problem

**complications** *plural noun* MED secondary medical problems developing as part of an existing medical condition ○ *The patient may develop complications after surgery.*

**comply** *verb* to be or do what is required by an instruction or law ○ *Equipment and furnishings of modern jet transports must comply with safety regulations.* (NOTE: **complying** – **complied**)

**component** *noun* **1.** ENG a part of an object, system or piece of equipment ○ *The undercarriage is made up of a number of different components.* **2.** PHYS one part of a force which consists of a number of different parts, e.g. wind **3.** CHEM a substance which forms part of a compound

**component density** *noun* ELEC the number of electronic components per unit area on a printed circuit board ○ *Component density is so high on this motherboard, that no expansion connectors could be fitted.*

**component error** *noun* COMPUT an error introduced by a malfunctioning device or component rather than incorrect programming

**Component Object Model** *noun* COMPUT a set of rules that define the way in which objects within the Windows OLE system interact with other documents, objects and applications. Abbreviation **COM**

**component video** *noun* a method of transmitting video information with separate signals for the luminance and two chrominance channels to avoid interference. Compare **composite video**

**compose** *verb* to make something from a number of parts ○ *Air is composed of a mixture of gases: 75% nitrogen, 23% oxygen, 1% argon and very small quantities of several other gases.*

**Compositae** *plural noun* BOT a common and very large family of plants whose flat flowers consist of many florets arranged around a central structure (NOTE: Dandelions and daisies belong to this family.)

**composite** *adjective* made up of a number of different parts ○ *a composite material* ■ *noun* a lightweight but very strong synthetic material used in aircraft manufacturing ○ *To make a composite it is necessary to combine the reinforcing glass fibres with special glue or resin.*

**composite circuit** *noun* ELEC an electronic circuit made up of a number of smaller circuits and components

**composite display** *noun* COMPUT a video display unit that accepts a single composite video signal and can display an infinite number of colours or shades of grey

**composite flower** *noun* BOT ◊ **Compositae**

**composite video** *noun* COMPUT a video signal that combines the colour signals and the monochrome signal into one single signal ○ *Most TV sets and video players expect a composite video feed.* Compare **component video**

**composition** *noun* the make-up or structure of something ○ *the composition of the atmosphere*

**compost** AGRIC *noun* **1.** rotted vegetation, used as fertiliser or mulch **2.** a prepared soil or peat mixture in which plants are grown in horticulture ■ *verb* to encourage the breaking down of organic waste, as in a compost heap

**compost activator** *noun* AGRIC a chemical added to a compost heap to speed up the decomposition of decaying plant matter

**compost heap** *noun* AGRIC a pile of rotting vegetation in the process of forming compost

**composting drum** *noun* AGRIC a cylindrical container in which organic waste is rotted down to make compost

**compound** *adjective* made up of two or more parts or substances ■ *noun* CHEM a substance made up of two or more components

COMMENT: Chemical compounds are stable (i.e. the proportions of the elements in them are always the same) but they can be split into their basic elements by chemical reactions.

**compound document** *noun* COMPUT a document that contains information created by several other applications

**compound eye** *noun* ZOOL an eye made up of a group of identical light-sensitive components (NOTE: This type of eye is found in insects and some crustaceans.)

**compound fertiliser** *noun* AGRIC a fertiliser that supplies two or more nutrients. Also called **mixed fertiliser**. Compare **straight fertiliser**

**compound file** *noun* COMPUT a file that consists of individual files grouped together

**compound lens** *noun* OPTICS a lens which contains more than one glass element (NOTE: A compound lens is more accurate than a single-element one.)

**compound statement** *noun* COMPUT a number of program instructions in one line of program ○ *The debugger cannot handle compound statements.*

**compress** *verb* to squeeze or put pressure on something so that it takes up less space or volume ○ *Use the archiving program to compress the file.*

**compressed video** *noun* a video signal that has been compressed to reduce the data rate required to transmit the information

**compressibility** *noun* the natural ability of a substance to change volume when under varying pressures ○ *In systems using very high pressure, the compressibility of the liquid becomes important.*

**compressible** *adjective* able to be compressed ○ *Air is compressible but water is not.*

**compression** *noun* **1.** the act or instance of putting pressure on something **2.** COMPUT a reduction in the size of a file by encoding the data in a more efficient form

**compression ratio** *noun* COMPUT the ratio of the size of an original uncompressed file to the size of its compressed version

**compression stroke** *noun* ENG the stage of an internal combustion cycle when the fuel–air mixture comes under pressure from the upwards-moving piston

**compression wave** *noun* PHYS a wave which travels through a body in the form of a compression of matter (NOTE: Compression waves are known from earthquakes and seem to form the spiral arms of galaxies.)

**compressive** *adjective* PHYS referring to forces caused by pressure on a surface

**compressive load** *noun* PHYS a load caused by forces acting in opposite directions towards each other ○ *A strut is designed to withstand compressive loads.*

**compressive stress** *noun* PHYS the resistance of something to crushing by two forces acting towards each other along the same straight line

**compressor** *noun* MECH ENG a device such as a pump that compresses air in order to increase its pressure ○ *A shaft connects the turbine to the compressor.*

**comprise** *verb* to be made up of different parts ○ *A simple fuel system comprises a tank, pipes, a filter, a pump and a carburettor.* (NOTE: The preferred use of **comprise** is as a synonym for the verb **consist of**. However it is sometimes used in an opposite sense: *tank, pipes, a filter, a pump and a carburettor comprise the fuel system* and in a passive form: *the fuel system is comprised of a tank, pipes, a pump and a carburettor*)

**Compton effect** *noun* PHYS the decrease in energy and increase in wavelength of a photon after it interacts with an electron

**compulsory** *adjective* forced or ordered by an authority ○ *the compulsory slaughter of infected animals*

**computable** *adjective* MATHS able to be calculated

**computation** *noun* MATHS a calculation

**computational error** *noun* MATHS a mistake made in calculating

**compute** *verb* MATHS to calculate something ○ *Connection charges were computed on an hourly rate.*

**computer** *noun* COMPUT **1.** a machine that receives, stores or processes data according to a stored program **2.** a programming language that consists of commands in binary code which can be directly understood by a central processing unit, without the need for translation

**computer-aided, computer-assisted** *adjective* COMPUT using a computer to make the work easier

**computer-aided design, computer-assisted design** *noun* COMPUT the use of computers and graphics terminals to help a designer in his or her work. Abbreviation **CAD**

**computer-aided engineering, computer-assisted engineering** noun COMPUT the use of a computer to help an engineer solve problems or to calculate design or product specifications. Abbreviation **CAE**

**computer-aided instruction, computer-assisted instruction** noun COMPUT the use of a computer to assist in teaching a subject. Abbreviation **CAI**

**computer-aided learning, computer-assisted learning** noun COMPUT the use of a computer to assist people to learn a subject. Abbreviation **CAL**

**computer-aided manufacture, computer-assisted manufacture** noun COMPUT the use of a computer to control machinery or to assist in a manufacturing process. Abbreviation **CAM**

**computer-aided testing, computer-assisted testing** noun COMPUT the use of a computer to test equipment or programs to find any faults. Abbreviation **CAT**

**computer-aided training, computer-assisted training** noun COMPUT the use of a computer to demonstrate to and assist pupils in learning a skill. Abbreviation **CAT**

**computer animation** noun COMPUT same as **animation**

**computer architecture** noun COMPUT **1.** the layout and interconnection of a computer's internal hardware **2.** the way in which the central processing unit, terminals, printers and network connections of a computer system are arranged

**computer-assisted** adjective COMPUT same as **computer-aided**

**computer conferencing** noun COMPUT the connecting of a number of computers together to allow a group of users to communicate ○ *The multi-user BBS has a computer conferencing facility.*

**computer crime** noun COMPUT theft, fraud or other crimes involving computers

**computer engineer** noun COMPUT a person who maintains, programs or designs computer equipment

**computer fraud** noun COMPUT the theft of data, dishonest use, or other crimes involving computers

**computer-generated** adjective COMPUT produced using a computer ○ *a computer-generated image*

**computer generation** noun COMPUT a stage in the advances in the field of computing

COMMENT: The development of computers has been divided into a series of 'generations'. First generation computers were constructed using valves and had limited storage. Second generation computers had transistors. Third generation computers had integrated circuits. Fourth generation computers have low-cost memory and use integrated circuit (IC) electronics. Fifth generation computers of the future will have very fast processors and large memories and allow human input/output.

**computer illiterate** adjective COMPUT not able to understand the basic principles of computers, related expressions and concepts, and to use computers for programming or applications. ♦ **computer literate**

**computer input microfilm** noun COMPUT microfilm used for computer data storage. Abbreviation **CIM**

**computer-integrated manufacturing** noun COMPUT the coordinated use of computers in every aspect of design and manufacturing. Abbreviation **CIM**

**computerisation** noun COMPUT the act of introducing a computer system or of changing from a manual to a computer system

**computerise** verb COMPUT to change something from a manual system to one using computers ○ *Our stock control has been completely computerised.*

**computerised tomography** noun MED a system for building up a three-dimensional image of the organs inside the body, using a scanning device that takes a number of X-ray photographs at slightly different angles as the scanner rotates

**computer language** noun COMPUT a language formed of figures or characters which is used to communicate with a computer

**computer literate** adjective COMPUT able to understand the basic principles of computers, related expressions and concepts, and to use computers for programming or applications

**computer logic** *noun* COMPUT the way in which the various sections of a computer's hardware are arranged

**computer-managed instruction** *noun* COMPUT the use of a computer to assist people in learning a subject. Abbreviation **CMI**

**computer-managed learning** *noun* COMPUT the use of a computer to teach people and assess their progress. Abbreviation **CML**

**computer network** *noun* COMPUT a number of computers, terminals and peripherals connected together to allow communications between each

**computer numeric control** *noun* COMPUT the control of a machine by a computer. Abbreviation **CNC**

**computer output on microfilm** *noun* COMPUT information output from a computer, stored directly onto microfilm. Abbreviation **COM**

**computer program** *noun* COMPUT a series of instructions to a computer, telling it to do a particular piece of work ○ *to write a computer program*

**computer programmer** *noun* COMPUT a person who writes computer programs

**computer science** *noun* COMPUT the scientific study of computers, the organisation of hardware and the development of software

**computer-telephony integration** *noun* COMPUT a system that allows normal audio telephone conversations to be transmitted over a computer data network and controlled by a computer. Abbreviation **CTI**

**computing** *noun* COMPUT the work done on computers

**computing power** *noun* COMPUT a measure of the speed and ability of a computer to perform calculations

**concatenate** *verb* to join together two or more things in a linked system

**concatenated data set** *noun* COMPUT more than one file or set of data joined together to produce one set

**concave** *adjective* MATHS **1.** curved inwards like the inner surface of a sphere **2.** referring to a polygon with an interior angle greater than 180°

**concentrate** *noun* a strong solution which is to be diluted ○ *orange juice made from concentrate* ■ *verb* **1.** to collect in a particular place rather than spread around ○ *Most of the mass of air is concentrated at the lowest levels of the atmosphere.* **2.** to give attention and thought to something in particular ○ *This chapter concentrates on charts.* **3.** to reduce the volume of a solution and increase its strength by evaporation. Opposite **dilute**

**concentration** *noun* **1.** a collection in a particular place rather than spread around ○ *The maximum concentration of ozone is between 20 and 25 km above the Earth's surface.* **2.** CHEM the amount of a substance in a particular volume or mass of a solution

**concentrator** *noun* COMPUT **1.** a device at the centre of a Token-Ring network which provides a logical star topology in which nodes are connected to the concentrator. Inside the device is a physical ring circuit that connects all the nodes together. **2.** a node which provides access for one or more stations to the network **3.** the device at the centre of a star-topology 10Base-T Ethernet network which receives signals from one port and regenerates them before sending them out to the other ports **4.** a device where all the cables from nodes are interconnected

**concentric** *adjective* having the same centre

**concentric circles** *plural noun* circles of different diameters but with the same centre point

**concept** *noun* an idea or abstract principle

**conception** *noun* BIOL the joining of egg and sperm to form an embryo

**conceptual model** *noun* COMPUT a description of a database or program in terms of the data it contains and its relationships

**concern** *noun* **1.** serious interest ○ *They showed concern for her training and development.* **2.** a worry or problem ○ *safety concerns* ○ *health concerns* □ **a matter for concern** something which must be taken very seriously ■ *verb* to be about something ○ *If there is serious vibration, the operator should shut down the machine concerned.* ○ *The report concerns existing safety regula-*

*tions and makes recommendations for upgrading.*

**concrete** *noun* INDUST a hard stone-like substance made by mixing cement, sand and water and letting it dry

**concrete shield** *noun* INDUST a protective cover made of concrete, e.g. around a nuclear reactor

**concretion** *noun* GEOL the formation of a solid mass of rock from pieces of stones and other sedimentary materials

**concurrency** *noun* COMPUT a resource that is accessed by more than one user or application at a time

**concurrent** *adjective* almost simultaneous ○ *Each concurrent process has its own window.*

**concurrently** *adverb* at almost the same time

**concurrent operating system** *noun* COMPUT an operating system that allows several programs or activities to be processed at the same time

**condensate** *noun* PHYS 1. a substance formed by condensation, e.g. a liquid formed from a vapour 2. a substance that is a gas when occurring naturally underground but becomes liquid when brought to the surface

**condensation** *noun* 1. PHYS the action of making vapour into liquid 2. the water that forms when warm damp air meets a cold surface such as a wall or window

**condensation aerosol** *noun* METEOROL the droplets of moisture that form in warm damp air as it cools, producing mist

**condensation nucleus** *noun* METEOROL a particle on which moisture condenses, forming a raindrop ○ *Moisture readily condenses on an existing surface and sulfate particles are ideal condensation nuclei.* (NOTE: The plural is **condensation nuclei**.)

**condensation pump** *noun* PHYS same as **diffusion pump**

**condensation reaction** *noun* CHEM a reaction between two molecules that creates a by-product of a third molecule, normally water

**condensation theory** *noun* ASTRON the theory that the Moon and the Earth both formed at about the same time, by aggregation of small particles into larger bodies

**condensation trail** *noun* AEROSP a white streak in the sky left by an aircraft flying at high altitude and caused by condensation and freezing of components of its exhaust gases, mainly water

**condense** *verb* 1. to make something compact or more dense 2. PHYS to make a vapour become liquid 3. PHYS (*of a vapour*) to become liquid

**condenser** *noun* a device that cools steam or other vapour and turns it back into liquid

COMMENT: Condensers are used in power stations to turn steam back into water, which goes back to the boilers for re-heating. On a smaller scale, they are used in domestic appliances such as clothes driers and refrigerators. They are also important in the distillation of substances such as alcohol.

**condition** *noun* 1. the present state of something 2. something on which another thing depends □ **on condition that** only if ■ *verb* COMPUT to modify data that is to be transmitted so as to meet set parameters ○ *Condition the raw data to a standard format.*

**conditional** *adjective* COMPUT 1. provided that particular things take place 2. referring to a process which is dependent on the result of another

**conditional branch** *noun* COMPUT same as **conditional jump**

**conditional breakpoint** *noun* COMPUT a breakpoint after which the programmer can jump to one of a number of sections, depending on data or program status

**conditional jump** *noun* COMPUT a programming instruction that provides a jump to a section of a program if a specific condition is met ○ *The conditional jump will select routine one if the response is yes and routine two if no.*

**conditional statement** *noun* COMPUT a program instruction that will redirect program control according to the outcome of an event

**conditional transfer** *noun* COMPUT same as **conditional jump**

**condition code register** *noun* COMPUT a register that contains the state of the central processing unit after the execution of the last instruction

**conditioned reflex** *noun* BIOL an automatic reaction by an animal to a stimulus, learned from past experience

**conditioning** *noun* the act of improving the quality of something

**conditions** *plural noun* variable environmental factors such as temperature and pressure ○ *The behaviour of the gas was observed under standard conditions.* ○ *The conditions in this environment are ideal for rapid plant growth.*

**conducive** *adjective* allowing something to happen more easily ○ *Atmospheric conditions conducive to the formation of ice are detected and these operate a warning system.*

**conduct** *verb* **1.** PHYS to carry out something such as an experiment, survey or review **2.** ELEC to allow an electrical current to flow through a material ○ *to conduct electricity* ○ *Copper conducts well.*

**conductance** *noun* PHYS a measure of the ability of an object to carry electricity (NOTE: This is the reciprocal of resistance.)

**conduction** *noun* PHYS the process by which heat or electricity passes through a substance ○ *Heat is transferred to the layer of air next to the Earth's surface by conduction.*

**conduction band** *noun* PHYS a range of electron energy levels within a semiconductor that allows electrons to flow when an electric field is applied

**conductive** *adjective* PHYS having the ability to allow heat or electricity to pass through ○ *Steel is a conductive material.* ○ *Land masses are less conductive than water.*

**conductivity** *noun* PHYS the ability of a material to heat or electricity ○ *Because of the poor conductivity of air, heat is transferred from the Earth's surface upwards by convection.*

**conductor** *noun* PHYS a substance through which heat or electricity can pass ○ *Water and steel are good conductors.*

**conduit** *noun* **1.** a channel along which a fluid flows **2.** ELEC a pipe or elongated box used to protect electrical cables

**cone** *noun* **1.** MATHS a solid body with a base in the shape of a circle, and with sides that narrow to a point **2.** any object shaped like a cone **3.** ANAT a cell in the retina of the eye which is sensitive to light. ♦ **rod** (NOTE: Cones are sensitive to bright light and colours and do not

function in bad light.) **4.** BOT a hard scaly structure containing the seeds of some plants, particularly conifers

**configuration** *noun* **1.** a pattern or way in which things are arranged **2.** COMPUT the way in which the hardware and software of a computer system are planned and set up

**configure** *verb* COMPUT to select hardware, software and interconnections to make up a special system ○ *This terminal has been configured to display graphics.*

**confine** *verb* to restrict something to a particular area ○ *Cooling is confined to the air in contact with the ground.*

**confined** *adjective* restricted or contained

**confined aquifer** *noun* GEOL an aquifer that has a layer of rock or soil above it

**confined space** *noun* a small space that does not allow free movement

**confirm** *verb* **1.** to agree that something is correct **2.** to repeat something to remove any uncertainty ○ *The increasing airspeed confirms that the aircraft is not in level flight.* ○ *Please confirm your last instruction.*

**confluence** *noun* **1.** EARTH SCI a place where two rivers join **2.** METEOROL a place where two streams of air join

**conform** *verb* **1.** to correspond to required standards ○ *Fuels must conform to strict requirements.* **2.** to do what is required by rules and regulations

**conformation** *noun* CHEM a structural arrangement of the atoms of a molecule, two or more of which may be possible by rotation around a single bond

**congenic** *adjective* GENETICS referring to animal cells that are genetically identical except for the arrangement of genes in a single region (**locus**) of a chromosome

**congenital** *adjective* BIOL existing at or before birth

COMMENT: A congenital condition is not always inherited from a parent through the genes. It may be due to abnormalities that develop in the foetus because of factors such as a disease which the mother has, as in the case of German measles, or a drug that she has taken.

**congenital defect** *noun* MED a defect which exists in a baby from birth

**congested** *adjective* blocked

**congestion** *noun* **1.** the blocking of a tube or a passage **2.** COMPUT a state that occurs when communication or processing demands are greater than the capacity of a system

**conglomerate** *noun* GEOL a sedimentary layer formed of small round stones

**congruent** *adjective* MATHS **1.** referring to two numbers whose difference is exactly divisible by a third number **2.** having identical geometric shapes

**conic** *adjective* based on the shape of a cone

**conical** *adjective* shaped like a cone

**conic projection** *noun* GEOG the standard two-dimensional representation of the Earth

**conic section** *noun* MATHS a shape produced by slicing through a cone at varying angles (NOTE: Conic sections include circles, ellipses, parabolas and hyperbolas.)

**conifer** *noun* BOT an evergreen tree with long thin leaves and fruit in the form of cones

   COMMENT: Conifers are members of the order Coniferales and include pines, firs and spruce. They are natives of the cooler temperate regions, are softwoods and often grow very fast. Their tough leaves are called needles and are resistant to cold and drought. They are frequently used in timber plantations.

**conifer monoculture** *noun* FORESTRY a system of afforestation where only one type of conifer is grown

**coniferous** *adjective* BOT referring to conifers

**coning** *noun* PHYS the effect of a plume of smoke from a chimney in which it widens into the shape of a cone as it leaves the chimney

**conjugated** *adjective* CHEM containing at least two double or triple chemical bonds alternating with single bonds

**conjugation** *noun* **1.** ZOOL a simple form of reproduction in single-celled organisms in which they join together, exchange genetic information and then separate **2.** BIOL in algae and fungi, the fusion of male and female nuclei **3.** CHEM the alternation in a molecule of two or more double or triple bonds with single bonds **4.** GENETICS the distribution of pairs of chromosomes into the four nuclei produced when a parent nucleus divides

**conjunct** *noun* COMPUT one of the variables in a logical AND function

**conjunction** *noun* **1.** COMPUT a logical function whose output is true if all inputs are true **2.** ASTRON the close apparent approach of two objects in the sky as seen from Earth (NOTE: It normally refers to the Sun and another planet.)

**connect** *verb* **1.** to join something or each other together ○ *Batteries are sometimes connected in series.* **2.** COMPUT to link together two points in a circuit or communications network

**connection** *noun* **1.** a point at which things are joined ○ *There is an electrical connection to the battery.* **2.** a link or feature which makes things interdependent ○ *There is a connection between temperature change and altitude.*

**connectionless network protocol** *noun* COMPUT an OSI transport protocol that provides an efficient way of routing information around a local area network using a datagram to carry the information. Abbreviation **CLNP**

**connection-oriented network services** *plural noun* COMPUT an OSI transport protocol that provides an efficient way of routing information around a wide area network. Abbreviation **CONS**

**connective** *noun* COMPUT a symbol between two operands that describes the operation to be performed

**connective tissue** *noun* ANAT the tissue that forms the main part of bones and cartilage, ligaments and tendons, in which a large amount of fibrous material surrounds the tissue cells

**connectivity** *noun* COMPUT the ability of a device to connect with others and transfer information

**connector** *noun* COMPUT a physical device with a number of metal contacts that allow devices to be easily linked together ○ *The connector at the end of the cable will fit any standard serial port.*

**CONS** *abbreviation* COMPUT connection-oriented network services

**consecutive** *adjective* following one another without a break ○ *4, 5 and 6 are three consecutive numbers.*

**consecutively** *adverb* one after the other ○ *The sections of the program run consecutively.*

**consequence** *noun* the result of an action

**consequent** *adjective* resulting ○ *As temperature rises, there will be a consequent increase in the volume of the gas.*

**consequently** *adverb* as a result ○ *He was late, consequently he missed the start of the examination.*

**conservancy** *noun* ENVIRON an official body which protects a part of the environment

**conservation** *noun* ENVIRON **1.** the process of keeping and protecting something from change **2.** the maintenance of environmental quality and resources by the use of ecological knowledge and principles

**conservationist** *noun* ENVIRON a person who promotes or works for conservation

**conservation laws** *plural noun* PHYS a set of laws of physics which state that energy, mass, angular momentum and other physical properties of systems are unvarying

COMMENT: The conservation laws mean that energy is not destroyed by use but merely degraded, and a car that wears out weighs as much as a new one until pieces start to fall off. In systems such as a star or a nuclear power station, matter can be changed into energy, but even then the total amount of both resources is conserved.

**conservation measure** *noun* ENVIRON a way in which environmental quality can be maintained

**conservation of energy** *noun* ENVIRON the process of making consumption of energy more efficient, preventing loss or waste of energy, e.g. by the loss of heat from buildings

**conservation of resources** *noun* ENVIRON the process of managing resources, e.g. fossil fuels and other natural materials, so as not to waste them, damage them or use them too quickly

**conserve** *verb* ENVIRON **1.** to keep and not waste something ○ *The sloth sleeps during the day to conserve energy.* **2.** to look after and keep something in the same state ○ *to conserve tigers' habitat*

**consider** *verb* to think carefully about something ○ *We need to consider the effects on the countryside.*

**considerable** *adjective* great or large ○ *a considerable amount of fuel* ○ *with considerable force*

**consideration** *noun* something important to remember and to think carefully about □ **to take something into consideration** to remember to include something when thinking about something, solving a problem or making a calculation

**consistency check** *noun* COMPUT a check to make sure that objects, data or items conform to their expected formats

**consistent** *adjective* always reacting or behaving in the same way ○ *Human hair responds in a consistent manner to changes in the relative humidity.*

**consist of** *verb* to be made up of something

**console** *noun* COMPUT a unit which allows an operator to communicate with a computer system consisting of an input device such as a keyboard and an output device such as a printer or screen

**consolidate** *verb* to make something more solid or strong

**consolidation** *noun* the process by which something is made more solid or strong

**constant** *noun* MATHS an item of data whose value does not change. Opposite **variable** ■ *adjective* COMPUT not changing ○ *The disk drive motor spins at a constant velocity.* □ **to remain constant** to stay the same ○ *The temperature of the gas remains constant.*

**constant angular velocity** *noun* COMPUT a constant speed of spinning of a CD-ROM. Abbreviation **CAV** (NOTE: The size of each data frame on the disc varies so as to maintain a regular data throughput of one frame per second.)

**constant bit rate** *noun* COMPUT a type of data transfer service that is used to guarantee a specific data transmission rate over a network even if there is a lot of traffic. Abbreviation **CBR**

**constant length field** *noun* COMPUT a data field that always contains the same number of characters

**constant linear velocity** *noun* COMPUT a disk technology in which the disk spins at different speeds according to the track that is being accessed. Abbreviation **CLV**

**constant pressure** noun PHYS pressure which stays the same

**constellation** noun ASTRON **1.** a group of stars that forms a distinct shape and has a name **2.** an area of the sky accepted by astronomers as a unit of the celestial sphere

COMMENT: Many constellations are still called after the familiar objects or mythological figures picked out by ancient astronomers in the patterns made by their prominent stars, an exception being the constellations of the extreme southern hemisphere, which were named in the last few hundred years. The International Astronomical Union now recognises 88 constellations.

**constituent** adjective forming part of a whole ○ the constituent elements of air ■ noun a substance or component which forms part of a whole

**constitute** verb to make up or form something ○ Oxygen and nitrogen together constitute most of the atmosphere.

**constrain** verb **1.** to restrict someone or something **2.** PHYS to set limits that define the maximum movement of an object **3.** MATHS to limit the value of a variable **4.** MATHS to define the maximum or minimum limits of a variable

**constraint** noun something that restricts something else

**constrict** verb **1.** to make something narrower **2.** to make the flow of gas or liquid more difficult by narrowing the passage through which it flows ○ In the carburettor venturi, the flow of air is constricted.

**constriction** noun a narrowing ○ A thermometer has a constriction in the base of the tube between the bulb and the beginning of the scale.

**construct** verb **1.** to put elements or factors together to make something ○ The table on page 4 can be used to construct the estimated time required for this experiment. **2.** to build or develop something ○ to construct a model

**construction** noun **1.** a way of putting things together ○ The basic construction of the lead-acid cell consists of a positive electrode and negative electrode. **2.** the building of something ○ The construction of the prototype took

two years. **3.** something built ○ an elegant construction of steel

**construction industry** noun ENVIRON the business or trade of constructing buildings

**consult** verb to ask an expert for advice ○ He consulted the maintenance manager about the disk fault.

**consultant** noun a specialist who gives advice ○ They called in a computer consultant to advise them on the system design.

**consumable goods** plural noun INDUST products that are used quickly and have to be bought often, e.g. food or stationery

**consumables** plural noun COMPUT small cheap extra items required in the day-to-day running of a computer system, e.g. paper and printer ribbons ○ Put all the printer leads and paper with the other consumables.

**consume** verb **1.** to use up or burn fuel ○ The new pump consumes only half the fuel which a normal pump would use. **2.** to eat foodstuffs ○ The population consumes ten tonnes of foodstuffs per week.

**consumer** noun **1.** a person or company which buys and uses goods and services ○ Gas consumers are protesting at the increase in prices. ○ The factory is a heavy consumer of water. **2.** ZOOL an organism such as an animal that eats other organisms

**consumption** noun **1.** the fact or process of using something as fuel ○ a car with low petrol consumption ○ The country's consumption of wood has fallen by a quarter. ○ Nearly 3% of all food samples were found to be unfit for human consumption through contamination by lead. **2.** BIOL the taking of food or liquid into the body

**consumption residues** plural noun MANUF waste matter left after manufactured goods are used

**contact** noun **1.** a touch ○ Don't allow the part to come into contact with water. □ **in contact with** touching ○ The air in contact with the surface cools. **2.** □ **to be in contact with someone** to be in a position to communicate with someone **3.** a person who can be contacted in order to get something done **4.** ELEC a section of a switch or connector that provides an electrical path when it touches another conductor ○ The circuit *is not working because the contact is dirty.* ■ *verb* to communicate with someone

**contact bounce** *noun* COMPUT same as **bounce**

**contact breaker** *noun* ELEC a mechanically operated switch which is timed to break the primary circuit when maximum current is flowing

**contact herbicide** *noun* AGRIC a substance such as paraquat which kills a plant whose leaves it touches

**contact image sensor** *noun* COMPUT a scanner in which the detectors touch the original, without any lens that might distort the image. Abbreviation **CIS**

**contact insecticide** *noun* AGRIC a substance such as DDT that kills insects which touch it

**contact weedkiller** *noun* AGRIC same as **contact herbicide**

**contagion** *noun* MED the spreading of a disease by touching an infected person, or objects which an infected person has touched. Compare **infection**

**contagious** *adjective* MED referring to a disease which can be transmitted by touching an infected person, or objects which an infected person has touched. Compare **infectious**

**contain** *verb* to hold or have something inside ○ *Most clouds contain some super-cooled water droplets.*

**container** *noun* **1.** a box or bottle which holds something else **2.** TRANSP a large case, with standard measurements, which can be transported by truck and then easily loaded on a ship **3.** COMPUT something that can be set to a value ○ *The programmer uses this variable as a container, storing the object's colour.*

**containment** *noun* **1.** PHYS the preventing of the nuclei and electrons generated in nuclear fusion from reaching the walls of the reaction chamber **2.** MED, ENVIRON the actions taken to stop the spread of something such as disease or contamination

**contaminant** *noun* ENVIRON a substance which causes contamination

**contaminate** *verb* ENVIRON to make something impure by touching it or by adding something to it ○ *Supplies of drinking water were contaminated by refuse from the factory.* ○ *A whole*

*group of tourists fell ill after eating contaminated food.*

**contaminated fuel** *noun* INDUST a fuel which contains an unwanted substance, e.g. water

**contamination** *noun* ENVIRON **1.** the action of making something impure ○ *the contamination of the water supply by runoff from the fields* **2.** the state of something such as water or food which has been contaminated and so is harmful to living organisms ○ *The level of contamination is dropping.*

**content** *noun* **1.** whatever is contained within something (NOTE: This is often expressed as a percentage.) □ **the moisture content of the atmosphere** the amount of water vapour in the air **2.** COMPUT information, ideas, text, images or data that form a letter, document, webpage, database or book

**content-addressable memory, content-addressable storage** *noun* COMPUT same as **associative memory**. abbreviation **CAM**

**contention** *noun* COMPUT a situation that occurs when two or more devices are trying to communicate with the same piece of equipment

**content provider** *noun* COMPUT a company that supplies information such as text, news stories, images, video or software for a publication or for use on a website

**content-rich** *adjective* COMPUT containing a lot of useful information

**contents** *plural noun* **1.** what is inside something ○ *The contents of the bottle poured out onto floor.* ○ *The officials inspected the contents of the box.* □ **the contents of the letter** the words written in the letter **2.** COMPUT a list of items in a file or document

**context-sensitive** *adjective* COMPUT depending on a particular situation

**context-sensitive help** *noun* COMPUT a help message that gives useful information about the particular function or part of the program you are in rather than general information about the whole program

**contig** *noun* GENETICS a continuous series of overlapping cloned DNA segments used to map the physical order of bases along the chromosome from which they were derived

**contiguous** *adjective* COMPUT touching

**contiguous file** *noun* COMPUT a file stored in a series of adjacent disk sectors

**contiguous graphics** *plural noun* COMPUT graphic cells or characters which touch each other ○ *Most display units do not provide contiguous graphics; their characters have a small space on each side to improve legibility.*

**continent** *noun* EARTH SCI one of the seven large landmasses on the Earth's surface (NOTE: The continents are Asia, Africa, North America, South America, Australia, Europe and Antarctica.)

**continental** *adjective* EARTH SCI referring to a continent

**continental climate** *noun* METEOROL a type of climate found in the centre of a large continent away from the sea, with long dry summers, very cold winters and not much rainfall

**continental crust** *noun* EARTH SCI the part of the Earth's crust under the continents and continental shelves, lying above the oceanic crust

**continental drift** *noun* EARTH SCI a geological theory that the present continents were once part of a single landmass and have gradually drifted away from each other over a period of millions of years

**continental margin** *noun* EARTH SCI an area of sea and seabed around a continent, extending to a depth of about 2000 m

**continental shelf** *noun* EARTH SCI a seabed surrounding a continent and covered with shallow water, usually taken to be the area between the shore and the 183 m deep line

**continental slope** *noun* EARTH SCI an area of the seabed which slopes down sharply from the edge of the continental shelf into deeper water

**continental terrace** *noun* EARTH SCI a level part of the Earth's crust including the continental shelf and the lower-lying areas of the continents themselves

**contingency** *noun* something which might happen in the future and therefore must be planned for

**contingency plan** *noun* a plan which will be put into action if something unexpected happens

**contingent valuation method** *noun* ENVIRON a survey-based economic method which is used to determine the monetary value of the benefits or costs of an environmental policy

**continual** *adjective* happening again and again ○ *The continual system breakdowns have slowed down the processing.*

**continually** *adverb* again and again

**continuation** *noun* the act of continuing

**continue** *verb* to go on doing something or to do something which you were doing earlier

**continuity** *noun* **1.** the situation of not stopping or being interrupted **2.** COMPUT a clear conduction path between two points

**continuous** *adjective* **1.** COMPUT with no end or with no breaks **2.** which goes on without stopping

**continuously** *adverb* without stopping ○ *The printer overheated after working continuously for five hours.*

**continuous spectrum** *noun* ASTRON a band of light of differing wavelengths against which dark absorption lines are seen

COMMENT: Stars exhibiting a continuous spectrum are those, like the Sun, where the surface of the star is seen rather than its atmosphere, the absorption lines providing information about the atoms in the atmosphere rather than the surface.

**continuous wave** *noun* PHYS an electromagnetic wave that has constant frequency and amplitude and is not produced in pulses

**continuum** *noun* MATHS a set of real numbers in which there are no gaps (NOTE: There is always an intermediate number between any two numbers in the set.)

**contour** *noun* **1.** the shape of something **2.** EARTH SCI same as **contour line**

**contour farming** *noun* AGRIC a method of cultivating sloping land in which the land is ploughed along a terrace rather than down the slope, so reducing soil erosion

COMMENT: In contour farming, the ridges of earth act as barriers to prevent soil being washed away and the furrows retain the rainwater.

**contouring** *noun* COMPUT a process that converts a wire-frame drawing into a solid-looking object by adding shadows and texture

**contour interval** *noun* GEOG the space between two contour lines on a map

**contour line** *noun* GEOG a line drawn on a map to show ground of the same height above sea level

**contour map** *noun* GEOG a map showing the contours of a geographical area

**contour ploughing** *noun* AGRIC the practice of ploughing across the side of a hill so as to create ridges along the contours of the soil which will hold water and prevent erosion

**contour strip cropping** *noun* AGRIC the planting of different crops in bands along the contours of sloping land so as to prevent soil erosion

**contraception** *noun* HEALTH the intentional prevention of pregnancy by the use of devices, drugs, sexual practices or surgical procedures

**contract** *noun* an agreement ■ *verb* to become smaller in volume or length ○ *Liquids contract as the temperature drops.* Opposite **expand**

**contractile vacuole** *noun* BIOL a membrane-surrounded cavity within a cell that fills with water from the cell and then contracts, expelling the water to the exterior

**contraction** *noun* 1. the decrease in volume of a substance brought about by cooling ○ *Due to contraction, the length of a mercury column shortens.* Opposite **expansion 2.** PHYSIOL a shortening ○ *a muscle contraction*

**contrail** *noun* AEROSP same as **condensation trail**

**contrast** *noun* 1. the degree of difference between light and dark tones ○ *Contrast and colour enable a pilot to identify ground features.* 2. the difference between two things ○ *There is an enormous contrast between the performance of the two aircraft.* □ **in contrast to** when compared with ■ *verb* to examine the differences between two sets of information ○ *The old data were contrasted with the latest information.*

**contrast enhancement filter** *noun* COMPUT a special filter put over a monitor to increase contrast and prevent eye-strain

**contribute** *verb* to give or provide something as part of the whole ○ *Exhaust gases contribute to engine power.* ○ *I contributed a paper to a special issue of the journal.*

**contribution** *noun* something given or provided as part of a whole ○ *The differences in the effect of solar radiation on land and sea make the biggest contribution to weather and climate.*

**contributor** *noun* a person or thing that contributes to something ○ *She was a contributor to the seminar.* ○ *The ozone effect is a major contributor to the division of the lower atmosphere into two layers.*

**control** *noun* 1. the action of directing or working in a specific way □ **to bring** *or* **keep something under control** to make sure that something is well regulated ○ *The authorities brought the epidemic under control.* □ **out of control** unregulated ○ *The epidemic appears to be out of control.* 2. the process of restraining something or keeping something in order 3. (*in experiments*) a sample used as a comparison with the one being tested 4. COMPUT a section of a computer or device which carries out instructions and processes signals 5. a key on a computer keyboard which sends a control character ■ *verb* to make a machine, system or procedure work in a specific way ○ *The purpose of the centrifugal switch is to control the starting and ignition circuits.*

**control block** *noun* COMPUT a reserved area of computer memory that contains control data

**control bus** *noun* COMPUT a set of connections to a microcomputer that carry the control signals between CPU, memory and input/output devices

**control cable** *noun* AVIAT a metal wire linking a pilot's cockpit controls to control surfaces such as the elevators and ailerons

**control character** *noun* COMPUT a special character that provides a control sequence rather than an alphanumeric character

**control computer** *noun* COMPUT a dedicated computer used to control a process or piece of equipment

**control cycle** *noun* COMPUT the events required to retrieve, decode and execute an instruction stored in memory

**control data** *plural noun* data that control the actions of a device

**control driven** *adjective* COMPUT referring to instructions that are executed once a control sequence has been received by a computer

**control field** *noun* COMPUT the storage area for control instructions

**control gene** *noun* GENETICS a gene that regulates the development and specialisation of cells

**control group** *noun* a group of organisms or substances that are not being tested, but whose test data are used as a comparison

**control instruction** *noun* COMPUT a program instruction that controls the actions of a device ○ *The next control instruction will switch to italics.*

**control language** *noun* COMPUT a system of commands that identify and describe the resources required by a job that a computer has to perform

**controlled tipping** *noun* ENVIRON the disposal of waste in special landfill sites (NOTE: The US term is **sanitary landfill**.)

**controller** *noun* **1.** a device which ensures that something operates in the correct way ○ *the propeller speed controller* **2.** a person who manages systems to ensure the smooth operation of procedures **3.** COMPUT a hardware or software device that controls a peripheral such as a printer or monitors and directs data transmission over a local area network

**control memory** *noun* COMPUT a memory that decodes control instructions into microinstructions that operate a computer or microcontroller

**control mode** *noun* COMPUT the state of a device in which control signals can be received to select options or functions

**control panel** *noun* COMPUT **1.** the control switches and status indicators of a main computer system **2.** a utility that displays user-definable options such as keyboard, country code and type of mouse

**control register** *noun* COMPUT the storage location only used for control data

**control rod** *noun* INDUST a rod or cylinder made of or containing a material such as graphite that absorbs neutrons and is used to control the rate of fission in a nuclear reactor

**controls** *plural noun* the manual or automatic devices used to control a machine or system to make it work in a correct way

**control sequence** *noun* COMPUT the codes containing a control character and various arguments, used to carry out a process or change mode in a device

**control signal** *noun* ELECTRONICS an electrical signal transmitted to control the actions of a circuit

**control statement** *noun* COMPUT **1.** a program instruction which directs a program somewhere, e.g. to another branch **2.** a program instruction which directs an electronic central processing unit to provide controlling actions or controls the actions of a central processing unit

**control structure** *noun* COMPUT a set of instructions that are run in a particular circumstance (NOTE: An IF.THEN statement selects a particular control structure depending on the value of a variable.)

**control system** *noun* COMPUT a system used to check that a computer system is working correctly

**control token** *noun* COMPUT a special sequence of bits transmitted over a LAN to provide control actions

**control total** *noun* COMPUT a result of summing specific fields in a computer file to provide error detection

**control transfer** *noun* COMPUT the redirection of the central processing unit when a jump or call instruction is encountered

**control unit** *noun* COMPUT a section of the central processing unit which selects and executes instructions. Abbreviation **CU**

**control word** *noun* a word which defines in a particular process the actions that are to be followed

**convection** *noun* PHYS the process by which hot air rises and cool air descends ○ *Heat is transferred from the Earth's surface upwards largely by convection.*

**convective** *adjective* PHYS referring to something which is affected by the vertical circulation of air

**convective clouds** *plural noun* METEOROL clouds formed as a result of warm moist air rising and condensing at altitude

**convenience** *noun* **1.** ease or comfort in doing something ○ *Reading lights are provided for passengers' convenience.* **2.** ease of understanding ○ *For convenience we will assume that the Earth is round.*

**convenient** *adjective* useful or easy to use ○ *The circular slide rule has a convenient scale for converting weights and volumes.*

**convention** *noun* **1.** an idea or mode of behaviour which, because of long usage, has become normal and accepted ○ *By convention, wind direction is given as the direction from which the wind blows.* **2.** a meeting of large numbers ○ *a convention of environmentalists* **3.** a formal agreement □ **by convention** by general agreement or custom

**conventional** *adjective* usual, accepted and familiar to most people ○ *Every scientist must know the conventional symbols used on charts.*

**conventional fuel** *noun* ENVIRON a traditional means of providing energy such as coal, wood or gas, as opposed to alternative energy sources such as solar power, tidal power or wind power

**conventional medicine** *noun* MED the generally accepted medical practice taught in hospitals and medical schools. Compare **alternative medicine**

**conventional memory** *noun* COMPUT the random access memory region installed in a PC from 0 up to 640 Kb (NOTE: This area of memory can be directly controlled by MS-DOS and it is where most programs are loaded when they are executed.)

**conventional power station** *noun* INDUST a non-nuclear power station

**conventional RAM** *noun* COMPUT same as **conventional memory**

**converge** *verb* to move towards, come together or meet at a point ○ *Meridians converge towards the poles.* Opposite **diverge**

**convergence** *noun* **1.** the movement towards or the act of coming together or meeting at a point ○ *There is convergence of meridians of longitude at the North and South Poles.* **2.** the combination of two or more technologies to pro-

duce a new technology (NOTE: Fax machines are the product of convergence of telephone, scanning and printing technologies.) **3.** COMPUT the accuracy with which the picture beam strikes the three colour dots that form each colour pixel **4.** METEOROL a phenomenon which occurs whenever there is a net inflow of air into a region of the atmosphere, resulting in the accumulation of air and an increase in density. Compare **divergence**

**conversational mode** *noun* COMPUT a computer system that provides immediate responses to a user's input

**converse** *noun* the opposite □ **warm air rises – the converse is also true** in other words, cool air descends ■ *verb* to have a conversation

**conversion** *noun* COMPUT a change from one system to another

**conversion factor** *noun* a formula or figure used for conversion of units, e.g. of temperatures or distances, from one system to another ○ *The conversion factor for converting UK gallons to litres is: x 4.546.*

**convert** *verb* to change something to a different system, set of rules or state ○ *to convert km into nm* ○ *How do you convert degrees C into degrees F?* ○ *Photochemical reactions convert oxygen to ozone.* ○ *He has converted his car to take unleaded petrol.*

**converter** *noun* **1.** a device which alters the form of something ○ *A backup converter converts the alternating current power into direct current.* **2.** COMPUT a device or program which translates data from one form to another ○ *The converter allowed the old data to be used on the new system.*

**convertibility** *noun* the ability to be changed

**convertible** *adjective* easily changed to fit in with a new system or set of standards ○ *The statute mile, unlike the nautical mile, is not readily convertible into terms of angular measurement.*

**convex** *adjective* curved outwards like the outer surface of a sphere or ellipsoid

**convey** *verb* to pass, carry or move something from one place to another ○ *A large number of tubes convey the cooling medium through the matrix.*

**cookie** *noun* COMPUT a tiny file stored on a computer when connected to a remote Internet site using a browser (NOTE: A cookie is used by the remote site to store information about options which can be read when the site is next visited.)

**cool** *adjective* rather cold ■ *verb* to make or become less hot ○ *The airflow is used to cool the oil.*

**coolant** *noun* **1.** CHEM, MECH ENG a substance used to cool something such as an engine **2.** INDUST a substance used to take the heat generated from a nuclear power station to the boilers ○ *Ordinary water is used as coolant in some types of nuclear reactor.*

**cooler** *noun* a device for cooling something ○ *A self-contained system, consisting of an oil tank, pump, filter, cooler, and oil jets, lubricates the auxiliary power unit.*

**cooling** *noun* the action of making something cool ○ *the cooling of the oil by the airflow* ■ *adjective* making cool

**cooling medium** *noun* CHEM a substance which reduces the temperature of another substance or material

**cooling pond** *noun* INDUST **1.** a part of a nuclear reactor where irradiated elements are cooled **2.** a part of an industrial process where water is allowed to cool in the open air

**cooling tower** *noun* INDUST a tall tower for cooling the water used in industrial processes such as at power stations

**cooling water** *noun* the water used to make something less hot, e.g. the irradiated elements from a nuclear reactor or the engine of a machine

**cooperation** *noun* the act of working together in harmony to achieve a common goal

**cooperative processing** *noun* COMPUT a system in which two or more computers in a distributed network can each execute a part of a program or work on a particular set of data

**coordinate** *verb* to organise complex tasks so that they fit together efficiently ○ *She has to coordinate the keyboarding of several parts of a file in six different locations.* ■ *noun* MATHS, NAVIG one of the values used to locate a point on a graph or map

**coordinate bond** *noun* CHEM a chemical bond in which a pair of electrons is shared by two atoms, both of which are supplied by one atom (NOTE: A coordinate bond is a type of covalent bond.)

**Coordinated Universal Time** *noun* the time based on the 24-hour clock system. Abbreviation **UTC** (NOTE: 7 p.m. is **1900 hours**, spoken as: 'nineteen hundred hours')

**coordinate graph** *noun* MATHS a means of displaying one point on a graph, using two values referring to axes which are usually at right angles to each other

**coordinate time** *noun* ASTRON time as measured by an observer far from a source of strong gravitation such as a black hole, providing a framework against which the effects of relativity can be measured

**coordination** *noun* **1.** the bringing together of the various parts of a procedure or plan to ensure that the operation works correctly ○ *A rescue coordination centre was set up to control the emergency.* **2.** PHYSIOL the ability to use different parts of the body together well ○ *A pilot must have good hand/eye coordination.*

**cope** *verb* to manage to do something, often with some difficulty ○ *In heavy rainstorms, the windscreen wipers may not be able to cope.* ○ *The structure must be able to cope with increased loads caused by turning movement.*

**Copernican system** *noun* ASTRON the theory of Nicolaus Copernicus (1479–1543) that the Earth and other planets revolve around the Sun (NOTE: This theory challenged the Ptolemaic system of astronomy that had prevailed since the second century.)

**copper** *noun* CHEM ELEM a metallic trace element, essential to biological life and used in making alloys and in electric wiring (NOTE: The chemical symbol is **Cu**; the atomic number is **29** and the atomic weight is **63.55**.)

**copper chloride** *noun* CHEM a chloride containing copper

**copper ore** *noun* CHEM a mineral containing copper

**copper oxide** *noun* CHEM a red or black powder, insoluble in water. Formula: $Cu_2O$.

**copper sulfate, copper sulphate**
noun CHEM a naturally occurring poisonous blue compound that is white when dehydrated. Formula: $CuSO_4$. (NOTE: It is used in textile dyeing, electroplating, fungicides and wood preservatives.)

**coppice** FORESTRY noun an area of trees which have been cut down to near the ground to allow shoots to grow which are then harvested ■ verb to cut trees down to near the ground to produce strong straight shoots which are then harvested ○ *Coppicing is a traditional method of wood management.* ○ *Coppiced wood can be dried for use in wood-burning stoves.* Compare **pollard**

COMMENT: The best trees for coppicing are those which naturally send up several tall straight stems from a bole, such as willow, alder or poplar. In coppice management, the normal cycle is about five to ten years of growth, after which the stems are cut back. Thick stems are dried and used as fuel, or for making charcoal. Thin stems are used for fencing.

**coprocessor** noun COMPUT an extra, specialised processor such as an array or numerical processor that can work with a main processor to increase execution speed

**copy** noun 1. COMPUT a document or object that looks the same as another 2. a duplicate of an original ○ *Make copies of the report for everyone.* 3. COMPUT a document ■ verb COMPUT to make a second document or object that is like the first ○ *He copied all the files and took them home.*

**copy protect** verb COMPUT to move a switch to prevent copies being made ○ *The program is not copy protected.* ○ *All the disks are copy protected.* ■ noun a switch used to prevent copies of a disk being made

**copy protection** noun the preventing of the making of copies ○ *A hard disk may crash because of faulty copy protection.* ○ *The new product will come without copy protection.*

**copyright** noun a legal right which writers or programmers have allowing them not to have their own work copied without the payment of royalties. ♦ **patent** ■ verb COMPUT to state the copyright of a written work by printing a copyright notice and publishing the work ■ adjective COMPUT covered by the laws of copyright ○ *It is illegal to take copies of a copyright work.*

**Copyright Act** noun an act of Parliament making copyright legal and controlling the copying of copyright material

**copyrighted** adjective legally protected from copying

**copyright infringement** noun the illegal copying of a work which is protected by copyright law

**copyright owner** noun COMPUT a person who owns the copyright in a work

**coral** noun MARINE BIOL a rock-like substance composed of the skeletons of dead polyps

**CORAL** noun COMPUT a computer programming language used in a real-time system. Full form **common real-time applications language**

**coral reef** noun MARINE BIOL a reef formed of coral

**coral sand** noun MARINE BIOL fine white particles which form tropical beaches, not sand at all but tiny pieces of dead coral

**CORBA** noun COMPUT full form of **common object request broker architecture**

**cord** noun ELEC a wire used to connect a device to a socket

**cordite** noun CHEM an explosive made of cellulose nitrate and nitroglycerine

**core** noun 1. the central part of something □ **the core of a problem** the most fundamental part of a problem 2. COMPUT the central conducting section of a cable ○ *The primary windings consist of heavy-gauge wire mounted on a soft iron core.* 3. EARTH SCI the central part of the Earth ○ *The Earth's core is believed to be formed of nickel and iron.* 4. INDUST the central part of a nuclear reactor, where the fuel rods are sited

**core memory** noun COMPUT 1. the central memory of a computer 2. a non-volatile magnetic storage method used in old computers

**core program** noun COMPUT a computer program stored in core memory

**coresident** adjective COMPUT referring to two or more programs stored in main memory at the same time

**core store** *noun* COMPUT same as **core memory**

**Coriolis effect** *noun* PHYS the sideways movement of particles as explained by the Coriolis force

**Coriolis force** *noun* PHYS a force which accelerates movement of a rotating mass perpendicular to its motion and towards the axis of rotation

COMMENT: The Coriolis force acts at a right angle to wind direction and is directly proportional to wind speed. It explains why wind patterns are clockwise in the northern hemisphere and anti-clockwise in the southern hemisphere. It is named after G. G. Coriolis, a French engineer who died in 1843.

**cork** *noun* BOT a protective outer layer that forms part of the bark in woody plants

**cork cambium** *noun* BOT the tissue near the outer surface of a woody plant stem that produces cork

**corm** *noun* BOT a swollen underground plant stem composed of fleshy leaf scales

COMMENT: Crocuses, gladioli and cyclamen have corms, not bulbs.

**corn** *noun* 1. wheat or barley (*informal*) 2. *US* maize

**cornification** *noun* BIOL the filling of skin cells with keratin to form horny tissue such as nails or scales

**corn oil** *noun* FOOD INDUST a vegetable oil obtained from maize grains, used for cooking and as a salad oil

**corolla** *noun* BOT a set of petals in a flower

**corona** *noun* 1. ASTRON the outermost portion of the Sun's atmosphere, extending more than 10 solar radii and maintaining a temperature of 1 000 000° C or more 2. ELEC an electric discharge used to charge the toner within a laser printer 3. BOT a trumpet-shaped, petal-like outgrowth in flowers such as narassi

**coronary artery** *noun* ANAT a blood vessel carrying blood away from the heart

**corona wire** *noun* COMPUT a thin wire that charges the powdered toner particles in a laser printer as they pass across it ○ *If your printouts are smudged, you may have to clean the corona wire.*

**coroutine** *noun* COMPUT a section of a program or procedure that can pass data and control to another coroutine, then halt itself

**corpus callosum** *noun* ZOOL the broad bundle of nerve fibres that connects the two hemispheres of the brain in higher mammals allowing communication between the hemispheres

**corpuscle** *noun* PHYSIOL a cell in the blood, especially a blood cell

**corpus luteum** *noun* ANAT a yellowish mass of tissue that forms after ovulation in the Graafian follicle of the ovary and secretes progesterone

**corrasion** *noun* EARTH SCI the wearing away of rock by material carried by ice, water or wind

**correct** *adjective* without error ■ *verb* 1. to adjust something to a particular standard ○ *corrected to three decimal places* ○ *A servo-motor fitted in the elevator trim system will automatically correct for loads.* 2. to remove mistakes from something

**correction** *noun* 1. the adjustment or changing of something to make it correct 2. an adjustment or change to something to make it correct 3. the use of a mathematical formula for adjusting a known inaccuracy of calculation ○ *In applying this correction the reading is converted to that which would occur at mean sea level.*

**corrective** *adjective* designed to correct something

**corrective action** *noun* action taken to improve something

**correlate** *verb* to compare two measurements in order to form a relationship between the two ○ *Power is measured not by the amount of work done, but by units of accomplishment correlated with time.*

**correlation** *noun* a measurable and predictable relationship ○ *At a given speed, there is a correlation between time and distance.*

**correspond** *verb* 1. to have a direct relationship with or fit with something ○ *Movements of the control surfaces correspond to movements of the pilots' flying controls.* 2. to be similar to something ○ *The ideal conditions to maintain would be those corresponding to sea level.* 3. to write to someone ○ *She cor-*

*responded with several Russian scientists.*

**corrie** *noun* EARTH SCI same as **cirque**

**corrode** *verb* CHEM **1.** to destroy something by a slow chemical process ○ *Turbine fuels tend to corrode the components of the fuel and combustion systems mainly as a result of the sulfur and water content of the fuel.* **2.** to suffer corrosion ○ *Aluminium will not corrode easily.*

**corrosion** *noun* CHEM a process in which the surface of a material, generally a metal, is changed by the action of moisture, air or a chemical

**corrosion protection** *noun* CHEM action taken to prevent corrosion such as rust

**corrosive** *adjective* CHEM causing corrosion ○ *Sulfuric acid is very corrosive.*

**corrupt** COMPUT *adjective* a program or data that contain errors ■ *verb* to introduce errors into data or a program ○ *Power loss during disk access can corrupt the data.*

**cortex** *noun* **1.** BOT the tissue in plants between the outer layer (**epidermis**) and the central core (**stele**) of the stem or root **2.** ANAT an outer layer of tissue in the brain, glands or cells

**corticosteroid** *noun* **1.** BIOCHEM a steroid hormone formed in the adrenal cortex **2.** PHARM a synthetic drug similar to a natural corticosteroid, used to reduce inflammation and allergic reactions

**corticotrophin** *noun* BIOCHEM ◊ **ACTH**

**cortisol** *noun* BIOCHEM a hormone produced in the adrenal glands that helps to control the synthesis of glucose, reduces or prevents inflammation and helps to regulate the way fat is deposited in the body. Also called **hydrocortisone** (NOTE: When used as a medical treatment, it helps control allergies, skin conditions and adrenal failure.)

**cortisone** *noun* BIOCHEM a biologically inactive steroid compound that is converted in the adrenal glands and other tissues to the active hormone cortisol

**corundum** *noun* MINERALS a hard crystalline form of aluminium oxide which has a range of colour forms

**cos** *abbreviation* MATHS cosine

**cosine** *noun* MATHS a trigonometric function defined as the length of the side adjacent to an angle in a right-angled triangle divided by the length of the hypotenuse

**cosmic** *adjective* ASTRON referring to the cosmos

**cosmic dust** *noun* ASTRON the small particles of solid matter found in outer space, often grouped in clouds

**cosmic radiation** *noun* ASTRON same as **cosmic ray**

**cosmic ray** *noun* ASTRON a high-energy particle stream entering Earth's atmosphere from space

COMMENT: Primary cosmic rays are of solar origin and their composition reflects the Sun's own, consisting mainly of neutrons and alpha particles, since the Sun consists mainly of hydrogen and helium. Other cosmic rays appear to come from deep space, especially from supernovae, which accounts for the appearance of heavier nuclei.

**cosmic string** *noun* ASTRON an extremely long thin defect in spacetime, supposedly formed in the instant following the birth of the universe

**cosmogony** *noun* ASTRON the study of the origin of the universe and the larger-scale objects within it, a subdivision of cosmology

**cosmological principle** *noun* ASTRON the theory that, on a very large scale, all the matter in the universe is distributed evenly, so that hypothetical astronomers a long way from the Earth would see the same universe, on the biggest scale, as we do. (NOTE: Observational tests of the principle are difficult to carry out and are complicated by the fact that looking into the universe over different distances also involves looking back over different time periods.)

**cosmology** *noun* ASTRON the study of the universe as a whole, including its structure and long-term development as well as its origins

**cosmos** *noun* ASTRON the whole universe

**cotangent** *noun* MATHS a trigonometric function equal to the length of the side adjacent to the angle divided by that of the side opposite, for a given angle in a right-angled triangle

**cotyledon** *noun* BOT the first leaf of a plant that appears as the seed sprouts, developing from an embryo in a seed

COMMENT: Cotyledons are thicker than normal leaves, and contain food for the growing plant. Plants are divided into two groups, those producing a single cotyledon (monocotyledons) and those producing two cotyledons (dicotyledons).

**coulomb** *noun* ELEC the SI unit of electric charge equal to the amount of electrical charge transported by a current of one ampere in one second. Symbol **C**

**count** *verb* MATHS to make a total of a number of items ■ *noun* the process of totalling a number of items

**counter** *noun* **1.** a device which counts automatically ○ *The loop will repeat itself until the counter reaches 100.* **2.** COMPUT a register or variable whose contents are increased or decreased by a set amount every time an action occurs ○ *The number of items changed are recorded with the counter.* ■ *verb* to work against something to remove the effect of it ○ *Some people find that swallowing hard counters the effects of changes in pressure.*

**counter-** *prefix* against

**counter-rotating ring** *noun* TELECOM the two signal paths transmitted in opposite directions around a ring network

**couple** *noun* two of something □ **a couple of** two or three, or a small number of ■ *verb* **1.** COMPUT to connect or join things together ○ *The auxiliary power unit is a self-contained unit which normally consists of a small gas turbine engine which is coupled to a gearbox.* **2.** to link ○ *Pilot error, coupled with poor weather conditions, resulted in an accident.*

**coupler** *noun* COMPUT a mechanical device used to connect three or more conductors

**coupling** *noun* a joining or connecting component ○ *When not in use, the coupling is sealed by a dust cap.*

**course** *noun* **1.** a formal period of study ○ *a meteorology course* **2.** NAVIG an imaginary line across the surface of the Earth which must be followed in order to arrive at a destination **3.** the set of actions taken in a particular situation ○ *The best course is to wait until we have done the tests.* ○ *What course of action*

do you recommend? **4.** the development of events over a period of time ○ *the usual course of the disease* □ **in the course of** during □ **in the normal course of events** usually **5.** a sequence of medical treatment given over a period of time ○ *a course of antibiotics*

**courseware** *noun* COMPUT software, manuals and videos that make up a training package or CAL product

**covalency** *noun* CHEM the chemical combining power of an atom in which electrons will be shared

**covalent bond** *noun* CHEM a chemical bond between two atoms in which a pair of electrons is shared

**covalent radius** *noun* PHYS the radius of an atom that has a covalent bond

**covariance** *noun* ASTRON the principle that the laws of the universe are everywhere the same

**cover** *verb* **1.** to include the complete extent of a period or a whole area ○ *The restriction covers the period from the 4th to the 8th of July.* □ **the area covered by the forecast** the area that the forecast deals with **2.** to deal with a subject ○ *The subject of central warning systems is covered in the systems book.* **3.** to be completely over something so as to hide what is underneath ○ *The area is covered in snow.* ■ *noun* something that goes over something else completely

**coverage** *noun* the amount of space or time given to a subject or an event ○ *More complete coverage of the one-in-sixty rule is given in the plotting section of these notes.*

**cover crop** *noun* AGRIC **1.** a crop sown to cover the soil and prevent it from drying out and being eroded (NOTE: When the cover crop has served its purpose, it is usually ploughed in, so leguminous plants which are able to enrich the soil are often used as cover crops.) **2.** a crop grown to give protection to another crop that is sown with it ○ *In the tropics, bananas can be used as a cover crop for cocoa.*

**Cowper's gland** *noun* ANAT one of a pair of small glands that lie beneath the prostate in mammals and secrete an alkaline fluid into the urethra just before ejaculation of semen

**cpi** *abbreviation* COMPUT characters per inch

**CPM** *abbreviation* COMPUT critical path method

**cps** *abbreviation* COMPUT characters per second

**CPU** *abbreviation* COMPUT central processing unit

COMMENT: In a file-handling program, CPU time might be minimal, since data retrieval from disk would account for a large part of the program run. In a mathematical program, the CPU time could be much higher in proportion to the total run time.

**CPU bound** *adjective* COMPUT the performance of a computer which is limited by the number of instructions the central processing unit can carry out (NOTE: Effectively, the memory and I/O devices can transfer data faster than the CPU can produce them.)

**CPU clock** *noun* COMPUT a clock inside a processor device which generates a regular signal millions of times every second to control operations and data transfer within the processor

**CPU cycle** *noun* COMPUT a period of time taken to fetch and execute an instruction, used as a measure of computer speed

**CPU element** *noun* COMPUT one of the main sections that make up a CPU, including ALU, control unit, I/O bus, memory and various registers

**CPU time** *noun* COMPUT the total period of time that a central processing unit is used to process instructions

**Cr** *symbol* CHEM ELEM chromium

**CR** *abbreviation* ENVIRON critically endangered

**cracking** *noun* INDUST the process by which crude oil is broken down into light oil

**craft** *noun* **1.** TRANSP a boat for carrying people or goods on water **2.** AEROSP an aircraft or spacecraft for carrying people or goods in the air or in space ○ *An airship is classified as a lighter-than-air craft.* **3.** a practical skill

**cranial nerve** *noun* ANAT one of the paired nerves that emerge directly from the brain to supply muscles and sense organs in the head, neck and viscera (NOTE: There are 12 pairs in mammals, birds and reptiles, and usually 10 pairs in fish and amphibians.)

**cranium** *noun* ANAT the part of the skull of a vertebrate that covers and protects the brain

**crankcase** *noun* MECH ENG the part of an engine that houses the crankshaft and usually the oil pump ○ *oil passages that allow lubricating oil to pass through*

**crankshaft** *noun* MECH ENG the part of a piston engine connecting the pistons, via the connecting rods, to the flywheel and gearbox

**crash** *noun* **1.** a collision **2.** COMPUT a failure of a component or a bug in a program during a run, which halts and prevents further use of the system ■ *verb* **1.** to collide **2.** COMPUT to come to a sudden stop ○ *The disk head has crashed and the data may have been lost.*

**crash-protected** *adjective* COMPUT referring to a computer disk which has a head protection or data corruption protection system ○ *If the disk is crash-protected, you will never lose your data.*

COMMENT: It is sometimes possible to recover data from a crashed hard disk before reformatting, if the crash was caused by a bad sector on the disk rather than contact between the access head and disk surface.

**crater** *noun* EARTH SCI a round depression at the top of a volcano

**crater lake** *noun* EARTH SCI a round lake that forms in a crater

**CRC** *abbreviation* COMPUT cyclic redundancy check

**cream of tartar** *noun* FOOD same as **potassium bitartrate**

**create** *verb* to make or produce something ○ *The velocity and pressure of the exhaust gas create the thrust in the turbojet engine.* ○ *A new file was created on disk to store the document.*

**creatine** *noun* BIOCHEM an amino acid that occurs chiefly as phosphocreatine, an energy storage compound in muscles

**creatinine** *noun* BIOCHEM a substance derived from the breakdown of creatine and found in urine. Formula: $C_4H_7ON_3$.

**creep** *noun* **1.** gradual change **2.** weakening and slow damage to something ○ *Creep is a particular feature of components which are subjected to operation at high temperatures.* **3.** a slight movement of a tyre on a wheel caused by landing ○ *Aligned white marks on the wheel and tyre indicate that there is no* *creep.* **4.** EARTH SCI a slow downhill movement of soil, caused by gravity ■ *verb* to move slowly or without being noticed

**creosote** *noun* CHEM a yellowish brown oily substance with a characteristic smell, derived from wood tar and used as a wood preservative

**crepuscular ray** *noun* METEOROL a separate vertical ray of sunlight which passes through a gap in clouds

**crest** *noun* **1.** EARTH SCI the highest point on the top of an object **2.** the highest point of a hill or mountain ridge

**crevasse** *noun* EARTH SCI a large crack in a glacier

**crevice** *noun* EARTH SCI a crack or little hole in rock

**crippled leapfrog test** *noun* COMPUT a standard leapfrog test that uses a single memory location rather than a changing location

**crisis** *noun* **1.** a time when things are in a very bad state ○ *a crisis caused by drought* **2.** MED a turning point in a disease after which the patient may start to become better or very much worse (NOTE: The plural is **crises**.)

**criterion** *noun* a standard by which something is defined, decided or judged (NOTE: The plural is **criteria**.)

**critical** *adjective* **1.** extremely important ○ *Temperature and oil pressure are critical to any type of system.* **2.** causing an important change ○ *As the angle of attack is increased, it reaches the critical point when the airflow over the upper surface of the wing begins to break down.* **3.** referring to a crisis ○ *critical conditions* **4.** making criticisms ○ *The report was critical of the steps taken to cut down pollution.*

**critical angle** *noun* OPTICS the angle at which a ray of light hits a surface and is completely reflected

**critical error** *noun* COMPUT an error which stops processing or causes a computer to crash

**critical factor** *noun* an extremely important factor which causes a change to occur

**critical load** *noun* ENVIRON the highest level of pollution which will not cause permanent harm to the environment

**critically** *adverb* **1.** in a way that criticises **2.** extremely ○ *critically ill*

**critically endangered** *adjective* ENVIRON referring to a species facing a high risk of becoming extinct, usually taken to be when there are fewer than 50 mature individuals. Abbreviation **CR**

**critical mass** *noun* PHYS the minimum amount of fissile matter that can produce a chain reaction

**critical path method** *noun* COMPUT the use of analysis and projection of each critical step in a large project to help a management team. Abbreviation **CPM**

**critical pH** *noun* CHEM the level of acidity at which a sudden change will occur

**critical point** *noun* PHYS a moment at which a substance undergoes a change in temperature, volume or pressure

**critical temperature** *noun* PHYS the temperature below which a gas will normally become liquid

**critical threshold** *noun* **1.** the point below which something will no longer take place ○ *The population will rapidly reach a critical threshold if steps are not taken to protect it from extinction.* **2.** ENVIRON the point at which a species is likely to become extinct

**criticise** *verb* to say what is wrong with something ○ *The report criticised the safety procedures.*

**Cromagnon** *noun* ANTHROP the earliest known form of modern human being found in Europe during the last Ice Age and dating from around 50 000 to 30 000 years ago

**crop** *noun* **1.** AGRIC a plant grown for food **2.** AGRIC a yield of produce from plants ○ *The tree has produced a heavy crop of apples.* ○ *The first crop was a failure.* ○ *The rice crop has failed.* **3.** ZOOL the bag-shaped part of a bird's throat where food is stored before digestion ■ *verb* **1.** (*of plants*) to produce fruit ○ *a new strain of rice which crops heavily* **2.** PRINTING to reduce the size or margins of an image or to cut out a rectangular section of an image

**crop breeder** *noun* AGRIC a person who specialises in developing new varieties of crops ○ *Crop breeders depend on wild plants to develop new and stronger strains.*

**crop breeding** *noun* AGRIC the developing of new varieties of crops

**crop dusting** *noun* AGRIC the putting of insecticide, herbicide or fungicide, onto crops in the form of a fine dust or spray

**cropland** *noun* AGRIC agricultural land which is used for growing crops

**crop mark** *noun* PRINTING a printed mark which shows the edge of a page or image and allows it to be cut accurately

**crop rotation** *noun* AGRIC a system of cultivation where three crops needing different nutrients are planted in three consecutive growing seasons to prevent the nutrients in the soil being totally used up (NOTE: The land is then allowed to lie fallow for the fourth year.)

**crop sprayer** *noun* AGRIC a machine or aircraft which sprays insecticide, herbicide or fungicide onto crops

**crop spraying** *noun* AGRIC same as **crop dusting**

**cross** *verb* **1.** to breed a plant or animal from two different breeds or varieties ○ *They crossed two strains of rice to produce a new strain which is highly resistant to disease.* **2.** to get from one side of an area to another **3.** (*of lines, roads, etc.*) to go across something or each other at an angle ○ *Meridians intersect at the poles and cross the equator at right angles.* ■ *noun* AGRIC **1.** the breeding of plants or animals from two different breeds or varieties ○ *a cross between two strains of cattle* **2.** a new form of plant or animal bred from two different breeds, varieties or species

**cross-** *prefix* COMPUT running from one side to another

**cross-assembler** *noun* COMPUT an assembler that produces machine-code code for one computer while running on another

**crossbred** *adjective* AGRIC having been bred from two parents with different characteristics ○ *a herd of crossbred sheep*

**crossbreed** AGRIC *noun* an animal bred from two different pure breeds ■ *verb* to produce new breeds of animals by mating animals of different pure breeds

**cross-check** *verb* to verify that something is correct

**cross-compiler** *noun* COMPUT an assembler or compiler that compiles programs for one computer while running on another

COMMENT: Cross-compilers and assemblers are used to compile programs for micros, but are run on larger computers to make the operation faster.

**cross-fertilisation** *noun* BOT the fertilising of one individual plant by another of the same species

**cross-flow turbine** *noun* ENG a turbine in which water flows at right angles to the turbine's axis of rotation

**crosshair** *noun* COMPUT a shape of a cursor that looks like a cross

**crossing-over** *noun* GENETICS the interchange of segments between homologous chromosomes during cell division (**meiosis**), resulting in new combinations of genes and therefore variability in inherited characteristics

**cross-linked files** *plural noun* COMPUT two files which claim to be using the same cluster on a disk, an error in MS-DOS

**crossover** *noun* COMPUT a change from one system to another ○ *The crossover to computerised file indexing was difficult.*

**cross-pollination** *noun* BOT the pollination of a flower with pollen from another plant of the same species. Compare **self-pollination** (NOTE: The pollen goes from the anther of one plant to the stigma of another.)

COMMENT: Cross-pollination, like cross-fertilisation and cross-breeding, avoids inbreeding, which may weaken the species. Some plants are self-fertile (i.e. they are able to fertilise themselves) and do not need pollinators, but most benefit from cross-fertilisation and cross-pollination.

**cross-section** *noun* **1.** a typical representative range ○ *The group included a cross-section of backgrounds and age groups.* **2.** a view of an object seen as if cut through ○ *The diagram is a cross-section of a turbojet engine.* **3.** PHYS a measure of the effective area or size of an atom or nucleus that represents a target for interaction with another particle or radiation prior to fission or ionisation

**crosstalk** *noun* COMPUT interference between two communication cables or channels

**crosswind component** *noun* AVIAT the part of the wind force that acts at an angle to the direction of flight

**crown** *noun* **1.** BOT the top part of a tree where the main growing point is ○ *The disease first affects the lower branches, leaving the crowns still growing.* **2.** DENT a covering for a tooth that is damaged

**crown-of-thorns** *noun* **1.** MARINE BIOL a type of large starfish which lives on coral and destroys reefs **2.** BOT one of various thorny plants

**CRT** *abbreviation* COMPUT cathode ray tube

**crucible** *noun* CHEM a heat-resistant container in which substances are melted or calcined

**crucifer** *noun* BOT a plant such as cabbage whose flowers have four petals. Family: Cruciferae.

**crude** *adjective* **1.** in a natural or original state and not treated or improved in any way ○ *crude results* ○ *crude products* **2.** simple and unsophisticated ○ *a crude timing mechanism*

**crude birth rate** *noun* MED the annual number of live births per 1000 population

**crude death rate** *noun* MED the annual number of deaths per 1000 population

**crude growth rate** *noun* MED the difference between the crude birth rate and the crude death rate

**crude oil** *noun* CHEM oil before it is refined and processed into petrol and other products

**crush** *verb* to compress something with force ○ *Excessive load on the beam may crush the core.*

**crusher** *noun* INDUST a machine for breaking down material such as rock, ore or seed into smaller pieces

**crust** *noun* **1.** a hard top layer **2.** the top layer of the surface of the Earth, which is formed of rock and lies above the asthenosphere

**crustacean** *noun* ZOOL an invertebrate animal with a hard chalky outer shell, several pairs of jointed legs and eyes on stalks. Subphylum: Crustacea. (NOTE: Crabs, lobsters, barnacles and woodlice are all crustaceans.)

**cryogenic memory** *noun* COMPUT a storage medium operating at very low temperatures (4° K) to use the superconductive properties of a material

**cryolite** *noun* MINERALS an uncommon white crystalline fluoride of sodium and aluminium

**cryophilous** *adjective* BOT referring to a plant that needs a spell of cold weather to grow properly

COMMENT: Cryophilous crops need a period of cold weather in order to produce flowers later in the growing period. If such crops do not undergo this cold period, their growth remains vegetative, or they only form abortive flowers with no seeds. Wheat, barley, oats, peas, sugar beet and potatoes are all cryophilous.

**cryosphere** *noun* EARTH SCI the frozen part of the Earth's surface

**cryptic coloration** *noun* ZOOL a pattern of colouring such as the stripes on a zebra which makes an animal less easy to see

**crypto-** *prefix* hidden

**cryptographic algorithm** *noun* COMPUT a set of rules used to encipher and decipher data

**cryptographic key** *noun* COMPUT a number or code that is used with a cipher algorithm to personalise the encryption and decryption of data

**cryptography** *noun* the study of the methods and techniques of encryption and decryption

**crystal** *noun* **1.** CHEM a regular geometric shape formed by minerals, or as water freezes **2.** ELECTRONICS a small slice of quartz crystal which vibrates at a specific frequency, used as a very accurate clock signal for computer or other high-precision timing applications

**crystal lattice** *noun* CHEM the regular array of positions in space that are occupied by the atoms, ions or molecules making up a crystal

**crystalline** *adjective* CHEM formed of crystals

**crystalloid** *adjective* CHEM having a structure, properties or an appearance like a crystal

**crystal shutter printer** *noun* COMPUT a page printer that uses a powerful light controlled by a liquid crystal display to produce an image on a photosensitive drum

**Cs** *symbol* CHEM ELEM caesium

**CS** *abbreviation* ELECTRONICS chip select

**CS gas** *noun* CHEM a gas that causes tears, salivation and painful breathing. Formula: $C_9H_5ClN_2$.

**CSM** *abbreviation* combined symbol matching

**CSMA-CD** *abbreviation* COMPUT carrier sense multiple access-collision detection

**CSS** *abbreviation* COMPUT cascading style sheet

**CT** *abbreviation* MED computerised tomography

**CTI** *abbreviation* COMPUT computer-telephony integration

**CTR** *abbreviation* COMPUT click through rate

**CTS** *abbreviation* COMPUT clear to send

**CT scan** *noun* MED a scan where a narrow X-ray beam, guided by a computer, photographs a thin section of the body or an organ from different angles; the results are fed into the computer which analyses them and produces a picture of a slice of the body or organ. Also called **CAT scan**

**Cu** *symbol* CHEM ELEM copper

**CU** *abbreviation* COMPUT control unit

**cubic centimetre, cubic foot, cubic inch, cubic metre, cubic yard** *noun* MEASURE the volume of a cube whose edge measures one centimetre, foot, inch, metre or yard, respectively

**cuesta** *noun* EARTH SCI a ridge that has both scarp and dip slopes

**CUG** *noun* COMPUT restricted access to a database or bulletin board system on a specific topic or subject to known and registered users, usually by means of a password. Full form **closed user group**

**cull** *verb* **1.** to reduce the numbers of something **2.** COMPUT to remove hidden or distant objects from a three-dimensional scene or storage space, reducing processing time

**culm** *noun* **1.** BOT a stem of a grass which bears flowers **2.** INDUST a type of waste from an anthracite processing plant

**cultivable acreage** *noun* AGRIC the number of acres on which crops can be grown

**cultivar** *noun* AGRIC a variety of a plant that has been developed under cultivation and that does not occur naturally in the wild

**cultivate** *verb* AGRIC **1.** to grow crops ○ *Bananas are cultivated as the main crop.* **2.** to dig and manure the soil ready for growing crops ○ *The fields are cultivated in the spring, ready for sowing corn.*

**cultivated land** *noun* AGRIC land that has been dug or prepared for growing crops

**cultivation** *noun* AGRIC the action of cultivating land or plants □ **to take land out of cultivation** to stop cultivating land or growing crops on it and allow it to lie fallow

**cultivator** *noun* AGRIC **1.** a person who cultivates land **2.** an instrument or small machine for cultivating small areas of land

**culture** BIOL *noun* a microorganism or tissues grown in a culture medium ■ *verb* to grow a microorganism or tissue in a culture medium

**cultured** *adjective* BIOL grown in a nutrient substance (**culture medium**)

**culture medium** *noun* BIOL an agar, liquid or gel on which a microorganism or tissue can be grown

**culvert** *noun* ENG a covered drain for waste water

**cumuliform** *adjective* METEOROL (*of clouds*) developing vertically ○ *cumuliform clouds such as cumulonimbus*

**cumulonimbus** *noun* METEOROL a dark low cumulus cloud associated with thunderstorms ○ *A cumulonimbus has a characteristic anvil shape.* Abbreviation **CB**

**cumulus** *noun* METEOROL a quantity of big, fluffy, white or grey clouds heaped or piled up, which develop at low altitude ○ *Grey cumulus often develop into cumulonimbus.* ○ *Cumulus clouds may develop because of thermal activity resulting from the warming of the surface.*

**cuprite** *noun* MINERALS a reddish-brown or black copper oxide ore

**curie** *noun* MEASURE a former unit of measurement of radioactivity, now replaced by the becquerel ○ *Discharges of more than 20 curies per year are not permitted.* Symbol **Ci**

**Curie point** *noun* PHYS the temperature at which there is a change in the magnetic properties of a substance such as iron

**Curie's law** *noun* PHYS the physical law that the effect of a magnetic field on a paramagnetic material is inversely proportional to its absolute temperature

**curium** *noun* CHEM ELEM a silvery-white metallic radioactive element in the actinide group artificially produced from plutonium (NOTE: The chemical symbol is **Cm**; the atomic number is **96** and the atomic weight is **247**.)

**curly brackets** *noun* COMPUT a pair of symbols, {}, used in some programming languages to enclose a routine

**current** *adjective* COMPUT referring to the present time ■ *noun* **1.** ELEC a movement of charge-carrying particles in a conductor **2.** PHYS a flow of water, air or electricity ○ *Dangerous currents make fishing difficult near the coast.* ○ *A warm westerly current of air is blowing across the country.* **3.** COMPUT a thicker line surrounding the border of a spreadsheet cell that is being edited

COMMENT: Mains electricity provides a 240 v AC supply at 50 Hz in the UK and 120 v at 60 Hz in the USA.

**current directory** *noun* COMPUT a directory within the directory tree which is currently being used

**current instruction register** *noun* COMPUT a register of a central processing unit that stores the instruction that is currently being executed. Abbreviation **CIR**

**cursor** *noun* COMPUT a marker on a display device which shows where the next character will appear

COMMENT: Cursors can take several forms, e.g. a square of bright light, a bright underline or a flashing light.

**cursor control key** *noun* COMPUT one of the keys on a keyboard which allow the cursor to be moved in different directions

**curvature** *noun* a degree of curving or roundness

**curvature of space** *noun* a property of space whereby, over large distances, it appears to obey the laws of spherical rather than plane geometry in terms of gravitation, the transmission of radiation and other effects

COMMENT: The curvature of space is predicted by the general theory of relativity, and it implies, e.g., that two lines cannot be parallel over cosmically large distances – or precisely parallel over shorter ones. Space-time curves so gradually that experiments to discover the size and direction of the curvature are almost impossible to devise.

**curve** *noun* a smoothly bending line, as on a graph

**cusp** *noun* **1.** DENT a ridge or projection on the grinding surface of a molar tooth **2.** ANAT a flap or fold of tissue that forms part of a valve in the heart, veins or lymph vessels **3.** MATHS the point where two arcs of a curve meet

**cuspate foreland** *noun* EARTH SCI a large triangular area of coastal deposition

**cut** *noun* **1.** COMPUT the removal of a piece from a file **2.** a piece removed from a file ■ *verb* COMPUT to remove sections of text from a file to make it shorter

**cut and paste** *noun* COMPUT the action of taking a section of text or data from one point and inserting it at another, often used in word-processors and DTP packages for easy page editing

**cuticle** *noun* **1.** BOT a thin waxy protective layer on plants **2.** ZOOL the epidermis, the outer layer of skin in animals

**cutin** *noun* BIOCHEM a network of fatty-acid polymers that forms the main component of the cuticle of plants

**cut sheet feeder** *noun* COMPUT a mechanism that automatically feeds single sheets of paper into a printer

**cutting** *noun* BOT a small piece of a plant used for propagation

COMMENT: Taking cuttings is a frequently used method of propagation which ensures that the new plant is an exact clone of the one from which the cutting was taken.

**cwm** *noun* EARTH SCI ◊ **cirque**

**cyan** *noun* COLOURS a primary blue colour

**cyanamide** *noun* CHEM a white crystalline unstable compound. Formula: $NH_2CN$.

**cyanide** *noun* CHEM a salt of hydrocyanic acid

**cyan-magenta-yellow-black** *noun* COMPUT full form of **CMYK**

**cyano-** *prefix* COLOURS blue

**cyanobacterium** *noun* MICROBIOL a bacterium of a large group that carry out photosynthesis. Family: Cyanophyta. (NOTE: Formerly classified as blue-green algae.)

**cyanocobalamin** *noun* BIOCHEM vitamin $B_{12}$

**cybernetics** *noun* COMPUT the study of the mechanics of human or electronic machine movements and the way in which electronic devices can be made to work and imitate human actions

**cyberspace** *noun* COMPUT the world in which computers and people interact, normally via the Internet

**cybersquatting** *noun* COMPUT an act by which someone registers a website address, normally a trademark or brand name, then tries to sell the name to the rightful owner (NOTE: Although this is not yet illegal in most countries, court cases almost always find in favour of the company trying to recover its name.)

**cycle** *noun* **1.** a series of actions which end at the same point as they begin ○ *With the piston engine, the cycle is intermittent, whereas in the gas turbine, each process is continuous.* **2.** a period of time when something leaves its original position and then returns to it **3.** one completed operation in a repeated process **4.** a series of events which recur regularly ○ *Industrial waste upsets the natural nutrient cycle.* ■ *verb* to repeat an operation or series of instructions until instructed to stop

**cycle availability** *noun* COMPUT a period of time in a cycle during which data can be accessed or transmitted

**cycle stealing** *noun* COMPUT a memory access operation by a peripheral that halts a central processing unit for one or more clock cycles while data are being transferred from memory to the device

**cyclic access** *noun* COMPUT access to stored information that can only occur at a specific point in a cycle

**cyclical** *adjective* occurring in cycles ○ *Off-shore and on-shore wind patterns are cyclical.*

**cyclic check** *noun* COMPUT an error detection method that uses or examines a bit of data every n bits (NOTE: One bit examined then n bits transmitted, then another bit is examined.)

**cyclic code** *noun* MATHS a coding system in which the binary representation of decimal numbers changes by only one bit at a time from one number to the next

**cyclic decimal code** *noun* MATHS a cyclic code that refers to decimal digits

**cyclic redundancy check** *noun* COMPUT an error detection code for transmitted data. Abbreviation **CRC**

**cyclo-** *prefix* cyclic

**cyclone** *noun* **1.** METEOROL an area of low pressure around which the air turns in the same direction as the Earth. ♦ **anticyclone 2.** INDUST a device which removes solid particles from waste gases produced during industrial processes

**cyclothymia** *noun* PSYCHIAT a mild form of bipolar disorder in which the patient suffers from alternating depression and excitement

**cyclotron** *noun* PHYS a circular particle accelerator in which charged particles are confined inside a vertical magnetic field and speeded up by an alternating high-frequency current

**cylinder** *noun* **1.** MATHS a solid tube shape formed by joining corresponding points on two parallel circles with straight lines **2.** MECH ENG a device shaped like a tube, in which a piston moves ○ *a static hydraulic system with a master cylinder and individual brake cylinders at each wheel* **3.** COMPUT the tracks in a multi-disk device that can be accessed without moving the read/write head

**cylinder block** *noun* MECH ENG a casing containing the cylinders in an internal-combustion engine

**cylinder capacity** *noun* MECH ENG the total volume of a reciprocating engine's cylinders, expressed in litres, cubic centimetres or cubic inches

**cylinder head** *noun* MECH ENG a removable top part of a piston engine cylinder containing plugs, inlet and exhaust connections and valves

**cylindrical** *adjective* with the shape of a cylinder

**cypher** *noun* COMPUT another spelling of **cipher**

**cyto-** *prefix* BIOL cell

**cytochemistry** *noun* BIOCHEM the study of the chemical activity of living cells

**cytochrome** *noun* BIOCHEM an iron-containing protein, several types of which are crucial to cell respiration

**cytogenetics** *noun* BIOL a branch of genetics which studies the structure and function of cells, especially chromosomes

**cytokinesis** *noun* BIOL the changes in the cytoplasm of a cell that occur during cell division

**cytokinin** *noun* BOT a plant growth factor, of a group derived from adenine, that stimulates cell division and delays senescence

**cytology** *noun* BIOL the study of the structure and function of cells

**cytolysis** *noun* BIOL the breaking down of cells

**cytoplasm** *noun* BIOL a jelly-like substance inside the cell membrane which surrounds the nucleus of a cell

**cytoplasmic** *adjective* BIOL referring to the cytoplasm of a cell

**cytoplasmic inheritance** *noun* GENETICS the inheritance from a female parent of genes that are found in organelles such as mitochondria and chloroplasts in the cell cytoplasm (NOTE: This type of inheritance is not controlled by Mendel's laws.)

**cytosine** *noun* BIOCHEM one of the four basic components of DNA

**cytotoxic** *adjective* IMMUNOL harmful or fatal to living cells (NOTE: Cells that kill other cells as part of the immune response are described as cytotoxic.)

**cytotoxin** *noun* BIOL a substance which has a toxic effect on living cells

# D

**D** *symbol* MATHS the hexadecimal figure equivalent to decimal number 13

**DAC** *abbreviation* COMPUT digital to analog converter ○ *Speech is output from the computer via a DAC.*

COMMENT: A DAC allows the computer to work outside the computer's environment, controlling machines, producing sound or speech, etc. An ADC allows real-world signals to be processed by a computer.

**D/A converter** *noun* COMPUT same as **digital to analog converter**

**daemon** *noun* COMPUT a utility program that performs its job automatically without the knowledge of the user

**daisy chain** *noun* COMPUT a method of connecting equipment with a single cable passing from one machine or device to the next rather than having separate cables to each device

**Dalton's law** *noun* PHYS the principle that the total pressure exerted by two or more mixed gases in a given volume is equal to the sum of the pressures that each would exert if it was occupying the same volume alone

**dam** *noun* ENG a construction built to block a river in order to channel the flow of water into a hydroelectric power station or to regulate the water supply to an irrigation scheme

**DAMA** *abbreviation* COMPUT demand assigned multiple access

**damage** *noun* harm done to something ■ *verb* COMPUT to harm something ○ *The faulty read/write head appears to have damaged the disks.* ○ *The wind and rain damaged the barley crop.*

**damaged** *adjective* having suffered damage ○ *Is it possible to repair the damaged files?*

**damage tolerance** *noun* the ability of a material or structure to withstand or resist damage ○ *The structural effi-*

ciency of bonded and machined structure is not achieved at the expense of damage tolerance.

**damp** *adjective* slightly wet ■ *noun* a slight wetness

**dampen** *verb* **1.** to make something slightly wet **2.** to decrease or reduce something ○ *An accumulator is fitted to store hydraulic fluid under pressure and dampen pressure fluctuations.*

**damper** *noun* a device to decrease or reduce something ○ *A yaw damper is used for rudder control.*

**damping** *noun* INDUST the closing down of a blast furnace by cutting off the air supply

**damp off** *verb* BOT to die from a fungus infection which spreads in warm damp conditions and attacks the roots and lower stems of seedlings

COMMENT: Damping off is a common cause of loss of material in greenhouses.

**dark adaptation** *noun* PHYSIOL the changes that occur in the eye in response to reduction in light conditions. Compare **light adaptation**

**dark energy** *noun* ASTRON a hypothetical force that opposes gravity throughout the universe and accelerates the expansion of the universe

**dark fibre** *noun* COMPUT an optical fibre that is not carrying a signal, especially a fibre-optic cable that has just been installed but has not yet been used

**dark matter** *noun* ASTRON material in the universe which cannot be observed directly

COMMENT: The rotational velocity of stars around the centres of galaxies reveals that they contain more material than can be observed directly. Many types of material, including small planet-sized objects of normal matter as well as concentrations of material unknown on Earth, have been proposed as possible solutions to the missing mass problem, whose solution is vital to such large problems as working out whether the universe will continue to expand indefinitely.

**dark star** *noun* ASTRON a star that is detectable only by its radio or infrared emissions or by its gravitational effect on other astronomical objects (NOTE: It is often a component of a binary star and can cause the brightness of its visible partner to vary periodically.)

**darmstadtium** *noun* CHEM ELEM an artificially produced chemical element (NOTE: The chemical symbol is **Ds**; the atomic number is **110** and the atomic weight is **269**.)

**Darrius Rotator** *noun* ENG a type of vertical-axis wind turbine that uses thin blades

**Darwin, Charles (1809–92)** a scientist best known for his theory of evolution proposed in *On the Origin of Species* that described how species gradually change and evolve to succeed in their environment

**Darwinian fitness** *noun* BIOL a measure of the success of organisms at passing on their genes to subsequent generations

**Darwinism, Darwinian theory** *noun* BIOL the theory of evolution, formulated by Charles Darwin (1809–82), which states that species of organisms arose by natural selection. ♦ **neo-Darwinism**

**DASD** *abbreviation* COMPUT direct access storage device

**DAT** *abbreviation* COMPUT digital audio tape

**data** *plural noun* COMPUT numbers, characters and symbols stored on a computer in such a way that they can be processed by the computer ○ *Data are input at one of several workstations.* ○ *The company stores data on customers in its main computer file.* ○ *Programs act upon data files.*

COMMENT: Data are different from information in that they are facts stored in machine-readable form. When the facts are processed by the computer into a form that can be understood by people, the data become information.

**data acquisition** *noun* COMPUT the gathering of data about a subject

**data analysis** *noun* COMPUT the extraction of information and results from data

**databank** *noun* COMPUT **1.** a large amount of data stored in a structured form **2.** a set of personal records stored in a computer

**database** *noun* COMPUT an integrated collection of files of data stored in a structured form in a large memory, which can be accessed by one or more users at different terminals

**database administrator** *noun* COMPUT a person in charge of running and maintaining a database system. Abbreviation **DBA**

**database engine** *noun* COMPUT a program that provides an interface between a program written to access the functions of a database management system and the system itself

**database language** *noun* COMPUT a set of languages such as data description language that make up a database management system

**database management system** *noun* COMPUT a series of programs that allow the user to create and modify databases easily. Abbreviation **DBMS**

**database schema** *noun* COMPUT the way in which a database is organised and structured

**database server** *noun* COMPUT a piece of database management software that runs on a server computer on a network and is used in a client-server system (NOTE: The user works with client software that formats and displays data that are retrieved by the server software.)

**data block** *noun* COMPUT all the data required for or from a process

**data buffer** *noun* COMPUT a temporary storage location for data received by a device that is not yet ready to process it

**data bus** *noun* COMPUT a bus carrying data between a central processing unit and memory and peripheral devices

**data capture** *noun* COMPUT the act of obtaining data by keyboarding, scanning or automatic means from a recording device or peripheral

**data carrier detect** *noun* COMPUT a signal from a modem to a computer, indicating that a carrier wave is being received ○ *The call is stopped if the* software does not receive a data carrier detect from the modem. Abbreviation **DCD**

**data channel** *noun* COMPUT a communications link able to carry data signals

**data check** *noun* COMPUT an error in reading data due to a fault in the magnetic medium

**data communications** *plural noun* TELECOM the transmission and reception of data rather than speech or images

**data communications equipment** *noun* TELECOM equipment such as a modem which receives or transmits data. Abbreviation **DCE**

**data compacting** *noun* COMPUT the reduction of the space taken by data by coding them in a more efficient way ○ *All the files were stored on one disk with this new data compacting routine.*

**data compression** *noun* COMPUT the means of reducing the size of blocks of data by removing spaces, empty sections and unused material

**data concentrator** *noun* COMPUT a means of combining intermittent data from various lines and sending them along a single line in one go

**data corruption** *noun* COMPUT the introduction of errors into data, due to noise or faulty equipment ○ *Acoustic couplers suffer from data corruption more than the direct connect form of modem.* ○ *Data corruption on the disk has made one file unreadable.*

**data delimiter** *noun* COMPUT a special symbol or character that marks the end of a file or data item

**data description language** *noun* COMPUT a part of database system software that describes the structure of the system and data. Abbreviation **DDL**

**data dictionary** *noun* COMPUT a file or piece of software that lists the structure and types of data used in a database

**data dictionary/directory** *noun* COMPUT full form of **DD/D**

**data-driven** *adjective* COMPUT referring to instructions that are executed once the relevant data have been received by a computer

**data encryption standard** *noun* COMPUT a standard developed by the US government for a high-security block data cipher system. Abbreviation **DES**

**data entry** *noun* COMPUT a method of entering data into a system usually using a keyboard but also direct from disks after data preparation

**data flowchart** *noun* COMPUT a diagram used to describe a computer or data processing system ○ *The data flowchart allowed us to improve throughput, by using a better structure.*

**datagram** *noun* COMPUT a packet of information in a packet switching system that contains its destination address and route

**data hierarchy** *noun* COMPUT a data structure organised hierarchically

**data input bus** *noun* COMPUT a bus used when transferring data from one section of a computer to another, e.g. between memory and CPU. Abbreviation **DIB**

**data integrity** *noun* COMPUT the state of data which has not been corrupted by damage or errors

**data interchange format** *noun* COMPUT a standard method of storing spreadsheet formulae and data in a file. Abbreviation **DIF**

**data item** *noun* COMPUT one unit of data, e.g. the quantity of items in stock, a person's name, age or occupation

**data link** *noun* COMPUT a connection between two devices to allow the transmission of data

**data link layer** *noun* COMPUT a second layer in the ISO/OSI defined network that sends packets of data to the next link and deals with error correction (NOTE: This layer is normally split into two further sub-layers: medium access control and logical link control.)

**data manipulation language** *noun* COMPUT a form of database software that allows the user to access, store and change data. Abbreviation **DML**

**dataplex** *noun* COMPUT a method of multiplexing a combination of data signals

**data processing** *noun* COMPUT the selection and operation of data to produce useful information. Abbreviation **DP**

**data protection** *noun* the act of making sure that data are not copied by an unauthorised user

**Data Protection Act** *noun* COMPUT a piece of legislation passed in 1984 in the UK that means any owner of a database that contains personal details must register with the government agency and cannot use the data for purposes other than its original use without the permission of the people on the list. It also allows an individual to request a copy of the information stored about them in the list.

**data record** *noun* COMPUT a record containing data for use with a program

**data register** *noun* COMPUT an area within a central processing unit used to store data temporarily before it is processed ○ *In this small micro, the data register is eight bits wide, an address register is sixteen bits wide.*

**data set ready** *noun* COMPUT a signal from a device that is ready to accept data, occurring after a DTR signal is received. Abbreviation **DSR**

**data sink** *noun* COMPUT a device in a data terminal that receives data

**data source** *noun* COMPUT a device in a data terminal that sends data

**data structure** *noun* COMPUT a number of related items that are treated as one by the computer (NOTE: In an address book record, the name, address and telephone number form separate entries which would be processed as one by the computer.)

**data terminal** *noun* COMPUT a device that is able to display and transmit or receive data ○ *A printer is a data terminal for computer output.*

**data terminal equipment** *noun* COMPUT a device at which a communications path starts or finishes. Abbreviation **DTE**

**data terminal ready** *noun* COMPUT a signal from a device that indicates that it is ready to send data. Abbreviation **DTR**

**data word** *noun* COMPUT a piece of data stored as a single word

**data word length** *noun* COMPUT a number of bits that make up a word in a computer

**date** *noun* a day, month and year ○ *I have received your message of yesterday's date.* ○ *The date of creation for the file was the 10th June 1994.* □ **to bring something up to date** to add the latest information to something □ **to keep something up to date** to keep adding information to something so that it is always up to date ○ *We spend a lot*

of time keeping our files up to date.* ■ *verb* COMPUT to put a date on a document

**dative bond** *noun* CHEM same as **coordinate bond**

**datum** *noun* a reference or base point of a scale or measurement

**daughter board** *noun* COMPUT an add-on board that connects to a system motherboard

**daughter cell** *noun* BIOL one of the cells that develop by mitosis from a single parent cell

**Dawes' limit** *noun* ASTRON the theoretical limit to the resolving power of a telescope, equal to 2/1000 times the wavelength of light in angstrom divided by the telescope aperture in centimetres, for a result in arc seconds

**daylight** *noun* TIME the light of the sun during the day

**dB** *abbreviation* MEASURE, ACOUSTICS decibel

**Db** *symbol* CHEM ELEM dubnium

**DBA** *abbreviation* COMPUT database administrator

**DBMS** *abbreviation* COMPUT database management system

**DC** *abbreviation* ELEC direct current

**DCA** *abbreviation* COMPUT document content architecture

**DCD** *abbreviation* COMPUT data carrier detect

**DCE** *abbreviation* COMPUT data communications equipment

**DCOM** *noun* COMPUT an enhanced version of the COM specification that allows applications to access objects over a network or over the Internet. Full form **distributed component object model**

**DCT** *abbreviation* COMPUT discrete cosine transform

**DD** *abbreviation* COMPUT double density

**DDC** *abbreviation* COMPUT direct digital control

**DD/D** *noun* COMPUT the software that gives a list of types and forms of data contained in a database. Full form **data dictionary/directory**

**DDE** *abbreviation* COMPUT **1.** direct data entry **2.** dynamic data exchange

**DDL** *abbreviation* COMPUT data description language

**DDP** *abbreviation* COMPUT distributed data processing

**DDR memory** *noun* COMPUT the set of electronic memory components that are used for RAM storage in computers and peripherals. Full form **double data rate memory**

**DDT** *noun* CHEM an insecticide used especially against malaria-carrying mosquitoes, now banned in many countries because of its toxicity and ability to accumulate in the environment. Formula: $C_{14}H_9Cl_5$. Full form **dichlorodiphenyltrichloroethane**

**de-** *prefix* to undo, remove or stop

**deactivate** *verb* to turn off a system or a piece of equipment, stopping it from being ready to operate ○ *On some aircraft, nose wheel steering must be de-activated before retraction.*

**dead** *adjective* **1.** BIOL not alive **2.** COMPUT not functioning at all

**deaden** *verb* to make a sound or colour less sharp ○ *Acoustic hoods are used to deaden the noise of printers.*

**dead halt** *noun* COMPUT a program instruction from the user or an error that causes the program to stop without allowing recovery

**dead key** *noun* COMPUT one of the keys on a keyboard that cause a function rather than a character to occur

**deadlock** *noun* COMPUT a situation that occurs when two users want to access two resources at the same time, in which one resource is assigned to each user but neither can use the other

**dead time** *noun* a period between two events, in which nothing happens, to ensure that they do not interfere with each other ○ *Efficient job management minimises dead time.*

**de-aerate** *verb* CHEM to remove gas, especially carbon dioxide or air, from a liquid such as fuel ○ *The pump helps to de-aerate the fuel before it enters the engine.*

**de-aerator** *noun* CHEM a device to remove gas from a liquid

**de-aerator tray** *noun* INDUST a device in a lubrication system to remove air bubbles from oil

**deal** *verb* to handle or manage something ○ *A computer can deal with the*

constant inputs required to control an unstable aircraft.

**deallocate** *verb* COMPUT to free resources previously allocated to a job, process or peripheral ○ *When a reset button is pressed all resources are deallocated.*

**deamination** *noun* PHYSIOL the removal of unwanted amino acids by the liver

**death** *noun* PHYSIOL the act of dying

**death rate** *noun* BIOL the number of deaths per year, shown per 1000 of the population ○ *a death rate of 15 per 1000* ○ *an increase in the death rate*

**debacle** *noun* EARTH SCI the breaking up of ice on a large river as it melts in spring

**debit** *noun* COMPUT a bit transmission rate that is twice the baud rate

**de-bounce** *noun* COMPUT the prevention of a single touch on a key giving multiple key contact

**debris** *noun* rubbish or waste matter ○ *volcanic debris from the eruption* ○ *Check that the area is free of stones and other debris.*

**debris flow** *noun* a landslide or mudslide of waste matter, as on a spoil heap

**de Broglie wavelength** *noun* PHYS the wavelength associated with the motion of an atomic or subatomic particle, given by Planck's constant divided by the mass and velocity of the particle (NOTE: The de Broglie wave can give rise to diffraction.)

**debug** *verb* COMPUT to test a program and locate and correct any faults or errors ○ *They spent weeks debugging the system.*

**Debye-Huckel theory** *noun* CHEM the theory that defines the behaviour of electrolytes

**decay** *noun* **1.** BIOL a process by which tissues become rotten, caused by the action of microbes and oxygen **2.** BIOL the formation of dental caries in teeth **3.** ACOUSTICS the process of a sound signal fading away ○ *With a short decay, it sounds very sharp.* ■ *verb* **1.** BIOL (*of organic matter*) to rot **2.** CHEM (*of radioactive matter*) to disintegrate

**decelerate** *verb* to slow down. Opposite **accelerate**

**deceleration** *noun* the process of slowing down ○ *Anti-skid braking systems units are designed to prevent the brakes locking the wheels during landing, thus reducing the possibility of wheel skid caused by the sudden deceleration of the wheel.*

**deceleration parameter** *noun* ASTRON a theory of the slowing down of the expansion of the universe, which may lead to a reversal of the expansion at some future time

**deceleration time** *noun* COMPUT the time taken for an access arm to come to a stop after it has moved to the correct location over the surface of a hard disk

**decentralized computer network** *noun* COMPUT a network where the control is shared between several computers

**dechlorination** *noun* CHEM removal of chlorine and its replacement with hydrogen or with hydroxide ions to detoxify a substance

**deci-** *prefix* MEASURE one tenth, $10^{-1}$. Symbol **d**

**decibel** *noun* ACOUSTICS **1.** a unit for measuring the power of a sound or the strength of a signal (the decibel scale is logarithmic). Abbreviation **dB 2.** a unit for comparing two power levels, especially the relative loudness of different sounds or relative strength of electrical signals. Symbol **dB** (NOTE: The difference in decibels is equal to ten times the common logarithm of the ratio of two levels.)

**deciding factor** *noun* the most important factor which influences someone's decision ○ *The deciding factor was the superb graphics.*

**deciduous** *adjective* BOT referring to a tree which loses its leaves or needles at some point during the year ○ *Deciduous woodlands grew up after the last Ice Age.*

**deciduous dentition** *noun* ANAT the first set of teeth of an animal which are gradually replaced by permanent teeth. Also called **deciduous teeth** (NOTE: In humans they are called milk teeth.)

**deciduous forest** *noun* BOT a forest containing only deciduous trees

**deciduous teeth** *noun* ANAT same as **deciduous dentition**

**decile** *noun* STATS one of a series of nine figures below which one tenth or several tenths of the total fall

**decilitre** *noun* MEASURE a unit of measurement of liquid equal to one tenth of a litre. Symbol **dl** (NOTE: The US spelling is **deciliter**.)

**decimal** *noun* MATHS an arithmetic and number representation using the decimal system ■ *adjective* referring to the decimal system □ **correct to three places of decimal** *or* **to three decimal places** correct to three figures after the decimal point ○ *2.754 is correct to three decimal places, 2.7 is correct to one decimal place.*

COMMENT: The decimal point is used in the USA and the UK In most European countries a comma (,) is used to show the decimal point, so 4.75% is written 4,75% in Germany.

**decimal fraction** *noun* MATHS a fraction as expressed in the decimal system ○ *0.50 is a decimal fraction that is equal to 1/2.*

**decimal notation** *noun* MATHS a number representation in base 10, using the digits 0–9

**decimal place** *noun* MATHS the position of a number to the right of the decimal point

**decimal point** *noun* MATHS the dot (.) used to separate a whole number from a decimal fraction

**decimal system** *noun* MATHS a system of counting based on the number 10 and using the digits 0 – 9

**decimate** *verb* to reduce something severely ○ *Overfishing has decimated the herring population in the North Sea.*

**decimetre** *noun* MEASURE a unit of measurement of length equal to one tenth of a metre. Symbol **dm** (NOTE: The US spelling is **decimeter**.)

**decipher** *verb* COMPUT to convert an encrypted or encoded message **ciphertext** into the original message **plaintext**

**decision** *noun* an act of making up your mind to do something ○ *to come to a decision* or *to reach a decision*

**decision box** *noun* a graphical symbol used in a flowchart to indicate that a decision is to be made and a branch or path or action carried out according to the result

**decision circuit, decision element**
*noun* COMPUT a logical circuit that operates on binary inputs, producing an output according to the function set in hardware

**decision framework** *noun* LOGIC a method of organising and evaluating information, leading eventually to the making of a decision

**decision instruction** *noun* COMPUT a conditional program instruction that directs control by providing the location of the next instruction to be executed if a condition is met. Also called **discrimination instruction**

**decision table** *noun* COMPUT a list of all possible events or states that could happen and the actions taken. It may sometimes be used instead of a flowchart.

**decision tree** *noun* LOGIC a graphical representation of a decision table showing possible paths and actions if different conditions are met

**declaration** *noun* COMPUT a statement within a program that informs the compiler or interpreter of the form, type and size of a particular element, constant or variable. Also called **declarative statement**

**declarative language** *noun* COMPUT a programming language, normally in a database application, in which you enter what you want to achieve, rather than instructions

**declarative statement** *noun* COMPUT same as **declaration**

**declare** *verb* COMPUT to define a computer program variable or to set a variable equal to a number ○ *He declared at the start of the program that X was equal to nine.*

**decline** *noun* a gradual reduction ○ *The decline in the number of cases of pollution is due to better policing of factory emissions.* ○ *The population of the birds now seems to be on the decline.* ○ *Ecologists are working to diagnose forest decline in its early stages.* ■ *verb* to become less ○ *The fish population declined sharply as the water became more acid.*

**decode** *verb* to change coded information into readable form

**decode unit** *noun* COMPUT a part of a microprocessor that translates a complex instruction into a simple form that the arithmetic logic unit can understand and process

**decompilation** *noun* COMPUT a conversion of a compiled program in object code into a source language ○ *fast incremental compilation and decompilation*

**decomposable** *adjective* CHEM referring to a substance which can be broken down into simple chemical compounds

**decompose** *verb* CHEM (*of organic material*) to break down into simple chemical compounds

**decomposer** *noun* BIOL an organism such as an earthworm, fungus or bacterium which feeds on dead organic matter and breaks it down into simple chemicals

**decomposition** *noun* CHEM the process of breaking down into simple chemical compounds

**decompression** *noun* COMPUT the expansion of a compressed image or data file so that it can be viewed

**decontaminate** *verb* ENVIRON to remove a harmful substance such as poison or radioactive material from a building, a watercourse, a person's clothes or some other place

**decontamination** *noun* ENVIRON the removal of a harmful substance such as poison or radioactive material from a building, a watercourse, a person's clothes, etc.

**decrease** *noun* a lessening or reduction ○ *A decrease in power results in the aircraft descending.* ■ *verb* to become less ○ *Air density and pressure decrease with an increase in altitude.* Opposite **increase**

**decrement** *verb* COMPUT to subtract a set number from a variable ○ *The register contents were decremented until they reached zero.*

**decrypt** *verb* COMPUT to convert encrypted data back into its original form

**decryption** *noun* COMPUT the conversion of encrypted data back into its original form ○ *Decryption is done using hardware to increase speed.*

**dedicated** *adjective* COMPUT reserved for a particular use ○ *There's only one dedicated graphics workstation in this network.*

**dedicated channel** *noun* TELECOM a communications channel reserved for a special purpose

**dedicated computer** *noun* COMPUT a computer which is only used for a single special purpose

**dedicated logic** *noun* COMPUT a logical function implemented in hardware design usually for only one task or circuit ○ *The person appointed should have a knowledge of micro-based hardware and dedicated logic.* ○ *The dedicated logic cuts down the chip count.*

**deduce** *verb* to reach a conclusion using information provided ○ *Sometimes, it is possible to estimate the depth of the layer of mist or fog from the ground observations and hence to deduce the ground range from any height.*

**deduct** *verb* to remove something from a total

**deductive reasoning** *noun* LOGIC the process of drawing conclusions from observations of the natural world by using logical reasoning. Compare **inductive reasoning**

**deep** *adjective* EARTH SCI referring to something which goes down a long way, e.g. a well or mine

**deep depository** *noun* INDUST a place where nuclear waste is stored in very deep holes in the ground

**deep ecology** *noun* ECOL an extreme form of ecological thinking in which humans are considered as only one species among many in the environment and large numbers of humans are seen as harmful to the environment in which they live

**deep-sea** *adjective* OCEANOG referring to the deepest part of the sea

**deep-sea fauna** *plural noun* MARINE BIOL fauna which live in the deepest part of the sea

**deep-sea plain** *noun* OCEANOG same as **abyssal plain**

**deep-sea trench** *noun* OCEANOG same as **oceanic trench**

**deep-sea zone** *noun* OCEANOG same as **abyssal zone**

**deep vein** *noun* ANAT a vein which is deep in tissue, near the bones

**de facto standard** *noun* a design, method or system which is so widely used that it has become a standard although not officially recognised by any committee

**default** *noun* COMPUT a predefined course of action or value that is assumed unless a conscious decision is taken to alter it

**default option** *noun* COMPUT a preset value or option that is to be used if no other value has been specified

**default palette** *noun* COMPUT a range of colours available on a system that a user or application can change to create an individualised range of colours. Also called **system colours**

**default value** *noun* COMPUT a value that is automatically used by the computer if no other value has been specified ○ *Screen width has a default value of 80.*

**defect** *noun* a fault or error ○ *a computer defect* or *a defect in the computer* ○ *Low oil pressure or excessive temperature indicate the development of a possible defect.*

**defective** *adjective* referring to something that is faulty or that is not operating correctly ○ *Loss of supply pressure is caused by either a defective booster pump or lack of fuel.*

**defective sector** *noun* COMPUT a fault with a hard disk in which data cannot be correctly read from a particular sector (NOTE: It could be caused by a damaged disk surface or faulty head alignment.)

**defensive computing** *noun* COMPUT a method of programming that takes into account any problems or errors that might occur

**deferred addressing** *noun* COMPUT indirect addressing, in which the location accessed contains the address of the operand to be processed

**deferred printing** *noun* COMPUT a delay in the printing of a document until a later time

**deficiency** *noun* a lack of something

**deficiency disease** *noun* MED a disease caused by the lack of an essential element in the diet, e.g. vitamins or essential amino and fatty acids

**deficient** *adjective* lacking something essential ○ *The soil is deficient in important nutrients.* ○ *Scrub plants are well adapted to this moisture-deficient habitat.* ○ *He has a calcium-deficient diet.*

**deficit** *noun* a situation in which the amount going out is larger than the amount coming in

**define** *verb* **1.** to give an exact explanation of something, as in a dictionary **2.** to set the limits of something ○ *Cloud tops are very difficult to define.*

**definite** *adjective* referring to something which is not in doubt ○ *Using a time scale on the track, the pilot should be prepared to look for a definite feature at a definite time.* Opposite **indefinite**

**definition** *noun* an exact explanation of what a word or expression means ○ *The definition of a year is the time taken for a planet to describe one orbit around the Sun.* □ **by definition** understood by the use of the word itself ○ *A sphere is, by definition, round.*

**definitive host** *noun* BIOL a host on which a parasite settles permanently

**deflate** *verb* to allow air to escape from something such as a tyre or balloon so that it becomes smaller or collapses ○ *To deflate a tyre, remove or depress the valve and allow the air to escape.*

**deflation** *noun* the act or an instance of allowing air to escape from something such as a tyre or balloon so that it becomes smaller or collapses ○ *Deflation of a tyre is done by depressing the valve.*

**deflect** *verb* **1.** to move something away from a neutral or central position ○ *During an out-of-balance turn, the indicator will be deflected to the left or right.* **2.** to move a ray or moving object, gas or liquid away from its intended path ○ *The windshield deflects the airflow over the driver's head.*

**deflection** *noun* **1.** a movement away from a central or neutral position ○ *Full deflection of the ailerons is sometimes needed on take-off to counteract a crosswind.* **2.** a movement of a beam or moving object, gas or liquid away from its intended path ○ *In the southern hemisphere the deflection of wind at the equator is to the left.*

**deflection of light** *noun* PHYS the movement of light away from a straight path as the effect of a mass (NOTE: The effect can only be observed for very large objects such as stars.)

COMMENT: The deflection is strong evidence of the special theory of relativity. It was first observed in 1919 by recording the positions of stars during a total solar eclipse, revealing that the Sun's mass drew passing starlight towards it.

**deflection yoke** *noun* ELEC the magnetic coils around a television tube used to control the position of the picture beam

**deflocculant** *noun* CHEM a substance added to break up lumps which have formed in a liquid

**deflocculation** *noun* CHEM the breaking up of lumps which have formed in a liquid

**defoliant** *noun* AGRIC a type of herbicide which makes the leaves fall off plants

**defoliate** *verb* AGRIC to make the leaves fall off a plant, especially by using a herbicide

**defoliation** *noun* AGRIC the removal of leaves from plants, especially by using a herbicide

**deforest** *verb* AGRIC to cut down forest trees from an area for commercial purposes or to make arable land ○ *Timber companies have helped to deforest the tropical regions.* ○ *About 40 000 square miles are deforested each year.*

**deforestation** *noun* AGRIC cutting down forest trees for commercial purposes or to make arable land

**deformation** *noun* a change of shape caused by stress ○ *Deformation of wing panels may be an indication of serious structural damage.*

**defragmentation** *noun* COMPUT the reorganisation of files scattered across non-contiguous sectors on a hard disk

COMMENT: When a file is saved to disk, it is not always saved in adjacent sectors thus increasing retrieval time. Defragmentation moves files back into adjacent sectors so that the read head does not have to move far across the disk, so increasing performance.

**deg** *abbreviation* MATHS degree

**degas** *verb* PHYS to remove gas from something, e.g. a borehole

**degassing** *noun* PHYS the removal of gas from something e.g.a borehole.

**degauss** *verb* to remove unwanted magnetic fields and effects from magnetic tape, disks or read/write heads ○ *The read/write heads have to be de-*

*gaussed each week to ensure optimum performance.*

**deglutition** *noun* PHYSIOL the physical action or process of swallowing

**degradable** *adjective* CHEM, BIOL referring to a substance which can be degraded. ◦ **biodegradable**

**degradation** *noun* **1.** PHYS loss of picture or signal quality **2.** COMPUT a loss of processing capacity because of a malfunction **3.** a reduction in the quality of something ○ *Chemical degradation of the land can be caused by overuse of fertilizers and by pollutants from industrial processes.* □ **degradation of air** the pollution of clean air **4.** CHEM the decomposition of a chemical compound into its elements

**degradative succession** *noun* BIOL a type of autogenic succession involving colonisation and subsequent decomposition of dead organic matter by fungi and other microbes

**degrade** *verb* **1.** to reduce the quality of something ○ *The land has been degraded through overgrazing.* ○ *Ozone may worsen nutrient leaching by degrading the water-resistant coating on pine needles.* **2.** CHEM to make a chemical compound decompose into its elements

**degree** *noun* **1.** a level, amount or quantity ○ *The degree of compression is insufficient.* ○ *Manufacturers aim for a high degree of safety.* □ **to a greater degree** more □ **to a lesser degree** less **2.** MEASURE a unit of temperature ○ *twenty degrees Centigrade (20° C)* Symbol ° **3.** MEASURE a unit of measurement of an angle equal to 1/360th of a circle. Symbol ° (NOTE: Each degree is divided into 60 minutes and each minute into 60 seconds.) □ **an angle of 90°** a right angle **4.** NAVIG a unit of direction as measured on a compass. Symbol ° (NOTE: East = 90° and west = 270°.)

**degree Celsius** *noun* MEASURE a unit of measurement on a scale of temperature where the freezing and boiling points of water are 0 and 100 respectively

**degree Fahrenheit** *noun* MEASURE a unit of measurement on a scale of temperature where the freezing and boiling points of water are 32 and 212 respectively

**degree of adaptability** *noun* BIOL the extent to which an organism can change to fit a new situation

**degree of freedom** *noun* PHYS one of the variables such as temperature and pressure that are needed to specify the state of a system according to the phase rule

**degree of saturation** *noun* CHEM the amount of a substance which can be absorbed

**dehisce** *verb* BOT (*of a ripe seed pod or fruit*) to burst open to allow seeds to scatter

**dehiscence** *noun* BOT the sudden bursting of a seed pod or fruit when it is ripe allowing the seeds to scatter

**dehiscent** *adjective* BOT referring to seed pods or fruit which burst open to allow the seeds to scatter

**dehumidifier** *noun* ENG a machine which removes the moisture from air, usually part of an air-conditioning system

**dehydrate** *verb* **1.** CHEM to lose water or to make something lose water **2.** BIOL to lose water from the body ○ *After two days without food or drink, he became severely dehydrated.*

**dehydration** *noun* **1.** CHEM loss of water or the removal of water from something **2.** BIOL loss of water from the body

**dehydrogenase** *noun* BIOCHEM an enzyme that accelerates the transfer of hydrogen between two compounds

**dejagging** *noun* COMPUT same as **anti-aliasing**

**delay** *noun* a situation when something happens later than planned ○ *There was a delay of thirty seconds before the printer started printing.* ○ *We are sorry for the delay in supplying your order, but the computer was not working.* ■ *verb* to cause something to have a delay

**delay line** *noun* TELECOM a device that causes a signal to take a certain time in crossing it

**delay vector** *noun* TELECOM the time that a message will take to pass from one packet switching network node to another

**delete** *verb* **1.** to cut out words in a document **2.** COMPUT to remove text, data or a file from a storage device ○

*The word-processor allows us to delete the whole file by pressing this key.*

**delimit** *verb* COMPUT to set up the size of data using delimiters

**delimited-field file** *noun* COMPUT a data file in which each field is separated by a special character such as a tab character or comma and each record is separated by a return or a second special character

**delimiter** *noun* COMPUT **1.** a character or symbol used to indicate to a language or program the start or end of data, a record or information **2.** the boundary between an instruction and its argument

**deliver** *verb* to provide something ○ *The motor will continue to run but will deliver only one-third of the rated power.* ○ *The pump can deliver fuel at the rate of 2000 gph.*

**delivery** *noun* the provision of something ○ *On some pumps, a depressurising valve is used to block delivery to the system.*

**delta** *noun* **1.** EARTH SCI a triangular piece of land at the mouth of a large river formed of silt carried by the river ○ *the Nile Delta* ○ *the Mississippi Delta* **2.** the fourth letter of the Greek alphabet

**deltaic deposit** *noun* EARTH SCI a deposit of silt in a river delta

**delta ray** *noun* PHYS an electron forced from an atom by the effect of ionising radiation

**demagnetize** *verb* PHYS to remove stray or unwanted magnetic fields from a disk, tape or recording head

**demagnetizer** *noun* PHYS a device which demagnetises something ○ *He used the demagnetiser to degauss the tape heads.*

**demand** *noun* **1.** a strong request for something to be done **2.** a need for something ○ *They are building more power stations to satisfy the increasing demand for electricity.* ○ *They calculate that demand will exceed supply within ten years.* ■ *verb* COMPUT to ask for something and expect to get it ○ *The suppliers are demanding immediate payment.*

**demand assigned multiple access** *noun* COMPUT a means of switching in circuits as and when they are required. Abbreviation **DAMA**

**demand processing** *noun* COMPUT the processing of data as soon as it appears

**demand protocol architecture** *noun* COMPUT a technique of loading protocol stacks in memory only if they are required for a particular session. Abbreviation **DPA**

**deme** *noun* ECOL a population of organisms in a small area

**-deme** *suffix* ECOL a section of a population which has distinct characteristics

**demersal** *adjective* MARINE BIOL referring to fish which live on or near the seabed. Compare **pelagic**

**demineralisation, demineralization** *noun* CHEM the removal of salts which are dissolved in water

**demineralize** *verb* CHEM to remove dissolved salts from water

**demo** *noun* COMPUT same as **demonstration**

**democratic network** *noun* COMPUT a synchronised network where each station has equal priority

**demodulation** *noun* TELECOM the recovery of an original signal from a received modulated carrier wave

**demographic** *adjective* ENVIRON referring to demography

**demographic transition** *noun* ENVIRON the pattern of change of population growth from high birth and death rates to low birth and death rates

**demography** *noun* ENVIRON the study of human populations and their development

**demonstrate** *verb* to show how something works ○ *He demonstrated the file management program.*

**demonstration** *noun* an act of showing how something works

**demonstration model** *noun* a piece of equipment used to show potential customers how the equipment works and then often sold cheaply

**demonstration software** *noun* COMPUT software that shows what an application is like to use and what it can do, without implementing all the functions ○ *The company gave away demonstration software that lets you do everything except save your data.*

**denary notation** *noun* MATHS a number system in base ten, using the digits 0 to 9

**denature** *verb* **1.** CHEM to add a poisonous substance to alcohol to make it unsuitable for humans to drink **2.** BIOCHEM to change the natural structure of a protein or nucleic acid by high temperature, chemicals or extremes of pH **3.** PHYS to add an isotope to fissile material to make it unsuitable for use in nuclear weapons

**denatured alcohol** *noun* CHEM ethyl alcohol with an additive, usually methyl alcohol, to make it unfit for people to drink

**dendrite** *noun* **1.** ANAT a branch of a nerve cell, which receives impulses from axons of other nerve cells at synapses **2.** CHEM a crystal that has branched in two as it grows

**dendritic** *adjective* with branched parts

**dendritic drainage** *noun* ENG a system of drainage where smaller channels branch out from larger ones

**dendrochronology** *noun* BOT a scientific method of finding the age of wood by the study of tree rings

**dendroclimatology** *noun* BOT the study of climate over many centuries, as shown in tree rings

COMMENT: Because tree rings vary in width depending on the weather during a specific year, it has been possible to show a pattern of yearly growth which applies to all wood from the same region. This method allows old structures to be dated even more accurately than with carbon-dating systems. It is also possible to chart past changes in climate in the same way, as rings vary in thickness according to climatic conditions, allowing scientists to compare the climatic changes in various parts of the world over a very long period of time.

**dengue** *noun* MED a tropical disease caused by an arbovirus, transmitted by mosquitoes, where the patient suffers a high fever, pains in the joints, headache and a rash. Also called **breakbone fever**

**denitrification** *noun* BIOCHEM the releasing of nitrogen from nitrates in the soil by the action of bacteria

**dense** *adjective* **1.** referring to a substance which is closely compacted **2.** PHYS referring to the amount of mass of a substance for a given unit of volume ○ *Air which contains water vapour is less dense than air which does not.* **3.** composed of closely associated items ○ *The animals live in dense tropical rainforest.*

**dense index** *noun* COMPUT a database index containing an address for every item or entry in the database

**density** *noun* **1.** PHYS the quantity of mass per unit of volume ○ *air density* **2.** COMPUT the amount of data that can be packed into a space on a disk or tape (NOTE: Scanner software produces various shades of grey by using different densities or arrangements of black and white dots and/or different size dots.) **3.** ECOL the number of species in a specific area

COMMENT: Density is usually measured in grams per millilitre, or cubic centimetre, a scale on which water has a density of one. On this scale the Earth's average density is 5.52 gm/cc and that of the Moon is 3.34, while the Sun is at 1.41 and a white dwarf star in the region of 100 000 gm/cc.

**density altitude** *noun* METEOROL pressure altitude corrected for non-ISA temperature

**density dependence** *noun* ECOL a situation in which a population of a species is regulated by its density

**density-dependent** *noun* ECOL controlled by its own size ○ *a density-dependent population*

**density-independent** *noun* ECOL not controlled by its own size ○ *a density-independent population*

**density wave theory** *noun* ASTRON a theory that the arms of spiral galaxies are caused by compression waves moving in a circular plane about the galaxy's centre through the disc containing most of its mass

**dental caries** *noun* DENT the formation of cavities in teeth due to the action of acid-forming bacteria and improper dental care causing decay

**dental formula** *noun* DENT a system that identifies the number and type of each kind of tooth in a mammal, normally written in order of incisors, canines, premolars, and molars for the upper and lower jaw on the left or right of the jaw

**dentine** *noun* DENT the hard part of a tooth lying underneath the enamel and surrounding the pulp and root canals

**denudation** *noun* ENVIRON the process of making land or rock bare by cutting down trees, or by erosion

**denude** *verb* ENVIRON to make land or rock bare by cutting down trees, or by erosion ○ *The timber companies have denuded the mountains.*

**deoxygenate** *verb* CHEM to remove oxygen from water or air

**deoxygenation** *noun* CHEM the removal of oxygen from water or air

**deoxyribonuclease** *noun* BIOCHEM an enzyme which breaks down DNA

**deoxyribonucleic acid** *noun* GENETICS full form of **DNA**

**deoxyribonucleotide** *noun* GENETICS a nucleotide containing deoxyribose that is a structural component of DNA

**deoxyribose** *noun* GENETICS a simple sugar with five carbon atoms per molecule that is a structural component of DNA

**departmental LAN** *noun* COMPUT a small local network used to connect a group of people who are working in the same department or office and allowing the users to share files, printers and other resources

**depend** *verb* **1.** to be controlled or affected entirely by something ○ *The final colour depends on how long you leave it in the solution.* **2.** to rely on somebody or something ○ *Pilots depend on air traffic controllers to help them conduct a safe flight.*

**dependable** *adjective* reliable or trustworthy ○ *Mercury barometers have largely been replaced by precision aneroid barometers which are smaller, simpler to use, and more dependable.*

**dependent** *adjective* affected by or varying with something else ○ *The height indicated by an altimeter is dependent on the pressure which is set on the sub-scale.* ○ *A process which is dependent on the result of another process.* ○ *The output is dependent on the physical state of the link.*

**dependent variable** *noun* MATHS a condition that may change when an independent variable is manipulated by an experimenter

**deplete** *verb* ENVIRON to remove a resource from something ○ *Runoff from hillsides depletes the soil of nutrients.*

**depletion** *noun* ENVIRON the removal of a resource from something ○ *a study of atmospheric ozone depletion* ○ *Production of ice crystals from methane can deplete ozone still further.*

**deploy** *verb* **1.** to use something ○ *They needed to deploy more resources to complete the review on time.* **2.** to work as expected ○ *The parachute failed to deploy.*

**depolarize** *verb* PHYS to reduce or prevent electric polarisation of a cell

**depollution** *noun* ENVIRON the removal of pollution from a contaminated area

**deposit** *noun* **1.** GEOL a layer of metal, coal or other substance that occurs in the ground ○ *Deposits of coal have been found in the north of the country.* **2.** GEOL a quantity of material moved from one place on the Earth's surface to another by natural agents such as wind or water ○ *deposits of silt* ○ *glacial deposits* **3.** a thin layer or coating on an inner or outer surface ○ *deposits of red dust* ○ *fatty deposits in the arteries* ■ *verb* **1.** to coat a surface with a thin layer of a substance **2.** COMPUT to write data into a register or storage location

**deposited matter** *noun* GEOL fragments of rock, sand, shells, mud and other material left by the action of rivers, the sea, a glacier or the wind

**deposition** *noun* **1.** ELEC a process by which a surface of a semiconductor is coated with a thin layer of a substance **2.** the process by which material is added to the surface of the Earth, including material moved from one place to another by natural agents such as wind and water ○ *the deposition of sediment at the bottom of a lake*

**depository** *noun* INDUST a place where something is stored, e.g. refuse or nuclear waste ○ *They carried out tests to establish the suitability of the rock formation as a waste depository.*

**depress** *verb* to push down on something such as a button or switch ○ *Switches on the control columns instantly disengage the autopilot when depressed.*

**depression** *noun* **1.** METEOROL an area of low atmospheric pressure **2.** a lower area on a surface that is often difficult to see ○ *A depression on the wing surface must be investigated in case it is* *an indication of more serious structural damage.*

**depression of freezing point**
*noun* PHYS the lowering of the freezing point of a liquid by dissolving a solid in the liquid

**depth** *noun* the distance from the top surface of something to the bottom ○ *The troposphere's depth is variable in temperate latitudes.*

**derelict** *adjective* **1.** ENVIRON referring to land which has been damaged and made ugly by mining or industrial processes, or which has been neglected and is not used for anything ○ *a plan to reconstruct derelict inner city sites* **2.** referring to a building which is neglected and in ruins

**dereliction** *noun* **1.** ENVIRON a state of being damaged or neglected **2.** a failure to do what you ought to do ○ *The council's officers were found guilty of gross dereliction of duty.*

**derivation graph** *noun* COMPUT a structure within a global database that provides information on the rules and paths used to reach any element or item of data

**derivative** *noun* CHEM a substance or product which is formed from something else

**derive** *verb* to get or obtain something ○ *Performance data is derived from flight tests.* ○ *Kepler derived the laws which relate to the motion of planets in their orbits.*

**dermapteran** *noun* INSECTS an insect that has appendages like forceps projecting from its abdomen, e.g. an earwig

**dermis** *noun* MED the thick sensitive layer of skin beneath the epidermis containing blood and lymph vessels, sweat glands and nerve endings

**derris** *noun* AGRIC a powdered insecticide extracted from the root of a tropical plant, used against fleas, lice and aphids

**DES** *abbreviation* COMPUT data encryption standard

**desalinate** *verb* CHEM to remove salt from water or soil

**desalination** *noun* CHEM the removal of salt from a substance such as sea water or soil

COMMENT: Desalination can refer simply to the removal of salts from soil by the action of rain. It is most commonly used to

mean the process of removing salt from sea water to make it drinkable. Desalination plants work by distillation, dialysis or by freeze drying. The process is very costly, and is only cost-effective in desert countries where the supply of fresh water is minimal.

**desalination plant** *noun* INDUST a factory which removes the salt from sea water to produce fresh drinking water

**Descartes, René (1596–1650)** ASTRON a French scientist and philosopher who developed theories of the origin of the planets. His view that planets are expired stars was proven wrong but his view of an infinite universe capable of logical explanation was original and far-sighted. He also worked on optics, including improved telescope manufacture, and the nature of light.

**descend** *verb* **1.** to go down **2.** to become lower **3.** (*of aircraft*) to lose altitude, usually in a planned manoeuvre. Opposite **climb, ascend**

**descender** *noun* PRINTING a part of a printed letter that is below the line

**descending aorta** *noun* ANAT the second section of the aorta as it turns downwards

**descent** *noun* **1.** the act of moving down to a lower place **2.** a planned loss of altitude in an aircraft ○ *The descent from cruise altitude took 40 minutes.*

**de-scramble** *verb* COMPUT to reassemble an original message or signal from its scrambled form

**describe** *verb* **1.** to give the particular features of something **2.** MATHS to draw or to make a geometric figure ○ *The definition of a year is the time taken for a planet to describe one orbit around the sun.* ○ *Its movement described an arc.*

**description** *noun* **1.** a statement of the particular features of something ○ *a detailed description of world climate* **2.** MATHS the act of drawing or making a geometric figure

**description list** *noun* COMPUT a list of data items and their attributes

**descriptor** *noun* COMPUT a code used to identify a filename, or a program name or pass code with a file

**desert** *noun* EARTH SCI an area of land with very little rainfall, arid soil and little or no vegetation

COMMENT: A desert will be formed in areas where rainfall is less than 25 cm per annum whether the region is hot or not. About 30% of all the land surface of the Earth is desert or in the process of becoming desert. The spread of desert conditions in arid and semi-arid regions is caused not only by climatic conditions, but also by human pressures. So overgrazing of pasture and the clearing of forest for fuel and for cultivation both lead to the loss of organic material, a reduction in rainfall by evaporation and to soil erosion.

**desert formation** noun ENVIRON same as **desertification**

**desertification** noun ENVIRON the process by which an area of land becomes a desert because of a change of climate or because of the action of humans, e.g. through intensive farming ○ *Changes in the amount of sunlight reflected by different vegetation may contribute to desertification.* ○ *Increased tilling of the soil, together with long periods of drought have brought about the desertification of the area.*

**desertify** verb ENVIRON to make land into a desert ○ *It is predicted that half the country will be desertified by the end of the century.*

**desert soil** noun EARTH SCI the typical soil of a desert, normally sandy with little organic matter

**desiccant** noun 1. CHEM a substance which dries something 2. AGRIC a type of herbicide which makes leaves wither and die

**desiccate** verb 1. FOOD INDUST to preserve food by removing moisture from it 2. EARTH SCI to dry out soil

**desiccation** noun 1. the act or process of removing water 2. EARTH SCI the act of drying out the soil ○ *The greenhouse effect may lead to climatic changes such as the vast desiccation of Africa.* □ **desiccation damage** harm done by the drying out of the soil

**design** noun 1. COMPUT the planning or drawing of a product before it is built or manufactured ○ *She works in design.* 2. a plan or drawing of a product before it is built or manufactured ○ *He showed them several designs to choose from.* ■ verb COMPUT to plan or draw something before it is built or manufactured ○ *He designed a new chip factory.* ○ *She designs typefaces.*

**designate** verb to name something officially or appoint someone to a position officially ○ *An area of woodland*

which has been designated a Site of Special Scientific Interest. ○ *The city centre has been designated a traffic-free zone.*

**designator** noun a group of letters and/or numbers which identify something

**designer** noun a person who has the idea for, and makes plans to produce something ○ *She is the designer of the new computer.*

**designer gene** noun GENETICS a gene popularly considered as capable of being introduced into an organism to control the presence or absence of a desired characteristic (*informal*)

**desirable** adjective having qualities that are attractive or wanted ○ *This variety has the desirable characteristics of high yield and disease resistance.*

**desktop** noun COMPUT a workspace on a computer screen that is a graphical representation of a desktop, with icons for items such as a telephone, diary, calculator, and filing cabinet

**desktop computer** noun COMPUT a small microcomputer system that can be placed on a desk

**desktop publishing** noun COMPUT the design, layout and printing of documents using special software, a small computer and a printer. Abbreviation **DTP**

**despool** verb COMPUT to print out spooled files

**despotic network** noun COMPUT a network synchronised and controlled by one single clock

**destination address** noun COMPUT the address of the node to which data is being transferred or sent

**destination object** noun COMPUT the object or icon onto which a computer user drops an object

**destroy** verb to damage something so severely that it cannot recover ○ *At this rate, all virgin rainforests will have been destroyed by the year 2020.* ○ *The building of the motorway will destroy several areas of scientific importance.*

**destruction** noun the act of severely damaging something ○ *The destruction of the habitat has led to the almost complete extinction of the species.*

**destructive** adjective causing severe damage ○ *the destructive power of a nuclear reaction*

**destructive addition** *noun* COMPUT an addition operation in which the result is stored in the location of one of the operands used in the sum, so overwriting it

**destructive cursor** *noun* COMPUT a cursor that erases the text as it moves over it ○ *Reading the screen becomes difficult without a destructive cursor.*

**destructive distillation** *noun* CHEM the heating of solid substances in the absence of air causing decomposition and obtaining useful products from the vapour and residues

**destructive read** *noun* COMPUT a read operation in which the stored data is erased as it is retrieved

**destructive readout** *noun* a display device that erases previous characters when displaying new ones

**desulfurisation, desulphurisation** *noun* CHEM the process of removing sulfur from a substance such as oil, iron ore or coal

**detach** *verb* **1.** to unfix and remove something ○ *They detached a fuselage panel which needed replacing.* **2.** to become unfixed ○ *The fuselage panel detached.*

**detachable** *adjective* referring to something which can be unfixed and removed

**detail** *noun* a small part of a description □ **in detail** giving many facts ○ *The catalogue lists all the products in detail.* ■ *verb* to list all the items or aspects possible ○ *The catalogue details the shipping arrangements for customers.* ○ *The terms of the licence are detailed in the contract.*

**detailed** *adjective* COMPUT including all possible items or aspects ○ *a detailed explanation of what went wrong*

**detailed account** *noun* COMPUT an account which lists every item

**detail file** *noun* COMPUT a file containing records that are to be used to update a master file

**detail paper** *noun* ENG thin transparent paper used for layouts and tracing

**detect** *verb* **1.** to notice something that is not obvious ○ *The equipment can detect faint signals from the transducer.* ○ *She detected a slight scratch on the surface.* **2.** to discover the existence of something using scientific methods and equipment

**detectable** *adjective* which can be detected ○ *The increase in the amount of carbon dioxide, together with trace gases such as methane and nitrogen oxide, is likely to cause a detectable global warming.*

**detected error** *noun* COMPUT an error noticed during a program run, but not corrected

**detection** *noun* the discovery of the presence of something

**detector** *noun* a device for discovering the existence of something

**detergent** *noun* INDUST a cleaning substance which removes grease and bacteria from the surface of something

COMMENT: The first detergents contained alkyl benzenesulfonate which does not degrade on contact with bacteria and so passed into sewage, creating large amounts of foam in sewers and rivers.

**detergent foam, detergent swans** *noun* ENVIRON a large mass of froth on the surface of rivers, canals and sewers, caused by detergent in effluent

**deteriorate** *verb* to become worse ○ *The quality of the water in the river has deteriorated since the construction of factories on its banks.* ○ *The electrolyte in the cells of a nickel-cadmium battery does not chemically react with the plates and so the plates do not deteriorate.*

**deterioration** *noun* the process of becoming worse ○ *The deterioration of the environment gives cause for concern.*

**determination** *noun* the process of finding something out by calculation or experiment ○ *determination of the maximum safe dose*

**determine** *verb* **1.** to discover something by calculation or experiment ○ *To determine the average age, divide the total number of years by the number of people.* **2.** to set or fix something precisely ○ *Have they determined the cause of death?* ○ *The experimental procedures have not yet been determined.* **3.** to control or have an effect on something ○ *These characteristics are genetically determined.* ○ *Health is significantly determined by diet.*

**deterministic** *adjective* COMPUT referring to a result of a process that depends on the initial state and inputs

**detinning** *noun* CHEM the removal of a coating of tin from something

**detonation** *noun* **1.** CHEM the extremely rapid combustion that occurs as part of an explosion **2.** AUTOMOT a sudden, explosive burning of the air/fuel mixture in the cylinders of a piston engine, possibly causing engine damage and resulting in engine failure ○ *Prior to the accident, engine detonation could be heard by people on the ground.*

**detoxication, detoxification** *noun* ENVIRON the removal of harmful or poisonous substances

**detoxify** *verb* ENVIRON to remove harmful or poisonous substances from something

**detrimental** *adjective* harmful ○ *Conservation groups have criticised the introduction of red deer, a species which is highly detrimental to local flora.*

**detrital** *adjective* **1.** BIOL formed from detritus **2.** EARTH SCI referring to a crystal which has been uncovered from weathered rock

**detrital food chain** *noun* BIOL the link between green plants and the decomposer organisms which feed on them

**detritivore** *noun* BIOL an organism such as an earthworm, fungus or bacterium which feeds on dead organic matter and breaks it down into simple chemicals

**detritivorous** *adjective* BIOL referring to an organism which feeds on dead organic matter and breaks it down into simple chemicals

**detritus** *noun* BIOL, INDUST waste matter which may be either organic or mineral

**deuterated compound** *noun* CHEM a substance in which the hydrogen has been replaced by deuterium

**deuterium** *noun* CHEM an isotope of hydrogen with a neutron as well as a proton in its nucleus. Symbol **D** (NOTE: It was discovered by Harold Urey (1893–1981) and is of importance to both nuclear technology and astrophysics.)

**deuterium oxide** *noun* CHEM water containing deuterium instead of the hydrogen atom, used as a coolant or moderator in some types of nuclear reactor. Formula: $D_2O$.

**deuteron** *noun* CHEM the nucleus of a deuterium atom, consisting of a neutron and a proton

**develop** *verb* **1.** to come into being, or cause something to come into being ○ *Icing may develop in any type of carburettor in relatively warm air temperatures.* ○ *Vertical motion and therefore turbulence suggest that thunderstorms may develop.* ○ *The plant soon develops branches.* **2.** to grow and change ○ *During the day, light breezes may develop into strong winds.* ○ *The embryo developed quite normally in spite of the mother's illness.* **3.** to plan and produce something ○ *The company is trying to develop a new pesticide to deal with the problem.*

**developer** *noun* ENVIRON a person or company that plans and builds structures such as roads, airports, houses, factories or office buildings ○ *The land has been acquired by developers for an industrial park.*

**development** *noun* **1.** something new, made as an improvement on something older ○ *Satellite navigation aids are a useful development.* **2.** growth and change ○ *To study weather and its development, the meteorologist has to be aware of the horizontal changes in atmospheric pressure both in space and time.* **3.** an area which has buildings on it

**development software** *noun* COMPUT a set of programs that help a programmer write, edit, compile and debug new software

**deviate** *verb* **1.** to be different from the usual or expected pattern or to do something that is different from the usual or expected pattern **2.** to move away from the normal position or path ○ *If the aircraft deviates beyond the normal ILS glide slope, the flight crew are alerted.*

**deviation** *noun* **1.** a difference from what is usual or expected **2.** the act of moving away from the usual position or path ○ *On final approach, any deviation from the extended centreline of the runway should be corrected immediately.* **3.** AEROSP a magnetic compass error caused by magnetic influences in the structure and equipment of the aircraft in which it is formed ○ *Deviation is not a constant value but varies from one aircraft to another.* **4.** STATS the difference between one value in a series and the average of all the values

**device** *noun* a machine or piece of equipment ○ *a device for controlling humidity* ○ *a labour-saving device*

**device address** *noun* COMPUT the location within the memory area that is used by a particular device (NOTE: The CPU can control the device by placing instructions at this address.)

**device code** *noun* COMPUT a unique identification and selection code for a peripheral

**device dependent** *noun* COMPUT a software program that will only work on a specific type of computer or with a specific type of device

**device driver** *noun* COMPUT a program or routine used to interface and manage an input/output device or peripheral

**device-independent** *adjective* COMPUT referring to a programming technique that results in a program that is able to run with any peripheral hardware

**device name** *noun* COMPUT an abbreviation that denotes a port or input/output device, e.g. COM for serial port, PRN for printer port and CON for keyboard and monitor

**device priority** *noun* COMPUT the importance of a peripheral device assigned by the user or central computer which dictates the order in which the central processing unit will serve an interrupt signal from it ○ *The master console has a higher device priority than the printers and other terminals.*

**device queue** *noun* COMPUT a list of requests from users or programs to use a device

**device status word** *noun* COMPUT a data word transmitted from the device that contains information about its current status ○ *This routine checks the device status word and will not transmit data if the busy bit is set.* Abbreviation **DSW**

**dew** *noun* METEOROL drops of condensed moisture left on surfaces overnight in cool places

**Dewar flask** *noun* CHEM a double-walled flask with a vacuum between the walls to give thermal insulation, generally made of silvered glass or

metal (NOTE: It is frequently used to store liquefied gases.)

**dew point** *noun* METEOROL the temperature at which air is saturated with water vapour and condensation begins

COMMENT: Weather reports may include the air temperature and dew point temperature. When the difference between temperature and dew point is small, there is a strong possibility of fog, clouds or precipitation.

**dew pond** *noun* EARTH SCI a small pond of rainwater which forms on high chalky soil

**dextrorotatory** *adjective* CHEM deviating the plane of polarisation of oncoming light to the right or in a clockwise direction. ♦ **laevorotatory**

**dextrose** *noun* BIOCHEM the most common form of glucose (NOTE: It occurs widely in nature, especially in many fruits, and in honey.)

**DFD** *noun* COMPUT a diagram used to describe the movement of data through a system. Full form **data flow diagram**

**DHCP** *noun* COMPUT TCP/IP a protocol that is used to assign an Internet address to nodes, workstations or servers in a network. Full form **dynamic host configuration protocol** (NOTE: A special server running DHCP software manages the process of assigning addresses and a client computer can then ask this server for the address of another node on the network.)

**Dhrystone benchmark** *noun* COMPUT a benchmarking system developed to measure and compare the performance of computers

**DIA** *abbreviation* COMPUT document interchange architecture

**diagnose** *verb* **1.** MED to identify a disease from symptoms **2.** COMPUT to find the cause and effect of a fault in hardware or an error in software **3.** SCI to use scientific methods to discover the cause of a problem or fault

**diagnosis** *noun* **1.** MED a disease or condition identified from symptoms **2.** COMPUT the discovery of a fault or the cause of a fault **3.** COMPUT the result of diagnosing faulty hardware or software

**diagnostics** *noun* SCI the use of scientific methods to discover the cause of a problem, fault or medical condition

**diagonal** *adjective* **1.** referring to a line that joins two opposite corners of a

**diagram** 178 **diaspore**

rectangle **2.** referring to a line, plane or structure that slopes halfway between the vertical and horizontal ○ *a diagonal strut* ■ *noun* **1.** a line joining two opposite corners of a rectangle **2.** a line sloping halfway between the vertical and horizontal

**diagram** *noun* an often simplified drawing showing the structure or workings of something ○ *The diagram shows a simple open-circuit system.*

**diagrammatic** *adjective* referring to something which is shown as a drawing of a system or structure □ **in diagrammatic form** in the form of a diagram ○ *The chart showed the sales pattern in diagrammatic form.*

**diagrammatic format** *noun* a representation of something as a diagram

**diakinesis** *noun* GENETICS the final stage of meiosis, during which the paired chromosomes begin to shorten, thicken and separate

**dial** *noun* the face of an instrument showing a scale ○ *A cup anemometer is connected to an instrument with a dial showing wind speed in knots.* ■ *verb* TELECOM to call a telephone number on a telephone or modem (NOTE: British English is **dialling – dialled**, but the US spelling is **dialing – dialed**.)

**dialect** *noun* COMPUT a slight variation of a standard language ○ *This manufacturer's dialect of BASIC is a little different to the one I'm used to.*

**dial into** *verb* COMPUT to call a telephone number which has a modem and computer at the other end ○ *With the right access code it is possible to dial into a customer's computer to extract the files needed for the report.*

**dial modifier** *noun* COMPUT a set of extra commands sent to a modem that instructs the modem to use a particular system when dialling a telephone number (NOTE: For example, the command 'ATDT123' tells the modem to use tone-dialling to dial the number '123'.)

**dialog box** *noun* COMPUT an on-screen message from a program to the user

**dialup** *noun* COMPUT an online information service that is accessed by dialling into the central computer. Also called **dial-up service**

**dial-up access** *noun* COMPUT a means of connection to the Internet that

is not permanent and uses a modem or ISDN adapter to dial a telephone access number

**dial-up service** *noun* COMPUT same as **dialup**

**dialysing membrane** *noun* CHEM a membrane used in dialysis

**dialysis** *noun* **1.** CHEM the use of a semi-permeable membrane as a filter to separate soluble waste substances from a liquid **2.** MED the process of filtering waste products from the blood of a patient with kidney malfunction

COMMENT: In dialysis, larger dispersed particles are not allowed through the membrane but small dissolved particles will pass through.

**diamagnetism** *noun* PHYS a tendency of some materials to be repelled by a magnetic field and align themselves at right angles to it

**diameter** *noun* MEASURE the distance across the widest part of a circle or a tube (NOTE: The diameter passes through the centre.) □ **less than 0.5mm in diameter** measuring less than 0.5 mm across the widest part

**diamond** *noun* MINERALS a very hard transparent crystalline form of carbon, used as a gemstone, in abrasives and in cutting tools

**diapause** *noun* ZOOL a period of reduced metabolic rate in some animals or insects during which growth and development are temporarily suspended, often linked to seasonal or environmental changes

**diaphragm** *noun* **1.** a thin sheet of material used to separate parts or chambers ○ *Some switches are operated by a diaphragm which flexes under fluid or air pressure.* **2.** ELEC a thin flexible sheet which vibrates in response to sound waves to create an electrical signal as in a microphone, or in response to electrical signals to create sound waves as in a speaker **3.** ANAT a thin layer of tissue stretched across an opening, especially the flexible sheet of muscle and fibre which separates the chest from the abdomen, and moves to pull air into the lungs in respiration

**diaspore** *noun* MINERALS a white, grey, or pink form of aluminium oxide used in abrasives and heat-resistant materials (NOTE: It is extracted from bauxite.)

**diastase** *noun* BIOCHEM the beta-amylase component of malt

**diastema** *noun* DENT an unusually large gap between two adjacent teeth

**diastole** *noun* PHYSIOL the rhythmic expansion of the chambers of the heart at each heartbeat, allowing them to fill with blood. ♦ **systole**

**diatom** *noun* MARINE BIOL a type of single-celled alga found in fresh and sea water that has a cell wall containing silica which forms two overlapping halves

COMMENT: Most of the producers in sea water food chains are diatoms. Bodies of diatoms have contributed to the formation of oil reserves.

**diatomaceous earth** *noun* GEOL same as **kieselguhr**

**diatomic** *adjective* CHEM containing two atoms per molecule

**diatomist** *noun* MARINE BIOL a scientist who studies diatoms

**diatomite** *noun* GEOL same as **kieselguhr**

**diatom ooze** *noun* GEOL a deposit formed from the fossil remains of diatoms

**diazine** *noun* CHEM an organic compound containing a ring of four carbon and two nitrogen atoms per molecule, which exists in three isomers

**diazo compound** *noun* CHEM an organic compound that has a basic structure of two nitrogen atoms, one attached to a carbon atom (NOTE: Diazo compounds form the basis of many drugs.)

**diazotisation, diazotization** *noun* CHEM the production of a diazo compound from an amine by the action of nitrous acid

**DIB** *abbreviation* COMPUT data input bus

**dibasic** *adjective* CHEM referring to an acid with two replaceable hydrogen atoms

**dibit** *noun* COMPUT a digit made up of two binary bits

**dibromochloropropane** *noun* AGRIC a powerful insecticide

**dicarboxylic acid** *noun* CHEM an acid containing two carboxyl groups

**dichlorine oxide** *noun* CHEM a dark yellow gas which can be dissolved in water to form hypochlorous acid, and explodes when heated. Formula: $Cl_2O$.

**dichlorodiphenyltrichloroethane** *noun* AGRIC full form of **DDT**

**dichotomizing search** *noun* COMPUT a fast search method for use on ordered lists of data (NOTE: The key word is compared with the data in the middle of the list and one half is discarded, this process being repeated until only one data item remains.)

**dichotomous** *adjective* BOT, ASTRON divided into two

**dichotomous branching** *noun* BOT a pattern of plant growth that develops when a growing point divides into two points that later divide into two and so on

**dichroic** *adjective* OPTICS referring to a chemical coating on the surface of a lens that selectively reflects different colours of light

**dichroic filter** *noun* OPTICS a filter that allows specific wavelengths of light to pass and reflects back those which are not transmitted

**dichroic head** *noun* OPTICS a coloured light source that is based on adjustable dichroic filters (NOTE: They are generally used with rostrum cameras and enlargers.)

**dichromate** *noun* CHEM a salt containing the $Cr_2O_7^{2-}$ ion, which is generally orange-red in colour

**dicotyledenous** *adjective* BOT referring to dicotyledons

**dicotyledon** *noun* BOT a plant having a cotyledon with two leaves ○ *Dicotyledons form the largest group of plants.* Compare **monocotyledon**

**dictionary** *noun* 1. a book which lists words and meanings 2. COMPUT a data management structure which allows files to be referenced and sorted 3. COMPUT a list of words against which a spellchecking program checks a text

**die** *verb* BIOL to stop living ○ *The fish in the lake died, poisoned by chemical discharge from the factory.* ○ *Scientists are trying to find out what is making the trees die.*

**die back** *verb* BIOL (*of plants*) to be affected by the death of a branch or shoot ○ *Roses may die back after pruning in frosty weather.*

**dieback** *noun* BOT 1. a fungal disease of some plants which kills shoots or branches 2. a gradual dying of trees starting at the ends of branches ○ *Half* *the trees in the forest are showing signs of dieback.*

COMMENT: There are many theories explaining the environmental cause of dieback. Sulphur dioxide, nitrogen oxides and ozone have all been suggested as causes, as well as acidification of the soil or acid rain on leaves.

**die down** *verb* to become less strong ○ *The strong winds eventually died down.* ○ *The food safety controversy shows no sign of dying down.*

**diel** *adjective* TIME referring to a period of 24 hours ○ *The diel cycle was due to the interaction of damage and repair processes.*

**dieldrin** *noun* AGRIC an organochlorine insecticide which kills on contact (NOTE: It is very persistent and can kill fish, birds and small mammals when it enters the food chain.)

**dielectric** *adjective* unable to conduct direct electric current ■ *noun* ELEC a dielectric substance or non-conductor of electricity

**dielectric constant** *noun* PHYS same as **relative permittivity**

**diesel** *noun* INDUST same as **diesel oil**

**diesel engine** *noun* ENG an engine in which air is compressed in a cylinder causing a rise in temperature before the introduction of oil which ignites on contact with the hot air

**diesel-engined** *adjective* ENG using a diesel engine to provide power

**diesel oil, diesel fuel** *noun* INDUST oil used as fuel in a diesel engine. Also called **diesel**

**diesel-powered** *adjective* ENG same as **diesel-engined**

**diet** *noun* 1. BIOL the amount and type of food eaten ○ *It lives on a diet of insects and roots.* ○ *The normal western diet is too full of fats.* 2. HEALTH a measured amount of food eaten, usually to try to lose weight □ **to be on a diet** to reduce the quantity or change the type of food eaten in order to lose weight or become healthier ■ *verb* HEALTH to reduce the quantity or change the type of food eaten in order to lose weight or to become healthier

**dietary** *adjective* BIOL, HEALTH referring to diet

**dietary fibre** *noun* BIOL fibrous matter in food, which cannot be digested

COMMENT: Dietary fibre is found in cereals, nuts, fruit and some green vegetables. It is believed to be necessary to help digestion and to avoid developing constipation, obesity and appendicitis.

**dietary reference values** *noun* HEALTH the nutrients that are essential for health published as a list by the British government. Abbreviation **DRV**

**dietetic** *adjective* BIOL, HEALTH referring to diet

**dietetics** *noun* BIOL, HEALTH the study of food, nutrition and health, especially when applied to food intake

**dietitian** *noun* HEALTH a specialist in dietetics

**DIF** *abbreviation* COMPUT data interchange format

**differ** *verb* to be unlike ○ *The two products differ considerably – one has an external hard disk, the other has internal hard disk and external magnetic tape drive.*

**difference** *noun* 1. the way in which two things are not the same ○ *Describe the major differences between plants and animals.* 2. MATHS the amount by which one number is bigger than another number ○ *The difference between 19 and 24 is five.*

**different** *adjective* not the same ○ *Living in the country is very different from living in town.* ○ *The landscape looks quite different since the mine was opened.*

**differential** *adjective* 1. referring to things which react differently when measured against a norm or standard 2. COMPUT, MATHS showing a difference

**differential calculus** *noun* MATHS the application of calculus to the determination of maximum and minimum points and rates of change

**differential equation** *noun* MATHS a mathematical equation relating functions to their derivatives

**differential expansion switch** *noun* ENG a switch which operates on the principle that the coefficients of expansion of dissimilar metals are different

**differential heating** *noun* METEOROL differences in the amount of heat received when different surfaces are heated by the Sun (NOTE: White surfaces such as snow heat less than dark ones such as soil.) □ **differential**

**heating of the atmosphere** the heating of the atmosphere to varying temperatures depending on the relative warmth of the land at the equator and the poles

**differential pulse coded modulation** *noun* COMPUT a method of encoding an analog signal into a digital form in which the value recorded is equal to the difference between the current and previous samples. Abbreviation **DPCM**

**differential reproduction** *noun* BIOL the ability to produce more offspring with the same adaptations as the parents, allowing the species to survive under changed environmental conditions

**differentiate** *verb* to recognise the difference between two or more things or to show two or more things to be different ○ *found it hard to differentiate different shades of green*

**differentiation** *noun* BIOL the developmental process from unspecified cells into complex tissues, organs or body parts

**diffraction** *noun* PHYS the breaking down of a beam of radiation ○ *Diffraction produces a surface wave which follows the curvature of the earth.* (NOTE: The longer the wave, the greater the diffraction produced.)

COMMENT: The different rates of diffraction of light of different wavelengths is the principle behind the diffraction grating.

**diffraction grating** *noun* OPTICS a glass plate or metal mirror engraved with a large number of parallel lines or grooves, which produces a spectrum when light passes through it

COMMENT: Tho diffraction grating has replaced the glass prism for most spectrum-gathering. A diffraction grating consists of an array of fine lines ruled parallel to each other on a flat surface which can either reflect or transmit the light falling on it, to give a transmission or reflection grating. The diffraction of light around the edges of the lines on the grating produces the spectrum.

**diffuse** *adjective* spread out in every direction ○ *Glare caused by diffuse reflection of sunlight from the top of a layer of fog or haze can seriously reduce air-to-ground visibility.* ■ *verb* **1.** to spread out in every direction ○ *Light diffuses as it passes through fog.* **2.** to spread through tissue or other matter ○

*Some substances easily diffuse through the walls of capillaries.*

**diffusion** *noun* **1.** the process of spreading out ○ *Gas from the turbine enters the exhaust system at high velocities but, because of high friction losses, the speed of flow is decreased by diffusion.* **2.** CHEM a means of transferring doping materials into an integrated circuit substrate **3.** PHYS the spreading of gas or light **4.** CHEM the mixing of a liquid with another liquid, or of a gas with another gas **5.** CHEM the passing of a liquid or gas through a membrane

**diffusion pump** *noun* PHYS a vacuum pump that achieves low pressures by condensing gas molecules carried in diffused vapour on its cool surfaces. Also called **condensation pump**

**digest** *verb* **1.** PHYSIOL to break down food in the alimentary tract and convert it into elements which can be absorbed by the body **2.** INDUST to process waste, especially organic waste such as manure, in order to produce biogas ○ *55% of UK sewerage sludge is digested.* ○ *Wastes from food processing plants can be anaerobically digested.*

**digester** *noun* INDUST a machine which takes refuse and produces gas such as methane from it

**digester gas** *noun* INDUST gas such as methane produced by a digester

**digestible** *adjective* PHYSIOL able to be digested ○ *Glucose is an easily digestible form of sugar.*

**digestible organic matter** *noun* INDUST a substance such as manure which can be processed to produce biogas. Abbreviation **DOM**

**digestion** *noun* **1.** PHYSIOL the process by which food is broken down in the alimentary tract and converted into elements which can be absorbed by the body **2.** BIOCHEM the conversion of organic matter into simpler chemical compounds, as in the production of biogas from manure

**digestive** *adjective* PHYSIOL referring to digestion

**digestive enzyme** *noun* BIOCHEM an enzyme which speeds up the process of digestion

**digestive system** *noun* ANAT the set of organs in the body associated with the digestion of food

**digestive tract** noun ANAT same as **alimentary canal**

**digit** noun MATHS a symbol or character which represents an integer that is smaller than the radix of the number base used ○ *a phone number with eight digits or an eight-digit phone number* ○ *the decimal digit 8* ○ *The decimal number system uses the digits 0123456789.*

**digital** adjective MATHS, COMPUT representing data or physical quantities in numerical form, especially using a binary system in computer-related devices

**digital audio tape** noun COMPUT a compact cassette, smaller than an audio cassette, that provides a system of recording sound as digital information onto magnetic tape with very high-quality reproduction. Abbreviation **DAT** (NOTE: It is also used as a high-capacity tape backup system that can store 1.33 Gb of data.)

**digital circuit** noun COMPUT an electronic circuit that operates on digital information providing logical functions or switching

**digital computer** noun COMPUT a computer which processes data in digital form

**digital data** noun COMPUT data represented in numerical form, usually binary

**digital display** noun COMPUT a video display that can only show a fixed number of colours or shades of grey

**digital logic** noun COMPUT the application of Boolean algebra to hardware circuits

**digital read-out** noun COMPUT data displayed in numerical form, e.g. a display of numbers on an LCD in a calculator

**digital resolution** noun COMPUT the smallest number that can be represented with one digit, the value assigned to the least significant bit of a word or number

**digital signal** noun ELEC an electric signal that has only a number of possible states, as opposed to an analog signal which is continuously variable

**digital signalling** noun ELEC ENG control and dialling codes sent down a telephone line in digital form

**digital signal processing** noun ELEC ENG a special integrated circuit used to manipulate digital signals. Abbreviation **DSP**

**digital signature** noun COMPUT a unique identification code sent by a terminal or device in digital form

**digital subscriber line** noun TELECOM a system of transmitting data at high speed over standard telephone wire. Abbreviation **DSL** (NOTE: One of the most popular DSLs is the asymmetric digital subscriber line scheme that provides a permanent, high-speed connection to the Internet over standard telephone lines.)

**digital switching** noun ELEC ENG the operation of communications connections and switches by digital signals

**digital to analog converter** noun ELEC ENG a circuit that outputs an analog signal that is proportional to the input digital number, and so converts a digital input to an analog form. Abbreviation **DAC**

**digital versatile disc, digital videodisc** noun COMPUT full form of **DVD**

**digital video interactive** noun COMPUT a system that defines how video and audio signals should be compressed and displayed on a computer. Abbreviation **DV-I**

**digitise, digitize** verb ELEC ENG to change analog movement or signals into a digital form which can be processed, e.g. by computers ○ *We can digitise your signature to allow it to be printed with any laser printer.*

**digitiser, digitizer** noun ELEC ENG an analog to digital device which converts an analog signal to a digital one which can be understood by a computer

**digit place, digit position** noun MATHS the position of a digit within a number

**dihybrid** noun GENETICS an organism that is heterozygous for two genes, each gene being represented by two variant forms (**alleles**)

**dihydrate** noun CHEM a chemical that contains two molecules of water of crystallisation

**DIL** noun ELEC a standard layout for integrated circuit packages using two parallel rows of connecting pins along each side. Full form **dual-in-line package**

**dilatation** noun MED same as **dilation**

**dilate** verb to increase in volume

**dilation** noun 1. an increase in volume 2. MED the process of widening, enlarging or stretching a hollow organ or body passage

**diluent** *noun* CHEM a substance which is used to dilute a liquid

**dilute** CHEM *adjective* with water or solvent added ○ *Bathe the wound in a solution of dilute antiseptic.* ■ *verb* to add water or solvent to a liquid to make it weaker ○ *The disinfectant must be diluted in four parts of water before it can be used on the skin.*

**dilute and disperse** *noun* ENVIRON a method of using unlined landfill sites in which the waste is allowed to leak gradually into the surrounding soil. Opposite **concentrate**

**diluted** *adjective* CHEM referring to a decreased strength or concentration of a liquid as a result of adding another liquid ○ *Spillage from a lead acid battery may be neutralised by washing with a diluted solution of sodium bicarbonate.*

**diluter** *noun* CHEM a device for decreasing the strength or concentration of a liquid or gas

**dilution** *noun* **1.** CHEM the action of diluting a liquid **2.** a liquid which has been diluted

**DIM** *abbreviation* COMPUT document image management

**dimension** *noun* **1.** a measurable distance such as height or length ○ *Variations of atmospheric pressure produce changes in the dimensions of the capsule chamber.* **2.** MATHS the power to which something is raised

**dimensional analysis** *noun* PHYS the use of knowledge about the physical dimensions of a system to infer information that is too complex to calculate

**dimensioning** *noun* COMPUT a definition of the size of something such as an array or matrix ○ *Array dimensioning occurs at this line.*

**dimer** *noun* CHEM a molecule made up of two simpler identical molecules or monomers

**dimethyl sulfide, dimethyl sulphide** *noun* CHEM a gas given off by water which is rich in sewage pollution

**diminish** *verb* to decrease or to reduce something ○ *Friction is greatest near the ground and diminishes with height.* ○ *Hammering diminishes the metal rod's strength.*

**diminished** *adjective* reduced ○ *At higher altitudes, ground objects are less easily seen because of diminished size.*

**diminished radix complement** *noun* MATHS a number representation in which each digit of the number is subtracted from one less than the radix

**DIMM** *abbreviation* COMPUT dual in-line memory module ○ *DIMM cards are used to expand the memory in high-performance computers.*

**dimorphism** *noun* BIOL the existence of two different forms within a species, as in sexual dimorphism in which there are distinct males and females or in the occurrence of sexual and asexual forms in some lower plants

**DIN** *noun* ELEC a German industry standards organisation; often referred to in the specification for plugs and sockets. Full form **Deutsche Industrienorm**

**dinitrogen oxide** *noun* CHEM same as **nitrous oxide**

**dinosaur** *noun* PALAEONT an extinct carnivorous or herbivorous reptile that lived in the Mesozoic Era. Order: Ornisthischia and Saurischia.

**diode** *noun* ELECTRONICS an electronic component that allows an electrical current to pass in one direction and not the other

**dioecious** *adjective* BOT referring to a plant species in which male and female flowers occur on different individuals. ♦ **monoecious**

**diol** *noun* CHEM an alcohol containing two hydroxyl groups in each molecule

**diopter** *noun* OPTICS US spelling of **dioptre**

**dioptre** *noun* OPTICS a unit of measurement of refraction of a lens. US spelling **diopter**

COMMENT: A one dioptre lens has a focal length of one metre; the greater the dioptre, the shorter the focal length.

**dioxide** *noun* CHEM an oxide containing two atoms of oxygen

**dioxin** *noun* CHEM an extremely poisonous gas formed as a by-product of the manufacture of the herbicide 2,4,5-T (NOTE: It is the gas that escaped in the disaster at Seveso in 1976.)

**dip** *noun* GEOG the angle between a magnetic needle and the horizontal plane

**DIP[1]** *noun* ELECTRONICS a standard layout for an integrated circuit package using two parallel rows of connecting pins along each side. Full form **dual-in-line package**

**DIP[2]** *abbreviation* document image processing

**dipl-, diplo-** *prefix* BIOL double

**diploblastic** *adjective* ZOOL referring to an invertebrate animal in which the body is made up of two cellular layers only, derived from the embryonic endoderm and ectoderm. Cnidarians are diploblastic.

**diploid** *adjective* GENETICS referring to an organism that has two matched sets of chromosomes in a cell nucleus, one set from each parent (NOTE: Each species has a characteristic diploid number of chromosomes.)

**diplont** *noun* GENETICS an organism whose cell nuclei have a diploid number of chromosomes, apart from in reproductive cells

**diplotene** *noun* GENETICS a stage in the first part of meiosis in which paired chromosomes start to move apart from each another but remain connected at points (**chiasmata**) (NOTE: At these connecting points, genetic information is exchanged.)

**dipole** *noun* PHYS two equal and opposite magnetic poles or electrical charges that are only a short distance apart

**dipole moment** *noun* PHYS the product of two equal and opposite magnetic poles or electric charges that are a short distance apart

**DIP switch** *noun* ELEC a small bank of switches that are used to configure a device. Full form **dual-inline-package switch**

**direct** *verb* to manage or organise something ■ *adjective* COMPUT straight or with no processing or going in a straight way ■ *adverb* COMPUT straight or with no third party involved ■ *noun* COMPUT a binary code which directly operates the central processing unit, using only absolute addresses and values (NOTE: This is the final form of a program after a compiler or assembler pass.)

**direct access** *noun* COMPUT storage and retrieval of data without the need to read other data first

**direct access storage device** *noun* COMPUT a storage medium whose memory locations can be directly read or written to. Abbreviation **DASD**

**direct addressing** *noun* COMPUT a method of addressing where the storage location address given in the instruction is the location to be used

**direct current** *noun* ELEC an electric current of constant value that flows in one direction. Abbreviation **DC**

**direct data entry** *noun* COMPUT the process of keying in data directly onto a magnetic disk or tape. Abbreviation **DDE**

**direct digital control** *noun* COMPUT a machine operated automatically by computer. Abbreviation **DDC**

**direct dye** *noun* CHEM a dye that can be applied directly to a fabric without needing an additional chemical (**mordant**) to fix the colour

**direction** *noun* the course taken by someone or something ○ *The Earth rotates about its own axis in an anticlockwise direction.*

**directive** *noun* COMPUT a programming instruction used to control something such as a language translator or compiler ■ *adjective* ELEC referring to the ability of a device to send or receive signals in straight lines ○ *The antenna is highly directive in transmission and reception.*

**direct memory access** *noun* COMPUT a direct, rapid link between a peripheral and a computer's main memory which avoids the use of accessing routines for each item of data required ○ *direct memory access transfer between the main memory and the second processor* Abbreviation **DMA**

**directory** *noun* COMPUT a unit of organisation of files stored on a disk, containing a group of files or further sub-directories

**directory services** *noun* COMPUT all the users and resources linked to a network recorded in a simple and easy-to-access way so that a user can locate another user by name rather than by a complex network address ○ *With directory services installed, it's much easier for our users to find and connect to the shared printers.*

**directory website** *noun* COMPUT a website that contains a list of other websites, normally organised into sections and often with a search feature

**direct page register** *noun* COMPUT a register that provides memory page access data to allow access to any part of memory when a central processing unit is carrying out a direct memory access

**direct reference address** *noun* COMPUT a virtual address that can only be altered by indexing

**direct transfer** *noun* COMPUT a bit for bit copy of the contents of one register into another register, including any status bits

**dirty bit** *noun* COMPUT a flag bit set by memory-resident programs to indicate that they have already been loaded into main memory

**disable** *verb* to prevent a device or function from operating ○ *He disabled the keyboard to prevent anyone changing the data.*

**disadvantage** *noun* a factor which makes someone or something less likely to succeed ○ *The disadvantage of a booster pump is that the output is constant so that when engine demand is high, fuel pressure tends to be low and vice versa.*

**disappear** *verb* **1.** to cease to exist ○ *If air blew at right angles to isobars, the horizontal pressure differences would eventually disappear.* **2.** to pass out of sight

**disarm** *verb* COMPUT to prevent an interrupt having any effect

**disassemble** *verb* COMPUT to translate machine code instructions back into assembly language mnemonics

**disc** *noun* **1.** a circular flat plate ○ *A turbine consists of a disc on which is mounted a number of blades.* **2.** a CD (NOTE: Magnetic media use the spelling 'disk'.)

**discard** *verb* to throw out something which is not needed

**discharge** *noun* **1.** ELEC a release of power from a source such as a battery ○ *A lightning flash is a large-scale example of an electrical spark, or discharge.* **2.** ENVIRON the action of passing waste material into the environment **3.** ENVIRON waste material, as from an industrial process or in the form of sewage, which is passed into the environment **4.** PHYS the rate of flow of a liquid in a channel ■ *verb* **1.** ELEC to release electrical supply from a source such as a battery ○ *The battery discharged overnight.* **2.** GEOG (*of a river*) to flow into a lake or the sea ○ *The river Rhine discharges into the North Sea.* **3.** ENVIRON to pass waste material into the environment ○ *The factory discharges ten tonnes of toxic effluent per day into the river.*

**discharge area** *noun* GEOG an area of land where there is a net annual transfer of water from the ground water to surface water

**discharge pipe** *noun* INDUST a pipe which carries waste material from an industrial process or in the form of sewage and deposits it somewhere else, e.g. in a tank or in the sea ○ *Discharge pipes used to take the liquid waste into the sea.*

**discharge tube** *noun* ELEC ENG a tube filled with gas at low pressure that glows on conduction of electricity when a voltage is applied (NOTE: It is used in neon and fluorescent lights.)

**disclimax** *noun* ENVIRON a stable ecological state which has been caused by human intervention, e.g. a desert caused by deforestation

**disclimax community** *noun* ENVIRON a stable plant community which is caused by human action, e.g. felling a rainforest for timber. Compare **climax**

**disclose** *verb* to reveal details of something which were supposed to be secret

**disclosing agent** *noun* a dye that is used to colour something that cannot otherwise be seen, e.g. plaque on teeth

**disclosure** *noun* the act of telling details about something, especially something that has been secret or confidential ○ *requested full disclosure of experimental procedures*

**discolor** *verb* US spelling of **discolour**

**discolour** *verb* to change the colour of something, usually by making it paler

**discolouration, discoloration** *noun* a change of colour, especially one reflecting deterioration

**discoloured** *adjective* with a changed colour, especially through deterioration

**disconnect** *verb* to separate two things attached to one another ○ *The* *electrical supply can be disconnected by pulling out the plug.*

**discontinuity** *noun* EARTH SCI a band in the interior of the Earth which separates two layers and through which seismic shocks do not pass

**discovery** *noun* **1.** an act of finding something which was not known before ○ *The discovery of penicillin completely changed hospital treatment.* **2.** something which was not known before ○ *New medical discoveries are reported each week.*

**discrete** *adjective* referring to values, events, energy or data which occur in small individual units ○ *The data word is made up of discrete bits.*

**discrete cosine transform** *noun* COMPUT an algorithm used to encode and compress images. Abbreviation **DCT**

**discretionary** *adjective* able to be used if wanted or not used if not wanted ○ *discretionary powers*

**discrimination** *noun* the ability to know or see the difference between two similar things ○ *Discrimination between the colour tones is difficult.*

**discrimination instruction** *noun* COMPUT a conditional program instruction that directs control by providing the location of the next instruction to be executed if a condition is met. Also called **decision instruction**

**discussion group** *noun* COMPUT a feature of a website that lets visitors discuss a particular subject by posting messages

**disease** *noun* MED, BOT an illness of people, animals or plants ○ *He caught a disease in the tropics.* ○ *She is suffering from a serious disease of the kidneys or from a serious kidney disease.* ○ *He is a specialist in occupational diseases.*

**diseased** *adjective* MED, BOT affected by a disease and so not functioning normally or not whole or normal ○ *a diseased kidney* ○ *To treat dieback, diseased branches should be cut back to healthy wood.*

**disengage** *verb* to switch off a system or device ○ *Switches on the control columns instantly disengage the autopilot when depressed.*

**dish** *noun* a shallow container

**dish antenna** *noun* TELECOM a circular aerial with a shape like a shallow bowl

**disinfect** *verb* MED to make something or somewhere free from germs or bacteria ○ *All utensils must be thoroughly disinfected.* (NOTE: **Disinfect**, **disinfection** and **disinfectant** are used for substances which destroy germs on instruments, objects or the skin.)

**disinfectant** *noun* MED a substance used to kill germs or bacteria

**disinfection** *noun* MED the process of making something or somewhere free from germs or bacteria

**disinfest** *verb* MED to get rid of vermin from a place

**disintegrate** *verb* to break into pieces ○ *In holocrine glands the cells disintegrate as they secrete.*

**disintegration** *noun* the process of breaking into pieces ○ *Electromagnetic radiations resulting from the disintegration of radioactive materials are known as gamma rays.*

**disintegration constant** *noun* PHYS the probability that a radioactive nucleus will decay inside a standard unit of time

**disjunction** *noun* MATHS a logical function that produces a true output if any input is true

**disjunctive search** *noun* COMPUT a search for data items that match at least one of a number of keys

**disk** *noun* COMPUT a flat circular plate coated with a substance that is capable of being magnetised (NOTE: Data is stored on the disk by magnetising selective sections to represent binary digits.)

COMMENT: The disk surface is divided into tracks which can be accessed individually. Magnetic tapes cannot be accessed in this way.

**disk cache** *noun* COMPUT a high speed section of memory that is used to temporarily store frequently used data that has been read from the disk (NOTE: The computer checks the cache to see if the data is there before it accesses the disk. This system can dramatically improve apparent disk performance.)

**disk compression** *noun* COMPUT a method of increasing the apparent capacity of a disk to store data, carried out by a special piece of software that compresses the data as it is being saved to disk and then decompresses the data when it is read back

**disk controller** *noun* COMPUT an integrated circuit or circuits used to translate a request for data by the central processing unit into control signals for the disk drive, including motor control and access arm movement

**disk crash** *noun* COMPUT a fault caused by the read/write head touching the surface of the disk

**disk directory** *noun* COMPUT a list of names and information about files in a backing storage device ○ *The disk directory shows file name, date and time of creation.*

**disk drive** *noun* COMPUT a device which spins a magnetic disk and controls the position of the read/write head

**diskette** *noun* COMPUT a light, flexible disk that can store data in a magnetic form, used in most personal computers

**disk file** *noun* COMPUT a number of related records or data items stored under one name on disk

**disk formatting** *noun* COMPUT the initial setting up of a blank disk with track and sector markers and other control information

**disk head** *noun* COMPUT a head which reads or writes on a floppy disk

**diskless** *adjective* COMPUT not having any disk drives for data storage ○ *a diskless system* ○ *They want to create a diskless workstation.*

**disk mirroring** *noun* COMPUT a data protection system in which all or part of a hard disk is duplicated onto another, separate, disk drive. Also called **duplexing**

**disk operating system** *noun* COMPUT a section of the operating system software that controls disk and file management. Abbreviation **DOS**

**disk partition** *noun* COMPUT ◊ **partition**

**disk sector** *noun* COMPUT the smallest area on a magnetic disk that can be addressed by a computer

**disk storage** *noun* COMPUT the use of disks as a backing store

**disk track** *noun* COMPUT one of a series of thin concentric rings on a magnetic disk, which the read/write head accesses and along which data is stored in separate sectors

**dislocation** *noun* **1.** CHEM an irregularity in the fine structure arrangement (**lattice**) of an otherwise normal crystal **2.** MED the displacement of a bone from its usual position in a joint ○ *a hip dislocation*

**dismantle** *verb* **1.** to take something apart into single components ○ *to dismantle an engine* (NOTE: There is no verb to 'mantle'.) **2.** to come apart into single components ○ *The supporting structure dismantles easily.*

**disomic** *adjective* GENETICS having an extra chromosome in the haploid state

**disorder** *noun* **1.** a disruption of a normal system or balanced state **2.** MED an illness ○ *a stomach disorder*

**disorderly close-down** *noun* COMPUT a system crash that did not provide enough warning to carry out a close-down in an orderly manner

**dispenser** *noun* **1.** INDUST a device or machine which gives out a particular thing ○ *a detergent dispenser* **2.** a person or an official group that provides something ○ *a major dispenser of research funds*

**dispersal** *noun* ECOL the moving of individual plants or animals into or from an area ○ *Aphids breed in large numbers and spread by dispersal in wind currents.*

**disperse** *verb* **1.** (*of organisms*) to separate and move away over a wide area **2.** to send something out over a wide area ○ *Power stations have tall chimneys to disperse the emissions of pollutants.*

**dispersed particles** *plural noun* PHYS particles which are not dissolved in a liquid but remain in suspension

**dispersing agent** *noun* CHEM a chemical substance sprayed onto an oil slick to try and break up the oil into smaller particles

**dispersion** *noun* **1.** ECOL the pattern in which animals or plants are found over a wide area **2.** PHYS the splitting of electromagnetic radiation such as light into its component wavelengths as it passes through a medium **3.** COMPUT a logical function whose output is false if all inputs are true, and true if any input is false

**dispersion aerosol** *noun* droplets of moisture which are blown into the air as spray

**dispersion model** *noun* ENVIRON a mathematical prediction of how pollutants from a source will be distributed in the surrounding area under specific conditions of wind, temperature, humidity and other environmental factors

**displace** *verb* to move something out of the normal position ○ *The atmosphere is said to be stable if, when a parcel of air is displaced vertically, it tends to return to its original level.*

**displacement** *noun* **1.** a movement away from a normal position **2.** COMPUT an offset used in an indexed address

**displacement reaction** *noun* CHEM same as **substitution reaction**

**display** COMPUT *noun* a device on which information or images can be presented visually ○ *Our names came up on the display.* ■ *verb* to show information ○ *The customer's details were displayed on the screen.* ○ *By keying HELP, the screen will display the options available to the user.*

**display adapter** *noun* COMPUT a device which allows information in a computer to be displayed on a CRTt (NOTE: The adapter interfaces with both the computer and CRT.)

**display attribute** *noun* COMPUT a variable which defines the shape, size or colour of text or graphics displayed

**display character** *noun* COMPUT a graphical symbol such as one of the letters of the alphabet or a number that appears in printed form

**display processor** *noun* COMPUT a processor which changes data to a format suitable for a display controller

**display register** *noun* COMPUT a register which contains character, control or graphical data that is to be displayed

**display resolution** *noun* COMPUT a number of pixels per unit area which a display can clearly show

**disposable** *adjective* INDUST thrown away after use ○ *disposable syringes*

**disposal** *noun* the process of getting rid of something ○ *The disposal of raw sewage into the sea contaminates shellfish.*

**disposal facility** *noun* INDUST a landfill, incinerator or other facility that receives waste for disposal

**dispose of** *verb* to get rid of something ○ *The problem with nuclear reactors is how to dispose of the radioactive waste.*

**disrupt** *verb* ENVIRON to upset a normal system or balanced state

**disruption** *noun* ENVIRON the process of upsetting a normal system or balanced state

**dissect** *verb* BIOL to cut and separate tissues in a body to examine them

**dissecting aneurysm** *noun* MED an aneurysm which occurs when the inside wall of the aorta is torn, and blood enters the membrane

**dissection** *noun* BIOL the cutting and separating of parts of a body or an organ as part of a surgical operation, autopsy or course of study

**disseminate** *verb* **1.** to make information or knowledge available ○ *Meteorological stations make routine weather observations at fixed intervals and disseminate this information locally.* **2.** to spread throughout something

**disseminated** *adjective* BIOL occurring in every part of an organ or in the whole body ○ *disseminated cancer*

**dissemination** *noun* the process of making information about something available ○ *the dissemination of new technology*

**dissimilar** *adjective* referring to something which is not the same as or is unlike something else ○ *Differential expansion switches operate on the principle that the coefficients of expansion of dissimilar metals are different.*

**dissipate** *verb* to spread out or cause something to spread out and lose power or strength ○ *Tropical storms often dissipate as they pass from sea to land.*

**dissipation** *noun* the process of spreading out with loss of power or strength ○ *The rubber covering forms a good electrical conductor for the safe dissipation of static electricity.*

**dissolvable** *adjective* CHEM able to be dissolved

**dissolve** *verb* CHEM **1.** to become part of a liquid and form a solution ○ *Sugar dissolves in water.* ○ *There is a possibility that in some types of accumulator,* gas may be dissolved into the fluid and thus introduced into the system. **2.** to cause something to dissolve ■ *noun* COMPUT a special effect that is used in presentation graphics software or multimedia to fade out one image and fade in the next

**dissolved** *adjective* CHEM having become part of a liquid and forming a solution

**dissolved oxygen** *noun* oxygen dissolved in water, needed by organisms that live in water

**distance** *noun* a measurement of the space between two points ○ *The distance from A to B on the diagram is 2 cm.*

**distance vector protocols** *plural noun* COMPUT information about the different routes over a wide area network that can be used by a router to find the shortest and fastest route to send information

**distil** *verb* **1.** CHEM to produce a pure liquid by heating a liquid and condensing the vapour, as in the production of alcohol or essential oils **2.** INDUST to produce by-products from coal

**distillate** *noun* CHEM a substance produced by distillation

**distillation** *noun* CHEM the process of producing a pure liquid by heating a liquid and condensing the vapour, as in the production of alcohol or essential oils

**distilled water** *noun* CHEM pure water, used in some industrial processes and in electric batteries

**distinct** *adjective* clearly separate ○ *When a lead-acid battery is fully charged, each cell displays three distinct indications.*

**distinction** *noun* a point of difference ○ *A clear distinction is made between showers and general precipitation.*

**distinctive** *adjective* easily recognised because of particular features or characteristics

**distinguish** *verb* to know or to see the difference between things ○ *The OCR has difficulty in distinguishing certain characters.*

**distinguishable** *adjective* easily recognised as different from other things ○ *distinguishable from their surroundings*

**distort** *verb* **1.** to go or put something out of shape ○ *Stress could cause the body to distort or change its shape.* **2.** PHYS to introduce unwanted differences between a signal input and output from a device

**distortion** *noun* **1.** the act of going out of shape or of putting something out of shape ○ *distortion of the airframe* **2.** PHYS unwanted differences in a signal before and after it has passed through a piece of equipment ○ *Distortion of the signal made it difficult for the controller to understand what the pilot said.*

**distributary** *noun* EARTH SCI a stream or river flowing out from a larger river, as in a delta

**distribute** *verb* **1.** to give something or send something out ○ *There are two basic configurations which are used to distribute electrical power, the parallel system and the split bus system.* **2.** to spread something over a wide area ○ *Multiple wheel undercarriage units distribute the weight of the aircraft.* **3.** COMPUT to send out data or information to users in a network or system

**distributed adaptive routing** *noun* COMPUT the directing of messages in a packet network switching system by an exchange of information between nodes

**distributed database system** *noun* COMPUT a database system in which the data is stored on several different computers but can be searched as if it is one single location

**distributed data processing** *noun* COMPUT operations to derive information from data which is kept in different places. Abbreviation **DDP**

**distributed file system** *noun* COMPUT a system that uses files stored in more than one location or backing store but processed at a central point

**distributed network** *noun* COMPUT a network in which each node can operate as a server storing files or working as a print server

**distributed processor** *noun* COMPUT a system with many small computers at different workstations instead of one central computer

**distribution** *noun* **1.** the process of giving or sending something out ○ *Parallel AC and DC power distribution systems are found on commercial aircraft* containing three or more engines. **2.** the act or an instance of spreading over a wide area ○ *There is a high distribution of used and disused airfields in the south of England.* **3.** ECOL the pattern in which a species is found in various areas, depending on factors such as climate or altitude ○ *The distribution of crops in various regions of the world is a result of thousands of years of breeding and testing.*

**distribution area** *noun* ECOL a number of places in which a species is found

**distribution network** *noun* ◊ **local area network**, **wide area network**

**distributor** *noun* ELEC ENG a device which sends an electrical charge to each spark plug in turn ○ *The distributor directs the high voltage impulses to the cylinders in turn as they reach their ignition point.*

**district** *noun* a part of an area, especially for administrative purposes

**district heating** *noun* INDUST a system of heating all houses in a district from a central source, as from hot springs in Iceland or by cooling water from a power station

**disturb** *verb* to alter the usual condition of something ○ *Small hills can disturb the flow of air.* ○ *The building of the road has disturbed the balance of the ecosystem.*

**disturbance** *noun* **1.** an alteration in the usual condition of something ○ *In general, the higher the mountain and the faster the air flow the greater is the resulting disturbance.* **2.** ENVIRON a change in an ecosystem caused by an alteration of the environmental conditions, by a process such as drought, pollution or felling of woodland

**disturbance threshold** *noun* ECOL the point at which an alteration of the environmental conditions causes change in an ecosystem

**ditch** *noun* AGRIC, ENG a channel to take away rainwater

**dither** *verb* COMPUT to create a curve or line that looks smoother by adding shaded pixels beside the pixels that make up the image

**dithered colour** *noun* COMPUT a colour that is made up of a pattern of different coloured pixels

**dithionate** *noun* CHEM a salt of sulfinic acid

**dithionic acid** *noun* CHEM an acid that is unstable and only found in solution. Formula: HSO.

**diuresis** *noun* MED an increase in the production of urine

**diuretic** *adjective*, *noun* MED referring to a substance which makes the kidneys produce more urine

**diurnal** *adjective* **1.** referring to the 24-hour cycle of day and night ○ *Diurnal changes in surface temperature over the sea are small.* **2.** happening every day **3.** happening in the daytime

**diurnal cycle** *noun* a pattern that recurs over a 24-hour period ○ *Air pollution shows a diurnal cycle.*

**diurnal rhythm** *noun* BIOL regularly recurring activities such as feeding and sleeping which take place every day

**divalent** *adjective* CHEM with a valency of 2

**diverge** *verb* to move further apart from something else ○ *Air diverges at low levels and converges at high levels, causing a sinking or subsiding effect in the atmosphere.* Opposite **converge**

**divergence** *noun* **1.** a difference ○ *a divergence of opinion on the cloning issue* ○ *a divergence between the preliminary report and the final results* **2.** METEOROL a phenomenon which occurs whenever there is a net outflow of air from a region of the atmosphere, resulting in the depletion of air and a reduction in density. Compare **convergence**

**divergent** *adjective* **1.** different **2.** moving apart from something else

**divergent duct** *noun* a duct which has an inlet area which is smaller than the outlet area

**divergent evolution** BIOL same as **adaptive radiation**

**diverging lens** *noun* OPTICS a lens, usually concave, that makes a parallel beam of light spread out

**diversify** *verb* to develop in different ways

**diversity** *noun* ECOL the richness of the number of species

**divide** *verb* **1.** to separate something into parts, or become separated into parts ○ *Air masses are divided into two types according to source region and these are known as polar and tropical air masses.* **2.** MATHS to calculate how many times a number is contained in another number ○ *Eight divided by four equals two (8 ÷ 4 = 2)*.

**dividend** *noun* MATHS an operand that is divided by a divisor in a division operation (NOTE: The dividend is divided by the divisor to form the quotient and a remainder.)

**division** *noun* **1.** a separation into parts **2.** MATHS a calculation of how may times a number is contained in another number ○ *learning multiplication and division* **3.** BIOL a traditional category in the scientific classification of plants, now replaced by **phylum**

**division sign** *noun* MATHS a printed or written sign (÷) used to show that numbers are to be divided

**divisor** *noun* MATHS an operand used to divide a dividend in a division operation

**dizygotic twins** *plural noun* BIOL two offspring who are not identical and not always of the same sex because they come from two different ova fertilised at the same time. Compare **monozygotic twins**. Also called **fraternal twins**

**D-lines** *plural noun* PHYS a pair of lines that are visible in the spectrum of sodium, used as a reference point

**DLL** *abbreviation* COMPUT dynamic link library ○ *The word-processor calls a spell-check program that is stored as a DLL.*

**dm** *symbol* MEASURE decimetre

**DMA** *abbreviation* COMPUT direct memory access

**DML** *abbreviation* COMPUT data manipulation language

**DMT** *noun* COMPUT technology that uses digital signal processors to create sound signals that carry digital video, sound, image and data over cable at high speed. Full form **discrete multi-tone**

**DNA** *noun* GENETICS a nucleic acid chain carrying genetic information that is a major constituent of chromosomes. Full form **deoxyribonucleic acid**

**DNA chip** *noun* GENETICS same as **gene chip**

**DNA fingerprinting** *noun* GENETICS the analysis of DNA patterns from body tissues such as blood, saliva or semen in order to establish somebody's identity. Also called **DNA profiling**

**DNA polymerase** *noun* GENETICS an enzyme that carries out repair and reproduction of DNA using single-stranded DNA

**DNA profiling** *noun* GENETICS same as **DNA fingerprinting**

**DNA sequencing** *noun* GENETICS the process of determining the exact order of the bases that make up a section of DNA

**DNA virus** *noun* MICROBIOL a virus with a genome that contains DNA

**DNS** *abbreviation* COMPUT **1.** domain name server **2.** domain name system

**dock** *verb* COMPUT to connect a laptop computer to a special docking station on a desk to give it the same resources as a normal desktop

**docking station** *noun* a hardware device into which a portable computer is inserted for recharging or downloading data

**document** *noun* **1.** a piece of paper or set of papers containing text **2.** COMPUT a computer file containing text created with a word-processor ■ *verb* to make a record of a process

**documentation** *noun* **1.** all the documents referring to something ○ *Please send all documentation concerning the product.* **2.** COMPUT the information, notes and diagrams that describe the function, use and operation of a piece of hardware or software

**document content architecture** *noun* COMPUT same as **document interchange architecture**. abbreviation **DCA**

**document image management** *noun* COMPUT the software that allows a user to capture, store and index printed text in a digital form. Abbreviation **DIM** (NOTE: It normally works in conjunction with a scanner and a high-capacity storage medium such as a recordable CD-ROM.)

**document image processing** *noun* COMPUT the process of scanning paper documents, performing OCR on the contents and storing this on disk so that it can be searched for. Abbreviation **DIP**

**document interchange architecture** *noun* COMPUT a standard method for the transmission and storage of documents, text and video over networks, which is part of the IBM SNA range of standards. Abbreviation **DIA**. Also called **document content architecture**

**document reader** *noun* COMPUT a device which converts written or typed information to a form that a computer can understand and process

**dodecanoic acid** *noun* CHEM same as **lauric acid**

**doldrums** *plural noun* METEOROL an area of low pressure over the ocean near the equator where there is little wind

**doline, dolina** *noun* EARTH SCI a round or oval depression in the ground, found in limestone regions

**dolomite** *noun* EARTH SCI an alkaline carbonate of magnesium or calcium rock

**dolphin** *noun* MARINE BIOL a marine mammal belonging to the family which also includes killer whales and pilot whales. Family: Delphinidae.

**dolphinarium** *noun* MARINE BIOL a display of dolphins

**DOM¹** *noun* COMPUT a scheme that describes how the different parts of a webpage are represented, in which each item is an object and has a set of attributes that defines how it is displayed and managed by a web browser. Full form **document object model** (NOTE: Dynamic HTML (DHTML) uses DOM to change how a webpage is displayed by a user's web browser.)

**DOM²** *abbreviation* **1.** ECOL digestible organic matter **2.** ENVIRON dry organic matter

**domain** *noun* **1.** a particular area of activity ○ *The subject is controversial outside the scientific domain.* **2.** COMPUT an area or group of nodes in a network □ **in the public domain** available to the public and not copyright ○ *All these programs are in the public domain and can be downloaded free of charge.*

**domain name** *noun* COMPUT a unique name that identifies the location of an Internet server or computer on the Internet

COMMENT: A domain name is in a convenient text format but refers to a physical address that locates the computer that stores the website for the domain name. This physical address is called the IP address. The domain name is made up of two or three parts, each separated by a 'dot'. Domain types include 'com' for a company (originally those based in the USA, but now worldwide), 'co' for company, 'edu' for an educational establishment, 'net' for a network or Internet supplier, 'gov' for a US government domain and 'mil' for a military site. The last two characters refer to the country of origin, e.g. 'au' for Australia, 'cn' for China, 'de' for Germany and 'uk' for the UK

**domain name server** *noun* COMPUT a computer on the Internet that stores part or all of the domain name system database. Abbreviation **DNS**

**domain name system** *noun* COMPUT a distributed database used in an Internet system to map names to addresses. Abbreviation **DNS** (NOTE: For example, you can use the name 'www.bloomsbury.com' to locate the Bloomsbury website rather than a complex **IP address**.)

**domestic** *adjective* referring to the home or used in the home

**domestic animal** *noun* AGRIC an animal such as a dog or cat which lives with human beings or an animal kept for food

**domesticated** *adjective* BIOL referring to a species which was formerly wild but has been selectively bred to fill human needs

**domestic heating oil** *noun* INDUST petroleum oil used as fuel in a central heating boiler

**domestic livestock** *noun* AGRIC pigs, goats, sheep, cows and other animals which are kept by human beings

**domestic refuse** *noun* ENVIRON waste material from houses. Also called **domestic waste, household refuse**

**domestic sewage** *noun* ENVIRON the sewage from houses

**domestic waste** *noun* ENVIRON same as **domestic refuse**

**dominance** *noun* **1.** ECOL a state where one species in a community is more abundant than others **2.** ZOOL the priority for food and reproductive mates that one animal has over another in a group **3.** GENETICS the characteristic of a gene form (**allele**) that leads to the trait which it controls being shown in any individual carrying it

**dominance hierarchy** *noun* ZOOL the system of priority given to specific individuals in terms of access to food and reproductive mates ○ *In many spe-*

*cies a male is at the top of the domi-nance hierarchy.*

**dominant** *adjective* **1.** important or powerful **2.** GENETICS (*of an allele*) hav-ing the characteristic that leads to the trait which it controls being shown in any individual carrying it **3.** ECOL (*of a species*) being more abundant than oth-ers in a community

COMMENT: For physical characteristics controlled by two alleles, if one allele is dominant and the other recessive, the re-sulting trait will be that of the dominant al-lele. Traits governed by recessive alleles appear only if alleles from both parents are recessive.

**dominate** *verb* to have the most effect or influence on something

**dongle** *noun* COMPUT a coded circuit or chip that has to be present in a system before a piece of copyright software will run

**donor** *noun* CHEM an atom, molecule, or group providing a pair of electrons in order to form a chemical bond

**do-nothing instruction** *noun* COMPUT a programming instruction that does not carry out any action except in-creasing the program counter to the next instruction address

**dopa** *noun* BIOCHEM a substance from which the body makes dopamine, and hence adrenaline and dopamine (NOTE: In a synthetic form it is used to treat Parkinson's disease.)

**dopamine** *noun* BIOCHEM a neuro-transmitter that is also used by the body to make adrenaline

**dopant** *noun* INDUST a chemical sub-stance that is diffused or implanted onto the substrate of a chip during manufac-ture, to provide it with n- or p-type properties

**dope** *verb* INDUST to introduce a dop-ant into a substance

**doped** *adjective* ELEC referring to a chip which has had a dopant added

**doping** *noun* INDUST the process or act of adding dopant to a chip

**Doppler effect** *noun* PHYS a per-ceived change in the frequency of a wave as its source moves relative to an observer (NOTE: For example, the sound of a siren on a moving vehicle appears to change as it approaches and passes, the size of the effect being related to its speed.)

**Doppler radar** *noun* TECH radar which can distinguish between fixed and moving targets or provide ground speed and track information from an air-borne installation

**dormancy** *noun* BIOL an inactive pe-riod ○ *In animals or plants metabolism slows during a certain period of the year.*

**dormant** *adjective* **1.** BIOL not active or developing **2.** EARTH SCI referring to a volcano which is not erupting but is still able to erupt. Compare **extinct**

**dorsal** *adjective* ANAT referring to the back of the body. Opposite **ventral**

**dorsal vertebra** *noun* ANAT one of the twelve vertebrae in the back, be-tween the cervical vertebrae and the lumbar vertebrae

**dorsum** *noun* ANAT same as **back**

**DOS** *abbreviation* COMPUT disk operat-ing system ○ *Boot up the DOS after you switch on the PC.*

**dose** *noun* MED the amount of a drug or of ionising radiation received by an organism ○ *The patients received more than the permitted dose of radiation.*

**dosemeter** *noun* PHYS same as **dosimeter**

**dose response** *noun* MED a response of an organism to a toxic substance, which alters as its overall exposure to the substance changes

**dosimeter** *noun* PHYS an instrument for measuring radiation absorbed by people or equipment in a work environ-ment. Also called **dosemeter**

**dot** *noun* **1.** PRINTING a small round spot **2.** COMPUT a small round punctua-tion mark used to separate parts of an Internet address

**dot-matrix printer** *noun* COMPUT a printer in which the characters are made up by a series of closely spaced dots, producing a page line by line. Also called **matrix printer**

**dot pitch** *noun* COMPUT the spacing between two adjacent pixels displayed on a monitor ○ *The smaller the dot pitch, the sharper the image displayed.* ○ *Typically the dot pitch is between .20 to .40 mm.*

**dots per inch** *noun* COMPUT full form of **d.p.i.**

**dotted-decimal-notation** *noun* COMPUT a method of writing a domain name, email address or other IP network address using a dot to separate the numeric parts of the address

**double** *adjective* involving two or twice

**double bond** *noun* CHEM a set of two covalent bonds between two atoms in which two pairs of electrons are shared

**double buffering** *noun* COMPUT the use of two buffers working together so that one can be read while the other is accepting data

**double-click** COMPUT *noun* the use of two rapid press-release actions on a mouse button, normally to start a program or select an option ○ *Move the pointer to the icon then start the program with a double-click.* ■ *verb* to click twice rapidly on a mouse button

**double cross** *noun* **1.** GENETICS the production of a new hybrid from parents each of which is a first-generation hybrid of pure strains **2.** a new hybrid produced by a double cross

**double decomposition** *noun* CHEM a chemical reaction in which two compounds are decomposed by the exchange of at least one of their components, with the formation of two new compounds

**double density** *noun* COMPUT a system to double the storage capacity of a disk drive by doubling the number of bits which can be put on the disk surface

**double helix** *noun* GENETICS the molecular structure of DNA, consisting of a pair of polynucleotide strands connected by a series of hydrogen bonds and twisted in opposing spirals

**double precision** *noun* COMPUT the use of two data words to store a number, providing greater precision

**double refraction** *noun* OPTICS the splitting of one ray of light into two by some crystals

**doublet** *noun* COMPUT same as **dyad**

**double word** *noun* COMPUT two bytes of data handled as one word, often used for address data

**Douglas fir** *noun* TREES an important North American softwood tree widely planted throughout the world, and yielding vast amounts of strong timber. Latin name: *Pseudotsuga menziesii.*

**down** *adverb* COMPUT (*of computers or programs*) not working ○ *The com-*

puter system went down twice during the afternoon.

**down draught** *noun* **1.** METEOROL the cool air which flows downwards as a rainstorm approaches **2.** EARTH SCI the air which flows rapidly down the lee side of a building or mountain **3.** the air which blows down a chimney

**downland** *noun* EARTH SCI an area of downs

**download** *verb* COMPUT **1.** to load a program or section of data from a remote computer via a telephone line ○ *There is no charge for downloading public domain software from the BBS.* **2.** to load data from a central processing unit to a small computer **3.** to send printer font data stored on a disk to a printer where it will be stored in temporary memory or RAM

**downpipe** *noun* ENG a pipe carrying rainwater from a roof into a drain or soakaway

**downs** *plural noun* EARTH SCI grass-covered chalky hills characterised by low bushes and few trees

**downstream** *adverb, adjective* EARTH SCI towards the mouth of a river ○ *The silt is carried downstream and deposited in the delta.* ○ *Pollution is spreading downstream from the factory.* ○ *Downstream communities have not yet been affected.*

**downtime** *noun* COMPUT a period of time during which a computer system is not working or usable. Opposite **uptime**

**downward** *adjective* moving to a lower level ○ *When flying in turbulent air conditions, an aircraft is subjected to upward and downward gust loads.* (NOTE: In US English, **downward** is used as an adverb as well as an adjective.)

**downward compatibility** *noun* COMPUT the ability of a complex computer system to work with a simple computer ○ *The mainframe is downward compatible with the micro.*

**downwards** *adverb* to a lower level or towards the bottom ○ *Pull the toggles downwards to inflate the lifejacket.*

**downwash** *noun* INDUST the action which brings smoke from a chimney down to the ground as it is caught in a down draught

**DP** *abbreviation* COMPUT data processing

**DPA** *abbreviation* COMPUT demand protocol architecture

**DPCM** *abbreviation* COMPUT differential pulse coded modulation

**d.p.i., dpi** *noun* COMPUT a standard method used to describe the resolution capabilities of a dot-matrix laser printer or scanner ○ *a 600 d.p.i. black and white laser printer* ○ *a 1200 dpi image scanner* Full form **dots per inch**

**draft** *noun* an early rough version of a document or drawing ■ *verb* to make an early rough version of a document or drawing ○ *He drafted out the details of the program on a piece of paper.*

**draft printing** *noun* COMPUT low quality, high speed printing

**drag** *noun* AEROSP the resistance of the air created by moving an aircraft through the air ○ *To reduce the effect of drag on an aircraft by the fixed undercarriage a retractable type was introduced.* ○ *If an engine failure occurs, the windmilling propeller may cause considerable drag.*

COMMENT: There are two basic types of drag, called parasite drag and induced drag. Parasite drag is caused by friction between the air and the aircraft surface or aerials, landing gear, and other parts. Induced drag is produced by lift.

**drag and click** *verb* COMPUT to hold down a mouse button while moving the mouse, so moving the object selected

**drag and drop** *verb* to drag a section of text, icon or object onto another program icon which starts this program and inserts the data ○ *Drag and drop the document icon onto the word-processor icon and the system will start the program and load the document.*

**drain** *noun* **1.** ENG an underground pipe which takes waste water from buildings or from farmland **2.** EARTH SCI, AGRIC an open channel for taking away waste water **3.** a device to allow fluid to escape from its container ○ *When the cabin is pressurised the drains close, preventing loss of pressure.* ■ *verb* **1.** to allow fluid to escape by providing a hole or tube or other means through which it can pass **2.** to remove liquid **3.** (*of liquid*) to flow into something ○ *The stream drains into the main river.*

**drainage** *noun* the removal of liquid from somewhere

**drainage area, drainage basin** *noun* EARTH SCI same as **catchment**

**drainage basin** *noun* same as **catchment**

**drainage channel** *noun* EARTH SCI, AGRIC a small ditch made to remove rainwater from the soil surface

**drainage ditch** *noun* EARTH SCI, AGRIC a channel to take away rainwater

**drainage trench** *noun* ENG a long hole cut in the ground to allow water to run away

**drainpipe** *noun* ENG a pipe carrying rainwater, sewage or other liquid into a drain or soakaway

**DRAM** *abbreviation* COMPUT dynamic RAM

**draught** *noun* a local current of air. US spelling **draft**

**draught animal** *noun* AGRIC an animal used to pull vehicles or carry heavy loads

**draw** *verb* **1.** to make a picture with lines ○ *Because there is a temperature gradient across each front it is possible to draw isotherms which reduce in value from warm to cold air.* **2.** to move something by pulling ○ *Fluid is drawn into the pump body.* (NOTE: **drawing – drew – drawn**)

**drawing program** *noun* COMPUT a piece of software that allows the user to draw and design on screen

**drift** *noun* EARTH SCI a slow movement or change

**drift current** *noun* METEOROL a current in the sea caused by the wind

**drift ice** *noun* EARTH SCI a large piece of ice floating in the sea

**drill** *noun* **1.** ENG a tool, often electrically powered, for making holes in metal, wood or other hard material **2.** a short series of actions carried out in a particular sequence

**drilling** *noun* INDUST the process of boring a hole or an oil well

**drilling mud** *noun* INDUST a mixture of clay, water and minerals, used as a lubricant and coolant when drilling into rock

**drilling rig, drilling platform** *noun* INDUST a large metal construction containing the drilling and pumping equipment for extracting oil or gas

**drilling ship** *noun* INDUST a ship which can bore an oil well

**drinkable** *adjective* ENVIRON safe to drink

**drinking water** *noun* ENVIRON water which is safe to drink

**drive** *noun* **1.** a device that transmits power to wheels or propellers ○ *Rotation of the engine for starting is done by an electric starter motor connected to a drive shaft in the accessories gearbox.* **2.** COMPUT a part of a computer which operates a tape or disk ■ *verb* **1.** to make something move or turn **2.** to control and guide a vehicle ○ *He's learning to drive.* **3.** COMPUT to make a tape or disk work ○ *The disk is driven by a motor.* (NOTE: **driving – drove – driven**)

**drive array** *noun* COMPUT a set of multiple hard disk drives linked together with an intelligent controller that uses the drives to store multiple copies of the data on each drive for reliability or parts of each data on each drive for speed

**drive letter** *noun* COMPUT a letter that denotes the disk drive currently being used. Also called **designator** (NOTE: A and B are normally floppy disks, C is normally the hard disk in a personal computer.)

**-driven** *suffix* COMPUT operated by ○ *steam-driven*

**driver** *noun* COMPUT a program or routine used to interface and manage an input/output device or other peripheral. Also called **device driver**

**drizzle** *noun* METEOROL a light persistent rain with drops of less than 0.5 mm in diameter

**drizzly** *adjective* METEOROL referring to weather with a lot of drizzle

**drop** *noun* **1.** a small amount of liquid that falls ○ *a drop of water* ○ *a few drops of rain* **2.** a lowering or reduction ○ *The passage of a cold front is usually followed by a drop in temperature.* ○ *A sudden drop in oil pressure is normally an indication of serious engine trouble.* **3.** BOT a fall of immature fruit ■ *verb* to become lower ○ *The temperature dropped by several degrees.*

**drop cable** *noun* COMPUT a section of cable that links an adapter fitted in a workstation to the main network cable or sometimes to a transceiver or T-connector in the main network cable

**drop-dead halt** *noun* COMPUT same as **dead halt**

**drop-down menu** *noun* COMPUT a menu that appears below a menu title when it is selected on a computer screen

**drop in** *noun* COMPUT a small piece of dirt that is on a disk or tape surface, which does not allow data to be recorded on that section

**droplet** *noun* a small drop of liquid ○ *Experiments show that smaller droplets of rain can remain supercooled to much lower temperatures than large droplets.*

**droppings** *plural noun* ZOOL excreta from animals ○ *The grass was covered with rabbit and sheep droppings.*

**drosophila** *noun* ZOOL, GENETICS a small two-winged fruit fly that is frequently used in genetic research

**drought** *noun* METEOROL a long period without rain at a time when rain normally falls

**drought stress** *noun* ECOL a lack of growth caused by drought

**drove** *verb* ◊ **drive**

**drowned valley** *noun* EARTH SCI a valley which has been submerged by the advance of the sea or a lake

**drug** *noun* **1.** PHARM a chemical substance, either natural or synthetic, which is used in medicine and affects the way in which organs or tissues function ○ *The doctors are trying to cure him with a new drug.* ○ *She was prescribed a course of pain-killing drugs.* ○ *The drug is being monitored for possible side-effects.* **2.** HEALTH a habit-forming, often illegal, substance

**drug addiction** *noun* HEALTH the condition of being mentally and physically dependent on taking a drug regularly. Also called **drug dependence**

**drug allergy** *noun* MED a reaction to a specific drug

**drug dependence** *noun* HEALTH same as **drug addiction**

**drug tolerance** *noun* PHYSIOL a condition where a drug has been given to a patient for so long that it is no longer effective and the dosage has to be increased

**drum** *noun* **1.** a cylindrical container used for storage, especially of liquids ○ *an oil drum* **2.** COMPUT an early type of magnetic computer storage

**drumlin** *noun* EARTH SCI a small oval hill formed by the action of ice, with one end blunt and the other tapered, similar to half of a hard-boiled egg, cut lengthways

**drupe** *noun* BOT a fruit such as a peach with a single seed and a fleshy body

**DRV** *abbreviation* MED dietary reference values

**dry** *adjective* with the smallest possible amount of moisture ■ *verb* to remove moisture from something

**dry adiabatic lapse rate** *noun* METEOROL the rate of temperature change in rising dry air

**dry cell** *noun* ELEC a current-generating electric device that contains an electrolyte in the form of a paste or within a porous material

**dry cell battery** *noun* ELEC a battery that cannot be recharged. Compare with **rechargeable battery**

**dry contact** *noun* ELEC a faulty electrical connection, often causing an intermittent fault

**dry deposition** *noun* ENVIRON the fall of dry particles from polluted air forming a harmful deposit on surfaces such as buildings or the leaves of trees

**dry farming** *noun* AGRIC a system of extensive agriculture, producing crops in areas of limited rainfall, without using irrigation

**dry ice** *noun* INDUST solid carbon dioxide, used as a refrigerant

**drying bed** *noun* INDUST an area where sewage sludge is spread out to dry

**drying out** *noun* ENVIRON a process whereby water is drained away from wetlands

**dryness** *noun* a state of not being wet ○ *the dryness of the atmosphere on very high mountains*

**dry organic matter** *noun* AGRIC organic matter such as sewage sludge or manure which has been dried out and may be used as a fertiliser. Abbreviation **DOM**

**dry rot** *noun* BOT a fungal disease causing rot in wood, potatoes or fruit

**dry run** *noun* COMPUT an act of running a program with test data to check everything works

**dry season** *noun* METEOROL the time of year in some countries when very little rain falls

**dry steam** *noun* PHYS steam that does not contain droplets of water

**dry up** *verb* (*of a river or lake*) to become dry ○ *The river dries up completely in summer.*

**Ds** *symbol* CHEM ELEM darmstadtium

**DSL** *abbreviation* COMPUT digital subscriber line

**DSP** *abbreviation* COMPUT digital signal processing

**DSR** *abbreviation* COMPUT data set ready

**DSW** *abbreviation* COMPUT device status word

**DTE** *abbreviation* COMPUT data terminal equipment

**DTMF** *abbreviation* COMPUT dual tone multi-frequency

**D to A converter** *noun* COMPUT same as **digital to analog converter**

**DTP** *abbreviation* COMPUT desktop publishing

**DTR** *abbreviation* COMPUT data terminal ready

**dual** *adjective* using two or a pair

**dual bus system** *noun* COMPUT a way of linking different parts of a system which keeps the memory bus separate from the input/output bus

**dual in-line memory module** *noun* COMPUT a system of arranging RAM memory chips on two sides of a tiny expansion card that can be inserted into a slot on the computer's motherboard to upgrade the main memory. Abbreviation **DIMM**

**dual-in-line package** *noun* COMPUT full form of **DIP, DIL**

**dual port memory** *noun* COMPUT a memory with two sets of data and memory lines to allow communications between central processing units

**dual processor** *noun* COMPUT a computer system with two processors for faster program execution

**dual tone multi-frequency** *noun* COMPUT a method of dialling in a telephone system in which each number on the telephone handset generates two tones. Abbreviation **DTMF**

**dub** *verb* to add sound effects to an animation, multimedia presentation, film or video

**dubnium** *noun* CHEM ELEM an extremely rare and unstable element produced by bombarding californium with carbon nuclei (NOTE: The chemical symbol is **Db**; the atomic number is **105** and the atomic weight is **262**.)

**duct** *noun* **1.** a channel or tube through which things such as fluids or cables can pass ○ *Air-conditioning ducts need regular cleaning* ○ *The modern jet engine is basically a duct into which the necessary parts are fitted.* **2.** ANAT a narrow passageway in a gland or bladder through which fluid leaves

**ductile** *adjective* PHYS (*of metals*) able to retain strength when bent and to be made into thin sheets or wires

**ductless gland** *noun* ANAT same as **endocrine gland**

**dumb terminal** *noun* COMPUT a peripheral that can only transmit and receive data from a computer, but is not capable of processing data

**dummy** *noun* COMPUT an imitation product to test the reaction of potential customers to its design

**dummy instruction** *noun* COMPUT an instruction in a program that is only there to satisfy language syntax or to make up a block length

**dump** *noun* **1.** COMPUT data which has been copied from one device to another for storage **2.** COMPUT the transferring of data to a disk for storage **3.** COMPUT a printout of the contents of all or selected data in memory **4.** ENVIRON a place where waste is thrown away ○ *The mine is surrounded with dumps of excavated waste.* ■ *verb* **1.** COMPUT to move data from one device or storage area to another ○ *The account results were dumped to the backup disk.* **2.** ENVIRON to throw away waste

**dumping** *noun* ENVIRON the disposal of waste ○ *The dumping of nuclear waste into the sea should be renewed.*

**dumping ground** *noun* ENVIRON a place where waste is thrown away

**dumpsite** *noun* ENVIRON a place where waste is dumped ○ *Sludge bacteria can survive in seawater for long periods and are widely dispersed from dumpsites.*

**dunes** *plural noun* EARTH SCI an area of sand blown by the wind into small hills and ridges which have very little soil or vegetation ○ *The village was threatened by encroaching dunes.*

**dung** *noun* AGRIC solid waste excreta from animals, especially cattle, often used as fertiliser

COMMENT: In some areas of the world dried dung is used as a cooking fuel, which has the effect of preventing the dung from being returned to the soil and leads to depletion of soil nutrients.

**duodecimal number system** *noun* MATHS a number system with a base of twelve

**duodenum** *noun* ANAT the first short section of the small intestine, into which food passes from the stomach

**duplex** *noun* COMPUT the simultaneous transmission of two signals on one line

**duplex computer** *noun* COMPUT a pair of two identical computer systems used in an on-line application, with one being used as a backup in case of the failure of the other

**duplexing** *noun* COMPUT same as **disk mirroring**

**duplication** *noun* **1.** the process of copying or repeating something **2.** a situation where two or more things have the same purpose ○ *Control surfaces are divided into sections operated by a separate control unit, thus providing duplication to guard against failure of a unit.*

**durability** *noun* the ability of a substance or device to last a long time in good condition ○ *High quality components have good durability.*

**durable** *adjective* COMPUT lasting a long time in good condition ○ *a durable cartridge*

**dura mater** *noun* ANAT the tough outer membrane of the three membranes that surround the brain and spinal cord of the vertebrate central nervous system

**duramen** *noun* BOT the hard dead wood in the centre of a tree's trunk which helps support the tree. Also called **heartwood**

**duration** *noun* the length of time for which something continues ○ *The duration of the examination is two hours.*

**durum** *noun* AGRIC a type of wheat grown in southern Europe and the USA and used in making semolina for processing into pasta. Latin name: *Triticum durum*.

**dust** *noun* a fine powder made of particles of dry dirt or sand

**dust bowl** *noun* EARTH SCI a large area of land where strong winds blow away the dry topsoil

**dust burden** *noun* PHYS the amount of dust which is found suspended in a gas

**dust cloud** *noun* METEOROL a mass of particles of dry dirt or sand suspended in the air

**dust devil** *noun* METEOROL a rapidly turning column of air which picks up sand over a desert or beach, and things such as dust, leaves and litter elsewhere

**dust discharge** *noun* ENVIRON a release of dust into the atmosphere, especially from an industrial process

**dust extractor** *noun* INDUST a machine which removes dust from a place

**dust storm** *noun* METEOROL a storm of wind which blows dust and sand with it, common in North Africa

**dust veil** *noun* ENVIRON a mass of dust in the atmosphere created by volcanic eruptions, storms and burning fossil fuels, which cuts off solar radiation and so reduces the temperature of the Earth's surface. Compare **greenhouse effect**

**Dutch elm disease** *noun* BOT a fungal disease that kills elm trees, caused by *Ceratoaptis ulmi* and spread by a bark beetle

**duty-rated** *adjective* COMPUT referring to the maximum number of operations which a device can perform in a set time to a given specification

**DVD** *noun* COMPUT a means of storing over 17 Gb of data onto a CD-ROM type disc. Full form **digital versatile disc, digital videodisc**

**DVD-R** *noun* COMPUT a DVD disc drive that allows a user to write data once on to a DVD disc. Full form **DVD-Recordable**

**DVD-RAM** *noun* COMPUT a DVD disc drive that allows a user to write, erase and rewrite data on to a DVD disc

**DVD-ROM** *noun* COMPUT a DVD disc drive that can read a DVD disc and provides data transfer rates equal to a standard nine-times CD-ROM

**DVD+RW** *noun* COMPUT a type of rewritable DVD disc that allows a user to store data on a disc with a capacity of 3 Gb per side

**DVD-video** *noun* COMPUT a standard that defines how full-length films can be compressed and stored on a DVD disc and played back on a dedicated player attached to a television set or viewed on a computer fitted with a DVD drive

**DV-I** *abbreviation* COMPUT digital video interactive

**DVI connector** *noun* COMPUT a connector on a monitor or graphics equipment for analogue and digital signals

**Dvorak keyboard** *noun* COMPUT a keyboard layout that is more efficient to use than a normal QWERTY keyboard layout

**dwarf** *noun* ASTRON same as **dwarf star**

**dwarf galaxy** *noun* ASTRON a small galaxy that contains no more than a few million stars and does not shine brightly

**dwarfing rootstock** *noun* AGRIC a plant which is normally low-growing so causing the plant grafted on to it to grow smaller than it would otherwise

**dwarf star** *noun* ASTRON a star with relatively low mass, size and luminosity. Also called **dwarf** (NOTE: The Sun is a dwarf star.)

**dyad** *noun* COMPUT a word made up of two bits

**dyadic Boolean operation** *noun* MATHS a logical operation producing a result from two words, e.g. AND

**dye** *noun* a substance used to change the colour of something ○ *Minute surface cracks which are difficult to detect by visual means may be highlighted by using penetrant dyes.*

**dye-polymer recording** *noun* COMPUT a recording method which creates minute changes in a thin layer of dye imbedded in a plastic optical disk (NOTE: Dye-polymer recording has the advantage that the data stored can be erased.)

**dye-sublimation printer** *noun* COMPUT a high-quality colour printer that produces images by squirting tiny drops of coloured ink onto paper ○ *The new dye-sublimation printer can pro-*

*duce colour images at a resolution of 300 dpi.*

**dyke** ENG *noun* **1.** a long wall of earth built to keep water out **2.** a ditch for drainage ■ *verb* to build walls of earth to help prevent water from flooding land

**dynamic** *adjective* **1.** referring to something in motion **2.** COMPUT referring to data which can change with time

**dynamic allocation** *noun* COMPUT a system where resources are allocated during a program run, rather than being determined in advance

**dynamic data exchange** *noun* COMPUT a method by which two active programs can exchange data. Abbreviation **DDE**

**dynamic data structure** *noun* COMPUT the structure of a data management system which can be changed or adapted

**dynamic electricity** *noun* ELEC electricity which is flowing in a current

**dynamic equilibrium** *noun* a situation which is fluctuating around an apparent average state, where that average state is also changing through time

**dynamic link library** *noun* COMPUT in some operating systems, a library of utility programs that can be called from a main program ○ *The word-processor calls a spell-check program that is stored as a dynamic link library.* Abbreviation **DLL**

**dynamic memory** *noun* COMPUT same as **dynamic RAM**

**dynamic pressure** *noun* AEROSP the pressure created by the forward movement of an aircraft ○ *If the dynamic pressure increases due to an increase in forward speed, the force required to move the control column will increase.*

**dynamic RAM** *noun* COMPUT random access memory that requires its contents to be updated regularly. Also called **dynamic memory**

**dynamic routing** *noun* COMPUT a process of selecting the shortest or most reliable path for data through exchanges at the time of the connection

**dynamics** *noun* PHYS the study of motion and the way in which forces produce it

**dynamic seal** *noun* ENG a seal which is part of a moving component, e.g. in a hydraulic system ○ *Dynamic seals require lubrication to remain effective.*

**dynamic storage allocation** *noun* COMPUT the allocation of memory to a program when it needs it rather than reserving a block in advance

**dynamite** *noun* CHEM a powerful explosive consisting of an inert porous material such as wood pulp or sawdust and nitroglycerine

**dynamo** *noun* PHYS a device that converts mechanical energy into electrical energy, usually producing direct current

**dynamometer** *noun* ENVIRON a machine which measures exhaust fumes from cars

**dyne** *noun* MEASURE the cgs unit of force, equivalent to $10^{-5}$ newtons

**dysenteric** *adjective* MED referring to dysentery

**dysentery** *noun* MED an infection and inflammation of the colon causing bleeding and diarrhoea

COMMENT: Dysentery occurs mainly in tropical countries. The symptoms include diarrhoea, discharge of blood and pain in the intestines. There are two main types of dysentery: bacillary dysentery, caused by the bacterium *Shigella* in contaminated food; and amoebic dysentery or amoebiasis, caused by a parasitic amoeba *Entamoeba histolytica* spread through contaminated drinking water.

**dysgenic** *adjective* GENETICS affecting later generations detrimentally as a result of transmitting undesirable characteristics

**dysgenics** *noun* GENETICS the study of factors associated with a decrease in the survival of the genetically well-adapted members of a line of descent

**dysphotic** *adjective* EARTH SCI referring to the area of water in a lake or the sea between the aphotic zone at the bottom of the water and the euphotic zone which sunlight can reach

**dysprosium** *noun* CHEM ELEM a soft silvery element of the lanthanide group that is paramagnetic and highly reactive (NOTE: It is extracted from monazite and bastnasite and used for laser materials, and in nuclear research. The chemical symbol is **Dy**; the atomic number is **66** and the atomic weight is **162.50**.)

**dystrophic** *adjective* ENVIRON referring to a pond or lake that contains very acidic brown water, lacks oxygen, and is unable to support much plant or animal life because of excessive humus content

**dystrophic lake** *noun* EARTH SCI a lake where the water is acid, brown and peaty, and the dead vegetation does not decompose but settles at the bottom forming a peat bog

**dystrophy** *noun* MED the wasting of an organ, muscle or tissue due to lack of nutrients in that part of the body

**DYUV** *noun* COMPUT a digital video encoding technique in which luminance of a pixel is calculated by the RGB (Red, Green, Blue) input signal. Full form **delta YUV** (NOTE: $Y0.6G + 0.3R + 0.1B$. From the value of Y it is possible to calculate the values of U and V as $UR - Y; VB - Y$.)

# E

**e** *abbreviation* MATHS exponential constant 2.71828… which is defined by the equation e = exp (I) ■ *symbol* PHYS the charge on an electron equal to 1.60219 x $10^{-19}$ coulombs

**E** *symbol* MEASURE exa- ■ *noun* MATHS the hexadecimal number equivalent to decimal number 14

**E¹** *noun* MATHS the hexadecimal number equivalent to decimal number 14

**E²** *symbol* MEASURE exa-

**EAPROM** COMPUT same as **electrically alterable, programmable read-only memory**

**ear** *noun* ANAT an organ which is used for hearing (NOTE: For terms referring to the ear, see words beginning with **auric-, ot-** or **oto-**.)

COMMENT: The outer ear is shaped in such a way that it collects sound and channels it to the eardrum. Behind the eardrum, the three ossicles in the middle ear vibrate with sound and transmit the vibrations to the cochlea in the inner ear. From the cochlea, the vibrations are passed by the auditory nerve to the brain.

**ear canal** *noun* ANAT one of several passages in or connected to the ear, especially the external auditory meatus, the passage from the outer ear to the eardrum

**eardrum** *noun* ANAT the membrane at the end of the external auditory meatus leading from the outer ear, which vibrates with sound and passes the vibrations on to the ossicles in the middle ear (NOTE: For terms referring to the eardrum, see words beginning with **auric-** or **tympan-**.)

**EAROM** *abbreviation* COMPUT electrically alterable read-only memory

**ear ossicle** *noun* ANAT one of three small bones, the malleus, the incus and the stapes, in the middle ear

**earth** *noun* **1.** soil **2.** the ground or land surface **3.** ELEC a connection in a circuit representing zero potential ○ *All loose wires should be tied to earth.* ■ *verb* ELEC to connect an electrical device to the ground ○ *All appliances must be earthed.* US term **ground**

**Earth** *noun* ASTRON, EARTH SCI the planet on which human beings developed and live

COMMENT: Earth is the third planet of the solar system and the only one known to house life. Earth is also remarkable for its seas of liquid water, for its oxygen-bearing atmosphere and for being geologically very active. Earth's equatorial radius is 6378 km, about a third of a per cent more than its polar radius because of Earth's rotation. About 4500 million years old, like the other planets, Earth rotates on its axis in a day, orbits the Sun in a year and has a satellite, the Moon, which orbits it once per lunar month. Earth can be divided into various zones: the lithosphere (solid rock and molten interior), the hydrosphere (the water covering the surface), the atmosphere (the gaseous zone rising above Earth's surface) and the biosphere (those parts of the other zones in which living organisms exist). The interior of the Earth is formed by a central core made of nickel and iron, part of which is solid. Above the core is the mantle, a layer about 2700 km thick of molten minerals. On top of the mantle is the crust, formed of solid rock between 6 and 70 km thick.

**earthquake** *noun* EARTH SCI a phenomenon where Earth's crust or the mantle beneath it shakes and the surface of the ground moves because of movement inside the crust along fault lines, often causing damage to buildings

**earth science** *noun* SCI a science that deals with the physical properties of Earth and its structure or development, e.g. geology or geophysics

**Earth Summit** *noun* ENVIRON the United Nations Conference on Environment and Development held in Rio de Janeiro, Brazil, in June 1992

COMMENT: The principal outcomes of the 'Earth Summit' were a declaration, conventions on controlling climate change and preserving biological diversity, and a lengthy agenda outlining the extent of global environmental problems and the measures needed to tackle them in order to achieve the agreed goal of 'sustainable development'. Opinion was divided as to how far the conference could be termed a success. Many environmentalists stressed its failure to set binding targets for resolving environmental problems, and to address adequately the links between poverty in developing countries and environmental degradation. Others stressed that it should be seen as a first step towards sustainable development and an important acknowledgement of the seriousness of the problem and of the fact that global co-operation is needed to overcome it.

**earth tremor** *noun* EARTH SCI a slight earthquake

**earth wire** *noun* ELEC a wire connecting an electrical device to the ground, representing zero potential

**earthworks** *plural noun* ENG constructions such as walls made from soil

**earthworm** *noun* ZOOL an invertebrate animal with a long thin body, living in large numbers in the soil

COMMENT: Earthworms provide a useful service by aerating the soil as they tunnel. They also eat organic matter and help increase the soil's fertility. They help stabilise the soil structure by compressing material and mixing it with organic matter and calcium. It is believed that they also secrete a hormone which encourages rooting by plants.

**east** *adjective, adverb, noun* NAVIG **1.** a compass point 90° clockwise from due north and directly opposite west ○ *London is east of New York.* ○ *The wind is blowing from the east.* ○ *The river flows east into the ocean.* **2.** the direction in which Earth rotates and the direction of the rising sun

**easterly** *adjective* NAVIG to or from the east ○ *The hurricane was moving in an easterly direction.* ■ *noun* METEOROL a wind which blows from the east

**eastern** *adjective* NAVIG referring to or in the east ○ *The main rain forests lie in the eastern half of the country.*

**east wind** *noun* METEOROL a wind which blows from the east

**easy-to-use** *adjective* simple to understand and operate

**eat** *verb* BIOL to chew and swallow food (NOTE: **eating – ate – eaten**)

**ebb tide** *noun* EARTH SCI a tide which is going down or which is at its lowest ○ *The plan is to build a barrage to generate electricity on the ebb tide.* Opposite **flood tide**

**EBCDIC** *abbreviation* COMPUT extended binary coded decimal interchange code

**EBNF** *abbreviation* COMPUT extended BNF

**ebony** *noun* TREES a black tropical hardwood, now becoming scarce

**ebook** *noun* COMPUT same as **electronic book**

**EBR** *abbreviation* COMPUT electron beam recording

**eccentric** *adjective* ASTRON referring to an orbit which is elliptical rather than circular

**eccentricity** *noun* ASTRON the amount by which an ellipse such as an orbit differs from an exact circle (NOTE: Eccentricity is measured as the difference between the large and small radii (the semi-major and semi-minor axes) divided by the semi-major axis.)

**ecdysis** *noun* ZOOL the regular shedding of the hard shell of arthropods or the skin of reptiles

**echinoderm** *noun* ZOOL a marine invertebrate animal with a radially symmetrical body, tube feet, and an internal skeleton of calcareous plates, e.g. a starfish, sea urchin, sea lily or sea cucumber. Phylum: Echinodermata.

**echo** PHYS *noun* **1.** the repetition of a sound by reflection of sound waves from a surface **2.** the return of a signal back to the source from which it was transmitted ○ *The strength of the returning echo from a radar transmission depends on a number of factors.* ■ *verb* to return a received signal along the same transmission path

**echo-** *prefix* PHYS referring to sound

**echo cancellation** *noun* TELECOM a technique used to remove echo signals from a communications line

**echolocation** *noun* PHYS the technique of finding a location by sending out a sound signal and listening to the reflection of the sound ○ *Bats and whales find their way by using echolocation.*

**echosounder** *noun* PHYS a device used to find the depth of water by sending a sound signal down to the bottom and calculating the distance from the time taken for the reflected sound to reach the surface again

**echosounding** *noun* PHYS the process of finding the depth of water using an echosounder

**ECL** *abbreviation* COMPUT emitter-coupled logic

**eclampsia** *noun* MED a serious condition of pregnant women at the end of pregnancy, where the patient has convulsions and high blood pressure and may go into a coma, caused by toxaemia of pregnancy

**eclipse** *noun* ASTRON a situation when the Moon passes between the Sun and the Earth (solar eclipse) or when the Earth passes between the Sun and the Moon (lunar eclipse), in both cases cutting off the light visible from Earth

COMMENT: In an eclipse of the Moon, Earth comes between the Moon and Sun, so that its shadow crosses the Moon's surface. The term is also used universally but in fact wrongly for occasions when the Sun's disc is blotted out by the Moon from the point of view of observers on Earth. These events are in fact occultations of the Moon, or eclipses of the Earth. The Moon and the Sun are almost exactly the same size – about half a degree – in the Earth's sky, making it possible, by coincidence, to observe the eclipsed Sun. This provides a powerful experimental tool for examining the Sun's atmosphere. The Moon's shadow on Earth is so narrow that any given solar eclipse is visible only from a narrow line on the Earth's surface. If the Moon is too far away in its orbit the full eclipse effect is not seen, but an **annular eclipse** is observed instead.

**ecliptic** *noun* ASTRON the apparent path of the Sun's annual motion relative to the stars, shown as a circle passing through the centre of the imaginary sphere (**celestial sphere**) containing all the planets and stars (NOTE: Eclipses of the Sun or Moon can occur only when the Moon crosses the ecliptic.)

**ECMA symbol** *noun* COMPUT one of a standard set of symbols used to draw flowcharts

**eco-** *prefix* ECOL, ENVIRON ecology, ecological

**ecocatastrophe** *noun* ENVIRON an event that results in very severe damage to the environment, especially one caused by human action

**ecoclimate** *noun* ECOL the climate seen as an ecological factor

**ecocline** *noun* ECOL the changes which take place in a species as individuals live in different habitats

**eco-efficiency** *noun* ENVIRON the efficient manufacture of goods at competitive prices without harm to the environment

**ecolabelling** *noun* ENVIRON the identification and labelling of products and services that are considered less harmful to the environment than other similar products or services

**E. coli** *abbreviation* MED Escherichia coli

**ecological** *adjective* referring to ecology

**ecological balance** *noun* ECOL the situation where relative numbers of different organisms living in the same ecosystem remain more or less constant

**ecological damage** *noun* ENVIRON harm done to an ecosystem

**ecological disaster** *noun* ENVIRON an event which seriously disturbs the balance of the environment

**ecological diversity** *noun* ECOL a variety of biological communities that interact with one another and with their physical and chemical environments

**ecological efficiency** *noun* ECOL a measurement of how much energy is used at different stages in the food chain or at different trophic levels

**ecological engineering** *noun* ENVIRON the construction of roads or harbours, the introduction of new plants or animals, or other actions which have an effect on the ecology of an area

**ecological factor** *noun* ECOL a factor which influences the distribution of a plant species in a habitat

**ecological footprint** *noun* an area of the Earth that supplies the ecosystem resources for an organism to exist ○ *Ecological footprints enable people to visualise the impact of their consumption patterns and activities on ecosystems.* ○ *You can alter the size of your ecological footprint by modifying your actions.*

**ecological indicator** *noun* ECOL a species that has particular nutritional or climatic requirements and whose presence in an area indicates that those requirements are satisfied

**ecological justification** *noun* ENVIRON grounds for nature conservation based on the idea that the environment provides specific functions necessary for human life

**ecological niche** *noun* ECOL all the chemical, physical or biological characters that determine the position of an organism or species in an ecosystem, commonly called the 'role' or 'profession' of an organism, e.g. an aquatic predator or a terrestrial herbivore

**ecological recovery** *noun* ECOL the return of an ecosystem to its former harmonious balance

**ecological restoration** *noun* ECOL the process of renewing and maintaining the health of an ecosystem

**ecological structure** *noun* ECOL the spatial and other arrangements of species in an ecosystem

**ecological succession** *noun* ECOL the series of stages by which a group of organisms living in a community reaches its final stable state or climax

**ecologist** *noun* 1. ECOL a scientist who studies ecology 2. ENVIRON a person who is in favour of maintaining a balance between living things and the environment in which they live in an attempt to improve the life of all organisms

**ecology** *noun* ECOL the study of the relationships among organisms as well as the relationships between them and their physical environment

**ecomovement** *noun* ENVIRON a grouping of individuals and organisations dedicated to the protection of the environment

**economic geology** *noun* EARTH SCI the study of rock or soil formation for the purpose of commercial mineral extraction

**economizer** *noun* INDUST a device which saves waste heat in a boiler, by transferring heat from waste gases to the water being heated or where water is pre-heated before it passes to the main boiler

**ecoparasite** *noun* BIOL a parasite which is adapted to a specific host

**ecophysiology** *noun* ECOL the study of organisms and their functions and how they exist in their environment

**ecospecies** *noun* BOT a subspecies of a plant

**ecosphere** *noun* EARTH SCI the part of the Earth and its atmosphere where living organisms exist, including parts of the lithosphere, the hydrosphere and the atmosphere. Also called **biosphere**

**ecosystem** *noun* ECOL a system which includes all the organisms of an area and the environment in which they live ○ *European wetlands are classic examples of ecosystems that have been shaped by humans.*

COMMENT: An ecosystem can be any size, from a pinhead to the whole ecosphere. The term was first used in the 1930s to describe the interdependence of organisms among themselves and their relationships with the living and non-living environment.

**ecotone** *noun* ECOL an area between two different types of vegetation such as the border between forest and moorland, which may share the characteristics of both

**ecotoxic** *adjective* ENVIRON likely to cause severe damage to organisms and their environment

**ecotoxicology** *noun* ENVIRON the study of how chemicals associated with human activities affect organisms and their environment

**ecotype** *noun* ECOL a species that has special characteristics which allow it to live in a specific habitat

**ECT** *abbreviation* MED electroconvulsive therapy

**ecto-** *prefix* outside. Compare **endo-**

**ectoderm** *noun* BIOL the outermost of three layers of cells of an embryo, which form the epidermis, nervous tissue and sense organs

**ectoparasite** *noun* BIOL a parasite which lives on the skin or outer surface of the host but feeds by piercing the skin

**ectopic** *adjective* MED not in the usual position

**ectoplasm** *noun* BIOL the outer and densest layer of the cytoplasm in cells

**ectotherm** *noun* ZOOL an organism which is largely reliant on external sources of heat to raise its body temperature ○ *Plants and reptiles are ectotherms.* Also called **poikilotherm**

**eczema** *noun* MED a non-contagious inflammation of the skin, with itchy rash and blisters

**EDAC** *abbreviation* COMPUT error detection and correction

**edaphic** *adjective* EARTH SCI referring to soil

**edaphic climax** *noun* EARTH SCI a climax caused by the type of soil in an area

**edaphic factors** *plural noun* ECOL the different soil conditions which affect the organisms living in a specific area

**edaphon** *noun* ECOL an organism living in soil

**eddy** *noun* PHYS a whirlpool of air or of water in a current

**eddy current** *noun* ELEC an electric current induced in the iron core of an electromagnet by an alternating magnetic field, frequently a source of wasted energy

**edge** *noun* the furthest point of something such as a flat object, a signal or a clock pulse

**edge connector** *noun* COMPUT a long connector with a slot containing metal contacts to allow it to make electrical contact with an edge card

**edge detection** *noun* COMPUT the process of using an algorithm and routines for image recognition to define the edges of an object

**edge-triggered** *adjective* ELEC referring to a process or circuit which is clocked or synchronised by the changing level (**edge**) of a clock signal rather than the level itself

**EDI** *abbreviation* COMPUT electronic data interchange

**edible** *adjective* BIOL able to be eaten

**edible fungus** *noun* FUNGI a fungus that is not poisonous to humans if eaten

**edit** *verb* COMPUT to change, correct and modify text or programs

**editor program** *noun* COMPUT a piece of software that allows the user to select sections of a file and alter, delete or add to them

**EDO memory** *noun* COMPUT memory technology that provides better performance by being able to find and read data from a memory location in one operation. Full form **extended data output memory** (NOTE: It can also store the last piece of data that was saved to memory in a cache ready to be read back from memory.)

**EDP** *abbreviation* COMPUT electronic data processing (NOTE: **EDP is more commonly used in US English**)

**EDP capability** *noun* COMPUT a word-processor able to carry out certain data processing functions

**edutainment** *noun* COMPUT software that is a cross between entertainment and educational products

**EEG** abbreviation **electroencephalogram**

**EEPROM** *abbreviation* ELEC electrically erasable programmable read-only memory

**EER** *abbreviation* MEASURE energy efficiency ratio

**EEROM** *abbreviation* COMPUT electrically erasable read-only memory

**EFA** *abbreviation* BIOCHEM essential fatty acid

**effect** *noun* **1.** something which happens because of a cause ○ *Ultra-violet radiation has the effect of warming the atmosphere.* ○ *Pressure patterns have an effect on weather.* **2.** the condition of being in full force □ **in effect** in operation □ **to take effect, to come into effect** to start to operate ○ *A new regulation comes into effect tomorrow.* ■ *verb* to carry out or bring about something ○ *Several modifications to the design were effected.* ○ *The accident effected a change in procedures.*

**effective** *adjective* **1.** having an expected and satisfactory result **2.** starting to work ○ *The regulation is effective immediately.*

**effective address** *noun* COMPUT an address resulting from the modification of an address

**effective instruction** *noun* COMPUT the instruction executed after the modification of an original instruction

**effectiveness** *noun* how well something works ○ *Ice covering reduces the effectiveness of an aerial.*

**effector** *noun* **1.** ANAT a muscle, gland or organ capable of responding to a nerve impulse **2.** ANAT a nerve that conducts an impulse **3.** BIOCHEM a substance that controls protein synthesis by binding to an enzyme and increasing or decreasing its activity

**efferent** *adjective* PHYSIOL referring to nerves that conduct impulses away from the brain or spinal cord, or blood vessels that remove blood from an organ

**efferent nerve** *noun* ANAT same as **motor nerve**

**effervescence** *noun* CHEM the escape of small bubbles of gas from a liquid

**efficiency** *noun* **1.** the ability to act or produce something with a minimum of waste, expense or unnecessary effort **2.** a comparison of the effective or useful output to the total input in any system ○ *Efficiency is a key component of a successful business.* **3.** MECH ENG a ratio of the energy delivered by a machine to the energy supplied for its operation ○ *mechanical efficiency*

**efficiency ratio** *noun* MECH ENG a number which shows the proportion of work done or energy produced by a machine or engine, to the energy supplied, usually expressed as a percentage

**efficient** *adjective* able to act or produce something with a minimum of waste, expense or unnecessary effort ○ *At certain speeds and altitudes the pure jet engine is less efficient than a piston engine.*

**efficient combustion** *noun* PHYS combustion in which fuel energy is used to its maximum capability with minimum waste

**efficiently** *adverb* in an efficient way

**efflorescence** *noun* CHEM the loss of some of the water of crystallisation from a crystalline salt

**effluent** *noun* INDUST sewage, especially liquid or solid waste from industrial processes or liquid, solid or gas waste material such as slurry or silage effluent from a farm

**effluent charge** *noun* INDUST a fee paid by a company to be allowed to discharge waste into the sea or a river

**effluent monitor** *noun* INDUST a device which monitors the radioactivity in liquid waste from nuclear power stations

**effluent purification process** *noun* INDUST any method of purifying sewage

**effluent standard** *noun* ENVIRON the amount of sewage which is allowed to be discharged into a river or the sea

**effort** *noun* **1.** the use of physical or mental energy to do something ○ *In order to qualify for a licence, it is necessary to put some effort into the training course.* **2.** PHYS the force applied against inertia

**effusion** *noun* PHYS the flow of a gas through a very small aperture under pressure

**egg** *noun* **1.** BIOL a reproductive cell which is produced in a female mammal by the ovary and which, if fertilised by male sperm, becomes an embryo **2.** ZOOL a fertilised ovum of an animal such as a bird, fish, reptile, amphibian or insect, protected by a membrane layer in which the embryo continues developing outside the mother's body until it hatches

**egg cell** *noun* BIOL an immature ovum or female cell

**EHO** *abbreviation* ENVIRON Environmental Health Officer

**EIA** *abbreviation* ENVIRON environmental impact assessment

**EIA interface** *noun* COMPUT a standard defining interface signals, transmission rate and power, usually used to connect terminals to modems

**EIDE** *noun* COMPUT an enhanced IDE specification that improves the performance and data transfer rates to and from a hard disk drive. Full form **extended integrated drive electronics**

**eigenvalue** *noun* PHYS (*in quantum mechanics*) the energy of a wave function of a system

**8-bit** *adjective* COMPUT referring to data that is transferred eight bits at a time along eight parallel conductors

**8-bit byte** *noun* COMPUT a byte made up of eight binary digits. Also called **octet**

**8-bit sample** *noun* COMPUT a single sample of an analog signal which is stored as an 8-bit digital number, meaning that there are 256 possible levels. ◊ **16-bit sample**

**Einstein, Albert (1879–1955)** a physicist of Swiss birth who lived most of his life in the USA. His work on relativity altered the face of modern physics.

**einsteinium** *noun* CHEM ELEM a synthetic radioactive element in the actinide group, produced by irradiation of plutonium and other elements. Symbol **Es** (NOTE: The chemical symbol is **Es**; the atomic number is **99** and the atomic weight is **254**.)

**EIS** *abbreviation* **1.** ENVIRON environmental impact statement **2.** COMPUT executive information system ○ *With this EIS software, we can see how every part of the company performs.*

**either-or operation** *noun* COMPUT a logical function that produces a true output if any input is true

**ejecta** *plural noun* EARTH SCI ash and lava thrown up by an erupting volcano

**elapse** *verb* (*of time*) to pass

**elapsed time** *noun* COMPUT the time taken by the user to carry out a task on a computer

**elasmobranch** *noun* FISH a fish with a cartilaginous skeleton and no true bone, e.g. a shark, ray or skate. Subclass: Elasmobranchii.

**elastance** *noun* ELECTRONICS the reciprocal of the capacitance of a device, measured in farad$^{-1}$

**elastic** *adjective* **1.** PHYS easily returning to original shape after being stretched or expanded ○ *At low values of stress, if the plot of stress and strain is a straight line, the indication is that the material is elastic within this range.* **2.** flexible

**elastic banding** *noun* COMPUT a method of defining the limits of an image on a computer screen by stretching a boundary around it

**elastic buffer** *noun* COMPUT a buffer size that changes according to demand

**elasticity** *noun* PHYS the property of returning to an original form or state following deformation ○ *Titanium falls between aluminium and stainless steel in terms of elasticity, density and elevated temperature strength.*

**elastic limit** *noun* PHYS the maximum stress that can be applied to a material without causing permanent change of form or state

**elastic modulus** *noun* PHYS the ratio of stress applied to a body compared to the strain produced inside the body

**elastomer** *noun* CHEM a material with elastic properties (NOTE: It may be a natural material such as rubber or a synthetic one such as neoprene.)

**electric** *adjective* ELEC worked by, charged with or producing electricity

**electrical** *adjective* ELEC **1.** referring to electricity ○ *an electrical fault* **2.** powered or worked by electricity ○ *Activation may be mechanical or electrical.*

**electrical actuation** *noun* ELEC a movement caused by an electric motor

**electrical appliance** *noun* ELEC a device or machine worked by electricity, e.g. a washing machine, vacuum cleaner, iron or toaster

**electrical equipment** *noun* devices, components or systems that use electricity

**electrically** *adverb* ELEC by electricity ○ *an electrically-powered motor*

**electrically alterable, programmable read-only memory** *noun* COMPUT a version of EAROM which can be programmed. Abbreviation **EAPROM**

**electrically alterable read-only memory** *noun* COMPUT a read-only memory chip whose contents can be programmed by applying a specific voltage to a write pin and can be erased by light or a reverse voltage. Abbreviation **EROM**

**electrically erasable programmable read-only memory** *noun* COMPUT a ROM storage chip which can be programmed and erased using an electrical signal. Abbreviation **EEPROM**

**electrically erasable read-only memory** *noun* COMPUT an EAROM memory chip whose contents can be programmed by applying a specific voltage to a write pin and can be erased by light or a reverse voltage. Abbreviation **EEROM**

**electrical polarity** *noun* ELEC a definition of whether an electrical signal is positive or negative, indicating whether a point is a source or collector of electrical current (NOTE: Positive polarity terminals are usually marked red, negative are black.)

**electrical power generation** *noun* ELEC the production of electricity

**electrical storm** *noun* METEOROL a storm with thunder and lightning

**electric battery** *noun* ELEC a small device for storing and releasing electric energy

**electric charge** *noun* PHYS a number of atoms that are charged because of an excess or deficiency of electrons

**electric current** *noun* ELEC the mass movement of electric charge in a conductor

**electric displacement** *noun* PHYS the charge per unit area in a dielectric material. Symbol **D**. Also called **electric flux density**

**electric field** *noun* PHYS the region or space around a charged body in which another charged particle will be affected by a force

**electric flux density** *noun* PHYS same as **electric displacement**

**electricity** *noun* ELEC an electric current used to provide light, heat or power ○ *The electricity was cut off and the computers crashed.*

COMMENT: Electricity, though clean and relatively cheap to use, is an inefficient form of energy since more than 50% of the heat needed to make it is wasted. On the other hand, electricity is used to drive machines which could not be operated by other means.

**electricity grid** *noun* ELEC a system for carrying electricity round a country, using power lines from power stations. Also called **national grid** (NOTE: The electricity is at a high voltage, which is reduced by transformers to low voltage by the time the electricity is brought into use.)

**electricity supply** *noun* ELEC the electric power provided for domestic and industrial use ○ *The electricity supply is often cut.*

**electric motor** *noun* ELEC a device for turning electrical energy into mechanical energy

**electric polarisation** *noun* PHYS polarisation of an electric signal or electromagnetic field

**electric potential** *noun* PHYS the work required to transfer a unit of positive electric charge from an infinite distance to a given point. Symbol **V**

**electro-** *prefix* electricity

**electrocardiogram** *noun* MED a visual record of the changes in electrical potential that occur with each heart beat, produced by an electrocardiograph

**electrocardiograph** *noun* MED a device that produces a visual record of the heart's electrical activity via electrodes placed on the patient's chest

**electrochemical cell** *noun* ELEC, CHEM a device that generates an electromagnetic force as a result of a chemical reaction. ⊕ **battery, cell**

**electrochemical equivalent** *noun* PHYS in electrolysis, the mass of an element separated from a solution by applying one coulomb of charge. Symbol **z**. ⊕ **Faraday's laws**

**electrochemical series** *noun* CHEM same as **electromotive series**

**electrochemistry** *noun* CHEM the study of chemical behaviour relating to electrolysis and electric cells

**electroconvulsive therapy** *noun* MED the treatment of severe depression and some mental disorders by giving the patient small electric shocks in the brain to make him or her have convulsions. Abbreviation **ECT**

**electrode** *noun* ELEC a solid electrical conductor through which an electric current enters or leaves an electrolytic cell ○ *A battery has a positive and a negative electrode.*

**electrodeposit** *noun* PHYS a substance deposited by electrolysis

**electrode potential** *noun* CHEM the potential difference generated between an electrode and the solution in which it is immersed

**electrodialysis** *noun* INDUST the process by which ions dissolved in sea water are removed, making the water fit to drink

**electroencephalogram** *noun* MED a graphic record of the electrical activity of the brain produced by an electroencephalograph

**electroencephalograph** *noun* MED a device that produces a graphic record of the electrical activity of the brain via electrodes placed on the patient's scalp

**electroforming** *noun* INDUST the process of manufacturing an object, often a very small or fragile one, by electrodeposition of a metal onto a pre-formed pattern or mould

**electroluminescence** *noun* PHYS light emitted from a phosphor dot when it is struck by an electron or charged particle

**electroluminescent** *adjective* PHYS capable of emitting light due to electroluminescence ○ *The screen coating is electroluminescent.*

**electroluminescent display** *noun* COMPUT a flat, lightweight display screen made up of two pieces of glass covered with a grid of conductors, separated by a thin layer of gas which luminesces when a point of the grid is selected by two electric signals

**electrolysis** *noun* CHEM a chemical reaction caused by the passage of electricity from one electrode to another

**electrolyte** *noun* CHEM a chemical solution of a substance which can conduct electricity

**electrolytic cell** *noun* CHEM a cell consisting of electrodes in an electrolyte solution

**electrolytic rectifier** *noun* PHYS a device made of two electrodes and an electrolyte that allows electric current to flow in only one direction

**electrolytic separation** *noun* PHYS the separation of isotopes using electrolysis

**electromagnet** *noun* PHYS a magnet consisting of a coil of insulated wire wrapped around a soft iron core that is magnetised only when electric current flows through the wire

COMMENT: In a practical electromagnet the magnetic field produced by the coil carrying the electric current is concentrated by the insertion of a ferrous core into the coil.

**electromagnetic** *adjective* PHYS **1.** having magnetic properties caused by a flow of electricity **2.** containing or worked by an electromagnet

**electromagnetic force** *noun* PHYS the force which acts between charged particles in chemical reactions and elsewhere

**electromagnetic interaction** *noun* PHYS the interaction between elementary particles arising from their electric and magnetic fields, with a strength between that of the strong and weak interactions

**electromagnetic interference** *noun* COMPUT the corruption of data due to nearby electrically generated magnetic fields. Abbreviation **EMI**

**electromagnetic radiation** *noun* PHYS a wave-like form of energy that can travel in a vacuum and consists of a magnetic and an electric field at right angles to each other and to the direction in which the wave travels (NOTE: It includes many familiar forms of energy such as visible light, X-rays, microwaves and radio waves, whose properties vary according to their wavelengths or frequencies.)

**electromagnetic spectrum** *noun* PHYS a range of energy capable of being transmitted through the universe by the propagation of electrical and magnetic fields, of which the visible spectrum experienced as light is only a minute fraction

COMMENT: The full electromagnetic spectrum starts with radio waves from very low frequency to extra high frequency. Below this come infrared wavelengths until the longest visible light, red, with a wavelength of some 780 nm. The visible runs from here to the end of the violet at 380 nm, after which the ultraviolet runs up to about 0.01 nm. After this come the gamma rays up to about a thousand trillionth of a metre wavelength. X-rays overlap the boundary between ultraviolet and gamma rays. Objects at different temperatures emit radiation preferentially at different wavelengths, getting shorter as the object gets hotter.

**electromagnetic wave** *noun* PHYS a wave of electromagnetic energy generated in an electromagnetic field

**electromagnetism** *noun* PHYS a force exerted by a magnetic field found around any conductor carrying current, the strength of which will depend on the amount of current flow

**electrometallurgy** *noun* METALL the range of metallurgical processes such as electroplating in which electricity is involved

**electromotive force** *noun* PHYS a source of electrical energy, from the movement of electrons, required to produce an electric current, produced by devices such as batteries or generators and measured in volts. Abbreviation **emf**

**electromotive series** *noun* CHEM an arrangement of chemical elements in the order of their electrode potentials, taking hydrogen as having zero electrode potential

**electron** *noun* PHYS a negatively charged sub-atomic particle within an atom ○ *Electrons in the outer orbits of an atom may not be strongly attracted to the nucleus and may be lost.*

**electron affinity** *noun* PHYS the amount of energy required to remove an electron from a negatively charged ion, giving a measure of the tendency of the molecule or atom to form a negative ion

**electron beam** *noun* PHYS a narrow, focused stream of electrons moving at high speed in the same direction, often in a vacuum ○ *The electron beam draws the image on the inside of a CRT screen.*

**electron beam recording** *noun* COMPUT the recording of the output from a computer directly onto microfilm using an electron beam. Abbreviation **EBR**

**electron capture** *noun* PHYS **1.** the process in the nucleus of an atom in which a proton is transformed into a neutron, reducing the atomic number by one **2.** the formation of a negative ion when an extra electron is acquired

**electronegative** *adjective* PHYS (*of atoms*) having negative electric charge and therefore tending to move towards a positive electric pole

**electron gun** *noun* PHYS a part of a cathode ray tube that produces a beam of electrons

**electronic** *adjective* ELECTRONICS referring to, based on, operated by or involving the controlled conduction of electrons, especially in a vacuum, gas or semi-conducting material ○ *Lightning does not often seriously damage aircraft but it may affect sensitive electronic equipment.*

**electronically** *adverb* ELECTRONICS by electronic methods ○ *The text is electronically transmitted to an outside typesetter.*

**electronic book** *noun* COMPUT a book published in electronic form

**electronic data interchange** *noun* COMPUT a system of sending orders, paying invoices or transferring company information over a network or telephone line using an electronic mail system. Abbreviation **EDI**

**electronic data processing** *noun* COMPUT data processing using computers and electronic devices. Abbreviation **EDP**

**electronic digital computer** *noun* COMPUT a digital computer constructed with electronic components (NOTE: The basic form uses a central processing unit, main memory, backing storage and input/output devices. These are all implemented with electronic components and integrated circuits.)

**electronic engineer** *noun* ELECTRONICS a person who specialises in work on electronic devices

**electronic publishing** *noun* COMPUT **1.** the use of desktop publishing packages and laser printers to produce printed matter **2.** the use of computers to write and display information such as viewdata

**electronic pulse** *noun* COMPUT a short voltage pulse

**electronics** *noun* ELECTRONICS the science of applying the study of electrons and their properties to manufactured products such as components, computers, calculators or telephones ○ *the electronics industry* ○ *an electronics specialist*

**Electronics Industry Association Interface** *noun* ELEC a standard defining interface signals, transmission rate and power, usually used to connect terminals to modems. Abbreviation **EIA**

**electronic smog** *noun* COMPUT excessive stray electromagnetic fields and static electricity generated by a lot of pieces of electronic equipment (NOTE: This can damage equipment *or* a person's health.)

**electronic traffic** *noun* COMPUT data transmitted in the form of electronic pulses

**electron lens** *noun* PHYS a machine that creates an electric or magnetic field that focuses an electron beam

**electron microscope** *noun* SCI a microscope that uses a beam of electrons instead of light. Abbreviation **EM**

**electron optics** *noun* PHYS the study of the properties and use of an electron beam in optical devices such as a cathode ray tube or electron microscope

**electron-spin resonance** *noun* PHYS a type of spectroscopy in which microwave radiation is used

**electronvolt** *noun* PHYS a measure of energy used in physics, equal to the energy accumulated by an electron passing through a one-volt electric potential. Symbol **eV**

**electrophile** *noun* CHEM an electron-attracting or electron-accepting atom, molecule or chemical group

**electrophilic addition** *noun* CHEM a chemical reaction caused by adding a molecule to the double or triple bond of an unsaturated organic compound

**electrophilic substitution** *noun* CHEM a chemical reaction that substitutes an atom in an organic compound

**electrophoresis** *noun* PHYS the movement of charged particles in a colloid or suspension when an electric field is applied (NOTE: It forms the basis of a common technique for analysing chemicals.)

**electrophorus** *noun* PHYS a machine for generating electrical charge from the friction between a spinning disc and a metal plate

**electrophotographic** *adjective* PRINTING referring to a printing technique used in many laser printers in which a laser beam creates an image on a charged drum (NOTE: The drum then attracts particles of fine black toner to the charged areas and transfers the image to paper which is then passed near a heater to melt the toner onto the paper.)

**electroplate** *verb* PHYS to use electrolysis to coat the surface of one metal with another

**electroporation** *noun* BIOTECH a method of genetic modification that uses an electric pulse to introduce DNA from one organism into a protoplast of another

**electropositive** *adjective* PHYS referring to an element that tends to lose an electron and so form a positive ion

**electrosensitive paper** *noun* PRINTING a metal-coated printing paper which can display characters using localised heating with a special dot-matrix print head

**electrosensitive printing** *noun* PRINTING printing using electrosensitive paper

**electroshock therapy** *noun* MED same as **electroconvulsive therapy**

**electrostatic** *adjective* PHYS referring to devices using the properties of static electrical charge

**electrostatic field** *noun* PHYS an electric field produced by a static electric charge

**electrostatic precipitator** *noun* PHYS a device for collecting minute particles of dust suspended in gas by charging the particles as they pass through an electrostatic field

**electrostatic printer** *noun* PRINTING a type of printer that forms an image on paper by charging some regions to provide character shapes and using ink with an opposite charge which sticks to the paper where required

**electrostatics** *noun* PHYS the study of electric charges at rest (**static electricity**)

**electrostatic screen** *noun* ELEC a metal cage surrounding sensitive equipment and connected to the ground to protect it from interference

**electrostatic storage** *noun* COMPUT the storage of data in the form of small electric charged regions on a dielectric material

**electrostriction** *noun* PHYS a change in the size of a dielectric material when it is near an electric field

**electrovalent bond** *noun* CHEM a chemical bond created by the transfer of electrons from one atom to another giving a structure in which oppositely charged ions are held together by attraction forces

**electrum** *noun* METALL a pale-coloured alloy of silver and gold often used for jewellery and ornaments

**elegant programming** *noun* COMPUT the writing of a well-structured program using the minimum number of instructions

**element** *noun* **1.** CHEM a basic simple chemical substance that cannot be broken down to a simpler substance (NOTE: There are 105 elements.) **2.** ELEC the resistance wire coil in an electrical device such as a heater **3.** a removable component or removable part such as in an air filter or oil filter **4.** a small part of an object which is made up of many similar parts **5.** MATHS one number or cell of a matrix or array

COMMENT: Chemical elements are the chemically discrete types of atom which make up the universe and of which chemical compounds are composed. Atoms of a particular element can vary in the number of neutrons in their nuclei. The variants are called isotopes and always have the same number of positively charged protons, and an equivalent number of electrons in orbit around the nucleus. The simplest example is the three isotopes of hydrogen: normal hydrogen, deuterium and tritium, which have no neutrons, one neutron and two neutrons respectively. Each has one proton, with one electron in orbit around the nucleus.

**elemental** *adjective* CHEM in the form of a pure element ○ *The snail stores elemental sulfur in its shell.*

**elementary** *adjective* 1. COMPUT made of many similar small sections or objects 2. fundamental or basic

**elementary particle** *noun* PHYS a particle that is smaller than an atom or forms part of an atom, e.g. an electron. Also called **subatomic particle**

**elevate** *verb* to move something to a higher place or position from a lower one ○ *In some light aircraft the magnetic compass is elevated to a position as far away from the interfering effect of other components as possible.*

**elevated** *adjective* 1. raised to a higher place or position 2. increased ○ *an elevated temperature*

**elevation** *noun* 1. the height at which something is above a point of reference such as the ground or sea level ○ *The highest point in a locality is marked by a dot with the elevation marked alongside.* 2. movement to a higher place or position

**elevation of boiling point** *noun* PHYS a rise in the boiling point of a liquid caused by dissolving a solid into the liquid

**elevator** *noun* COMPUT a small, square indicator displayed within a scroll bar that indicates the current position within a long document or image ○ *The user can scroll through the image* or *text by dragging the elevator up* or *down the scroll bar.*

**eliminate** *verb* 1. to get rid of or remove something ○ *To eliminate the need for complex mechanical linkage, the selector is operated electrically.* ○

*The spelling checker does not eliminate all spelling mistakes.* ○ *Mosquitoes were eliminated by a programme of spraying breeding grounds with oil.* **2.** to rule out a possibility ○ *Bacteria were eliminated as a possible cause of the illness.*

**elimination** *noun* 1. BIOL removal of waste matter from the body 2. the process of eliminating something □ **by a process of elimination** by removing possibilities one by one until only the most likely cause or answer is left

**elimination factor** *noun* COMPUT a section of data that is not used during a search

**ELISA** *noun* IMMUNOL a technique for detecting and measuring proteins in biological materials. Full form **enzyme-linked immunosorbent assay**

**ellipse** *noun* MATHS an oval shape or course ○ *Each planet moves in an ellipse and the sun is at one of the foci.*

**ellipsoid** *noun* MATHS a curved surface or body

**elliptical** *adjective* MATHS having an oval shape ○ *The path of the Earth around the sun is elliptical.*

**elliptical galaxy** *noun* ASTRON a galaxy with no arms or internal structure and an overall elliptical or spherical shape

**elm** *noun* TREES a large hardwood tree which grows in temperate areas. Genus: *Ulmus*.

**El Niño** *noun* EARTH SCI a phenomenon occurring every few years in the Pacific Ocean, where a mass of warm water moves from west to east, rising as it moves, giving very high tides along the Pacific coast of South America

COMMENT: El Niño not only brings high tides but also influences rainfall patterns around the Pacific basin, most rain falling along the Pacific coast of South America, in southern South Asia and in the Pacific Islands, but making northern South Asia, Africa and Australia drier than usual. The phenomenon seems to occur as a cycle, every two to five years.

**else rule** *noun* COMPUT a logical rule used with an IF-THEN instruction to provide an alternative if the IF-THEN condition is not met

**eluant** *noun* CHEM another spelling of **eluent**

**eluate** *noun* CHEM a liquid that has removed adsorbed material from an adsorbent using an elution process, consisting of the solvent and the previously adsorbed material

**eluent, eluant** *noun* CHEM a solvent

**elution** *noun* CHEM the removal of an adsorbed substance by washing with a solvent

**eluviation** *noun* EARTH SCI the action of leaching out particles and chemicals from the topsoil down into the subsoil

**eluvium** *noun* EARTH SCI a gravel formed as rocks are broken down into fragments where they are lying. Compare **alluvium**

**em** *noun* PRINTING a measure equal to the width of the letter m in a particular font. Compare **en**

**EM** *abbreviation* PHYS electron microscope

**email, e-mail** *noun* 1. COMPUT a system of sending messages to and receiving messages from other users on an electronic network 2. a message sent by e-mail. Full form **electronic mail**

**embankment** *noun* ENG a wall made along a river bank to prevent a river from overflowing

**embed** *verb* to fix something firmly in a surrounding mass ○ *A temperature probe is embedded into the stator of the generator.* ○ *Water outlets have heater elements embedded in rubber seals in the outlet pipe.*

**embedded code** *noun* COMPUT a set of sections or routines written in machine code, inserted into a high-level program to speed up or perform a special function

**embedded computer, embedded system** *noun* COMPUT a dedicated computer controlling a machine or, within a larger system, performing one fixed function

**embolism** *noun* MED 1. the obstruction of a blood vessel by an embolus 2. same as **embolus**

**embolus** *noun* MED an obstruction in a blood vessel, usually a lodged blood clot

**embryo** *noun* BIOL a living organism that develops from a fertilised egg or seed, e.g. an animal in the first weeks of gestation or a seedling plant with cotyledons and a root (NOTE: After eight weeks an unborn baby is called a **fetus**.) □ **in embryo** not yet developed

**embryogenesis** *noun* BIOL the formation and development of an embryo

**embryology** *noun* BIOL the scientific study of embryos, their growth and development

**embryonic** *adjective* 1. BIOL referring to an embryo 2. in the first stages of development

**embryonic abortion** *noun* BIOL the termination of pregnancy while the fetus is still an embryo (NOTE: A human baby is considered to be an embryo in the first eight weeks from conception.)

**embryo sac** *noun* BOT a large cell inside a female reproductive organ (**ovule**) of a flowering plant in which the egg cell is fertilised and the embryo develops

**embryo transfer** *noun* BIOTECH the transplanting of an embryo from a female into the womb of a surrogate mother

**emergence** *noun* 1. EARTH SCI a gradual upward movement of a land mass 2. BOT the germination of a seed

**emergency** *noun* a dangerous situation where immediate action needs to be taken ○ *a state of emergency exists*

**emergency shutdown** *noun* INDUST the closure of stopping a nuclear reactor when it seems that something dangerous may happen

**emergency ward** *noun* MED a hospital ward that deals with urgent cases such as accident victims

**emergent** *adjective* 1. BOT, ENVIRON referring to a plant that is just starting to grow 2. referring to a country that is starting to become developed industrially

**emery** *noun* MINERALS a variety of the mineral corundum used as an abrasive

**emf** *abbreviation* PHYS electromotive force

**EMI** *abbreviation* COMPUT electromagnetic interference

**emigration** *noun* ECOL the movement of a species out of an area. Opposite **immigration**

**emission** *noun* 1. the sending out of matter, energy or signals ○ *light emissions* ○ *One factor on which the operational range of a radio emission depends is the transmitted power.* 2. EN-

VIRON a substance discharged into the air, as by an internal combustion engine ○ *Exhaust emissions contain pollutants.* ○ *Gas emissions can cause acid rain.*

**emission line** *noun* ASTRON a bright line seen in an emission spectrum, usually caused by radiation from a hot gas superimposing its spectrum on the radiation from a cooler object, as with the Sun's outer atmosphere modifying radiation from the Sun's surface (NOTE: If emission processes in the gas are using all the energy passing through it, a spectrum can consist entirely of bright lines on a dark background. Otherwise the observer sees bright lines on a background which also contains radiation, but at a lower level.)

**emission spectrum** *noun* ASTRON a spectrum consisting wholly or mainly of emission lines

**emission standard** *noun* ENVIRON the amount of an effluent or pollutant that is permitted to be released into the environment, e.g. the amount of sewage which can be discharged into a river or the sea

**emit** *verb* to send out matter, energy or a signal ○ *radiation emitted by the sun* ○ *an X-ray tube emits radiation* ○ *Latent heat is emitted when condensation takes place.* (NOTE: **emitting – emitted**)

**emitter** *noun* **1.** a device or other means of emitting something **2.** ELECTRONICS a layer of semiconductor material in a transistor from which the electrons carrying the charge originate

**emitter-coupled logic** *noun* ELECTRONICS a high-speed logic circuit design using the emitters of transistors as output connections to other stages. Abbreviation **ECL**

**emoticon** *noun* COMPUT same as **smiley**

**emphasis** *noun* **1.** the force of expression that gives importance to something ○ *It is only in recent years that much emphasis has been placed on determining the causes of metal fatigue.* **2.** ACOUSTICS a filter that helps cut down the background noise and so boost a signal **3.** COMPUT a special effects function in a paint program that will increase the value of a range of colours so that they appear brighter

**emphysema** *noun* **1.** MED a chronic lung disease characterised by enlargement and loss of elasticity of the air spaces, resulting in breathing difficulties **2.** PHYSIOL an unusual enlargement of an organ or body tissue caused by retention of air or other gas

**empirical** *adjective* referring to a result that is obtained by observation or experiment rather than from theory and mathematical equations

**empirical formula** *noun* CHEM a chemical formula showing the relative proportion of elements in a compound rather than the structural arrangement and giving no indication of molecular weight, e.g. the formula $H_2O$

**empty¹** *adjective* with nothing inside

**empty²** *noun* COMPUT **1.** a reserved area for related data items, containing no data **2.** a variable containing no characters

**empty set** *noun* a set that contains no numbers, represented by the symbol emptyset ○ *A set containing prime numbers less than 1 is an empty set.* Also called **null set**

**emulate** *verb* to copy or behave like something else ○ *Some laser printers are able to emulate the more popular office printers.*

**emulator** *noun* COMPUT a piece of software or hardware that allows a machine to behave like another

**emulsifier** *noun* FOOD INDUST a substance added to mixtures of food such as water and oil to hold them together. ♦ **stabiliser**. Also called **emulsifying agent** (NOTE: Emulsifiers are used in sauces and added to meat to increase the water content so that the meat is heavier. In the European Union, emulsifiers and stabilisers have E numbers E322 to E495.)

**emulsify** *verb* PHYS, FOOD INDUST to mix two liquids so thoroughly that they will not separate

**emulsifying agent** *noun* FOOD INDUST same as **emulsifier**

**emulsion** *noun* **1.** CHEM a suspension of one liquid such as oil in another such as water **2.** CHEM a part of photographic film which reacts chemically to incident light to produce an image **3.** a type of water-based paint, usually giving a matt finish

**emulsion laser storage** *noun* COMPUT a digital storage technique using a laser to expose light-sensitive material

**en** *noun* PRINTING a measure equal to half the width of a letter m in a particular font. Compare **em**

**EN** *abbreviation* ENVIRON endangered species

**enable** *verb* **1.** to make it possible for someone to do something ○ *Isolation valves are fitted to enable servicing and maintenance to be carried out.* ○ *A spooling program enables editing work to be carried out while printing is going on.* **2.** ELECTRONICS to use an electronic signal to start a process or access a function on a chip or circuit

**enabled** *adjective* COMPUT referring to a function or menu item that is available to the user ○ *If an option on a menu appears in grey text rather than black, this indicates that these are not enabled and that you cannot use the option.*

**enabling signal** *noun* a signal that starts a process or allows one to take place

**enamel** *noun* the smooth, white, hard coating over the visible part of a tooth that protrudes out of the gum

**encapsulated** *adjective* COMPUT referring to something contained within something else

**encapsulated Postscript** *noun* COMPUT Postscript commands that describe an image or page contained within a file that can be placed within a graphics or DTP program

**encapsulation** *noun* **1.** COMPUT a system of sending a frame of data in one format within a frame of another format **2.** the enclosure of something inside something else, especially for protection

**encipher** *verb* to convert plain text into a secure coded form by means of a cipher system ○ *Our competitors cannot understand our files – they have all been enciphered.* Opposite **decipher**

**enclose** *verb* to surround something on all sides or close something in ○ *The housing encloses the various mechanical parts.* ○ *Fuses form a weak link in a circuit and are usually made of a strip of tinned copper enclosed in a glass tube.*

**enclosed object** *noun* a graphic object that is closed on all sides and so can be filled with a colour or pattern

**enclosure** *noun* **1.** an area surrounded by a fence **2.** COMPUT a protective casing for equipment

**encode** *verb* to put data into code ○ *Weather information is encoded to allow large amounts of information to be given in a short time.*

**encoder** *noun* COMPUT a device that can translate data from one format to another

**encounter** *verb* to meet something unexpected or unwanted ○ *Severe icing can be encountered in wave cloud.*

**encroach on** *verb* to come close to and gradually cover something ○ *The town is spreading beyond the by-pass, encroaching on good quality farming land.* ○ *Trees are spreading down the mountain and encroaching on the lower more fertile land in the valleys.*

**encrypt** *verb* to convert plain text to a secure coded form using a cipher system ○ *The encrypted text can be sent along ordinary telephone lines, and no-one will be able to understand it.* Also called **encipher**

**end** *noun* **1.** a final point or last part ○ *at the end of the data transmission* **2.** COMPUT a statement or character to indicate the last word of a source file ■ *verb* COMPUT to finish something or to stop

**end about carry** *noun* COMPUT the most significant digit added into the least significant place, used in BCD arithmetic. Also called **end around carry**

**end about shift** *noun* COMPUT data movement to the left or right in a word during which the bits falling outside the word boundary are discarded and replaced with zeros

**endanger** *verb* to put something in danger ○ *Pollution from the factory is endangering the aquatic life in the lakes.*

**endangered species** *noun* ENVIRON a species that is facing a risk of extinction in the wild, usually taken to be when fewer than 250 mature individuals exist. Abbreviation **EN** (NOTE: The plural is **endangered species**.)

COMMENT: The categories of the degree of risk of extinction as drawn up by the IUCN are: 1. Critically Endangered (CR) – in danger of extinction (fewer than 50 mature individuals) and unlikely to survive if the causal factors continue to operate. 2. Endangered (EN) – in danger of extinction (fewer than 250 mature individuals). 3. Vulnerable (VU) – fewer than 1,000 mature individuals, and will move into the endangered category in the near future if the causal factors continue to operate.

**end around carry** *noun* COMPUT same as **end about carry**

**endemic** *adjective* **1.** ECOL referring to an organism that exists or originated from a specific area ○ *The isolation of the islands has led to the evolution of endemic forms.* ○ *The northern part of the island is inhabited by many endemic mammals and birds.* **2.** MED referring to a disease that occurs within a specific area ○ *This disease is endemic to Mediterranean countries.* Compare **epidemic, pandemic** ■ *noun* MED an endemic disease

**endemic population** *noun* ECOL a group of organisms existing in a specific area

**endemic species** *noun* ECOL a species that is native to a specific geographic region

**ending** *noun* **1.** the action of coming to an end or of stopping something **2.** COMPUT the end part of something

**endless** *adjective* with no end

**endless loop** *noun* **1.** a continuous piece of recording tape or a number of computer instructions that are continuously repeated **2.** COMPUT a loop that has no end, except when the program is stopped ▶ also called **infinite loop**

**endo-** *prefix* inside or within. Compare **ecto-**

**endocarp** *noun* BOT the innermost of the layers of the wall (**pericarp**) of a fruit (NOTE: Sometimes it is toughened or hardened, as in a cherry stone or peach stone.)

**endocrine gland** *noun* ANAT a gland without a duct such as the pituitary gland which produces hormones introduced directly into the bloodstream

**endocrinology** *noun* MED the study of endocrine glands and the hormones they secrete

**endoderm** *noun* BIOL the innermost cell layer of an animal embryo, which develops into the respiratory and digestive tract linings

**endodermis** *noun* BOT a layer of cells in a plant root that divides the inner core (**stele**) from the outer surrounding tissue (**cortex**) (NOTE: An endodermis also occurs in the stems of some plants such as ferns.)

**end of address** *noun* COMPUT a transmitted code which indicates that address data have been sent. Abbreviation **EOA**

**end of block** *noun* COMPUT a code which indicates that the last byte of a block of data has been sent. Abbreviation **EOB**

**end of data** *noun* COMPUT a code which shows that the end of a stored data file has been reached. Abbreviation **EOD**

**end of document, end of file** *noun* COMPUT a marker after the last record in a file

**end of job** *noun* COMPUT a code used in batch processing to show that a job has been finished. Abbreviation **EOJ**

**end of line** *noun* COMPUT a code to indicate the end of a line, usually a CR or LF character. Abbreviation **EOL**

**end of medium** *noun* COMPUT a code that indicates the end of a usable physical medium. Abbreviation **EM**

**end of message** *noun* COMPUT a code used to separate the last character of one message from the first of another message. Abbreviation **EOM**

**end of record** *noun* COMPUT a code used to show the end of a record. Abbreviation **EOR**

**end of text** *noun* COMPUT a code sent after the last character of text. Abbreviation **EOT, ETX**

**end of transmission** *noun* COMPUT a sequence of characters indicating that all the data from a terminal or peripheral have been transmitted. Abbreviation **EOT**

**endogenous** *adjective* BIOL originating within an organism

**endolymph** *noun* ANAT the fluid contained within the membranous labyrinth of the inner ear

**endometrial laser ablation** *noun* MED a gynaecological surgical procedure using a laser to treat fibroids or other causes of thickening of the lining of the uterus

**endomitosis** *noun* GENETICS a process by which chromosomes divide within a cell but the nucleus does not divide, leading to an increase in chromosome number

**endoparasite** *noun* BIOL a parasite that lives inside the host

**endoplasm** *noun* BIOL the cytoplasm in the core of a cell within a plasma membrane

**endoplasmic reticulum** *noun* BIOL a network of tubular membranes in the cytoplasm of a cell that is responsible for processing materials made in or entering or leaving the cell

**endorphin** *noun* BIOCHEM a substance that attaches to the same cell receptors in the brain as morphine does (NOTE: Endorphins are natural painkillers released after severe injury.)

**endoskeleton** *noun* ZOOL the internal skeleton of an animal such as a vertebrate

**endosperm** *noun* BOT a storage tissue in plant seeds that provides nourishment for the developing embryo

**endospore** *noun* MICROBIOL the inner layer of the wall around a spore

**endothelium** *noun* ANAT a membrane of special cells that lines the internal passages and organs in the body such as the heart and blood vessels. Compare **epithelium, mesothelium**

**endotherm** *noun* BIOL an organism that is able to generate heat internally in order to raise its body temperature ○ *Birds and mammals are endotherms.* Also called **homoiotherm**

**endothermic** *adjective* **1.** CHEM used to describe a reaction or process that absorbs heat energy. Compare **exothermic 2.** ZOOL maintaining a constant body temperature irrespective of environmental temperature

**endothermic reaction** *noun* CHEM a chemical reaction in which heat is removed from the surroundings

**endotoxin** *noun* MED a poison from bacteria which passes into the body when contaminated food is eaten

**end product** *noun* INDUST an item or state produced by a manufacturing process or by radioactive decay

**endrin** *noun* AGRIC a type of broad-based organochlorine insecticide which is extremely toxic and persistent

**end system** *noun* COMPUT a server or host computer connected to the Internet

**end system to intermediate system** *noun* COMPUT an OSI protocol standard that allows host computers, the end system, to locate a router, the intermediate system. Abbreviation **ES-IS**

**end-use efficiency** *noun* INDUST an efficient way of using a form of energy by the end user

**end user** *noun* **1.** COMPUT a person who will use a device, program or product ○ *The company is creating a computer with a specific end user in mind.* **2.** INDUST a person who uses a manufactured product

**energise** *verb* PHYS to supply energy such as electricity to a machine or system to make it work

**energy** *noun* **1.** PHYS, PHYSIOL the force or strength to carry out activities ○ *You need to eat certain types of food to give you energy.* **2.** INDUST electricity or other fuel ○ *We have to review our energy requirements regularly.*

COMMENT: Energy is the capacity to do useful work and includes setting a process in motion, the production of heat and light, the emission of heat and light and the making of electricity. It is measured in joules or calories. One joule is the amount of energy used to move one kilogram the distance of one metre; one calorie is the amount of heat needed to raise the temperature of one gram of water by one degree Celsius The calorie is also used as a measurement of the energy content of food and to show the amount of energy needed by an average person.

**energy analysis, energy audit** *noun* INDUST a check of how much energy is used within a specific period

**energy balance** *noun* ECOL, BIOL a series of measurements showing the movement of energy between organisms and their environment

**energy budget** *noun* INDUST, ECOL the level of energy at different points in an ecosystem or an industrial process

**energy conservation** *noun* ENVIRON the avoidance of wasting energy

COMMENT: Energy conservation is widely practised to reduce excessive and costly consumption of energy. Reduction of heating levels in houses and offices, insulating buildings against loss of heat, using solar power instead of fossil fuels and increasing the efficiency of car engines are all examples of energy conservation.

**energy consumption** *noun* PHYS, PHYSIOL the amount of energy consumed by a person or apparatus, shown as a unit

**energy crop** *noun* INDUST a crop such as fast-growing trees which is grown to be used to provide energy

**energy efficiency ratio** *noun* INDUST a measure of the efficiency of a heating or cooling system such as a heat pump or an air-conditioning system, shown as the ratio of the output in Btu per hour to the input in watts. Abbreviation **EER**

**energy-efficient** *adjective* ENVIRON using energy carefully and with minimum waste

**energy farm** *noun* INDUST an area of land or water where plants such as cassava or sugar cane are cultivated to produce biofuels such as ethanol and methane

**energy flow** *noun* ECOL a flow of energy from one trophic level to another in a food chain

**energy gain** *noun* PHYS an increase in the amount of energy or heat. Also called **heat gain**

**energy level** *noun* PHYS a possible state at which an electron can exist in an atom (NOTE: The fact that any particular atom can house electrons only at specific energy levels gives rise to the lines in spectra, which exist as sharp features because they reflect the difference in energy between two energy levels.)

**energy loss** *noun* PHYS the amount of energy lost

**energy of mass** *noun* PHYS the amount of energy which can be released by converting a given amount of matter entirely to energy, given by the amount of matter multiplied by the velocity of light squared, in Einstein's famous equation $e = mc^2$ (NOTE: The huge amount of energy obtainable from tiny amounts of matter accounts for the long lives of the stars and for the portable size of highly destructive nuclear weapons.)

**energy output** *noun* PHYS the amount of energy produced

**energy recovery** *noun* INDUST the production of energy from synthetic materials, e.g. by using the heat from incineration of solid waste to generate electricity

**energy reserves** *plural noun* INDUST the amount of energy stored, especially the stocks of non-renewable fuel such as oil which a nation possesses

**energy resources** *plural noun* INDUST potential supplies of energy not yet used, e.g. coal lying in the ground, solar heat, wind power or geothermal power

**energy value** *noun* PHYS, PHYSIOL the heat value of a substance measured in joules. Also called **calorific value**

**engage** *verb* **1.** to switch something on and use it. Opposite **disengage 2.** to fit in with something else ○ *The large wheel engages with the smaller wheel and starts to turn.*

**engage in** *verb* to take part in something ○ *The research group is engaged in a long series of diagnostic tests.*

**engine** *noun* **1.** MECH ENG a machine that converts energy into mechanical force or motion, different from an electric or hydraulic motor because of its use of a fuel ○ *a jet engine* ○ *a piston engine* ○ *internal combustion engine* **2.** COMPUT a part of a software package that carries out a particular function ○ *A search engine is the part of a multimedia title that lets a user search for text in a multimedia book.*

COMMENT: In British usage there is a clear distinction between the terms engine and motor, the term motor only being used for electric power units. In American usage engine is used for all types of power unit including internal combustion.

**engine block** *noun* MECH ENG a cylinder block with an integral crankcase

**engine capacity** *noun* MECH ENG the swept volume of the cylinders in an engine

**engineer** ENG *noun* a person who works in engineering ■ *verb* to design and make something

**engineering** *noun* ENG the application of the principles of science to the design, construction and use of machines or buildings

**engineering industry** *noun* INDUST the factories or companies that manufacture machinery and machine parts

**engine failure** *noun* MECH ENG the unwanted stoppage of an engine during running

**engine housing** *noun* MECH ENG an engine compartment

**engine intake** *noun* MECH ENG the front part of an engine where air enters the engine

**engine performance** *noun* MECH ENG a description of how well an engine works or detailed statistical information about the capabilities of an engine

**engine surge** *noun* MECH ENG an instability in the power output of an engine

**enhance** *verb* to improve something or make something clearer

**enhanced small device interface** *noun* COMPUT an interface standard between a central processing unit and peripherals such as disk drives. Abbreviation **ESDI**

**enhancer** *noun* FOOD INDUST an artificial substance that increases the flavour of food or of artificial flavouring that has been added to food (NOTE: In the European Union, flavour enhancers added to food have the E numbers E620 to E637.)

**enlarge** *verb* to make something bigger or larger

**ENQ** *abbreviation* COMPUT enquiry

**enquire** *verb* another spelling of **inquire**

**enquiry** *noun* **1.** a question, or the process of asking a question **2.** COMPUT a request for data or information from a device or database **3.** COMPUT the accessing of data in a computer memory without changing the data

**enquiry character** *noun* COMPUT a special control code that is a request for identification, status or data from a device

**enrich** *verb* **1.** to make something richer or stronger **2.** to improve the nutritional quality of food ○ *enriched with vitamins* **3.** INDUST to increase the amount of uranium-235 in the fuel of a nuclear reactor ○ *Fuel is enriched to 15% with fissile material.*

**enriched plutonium** *noun* CHEM, INDUST plutonium to which uranium-235 has been added and which is used as a fuel in nuclear reactors

**enrichment** *noun* INDUST the action of enriching the proportion of uranium-235 in nuclear fuel

**ensilage, ensiling** *noun* AGRIC the process of making silage for cattle by cutting grass and other green plants and storing it in silos

**ensure** *verb* COMPUT to make sure that something happens ○ *Pushing the write-protect tab will ensure that the data on the disk cannot be erased.*

**enter** *verb* **1.** to come or go into a place **2.** to write down or record something ○ *Enter your name in the correct place in the form.* **3.** COMPUT to type in information on a terminal or keyboard ○ *The data have been entered on data capture forms.*

**enter-** *prefix* ANAT same as **entero-**

**enteric** *adjective* ANAT referring to the intestine

**enteric fermentation** *noun* BIOL the breaking down of food in the gut of ruminant animals, especially cattle, producing methane which is eliminated from the animal's body

**enteritis** *noun* MED an inflammation of the mucous membrane of the intestine

**enter key** *noun* COMPUT a key pressed to indicate the end of an input or line of text

**entero-** *prefix* ANAT referring to intestine

**Enterobacteria** *plural noun* BIOL a family of bacteria, including *Salmonella* and *Escherichia*

**Enterobius** *noun* ZOOL a threadworm or nematode which infests the intestine

**enterokinase** *noun* BIOCHEM an enzyme in the upper small intestine that converts trypsinogen to trypsin

**enterotoxin** *noun* MED a bacterial exotoxin which particularly affects the intestine

**enterprise network** *noun* COMPUT a network that connects all the workstations, terminals or computers in a company (NOTE: It can be within one building or linking several buildings in different countries.)

**enthalpy** *noun* PHYS the heat content of a system, equal to the sum of its internal energy and the product of its pressure and volume

**entire** *adjective* having no part excluded or left out ○ *spilt the entire contents of the container*

**entity** *noun* **1.** something which is distinct and separate from something else ○ *The institutes are closely connected*

*but are separate legal entities.* **2.**
COMPUT a subject to which the data
stored in a file or database refers

**entomological** *adjective* ZOOL referring to insects

**entomologist** *noun* ZOOL a scientist
who specialises in the study of insects

**entomology** *noun* ZOOL the study of
insects

**entrap** *verb* to catch and retain something ○ *Up to 90% of sulfur emissions
can be entrapped.* ○ *Coal-fired power
stations should be equipped with the
means of entrapping sulfur.*

**entropy** *noun* **1.** PHYS a measure of
the energy in a system or process that is
unavailable to do work **2.** a measure of
the degree of disorder in a closed system

**entry** *noun* **1.** a place where you can
enter **2.** COMPUT a single record or a
piece of data about one action or object
in a database or library

**entry condition** *noun* COMPUT a condition that must be satisfied before a
routine can be entered

**entry point** *noun* **1.** a place where
you can enter **2.** COMPUT the address
from which a program or subroutine is
to be executed

**E number** *noun* a classification of additives to food approved by the European Union

COMMENT: Additives are classified as follows: colouring substances E100-E180;
preservatives E200-E297; antioxidants
E300-E321; emulsifiers and stabilisers
E322-E495; acids and bases E500-E529;
anti-caking additives E530-E578; flavour
enhancers and sweeteners E620-E637.

**enumerated type** *noun* COMPUT a
system of data storage or classification
using numbers to represent chosen convenient labels

COMMENT: If 'man', 'horse', 'dog' and
'cat' are items of data, stored by machine
simply as 0, 1, 2, 3, they can still be referred to in the program as man or horse
to make it easier for the user to recognise
them.

**enumeration** *noun* COMPUT a method
of identifying resources or objects using
a unique number

**envelop** *verb* to surround and cover
something ○ *The atmosphere envelops
the Earth.*

**envelope** *noun* **1.** a paper packet that
contains a letter or document **2.** a cover
○ *The atmosphere is the gaseous envelope surrounding the Earth.* **3.** COMPUT
a transmitted packet of data containing
error-detection and control information
**4.** PHYS the shape of the decay curve of
a sound **5.** COMPUT the name for the data
which contain a mail message with the
destination address information **6.**
AEROSP the set of limitations within
which a technological system, especially an aircraft, can perform safely and
effectively

**envelope feeder** *noun* COMPUT a
special add-on to a printer used to print
on an envelope instead of on a sheet of
paper

**environment** *noun* **1.** ECOL the surroundings of any organism, including
the physical world and other organisms
**2.** COMPUT a condition in a computer
system of all the registers and memory
locations

COMMENT: The environment is anything
outside an organism in which the organism lives. It can be a geographical region,
a climatic condition, a pollutant or the
noises which surround an organism. The
human environment includes the country
or region or town or house or room in
which a person lives. A parasite's environment includes the body of the host. A
plant's environment includes the type of
soil at a specific altitude.

**environmental** *adjective* ENVIRON
referring to the environment

**environmental annoyance** *noun*
ENVIRON a nuisance caused by environmental factors such as traffic noise

**environmental assessment** *noun*
ENVIRON the identification of the expected environmental effects of a proposed action

**environmental audit** *noun* ENVIRON
an assessment made by a company or
organisation of the financial benefits
and disadvantages of adopting an environmentally sound policy

**environmental biology** *noun* ECOL
the study of living organisms in relationship to their environment

**environmental control** *noun* ENVI-
RON the means of protecting an
environment

**environmental damage** *noun* ENVIRON harm done to the environment, e.g. pollution of rivers

**environmental degradation** *noun* ENVIRON a reduction in the quality of the environment

**environmental disorder** *noun* ECOL a disruption of the normal balance of the environment

**environmental equity** *noun* ENVIRON environmental protection for everyone so that no section of the population suffers a disproportionate effect of environmental pollution. Also called **environmental justice**

**environmental ethics** *noun* ENVIRON a discipline that examines people's environmental obligations

**environmental forecasting** *noun* ENVIRON the prediction of the effects on the surrounding environment of new construction programmes

**environmental geology** *noun* GEOL the study of geology in relation to problems concerned with the environment

**environmental health** *noun* HEALTH public health in the local environment, including aspects such as water and air quality, hygiene in restaurants and shops, and pest control (NOTE: Environmental health is a responsibility of local government.)

**Environmental Health Officer** *noun* HEALTH an official of a local authority who examines the environment and tests for such aspects as air pollution, bad sanitation or noise pollution. Abbreviation **EHO**

**environmental hygiene** *noun* MED the study of health and how it is affected by the environment

**environmental impact** *noun* ENVIRON the effect upon the environment of large construction programmes such as draining of marshes

**environmental impact assessment** *noun* ENVIRON an evaluation of the effect upon the environment of a large construction programme. Abbreviation **EIA**

**environmental impact statement** *noun* ENVIRON a statement required under US law for any major federal project, evaluating the effect of the project on the environment. Abbreviation **EIS**

**environmentalism** *noun* ENVIRON concern for the environment and its protection

**environmentalist** *noun* ENVIRON a person who is concerned with protecting the environment

**environmentalist group** *noun* ENVIRON an association or society dedicated to the protection of the environment and to increasing people's awareness of environmental issues

**environmentalist lobby** *noun* ENVIRON a group of people who try to persuade politicians that the environment must be protected and that pollution must be stopped

**environmental justice** *noun* ENVIRON same as **environmental equity**

**environmental labelling** *noun* ENVIRON same as **ecolabelling**

**environmentally friendly** *adjective* ENVIRON intended to minimise harm to the environment, e.g. by using biodegradable ingredients

**environmental policy** *noun* ENVIRON a plan for dealing with all matters affecting the environment on a national or local scale

**environmental pollution** *noun* ENVIRON the pollution of the environment by human activities

**environmental protection** *noun* ENVIRON an act of protecting the environment by regulating the discharge of waste, the emission of pollutants and other human activities

**environmental protection association** *noun* ENVIRON an organisation dedicated to protecting the environment from damage and pollution

**Environmental Protection Act 1990** *noun* ENVIRON a UK act to allow the introduction of integrated pollution control, regulations for the disposal of waste and other provisions

**environmental quality standard** *noun* ENVIRON the concentration of an effluent or pollutant which is accepted in a specific environment, e.g. the amount of trace elements in drinking water or the amount of additives in food

**environmental radioactivity** *noun* ENVIRON the energy in the form of radiation that is emitted into the environment by radioactive substances

**environmental resistance** *noun* ECOL the ability to withstand pressures such as predation, competition, weather or food availability, which inhibit the potential growth of a population

**environmental science** *noun* ENVIRON the study of the relationship between humans and the environment, the problems caused by pollution or loss of habitats and the proposed solutions

**environmental set-aside** *noun* ENVIRON a scheme that may improve the environment, e.g. paying farmers to sow grass seed mixtures for a green cover and cutting a strip15 m wide along the side of footpaths at the edge of cereal fields

**environmental studies** *noun* ENVIRON a course of academic study that includes a range of disciplines focusing on the natural environment

**environmental variation** *noun* ECOL continual changes in the environment over a period

**environment-friendly** *adjective* ENVIRON same as **environmentally friendly**

**environment space** *noun* COMPUT the amount of memory free to be used by a program

**environment variable** *noun* COMPUT a variable set by the system or by a user at the system command line which can be used by any program

**enzymatic** *adjective* BIOCHEM referring to an enzyme

**enzyme** *noun* BIOCHEM a protein substance produced by living cells which catalyses a biochemical reaction in living organisms (NOTE: The names of enzymes mostly end with the suffix **-ase**.)

COMMENT: Many different enzymes exist in organisms, working in the digestive system, metabolic processes and the synthesis of certain compounds. Some pesticides and herbicides work by interfering with enzyme systems or by destroying them altogether.

**enzyme-linked immunosorbent assay** *noun* full form of **ELISA**

**EOA** *abbreviation* COMPUT end of address

**EOB** *abbreviation* COMPUT end of block

**EOD** *abbreviation* COMPUT end of data

**EOJ** *abbreviation* COMPUT end of job

**EOL** *abbreviation* COMPUT end of line

**eolian** *adjective* METEOROL caused by wind

**EOM** *abbreviation* COMPUT end of message

**EOR** *abbreviation* COMPUT end of record

**EOT** *abbreviation* COMPUT **1.** end of text **2.** end of transmission

**epact** *noun* ASTRON a period of about 11 days that is the difference between the lunar year and the solar year

**ephemeral** *noun* BIOL a plant or insect that has a short life cycle and may complete several life cycles within a season

**ephemeral stream** *noun* EARTH SCI a stream that flows only after rain or snowmelt

**epibiont** *noun* BIOL an organism that lives on the surface of another

**epibiosis** *noun* BIOL a state where an organism lives on the surface of another, but is not a parasite

**epicarp** *noun* BOT the outer skin of a fruit. Also called **exocarp**

**epicentre** *noun* EARTH SCI a point on the surface of the Earth above the focus of an earthquake or in the centre of a nuclear explosion

**epicycloid** *noun* MATHS the curve traced out by a fixed point on an epicycle

**epidemic** *noun* MED **1.** an infectious disease that spreads quickly through a large part of the population ○ *The health authorities are taking steps to prevent an epidemic of cholera* or *a cholera epidemic.* **2.** referring to a rapidly spreading infection or disease. ♦ **endemic, pandemic**

**epidemiological** *adjective* MED referring to epidemiology

**epidemiologist** *noun* MED a person who studies the factors involved in the incidence, distribution and control of disease in a population

**epidemiology** *noun* MED the study of diseases in a population, how they spread and how they can be controlled

**epidermis** *noun* ANAT an outer layer of cells of a plant or animal

**epididymis** *noun* ANAT a tightly coiled tube, attached to the testis, that stores sperm and leads into the sperm duct

**epidural anaesthesia** *noun* MED local anaesthesia in which anaesthetic is injected into the space between the vertebral canal and the dura mater

**epigamic** *adjective* ZOOL referring to a characteristic such as large antlers or bright colours that attracts a mate

**epigeal** *adjective* BOT occurring or developing above ground. Compare **hypogeal**

**epigenetic** *adjective* GENETICS relating to the control of changes in gene function that are not associated with changes in DNA sequences

**epigenetics** *noun* GENETICS the control of changes in gene function that are not associated with changes in DNA sequences

**epigenome** *noun* GENETICS a subset of genes whose function is under the control of specific biochemical factors as well as their DNA sequence

**epigenomics** *noun* GENETICS the study of the biochemical relationships controlling the function of genes within the epigenome

**epigenous** *adjective* BIOL developing or growing on a surface

**epiglottis** *noun* ANAT a flap of cartilage at the base of the tongue that seals off the windpipe (**trachea**) when swallowing food or liquids

**epigynous** *adjective* BOT referring to a flower structure in which the stamens, calyx and corolla are on the top of the ovary

**epilimnion** *noun* EARTH SCI the top layer of water in a lake, which contains more oxygen and is warmer than the water below. Compare **metalimnion**, **hypolimnion**

**epilithic** *adjective* BIOL growing on or attached to the surface of rocks or stones

**epinephrine** *noun* BIOCHEM the hormone adrenaline

**epiphysis** *noun* ANAT same as **pineal gland**

**epiphyte** *noun* BOT a plant that lives on another plant for physical support, but is not a parasite of it

**epiphytic** *adjective* BOT attached to another plant for support, but not parasitic

**episode** *noun* **1.** an event, or a group of related events **2.** an occurrence or time when a particular phenomenon takes place ○ *There have been three serious acid rain episodes in the last four months.* ○ *High sulfur dioxide episodes have killed several hundred birds at one time.*

**episodic** *adjective* happening sometimes but not regularly

**episome** *noun* GENETICS a genetic unit capable of multiplying independently in host cells or when integrated into a chromosome (NOTE: Bacterial plasmids are examples of episomes.)

**epistasis** *noun* GENETICS the nonappearance of a characteristic because the activity of another gene has suppressed or masked the gene that controls it

**epithelial** *adjective* ANAT referring to the epithelium

**epithelium, epithelial layer** *noun* ANAT a layer of cells covering an organ, including the skin and the lining of hollow cavities. Compare **endothelium**, **mesothelium**

**epithermal neutron** *noun* PHYS a neutron that has a high energy level between $10^{-2}$ and $10^2$ eV

**epixylous** *adjective* BIOL growing on wood

**epizoite** *noun* ZOOL an animal that lives on the surface of another, without being a parasite

**epoch** *noun* GEOL an interval of geological time, the subdivision of a period

**epoxy resin** *noun* CHEM a tough synthetic resin that sets following the application of heat or pressure, used in adhesives and surface coatings

**EPROM** *abbreviation* COMPUT erasable programmable read-only memory

**EPS** *abbreviation* COMPUT encapsulated Postscript

**Epsom salts** *noun* PHARM a white powder, magnesium sulfate, which when diluted in water is used as a laxative. Formula: $MgSO_4.7H_2O$.

**equal** *adjective* having the same quantity, measure, or value as another ○ *For every action, there is an equal and opposite reaction.* ■ *verb* MATHS to be the same in value as a number ○ *Two plus two equals four (2 + 2 = 4).*

**equalise** *verb* to become or make something the same in quantity, measure or value as another ○ *Fluid pressure and gas pressure equalise at normal system pressure.* ○ *The received signal was equalised to an optimum shape.*

**equality** *noun* MATHS a logical function whose output is true if either of two inputs is true, and false if both inputs are the same

**equally** *adverb* in the same way or to the same extent ○ *They were both equally responsible for the successful launch of the new system.*

**equate** *verb* to be or make something the same as another ○ *The variable was equated to the input data.*

**equation** *noun* 1. MATHS a statement, usually in symbols, that two quantities or mathematical expressions are equal ○ *The equation $Vg = P$ can be used to calculate the geostrophic wind.* □ Same as 2. CHEM same as **chemical equation**

**equation of motion** *noun* PHYS a mathematical equation used to describe the motion of an object

**equation of state** *noun* PHYS an equation that gives the mathematical relation between the pressure, temperature and volume of a gas or liquid

**equation of time** *noun* ASTRON the time that must be added to mean solar time, as given by a clock, to make it equal to apparent solar time, as given by a sundial (NOTE: It varies from about −14 minutes in February to about +16 minutes in October.)

**equator** *noun* 1. EARTH SCI an imaginary circle around the Earth's surface, equidistant from the poles and perpendicular to the axis of rotation, which divides the Earth into the northern and southern hemispheres ○ *Every point on the equator is equidistant from the poles.* 2. ASTRON an imaginary circle around an astronomical object, equidistant from the poles now 3. ASTRON same as **celestial equator**

**equatorial** *adjective* EARTH SCI referring to the equator

**equatorial current** *noun* EARTH SCI a westward-moving current in the Atlantic Ocean

**equatorial diameter** *noun* the distance from the equator, through the centre of the Earth to the equator on the opposite side of the globe

**equatorial region** *noun* EARTH SCI the land area near the equator, mostly with a very hot and humid climate, except for land at high altitudes as in South America

**equatorial trough** *noun* METEOROL a shallow low-pressure zone around the equator

**equatorial zone** *noun* EARTH SCI an area near the equator, mostly with a very hot and humid climate, except for land at high altitudes as in South America

**equilateral** *adjective* MATHS referring to an object or structure in which all the sides are of equal length

**equilibrium** *noun* a state of balance

**equilibrium constant** *noun* CHEM the relationship between the concentration of products and starting materials in a reversible chemical reaction that is at equilibrium (NOTE: It is strongly dependent on temperature and pressure.)

**equinox** *noun* EARTH SCI either of the two occasions in the year, spring and autumn, when the sun crosses the celestial equator and night and day are each 12 hours long

COMMENT: The two equinoxes are the spring or vernal equinox, which occurs about 21 March and the autumn equinox, which occurs about 22 September.

**equip** *verb* COMPUT to provide a person, organisation or place with machinery or equipment ○ *The operating theatre is equipped with the latest scanning devices.*

**equipment** *noun* the devices, systems or machines that are needed for a particular purpose ○ *drilling equipment* (NOTE: no plural: for one item say a **piece of equipment**.)

**equivalence** *noun* MATHS a logical operation that is true if all the inputs are the same

COMMENT: Output is 1 if both inputs are 1 or if both are 0. If the two inputs are different, the output is 0.

**equivalence function** *noun* MATHS a logical function whose output is true if both inputs are the same. Also called **equivalence operation**

**equivalence gate** *noun* ELEC a gate which performs an equivalence function

**equivalence operation** *noun* MATHS same as **equivalence function**

**equivalent** *adjective* being equal, all things considered ○ *The function of a logic gate is equivalent to that of a switch.* ○ *A metal part could be as much as 25 times heavier than an equivalent plastic part.* □ **to be equivalent to** to have the same value as something or to be the same as something ■ *noun* an equal thing or amount

**equivalent weight** *noun* MEASURE, CHEM the mass of a substance that will combine with or replace 8 parts by mass of oxygen or 1.008 parts of hydrogen

**era** *noun* GEOL a major interval of geological time, divided into periods

**eradicate** *verb* to remove something completely ○ *international action to eradicate glaucoma*

**eradication** *noun* **1.** complete removal **2.** BIOL the total extinction of a species

**erasable** *adjective* COMPUT able to be erased

**erasable memory** *noun* COMPUT same as **erasable storage**

**erasable programmable read-only memory** *noun* COMPUT a read-only memory chip which can be programmed by a voltage applied to a write pin and data applied to its output pins, usually erasable with ultraviolet light. Abbreviation **EPROM**

**erasable storage** *noun* COMPUT a temporary storage medium which can be re-used. Also called **erasable memory**

**erase** *verb* **1.** to remove all signs of something **2.** COMPUT to remove any signal from a magnetic medium **3.** COMPUT to set all the digits in a storage area to zero

**erase head** *noun* ELEC a small magnet that clears a magnetic tape or disk of recorded signals

**eraser** *noun* ELEC a device that erases the contents of something, as by using ultraviolet light to erase an EPROM

**eraser tool** *noun* COMPUT a function that allows areas of an image to be erased or set to the background colour

**erbium** *noun* CHEM ELEM a soft silvery metallic element of the lanthanide group used in alloys and pigments (NOTE: The chemical symbol is **Er**; the atomic weight is **68** and the atomic weight is **167.26**.)

**erg** *noun* MEASURE, PHYS the cgs unit equal to the work done by a force of one dyne acting over a distance of one centimetre (NOTE: 1 erg is equivalent to $10^{-7}$ joules.)

**ergodicity** *noun* STATS a system in which conditions of a stochastic process are such that time and space averages will coincide for infinite realisations

**ergonomics** *noun* the study of people at work

**ergosterol** *noun* BIOCHEM a substance found in yeast and moulds that forms vitamin $D_2$ when exposed to ultraviolet light

**ergot** *noun* BOT a fungus that grows on cereals, especially rye. Genus: *Claviceps*.

**ergotamine** *noun* MED the poison which causes ergotism

**ergotism** *noun* MED poisoning by eating cereals or bread contaminated by ergot

**erode** *verb* BIOL to wear something away ○ *The cliffs have been eroded by the sea.*

**EROM** *abbreviation* COMPUT electrically alterable read-only memory

**erosion** *noun* EARTH SCI the wearing away of soil or rock by rain, wind, sea or rivers or by the action of toxic substances ○ *Grass cover provides some protection against soil erosion.*

COMMENT: Accelerated erosion is caused by human activity in addition to the natural rate of erosion. Cleared land in drought-stricken areas can produce dry soil which may blow away. Felling trees removes the roots which bind the soil particles together and so exposes the soil to erosion by rainwater. Ploughing up and down slopes as opposed to contour ploughing, can lead to the formation of rills and serious soil erosion.

**error** *noun* **1.** a mistake **2.** a known inaccuracy of an instrument or system which has to be corrected by calculating the true value **3.** COMPUT a mistake due to an operator or caused by a hardware or software fault

**error box** *noun* COMPUT a dialog box displayed with a message alerting the user that an error has occurred

**error burst** *noun* COMPUT a group of several consecutive errors in a transmission

**error checking code** *noun* COMPUT a coding system that detects or corrects errors

**error code** *noun* COMPUT a code that indicates that a particular type of error has occurred

**error condition** *noun* COMPUT a state that is entered if an attempt is made to operate on data containing errors

**error correcting code** *noun* COMPUT a coding system that allows bit errors occurring during transmission to be rapidly corrected by logical deduction methods

**error correction** *noun* COMPUT hardware or software that can detect and correct an error in a transmission

**error detecting code** *noun* COMPUT a coding system that allows bit errors occurring during transmission to be detected, but is not complex enough to correct them

**error detection** *noun* COMPUT the use of special hardware or software to detect errors in a data entry or transmission, then usually to ask for re-transmission

**error detection and correction** *noun* COMPUT a forward error correction system for data communications. Abbreviation **EDAC**

**error handler** *noun* COMPUT a software routine that controls and reports an error when it occurs

**error handling, error management** *noun* COMPUT same as **exception handling**

**error rate** *noun* COMPUT 1. the number of mistakes per thousand entries or per page ○ *The error rate is less than 1%.* 2. the number of corrupt bits of data in relation to the total transmission length

**error routine** *noun* COMPUT a short routine within a main program that handles any errors when they occur

**error trapping** *noun* COMPUT the detection and correction of errors before they cause any problems

**erupt** *verb* EARTH SCI (*of a volcano*) to become active and produce lava, smoke and hot ash

**eruptive** *adjective* 1. EARTH SCI referring to a volcano that produces lava, smoke and hot ash 2. EARTH SCI referring to rock formed by the solidification

of magma 3. MED causing boils or spots on the skin

**erythrocyte** *noun* BIOL a red blood cell

**escape** *noun* 1. the action of allowing toxic substances to leave a container ○ *The area around the reprocessing plant was evacuated because of an escape of radioactive coolant.* 2. BOT a cultivated plant that now reproduces in the wild 3. ZOOL a domesticated animal that has become wild ■ *verb* 1. to move from a container 2. to move from a cultivated or domestic area ○ *Feral cats have escaped from households and become wild.* 3. to get out of captivity

**escape character** *noun* COMPUT a character used to represent an escape code

**escape code** *noun* COMPUT a transmitted code sequence which informs the receiver that all following characters represent control actions

**escapement** *noun* COMPUT a preset vertical movement of a sheet of paper in a printer

**escape sequence** *noun* COMPUT a method of switching a Hayes-compatible modem into command mode by sending the three characters '+++' allowing a user to enter new commands while still online

**escape velocity** *noun* PHYS the speed that an object must reach to escape a gravitational field (NOTE: A spacecraft needs to travel at about 25 000 mph/40 000 kph to escape Earth's gravity and travel into space.)

**escarpment** *noun* EARTH SCI a steep slope of a cuesta

**Escherichia coli** *noun* MICROBIOL a gram-negative bacterium commonly found in faeces and associated with acute gastroenteritis if it is ingested

**ESDI** *abbreviation* COMPUT enhanced small device interface

**ES-IS** *abbreviation* COMPUT end system to intermediate system

**esker** *noun* EARTH SCI a long winding ridge formed of gravel

**esophagus** *noun* ANAT US spelling of **oesophagus**

**essence** *noun* CHEM a concentrated oil from a plant, used in cosmetics, analgesics and antiseptics

**essential** *adjective* **1.** extremely important or necessary **2.** MED referring to a disease with no obvious cause

**essential amino acid** *noun* BIOCHEM an amino acid necessary for growth but which cannot be synthesised by the body and has to be obtained from the food supply

COMMENT: The essential amino acids are: isoleucine, leucine, lysine, methionine, phenylalanine, threonine, tryptophan and valine.

**essential element** *noun* BIOCHEM a chemical element necessary for an organism's growth and function

**essential fatty acid** *noun* BIOCHEM an unsaturated fatty acid essential for growth but which cannot be synthesised by the body and has to be obtained from the food supply. Abbreviation **EFA**

COMMENT: The essential fatty acids are linoleic acid, linolenic acid and arachidonic acid.

**essential hypertension** *noun* MED high blood pressure without any obvious cause

**essential oil** *noun* CHEM a concentrated oil from scented plants used in cosmetics, analgesics and antiseptics. Also called **volatile oil**

**establish** *verb* **1.** to work out or calculate something □ **to establish a position** to find out where you are **2.** to start or set up something ○ *We established routine procedures very quickly* □ **to establish communication** to make contact □ **to establish control** to get control **3.** ECOL to settle permanently ○ *The starling has become established in all parts of the USA.* ○ *Even established trees have been attacked by the disease.*

**established** *adjective* BOT, ZOOL living or growing successfully

**ester** *noun* CHEM an organic compound formed during the reaction between an acid and an alcohol with loss of water, often having a fragrant smell

**estimate** *noun* **1.** an approximate calculation of size, weight or extent **2.** a document giving details of how much a job is likely to cost ■ *verb* to make an approximate calculation of size, weight or extent

**estimation** *noun* **1.** an approximate calculation ○ *an estimation of ground speed* ○ *Estimation of visibility is achieved by noting the distances at* which lights of known candle power can be observed and relating these distances to visibility-by-day values. **2.** an opinion □ **in my estimation** in my opinion

**estivation** *noun* ZOOL US spelling of **aestivation**

**estrogen** *noun* BIOCHEM US spelling of **oestrogen**

**estuarine** *adjective* EARTH SCI, BIOL referring to estuaries

**estuarine plant** *noun* BOT a plant which lives in an estuary where the water is alternately fresh and salty as the tide comes in and goes out

**estuary** *noun* EARTH SCI a part of a river where it meets the sea and is partly composed of salt water

**ethanal** *noun* CHEM same as **acetaldehyde**

**ethanamide** *noun* CHEM same as **acetamide**

**ethane** *noun* CHEM a highly flammable gas that is colourless and odourless used as a fuel and in refrigeration. Formula: $C_2H_6$. (NOTE: It occurs naturally in petroleum and natural gas.)

**ethanedioic acid** *noun* CHEM same as **oxalic acid**

**ethanoate** *noun* CHEM same as **acetate**

**ethanoic acid** *noun* CHEM same as **acetic acid**

**ethanol** *noun* CHEM colourless inflammable liquid, produced by the fermentation of sugars and used as an ingredient of organic chemicals, intoxicating drinks and medicines. Formula: $C_2H_5OH$. Also called **ethyl alcohol**

**ethene** *noun* CHEM same as **ethylene**

**ether** *noun* **1.** MED an anaesthetic substance, now rarely used **2.** CHEM a volatile, flammable organic compound belonging to a class that contains -O- in its molecules

**Ethernet** *trademark* COMPUT a standard defining the protocol and signalling method of a local area network

COMMENT: The standard is IEEE 802.3. Ethernet has several implementations: 10Base5, the most common, is a bus-based topology running over coaxial cable. 10BaseT uses unshielded-twisted-pair cable in a star-based topology. Ethernet normally has a data transmission rate of 10 Mbps.

**ethical** *adjective* concerning accepted standards of behaviour and practice

**ethical committee** *noun* a group of specialists who monitor experiments involving humans or who regulate the way in which members of the medical profession conduct themselves

**ethics** *noun* a code of practice which shows how a professional group such as doctors and nurses should work and what type of relationship they should have with their patients

**Ethiopian Region** *noun* EARTH SCI a biogeographical region, part of Arctogea, comprising Africa south of the Sahara

**ethno-** *prefix* BIOL referring to humans

**ethnobotany** *noun* BOT the study of the way plants are used by humans

**ethology** *noun* BIOL the study of the behaviour of living organisms

**ethyl acetate** *noun* CHEM a colourless liquid that evaporates readily and has a pleasant fruity smell, used in perfume manufacture and as a solvent. Formula: $C_4H_8O_2$.

**ethyl alcohol** *noun* CHEM same as **ethanol**

**ethylbenzene** *noun* CHEM a colourless flammable liquid used in making phenylethene for polystyrene manufacture

**ethylene** *noun* CHEM a hydrocarbon occurring in natural gas and ripening fruits, used in the production of polythene and as an anaesthetic. Also called **ethene**

**ethylene glycol** *noun* CHEM a colourless viscous liquid with a sweet taste used as antifreeze and in polyester manufacture. Formula: $C_2H_6O_2$.

**ethyne** *noun* CHEM same as **acetylene**

**etiolation** *noun* BOT the process by which a green plant grown in insufficient light becomes yellow and grows long shoots

**etiology** *noun* BIOL the cause or origin of a disease

**ETX** *abbreviation* COMPUT end of text

**eucalyptus** *noun* TREES a quick-growing Australian hardwood tree with strong-smelling resin. Genus: *Eucalyptus*.

**eucaryote** *noun* BIOL another spelling of **eukaryote**

**eucaryotic** *adjective* BIOL another spelling of **eukaryotic**

**euchromatin** *noun* GENETICS an expanded form of the material of which chromosomes are composed (NOTE: It occurs when DNA is being actively copied and stains lightly only with basic dyes.)

**eugenics** *noun* SOC SCI the proposed improvement of the human species by encouragement to reproduce only among those with genetic characteristics regarded as desirable and discouragement among those with characteristics regarded as undesirable

**Euglenophyta** *noun* MARINE BIOL a type of algae

**eukaryote, eucaryote** *noun* BIOL an organism with a cell or cells with visible nuclei and organelles

**eukaryotic, eucaryotic** *adjective* BIOL referring to eukaryotes

**euphotic zone** *noun* EARTH SCI the top layer of water in the sea or a lake, which sunlight can penetrate and in which photosynthesis takes place

**euploid** *adjective* GENETICS relating to a cell or organism with a chromosome number that is an even multiple of the basic chromosome set for the species

**europium** *noun* CHEM ELEM a soft silvery-white metallic element of the lanthanide group, derived from monaziteand bastnasite and used in lasers (NOTE: The chemical symbol is **Eu**; the atomic number is **63** and atomic weight is **151.96**.)

**euryhaline** *adjective* BIOL referring to an organism which can survive a wide range of salt levels in its environment

**eurythermous** *adjective* BIOL referring to an organism which can survive a wide range of temperatures in its environment

**eusocial society** *noun* ZOOL a group of animals such as ants, bees and wasps in which some individuals are workers and do not reproduce, while others are fertile

**Eustachian tube** *noun* ANAT a canal extending from the middle ear to the nasopharynx that equalises air pressure on both sides of the eardrum

**eustatic change** *noun* EARTH SCI a change resulting from worldwide variations in sea level, as distinct from regional change caused by earth movements in a particular area

**eutectic mixture** *noun* CHEM a mixture that has the lowest freezing point of any combination of its constituents

**eutectic point** *noun* the temperature at which a eutectic mixture freezes, which is the lowest freezing point of any constituent of the mixture

**eutherian** *noun* ZOOL a mammal whose young develop within the womb attached to maternal tissues by a placenta. Subclass: Eutheria.

**eutrophic** *adjective* EARTH SCI referring to water which is rich in dissolved organic and mineral nutrients

**eutrophication** *noun* EARTH SCI the process by which water becomes full of phosphates and other nutrients which encourage the growth of algae and kill other organisms. Also called **eutrophy**

**eutrophic lake** *noun* EARTH SCI a lake which has a high decay rate in the top layer of water, and so contains little oxygen at the lowest levels (NOTE: It has few fish but is rich in algae.)

**eutrophy** *noun* EARTH SCI same as **eutrophication** ■ *verb* BIOCHEM to fill something up with nutrients ○ *The sea is becoming eutrophied with nutrients.*

**eV** *symbol* PHYS electronvolt

**evacuate** *verb* **1.** to remove all the people from a place in the event of an emergency ○ *procedures for evacuating all passengers from the airport* **2.** PHYS to create a vacuum in something by removing all the air ○ *evacuate a glass jar*

**evaluate** *verb* **1.** to judge the value or importance of something ○ *We'll evaluate the new treatment over 6 months.* **2.** to calculate a value or a quantity

**evaluation** *noun* an examination and judgement of something ○ *The ice detector system provides continuous evaluation of conditions conducive to the formation of ice.*

**evaluation copy** *noun* COMPUT a demonstration version of a software product that allows a user to try the main functions of a software product before buying it

**evaporate** *verb* PHYS to change from being a liquid to being a vapour, or to change a liquid into a vapour ○ *In the heat of the day, water evaporates from the surface of the earth.* ○ *The sun evaporated all the water.*

**evaporation** *noun* PHYS the process of changing from a liquid into a vapour

**evaporative** *adjective* PHYS able to evaporate

**evapotranspiration** *noun* BOT the movement of water from soil through a plant until it is released into the atmosphere from leaf surfaces

**even** *adjective* **1.** flat or smooth, with no bumps or dents **2.** uniform (*of distribution*) ○ *an even distribution of passengers* ○ *an even application of paint* ■ *adverb* used to emphasise a comparison with something stated ○ *It will be even higher than the new building.*

**even number** *noun* MATHS a number that is a multiple of two ○ *The first three even numbers are 2, 4 and 6.*

**even parity check** *noun* an error checking method that only transmits an even number of binary ones in each word. Compare **odd parity check**

**event** *noun* an action or activity

**event-driven** *adjective* COMPUT referring to a computer program or process where each step of the execution relies on external actions

**event focus** *noun* COMPUT an object that is currently receiving messages from an action or event

**event handler** *noun* COMPUT a routine that responds to an event or message within an object-oriented programming environment ○ *If a user clicks the mouse button this generates a message which can be acted upon by the event handler.*

**event horizon** *noun* ASTRON the boundary of a black hole, at which its gravitational field is strong enough to prevent the escape of electromagnetic radiation

**eventual** *adjective* happening at an unspecified time in the future ○ *Water in the fuel may lead to eventual engine stoppage.*

**eventually** *adverb* at an unspecified time in the future ○ *Vapour cools and eventually condenses.*

**evergreen** BOT *adjective* referring to a plant which does not lose its leaves in winter. Compare **deciduous** ■ *noun* a tree or shrub which does not lose its leaves in winter

**evidence** *noun* something which can be seen on the surface which suggests that there is a deeper structural problem ○ *no external evidence of cracking* ○ *Deformed wing panels may be evidence of an over-stressed airframe.*

**evident** *adjective* easily seen or understood ○ *It is evident from the information available that these problems played a part in the cause of the accident.*

**evolution** *noun* BIOL heritable changes in organisms which take place over a long period involving many generations

**evolutionary** *adjective* BIOL referring to evolution ○ *Evolutionary changes have taken place over millions of years.*

**evolutionary ecology** *noun* ECOL the study of the impact of evolution on current ecological patterns

**evolve** *verb* **1.** to develop gradually **2.** BIOL to change and develop gradually over millions of years from primitive forms into the range of plant and animal species known on Earth **3.** PHYS to give off a physical quantity or chemical substance such as heat, gas or vapour

**exa-** *prefix* MEASURE $10^{18}$. Symbol **E**

**exact** *adjective* completely accurate or correct ○ *The exact fuel flow and pressure is adjusted.* ○ *The calculation is not exact.*

**exactly** *adverb* **1.** accurately ○ *measure the quantity exactly* **2.** completely ○ *A fuel injection system performs exactly the same function as a carburettor.*

**examination** *noun* **1.** a set of questions or exercises testing knowledge or skill ○ *The examination includes multiple-choice questions.* **2.** a careful observation or inspection ○ *examination of a faulty component* ○ *Examination of the house revealed traces of radon.*

**examine** *verb* **1.** to test someone's knowledge or skills by means of questions or exercises ○ *Students will be examined in four subjects.* **2.** MED to test or check the condition or health of someone ○ *to examine a patient* **3.** to study or analyse something ○ *to examine charts*

**exceed** *verb* to be more than something ○ *The concentration of radioactive material in the waste exceeded the government limits.* □ **it is dangerous to exceed the stated dose** do not take more than the stated dose

**except** *preposition* not including ○ *All the text has been keyboarded, except the last ten pages.*

**except gate** *noun* COMPUT a logical function whose output is true if either of two inputs is true and false if both inputs are the same

**exception** *noun* something or someone not included □ **an exception to the rule** an example which does not conform to a general statement □ **with the exception of** not including

**exceptional** *adjective* **1.** being an exception **2.** well above average

**exception handling** *noun* COMPUT the routines and procedures that diagnose and correct errors or minimise the effects of errors, so that a system will run when an error is detected. Also called **error handling, error management**

**excess** *noun* an amount or quantity beyond what is normal or sufficient □ **in excess of** more than

**excess-3 code** *noun* MATHS a code in which decimal digits are represented by the binary equivalent of three greater than the number ○ *The excess-3 code representation of 6 is 1001.*

**excess electron** *noun* PHYS an electron added to a semiconductor by adding an impurity to the semiconductor

**excessive** *adjective* more than usual or sufficient ○ *Excessive ultraviolet radiation can cause skin cancer.*

**excess power** *noun* MECH ENG the difference between horsepower available and horsepower required

**exchange** *verb* to take one thing and put another in its place ○ *Meteorological stations exchange information with other meteorological stations.*

**exchangeable** *adjective* able to be exchanged

**exchanger** *noun* a device which exchanges things

**exchange selection** *noun* a sorting method which repeatedly exchanges various pairs of data items until they are in order

**excitation** *noun* **1.** PHYS the process during which a nucleus, electron, atom or ion acquires enough energy to raise it to a quantum or excited state. The difference of energy between ground level and the excited state is the excitation energy. **2.** ELEC the act of supplying a small current to the windings of larger electrical motors

**excite** *verb* PHYS to raise a particle, atom, molecule or system from its lowest energy level (**ground state**) to a higher energy level

**excited state** *noun* PHYS a state in which a particle, atom, molecule or system has a higher energy level than its ground state

**exciter** *noun* ELEC a device that supplies a small current to the windings of a larger electrical motor

**exclude** *verb* to keep something out ○ *Joints and interfaces should exclude moisture and improve fatigue life.*

**excluding** *preposition* COMPUT not including

**exclusion** *noun* **1.** the act of not including something or someone **2.** COMPUT restriction of access to a system

**exclusion principle** *noun* PHYS the rule that not more than one particle can have the same quantum conditions in the same atom and they must differ in energy level, spin or some other characteristic. Also called **Pauli exclusion principle**

**exclusive** *adjective* COMPUT not including ○ *service exclusive* □ **exclusive of** not including □ **mutually exclusive** not possible simultaneously

**exclusive NOR** *noun* MATHS a logical function whose output is true if all inputs are the same level and false if any are different. Abbreviation **EXNOR**

**exclusive OR** *noun* MATHS a logical function whose output is true if any input is true and false if all the inputs are the same. Abbreviation **EXOR**

**excrement** *noun* BIOL faeces

**excreta** *plural noun* BIOL waste material from the body

**excrete** *verb* BIOL to pass waste matter out of the body ○ *The urinary system separates waste liquids from the blood and excretes them as urine.*

**excretion** *noun* BIOL the passing of waste matter, faeces, urine, sweat or carbon dioxide out of the body. Compare **secrete, secretion**

**executable file** *noun* COMPUT a file that contains a program rather than data

**execute** *verb* COMPUT to run or carry out a computer program or process

**execute cycle** *noun* COMPUT the series of events required to fetch, decode and carry out an instruction stored in memory

**execute phase** *noun* COMPUT a section of the execute cycle when the instruction is carried out

**execution** *noun* COMPUT the process of carrying out a computer program or process

**execution cycle** *noun* COMPUT a period of time during which an instruction is executed

**executive** *adjective* **1.** referring to making decisions and managing situations **2.** COMPUT referring to the operating system of a computer

**executive control program** *noun* COMPUT same as **operating system**

**executive information system** *noun* COMPUT an easy-to-use piece of software providing information to managers or executives about their company. Abbreviation **EIS**

**exercise** *verb* to use something ○ *Exercise special care when handling chemicals.*

**exert** *verb* □ **to exert an influence** to have an influence □ **to exert pressure** to put pressure onto something

**exhalation** *noun* BIOL the action of breathing out. Compare **inhalation**

**exhale** *verb* BIOL to breathe out. Compare **inhale**

**exhaust** *verb* **1.** to tire someone out **2.** to use something up completely ○ *The supplies are exhausted.* ■ *noun* **1.** ENG waste gases from an engine **2.** AUTOMOT the part of an engine through which waste gases pass ○ *Fumes from vehicle exhausts contribute a large percentage of air pollution in towns.*

**exhausted fallow** *noun* AGRIC fallow land which is no longer fertile

**exhaust fumes, exhaust gases** *plural noun* AUTOMOT gases, including carbon dioxide and carbon monoxide, produced by the engine of a car or truck as it burns petrol or fuel

**exhaust gas filter system** *noun* AUTOMOT a means of removing some or all of the harmful emissions from the exhaust gases of an engine by filtration or catalytic action

**exhaustion** *noun* **1.** the complete utilisation of something ○ *the exhaustion* of the Earth's natural resources **2.** extreme tiredness or fatigue

**exhaustive** *adjective* complete and thorough ○ *an exhaustive reply to the safety concerns* ○ *an exhaustive search for the information*

**exhaust purification device** *noun* AUTOMOT same as **exhaust gas filter system**

**exhaust system** *noun* AUTOMOT a part of an engine through which waste gases pass

**exhaust valve** *noun* AUTOMOT a valve in a piston engine which allows exhaust gases to leave the cylinder

**exhibit** *verb* to have something as a characteristic ○ *Composites, due to their construction, exhibit good fatigue behaviour.* ○ *Altocumulus cloud frequently exhibits a waved appearance.*

**exist** *verb* to be present under particular circumstances or in a particular place ○ *Water can exist in the atmosphere in three forms.* ○ *A fire risk may exist following failure or leakage of any component.*

**existence** *noun* the fact or state of being ○ *Warning systems are provided to give an indication of the existence of a dangerous condition.*

**exit** *noun* the act of going out of a place ○ *The exhaust valve opens to allow for the exit of exhaust gases.* ■ *verb* COMPUT to stop program execution or to leave a program and return control to the operating system or interpreter

**exitance** *noun* a measure of the level of flux emitted per unit area of a surface (NOTE: Radiant exitance ($M_e$) is measured in watts per square metre (W m$^{-2}$ while luminous exitance ($M_v$) is measured in lumens per square metre (1m m$^{-2}$)).)

**exit point** *noun* COMPUT a point in a subroutine where control is returned to the main program ○ *You have to exit to another editing system to add headlines.*

**exjunction** *noun* COMPUT a logical function whose output is true if either of two inputs is true and false if both inputs are the same

**EXNOR** *abbreviation* MATHS exclusive NOR

**exobiology** *noun* ASTRON the study of possible life in the universe other than on the Earth

**exocarp** *noun* BOT same as **epicarp**

**exocrine gland** *noun* ANAT a gland that discharges its secretion through a duct into a body cavity or to the exterior, e.g. the sweat glands and salivary glands

**exogamous** *adjective* BIOL referring to a zygote produced by gametes from two unrelated parents

**exogenous** *adjective* BIOL originating outside an organism

**exon** *noun* GENETICS a discontinuous sequence of DNA that carries the genetic code for the final messenger RNA molecule

**EXOR** *abbreviation* MATHS exclusive OR

**exoskeleton** *noun* ZOOL a hard covering or skeleton situated on the outside of organisms such as crustaceans, insects, turtles and armadillos, giving support and protection

**exosphere** *noun* EARTH SCI the highest layers of Earth's atmosphere, more than 650 km above the surface and composed almost entirely of hydrogen

**exothermic** *adjective* CHEM relating to a chemical reaction that is a net producer of heat energy. Compare **endothermic**

**exothermic reaction** *noun* CHEM a chemical reaction in which heat is given out to the surroundings

**exotoxin** *noun* MED a poison produced by bacteria which affects parts of the body away from the place of infection

**expand** *verb* to increase in size, volume or quantity ○ *Air expands when heated and contracts when cooled.* (NOTE: The opposite is **contract**; but when it is caused by factors other than temperature it is **compress**.)

**expandable** *adjective* able to be expanded

**expandable system** *noun* COMPUT a computer system that is designed to be able to grow in power or memory by hardware or software additions

**expanded** *adjective* INDUST (*of plastic or polystyrene*) made into a hard lightweight foam by blowing air or gas into it

COMMENT: Expanded polystyrene and other plastics are extensively used for packaging. CFCs are sometimes used in their manufacture.

**expansion** *noun* **1.** an increase in size, volume or quantity ○ *There is an expansion of the gas when it is heated.* **2.** COMPUT an increase in computing power or storage size **3.** MATHS (*of a mathematical expression*) the rewriting of a mathematical function as a series of terms

**expansion bus** *noun* COMPUT data and address lines leading to a connector and allowing expansion cards to control and access the data in main memory

**expansion card** *noun* COMPUT a printed circuit board connected to a system to increase its functions or performance

**expansion chamber** *noun* PHYS a container which allows for expansion of a fluid caused by increase in temperature or some other factor

**expansion of the universe** *noun* ASTRON the process by which the universe is moving outwards after the Big Bang some 20 billion years ago

COMMENT: The expansion is seen by terrestrial observers in the form of the redshift in the radiation from distant galaxies. The Hubble Constant which tells us how fast objects recede for their distance is today put at 55 kilometres per second per million parsecs of distance. Distance has been determined from looking at Cepheid variables in nearby galaxies and by other means for more distant ones, while the velocities are found from redshifts in optical or other wavelengths.

**expansion slot** *noun* COMPUT a connector inside a computer into which an expansion card can be plugged ○ *Insert the board in the expansion slot.*

**expansivity** *noun* PHYS the measure of how much a solid or liquid expands or contracts in different temperatures

**expect** *verb* to hope or assume that something is going to happen ○ *the weather to be expected around the equinox*

**expectancy** *noun* the state of expecting something

**expected** *adjective* hoped for as a possibility ○ *the expected number of passengers*

**expel** *verb* to force something out ○ *Exhaust gases are expelled from the cylinder by the upward movement of the piston.* ○ *The piston expels fluid into the system on the inward stroke.*

**expenditure** *noun* **1.** the spending of money ○ *The expenditure of public funds for this project.* **2.** the amount of money spent

**experience** *noun* **1.** the building up of knowledge or skill over a period of time by an active participation in events or activities ○ *a teacher with 20 years' experience* **2.** an event ○ *The first solo flight is an experience most pilots never forget.* ■ *verb* to participate in something or find yourself in a particular situation ○ *It is not unusual to experience traffic delays.* ○ *Turbulence can be experienced when flying through a trough.*

**experiment** *noun* a scientific test under controlled conditions that is made to demonstrate or discover something ○ *Experiments have shown that left-handed people often have better hand/eye coordination than right-handed people.* □ **to conduct an experiment** to carry out an experiment ■ *verb* to carry out a scientific test under controlled conditions in order to demonstrate or discover something □ **to experiment with something** to try something to see how it performs or affects you ○ *experimenting with new drug delivery systems* □ **to experiment on someone or something** to use someone or something in an experiment ○ *experimented on laboratory mice*

**experimental** *adjective* referring to something still at an early stage of development ○ *the experimental and testing stages of a new type of aircraft*

**experimentally** *adverb* by carrying out experiments

**expert** *noun* a person who knows a lot about something ○ *He is a computer expert.* ○ *She is an expert in programming languages.*

**expert system** *noun* COMPUT a piece of software which applies the knowledge, advice and rules defined by experts in a particular field to a user's data to help solve a problem

**expire** *verb* **1.** PHYSIOL to breathe out **2.** BIOL to die

**explanatory** *adjective* giving an explanation ○ *an explanatory paragraph*

**explicit address** *noun* COMPUT an address provided in two parts, the reference point and a displacement or index value

**explicit reference** *noun* COMPUT a way of identifying a particular object, e.g. a field or button, by a unique name

**explode** *verb* PHYS to burst, or to make something burst, violently

**exploit** *verb* **1.** to take advantage of something ○ *Ladybirds have exploited the sudden increase in the numbers of insects.* **2.** to use a natural resource ○ *exploiting the natural wealth of the forest* **3.** to treat something or someone unfairly for personal benefit

**exploitation** *noun* **1.** the action of taking advantage of something **2.** the utilisation of natural resources ○ *Further exploitation of the coal deposits is not economic.* **3.** the using of something or someone for personal benefit

**explosion** *noun* **1.** a release of energy in a sudden and often violent way ○ *an explosion caused by a bomb* **2.** the action of bursting as a result of internal pressure ○ *tyre explosion due to overheating* **3.** the loud sound made as a result of an explosion ○ *The passengers heard an explosion.*

**explosive** *adjective* **1.** able to or designed to explode ○ *an explosive device* **2.** causing a rapid expansion ○ *explosive growth* ■ *noun* a substance which can explode

**explosive hazard** *noun* the risk that a substance may blow up

**exponent** *noun* MATHS a number indicating the power to which a base number is to be raised

**exponential** *adjective* **1.** increasing more and more rapidly **2.** referring to a mathematical function that varies in relation to the power of another value. If $x = n^y$, then x is said to vary exponentially with y.

**exponentially** *adverb* more and more rapidly ○ *We can expect this population to increase exponentially over the next years.*

**exponentiation** *noun* MATHS the action of raising a base number to a particular power

**export** *verb* COMPUT to save data in a different file format from the default ○ *To use this data with dBASE, you will have to export it as a DBF file.*

**expose** *verb* **1.** to subject something, or allow something to be subjected, to an action or an effect ○ *When the slope of a hill is exposed to solar radiation,* wind currents are set up. **2.** to show something which was covered or hidden ○ *The report exposed a lack of supervision in maintenance of the reactor.*

**exposed** *adjective* **1.** not covered or hidden ○ *painted all the exposed surfaces* **2.** ENVIRON not protected from environmental effects □ **exposed to the sun** in sunlight without covering

**exposure** *noun* **1.** the act or process of being exposed ○ *his exposure to radiation* **2.** MED the harmful effect on someone of having no protection from the weather ○ *suffering from exposure after spending a night in the snow*

**exposure dose** *noun* MED the amount of radiation to which someone has been exposed

**express** *verb* to put something into words, symbols or signs ○ *An angle may be expressed in degrees, minutes and seconds.* ○ *Pressure altitudes are expressed in hundreds of feet.*

**expression** *noun* **1.** MATHS a mathematical formula or relationship **2.** COMPUT a definition of a value or variable in a program

**expressivity** *noun* GENETICS the extent to which a gene affects the observable characteristics (**phenotype**) of an organism

**extend** *verb* to make something longer

**extended arithmetic element** *noun* COMPUT a section of a central processing unit that provides hardware implementations of various mathematical functions

**extended binary coded decimal interchange code** *noun* COMPUT an 8-bit character coding system. Abbreviation **EBCDIC**

**extended BNF** *noun* COMPUT a more flexible way of defining the syntax of a language. Abbreviation **EBNF**

**extended family** *noun* SOC SCI a family group which includes not only parents and their offspring but also other blood relatives. Compare **nuclear family**

**extensible language** *noun* COMPUT a computer programming language that allows the user to add data types and commands

**extensification** *noun* AGRIC the use of less intensive farming methods

**extension** *noun* something added to something else to make it longer

**extension cable** *noun* ELEC a cable that allows a device located at some distance to be connected

**extensive** *adjective* large in range or amount ○ *Extensive use is made of volunteers.*

**extensive farming** *noun* AGRIC a way of farming which is characterised by a low level of inputs per unit of land

COMMENT: Extensive farming involves practices such as using fewer chemical fertilisers, leaving uncultivated areas at the edges of fields and reducing the size of herds of cattle. This allows lower yields from the same area of farmland, which is necessary if production levels are too high. Extensive farms are usually very large.

**extensive system** *noun* AGRIC a farming system which uses a large amount of land per unit of stock or output ○ *an extensive system of pig farming*

**extent** *noun* a range or amount of something ○ *The horizontal extent of the cloud averages about 50 km.* ○ *Clouds of great vertical extent are not uncommon.* □ **to a certain extent**, **to some extent** partly ○ *The accident was caused, to a certain extent, by the poor weather.* □ **to a lesser** *or* **greater extent** not as much as *or* more than something previously stated

**external** *adjective* 1. on or from the outside of something ○ *external appearance* □ **for external use** referring to medication that is to be used only on the outside of the body and not swallowed. Compare **internal** 2. COMPUT outside a program or device

**external clock** *noun* COMPUT a clock or synchronising signal supplied from outside a device

**external device** *noun* COMPUT 1. an item of hardware such as a terminal or printer that is attached to a main computer 2. a device that allows communications between the computer and itself, but which is not directly operated by the main computer

**external disk drive** *noun* COMPUT a device that is not built into the computer, but is added to increase its storage capabilities

**external effects** *plural noun* INDUST the costs to society of industrial processes which are not reflected in the price of the product sold, e.g. the environmental costs associated with a power station. Also called **externalities**

**external iliac artery** *noun* ANAT an artery which branches from the aorta in the abdomen and leads to the leg

**external interrupt** *noun* COMPUT an interrupt signal from a peripheral device indicating that attention is required

**externalities** *plural noun* INDUST same as **external effects**

**external maxillary artery** *noun* ANAT a branch of the external carotid artery, in the face

**external register** *noun* COMPUT a user's register located in main memory rather than within the CPU

**external respiration** *noun* PHYSIOL the process of oxygen in the air being exchanged in the lungs for carbon dioxide from the blood

**external schema** *noun* COMPUT the user's view of the structure of data or a program

**exteroceptor** *noun* BIOL a sensory organ such as the eye or ear which is affected by stimuli from outside the body

**extinct** *adjective* 1. ECOL referring to a species which has died out ○ *Several native species have become extinct since sailors in the nineteenth century introduced dogs to the island.* 2. EARTH SCI referring to a volcano which is no longer able to erupt. Compare **dormant**

**extinction** *noun* 1. ECOL the process of a species dying out 2. PHYS the effect by which a beam of light is reduced in intensity as it passes through a solution

**extinguish** *verb* to put out a fire

**extinguisher** *noun* a portable mechanical device for spraying and putting out a fire with chemicals

**extinguishing agent** *noun* CHEM 1. one of several substances used to put out fires 2. a chemical substance which makes another substance react

**extra** COMPUT *adjective* more than usual ○ *extra checking* ■ *noun* an item which is additional to a basic product ○ *The mouse and cabling are sold as extras.*

**extracellular** *adjective* BIOL taking place or situated outside a cell or cells

**extrachromosomal** *adjective* GENETICS referring to the inheritance of characteristics controlled by factors that are not carried on chromosomes

**extracode** *noun* COMPUT a short routine within the operating system that emulates a hardware function

**extract** *noun* a part taken from a longer text ○ *The following paragraph is an extract from the safety regulations.* ■ *verb* **1.** to remove something from a place ○ *extracted the book from a large pile* **2.** to obtain information from something ○ *Extract the important information from the report and make a summary.* **3.** CHEM, INDUST to obtain something from a substance by a chemical or industrial process ○ *A dehumidifier extracts moisture from the atmosphere.*

**extraction** *noun* INDUST the act or process of extracting something ○ *The extraction of coal from the mine is becoming too costly.*

**extractor** *noun* ENG a machine which extracts something, e.g. a machine which removes fumes or gas

**extractor fan** *noun* ENG a small fan which removes fumes or smoke from a kitchen or factory

**extragalactic** *adjective* ASTRON existing, originating or happening outside the galaxy that contains Earth

**extranet** *noun* COMPUT an internal company network (**intranet**) that has a connection to the public Internet and allows users to gain access via the Internet (NOTE: It is often used to provide access to people in the company who are working away from the office.)

**extrapolate** *verb* to estimate something by using known facts ○ *Information given on a synoptic chart can be extrapolated, by the use of some simple guidelines.*

**extrasolar** *adjective* ASTRON existing in or relating to space outside the solar system that contains Earth

**extreme** *adjective* **1.** most distant in any direction ○ *the most extreme point on the map* **2.** to the greatest or highest degree ○ *extreme difficulty* ○ *Extreme care must be taken in handling the specimens.* ■ *noun* either of the two things situated at opposite ends of a range ○ *the extremes of boiling and freezing* ○ *The region experiences extremes of temperature.*

**extrinsic factor** *noun* BIOCHEM a form of vitamin $B_{12}$

**extrinsic semiconductor** *noun* PHYS a semiconductor material that has had impurities added to change its conductive properties

**extrusive** *adjective* EARTH SCI referring to rock formed from molten lava which has pushed up through Earth's crust

**eye** *noun* **1.** ANAT a sense organ which is used for seeing **2.** METEOROL the central point of a tropical storm, where pressure is lowest (NOTE: The eye can be several kilometres wide and may take some minutes to pass.)

**eye-dropper** *noun* COMPUT a tool in a graphics software application that allows a user to click on a pixel in an image and select the colour of the pixel

**eyepiece** *noun* ASTRON the small lens of a telescope or microscope through which the image is viewed

**eyesight** *noun* BIOL same as **vision**

**eyespot** *noun* ZOOL a marking in the shape of an eye, e.g. on some butterflies wings or on a peacock's tail

**eye tooth** *noun* DENT a canine tooth

# F

**F** *symbol* **1.** PHYS Fahrenheit **2.** PHYS, MEASURE farad **3.** ELEC, MEASURE faraday **4.** CHEM ELEM fluorine ■ *noun* MATHS the hexadecimal number equivalent to decimal number 15

**f-** *prefix* one thousandth of a million millionth ($10^{-15}$). Full form **femto-**

**F₁** *noun* GENETICS (*in breeding experiments*) the first generation of offspring

**F₁ hybrid** *noun* GENETICS, BOT a plant produced by breeding two parent plants, which is stronger than the parents, but which will not itself breed true

COMMENT: $F_1$ hybrids can be crossbred to produce $F_2$ hybrids and the process can be continued for many generations

**fabric** *noun* cloth produced especially by knitting or weaving

**fabricate** *verb* INDUST to manufacture something ○ *The ease with which aluminium can be fabricated into any form is one of its most important qualities.*

**face** *noun* **1.** ANAT the front of the head, including the eyes, nose and mouth **2.** the surface of an object ○ *the face of the Earth* ○ *The exhaust cone prevents the hot gases from flowing across the rear face of the turbine disc.* □ **the north face of a mountain** the vertical or near-vertical side facing north **3.** (*of a clock or instrument*) the part with a dial and indicators ○ *the face of an instrument* ■ *verb* to turn towards a particular direction ○ *The window faces east.*

**facet** *noun* a surface or plane

**faceted code** *noun* COMPUT a code which indicates various details of an item by assigning each one a value

**facial artery** *noun* ANAT an artery which branches off the external carotid into the face and mouth

**facial nerve** *noun* ANAT the seventh cranial nerve which governs the muscles of the face, the taste buds on the front of the tongue and the salivary and lacrimal glands

**facies** *noun* BIOL the characteristic appearance of something, e.g. an animal or plant

**facilitate** *verb* to enable something to happen more easily or quickly ○ *A ramp is used to facilitate access to the wing.*

**facilities** *plural noun* the building, equipment or resources which can be used to do something ○ *research facilities*

**facility** *noun* **1.** a natural aptitude or ability ○ *a facility for logical thinking* **2.** an installation or building with a specific function ○ *a processing facility* **3.** a mode of operation which allows the user of equipment to do something ○ *The printer has a self-test facility.*

**facsimile** *noun* **1.** COMPUT an exact copy of an original **2.** TELECOM a fax message

**facsimile transmission** *noun* TELECOM the sending and receiving of images by fax

**fact** *noun* a piece of information ○ *interesting scientific facts*

**factor** *noun* **1.** something that has an influence on something else ○ *Even with modern instruments, visibility remains a very important factor in aviation.* **2.** MATHS the amount by which something is multiplied □ **by a factor of** indicating a quantity by which a stated quantity is multiplied or divided, so as to indicate an increase or decrease in a measurement **3.** MATHS either of two numbers or quantities that can be multiplied together to give a particular number **4.** MED a substance in the plasma which makes the blood coagulate when a blood vessel is injured

**factorial** *noun* MATHS the product of all the numbers below a number (NOTE: For example, 4 factorial (written 4!) = 1x2x3x4 = 24.)

**factorise** *verb* MATHS to break down a number into two whole numbers which when multiplied will give the original number ○ *When factorised, 15 gives the factors 1, 15 or 3, 5.*

**Factor IX** *noun* MED same as **Christmas factor**

**Factor VIII** *noun* MED a substance in plasma that makes blood coagulate and which is lacking in haemophiliacs

**factor XII** *noun* BIOCHEM same as **Hageman factor**

**factory** *noun* INDUST a building where products are manufactured ○ *a chemical factory*

**factory farming** *noun* AGRIC a highly intensive method of rearing animals characterised by keeping large numbers of animals indoors in confined spaces and feeding them processed foods, with the use of drugs to control diseases

**fade** *noun* **1.** a periodic reduction in the received strength of a radio transmission ○ *Surface wave at night causes fade of the signal.* **2.** a periodic reduction in braking power ○ *Hard braking can cause fade and tyre burst through overheating.* ■ *verb* to lose brightness, loudness or brilliance gradually ○ *The radio signal faded.*

**faecal** *adjective* BIOL referring to faeces. US spelling **fecal**

**faecal matter** *noun* BIOL same as **faeces**

**faeces** *plural noun* BIOL solid waste matter passed from the bowels after food has been eaten and digested. US spelling **feces**

**Fahrenheit** *noun* MEASURE a scale of temperatures on which the freezing and boiling points of water are 32° and 212° respectively (NOTE: Fahrenheit is used in the USA but is now less common in the UK)

COMMENT: To convert Fahrenheit temperatures to Celsius, subtract 32, multiply by 5 and divide by 9. So 68°F is equal to 20° C. As a quick rough estimate, subtract 30 and divide by two.

**fail** *verb* **1.** to be unsuccessful ○ *Attempts to reach agreement on the environmental agenda failed.* **2.** to stop working properly ○ *The car's brakes must have failed.*

**fail safe system** *noun* **1.** a system or device which has in-built safeguards against total failure ○ *The term 'fail safe' means in this case that the structure, though damaged, is capable of supporting a reasonable percentage of its design load.* **2.** COMPUT a system which has a predetermined state it will go to if a main program or device fails, so avoiding the problems that a complete system shutdown would produce

**fail soft system** *noun* a system which will still be partly operational even after a part of the system has failed

**failure** *noun* **1.** breakdown ○ *Engine failure is sometimes accompanied by fire.* **2.** the fact of not achieving the desired end or ends ○ *the failure of an experiment* □ **failure to do something** not having done something ○ *criticised their failure to comply with the safety regulations*

**failure annunciation** *noun* ELEC a set of signals on an annunciator panel that indicate the failure of a system

**failure logging** *noun* COMPUT a section of an operating system that automatically saves the present system states and relevant data when an error or fault is detected

**failure rate** *noun* a number of failures of a specific type within a specific period of time

**failure recovery** *noun* the return to normal activity of a process or program after a failure has occurred and been corrected

**fairing** *noun* AEROSP a device to improve the flow of air over a surface ○ *There is a dorsal fairing at the base of the fin or vertical stabiliser.* ○ *Wheel fairings, called spats, are fitted to light aircraft to reduce drag.*

**fairly** *adverb* moderately

**Fajans' rules** *plural noun* CHEM the rules that state when a chemical compound will have ionic rather than covalent bonds

**fall** *noun* **1.** a reduction ○ *a fall in pressure* **2.** METEOROL the amount of rain or snow which comes down at any one time ○ *an overnight fall of snow* **3.** *US* autumn ■ *verb* **1.** to become less in amount ○ *atmospheric pressure is falling* **2.** to be included within the range of something ○ *Design methods fall into four groups.* ○ *Long-range high-frequency communications fall in the frequency bracket 2–25 MHz.* **3.** to come down freely because of gravity ○ *Light rain may fall occasionally.* **4.** to occur at a particular time ○ *The vernal equinox falls in March.* (NOTE: **falling – fell – fallen**)

**fall back recovery** *noun* COMPUT the return to normal activity of a program after a fault has been fixed, from the point at which fall back routines were called

**fallopian tube** *noun* ANAT in mammals, a tube that conveys eggs from an ovary to the womb

**fallout** *noun* ENVIRON the radioactive matter which falls from the atmosphere as particles, either in rain or as dust

**fallow** AGRIC *adjective* referring to land which is not being used for growing crops for a period so that the nutrients can build up again in the soil ○ *letting the land lie fallow* ■ *noun* a period when land is not used for cultivation ○ *Shifting cultivation is characterised by short cropping periods and long fallows.*

**fallow crop** *noun* AGRIC a crop grown in widely spaced rows, so that it is possible to hoe and cultivate between the rows

**fallow cultivation** *noun* AGRIC a type of cultivation in which the period under crops is increased and the length of the fallow is reduced

**fallspeed** *noun* METEOROL the speed at which raindrops or dry particles fall through the air

**fallstreak** *noun* METEOROL a column of ice particles which are falling through a cloud

**false** *adjective* not true or not correct ○ *Lightning may cause false readings from sensitive instruments.*

**false code** *noun* COMPUT a code that contains values not within specified limits

**false drop** *noun* COMPUT the retrieval of unwanted files from a database through the use of incorrect search codes

**false error** *noun* COMPUT an error warning given when no error has occurred

**false fruit** *noun* BOT same as **pseudocarp**

**FAM** *abbreviation* COMPUT fast access memory

**familiar** *adjective* **1.** common ○ *Clouds are the most familiar visible me-*teorological feature. **2.** well known or easily recognised □ **to be familiar with** to have some knowledge of something ○ *He is familiar with the procedure.*

**familiarise** *verb* □ **to familiarise yourself with** to get to know something well

**family** *noun* **1.** BIOL a group composed of parents and offspring **2.** BIOL a group of genera which have specific characteristics in common ○ *Tigers and leopards are members of the cat family.* (NOTE: Scientific names of families of animals end in **-idae** and those of families of plants end in **-ae**.) **3.** COMPUT a range of different designs of a particular typeface **4.** ENG a range of machines from one manufacturer that are compatible with other products in the same line from the same manufacturer

**fan** *noun* **1.** ENG a mechanism which circulates air for cooling ○ *If the fan fails, the system will rapidly overheat.* **2.** COMPUT a spread of data items or devices ■ *verb* **1.** ENG to cool a device by blowing air over it **2.** COMPUT to spread out a series of items or devices

**fan-in** *noun* ELECTRONICS the maximum number of inputs that a circuit or chip can deal with

**fanning** *noun* ENVIRON the spreading out of a horizontal layer of smoke and other pollutants from a chimney

**fan out** *verb* to spread out from a central point

**fan-out** *noun* ELEC the maximum number of outputs that a circuit or chip can drive without exceeding its power dissipation limit

**FAO** *abbreviation* FOOD INDUST, AGRIC Food and Agriculture Organization

**FAQ** *abbreviation* COMPUT frequently asked questions

**farad** *noun* MEASURE the SI derived unit of electric capacitance. Symbol **F** (NOTE: A capacitor carrying one coulomb of charge when a potential difference of one volt is applied has a capacitance of one farad.)

**faraday** *noun* MEASURE, PHYS a unit of electric charge equal to that required to deposit a unit amount of singly charged substance during electrolysis. Symbol **F** (NOTE: Its approximate SI equivalent is 96 485 coulombs.)

**Faraday cage** *noun* ELEC a wire or metal screen, connected to ground, that completely encloses sensitive equipment to prevent any interference from stray electromagnetic radiation

**Faraday constant** *noun* the electric charge carried by one mole of electrons, equal to 9.64853 x $10^4$ coulombs per mole. Symbol **F**

**Faraday's law of electrolysis** *noun* PHYS a law developed by Michael Faraday describing the chemical changes caused by changing electrical charge

**Faraday's law of electromagnetic induction** *noun* PHYS a law developed by Michael Faraday describing the electromotive force generated in a conductor by a changing magnetic flux

**Faraday's laws** *noun* PHYS a law developed by Michael Faraday describing the electromagnetic induction of an e.m.f. or electrical charge in a conductor when near a changing magnetic flux

**farm** AGRIC *noun* **1.** an area of land used for growing crops and keeping animals to provide food and the buildings associated with it **2.** an area of land or water where particular animals or crops are raised commercially ○ *a fish farm* ○ *a butterfly farm* ■ *verb* **1.** to run a farm **2.** to grow crops and keep animals on a particular piece or size of land ○ *farms 100 acres in Devon* **3.** to raise a particular animal or crop commercially ○ *He intends to farm salmon and sea bass.*

**farmed** *adjective* AGRIC **1.** grown or produced on a farm and not in the wild **2.** referring to meat from fish grown in a fish farm or from animals kept on a farm ○ *farmed venison*

**farmer** *noun* AGRIC someone who runs or owns a farm

**farmer's lung** *noun* MED a type of asthma caused by an allergy to rotting hay

**farm produce** *noun* AGRIC food such as fruit, vegetables, meat, milk and butter, which is produced on a farm

**fascicle** *noun* BOT a bundle of branches, leaves or stems arising from the same point

**fast** *adjective* **1.** COMPUT (*of a storage or peripheral device*) performing its functions very rapidly ○ *fast program execution* ○ *This hard disk is fast, it has an access time of 28 mS.* **2.** PHYS taking place in a short period of time **3.** PHYS (*of a neutron*) having a lot of energy

**fast access memory** *noun* COMPUT a storage location which can be read from or written to very rapidly. Abbreviation **FAM**

**fast breeder reactor, fast breeder** *noun* INDUST a nuclear reactor which produces more fissile material than it consumes, using fast-moving neutrons and making plutonium-239 from uranium-238, thereby increasing the reactor's efficiency. Abbreviation **FBR**

**fast core** *noun* COMPUT a high speed, low access time working memory for a CPU ○ *The fast core is used as a scratchpad for all calculations in this system.*

**fast fission** *noun* PHYS nuclear fission of the uranium-238 isotope, which is much faster than that of uranium-235

**fast line** *noun* TELECOM a special telecommunications line which allows data to be transmitted at 48 K or 96 K baud rates

**fast neutron** *noun* PHYS a neutron with energy in excess of 1.5 MeV, sufficient to produce fission in uranium 238

**fat** *noun* **1.** BIOCHEM a water-soluble component of food (NOTE: **Fat** has no plural when it means the substance; the plural **fats** is used to mean different types of fat. For other terms referring to fats, see also **lipid** and words beginning with **steato-**.) **2.** BIOL A white oily substance in the body of mammals, which stores energy and protects the body against cold ■ *adjective* BIOL big and round in the body (NOTE: **fat – fatter – fattest**)

COMMENT: Fat is a necessary part of diet because of the vitamins and energy-giving calories which it contains. Fat in the diet comes from either animal fats or vegetable oils. Animal fats such as butter, fat meat or cream, are saturated fatty acids. It is believed that the intake of unsaturated and polyunsaturated fats, mainly vegetable oils and fish oil, in the diet, rather than animal fats, helps keep down the level of cholesterol in the blood and so lessens the risk of atherosclerosis. A low-fat diet does not always help to reduce weight.

**FAT** *abbreviation* COMPUT file allocation table

**fatal** *adjective* BIOL causing death ○ *a fatal accident*

**fatal error** *noun* COMPUT a fault in a program or device that causes the system to crash

**father** *noun* a man who has a son or daughter

**father file** *noun* COMPUT a backup of the previous version of a file

**fatigue** *noun* **1.** physical or mental tiredness resulting from exertion ○ *Fatigue was a contributing factor in the accident.* **2.** the weakening or failure of a material such as metal resulting from stress ○ *Fan blades must be resistant to fatigue and thermal shock.* ○ *Titanium has good fatigue resistance.*

**fatigue crack** *noun* a crack caused by fatigue of materials

**fat-soluble** *adjective* CHEM able to be dissolved in fat ○ *Vitamin D is fat-soluble.* ○ *PCBs are fat-soluble and so collect in the blubber of seals.*

**fatstock** *noun* AGRIC livestock which has been fattened for meat production

**fatten** *verb* AGRIC to give animals more food so as to prepare them for slaughter

**fatty** *adjective* BIOL containing fat

**fatty acid** *noun* **1.** BIOCHEM an acid found in plants and animals that consists of a straight chain of carbon atoms ending in a carboxyl group which is an important substance in the body **2.** CHEM ◊ **carboxylic acid**

**fatty degeneration** *noun* MED the accumulation of fat in the cells of an organ such as the liver or heart, making the organ less able to perform

**fault** *noun* **1.** a feature that spoils the overall quality of something ○ *a design fault* **2.** an error **3.** COMPUT a situation where something has gone wrong with software or hardware, causing it to malfunction ○ *The technical staff are trying to correct a programming fault.* **4.** EARTH SCI a line of a crack in the Earth's crust along which movements can take place leading to major earthquakes

**fault diagnosis** *noun* COMPUT the process by which the cause of a fault is located

**fault line** *noun* EARTH SCI a line of a crack in the Earth's crust

**fault management** *noun* COMPUT one of the five categories of network management specified by the ISO that will detect, isolate and correct network faults

**fault plane** *noun* EARTH SCI the face of the rock at a fault where one mass of rock has slipped against another

**fault-tolerant** *adjective* COMPUT able to continue functioning even when a fault occurs ○ *They market a highly successful range of fault-tolerant minis.*

**faulty sector** *noun* COMPUT a sector of a magnetic disk that cannot be written to or read from correctly

**fauna** *noun* **1.** ECOL the wild animals and birds which live naturally in a specific area. Compare **flora 2.** EARTH SCI a book or list describing the animals and birds of a specific area. ♦ **flora**

**fax, FAX** *noun* TELECOM **1.** a method of sending and receiving images in digital form over a telephone or radio link. Full form **facsimile transmission 2.** an image sent in digital form over a telephone or radio link. Full form **facsimile** ■ *verb* to send a fax

**FBC** *abbreviation* INDUST fluidised-bed combustion

**FBR** *abbreviation* INDUST fast breeder reactor

**FC** *abbreviation* INDUST fibre-concrete

**FCB** *abbreviation* COMPUT file control block

**FD, fd** *abbreviation* COMPUT full duplex

**FDA** *abbreviation* INDUST Food and Drug Administration

**fdc** *abbreviation* COMPUT floppy disk controller

**FDD** *abbreviation* COMPUT floppy disk drive

**FDDI** *abbreviation* COMPUT fibre distributed data interface

**FDM** *abbreviation* COMPUT frequency division multiplexing

**fdx, FDX** *abbreviation* COMPUT full duplex

**Fe** *symbol* CHEM ELEM iron

**feathers** *plural noun* ZOOL the fringes of hair that some dogs and horses have on their legs or tails

**feature** *noun* an important, noticeable or distinctive aspect, quality, or characteristic ○ *Sea breeze is a regular feature of coastal climates.* ■ *verb* to have something as a particular characteristic

○ *The machine features voice-activated control.*

**fecal** *adjective* BIOL US spelling of **faecal**

**feces** *plural noun* BIOL US spelling of **faeces**

**fecundity** *noun* BIOL fertility

**FED** *abbreviation* COMPUT field emission display

**feed** *verb* 1. BIOL to take food ○ *The herd feeds here at dusk.* 2. BIOL to give food to a person or an animal 3. AGRIC to provide fertiliser for plants or soil 4. COMPUT to put paper into a machine or information into a computer ○ *This paper should be manually fed into the printer.* ○ *Data is fed into the computer.* 5. to supply or add to something ○ *Several small streams feed into the river* ■ *noun* 1. AGRIC food given to animals and birds ○ *Traces of pesticide were found in the cattle feed.* 2. AGRIC fertiliser for plants or soil ○ *Tomatoes need liquid feed twice a week at this time of year.* 3. a supply of something 4. COMPUT a device which guides paper or other materials into and through a machine

**feed additive** *noun* AGRIC a supplement added to the feed of farm livestock, particularly pigs and poultry, to promote growth

**feedback** *noun* COMPUT the return of part of the output of a process or system to the input, especially when used to maintain performance or to control a system ○ *The LC ensures that a feedback signal of the monitored output frequency is sent back to the CSDU.*

**feedback control** *noun* COMPUT information about the effects of a controlling signal on a machine or device, returned to the controlling computer

**feed concentrate** *noun* AGRIC animal feed which has a high food value relative to volume

**feeder** *noun* 1. BIOL an animal that eats particular food or eats in a particular way ○ *a night feeder* 2. a device which supplies something ○ *a bird feeder* ○ *a paper feeder* 3. something which supplies or adds to something else of the same type

**feeder reservoir** *noun* ENG a small reservoir from which water flows into another reservoir

**feeder stream** *noun* EARTH SCI a small stream which leads into a river

**feed grain** *noun* AGRIC a cereal such as wheat or maize which is fed to animals and birds

**feeding ground** *noun* ZOOL an area where animals come to feed ○ *Estuaries are the winter feeding grounds for thousands of migratory birds.*

**feedingstuff** *noun* AGRIC same as **feedstuff**

**feed intake** *noun* AGRIC, BIOL the amount of food eaten by an animal

**feedlot** *noun* AGRIC a field with small pens in which cattle are fattened

**feed reel** *noun* COMPUT a reel of tape which is being fed into a machine

**feedstuff** *noun* AGRIC food for farm animals. Also called **feedingstuff**

**Fehling's test** *noun* BIOCHEM a test for detecting dissolved reducing sugars such as glucose and aldehydes

**feldspar, feldspath** *noun* EARTH SCI a common type of crystal rock formed of silicates

**fell** *noun* EARTH SCI a high moor and mountain in the North of England ■ *verb* FORESTRY to cut down a tree

**female** *adjective* 1. ZOOL referring to an animal that produces ova and bears young 2. BOT referring to a flower which has carpels but not stamens, or a plant that produces such flowers

**female connector** *noun* COMPUT a connector with connecting sockets into which the pins or plugs of a male connector can be inserted

**femoral** *adjective* ANAT of or concerning the thigh or femur

**femoral artery** *noun* ANAT a continuation of the external iliac artery, which runs down the front of the thigh and then crosses to the back

**femoral nerve** *noun* ANAT a nerve which governs the muscle at the front of the thigh

**femoral pulse** *noun* MED a pulse taken in the groin

**femto-** *prefix* MEASURE $10^{-15}$. Symbol **f**

**femtosecond** *noun* MEASURE a thousandth of a picosecond

**femur** *noun* ZOOL a bone in vertebrates that is equivalent to the human thighbone

**fen** *noun* EARTH SCI an area of flat marshy land, with reeds and mosses growing in alkaline water

**fenland** *noun* EARTH SCI a large area of flat marshy land

**FEP** *abbreviation* COMPUT front-end processor

**feral** *adjective* ZOOL referring to an animal which was formerly domesticated and has since reverted to living wild ○ *The native population of rabbits was exterminated by feral cats.*

**fermentation** *noun* CHEM the process by which organic compounds such as carbohydrates are broken down by enzymes from microorganisms such as yeasts to produce energy

**fermi** *noun* PHYS a unit of length used to measure nuclear distances, equal to $10^{-15}$ m

**fermium** *noun* CHEM ELEM an artificially produced radioactive element in the actinide group of the periodic table, produced by neutron-bombardment of plutonium (NOTE: The chemical symbol is **Fm**; the atomic number is **100** and the atomic weight is **257**.)

**fern** *noun* BOT a type of green plant which propagates itself by spores from its leaves, and not seeds, and therefore has no flowers

**ferric oxide** *noun* CHEM a red insoluble oxide of iron that can be magnetised to store data or signals and is used as tape or disk coating. Formula: $Fe_2O_3$.

**ferrite** *noun* MINERALS a mineral containing iron oxide that occurs as small grains in a variety of rocks

**ferrite core** *noun* PHYS a small bead of magnetic material that can hold an electromagnetic charge used in the first type of computer

**ferro-** *prefix* CHEM referring to or containing iron

**ferrocene** *noun* CHEM an orange-red crystalline solid containing an atom of iron situated between two rings each consisting of five carbon and five hydrogen atoms. Formula: $Fe(C_5H_5)_2$.

**ferrocyanide** *noun* CHEM a salt of ferrocyanic acid containing an anion of iron and six cyanide groups, used in dyes and pigments

**ferromagnetic material** *noun* PHYS any ferrite material that can be magnetised

**ferromagnetism** *noun* PHYS the ability of some substances such as iron to become highly magnetic when exposed to a weak magnetic field within a specific temperature range

**ferrous** *adjective* CHEM referring to or containing iron

**ferruginous** *adjective* EARTH SCI referring to rock or water which contains iron

**fertile** *adjective* **1.** ZOOL referring to an animal which is able to produce young. Opposite **sterile 2.** AGRIC referring to a plant which is able to produce fruit. Opposite **sterile 3.** BIOL referring to soil which is able to produce good crops

**fertilisation** *noun* BIOL the joining of an ovum and a sperm to form a zygote and so start the development of an embryo

**fertilise** *verb* **1.** BIOL (*of a sperm*) to join with an ovum **2.** BIOL (*of a male*) to make a female pregnant **3.** AGRIC to put fertiliser on crops or soil

**fertiliser** *noun* AGRIC a chemical or natural substance spread and mixed with soil to make it richer and stimulate plant growth

COMMENT: Organic materials used as fertilisers include manure, slurry, rotted vegetable waste, bonemeal, fishmeal and seaweed. Inorganic fertilisers such as powdered lime or sulphur are also used. In commercial agriculture, artificially prepared fertilisers (manufactured compounds containing nitrogen, potassium and other chemicals) are most often used, but if excessive use of them is made, all the chemicals are not taken up by plants and the excess is leached out of the soil into rivers where it may cause algal bloom.

**fertility** *noun* BIOL the state of being fertile

**fertility rate** *noun* the number of births per year, shown, in humans, per thousand females aged between 15 and 44

**FET** *abbreviation* ELEC field-effect transistor

**fetch** *noun* COMPUT same as **fetch instruction**

**fetch cycle** *noun* COMPUT the set of events that retrieve the next instruction to be executed from memory by placing the program counter contents on the address bus

**fetch-execute cycle** noun COMPUT the set of events required to retrieve, decode and carry out an instruction stored in memory

**fetch instruction** noun COMPUT a computer instruction to select and read the next instruction or data to be processed. Also called **fetch**

**fetus, foetus** noun BIOL an unborn animal in the womb at the stage when all the structural features are visible, i.e. after eight weeks in humans (NOTE: The usual scientific spelling is 'fetus', although 'foetus' is common in non-technical British English usage.)

**Feulgen's test** noun GENETICS a test that determines the presence of DNA

**FF** abbreviation COMPUT **1.** form feed **2.** flip-flop

**FGD plant** abbreviation INDUST flue gas desulfurisation plant

**fiber** US spelling of **fibre**

**fibre** noun **1.** INDUST a natural or synthetic filament like cotton or nylon **2.** BOT a long narrow plant cell with thickened walls that forms part of a plant's supporting tissue, especially in the outer region of a stem **3.** COMPUT a very thin glass or plastic strand that can carry data in the form of light signals ▶ US spelling **fiber**

**fibre channel** noun COMPUT an ANSI standard that defines a high-speed serial interface that can transfer data at up to 1.06 Gbps and is often used as a backbone technology to link servers or high-speed devices (NOTE: The technology is normally used over optic fibre, but will work over twisted-pair cable or coax cable.)

**fibre-concrete** noun INDUST a construction material made of sand, cement and fibre, used for making things such as roofing tiles and light walls. Abbreviation **FC**

**fibre connector** noun COMPUT a type of connector that can be used to connect two fibre optic cables together

**fibre distributed data interface** noun COMPUT an ANSI standard for high-speed networks that uses fibre optic cable in a dual ring topology. Abbreviation **FDDI** (NOTE: Data is transmitted at 100 Mbps.)

**fibreglass** noun INDUST a material made of fine fibres of glass, used as a heat and sound insulator and for building bodies of cars, boats and other vehicles

**fibre optic cable** noun COMPUT a bundle of fine strands of glass or plastic protected by a surrounding material, used for transmission of light signals that carry data at very high speeds

**fibre optics** noun COMPUT the use of thin strands of glass or plastic to transmit light signals at the speed of light (NOTE: The light or laser signal is pulsed or modulated to represent data being transmitted.)

**fibre over Ethernet** noun COMPUT an enhanced version of the 802.3 Ethernet network protocol standard that allows data to be transferred at 10 Mbits/second (10 BaseFX) or 100 Mbits/second (100 BaseFX)

**fibrin** noun BIOCHEM an insoluble protein, formed from fibrinogen by the action of thrombin, that starts a blood clot by forming a network of fibres in which blood cells become trapped

**fibrinogen** noun BIOCHEM a soluble blood protein and clotting factor that forms fibrin when activated by thrombin

**fibroblast** noun ANAT a star-shaped or spindle-shaped cell that secretes collagen and elastic fibres in connective tissue

**fibroid** noun MED a benign tumour in the muscle fibres of the uterus ■ adjective like fibre

**fibrous** adjective made of a mass of fibres

**fibrous-rooted plant** noun BOT a plant with roots which are masses of tiny threads, with no major roots like taproots

**fibula** noun ANAT the thinner outer bone of two bones situated between the knee and ankle in the lower or hind leg of terrestrial vertebrates

**fidelity** noun ECOL the degree to which an organism stays in one type of environment

**field** noun **1.** ELEC an area of force and energy distribution, caused by magnetic or electric energy sources **2.** COMPUT a section containing individual data items in a record ○ *The employee record has a field for age.* **3.** PHYS the force which one object exerts on another **4.** AGRIC an area of cultivated land, usually surrounded by a fence or hedge, used for growing crops or for pasture **5.** GEOL an area of natural resources such as an oil-field or coalfield **6.** an area of interest ○ *He specialises in the field of environmental health.*

COMMENT: The main types of physical field are gravitational, magnetic and electric. Any mass has a gravitational field, which like electric and magnetic fields is subject to an inverse square law. Electric fields are found surrounding electric charges, and can involve objects being attracted (if they have a charge opposite to that of the object whose field they are in), repelled (if they bear the same charge) or not affected at all (if they are electrically neutral). An electric field can be produced by flowing electric current or by a static electric charge. Electric and magnetic fields are essentially manifestations of the same effect, and electricity is generated by movement in magnetic fields. Magnetic fields affect mainly iron, nickel and similar magnetic materials as well as ionised materials like charged particles in the Sun or the Earth's outer atmosphere.

**field botanist** *noun* BOT a botanist who examines plants in their growing habitat

**field botany** *noun* BOT the scientific study of plants in their growing habitat

**field capacity** *noun* EARTH SCI the maximum possible amount of water remaining in the soil after excess water has drained away

**field coil** *noun* ELEC ENG a coil of wire that produces the magnetisation required to operate an electrical motor or generator when carrying an electrical current

**field crop** *noun* AGRIC a crop grown over a wide area, such as most agricultural crops and some market-garden crops

**field-effect transistor** *noun* ELECTRONICS a transistor, with at least three electrodes, in which a variable electric field controls the output current. Abbreviation **FET**

**field emission display** *noun* ELEC a method of producing thin, flat displays for laptop computers in which a miniature colour CRT is located at each pixel point. Abbreviation **FED**

**field-grown** *noun* AGRIC referring to a crop which is grown in a field as opposed to in a greenhouse

**field label** *noun* COMPUT a series of characters used to identify a field or its location. Also called **field name**

**field magnet** *noun* ELEC ENG a magnet that provides the magnetic field in an electric machine, e.g. a motor or dynamo

**field name** *noun* COMPUT same as **field label**

**field observation** *noun* BIOL an examination made in the open air, looking at organisms in their natural habitat, as opposed to in a laboratory

**field programmable device** *noun* COMPUT an integrated circuit that can be permanently programmed to perform logic operations on data

**field programming** *noun* COMPUT the writing of data into a PROM

**field research** *noun* SCI a scientific study made in the open air as opposed to in a laboratory. Also called **field study**

**field station** *noun* SCI a scientific research centre located in the area being researched

**field study** *noun* SCI also called **field research**

**field test** *noun* SCI a test carried out on a substance or on an organism in the open air as opposed to in a laboratory

**field tested** *adjective* COMPUT referring to a product tested outside a company or research laboratory, in a real situation

**fieldwork** *noun* SCI a scientific study made in the open air as opposed to in a laboratory

**FIFO** *abbreviation* COMPUT first in first out

**FIFO queue** *noun* COMPUT a temporary storage method, in which the first item written to the queue is the first to be read

**fifth generation computer** *noun* COMPUT a stage of computer system design using fast VLSI circuits and powerful programming languages to allow human interaction

**figure** *noun* **1.** MATHS a number, especially in mathematical calculations □ **to have a head for figures** to be good at arithmetic □ **in round figures** not totally accurate, but correct to the nearest 10 or 100 ○ *They have a workforce of 2500 in round figures.* **2.** MATHS a form consisting of any combination of points or lines, e.g. a triangle **3.** a diagram or drawing ○ *Figure 1 shows a cross-section of an internal combustion engine.*

**filament** *noun* BOT the stalk of a stamen

**filariasis** *noun* MED a tropical disease caused by parasitic threadworms in the lymph system, transmitted by mosquito bites

**file** *noun* **1.** documents kept for reference □ **to place something on file** to keep a record of something **2.** COMPUT a section of data on a computer in the form of individual records which may contain data, characters, digits or graphics

**file activity ratio** *noun* COMPUT a ratio of the number of different records accessed within a file compared to the total number in store

**file allocation table** *noun* COMPUT a data file stored on disk containing the names of each file stored on the disk, together with its starting sector position, date and size. Abbreviation **FAT**

**file attribute** *noun* COMPUT a control bit of data stored with each file which controls a particular function or aspect of the file such as read-only, archived or system file ○ *The read-only file attribute is set, so you cannot change the contents.*

**file control block** *noun* COMPUT an area of memory used by the operating system that contains information about the files in use or those stored on a disk drive. Abbreviation **FCB**

**file conversion** *noun* COMPUT a change of format or structure of a file system, usually when using a new program or file handling routine

**file copy** *noun* a copy of a document which is filed in an office for reference

**file defragmentation** *noun* COMPUT ◊ **defragmentation**

**file deletion** *noun* COMPUT the erasing of a stored file

**file fragmentation** *noun* COMPUT a file that is stored in non-contiguous sectors on a disk

**file handle** *noun* COMPUT a number by which an open file is identified within a program ○ *The new data is written to the file identified by file handle 1.*

**file handling routine** *noun* COMPUT a short computer program that manages the reading/writing and organisation of stored files

**file header** *noun* COMPUT a section of information about the file stored at the beginning of the file ○ *The file header in the database file shows the total number of records and lists the index fields.*

**file locking** *noun* COMPUT a software mechanism that prevents data in a file being updated by two different users at the same time

**filename** *noun* COMPUT a unique identification code allocated to a program

**filename extension** *noun* COMPUT a set of three or four characters given after a filename, indicating the type or use of the file

**file queue** *noun* COMPUT a number of files temporarily stored in order before being processed ○ *Output devices such as laser printers are connected on-line with an automatic file queue.*

**file server** *noun* COMPUT a computer connected to a network that runs a network operating system software to manage user accounts, file sharing and printer sharing

**file sharing** *noun* COMPUT a file that can be used by two or more users or programs in a network often using file locking

**file transfer, access and management** *noun* COMPUT full form of **FTAM**

**file transfer protocol** *noun* COMPUT the TCP/IP standard for transferring files between computers. Abbreviation **FTP** (NOTE: It is a file sharing protocol that operates at layers 5, 6 and 7 of an OSI model network.)

**filial generation** *noun* GENETICS the offspring that result from crossing two parental lines ○ *the first filial generation*

**filing** *noun* COMPUT **1.** the act of putting documents in order **2.** a set of documents which have to be put in order

**fill** *verb* **1.** to make something full ○ *The screen was filled with flickering images.* **2.** COMPUT to draw an enclosed area in one colour or shading **3.** COMPUT to put characters into gaps in a field so that there are no spaces left

**filler** *noun* CHEM **1.** a substance used to add bulk or strength to a material **2.** a

**film** *noun* **1.** a thin layer ○ *An electrical element made of gold film is sandwiched between the layers of glass.* **2.** a thin covering or coating ○ *There is a film of oil between the piston and cylinder wall.*

**filter** *noun* **1.** a material or device through which a liquid or a gas is passed in order to separate the fluid from solid matter or to remove unwanted substances ○ *fuel filter* ○ *oil filter* **2.** an electric, electronic, acoustic, or optical device used to reject signals, vibrations, or radiation of specific frequencies while passing others ○ *The tuner is a band pass filter which confines the bandwidth passed to the receiver to that required.* **3.** COMPUT a pattern of binary digits used to select various bits from a binary word ■ *verb* **1.** to remove unwanted elements from a signal or file **2.** COMPUT to select various bits from a binary word ○ *Filter the top three bits of the video attribute word.* **3.** COMPUT to select various records from a database file ○ *We filtered the data to select those customers based in New York.* **4.** to pass a liquid or gas through a filter in order to remove unwanted substances ○ *Fuel is filtered before entering the carburettor.*

**filter basin** *noun* ENVIRON a large tank through which drinking water is passed to be filtered

**filter bed** *noun* INDUST a layer of charcoal, clinker or similar material through which liquid sewage is passed to clean it

**filter cake** *noun* ENVIRON a deposit of semisolids or solids that separates out between layers of filtering material

**filter cartridge, filter element** *noun* a removable paper or metal component in a filter housing which must be replaced periodically ○ *From time to time the filter element must be removed and cleaned or replaced.*

**filter-feeder** *noun* ZOOL a fish which eats particles of detritus floating in water

**filtrate** *noun* CHEM a liquid which has passed through a filter

**filtration** *noun* CHEM the process of passing a liquid through a filter to remove solid substances

**fin** *noun* **1.** ZOOL a thin flat projection on the body of a fish **2.** AEROSP a fixed vertical aerofoil at the rear of an aircraft

○ *The fin provides directional stability about the vertical axis.*

**final** *noun* the end part of a series or process ■ *adjective* coming at the end

**find** COMPUT *verb* to get something back which has been lost ○ *It took a lot of time to find the faulty chip.* ○ *The debugger found the error very quickly.* ■ *noun* a command to locate a piece of information

**find and replace** *noun* COMPUT a feature on a word-processor that allows a word or section of text to be located and replaced with another

**fine** *adjective* **1.** of superior quality, skill or appearance **2.** very small in size, thickness or weight **3.** METEOROL warm, sunny, with few clouds and no rain or fog

**fine chemical** *noun* INDUST a chemical that is manufactured in relatively small quantities and is generally high in cost to the user, e.g. a flavouring or vitamin

**fine powder** *noun* a powder consisting of very small particles

**fine spray** *noun* a spray consisting of very small drops of liquid

**fine structure** *noun* PHYS the splitting of lines in a spectrum into two or more closely spaced fine lines (NOTE: This effect is caused by magnetic interactions within atoms.)

**fine tune** *verb* COMPUT to adjust by small amounts the features or parameters of hardware or software to improve performance ○ *Fine-tuning improved the speed by ten per cent.*

**fine wire** *noun* very thin wire

**finger** *noun* **1.** ANAT one of the slender jointed parts at the end of the hand **2.** COMPUT a software program that will retrieve information about a user based on his or her electronic mail address

**finish** *verb* **1.** to do or make something completely ○ *The order was finished in time.* ○ *She finished all the keyboarding before lunch.* **2.** COMPUT to come to an end ○ *The contract is due to finish next month.* ■ *noun* COMPUT **1.** the end of a process or function **2.** a final appearance ○ *The product has an attractive finish.*

**finished** *adjective* having been completed

**finite** *adjective* having an end ○ *Coal supplies are finite and are forecast to run out in 2020.*

**finite-precision number** *noun* COMPUT a number represented by a fixed number of bits

**finite resources** *plural noun* ENVIRON natural resources such as coal or oil which will in the end be used up. Opposite **renewable resources**

**finite series** *noun* MATHS a sequence of numbers represented by an algebraic function that has a fixed number of terms

**fiord** EARTH SCI another spelling of **fjord**

**fir** *noun* TREES a common evergreen softwood tree

**fir cone** *noun* BOT the hard structure containing the seeds of a fir tree (NOTE: Sometimes applied to the cones of other trees such as pines.)

**fire** *noun* an area of burning ■ *verb* **1.** to shoot with a gun **2.** to launch something such as a flare or a rocket

COMMENT: In shifting cultivation, the practice of clearing vegetation by burning is widespread. One of the simplest forms involves burning off thick and dry secondary vegetation. Immediately after burning, a crop such as maize is planted and matures before the vegetation has recovered. Where fire clearance methods are used, the ash acts as a fertiliser.

**firebreak** *noun* FORESTRY an area where no trees are planted, so that a forest fire cannot pass across and spread to other parts of the forest

**-fired** *suffix* INDUST burning as a fuel ○ *coal-fired power station* ○ *gas-fired central heating*

**firedamp** *noun* CHEM same as **methane**

**fire deluge system** *noun* a system that extinguishes fire by spraying large quantities of water on it ○ *A lever actuates the fire deluge system.*

**fire extinguisher** *noun* a portable device for putting out fires

**fire hazard** *noun* **1.** the risk of something catching fire **2.** something that increases the risk of fire ○ *This pile of paper is a fire hazard.*

**fireproof** *adjective* designed to resist the effect of fire ○ *A fireproof bulkhead*

is provided to separate the cool area of the engine from the hot area.

**fire protection** *noun* the action and/or measures taken to prevent fire

**fire-retardant** *adjective* CHEM referring to a substance which slows down the rate at which a material burns

**fire triangle** *noun* CHEM the illustration of the chemistry of fire as the three sides of a triangle representing fuel, oxygen and heat ○ *If fuel, oxygen or heat is removed from the fire triangle, combustion will cease.*

**firewall** *noun* COMPUT a hardware or software security system between a server or intranet and the public Internet ○ *We have installed a firewall in our intranet to prevent hackers accessing company data via the Internet link.* (NOTE: The system allows information to pass out to the Internet but checks any incoming data before passing it on to the private server.)

**firmware** *noun* COMPUT a computer program or data that is permanently stored in a hardware memory chip such as a ROM or EPROM

**firn** *noun* METEOROL spring snow on high mountains which becomes harder during the summer

**first aid** *noun* MED temporary help given rapidly to someone who is injured or ill until full-scale medical treatment can be given

**first fit** *noun* COMPUT a routine or algorithm that selects the first, largest section of free memory in which to store a virtual page

**first generation** *noun* COMPUT the earliest type of computer technology. ♦ **computer generation**

**first in first out** *noun* COMPUT a temporary queue where the first item stored is the first read. Abbreviation **FIFO**

**first law of thermodynamics** PHYS ◊ **thermodynamics**

**fish** *noun* ZOOL a cold-blooded aquatic vertebrate (NOTE: Some species are eaten for food. Fish are high in protein, phosphorus, iodine and vitamins A and D. White fish have very little oil.) ■ *verb* BIOL to try to catch fish for food

**fish farm** *noun* AGRIC a place where edible fish are bred or reared in special pools for sale as food

**fishing zone** *noun* FISHERY an area of sea that can be fished

**fish kill** *noun* ENVIRON an instance of a lot of fish being killed ○ *Aluminium is a critical factor in fish kills.*

**fish ladder** *noun* ENVIRON a series of pools, each one higher than the other, specially built to allow fish such as salmon to swim up or down a river on migration

**fishmeal** *noun* AGRIC dried fish reduced to a powder and used as an animal feed or as a fertiliser

**fish pass, fish way** *noun* ENVIRON a channel near a dam, built to allow fish to bypass the dam

**fishway** same as **fish pass**

**fissile** *adjective* **1.** EARTH SCI referring to rock which can split or can be split **2.** CHEM referring to an isotope which can split on impact with a neutron

**fission** *noun* **1.** PHYS ◊ **atomic fission 2.** BIOL the process of splitting ■ *verb* CHEM, BIOL (*in nuclear fission*) to split an atomic nucleus ○ *When the plutonium is fissioned, fast neutrons are produced.*

**fissionable** *adjective* PHYS same as **fissile**

**fissiparous** *adjective* BIOL referring to an organism that reproduces by dividing into two equal parts, each of which grows into a complete organism

**fissure** *noun* a crack or groove

**fit** *adjective* **1.** HEALTH in good physical condition ○ *Keep fit with diet and exercise.* **2.** suitable for its purpose ○ *This food is fit to eat.* **3.** BIOL well adapted or evolutionarily successful ○ *Only the fit individuals will survive here.* ■ *noun* ENG the exactness with which surfaces are adjusted to each other in a machine ○ *There should be a loose fit between the cylinder and the piston, the difference being taken up by the piston rings.* ■ *verb* **1.** to be the correct size and shape for someone or something ○ *Oxygen masks should fit the wearer properly.* **2.** to attach ○ *Wheel fairings, called spats, are fitted to some light aircraft to reduce drag.* **3.** MATHS to plot or calculate a curve that most closely approximates a number of points or data (NOTE: **fitting – fitted**)

**fitment** *noun* **1.** the act of attaching or fixing something ○ *Attachment points are supplied for the fitment of heavy equipment.* **2.** something attached or fixed

**fitness** *noun* BIOL a measure of the evolutionary success of genes, traits, organisms or populations

**fix** *verb* **1.** to make something permanent ○ *The dye is fixed to stop it fading.* **2.** to mend something ○ *The technicians are trying to fix the switchboard.* **3.** to attach something permanently ○ *The barnacles fix their shells to the rock.*

**fixation** *noun* the act of fixing something

**fixed disk storage** *noun* COMPUT a hard disk or magnetic disk that cannot be removed from the disk drive

**fixed-field file** *noun* COMPUT a data file in which each field consists of a pre-defined and fixed number of characters. Compare **delimited-field file**

**fixed-frequency monitor** *noun* COMPUT a monitor that can only accept one frequency and type of video signal

**fixed-length field** *noun* COMPUT a field whose size cannot be changed

**fixed-length record** *noun* COMPUT a record whose size cannot be changed

**fixed-length word** *noun* COMPUT a preset number of bits that make up a computer word

**fixed oil** *noun* CHEM oil that is liquid at 20° C

**fixed point** *noun* PHYS a temperature that is always the same under specific conditions (NOTE: A fixed point such as the boiling or freezing point of a substance can be used for calibrating measuring instruments.)

**fixed-point arithmetic** *noun* COMPUT arithmetic rules and methods using fixed-point numbers

**fixed-point notation** *noun* COMPUT a number representation that retains the position of the digits and decimal points in the computer, so limiting the maximum manageable numbers. Compare **floating point notation**

**fixed-point number** *noun* COMPUT a number represented by using fixed-point notation ○ *Storage of fixed-point numbers has two bytes allocated for the whole number and one byte for the fraction part.*

**fixed routing** *noun* COMPUT communications direction routing that does not consider traffic or efficient paths

**fixed wing aircraft** *noun* AVIAT an aeroplane with rigidly attached wings

**fjord, fiord** *noun* EARTH SCI a long inlet of the sea among mountains in temperate or arctic regions

**flaccid** *noun* BIOL soft or limp ○ *Without water, plant stems become flaccid and droop.* ■ *adjective* BOT referring to plant tissue that has become limp through loss of water. Opposite **turgid**

**flag** COMPUT *noun* **1.** a way of showing the end of a field or of labelling something special in a database ○ *If the result is zero, the zero flag is set.* **2.** a method of reporting the status of a register after a mathematical or logical operation ■ *verb* to attract the attention of a program while it is running to provide a result or to report an action

**flag bit** *noun* COMPUT a single bit of a word used as a flag for some operations

**flagellum** *noun* BIOL a long thin tapering outgrowth of some cells that waves or rotates to propel the cell (NOTE: Flagella are found in some bacteria and protozoa, and in sperm cells.)

**flagging** *noun* COMPUT the insertion of an indicator against an item so that it can be found later

**flake** *noun* **1.** a small piece of a solid ○ *a flake of rock* **2.** METEOROL a small piece of snow which falls from the sky

**flame** *noun* the area of burning gases seen when something is burning ○ *Flames were seen coming from number 2 engine.* ■ *verb* COMPUT to send a rude or angry message to a user

**flame arrester** *noun* ENG a device to prevent flame from an external source from entering a fuel tank

**flame out** *verb* (*of combustion in a gas turbine engine*) to cease from some cause other than the shutting off of fuel ○ *Air in the fuel line can cause an engine to flame out or stop.*

**flame test** *noun* CHEM a test to see which metal is present in a substance by placing a small amount in a flame and noting the colours produced

**flammability** *noun* CHEM the ability of a material to catch fire

**flammable** *adjective* easily set on fire and capable of burning fiercely and rapidly ○ *Aviation gasoline is a flammable liquid.* (NOTE: **Flammable** and **inflammable** mean the same thing. To avoid confusion, it is recommended to use **flammable**.)

**flange** *noun* ENG the outside edge or rim of a part such as a beam or wheel ○ *The web connects the upper and lower flanges of a beam.*

**flare** *noun* **1.** INDUST a device that burns surplus gases to prevent them from being released into the environment ○ *Flares are usually found on top of stacks.* **2.** a firework that burns with a bright light and can be fired into the air to summon help

**flash** *noun* a sudden or periodic burst of light ○ *Lightning is accompanied by a brilliant flash.* ■ *verb* **1.** to give off light in regular bursts **2.** to switch a light on and off **3.** to appear or to happen suddenly ○ *The image flashed onto the screen.* **4.** COMPUT to increase and lower the brightness of a cursor to provide an indicator

**flashing character** *noun* COMPUT a character intensity that is switched on and off as an indicator

**flash memory** *noun* COMPUT a non-volatile memory that operates with blocks of data rather than single bytes

**flash point** *noun* PHYS the temperature at which fuel vapour or oil vapour will burst into flame

**flat** *adjective* **1.** having a horizontal surface without a slope, tilt or curvature **2.** (*of a tyre*) having no air inside ○ *The flat tyre had to be changed because it had a puncture.* **3.** ELEC (*of a battery*) electrically discharged or with no electrical charge left in it ○ *The engine wouldn't start because the battery was flat.*

**flatbed** *noun* COMPUT a printing or scanning machine that holds the paper or image on a flat surface while processing ○ *Paper cannot be rolled through flatbed scanners.*

**flat file** *noun* COMPUT a two-dimensional file of data items

**flatfish** *noun* ZOOL a type of fish with a flattened back that lives on the bed of the sea or of a lake and has both eyes on the top of its body (NOTE: The body of a flatfish is flattened in such a way that the fish is lying on its side. As the young fish grows, the eye underneath moves round its head to join the one on top.)

**flat pack** *noun* ELEC an integrated circuit package whose leads extend horizontally, allowing the device to be mounted directly onto a circuit board without the need for holes

**flat panel** a display monitor that is manufactured using a thin, flat liquid crystal display device

**flat screen** *noun* COMPUT a display monitor that has been manufactured with a flat, square-edged front to the monitor

**flatten, flatten out** *verb* to become flat or make something flat ○ *As altitude increases, the countryside appears to flatten out.*

**flatworm** *noun* ZOOL any worm with a flat body, a single gut opening, and no circulatory system. Phylum: Platyhelminthes. (NOTE: Flatworms include both free-living species and parasites such as flukes and tapeworms.)

**flavonoid** *noun* BIOCHEM a natural compound derived from phenol and belonging to a group that includes many plant pigments

**flavoprotein** *noun* BIOCHEM an enzyme belonging to a group that includes some vital components of cell respiration

**flavouring agent** *noun* FOOD INDUST a substance added to give flavour

**flaw** *noun* **1.** a fault or error **2.** INDUST an imperfection in a material, often hidden, that may be an indication of future structural failure

**flaw detection** *noun* INDUST the process or system by which small weaknesses in metal structures are found

**flea** *noun* ZOOL a small jumping insect which lives as a parasite on animals, sucking their blood and spreading diseases such as bubonic plague. Order: Siphonaptera.

**fleet** *noun* ENG a number of vehicles such as ships, aircraft or buses

**flew** *verb* ◊ **fly**

**flex** *noun* ELEC a wire or cable used to connect an appliance to the mains electricity supply (NOTE: no plural: for one item, say **a piece of flex**)

**flexibility** *noun* **1.** the amount or extent to which something can be bent or flexed ○ *Wing structures must have flexibility in order to absorb sudden changes in loading.* **2.** the extent to which a system or device can change or respond to a variety of conditions or situations ▶ opposite **rigidity**

**flexible** *adjective* **1.** not rigid or stiff **2.** capable of responding to a variety of conditions or situations ○ *AC electrical energy is more flexible and more efficient than DC.* **3.** COMPUT able to be altered or changed

**flexible array** *noun* COMPUT an array whose size and limits can be altered

**flexible pipe** *noun* a pipe made of soft material such as rubber or plastic

**flicker** COMPUT *noun* a computer graphic image whose brightness alternates owing to a low image refresh rate or signal corruption ■ *verb* to move very slightly ○ *The image flickers when the printer is switched on.*

**flicker-free** *noun* COMPUT (*of a screen display*) not flickering

**flight** *noun* **1.** the motion of an object or organism in or through the Earth's atmosphere or through space **2.** the distance covered by a body, e.g. the distance covered by an aircraft through the atmosphere

**flightless bird** *noun* ZOOL a bird such as an ostrich or a penguin which has small wings and cannot fly

**flight simulator** *noun* AEROSP, COMPUT a computer program that allows a user to pilot a virtual plane (NOTE: It shows a realistic control panel and moving scenes and is used either as a training programme or as a computer game.)

**flint** *noun* GEOL a very hard smooth form of quartz that produces a spark when struck with steel and breaks to form a sharp edge (NOTE: Prehistoric humans used flint to make tools.)

**flip-flop** *noun* **1.** ELEC ENG, MECH ENG an electronic circuit or mechanical device that can be switched between two stable states **2.** ELECTRONICS an electronic circuit or chip whose output can be one of two states, which is determined by one or two inputs and can be used to store one bit of digital data. Abbreviation **FF**

**float** *noun* **1.** a floating ball attached to a lever to regulate the level of a liquid in a container such as a tank **2.** COMPUT the addition of the origin address to all indexed or relative addresses to check the amount of memory a program will require ■ *verb* to remain on the surface of a fluid without sinking ○ *Because of the air-tight nature of the fuselage, most large aircraft will float for some time before sinking.*

**float chamber** *noun* AUTOMOT a part of a carburettor which houses the float

**float charging** *noun* ELEC a way of charging a battery by varying the charging current

**float factor** *noun* COMPUT the location in memory at which the first instruction of a program is stored

**floating** *adjective* 1. COMPUT not fixed 2. COMPUT, PRINTING (*of a character*) separate from the character it should be attached to

**floating address** *noun* COMPUT a location specified in relation to a reference address

**floating point arithmetic** *noun* MATHS arithmetic operations on floating point numbers (NOTE: The fixed number 56.47 in floating point arithmetic would be 0.5647 and a power of 2.)

**floating point notation** *noun* MATHS a numerical notation in which a fractional number is represented with a point after the first digit and a power, so that any number can be stored in a standard form. Compare **fixed-point notation**

**floating point number** *noun* MATHS a number represented by using floating point notation

**floating point operation** *noun* MATHS a mathematical operation carried out on a floating point number. Abbreviation **FLOP**

**floating point processor** *noun* COMPUT same as **floating point unit**

**floating point routines** *noun* COMPUT a set of routines that allow floating point numbers to be handled and processed

**floating point unit** *noun* COMPUT a specialised computer that can process floating point numbers very rapidly ○ *The floating point unit speeds up the processing of the graphics software.* Abbreviation **FPU**. Also called **floating point processor**

**floating symbolic address** *noun* COMPUT a symbol or label that identifies a particular instruction or word, regardless of its location

**floating window** *noun* COMPUT a window that can be moved anywhere on screen

**float-operated switch** *noun* ENG a shut-off valve operated by a float

**float relocation** *noun* COMPUT the conversion of a floating address to an absolute address

**flocculant** *noun* INDUST a substance added to water as it is treated to encourage impurities to settle

**flocculation** *noun* 1. INDUST the gathering together in lumps of particles 2. EARTH SCI the grouping of small particles of soil together to form larger ones ○ *The flocculation of particles is very important in making clay soils easy to work.*

**flocculus** *noun* ASTRON a mass of gas seen as either a dark or a bright spot on the surface of the Sun, often near to a sunspot

**flock** *noun* ZOOL a large group of birds or herbivorous animals ○ *a flock of geese* ○ *a flock of sheep* (NOTE: The word **flock** is used for sheep, goats and domesticated birds such as chickens or geese. The word used for cattle is **herd**.)

**flood** METEOROL *noun* a large amount of water covering land that is normally dry, caused by phenomena such as melting snow, heavy rain, high tides or storms ■ *verb* to cover dry land with a large amount of water ○ *The river bursts its banks and floods the whole valley twice a year in the rainy season.*

**flood alleviation, flood control** *noun* ENVIRON the avoidance of the possibility of flooding by controlling the flow of water in rivers

**flood damage** *noun* ENVIRON damage caused by floodwater

**flooded cell battery** *noun* ELEC a form of rechargeable battery where the plates are completely immersed in a liquid electrolyte (NOTE: Flooded cell batteries are commonly used as a power supply for independent and remote areas.)

**floodgate** *noun* ENG a gate in a weir or dyke, designed to regulate water flow

**flooding** *noun* METEOROL the action of covering land with a large amount of water ○ *Severe flooding has been reported after the heavy rain overnight.*

**flood plain** *noun* EARTH SCI a wide flat part of the bottom of a valley which is usually covered with water when the river floods

**flood tide** *noun* OCEANOG a tide that is rising. Opposite **ebb tide**

**flood warning** *noun* ENVIRON an alert that there is likely to be a flood

**floodwater** *noun* METEOROL water that floods land ○ *After the floodwater receded the centre of the town was left buried in mud.*

**floodwater level** *noun* METEOROL the highest point that the water reaches in a flood

**floor** *noun* EARTH SCI the ground at the bottom of something ○ *fish that live on the floor of the ocean* ○ *The forest floor is covered with decaying vegetation.*

**FLOP** *abbreviation* MATHS floating point operation

**floppy disk** *noun* COMPUT a small disk for storing information which can be removed from a computer

**floppy disk controller** *noun* COMPUT a combination of hardware and software devices that control and manage the operations of a disk drive from a computer. Abbreviation **fdc**

**floppy disk drive** *noun* COMPUT a disk drive for floppy disks. Abbreviation **FDD**

**FLOPs per second** *noun* COMPUT the number of floating point operations that a computer can execute every second

**flora** *noun* BOT **1.** the wild plants that grow naturally in a specific area **2.** a book or list describing the plants of a specific area ▶ compare **fauna**

**floral** *adjective* BOT referring to plants or flowers

**floret** *noun* BOT a little flower that forms parts of a larger flower head

**flotation** *noun* CHEM a separation process in which a component of a mixture may be recovered according to its ability to float on a given liquid, often applied to minerals in an ore

**flourish** *verb* BIOL to live well and spread ○ *The colony of rabbits flourished in the absence of any predators.*

**flow** *verb* **1.** to move or run smoothly with continuity ○ *Air flows over the wing surfaces and lift is produced.* **2.** to circulate ○ *Liquid coolant flows around*

*the engine.* ■ *noun* **1.** continuous movement of a fluid in a particular direction ○ *The flow of fuel from the fuel tanks to the engines.* **2.** COMPUT a regular movement ○ *automatic text flow across pages* **3.** the amount of a substance that is moving ○ *The meter measures the flow of water through the pipe.*

**flowchart** *noun* COMPUT a chart that shows the arrangement of the steps in a process or program. Also called **flow diagram**

**flow control** *noun* COMPUT the management of the flow of data into queues and buffers, to prevent heavy traffic

**flow diagram** *noun* same as **flowchart**

**flower** *noun* BOT the reproductive part of a seed-bearing plant (NOTE: Flowers are often brightly coloured to attract pollinating insects and usually consist of protective sepals and bright petals surrounding the stamens and stigma. Many flowers are cultivated for their colour and perfume.)

**flowering plant** *noun* PLANTS a plant that produces flowers

COMMENT: Flowering plants include trees and grasses as well as shrubs, herbs and bulbs. They all reproduce by seeds, unlike ferns, mosses and other so-called lower plants, which have no flowers and reproduce by spores.

**flowline** *noun* COMPUT a line connecting symbols to show the direction of flow within a flowchart

**flowmeter** *noun* MEASURE a meter attached to a pipe to measure the speed at which a liquid or gas moves through the pipe

**fluctuate** *verb* to vary or change irregularly ○ *The magnetic field will fluctuate at the supply frequency.*

**fluctuation** *noun* an irregular variation or change ○ *Small fluctuations in the Earth's average temperature can have important climatic results.*

**flue** *noun* INDUST a tube through which gas or smoke is released from a furnace or stove ○ *Flue gases are passed directly into the atmosphere.*

**flue gas desulfurisation plant** *noun* INDUST a device that traps sulfur in emissions from coal-burning furnaces and prevents it reaching the atmosphere. Abbreviation **FGD plant**

**flue gas scrubber** *noun* INDUST a device for cleaning flue gas of particles of pollutant

**fluid** *noun* PHYS a substance whose molecules move freely past one another and that takes the shape of its container (NOTE: Both liquids and gases are fluids.)

**fluidise** *verb* INDUST to make a solid move in the manner of a fluid (NOTE: One way to do this is by pulverising it into a fine powder and passing a gas through to induce flow.)

**fluidised-bed combustion** *noun* INDUST a method of burning fluidised low-grade fuel while keeping the emission of pollutant gases to a minimum. Abbreviation **FBC**

**fluke** *noun* ZOOL a parasitic flatworm (NOTE: Flukes may settle inside the liver (liver fluke), in the bloodstream (*Schistosoma*) or in other parts of the body.)

**fluorescein** *noun* CHEM an orange-red crystalline compound that fluoresces bright green in blue light (NOTE: It is used in solution to show up damage to the surface of the cornea.)

**fluorescence** *noun* PHYS **1.** the sending out of light from a substance which is receiving radiation **2.** radiation emitted by a substance at one wavelength following illumination at another wavelength (NOTE: When the original illumination is removed, no more radiation is emitted.)

**fluorescent** *adjective* PHYS referring to the emission of visible light ○ *The fluorescent penetrant process of flaw detection uses a penetrant containing a dye that fluoresces in ultraviolet light.*

**fluorescent light** *noun* INDUST a long thin tube of glass containing mercury vapour and phosphor powder that produces white light when connected to an electricity supply

**fluoridate** *verb* HEALTH to add sodium fluoride to drinking water to help prevent tooth decay □ **water fluoridated to 1 ppm** water which has had one part per million of fluoride added to it

**fluoridation** *noun* HEALTH the addition of sodium fluoride to drinking water to help prevent tooth decay

**fluoride** *noun* CHEM a chemical compound of fluorine, usually with sodium, potassium or tin

COMMENT: Fluorides such as hydrogen fluoride are emitted as pollutants from certain industrial processes and can affect plants, especially citrus fruit, by reducing chlorophyll. They also affect cattle by reducing milk yields. On the other hand, sodium fluoride will reduce decay in teeth and is often added to drinking water or to toothpaste. In some areas, the water contains fluoride naturally and here fluoridation is not carried out. Some people object to fluoridation, although tests have proved that instances of dental decay are fewer in areas where fluoride is present in drinking water.

**fluorinate** *verb* CHEM to treat or combine a substance with fluorine

**fluorine** *noun* CHEM ELEM a yellowish gas (NOTE: The chemical symbol is **F**; the atomic number is **9** and the atomic weight is **19.00**.)

**fluorocarbon** *noun* CHEM an inert compound of fluorine and carbon, with high temperature stability. ◆ **chlorofluorocarbon**

**fluorosis** *noun* MED a condition caused by excessive fluoride in drinking water or food (NOTE: It causes discoloration of teeth and affects the milk yields of cattle.)

**flush** *verb* **1.** ENG to clear a tube such as a sewer by sending water through it **2.** COMPUT to clear or erase all the contents of a queue, buffer, file or section of memory ■ *adjective* level or in line with something

**flutter** *noun* ACOUSTICS a repeated change in tape speed owing to mechanical or circuit problems, causing signal distortion

**fluvial, fluviatile** *adjective* EARTH SCI referring to rivers

**fluvial deposit** *noun* GEOL sediment deposited by a river

**fluviatile** *adjective* EARTH SCI same as **fluvial**

**flux** *noun* **1.** PHYS the rate at which heat, energy or radiation flows **2.** CHEM a substance applied to the surface of metals when soldering them together **3.** CHEM a substance used in ore smelting to aid the removal of impurities

**flux density** *noun* PHYS flux per unit area

**fly** *noun* ZOOL a small insect with two wings. Order: Diptera. ■ *verb* BIOL,

AEROSP to move through the air (NOTE: **fly – flew – flown**)

**fly ash** *noun* INDUST a fine ash that is carried in smoke and fumes from burning processes ○ *The cloud contained particles of fly ash.* (NOTE: It can be collected and used to make bricks.)

**flyback** *noun* COMPUT an electron picture beam return from the end of a scan to the beginning of the next. Also called **line flyback**

**fly-by-wire** *noun* AEROSP technology that interprets movements of a pilot's controls and, with the aid of computerised electronics, moves the control surfaces accordingly ○ *Using fly-by-wire technology, the stalling angle cannot be exceeded regardless of stick input.*

**flying head** *noun* COMPUT a hard disk read/write head that is wing-shaped to fly just above the surface of the spinning disk

**FM** *noun* PHYS a method of changing the frequency of one signal according to that of another signal. Full form **frequency modulation** (NOTE: It is often used as a method of carrying data over fibre-optic or telephone cables. Many modem standards use FM to transmit data.)

**f-number** *noun* PHOTOGRAPHY the ratio of the focal length of a camera lens to its effective diameter

**foam** *noun* **1.** a mass of bubbles of air or gas in a liquid film ○ *foam fire extinguishers* **2.** INDUST a light, porous, semi-rigid or spongy material used for thermal insulation or shock absorption ○ *Polyurethane foam is used in packaging.*

**foam plastic** *noun* plastic with bubbles blown into it to make a light material used for packing. Also called **plastic foam**

**focal length** *noun* OPTICS **1.** the distance at which a converging mirror or lens will bring parallel light to a point **2.** the distance from which a parallel beam will appear to diverge after passing through a diverging lens or mirror (NOTE: For a simple mirror with a surface which is part of a sphere, the focal length is half of the radius of curvature. Because astronomical objects are in effect infinitely far away, a mirror or lens will focus light from them at its own focal length, near which an eyepiece can form a visible image.)

**focal point** *noun* same as **focus**

**focus** *noun* **1.** OPTICS, PHYS a point at which rays of light or other radiation converge ○ *The focus of a lens is also called the focal point.* Also called **focal point** □ **to come into focus** to become clearer, as through the viewfinder of a camera **2.** COMPUT a particular window or field that is currently ready to accept a user's command ○ *The object that currently has the user's focus has a dotted line around it.* **3.** EARTH SCI a point in the interior of the Earth which is the centre of an earthquake. Also called **epicentre** ■ *verb* **1.** OPTICS, PHYS to make things such as light rays converge on a central point ○ *A parabolic reflector focuses the transmission into a narrow beam.* **2.** OPTICS to give an object or image a clear outline or detail by adjustment of an optical device ○ *Focus the microscope in order to make the image easier to see.* **3.** to direct something towards a particular point or purpose ○ *The crew focused all their attention on finding a solution to the problem.*

**focusing** *noun* PHYSIOL the process of changing the shape of the lens at the front of the eye to focus on objects at different distances

**fodder, fodder crop** *noun* AGRIC a crop such as grass or clover which is grown to give to animals as food

**foehn** *noun* METEOROL another spelling of **föhn**

**foetus** *noun* BIOL an unborn animal in the womb at the stage when all the structural features are visible, i.e. after eight weeks in humans. Another spelling of **fetus** (NOTE: The usual scientific spelling is 'fetus', although 'foetus' is common in non-technical British English usage.)

**fog** *noun* METEOROL a thick mist made up of millions of tiny drops of water

COMMENT: Fog is caused by a fall in the temperature of damp air, making the moisture in the air condense into droplets. This can happen when a warmer, moist air mass moves over a colder surface (advection fog), or when the air just above ground level is cooled as the land surface immediately beneath it cools at night due to radiation (radiation fog). Technically speaking, a fog occurs when visibility falls to below 1000 m. Above this, moisture in the atmosphere is called **mist**. Fog may be classified as: thick fog, with visibility down to 200 m, where road traffic is affected, and dense fog, with visibility down to 50 m, where it is not safe for any vehicles to move about.

**fogging** noun COMPUT a graphic effect that is used to simulate atmospheric fog or haze, used to make a three-dimensional scene more realistic. Also called **haze**

**foggy** adjective METEOROL referring to weather conditions when there is fog

**föhn, foehn** noun METEOROL a warm dry wind which blows down the lee side of a mountain, caused when moist air rises up the mountain on the windward side, loses its moisture as precipitation and then goes down the other side as a dry wind

**folder** noun COMPUT a group of files stored together under a single name

**folding** noun COMPUT a method of creating a hash address by splitting the key into parts and adding them together

**foliage** noun BOT leaves on plants ○ In a forest, animals are hard to see through the thick foliage on the trees.

**foliar** adjective BOT referring to leaves

**foliar feed** noun AGRIC a liquid nutrient used by gardeners to spray onto the leaves of plants which then absorb it

**foliar spray** noun AGRIC a method of applying liquid nutrient to plant leaves

**folic acid** noun BIOCHEM a vitamin in the vitamin B complex found in milk, liver, yeast and green vegetables such as spinach

COMMENT: Folic acid is essential for creating new blood cells. A lack of folic acid can cause anaemia and neural tube defects in the developing fetus. In the UK all pregnant women are given regular folic acid supplements.

**follicle** noun 1. BOT a fruit in the form of a dry case that splits along one side to release the seeds 2. ANAT the small structure in the skin from which each hair develops 3. BIOL one of many small structures in the ovaries where egg cells develop

**follicle-stimulating hormone** noun BIOCHEM a hormone that regulates the growth of egg follicles in the ovaries and the making of sperm in the testes

**font, fount** noun COMPUT, PRINTING a set of characters all of the same style. Also called **typeface**

**foobar** noun COMPUT whatever is being discussed by programmers (informal) (NOTE: You will often see this term used in books and lessons about software and systems.)

**food** noun 1. BIOL nutrient material eaten by animals for energy and growth 2. AGRIC nutrient material applied to plants as fertiliser

**food additive** noun FOOD INDUST a chemical substance added to food to improve its appearance or taste, or to prevent it from going bad

**food allergen** noun MED a substance in food that produces an allergy

**food allergy** noun MED a reaction caused by sensitivity to some foods (NOTE: Some of the commonest food allergies are to strawberries, chocolate, milk, eggs and wheat protein. Nut allergies are also common and may be severe.)

**Food and Agriculture Organization** noun AGRIC an international organisation that is an agency of the United Nations established with the purpose of encouraging higher standards of nutrition and eradicating malnutrition and hunger. Abbreviation **FAO**

**Food and Drug Administration** noun FOOD INDUST, PHARM a US government department that protects the public against unsafe foods, drugs and cosmetics. Abbreviation **FDA**

**food balance** noun ENVIRON the balance between food supply and the demand for food from a population

**food chain** noun ECOL a series of organisms that pass energy from one to another as each provides food for the next (NOTE: The first organism in the food chain is the producer and the rest are consumers.)

COMMENT: Two basic kinds of food chain exist: the grazing food chain and the detrital food chain, based on plant-eaters and detritus-eaters respectively. In practice, food chains are interconnected, making up food webs.

**food colouring** noun FOOD INDUST a substance used to colour food

**food crop** noun AGRIC a plant grown for food

**food grain** noun AGRIC a cereal crop such as wheat, barley or rye used as food for humans

**food poisoning** *noun* MED an illness caused by eating food that is contaminated with bacteria

**food processing industry** *noun* FOOD INDUST the industry involved in the treating of raw materials to produce foodstuffs

**food pyramid** *noun* ECOL a chart of a food chain showing the number of organisms at each level

**foodstuff** *noun* FOOD INDUST something that can be used as food ○ *cereals, vegetables and other foodstuffs*

**food supply** *noun* **1.** FOOD INDUST the production of food and the way in which it gets to the consumer **2.** a stock of food ○ *The ants will vigorously defend their food supply.*

**food value** *noun* BIOL the amount of energy produced by a specific amount of a type of food

**food web** *noun* ECOL a series of food chains that are linked together in an ecosystem

**foot** *noun* **1.** ANAT the bottom part of a leg which supports the body **2.** MEASURE a unit of length in the US and British Imperial Systems equal to 12 inches or 30.48 centimetres. Abbreviation **ft** (NOTE: The plural is **feet**.)

**footer, footing** *noun* COMPUT a message at the bottom of all the pages in a printed document. Compare **header**

**footnote** *noun* PRINTING a note at the bottom of a page, which refers to the text above it, usually using a superscript number as a reference

**foot-pound** *noun* MEASURE the ability to lift a one pound weight a distance of one foot

**footprint** *noun* **1.** TELECOM the area covered by a transmitting device such as a satellite or antenna **2.** COMPUT the area that a computer takes up on a desk **3.** ECOL the resources that an individual or organisation consumes

**forage** *noun* AGRIC a crop planted for animals to eat in the field ■ *verb* BIOL to look for food ○ *The woodpecker forages in the forest canopy for insects.*

**forbid** *verb* to say that something must not be done

**forbidden character, forbidden combination** *noun* COMPUT a bit combination in a computer word that is not

allowed according to the rules defined by the programmer or system designer

**force** *noun* PHYS **1.** the capacity to do work or cause physical change ○ *the force of an explosion* **2.** a vector quantity that produces an acceleration of a body in the direction of its application ■ *verb* to use power against resistance ○ *Because of distortion to the airframe, the pilot had to force the door open in order to exit the aircraft.*

COMMENT: There are four types of force in the universe. The strong force, which binds atomic nuclei together; the weak force, encountered in particle physics; the electromagnetic force; and the gravitational force. These four forces appear to account for all the interactions of matter which we know about. Strong force is expressed by a variety of particles called quarks and is some hundred times as powerful as the electromagnetic force, which governs chemical reactions and the emission of electromagnetic radiation. Electromagnetic forces are some 100 billion times as strong as the weak force, which is itself 100 trillion trillion times as strong as gravitation. This is why a minute pocket magnet can hold a lump of iron in mid-air, defying the whole of the Earth's gravitation.

**force of gravity** *noun* PHYS same as **gravity**

**forceps** *plural noun* MED a surgical instrument like a pair of scissors, made in different sizes and with differently shaped ends, used for holding and pulling

**force ratio** *noun* PHYS the ratio between the output force **load** and the input force **effort**. Also called **mechanical advantage** (NOTE: It is often described as a percentage. A machine can have a force ratio of more than one if a small effort can work a large load.)

**forcing mechanism** *noun* EARTH SCI a process that alters the relative balance between incoming solar radiation and outgoing infrared radiation from Earth

**fore** *adjective* located at or towards the front □ **the fore and aft axis of an aircraft** the longitudinal axis of an aircraft □ **to come to the fore** to take a leading part ○ *The jet engine came to the fore in the late forties.* Opposite **aft**

**forebrain** *noun* ANAT the frontmost of the three parts of the brain in an embryo. Compare **midbrain, hindbrain**

**forecast** *noun* a description of what it is thought will happen in the future ○ *the weather forecast* ■ *verb* to describe what it is thought will happen in the future

**foreground** *noun* COMPUT **1.** the front part of an illustration **2.** a high-priority task done by a computer

**foreign** *adjective* GEOG belonging to or coming from another country

**foreign body** *noun* MED a piece of material that is not part of the surrounding body tissue and should not be there, e.g. sand in a cut, dust in the eye or a pin which has been swallowed ○ *The X-ray showed the presence of a foreign body.*

**foreign matter** *noun* something unwanted which is found in a substance or a device ○ *Turbine blades can be damaged by foreign matter such as stones entering through the engine intake on take-off.*

**foreshock** *noun* EARTH SCI a small shock that comes before a main earthquake

**foreshore** *noun* EARTH SCI an area of sand or pebbles which is only covered by the sea when there are very high tides

**forest** *noun* **1.** ECOL a large area of land on which trees and other plants grow naturally ○ *The whole river basin is covered with tropical forest.* **2.** FORESTRY same as **plantation 3.** COMPUT a number of interconnected data structure trees ■ *verb* FORESTRY to manage a forest, by cutting wood as necessary, and planting new trees

**forest conservation** *noun* FORESTRY the active maintenance of forests by controlled felling and planting

**forest dieback** *noun* ENVIRON a disease affecting pine trees in which the pine needles turn yellow. Also called **Waldsterben**

COMMENT: There are many different theories about the cause of forest dieback: sulfur dioxide, nitrogen oxides and ozone are all possible causes, as are acid rain or acidification of the soil which makes the trees weak, and prevents them from taking up nutrients from the soil.

**forester** *noun* FORESTRY a person who manages woods and plantations of trees

**forest floor** *noun* ECOL the ground at the base of the trees in a forest

**forestry** *noun* FORESTRY the management of forests, woodlands and plantations of trees

**forest tree** *noun* BOT a large tree of the type that grows in a forest

**form** *noun* **1.** a document with blanks for the insertion of details or information ○ *an application form* **2.** a kind or type ○ *The ground automatic relief valve is a form of discharge valve.* ○ *Drizzle is the lightest form of precipitation.* **3.** the shape of an object ○ *Fluids take on the form of the container in which they are found.* □ **in the form of** having the shape of ○ *arranged in the form of a triangle* **4.** the particular way in which a thing exists, acts or shows itself ○ *fuel in solid form* □ **in the form of** having the characteristic of something ○ *water in the form of ice* ■ *verb* **1.** to come into being ○ *In certain conditions, ice forms on the leading edge of the wing.* **2.** to make a shape ○ *Three points on the chart form a triangle.* **3.** to make up or constitute something ○ *The classroom and accommodation building form the main part of the college.*

**formaldehyde** *noun* CHEM a colourless gas with an unpleasant smell, used in the manufacture of resins, fertilisers, dyes and in the preservation of organic specimens. Formula: HCHO.

**formalin** *noun* CHEM a 40% solution of formaldehyde in water, used as a disinfectant and in the preservation of organic specimens

**formal logic** *noun* LOGIC the treatment of form and structure, ignoring content

**format** COMPUT *noun* **1.** a specific method of arranging text or data **2.** the precise syntax of instructions and arguments ■ *verb* to arrange text as it will appear in printed form on paper ○ *Style sheets are used to format documents.* ◇ **to format a disk** COMPUT **1.** to set up a blank disk so that it is ready for data, by writing control and track location information on it **2.** to define the areas of a disk reserved for data and control

**formation** *noun* **1.** the coming or bringing into being of something **2.** □ **to fly in formation** (*of a number of aircraft*) to fly in a group which maintains a particular pattern or arrangement in the air

**former** *adjective* **1.** having been in the past ○ *the former president of the society* **2.** referring to the first of two things mentioned earlier ○ *Of the two proposed explanations, the former is unconvincing and the latter absurd.* ■ *noun* AVIAT a light secondary structure of the airframe which gives improved shape

**form factor** *noun* COMPUT the size and shape of a device, especially a computer's motherboard or other printed circuit board

**form feed** *noun* COMPUT to advance the paper in a printer to the top of the next page or sheet (NOTE: If you are using a laser or inkjet printer this has the effect of ejecting the current piece of paper.)

**formic acid** *noun* CHEM a colourless corrosive liquid with an unpleasant smell that is naturally present in ants and in some plants. Formula: HCOOH. Also called **methanoic acid** (NOTE: It is used in tanning, electroplating, paper, textiles, insecticides and refrigerants.)

**form mode** *noun* COMPUT a display method on a data entry terminal in which a form is displayed on the screen and the operator enters relevant details

**form overlay** *noun* COMPUT a heading or other matter held in store and printed out at the same time as the text

**formula** *noun* **1.** MATHS a mathematical rule expressed in symbols ○ *The formula for calculating speed is D ÷ T = S (where D = distance, T = time and S = speed).* (NOTE: The plural is **formulas or formulae**.) **2.** CHEM a representation of the chemical composition of a compound in terms of its atoms (NOTE: plural is **formulas** or **formulae**)

**formula translator** *noun* COMPUT full form of **FORTRAN**

**for–next loop** *noun* COMPUT a loop or routine that is repeated until a condition no longer occurs (NOTE: For X = 1 to 5: print X: next X – this will print out 1 2 3 4 5.)

**FORTH** *noun* COMPUT a computer programming language mainly used in control applications

**Fortin barometer** *noun* PHYS a mercury barometer that accurately measures atmospheric pressure

**FORTRAN** *noun* COMPUT a programming language developed originally for scientific use. Full form **formula translator**

**forward** *adjective* moving in advance or in front ■ *verb* **1.** to send a letter or email on to another address ○ *I did not know the answer to the question, so I have forwarded your message to my colleague.* **2.** to improve or progress something **3.** COMPUT (*in a network*) an action by a bridge to copy a packet of data from one segment to another

**forwards** *adverb* towards a position in front ○ *The throttles are moved forwards for take-off.* (NOTE: In US English, **forward** is used as an adverb as well as an adjective.)

**fossil** *noun* BIOL the remains of an ancient animal or plant found preserved in rock

**fossil fuel** *noun* INDUST a fuel such as coal, oil or gas, formed from the remains of plants in rock

**fossil fuel combustion** *noun* INDUST the burning of coal, oil or natural gas

**fossil-fuelled power station** *noun* INDUST a power station that burns fossil fuel to generate electricity

**fossil-fuel power** *noun* INDUST power, especially electricity, generated from fossil fuels

**fossilised** *adjective* BIOL referring to an animal or plant that has become a fossil

**fossil water** *noun* ENVIRON water that has accumulated in underground strata over millions of years and is therefore not a renewable resource

**Foucault pendulum** *noun* PHYS a heavy pendulum suspended by a long thin wire that can swing in any direction (NOTE: The plane of motion of the pendulum appears to change as the Earth rotates.)

**foul air** *noun* INDUST the air that has been circulated in a building or mine without being changed

**fouling** *noun* AUTOMOT the contamination of spark plugs with oil or petrol so that they do not fire correctly ○ *The engine should be run at a positive idling speed to prevent spark plug fouling.*

**foul water** *noun* ENVIRON water containing waste or sewage

**founder effect** *noun* BIOL the existence of low levels of genetic variation due to a new population being established by only a few original individuals

**fount** *noun* COMPUT, PRINTING another spelling of **font**

**4:3** *noun* COMPUT the aspect ratio of a conventional TV or computer display

**four-address instruction** *noun* COMPUT a program instruction that contains four addresses within its address field

**fourcc** *noun* COMPUT a method of identifying the type of data within a RIFF file. Full form **four-character code**

**four-fold** *adjective, adverb* MATHS four times

**4GL** *abbreviation* COMPUT fourth generation language

**Fourier analysis** *noun* MATHS the analysis of a periodic function by using the terms of a Fourier series as an approximation

**Fourier series** *noun* MATHS an infinite series of terms consisting of constants multiplied by sines or cosines (NOTE: It is used in the analysis of periodic functions.)

**four-plus-one address** *noun* COMPUT an instruction that contains the locations of four registers and the location of the next instruction

**four-stroke combustion engine** *noun* AUTOMOT an engine that operates in accordance with the four-stroke cycle

**four-stroke cycle** *noun* AUTOMOT the cycle of induction, compression, power and exhaust phases in the operation of a four-stroke combustion engine

**fourth generation computer** *noun* COMPUT a computer that uses large scale integration circuits, developed around 1970 and still in current use. ♦ **computer generation**

**fourth generation language** *noun* COMPUT a computer language that is user-friendly and has been designed with the non-expert in mind. Abbreviation **4GL**

**fovea, fovea centralis** *noun* a shallow pit

**fovea centralis** *noun* ANAT an area of the eye that is specialised for the recognition of colour

**fowl** *noun* AGRIC a bird, especially a hen, raised on a farm for food

**fowl pest** *noun* VET a viral disease of chickens

**fps** *plural noun* COMPUT the number of individual frames of a video sequence that can be displayed each second to give the impression of movement. Full form **frames per second**

COMMENT: To give the impression of smooth, continuous movement, a computer needs to display at least 25 separate frames each second. If the frames are large the computer has to update the hundreds of thousands of pixels that make up each image 25 times per second. To do this needs a fast graphics adapter or special video display hardware.

**FPU** *abbreviation* COMPUT floating point unit

**FQDN** *noun* COMPUT a full domain name that can be used to identify a server. Full form **fully qualified domain name**

**Fr** *symbol* CHEM ELEM francium

**fractal** *noun* MATHS a geometric shape that repeats itself within itself and always appears the same, however much the image is magnified

**fractal compression** *noun* COMPUT a technique used to compress images by reducing an image to a fractal that can be represented by a mathematical equation

**fraction** *noun* **1.** MATHS a part of a whole unit, expressed as one figure above another, e.g. 1/4 or 1/2 **2.** MATHS the mantissa of a floating point number **3.** CHEM a component of a mixture separated out by a fractional process ○ *The fraction of petroleum which is a gas is natural gas.*

**fractional** *adjective* MATHS referring to fractions ○ *The root is the fractional power of a number.*

**fractional distillation** *noun* CHEM a distillation process in which different fractions of a mixture of liquids are collected at different points during the process

**fractional part** *noun* MATHS the mantissa of a floating point number

**fractional process** *noun* CHEM a process that separates out the components of a mixture

**fractional service** *noun* COMPUT the allocation of parts of a bandwidth to different signals or customers ○ *The com-*

*mercial carrier will sell you fractional services that provide 64 Kbps data transmission.*

**fractionate** *verb* CHEM to separate a mixture into its constituents by a method such as crystallisation or distillation

**fracture** *noun* **1.** MED a break in a bone ○ *a multiple fracture of the skull* **2.** EARTH SCI the breaking of rock

**fragile** *adjective* easily broken or destroyed ○ *The desert is a fragile environment.*

**fragment** *noun* **1.** a small piece of something ○ *a fragment of rock* **2.** COMPUT a piece of information that has had to be split up into several smaller units of information before being sent over the Internet **3.** GENETICS a piece of DNA, especially one cut by an enzyme ○ *a restriction fragment* ■ *verb* to break into pieces ○ *The windscreen fragmented on impact.*

**fragmentation** *noun* COMPUT memory allocation that results in related files being scattered all over a hard disk instead of being stored next to one another

**frame** *noun* **1.** a structure that gives shape or support ○ *Early aircraft fuselages were made of a frame covered by a fabric.* **2.** an open structure for holding or making a border ○ *a door or window frame* **3.** COMPUT a space on magnetic tape for one character code **4.** COMPUT a packet of transmitted data including control and route information **5.** COMPUT a single image within a sequence of different images that together show movement or animation **6.** COMPUT a set of commands that allow the main window of a browser to be split into separate sections, each of which can be scrolled independently

**frame buffer** *noun* COMPUT a section of memory used to store an image before it is displayed on screen

**frame grabber** *noun* COMPUT a high-speed electronic circuit that samples one complete frame of a video sequence, converts it to digital format and stores it in memory so that it can then be processed

**frame of reference** *noun* MATHS a set of geometric axes used to describe the location of a point in space

**frame rate** *noun* COMPUT the speed at which frames in a video sequence are displayed (NOTE: It is measured in

frames displayed per second. PAL is 25 fps, NTSC is 30 fps and film is 24 fps.)

**frames per second** *plural noun* COMPUT full form of **fps**

**framework** *noun* **1.** the supporting structure round which something is made or built ○ *This house has a timber framework.* **2.** COMPUT the basic structure of a database process or program ○ *The program framework was designed first.*

**francium** *noun* CHEM ELEM a naturally radioactive element (NOTE: The chemical symbol is **Fr**; the atomic number is **87** and the atomic weight is **223**.)

**Frasch process** *noun* MIN EXTRACT the process used to extract sulfur from underground (NOTE: Superheated water is pumped through a tube into the underground deposit, melting the sulfur, which is then forced to the surface with hot air.)

**fraternal twins** *plural noun* BIOL two offspring that come from two different egg cells fertilised at the same time (NOTE: Fraternal twins are not identical and not always of the same sex.)

**free** *adjective* **1.** not attached, confined or controlled **2.** COMPUT available for use or not currently being used ○ *free memory space* **3.** CHEM chemically uncombined ■ *verb* **1.** to release something or someone from constraint **2.** COMPUT to erase or back up programs or files to provide space in memory

**free electron** *noun* PHYS an electron that is not bonded to an atom or molecule (NOTE: Free electrons can move about under the influence of external electric or magnetic fields.)

**free energy** *noun* PHYS a measure of the capacity of a system to do work. Also called **Gibbs free energy**. Symbol $g$

**free fall** *noun* PHYS an ideal state in which the only force acting on an object is the Earth's gravitational attraction

**free form database** *noun* COMPUT a database that can store any type of data and does not have a fixed record structure

**free heat** *noun* ENVIRON the heat that is present in a building, coming not from heating but from other sources such as appliances, people and heat retained in walls or floors

**free-living animal** *noun* ECOL an animal that exists in its environment without being a parasite on another

**freely** *adverb* with no restrictions

**free oxygen** *noun* CHEM oxygen not combined with any other element

**free radical** *noun* CHEM an atom or group of atoms that is highly reactive due to the presence of an unpaired electron

**free-swimming** *adjective* MARINE BIOL same as **pelagic**

**free temperature rise** *noun* ENVIRON the difference between the temperature outside a building and the free heat inside it (NOTE: If the building is well insulated, it can be as much as 10 K.)

**freeware** *noun* COMPUT software that is in the public domain and can be used by anyone without having to pay

**freeze** *verb* **1.** PHYS to pass from the liquid to the solid state by loss of heat **2.** FOOD, INDUST to preserve something such as food by freezing it **3.** METEOROL (*of weather*) to be so cold that water turns to ice ○ *They say it will freeze tomorrow.* Compare **melt 4.** COMPUT same as **hang 5.** ZOOL to become or remain motionless to avoid the attention of predators ○ *These small birds freeze if a hawk passes overhead.* (NOTE: **freeze – froze – frozen**)

**freeze drying** *noun* INDUST a method of preserving food or tissue specimens by freezing rapidly and drying in a vacuum

**freeze frame** *verb* COMPUT to stop a video sequence so that only one frame is displayed

**freezer** *noun* an appliance for preserving perishable items by freezing them

**freezing fog** *noun* METEOROL fog formed from supercooled vapour droplets, which remain liquid in the air but turn to ice when they touch a surface

**freezing level** *noun* METEOROL the altitude at which the atmospheric temperature has fallen to 0° C

**freezing mixture** *noun* CHEM a mixture of a salt and water or ice that produces a significant decrease in temperature (NOTE: Such mixtures are used in laboratories to produce a temperature below the freezing point of water.)

**freezing point** *noun* PHYS the temperature at which a liquid becomes solid ○ *The freezing point of water is 0° C or 32°F under a pressure of one atmosphere.*

**F region, F layer** *noun* METEOROL the highest part of the ionosphere, capable of reflecting radio waves of up to 50 MHz back to Earth (NOTE: Two layers are distinguished within it and their relative heights differ from day to night.)

**Freon** *trademark* CHEM chlorofluorocarbon

**frequency** *noun* **1.** the number of times something happens in a given period of time **2.** PHYS the number of repetitions per unit time of a complete waveform such as an electric or sound wave (NOTE: The frequency of electromagnetic radiation is inversely proportional to the wavelength of the radiation.) **3.** ECOL the number of species in a specific area **4.** STATS the number of occurrences of something in a group or sample

**frequency allocation** *noun* the frequency or range of radio frequencies set aside for particular use ○ *The frequency allocation for VOR is 108–117.975 MHz.*

**frequency division multiplexing** *noun* the assignation of a number of different signals to different frequencies or bands to allow many signals to be sent along one channel ○ *Using FDM we can transmit 100 telephone calls along one main cable.* Abbreviation **FDM**

**frequency modulation** *noun* PHYS a radio transmission method in which the frequency of the wave carrying the signal is varied according to the characteristics of the sound being broadcast

**frequent** *adjective* happening or appearing often ○ *frequent inspection*

**frequently** *adverb* COMPUT often

**frequently asked questions** *noun* COMPUT a document that contains common questions and their answers related to a particular subject ○ *The website has a section for FAQ about the new disk drive.* Abbreviation **FAQ**

**fresh air** *noun* ENVIRON open air ○ *They came out of the mine into the fresh air.*

**fresh water** *noun* EARTH SCI water in rivers and lakes which contains almost no salt. Compare **salt water**

**freshwater** *adjective* **1.** EARTH SCI containing fresh water **2.** ZOOL living in fresh water ○ *freshwater fish such as pike*

**freshwater limit** *noun* EARTH SCI the place in the course of a river at which the salinity of the water has decreased and upstream of which the water contains almost no salt

**Fresnel lens** *noun* OPTICS a thin lens made up of concentric rings, each having a curvature corresponding to a similar ring of a plain convex lens (NOTE: A Fresnel lens in the rear window of a bus allows the driver a wide view of what is behind the vehicle.)

**friable** *adjective* EARTH SCI, AGRIC referring to soil which is light and crumbles easily into fragments

**friction** *noun* PHYS a force that resists the relative motion or tendency to such motion of two bodies in contact ○ *Energy is converted to heat through friction.*

**FROM** *abbreviation* COMPUT fusible read only memory

**front** *noun* **1.** the forward part or surface ○ *The entrance is at the front.* **2.** the area, location, or position directly before or ahead □ **in front** in a forward position relative to something else ○ *Row 23 is in front of row 24.* **3.** METEOROL the mixed area between air masses of different temperatures or densities ○ *There is a warm front advancing from the south.*

**frontal** *adjective* **1.** referring to the forward part or surface area of something ○ *the frontal area* **2.** METEOROL relating to a weather front ○ *a frontal storm*

**frontal surface** *noun* METEOROL the boundary between two air masses

**frontal system** *noun* METEOROL a series of cold or warm fronts linked together

**frontal wave** *noun* METEOROL a movement of air at the edge of a warm front

**front-end** COMPUT *adjective* located at the start or most important point of a circuit or network ■ *noun* the visible part of an application that is seen by a user and is used to view and work with information ○ *The program is very easy to use thanks to the uncomplicated front-end.*

**front-end processor** *noun* COMPUT a processor placed between an input source and the central computer whose function is to preprocess received data to relieve the workload of the main computer. Abbreviation **FEP**

**front feed** *noun* COMPUT a device that can be attached to a line printer to allow individual sheets of paper to be fed in automatically

**frost** *noun* METEOROL **1.** ice that forms on outdoor surfaces when the temperature is below the freezing point of water ○ *There was a frost last night.* **2.** a deposit of crystals of ice on surfaces

**frostbite** *noun* MED an injury caused by very severe cold which freezes tissue

**frostbitten** *adjective* MED suffering from frostbite

COMMENT: In very cold conditions, the outside tissue of the fingers, toes, ears and nose can freeze, becoming white and numb. Thawing of frostbitten tissue can be very painful and must be done very slowly.

**frost-free region** *noun* METEOROL a region where there are no frosts

**frost hollow, frost pocket** *noun* METEOROL a low-lying area where cold air collects and frosts are frequent

**frost point** *noun* METEOROL the temperature at which moisture in saturated air turns to ice

**frosty** *adjective* METEOROL at an air temperature below 0° C

**fructification** *noun* BOT the production of fruit or fruits by a plant

**fructose** *noun* BIOCHEM a fruit sugar found in honey and some fruit, which together with glucose forms sucrose. Also called **fruit sugar**

**frugivore** *noun* ZOOL an animal that mainly eats fruit ○ *Many bats and birds are frugivores.*

**fruit** BOT *noun* **1.** the ripe ovary of a plant usually containing seeds **2.** the fleshy material round the fruit which is eaten as food ○ *a diet of fresh fruit and vegetables* ■ *verb* (*of a tree*) to have fruit ○ *Some varieties of apple fruit very early.*

COMMENT: Fruit contains fructose which is a good source of vitamin C and some dietary fibre. Dried fruit has a higher sugar content but less vitamin C than fresh fruit.

**fruit fly** *noun* INSECTS a small fly that feeds on fruit. Genus: *Drosophila*. (NOTE: Fruit flies are often used in genetics experiments because they are easy to keep and have a short generation time.)

**fruiting season** *noun* BOT the time of year when a particular tree has fruit

**fruit sugar** *noun* BIOCHEM same as **fructose**

**fruit tree** *noun* BOT a tree that produces edible fruit

**fruitwood** *noun* BOT, INDUST the wood from a fruit tree such as apple or cherry, which may be used to make furniture

**ft** *abbreviation* MEASURE foot

**FTAM** *noun* COMPUT a standard method of transferring files between different computer systems. Full form **file transfer, access and management**

**FTP** *abbreviation* COMPUT file transfer protocol (NOTE: It is a file-sharing protocol that operates at layers 5, 6 and 7 of an OSI model network.)

**fucoxanthin** *noun* BIOCHEM a brown pigment found in some algae such as brown seaweeds

**fuel** INDUST *noun* a substance such as wood, coal, gas or oil that can be burnt to provide heat or power ■ *verb* to use a fuel to power something ○ *The boilers are fuelled by natural gas.*

**fuel additive** *noun* AUTOMOT a substance such as tetraethyl lead which is added to petrol to prevent knocking

**fuel/air mixture** *noun* AUTOMOT a combination of fuel and air which is ignited in a piston engine to provide power

**fuel cell** *noun* ELEC a device that converts the chemical energy of a fuel and an oxidant to electrical energy

**fuel contamination** *noun* INDUST the act or an instance of fuel being made unusable because of an unwanted substance such as water in it

**fuel efficiency** *noun* PHYS the percentage of the heat from burning a fuel which is actually converted into energy

**fuel-efficient** *adjective* INDUST using fuel efficiently

**fuel element** *noun* INDUST a piece of nuclear fuel in a reactor

**fuel gauge** *noun* AUTOMOT an instrument to indicate how much fuel is left in a fuel tank

**fuel injection** *noun* AUTOMOT the spraying of pressurised liquid fuel into the combustion chambers of an internal combustion engine to increase the engine's performance

**fuel injector** *noun* AUTOMOT an injector that sprays fuel into the combustion chamber of an engine

**fuel oil** *noun* INDUST petroleum oil used as fuel in a domestic heating boiler or industrial furnace

**fuel rod** *noun* INDUST a piece of nuclear fuel, in the form of a rod, placed in the core of a nuclear reactor

**fuel-saving** *adjective* INDUST able to use less fuel than others of the same type

**fuel tank** *noun* ENG a container for holding liquid fuel

**fuelwood** *noun* INDUST wood that is grown to be used as fuel

**full** *adjective* **1.** with as much inside as possible ○ *The disk is full, so the material will have to be stored on another disk.* **2.** complete or including everything ○ *a full list of contents*

**full adder** *noun* COMPUT a binary addition circuit that can produce the sum of two inputs and can also accept a carry input, producing a carry output if necessary

**full duplex** *noun* COMPUT data transmission down a channel in two directions simultaneously

**fuller's earth** *noun* GEOL, INDUST an absorbent clay used for treating cloth and filtering liquids

**full handshaking** *noun* COMPUT the process of transmitting signals between two communicating devices where both devices use control signals to indicate when they are ready to receive data or have received data

**full moon** *noun* ASTRON the middle point of a lunar cycle, when the whole face of the Moon is lit by the Sun

**full-motion video** *noun* COMPUT a sequence of images that gives the impression of continuous movement

**full-wave rectifier** *noun* ELECTRONICS a device for converting an alternating current into a direct current operating on both the positive and negative cycles of the alternating current (NOTE: Such rectifiers are used in the design of electronic equipment such as radios, computers and televisions.)

**fully** *adverb* completely

**fully populated** *adjective* COMPUT with all the possible options or memory fitted, or with components in all free sockets

**fumarole** *noun* EARTH SCI a small hole in the Earth's crust near a volcano from which gases, smoke or steam are released

**fumes** *plural noun* **1.** PHYS gas or vapour **2.** CHEM solid particles produced by a chemical reaction which pass into the air as smoke

**fumigant** *noun* MED, AGRIC a chemical compound that becomes a gas or smoke when heated and is used to kill insects

**fumigate** *verb* MED, AGRIC to kill microbes or insects by using a fumigant

**fumigation** *noun* **1.** MED, AGRIC the killing of germs or insects by means of a fumigant **2.** ENVIRON a high amount of air pollution near the ground, caused when the morning sun heats the air and forces polluted air down from higher levels

**function** *noun* **1.** the use or purpose of something ○ *The function of a wing is to provide lift.* **2.** MATHS a mathematical formula where a result is dependent upon several other numbers **3.** COMPUT a sequence of computer program instructions in a main program that perform a specific task **4.** COMPUT a special feature available on a computer or word-processor ○ *a spelling-checker function* ■ *verb* to operate or perform correctly ○ *The new system has not functioned properly since it was installed.*

**functional** *adjective* **1.** COMPUT referring to the way something works **2.** useful or serving a practical purpose **3.** MED having no apparent organic cause

**functional food** *noun* HEALTH a food designed to be medically beneficial, helping to protect against serious conditions such as diabetes, cancer or heart disease

**functional genomics** *noun* GENETICS the study of the relationships between the structure of genes and their biological function in organisms

**functional group** *noun* CHEM a group of atoms that reacts as a single unit and determines the properties and

structure of a class of chemicals (NOTE: For example, the hydroxyl group is the functional group in alcohols.)

**function call** *noun* COMPUT a program instruction that moves execution to a predefined function or named sequence of instructions

**function key** *noun* COMPUT one of several special keys placed along the top of a PC keyboard that have different uses according to different applications ○ *Tags can be allocated to function keys.*

COMMENT: Function keys often form a separate group of keys on the keyboard, and have specific functions attached to them. They may be labelled F1, F2 etc. Most applications use the F1 key to display help information and Alt-F4 to quit an application.

**function library** *noun* COMPUT a collection of functions that can be used by a program

**function overloading** *noun* COMPUT a programming system in which several different functions can have the same name, but are differentiated because they operate on different data types

**fundamental** *adjective* **1.** referring to or forming the foundation or base ○ *the fundamental laws of aerodynamics* **2.** forming or serving as an essential component of a system or structure ○ *Electricity is one of the fundamental types of energy that exist in nature.*

**fundamental niche** *noun* ECOL the full range of physical, chemical and biological factors each species could use if there were no competition from other species

**fundamental particle** *noun* PHYS same as **elementary particle**

**fundamental unit** *noun* MEASURE a basic unit of length, mass or time

**fungal** *adjective* BIOL referring to fungi ○ *a fungal disease* ○ *He had a fungal skin infection.*

**fungi** *noun* BIOL ◊ **fungus**

**fungicidal** *adjective* AGRIC referring to a substance which kills fungi

**fungicide** *noun* AGRIC a substance used to kill fungi

**fungoid** *adjective* BIOL shaped like a fungus ○ *a fungoid growth on the skin*

**fungus** *noun* FUNGI an organism that has thread-like cells with walls made of chitin and no green chlorophyll (NOTE: The plural is **fungi.** For other terms referring to fungi, see words beginning with **myc -**.)

COMMENT: Fungi grow in almost every environment and are vital in nutrient cycling as they can digest the cellulose in dead plants. Mushrooms are the spore-producing structures of a large group of otherwise threadlike fungi; many are edible although some are deadly poisonous. Fungi are used in brewing, cheese-making and the production of antibiotics such as penicillin. Some fungi can cause diseases of animals and plants.

**funicle** *noun* BOT the stalk that attaches an ovule to the carpel wall

**funnel cloud** *noun* METEOROL a rotating, visible extension of a cloud, with the top attached to the cloud but without the bottom tip touching the ground ○ *When a funnel cloud touches the ground it becomes a tornado.*

**fur** *noun* **1.** ZOOL a coat of hair covering an animal ○ *The rabbit has a thick coat of winter fur.* **2.** INDUST skin and hair removed from an animal, used to make clothes ○ *She wore a fur coat and fur gloves.*

**furan** *noun* CHEM a colourless flammable liquid of low boiling point with a five-membered ring structure, used as a solvent and in polymer manufacture. Formula: $C_4H_4O$.

**furanose** *noun* BIOCHEM a sugar containing a ring made up of one oxygen atom and four carbon atoms

**furnace** *noun* INDUST a container for burning fuel and ore

**furrow** *noun* AGRIC a long trench cut in the soil by a plough

**fuse** *noun* ELEC an electrical protection device consisting of a small piece of metal, which will melt when too much power passes through it □ **to blow a fuse** to melt a fuse by passing too much current through it ■ *verb* **1.** to join together to form a whole ○ *The bones of the skull fuse together to enclose the brain.* **2.** ELEC to draw too much current, causing a fuse to melt ○ *When the air-conditioning was switched on, it fused the whole system.*

**fuselage** *noun* AEROSP the central body of an aircraft, to which the wings and tail assembly are attached and which accommodates the crew, passengers and cargo ○ *The fire started in the wing but soon spread to the fuselage.*

**fusible link** *noun* COMPUT a small link in a programmable logic array that can be blown to program the device permanently

**fusible read only memory** *noun* COMPUT a type of memory that is made up of a matrix of fusible links which are selectively blown to program it. Abbreviation **FROM**

**fusion reactor** *noun* PHYS a nuclear reactor producing energy from the fusion of two atoms such as deuterium and tritium

**fuzzy logic, fuzzy theory** *noun* COMPUT a type of logic applied to computer programming which tries to replicate the reasoning methods of the human brain

**FYI** *noun* COMPUT a document file that contains general background information related to the Internet or protocols. Full form **for your information**

# G

**g** *symbol* PHYS acceleration due to Earth's gravity

**g** *symbol* **1.** Gibbs free energy **2.** gravitational constant

**G** *abbreviation* **1.** MEASURE gauss **2.** MATHS giga- **3.** MEASURE gram ■ *symbol* COMPUT $2^{30}$, equal to 1 073 741 824

**Ga** *symbol* CHEM ELEM gallium

**gadolinium** *noun* CHEM ELEM a rare silvery-white metallic element in the lanthanide group of the periodic table (NOTE: It is used in high-temperature alloys and as a neutron absorber in nuclear reactors and fuels. The chemical symbol is **Gd**; the atomic number is **64** and atomic weight is **157.93**.)

**Gaia hypothesis, Gaia theory** *noun* ECOL a theory that the biosphere is like a single organism where the living fauna and flora of Earth, its climate and geology, all function together and are interrelated, influencing the development of the whole environment

**gain** *noun* **1.** an increase ○ *a gain in altitude* ○ *There is a gain of heat by the Earth due to solar radiation.* **2.** ELEC an increase in signal power, voltage, or current ○ *The amplifier boosts the gain of the incoming signal.* **3.** a benefit or advantage ○ *An additional gain from the horizontally opposed arrangement of cylinders is a smoother running engine.* ■ *verb* **1.** to increase by a particular amount ○ *He failed the test because the aircraft gained 100 ft in the 360° level turn.* **2.** to get or obtain a result in an examination ○ *He gained a good mark in his meteorology exam.* □ **to gain access to** to be able to access a file or information in it ○ *The user cannot gain access to the confidential information in the file without a password.*

**galactic** *adjective* ASTRON referring to a galaxy

**galactic equator** *noun* ASTRON the imaginary circle formed by extending the plane that passes through the centre of the galaxy (NOTE: It is inclined at approximately 62° to the celestial equator.)

**galactic halo** *noun* ASTRON the large region of space outside the Milky Way, including the main spiral arms, older fainter stars and globular clusters, and the outer regions of the galactic magnetic field

**galactose** *noun* BIOCHEM a six-carbon sugar found mainly in lactose

**galaxy** *noun* ASTRON a massive assembly of stars, dust, gas and other components held together by gravity

COMMENT: The main types (see **Hubble Classification**) are spiral galaxies, barred spirals, elliptical, irregular and peculiar. It appears that only about 10% of the mass of galaxies is in the form of visible matter, and that they contain a much larger amount of dark matter. Our own galaxy is known as the Milky Way galaxy because the path of the Milky Way across the sky marks the main mass of the galaxy, whose centre is in the constellation Scorpius.

**gale** *noun* METEOROL a very strong wind usually blowing from a single direction (NOTE: A gale is force 8 on the Beaufort scale.)

**galena** *noun* MINERALS a shiny blue-grey crystalline mineral consisting of lead sulfide. Symbol **Pbs** (NOTE: It is a source of lead and silver.)

**gale warning** *noun* METEOROL an alert that there is going to be a gale

**Galileo Galilei (1564–1642)** ASTRON an Italian astronomer who was one of the first people to look at the sky through a telescope

COMMENT: He concluded that the Earth moves like other astronomical objects, a conclusion that led him to a showdown with the Church of Rome in which he was forced to retract. He observed Neptune without recognising it as a planet. He also applied mathematical analysis to the movement of bodies in a way which was a precursor to Newton's work on motion, and was an inventor whose devices ranged from clocks to artillery.

**gall** *noun* BOT a hard growth on a plant caused by a parasitic insect

**gall bladder** *noun* ANAT a small muscular sac on the underside of the liver in which bile secreted by the liver is stored until needed for digestion

**gallium** *noun* CHEM ELEM a rare blue-grey metal element used in high-temperature thermometers, semiconductors and alloys (NOTE: The chemical symbol is **Ga**; the atomic number is **31** and the atomic weight is **69.72**.)

**gallium arsenide** *noun* ELEC a semiconductor compound used in chip construction. Symbol **GaAs** (NOTE: It allows faster operation than silicon chips.)

**gallon** *noun* a unit of liquid volume in the Imperial System, approximately equal to 4.5 litres

**galvanic** *adjective* ELEC referring to electricity produced by chemical reaction

**galvanic cell** *noun* ELEC same as **primary cell**

**galvanisation, galvanization** *noun* INDUST the coating of iron or steel with zinc to prevent it from rusting

**galvanise, galvanize** *verb* INDUST to coat iron or steel with zinc to prevent it from rusting

**galvanised iron** *noun* INDUST iron that has been coated with zinc to prevent it from rusting (NOTE: Galvanised iron sheeting is widely used for roofs.)

**galvanometer** *noun* ELEC ENG an instrument used to detect or measure small electric currents using a coil in a magnetic field to move a pointer or light in a manner that is proportional to the strength and direction of the current

**game** *noun* AGRIC animals that are hunted and killed for sport or food or both

**game bird** *noun* AGRIC a bird that is hunted and killed for sport or food or both

**game reserve** *noun* AGRIC an area of land where wild animals are kept to be hunted and killed for sport

**gametangium** *noun* BOT a cell or organ that produces sex cells (**gametes**), especially in algae and fungi

**gamete** *noun* BIOL a sex cell

COMMENT: In animals the male and female gametes are a spermatozoon and an ovum respectively, in plants they are a pollen grain and an ovule. Gametes are produced by a special sort of cell division called meiosis and each contains only half the number of chromosomes found in ordinary body cells.

**gametocide** *noun* BIOCHEM a drug that kills gametocytes

**gametocyte** *noun* BIOL a cell that develops into a gamete

**gametogenesis** *noun* BIOL the production of gametes from gametocytes by cell division (**meiosis**)

**gametophyte** *noun* BOT the part of a plant's life cycle when sex organs and sex cells (**gametes**) are produced

**gamma** *noun* the third letter of the Greek alphabet

**gamma globulin** *noun* IMMUNOL a protein component of blood serum that contains the antibodies (NOTE: It is produced commercially from human plasma and used in vaccines against diseases such as measles and poliomyelitis.)

**gamma radiation** *noun* PHYS radiation from gamma rays

**gamma ray** *noun* PHYS a high-energy form of electromagnetic radiation

COMMENT: Gamma rays form part of the high-energy radiation which the Earth receives from the Sun. Gamma rays are also given off by radioactive substances and can penetrate very thick metal. They have no electric charge or mass and their frequency is higher than that of X-rays.

**gamogenesis** *noun* BIOL sexual reproduction

**ganged** *adjective* ELEC mechanically linked and operated by a single action

**ganged switch** *noun* ELEC a series of switches that operate on different parts of a circuit, but which are all switched by a single action ○ *A ganged switch is* *used to select which data bus a printer will respond to.*

**ganglion** *noun* ANAT **1.** a mass of nerve cell bodies and synapses, usually covered in connective tissue, found along the peripheral nerves with the exception of the basal ganglia **2.** a cyst of a tendon sheath or joint capsule, usually at the wrist, which results in a painless swelling containing fluid (NOTE: The plural is **ganglia**.)

**gap** *noun* **1.** a space between objects or points **2.** a difference between things or groups of things ○ *a gap between theory and practice* **3.** a period of time ○ *started again after a gap of five years* **4.** COMPUT a space between recorded data **5.** COMPUT a space between a read head and the magnetic medium

**gap character** *noun* COMPUT an extra character added to a group of characters for parity or another purpose, but not data or instructions

**gap loss** *noun* COMPUT a signal weakening due to incorrect alignment of the read/write head with the storage medium

**garbage** *noun* **1.** *US* ENVIRON rubbish or household waste **2.** MEDIA radio interference from adjacent channels **3.** COMPUT data or information that is no longer required because it is out of date or contains errors

**garbage in garbage out** *noun* COMPUT an expression meaning that the accuracy and quality of information that is output depends on the quality of the input. Abbreviation **GIGO**

**gas** *noun* **1.** CHEM a substance which is not a liquid or a solid, which will completely fill a container it occupies, and which becomes liquid when it is cooled ○ *Heating turned the liquid into a gas.* ○ *If a gas is cooled it will become liquid.* **2.** INDUST a substance found underground or produced from coal and used to cook or heat ○ *a gas cooker* ○ *We heat our house by gas.* **3.** *US* INDUST same as **gasoline** (NOTE: The UK term is **petrol**.) **4.** MED gas which accumulates in the stomach or alimentary canal and causes pain

**gas carrier** *noun* CHEM an inert gas used to transport the sample in gas chromatography

**gas chromatography** *noun* CHEM a scientific method for analysing a mixture of volatile substances

**gas cleaning** *noun* ENVIRON the removal of pollutants from gas, especially from emissions from factories and power stations

**gas coal** *noun* INDUST coal used for making coal gas

**gas coke** *noun* INDUST coke resulting from the processing of coal for gas

**gas constant** *noun* PHYS the constant in the equation that describes the mathematical relation between the pressure and volume of a gas and its absolute temperature (NOTE: Its value is 8.314 joules per kelvin.)

**gas-cooled reactor** *noun* INDUST a nuclear reactor in which carbon dioxide or helium is used as a coolant and is passed into water tanks to create the steam which will drive the turbines

**gas discharge, gas electroluminescent display** *noun* COMPUT a flat lightweight display screen that is made up of two flat pieces of glass covered with a grid of conductors, separated by a thin layer of gas which luminesces when a point of the grid is selected by two electrical signals. Also called **gas plasma**

**gas engine** *noun* ENG a type of internal combustion engine using a flammable gas as a fuel

**gaseous** *adjective* PHYS formed or in the form of gas ○ *a gaseous pollutant* □ **water in the gaseous state** steam

**gas exchange** *noun* ECOL the transfer of gases between an organism and its environment

**gas extraction** *noun* INDUST the process of pumping gas out of a landfill site to use as fuel

**gas-fired power station** *noun* INDUST a power station which burns gas, as opposed to a coal-fired station or nuclear power station

**gas gangrene** *noun* MED a complication of severe wounds in which the bacterium *Clostridium welchii* breeds in the wound and then spreads to healthy tissue which is rapidly decomposed with the formation of gas

**gasholder** *noun* INDUST same as **gasometer**

**gasification** *noun* INDUST the process of converting coal into gas to be used as fuel in gas-fired power stations

**gasifier** *noun* INDUST a factory which can convert coal into gas to be used as fuel

**gasket** *noun* ENG a seal or packing used between matched machine parts or around pipe joints to prevent the escape of a gas or fluid

**gas laws** *plural noun* PHYS laws describing alterations in the volume of a gas as the pressure and temperature are changed (NOTE: These laws are not perfectly obeyed in practice.)

**gasohol** *noun* INDUST a mixture of petrol and ethyl alcohol, used as a fuel in internal combustion engines

**gasoline** *noun* US INDUST a liquid made from petroleum, used as a fuel in internal combustion engines (NOTE: The UK term is **petrol**.)

**gasoline-powered** *adjective* ENG working on gasoline

**gasometer** *noun* INDUST a large tank for storing coal gas or natural gas. Also called **gasholder**

**gas plasma** *noun* same as **gas discharge**

**gas poisoning** *noun* MED poisoning by breathing in carbon monoxide or other toxic gas

**Gasserian ganglion** *noun* ANAT same as **trigeminal ganglion**

**gas supply line** *noun* INDUST a pipe which carries gas from its source to the consumer

**gastr-** *prefix* ANAT same as **gastro-**

**gastric** *adjective* ANAT referring to the stomach

**gastric acid** *noun* BIOCHEM hydrochloric acid secreted into the stomach by acid-forming cells

**gastric artery** *noun* ANAT an artery leading from the coeliac trunk to the stomach

**gastric juice** *noun* PHYSIOL a mixture of hydrochloric acid, pepsin, intrinsic factor and mucus secreted by the cells of the lining membrane of the stomach to help the digestion of food

**gastro-** *prefix* ANAT the stomach

**gastroenteritis** *noun* MED an inflammation of the membrane lining the intestines and the stomach, caused by a viral infection and resulting in diarrhoea and vomiting

**gastrointestinal tract** *noun* ANAT same as **alimentary canal**

**gastropod** *noun* ZOOL a mollusc that has a head with eyes, tongue and tentacles, a large flattened muscular foot and often a single shell. Class: Gastropoda. (NOTE: Limpets, snails and slugs are gastropods.)

**gastrula** *noun* BIOL the stage in embryonic development following the blastula when the embryo develops two layers

**gas turbine** *noun* ENG an internal combustion engine where expanding gases from combustion chambers drive a turbine (NOTE: A rotary compressor driven by the turbine sucks in the air used for combustion.)

**gasworks** *noun* INDUST a place where gas, especially coal gas, is made

**gate** *noun* 1. ENG a device for controlling the passage of water or gas through a pipe ○ *During a descent from altitude, with low power set, the turbocharger waste gate is fully closed.* 2. ENG a device to prevent a lever from being moved to an incorrect setting ○ *It is necessary to move the rpm control lever through a feathering gate to the feathering position.* 3. ELECTRONICS a logical electronic switch whose output depends on the states of the inputs and the type of logical function implemented

**gate array** *noun* ELECTRONICS a number of interconnected logic gates built into an integrated circuit to perform a complex function

**gate circuit** *noun* ELECTRONICS a series of electronic components that implement a logical function

**gated** *noun* COMPUT software that redirects network traffic, normally Internet traffic, according to a set of rules (NOTE: It can also be used to limit access to a site or to route traffic to another site. Pronounced 'gate-dee'.)

**gated quadrant** *noun* ENG a quadrant with a device preventing a lever from being moved to an incorrect setting ○ *The throttles, usually known as power levers, operate in a gated quadrant.*

**gateway** *noun* 1. an entrance that is accessible through a gate 2. a means of doing or achieving something ○ *a gateway to success* 3. COMPUT a device that links two dissimilar networks ○ *We use a gateway to link the LAN to a WAN.* 4.

COMPUT a software protocol translation device that allows users working in one network to access another **5.** COMPUT software that allows mail messages to be sent via a different route or to another network ○ *To send messages by fax instead of across the network, you'll need to install a fax gateway.*

**gather** *verb* **1.** to collect things together from different sources ○ *We gathered information from several reports and reviews.* **2.** COMPUT to receive data from various sources and sort and insert it in correct order into a database

**gather write** *verb* COMPUT to write a group of separate records as one block of data

**gauge** *noun* **1.** an instrument for measuring or testing ○ *a temperature gauge* ○ *a pressure gauge* **2.** MEASURE a unit of diameter or width ■ *verb* to calculate something approximately by using the senses ○ *In fog, it is difficult to gauge horizontal distances.* (NOTE: **gauging – gauged**)

**gauss** *noun* MEASURE, PHYS the cgs unit of magnetic flux density, equivalent to $10^{-4}$ tesla

**Gay-Lussac's law** *noun* CHEM the principle that in a reaction between gases, they combine in simple ratios of their volumes, with any gaseous product also produced in a simple ratio

**Gb** *abbreviation* COMPUT gigabyte

**GCV** *abbreviation* PHYS gross calorific value

**Ge** *symbol* CHEM ELEM germanium

**GE** *abbreviation* BIOTECH genetic engineering

**gear** *noun* MECH ENG, AUTOMOT a toothed wheel that turns with another toothed part to transmit motion or change speed or direction

**gearbox** *noun* MECH ENG, AUTOMOT a device to allow changes in the ratio of engine speed to final drive speed ○ *The auxiliary power unit is a small gas turbine engine which is connected to a gearbox.*

**Geiger counter, Geiger-Muller detector** *noun* PHYS an instrument for the detection and measurement of radiation

COMMENT: A Geiger counter is made of a tube forming a negative electrode, with a wire running through the centre which forms the positive electrode. The presence of radiation causes a discharge of electricity between the electrodes which creates an audible pulse which is used as a measure of the radiation. The greater the frequency of the pulses, the higher the level of radiation.

**gel** *noun* CHEM a substance that has coagulated to form a jelly-like solid

**gelatin** *noun* BIOCHEM a protein which is soluble in water, made from collagen

COMMENT: Gelatin is used in foodstuffs such as desserts or meat jellies and is also used to make capsules in which to put medicine.

**gelignite** *noun* CHEM an explosive consisting of nitroglycerine contained in a gel with cellulose nitrate, potassium nitrate, and wood pulp or guncotton

**gender** *noun* BIOL the sex of a person ○ *She's just had a baby but I don't know what gender it is.*

**gender changer** *noun* ELEC a device for changing a female connection to a male or vice versa (*informal*)

**gene** *noun* GENETICS a unit of DNA on a chromosome which governs the synthesis of one protein, usually an enzyme, and may combine with other genes to determine a particular characteristic

COMMENT: Genes exist in different forms, called alleles. They are either dominant, in which case the characteristic is always passed on to the offspring, or recessive, where the characteristic only appears if both parents have contributed a copy of the same allele.

**gene amplification** *noun* BIOTECH a method for the repeated duplication of a specific length of DNA to produce an amount suitable for gene analysis, usually using the technique of polymerase chain reaction (NOTE: It can be used to test for genetic defects such as those arising from a single cell.)

**gene bank** *noun* GENETICS a collection of seeds from potentially useful wild plants, which may be used in the future for breeding new varieties

**gene chip** *noun* BIOTECH a substrate containing an array of DNA used to perform genetic testing

**gene cloning** *noun* BIOTECH the process of producing identical copies of a gene by the technique of polymerase chain reaction

**gene expression** *noun* GENETICS the process by which the coded information carried in a gene is converted into a biological function

**gene flow** *noun* GENETICS a movement of genes among populations through interbreeding, dispersal and migration

**gene frequency** *noun* GENETICS the ratio of a specific variant form (**allele**) of a gene to the total number of alleles in a specific population

**gene gun** *noun* BIOTECH a device for inserting DNA directly into cells, used as a method of genetic modification

**gene mutation** *noun* GENETICS a change in a single base or base pair in the DNA sequence of a gene

**gene pool** *noun* GENETICS the total of all the genes carried by the individual organisms in a population

**gene probe** *noun* BIOTECH a fragment of DNA or RNA marked by a chemical or radioactive substance that will bind to a specific gene, used as a method of identifying or isolating that gene

**genera** *noun* BIOL plural of **genus**

**general** *adjective* **1.** ordinary or not special **2.** dealing with everything

**general anaesthesia** *noun* MED loss of feeling and loss of consciousness

**general anaesthetic** *noun* MED a substance such as nitrous oxide given to make a patient lose consciousness so that a major surgical operation can be carried out

**general circulation model** *noun* METEOROL a complex computer simulation of climate and its various components ○ *General circulation models are used by researchers and policy analysts to predict climate change.*

**general fertility rate** *noun* MED the number of live births per 1000 women of childbearing age per year

**generalist** *noun* **1.** BIOL a species which can live in many different environments **2.** a person who studies many different subjects, rather than specialising in one

**general packet radio service** *noun* TELECOM full form of **GPRS**

**general purpose** *adjective* for all-round or general use

**general purpose interface adapter** *noun* COMPUT an adapter usually used to interface a processing unit to an IEEE-488 bus. Abbreviation **GPIA**

**general purpose interface bus** *noun* COMPUT a standard for an interface bus between a computer and laboratory equipment. Abbreviation **GPIB**

**general purpose register** *noun* COMPUT full form of **GPR**

**general register** *noun* COMPUT a data register in a computer processing unit that can store items of data for many different mathematical or logical operations

**general theory of relativity** *noun* PHYS ◊ **relativity**

**generate** *verb* **1.** to bring something into being ○ *The exhibition aims to generate interest in the study of science.* **2.** PHYS, CHEM to produce something such as heat or electricity as a result of a chemical or physical process ○ *The passage of air around the wing generates lift.* ○ *Carbon monoxide is generated by car engines.* ○ *The nuclear reaction generates a huge amount of heat.* **3.** COMPUT to use software or a device to produce codes or a program automatically ○ *to generate an image from digitally recorded data* ○ *The graphics tablet generates a pair of coordinates each time the pen is moved.*

**generated address** *noun* COMPUT the location used by a program that has been produced by instructions within the program

**generating plant** *noun* INDUST a factory which produces something such as electricity or a chemical substance

**generation** *noun* **1.** the act or process of creating or making something ○ *the generation of ideas* ○ *the generation of electricity* **2.** COMPUT production of data, software or programs using a computer ○ *The computer is used in the generation of graphic images.* ○ *Code generation is automatic.* **3.** COMPUT a state or age of the technology used in the design of a system. See Comment at **computer generation 4.** COMPUT the distance between a file and the original version, used when making backups ○ *The father file is a first generation backup.* **5.** GENETICS a group of individual organisms which have usually derived from the same parents, leading back to a common ancestor

**generation loss** *noun* PHYS a degradation of signal quality with each successive recording of a video or audio signal

**generation time** *noun* BIOL the time taken for cells to divide and double to form a pair of daughter cells

**generator** *noun* **1.** ELEC, INDUST a device that generates electricity ○ *The computer centre has its own independent generator, in case of mains power failure.* **2.** COMPUT a device that generates new programs according to rules or specifications set out by the user

**generator lock** *noun* COMPUT a device that synchronises the timing signals of two video signals from different sources so that they can be successfully combined or mixed. Also called **genlock** (NOTE: It is often used to synchronise the output of a computer's display adapter with an external video source when using the computer to create overlays or titling.)

**gene replacement therapy** *noun* BIOTECH the treatment of a disease caused by a genetic defect by manipulating the faulty gene outside the body and replacing the repaired gene into the individual. Also called **gene therapy**

**generic** *adjective* **1.** relating to or suitable for a broad range of things or situations **2.** COMPUT compatible with a whole family of hardware or software devices from one manufacturer **3.** BIOL referring to a genus **4.** PHARM referring to a drug that does not have a proprietary name used by a manufacturer

COMMENT: Organisms are usually identified by using their generic and specific names, e.g. *Homo sapiens* (human) and *Felis catus* (domestic cat). The generic name is written or printed with a capital letter. Both names are usually given in italics or are underlined if written or typed.

**gene sequence** *noun* GENETICS a set of nucleotides in a section of DNA with a specific function

**gene sequencing** *noun* GENETICS the process of determining the set of nucleotides in DNA that make up a specific gene. Also called **genetic sequencing**

**gene splicing** *noun* BIOTECH a technique in which segments of DNA or RNA, often from different organisms, are combined, in order to be introduced into an organism

**genet** *noun* **1.** BIOL an individual organism which is genetically different from others **2.** EARTH SCI a clone from a genetically distinct organism

**gene therapy** *noun* GENETICS same as **gene replacement therapy**

**genetic, genetical** *adjective* GENETICS referring to genes or genetics ○ *Breeders of new crop plants are dependent on genetic materials from wild forms of maize and wheat.*

**genetically modified** *adjective* BIOTECH referring to an organism that has received genetic material from another in a laboratory procedure, leading to a permanent change in one or more of its characteristics. Abbreviation **GM**

**genetically modified organism** *noun* BIOTECH a plant, animal or microorganism produced by genetic modification. Abbreviation **GMO**

**genetic bottleneck** *noun* GENETICS a change in gene frequencies and decline in total genetic variation where there is a sharp decrease in population numbers

**genetic code** *noun* GENETICS information carried by DNA which determines the synthesis of proteins by cells and which is passed on when the cell divides. Also called **code**

**genetic damage** *noun* GENETICS damage to an organism's gene by external agents such as radiation or chemicals

**genetic diversity** *noun* GENETICS, ECOL the richness of the variety and range of genes

**genetic drift** *noun* GENETICS a random change in gene frequency

**genetic engineering** *noun* BIOTECH same as **genetic modification**. abbreviation **GE**

**genetic fingerprint** *noun* GENETICS the pattern of sequences of genetic material unique to an individual

**genetic fingerprinting** *noun* BIOTECH a method of revealing an individual's genetic fingerprint, used in paternity queries and criminal investigation

**genetic information** *noun* GENETICS same as **genetic code**

**geneticist** *noun* GENETICS a person who specialises in the study of genetics

**genetic load** *noun* GENETICS the average number of unfavourable recessive genetic mutations per individual in a population

**genetic manipulation** *noun* BIOTECH same as **genetic modification**

**genetic map** *noun* GENETICS a diagram of the arrangement of genes on a specific chromosome

**genetic mapping** *noun* GENETICS the identification of the arrangement of genes on a specific chromosome

**genetic marker** *noun* GENETICS a known, usually dominant, gene that is used in the identification of genes, chromosomes and characteristics already known to be associated with that gene

**genetic material** *noun* the parts of a cell that carry heritable information, e.g. DNA, genes or chromosomes

**genetic modification** *noun* BIOTECH the alteration and recombination of genetic material under laboratory conditions, resulting in transgenic organisms. Abbreviation **GM**. Also called **genetic manipulation, genetic engineering**

**genetic profiling** *noun* BIOTECH same as **DNA fingerprinting**

**genetic resources** *plural noun* GENETICS the genes found in plants and animals that have value to humans

**genetics** *noun* BIOL the study of the way in which the characteristics of an organism are inherited

**genetic screening** *noun* GENETICS the testing of people to see if they have a specific genetic disorder

**genetic sequencing** *noun* GENETICS same as **gene sequencing**

**genetic variation** *noun* GENETICS the inherited differences between the members of a species

**gene tracking** *noun* GENETICS the method used to trace the inheritance of a particular gene through a family in order to diagnose and predict genetic disorders

**gene transfer** *noun* BIOTECH the insertion of genetic material from one organism into another in a laboratory procedure

**-genic** *suffix* produced by or producing

**genlock** *noun* COMPUT same as **generator lock**

**genome** *noun* GENETICS **1.** the set of all the genes in an individual **2.** the set of genes which are inherited from one parent

**genomic** *adjective* GENETICS relating to a genome

**genomic imprinting** *noun* GENETICS the transfer of the complete set of genes from a parent to an offspring's chromosomes

**genomics** *noun* GENETICS the identification and study of sections of DNA with a specific function

**genotoxicity** *noun* GENETICS the degree to which a physical or chemical agent damages DNA or causes mutation

**genotoxin** *noun* GENETICS a substance that can cause damage to or mutation in DNA

**genotype** *noun* GENETICS **1.** the genetic constitution of an organism. ♦ **phenotype 2.** an individual organism

**genotypic** *adjective* relating to a genotype

**genuine** *adjective* real or correct ○ *Authentication allows the system to recognise that a sender's message is genuine.*

**genus** *noun* BIOL a group of closely related species (NOTE: The plural is **genera**.)

**geo-** *prefix* EARTH SCI Earth

**geocentric** *adjective* ASTRON referring to the solar system when it is regarded as having Earth as its centre

**geochemical** *adjective* CHEM relating to geochemistry

**geochemist** *noun* CHEM a scientist who specialises in the study of geochemistry

**geochemistry** *noun* CHEM the scientific study of the chemical composition of Earth

**geocline** *noun* ECOL the set of changes that take place in a species across different geographical environments

**geodesic** *adjective* **1.** EARTH SCI same as **geodetic 2.** MATHS referring to the geometry of curved surfaces

**geodesic dome** *noun* MATHS a dome composed of many flat faces intersected by bars to form equilateral triangles or polygons

**geodesy** *noun* EARTH SCI the science of the measurement of Earth or of very large sections of it to determine the exact location of points on Earth's surface through precise observation of distances and angles

**geodetic, geodesic** *adjective* EARTH SCI referring to geodesy ○ *Geodetic surveys employ precise observations of angles and distances to determine the exact location of points on the Earth's surface.*

**geographer** *noun* EARTH SCI a person who specialises in the study of geography

**geographic, geographical** *adjective* EARTH SCI referring to geography

**geographical pole** *noun* EARTH SCI one of two points, the North and South Poles, where longitudinal lines meet and which are the most northerly or southerly points on Earth

**geographic information system** *noun* COMPUT a computer system for capturing, manipulating, analysing and displaying all forms of geographic information. Abbreviation **GIS**

**geography** *noun* EARTH SCI the scientific study of the Earth's surface, climate and physical features

**geological** *adjective* EARTH SCI referring to geology

**geological era, geological period** *noun* EARTH SCI a span of millions of years during which Earth's surface and its underlying strata underwent changes

**geologist** *noun* EARTH SCI a scientist who specialises in the study of geology

**geology** *noun* EARTH SCI the scientific study of the composition of Earth's surface and its underlying strata

**geomagnetic** *adjective* EARTH SCI referring to Earth's magnetic field

**geomagnetic pole** *noun* EARTH SCI same as **magnetic pole**

**geomagnetism** *noun* EARTH SCI the study of Earth's magnetic field

**geometric, geometrical** *adjective* MATHS referring to geometry ○ *A triangle is a geometric figure.*

**geometry** *noun* MATHS **1.** the study of the properties, measurement, and relationships of points, lines, angles, surfaces and solids ○ *An understanding of geometry is essential to the student of navigation.* **2.** a configuration or arrangement ○ *the geometry of the engine nacelle*

**geometry processing** *noun* COMPUT a process required to calculate the x, y and z coordinates of a three-dimensional object that is to be displayed on screen ○ *Geometry processing is usually carried out by the central processing unit or by a specialised graphics processor.*

**geomorphology** *noun* EARTH SCI the study of the physical features of Earth's surface, their development and how they are related to the core beneath

**geophone** *noun* EARTH SCI a sensitive device which records sounds of seismic movements below Earth's surface

**geophysicist** *noun* EARTH SCI a scientist who specialises in the study of geophysics

**geophysics** *noun* EARTH SCI the scientific study of the physical properties of Earth

**geophyte** *noun* BOT a perennial plant propagated by underground buds

**geoscience** *noun* EARTH SCI any science which is concerned with the physical aspects of Earth, e.g. geochemistry, geodesy, geography, geology, geomorphology, geophysics or meteorology

**geoscientist** *noun* EARTH SCI a person who specialises in one or several of the geosciences

**geosphere** *noun* EARTH SCI the central part of Earth, which contains no living organisms

**geostationary** *adjective* AEROSP referring to an object in Earth's orbit such as a satellite which travels at the same speed as Earth and is therefore stationary with reference to a point on Earth

**geostrophic wind** *noun* METEOROL a wind which blows horizontally along the isobars, across the surface of the earth

**geosyncline** *noun* EARTH SCI a long fold in Earth's crust, forming a basin filled with a sediment of volcanic rocks

**geothermal** *adjective* EARTH SCI referring to heat from the interior of the Earth

**geothermal deposit** *noun* EARTH SCI heat-producing matter inside the Earth

**geothermal energy** *noun* INDUST energy or electricity generated from the heat inside the Earth, e.g. in hot springs. Also called **geothermal power**

COMMENT: Apart from channelling water from hot springs, geothermal energy can also be created by pumping cold water into deep holes in the ground at points where hot rocks lie relatively close to the surface. The water is heated and becomes steam which returns to the surface and is used for domestic heating.

**geothermal field** *noun* GEOG an area of the Earth where there is heat beneath the surface, e.g. near hot springs or a volcano

**geothermal gradient** *noun* GEOL an increase in temperature with the increase of depth inside the Earth

**geothermal installation** *noun* INDUST an establishment or equipment that extracts hot water and steam from inside the Earth to heat buildings or generate electricity

**geothermally** *adverb* INDUST from geothermal sources ○ *Geothermally heated water can be used for domestic heating.*

**geothermal power** *noun* INDUST same as **geothermal energy**

**geothermal power plant** *noun* INDUST a power station generating electricity from the heat inside the Earth such as that (heat) in hot springs

**geotropism** *noun* BOT the growth or movement of a plant in response to gravity (NOTE: Stems and other parts that grow upwards against gravity show negative geotropism. The downwards growth of roots is positive geotropism.)

**germ** *noun* **1.** MICROBIOL a microorganism such as a virus or bacterium that causes a disease ○ *Germs are not visible to the naked eye.* **2.** BIOL a part of an organism that develops into a new organism

**germanium** *noun* CHEM ELEM a brittle grey crystalline element with both metallic and non-metallic properties used in semiconductors and alloys (NOTE: The chemical symbol is **Ge**; the atomic number is **32** and the atomic weight is **72.59**.)

**germ carrier** *noun* MED a person who carries bacteria of a disease in his or her body and who can transmit the disease to others without showing any signs of it himself (*informal*)

**germ cell** *noun* BIOL a cell which is capable of developing into a spermatozoon or ovum

**germ-free** *noun* MICROBIOL sterile, without any microbes present

**germicide** *adjective, noun* PHARM a substance that can kill germs

**germinate** *verb* BOT (*of a seed or spore*) to start to grow

**germination** *noun* BOT the point at which a seed or spore is starting to grow

**germ layer** *noun* ZOOL one of the layers of cell which form the organs of an animal embryo

**germplasm** *noun* GENETICS the genetic material that is transmitted from one generation of an organism to another

**germ warfare** *noun* MIL a strategy of war where one side tries to kill or affect the people of the enemy side by infecting them with microorganisms that cause disease

**gestation period, gestation** *noun* BIOL the period from conception to birth, when a female mammal has live young in her womb (NOTE: In humans, it is referred to as pregnancy.)

**geyser** *noun* EARTH SCI a phenomenon which happens when hot water and steam are sent out of a hole in the ground at regular intervals

COMMENT: A geyser such as Old Faithful in Yellowstone National Park in the USA is caused when water deep below the Earth's surface is heated to steam and rises rapidly up the pipe leading to the surface, pushing the water already in the channel up with it.

**geyser field** *noun* EARTH SCI an area of land where there are geysers

**ghost cursor** *noun* COMPUT a second cursor which can be used in some programs

**GHz** *abbreviation* MEASURE gigahertz

**giant star, giant** *noun* ASTRON a low-density star with a diameter that is up to 100 times greater than that of the Sun

**gibberellin** *noun* BIOCHEM a plant hormone that stimulates growth and triggers seed germination

**Gibbs free energy** *noun* PHYS same as **free energy**

**giga-** *prefix* MEASURE one thousand million, $10^9$. Symbol **G**

**gigabyte** *noun* COMPUT a unit of $2^{30}$ bytes

**gigaflop** *noun* COMPUT a unit of one thousand million floating point operations per second

**gigahertz** *noun* MEASURE a frequency of one thousand million cycles per second. Abbreviation **GHz**

**gigawatt** *noun* ELEC a unit of one thousand million watts ○ *Air-conditioning accounts for one-third of the 500 gigawatt peak demand in the USA.* Abbreviation **GW**

**gigawatt-hour** *noun* ELEC a unit of one thousand million watts of electricity used for one hour. Abbreviation **GWh**

**GIGO** *abbreviation* COMPUT garbage in garbage out

COMMENT: GIGO is sometimes taken to mean 'garbage in gospel out': i.e. that whatever wrong information is put into a computer, people will always believe that the output results are true.

**gilbert** *noun* MEASURE the cgs unit of magnetomotive force, approximately equal to 0.7958 ampere-turns

**gills** *plural noun* **1.** ZOOL the breathing apparatus of fish and other animals living in water, consisting of a series of layers of tissue which extract oxygen from water as it passes over them **2.** FUNGI a series of thin structures on the underside of the cap of a fungus, carrying the spores

**GIS** *abbreviation* EARTH SCI geographic information system

**given** *adjective* specified or fixed ○ *At high altitudes, less fuel is consumed for a given airspeed than for the same airspeed at a lower altitude.* ■ *preposition* taking into account, considering □ **given that** taking into account the fact that, considering that ○ *Given the condition of the engine, it is surprising that it starts.*

**gizzard** *noun* ZOOL a thick-walled muscular part of the gut of many birds where food is mechanically crushed. Also called **proventriculus** (NOTE: A gizzard is also present in some insects, fish and crustaceans.)

**glacial** *adjective* EARTH SCI referring to a glacier ○ *The rocks are marked by glacial action.*

**glacial climatologist** *noun* METEOROL a scientist who studies climate as recorded in the ice of glaciers

**glacial deposits** *plural noun* EARTH SCI the material such as sand, soil or gravel left behind by a glacier

**glacial drift** *noun* EARTH SCI the material such as sand, soil or gravel left behind by a glacier

**glacial stratigraphy** *noun* METEOROL the science of studying layers of polar ice to discover information about climatic conditions when the ice was formed thousands of years ago

**glacial striation** *noun* EARTH SCI the marking made on rocks by a moving glacier

**glaciation** *noun* **1.** EARTH SCI the formation of glaciers **2.** METEOROL the formation of ice crystals at the top of a rain cloud

**glacier** *noun* EARTH SCI **1.** a mass of ice moving slowly across land, like a frozen river **2.** a large amount of stationary ice covering land in the Arctic regions

COMMENT: During the Ice Ages, glaciers covered large parts of the northern hemisphere, depositing sand in the form of glacial moraines and boulder clay. Glaciers are still found in the highest mountain areas and in the Arctic and Antarctic regions.

**glaciologist** *noun* EARTH SCI a scientist who specialises in the study of glaciers

**glaciology** *noun* EARTH SCI the study of glaciers

**gland** *noun* ANAT (*in animals and plants*) a cell or group of cells that secrete a specific substance

**glare** *noun* a strong blinding light ○ *Glare can be caused by diffuse reflection of sunlight from the top of a layer of fog.*

**glare filter** *noun* a coated glass or plastic sheet placed in front of a screen to cut out bright light reflections

**glass** *noun* **1.** CHEM any solid with a noncrystalline structure **2.** INDUST a substance made from sand and soda or lime, usually transparent and used for making windows, bottles and other objects

**glass electrode** *noun* CHEM an electrode made of very thin glass, often used to measure pH value

**glass fibre, glass filament** *noun* CHEM a very thin fibre drawn from melted glass which may be made into threads or fabric

**Glauber's salt** *noun* CHEM a white soluble crystalline sodium sulfate, used in solar energy systems, and in dye, glass, and paper manufacture

**glaucoma** *noun* OPHTHALMOL a condition of the eyes, caused by an unusually high pressure of fluid inside the eyeball, resulting in disturbances of vision and blindness

**glauconite** *noun* MINERALS a green mineral composed of iron, potassium, aluminium and magnesium

**glen** *noun* GEOG (*in Scotland*) a long narrow mountain valley with a stream running along it

**gley** *noun* GEOG a thick rich soil found in waterlogged ground

**gleyed soil** *noun* GEOG soil which is waterlogged

**gleying** *noun* GEOG a set of properties of soil which indicate poor drainage and lack of oxygen (NOTE: The signs are a blue-grey colour, rusty patches and standing surface water.)

**glitch** *noun* COMPUT anything which causes the sudden unexpected failure of a computer or equipment (*informal*)

**global** *adjective* **1.** referring to the whole Earth ○ *the global economy* ○ *Global temperatures will rise over the next fifty years.* **2.** covering everything

**global backup** *noun* COMPUT **1.** a backup of all data stored on all nodes or workstations connected to a network **2.** a backup of all files on a hard disk or file server

**global ecology** *noun* ECOL the study of the relationship of organisms to each other and to their environment on a global scale

**global exchange** *noun* COMPUT a replace function which replaces one piece of text such as a word with another throughout a whole text

**globalisation** *noun* the development of a single culture and economy across the whole world as a result of technological advances in communications

**global knowledge** *noun* COMPUT all the knowledge about one problem or task

**global positioning system** *noun* NAVIG a satellite-based navigation system. Abbreviation **GPS**

**global search and replace** *noun* COMPUT a word-processor search and replace function covering a complete file or document

**global solar radiation** *noun* PHYS the rays emitted by the Sun which fall on the Earth. Abbreviation **GSR**

**global stability** *noun* ECOL the ability of an ecological or taxonomic unit to be unaffected by large disturbances

**global system for mobile communications** *noun* TELECOM full form of **GSM**

**global temperature** *noun* METEOROL the temperature over the Earth as a whole

**global variable** *noun* COMPUT a number that can be accessed by any routine or structure in a program

**global warming** *noun* ENVIRON a gradual rise in temperature over the whole of the Earth's surface, caused by the greenhouse effect

**global warming potential** *noun* ENVIRON a concept that takes into account the differing times that gases remain in the atmosphere, in order to find out the potential climate effects of equal emissions of each of the greenhouse gases

**globe** *noun* **1.** an object shaped like a ball **2.** the Earth (*literary*)

**globular cluster** *noun* ASTRON a cluster of densely packed stars, approximately spherical in shape, located within a spherical halo around the Milky Way galaxy

**globule** *noun* a round drop of liquid

**globulin** *noun* BIOCHEM a globular protein, various types of which are found in blood

**glomerulus** *noun* ANAT a cluster of capillaries found in the nephron of the kidney, which filters wastes from the blood to be excreted as urine

**gloom** *noun* METEOROL dark and miserable weather

**glossopharyngeal nerve** *noun* ANAT the ninth cranial nerve which controls the pharynx, the salivary glands and part of the tongue

**glottis** *noun* ANAT **1.** the opening of the upper portion of the larynx between the vocal cords (NOTE: The plural is **glottises** or **glottides**.) **2.** the portion of the larynx that produces voice

**glove box** *noun* CHEM, BIOL a sealed container with gloved openings on its sides that is used for handling radioactive or toxic substances safely without contamination

**glow-worm** *noun* INSECTS a beetle of which the females and larvae produce a greenish light

**glucagon** *noun* BIOCHEM a hormone produced by islet cells in the pancreas that stimulates the breakdown of glycogen to glucose and so raises raises blood sugar

**glucosamine** *noun* BIOCHEM a glucose derivative found in supportive tissues and plant cell walls

**glucose** *noun* BIOCHEM a simple sugar found in some fruit, but also broken down from white sugar or carbohydrate and absorbed into the body or secreted by the kidneys

COMMENT: Combustion of glucose with oxygen to form carbon dioxide and water is the body's main source of energy.

**glucose tolerance test** *noun* MED a test for diabetes mellitus in which the patient eats glucose and has urine and blood tests at regular intervals

**gluon** *noun* PHYS a theoretical elementary particle that has no mass (NOTE: Gluons may be involved in binding quarks together.)

**glutamic acid, glutamine** *noun* BIOCHEM an amino acid in protein

**gluten** *noun* BIOCHEM a protein found in some cereals which makes a sticky paste when water is added

**gluten enteropathy** *noun* **1.** MED an allergic disease, mainly affecting children in which the lining of the intestine is sensitive to gluten, preventing the small intestine from digesting fat **2.** BIOL a condition in adults where the villi in the intestine become smaller, and so reduce the surface which can absorb nutrients ▶ also called **coeliac disease**

**gluten-free diet** *noun* MED a diet consisting only of food containing no gluten

**glyceride** *noun* CHEM an ester that is formed by the reaction of glycerol with an acid (NOTE: It occurs widely in animal and vegetable fats and oils.)

**glycerin, glycerine, glycerol** *noun* BIOCHEM a colourless viscous sweet-tasting liquid present in combination with fats and oils

COMMENT: Synthetic glycerin is used in various medicinal preparations and also as a lubricant in toothpaste and cough medicines. A mixture of glycerin and honey is useful to soothe a sore throat.

**glycine** *noun* BIOCHEM an amino acid in protein

**glycogen** *noun* BIOCHEM a type of starch that is converted from glucose by the action of insulin and stored in the liver as a source of energy

**glycol** *noun* CHEM same as **diol**

**glycolipid** *noun* BIOCHEM a sugar-containing lipid found in cell membranes

**glycolysis** *noun* BIOCHEM the process by which living cells break down glucose to pyruvate in order to release usable energy

**glycoprotein** *noun* BIOCHEM a protein that is linked to a carbohydrate

**GM** *abbreviation* BIOTECH **1.** genetically modified **2.** genetic modification

**GMO** *abbreviation* BIOTECH genetically modified organism

**GMT** *abbreviation* TIME Greenwich Mean Time

**gnathostome** *noun* ZOOL a vertebrate with a mouth that has jaws. Superclass: Gnathostomata. (NOTE: The classification includes all vertebrates except agnathans.)

**GND** *abbreviation* ELEC ground

**gneiss** *noun* EARTH SCI a rough rock with layers of different minerals

**gnotobiotics** *noun* BIOL the study of organisms living either in a germ-free environment or a controlled environment into which a known contaminant has been introduced

**goal** *noun* **1.** an aim or something you are trying to do **2.** a final state reached when a task has been finished or has produced satisfactory results

**gob** *noun* INDUST waste matter from coal processing plants which use bituminous coal

**goblet cell** *noun* BIOL a tube-shaped cell in the epithelium which secretes mucus

**gold** *noun* CHEM ELEM a heavy yellow metal, used in jewellery (NOTE: The chemical symbol is **Au**; the atomic number is **79** and the atomic weight is **196.97**.)

**gold contact** *noun* ELEC an electrical contact, usually for low-level signals, that is coated with gold to reduce the electrical resistance

**gold mine** *noun* MIN EXTRACT a hole dug in the ground to extract gold

**Golgi apparatus** *noun* BIOL a stack of flattened sacs in the cytoplasm of cells in which proteins are sorted and packaged, especially for secretion

**gonad** *noun* ANAT an organ in animals that produces reproductive cells or gametes, e.g. a testis or an ovary

**Gondwanaland** *noun* EARTH SCI an ancient landmass that included South America, Africa, India, Australia and Antartica

**Gopher** *noun* COMPUT a system that allows a user to find information and files stored on the Internet using a series of commands

**gorge** *noun* EARTH SCI a narrow valley with steep sides

**GOSUB** *noun* COMPUT a programming command which executes a routine then returns to the following instruction

**GOTO** *noun* COMPUT a programming command which instructs a jump to another point or routine in the program ○ *GOTO 105 instructs a jump to line 105.*

COMMENT: GOTO statements are frowned upon by software experts since their use discourages set structured programming techniques

**Gouraud shading** *noun* MATHS a mathematical equation that is used to create shading within a three-dimensional scene (NOTE: The equation is applied to each side of each object and produces a gradual change in colour to give the impression of light and shade.)

**govern** *verb* ENG to control or limit the speed, size or amount of something ○ *The type of undercarriage fitted to an aircraft is governed by the operating weight.*

**governor** *noun* ENG a device for controlling or limiting the speed, size or amount of something ○ *Excessive speeding of the engine is prevented by a governor in the fuel system.*

**GPIA** *abbreviation* COMPUT general purpose interface adapter

**GPIB** *abbreviation* COMPUT general purpose interface bus

**GPR** *noun* COMPUT a data register in a computer-processing unit that can store items of data for many different mathematical or logical operations. Full form **general purpose register**

**GPRS** *noun* TELECOM a standard system for wireless radio and mobile telephone communications that is due to replace the existing GSM system. Full form **general packet radio service** (NOTE: GPRS supports high-speed data transfer rates of up to 150 Kbps compared to the GSM limit of 9.6 Kbps.)

**GPS** *abbreviation* NAVIG global positioning system

**gr** *abbreviation* MEASURE grain

**Graafian follicle** *noun* ANAT a fluid-filled sac or vesicle that surrounds and protects a maturing ovum in the ovary of a mammal

**graben** *noun* EARTH SCI a type of rift valley, formed where land between fault lines has sunk

**grab sample** *noun* EARTH SCI a single sample of soil or of water taken without considering factors such as time or flow

**graceful degradation** *noun* COMPUT the process of allowing some parts of a system to continue to function after a part has broken down

**grade** *noun* a position on a scale of size, quality, amount or academic achievement

**gradient** *noun* **1.** PHYS the rate at which a physical quantity such as temperature or pressure changes relative to change in a given variable, especially distance ○ *Because there is a temperature gradient across each front it is possible to draw isotherms which reduce in value from warm to cold air.* ○ *A pressure gradient occurs aloft from land to sea.* **2.** COMPUT a smooth change of colour from one colour to another or from black to white **3.** the angle of a slope ○ *Plant roots cannot retain the soil on very steep gradients.* **4.** MATHS the rate of increase or decrease of a measurement

**gradual** *adjective* progressing with continuous but unhurried certainty ○ *a gradual change* ○ *Loss of cabin pressure may be gradual rather than sudden.*

**graduate** *verb* **1.** to be granted an academic degree or diploma ○ *She gradu-*

*ated from Oxford University with a first class honours degree.* **2.** to advance to a new level of skill, achievement or activity ○ *After 50 hours of flying the single engine trainer, the student pilots graduate to flying the twin engine aircraft.* **3.** to divide into marked intervals, especially for use in measurement ○ *A thermometer has a scale that is graduated in degrees Celsius.*

**graft** BIOL *noun* a piece of plant or animal tissue transplanted onto another plant or animal and growing there ■ *verb* to transplant a piece of tissue from one plant or animal to another

COMMENT: Many cultivated plants are grafted. The piece of tissue from the original plant (the scion) is placed on a cut made in the outer bark of the host plant (the stock) so that a bond takes place. The aim is usually to ensure that the hardy qualities of the stock are able to benefit the weaker cultivated scion.

**Graham's law** *noun* CHEM a chemical rule in which the diffusion rate of a gas is related to the inverse square root of its density

**grain** *noun* **1.** the seed of a cereal crop such as wheat or maize **2.** AGRIC a cereal crop, such as wheat, of which the seeds are dried and eaten **3.** GEOL the size of crystals in a rock or the size of particles of sand **4.** MEASURE a measure of weight equal to 0.0648 grams. Abbreviation **gr**

**grain storage** *noun* AGRIC the practice or means of keeping grain until it is sold or used (NOTE: Most grain is stored on the farm until it is sold, and is kept in bins or in bulk on the floor of the granary. The system of storage depends on whether the grain is to be used for feeding animals on the farm or is to be sold.)

**gram** *noun* MEASURE a metric measure of weight equal to one thousandth of a kilogram. Abbreviation **g**

**-gram** *suffix* a record in the form of a picture

**Gramineae** *plural noun* BOT the grasses, a very large family of plants including cereals such as wheat and maize

**grammar checker** *noun* COMPUT a software utility used to check a document or letter to make sure it is grammatically correct

**Gram-negative bacterium** *noun* MICROBIOL a bacterium which takes up

the red counterstain, after alcohol has washed out the first violet dye

**Gram-positive bacterium** *noun* MICROBIOL a bacterium which retains the first violet dye and appears blue-black when viewed under the microscope

**Gram's stain, Gram's method** *noun* BIOTECH a method of staining bacteria so that the two main types can be distinguished

COMMENT: The bacterial sample is first stained with a violet dye, treated with alcohol, and then counterstained with a red dye.

**grandfather file** *noun* COMPUT the third most recent version of a backed up file, after father and son files

**granite** *noun* GEOL a hard grey rock with pieces of quartz, feldspar and other minerals in it

**grant** *noun* an amount of money given to support a specific person or project

**granular** *adjective* in the form of granules

**granularity** *noun* COMPUT the size of memory segments in a virtual memory system

**granule** *noun* **1.** CHEM a small particle of a mineral **2.** EARTH SCI a small artificially made particle ○ *Fertilisers are produced in granule form, which is easier to handle and distribute than powder.*

**grape sugar** *noun* BIOCHEM a sugar that is obtained from grapes

**graph** *noun* MATHS a diagram that shows a relationship between two sets of numbers as a series of points often joined by a line ○ *The graph shows the relationship between lift and drag at various airspeeds.*

**-graph** *suffix* a machine which records by drawing

**-grapher** *suffix* **1.** a person skilled in a subject **2.** a technician who operates a machine which records

**graphic** *adjective* **1.** in the form of pictures or diagrams ○ *a graphic representation of age group response* **2.** described in vivid detail ○ *The eyewitness provided a graphic description of the events leading to the accident.* ■ *noun* COMPUT a picture used in a computer application ○ *The instructor's worksheets were greatly improved by* several graphics which highlighted the subject matter.

**graphical** adjective COMPUT referring to something represented by graphics

**graphically** adverb by using pictures ○ The sales figures are graphically represented as a pie chart.

**graphical user interface** noun COMPUT an interface between an operating system or program and the user that uses graphics or icons to represent functions or files. Abbreviation **GUI**

COMMENT: A graphical user interface normally uses a combination of windows, icons and a mouse to control the operating system. In many GUIs, for example Microsoft Windows and the Apple Macintosh System, you can control all the functions of the operating system just using the mouse. Icons represent programs and files; instead of entering the file name, you select it by moving a pointer with a mouse.

**graphic data** noun COMPUT stored data that represents graphical information when displayed on a screen

**graphic display** noun COMPUT a computer screen able to present graphical information

**graphic display resolution** noun COMPUT the number of pixels that a computer is able to display on the screen

**graphic language** noun COMPUT a computer programming language with commands that are useful when displaying graphics ○ This graphic language can plot lines, circles and graphs with a single command.

**graphics** plural noun COMPUT illustrations which represent information ○ graphics such as bar charts, pie charts and line drawings

**graphics accelerator** noun COMPUT a special card that fits inside a computer and uses a dedicated processor chip to speed up the action of drawing lines and images on the screen

**graphics coprocessor** noun COMPUT a high-speed display adapter that is dedicated to graphics operations such as line drawing and plotting. ♦ **graphics processor**

**graphics library** noun COMPUT a number of routines stored in a library file that can be added to any user program to simplify the task of writing graphics programs

**graphic solution** noun MATHS a technique of using geometric constructions to solve problems ○ One side of the calculator has a moveable slide which is used for the graphic solution of triangle of velocities problems.

**graphics primitive** noun COMPUT a basic shape such as an arc, line or filled square that is used to create other shapes or objects

**graphics processor** noun COMPUT a secondary processor used to speed up the display of graphics. ♦ **graphics coprocessor** (NOTE: It calculates the position of pixels that form a line or shape and displays graphic lines or shapes.)

**graphite** noun CHEM a mineral form of carbon occurring naturally as crystals or as a soft black deposit (NOTE: It is used as a moderator in some types of nuclear reactor and is mixed with clay to make lead pencils.)

**graph plotter** noun COMPUT a printing device with a pen which takes data from a computer and plots it in graphic form

**-graphy** suffix ENG the process of drawing

**grass** noun BOT a flowering monocotyledon of which there are a great many genera, including wheat, barley, rice and oats. Latin name: Gramineae. (NOTE: Grasses are an important food for herbivores and humans.)

**grassland** noun EARTH SCI land covered by grasses, especially wide open spaces such as the prairies of North America or the pampas of South America

**graticule** noun 1. OPTICS a series of fine lines in an optical instrument such as a telescope, used for measuring 2. NAVIG the network of lines formed by the meridians and parallels of longitude and latitude of the Earth on a flat sheet of paper ○ A graticule of lines of latitude and longitude is imagined to cover the Earth.

**gravel** noun EARTH SCI sand and small pebbles occurring as deposits (NOTE: On the Wentworth-Udden scale, gravel has a diameter of between 2 and 4 millimetres.)

**gravel pit** noun INDUST an area of land from which gravel is extracted

**graveyard** *noun* INDUST, ENVIRON a place where nuclear waste is buried

**gravitation** *noun* ASTRON, PHYS the apparently universal attractive force between matter, increasing according to the two masses multiplied together and decreasing with the square of their distance apart, according to the law of gravitation set out by Isaac Newton (NOTE: The size of the force for any particular combination of distance and mass is given by the gravitational constant.)

**gravitational** *adjective* PHYS referring to gravity

**gravitational constant** *noun* PHYS the numerical factor that relates force, mass and distance in Newton's theory of gravitation (NOTE: It has the value $6.673 \times 10^{-11}$ N m$^2$kg$^{-2}$.)

**gravitational field** *noun* PHYS an area of space in which gravity is felt ○ *Tides are caused by the Moon's gravitational pull.*

**gravitational lens** *noun* ASTRON a concentration of matter dense enough to refract light into an image

**gravitational radiation** *noun* ASTRON a form of energy whose existence is predicted by general relativity and which has been looked for using instruments such as large metal cylinders suspended in caverns below the Earth's surface (NOTE: Gravitational radiation would be observed, if at all, in the form of very long waves of fluctuating gravitational attraction (**gravity waves**).)

**gravitational redshift** *noun* PHYS, ASTRON the redshift of light or other electromagnetic radiation caused by its passing through a strong gravitational field, rather than being due to a Doppler effect

**gravitino** *noun* PHYS (*in unified field theory physics*) a proposed particle which carries gravitational energy, in the same way as neutrinos are the carriers of angular momentum

**graviton** *noun* PHYS a proposed subatomic particle which carries gravitational forces between massive particles, in the same way as photons carry electromagnetic energy

**gravity** *noun* a natural force of attraction which pulls bodies towards each other and which pulls objects on Earth towards its centre ○ *In order for an*

*aeroplane to fly, lift must overcome gravity.* Also called **force of gravity**

**gravity feed** *noun* AUTOMOT the use of the force of gravity to move fuel from the tank to the carburettor

**gravity wave** *noun* PHYS a long wave of fluctuating gravitational attraction

**gray** *noun* PHYS, MEASURE an SI unit of measurement of absorbed radiation equal to 100 rads. Symbol **Gy**

**Gray code** *noun* COMPUT a coding system in which the binary representation of decimal numbers changes by only one bit at a time from one number to the next

COMMENT: It is used in communications systems to provide error detection facilities.

**graze** *verb* ZOOL (*of animals*) to feed on grass

**grazer** *noun* ZOOL a grazing animal

**grazing** *noun* AGRIC **1.** the action of feeding animals on growing grass **2.** land covered with grass, suitable for animals to feed on ○ *There is good grazing on the mountain pastures.*

**grazing food chain** *noun* ECOL a food chain in which the energy in vegetation is eaten by animals, digested, then passed into the soil as dung and so taken up again by plants which are eaten by animals

**grazing season** *noun* AGRIC the time of year when animals can feed outside on grass

**great** *adjective* large in size, quantity, number, quality or importance □ **a great deal of** a large amount of

**great year** *noun* ASTRON a period of about 25 800 years that is a complete cycle of the precession of the equinoxes

**greeked** *adjective* COMPUT (*in a DTP program*) referring to a font with a point size too small to display accurately, shown as a line rather than individual characters

**green** *adjective* **1.** of a colour like that of leaves ○ *The green colour in plants is provided by chlorophyll.* **2.** BIOL immature ○ *green shoots* **3.** ECOL, ENVIRON referring to an interest in ecological and environmental problems ■ *noun* **1.** a colour like that of leaves **2.** ECOL, ENVIRON a person with an interest in ecological and environmental problems

**green algae** *plural noun* BIOL green organisms that live in water. Division: *Chlorophyta.*

**green audit** *noun* ENVIRON same as **environmental audit**

**green electricity** *noun* INDUST electricity produced from renewable sources, such as tidal power or wind power. Compare **brown electricity**

**green energy** *noun* INDUST power produced by alternative technology such as wind power or tidal power

**greenhouse effect** *noun* ENVIRON the effect produced by the accumulation of carbon dioxide crystals and water vapour in the upper atmosphere, which insulates the Earth and raises the atmospheric temperature by preventing heat loss

COMMENT: Carbon dioxide particles allow solar radiation to pass through and reach the Earth, but prevent heat from radiating back into the atmosphere. This results in a rise in the Earth's atmospheric temperature. Even a small rise of less than 1° C in the atmospheric temperature could have serious effects on the climate of the Earth as a whole. The polar ice caps would melt, causing sea levels to rise everywhere with consequent flooding. Temperate areas in Asia and America would experience hotter and drier conditions, causing crop failures. Carbon dioxide is largely formed from burning fossil fuels. Other gases contribute to the greenhouse effect, for instance, methane is increasingly produced by rotting vegetation in swamps, from paddy fields and even from the stomachs of cows. Chlorofluorocarbons also help create the greenhouse effect.

**greenhouse gas** *noun* ENVIRON a gas such as carbon dioxide, methane, CFC or nitrogen oxide which is produced by burning fossil fuels and which rises into the atmosphere, forming a barrier which prevents heat loss ○ *The EU is planning to introduce a tax to inhibit greenhouse gas emissions.*

**green manure** *noun* AGRIC rapid-growing green vegetation such as mustard or rape which is grown and ploughed into the soil to rot and act as manure

**green mud** *noun* EARTH SCI a deposit found on the seabed off the southeastern USA and elsewhere, containing fine clay and glauconite, the latter giving it its green colour

**green petrol** *noun* INDUST, ENVIRON petrol containing fewer pollutants than ordinary petrol

**green phosphor** *noun* COMPUT the most commonly used phosphor for monochrome screen coating, which displays green characters on a black background

**Green Revolution** *noun* BIOTECH the development of new forms of cereal plants such as wheat and rice, which gave much higher yields and increased food production especially in tropical countries

**Greenwich Mean Time** *noun* local time on the Greenwich meridian. Abbreviation **GMT**

COMMENT: Greenwich Mean Time is now called Coordinated Universal Time or Universal Coordinated Time (UTC) and is also known as Zulu time. UTC is expressed in 24-hour format; for example, 7:00 p.m. is 1900 hours (say: nineteen hundred hours).

**Greenwich meridian** *noun* GEOG a line of longitude situated at 0° and passing through Greenwich, England. Also called **prime meridian**

**green wood** *noun* BOT new shoots on a tree, which have not ripened fully

**Gregorian telescope** *noun* ASTRON an astronomical telescope in which the primary mirror has a central hole through which light reflected from the smaller secondary mirror passes to the eyepiece

**gremlin** *noun* COMPUT an unexplained fault in a system (*informal*)

**grey hole** *noun* ASTRON an object which might be formed by the collapse of a massive star too small to form a black hole but too large to form a neutron star

**grey scale** *noun* **1.** PHOTOGRAPHY a set of shades of grey used to measure the correct exposure when filming **2.** COMPUT the set of shades which are produced by displaying what should be colour information on a monochrome monitor

**grid** *noun* **1.** a pattern of equally spaced vertical and horizontal lines **2.** PHYS a metal cylinder in a cathode ray tube **3.** a pattern of equally spaced vertical and horizontal metal rods or bars ○

*Lead-antimony alloy grid plates are components in a lead-acid battery.*

**grid snap** *noun* COMPUT a set of patterns or lines drawn on screen limited to the points of a grid ○ *If you want to draw accurate lines, you'll find it easier with grid snap turned on.*

**Grignard reagent** *noun* CHEM an alkyl magnesium halide dissolved in diethyl ether used in the preparation of organic compounds

**grind** *verb* **1.** INDUST to reduce a substance to fine particles by crushing **2.** to move or work noisily and with difficulty

**grinder** *noun* INDUST a device or machine which reduces a substance to fine particles by crushing

**grinding** *noun* INDUST the reducing of a substance to fine particles by crushing

**grip** *verb* to hold something tightly ○ *In friction feed, the paper is gripped by the rollers.*

**grit** *noun* **1.** EARTH SCI sharp-grained sand **2.** METEOROL a tiny solid particle in the air, larger than dust

**groove** *noun* a long shallow depression in a surface

**gross** *adjective* total, with no deductions

**gross calorific value** *noun* PHYS the total number of calories which a specific amount of a substance contains. Abbreviation **GCV**

**gross output** *noun* INDUST the total amount produced

**gross primary production** *noun* ECOL the rate at which a biomass assimilates organic matter

**gross primary productivity** *noun* ECOL the rate at which producers in an ecosystem capture and store chemical energy as biomass

**gross productivity** *noun* BOT the rate at which energy is produced by plants through photosynthesis, before the plant uses any of the energy itself

**ground** *noun* **1.** the solid surface of the Earth **2.** a surface layer of soil or earth **3.** an area of land

**ground clearance** *noun* ENVIRON the removal of trees and undergrowth in preparation for an activity such as ploughing or building

**ground cover** *noun* BOT plants which cover the surface of the soil

**ground frost** *noun* METEOROL the condition where the air temperature at ground level is below 0° C

**ground level** *noun* GEOG the height of the ground

**ground-level concentration** *noun* ENVIRON the amount of a pollutant measured at the height of the ground just above it or just below it

**ground moraine** *noun* GEOL a deposit of gravel and sand left under a glacier

**ground pollution** *noun* ENVIRON the presence of unusually high concentrations of harmful substances in the soil

**ground speed** *noun* AVIAT the speed of an aircraft in relation to the ground

**ground state** *noun* PHYS the state in which a particle, atom, molecule or system has the lowest energy

**ground water** *noun* GEOL water which stays in the top layers of soil or in porous rocks and can collect pollution

**ground-water basin** *noun* GEOL an area of land where water stays in the top layers of soil or in porous rocks and can collect pollution

**ground-water level** *noun* GEOL a point below the surface of the Earth where ground water lies

**ground-water runoff** *noun* GEOL water which enters streams and rivers from below ground

**group** *noun* **1.** a number of individual items or people brought together **2.** COMPUT a set of computer records containing related information **3.** CHEM a vertical column in the periodic table that contains elements with similar properties ■ *verb* to bring several things together

**groupware** *noun* COMPUT software specially written to be used by a group of people connected to a network and to help them carry out a particular task (NOTE: It provides useful functions such as a diary or electronic mail that can be accessed by all users.)

**grove** *noun* BOT a small group of trees

**grow** *verb* **1.** BIOL (*of plants*) to exist and flourish ○ *Bananas grow only in warm humid conditions.* ○ *Tomatoes grow well in greenhouses.* **2.** BIOL (*of plants and animals*) to increase in size ○ *The tree grows slowly.* ○ *A sunflower can grow three centimetres in one day.*

**3.** AGRIC to cultivate plants ○ *Farmers here grow two crops in a year.* ○ *He grows peas for the local canning factory.* **4.** to become ○ *It's growing colder at night now.* ○ *She grew weak with hunger.*

**growing point** *noun* BOT a point on the stem of a plant where growth occurs, often at the tip of the stem or branch

**growing season** *noun* BOT the time of year when a plant grows ○ *Alpine plants have a short growing season.*

**growth** *noun* **1.** an increase in size ○ *the growth in the population since 1960* **2.** the amount by which something increases in size ○ *The disease stunts the conifers' growth.* ○ *The rings show the annual growth of the tree.*

**growth factor** *noun* BIOCHEM a chemical substance which encourages the growth of a type of cell

**growth hormone** *noun* BIOCHEM a natural or artificial chemical that makes an organism grow

**growth inhibitor** *noun* BIOCHEM a chemical which stops an organism growing

**growth promoter** *noun* BIOCHEM a chemical which makes an organism grow

**growth rate** *noun* the amount or speed of increase in size

**growth regulator** *noun* AGRIC a chemical used to control the growth of plants, mainly used for weed control in cereals and grassland

**growth retardant** *noun* BIOCHEM a chemical used to make an organism grow more slowly

**growth ring** *noun* BOT same as **annual ring**

**growth stimulant** *noun* BIOCHEM a chemical which makes an organism start to grow

**growth substance** *noun* BIOCHEM same as **hormone**

**grub** *noun* INSECTS a small caterpillar or larva

**grub up** *verb* AGRIC to dig up a plant with its roots ○ *Miles of hedgerows have been grubbed up to make larger fields.*

**GSM** *noun* COMPUT a system used for wireless cellular telephone communications throughout Europe, Asia and parts of North America. Full form **global system for mobile communications**

COMMENT: The GSM system allows eight calls to share the same radio frequency and carries the digital data that represents voice signals transmitted by each user's telephone. The main drawback of GSM is that it does not offer very fast data transfer rates, which has become more important as users want to access the Internet and read email via a mobile telephone connection. GSM provides data transfer at up to 9.6 Kbps, but it is due to be replaced by the GPRS system, which can support high-speed data transfer at up to 150 Kbps.

**GSR** *abbreviation* ASTRON global solar radiation

**guanidine** *noun* CHEM an alkaline substance found in urine produced by protein metabolism and also in plant tissues. Formula: $CH_5N_3$. (NOTE: It is used in the plastics and resins manufacture.)

**guanine** *noun* BIOCHEM one of the four basic components of DNA

**guano** *noun* AGRIC a mass of accumulated bird droppings, found especially on small islands and used as fertiliser

**guard** *noun* a device to prevent injury or damage ■ *verb* to watch over and protect something or someone from harm

**guard band** *noun* COMPUT a section of magnetic tape between two channels recorded on the same tape

**guard bit** *noun* COMPUT one bit within a stored word that indicates to the computer whether it can be altered or if it is protected

**guard cell** *noun* BOT either of a pair of cells that border a leaf pore and control its size (NOTE: The guard cells and pore are called a stoma, and are most common on the underside of leaves.)

**GUI** *abbreviation* COMPUT graphical user interface

**guidance** *noun* **1.** helpful advice ○ *Guidance is provided to assist people in filling in the form.* ○ *The booklet contains guidance on the safe handling of chemicals.* **2.** AVIAT the giving of flying directions to an aircraft ○ *Systems which are designed to carry out automatic landings under all visibility conditions must provide better guidance and control than a pilot.*

**guidance system** *noun* AEROSP a system which provides signals to the flight control system for steering an aircraft

**guide** *noun* something that directs or indicates ■ *verb* to direct something or someone

**guide bar** *noun* COMPUT a line in a bar code that shows the start or finish of the code (NOTE: The standard guide bars are two thin lines that are a little longer than the coding lines.)

**guideline** *noun* a general rule laid down, telling people how something should be done ○ *guidelines for the conduct of experiments*

**guild** *noun* ECOL a group of plants or animals of the same species which live in the same type of environment

**gulf** *noun* EARTH SCI a very large area of sea enclosed partly by land

**Gulf Stream** *noun* EARTH SCI a current of warm water in the Atlantic Ocean, which flows north along the east coast of the USA, then crosses the Atlantic to hit northern Europe

**gulfweed** *noun* MARINE BIOL floating seaweed which grows in the Sargasso Sea

**gull** *noun* ZOOL a seabird, having a stout build, usually white plumage, hooked bill and webbed feet, belonging to a number of different species

**gully** *noun* **1.** EARTH SCI a deep channel formed by soil erosion and unable to be filled in by cultivation **2.** ENG, GEOL a small channel dug for water, e.g. an artificial channel at the edge of a field or a natural channel in rock

**gulp** *noun* COMPUT a group of words, usually two bytes. ♦ **byte, nibble**

**gum** *noun* BOT, INDUST a substance existing in a liquid state in the trunks and branches of trees, which hardens on contact with air and is used in confectionery, pharmacy and stationery

**gust** *noun* METEOROL a strong sudden rush of wind ○ *Strong gusts blew them off course.* ■ *verb* (*of wind*) to increase in strength suddenly ○ *Wind is at 10 knots gusting to 20 knots.*

**gusty** *adjective* METEOROL referring to wind which is blowing in gusts

**gut** *noun* ANAT same as **alimentary canal**

**Gutenberg discontinuity** *noun* EARTH SCI a boundary between the mantle and the core inside the Earth

**gutter** *noun* PRINTING a blank space or inner margin between two facing pages

**GW, gW** *abbreviation* ELEC gigawatt

**GWh** *abbreviation* ELEC gigawatt-hour

**Gy** *abbreviation* PHYS gray

**gymnosperm** *noun* BOT a seed-bearing plant such as a conifer, cycad or ginkgo in which the seeds are carried naked on the scales of a cone rather than being inside a fruit. ♦ **angiosperm**

**gynoecium** *noun* BOT the female sex organs (**carpels**) of a plant

**gynogenesis** *noun* GENETICS the development of an embryo that has only maternal chromosomes because fusion of an egg and sperm nuclei has not occurred

**gypsum** *noun* MINERALS a soft white or colourless mineral consisting of hydrated calcium sulfate, used in cement, plaster and fertilisers

**gyre** *noun* OCEANOG a circular or spiral motion of ocean water

**gyro** *noun* PHYS same as **gyroscope**

**gyrocompass** *noun* NAVIG same as **gyroscopic compass**

**gyroscope** *noun* PHYS, NAVIG a device consisting of a spinning wheel, mounted on a base so that its axis can turn freely in one or more directions and thereby maintain its own direction even when the base is moved. Also called **gyro**

**gyroscopic compass** *noun* NAVIG a compass which uses gyroscopic directional stability rather than magnetism to indicate direction. Also called **gyrocompass**

**gyroscopic precession** *noun* PHYS, NAVIG a characteristic of a gyroscope, that the force applied to a spinning gyroscope will act at a point 90° in the direction of rotation, not at the point where the force is applied ○ *Forces of gyroscopic precession act on the direction indicator to keep it aligned vertically and horizontally.*

# H

**h** *symbol* hecto-

**H** *symbol* **1.** PHYS, MEASURE henry **2.** CHEM ELEM hydrogen

**ha** *symbol* MEASURE, AGRIC hectare

**haar** *noun* METEOROL a sea mist occurring during the summer in the north of the British Isles

**Haber process** *noun* INDUST a commercial process in which ammonia is produced from atmospheric nitrogen and hydrogen using a catalyst at high temperature and pressure

**habit** *noun* BOT the characteristic way in which a specific plant grows ○ *a bush with an erect habit* ○ *a plant with a creeping habit*

**habitat** *noun* ECOL the type of environment in which a specific organism lives

**habitat loss** *noun* ECOL a permanent disappearance of, or decrease in, the amount of suitable environment available to an organism. Also called **habitat reduction**

**habitat management** *noun* ENVIRON same as **nature management**

**habitat reduction** *noun* ECOL same as **habitat loss**

**haboob** *noun* METEOROL a violent dust storm or sand storm of a type found in North Africa, especially in Sudan (NOTE: Such dust storms are associated with cumulonimbus clouds.)

**hack** *verb* COMPUT **1.** to experiment and explore computer software and hardware **2.** to break into a computer system for criminal purposes

**hacker** *noun* COMPUT a person who hacks

**hadal zone** *noun* OCEANOG a zone of the ocean at depths greater than the abyssal zone, i.e. below 6000 m

**hadron** *noun* PHYS a particle that is subject to the strong nuclear interaction

**haem-** *prefix* BIOL blood (NOTE: The US spelling for words beginning with the prefix **haem-** is **hem-**.)

**haematite** *noun* MINERALS iron oxide, the most common form of iron ore. Formula: $Fe_2O_3$.

**haemoglobin** *noun* BIOCHEM a red protein in red blood cells that combines reversibly with oxygen and transports it round the body. Abbreviation **Hb**

COMMENT: Haemoglobin absorbs oxygen in the lungs and carries it in the blood to the tissues. Haemoglobin is also attracted to carbon monoxide and readily absorbs it instead of oxygen, causing carbon monoxide poisoning.

**haemolytic anaemia** *noun* MED anaemia caused by the destruction of red blood cells

**hafnium** *noun* CHEM ELEM a silvery metallic element, used to absorb neutrons in nuclear reactor rods and in the manufacture of tungsten filaments (NOTE: The chemical symbol is **Hf**; the atomic number is **72** and the atomic weight is **178.49**.)

**Hageman factor** *noun* BIOCHEM a protein found in plasma, one of the factors that causes blood to clot. Also called **factor XII**

**hail** METEOROL *noun* water falling from clouds in the form of small round pieces of ice ■ *verb* to fall as small pieces of ice

COMMENT: Hail occurs when rain forms in cumulonimbus clouds and is carried upwards into colder air where it freezes. It then falls back through the cloud, growing in size as it accumulates moisture.

**hailstone** *noun* METEOROL a piece of ice which falls from clouds like rain

**hailstorm** *noun* METEOROL a storm in which the precipitation is hail and not rain

**hair** *noun* BIOL **1.** a slender outgrowth on the surface of a plant or animal **2.** a mass of outgrowths on an animal's skin or a person's head

**hairline fracture** *noun* MED a very thin crack in a bone

**half** *noun* MATHS one of two equal parts ○ *Half the data was lost in transmission.* ○ *The second half of the program contains some errors.*

**half adder** *noun* ELECTRONICS a binary adder that can produce the sum of two inputs, producing a carry output if necessary, but cannot accept a carry input

**half duplex** *noun* COMPUT data transmission in one direction at a time over a bidirectional channel. Abbreviation **HD**

**half-hardy** *adjective* BOT (*of a plant*) able to withstand a mild degree of frost

**half-life, half-life period** *noun* PHYS the time taken for half the atoms in a radioactive isotope to decay. Also called **half-value period**

COMMENT: Radioactive substances decay in a constant way and each has a different half-life: strontium-90 has a half-life of 28 years, radium-226 one of 1 620 years and plutonium-239 one of 24 360 years.

**halftone** *noun* PHOTOGRAPHY, COMPUT a photograph or image that originally had continuous tones, displayed or printed by using groups of dots to represent the tones

**half-value period** *noun* PHYS same as **half-life**

**half word** *noun* COMPUT a sequence of bits occupying half a standard computer word, but able to be accessed as a single unit

**halide** *noun* CHEM a compound of halogen with another element or group, e.g. fluoride

**halite** *noun* CHEM sodium chloride occurring naturally in the ground. Also called **rock salt**

**Hall effect** *noun* PHYS a description of the effect of a magnetic field on electron flow

**Hall effect switch** *noun* ELEC a solid-state electronic switch operated by a magnetic field

**Halley, Edmond (1656–1742)** ASTRON English astronomer best remembered for the comet named after him. He realised that the great comet of 1682 was in fact a periodic comet identical to others seen at 76-year intervals throughout history. Halley later became Astronomer Royal and was one of the circle including Newton and others which produced many discoveries in mathematics, physics and astronomy.

**Halley's Comet** *noun* ASTRON a comet with a 76-year orbit, which is bright enough to be seen with the naked eye (NOTE: Its brightness and the fact that it spends almost all of its orbit in deep space mean that Halley's Comet is an almost unaltered chunk of material from the earliest days of the solar system.)

**halo** *noun* METEOROL a circle of light seen round the Sun or Moon, caused by ice crystals in Earth's atmosphere

**halo-** *prefix* CHEM salt

**halobiotic** *adjective* BIOL referring to organisms which live in salt water

**halocarbon** *noun* CHEM a chemical consisting of carbon, sometimes hydrogen, and a halogen such as chlorine, fluorine, bromine or iodine

**halocline** *noun* EARTH SCI a salinity gradient where two masses of water meet, as between a mass of fresh water and the sea

**halogen** *noun* CHEM a non-metallic element belonging to a series of chemically related non-metallic elements that includes fluorine, chlorine, iodine, bromine and astatine

**halogenated** *adjective* CHEM referring to a chemical compound which contains one of the halogens

**halogenation** *verb* CHEM the process of treating or combining something with a halogen

**halogen lamp** *noun* INDUST a light bulb containing a halogen that runs at a much higher temperature than a conventional incandescent lamp

**halogenous** *adjective* CHEM ELEM referring to or containing a halogen

**halomorphic soil** *noun* GEOL soil that contains large amounts of salt

**halon** *noun* CHEM a chemical compound that contains bromine and resembles a chlorofluorocarbon

**halophile** *noun* BIOL a species that can live in salty conditions

**halophyte** *noun* BOT a plant that grows in salty soil

**halt** COMPUT *noun* same as **halt instruction** ■ *verb* to stop or bring something to a stop ○ *Hitting CTRL S will halt the program.*

**halt condition** *noun* COMPUT the operating state reached when a computer comes across a fault, faulty instruction or halt instruction in the program that is being run

**halt instruction** *noun* COMPUT an instruction to stop a computer carrying out any further instructions until restarted. Also called **halt**

**hand-held** COMPUT *adjective* able to be held in the hand ○ *Nowadays, headsets are usually used in preference to hand-held microphones.* ■ *noun* a device that can be held in the hand

**handle** *noun* 1. a device for taking in, or being operated by, the hand ○ *a door handle* 2. COMPUT a number used to identify an active file within the program that is accessing the file 3. COMPUT a small square that can be dragged to change the shape of a window or graphical object ○ *To stretch the box in the DTP program, select it once to display the handles then drag one handle to change its shape.* ■ *verb* 1. to touch something with the hands ○ *Do not handle unwrapped food.* 2. to control or operate something by hand ○ *The student pilot handled the aircraft well in the turbulent conditions.* 3. to deal with a situation ○ *I've been asked to handle the department's grant application.*

**handler** *noun* COMPUT a part of an operating system software or a special software routine which controls a device or function ○ *The scanner handler routines are supplied on disk.*

**handling** *noun* 1. the act of touching something with the hands ○ *guidelines for the handling of chemicals* 2. the act of controlling or operating something 3. AUTOMOT the way in which a car behaves when it is driven ○ *The handling is superb.*

**handshake,** **handshaking** *noun* COMPUT a standardised set of signals between two devices to make sure that the system is working correctly, the equipment is compatible and data transfer is correct

**hands off** *adjective, adverb* (*of a working system*) not controlled by an operator because the operation is automatic ○ *an automatic flight control system capable of landing an aircraft hands off* ■ *noun* 1. COMPUT a working system where the operator does not control the operation, which is automatic 2. a working system where the operator does not need to touch the device in use

**hands on** *noun* COMPUT a working system where the operator controls the operations by keying instructions on the keyboard ■ *adjective* being actively involved in something ○ *hands-on experience of the system* ○ *The computer firm gives a two-day hands on training course.*

**hang** *verb* COMPUT to enter an endless loop and not respond to further instruction

**hanging valley** *noun* EARTH SCI a valley formed when a glacier flows into a larger glacier

COMMENT: Hanging valleys are the result of glaciation. The main valley has been cut deeper by the larger glacier, leaving the smaller valley to join it at a cliff. This is one of the ways in which waterfalls are formed.

**hangup** *noun* COMPUT the sudden stop of a working program (NOTE: Hangups are often due to the computer's executing an illegal instruction or entering an endless loop.)

**haploid** *adjective* GENETICS referring to an organism that has a single set of unpaired chromosomes in a cell nucleus

**hard** *adjective* 1. not soft ○ *A diamond is one of the hardest minerals.* 2. difficult ○ *It is hard for grazing animals to find enough to eat in drought conditions.* 3. COMPUT (*of parts of a computer system*) not able to be programmed or altered

**hard copy** *noun* COMPUT a printed version of information contained in a computer or system

**hard detergent** *noun* CHEM a detergent that is not broken down in water

**hard disk** *noun* COMPUT a rigid magnetic disk that is able to store many times more data than a floppy disk, and usually cannot be removed from the disk drive

**hard disk drive** *noun* COMPUT a unit used to store and retrieve data from a spinning hard disk. Abbreviation **HDD**

**harden** *verb* to make something hard or become hard

**hardener** *noun* CHEM a substance that causes another to become hard by chemical reaction

**harden off** *verb* AGRIC to make plants become gradually more used to cold ○ *After seedlings have been grown in the greenhouse, they need to be hardened off before planting outside in the open ground.*

**hard frost** *noun* METEOROL weather when the temperature falls well below 0° C

**hardness** *noun* CHEM **1.** an indication of the percentage of calcium in water **2.** a measurement of how hard a mineral is

COMMENT: Hardness of minerals is shown on a scale of 1 to 10: diamond is the hardest (i.e. it has hardness 10) and talc is the softest. A mineral of one grade is able to scratch or mark a mineral of the grade below.

**hardpan** *noun* EARTH SCI a hard soil surface, usually formed of dried clay

**hard reset** *noun* COMPUT a switch that generates an electrical signal to reset the central processing unit and all devices, equivalent to turning a computer off and back on again. Also called **hardware reset**

**hard return** *noun* COMPUT a code in a word-processing document that normally indicates the end of a paragraph

**hard-sectored** *adjective* COMPUT referring to a disk with sector start locations described by holes or other physical marks on the disk, which are set when the disk is manufactured

**hardware** *noun* COMPUT the equipment and devices that make up a computer system

COMMENT: Computer hardware can include the computer itself, the disks and disk drive, printer, VDU, etc.

**hardware compatibility** *noun* COMPUT the architecture of two different computers that allows one to run the programs or use the add-on boards of the other without changing any device drivers or memory locations

**hardware interrupt** *noun* COMPUT an interrupt signal generated by a piece of hardware rather than by software

**hardware platform** *noun* COMPUT the standard of a particular make of computer

**hardware reset** *noun* COMPUT same as **hard reset**

**hard water** *noun* CHEM tap water that contains a high percentage of calcium and magnesium (NOTE: Hard water makes it difficult for soap to lather and also causes deposits in pipes, boilers and kettles.)

**hard winter** *noun* METEOROL a very cold winter ○ *In a hard winter, many smaller birds may be killed.*

**hardwired connection** *noun* COMPUT a permanent phone line connection, instead of a plug and socket

**hardwired logic** *noun* COMPUT a logical function or software program that is built using electronic hardware devices such as logic components, rather than written in software

**hardwired program** *noun* COMPUT a computer program built into the hardware, which cannot be changed

**hardwood** *noun* **1.** TREES a slow-growing broad-leaved tree such as oak or teak **2.** INDUST the fine-grained wood produced by a tree such as oak or teak. Compare **softwood**

**hardy** *adjective* BOT (*of a plant*) able to withstand cold weather, especially below 5° C. ♦ **half-hardy**

**Hardy-Weinberg law** *noun* GENETICS a principle of genetics stating that gene frequencies remain constant from generation to generation if mating is random and there are no external influences such as mutation and immigration

**harmattan** *noun* METEOROL a hot dry winter wind that blows from the northeast and causes dust storms in the Sahara

**harmonic** *noun* PHYS a single oscillation whose frequency is a whole multiple of a fundamental frequency

**harmonic motion** *noun* PHYS a periodic vibration that has a single frequency or an even multiple of one or is symmetrical about a point of equilibrium (NOTE: It is seen in the movement of a pendulum or the vibration of a violin string.)

**harmonics** *noun* MATHS same as **harmonic series**

**harmonic series** *noun* MATHS an infinite series constructed by adding together all the numbers in a harmonic progression

**harness** *verb* ENVIRON to control a natural phenomenon and make it produce energy ○ *A tidal power station harnesses the power of the tides.*

**harrow** AGRIC *noun* a piece of equipment with teeth or discs, used for breaking up soil or levelling the surface of ploughed soil ■ *verb* to level the surface of ploughed soil with a harrow, covering seeds that have been sown in furrows

**hartley** *noun* COMPUT a unit of information, equal to 3.32 bits, or the probability of one state out of ten equally probable states

**harvest** *noun* AGRIC **1.** the time when a crop is gathered **2.** a crop that is gathered ■ *verb* **1.** AGRIC to gather a crop that is ripe ○ *They are harvesting the rice crop.* **2.** AGRIC to gather a natural resource **3.** MED to remove an organ for transplanting

**hash** *noun* TELECOM, COMPUT the symbol ( # ) on a computer keyboard or telephone keypad. Also called **hashmark** ■ *verb* COMPUT to produce a unique number derived from the entry itself, for each entry in a database

**hash index** *noun* COMPUT a list of entries according to their hashed numbers

**hashmark, hash mark** *noun* COMPUT, TELECOM same as **hash**

COMMENT: In US usage # means number; #32 = number 32 (apartment number in a postal address, paragraph number in a text, etc.).

**hash table** *noun* COMPUT a list of all entries in a file with their hashed key addresses

**hash total** *noun* COMPUT the total of a number of hashed entries used for error detection

**hash value** *noun* COMPUT a number arrived at after a key is hashed

**hassium** *noun* CHEM ELEM an extremely rare and unstable chemical element produced in high-energy atomic collisions (NOTE: The chemical symbol is **Hs**; the atomic number is **108** and the atomic weight is **269**.)

**hatch** *verb* ZOOL (*of an animal in an egg*) to become mature and break out of the egg

**hatchery** *noun* AGRIC a place where eggs are kept warm artificially until the animal inside becomes mature and breaks out

**Haversian canal** *noun* ANAT a tiny longitudinal channel in bone tissue forming part of a network that contains blood vessels and nerve fibres

**Hawking, Stephen (born 1942)** ASTRON British cosmologist based in Cambridge, best known for work on relativistic phenomena such as black holes and as the author of *A Brief History of Time*

**hay** *noun* AGRIC grass mowed and dried before it has flowered

COMMENT: Hay is cut before the grass flowers and at this stage in its growth it is a nutritious fodder. If it is mowed after it has flowered it is called straw, and is of less use as a food and so is used for bedding.

**hay fever** *noun* MED an inflammation of the nose and eyes caused by an allergic reaction to pollen, fungus spores or dust in the atmosphere

COMMENT: Tree pollen is most prevalent in spring, followed by the pollen of flowers and grasses during the summer months and fungal spores in the early autumn. The pollen released by the stamens of a flower floats in the air until it finds a female flower. Pollen in the air is a major cause of hay fever. It enters the nose and eyes and chemicals in it irritate the mucus and force histamines to be released by the sufferer, causing the symptoms of hay fever to appear.

**hazard** *noun* a possible danger ○ *a fire hazard* ○ *a health hazard* ○ *Thunderclouds may pose hazards to aircraft.*

**hazardous** *adjective* dangerous ○ *hazardous chemicals* ○ *Flying over mountainous terrain can be hazardous.* □ **hazardous to health** likely to damage somebody's health

**hazardous waste** *noun* ENVIRON waste materials that can damage people's health if not treated correctly

**haze** *noun* **1.** METEOROL dust or smoke in the atmosphere ○ *Haze can seriously reduce air-to-ground visibility.* **2.** COMPUT same as **fogging**

**Hb** *abbreviation* BIOCHEM haemoglobin

**HD** *abbreviation* **1.** COMPUT half duplex **2.** high-density

**HDD** *abbreviation* COMPUT hard disk drive

**HDLC** *abbreviation* COMPUT high-level data link control

**HD polythene** *noun* INDUST same as **high-density polythene**

**HDTV** *abbreviation* TECH high-definition television

**He** *symbol* CHEM ELEM helium

**head** *noun* **1.** ANAT the top part of the body above the shoulders **2.** a person ○ *Allow three pieces per head.* **3.** the top part of a device, network or body **4.** a main end part or top of something **5.** COMPUT data that indicates the start address of a list of items stored in memory **6.** the start of a reel of recording tape **7.** GEOG a point where a river starts to flow **8.** INDUST pressure shown as the vertical distance that water falls from the inlet of the collection pipe to the water turbine in a hydroelectric power system **9.** pressure shown as the vertical distance of a water tank above the taps in a house ■ *verb* **1.** to be in charge of an organisation or group of people **2.** to be the first item in a list or queue **3.** to move or move something in a particular direction

**head alignment** *noun* COMPUT the correct position of a tape or disk head in relation to the magnetic surface, to give the best performance and correct track location

**head count** *noun* a count of how many people are present

**head crash** *noun* COMPUT a component failure in a disk drive, where the head is allowed to hit the surface of the spinning disk, causing disk surface damage and data corruption

**head end** *noun* interconnection equipment between an antenna and a cable television network

**header** *noun* COMPUT **1.** a packet of data that is sent before a transmission to provide information on destination and routing **2.** the set of words that appear at the top of each page of a document, e.g. title, author's name or page number. Also called **heading, headline**. Compare **footer**

**header block** *noun* COMPUT a block of data at the beginning of a file containing data about file characteristics

**heading** *noun* **1.** the title or name of a document or file **2.** COMPUT same as

**header 3.** NAVIG the direction in which a ship or aircraft is travelling

COMMENT: Wind affects an aircraft in flight. Therefore heading does not always coincide with the aircraft's track. The pilot must head the aircraft slightly into the wind to correct for drift.

**heading indicator** *noun* NAVIG an instrument that gives course or direction information

**headland** *noun* **1.** EARTH SCI a high mass of land sticking into the sea **2.** AGRIC an uncultivated area of soil at the edge of a field, where the tractor turns when ploughing

**headlife** *noun* COMPUT the length of time that a video or tape head can work before being serviced or replaced

**headline** *noun* COMPUT same as **header**

**head park** *noun* COMPUT the act of moving the read/write head in a hard disk drive to a safe position, not over the disk, so that if the unit is knocked or jarred the head will not damage the disk surface

**headphones** *plural noun* TELECOM a pair of listening devices, one for each ear, joined by a bar that goes over the head

**headset** *noun* TELECOM a set of headphones with a microphone attached ○ *Headsets are usually used in preference to hand-held microphones.*

**headstream** *noun* EARTH SCI a stream that flows into a river near its source

**headwaters** *plural noun* EARTH SCI the area at which tributary streams feed into a river near its source

**health** *noun* MED the state of being well ○ *Fumes from the factory were a danger to health.*

**health education** *noun* HEALTH the teaching of people to do things to improve their health, such as taking more exercise or stopping smoking

**health food** *noun* FOOD INDUST a food that is regarded as contributing to good health, especially one with no additives (NOTE: Health foods include natural cereals, dried fruit and nuts.)

**health risk assessment** *noun* MED a prediction of the potential health effects of being exposed to hazardous substances

**healthy** *adjective* **1.** not ill **2.** likely to keep or make you well ○ *a healthy diet*

**heap** *noun* **1.** a large pile of something **2.** COMPUT a temporary data storage area that allows random access **3.** COMPUT a binary tree

**hearing threshold** *noun* same as **audibility threshold**

**heart** *noun* **1.** ANAT a muscular organ that pumps blood round an animal's body **2.** BOT the compact central part of a vegetable such as lettuce, cabbage or celery, where new leaves or stalks form **3.** the innermost part of something ○ *This tree grows only in the heart of the forest.*

**heart rate** *noun* MED the number of times a heart beats per minute

**heartwood** *noun* BOT the hard dead wood in the centre of a tree's trunk which helps support the tree. Compare **sapwood**

**heat** *noun* **1.** PHYS energy which is moving from a source to another point ○ *The heat of the Sun made the surface of the road melt.* **2.** ZOOL the period when a female animal will allow mating □ **an animal on heat** a female animal in the period when she will accept a mate ■ *verb* PHYS to make something hot ○ *The solution should be heated to 25 ° C.*

**heat accumulator** *noun* PHYS a vessel for storing hot liquid. Also called **thermal accumulator**

**heat balance** *noun* EARTH SCI a state in which Earth loses as much heat by radiation and reflection as it gains from the Sun, making Earth's temperature constant from year to year

**heat capacity** *noun* PHYS the amount of heat required to raise the temperature of a substance by one degree

**heat conduction** *noun* PHYS the passing of heat from one part to another

**heat discharge** *noun* INDUST a release of waste heat into the atmosphere, especially from an industrial process. Also called **thermal discharge**

**heat engine** *noun* **1.** PHYS a machine or organism that consumes fuel and produces heat which can be converted into work **2.** EARTH SCI a phenomenon that produces Earth's climatic pattern, caused by the difference in temperature between the hot equatorial zone and the cold polar regions, making warm water

and air from the tropics move towards the poles

**heater** *noun* ENG a device for producing heat

**heat exchanger** *noun* ENG a device that takes heat from one source and gives it to another (NOTE: An example is in a heating system where a hot pipe goes through a water tank to heat it.)

**heat exhaustion** *noun* MED a state of collapse as a result of overexertion in hot conditions

**heat flow** *noun* PHYS a movement of heat, as through a metal or from the Earth into space

**heat flux** *noun* PHYS the flow of heat during heat exchange

**heat gain** *noun* PHYS same as **energy gain**

**heath** *noun* EARTH SCI an area of dry sandy acid soil with low shrubs such as heather and gorse growing on it

**heat haze** *noun* METEOROL a reduction in visibility caused by warm air rising from the ground

**heathland** *noun* EARTH SCI a wide area of heath

**heating** *noun* **1.** the process of making something hot **2.** INDUST a system that supplies heat

**heating appliance** *noun* ENG, INDUST a device that supplies heat, usually in a building

**heating oil** *noun* INDUST petroleum oil used as fuel in a central heating boiler

**heating power, heating value** *noun* PHYS a measurement of the amount of heat that a substance or process can supply

**heat insulation** *noun* PHYS the prevention of the escape of heat

**heat island** *noun* ENVIRON an increase in temperature experienced in the centre of a large urban area, caused by the release of heat from buildings

**heat loss** *noun* PHYS the amount of heat lost, as through inadequate insulation

**heat of atomisation** *noun* PHYS the amount of heat required to convert one mole of a substance into its gaseous form

**heat of combustion** *noun* PHYS the amount of heat produced by one mole of a substance when it is burned in oxygen

**heat of neutralisation** *noun* PHYS the heat that is released when one mole of hydrogen ions is neutralised by a base

**heat-proof** *adjective* **1.** not affected by heat **2.** through which heat cannot pass

**heat pump** *noun* INDUST a device that cools or heats by transferring heat from cold areas to warm ones (NOTE: Heat pumps are used in refrigerators or for heating large buildings.)

**heat reclamation, heat recovery** *noun* INDUST the process of collecting heat from substances heated during a process and using it to heat further substances, so as to avoid heat loss

**heat-sealing** *noun* FOOD INDUST a method of closing plastic food containers (NOTE: The air is removed from a plastic bag with the food inside and the bag is then pressed by a hot plate, which melts the plastic and seals the contents in the vacuum.)

**heat sink** *noun* **1.** COMPUT a metal device used to conduct heat away from an electronic component to prevent damage **2.** PHYS a place that can absorb extra heat ○ *The oceans may delay global warming by acting as a heat sink.*

**heat storage** *noun* INDUST the storage of heat produced during a period of low consumption until a peak period when it is needed. Also called **thermal storage**

**heat transfer** *noun* PHYS the process of passing heat from one medium or substance to another

**heat-treated alloy** *noun* an alloy that has undergone a process of hardening by using heat

**heavenly body** *noun* ASTRON same as **celestial body** (*literary*)

**heavy** *adjective* **1.** weighing a lot **2.** severe, difficult or unpleasant **3.** involving a lot of effort

**heavy-duty** *adjective* referring to something designed for long or hard wear or use ○ *a heavy-duty battery*

**heavy gauge wire** *noun* ELEC a thick wire

**heavy goods vehicle** *noun* AUTOMOT a large truck for moving objects

**heavy hydrogen** *noun* CHEM same as **deuterium**

**heavy industry** *noun* INDUST **1.** an industry such as steelmaking or engineering that takes raw materials and makes them into large finished products **2.** an industry that extracts raw materials such as coal

**heavy metal** *noun* CHEM a metal that has a high relative atomic mass and density and is toxic to humans, e.g. copper, lead and zinc

**heavy oil** *noun* CHEM a mixture of hydrocarbons that is distilled from coal tar and is heavier than water

**heavy water** *noun* CHEM water containing deuterium instead of hydrogen. Formula: $D_2O$. (NOTE: It is used as a coolant or moderator in some types of nuclear reactor.)

**hectare** *noun* MEASURE an area of land measuring 100 by 100 metres, i.e. 10 000 square metres or 2.47 acres. Symbol **ha**

**hecto-** *prefix* MEASURE one hundred, $10^2$. Symbol **H**

**height** *noun* the vertical distance of a point, level or object measured from a particular place such as sea level ○ *Pressure decreases with increasing height.*

**helical scan** *noun* COMPUT a method of storing data on magnetic tape in which the write head stores data in diagonal strips rather than parallel with the tape edge

**helio-** *prefix* ASTRON the Sun

**heliocentric** *adjective* ASTRON **1.** relating to the solar system when it is regarded as having the Sun at its centre **2.** measured from the centre of the Sun

**heliophyte** *noun* BOT a plant that prefers to grow in sunlight

**heliotropic** *adjective* BOT referring to a plant that grows or turns towards the light

**helium** *noun* CHEM ELEM a light inert gas, used in balloons and as a coolant in some types of nuclear reactor (NOTE: The chemical symbol is **He**; the atomic number is **2** and the atomic weight is **4.00**.)

**helophyte** *noun* BOT a plant that typically grows in marshy or lake-edge environments

**help** noun **1.** anything that makes it easier to do something ○ *He finds his word processor a great help in the office.* **2.** COMPUT a function in a program or system that provides useful information about the program in use ○ *Hit the HELP key if you want information about what to do next.*

**helper T cell** noun IMMUNOL (*in the lymphocyte system*) a lymphocyte that helps provide immunity against diseases by recognising foreign antigens

**hemihydrate** noun CHEM a hydrated salt consisting of two parts of an anhydrous compound to one part water (NOTE: Plaster of Paris is a hemihydrate.)

**hemipteran** noun INSECTS an insect that has mouthparts adapted for piercing and sucking and two pairs of wings. Order: Hemiptera. (NOTE: Hemipterans are generally parasitic in nature and include bedbugs and other true bugs.)

**hemisphere** noun **1.** one half of a sphere **2.** one half of the Earth north or south of the equator ○ *the northern hemisphere*

**hemizygous** adjective GENETICS having only one of a pair of genes (NOTE: An example of this occurs in males, which have an unpaired X chromosome and therefore only one of a pair of genes.)

**hemlock** noun **1.** TREES a North American softwood tree. Genus: *Tsuga.* **2.** PLANTS a deadly poisonous plant. Latin name: *Conium maculatum.*

**hemp** noun PLANTS a plant used to make rope and that also produces an addictive drug. Latin name: *Cannabis sativa.*

**henry** noun PHYS, MEASURE the SI unit of electrical inductance. Symbol **H** (NOTE: It is equal to an electrical potential of one volt induced in a closed circuit by a current varying uniformly by one ampere per second.)

**Henry's law** noun CHEM the principle that the amount of gas dissolved at equilibrium in a volume of liquid is directly proportional to the pressure of that gas in contact with the liquid surface (NOTE: This is only applicable to gases that do not react with the solvent.)

**hepatic** adjective ANAT referring to the liver

**hepatic artery** noun ANAT an artery that takes the blood to the liver

**hepatic portal system** noun ANAT the network of blood vessels around the intestine that absorb food from the intestine lining into the blood

**hepatic vein** noun ANAT a vein that carries blood from the liver to the vena cava

**heptane** noun CHEM an organic hydrocarbon liquid of the alkane family, that is colourless and flammable. Formula: $C_7H_{16}$. (NOTE: It is obtained from petroleum and used as a solvent and anaesthetic and in octane rating measurement.)

**herb** noun **1.** a plant that is used to add flavour in cooking **2.** PHARM a plant that has medicinal properties **3.** BOT a plant that has no perennial stem above the ground during the winter period

**herb-** prefix BOT referring to plants or vegetation

**herbaceous** adjective BOT (*of plants*) without perennial stems above the ground

**herbage** noun AGRIC the green foodstuffs eaten by grazing animals

**herbal** adjective BOT referring to plants

**herbalism** noun PHARM the treatment of illnesses or disorders by the use of herbs or by medicines extracted from herbs

**herbalist** noun PHARM a person who treats illnesses or disorders by the use of herbs

**herbal remedy** noun PHARM a remedy made from plants, e.g. an infusion made from dried leaves or flowers in hot water

**herbarium** noun BOT a collection of preserved plant or fungal specimens, especially one that is used for scientific study and classification

**herbicide** noun AGRIC a chemical that kills plants, especially weeds

**herbivore** noun ZOOL an animal that feeds only on plants

**herbivorous** adjective ZOOL referring to an animal that feeds only on plants

**herd** noun ZOOL a group of herbivorous animals that live together ○ *a herd of wildebeest* (NOTE: The word **herd** is usually used with cattle; for sheep, goats, and birds such as hens or geese, the word to use is **flock**.) ■ *verb* **1.** AGRIC to tend a herd of animals **2.** to crowd animals together

**hereditary** *adjective* GENETICS transmitted from parents to offspring

**heredity** *noun* GENETICS the transmission of genes or characteristics from parents to offspring

**hermaphrodite** *noun* **1.** ZOOL an animal that has both male and female sexual organs **2.** BOT a plant whose flowers contain both male and female sexual organs

**hertz** *noun* PHYS, MEASURE the SI unit of frequency. Symbol **Hz** (NOTE: One hertz is equal to one cycle per second.)

**Hess's law** *noun* CHEM the law that states that the total quantity of heat absorbed or released during a chemical reaction is the same whether the reaction occurs in one or in several steps

**hetero-** *prefix* different. Compare **homo-**

**heterochromatin** *noun* GENETICS the material that appears in a cell nucleus as nodules between chromosomes but contains few genes

**heterochromosome** *noun* GENETICS a chromosome consisting mainly of heterochromatin, especially a sex chromosome

**heterogeneous** *adjective* BIOL having different characteristics or qualities (NOTE: Do not confuse with **heterogenous**.)

**heterogeneous network** *noun* COMPUT a computer network joining computers of many different types and makes

**heterogenesis** *noun* GENETICS the appearance of a mutation in a population

**heterogenic** *adjective* GENETICS having more than one variant form (**allele**) of a specific gene

**heterogenous** *adjective* BIOL coming from a different source (NOTE: Do not confuse with **heterogeneous**.)

**heterologous** *adjective* BIOL differing in structural features or origin

**heterolytic fission, heterolysis** *noun* CHEM the process of breaking a covalent bond in a compound to form two ions, one positive, one negative, of each of the elements

**heteromorphic** *adjective* differing in size or shape (NOTE: The X and Y sex chromosomes are heteromorphic.)

**heterophyte** *noun* BOT **1.** a plant that grows in a wide range of habitats **2.** a plant that lacks chlorophyll and is parasitic

**heteroploid** *adjective* GENETICS relating to an organism that has a chromosome number in a cell nucleus that is not an exact multiple of the basic chromosome number for that species

**heterosis** *noun* GENETICS an increase in size or rate of growth, fertility or resistance to disease found in offspring of a cross between organisms with different genotypes. Also called **hybrid vigour**

**heterotroph** *noun* BIOL an organism that requires carbon in organic form and cannot manufacture it (NOTE: Animals, fungi and some algae and bacteria are heterotrophs.)

**heterotrophic** *adjective* BIOL referring to a heterotroph

**heterotypic** *adjective* GENETICS referring to a form of cell nucleus division in which the new nuclei produced contain only half the number of chromosomes of the parent cell, characteristic of the first division of meiosis

**heterozygote** *noun* GENETICS an organism that has two dissimilar forms (**alleles**) of a gene and which may therefore produce offspring different from the parents and from each other for that characteristic

**heuristic** *adjective* COMPUT learning from past experiences ○ *A heuristic program learns from its previous actions and decisions.*

**hex** *abbreviation* hexadecimal notation

**hexachlorocyclohexane** *noun* AGRIC a white or yellow powder used as an insecticide. Formula: $C_6H_6Cl_6$. Also called **lindane**

**hexadecimal notation** *noun* MATHS a number system using base 16 and the digits 0–9 and A–F

**hexahydrate acid** *noun* CHEM same as **chloroplatinic acid**

**hex dump** *noun* COMPUT a display of a section of memory in hexadecimal form

**hex keypad** *noun* COMPUT a set of sixteen keys with all the figures needed to enter hexadecimal numbers

**Hf** *symbol* CHEM ELEM hafnium

**HF** *abbreviation* PHYS high frequency

**HFC** *abbreviation* CHEM hydrofluorocarbon

**HFS** *abbreviation* COMPUT hierarchical filing system

**Hg** *symbol* CHEM ELEM mercury

**hibernaculum** *noun* ZOOL a place such as a nest where an animal hibernates (NOTE: The plural is **hibernacula.**)

**hibernate** *verb* ZOOL (*of an animal*) to survive the cold winter months by a big reduction in metabolic rate and activity, and by using up stored body fat for food

COMMENT: During the cold weather, many small mammals and reptiles hibernate. Their blood temperature falls and their metabolism slows.

**hibernation** *noun* ZOOL a big reduction in metabolic rate and activity, and the using up of stored body fat to survive the cold winter months

**hickory** *noun* TREES a North American hardwood tree. Genus: *Carya*.

**hidden** *adjective* unable to be seen □ **a hidden defect in a program** a defect that was not seen when the computer program was tested

**hidden line removal** *noun* COMPUT the erasure of lines which should not be visible when looking at a two-dimensional image of a three-dimensional object

**hide** *noun* ZOOL 1. the skin of a large animal 2. a shelter where humans can stay hidden while watching birds or animals

**hierarchical** *adjective* COMPUT organised with the most important or highest-priority item at the top, then working down a tree structure

**hierarchical computer network** *noun* COMPUT a method of allocating control and processing functions in a network to the computers that are most suited to the task

**hierarchical database** *noun* COMPUT a database in which records can be related to each other in a defined structure

**hierarchical filing system** *noun* COMPUT a method used to store and organise files on a disk. Abbreviation **HFS**

**hierarchy** *noun* COMPUT the way in which objects or data are organised

**high** *adjective* 1. reaching far from ground level ○ *Altocumulus clouds form at higher levels than cumulus.* 2. of greater than average amount ○ *The sample gave a high reading of radioactivity.* ○ *The soil is red and high in aluminium and iron oxide.* 3. at the top of something ■ *noun* METEOROL an area of high pressure

**high-alumina cement** *noun* INDUST cement made of bauxite and limestone, used because it resists heat

**high-definition television** *noun* TECH a broadcast television standard that displays images at a different aspect ratio and with much better definition than existing television sets. Abbreviation **HDTV**

**high-density** *adjective* 1. PHYS having a large mass per unit of volume 2. ECOL having a lot of people or organisms living closely together ▶ abbreviation **HD**

**high-density polythene** *noun* INDUST very thick heavy-duty plastic. Abbreviation **HD polythene**

**high-density storage** *noun* COMPUT a very large number of bits stored per area of storage medium ○ *A hard disk is a high-density storage medium compared to paper tape.*

**high-end** *noun* ENG an expensive or high-performance device

**high-energy food** *noun* HEALTH food such as fats or carbohydrates which gives a lot of energy when broken down by the digestive system

**high-fibre diet** *noun* HEALTH a diet that contains a large amount of cereals, nuts, fruit and vegetables

**high fidelity** *noun* ACOUSTICS very good quality sound (NOTE: It normally refers to stereo sound recorded in 16 bits at a sample rate of 44.1 kHz.)

**high forest** *noun* EARTH SCI a forest made up of tall trees that block the light to the forest floor

**high frequency** *noun* PHYS a radio frequency ranging from 3 to 30 MHz or with a wavelength of 10–100 metres. Abbreviation **HF**

**high frequency band** *noun* TELECOM a radio communications range between 3 MHz and 30 MHz

**high-grade** *adjective* of very high quality

**high-grade ore** *noun* METALL ore that contains a large percentage of metal

**highland** EARTH SCI *noun* an area of high land or mountains. Opposite **lowland** ■ *adjective* referring to a hilly or mountainous area ○ *Highland vegetation is mainly grass, heather and herbs.*

**high latitudes** *plural noun* EARTH SCI the areas of Earth near the Poles

**high-level data link control** *noun* COMPUT an ISO/OSI standard that provides a data link layer protocol and defines how data is formatted before being transmitted over a synchronous network. Abbreviation **HLDLC**

**high-level inversion** *noun* METEOROL a situation where warm air lies above cold air relatively high above the ground

**high-level language** *noun* COMPUT a computer programming language that is easy to learn and allows the user to write programs using words and commands that are easy to understand and look like English words. Abbreviation **HLL** (NOTE: The program is then translated into machine code, with one HLL instruction often representing more than one machine code instruction.)

**high-level nuclear waste** *noun* ENVIRON same as **high-level waste**

**high-level radiation** *noun* PHYS radiation from a very radioactive substance

**high-level waste, high-level radioactive waste** *noun* ENVIRON waste that is hot and emits strong radiation. Also called **high-level nuclear waste**

COMMENT: High-level waste is potentially dangerous and needs special disposal techniques. It is sealed in special containers, sometimes in glass, and is sometimes disposed of by dumping at sea.

**highlight** COMPUT *noun* the treatment of characters or symbols to make them stand out from the rest of the text, often by using bold type ■ *verb* to make part of the text stand out from the rest ○ *The headings are highlighted in bold.*

**high memory** *noun* COMPUT the memory area between 640 kb and 1 Mb in a PC

**high order** *noun* MATHS a digit with the greatest weighting within a number

**high-performance** *adjective* **1.** designed to operate very efficiently **2.** of high quality or with a high specification ○ *high-performance equipment*

**high-pressure belt** *noun* METEOROL a long narrow area of high pressure

**high-priority program** *noun* COMPUT a program that is important or urgent and is processed before others

**high-quality** *adjective* of the very best quality ○ *The store specialises in high-quality imported items.*

**high-res** *adjective* COMPUT same as **high-resolution** (*informal*)

**high-resolution** *adjective* COMPUT having the ability to display or detect a very large number of pixels per unit area ○ *high-resolution graphics* Also called **hi-res, high-res**

**high-risk** *adjective* HEALTH having a strong likelihood of damage or injury ○ *high-risk occupations*

**high-spec** *adjective* COMPUT having a high specification (*informal*) ○ *high-spec cabling*

**high specification** *noun* ENG the quality of a high degree of accuracy and performance

**high-speed** *adjective* COMPUT operating faster than normal

**high-speed carry** *noun* COMPUT an operation when a carry into an adder results in a carry

**high-speed skip** *noun* COMPUT a rapid movement in a printer to miss the perforations in continuous stationery

**high-sulfur coal, high-sulphur coal** *noun* INDUST coal with a lot of sulfur in it, therefore producing more sulfur dioxide when it is burnt

**high-tech** *adjective* same as **high technology** (*informal*)

**high technology** *adjective* COMPUT technologically advanced

**high-tension** *adjective* INDUST (*of electricity cable*) carrying a high voltage

**high tide, high water** *noun* OCEANOG the point when the level of the sea is at its highest

**highway** *noun* a main public road

**high-yielding** *adjective* AGRIC producing a large crop ○ *They have started to grow high-yielding varieties of wheat.*

**hill** *noun* EARTH SCI an area of ground higher than the surrounding areas but not as high as a mountain

**hill farm** *noun* AGRIC a farm in mountainous country, with 95% or more of its land classified as rough grazing, mainly for breeding ewe flocks

**hillside** *noun* EARTH SCI the sloping side of a hill

**hindbrain** *noun* ANAT the rearmost of the three parts of the brain in an embryo. Compare **forebrain, midbrain**

**hinder** *verb* to make progress difficult for something ○ *Free flow of fuel may be hindered by a blockage in the fuel line.*

**hinge** *noun* a device that allows a door, flap or lid to open and close on a stationary frame ■ *verb* (*of a surface such as a door*) to move against a stationary frame

**hinged** *adjective* having a hinge to permit opening and closing ○ *a hinged panel*

**hinterland** *noun* EARTH SCI an area of land lying behind the shore of the sea or of a river

**hippocampus** *noun* ANAT a curved ridge in each cerebral hemisphere of the brain consisting of grey matter that functions in short-term memory and forms part of the limbic system (NOTE: The plural is **hippocampi**.)

**hi-res** *adjective* COMPUT same as **high-resolution** (*informal*)

**histamine** *noun* BIOCHEM a substance released from mast cells throughout the human body which stimulates tissues in various ways ○ *The presence of substances to which someone is allergic releases large amounts of histamine into the blood.* ◆ **antihistamine**

**histaminic** *adjective* BIOCHEM referring to histamine

**histo-** *prefix* BIOL biological tissue

**histochemistry** *noun* BIOCHEM the study of the chemical constituents of cells and tissues and also their function and distribution

**histogram** *noun* MATHS a graph on which values are represented as vertical or horizontal bars

**histology** *noun* BIOL the study of the anatomy of tissue cells and minute cellular structures, using a microscope after the cells have been stained

**histone** *noun* GENETICS a simple protein bound to DNA that is involved in the coiling of chromosomes (NOTE: There are five types, together constituting about half the mass of chromosomes.)

**history** *noun* **1.** the study of what happened in the past ○ *the history of science* **2.** a record of past events and experiences ○ *We don't know much about his medical history* ○ *the history of the discovery of DNA*

**hit** *noun* **1.** an impact or blow **2.** COMPUT a successful match or search of a database ○ *There was a hit after just a few seconds.* □ **a hit on the line** a short period of noise on a communications line, causing data corruption ■ *verb* COMPUT to press a key ○ *to save the text, hit ESCAPE S*

**HLDLC** *abbreviation* COMPUT high-level data link control

**HLL** *abbreviation* COMPUT high-level language

**HMI** *abbreviation* COMPUT human-machine interface

**hoar frost** *noun* METEOROL the frozen dew that forms on outside surfaces when the temperature falls below freezing point

**holandric** *adjective* GENETICS referring to genetic characteristics that are carried on the Y chromosome and are therefore inherited only by males. Compare **hologynic**

**Holarctic region** *noun* EARTH SCI a biogeographical region which includes the Nearctic region, i.e. North America, and the Palaearctic region, i.e. Europe, North Africa and North Asia

**hole** *noun* PHYS a vacancy in an energy band that is normally filled by an electron (NOTE: Such holes are mobile and help in the movement of electric current through a material.)

**holistic** *adjective* **1.** HEALTH involving all the patient's mental and family circumstances rather than just dealing with the illness **2.** dealing with a subject as a whole rather than looking at just one aspect

**hollow** *adjective* with nothing inside ○ *hollow plant stems* ■ *noun* a place which is lower than the rest of the surface ○ *Pour the liquid into the hollow.*

**holmium** *noun* CHEM ELEM a silvery-white metallic element of the lanthanide group of the periodic table (NOTE: The chemical symbol is **Ho**; the atomic number is **67** and the atomic weight is **164.26.**)

**holoenzyme** *noun* BIOCHEM a complete active enzyme, consisting of an apoenzyme and coenzyme

**hologram** *noun* OPTICS an imaginary three-dimensional image produced by the interference pattern when a part of a coherent light source, e.g. a laser, is reflected from an object and mixed with the main beam

**holography** *noun* OPTICS a method of producing a three-dimensional image by scanning an object with light from a laser

**hologynic** *adjective* GENETICS referring to genetic characteristics that are inherited only by females. Compare **holandric**

**holophytic** *adjective* BOT referring to organisms such as plants that can make complex organic molecules by photosynthesis

**holoplankton** *plural noun* MARINE BIOL organisms such as algae and diatoms which remain as plankton throughout their entire life cycle

**holozoic** *adjective* BIOL referring to organisms such as animals that feed on other organisms or organic matter

**home** *noun* **1.** ENVIRON a place where a person or animal lives **2.** an environment or habitat **3.** COMPUT the starting point or initial point

**home computer** *noun* COMPUT same as **personal computer**

**homeo-** *prefix* similar

**homeobox** *noun* GENETICS a set of nucleotides with a sequence of bases that is almost identical in all the genes that contain it

**homeostasis** *noun* **1.** the tendency of a system to resist change and maintain itself in a state of equilibrium **2.** BIOCHEM the process by which the functions and chemistry of a cell or organism are kept stable, even when external conditions vary greatly

**homeotherm** *noun* ZOOL another spelling of **homoiotherm**

**home page** *noun* COMPUT the opening page of a website ○ *The home page is formatted using HTML and stored in a file called index.html.*

**home range** *noun* ZOOL an area occupied by an animal during the day-to-day course of activity (NOTE: It is not to be confused with territory, which is a defended area and may be part or all of the home range.)

**homing** *noun* ZOOL an animal's return to a particular site which is used for sleeping or breeding

**hominoid** *adjective* BIOL referring to the primates including humans and apes. Superfamily: Hominoidea.

**homo-** *prefix* same. Compare **hetero-**

**homoeo-** *prefix* same as **homeo-**

**homogametic** *adjective* GENETICS referring to organisms that produce gametes with the same type of sex chromosome

**homogamy** *noun* BOT the maturation of a flower's male and female organs at the same time, so permitting self-fertilisation

**homogeneous** *adjective* evenly mixed or unvarying ○ *The atmosphere is not homogeneous and pressure, temperature and humidity can all change with height.* Also called **homogenous**

**homogeneous computer network** *noun* COMPUT a network made up of similar machines that are compatible or from the same manufacturer

**homogenous** *adjective* same as **homogeneous**

**homograft** *noun* BIOL a graft of tissue from one specimen to another of the same species

**homoiotherm, homoeotherm** *noun* ZOOL same as **endotherm**

**homologous** *adjective* BIOL **1.** having the same structural features **2.** having biological structures that share the same origin but with a different function, e.g. the wing of a bird and the fin of a fish

**homologous pair** *noun* GENETICS a pair of chromosomes in a diploid organism that are structurally similar and have the same arrangement of genes, although they may carry different alleles (NOTE: One member of each pair is inherited from each parent.)

**homologous series** *noun* CHEM a group of compounds, each with the same basic elements and similar atomic structure, in which each compound in the series differs from the next one by a fixed number of atoms

**homologue** *noun* BIOL a part or organ with the same origin in evolution as another but with a different function, e.g. a bird's wing in relation to the fin of a fish

**homolytic fission** *noun* CHEM the process of breaking a covalent bond in a compound to form two free radicals

**Homo sapiens** *noun* BIOL the species that consists of modern human beings and the only species of the genus with living individuals

**homosphere** *noun* EARTH SCI the zone of Earth's atmosphere, including the troposphere, the stratosphere and the mesosphere, where the composition of the atmosphere remains relatively constant

**homozygote** *noun* GENETICS an organism that has two identical forms (**alleles**) of a gene at the same place on two corresponding chromosomes

**homozygous** *adjective* GENETICS relating to a cell or organism that has two identical forms (**alleles**) of a gene

**hook** *noun* COMPUT a point in a program at which a programmer can insert test code or debugging code

**hookworm** *noun* ZOOL a parasitic worm in the intestine which holds onto the wall of the intestine with its teeth and lives on the blood and protein of the carrier

**hop** *noun* **1.** COMPUT the path taken by a packet of data as it moves from one server or router to another **2.** PLANTS a climbing plant that has long thin groups of green flowers which are used dried in brewing to add flavour to beer. Latin name: *Humulus lupulus*.

**horizon** *noun* **1.** the line where the sky and the ground appear to join **2.** GEOL a layer of soil which is of a different colour or texture from the rest

**horizontal** *adjective* lying flat or going from side to side, not up and down

**horizontal axis** *noun* MATHS a reference line used for horizontal coordinates on a graph ○ *The plot shows the effect of airspeed on lift with airspeed shown on the horizontal axis and lift on the vertical axis.* Also called **X-axis**

**horizontal-axis wind turbine** *noun* INDUST a wind turbine with two or three blades attached to a central hub that drives a generator and where the main shaft is parallel with the surface of the ground ○ *Horizontal-axis wind turbines are the most common form of wind turbine.*

**horizontal blanking period** *noun* COMPUT the time taken for the picture beam in a monitor to return to the start of the next line from the end of the previous line

**horizontal motion** *noun* a movement from side to side

**horizontal scan frequency** *noun* COMPUT the number of lines on a video display that are refreshed each second

**horizontal stabiliser** *noun* a device to provide longitudinal stability about the lateral axis of an aircraft

**hormonal** *adjective* BIOCHEM referring to hormones

**hormonal deficiency** *noun* BIOCHEM a lack of necessary hormones

**hormone** *noun* **1.** BIOCHEM a substance produced in animals in one part of the body which has a particular effect in another part of the body **2.** BOT a plant growth factor

**hornblende** *noun* MINERALS a dark green to black mineral consisting of the aluminium silicates of calcium, iron, magnesium and sodium

**horsepower** *noun* MEASURE a unit of power equal in the UK to 550 foot-pounds per second and in the USA to 745.7 watts. Abbreviation **h.p., HP** (NOTE: This obsolete unit is still used to measure the power output of car engines.)

**horticultural** *adjective* AGRIC referring to horticulture

**horticulture** *noun* AGRIC the growing of flowers, fruit and vegetables in gardens or glasshouses

**horticulturist** *noun* AGRIC a person who specialises in horticulture

**hose** *noun* a long flexible pipe usually made of fabric, plastic or rubber for pumping gases or liquids

**host** *noun* **1.** BIOL the plant or animal on which a parasite lives **2.** COMPUT same as **host computer** ■ *adjective* BIOL on which a parasite lives

**host adapter** *noun* COMPUT an adapter which connects to a host computer ○ *The cable to connect the scanner to the host adapter is included.*

**host address** *noun* COMPUT same as Internet address

**host computer** *noun* COMPUT **1.** the main controlling computer in a multi-user or distributed system **2.** a computer used to write and debug software for another computer, often using a cross-compiler **3.** a computer in a network that provides special services or programming languages to users

**hosting service provider** *noun* COMPUT same as **host service provider**

**host number** *noun* COMPUT same as Internet address

**host–parasite interaction** *noun* BIOL a relationship between a host and a parasite

**host plant** *noun* BOT the plant on which a parasite lives

**host service provider** *noun* COMPUT a company that provides connections to the Internet and storage space on its computers which can store the files for a user's website ○ *We rent storage space on this host service provider's server for our company website.* Also called **hosting service provider**

**hot** *adjective* **1.** having a high temperature **2.** dangerously radioactive (*informal*) **3.** ELEC electrically charged **4.** MED extremely infectious **5.** PHYS (*of an atom*) having a raised energy level

**hot chassis** *noun* COMPUT a metal framework or case around a computer that is connected to a voltage supply rather than being earthed

**hot desert** *noun* EARTH SCI a desert situated in the tropics, e.g. the Sahara Desert or the Arabian Desert. Also called **tropical desert**

**hot fix** *verb* COMPUT to detect and repair a fault such as a corrupt sector on a hard disk without affecting normal operations

**hot key** *noun* COMPUT a special key or key combination that starts a process or activates a program

**hot link** *noun* (*in a hypertext document*) a word or image that will display new information when a user clicks on it

**hot plugging** *noun* COMPUT a feature of a computer that allows a device or peripheral to be plugged in or connected while the computer is working. Also called **hot swapping**

**hot rock** *noun* rock with a high temperature beneath Earth's surface (NOTE: It can be used to create geothermal energy by pumping down cold water and making use of the rising hot water which the rocks have heated.)

**hotspot** *noun* **1.** COMPUT a special area on an image or display that does something when the cursor is moved onto it ○ *The image of the trumpet is a hotspot and will play a sound when you move the pointer over it.* **2.** ENVIRON a place where background radiation is particularly high

**hot spring** *noun* GEOG a stream of hot water running out of the ground continuously

**hot swapping** *noun* COMPUT same as **hot plugging**

**hotword** *noun* COMPUT a word within displayed text that does something when the cursor is moved onto it or it is selected ○ *Click on the hotword to see the image.*

**hour** *noun* a period of time which lasts sixty minutes ○ *It's a three-hour flight to Greece from London.*

**hours** *plural noun* MEASURE a particular time of day using the 24-hour clock ○ *The experiment started at 13:20 hours.*

**house** *noun* a building where a person lives ■ *verb* **1.** to contain or provide space for something ○ *The areas between the ribs in the wings are utilised to house fuel tanks.* **2.** to put a device in a case ○ *The magnetic tape is housed in a solid plastic case.*

**housefly** *noun* INSECTS a common fly living in houses, which can spread disease by laying its eggs in decaying meat and vegetables

**household** *noun* a group of people living together in a single home ■ *adjective* **1.** ENVIRON referring to or used in houses where people live ○ *household appliances such as fridges and TVs* **2.** familiar ○ *household knowledge*

**household refuse, household waste** *noun* ENVIRON same as **domestic refuse**

**housekeeping** *noun* COMPUT the tasks that have to be regularly carried out to maintain a computer system, e.g. checking backups or deleting unwanted files

**housing** *noun* **1.** a container ○ *The crankcase is the housing that encloses the various mechanical parts surrounding the crankshaft.* **2.** ENVIRON buildings where people live

**hover** *verb* to remain stationary relative to the ground while in the air ■ *noun* an act of remaining stationary relative to the ground while in the air ○ *During a hover, helicopter pilots must be able to coordinate movements of both hands and feet.*

**howler** *noun* **1.** a very bad and obvious mistake ○ *What a howler, no wonder your program won't work.* **2.** TELECOM a buzzer that indicates to a telephone exchange operator that a user's telephone handset is not on the receiver

**h.p., HP** *abbreviation* MEASURE horsepower

**Hs** *symbol* CHEM ELEM hassium

**HSB** *abbreviation* COMPUT hue, saturation, brightness

**HSI** *abbreviation* COMPUT hue, saturation, intensity

**HSL** *abbreviation* PHYS hue, saturation, level

**HST** *abbreviation* ASTRON Hubble Space Telescope

**HSV** *abbreviation* COMPUT hue, saturation and value

**HTML** *noun* COMPUT a series of special codes that define the typeface and style that should be used when displaying the text of a document and also allow hypertext links to other parts of the document or to other documents ○ *HTML is normally used to create documents for the World Wide Web.* Full form **hypertext markup language**

**HTTP** *noun* COMPUT a set of commands used by a browser to ask an Internet web server for information about a webpage. Full form **hypertext transfer protocol**

**HTTPd** *noun* COMPUT server software that sends webpage files to a client in response to a request from a user's web browser ○ *When you type a website address into your web browser, this sends a request to the HTTPd server software that replies with the HTML code of a formatted web page.* Full form **hypertext transfer protocol daemon**

**hub** *noun* COMPUT **1.** the central part of a disk, usually with a hole and ring which the disk drive grips to spin the disk **2.** the central ring or wiring cabinet where all circuits meet and form an electrical path for signals

**Hubble, Edwin P. (1889–1953)** ASTRON a US astronomer who revolutionised thinking about the large-scale structure of the universe by methodical study of the galaxies. He discovered that they are receding at a rate dependent on their distance from Earth, which led to the idea of the expansion of the universe. He also developed the now standard classification of galactic types.

**Hubble Classification** *noun* ASTRON a classification of the galaxies into elliptical, spiral and barred spiral types, which is used to describe all but the most unusual types of galaxy

COMMENT: Within these overall headings are subdivisions. The ellipticals are classed as E0 to E7, becoming steadily more elongated as the number increases. Spirals are classed as Sa, Sb or Sc, with the spirals less tightly wound for the later letters, and the same system is adopted for the barred spirals, which are classed as SBa, SBb and SBc. Type S0 indicates a regular ellipse apparently intermediate between the three categories. Galaxies that fall between the categories are sometimes classed as Sbc or some similar hybrid. It is important to note that the actual relation between the different types of galaxy may well be less neat than this family tree implies.

**Hubble Constant** *noun* ASTRON the number linking the rate of recession of the galaxies with their distance from Earth (NOTE: The value of the Hubble Constant is between 50 and 100 km/s of recession velocity per megaparsec of distance. Observation with the Hubble Space Telescope suggests a figure of about 80 km/s per megaparsec.)

**Hubble Diagram** *noun* ASTRON a graph showing the distance of galaxies against their velocity of recession from Earth (NOTE: The steepness of the graph gives the **Hubble Constant**.)

**Hubble Space Telescope** *noun* ASTRON a telescope mounted on a satellite orbiting Earth, launched in 1990. Abbreviation **HST**

COMMENT: The 12-tonne spacecraft has a telescope with a 2.4 m main mirror, which by being placed above Earth's atmosphere can be used to see objects as faint as the 31st magnitude. The HST's instruments include faint-object and wide-field cameras and photometers and spectrographs. It is used mainly to examine objects in deep space, but has also produced startling images of solar system objects such as Mars, and Jupiter during the 1994 impact of Comet Shoemaker Levy 9.

**hue** *noun* COMPUT the colour of an image or pixel

**hue, saturation, brightness** *noun* PHYS same as **hue, saturation, intensity**. abbreviation **HSB**

**hue, saturation, intensity** *noun* PHYS a method of defining a colour through its three properties: hue, colour defined by its wavelength; saturation, the purity of the colour and the amount of white. Abbreviation **HSI**

**hue, saturation, level** *noun* PHYS same as **hue, saturation, intensity**. abbreviation **HSL**

**Huffman code** *noun* COMPUT a data compression code in which frequent characters occupy less bit space than less frequent ones

**human** BIOL *adjective* referring to a man, woman or child. Also called **human being** ■ *noun* a man, woman or child ○ *Most animals are afraid of humans.*

**human anatomy** *noun* BIOL the study of the the structure, shape and functions of the human body

**human being** *noun* BIOL a man, woman or child

**human-caused** *adjective* ENVIRON referring to a disaster or event which has been brought about by human beings

**human-computer interface** *noun* COMPUT same as **human-machine interface**

**human ecology** *noun* ENVIRON the study of communities of people, the place which they occupy in the natural world and the ways in which they adapt to or change the environment

**Human Genome Project** *noun* GENETICS an international research initiative to sequence and identify all human genes and record their positions on chromosomes, officially completed in 2003

**human geography** *noun* ENVIRON the study of the distribution of human populations with reference to their geographical environment

**human-induced stress** *noun* ENVIRON stress in animals caused by interactions with humans

**humankind** *noun* all human beings considered as a whole

**human-machine interface** *noun* COMPUT a set of facilities provided to improve the interaction between a user and a computer system. Abbreviation **HMI**. Also called **human-computer interface**

**human nature** *noun* BIOL the general characteristics of behaviour shared by all human beings

**human physiology** *noun* PHYSIOL the study of the functions of the human body

**human race** *noun* BIOL same as **humankind**

**humate** *noun* CHEM a salt that is derived from humus

**humerus** *noun* ANAT the long bone of the forelimb in vertebrate animals

**humid** *adjective* METEOROL relating to air that contains moisture vapour ○ *Decomposition of organic matter is rapid in hot and humid conditions.*

**humidifier** *noun* INDUST a device for making dry air moist, e.g. in air conditioning or central heating systems

**humidify** *noun* to make something moist

**humidity** *noun* METEOROL a measurement of how much water vapour is contained in the air

**humification** *noun* BIOL the breaking down of rotting organic waste to form humus

**humify** *verb* BIOL to break down rotting organic waste to form humus

**humus** *noun* **1.** EARTH SCI the fibrous organic matter in soil, formed from decomposed plants and animal remains, which makes the soil dark and binds it together **2.** INDUST a dark organic residue left after sewage has been treated in sewage works

**hurricane** *noun* METEOROL a tropical storm in the Caribbean or Eastern Pacific Ocean with extremely strong winds

**hurricane force wind** *noun* METEOROL a wind blowing at force 12 on the Beaufort scale

**husbandry** *noun* AGRIC the process of looking after farm animals and crops ○

*a new system of intensive cattle husbandry*

**hybrid** *noun* BIOL a new form of plant or animal resulting from a cross between organisms that have different genotypes ○ *high-yielding maize hybrids* ■ *adjective* BIOL being the result of a cross between organisms that have different genotypes ■ *adjective, noun* made up of differing elements

**hybrid circuit** *noun* COMPUT the connection of a number of different electronic components such as integrated circuits, transistors, resistors and capacitors in a small package

**hybridisation, hybridization** *noun* GENETICS the production of hybrids

**hybridise, hybridize** *verb* GENETICS to produce a new form of plant or animal by combining the genes of two organisms that have different genotypes

**hybrid vigour** *noun* GENETICS same as **heterosis**

**hydr-** *prefix* same as **hydro-** (NOTE: used before vowels)

**hydrate** *noun* CHEM a chemical compound, frequently a salt, containing bound water molecules that can usually be expelled by heating, without decomposition of the compound

**hydrated** *adjective* CHEM referring to a chemical compound in which water is bound

**hydraulic** *adjective* MECH ENG referring to a system or device that uses fluids such as oil to transmit a force from one place to another using pipes ○ *a hydraulic pump*

**hydraulic gradient** *noun* EARTH SCI the direction of ground water flow due to changes in the depth of the water table

**hydraulic pressure** *noun* MECH ENG the pressure exerted by hydraulic fluid

**hydraulic tubing** *noun* MECH ENG a system of tubes or thin pipes connecting the main components of a hydraulic system

**hydrazine** *noun* CHEM a highly reactive fuming colourless liquid that is strongly alkaline. Formula: $H_2N.NH_2$. (NOTE: It is used as rocket fuel.)

**hydric** *adjective* ECOL referring to an environment that is wet. Compare **xeric**

**hydro-** *prefix* water

**hydrobromic acid** *noun* CHEM a colourless solution of hydrogen bromide in water. Formula: HBr.

**hydrocarbon** *noun* CHEM a compound formed of hydrogen and carbon

COMMENT: Hydrocarbons are found in fossil fuels such as coal, oil, petroleum and natural gas. They form a large part of exhaust fumes from cars and contribute to the formation of smog. When released into the air from burning coal or oil they react in the sunlight with nitrogen dioxide to form ozone. Hydrocarbons are divided into aliphatic hydrocarbons (paraffins, acetylenes and olefins) and aromatic hydrocarbons (benzenes).

**hydrochloric acid** *noun* CHEM a colourless strong acid solution consisting of hydrogen chloride gas dissolved in water. Formula: HCl. (NOTE: It is used in industrial and laboratory processes.)

**hydrocortisone** *noun* BIOCHEM same as **cortisol**

**hydrocyanic acid** *noun* CHEM a colourless solution of hydrogen cyanide in water, which is highly toxic and smells of almonds. Formula: HCN.

**hydroelectric** *adjective* INDUST relating to hydroelectricity ○ *The valley was flooded to construct the hydroelectric scheme.*

**hydroelectric energy** *noun* INDUST electricity produced by using a flow of water to drive the turbines

**hydroelectricity** *noun* INDUST electricity produced by water power

**hydroelectric power** *noun* INDUST electricity produced by using a flow of water to drive the turbines. Also called **hydropower**

**hydroelectric power station** *noun* INDUST a power station that produces electricity using a flow of water to drive the turbines

**hydrofluoric acid** *noun* CHEM a solution of hydrogen fluoride in water that is extremely corrosive and attacks glass and stone. Formula: HF.

**hydrofluorocarbon** *noun* CHEM a chemical that is emitted as a by-product of industrial processes and contributes to global warming, although it does not damage the ozone layer. Abbreviation **HFC**

**hydrogen** *noun* CHEM ELEM a gaseous chemical element that combines with oxygen to form water, with other elements to form acids, and is present in all animal tissue (NOTE: Hydrogen is also used as a moderator in some nuclear reactors. The chemical symbol is **H**; the atomic number is **1** and the atomic weight is **1.01**.)

**hydrogen bomb** noun MIL an explosive weapon of mass destruction in which huge amounts of energy are suddenly released by the fusion of hydrogen nuclei

**hydrogen bond** noun CHEM a weak electrostatic interaction between molecules in which hydrogen atoms are bound to electronegative atoms such as oxygen or nitrogen in which the hydrogen atom is attracted to the electronegative atom (NOTE: The attraction between water molecules due to hydrogen bonds accounts for the relatively high boiling point of water.)

**hydrogen bromide** noun CHEM a colourless or brown fuming gas with a distinctive unpleasant smell. Formula: HBr.

**hydrogen carbonate** noun CHEM a salt of carbonic acid in which one hydrogen atom has been replaced, usually by a metal. Also called **bicarbonate**

**hydrogen chloride** noun CHEM a colourless fuming corrosive gas with an unpleasant choking smell. Formula: HCl. (NOTE: It is used in PVC manufacture and chemical synthesis.)

**hydrogen cyanide** noun CHEM a liquid or gas with a smell of almonds which kills very rapidly when drunk or inhaled. Formula: HCN.

**hydrogen electrode** noun PHYS an electrode created by adsorbing hydrogen onto a platinum electrode, which is then set to zero potential and used to compare other results. Also called **hydrogen half cell**

**hydrogen fluoride** noun CHEM a colourless poisonous strong-smelling gas. Formula: HF.

**hydrogen fuel** noun INDUST liquid hydrogen, proposed as an alternative fuel for use in cars and aircraft

**hydrogen half cell** noun PHYS same as **hydrogen electrode**

**hydrogen ion** noun CHEM a positively charged hydrogen atom that is formed by the removal of an electron and is present in solutions of acids in water (NOTE: The concentration of hydrogen ions in solution is measured using the pH scale.)

**hydrogen peroxide** noun CHEM a colourless viscous liquid that readily decomposes to give off oxygen, used as a bleach, antiseptic and rocket fuel component. Formula: $H_2O_2$.

**hydrogen spectrum** noun PHYS the light spectrum produced when a strong electric current is passed through hydrogen gas

**hydrogen sulfate, hydrogen sulphate** noun CHEM a salt formed when one hydrogen atom is removed from sulfuric acid by reaction with a metal, metal salt or organic group. Also called **bisulfate**

**hydrogen sulfide, hydrogen sulphide** noun CHEM a colourless gas with an unpleasant smell, produced during industrial processes, which corrodes metal and is toxic to animals. Formula: $H_2S$.

**hydrograph** noun EARTH SCI a graph showing the level or flow of water in a river or lake

**hydrography** noun EARTH SCI the science of measuring and charting rivers, lakes and seas

**hydrological** adjective EARTH SCI referring to hydrology

**hydrology** noun EARTH SCI the study of water, its composition and properties and in particular the place of water in the environment

**hydrolysis** noun CHEM a chemical reaction in which a substance reacts with water, causing decomposition of both the original substance and the water and the production of two or more other compounds (NOTE: The conversion of starch to glucose is an example of hydrolysis.)

**hydrometer** noun PHYS an instrument that measures the density of a liquid

**hydromorphic soil** noun EARTH SCI waterlogged soil found in bogs and marshes

**hydrophilic** adjective CHEM displaying a tendency to dissolve in, absorb or mix easily with water

**hydrophobic** adjective CHEM not soluble in, mixing easily with or able to absorb water

**hydrophyte** *noun* BOT a plant that lives in water or in marshy conditions

**hydroponics** *noun* AGRIC the practice of growing plants in a nutrient liquid with or without sand, vermiculite or other granular material

**hydropower** *noun* INDUST same as **hydroelectric power**

**hydrosere** *noun* BOT a series of plant communities growing in water or in wet conditions

**hydrosol** *noun* CHEM a solvent of water

**hydrosphere** *noun* EARTH SCI all the Earth's water in the sea, the atmosphere and on land

**hydrostatic** *adjective* EARTH SCI referring to water that is not moving

**hydrostatic pressure** *noun* EARTH SCI the pressure of water that is not moving

**hydrothermal** *adjective* EARTH SCI referring to water and heat under the Earth's crust

**hydrothermal formation** *noun* EARTH SCI a rock formation where water pockets or porous water-filled rock come into contact with magma, so creating steam

**hydrothermal vent** *noun* EARTH SCI a place on the ocean floor where hot water and gas flow out of the Earth's crust

**hydrotropism** *noun* PLANTS a movement of a root or other plant part towards or away from moisture

**hydroxide** *noun* CHEM a metallic compound containing inorganic OH⁻ groups giving it basic properties

**hydroxonium ion** *noun* CHEM a positive ion formed by the addition of a hydrogen ion or proton to a water molecule, usually in acid solution. Formula: $H_3O^+$.

**hydroxyproline** *noun* BIOCHEM an amino acid present in some proteins, especially in collagen

**hygiene** *noun* HEALTH **1.** the state or practice of being clean and keeping healthy conditions **2.** the science of health

**hygienic** *adjective* HEALTH **1.** clean ○ *Don't touch the food with dirty hands – it isn't hygienic.* **2.** producing healthy conditions

**hygro-** *prefix* CHEM wet

**hygrometer** *noun* METEOROL an instrument used for the measurement of humidity ○ *The most common type of hygrometer is the wet and dry bulb thermometer arrangement.*

**hygroscope** *noun* CHEM a device or substance which gives an indication of humidity, often by changing colour

**hygroscopic** *adjective* CHEM referring to a substance which absorbs moisture from the atmosphere

**hyp-** *prefix* same as **hypo-** (NOTE: used before vowels)

**hypalgesia** *noun* MED a low sensitivity to pain

**hyper-** *prefix* over, above, higher or too much. Opposite **hyp-, hypo-**

**hyperaccumulate** *verb* ENVIRON to take up and retain an unusually high concentration of metal from the environment

**hyperactive** *adjective* BIOL being unusually active and restless

**hyperfine structure** *noun* PHYS the splitting of lines in a spectrum on an even smaller scale than fine structure

**hyperinsulinism** *noun* MED the reaction of a diabetic to an excessive dose of insulin or to hypoglycaemia

**hyperlink** *noun* COMPUT a word, image or button in a webpage or multimedia title that moves the user to another page when clicked

**hypermetropia** *noun* OPHTHALMOL same as **hyperopia**

**hyperon** *noun* PHYS a baryon with a large mass and a short life (NOTE: Hyperons may be unstable.)

**hyperopia** *noun* OPHTHALMOL the ability to see distant objects more clearly than close objects. Also called **hypermetropia, long-sightedness**

**hyperparasite** *noun* BIOL a parasite which is a parasite on other parasites

**hyperploid** *adjective* GENETICS referring to an organism that has an extra chromosome or section of a chromosome (NOTE: An extra copy or segment of chromosome 21 occurs in people with Down's syndrome.)

**hypersensitive** *adjective* MED reacting more strongly than usual to sources of stress such as an antigen or disease agent

**hypersensitivity** *noun* BIOL a condition where an organism reacts unusually strongly to a source of stress such as an antigen or disease agent

**hypertension** *noun* MED a condition where the pressure of the blood in the arteries is higher than 160/95 for adults without heart disease or diabetes

**hypertext** *noun* COMPUT a multimedia system of organising information in which some words in a document link to other documents and display the text when the word is selected ○ *Hypertext allows you to click once on the word 'computer' and jump to a page where it will tell you what a computer is.* ■ *adjective* referring to hypertext ○ *a hypertext page*

**hypertext markup language** *noun* COMPUT full form of **HTML**

**hypertext transfer protocol** *noun* COMPUT full form of **HTTP**

**hypertext transfer protocol daemon** *noun* COMPUT full form of **HTTPd**

**hypertonic** *adjective* CHEM referring to a solution with a higher osmotic pressure than that of another solution that it is compared to

**hypha** *noun* FUNGI a long thin structure containing cytoplasm that is part of the network forming the vegetative body of a fungus (NOTE: The plural is **hyphae**.)

**hypo-** *prefix* under, less, too little or too small. Opposite **hyper-**

**hypochlorite** *noun* CHEM a salt of hypochlorous acid

**hypochlorous acid** *noun* CHEM a weak greenish-yellow acid that is unstable and occurs only in solution or as salt. Formula: HOCl.

**hypodermic injection** *noun* MED an injection of a liquid beneath the skin. Also called **subcutaneous injection**

**hypodermic syringe** *noun* MED an instrument for injecting liquids under the skin

**hypogeal** *adjective* ZOOL occurring or developing below ground. Compare **epigeal**

**hypoglossal nerve** *noun* ANAT the twelfth cranial nerve which governs the muscles of the tongue

**hypoglycaemia** *noun* MED a low concentration of glucose in the blood

**hypoglycaemic** *adjective* MED suffering from hypoglycaemia

**hypolimnion** *noun* EARTH SCI the lowest layer of water in a lake, which is cold and stationary and contains less oxygen than the epilimnion. ♦ **epilimnion, metalimnion**

**hypophysis** *noun* ANAT same as **pituitary gland**

**hypoploid** *adjective* GENETICS referring to an organism that has a chromosome number that is slightly less than the diploid number

**hypotension** *noun* MED a condition where the pressure of the blood is unusually low

**hypotenuse** *noun* MATHS the longest side of a right-angled triangle located opposite the right angle

**hypothalamus** *noun* ANAT the part of the brain above the pituitary gland, which controls the production of hormones by the pituitary gland and regulates important bodily functions such as hunger, thirst and sleep

**hypothermia** *noun* MED a reduction in body temperature below 35° C

**hypothesis** *noun* a suggestion that something is true, though without proof (NOTE: The plural is **hypotheses**.)

**hypotonic** *adjective* CHEM, BIOL referring to a solution with lower osmotic pressure than that of another solution that it is compared to

**hysteresis** *noun* PHYS a delay in the response of an object to changes in the forces acting on it, especially magnetic forces

**Hz** *abbreviation* MEASURE hertz

# I

**I** *symbol* CHEM ELEM iodine

**IAB** *abbreviation* COMPUT **1.** Internet Activities Board **2.** Internet Architecture Board

**IAM** *abbreviation* COMPUT intermediate access memory

**IANA** *abbreviation* COMPUT Internet Assigned Numbers Authority

**IAR** *abbreviation* COMPUT instruction address register

**IAS¹** *noun* COMPUT a high-speed main memory area in a computer system. Full form **immediate access store**

**IAS²** *abbreviation* AEROSP indicated airspeed

**-iasis** *suffix* MED disease caused by a particular agent

**I-beam** *noun* COMPUT a cursor shaped like the letter 'I' used in a graphical user interface to edit text or indicate text operations

**IBG** *abbreviation* COMPUT interblock gap

**IC** *abbreviation* COMPUT integrated circuit

**icand** *noun* COMPUT same as **multiplicand**

**ice** *noun* METEOROL frozen water

COMMENT: Ice is formed when water freezes at 0° C. Ice is less dense than water and so floats. Because the ice in the polar ice caps is very thick and has been formed over many thousands of years, scientists are able to discover information about the climate over a very long period of time by examining core samples obtained by drilling into the ice.

**Ice Age** *noun* GEOL a long period of time when Earth's temperature was cool and large areas of the surface were covered with ice

**iceberg** *noun* OCEANOG a very large block of ice floating in the sea, formed when ice breaks away from an Arctic glacier or ice sheet

**ice cap** *noun* EARTH SCI a large area of thick ice covering the north and south polar regions

**ice crystal** *noun* METEOROL a type of precipitation composed of crystals in the form of needles, plates or columns

**ice floe** *noun* OCEANOG a sheet of ice floating in the sea

**ice formation** *noun* EARTH SCI the natural production and development of ice

**ice point** *noun* PHYS the freezing point of water

**ice sheet** *noun* EARTH SCI a large area of thick ice covering the north or south polar regions

**ice shelf** *noun* EARTH SCI an outer margin of an ice cap or ice sheet that extends into and over the sea

**ice storm** *noun* METEOROL freezing rain that creates a sheet of ice on structures such as trees and electric wires

**-icide** *suffix* BIOL substance which destroys a particular organism

**ICMP** *noun* COMPUT an extension to the Internet Protocol that provides error detection and control messages ○ *The Internet command 'ping' uses ICMP to test if a named node is working correctly.* Full form **Internet control message protocol**

**icon** *noun* COMPUT a graphic symbol or small picture displayed on screen, used in an interactive computer system to provide an easy way of identifying a function ○ *The icon for the graphics program is a small picture of an artist's palette.*

**ICSH** *abbreviation* BIOL interstitial-cell-stimulating-hormone

**IDE** *abbreviation* COMPUT integrated device electronics ○ *IDE drives are fitted to most home PCs.*

**ideal** *adjective* referring to a situation that is as good as can be expected or the best possible

**ideal gas** *noun* CHEM a theoretical concept of a gas that obeys the gas laws exactly at all temperatures and pressures

**ideal solution** *noun* CHEM a solution described by the equation $p = p_0 X$ where p is the vapour pressure of the solvent with a substance dissolved in it, X is the mole fraction of the solvent and $p_0$ is the vapour pressure of the pure solvent

**identical** *adjective* exactly the same

**identical twins** *noun* BIOL same as **monozygotic twins**

**identification** *noun* 1. the action or process of establishing the identity of somebody or something 2. the action or process of understanding or establishing the nature of something

**identification character** *noun* COMPUT a single character sent to a host computer to establish the identity and location of a remote computer or terminal

**identification division** *noun* COMPUT a section of a COBOL program source code in which the identifiers and formats for data and variables to be used within the program are declared

**identifier** *noun* COMPUT a grouped number/letter code by which a device, block or file can be recognized

**identify** *verb* 1. to recognize somebody or something as different from somebody or something else ○ *The team has identified a new species.* 2. to be the means of recognising somebody or something ○ *The pelvic structure identified the skeleton as female.* 3. to understand the nature of something ○ *We soon identified the problem.*

**identity** *noun* something that distinguishes who someone or what something is

**identity burst** *noun* COMPUT a pattern of bits before the first block of data on a magnetic tape that identifies the tape format used

**identity gate, identity element** *noun* COMPUT a logical gate that provides a single output that is true if the inputs are both the same

**idiogram** *noun* GENETICS a photograph or diagram showing chromosomes arranged in their homologous

pairs according to the standard numbering system for that organism

**idle** *noun* 1. not being used, but ready and waiting to be used 2. MECH ENG the state of an engine when it is running but not delivering power to move the vehicle or aircraft ■ *verb* MECH ENG (*of an engine*) to turn over slowly without providing enough power to move a vehicle or aircraft ○ *After starting a piston engine from cold, allow it to idle for a short time before opening the throttle wide.*

**idle character** *noun* COMPUT a symbol or code that means 'do nothing' or a code which is transmitted when there is no data available for transmission at that time

**idle cut-off** *noun* AVIAT a position on the mixture control of a light aircraft that allows the engine to be shut down without leaving a combustible fuel/air mixture in the engine

**idling speed, idle rpm** *noun* MECH ENG the speed at which a piston engine turns when it is not running fast enough to move the vehicle or aircraft, i.e. on a light aircraft when the throttle is closed ○ *After start-up, the engine accelerates up to idling speed.* ○ *Before the engine is stopped, it should normally be allowed to run for a short period at idling speed to ensure gradual cooling.*

**IDP** *abbreviation* COMPUT integrated data processing

**IEE** *abbreviation* ELEC ENG Institution of Electrical Engineers

**IEEE** *abbreviation US* ELEC ENG Institute of Electrical and Electronic Engineers

**IEEE-488** *noun* COMPUT an interfacing standard as laid down by the US Institute of Electrical and Electronic Engineers, in which only data and handshaking signals are involved (NOTE: It is mainly used in laboratories to connect computers to measuring equipment.)

**IEEE-802.2** *noun* COMPUT a standard defining data links used with 802.3, 802.4 and 802.5

**IEEE-802.3** *noun* COMPUT a standard defining the Ethernet network system

**IEEE-802.4** *noun* COMPUT a standard defining Token Bus

**IEEE-802.5** *noun* COMPUT a standard defining IBM Token-Ring network system in which access is using a token passed around a ring network

**IEEE bus** *noun* COMPUT an interface that conforms to IEEE standards

**IEN** *abbreviation* COMPUT Internet experiment note

**IESG** *abbreviation* COMPUT Internet Engineering Steering Group

**IETF** *abbreviation* COMPUT Internet Engineering Task Force

**IFF** *noun* COMPUT a standard for compressed files stored on a CD-I. Full form **international file format**

**IF statement** *noun* COMPUT a computer programming statement, meaning do an action IF a condition is true (NOTE: It is usually followed by THEN.)

**IF-THEN-ELSE** *noun* COMPUT a high-level programming language statement, meaning IF something cannot be done, THEN do this, or ELSE do that

**Ig** *abbreviation* BIOCHEM immunoglobulin

**IGMP** *noun* COMPUT a standard that helps manage how data is transferred during an IP Multicast operation in which one server computer sends each packet of data to several destinations at the same time. Full form **Internet group management protocol** (NOTE: The IGMP standard is defined in RFC1112.)

**igneous** *adjective* EARTH SCI referring to rock such as basalt or granite formed from molten lava

COMMENT: Igneous rocks are formed from lava which has either broken through Earth's crust, as in a volcanic eruption, or has entered the crust from below and formed a layer inside the crust.

**igneous intrusion** *noun* EARTH SCI molten rock that solidified before reaching Earth's surface and remains as a layer among other rocks

**igneous rock** *noun* EARTH SCI a rock such as basalt or granite formed from molten lava

**ignite** *verb* to begin to burn or cause something to burn ○ *The spark plug ignites the fuel/air mixture.* ○ *The air/fuel mixture ignites.*

**igniter** *noun* MECH ENG a device for starting gas turbine engines ○ *An electric spark from the igniter plug starts combustion.*

**ignition** *noun* **1.** PHYS the starting of burning of a substance ○ *Satisfactory ignition depends on the quality of the fuel.* **2.** MECH ENG the moment when a spark from the spark plug in an internal combustion engine causes the fuel/air mixture to burn ○ *Ignition should occur just before top-dead-centre.* **3.** ELEC ENG an electrical system, usually powered by a battery or magneto, that provides the spark to ignite the fuel mixture in an internal-combustion engine ○ *Ignition problems are a source of many engine failures.* **4.** MECH ENG a switch that activates the ignition system of a vehicle or aircraft

**ignition key** *noun* MECH ENG a key used to switch on the ignition of a vehicle or aircraft

**ignition lock** *noun* MECH ENG a key-operated switch for activating the ignition circuit of an aircraft or a vehicle

**ignition temperature** *noun* PHYS the temperature at which a substance will start to burn

**IGP** *abbreviation* COMPUT interior gateway protocol

**IH** *abbreviation* COMPUT interrupt handler

**IIL** *abbreviation* COMPUT integrated injection logic

**IKBS** *abbreviation* COMPUT intelligent knowledge-based system

**ileocaecal valve** *noun* ANAT a valve at the end of the ileum, which allows food to pass from the ileum into the caecum

**ileocolic artery** *noun* ANAT a branch of the superior mesenteric artery

**ileum** *noun* ANAT the third and last part of the small intestine, between the jejunum and the beginning of the large intestine

**ilium** *noun* ANAT the wide flat upper portion of the pelvis that is connected to the base of the spine (NOTE: At birth it is a separate bone, later becoming fused with two other bones in the formation of the hip bone.)

**illegal** *adjective* **1.** not legal **2.** COMPUT against the rules of programming syntax

**illegal instruction** *noun* COMPUT an instruction code not within the repertoire of a language

**illuminance** *noun* PHYS the visible radiation that reaches a unit of surface area in a unit of time

**illuminate** *verb* 1. to give light to an otherwise dark area ○ *A flare illuminates the ground below it.* 2. to light a lamp

**illumination** *noun* 1. the provision of light 2. PHYS the extent to which a surface is illuminated

**illustrate** *verb* 1. to explain something clearly, often by using pictures ○ *Contour charts illustrate the horizontal distribution of height above mean sea level.* 2. to show something by being an example of it ○ *The accident illustrates the need for improved safety procedures in this area.*

**illustration** *noun* 1. a picture which explains something ○ *The illustration on page 23 shows a cross section of a typical gas-turbine engine.* 2. an example ○ *The mechanics of the föhn wind provide a good illustration of the adiabatic process in action.*

**illuviation** *noun* EARTH SCI a deposition of particles and chemicals leached out from the topsoil into the subsoil

**IMA** *abbreviation* COMPUT Interactive Multimedia Association

**image** *noun* 1. a picture, photograph, design or other piece of artwork 2. COMPUT an exact duplicate of an area of memory

**image buffer** *noun* COMPUT an area of memory that is used to build up an image before it is transferred to screen

**image compression** *noun* COMPUT the process of compressing the data that forms an image

**image converter** *noun* PHYS an optical-electronic device that turns an image formed by invisible radiation into an image that can be seen

**image degradation** *noun* ELEC loss of picture contrast and quality due to signal distortion or bad copying of a video signal

**image editing** *noun* COMPUT the altering or adjusting of an image using a paint package or special image editing program

**image editor** *noun* COMPUT a piece of software that allows a user to edit, change or create a bit-map image

**image enhancement** *noun* COMPUT the adjustment of parts of an image using special image processing software to change the brightness or sharpness of an image

**image intensifier** *noun* ASTRON an opto-electronic device using materials that emit large numbers of photons in response to the arrival of a single photon (NOTE: This allows image intensifiers to produce increased light fluxes from weak sources under observation.)

**imagemap** *noun* COMPUT a graphic image that has areas of the image defined as hyperlink hotspots that link to another webpage

**image processing** *noun* COMPUT the analysis of information contained in an image, usually by electronic means, by using a computer which provides the analysis or by recognition of objects in the image

**image processing software** *noun* COMPUT software that allows a user to adjust contrast, colour or brightness levels or apply special effects to a bit-map image

**image processor** *noun* COMPUT an electronic or computer system used for image processing, and to extract information from the image

**image scanner** *noun* COMPUT an input device which converts documents, drawings or photographs into a digitized, machine-readable form

**image sensor** *noun* PHYS a photoelectric device that produces a signal related to the amount of light falling on it

**image stability** *noun* COMPUT the ability of a display screen to provide a flicker-free picture

**image storage space** *noun* COMPUT a region of memory in which a digitized image is stored

**image table** *noun* COMPUT either of two bit-mapped tables used to control input and output devices or processes

**imaginary** *adjective* not real ○ *The equator is an imaginary line around the Earth.*

**imaginary number** *noun* MATHS a complex number written as $a + ib$, where $i$ is the square root of minus one, and $b$ is not equal to zero

**imago** *noun* INSECTS an insect in the final adult stage after metamorphosis

**IMAP** *noun* COMPUT a standard that defines how electronic mail messages can be accessed and read over a network. Full form **Internet message access protocol**

COMMENT: The IMAP standard, currently at version four, provides an alternative to the common POP3 standard. It stores a user's messages on a shared server, for example at an ISP, and allows a user to connect from any computer and read, send or manage messages. In contrast, the POP3 protocol downloads all messages from a shared server onto the user's computer. This makes it difficult for a user to access messages from a different computer – for example when travelling. Regardless of whether IMAP or POP3 is used to read messages, the SMTP protocol is normally used to send messages.

**imbalance** *noun* a situation where the balance between a set of things is unequal ○ *Lack of vitamins A and E creates hormonal imbalances in farm animals.*

**imino group** *noun* CHEM a group of compounds containing the basic structure -NH- where the nitrogen atom is not joined to any other hydrogen atoms or carbonyl groups

**immature** *adjective* BIOL still developing

**immediate** *adjective* **1.** COMPUT happening at once **2.** nearby ○ *The immediate area surrounding the Earth is known as the atmosphere.*

**immediate access store** *noun* COMPUT full form of **IAS**

**immediate address** *noun* COMPUT same as **zero-level address**

**immediate mode** *noun* COMPUT a mode in which a computer executes an instruction as soon as it is entered

**immediate processing** *noun* COMPUT the processing of data when it appears, rather than waiting for a synchronising clock pulse or time. Compare **batch processing**

**immerse** *verb* to cover something completely in liquid ○ *The booster pumps mounted on the base of the fuel tank are fully immersed.*

**immigrant species** *noun* ECOL a species that migrates into or is introduced into an ecosystem, deliberately or accidentally, by humans

**immigration** *noun* ECOL the movement of an organism into a new area. Opposite **emigration**

**imminent** *adjective* which will happen in a very short time

**immune** *adjective* IMMUNOL protected against an infection or disease ○ *This barley strain is not immune to the virus.*

**immune body** *noun* IMMUNOL a substance which protects against an infection or disease

**immune response** *noun* IMMUNOL the way in which an organism defends itself against pathogenic organisms and other foreign material

**immune system** *noun* IMMUNOL the arrangement of organs, cells and substances that protects the body against an infection or against an allergic disease (NOTE: The spleen, lymph tissue and white blood cells are part of the immune system.)

**immunisation** *noun* IMMUNOL the production of immunity to a specific disease in a person, either by injecting an antiserum or by giving the body the disease in such a small dose that the body does not develop the disease, but produces antibodies to counteract it

**immunise** *verb* IMMUNOL to make a person immune to a specific infection

**immunity** *noun* IMMUNOL **1.** the natural or acquired ability of an animal to resist a microorganism ○ *The vaccine gives immunity to tuberculosis.* **2.** the ability of a plant to resist disease through a protective covering on leaves, through the formation of protoplasts or through the development of inactive forms of viruses

**immunodeficiency** *noun* IMMUNOL lack of immunity to a disease

**immunogenetics** *noun* GENETICS, IMMUNOL the study of the genetic basis of the immune system (NOTE: This study is especially important in organ transplantation, where a close genetic match of tissue improves the chances of success.)

**immunoglobulin** *noun* IMMUNOL a protein produced by specific white blood cells that acts as an antibody in immune responses. Abbreviation **Ig** (NOTE: Immunoglobulins occur in blood serum and other body fluids, and are grouped into five classes with differing structures and immune functions. They are IgG, IgA, IgD, IgE and IgM.)

**immunology** *noun* MED the study of immunity and immunisation

**impact** *noun* **1.** a collision or the striking of one object against another **2.** an effect or impression made on something or someone

**impact assessment** *noun* ENVIRON an evaluation of the effect upon the environment of an activity such as a large construction programme or draining of marshes. Also called **impact study**

**impacted area** *noun* ENVIRON an area of land affected or concerned by something such as a large-scale building project

**impact printer** *noun* COMPUT a printer that prints text and symbols by striking an inked ribbon onto paper with a metal character

**impact resistance** *noun* INDUST the ability of a material to withstand impact without breaking or shattering ○ *Kevlar 49 has high impact resistance.*

**impact study** *noun* ENVIRON same as **impact assessment**

**impair** *verb* to cause something to become less effective ○ *An incorrect grade of fuel impairs engine performance.*

**impaired vision** *noun* OPHTHALMOL eyesight which is not fully clear

**impairment** *noun* **1.** the inability of something to function effectively ○ *hearing impairment* **2.** the process of damaging something so that it does not function effectively

**impart** *verb* **1.** to give a particular characteristic or quality ○ *A rotating propeller imparts rearward motion to a mass of air.* **2.** to communicate something

**impedance** *noun* ELEC total electrical resistance to current flow in an alternating current circuit ○ *Impedance will vary with changes in frequency.*

COMMENT: Network cables need to have the correct impedance for the type of network card installed. 10BaseT unshielded twisted-pair cable normally has an impedance between 100–105 ohms, while 10Base2 coaxial cable has an impedance of 50 ohms.

**impede** *verb* to obstruct or hinder progress

**impeller** *noun* MECH ENG a rotor used to force a fluid in a particular direction ○ *A turbocharger consists of a turbine wheel and an impeller fitted on the same shaft.*

**imperial gallon** *noun* MEASURE a unit of volume in the British Imperial System, usually used in liquid measure and equal to 4.546 litres ○ *The system delivers fuel at the rate of 100 to 2000 gallons per hour.*

**Imperial System** *noun* MEASURE a nonmetric system of weights and measures used in the United Kingdom, incuding the foot, pound and gallon

**imperial unit** *noun* a unit in a system measuring weight, distance and volume in pounds, yards and gallons and their subunits, now generally replaced by SI units

**impermeable** *adjective* **1.** PHYS referring to a substance which does not allow a liquid or gas to pass through ○ *rocks which are impermeable to water* **2.** referring to a membrane which allows a liquid to pass through, but not solid particles suspended in the liquid

**impervious** *adjective* PHYS not allowing a liquid to enter

**implantation** *noun* BIOL the process in which an embryo becomes attached to the lining of the womb in higher mammals or to the yolk in other vertebrates

**implement** *verb* to carry out or put a plan into action

**implementation** *noun* **1.** the process of carrying out a plan **2.** COMPUT a version of something that works ○ *The latest implementation of the software runs much faster.*

**implication** *noun* **1.** a suggestion rather than a direct statement ○ *There was an implication that the method was unsound.* **2.** the effect that one thing has on another ○ *The recent cuts in funding carry serious implications for research.* **3.** COMPUT a logical operation that uses an IF-THEN structure by which if A is true and if B is true this implies that the AND function of A and B will be true

**implicit reference** *noun* **1.** something that is suggested rather than stated directly **2.** COMPUT a reference to an object that does not give its exact page location, but assumes that the object is on the current page or is currently visible

**implied addressing** *noun* COMPUT an assembler instruction that operates on only one register that is preset at manufacture ○ *Implied addressing for the accumulator is used in the instruction LDA,16.*

**implosion** *noun* PHYS the sudden and violent inward collapse of a hollow structure that occurs when the pressure outside is greater than that inside

**import** *verb* 1. to bring goods into a country to resell 2. to introduce new things from elsewhere 3. COMPUT to bring something in from outside a computer system ○ *You can import images from the CAD package into the DTP program.* 4. COMPUT to convert a file stored in one format to the default format used by a program ○ *Select import if you want to open a TIFF graphics file.*

**importance** *noun* strong effect or influence ○ *Upper winds are of great importance in meteorology.* (NOTE: The expressions of **fundamental importance, of great importance, of prime importance, of utmost importance, of vital importance** all mean **very important**.)

**important** *adjective* having a major effect ○ *an important decision* ○ *a discovery with important consequences*

**impose** *verb* to introduce something difficult or restricting ○ *Restrictions have been imposed on field trials.* ○ *The trimmer is used to ease the loads imposed on the flying controls during flight.*

**impoundment** *noun* ENG a body of water or sludge confined by a dam, dyke, floodgate or other barrier

**impoverish** *verb* to reduce the quality or fertility of something ○ *If impoverished soil is left fallow for some years, nutrients may build up in the soil again.*

**impoverishment** *noun* a reduction in quality or fertility ○ *Overexploitation led to the impoverishment of the soil.*

**impregnate** *verb* 1. to fill something with a substance by passing it inside through the outer surface ○ *Fruits on sale may be impregnated with pesticides even if they have been washed.* ○ *They impregnated the wooden posts with creosote.* 2. ZOOL to fertilize a female, by introducing male spermatozoa into the

female's body so that they link with the female's ova

**imprinting** *noun* ZOOL the very early learning in an animal's social development in which strong patterns of attraction to members of its own species are developed, especially to parents

**improve** *verb* to make something better or become better ○ *Turbochargers improve aircraft performance.*

**improvement** *noun* the act or an instance of something becoming or being made better ○ *the improvement of crop varieties by selection* ○ *There is still room for improvement in performance.* ○ *We need to achieve improvements in efficiency.* ○ *An improvement in weather conditions allowed the flight to depart.*

**impulse** *noun* 1. ELEC a voltage pulse which lasts a very short time ○ *A magneto is designed to produce electrical impulses one after another at precise intervals, so that each separate impulse can be used to provide a spark at a spark plug.* 2. PHYS a force of short duration

**impulse magneto** *noun* ELEC a magneto with a mechanism to give a sudden rotation and thus produce a strong spark

**impulse turbine** *noun* ENG a turbine where jets of water are directed at bucket-shaped blades which catch the water

**impulsive** *adjective* 1. done suddenly 2. COMPUT lasting a very short time 3. propelling or having the power to propel

**impulsive noise** *noun* TELECOM interference on a signal caused by short periods of noise

**impure** *adjective* CHEM not pure

**impurity** *noun* CHEM a foreign substance present at a low concentration in a another substance ○ *a filter which removes impurities from drinking water*

**In** *symbol* CHEM ELEM indium

**in.** *abbreviation* MEASURE inch

**inability** *noun* the lack of ability to do something ○ *An inability of the engine to accelerate may be an indication of serious mechanical problems.*

**in accordance with** *preposition* in a way that follows rules, instructions or laws ○ *Fuels must be used in accordance with instructions.*

**inaccurate** *adjective* not correct ○ *He entered an inaccurate password.*

**inactivate** *verb* to make something inactive ○ *Biopesticides are easily inactivated in sunlight.*

**inactive** *adjective* **1.** not doing anything **2.** (*of a system*) not switched on, not responding or not being used ○ *At the time of the accident the radar was inactive.* **3.** COMPUT (*of a volcano*) not erupting or likely to erupt, though not necessarily extinct **4.** CHEM (*of a chemical*) not reacting with other substances **5.** MED (*of a disease*) not producing symptoms **6.** BIOL biologically inert

**inactive window** *noun* COMPUT a window that is still displayed, but not currently being used

**inactivity** *noun* the state of not being active

**inadvertent** *adjective* not intended ○ *A safety mechanism prevents inadvertent retraction of the undercarriage while the aircraft is on the ground.*

**in alignment** *adverb, adjective* correctly aligned

**in ascending order** *adverb, adjective* in order of number or rank with the smallest or less important at the bottom and the largest or more important at the top

**in-band signalling** *noun* COMPUT data transmission in which the signal carrying the data is within the bandwidth of the cable or transmission media

**inbound** *adverb, adjective* moving towards a destination

**inbred** *adjective* GENETICS resulting from inbreeding

**inbreed** *verb* GENETICS to cross or mate closely related individuals with each other over several generations

**inbreeding** *noun* GENETICS the process of mating or crossing between closely related individuals, leading to a reduction in variation. Compare **outbreeding** (NOTE: Inbreeding as a result of self-fertilisation occurs naturally in many plants. In humans, congenital defects may occur when parents are closely related.)

**inbreeding depression** *noun* GENETICS a reduction in variation and vigour arising in an outbreeding population that is repeatedly inbred

**inbuilt** *adjective* **1.** which is a basic or naturally occurring part of something ○ *an inbuilt instinct for survival* ○ *This software has inbuilt error correction.* **2.** fitted inside or provided as part of something

**incandescent lamp** *noun* INDUST the most common form of light in the home, usually consisting of a glass bulb containing a wire filament that glows when electricity is passed through it ○ *Incandescent lamps are the least efficient of all electrical lighting systems.*

**incapacity** *noun* **1.** an inability to do what is needed **2.** not having the necessary power to do something

**incentive** *noun* something which encourages someone to do something

**incentive-based regulation** *noun* ENVIRON the use of rules to affect the economic behaviour of companies and households to achieve environmental goals ○ *Emission taxes are a form of incentive-based regulation.*

**inch** *noun* a British Imperial System unit of length, also used in the USA, equal to 25.4 millimetres or 2.54 centimetres or 1/12 of a foot. Abbreviation **in.** (NOTE: The plural is **inches**.)

**inches-per-second** *noun* COMPUT a measurement of the speed of tape past the read/write heads. Abbreviation **ips**

**incidence** *noun* the frequency of occurrence of something ○ *The incidence of structural failure has decreased with the introduction of modern construction materials and techniques.*

**incidence rate** *noun* MED the number of new cases of a disease during a given period, per thousand of population

**incident** *noun* an event or happening which interrupts normal procedure □ **without incident** without any problems occurring ○ *The research review passed without incident.*

**incinerate** *verb* ENVIRON to burn waste

**incineration** *noun* ENVIRON the burning of waste ○ *Uncontrolled incineration can contribute to atmospheric pollution.* ○ *Controlled incineration of waste is one of the most effective methods of disposal.*

**incineration ash** *noun* ENVIRON a powder left after a substance has been burnt

**incineration facility, incineration plant** *noun* INDUST an establishment where waste is burnt

**incinerator** *noun* INDUST a device which burns waste

**incipient** *adjective* in the early stages of development

**incipient lethal level** *noun* ENVIRON the level of toxic substances at which 50% of affected organisms will die

**in-circuit emulator** *noun* ELEC a circuit that emulates a device or integrated circuit and is inserted into a new or faulty circuit to test if it is working correctly ○ *This in-circuit emulator is used to test the floppy disk controller by emulating a disk drive.*

**incisor** *noun* DENT a flat sharp-edged tooth in the front of the mouth for cutting and tearing food

**inclination** *noun* a slope or slant from the horizontal or vertical

**incline** *verb* to slope or slant from the horizontal or vertical ■ *noun* a slope or slant

**include** *verb* 1. to have something as a part ○ *Solid particles in the atmosphere include dust, sand, volcanic ash and atmospheric pollution.* ○ *A fuel system includes tanks, fuel lines, fuel pumps, fuel filters and a carburettor or fuel injection system.* 2. to add as a part with others ○ *Please include full bibliographical details in your report.*

**inclusion** *noun* 1. the state of having or an act of adding something as a part ○ *the inclusion of checks at each stage* 2. COMPUT a logical operation that uses an IF-THEN structure so that if A is true and if B is true this implies that the AND function of A and B will be true

**inclusive** *adjective* taking in the extremes in addition to the part in between ○ *The migration takes from February to June inclusive.*

**inclusive fitness** *noun* BIOL the sum of an organism's Darwinian fitness with the fitness of its relatives

**incoming** *adjective* referring to signals such as radio waves or solar radiation being received ○ *incoming transmissions* ○ *an incoming signal*

**incoming message** *noun* COMPUT a message received in a computer

**incoming traffic** *noun* COMPUT the amount of data or messages received

**incompatibility** *noun* the state of being incompatible

**incompatible** *adjective* having basic differences that prevent effective joint working ○ *Our ideas were incompatible with their outline plans.*

**incomplete dominance** *noun* GENETICS a condition that occurs when neither of a pair of alleles is dominant

**incorporate** *verb* to include something ○ *Some types of outflow valve incorporate safety valves.*

**incorrect** *adjective* not correct ○ *If the positioning is incorrect, a warning horn will sound.*

**incorrectly** *adverb* not correctly or with mistakes ○ *The data was incorrectly keyboarded.*

**increase** *noun* the act or an instance of becoming greater or more ○ *Decreasing engine rpm results in an increase in the rate of descent.* Opposite **reduction** ■ *verb* to become greater or more or make something greater or more ○ *As you increase in height, the countryside below you appears to flatten out.* ○ *Efforts are being made to increase productivity.* Opposite **reduce** ▶ opposite (all senses) **decrease**

**increment** *noun* 1. an addition of a set number, usually one, to a register, often for counting purposes ○ *An increment is added to the counter each time a pulse is detected.* 2. the value of the number added to a register ○ *Increase the increment to three.* ■ *verb* 1. to add something or to increase a number ○ *The counter is incremented each time an instruction is executed.* 2. to move forward to the next location 3. to move a document or card forward to its next preset location for printing or reading

**incremental backup** *noun* COMPUT a backup procedure that only backs up the files which have changed since the last backup

**incubate** *verb* 1. ZOOL to hatch eggs either by a sitting bird or by artificial means in an incubator 2. MED (*of a disease caused by microorganisms*) to develop until symptoms appear 3. MICROBIOL to culture microorganisms at a temperature that promotes their growth

**incubation** *noun* 1. ZOOL the hatching of eggs either by a sitting bird or by artificial means in an incubator **2.** MICROBIOL the growing of bacteria

**incubation period** noun MED the time during which a virus or bacterium develops in the body after contamination or infection, before the appearance of the symptoms of the disease

**incubator** noun MICROBIOL, MED, AGRIC a container that keeps a constant temperature and controls other environmental conditions (NOTE: Incubators are used for allowing premature babies to grow, hen's eggs to hatch, or microorganisms to develop.)

**incur** verb to experience something unpleasant as a result of an action ○ incur disapproval ○ incur a fine (NOTE: **incurring – incurred**)

**indefinite** adjective **1.** without limits **2.** not exact ○ an indefinite number of sources **3.** unclear ○ indefinite plans □ **for an indefinite period of time** for a period of time which may have no end

**indent** COMPUT, PRINTING noun a space or series of spaces from the left margin, when starting a line of text ■ verb to start a line of text with a space in from the left margin ○ The first line of the paragraph is indented two spaces.

**indentation** noun **1.** a hollow in the surface of something **2.** a gap in the edge of something **3.** COMPUT, PRINTING the leaving of a space at the beginning of a line of text

**independent** adjective free from the influence or effects of other people or things ○ Airspeed is independent of wind and is the same regardless whether the aircraft is flying upwind, downwind or at any angle to the wind.

**independent assortment** noun GENETICS a principle stating that during meiosis the two variant forms (**alleles**) of a gene are distributed to the gametes independently of the distribution of alleles of other genes, although alleles located on the same chromosome are often inherited together

**independently** adverb without being controlled or connected ○ In spooling, the printer is acting independently of the keyboard.

**independent power system** noun ELEC a power generation system that is separate from the mains grid

**independent system** noun a system that can operate by itself

**independent variable** noun a condition that is deliberately manipulated by an experimenter to test response

**index** noun **1.** an alphabetical list of references to page numbers found at the end of a book or long document **2.** a list of terms classified into groups or put in alphabetical order **3.** COMPUT an address to be used that is the result of value added to a start location **4.** a series of guide marks along the edge of a piece of film or a strip of microfilm ■ verb to put marks against items, so that they will be selected and sorted to form an index

**indexed address** noun COMPUT the address of the location to be accessed, which is found in an index register

**indexed instruction** noun COMPUT an instruction that contains an origin and offset that are added to provide the location to be accessed

**indexed sequential access method** noun COMPUT a data retrieval method using a list containing the address of each stored record, where the list is searched and the record retrieved from the address in the list. Abbreviation **ISAM**

**indexed sequential storage** noun COMPUT a method of storing records in a consecutive order, but in such a way that they can be accessed rapidly

**indexing** noun **1.** COMPUT the use of indexed addressing in software or a computer **2.** COMPUT the process of building and sorting a list of records **3.** the process of making an index for a document or book

**index key** noun COMPUT one field that is used to index a record

**index register** noun COMPUT a computer address register that is added to a reference address to provide the location to be accessed. Abbreviation **IR**

**indicate** verb **1.** to show something ○ A lamp on the instrument panel will indicate when the pump is operating. ○ The needle indicated zero. **2.** to point to something **3.** to serve as a sign or symptom of something ○ Black smoke from the exhaust may indicate a rich mixture or worn piston rings.

**indicated airspeed** noun AEROSP the airspeed shown on the cockpit or flight-deck instrument. Abbreviation **IAS**

**indication** noun 1. the act of showing something ○ *Indication of altitude is given on the altimeter.* 2. a sign ○ *A drop in engine rpm is an indication of ice forming in the carburettor.*

**indicator** noun 1. something which shows the state of a process, usually a light or buzzer 2. CHEM a substance which shows that another substance is present ○ *Lichens act as indicators for atmospheric pollution.* 3. BIOL an organism which shows the presence of something in its environment

**indicator chart** noun COMPUT a graphical representation of the location and use of indicator flags within a program

**indicator flag** noun COMPUT a register or single bit that indicates the state of the processor and its registers, e.g. a carry or overflow

**indicator light** noun a light used to warn or indicate the condition of equipment

**indicator species** noun ENVIRON a species which is very sensitive to changes in the environment, which can warn that environmental changes are taking place

**indigenous** adjective ECOL native to a place ○ *There are six indigenous species of monkey on the island.* ○ *Oaks are indigenous to the British Isles.*

**indigo** noun PLANTS a tropical plant of the pea family which is a source of blue dye. Genus: *Indigofera*.

**indirect address** noun COMPUT same as **relative address**

**indirect addressing** noun COMPUT a way of addressing data in which the first instruction refers to an address which contains a second address

**indium** noun CHEM ELEM a soft silvery metal, used in alloys, transistors and electroplating (NOTE: The chemical symbol is **In**; the atomic number is **49** and the atomic weight is **114.82**.)

**individual** adjective existing as a separate thing ○ *The hydraulic braking system consists of a master cylinder with individual brake cylinders at each wheel.* ○ *The individual workstations are all linked to the mainframe.* ■ noun BIOL a single human being or other organism considered as one rather than as a member of a larger group

**induce** verb 1. to cause something to happen ○ *Unequal deposits on moving parts can induce severe vibration, especially on propellers and helicopter rotors.* ○ *Doctors had to induce the birth.* 2. ELEC to generate an electrical current in a coil of wire by electromagnetic effects

**induced drag** noun AEROSP the part of total drag created by lift

COMMENT: Induced drag is created when high-pressure air below a wing rotates around the tip to the low-pressure area above and increases as airspeed decreases and angle of attack increases. The other basic type of drag is parasite drag.

**induced failure** noun the failure of a device due to external effects

**induced interference** noun ELEC electrical noise on a signal due to induced signals from nearby electromagnetic sources

**inducer** noun 1. BIOL, BIOCHEM a substance which changes the way in which an enzyme acts 2. GENETICS a substance which activates a structural gene within a cell

**inductance** noun ELEC a measure of the ability of a conductor to bring a voltage into itself when carrying an alternating current, e.g. during short times when the circuit is switched on or off ○ *At low frequencies, the rate of collapse of the magnetic field will be slow and the inductance will be low.*

**induction** noun 1. MECH ENG the process by which the fuel/air mixture is drawn into the cylinders of an internal combustion engine ○ *The four strokes of the engine are induction, compression, combustion and exhaust.* 2. ELEC the generation of an electrical current due to electromagnetic effects from a nearby source ○ *A transformer is a static device that changes the amplitude or phase of an alternating voltage or current by electro-magnetic induction.* 3. BIOL the process of changing the way in which an enzyme acts

**induction coil** noun ELEC ENG a transformer that produces an intermittent high-voltage current from a low-voltage source by means of several wire windings generally around a soft iron core

**induction heating** noun ELEC a process by which the temperature of a metal is increased by an alternating magnetic field which induces an electric current within it

**induction motor** *noun* ELEC ENG an electric motor in which interactions between alternating currents in its windings create a varying magnetic field and induce a rotor to turn

**inductive** *adjective* ELEC referring to the production of electrical current in a conductor by a change of magnetic field ○ *One side effect of low frequency in an inductive circuit is that excess heat may be produced.*

**inductive reasoning** *noun* the drawing of a general conclusion based on a limited set of observations. Compare **deductive reasoning**

**inductor** *noun* ELEC an electrical component consisting of a coil of wire used to introduce inductance effects into a circuit by storing energy in its magnetic field

**industrial** *adjective* INDUST referring to industries or factories

**industrial dereliction** *noun* ENVIRON an ugly and neglected state of the landscape and environment damaged by industrial processes

**industrial disease** *noun* MED a disease which is caused by the type of work done by a worker, e.g. by dust produced or chemicals used in a factory

**industrial effluent** *noun* ENVIRON liquid industrial waste. Also called **industrial sewage**

**industrialisation, industrialization** *noun* INDUST the process of developing industry in a country

**industrial melanism** *noun* BIOL a phenomenon where forms of some animals such as butterflies and moths that are darker in colour become more common in industrial areas, allowing them to match the trees and leaves that are covered with soot

**industrial sewage** *noun* ENVIRON same as **industrial effluent**

**industrial waste** *noun* ENVIRON waste from industrial processes

**industry** *noun* INDUST all factories, companies or processes involved in the manufacturing of products

**Industry Standard Architecture** *noun* COMPUT a standard used for the 16-bit expansion bus in an IBM PC or compatible. Abbreviation **ISA**

**inequality operator** *noun* COMPUT a symbol used to indicate that two variables or quantities are not equal ○ *The C programming language uses the symbol '!=' as its inequality operator.*

**inequivalence** *noun* COMPUT a logical function whose output is true if the inputs are not the same, otherwise the output is false

**inert** *adjective* CHEM referring to a chemical substance or gas that does not react with other chemicals

**inert gas** *noun* CHEM helium, neon, argon, krypton or xenon ○ *Inert gases, dust, smoke, salt, volcanic ash, oxygen and nitrogen together constitute 99% of the atmosphere.* Also called **noble gas**

**inertia** *noun* PHYS the tendency of a body at rest to stay at rest or of a moving body to continue moving in a straight line unless acted on by an outside force

**infect** *verb* **1.** MICROBIOL (*of an organism*) to enter a host organism and cause disease ○ *The new strain has infected many people and the disease is spreading fast.* ○ *All these plants have been infected by a virus.* **2.** MICROBIOL to contaminate something with a microorganism that causes disease **3.** COMPUT (*of a computer virus*) to enter a computer and cause problems in normal working

**infected computer** *noun* COMPUT a computer that carries a virus program

**infection** *noun* MED **1.** the process of a microorganism entering a host organism and causing disease ○ *As a carrier he was spreading infection to other people in the office.* **2.** a disease caused by a microorganism ○ *She is susceptible to minor infections.*

**infectious** *adjective* MED referring to a disease which is caused by microorganisms and can be transmitted to other individuals by direct means ○ *This strain of flu is highly infectious.* Compare **contagious**

**infectious virus hepatitis** *noun* MED hepatitis transmitted by a carrier through food or drink

**infective** *adjective* MED referring to a disease caused by a microorganism, which can be caught from another person but which cannot always be directly transmitted

**infective enteritis** *noun* MED enteritis caused by bacteria

**inference** *noun* **1.** a deduction of results from data according to specific rules **2.** COMPUT a method of deducing a result about confidential information concerning a specific individual by using various data related to groups of people

**inference control** *noun* COMPUT the process of determining which information may be released without disclosing personal information about a specific individual

**inference engine, inference machine** *noun* COMPUT a set of rules used in an expert system to deduce goals or results from data

**inferential** *adjective* obtained by deduction ○ *inferential results*

**inferior** *adjective* **1.** of lower quality **2.** ASTRON between Earth and the Sun (NOTE: Mercury and Venus are designated as inferior planets.)

**inferior figure** *noun* MATHS, CHEM (*in mathematical and chemical formulae*) one of the smaller numbers or characters that are printed slightly below normal characters (NOTE: It is used with figures and letters: $CO_2$.)

**inferior gluteal artery** *noun* ANAT an artery supplying the buttocks

**infertile** *adjective* **1.** BOT not able to bear fruit **2.** ZOOL not able to produce young **3.** AGRIC (*of soil*) not able to produce good crops

COMMENT: An infertile soil is one which is deficient in plant nutrients. The fertility of a soil at any one time is partly due to its natural makeup, and partly to its condition, which is largely dependent on its management in recent times. Application of fertilisers can raise soil fertility and bad management can decrease it.

**infertility** *noun* ZOOL the inability to reproduce or have offspring

**infest** *verb* BIOL (*of parasites*) to be present somewhere in large numbers ○ *Pine forests have been infested with beetles.* ○ *Infested plants should be dug up and burnt.* ○ *The child's hair was infested with lice.*

**infestation** *noun* BIOL the presence of large numbers of parasites ○ *The crop showed serious infestation with greenfly.* ○ *The condition is caused by an infestation of lice.*

**infiltration** *noun* ENVIRON the passing of water into the soil or into a drainage system

**infiltration basin** *noun* EARTH SCI a depression in the ground where infiltration occurs

**infiltration capacity** *noun* EARTH SCI the maximum rate at which water is absorbed by soil

**infiltration water** *noun* ENVIRON water which passes into the soil or into a drainage system

**infinite** *adjective* with no end

**infinite loop** *noun* COMPUT same as **endless loop**

**infinitesimal** *adjective* MATHS with a value very close to but greater than zero

**infinity** *noun* **1.** MATHS a very large quantity **2.** OPTICS the distance of an object from a viewer where beams of light from the object would be seen to be parallel, i.e. very far away

**infix notation** *noun* COMPUT a method of computer programming syntax where operators are embedded inside operands, e.g. $C - D$ or $X + Y$. Compare **postfix notation**

**inflammable** *adjective* easily set on fire ○ *Petrol is an inflammable liquid.* Opposite **nonflammable** (NOTE: **Flammable** and **inflammable** mean the same thing. To avoid confusion, it is recommended to use **flammable**.)

**inflammation** *noun* MED a reaction of the body to injury or infection characterised by swelling, redness, heat and pain

**inflate** *verb* to blow air into something and thereby increase its size ○ *A sharp pull on the cord will discharge the gas bottle and inflate the life jacket.* Opposite **deflate**

**inflation** *noun* the act of blowing air into something such as a balloon or a tyre and so increasing its size ○ *Tyre inflation pressures should be maintained within 4% limits.*

**inflorescence** *noun* BOT a flower or group of small flowers, together with the stem

**inflow** *noun* the action of flowing in ○ *an inflow of effluent into a river*

**influence** *noun* a power which affects people or things ■ *verb* to have an effect on something or someone ○ *Day length influences plant growth.*

**influent** *noun* **1.** EARTH SCI a stream or river flowing into a larger river **2.** ECOL an organism which has an important effect on the balance of its community

**inform** *verb* **1.** to tell somebody something **2.** to influence something ○ *The feedback will inform our planning.*

**informatics** *noun* COMPUT the science and study of ways and means of information processing and transmission

**information** *noun* **1.** knowledge presented to a person in a form that can be understood **2.** COMPUT data that have been processed or arranged to provide facts which have a meaning

**information bearer channel** *noun* COMPUT a communications channel that is able to carry control and message data, usually at a higher rate than a data-only channel

**information content** *noun* COMPUT a measurement of the amount of information conveyed by the transmission of a symbol or character, often measured in shannons

**information flow control** *noun* COMPUT a regulation of access to specific information

**information input** *noun* COMPUT information received from an input device

**information line** *noun* COMPUT a line running across the screen which gives the user information about the program being executed or the file being edited

**information management system** *noun* COMPUT a computer program that allows information to be easily stored, retrieved, searched and updated

**information network** *noun* COMPUT a number of databases linked together, usually by telephone lines and modems, allowing a large amount of data to be accessed by a wider group of users

**information output** *noun* COMPUT a display of information on an output device

**information processing** *noun* COMPUT the process of organizing, processing and extracting information from data

**information processor** *noun* COMPUT a machine that processes a received signal, according to a program, using stored information, and provides an output (NOTE: This is an example of a computer that is not dealing with mathematical functions.)

**information provider** *noun* COMPUT a company or user who provides an information source for use in a videotext system, e.g. a company providing weather information or stock market reports. Abbreviation **IP**

**information rate** *noun* COMPUT the amount of information content per character multiplied by the number of characters transmitted per second

**information retrieval** *noun* COMPUT the location of quantities of data stored in a database and production of useful information from the data. Abbreviation **IR**

**information storage** *noun* COMPUT the storage of data in a form which allows it to be processed at a later date

**information storage and retrieval** *noun* COMPUT the techniques involved in storing information and retrieving data from a store. Abbreviation **ISR**

**information structure** *noun* COMPUT same as **data structure**

**information system** *noun* COMPUT a computer system which provides information according to a user's requests

**information technology** *noun* COMPUT the technology involved in acquiring, storing, processing and distributing information by electronic means. Abbreviation **IT**

**information theory** *noun* MATHS the formulae and mathematics concerned with data transmission equipment and signals

**information transfer channel** *noun* COMPUT a connection between a data transmitter and a receiver

**infra-** *prefix* below or beneath

**infrared, infra-red** *adjective* PHYS referring to the range of invisible radiation wavelengths from about 0.7 micrometres to 1 millimetre

**infrared astronomy** *noun* ASTRON the study of infrared radiation emitted by astronomical objects (NOTE: Infrared sources include cool gas giants and the galactic centre.)

**infrared photography** *noun* PHOTOGRAPHY photography using an infrared camera, which shows up heat sources and so can be used to take pictures at night

**infrared radiation** noun PHYS electromagnetic radiation outside the visible spectrum, with wavelengths in the range 0.7 micrometres to 1 millimetre

**infrared rays** plural noun the long invisible rays below the visible red end of the colour spectrum, that form part of the warming radiation which Earth receives from the Sun

**infrasound** noun PHYS sound at frequencies below 20 Hz (NOTE: Humans cannot hear infrasound but they can feel it as vibration. Elephants use it for communication.)

**infrastructure** noun 1. the basic framework of a system or organisation 2. GEOG the basic facilities and systems of a country or city, e.g. roads, pipelines, electricity and telecommunications networks, schools or hospitals

**infrequent** adjective not happening often ○ In northern Europe, thunderstorms are infrequent in winter time.

**ingest** verb PHYSIOL to take in or absorb food

**ingestion** noun PHYSIOL the process of taking in or absorbing food

**inhabit** verb ENVIRON to live in a place

**inhabitant** noun ECOL a plant or animal which lives in a place

**inhalation** noun PHYSIOL the act of breathing in. Compare **exhalation**

**inhale** verb PHYSIOL to breathe in ○ He inhaled some toxic gas fumes and was rushed to hospital. Compare **exhale**

**inherent** adjective existing as a basic or fundamental characteristic ○ A boiling point of 100° C is an inherent characteristic of water.

**inherent addressing** noun COMPUT an instruction that contains all the data required for the address to be accessed with no further operation

**inherit** verb 1. GENETICS to receive a genetically controlled characteristic from a parent ○ Flower colour is inherited. ○ He inherited haemophilia. 2. COMPUT (in object-oriented programming) to acquire the characteristics of another class or data type

**inheritance** noun 1. GENETICS the transmission of genetically controlled characteristics from one generation to the next 2. COMPUT the passing on of the characteristics of one class or data type to another, called its descendant

**inherited** adjective 1. GENETICS relating to a genetically controlled characteristic passed on from parent to offspring 2. COMPUT relating to passing on characteristics of a class or data to another derived class or type of data

**inhibit** verb to prevent or limit the effect of something ○ Cloud cover inhibits cooling of the Earth's surface at night.

**inhibiting input** noun COMPUT one input of a gate which blocks the output signal

**inhibition** noun 1. the prevention or limitation of the effect of something ○ Fuel contains chemicals for the inhibition of fungal growth. 2. CHEM the reduction in the rate of chemical reaction due to the presence of an inhibitor substance

**inhibitor** noun 1. a device or substance which prevents or limits the effect of something 2. CHEM a substance that slows down a reaction

**initial** adjective being or happening at the beginning ■ noun COMPUT the first letter of a word, especially of a name

**initialisation, initialization** noun COMPUT the process of initialising ○ Initialisation is often carried out without the user knowing.

**initialise** verb COMPUT to set values, parameters or control lines to their initial values, to allow a program or process to be started

**initiate** verb to cause something to start

**initiation** noun the process of causing something to start ○ the initiation of emergency procedures

**inject** verb 1. ENG to force or drive a fluid into something ○ An accelerator pump, operated by the movement of the throttle lever, injects fuel into the choke tube. 2. MED to inject a liquid into the body using a syringe 3. to introduce something new and stimulating

**injection** noun 1. ENG the forcing of fluid into something ○ Power output can be boosted to a value over 100% maximum power, by the injection of a water methanol mixture at the compressor inlet or at the combustion chamber inlet. 2. MED the act of injecting a liquid into the body using a syringe 3. MED a preventative measure against a particular disease ○ a TB injection 4. the introduction of something new and stimulating

**injector** *noun* ENG a device that will force or drive a fluid into something

**ink cartridge** *noun* COMPUT a plastic module that contains ink for use in bubble-jet or ink-jet printers

**ink-jet printer** *noun* COMPUT a printer that produces characters by sending a stream of tiny drops of ink onto paper

**inlet** *noun* 1. an opening which allows an intake of something ○ *a turbine inlet* ○ *a combustion chamber inlet* ○ *Air enters the cabin through an inlet.* 2. GEOG a coastal feature such as the mouth of a river

**inlet valve** *noun* AUTOMOT a valve in a piston engine which allows the fuel/air mixture to enter the cylinder

**in-line chip** *noun* COMPUT an electronic component with a set of connection pins on a chip arranged in one or two rows

**in-line image** *noun* COMPUT a graphical image that is part of a webpage

**inner** *adjective* further inside or further towards the centre

**inner ear** *noun* ANAT the part of the ear inside the head containing the vestibule, the cochlea and the semicircular canals

**inner loop** *noun* COMPUT a loop contained inside another loop

**inner planet** *noun* ASTRON one of the four planets, Mercury, Venus, Earth and Mars, whose orbits lie closest to the Sun and are within the asteroid belt

**innominate artery** *noun* ANAT the largest branch of the arch of the aorta, which continues as the right common carotid and right subclavian arteries

**innovative technology** *noun* ENVIRON new or inventive methods to treat hazardous waste, prevent pollution or conserve energy

**inoculate** *verb* 1. IMMUNOL to introduce vaccine into a person's body in order to make the body create antibodies, so making the person immune to the disease ○ *The baby was inoculated against diphtheria.* 2. MICROBIOL to introduce a microorganism into a plant or a growth medium

**inoculation** *noun* 1. IMMUNOL the act of inoculating someone 2. MED an injection against a particular disease ○ *a diphtheria inoculation*

**inoperative** *adjective* not functioning

**inorganic** *adjective* 1. referring to a substance which does not come from an animal or a plant ○ *Inorganic substances include acids, alkalis and metals.* 2. CHEM referring to a substance which does not contain carbon

**inorganic acid** *noun* CHEM an acid which comes from a mineral

**inorganic chemistry** *noun* CHEM the branch of chemistry dealing with compounds not including carbon

**inorganic fertiliser** *noun* AGRIC an artificial synthesised fertiliser

**inorganic fungicide** *noun* AGRIC a fungicide made from inorganic substances such as sulphur

**inorganic herbicide** *noun* AGRIC a herbicide made from inorganic substances such as sulphur

**inorganic matter** *noun* 1. a substance which does not come from an animal or a plant 2. CHEM a substance which does not contain carbon

**inorganic pesticide** *noun* AGRIC a pesticide made from inorganic substances such as sulfur

**input** *noun* 1. COMPUT something, e.g. energy, electrical power or information, put into a system to achieve output or a result ○ *Pumps require high input current.* ○ *If the number of turns on the secondary winding is greater than the number of turns on the primary, the output voltage from the secondary will be greater than the input voltage to the primary.* 2. ELECTRONICS the action of transferring information into a computer 3. COMPUT data or information that is transferred into a computer 4. electrical signals which are applied to relevant circuits to perform an operation ■ *verb* COMPUT to transfer data or information from outside a computer to its main memory ○ *The data was input via a modem.*

**input area** *noun* COMPUT a section of main memory that holds data transferred from backing store until it is processed or distributed to other sections. Also called **input section, input storage**

**input block** *noun* COMPUT a block of data transferred to an input area

**input bound** *noun* COMPUT a computer or device in which the slowest part is data transfer

**input buffer register** *noun* COMPUT a temporary store for data from an input device before it is transferred to main or backing store

**input device** *noun* COMPUT a device such as a keyboard or bar code reader which converts actions or information into a form which a computer can understand and transfers the data to the processor. Also called **input unit**

**input lead** *noun* COMPUT a lead which connects an input device to a computer

**input limited program** *noun* COMPUT a program which is not running as fast as it could, due to limiting input rate from a slower peripheral

**input mode** *noun* COMPUT a mode in which a computer is receiving data

**input/output¹** *noun* COMPUT **1.** the receiving or transmitting of data between a computer and its peripherals and other points outside the system **2.** all data received or transmitted by a computer ▶ abbreviation **I/O**

**input/output²** *noun* COMPUT DELETE. Abbreviation **I/O**

**input/output bus** *noun* COMPUT a link allowing data and control transfer between a computer and external peripherals

**input/output channel** *noun* COMPUT the link between a processor and a peripheral allowing data transfer

**input/output controller** *noun* COMPUT an intelligent device that monitors, directs and controls data flow between a central processing unit and I/O devices

**input/output device** *noun* COMPUT same as **input/output unit**

**input/output interrupt** *noun* COMPUT an interrupt signal from a peripheral device or to indicate that an input or output operation is required

**input/output unit** *noun* COMPUT a peripheral such as a terminal or a workstation which can be used both for inputting and outputting data to a processor. Also called **input/output device**

**input port** *noun* COMPUT a circuit or connector which allows a computer to receive data from other external devices

**input register** *noun* COMPUT a temporary store for data received at slow speeds from an I/O unit (NOTE: The data is then transferred at high speed to main memory.)

**input routine** *noun* COMPUT a short section of code that accepts data from an external device, e.g. reading an entry from a keyboard. Also called **input section**

**input section** *noun* **1.** same as **input routine 2.** same as **input area**

**input statement** *noun* COMPUT a computer programming command that waits for data entry from a port or keyboard

**input storage** *noun* COMPUT same as **input area**

**input unit** *noun* same as **input device**

**input work queue** *noun* COMPUT a list of commands to be carried out in the order they were entered or in order of priority

**inquire** *verb* to ask questions about something ○ *He inquired about the environmental effects of the proposed scheme.*

**inquiry** *noun* **1.** a question (NOTE: The plural is **inquiries**.) **2.** the act of asking a question **3.** COMPUT the accessing of data held in a computer system

**inquiry/response** *noun* COMPUT an interactive computer mode in which a user's commands and inquiries are responded to very quickly

**inquiry station** *noun* COMPUT a terminal that is used to access and interrogate files stored on a remote computer

**in round figures** *adverb* in a way that is not totally accurate, but correct to the nearest 10 or 100 ○ *They have a workforce of 2500 in round figures.*

**insanitary** *adjective* HEALTH unhygienic ○ *Cholera spread rapidly because of the insanitary conditions in the town.*

**insect** *noun* ZOOL a small animal with six legs and a body in three parts ○ *Insects were flying round the lamp.* ○ *He was stung by an insect.*

COMMENT: Insects form the class Insecta. The body of an insect is divided into three distinct parts: the head, the thorax and the abdomen. The six legs are attached to the thorax and two antennae are on the head.

**insect bite** *noun* BIOL a sting caused by an insect which punctures the skin and in so doing introduces irritants

**insect-borne** *adjective* MED referring to infection which is carried and transmitted by insects ○ *insect-borne viruses* ○ *Malaria is an insect-borne disease.*

**insecticide** *noun* AGRIC a substance which kills insects

COMMENT: Natural insecticides produced from plant extracts are regarded as less harmful to the environment than synthetic insecticides which, though effective, may be persistent and kill not only insects but also other larger animals when they get into the food chain. In agriculture, most pesticides are either chlorinated hydrocarbons, organophosphorus compounds or carbamate compounds. Insecticides may be sprayed or dusted on, or used in granular form as seed dressings. In the form of a gas, insecticides are used to fumigate greenhouses and granaries.

**insectivore** *noun* ZOOL an animal that feeds mainly on insects

**insectivorous** *adjective* ZOOL feeding mainly on insects

**insectivorous plant** *noun* BOT a plant such as sundew which attracts insects, traps them and digests them

**insect pollination** *noun* BOT pollination of a flower by an insect

**insect repellent** *noun* INDUST a chemical which protects by repelling insects

**inselberg** *noun* EARTH SCI a steep-sided isolated hill that stands above nearby hills

**insert** *verb* **1.** to put one thing into another ○ *First insert the system disk in the left slot.* **2.** COMPUT to add new text inside a word or sentence

**inserted subroutine** *noun* COMPUT a series of instructions that are copied directly into the main program where a call instruction appears or where a user requires

**insertion** *noun* **1.** the process of putting one thing into another **2.** COMPUT the addition of new text inside a word or sentence **3.** ANAT the end of a muscle that is attached to a part of the skeleton that moves as a result of a contraction. Compare **origin** **4.** GENETICS the addition of a segment of DNA within a gene sequence

**insertion loss** *noun* COMPUT attenuation of a signal caused by adding a device into an existing channel or circuit

**insertion point** *noun* COMPUT a cursor positioned to show where any text typed in will be entered within a document

**insert key** *noun* COMPUT a key that switches a word-processor or editor program into insert mode rather than overwrite mode. Abbreviation **Ins key**

**insert mode** *noun* COMPUT an interactive computer mode used for editing and correcting documents

COMMENT: This is a standard feature on most word-processing packages where the cursor is placed at the required point in the document and any characters typed will be added, with the existing text moving on as necessary.

**inshore** *adjective* EARTH SCI on the sea, but near the coast

**in situ** *adjective, adverb* in place

**Ins key** *abbreviation* COMPUT insert key

**insolation** *noun* ASTRON radiation from the Sun

**insoluble** *adjective* CHEM not able to be dissolved in liquid

**insoluble fibre** *noun* BIOL the fibre in bread and cereals, which is not digested, but which swells inside the intestine

**inspect** *verb* to look at something closely and check for problems

**inspection** *noun* a careful check for problems

**inspection chamber** *noun* ENG a large hole built above a drain, allowing someone to look at the inside of the pipes to see if they are blocked

**instability** *noun* PHYS a condition in which a body or mass moves easily, and with increasing speed, away from its original position

**install** *verb* **1.** to put something in position, connect and make ready for use ○ *Most carburettors are installed in a warm position to help against icing.* **2.** to put a machine into an office or factory ○ *The system is easy to install and simple to use.* **3.** COMPUT to set up a new computer system to the user's requirements or to configure a new program to the existing system capabilities

**installation** *noun* **1.** the act of putting equipment or devices into position and connecting them for use ○ *The installation of the computer took three hours.* **2.** equipment or devices which are installed ○ *In some auxiliary-power-unit installations the air intake area is protected against ice formation.*

**installation manual** *noun* a booklet showing how a system should be installed

**install program** *noun* COMPUT a software utility that transfers program code from the distribution disks onto a computer's hard disk and configures the program

**instance** *noun* **1.** an example which is used to support or contest a statement ○ *Failure to check fuel levels regularly is an instance of bad practice.* **2.** COMPUT an object or duplicate object that has been created

**instant** *adjective* happening immediately ■ *noun* a very short period of time

**instantaneous access** *noun* COMPUT an extremely short access time to a random access device

**instar** *noun* INSECTS a developmental stage of insects and other arthropods between two moults

**instinct** *noun* ZOOL an inborn behaviour pattern particular to a species and developed according to necessities such as survival and reproduction

**instinctive** *adjective* ZOOL natural, rather than thought-out ○ *an instinctive response*

**instruct** *verb* to give information or knowledge to someone, usually in a formal setting such as a lesson or briefing ○ *The safety officer instructs employees on the use of the breathing equipment.*

**instruction** *noun* **1.** the act of giving information or knowledge, usually in a formal setting such as a lesson or briefing ○ *Trainees receive first-aid instruction.* **2.** a piece of information on how something should be operated or used ○ *You must follow the instructions.* **3.** COMPUT a word used in a programming language that is understood by the computer to represent an action ○ *The instruction PRINT is used in this BASIC dialect as an operand to display the following data.*

COMMENT: In a high level language the instructions are translated by the compiler or interpreter to a form that is understood by the central processing unit.

**instruction address register** *noun* COMPUT a register in a central processing unit that contains the location of the next instruction to be processed. Abbreviation **IAR**

**instruction cache** *noun* COMPUT a section of high-speed memory which stores the next few instructions to be executed by a processor in order to speed up operation

**instruction cycle** *noun* COMPUT a sequence of events and their timing that is involved when fetching and executing an instruction stored in memory

**instruction decoder** *noun* COMPUT **1.** a piece of hardware that converts a machine-code code instruction in binary form into actions **2.** a program that decodes instructions in machine code

**instruction manual** *noun* a book containing information on how something should be operated or used

**instruction pipelining** *noun* COMPUT the process of beginning to work on a second instruction while still processing the present one, increasing program speed of execution

**instruction processor** *noun* COMPUT a section of the central processing unit that decodes the instruction and performs the necessary arithmetic and logical functions

**instruction register** *noun* COMPUT a register in a central processing unit that stores an instruction during decoding and execution operations. Abbreviation **IR**

**instruction sheet** *noun* a piece of paper on which special instructions are written or printed

**instructor** *noun* a person who gives information or knowledge, usually in a formal setting such as a lesson or briefing

**instrument** *noun* ENG a device for recording, measuring or controlling something, especially as part of a control system

**instrumentation** *noun* ENG a set of specialized instruments for operating a machine or vehicle

**instrument error** *noun* ENG the difference between indicated instrument value and true value

**insufficient** *adjective* not enough ○ *insufficient information*

**insulate** *verb* **1.** to prevent the passing of heat, cold or sound into or out of an area **2.** ELEC to prevent the passing of electricity to where it is not required, especially by using a non-conducting material ○ *Bus bars are insulated from the main structure and are normally provided with some form of protective covering.*

**insulating** *adjective* providing insulation

**insulating tape** *noun* ELEC a special adhesive tape which is used to insulate electrical wires ○ *Insulating tape was used to prevent the electrical wires from touching.*

**insulation** *noun* **1.** the act of of preventing the passing of heat, cold, sound or electricity from one area to another **2.** the state of being protected against the passing of heat, cold, sound or electricity from one area to another **3.** a material or substance used to insulate something

**insulator** *noun* a substance which will insulate, especially one which will not conduct electricity ○ *Wood is a good insulator.*

**insulin** *noun* BIOCHEM a hormone produced by the islets of Langerhans in the pancreas

COMMENT: Insulin controls the way in which the body converts sugar into energy and regulates the level of sugar in the blood. A lack of insulin caused by diabetes mellitus makes the level of glucose in the blood rise. Insulin injections are regularly used to treat diabetes mellitus, but care has to be taken not to exceed the dose as this will cause hyperinsulinism and hypoglycaemia.

**intake** *noun* same as **air intake**

**intake guide vane** *noun* AEROSP a device to direct the flow of air at the air intake of a jet engine

**intake lip** *noun* AEROSP the rim or edge of the air intake of a jet engine ○ *As sonic speed is approached, the efficiency of the intake begins to fall because of shock waves at the intake lip.*

**intake temperature gauge** *noun* an instrument to indicate the temperature of air entering a jet engine

**integer** *noun* MATHS a mathematical term to describe a whole number, which may be positive, negative or zero

**integral** *adjective* completing the whole or belonging to a whole as a necessary part ○ *Meteorology is an integral part of a flying training course.*

**integral calculus** *noun* MATHS the application of calculus to determining areas, volumes and lengths

**integrated** *adjective* COMPUT referring to a system that contains parts organised together to provide a complete system

**integrated circuit** *noun* COMPUT a circuit where all the active and passive components are formed on one small piece of semiconductor, by means of etching and chemical processes. Abbreviation **IC**

COMMENT: Integrated circuits can be classified as follows: Small Scale Integration (SSI), 1 to 10 components per IC; Medium Scale Integration (MSI), 10 to 100 components per IC; Large Scale Integration (LSI), 100 to 5000 components per IC; Very Large Scale Integration (VLSI), 5000 to 50 000 components per IC; Ultra Large Scale Integration (ULSI), over 100 000 components per IC.

**integrated data processing** *noun* COMPUT an organisational method for the entry and retrieval of data to provide maximum efficiency. Abbreviation **IDP**

**integrated device electronics** *noun* COMPUT a popular standard for a hard disk drive controller unit that allows data transfer rates up to 4.1 MBps and can support two hard disk drives on each controller. Abbreviation **IDE** (NOTE: Enhanced versions of the IDE standard provide flexibility and speed.)

**integrated injection logic** *noun* COMPUT a type of circuit design able to produce very small, low-power components. Abbreviation **IIL**

**integrated pest management** *noun* AGRIC an appropriate combination of all methods of pest control, involving good cultivation practices, use of chemical pesticides, resistant crop varieties and biological control. Abbreviation **IPM**

**integrated services digital network** *noun* COMPUT full form of **ISDN**

**integrated software** *noun* COMPUT software such as an operating system or word-processor that is stored in the computer system and has been tailored to the requirements of the system

**integration** *noun* the process of bringing several operations together ○ *small-scale integration*

**integrity** *noun* the state of being complete and in good working condition ○ *The engine fire warning system is checked to test its integrity.* ○ *The integrity of an aid used to conduct procedural approaches must be high.*

**integument** *noun* BIOL an outer protective layer of an organism, e.g. a shell, husk or skin

**intelligence** *noun* 1. the ability to reason 2. COMPUT the ability of a device to carry out processing or run a program

**intelligence quotient** *noun* the result of an intelligence test shown as the ratio of mental age to the actual age of the person tested, the average being 100. Abbreviation **IQ**

**intelligent** *adjective* 1. able to understand quickly and easily 2. COMPUT (*of a machine*) capable of limited reasoning facilities, giving it human-like responses

**intelligent knowledge-based system** *noun* COMPUT software that applies the knowledge, advice and rules defined by an expert in a particular field to a user's data to help solve a problem. Abbreviation **IKBS**

**intend** *verb* to have a particular plan, aim or purpose ○ *A battery is intended to supply only limited amounts of power.*

**intense** *adjective* extreme or strong ○ *intense heat* ○ *intense wind*

**intense concentration** *noun* very hard or deep concentration

**intensification** *noun* 1. the process of becoming stronger or greater 2. the act of doing something in an intensive way ○ *Intensification of farming has contributed to soil erosion.*

**intensify** *verb* 1. to become stronger or greater 2. to make something stronger or greater 3. to start doing something intensively

**intensity** *noun* 1. PHYS a measure of the strength of a signal or the brightness of a light source 2. ENVIRON the degree to which land is used

**intensive** *adjective* 1. requiring much effort in a short time ○ *intensive preparation* 2. AGRIC achieving maximum production from land or animals ○ *intensive agriculture*

**intensive animal breeding** *noun* AGRIC a specialised system of breeding animals where the livestock are kept indoors and fed on concentrated foodstuffs, with frequent use of drugs to control diseases, which are a constant threat under these conditions

**intensive farming, intensive cultivation** *noun* AGRIC farming in which as much use is made of the land as possible by growing crops close together, growing several crops in a year or using large amounts of fertiliser. Opposite **extensive**

**intensively** *adverb* in an intensive way

**intention** *noun* a course of action planned to be followed ○ *It is not the intention of this chapter to give a detailed description of world weather.* ○ *Our intention is to provide safe, cost-effective flying.*

**inter-** *prefix* between

**interact** *verb* to act on each other ○ *Angle of attack and the profile of the wing section interact to produce lift.* ○ *Direct and reflected path signals can interact to cause bending of the localiser and generation of a false glidepath.*

**interaction** *noun* a relationship between two or more organisms or things

**interactive** *adjective* 1. involving people reacting to and communicating with other people or situations 2. COMPUT allowing communication between a user and a computer, TV or video

**Interactive Multimedia Association** *noun* COMPUT a professional organisation that covers subjects including authoring languages, formats and intellectual property. Abbreviation **IMA**

**interactive TV** *noun* TELECOM a channel that allows two-way communication between the viewer and broadcasting station (NOTE: This feature often allows the user to choose which programme to watch or to respond directly to questions displayed on-screen.)

**interblock** *adjective* COMPUT situated between blocks

**interblock gap** *noun* COMPUT a space between two blocks of stored data. Abbreviation **IBG**

**interbreed** *verb* BIOL to mate animals with some different characteristics together (NOTE: Individuals from the same species can interbreed, those from different species cannot.)

**intercellular** *adjective* BIOL taking place or situated between cells

**intercept** *verb* to stop or interrupt the intended path of something ○ *When a radio transmission is made from a moving platform, there will be a shift in frequency between the transmitted and intercepted radio signals.*

**interchange** COMPUT *noun* an exchange of one thing for another ○ *The machine allows document interchange between it and other machines without reformatting.* ■ *verb* to exchange one thing for another

**interchangeable** *adjective* COMPUT which can be exchanged without changing an outcome

**intercharacter spacing** *noun* COMPUT a word-processor feature that provides variable spacing between words to create a justified line

**interconnect** *verb* to connect several devices together or be connected together ○ *The fire extinguishers for each engine are interconnected, so allowing two extinguishers to be used on either engine.*

**interconnection** *noun* COMPUT a section of connecting material between two devices

**intercostal muscle** *noun* ANAT a muscle between the ribs of a mammal, used when breathing

**interdependence** *noun* a state of two or more organisms or processes that depend on each other

**interdependent** *adjective* being dependent on each other

**interest group** *noun* ENVIRON a group of people who are all concerned about the same issue and who try to influence the opinions of politicians, local officials and business people on this particular issue

**interface** COMPUT *noun* 1. a point at which one computer system ends and another begins 2. a circuit, device or port that allows two or more incompatible units to be linked together in a standard communication system, allowing data to be transferred between them 3. a section of a program which allows transmission of data to another program ■ *verb* 1. to modify a device by adding

a circuit or connector to allow it to conform to a standard communications system 2. to connect two or more incompatible devices together with a circuit, to allow them to communicate

**interfacing** *noun* COMPUT hardware or software used to interface two computers, programs or devices

**interference** *noun* 1. TELECOM the prevention of reception of a clear radio signal 2. noise on a signal ○ *Certain equipment, such as generators and ignition systems, will cause unwanted radio frequency interference.*

**interfere with** *verb* 1. to create a problem with something 2. to get in the way of something 3. to stop something working properly

**interferon** *noun* BIOL a protein that is produced by cells, usually in response to a virus, and then reduces the spread of viruses

**interfluve** *noun* EARTH SCI the land area between two rivers

**intergalactic** *adjective* ASTRON referring to two or more galaxies

**intergenerational equity** *noun* ENVIRON the fairness of the distribution of the costs and benefits of an environmental policy when they are experienced by different generations

**interglacial period**, **interglacial** *noun* EARTH SCI the period between two Ice Ages when the climate becomes warmer

**interior** *noun* the inside of something ○ *reserves in the interior of the continent* ■ *adjective* situated inside ○ *The interior walls of the intestine.*

**interior gateway protocol** *noun* COMPUT a protocol that distributes information to gateways, now normally called routers, within a particular network. Abbreviation **IGP**

**interlace** *verb* TELECOM to build up an image on a television screen using two passes, each displaying alternate lines

COMMENT: This system uses two picture fields made up of alternate lines to reduce picture flicker effects.

**interlaced video** *noun* COMPUT a video signal made up of two separate fields (NOTE: This is the normal display mode for home video.)

**interleaved memory** *noun* COMPUT two separate banks of memory used together in sequence

**interleave factor** *noun* COMPUT a ratio of sectors skipped between access operations on a hard disk

**interleaving** *noun* COMPUT **1.** a processor dealing with slices or sections of processes alternately, so that they appear to be executed simultaneously **2.** the dividing of data storage into sections so that each can be accessed separately

**interlobar artery** *noun* ANAT an artery running towards the cortex on each side of a renal pyramid to the glomeruli of the kidneys

**interlock** *noun* COMPUT a security device which is part of the logon prompt and requires a password ■ *verb* **1.** COMPUT to prevent a device from performing another task until the present one has been completed **2.** (*of parts of a mechanism*) to connect together so that the movement or operation of one affects others ○ *The two parts interlock to create a solid structure.*

**interlude** *noun* **1.** a period of time between two events **2.** COMPUT a small initial routine at the start of a program that carries out housekeeping tasks

**intermediate** *adjective* at a stage between two others

**intermediate access memory** *noun* COMPUT memory storage that has an access time between that of main memory and disk-based systems. Abbreviation **IAM**

**intermediate code** *noun* COMPUT a code used by a computer or assembler during the translation of a high-level code to machine code

**intermediate file** *noun* COMPUT a series of records that contain partially processed data, which will be used at a later date to complete that task

**intermediate frequency** *noun* ELECTRONICS the frequency that an incoming carrier wave signal is changed to in a heterodyne radio receiver before it is amplified

**intermediate host** *noun* BIOL a host on which a parasite lives for a time before passing on to another host

**intermediate neutron** *noun* PHYS a neutron with energy between that of a fast neutron and a thermal neutron

**intermediate storage** *noun* COMPUT a temporary area of memory for items that are currently being processed

**intermediate system to intermediate system** *noun* COMPUT an OSI protocol that allows data to be transferred between routers. Abbreviation **IS-IS**

**intermediate technology** *noun* TECH the technology between the advanced electronic technology of industrialised countries and the local technology of developing countries

**intermediate waste** *noun* INDUST waste from a nuclear reactor in the form of sludge or metal parts, which are more radioactive than low-level waste and less radioactive than high-level waste

**intermittent** *adjective* stopping and starting at intervals ○ *The cycle of induction, compression, combustion and exhaust in the piston engine is intermittent, whereas in the gas turbine each process is continuous.*

**intermittent error** *noun* an error which apparently occurs randomly in a computer or communications system due to a program fault or noise

**internal** *adjective* on or from the inside of something. Compare **external**

**internal arithmetic** *noun* COMPUT arithmetic operations performed by the arithmetic logic unit

**internal combustion engine** *noun* ENG a type of engine used in motor vehicles, where the fuel is a mixture of petrol and air burnt in a closed chamber to give energy to the pistons

**internal command** *noun* COMPUT a command that is part of the operating system, rather than a separate utility program ○ *In MS-DOS, the internal command DIR is used frequently.*

**internal font** *noun* COMPUT, PRINTING a font that is stored on a ROM in a printer. Also called **resident font**

**internal format** *noun* COMPUT the way in which data and instructions are represented within a central processing unit or backing store

**internal hard disk** *noun* COMPUT a hard disk drive mounted inside the main case of a computer

**internal iliac artery** *noun* ANAT an artery that branches from the aorta in the abdomen and leads to the pelvis

**internalise** *verb* □ **to internalise the externality** to bring external factors under the control of the relevant authority

**internal language** *noun* COMPUT a language used in a computer system that is not under the direct control of the operator

COMMENT: Many compiled languages are translated to an internal language.

**internally stored program** *noun* COMPUT a computer program code that is stored in a ROM device and does not have to be loaded from backing store

**internal maxillary artery** *noun* ANAT a branch of the external carotid artery, in the face

**internal memory/store** *noun* COMPUT a section of RAM and ROM to which the central processing unit is directly connected without the use of an interface, as in external memory devices such as disk drives

**internal regulation** *noun* BIOL the process by which organisms maintain a constant internal environment

**internal resistance** *noun* ELEC the resistance exerted within a source of electrical current such as a battery or generator

**internal respiration** *noun* PHYSIOL the part of respiration concerned with the passage of oxygen from the blood to the tissues and the passage of carbon dioxide from the tissues to the blood

**internal store** *noun* COMPUT also called **internal store**

**international** *adjective* referring to more than one country

**international candle** *noun* MEASURE an obsolete unit of luminous intensity, now replaced by the candela

**international standard atmosphere** *noun* PHYS a model atmosphere defined in terms of pressure, density and temperature for all heights, with perfect gases and without any form of water or solid matter. Abbreviation **ISA** (NOTE: It is used in the calibration of instruments and descriptions of aircraft performance.)

**International Standards Organisation Open System Interconnection** *noun* COMPUT a standardised ISO network design that is constructed of layers, each with a specific task, allowing different systems to communicate if they conform to the standard. Abbreviation **ISO/OSI**

**International Standards Organisation** *noun* COMPUT an organisation

which creates and regulates standards for many types of computer and networking products. Full form of **ISO**

**Internet** *noun* COMPUT an international wide area network that provides file and data transfer together with electronic mail functions for millions of users around the world. ♦ **www**

**Internet Activities Board** *noun* COMPUT an independent committee that is responsible for the design, engineering and management of the Internet. Abbreviation **IAB**

**Internet address** *noun* COMPUT a unique number that identifies the precise location of a particular node on the Internet. Also called **IP address, host address, host number** (NOTE: This is a 32-bit number usually written in dotted decimal format. It used by the TCP/IP protocol and is normally of the form '123.33.22.32'. A domain name system is used to convert a domain name, e.g. 'bloomsbury.com' into its full Internet address.)

**Internet Architecture Board** *noun* COMPUT a group that monitors and manages the development of the Internet (NOTE: It includes the IETF and the IRTF.)

**Internet Assigned Numbers Authority** *noun* COMPUT a group that assigns unique identifying numbers to the different protocols and network products used on the Internet. Abbreviation **IANA**

**Internet Engineering Steering Group** *noun* COMPUT a group that reviews Internet standards and manages the IETF. Abbreviation **IESG**

**Internet Engineering Task Force** *noun* COMPUT a committee that is part of the IAB and determines Internet standards. Abbreviation **IETF**

**Internet message access protocol** *noun* COMPUT full form of **IMAP**

**Internet protocol** *noun* COMPUT a part of the TCP/IP standard that defines how data is transferred over a network. Abbreviation **IP**

**Internet protocol address** *noun* COMPUT a unique 32-bit number that identifies computers that want to connect to a TCP/IP network

**Internet protocol next generation** *noun* COMPUT full form of **IPng**

**Internet relay chat** *noun* COMPUT a system that allows many users to participate in a chat session in which each user can send messages and see the text of any other user. Abbreviation **IRC** (NOTE: It is part of the Internet Society.)

**Internet research steering group** *noun* COMPUT a group that manages the Internet research task force. Abbreviation **IRSG**

**Internet research task force** *noun* COMPUT a committee that is part of the IAB and researches new Internet standards before referring them to the IETF for approval. Abbreviation **IRTF**

**Internet service provider** *noun* COMPUT a company that provides one of the permanent links that make up the Internet and sells connections to private users and companies to allow them to access the Internet. Abbreviation **ISP**

**Internet Society** *noun* COMPUT an organisation that looks after maintaining and enhancing the Internet (NOTE: It is not linked to any government or company and so provides an independent view. It is made up of committees such as the Internet Advisory Board and the Internet Engineering Task Force.)

**Internetwork** *noun* COMPUT a number of networks connected together using bridges or routers to allow users on one network to access any resource on any other of the connected networks

**internode** *noun* BOT the part of a plant stem between two adjacent nodes

**interoceptor** *noun* ANAT a nerve cell that reacts to a change taking place inside the body

**interoperability** *noun* COMPUT the ability of two devices or computers to exchange information

**interphase** *noun* BIOL the period when a cell is not dividing

**interplanetary** *adjective* ASTRON referring to two or more planets

**interpolation** *noun* the estimation of a middle value by reference to known values on each side ○ *Spot temperatures at positions other than those printed are obtained by interpolation.*

**interpret** *verb* **1.** to understand something presented in code or symbolic form ○ *Aircrew must be able to interpret information printed on a contour chart.* **2.** to translate what is said in one language into another

**interpretation** *noun* an explanation of the meaning of something ○ *Synoptic charts require interpretation in order to understand the information given.*

**interpretative code** *noun* COMPUT a code used with an interpretative program

**interpretative program** *noun* COMPUT a piece of software that translates high level interpretative code into machine code instructions at run-time

**interpreted language** *noun* COMPUT a programming language that is executed by an interpreter

**interpreter** *noun* **1.** a person who translates or explains something **2.** COMPUT a piece of software used to translate a user's high-level program into machine code in real time

**interrupt** *verb* to stop something while it is happening ■ *noun* **1.** TELECOM the stopping of a transmission due to an action at the receiving end of a system **2.** COMPUT a signal that diverts a central processing unit from one task to another which has higher priority, allowing the central processing unit to return to the first task later ○ *This printer port design uses an interrupt line to let the CPU know it is ready to receive data.*

**interrupt-driven** *adjective* COMPUT working in response to an interrupt

**interrupt handler** *noun* COMPUT a piece of software that accepts interrupt signals and acts on them, e.g. running a special routine or sending data to a peripheral. Abbreviation **IH**

**interrupt mask** *noun* COMPUT a data word in a computer that selects which interrupt lines are to be activated

**interrupt request** *noun* COMPUT a signal from a device that indicates to the central processing unit that it requires attention. Abbreviation **IRQ**

**intersect** *verb* (*of a line*) to cut across another line ○ *Meridians intersect at the poles and cross the equator at right angles.*

**intersection** *noun* **1.** a point at which two lines cross each other ○ *The intersection of the drift line and the wind vector gives the drift point.* **2.** MATHS a set containing all the elements that are common to two or more sets **3.** COMPUT a logical function whose output is only true if both its inputs are true

**interspecific** *adjective* BIOL referring to two or more species

**interspecific competition** *noun* ECOL competition between species for one or more of the same limited resources of food, sunlight, water, soil, nutrients or space

**interstellar** *adjective* ASTRON referring to two or more stars

**interstitial** *adjective* ANAT referring to the spaces between parts of something such as the tissue in an organ

**interstitial cells** *plural noun* ANAT the testosterone-producing cells between the tubules in the testes. Also called **Leydig cells**

**interstitial-cell-stimulating hormone** *noun* BIOCHEM same as **luteinising hormone**. abbreviation **ICSH**

**intertidal zone** *noun* EARTH SCI an area of sea water and shore between the high and low water marks

**intertropical convergence zone** *noun* EARTH SCI a boundary between the trade winds and tropical air masses of the northern and southern hemispheres. Abbreviation **ITCZ**

**interval** *noun* **1.** the amount of space between places or points ○ *The intervals at which contours are drawn depends on the scale of the chart and this interval, known as the vertical interval, is noted on the chart.* **2.** the period of time between two events ○ *A precise interval is essential to obtain correct ignition timing on all cylinders.*

**intervention** *noun* COMPUT the act of making a change in a system

**intestine** *noun* ZOOL the digestive canal between the stomach and the anus or cloaca in which food is digested and absorbed (NOTE: In mammals, the small intestine digests and absorbs food from the stomach, and the large intestine then absorbs most of the remaining water.)

**intimate** *adjective* COMPUT referring to software that operates and interacts closely with hardware in a system

**intra-** *prefix* inside or within

**intracellular** *adjective* BIOL occurring within a cell or cells

**intracutaneous injection** *noun* MED an injection of a liquid between the layers of skin, e.g. in a test for an allergy

**intragenic** *adjective* GENETICS occurring within the same gene sequence

**intramuscular injection** *noun* MED an injection of liquid into a muscle, e.g. for a slow release of a drug

**intranet** *noun* COMPUT a private network of computers within a company that provide similar functions to the Internet e.g. electronic mail, newsgroups and the WWW, without the associated security risks of making the information public or linking the company to a public network

**intraspecific** *adjective* BIOL occurring among species

**intravenous** *adjective* MED administered into into a vein

**intravenous feeding** *noun* MED the process of giving liquid food to a patient by means of a tube inserted into a vein

**intravenous injection** *noun* MED an injection of liquid into a vein, e.g. for fast release of a drug

**intra vitam** *adverb* BIOL during life

**intrinsic factor** *noun* BIOCHEM a protein produced in the gastric glands which reacts with vitamin B12 controls the absorption of extrinsic factor, and which, if lacking, causes pernicious anaemia

**intrinsic value** *noun* ENVIRON the value placed on the inherent qualities of a species, as opposed to its value to humans

**introduce** *verb* **1.** to bring something into being or start to use something new ○ *The lab introduced a new rapid method of testing.* **2.** ENVIRON to bring something to a new place ○ *Several of the species of plant now common in Britain were introduced by the Romans.* ○ *Starlings were introduced to the USA in 1891.*

**introduction** *noun* **1.** the process of bringing something into being or using something new ○ *the introduction of a new rapid testing method* **2.** the bringing of something to a new place ○ *Before the introduction of grey squirrels, the red squirrel was widespread.* ○ *The death rate from malaria was very high before the introduction of new anti-malarial techniques.* **3.** ENVIRON a plant or animal that has been brought to a new place ○ *It is not an indigenous species but a 19th-century introduction.* **4.** the first part of a report, book or talk

**introgression** *noun* GENETICS the transfer of genes from one species into the gene pool of another as a result of hybridisation

**intruder** *noun* a person who is not authorised to be in a place

**intrusion** *noun* EARTH SCI an area of rock which has pushed into other rocks

**invalid** *adjective* not valid ○ *He tried to use an invalid password.* ○ *The message was that the instruction was invalid.* ■ *noun* HEALTH a person who is ill

**invasion** *noun* **1.** AGRIC the arrival of large numbers of pests in an area **2.** MED the entry of bacteria into a body

**inventory** *noun* ECOL a list of items in a place

**inverse** *adjective* **1.** reversed in order or effect ○ *There is an inverse relationship between altitude and temperature: temperature decreases as altitude increases.* **2.** COMPUT changing the logical state of a signal or device to its logical opposite ■ *noun* the opposite of something in order or effect ○ *The inverse of true is false.* ○ *The inverse of 1 is 0.*

**inversely proportional** *adjective* referring to a relationship in which one thing increases as another decreases to the same extent ○ *Temperature is inversely proportional to altitude.*

**inverse-square law** *noun* PHYS a law stating that a physical quantity varies inversely with the square of the distance from its source (NOTE: Gravitation, electromagnetism, radiation and sound follow this law)

**inverse video** *noun* TELECOM a television effect created by swapping the background and foreground text display colours

**inversion** *noun* **1.** METEOROL an atmospheric phenomenon in which cold air is nearer the ground than warm air ○ *Smog is smoke or pollution trapped on the surface by an inversion of temperature with little or no wind.* **2.** the act of turning something upside down ○ *Inversion of the aircraft in flight may result in fuel stoppage.* **3.** COMPUT the changing over of numbers in a binary word, e.g. one to zero, zero to one ○ *The inversion of a binary digit takes place in one's complement.*

COMMENT: Air normally cools at a rate of 6.4° C per 1000 m of altitude. During the night, the ground cools as it loses heat by radiation and the air at ground level becomes cooler than the air above. This thermal inversion can cause smog, when the cooler ground-level air cannot move because there is no wind and remains trapped with its pollutants between the ground and the warm air above it.

**inversion layer** *noun* METEOROL a layer of the atmosphere in which the temperature increases as altitude increases

**invert** *verb* **1.** to turn something upside down ○ *A glass tube is sealed at one end, filled with mercury and then inverted so that the open end is immersed in a bowl containing mercury.* **2.** COMPUT to change all binary ones to zeros and zeros to ones

**invertase** *noun* BIOCHEM an enzyme that speeds up the breakdown of sucrose

**invertebrate** *noun* ZOOL an animal that has no backbone. Compare **vertebrate** ■ *adjective* referring to animals that have no backbone

**inverted backbone** *noun* COMPUT a network architecture in which the hub is the centre of the network and all subnetworks connect to the hub (NOTE: In a traditional backbone network, the subnetworks connect to the cable that is the main backbone.)

**inverted file** *noun* COMPUT a file with an index entry for every data item

**inverter** *noun* **1.** COMPUT a logical gate that provides inversion facilities **2.** ELEC a circuit used to provide alternating current supply from a DC battery source

**investigate** *verb* to examine or find out about something in great detail ○ *The cause of the blockage must be investigated.*

**invisible** *adjective* unable to be seen ○ *Oxygen is an invisible gas.*

**invitation** *noun* an opportunity offered to someone to do something

**invite** *verb* to offer someone an opportunity to do something

**in vitro** *adjective*, *adverb* BIOL occurring outside a living organism, in laboratory conditions ○ *in vitro experiments* ○ *The tissue was cultured in vitro.*

**in vitro fertilisation** *noun* BIOTECH the fertilisation of an ovum in laboratory conditions. Abbreviation **IVF**

**in vivo** *adjective, adverb* BIOL occurring within or taking place on a living organism ○ *The experiments were carried out in vivo.*

**invoke** *verb* COMPUT to start or run a program, often a memory resident utility

**involve** *verb* to have to do with something or to include something in a process ○ *Backing up involves copying current working files onto a separate storage disk.*

**inward** *adjective* directed to or moving towards the inside or interior

**inwards** *adverb* towards the inside or interior (NOTE: American English is **inward.**)

**I/O** *abbreviation* COMPUT input/output

**I/O bound** *noun* COMPUT a processor that is doing very little processing since its time is taken up reading or writing data from a I/O port

**I/O buffer** *noun* COMPUT a temporary storage area for data waiting to be input or output

**I/O bus** *noun* COMPUT a set of links allowing data and control signal transfer between a central processing unit and memory or peripheral devices

**I/O device** *noun* a peripheral such as a terminal that can be used for inputting or outputting data to a processor

**iodide** *noun* CHEM a salt of hydriodic acid containing the univalent anion ion I⁻ (NOTE: Silver iodides are used in photography, and sodium and potassium iodides are used in iodised table salt.)

**iodine** *noun* CHEM ELEM a chemical element essential to the body, especially to the functioning of the thyroid gland, found in seaweed (NOTE: The chemical symbol is **I**; the atomic number is **53** and the atomic weight is **126.90.**)

**iodise** *verb* CHEM to treat or impregnate something with iodine

**iodoform** *noun* CHEM a yellow crystalline compound with a penetrating odour, used as an antiseptic, and in the treatment of minor skin diseases. Formula: $CHI_3$.

**ion** *noun* CHEM an atom or a group of atoms that has obtained an electric charge by gaining or losing one or more electrons ○ *negative ion* ○ *Ions with a positive charge are called cations and those with a negative charge are anions.*

COMMENT: It is believed that living organisms, including human beings, react to the presence of ionised particles in the atmosphere. Hot dry winds contain a higher proportion of positive ions than normal and cause headaches and other illnesses. If negative ionised air is introduced into an air-conditioning system, the incidence of headaches and nausea among people working in the building may be reduced.

**ion deposition** *noun* PRINTING a printing technology that uses a printhead that deposits ions to create a charged image that attracts the toner

**ion drive** *noun* ASTRON, AEROSP a type of rocket motor that drives spacecraft with a stream of ions instead of a jet of hot gas as in normal rockets (NOTE: Ion drives are powered by electricity and have been tested in orbit.)

**ion engine** *noun* AEROSP a theoretical rocket engine that obtains thrust from a stream of high-speed ions (NOTE: The engine would be used only in space because it does not produce enough thrust to escape Earth's gravity.)

**ion exchange** *noun* CHEM the exchange of ions between a solid and a solution

**ion-exchange filter** *noun* a water-softening device attached to the water supply to remove nitrates or calcium from the water

**ionic crystal** *noun* PHYS a crystal composed of ions

**ionic product** *noun* CHEM water that contains the combination of hydrogen ions and hydrogen-oxide ions $H^+OH^-$, caused by ionisation

**ionic radius** *noun* CHEM a measure of the effective radius of an ion in a compound

**ionisation, ionization** *noun* CHEM **1.** the production of atoms with electric charges **2.** the process of producing ions by heat or radiation ○ *The intensity of ionisation depends on the strength of the ultraviolet radiation and the density of the air.*

**ionisation chamber** *noun* PHYS a piece of equipment for detecting and measuring ionising radiation (NOTE: It consists of a gas-filled tube with electrodes at each end between which a voltage is maintained.)

**ionisation potential** *noun* PHYS the energy needed to remove an electron from an atom or molecule and move it infinitely far away

**ionise** *verb* CHEM to give an atom an electric charge

**ioniser** *noun* INDUST a machine that increases the concentration of negative ions in the atmosphere of a room, so counteracting the effect of positive ions. Also called **negative ion generator**

**ionising radiation** *noun* PHYS radiation such as alpha particles or X-rays that produces atoms with electrical charges as it passes through a medium

**ionosphere** *noun* METEOROL the part of the atmosphere 50 km above Earth's surface ○ *Since the strength of the Sun's radiation varies with latitude, the structure of the ionosphere varies over the surface of the Earth, composed of 70% nitrogen, 15% oxygen and 15% helium, in which atoms are ionised by solar radiation.*

COMMENT: The uppermost layer of Earth's atmosphere is where most of the atoms are ionised. Some 350 km above sea level, the ionosphere has high temperatures because high-energy solar photons are captured there, including those in X-ray wavelengths. This prevents radiation which would otherwise be fatal to human and other life from reaching sea level, so that without the ionosphere any life on Earth would have evolved very differently. The ionosphere is also useful for communications and radar, since it is possible to bounce radio signals off it for transmission beyond the visible horizon.

**ionospheric** *adjective* METEOROL referring to the ionosphere

**ionospheric attenuation** *noun* PHYS loss of signal strength to the ionosphere

**ionospheric refraction** *noun* PHYS a change in direction as a wave passes through an ionised layer

**ion pump** *noun* PHYS a device that removes a gas by ionising the gas atoms and adsorbing these ions

**ion tail** *noun* ASTRON the ionised portion of the tail of a comet (NOTE: It is synonymous with the gas tail since most gas in comet tails is ionised near the Sun where comet tails are observed.)

**I/O port** *noun* COMPUT a circuit or connector that provides an input/output channel to another device

**ip** *abbreviation* COMPUT information provider

**IP** *abbreviation* COMPUT Internet protocol

**IP address** *noun* COMPUT same as **Internet address**

**IPCC** *abbreviation* ENVIRON Intergovernmental Panel on Climate Change

**IP datagram** *noun* COMPUT a packet of data transferred across a TCP/IP network

**IPM** *abbreviation* AGRIC integrated pest management

**IP multicast** *noun* COMPUT a process of sending out one set of data to several recipients simultaneously

**IPng** *noun* COMPUT a new version of the Internet protocol that allows more computers to connect to the Internet and supports more data traffic. Full form **Internet protocol next generation.** ♦ **IP**

**ips** *abbreviation* MEASURE inches-per-second

**IP spoofing** *noun* COMPUT a method of gaining unauthorised access to a computer or network by pretending to be an authorised computer or device (NOTE: Each device on the network has its own unique address and many security systems block or allow access to networks based on the computer's IP address. A hacker needs to find out which IP address is allowed or trusted, then modifies the header information in the data packets from the computer to include this IP address, so gaining access to the target computer. Newer routers and firewalls use a range of techniques to spot this scheme and block the data.)

**ip terminal** *noun* COMPUT a special visual display unit that allows users to create and edit videotext pages before sending them to the main videotext page database

**IQ** *abbreviation* BIOL intelligence quotient

**Ir** *symbol* CHEM ELEM iridium

**IR** *abbreviation* COMPUT **1.** information retrieval **2.** index register **3.** instruction register

**IRC** *abbreviation* COMPUT Internet relay chat

**IrDA** *noun* COMPUT a standard method of transferring information via an infrared light beam, often used to transfer information from a laptop or PDA to a printer or desktop computer. Full form **infrared data association** (NOTE: To use this feature, the computer or printer needs to have an IrDA port.)

**iridium** *noun* CHEM ELEM a hard, corrosion-resistant, silver-white metal, similar to and occurring with platinum and used in alloys (NOTE: The chemical symbol is **Ir**; the atomic number is **77** and the atomic weight is **192.22**.)

**iris** *noun* **1.** OPTICS a small hole in a camera between the lens and the film, normally variable in size to adjust the amount of light passing through it to the film **2.** ANAT the coloured part of the eye, which expands and contracts the pupil **3.** BIOL, BOT a plant with coloured flowers and sword-shaped leaves. Genus: *Iris*.

**iroko** *noun* INDUST an African hardwood, formerly widely used but becoming rarer

**iron** *noun* CHEM ELEM a metallic element essential to biological life and an essential part of human diet (NOTE: The chemical symbol is **Fe**; the atomic number is **26** and atomic weight is **55.85**.)

COMMENT: Iron is an essential part of the red pigment in red blood cells. Lack of iron in haemoglobin results in iron-deficiency anaemia. The metal and alloys made from iron are magnetic. Compass needles made from iron point to magnetic north.

**iron chloride** *noun* CHEM a compound of iron and chlorine. Formula: $FeCl_2$.

**iron-deficiency anaemia** *noun* MED anaemia caused by lack of iron in red blood cells

**iron ore** *noun* GEOL a rock that contains iron compounds, and from which iron can be extracted

**iron oxide** *noun* CHEM same as **ferric oxide**

**iron pyrites** *noun* CHEM same as **pyrite**

**iron sulfate, iron sulphate** *noun* CHEM a compound of iron, sulfur and oxygen. Formula: $Fe_2(SO_4)_3$.

**ironworks** *noun* INDUST a place where iron is smelted and worked

**IRQ** *abbreviation* COMPUT interrupt request

**irradiate** *verb* PHYS to subject something to radiation

COMMENT: Food is sometimes irradiated with gamma rays which kill bacteria as a method of preservation. It is not certain that irradiated food is safe for humans to eat, as the effects are not known. In some countries irradiation is only permitted as a treatment of specific foods.

**irradiation** *noun* **1.** the spread of something from a centre **2.** exposure to radiation, especially ionising radiation **3.** PHYS the use of rays to treat patients or to kill bacteria in food

**irradiation dose** *noun* PHYS the amount of radiation to which an organism is exposed

**irrational number** *noun* MATHS a real number that cannot be expressed as an exact ratio of two whole numbers

**irregular** *adjective* not regular

**irrespective** *adverb* taking no account of something ○ *irrespective of age* ○ *They noted the warning, but decided to go ahead irrespective.*

**irretrievable** *adjective* COMPUT unable to be retrieved ○ *The files are irretrievable since the computer crashed.*

**irreversible** *adjective* unable to be reversed ○ *an irreversible process*

**irreversible reaction** *noun* CHEM a chemical reaction that cannot be reversed

**irrigate** *verb* AGRIC to supply water to land to allow plants to grow, usually through a system of constructed channels

**irrigation** *noun* AGRIC the supplying of water to land to allow plants to grow, usually through a system of constructed channels ○ *New areas of land must be brought under irrigation to meet the rising demand for food.*

COMMENT: Irrigation can be carried out using sprinklers or by channelling water along small irrigation canals from reservoirs or rivers. Irrigation can cause salinisation of the soil. The soil becomes waterlogged and salts rise to the surface. At the surface, the irrigated water rapidly evaporates, leaving the salts behind as a saline crust. Irrigation can also increase the spread of disease. Water insects are easily spread through irrigation canals and reservoirs.

**irritability** *noun* PHYSIOL same as **sensitivity**

**irritant** *noun* MED a substance or object that can cause irritation (NOTE: An irritant can have an acute effect on respiration from a single high-level exposure, or chronic effects from repeated low-level exposures.)

**IRSG** *abbreviation* COMPUT Internet research steering group

**IRTF** *abbreviation* COMPUT Internet research task force

**ISA** *abbreviation* **1.** COMPUT Industry Standard Architecture **2.** AEROSP international standard atmosphere

**ISAM** *abbreviation* COMPUT indexed sequential access method

**ischium** *noun* ANAT the rearmost of the three bones that form each half of the pelvis

**ISDN** *abbreviation* COMPUT integrated services digital network

**IS-IS** *abbreviation* COMPUT intermediate system to intermediate system

**island** *noun* GEOG a piece of land surrounded by water, in a sea, river or lake

**island biogeography** *noun* ECOL a theory stating that the number of species on an island or any area results from a dynamic equilibrium between colonisation and extinction

**islets of Langerhans** *plural noun* ANAT the clusters of cells in the pancreas that secrete the hormones insulin and glucagon

**ISO** *abbreviation* COMPUT International Standards Organisation

**iso-** *prefix* equal

**isobar** *noun* METEOROL a line on a map linking points which are of equal barometric pressure at a given time

**isobaric chart** *noun* METEOROL a weather map showing the isobars at a given time

**isochronous network** *noun* COMPUT a network in which all the components on the network run from a common clock so that their timing is uniform

**isochronous transmission** *noun* COMPUT the transfer of asynchronous data over a synchronous link

**isocyanide** *noun* CHEM same as **isonitrile**

**isoelectric point** *noun* CHEM the pH value at which there is no electric force on a molecule in a solution

**isogenic, isogenous** *adjective* GENETICS with identical genes

**isohaline** *noun* EARTH SCI a line on a map linking areas of equal salt content

**isohyet** *noun* METEOROL a line on a map linking points of equal rainfall

**isolate** *verb* **1.** to separate and keep something or someone apart from other things or people ○ *The low-pressure fuel cock isolates the airframe fuel system from the engine fuel system to enable maintenance and engine removals to be carried out.* **2.** ELEC to separate something from a system **3.** ELEC to insulate something electrically **4.** MED to keep one patient apart from others usually because he or she has a dangerous infectious disease **5.** MICROBIOL to separate a microorganism from its host or the material on which it grows ○ *Scientists have been able to isolate the virus which causes legionnaires' disease.* ○ *Candida is easily isolated from the mouths of healthy adults.* ■ *noun* MICROBIOL a pure culture of a microorganism

**isolation** *noun* a state or the process of being separated and kept apart from other things or people

**isolation hospital** *noun* MED a special hospital where patients suffering from dangerous infectious diseases can be isolated

**isolation transformer** *noun* ELEC a transformer used to isolate equipment from direct connection with the mains electricity supply, in case of voltage spikes

**isolation ward** *noun* a special ward in a hospital where patients suffering from dangerous infectious diseases can be isolated

**isoleucine** *noun* BIOCHEM an essential amino acid

**isomer** *noun* CHEM one of two or more nuclides with the same mass number and atomic number but different energy states and half-lives

**isomerism** *noun* CHEM the existence of two or more nuclides as isomers

**isometric view** *noun* COMPUT a drawing that shows all three dimensions of an object in equal proportion ○ *An isometric view does not show any perspective.*

**isomorphism** *noun* MATHS a one-to-one correspondence between sets such that an operation such as addition or multiplication in one produces the same result as the analogous operation in the other

**isonitrile** *noun* CHEM a colourless organic compound with an unpleasant smell, containing the group -NC. Also called **isocyanide**

**ISO/OSI** *abbreviation* COMPUT International Standards Organisation Open System Interconnection

**isoprene** *noun* CHEM a colourless liquid hydrocarbon that is flammable and may react to give a polymer. Formula: $C_5H_8$. (NOTE: It is used in synthetic rubber manufacture.)

**isotach** *noun* METEOROL a line on a map linking points where the wind is blowing at the same speed

**isotherm** *noun* METEOROL a line on a map linking points of equal temperature

**isotonic** *adjective* CHEM referring to solutions that exert the same osmotic pressure

**isotope** *noun* CHEM a form of a chemical element which has the same chemical properties as other forms, but a different atomic mass

COMMENT: Uranium exists in several isotopes: uranium-238 is the commonest and is used in fast breeder reactors because of its property of releasing energy very slowly under normal conditions; uranium-235 is the isotope used in fission, because of its ability to release energy rapidly.

**isotopic number** *noun* PHYS the difference between the number of neutrons and the number of protons in an atom

**isotropic** *adjective* CHEM referring to something that has physical properties that do not differ according to direction

**isotropy** *noun* CHEM the property of a material whereby it has the same properties from different directions (NOTE: Some crystals are anisotropic rather than isotropic because they refract light differently depending on which face the light falls upon. Isotropy is significant in optics and on a larger scale as a property of the universe in general.)

**isozyme** *noun* BIOCHEM a form of an enzyme that is chemically different from other forms but functions in the same way

**ISP** *abbreviation* COMPUT Internet service provider

**ISR** *abbreviation* COMPUT information storage and retrieval

**issue** *noun* a copy of a publication ○ *The article was in last month's issue of the journal.* ■ *verb* **1.** to give something out officially ○ *issued a warning* ○ *will be issuing security passes* **2.** to arise from somewhere ○ *A dark liquid was issuing from the crack.*

**isthmus** *noun* EARTH SCI a narrow piece of land linking two larger areas of land

**IT** *abbreviation* COMPUT information technology

**italic** *adjective, noun* PRINTING (a character font) in which the characters slope to the right ○ *The species name is printed in italic font.*

**italics** *plural noun* PRINTING italic characters ○ *All the footnotes are printed in italics.* ○ *Hit CTRL I to print the text in italics.*

**ITCZ** *abbreviation* EARTH SCI intertropical convergence zone

**item** *noun* a single thing among many ○ *An item of data can be a word, a series of figures or a record in a file.*

**item size** *noun* COMPUT a number of characters or digits in an item of data

**iteration** *noun* **1.** a repetition **2.** COMPUT the repeated application of a program to solve a problem

**iterative process** *noun* a process that is continuously repeated until a condition is met

**iterative routine, iterate** *noun*
COMPUT a loop or series of instructions
in a program which repeats over and
over again until the program is
completed

**IV** *abbreviation* MED intravenous

**IVF** *abbreviation* MED in vitro
fertilisation

**ivory** *noun* ZOOL a smooth whitish substance forming the tusks of animals such
as elephants and walruses, formerly
used to make piano keys and ornaments

COMMENT: The main source of ivory is
the African elephant, which is an endangered species. Opinion is divided on
whether there should be a total ban or
only a partial ban on the trade in ivory.
There are several ivory substitutes including plastic, ceramic and the ivory nut.

**ivory nut** *noun* BOT the seed of a
South American palm tree, used as a
substitute for real ivory

# J

**J** *abbreviation* MEASURE joule

**jabber** *noun* COMPUT a continuous random signal transmitted by a faulty adapter card or node on a network

**jack** *noun* **1.** ENG a powered device to lift or move heavy components **2.** ELEC a plug that consists of a single pin

**jacket** *noun* an outer covering or casing ○ *a cylinder jacket*

**jaggies** *plural noun* COMPUT jagged edges which appear along diagonal or curved lines displayed on a computer screen, caused by the size of each pixel

**jam** *noun* a stoppage in a process or mechanism due to a fault ○ *a jam in the paper feed* ■ *verb* to stop working because something is causing a blockage ○ *The recorder is not working because the tape is jammed in the motor.* ○ *Lightweight copier paper will feed without jamming.*

**jar** *verb* COMPUT to give a sharp shock to a device ○ *You can cause trouble by turning off or jarring the PC while the disk read heads are moving.* ○ *Hard disks are very sensitive to jarring.* ■ *noun* a glass container

**Java** *trademark* COMPUT a programming language and program definition used to create small applications to enhance the functionality of a webpage (NOTE: The language is similar to object-oriented languages such as C++ and can run on any compatible platform.)

**JavaScript** *noun* COMPUT a set of programming commands that can be included within a normal webpage, written using HTML commands (NOTE: When the web browser loads the webpage, it runs the JavaScript commands, usually used to create special effects to a webpage.)

**JCL** *abbreviation* COMPUT job control language

**JD** *abbreviation* Julian date

**jejunum** *noun* ANAT the part of the small intestine between the duodenum and ileum, concerned mainly with absorbing nutrients from digested food

**jet** *noun* **1.** a strong fast stream of fluid forced out of an opening ○ *a jet of water from a pipe* **2.** same as **jet engine 3.** AEROSP an aircraft which has jet engines

**jet engine** *noun* AEROSP an engine used on aircraft which produces forward motion by sending out a jet of hot gases backwards ○ *The jet engine was invented by Frank Whittle in 1941.*

**jet fuel** *noun* AEROSP same as **kerosene**

**jet-powered, jet-propelled** *adjective* driven by jet propulsion

**jet propulsion** *noun* **1.** ENG the act of making something move forward by sending out backwards a jet of hot gases, air or water **2.** AEROSP power that provides thrust for an aircraft by taking in air at the front, mixing it with fuel, burning the mixture and causing expansion of gases

**jet stream** *noun* **1.** METEOROL a wide belt of fast-moving air occurring at the top limit of the troposphere, about 15 km above Earth's surface **2.** AEROSP a flow of gases from a jet engine

**jettison** *verb* to throw off or release something from a moving aircraft or ship

**jitter** *noun* COMPUT **1.** a fault where there is rapid small up-and-down movement of characters or pixels on a screen of image bits in a facsimile transmission ○ *Looking at this screen jitter is giving me a headache.* **2.** a fault in a transmission line that causes some of the data bits being transmitted to be corrupted

**JK-flip-flop** *noun* ELEC a flip-flop device with two inputs, J and K, and two complementary outputs that are dependent on the inputs

**job** *noun* a task, set of tasks or work to be processed as a single unit ○ *The next job to be processed is to sort all the records.*

**job control language** *noun* COMPUT a set of commands that describe the identification of and resources required for a job that a computer has to process. Abbreviation **JCL**

**job priority** *noun* COMPUT the importance of a job compared to others

**job statement control** *noun* COMPUT the use of instructions and statements to control the actions of the operating system of a computer

**join** *verb* **1.** to connect or bring things together ○ *Join the two wires.* ○ *With a pencil and ruler, join point A to point B.* **2.** to combine two or more pieces of information to produce a single unit of information ■ *noun* **1.** a place at which two or more things are connected **2.** COMPUT a logical function that produces a true output if any input is true

**join files** *noun* COMPUT an instruction to produce a new file consisting of one file added to the end of another

**joint** *noun* **1.** a place at which two or more things are joined together ○ *Fuselage frame rings are formed with only one joint.* **2.** ANAT a place at which two bones are connected ■ *adjective* **1.** with two or more things linked together **2.** shared by two or more people ○ *a joint effort* ○ *a joint venture* **3.** ANAT referring to a joint in the body ○ *joint pains*

**joint denial** *noun* COMPUT a logical function whose output is false if any input is true

**Joint Implementation** *noun* ENVIRON a set of agreements made between two or more nations under the Framework Convention on Climate Change to help reduce greenhouse gas emissions

**joule** *noun* MEASURE an SI unit of measurement of energy. Symbol **J**

COMMENT: One joule is the amount of energy used to move one kilogram the distance of one metre, using the force of one newton 4.184 joules equal one calorie.

**journal** *noun* **1.** a scientific publication **2.** COMPUT a record of all communications to and from a terminal **3.** COMPUT a list of any changes or updates to a file ○ *The modified records were added to the master file and noted in the journal.*

**joystick** *noun* COMPUT a device that allows a user to move a cursor around the screen by moving an upright rod connected to an I/O port on the computer

**JPEG** *noun* COMPUT a standard that defines a way of storing graphic images in a compressed format in a file on disk. Full form **Joint Photographic Experts Group**

**jugular vein** *noun* ANAT one of several paired veins that pass through the neck to drain blood from the head (NOTE: In humans, on either side of the neck there is a larger internal vein flanked by an external vein.)

**jukebox** *noun* COMPUT a CD-ROM drive that can hold several CD-ROM disks and select the correct disk when required

**Julian calendar** *noun* ASTRON a calendar system with a leap year every four years (NOTE: It is so-called because it was introduced during Julius Caesar's period as ruler of Rome in 46 BC. The Julian calendar ceased to be used between the 16th and 20th centuries as the more accurate Gregorian calendar entered use.)

**Julian date** *noun* ASTRON a date in years, days and decimals of a day, taken from an arbitrary start date of 465 BC and with the days counted from noon rather than midnight. Abbreviation **JD** (NOTE: Julian dates occur in astronomical calculation and reckoning. They are unrelated to the Julian calendar.)

**jumbo chip** *noun* COMPUT an integrated circuit made using the whole of a semiconductor wafer

**jump** COMPUT *noun* a programming command to end one set of instructions and direct the processor to another section of the program. Also called **jump instruction** ■ *verb* to direct a central processing unit to another section of a program

**jumper** *noun* ELEC a temporary wire connection on a circuit board

**jumper-selectable** *noun* ELEC a circuit or device whose options can be selected by positioning various wire connections ○ *The printer's typeface was jumper-selectable.*

**jumping gene** *noun* GENETICS same as **transposon**

**jump instruction** *noun* COMPUT same as **jump**

**jump on zero** *noun* COMPUT a conditional jump executed if a flag or register is zero

**jump operation** *noun* COMPUT a situation where the central processing unit is sent from the instruction it is currently executing to another point in the program

**junction** *noun* a place where two things meet ○ *the junction of two wires*

**junction box** *noun* ELEC an electrical unit where a number of wires can be connected together

**jungle** *noun* ECOL a tropical rainforest (*informal*)

**juniper** *noun* TREES a small coniferous tree of the northern hemisphere, whose cones are like berries. Genus: *Juniperus.*

**juniper berry** *noun* FOOD INDUST the purple cone of the juniper, used as a flavouring

**junk** *noun* **1.** useless things **2.** COMPUT information or hardware which is useless or out-of-date or non-functional ■ *verb* COMPUT to get rid of something

useless or redundant □ **to junk a file** to erase or delete from storage a file that is no longer used

**Jupiter** *noun* ASTRON the largest planet of the solar system, 318 times as massive as the Earth and eleven times as large, with an equatorial radius of 72 000 km (NOTE: Jupiter is a mean distance of 778 million km from the Sun, which it takes 12 years to orbit. Jupiter is accompanied by a thin ring system and a huge array of satellites.)

**justify** *verb* **1.** COMPUT, PRINTING to change the spacing between words or characters in a document so that the left and right margins are straight **2.** COMPUT to shift the contents of a computer register by a set amount **3.** to argue a logical case for something

**juvenile** BIOL *noun* a young animal or plant ■ *adjective* not yet adult

**juvenile hormone** *noun* BIOCHEM a hormone in an insect larva that regulates its development into an adult

**juvenile phase** *noun* BIOL the period of development of a plant before it flowers or of an animal before it becomes adult

# K

**k** *symbol* MEASURE kilo-

**K** *symbol* **1.** PHYS, MEASURE kelvin **2.** CHEM ELEM potassium

**kainite** *noun* MINERALS a white mineral containing potassium chloride and magnesium sulfate that is a source of potassium

**kala-azar** *noun* MED a severe infection, occurring in tropical countries

COMMENT: Kala-azar is a form of leishmaniasis, caused by the infection of the intestines and internal organs by a parasite *Leishmania* spread by flies. Symptoms are fever, anaemia, general wasting of the body and swelling of the spleen and liver.

**kalium** *noun* CHEM same as **potassium**

**kaolin** *noun* INDUST a fine white clay used for making china, for coating shiny paper and in medicines ○ *Spoil heaps from kaolin workings are bright white.*

**Karnaugh map** *noun* COMPUT a graphical representation of states and conditions in a logic circuit ○ *The prototype was checked for hazards with a Karnaugh map.*

**karst** *noun* EARTH SCI a terrain typical of limestone country, with an uneven surface and holes and cracks due to weathering

**karyogram** *noun* GENETICS a photograph or diagram of the chromosomes of a cell

**karyology** *noun* GENETICS the study of cell nuclei, especially chromosomes

**karyotype** *noun* GENETICS the chromosome make-up of a cell, shown as a diagram or as a set of letters and numbers

**katabatic wind** *noun* METEOROL a cold wind which blows downhill as the ground surface cools at night. Compare **anabatic wind**

**katadromous** *adjective* MARINE BIOL another spelling of **catadromous**

**Kb** *abbreviation* COMPUT kilobyte ○ *The new disk drive has a 100 Kb capacity.*

**Kbit** *abbreviation* COMPUT kilobit

**Kbps** *abbreviation* COMPUT kilobits per second ○ *A fast modem can transfer data at a rate of 33.6 Kbps, whereas an ISDN adapter can transfer data at a rate of 64 Kbps.*

**Kbyte** *abbreviation* COMPUT kilobyte

**kcal** *abbreviation* MEASURE kilocalorie

**Kekulé structure** *noun* CHEM the representation of a benzene molecule as a hexagonal ring in which single and double bonds alternate, linking six carbon atoms, each of which is bound to one hydrogen atom

**kelp** *noun* MARINE BIOL a large brown seaweed which is a source of iodine and potash

**kelp forest** *noun* MARINE BIOL a marine ecosystem dominated by kelp ○ *Kelp forests are restricted to cold and temperate waters.*

**kelvin** *noun* MEASURE, PHYS a base SI unit of measurement of thermodynamic temperature. Symbol **K** (NOTE: 0° C is equal to 273.15 K. Temperatures are shown in kelvin without a degree sign: **20 K.**)

**Kelvin scale** *noun* MEASURE, PHYS a temperature scale on which zero is the lowest attainable temperature and the triple point of water is defined as 273.16 K

**Kepler, Johannes (1571–1630)** ASTRON a German astronomer who produced three laws describing the motion of the planets around the Sun. He was also a pioneer of optics and calculus.

**Kepler's laws** *plural noun* ASTRON three mathematical statements describing the movement of the planets in their orbits around the Sun, the first two of which were published in 1609 and the third in 1619

COMMENT: The first law states that the orbit of a planet is an ellipse, with the Sun at one focus. The second states that a line between the Sun and a particular planet sweeps out equal areas in equal times. The line is termed the radius vector. This law means that the nearer a planet is to the Sun, the faster it moves. The third law states that the square of the orbital period of a planet is proportional to the cube of its distance from the Sun. Neptune is on average 30 times as far from the Sun as Earth, but takes 165 times as long to orbit the Sun. This law means that more distant planets have much longer years. Kepler's laws also apply to the orbits of artificial and natural satellites, binary stars and other celestial objects including comets and asteroids.

**keratin** *noun* BIOCHEM a fibrous protein that gives strength and elasticity to hair, nails, feathers and hooves

**kern** *verb* PRINTING to adjust the space between pairs of letters so that they are printed closer together ○ *We have kerned 'T' and 'o' so they are closer together.*

**kernel** *noun* 1. BOT the soft edible part of a nut 2. BOT the seed and husk of a cereal grain 3. COMPUT the set of basic essential instruction routines required for any operations in a computer system

COMMENT: Kernel routines are usually hidden from the user. They are used by the operating system for tasks such as loading a program or displaying text on a screen.

**kerosene, kerosine** *noun* a thin fuel oil made from petroleum ○ *Kerosene will only burn efficiently at, or close to, a ratio of 15:1.* Also called **jet fuel**

**Kerr black hole** *noun* ASTRON a black hole with rotation but no electric charge

**ketone** *noun* CHEM an organic compound containing the group -CO- attached to two hydrocarbons

**ketose** *noun* BIOCHEM a simple sugar

**Kevlar** *trademark* INDUST a light and very strong composite material ○ *Kevlar and carbon fibre account for a*

*large percentage of a modern jet airliner's structure.*

**key** *noun* 1. COMPUT a button on a keyboard that operates a switch ○ *There are 64 keys on the keyboard.* 2. COMPUT an important object or group of characters in a computer system, used to represent an instruction or set of data 3. COMPUT a special combination of numbers or characters that is used with a cipher to encrypt or decrypt a message ○ *Type this key into the machine, it will decode the last message.* 4. COMPUT an identification code or word used for a stored record or data item ○ *We selected all the records with the word disk in their keys.* 5. a set of questions to enable something to be identified

**keyboard** COMPUT *noun* a number of keys fixed together in some order, used to enter information into a computer or to produce characters on a typewriter ■ *verb* to enter information by using a keyboard ○ *It was cheaper to have the manuscript keyboarded by another company.*

**key click** *noun* COMPUT a sound produced by a computer to allow the operator to know that the key pressed has been registered

**keyed sequential access method** *noun* COMPUT a file structure that allows data to be accessed using key fields or key field content. Abbreviation **KSAM**

**key field** *noun* COMPUT a field which identifies entries in a record

**key matrix** *noun* COMPUT the way in which the keys of a keyboard are arranged as an array of connections

**key number** *noun* COMPUT a numeric code used to identify which key has been pressed

**keypad** *noun* COMPUT a group of special keys used for certain applications ○ *You can use the numeric keypad to enter the figures.*

**keystone species** *noun* ECOL a species that plays a significant role in helping to maintain the ecosystems that it is part of

**keystroke** *noun* COMPUT an act of pressing a key ○ *He keyboards at a rate of 3500 keystrokes per hour.*

**keyword** *noun* COMPUT **1.** a command word used in a programming language to provide a function ○ *The BASIC keyword PRINT will display text on the screen.* **2.** an important or informative word in a title or document that describes its contents ○ *Computer is a keyword in IT.* **3.** a word that is relevant or important to a text

**kg** *symbol* MEASURE kilogram

**khamsin** *noun* METEOROL a hot wind that brings dust storms in North Africa

**kHz** *symbol* MEASURE kilohertz

**kidney** *noun* ANAT an organ in vertebrates that regulates and filters waste for excretion

**kieselguhr** *noun* a mineral deposit formed from the bodies of diatoms, used in filters and in the manufacture of polishes

**kill** *verb* **1.** to make someone or something die ○ *She was given the kidney of a person killed in a car crash.* ○ *Heart attacks kill more people every year.* ○ *Antibodies are formed to kill bacteria.* **2.** COMPUT to erase a file or stop a program during execution ■ *noun* **1.** an act of making someone or something die ○ *Pollutants in water are one of the main causes of fish kills.* **2.** prey which has been killed ○ *The vultures surrounded the remains of the lion's kill.*

**kill off** *verb* BIOL to kill all the individual members of a species, usually one by one ○ *Dodos were killed off by 18th-century sailors.*

**kiln** *noun* INDUST a furnace used for making something such as pottery or bricks ○ *The smoke from the brick kilns was taken away by the prevailing winds.*

**kilo** *noun* MEASURE same as **kilogram**

**kilo-** *prefix* **1.** MEASURE one thousand, $10^3$. Symbol **K 2.** MEASURE, COMPUT (*in computer and electronics applications*) 1024 units, equal to $2^{10}$. Symbol **k**

**kilobaud** *noun* COMPUT a unit of 1000 bits per second

**kilobit** *noun* COMPUT a unit of 1024 bits of data. Abbreviation **Kbit**

**kilobits per second** *noun* COMPUT a measure of the amount of data that a device can transfer each second. Abbreviation **Kbps**

**kilobyte** *noun* COMPUT a unit of measurement for high-capacity storage devices equal to 1024 bytes of data. Abbreviation **Kbyte**. Symbol **Kb**

COMMENT: In computer or electronics applications, 1024 is the strict definition of kilobyte, being equal to a convenient power of two. It can also be taken to equal approximately 1000, even in computing applications. 1 Kb is roughly equal to 1000 output characters in a PC.

**kilocalorie** *noun* MEASURE a unit of measurement of heat equal to 1000 calories. See Comment at **calorie** (NOTE: In scientific use, the SI unit **joule** is now more usual. 1 calorie = 4.186 joules.)

**kilogram** *noun* MEASURE the base unit of mass in the SI system, equal to 1000 grams or 2.2046 pounds. Symbol **kg**. Also called **kilo**

**kilogray** *noun* MEASURE an SI unit of measurement of absorbed radiation equal to 1000 grays

**kilohertz** *noun* MEASURE an SI unit of frequency measurement equal to 1000 Hertz or one thousand cycles per second. Symbol **kHz**

**kilo instructions per second** *noun* COMPUT a measure of power, 1000 computer instructions processed every second. Abbreviation **KIPS**

**kilojoule** *noun* MEASURE an SI unit of measurement of energy or heat equal to 1000 joules. Symbol **kJ**

**kilometer** US spelling of **kilometre**

**kilometre** *noun* a measure of length equal to 1000 metres or 0.621 miles. Symbol **km** (NOTE: The US spelling is **kilometer**.)

**kilopascal** *noun* MEASURE an SI unit of measurement of pressure equal to 1000 pascals. Symbol **kPa**

**kilowatt** *noun* MEASURE a unit of measurement of electricity equal to 1000 watts. Symbol **kW**

**kilowatt-hour** *noun* MEASURE a unit of 1000 watts of electricity used for one hour. Symbol **kWh**

**kiloword** *noun* COMPUT a unit of measurement of 1024 computer words. Abbreviation **KW**

**kinase** *noun* BIOCHEM an enzyme that transfers a phosphate group from ATP

**kinematics** noun BIOL the science of movement, especially of body movements

**kinesis** noun BIOL the movement of a cell or organism in response to the intensity of a stimulus rather than its direction

**kinetic** adjective PHYS referring to motion or something produced by motion

**kinetic energy** noun PHYS energy possessed by an object because of its motion ○ *The greater the velocity of the car, the greater its kinetic energy.* (NOTE: The energy is equal to 1/2 $mv^2$ where m = mass of the object and v = velocity.)

**kinetic heating** noun AEROSP the heating of an aircraft skin by friction with the air as it moves through it

**kinetics** noun PHYS the scientific study of bodies in motion

**kinetic temperature** noun PHYS the temperature of a material, usually a gas, due to the motion of its particles

**kinetic theory** noun PHYS a theory that explains the behaviour of gases by assuming that heat is a process of energy transfer and that the internal energy of a gas is the sum of the energy of its particles

**kingdom** noun BIOL the largest category in the classification of organisms ○ *The largest species in the animal kingdom is the whale.*

COMMENT: The different kingdoms are: Kingdom Monera, Kingdom Protista, Kingdom Plantae, Kingdom Fungi and Kingdom Animalia.

**kinin** noun BIOCHEM same as **cytokinin**

**KIPS** abbreviation COMPUT kilo instructions per second

**kit** noun a set of items used for a specific purpose ○ *A physician's kit containing surgical equipment would be available to a qualified doctor assisting crew with major medical problems.*

**kJ** abbreviation MEASURE kilojoule

**kludge, kluge** noun COMPUT (*informal*) **1.** a temporary correction made to a badly written or constructed piece of software or to a keyboarding error **2.** hardware which should be used for demonstration purposes only

**km** abbreviation MEASURE kilometre

**knob** noun **1.** a rounded handle ○ *door knob* **2.** a rounded part that controls something ○ *When the control knob is moved from the central position, the ailerons are moved.*

**knock** verb ENG to make a loud noise as the mixture of petrol and air in a petrol engine explodes, caused when the mixture is not rich enough in petrol

**knot** noun **1.** MEASURE a unit of speed equal to one nautical mile per hour, approximately 1.85 km or 1.15 statute miles per hour ○ *Wind speeds in aviation are usually given in knots.* Abbreviation **kt 2.** a structure formed when several strands are joined together or a single strand is looped on itself **3.** BOT a dark area in a piece of wood where a branch formerly grew

**knowledge** noun what is known

**knowledge-based system** noun COMPUT a computer system that applies the stored reactions, instructions and knowledge of experts in a particular field to a problem

**Köppen classification** noun METEOROL a standard classification of climate

COMMENT: The classification of climate types was drawn up by Wladimir Köppen in 1900 and has been much modified since then. The classification divides the Earth into five climate types: A, B, C, D and E, according to temperature and rainfall.

**Kr** symbol CHEM ELEM krypton

**Krebs cycle** noun BIOCHEM a series of reactions in which the intermediate products of fats, carbohydrates and amino acid metabolism are converted to carbon dioxide and water in mitochondria. Also called **citric acid cycle**

**krill** noun MARINE BIOL a mass of tiny shrimps that live in cold seas and form the basic diet of many marine animals including whales

**krotovina** noun EARTH SCI an animal burrow that has been filled with organic or mineral material from another soil horizon

**krypton** noun CHEM ELEM an inert gas found in very small quantities in the atmosphere (NOTE: The chemical symbol is **Kr**; the atomic number is **36** and atomic weight is **83.80**.)

**KSAM** abbreviation COMPUT keyed sequential access method

**kt** *abbreviation* MEASURE knot

**Kuiper, Gerald (1905–73)** ASTRON a US astronomer born in the Netherlands who worked in all aspects of planetary astronomy, especially the study of Mars and the Moon. Kuiper is regarded by many as the founder of the present-day scientific study of the solar system.

**Kuiper Belt** *noun* ASTRON a zone beyond the orbits of Neptune and Pluto, some 30–60 AU distant and mainly in the plane of the ecliptic, in which many millions of comets are postulated to exist

**kW** *abbreviation* MEASURE kilowatt

**KW** *abbreviation* COMPUT kiloword

**kwashiorkor** *noun* MED malnutrition of small children, mostly in tropical countries, causing anaemia, wasting of the body and swollen liver (NOTE: It is caused by protein deficiency in the diet, especially where cassava is the staple foodstuff, since the protein content of cassava is almost nil.)

**kWh** *abbreviation* MEASURE kilowatt-hour

# L

**l, L** *symbol* MEASURE litre

**La** *symbol* CHEM ELEM lanthanum

**lab** *noun* TECH same as **laboratory** (*informal*) ○ *We'll send the specimens away for a lab test.* ○ *The samples have been returned by the lab.*

**label** *noun* **1.** a piece of paper or card attached to something to show instructions for use or an address **2.** COMPUT a characters or set of characters used to identify a variable or piece of data or a file **3.** COMPUT a word or other symbol used in a computer program to identify a routine or statement ○ *BASIC uses many program labels such as line numbers.* ■ *verb* **1.** to identify something by using a label ○ *Parts are labelled with the manufacturer's name.* **2.** to add identifying words and numbers to a diagram ○ *There is a standard way of labelling the navigation vector.*

**labile** *adjective* CHEM unstable and readily undergoing chemical or physical change

**labium** *noun* BOT the lower lip of the flower tube of some plants

**laboratory** *noun* TECH a special room where scientists can do experimental research and testing ○ *The samples of water have been sent to the laboratory for testing.* ■ *adjective* referring to laboratories ○ *The new drug has passed its laboratory tests.*

**laboratory officer** *noun* TECH a qualified person in charge of a laboratory

**laboratory technician** *noun* TECH a person who does practical work in a laboratory and has particular care of equipment

**laboratory technique** *noun* TECH a method or skill needed to perform experiments in a laboratory

**labrum** *noun* ZOOL an upper mouthpart found in some arthropods such as insects

**lack** *noun* the absence or need of something ○ *The engine stopped because of a lack of fuel.*

**lacrimal gland, lacrymal gland** *noun* ANAT a gland in the eyelids of some vertebrate animals, including humans, that produces tears

**lactase** *noun* BIOCHEM an enzyme, secreted in the small intestine, that converts milk sugar into glucose and galactose

**lactate** *verb* BIOL to produce milk as food for young

**lactation** *noun* BIOL the production of milk as food for young

**lactic acid** *noun* BIOCHEM a sugar which forms in cells and tissue, and is also present in sour milk, cheese and yoghurt

COMMENT: Lactic acid is produced as the body uses up sugar during exercise. Excessive amounts of lactic acid in the body can produce muscle cramp.

**lactose** *noun* BIOCHEM a sugar found in milk

**lactose intolerance** *noun* MED an inability to digest lactose because lactase is absent in the intestine, or because of an allergy to milk, causing diarrhoea

**lacustrine** *adjective* EARTH SCI referring to a lake or pond

**laevorotatory** *adjective* OPTICS deviating the plane of polarisation of oncoming light to the left or in an anticlockwise direction. Compare **dextrorotatory**

**laevulose** *noun* BIOCHEM same as **fructose**

**lag** *noun* a delay ○ *There is a time lag between the piston moving down and the mixture flowing into the cylinder.* ■ *verb* to cover something with an insulating material to protect against cold or to stop heat escaping ○ *Boilers and pipes* *should be carefully lagged to prevent heat loss.*

**lagging** *noun* INDUST material used to insulate pipes

**lagoon** *noun* **1.** EARTH SCI a shallow part of the sea in the tropics, surrounded or almost surrounded by reefs **2.** INDUST an artificial lake used for purifying sewage or the runoff from silage

**lagooning** *noun* INDUST the creation of artificial lakes for purifying sewage

**lake** *noun* EARTH SCI a large area of fresh water surrounded by land

**lake bloom** *noun* BIOL a mass of algae which develops rapidly in a lake due to eutrophication

**lake deposits** *plural noun* EARTH SCI deposits of silt on the bed of a lake

**Lamarckism** *noun* BIOL the theory of Jean Baptiste Lamarck that evolution occurs through the inheritance of characteristics acquired by individual organisms as a response to their environmental conditions

**lambert** *noun* MEASURE the cgs unit of surface brightness (**luminance**), equal to one lumen per square centimetre

**Lambert's law** *noun* PHYS a law defining the rate of absorption of all types of radiation, including light, as it travels within a medium

**Lambert's projection** *noun* EARTH SCI a map projection of the Earth based around two standard parallels of latitude

**lamella** *noun* FUNGI one of the gills on the underside of the cap of a fungus

**lamina** *noun* ZOOL (*in mammals with hooves*) one of several layers of sensitive tissue just inside the hard exterior of the hoof

**laminar flow** *noun* PHYS a flow in a liquid or gas which consists of separate layers flowing at different velocities and not mixing

**laminate** *noun* a sheet of manufactured material made up of bonded layers ○ *Direction of the fibres and types of cloth used in the laminate are all very important factors.* ■ *verb* to make something by using bonded layers of material ○ *laminated windscreens*

**lampblack** *noun* INDUST a fine powdery form of carbon that is deposited when organic oils are burned, used as a pigment and in electrodes

**lampbrush chromosome** *noun* GENETICS an enlarged chromosome covered with fine loops of chromatin that is observed during the initial stage of meiosis

**LAN, lan** *abbreviation* COMPUT local area network

**land** *noun* EARTH SCI the solid part of the Earth's surface

**land breeze** *noun* METEOROL a light wind which blows from the land to the sea, usually during the day when the land is warm

**land burial** *noun* ENVIRON same as **land disposal**

**land clearance** *noun* ENVIRON the removal of trees or undergrowth in preparation for ploughing or building

**land disposal** *noun* ENVIRON the act of depositing waste in a hole in the ground. Also called **land burial**

**land erosion control** *noun* ENVIRON a method of preventing the soil from being worn away by irrigation, planting or mulching

**landfill** *noun* ENVIRON **1.** the disposal of waste by putting it into holes in the ground and covering it with earth (NOTE: The US term is **sanitary landfill**.) **2.** same as **landfill site**

**landfilling** *noun* ENVIRON the disposal of waste by putting it into holes in the ground and covering it with earth

**landfill site** *noun* ENVIRON an area of land where domestic rubbish is put into holes in the ground and covered with earth ○ *The council has decided to use the old gravel pits as a landfill site.* ○ *Landfill sites can leak pollutants into the ground water.* ○ *Landfill sites, if properly constructed, can be used to provide gas for fuel.* Also called **landfill**

**land improvement** *noun* AGRIC the process of making the soil more fertile

**landing zone** *noun* COMPUT an area of a hard disk which does not carry data (NOTE: The head can come into contact with the disk in this area without damaging the disk or data.)

**landline** *noun* TELECOM a communications link that uses cable to physically and electrically link two devices

**landlocked** *adjective* EARTH SCI entirely surrounded by land

**landmass** *noun* EARTH SCI a large area of land ○ *the continental landmass of the USA*

**landrace** *noun* ECOL a native species of plant or animal which has not been cultivated

**land reclamation, land restoration** *noun* AGRIC the bringing back into productive use of a piece of land such as a waste site

**Landsat** *noun* AEROSP a US satellite belonging to a set which scan the land surface of the Earth, particularly the vegetation cover

**landscape** *noun* **1.** EARTH SCI the scenery, general shape, structure and contents of the surface of an area of land **2.** PRINTING the orientation of a page or piece of paper where the longest edge is horizontal. Compare **portrait**

**landslide, landslip** *noun* EARTH SCI a sudden fall of large amounts of soil and rocks down the side of a mountain or of waste matter down the side of a spoil heap

**land use** *noun* ENVIRON the way in which the land is used ○ *They are carrying out a study of land use in northern areas.*

**language** *noun* COMPUT a system of words or symbols which allows communication with computers, e.g. one that allows computer instructions to be entered as words which are easy to understand and then translates them into machine code

COMMENT: There are three main types of computer languages: machine code, assembler and high-level language. The higher the level the language is, the easier it is to program and understand, but the slower it is to execute. The following are the commonest high-level languages: ADA, ALGOL, APL, BASIC, C, C++, COBOL, COMAL, CORAL, FORTH, FORTRAN, LISP, LOGO, PASCAL, PL/1, POP-2, PROLOG and Visual Basic. Assembly language uses mnemonics to represent machine code instructions. Machine code is the lowest level of programming language and consists of basic binary patterns that instruct the processor to perform various tasks.

**language processor** *noun* COMPUT a program that translates from an assembler or high-level language to machine code (NOTE: There are three types: assemblers, compilers and interpreters.)

**lanolin** *noun* PHARM a fat extracted from sheep's wool used in making soaps, skin creams and shampoos

**lanthanide** *noun* CHEM an element belonging to a series of rare-earth elements with atomic numbers in the range 57 to 71 and in which the f-shell is not completely full

**lanthanum** *noun* CHEM ELEM a silvery metallic element similar to aluminium belonging to the rare-earth group, used in glass manufacture (NOTE: The chemical symbol is **La**; the atomic number is **139** and the atomic weight is **138.91**.)

**LAP** *noun* COMPUT a CCITT standard protocol used to start and maintain links over an X.25 network. Full form **link access protocol**

**lapis lazuli** *noun* MINERALS a deep blue rock, used in making jewellery

**lapse** *noun* a short period of time which separates two events

**lapse rate** *noun* EARTH SCI the rate at which temperature changes according to altitude

**laptop computer, laptop** *noun* COMPUT a computer that is light enough to carry but not so small as to fit in a pocket, usually containing a screen, keyboard and disk drive

**large intestine** *noun* ANAT the latter part of the vertebrate alimentary canal, extending from ileum to anus and consisting of the caecum, colon and rectum (NOTE: It extracts water from the gut contents to form faeces.)

**large-scale** *adjective* working with large amounts of data. Compare **small-scale**

**large-scale computer** *noun* COMPUT a high-powered computer system that can access high capacity memory and backing storage devices as well as multiple users

**large-scale integration** *noun* COMPUT an integrated circuit with 500 to 10 000 components. Abbreviation **LSI**

**larva** *noun* ZOOL the form of an insect or other animal in the stage of development after the egg has hatched but before the animal becomes adult (NOTE: The plural is **larvae**.)

**larval** *adjective* ZOOL referring to larvae

**larval stage** *noun* ZOOL an early stage in the development of an insect or other animal after it has hatched from an egg

**larynx** *noun* ANAT the part of the respiratory tract at the entrance to the windpipe that, in humans and some other vertebrates, contains vocal cords and is the organ of voice production

**laser** *noun* PHYS a device that produces coherent light of a single wavelength in a narrow beam, by exciting a material so that it emits photons of light. Full form **light amplification by stimulated emission of radiation**

**laser disc** *noun* COMPUT same as **compact disc**

**laser printer** *noun* COMPUT a high-resolution computer printer that uses a laser source for high-quality printing

**Lassa fever** *noun* MED a highly infectious and often fatal virus disease found in Central and West Africa

**last** *adjective* **1.** coming or placed after all the others **2.** most recent ■ *verb* **1.** to continue for a period of time ○ *A gust is a sudden increase in wind speed above the average speed lasting only a few seconds.* **2.** to stay in good or usable condition ○ *A piston engine lasts longer if it is handled carefully and serviced regularly.*

**last in first out** *noun* COMPUT a queue system in which the last item stored is the first read ○ *This computer stack uses a last in first out data retrieval method.* Abbreviation **LIFO**

**latch** *verb* COMPUT to set an output state ○ *The output latched high until we reset the computer.*

**latency** *noun* COMPUT the time delay between the moment when an instruction is given to a computer and the execution of the instruction or return of a result, e.g. the delay between a request for data and the data being transferred from memory

**latent** *adjective* present but not yet developed

**latent heat** *noun* PHYS the heat taken in or given out when a solid changes into a liquid or vapour, or when a liquid changes into a vapour at a constant temperature and pressure

**latent heat of fusion** *noun* the quantity of heat required to convert ice

at its melting point into liquid at the same temperature

**latent heat of sublimation** *noun* the quantity of heat required to convert ice to vapour at the same temperature

**latent heat of vaporisation** *noun* PHYS the quantity of heat required to convert liquid to vapour at the same temperature

**lateral** *adjective* referring to the side ○ *Drift is lateral movement caused by wind.*

**lateral aspect** *noun* ANAT a view of the side of part of the body. Also called **lateral view**

**lateral moraine** *noun* EARTH SCI a deposit of sand and gravel left at the sides of a glacier as it moves forwards

**lateral view** *noun* ANAT same as **lateral aspect**

**laterisation** *noun* EARTH SCI the process of weathering tropical soil into hard laterite

**laterise** *verb* EARTH SCI to weather tropical soil into hard laterite

**laterite** *noun* EARTH SCI a hard rock-like clay found in the tropics, formed when latosol dries out

COMMENT: When tropical rainforests are cleared, the soil beneath rapidly turns to laterite as nutrients are leached out by rain. The land is incapable of cultivation and such areas turn to desert.

**lateritic** *adjective* EARTH SCI referring to soil that contains laterite

**latex** *noun* **1.** BOT a white fluid from a plant such as the poppy **2.** BIOL a thick white fluid from a rubber tree, which is treated and processed to make rubber

**latitude** *noun* EARTH SCI, NAVIG an angular distance north or south of the Earth's equator, measured in degrees, minutes and seconds, along a meridian ○ *Parallels of latitude are imaginary circles on the surface of the Earth, their planes being parallel to the plane of the equator.* □ **at a latitude of 46°N** at a position on the Earth's surface which is 46 degrees north of the equator

COMMENT: Together with longitude, latitude is used to indicate an exact position on the Earth's surface. Latitude is measured in degrees, minutes and seconds. The centre of London is latitude 51°30'N, longitude 0°5'W. The lines of latitude are numbered and some of them act as national boundaries: the 49th parallel marks most of the border between the USA and Canada.

**latosol** *noun* EARTH SCI a type of reddish soft soil found in tropical areas that is characterised by deep weathering and hydrous oxide material

**latter** *adjective* **1.** referring to the second of two things mentioned earlier. Compare **former 2.** referring to something coming at the end ○ *in the latter part of the report* ■ *noun* the second of two things mentioned earlier

**lattice** *noun* CHEM a regular geometrical arrangement of points or objects in three dimensions, e.g. the atoms in a crystal

**laughing gas** *noun* CHEM same as **nitrous oxide**

**launch** *noun* **1.** the introduction of a new product into a market ○ *The launch of the new PC has been put back six months.* ○ *The launch date for the network will be September.* **2.** the start of a planned activity ○ *the launch of their public awareness campaign* ■ *verb* **1.** to begin a planned activity, especially by announcing it publicly ○ *to launch a new research initiative* **2.** to put a new product on the market ○ *The new PC was launched at the Computer Show.* ○ *Launching costs for the computer range were calculated at $250 000.* **3.** COMPUT to start or run a program ○ *You launch the word-processor by double-clicking on this icon.*

**lauric acid** *noun* CHEM a white crystalline fatty acid that is insoluble in water, used in the manufacture of soaps, insecticides and cosmetics. Formula: $C_{12}H_{24}O_2$. Also called **dodecanoic acid**

**lava** *noun* EARTH SCI molten rock and minerals which flow from an erupting volcano and solidify into various types of igneous rock

**lava flow** *noun* EARTH SCI a stream of lava moving down the sides of a volcano ○ *Lava flows from the volcano destroyed sugar plantations.*

**law** *noun* **1.** a rule or set of rules by which a country is governed □ **by law** legally **2.** a basic principle of science or mathematics

**law of gravitation** *noun* PHYS a basic principle of physics that any two masses attract each other with a force equal to a

constant multiplied by the product of the two masses and divided by the square of the distance between them

**lawrencium** *noun* CHEM ELEM one of the transuranic elements (NOTE: The chemical symbol is **Lr**; the atomic number is **103** and the atomic weight is **256**.)

**layer** *noun* **1.** one of several or more horizontal parts ○ *The lowest layer of the atmosphere is called the troposphere.* **2.** a thickness of something ○ *Layers of fluid next to the surface over which it is flowing travels more slowly than layers further from the surface.* **3.** COMPUT one of the ISO/OSI standards defining the stages a message has to pass through when being transmitted from one computer to another over a local area network **4.** a flat area of a substance under or over another area (NOTE: In geological formations, layers of rock are called **strata**; layers of soil are called **horizons**.) **5.** BOT a stem of a plant which has made roots where it touches the soil ■ *verb* BOT to propagate a plant by bending a stem down until it touches the soil and letting it form roots there

**layer cloud** *noun* METEOROL a stratus cloud

**layout** *noun* the way in which things are arranged

**lb** *symbol* MEASURE pound

**LC₅₀** *abbreviation* BIOL lethal concentration 50

**LCD** *abbreviation* COMPUT liquid crystal display

**LCP** *abbreviation* COMPUT link control procedure

**LD₅₀** *abbreviation* BIOL lethal dose 50%

**leach** *verb* ENVIRON to be washed out of the soil by water ○ *Excess chemical fertilisers on the surface of the soil leach into rivers and cause pollution.* ○ *Nitrates have leached into ground water and contaminated the water supply.*

**leachate** *noun* ENVIRON **1.** a substance which is washed out of the soil **2.** a liquid which forms at the bottom of a landfill site

**leaching** *noun* ENVIRON the process by which a substance is washed out of the soil by water passing thought it

**leaching field** *noun* INDUST an area round a septic tank with pipes which allow the sewage to drain away underground

**lead**[1] *noun* CHEM ELEM a very heavy soft metallic element (NOTE: The chemical symbol is **Pb**; the atomic number is **82** and the atomic weight is **207.20**.)

COMMENT: Small children are particularly vulnerable to lead pollution, as lead affects brain development. Lead can enter the body through drinking water which has been kept in lead pipes or through paint (children's toys must be painted with lead-free paint). Lead is added to petrol to prevent knocking and give more power, but it causes lead fumes which are toxic and can be avoided by using lead-free petrol. Lead poisoning also occurs in birds, e.g. swans, which have eaten the lead pellets used by fishermen to weight their lines.

**lead**[2] *noun* ELEC ENG an electrical wire or narrow cable ○ *A lead connects the monitor to the computer.*

**lead-acid battery, lead-acid accumulator** *noun* ELEC a type of battery consisting of lead and lead-oxide plates, surrounded by a sulfuric acid electrolyte

**lead-based additive** *noun* INDUST same as **fuel additive**

**lead dioxide** *noun* CHEM a toxic dark brown crystalline substance used in batteries and explosives. Formula: $PbO_2$.

**leaded petrol** *noun* INDUST petrol to which a fuel additive such as tetraethyl lead has been added to prevent knocking

**leader** *noun* a section of magnetic tape that contains no signal, used at the beginning of a reel for identification and to aid the tape machine to pick up the tape

**leader stroke** *noun* METEOROL the first lightning flash, which makes a path for other flashes to follow

**lead-free** *adjective* INDUST referring to something such as paint or fuel which has no lead in it ○ *lead-free petrol* ○ *Lead-free fuel is used in most modern piston engines.*

**lead in** *noun* COMPUT a section of a CD-ROM before the data starts, normally used to store the table of contents

**lead monoxide** *noun* CHEM a toxic yellow or reddish-yellow substance used in storage batteries, pottery, glass, rubber and pigments. Formula: $PbO$. Also called **litharge**

**lead paint** *noun* INDUST a paint containing lead, which makes it more durable, but which is largely forbidden for use, particularly on children's toys and furniture

**lead poisoning** *noun* MED poisoning caused by taking in lead salts

**leaf** *noun* **1.** BOT a green, usually flat part of a plant, growing from a stem node, whose purpose is to activate photosynthesis **2.** COMPUT a final node in a tree structure

**leaf cutting** *noun* AGRIC a piece of a leaf or root or stem cut from a living plant and put in soil where it will sprout

**leaf litter** *noun* BOT dead leaves lying on the floor of a forest. Also called **litter**

**leaf mould** *noun* BOT a soft fibrous material formed of decomposed organic matter such as leaves

**leak** *noun* an escape of liquid or gas from a sealed container ○ *a gas leak* ■ *verb* (*of liquid or gas*) to escape from a sealed container ○ *Fuel may leak from a fuel tank if the drain plug is not seated correctly.*

**leakage** *noun* an escape of liquid or gas from a sealed container ○ *Any internal or external leakage of fuel will cause a reduction in the operating period.*

**lean** *adjective* AUTOMOT referring to a fuel/air mixture in which the ratio of air to fuel is greater than usual ○ *Moving the mixture control lever aft to the lean position reduces the amount of fuel mixing with the air.*

**lean-burn engine** *noun* INDUST a type of internal combustion engine adapted to use less fuel than normal engines, and so release less carbon monoxide and nitrogen oxide into the atmosphere

**leap-frog test** *noun* COMPUT a memory location test in which a program skips from one location to another random location, writing data then reading and comparing for faults, until all locations have been tested

**leap second** *noun* an extra second inserted into clock time to allow for the fact that Earth's rotation is less regular than the atomic clocks by which it is measured (NOTE: Leap seconds have to be placed into clock time rather than being taken out of it because Earth's rotation is gradually slowing.)

**leap year** *noun* a year occurring every four years in which an extra day has to be added because there are 365.25 days in a year (NOTE: The extra day is omitted when the year is a round century not divisible by 400, for extra accuracy.)

**learning curve** *noun* a graphical description of how someone can acquire knowledge over time

**lease** *noun* a written contract for letting or renting a piece of equipment for a period against payment of a fee ■ *verb* **1.** to let or rent equipment for a period ○ *The company has a policy of only using leased equipment.* **2.** to use equipment for a time and pay a fee ○ *The company leases all its computers.*

**leased line** *noun* TELECOM a communications channel such as a telephone line which is rented for the exclusive use of the subscriber

**least cost design** *noun* COMPUT the best money-saving use of space or components ○ *The budget is only £5000 so we need the least cost design for the new circuit.*

**least recently used algorithm** *noun* COMPUT an algorithm which finds the page of memory that was last accessed before any other and erases it to make room for another page. Abbreviation **LRU**

**least significant bit** *noun* COMPUT a binary digit occupying the right hand position of a word and carrying the least power of two in the word usually equal to two raised to zero = 1. Abbreviation **LSB**

**least significant digit** *noun* COMPUT a digit which occupies the right hand position in a number and so carries the least power, equal to the number radix raised to zero = 1. Abbreviation **LSD**

**Le Chatelier's principle** *noun* CHEM the principle that if a chemical system is in equilibrium, any change to it is offset by compensatory changes that oppose the original change

**lecithin** *noun* BIOCHEM a constituent of all animal and plant cells, involved in the transport and absorption of fats

**Leclanché cell** *noun* ELEC a primary cell that has a carbon anode, a zinc cathode and sal ammoniac as the electrolyte

**lectin** *noun* BIOCHEM a protein found widely in nature, especially in seeds, that belongs to a group that bind to specific carbohydrates and cause clumping of blood cells (NOTE: Lectins might sometimes trigger immune reactions and dietary intolerance. They are used in testing for blood type.)

**LED** *abbreviation* ELEC light-emitting diode

COMMENT: LED displays are used to display small amounts of information, e.g. in pocket calculators, watches and indicators.

**lee** *noun* EARTH SCI the side of something which is protected from the wind ○ *The trees in the lee of the hill grow better than those on the windward side.* □ **on the lee side** on the side away from the wind

**leeward** *adjective* EARTH SCI protected from the wind

**left justification** *noun* COMPUT the shifting of a binary number to the left hand end of the word containing it

**left justify** *noun* COMPUT a printing command that makes the left hand margin of the text even

**left shift** *noun* COMPUT a left arithmetic shift by one bit of data in a word (NOTE: A binary number is doubled for each left shift.)

**leg** *noun* ANAT a part of the body with which a person or animal walks and stands

COMMENT: The leg is formed of the thigh including the thighbone or femur, the knee including the kneecap or patella, and the lower leg including the tibia and fibula.

**legacy** *adjective* COMPUT referring to older technology or a previous version of software or hardware that is still supported in new developments to allow existing applications and hardware to still be used

**legal** *adjective* COMPUT acceptable within language syntax rules

**legend** *noun* a list explaining the symbols on a chart, map or diagram

**legionnaires' disease** *noun* MED a bacterial disease similar to pneumonia (NOTE: The bacteria develop in warm, moist areas such as air-conditioning systems and are transmitted through droplets of moisture in the air, often affecting many people at once.)

**legume** *noun* PLANTS a member of the plant family which produces seeds in pods, e.g. peas and beans. Family: Leguminosae. ○ *Grass and legume as-*

*sociations are common in European pastureland.*

COMMENT: There are many species of legume and some are particularly valuable because they have root nodules that contain nitrogen-fixing bacteria. Such legumes have special value in maintaining soil fertility and are used in crop rotation. Peas, beans, clover and vetch are all legumes.

**leguminous** *adjective* BOT producing seeds in pods

**leishmaniasis** *noun* MED any of several diseases caused by the parasite *Leishmania*, one form giving disfiguring ulcers, another attacking the liver and bone marrow

**length** *noun* 1. a measurement along something's greatest dimension 2. a piece that is normally measured along its greatest dimension ○ *a length of pipe* 3. the extent from beginning to end ○ *the length of a book* 4. the amount of time between particular points in time 5. the distance between two points 6. COMPUT the number of data items in a variable or list

**lengthen** *verb* to become long or longer or to make something long or longer ○ *The mercury column shortens when cooled and, due to expansion, lengthens when heated.* Opposite **shorten**

**lengthways, lengthwise** *adjective, adverb* along the length ○ *in a lengthwise direction*

**lengthy** *adjective* 1. long ○ *He wrote a lengthy report.* 2. lasting for a long time

**lens** *noun* 1. OPTICS a normally round piece of glass with curved surfaces found in microscopes, telescopes, cameras or spectacles 2. ANAT the part of the eye that causes light to bend and produce an image on the retina

COMMENT: The lens in the eye is elastic and can change its shape under the influence of the ciliary muscle, to allow the eye to focus on objects at different distances.

**lens-shaped cloud** *noun* METEOROL a cloud with outwardly curved upper and lower surfaces. Also called **lenticular cloud**

**lentic** *adjective* EARTH SCI referring to stagnant water

**lenticular cloud** *noun* METEOROL same as **lens-shaped cloud**

**Lepidoptera** *noun* ZOOL an order of insects which includes butterflies and moths

**-less** *suffix* without

**lessen** *verb* to make something less or to become less ○ *Clean filters lessen the possibility of blockage.*

**lesser circulation** *noun* PHYSIOL same as **pulmonary circulation**

**lethal** *adjective* BIOL which can kill ○ *These fumes are lethal if inhaled.*

**lethal concentration 50** *noun* ENVIRON the concentration of a pollutant or effluent at which 50% of the test organisms die. Abbreviation **LC50**

**lethal dose 50%** *noun* BIOL the dose of a substance which will kill half the organisms which absorb it. Abbreviation **LD50**

**lethal gene** *noun* GENETICS a gene which can kill the organism that inherits it

**leucine** *noun* BIOL an essential amino acid

**leucocyte** *noun* ANAT a white blood cell

**leucoplast** *noun* BIOL a tiny colourless sac (**plastid**) in which food is stored inside plant cells

**levee** *noun* EARTH SCI (*in the USA*) an embankment built up along the bank of a river to prevent flooding

**level** *adjective* 1. □ **level with** at the same height or position as something else ○ *In most light aircraft, the aeroplane will be in a climb if the engine cowling is level with the horizon.* 2. having a flat, smooth surface 3. on a horizontal plane 4. referring to something with no sudden changes □ **the level tone of an engine** the unchanging sound of an engine ■ *noun* 1. a position along a vertical axis ○ *ground level* ○ *reference level* ○ *The tropopause is the level at which the lapse rate ceases to be so important.* □ **the fluid level in the reservoir** the point up to which the surface of the fluid reaches 2. a position on a scale ○ *an advanced level of study* 3. a relative amount, intensity or concentration ○ *an unsafe level of contamination* ○ *a reduced level of noise* ○ *A gas turbine engine has an extremely low vibration level.* 4. COMPUT a quantity of bits that make up a digital transmitted signal

**lever** *noun* MECH ENG 1. a device with a rigid bar balanced on a fixed point, used to transmit force, as in raising a weight at one end by pushing down on the other ○ *Push the lever fully up to activate the brake mechanism.* **2.** a handle used to adjust or operate a mechanism ○ *control lever* ■ *verb* to move something with a lever ○ *The door was stuck and they had to lever it open.*

**Lewis acid** *noun* CHEM a substance that can form a covalent bond by accepting a pair of electrons from a base

**Lewis base** *noun* CHEM a substance that can form a covalent bond by donating a pair of electrons to an acid

**lexical analysis** *noun* COMPUT a stage in program translation when the compiling or translating software replaces program keywords with machine code instructions

**ley** *noun* AGRIC a field in which crops are grown in rotation with periods when the field is under pasture

COMMENT: Leys are an essential part of organic farming. Pasture land is fertilised by the animals which graze on it and then is ploughed for crop growing. When the land has been exhausted by the crops, it is put back to pasture to recover.

**Leyden jar** *noun* ELEC a historical form of electrostatic capacitor comprising a glass jar coated inside and outside with metal foil with a conducting rod passing through an insulated stopper

**Leydig cells** *noun* ANAT same as **interstitial cells**

**LF** *abbreviation* COMPUT line feed

**LH2** *noun* INDUST liquid hydrogen, proposed as an alternative fuel for use in cars and aircraft

**Li** *symbol* CHEM ELEM lithium

**liana** *noun* BOT a climbing plant found in tropical rainforests

**lias** *noun* EARTH SCI a type of rock formation consisting of shale and limestone

**library** *noun* a collection of files, documents, books, records or other materials which can be consulted or borrowed by the public, usually kept in a public place

**library function** *noun* COMPUT a software routine that a user can easily insert into a program

**library routine** *noun* COMPUT a routine that can be inserted into a main program and called up when required

**libration** *noun* ASTRON a real or apparent oscillation in the orbit of one astronomical object, especially as observed in the orbit of the Moon from Earth

**lice** ZOOL plural of **louse**

**licence** *noun* the permission given by one manufacturer to another to make copies of products against payment of a fee ○ *The software is manufactured in this country under licence.*

**lichen** *noun* BOT a complex organism that grows on the surface of stones or trunks of trees and can survive in cold or exposed conditions

COMMENT: Lichens are formed of two organisms growing in symbiosis: a fungus which provides the outer shell and an alga or a cyanobacterium which provides chlorophyll and gives the plant its colour. Many lichens are very sensitive to pollution, especially sulphur dioxide, and act as indicators for atmospheric pollution. They also provide food for many arctic animals.

**lidar** *noun* METEOROL a device that uses pulses of laser light to analyse atmospheric phenomena

**life** *noun* **1.** the time from birth to death □ **someone's adult life** the time when someone is an adult **2.** BIOL a state of active metabolism or being alive ○ *The medicine saved his life.* ○ *Their lives were put at risk by the contamination.* **3.** BIOL living organisms ○ *bird life* ○ *plant life*

**life cycle** *noun* BIOL all the changes an organism goes through between a certain stage in its development and the same stage in the next generation

**life expectancy** *noun* BIOL the number of years a person, animal, or other organism is likely to live

**life form** *noun* BIOL a living thing, e.g. a plant, animal or microorganism

**life history** *noun* BIOL all the changes an organism goes through from fertilisation to death

**life science** *noun* BIOL a science such as biology or botany which studies living organisms

**lifestyle** *noun* PSYCHIAT the way in which a person or group of people live their daily lives, including habits, behaviour and activities

**life system** *noun* ECOL a part of an ecosystem which is formed of a living organism and the parts of the environment which support it

**life table** *noun* BIOL a chart showing how long a person, animal or plant is likely to live

**life-threatening disease** *noun* MED a disease which may kill a person or animal

**lifetime** *noun* 1. BIOL the time during which an organism is alive 2. ENVIRON the approximate time it would take for that part of an atmospheric pollutant concentration created by humans to return to its natural level assuming emissions cease ○ *Average lifetimes can vary from about a week (sulfate aerosols) to more than a century (CFCs, carbon dioxide).* 3. a period of time during which a device is useful or not outdated ○ *This new computer has a four-year lifetime.*

**life zone** *noun* ECOL a place or area in which the type and number of organisms differ slightly from neighbouring areas because of variations in environmental conditions

**LIFO** *abbreviation* COMPUT last in first out ○ *This computer stack uses a LIFO data retrieval method.*

**lift** *noun* 1. AVIAT a component of the total aerodynamic force acting on an aerofoil which causes an aeroplane to fly ○ *In level flight, a lift force equal to the weight must be produced.* 2. ENG an electrically operated machine for moving people or goods between the floors of a building (NOTE: The US term is **elevator**.) ■ *verb* to move to a higher position

COMMENT: Bernoulli's principle states that if the speed of a fluid speed increases, its pressure decreases; if its speed decreases, its pressure increases. Wings are shaped so that the high-speed flow of air that passes over the curved upper surface results in a decrease in pressure. Lift is created because of the pressure differential between upper and lower surfaces of the wing. Lift is also created because the angle of attack allows the airflow to strike the underside of the wing.

**ligament** *noun* ANAT a sheet or band of tough, fibrous connective tissue that connects bones or cartilages at a joint or holds organs in place

**ligand** *noun* CHEM a molecule, part of a molecule or an ion that is bound to

something such as a metal atom or ion, forming a complex

**light** *noun* 1. brightness produced by the Sun, the Moon or a lamp 2. a source of light such as a lamp ○ *Switch off the navigation lights.* 3. PHYS electromagnetic radiation which can be sensed by the eyes ■ *adjective* 1. without much weight ○ *Aluminium is a light metal.* 2. of little force or requiring little force ○ *a light touch* ○ *a light wind* ○ *The plane had light controls.* 3. of little quantity ○ *light rain* ○ *light snow* 4. of thin consistency ○ *light oil* 5. bright so that people can see well ○ *At six o'clock in the morning it was just getting light.*

**light adaptation** *noun* PHYSIOL a series of changes in the eye to adapt to an abnormally bright or dim light, or to adapt to normal light after being in darkness. Compare **dark adaptation**

**light aircraft** *noun* AVIAT a small, single engine aircraft for private not commercial use

**light-emitting diode** *noun* ELEC a semiconductor diode that emits light when a current is applied, used in clock and calculator displays and as an indicator. Abbreviation **LED**

**light industry** *noun* INDUST an industry which makes small or lightweight products

**lightning** *noun* METEOROL a discharge of electricity between clouds and the Earth, which gives a bright flash and makes the sound of thunder

**lightning arrester** *noun* ELEC a device that prevents surges of the electrical current which are caused when lightning strikes a building and which can damage equipment

**lightning conductor, lightning rod** *noun* ELEC a length of metal running down the outside wall of a building to the ground, which acts as a channel for the electric current when lightning strikes the building

**light pen** *noun* COMPUT a computer accessory in the shape of a pen that contains a light-sensitive device that can detect pixels on a video screen (NOTE: It is often used with suitable software to draw graphics on a screen or position a cursor.)

**light pollution** *noun* ENVIRON the effect of street lighting which makes the sky red or orange at night, and so reduces the visibility of stars

**light reflex** *noun* PHYSIOL a reaction of the pupil of the eye which changes size according to the amount of light going into the eye

**light water** *noun* CHEM ordinary water used as a coolant in some types of power station. Compare **heavy water**

**light water reactor** *noun* INDUST a nuclear reactor which uses ordinary water as a coolant. Abbreviation **LWR**

**light wave** *noun* PHYS **1.** a wave of electromagnetic radiation that travels from a source of light and is capable of stimulating the retina, and is visible **2.** any wave of electromagnetic radiation, including ultraviolet and infrared

**light year** *noun* ASTRON an astronomical unit of distance equal to the space covered by light in a year in a vacuum, equal to 9.3 billion km or 0.3 parsec

**lignin** *noun* BIOCHEM the material in plant cell walls that makes plants woody and gives them rigidity and strength

**lignite** *noun* INDUST a type of soft coal with a low carbon content

**limb** *noun* ANAT a leg or arm

**lime** *noun* **1.** INDUST calcium oxide made from burnt limestone, used to spread on soil to reduce acidity and add calcium (NOTE: It is used in the composition of cement and in many industrial processes.) **2.** TREES a common European hardwood tree. Genus: *Tilia*. **3.** TREES a citrus fruit tree, with green fruit similar to, but smaller than, a lemon. Latin name: *Citrus aurantifolia*. ■ *verb* AGRIC to treat acid soil by spreading lime on it

**lime slurry** *noun* INDUST a mixture of lime and water added to hard water to make it softer

**limestone** *noun* EARTH SCI a common sedimentary rock

COMMENT: Limestone is formed of calcium minerals and often contains fossilised shells of sea creatures. It is used in agriculture and building. Limestone is porous in its natural state and may form large caves by being weathered by water.

**lime treatment** *noun* AGRIC same as **liming**

**limewater** *noun* CHEM a solution of calcium hydroxide in water

**liming** *noun* AGRIC the spreading of lime on soil to reduce acidity and add calcium. Also called **lime treatment**

**limit** *noun* a furthest point or place beyond which you cannot go ○ *They have set a strict limit on the amount of fish which foreign fishing boats are allowed to catch.* ■ *verb* to set a limit to something ○ *The government has limited the number of barrels of oil to be extracted each day.*

**limiter** *noun* ELEC a device that removes the part of an input signal that is greater than or less than a predefined limit (NOTE: Limiters are used with audio and video signals to prevent overloading of an amplifier.)

**limiting factor** *noun* BIOL a factor which limits the growth of an organism

**limiting factor principle** *noun* BIOL a general rule that too much or too little of any abiotic factor can limit or prevent growth of a population

**limiting friction** *noun* PHYS friction between two objects before they slip at the limiting point

**limiting similarity** *noun* ECOL the extent of niche differentiation required for species to coexist

**limits** *plural noun* COMPUT a predefined maximum range for numbers in a computer

**limn-** *prefix* EARTH SCI fresh water

**limnetic** *adjective* EARTH SCI referring to deep fresh water

**limnetic zone** *noun* EARTH SCI an area of deep water away from the edge of a lake, in which plants cannot live but where phytoplankton can exist

**limnic** *adjective* EARTH SCI referring to deposits in fresh water

**limnology** *noun* EARTH SCI the study of fresh water such as rivers and lakes

**limonite** *noun* GEOL a brown or yellow hydrated iron oxide ore

**lindane** *noun* AGRIC an organochlorine pesticide that is harmful to some animals such as bees and fish. Also called **hexachlorocyclohexane** (NOTE: Lindane is used in Britain as a farm insecticide and as a chemical for treating wood. It is banned in some countries, e.g. Finland, New Zealand and Sweden.)

**line** *noun* **1.** a thin continuous mark as made by a pencil, pen or printer ○ *Draw a line from point A to point B.* **2.** a real or imaginary mark placed in relation to points of reference ○ *An isobar is a line* *joining points of equal pressure.* **3.** a row of written or printed words ○ *Look at line 4 on page 26.* **4.** TELECOM a telephone connection to another telephone or system ○ *Dial 9 to get an outside line.* **5.** ENG a system of pipes ○ *a fuel line* **6.** COMPUT a physical connection for data transmission **7.** COMPUT one trace by the electron picture beam on a screen or monitor **8.** COMPUT, PRINTING a row of characters printed on a page or displayed on a computer screen ○ *Each page has 52 lines of text.* ○ *Several lines of manuscript seem to have been missed by the keyboarder.* ○ *Can we insert an extra line of spacing between the paragraphs?* **9.** COMPUT one row of commands or arguments in a computer program ■ *verb* to cover the inside of a container to prevent the contents escaping ○ *Landfill sites are lined with nylon to prevent leaks of dangerous liquids.*

**line adapter** *noun* ELECTRONICS an electronic circuit that matches the correct signal voltage and impedance for a particular line

**line analyser** *noun* ELEC a piece of test equipment that displays the characteristics of a line or the signals carried on the line

**linear** *adjective* referring to a straight line

**linear absorption coefficient** *noun* PHYS a measurement of the absorption of a beam of radiation passing through something

**linear accelerator** *noun* PHYS a machine that makes charged particles travel very fast in straight paths by using alternating high-frequency voltages

**linear actuator** *noun* ENG an actuator which operates in a straight back and forth manner e.g. to open undercarriage doors

**linear equation** *noun* MATHS an equation in which none of the variables is raised to a power

**linearity** *noun* COMPUT the shape of the frequency response curve of a device such as a microphone or A/D converter (NOTE: If the curve is straight, the device is very accurate, but if it is not, the device is introducing frequency distortion.)

**linear list** *noun* a list that has no free space for new records within its structure

**linear molecule** *noun* PHYS a molecule in which the atoms are arranged in a line

**linear momentum** *noun* PHYS same as **momentum**

**linear motor** *noun* ENG an electric motor in which there is linear motion between the rotor and stator, producing thrust along a straight line

**linear program** *noun* COMPUT a computer program that contains no loops or branches

**linear programming** *noun* COMPUT a method of mathematically breaking down a problem so that it can be solved by computer

**linear scale** *noun* MEASURE a horizontal or vertical straight-line scale on an instrument

**linear search** *noun* a search method which compares each item in a list with the search key until the correct entry is found by starting with the first item and working sequentially towards the end

**line breeding** *noun* GENETICS the deliberate crossing or mating of closely related individuals in order to retain characteristics of a common ancestor

**line busy tone** *noun* TELECOM a signal generated to indicate that a connection or telephone line is already in use

**line communication** *noun* TELECOM a signal transmission using a cable link or telegraph wire

**line conditioning** *noun* TELECOM the keeping of the quality of data transmissions or signals on a line to a certain standard

**line control** *noun* TELECOM a special code used to control a communications link

**lined landfill** *noun* ENVIRON a hole in the ground covered on the inside with nylon sheets to prevent leaks of dangerous liquids from waste deposited there

**line driver** *noun* ELEC a high power circuit and amplifier used to send signals over a long distance line without too much loss of signal

**line editor** *noun* COMPUT a piece of software that allows the operator to modify one line of text from a file at a time

**line ending** *noun* COMPUT a character which shows that a line has ended, instructed by pressing the return key

**line feed** *noun* COMPUT a control on a printer or computer terminal that moves the cursor down by one line. Abbreviation **LF**

**line flyback** *noun* an electron beam returning from the end of one line to the beginning of the next

**line frequency** *noun* COMPUT the number of times that the picture beam scans a horizontal row of pixels in a monitor

**line in** *noun* ELEC an input connection to audio equipment, e.g. an amplifier, that accepts a low voltage audio signal

**line length** *noun* a number of characters contained in a displayed line (NOTE: On a computer screen this is normally 80 characters. On a printer it is often 132 characters.)

**line level** *noun* TELECOM an amplitude of a signal transmitted over a cable

**line noise** *noun* TELECOM unwanted interference on a telephone or communications line that causes errors in a data transmission

**line number** *noun* COMPUT a number that refers to a line of program code in a computer program

COMMENT: The programming language will sort out the program into order according to line number.

**line of latitude** *noun* EARTH SCI an imaginary line running round the Earth, linking points at an equal distance from the equator

**line of longitude** *noun* EARTH SCI an imaginary line on the surface of the Earth running from the North Pole to the South Pole, at right angles to the equator

**line of sight** *noun* a clear path between sending and receiving antennas. Abbreviation **LOS**

**line printer** *noun* COMPUT a device for printing draft quality information at high speeds, with a typical output of 200 to 3000 lines per minute

COMMENT: Line printers print a whole line at a time, running from right to left and left to right, and are usually dot matrix printers with not very high quality print. Compare page printers, which print a whole page at a time.

**liner** *noun* INDUST material such as nylon sheets used to line something

**line spacing** *noun* PRINTING the distance between two rows of characters

**line spectrum** *noun* PHYS a spectrum that appears as a series of distinct parallel lines, produced by a gas emitting light or a gas selectively absorbing light from another source

**lingual artery** *noun* ANAT an artery which supplies blood to the tongue

**lingual vein** *noun* ANAT a vein which takes blood away from the tongue

**link** *noun* COMPUT a connection between two things ○ *To transmit faster, you can use the direct link with the mainframe.* ■ *verb* **1.** to connect two things to each other ○ *The two computers are linked.* **2.** to be related or associated ○ *Health is linked to diet.* ○ *Health and diet are linked.*

**linkage** *noun* **1.** MECH ENG a system or series of mechanical connections such as rods, levers and springs **2.** GENETICS the process of two or more genes situated close together on a chromosome being inherited together

**linkage group** *noun* GENETICS a set of two or more genes on a chromosome that are usually inherited together

**link control procedure** *noun* COMPUT a set of rules defining the transmission of data over a channel. Abbreviation **LCP**

**linked list** *noun* COMPUT a list of data where each entry carries the address of the next consecutive entry

**linked object** *noun* COMPUT one piece of data that is referred to in another file or application

**linked subroutine** *noun* COMPUT a number of computer instructions in a program that can be called at any time, with control being returned on completion to the next instruction in the main program

**link files** *noun* COMPUT a command to merge together a list of separate files

**link-layer protocol** *noun* COMPUT within the standard OSI network model defined by the ISO, a layer that sends data packets to a connected device and manages error detection

**link trial** *noun* COMPUT a test of computer programs so as to see if each module works in conjunction with the others

**Linnaean system** *noun* BIOL the scientific system of naming organisms devised by the Swedish scientist Carolus Linnaeus (1707–78). See Comment at **binomial classification**

**linoleic acid** *noun* BIOCHEM one of the essential fatty acids which cannot be synthesised and has to be taken into the body from food such as vegetable oil

**linolenic acid** *noun* CHEM one of the essential fatty acids which cannot be synthesised and has to be taken into the body from food such as vegetable oil, particularly linseed oil. Formula: $C_{25}H_{30}O_2$. (NOTE: It is also used in paints and in synthetic resin manufacture.)

**linseed oil** *noun* INDUST an oil that is obtained from the seeds of flax plants, used in paints and inks to help them dry more quickly

**Linux** *trademark* COMPUT a popular version of the UNIX operating system originally developed by Linus Torvalds, who then distributed it free of charge over the Internet (NOTE: normally pronounced 'lee-nucks')

**lipase** *noun* BIOCHEM an enzyme that breaks down fats

**lipid** *noun* BIOCHEM an organic compound belonging to a group of compounds that are not water-soluble and include animal fat, plant oils and waxes

**lipid metabolism** *noun* CHEM the set of chemical changes by which lipids are broken down into fatty acids

**lipoprotein** *noun* BIOCHEM a complex of lipids and proteins involved in transportation of lipids around the body

**liposoluble** *adjective* BIOCHEM which can dissolve in fat

**liposome** *noun* BIOCHEM a microscopic spherical sac bounded by a double layer of lipids, sometimes used to carry a drug to targeted body tissues

**LIPS** *abbreviation* COMPUT logical inferences per second

COMMENT: One inference often requires thousands of computer instructions.

**liquefaction** *noun* PHYS the process of making a solid or gas into liquid

**liquefaction of gases** *noun* PHYS a change of state from gas to a liquid

**liquefied natural gas** *noun* INDUST a natural gas, extracted from under ground, that is cooled and transported in containers. Abbreviation **LNG**

**liquefied petroleum gas** *noun* INDUST propane or butane or a combination of both produced by refining crude petroleum oil. Abbreviation **LPG** (NOTE: It is used for domestic heating and cooking and for powering vehicles.)

**liquefy** *verb* PHYS to make a gas into liquid or to become liquid

**liquid** *adjective* PHYS having a consistency like that of water ○ *Liquid oxygen is stored in cylinders.* ■ *noun* a substance with a consistency like water ○ *Water is a liquid, ice is a solid.*

**liquid crystal** *noun* CHEM a liquid that varies being cloudy or clear according to temperature or applied voltage, used in visual display units

**liquid crystal display** *noun* COMPUT a screen that uses a liquid crystal material to display information when a voltage is applied. Abbreviation **LCD**

**liquid fertiliser** *noun* a solution of a solid fertiliser (NOTE: Liquid fertilisers are easier, quicker and cheaper to handle and apply than solid fertilisers.)

**liquid hydrocarbon** *noun* CHEM an organic compound in liquid form, e.g. kerosene

**liquid hydrogen** *noun* INDUST an alternative fuel proposed for use in cars and aircraft. Abbreviation **LH2**

**liquid manure** *noun* AGRIC a manure consisting of dung and urine in a liquid form (NOTE: Manure in semi-liquid form is slurry.)

**liquid paraffin** *noun* INDUST an oil distilled from petroleum and used as a fuel, lubricant or as a laxative (NOTE: The US term is **mineral oil**.)

**LISP** *noun* COMPUT a high-level language used mainly in processing lists of instructions or data and in artificial intelligence work. Full form **list processing**

**Lissajous figure** *noun* PHYS the course of displacement of a point when two or more periodic wave motions are superimposed, commonly used to describe two sinusoidal waves at right angles

**list** *noun* **1.** a set of short pieces of information, each one given on a separate line **2.** COMPUT a series of ordered items of data ■ *verb* COMPUT to record, display or print a set of items one above the other □ **to list a program** to display a program line by line in correct order

**list box** *noun* COMPUT a number of items or options displayed in a list

**listeria** *noun* MICROBIOL a bacterium found in human and animal faeces, one species of which can cause meningitis if ingested in contaminated food. Genus: *Listeria*.

**listing** *noun* COMPUT an ordered presentation of program lines

**list processing** *noun* COMPUT **1.** the computation of a series of items of data such as adding, deleting, sorting or updating entries **2.** full form of **LISP**

**liter** *noun* MEASURE US spelling of **litre**

**literal** *noun* **1.** COMPUT a computer instruction that contains the actual number or address to be used, rather than a label or its location **2.** PRINTING a printing error when one character is replaced by another or when two characters are transposed

**literal operand** *noun* COMPUT an actual number or address to be used rather than a label or its location

**lith-** *prefix* EARTH SCI stone

**litharge** *noun* CHEM same as **lead monoxide**

**lithium** *noun* CHEM ELEM a soft silvery metallic element, the lightest known metal, used in batteries (NOTE: The chemical symbol is **Li**; the atomic number is **3** and the atomic weight is **6.94**.)

**Lithium-ion battery, lithium battery** *noun* ELEC a type of rechargeable battery that provides high output power in a compact and lightweight unit (NOTE: This type of battery is often used in mobile telephones, PDAs and laptop computers. The main advantages of Lithium-ion batteries are that they are light, powerful, and do not suffer from memory effects.)

**lithosere** *noun* ECOL a succession of communities growing on rock

**lithosol** *noun* EARTH SCI soil which forms on the surface of rock, with no soil horizons

**lithosphere** *noun* EARTH SCI the Earth's solid surface, together with the molten interior above the core

**lithospheric plates** *plural noun* EARTH SCI the solid masses of Earth's surface, of the size of continents, which move slowly

**litmus** *noun* CHEM organic matter used to indicate acidity (NOTE: It becomes red when the pH falls below 7, indicating acid, and becomes blue when pH is above 7, indicating alkaline.)

**litmus paper** *noun* CHEM a strip of paper that has been treated with litmus, used to determine the acidity or alkalinity of a solution

**litre** *noun* MEASURE a measure of capacity equal to 1000 cc or 1.76 pints. Symbol **l, L** (NOTE: It is the volume of one kilogram of water at 4° C.)

**litter** *noun* **1.** BIOL dead leaves lying on the floor of a forest. Also called **leaf litter 2.** ENVIRON rubbish left by people **3.** ZOOL a group of young mammals born to one mother at the same time ○ *The sow had a litter of ten piglets.* **4.** AGRIC bedding for livestock ○ *Straw is the best type of litter.* ■ *verb* **1.** to lie all over the place ○ *The valley is littered with huge boulders.* **2.** ZOOL to give birth ○ *Bears litter in early spring.*

**littoral** EARTH SCI *adjective* referring to the coast ■ *noun* a coast

**littoral current** *noun* EARTH SCI a current which moves along the shore

**littoral drift** *noun* EARTH SCI a movement of sand as it is carried by the sea along the coastline

**littoral zone** *noun* EARTH SCI **1.** an area of fresh water at the edge of a lake where plants can exist **2.** an area of the sea and shore between the high and low water marks

**live** *adjective* **1.** BIOL carrying out metabolism **2.** ELEC carrying electricity ○ *He was killed when he touched a live wire.* **3.** EARTH SCI (*of a volcano*) erupting from time to time **4.** in active use ■ *verb* **1.** BIOL to be or remain alive ○ *They thought she would not live through the night.* **2.** to exist or make a home ○ *Animals which live partly in water and partly on land are amphibians.*

**live off** *verb* BIOL to exist by eating something ○ *These fish live off the debris which sinks to the bottom of the lake.*

**live on** *verb* BIOL **1.** to exist by eating something ○ *Most apes live on berries and roots.* **2.** to exist on the surface of something ○ *Lice live on the skin of their host.*

**liver** *noun* ANAT a large gland in the upper part of the abdomen (NOTE: For other terms referring to the liver, see words beginning with **hepat-**)

COMMENT: The liver is situated in the top part of the abdomen on the right side of the body next to the stomach. It is the largest gland in the body, weighing almost 2 kg. Blood carrying nutrients from the intestines enters the liver by the hepatic portal vein; the nutrients are removed and the blood returned to the heart through the hepatic vein. The liver is the major detoxicating organ in the body. It destroys harmful organisms in the blood, produces clotting agents, secretes bile, stores glycogen and metabolises proteins, carbohydrates and fats. Diseases affecting the liver include hepatitis and cirrhosis. The symptom of liver disease is often jaundice.

**livestock** *noun* AGRIC cattle and other farm animals which are reared to produce meat, milk or other products ○ *Livestock production has increased by 5%.*

**live well** *noun* a well from which water or oil is being extracted

**living environment** *noun* BIOL the part of the environment made up of living organisms

**LLC** *abbreviation* COMPUT logical link control

**LLL** *abbreviation* COMPUT low-level language

**Lloyd's mirror** *noun* OPTICS a mirror used to reflect part of a direct light source so that the reflection interferes with the direct source, producing fringes

**lm** *symbol* PHYS, MEASURE lumen

**LNG** *abbreviation* INDUST liquefied natural gas

**load** *noun* 1. a weight or mass which is supported ○ *The load on the undercarriage decreases as lift increases and, when the aircraft rises into the air, the aircraft is supported by the wings.* 2. PHYS the force which a structure is subjected to when resisting externally applied forces ○ *The load on the control column is increased when the aircraft is flown out of trim.* 3. ELEC the power output of an electrical generator or power plant 4. COMPUT a job or piece of work to be done 5. something that is loaded or transported 6. the amount of something that a vehicle can carry or a machine can deal with at one time ■ *verb* 1. to put something into a vehicle or into a piece of equipment 2. COMPUT to transfer a file or program from disk or tape to

main memory 3. COMPUT to put a disk or tape into a computer, so that it can be run

**load and run** *noun* COMPUT a computer program that is loaded into main memory and then starts to execute itself automatically

**load bearing** *adjective* ENG which supports some weight

**load-bearing structure** *noun* a structure which supports the weight of something

**load controller** *noun* a device which monitors the output of a generator

**loader** *noun* COMPUT a program which loads another file or program into computer memory

**load factor** *noun* stress applied to a structure as a multiple of stress applied in flight under 1 g of acceleration due to Earth's gravity ○ *If a structure fails at 10 000 pounds load, an aircraft weighing 4000 pounds will reach this load at a load factor of 2.5.*

**loading** *noun* COMPUT the action of transferring a file or program from disk to memory ○ *Loading can be a long process.*

**load sharing** *noun* COMPUT the use of more than one computer in a network to even out the work load on each processor

**load up** same as **load**

**loam** *noun* EARTH SCI dark soil, with medium-sized grains of sand, which crumbles easily and is very fertile

**loamy** *adjective* EARTH SCI referring to soil that is dark, crumbly and fertile

**local** *adjective* 1. COMPUT referring to a device that is physically attached and close to the controlling computer 2. COMPUT referring to a variable argument that is only used in a certain section of a computer program or structure 3. COMPUT referring to a system with limited access 4. ENVIRON referring to a particular area

**local anaesthesia** *noun* PHYSIOL, MED loss of feeling in a specific part of the body

**local anaesthetic** *noun* PHARM a substance which removes the feeling in a specific part of the body only

**local area network** *noun* COMPUT a network where the various terminals and equipment are all within about

500 m of one another and can be interconnected by cables. Abbreviation **LAN**. Opposite **wide area network**

**local declaration** *noun* COMPUT an assignment of a variable that is only valid in a section of a computer program or structure

**localised** *adjective* restricted in area or influence

**localised fire** *noun* a fire which has not spread

**localiser** *noun* AEROSP a component of an aircraft's instrument landing system that provides horizontal guidance to the runway

**local printer** *noun* COMPUT a printer physically attached to a computer rather than a shared resource available on a network

**local variable** *noun* COMPUT a variable which can only be accessed by specific routines in a one section of a computer program

**locate** *verb* 1. to find the position of something 2. to position something

**location** *noun* 1. a place where something can be found 2. the process of finding where something is 3. COMPUT a number or absolute address which specifies the point in memory where a data word can be found and accessed

**loch** *noun* EARTH SCI (*in Scotland*) a lake

**loci** *noun* GENETICS plural of locus

**lock** *noun* a device operated by a key for securing a door, window or lid ■ *verb* 1. to secure a door by turning a key in the lock ○ *Lock the door before leaving the building.* 2. to be in or to move into a secure position 3. to block or stop the movement of something ○ *Anti-skid braking systems units are designed to prevent the brakes locking the wheels during landing.* 4. COMPUT to prevent access to a system or file

**locking pin** *noun* ENG a short metal device to prevent a nut from turning

**lockjaw** *noun* MED same as **tetanus**

**lock on** *verb* 1. to search for, find and follow a target with a thin radar beam 2. COMPUT to synchronise an internal clock with a received signal

**lock up** *noun* COMPUT a faulty operating state of a computer that cannot be recovered from without switching off

the power (NOTE: It can be caused by an infinite program loop or a deadlock.)

**locomotion** *noun* movement or travel from one place to another

**locus** *noun* GENETICS the position of a gene on a chromosome (NOTE: The plural is **loci**.)

**locust** *noun* ZOOL a flying insect which occurs in subtropical areas, flies in swarms and eats large amounts of vegetation

**lode** *noun* EARTH SCI a deposit of metallic ore

**lodestone** *noun* GEOL magnetite or magnetic natural iron oxide, or a piece of this

**loess** *noun* EARTH SCI a fine fertile soil formed of tiny clay and silt particles deposited by the wind

**log** *noun* 1. a full record of a set of actions or events 2. COMPUT a record of computer processing operations 3. FORESTRY a large piece of wood cut from the trunk or from a main branch of a tree ■ *verb* COMPUT 1. to record a series of actions or events □ **to log calls** to keep a record of telephone calls 2. to make a connection and start using a remote device such as a network server

**logarithm** *noun* MATHS the power to which a base must be raised to equal a given number

**logarithmic** *noun* MATHS referring to logarithms

**logarithmic scale** *noun* MEASURE a method of measuring using a logarithmic series of numbers (NOTE: It is often used as a scale on the axis of a graph.)

**logger** *noun* 1. COMPUT a device which keeps a record of a series of actions 2. FORESTRY a person who cuts down trees

**logging** *noun* FORESTRY the cutting down of trees

**logging residues** *plural noun* FORESTRY material left on the ground after cut logs have been removed

**logic** *noun* 1. a science which deals with thought and reasoning 2. MATHS a mathematical treatment of formal logic operations such as AND and OR and their transformation into various circuits 3. COMPUT a system for deducing results from binary data 4. COMPUT the components of a computer or digital system

**logical** *adjective* **1.** referring or according to logic **2.** COMPUT using logic ○ *Logical reasoning can be simulated by an artificial intelligence machine.*

**logical channel** *noun* COMPUT an electronic circuit between a terminal and a network node in a packet switching system

**logical error** *noun* COMPUT a fault in a program design causing incorrect branching or operations

**logical expression** *noun* COMPUT a function made up from a series of logical operators such as AND and OR

**logical high** *noun* LOGIC a state equal to logic TRUE or 1

**logical inferences per second** *noun* COMPUT a standard for the measurement of processing power of an inference engine. Abbreviation **LIPS**

**logical link control** *noun* COMPUT an IEEE 802.2 standard defining the protocol for data-link-level transmissions. Abbreviation **LLC**

**logical low** *noun* COMPUT a state equal to logic false or 0

**logical operator** *noun* COMPUT a character or word that describes the logical action it will perform (NOTE: The most common logical operators are AND, NOT, and OR.)

**logical unit** *noun* COMPUT a set of protocols developed by IBM to allow communication over an SNA network. Abbreviation **LU** (NOTE: LU1, LU2 and LU3 provide control of the session, LU4 supports communication between the devices and LU6.2 is a peer-to-peer protocol.)

**logic circuit** *noun* ELECTRONICS an electronic circuit made up of various logical gates, e.g. AND, OR and EXOR

**logic gate** *noun* ELECTRONICS an electronic circuit that applies a logical operator to an input signal and produces an output

**logic level** *noun* ELECTRONICS the voltage used to represent a particular logic state

**logic map** *noun* ELECTRONICS a graphical representation of states and conditions in a logic circuit

**logic operation** *noun* COMPUT a computer operation or procedure in which a decision is made

**logic state** *noun* ELECTRONICS one out of two possible levels in a digital circuit, the levels being 1 and 0 or TRUE and FALSE

**logic state analyser** *noun* ELECTRONICS a piece of test equipment that displays the logic states of a number of components or circuits

**logic symbol** *noun* COMPUT a graphical symbol used to represent a type of logic function in a diagram

**log in** *verb* COMPUT to enter various identification data, e.g. a password, usually by means of a terminal, to the central computer before accessing a program or data (NOTE: This is used as a means of making sure that only authorised users can access the computer system.)

**login, log-in** *noun* COMPUT an act of logging in at the beginning of a computer session. Also called **logon**

**LOGO** *noun* COMPUT a high-level programming language used mainly for educational purposes, with graphical commands that are easy to use

**log off** *verb* COMPUT to enter a symbol or instruction at the end of a computing session to close all files and break the channel between the user's terminal and the main computer

**logoff, log-off** *noun* COMPUT an act of logging off at the end of a computer session. Also called **logout**

**logon, log-on** *noun* COMPUT same as **login**

**log out** *verb* COMPUT same as **log off**

**logout, log-out** *noun* COMPUT same as **logoff**

**lone pair** *noun* CHEM a pair of unshared electrons on an atom in a molecule that are not involved in bonding within that molecule

**long-grass prairie** *noun* EARTH SCI an area in the east of the North American prairies where mainly varieties of tall grasses grow. Also called **tall-grass prairie**

**long integer** *noun* COMPUT an integer represented by several bytes of data

**longitude** *noun* EARTH SCI, NAVIG an angular distance on the Earth's surface, measured east or west from the prime meridian to the meridian passing through a position, expressed in degrees, minutes and seconds

COMMENT: Longitude is measured from Greenwich, just east of London, and, together with latitude, is used to indicate an exact position on the Earth's surface. Longitude is measured in degrees, minutes and seconds. The centre of London is latitude 51°30'N, longitude 0°5'W

**longitudinal** *adjective* in a lengthwise direction

**longitudinal axis** *noun* AEROSP the axis of the aircraft which extends from the nose to the tail

**longitudinal redundancy check** *noun* COMPUT a check on received blocks of data to detect any errors

**longitudinal time code** *noun* COMPUT a method of recording a time code signal on a linear audio track along a video tape. Abbreviation **LTC** (NOTE: The disadvantage of this method is that the code is not readable at slow speeds or when the tape has stopped.)

**longitudinal wave** *noun* PHYS a wave that is propagated in the same direction as that in which the particles of the medium vibrate

**long-lived** *adjective* BIOL living for a long time

**long-range weather forecast** *noun* METEOROL a forecast covering a period more than five days ahead

**longshore bar** *noun* OCEANOG a bank of sand submerged at high tide and running parallel with the coast

**longshore drift** *noun* OCEANOG a movement of sand particles along the shore, caused by currents flowing along the shore

**long-sightedness** *noun* MED same as **hyperopia**

**long-term** *adjective* lasting for a long time ○ *The long-term effects of exposure to radiation from power lines are not yet known.*

**long ton** *noun* MEASURE a unit of measurement of weight equal to 1016 kilograms

**look ahead** *noun* COMPUT the action by some central processing units of fetching instructions and examining them before they are executed in order to speed up operations

**lookup table** *noun* COMPUT a collection of stored results which can be accessed very rapidly ○ *This is the value of the key pressed, use a lookup table to find its ASCII value.*

**loop** COMPUT *noun* a procedure or series of instructions in a computer program that are performed again and again until a test shows that a specific condition has been met or until the program is completed ■ *verb* to make a piece of wire or tape into a circle

**loopback** *noun* COMPUT a diagnostic test that returns the transmitted signal to the sending device after it has passed through a device or across a link

**looping** *noun* METEOROL a situation in which a plume of smoke from a tall chimney is brought down to ground level by air currents and then rises again

**Lorentz-Fitzgerald contraction** *noun* PHYS the consequence of relativity that causes an object to become shorter as its speed approaches that of light

**lo-res** *adjective* COMPUT same as **low-resolution** (*informal*)

**LOS** *abbreviation* line of sight

**loss** *noun* the state of not having something any more or of having less of something □ **loss of a signal** disappearance of a signal ○ *The term attenuation means the loss of strength of a radio signal.*

**lossless compression** *noun* COMPUT image compression techniques that can reduce the number of bits used for each pixel in an image, without losing any information or quality

**lossy compression** *noun* COMPUT image compression techniques that can reduce the number of bits used for each pixel in an image, but in doing so lose information

**lost cluster** *noun* COMPUT a number of sectors on a disk whose identification bits have been corrupted (NOTE: The operating system has marked this area of disk as being used by a file, but the data they contain can no longer be identified with a particular file.)

**Lotka-Volterra predator-prey model** *noun* ECOL a simple mathematical model representing the interaction between predators and their prey

**loudness** *noun* PHYS the magnitude of the physiological stimulation due to a sound

**loudspeaker** *noun* ACOUSTICS an electromagnetic device that converts electrical signals into audible noise. Also called **speaker**

**lough** *noun* EARTH SCI (*in Ireland*) a lake

**louse** *noun* ZOOL a small wingless insect that sucks blood and lives on the skin as a parasite on animals and humans. Genus: *Pediculus*. (NOTE: The plural is **lice**.)

COMMENT: There are several forms of louse. The commonest are the body louse, the crab louse and the head louse. Some diseases can be transmitted by lice.

**louvre** *noun* a thin, horizontal opening for air cooling

**low** *adjective* 1. not high or tall ○ *a low building* 2. below a usual or expected value or amount ○ *The temperature is too low here for oranges to grow.* 3. not loud 4. near the bottom or towards the bottom □ **an area of low pressure** an area in which the atmospheric pressure is low and around which the air turns in the same direction as Earth. Also called **cyclone** ■ *noun* METEOROL an area of low atmospheric pressure usually accompanied by rain ○ *A series of lows are crossing the North Atlantic towards Ireland.* Also called **depression**

**low blood pressure** *noun* MED a condition where the pressure of the blood is unusually low. Also called **hypotension**

**low-calorie diet** *noun* MED a diet with few calories which can help a person to lose weight

**low end** *noun* COMPUT hardware or software that is not very powerful or sophisticated and is designed for beginners

**lower** *adjective* 1. referring to something that is at a low level or towards the bottom ○ *the lower layers of the atmosphere* 2. referring to something which is below something ○ *Air is cooler high up than at lower levels.* ▶ opposite **upper** ■ *verb* 1. to let something down to a lower position 2. to reduce something in amount or intensity ○ *lowered the temperature* ○ *lowered the pressure* □ **to lower the volume** to make a sound less loud

**lower atmosphere** *noun* METEOROL a layer of the atmosphere in which changes in the weather take place. Also called **troposphere**

**lower case** *noun* PRINTING small characters such as a, b, c, as opposed to upper case A, B, C

**lower limb** *noun* ANAT a leg

**lower motor neuron** *noun* ANAT a neuron which carries motor impulses from the spinal cord to the muscles

**low-fat diet** *noun* HEALTH a diet with little animal fat e.g. to help skin conditions

**low frequency** *noun* PHYS a radio frequency of 30 to 300 kilohertz

**low-grade** *adjective* not of high quality

**low-grade ore** *noun* EARTH SCI ore which contains a small percentage of metal

**low-grade petrol** *noun* INDUST petrol which does not contain very much octane and therefore produces less pollution. Also called **low-octane petrol**

**low-intensity land** *noun* AGRIC land on which crops are not intensively cultivated

**lowland** *noun* EARTH SCI an area of low-lying land as opposed to hills and mountains or highlands

**low latitudes** *plural noun* GEOG areas near the equator

**low-level format** *noun* COMPUT a process that defines the physical pattern and arrangement of tracks and sectors on a disk

**low-level language** *noun* COMPUT a programming language similar to an assembler, in which each instruction has a single equivalent machine code instruction. Abbreviation **LLL** (NOTE: The language is specific to one system or computer.)

**low-level radiation** *noun* PHYS radiation from a substance which is slightly radioactive

**low-level waste** *noun* ENVIRON waste which is only slightly radioactive and does not cause problems for disposal

**low-octane petrol** *noun* INDUST same as **low-grade petrol**

**low-order digit** *noun* MATHS a digit in the position within a number that represents the lowest weighting of the number base ○ *The number 234156 has a low-order digit of 6.*

**low-res** *adjective* COMPUT same as **low-resolution** (*informal*)

**low-resolution** *adjective* COMPUT not having a high number of pixels per unit area and so not sharply defined. Also called **lo-res, low-res**

**Lowry-Bronsted theory** *noun* CHEM a theory that defines an acid as a substance with a tendency to lose a proton

**low-sulfur coal, low-sulphur coal** *noun* INDUST coal with little sulfur in it, therefore producing less sulfur dioxide when it is burnt

**low tide** *noun* OCEANOG the point when the sea is lowest. Also called **low water**

**low-velocity zone** *noun* an area below the crust of the Earth where earthquake shock waves travel slowly

**low-waste technology** *noun* ENVIRON efficient technology which produces little waste

**low water** *noun* EARTH SCI same as **low tide**

**LPG** *abbreviation* CHEM liquefied petroleum gas

**Lr** *symbol* CHEM ELEM lawrencium

**LRU** *abbreviation* COMPUT least recently used algorithm

**LSB** *abbreviation* COMPUT least significant bit

**LSD** *abbreviation* COMPUT least significant digit

**LSI** *abbreviation* ELECTRONICS large-scale integration

**LTC** *abbreviation* COMPUT longitudinal time code

**LU** *abbreviation* COMPUT logical unit

**lubricant** *noun* MECH ENG an oily or greasy substance applied to moving parts, e.g. in an engine, to make them run smoothly

**lubricate** *verb* MECH ENG to oil or to grease moving parts in order to reduce friction ○ *Oil passes through the hollow crankshaft to lubricate the big-end bearings.* ○ *Turbo chargers are lubricated by the engine oil system.*

**lubricating oil** *noun* MECH ENG an oil applied to moving parts as in an engine to make them run smoothly

**lubrication** *noun* MECH ENG the act or process of covering moving surfaces with oil or grease to reduce friction

**lubrication system** *noun* MECH ENG a set of tanks, pipes, pumps and filters which together supply oil to moving parts of the engine

**lucerne** *noun* PLANTS a leguminous plant grown as fodder. Latin name: *Medicago sativa*.

COMMENT: Lucerne is the most important forage legume. It is called lucerne in Europe, Oceania and South Africa, and elsewhere it is called alfalfa. Lucerne is perennial, drought-resistant and rich in protein. It is mainly used for cutting, either for green feed or for hay or silage.

**luma** *noun* COMPUT the black and white parts of an image or video signal, represented by the symbol Y

**lumbar artery** *noun* ANAT one of four arteries which supply blood to the back muscles and skin

**lumber** *noun* (*in the USA and Canada*) FORESTRY trees which have been cut down

**lumberjack** *noun* (*in the USA and Canada*) FORESTRY a person who cuts down trees

**lumen** *noun* **1.** MED an inside width of a passage in the body or of an instrument such as an endoscope **2.** MED a hole at the end of an instrument such as an endoscope **3.** PHYS, MEASURE an SI unit of light emitted per second. Symbol **lm**

**luminance** *noun* COMPUT a part of a video signal or image that defines the brightness at each point

**luminescence** *noun* PHYS light produced by means other than heat, by processes such as phosphorescence, fluorescence or bioluminescence

**luminosity** *noun* ASTRON the light output of an astronomical object corrected to allow for its distance from Earth, and measured by means of absolute magnitude

**luminous** *adjective* PHYS giving the visual sensation of light

**luminous flux** *noun* PHYS a measure of the rate of flow of light from a standard source

**luminous intensity** *noun* PHYS the amount of light emitted by a source in a particular direction (NOTE: It is measured in candelas.)

**lunar** *adjective* ASTRON referring to the moon

**lunar eclipse** *noun* ASTRON a situation when Earth passes between the Sun and the Moon causing the shadow of Earth to fall across the Moon, so cutting off its light

**lunar phase** *noun* ASTRON a change in the appearance of the Moon as it moves from new to full and back again every 29 days (NOTE: The phases are: new moon, first quarter, full moon and last quarter.)

**lung** *noun* ANAT **1.** the organ of respiration of vertebrates that breathe air **2.** an organ for breathing air in invertebrate animals, positioned in the highly vascular region of the mantle cavity in some terrestrial snails

**lush** *adjective* BOT referring to vegetation which is thick and green ○ *The cattle were put to graze on the lush grass by the river.* ○ *Lush tropical vegetation rapidly covered the clearing.*

**luteinising hormone** *noun* BIOCHEM a hormone produced by the pituitary gland. Also called **interstitial-cell-stimulating hormone** (NOTE: In females it stimulates ovaries to release one or more eggs and causes the secretion of progesterone and the formation of the corpus luteum. In males it causes testes to secrete male sex hormones.)

**lutetium** *noun* CHEM ELEM a silvery-white metallic element in the lanthanide group of the periodic table, used as a catalyst in the nuclear industries (NOTE: The chemical symbol is **Lu**; the atomic number is **71** and the atomic weight is **174.97**.)

**lux** *noun* MEASURE, PHYS an SI unit of brightness of light shining on a surface. Symbol **lx**

**luxon** *noun* PHYS an elementary particle such as a photon or a neutrino travelling at the speed of light and therefore possessing no mass

**LWR** *abbreviation* INDUST light water reactor

**lx** *symbol* PHYS, MEASURE lux

**Lyman series** *noun* PHYS a series of lines in the ultraviolet spectrum, caused by excited hydrogen atoms

**lymph** *noun* PHYSIOL a colourless liquid containing white blood cells, which circulates in the body, carrying waste matter away from tissues to the veins (NOTE: It is an essential part of the body's defence against infection)

**lymphatic system** *noun* PHYSIOL a network of vessels through which lymph circulates removing microorganisms and other debris from tissues

**lymph node, lymph gland** *noun* ANAT a mass of tissue which produces white blood cells and filters waste matter from the lymph as it passes through

**lymphocyte** *noun* ANAT a white blood cell that forms part of the immune system (NOTE: Lymphocytes produce antibodies to destroy infected and cancerous cells and cause the rejection of foreign tissue.)

**lyophilic** *adjective* CHEM referring to a solid that will disperse finely in a colloid forming a stable dispersion and will redisperse following separation from the solvent

**lyophilise** *verb* FOOD INDUST to preserve food by freezing it rapidly and drying in a vacuum

**lyophobic** *adjective* CHEM referring to a solid distributed in a colloid that forms an unstable dispersion and that will not redisperse following separation

**Lysenkoism** *noun* GENETICS a biological doctrine maintaining that characteristics acquired by an organism during its lifetime can be inherited by its offspring (NOTE: This form of neo-Lamarckism, put forward by Trofim Denisovich Lysenko in the 1930s and disputed by most biologists, had an influence over Soviet genetics until the mid-1960s.)

**lysine** *noun* BIOCHEM an essential amino acid in protein foodstuffs, essential for animal growth

**lysis** *noun* BIOL the destruction of a cell by disrupting its outer membrane, allowing the cell contents to escape

**lysosome** *noun* BIOL a membrane-surrounded sac found in some cells that contains enzymes and functions in breaking down and recycling molecules (NOTE: Lysosomes occur in animal cells and in some protists, and are especially important in the immune cells that take in and destroy bacteria.)

# M

**m** *symbol* MEASURE **1.** metre **2.** milli-

**M 1.** MEASURE symbol **mega- 2.** COMPUT, ELECTRONICS (*in computer and electronic applications*) 1 048 576, equal to $2^{20}$

**mA** *abbreviation* MEASURE milliampere

**MAB** *abbreviation* ENVIRON Man and the Biosphere Programme

**MAC¹** COMPUT *noun* a special code transmitted at the same time as a message as proof of its authenticity. Full form **message authentication code** ■ *abbreviation* media access control

**MAC²** *abbreviation* ENVIRON maximum allowable concentration

**macerate** *verb* BIOL to make something soft by letting it remain in a liquid for a time

**Mach** *noun* PHYS a ratio of the speed of an object to the speed of sound in the same atmospheric conditions ○ *Mach 2 equals twice the speed of sound.*

**machine** *noun* **1.** MECH ENG a device with fixed and moving parts that takes mechanical energy and uses it to do useful work ○ *An electrical circuit carries energy to a machine which can then operate.* **2.** COMPUT a computer, system or processor made of various components connected together to provide a function or to perform a task

**machine address** *noun* COMPUT same as **absolute address**

**machine code** *noun* COMPUT a programming language that consists of commands in binary code that can be directly understood by the central processing unit without the need for translation. Also called **machine language**

**machine intelligence** *noun* COMPUT the design of computer programs and devices that attempt to imitate human intelligence and decision-making functions, providing basic reasoning and other human characteristics

**machine language** *noun* COMPUT **1.** the way in which machine code is written **2.** same as **machine code**

**machine-readable code** *noun* COMPUT a set of signs or letters such as bar codes or postcodes that can be read by computers

**Mach number** *noun* PHYS the speed of an object relative to the speed of sound (NOTE: An aircraft travelling at Mach 2 is going twice as fast as sound.)

**mackerel sky** *noun* METEOROL a pattern of wavy cirrocumulus or altocumulus cloud with holes which looks like the body markings of mackerel fish

**macro** *noun* COMPUT a program routine or block of instructions identified by a single word or label

**macro-** *prefix* large. Opposite **micro**

**macro assembler** *noun* COMPUT an assembler program that is able to decode macro instructions. Also called **assembly program**

**macrobiotic** *adjective* HEALTH without artificial additives or preservatives ○ *a macrobiotic diet*

**macrobiotics** *noun* HEALTH a dietary system based on vegetarian foods without artificial additives or preservatives, especially organically grown whole grains, fruit and vegetables

**macroclimate** *noun* METEOROL the climate of a large area

**macro definition** *noun* COMPUT a description of the structure, function and instructions that make up a macro operation

**macroelement** *noun* COMPUT a number of data items treated as one element

**macro instruction** *noun* COMPUT one programming instruction that refers to a number of instructions within a routine or macro

**macro language** *noun* COMPUT a programming language that allows the programmer to define and use macro instructions

**macromolecule** *noun* CHEM a large molecule such as a protein or a polymer

**macronutrient** *noun* BIOL a nutrient that an organism uses in very large quantities, e.g. oxygen, carbon, hydrogen, nitrogen, phosphorus, potassium, calcium, magnesium and iron

**macrophage** *noun* IMMUNOL a large cell that removes foreign material and bacteria from the bloodstream, lymph nodes and other tissues by phagocytosis (NOTE: Macrophages are found in the lymph and connective tissues as well as in the blood.)

**macrophyte** *noun* BOT a plant that is large enough to to be studied without the aid of a microscope

**macroplankton** *plural noun* BIOL plankton of about 1 mm in length

**macroscopic** *adjective* BIOL able to be seen without the aid of a microscope

**macro virus** *noun* COMPUT a computer virus that is stored as a macro attached to a document or email message

COMMENT: A macro virus will run when a document is opened. Some viruses are benign, others carry out malicious damage on files and data. The virus will also try and spread to other compatible documents and applications on your computer, so that any new documents you create are also infected. The best way to avoid a macro virus is to regularly run virus detection software that can check and remove viruses attached to documents and new email messages.

**macula** *noun* **1.** ASTRON same as **sunspot 2.** BIOL a change in the colour of a small part of the body without changing the surface as in freckles **3.** ANAT an area of hair cells inside the utricle and saccule of the ear

**macula lutea** *noun* ANAT a yellow spot on the retina, surrounding the fovea, the part of the eye which sees most clearly (NOTE: The plural is **maculae**.)

**mad cow disease** VET same as **BSE** (*informal*)

**magic number** *noun* PHYS any of the numbers 2, 8, 20, 28, 50, 82, and 126

(NOTE: Nuclides with these numbers of nucleons are very stable.)

**magma** *noun* EARTH SCI a molten substance in the Earth's mantle, which escapes as lava during volcanic eruptions and solidifies to form igneous rocks

COMMENT: Magma is formed of silicate materials which include crystals and dissolved gases.

**magmatic** *adjective* EARTH SCI referring to magma

**magnesite** *noun* MINERALS a white or colourless magnesium carbonate mineral used in insulation, furnace linings and as a source of magnesium oxide

**magnesium** *noun* CHEM ELEM a light, silvery-white metallic element that burns with a brilliant white flame (NOTE: It is also found in green vegetables and is essential especially for the correct functioning of human muscles. The chemical symbol is **Mg**; the atomic number is **12** and the atomic weight is **24.31**.)

**magnesium carbonate** *noun* CHEM a crystalline white salt used in glass making and in indigestion remedies. Formula: $MgCO_3$.

**magnesium chloride** *noun* CHEM a white or colourless crystalline compound used in fire extinguishers, papermaking, pottery and as a source of magnesium. Formula: $MgCl_2 \cdot 6H_2O$.

**magnesium hydroxide** *noun* CHEM a white powder used as an indigestion remedy and laxative. Formula: $Mg(OH)_2$.

**magnesium oxide** *noun* CHEM a white powder used in indigestion remedies and laxatives, fire bricks, electrical insulation, fertilisers and cement. Formula: $MgO$.

**magnesium sulfate, magnesium sulphate** *noun* CHEM a magnesium salt which when diluted in water is used as a laxative. Formula: $MgSO_4 \cdot 7H_2O$. Also called **Epsom salts**

**magnesium trisilicate** *noun* CHEM a magnesium compound used to treat peptic ulcers

**magnet** *noun* PHYS an object that produces a magnetic field and attracts iron and steel

COMMENT: A freely suspended magnet, uninfluenced by outside forces, will align itself with the Earth's magnetic lines of force, which run from the north magnetic pole to the south magnetic pole.

**magnetic** *adjective* PHYS referring to a magnet or a magnetic field

**magnetic anomaly** *noun* PHYS the way in which the local magnetic field differs from the normal magnetic field in a specific area

**magnetic attraction** *noun* PHYS the power of a body to attract other substances to it

**magnetic bearing** *noun* NAVIG the angle measured in a clockwise direction of a distant point, relative to magnetic north

**magnetic declination** *noun* NAVIG the angle of difference between the direction of the North Pole and that of the north magnetic pole. Also called **magnetic variation**

**magnetic dip** *noun* PHYS the angle of magnetic particles in rocks relative to the centre of the Earth (NOTE: It varies according to whether the rocks lie north or south of the equator.)

**magnetic disk** *noun* COMPUT a flat circular piece of material coated with a substance, on which signals and data can be stored magnetically

**magnetic field** *noun* PHYS an area round a body which is under the influence of its magnetic effect ○ *The Earth's magnetic field is concentrated round the two magnetic poles.*

**magnetic field strength** *noun* PHYS a quantity that indicates the strength of a magnetic field at a point in the direction of the line of force, measured in amperes per metre. Symbol **H**

**magnetic flux** *noun* MEASURE, PHYS a measure of the strength and extent of a magnetic field per unit area

**magnetic flux density** *noun* MEASURE, PHYS the strength of a magnetic field at a given point. Also called **magnetic induction** (NOTE: Its units are the tesla or the gauss.)

**magnetic head** *noun* ELEC an electromagnetic component that converts electrical signals into a magnetic field, allowing them to be stored on a magnetic medium

**magnetic induction** *noun* PHYS same as **magnetic flux density**

**magnetic intensity** *noun* PHYS same as **magnetic field strength**

**magnetic memory** *noun* COMPUT storage that uses a medium that can store data bits as magnetic field changes. Also called **magnetic store**

**magnetic mirror** *noun* PHYS a device that changes the direction of ions moving in a magnetic field

**magnetic moment** *noun* PHYS a vector expressing the torque experienced by a magnetic system in a magnetic field

**magnetic monopole** *noun* PHYS a particle with a single magnetic pole rather than the paired north and south poles of a normal magnet

**magnetic north** *noun* NAVIG the direction in which the needle of a compass points, as opposed to true north

**magnetic polarity** *noun* PHYS a method of indicating whether a point is a source or a collector of magnetic flux patterns

**magnetic pole** *noun* EARTH SCI one of the two poles of the Earth, near to but not identical with the geographical poles, which are the centres of Earth's magnetic field and to which a compass points. Also called **geomagnetic pole**

**magnetic recording** *noun* ELEC the transfer of an electrical signal onto a moving magnetic tape or disk by means of a magnetic field generated by a magnetic head

**magnetic resonance imaging** *noun* MED a technique that uses electromagnetic radiation to obtain images of invisible parts of a structure or the body's soft tissues. Abbreviation **MRI** (NOTE: The object is subjected to a powerful magnetic field which allows signals from atomic nuclei to be detected and converted into images by computer.)

**magnetic screen** *noun* PHYS a metal screen that prevents magnetic fields affecting electronic components ○ *Without the magnetic screen over the power supply unit, the computer just produced garbage.*

**magnetic storage** *noun* COMPUT a method of storing information as magnetic changes on a sensitive tape or disk, e.g. a floppy disk or hard disk

**magnetic store** *noun* COMPUT same as **magnetic memory**

**magnetic storm** *noun* METEOROL a sudden disturbance of Earth's magnetic field which affects compasses and radio and TV waves

**magnetic susceptibility** *noun* PHYS the relative degree of magnetisation of a substance when subjected to a magnetic field

**magnetic tape** *noun* TECH a thin ribbon of plastic coated with iron oxide that can store information by becoming magnetised (NOTE: It was formerly widely used to record sound, video pictures or computer data but is now largely replaced by digital media such as compact discs.)

**magnetic variation** *noun* NAVIG same as **magnetic declination**

COMMENT: To convert magnetic bearing into true bearing it is necessary to apply magnetic variation at the point at which the bearing was taken.

**magnetise** *verb* PHYS to convert an object or material into a magnet

**magnetism** *noun* PHYS **1.** property of attraction possessed by a naturally magnetic substance or by a conductor carrying an electric current (**electromagnet**) **2.** the study of properties associated with magnetic fields

**magnetite** *noun* MINERALS a common black magnetic mineral made of iron oxide that is a source of iron

**magneto** *noun* ELEC a device that produces electrical current for distribution to the spark plugs of piston aero-engines

COMMENT: The crankshaft turns the magnetos, which provide the electrical energy to create a spark from the spark plugs. This ensures that the spark plugs work even if the battery and electrical system fail.

**magnetograph** *noun* PHYS a device for measuring magnetic fields

COMMENT: A network of magnetographs has been installed all over the Earth for decades, yielding huge amounts of data, and versions of these instruments have been sent into orbit and to other planets since the 1960s.

**magnetohydrodynamics** *noun* PHYS the study of the way in which electrically conducting fluids behave in magnetic fields. Abbreviation **MHD**

**magneton** *noun* MEASURE the unit of measurement of the magnetic moment of a magnetic field

**magneto-optical recording** *noun* COMPUT a storage medium that uses an optical disc

COMMENT: An optical disc has a thin layer of magnetic film which is heated by a laser. The magnetic particles are then polarised by a weak magnetic field. Magneto-optical recording has very high capacity (over 600 Mb) and is rewritable.

**magnetosphere** *noun* EARTH SCI a region surrounding Earth, extending from about 500 to several thousand kilometres above the surface, in which charged particles are controlled by Earth's magnetic field

**magnetron** *noun* ENG an electronic valve used to generate microwaves

**magnification** *noun* OPTICS a measure of increase in size, especially in the apparent size of an image seen through a microscope

**magnify** *verb* OPTICS **1.** to increase the size of something, especially by using a lens or microscope ○ *It was only after the image was magnified that it was possible to see the flaw.* **2.** to increase the effect of something ○ *The stress level is magnified at times of high work load, for example, preparation for landing.* (NOTE: **magnifying – magnified**)

**magnitude** *noun* **1.** greatness of size, extent, level or strength of a variable ○ *When the surface wind speed reaches this magnitude the term gale is used.* **2.** ASTRON a measure of the brightness of any object in the sky

COMMENT: In astronomy, the basis of the magnitude system is a 100-fold difference in brightness between objects separated by five magnitudes. This means that each magnitude is equivalent to a change of just over 2.5-fold in the amount of light received by an observer. The numbers get smaller as the objects get brighter. The Sun has a magnitude of −26.8 and the full Moon −12.6. The largest telescopes now in use will reach objects below the 25th magnitude and the Hubble Space Telescope can stretch this to about the 31st magnitude.

**magnox** *noun* INDUST an alloy of magnesium, aluminium and other metals, used to surround uranium fuel rods in a nuclear reactor

**magnox power station** *noun* INDUST a nuclear power station with a magnox reactor

COMMENT: The first magnox power station was built in the UK in 1956. The safety record has been very good, but magnox power stations are now coming to the end of their commercial life and decommissioning began in 1990.

**magnox reactor** *noun* INDUST a type of gas-cooled nuclear reactor in which the uranium fuel rods are surrounded with magnox

**mail** *noun* **1.** a system for sending letters and parcels from one place to another **2.** letters sent or received **3.** COMPUT electronic messages to and from users of a bulletin board or network. Also called **email**

**mailbox** *noun* COMPUT an electronic storage space with an address in which a user's incoming e-mail messages are stored

**mail exchange record** *noun* COMPUT information stored in a database that tells a mail system how to deliver a mail message to a particular domain. Abbreviation **MX record**

**mail server** *noun* COMPUT a computer that stores incoming mail before sending it to the correct recipient and stores outgoing mail before transferring it to the correct destination server on the Internet

**mail transfer agent** *noun* COMPUT a software program that manages the way electronic mail messages are transferred over a network. Abbreviation **MTA**

COMMENT: A user would never normally see mail transfer software and would use an e-mail application (**mail user agent**) to create and read messages. On computers running the Unix operating system and the Internet, the 'sendmail' software is the most popular mail transfer agent.

**mail user agent** *noun* COMPUT software used to create and read electronic mail messages. Abbreviation **MUA** (NOTE: This software creates a message in the correct format and standard and passes this to the mail transfer agent that is responsible for transferring the message over the network.)

**main** *adjective* most important or principal ■ *noun* ENG a principal pipe or cable

**mainframe, mainframe computer** *noun* COMPUT a large-scale high-power computer system that can handle high-capacity memory and backing storage devices as well as a number of operators simultaneously

**main loop** *noun* COMPUT a series of instructions performed repeatedly that carry out the main action of a program (NOTE: This loop is often used to wait for user input before processing the event.)

**main memory** *noun* COMPUT a fast access RAM whose locations can be directly and immediately addressed by the central processor unit ○ *The 16-bit system includes up to 3 Mb of main memory.* Also called **main storage**

**mains** *noun* **1.** ENG a system of pipes which bring gas, water or electricity to a house **2.** INDUST the national electricity supply ○ *The farm is on the mains but still has its own generator for emergencies.*

**mains electricity** *noun* ELEC a normal domestic electricity supply to consumers

COMMENT: In Europe, this is 240 volts at 50 Hz. In the USA, it is 110 volts at 60 Hz.

**mains gas** *noun* ENG gas brought to a house by a pipe or cable connected to an extensive system

**main storage** *noun* COMPUT same as **main memory**

**maintenance ration** *noun* AGRIC the quantity of food needed to keep a farm animal healthy but not productive

**maintenance release** *noun* COMPUT a revision to a software program that corrects a minor problem or bug but does not offer any major new features ○ *The maintenance release of the database program, version 2.01, corrects the problem with the margins.*

**maintenance routine** *noun* COMPUT a software diagnostic tool used by an engineer during preventative maintenance operations

**maize** *noun* PLANTS a tall cereal crop grown in warmer climates. Latin name: *Zea mays.* (NOTE: The US term is **corn**.)

**majority** *noun* the greater number or larger part. Opposite **minority**

**make up water** *noun* ENVIRON water introduced into an irrigation or sewage system to make up for water lost by leaking or evaporation

**malachite** *noun* MINERALS a green rock made of copper carbonate that often has an attractive striped pattern when sectioned and polished and is used for jewellery

**malaria** *noun* MED a tropical disease caused by the parasite *Plasmodium* which enters the body after a bite from a mosquito. Also called **paludism**

COMMENT: Malaria is a recurrent disease which produces regular periods of shivering, vomiting, sweating and headaches as the parasites develop in the body. The patient also develops anaemia.

**malarial** *adjective* MED referring to malaria

**malarial parasite** *noun* MED the plasmodium parasite that causes malaria

**malarious** *adjective* MED referring to a region where malaria is endemic

**malathion** *noun* AGRIC an organophosphorus insecticide used to kill small aphids and mites

**male** *noun* ZOOL referring to an animal that produces sperm ■ *adjective* referring to a flower that produces pollen, or a plant that produces such flowers

**male connector** *noun* ELEC a plug with conducting pins that can be inserted into a female connector to provide an electrical connection

**malfunction** *noun* a failure to work correctly ○ *The data were lost owing to a software malfunction.* ■ *verb* COMPUT not to work properly ○ *Some of the keys on the keyboard have started to malfunction.*

**malfunctioning** *adjective* COMPUT not working correctly

**malfunction routine** *noun* COMPUT a software routine used to find and help diagnose the cause of an error or fault

**malic acid** *noun* CHEM a colourless crystalline solid found in fruits, particularly apples. Formula: $C_4H_6O_5$.

**malignant** *adjective* MED likely to lead to death. Opposite **benign**

**malignant hypertension** *noun* MED dangerously high blood pressure

**malignant melanoma** *noun* MED a dark tumour that develops on the skin from a mole, caused by exposure to strong sunlight ○ *Cases of malignant melanoma could rise by between 5 and 7 per cent for each percentage decrease in ozone in the atmosphere.*

**malignant tumour** *noun* MED a tumour that is cancerous and can reappear

or spread into other tissue, even if removed surgically

**malleus** *noun* ANAT a tiny hammer-shaped bone in the middle ear, one of a set of three that help sound to pass from the eardrum to the inner ear

**malnutrition** *noun* HEALTH the effect of an inadequate or unhealthy diet

**maltase** *noun* BIOCHEM an enzyme in the small intestine that converts maltose into glucose

**maltose** *noun* BIOCHEM a sugar formed by digesting starch or glycogen

**mammal** *noun* ZOOL an animal of the that gives birth to live young, secretes milk to feed them, keeps a constant body temperature and is covered with hair. Class: Mammalia.

**mammary gland** *noun* ANAT a large milk-producing gland in female mammals in which a network of ducts and cavities leads to a nipple or teat (NOTE: Mammary glands generally occur in pairs.)

**mammoth** *noun* ZOOL a large extinct mammal that had long curved tusks and a hairy body

**man** *noun* BIOL **1.** an adult male human being **2.** all human beings considered as a whole ○ *Man has existed for a very short time compared with fish.* Also called **mankind, humankind**

**MAN** *abbreviation* COMPUT metropolitan area network

**manage** *verb* **1.** to be in charge of something ○ *The department is in charge of managing land resources.* **2.** to succeed in doing something ○ *We managed to prevent further damage occurring.*

**managed woodland** *noun* FORESTRY woodland that is controlled by felling, coppicing or planting

**management** *noun* the organised use of resources or materials

**management information system** *noun* COMPUT software that allows managers in a company to access and analyse data. Abbreviation **MIS**

**manager** *noun* a person who is in charge of an organisation or part of one

**Man and the Biosphere Programme** *noun* ENVIRON an interdisciplinary programme of research and training to promote rational use and conservation of the biosphere's resources and to improve the global relationship between people and the environment. Abbreviation **MAB** (NOTE: It is organised by UNESCO.)

**man-caused** *adjective* ENVIRON same as **human-caused**

**Manchester coding** *noun* COMPUT a method of encoding data and timing signals that is used in communications (NOTE: The first half of the bit period indicates the value of the bit (1 or 0) and the second half is used as a timing signal.)

**mandatory** *adjective* required or ordered by an official organisation or authority

**Mandelbrot set** *noun* MATHS a mathematical equation that is called recursively to generate a set of values that form a fractal image when plotted

**mandible** *noun* ANAT **1.** the lower jaw of vertebrates **2.** a biting mouthpart in insects and other invertebrates

**manganese** *noun* CHEM ELEM a metallic trace element that is used in making steel and is essential for biological life (NOTE: The chemical symbol is **Mn**; the atomic number is **25** and the atomic weight is **54.94**.)

COMMENT: Manganese deficiency is associated with high pH and soils that are rich in organic matter.

**mangrove** *noun* TREES a tropical shrub or tree that grows in saltwater swamps in the estuaries of rivers in Asia and America ○ *Mangrove forests cover muddy tidal marshes, lagoons and estuaries.*

COMMENT: Some mangrove trees produce adventitious roots which take root near the parent tree and form new trees. Others produce seeds which have roots even before they fall from the tree. The result is that mangrove swamps are very thick and spread quickly.

**mangrove swamp** *noun* ECOL a swamp covered with mangroves

**manhole** *noun* ENG a hole in a roadway or pavement leading to a shaft down which workmen can go to inspect the sewers

**manifestation** *noun* BIOL a sign or indication of something

**manifold** *noun* ENG a system of pipes for a fluid from single input to multiple output or multiple input to single output

○ *inlet and exhaust manifolds of a piston engine*

**manifold pressure** *noun* ENG the absolute pressure in the induction system of a piston engine measured in inches of mercury

**manipulate** *verb* COMPUT to move, edit and change text or data ○ *An image processor captures, displays and manipulates video images.*

**manipulation** *noun* COMPUT the moving, editing or changing of text or data ○ *The high-speed database management program allows the manipulation of very large amounts of data.*

**mankind** *noun* BIOL all human beings considered as a whole. Also called **humankind, man**

**man machine interface** *noun* COMPUT hardware and software designed to make it easier for users to communicate effectively with a machine. Abbreviation **MMI**

**man-made** *adjective* ENVIRON made or caused by human beings

**manner** *noun* a way of doing something ○ *Safety checks should be done in the approved manner.*

**mannitol** *noun* BIOCHEM a clear, sweet-tasting alcohol found in many plants, used as a diuretic and sweetener

**manometer** *noun* PHYS an apparatus used to measure gas pressure

**mantissa** *noun* MATHS the fractional part of a number ○ *The mantissa of the number 45.897 is 0.897.*

**mantle** *noun* EARTH SCI a layer of the interior of the Earth, between the solid crust and the core, formed of magma

**manual** *noun* a document containing instructions about the operation of a system or piece of software ○ *The manual is included with the system.* ■ *adjective* **1.** done by hand **2.** carried out by someone without the help of a machine

**manual data processing** *noun* the sorting and processing of information without the help of a computer

**manual entry, manual input** *noun* COMPUT the act of entering data into a computer, by an operator via a keyboard

**manually** *adverb* COMPUT by hand, not automatically ○ *The paper has to be fed into the printer manually.*

**manufacture** *verb* **1.** INDUST to make a product using machines **2.** CHEM to produce a chemical naturally ○ *Ozone is constantly being manufactured and destroyed by natural processes in the atmosphere.*

**manufacturer** *noun* INDUST a person or company that produces machine-made products for sale ○ *The company is a large manufacturer of farm machinery.*

**manufacturing** *noun* INDUST the production of machine-made products for sale

**manufacturing industry** *noun* INDUST an industry that takes raw materials and makes them into finished products

**manure** AGRIC *noun* animal dung used as fertiliser (NOTE: In liquid form it is called 'slurry'.) ■ *verb* to spread animal dung on land as fertiliser

COMMENT: All farm manures and slurries are valuable, and should not be regarded as a problem for disposal, but rather as assets to be used in place of expensive fertilisers which would otherwise need to be bought. Manure and slurry have to be spread in a controlled way, or pollution can result from runoffs into streams after rainfall.

**map** *noun* 1. NAVIG a drawing that shows geographical and urban features 2. COMPUT a diagram representing the internal layout of a computer's memory or communications regions 3. ASTRON a diagram showing the position of stars 4. GENETICS same as **genetic map** ■ *verb* 1. to make a map of a place or area 2. COMPUT to display how things are connected, related or derived 3. COMPUT to retrieve data and display it as a map 4. COMPUT to represent a network directory path on a remote computer with a local drive letter, enabling a user to view the contents of the remote directory by simply typing in the drive letter rather than the often long and complex directory path 5. COMPUT to represent a network printer connected to another computer on a network with a local printer identifier, so a user can treat the remote network printer as if it is directly connected to their computer 6. COMPUT to transform a two-dimensional image into a three-dimensional form that can then be rotated or manipulated

**maple** *noun* TREES a hardwood tree of northern temperate regions, some varieties of which produce sweet sap which is used for making sugar and syrup. Genus: *Acer.*

**MAPPS model** *noun* ECOL a global biological and geographical model that simulates the potential natural vegetation that will grow at any site in the world. Full form **mapped atmosphere–plant–soil model**

**MAR** *abbreviation* COMPUT memory address register

**marble** *noun* EARTH SCI a form of limestone that has been metamorphosed, used especially in building and sculpture as it can be polished to give a flat shiny surface

**mare** a circular plain on the surface of the Moon (NOTE: The plural is **maria**.)

**margarine** *noun* FOOD INDUST a substance made from vegetable fat, which is used instead of butter

**margin** *noun* 1. PRINTING a blank space around a section of printed text ○ *The left margin and right margin are the two sections of blank paper on either side of the page.* □ **to set the margin** to define the width of a margin 2. COMPUT an amount of extra time or space

**marginal** *adjective* 1. AGRIC referring to land which is at the edge of cultivated land, e.g. edges of fields or banks beside roads 2. BOT referring to a plant which grows at the edge of two types of habitat 3. AGRIC referring to land of poor quality which results from bad physical conditions, e.g. poor soil, high rainfall or steep slopes, and where farming is often hazardous ○ *Cultivating marginal areas can lead to erosion.* 4. situated in the margins of a document ○ *marginal notes*

**mariculture** *noun* FISHERY a type of fish farming where sea fish or shellfish are grown in sea-water farms

**marijuana** *noun* MED an addictive drug made from the leaves or flowers of the Indian hemp plant

**marine** *adjective* MARINE BIOL 1. referring to the sea ○ *seals and other marine mammals* 2. an animal or plant which lives in the sea

**marine biocoenosis** *noun* MARINE BIOL a varied community of organisms living in the sea

**marine biology** *noun* MARINE BIOL the scientific study of ocean life

**marine disposal** *noun* ENVIRON the depositing of waste at sea

**marine ecology** *noun* ECOL, MARINE BIOL the study of the relationship between organisms that live in the sea and their environment

**marine fauna** *noun* MARINE BIOL the animals that live in the sea

**marine flora** *noun* MARINE BIOL the plants that live in the sea

**marine life** *noun* MARINE BIOL animals and plants which live in the sea

**marine park** *noun* ENVIRON a natural park created on the bottom of the sea where visitors can go into observation chambers to look at the fish and plant life. Compare **oceanarium**

**marine science** *noun* MARINE BIOL, OCEANOG a science that studies all aspects of the sea, including its biology, chemistry, geology and physics

**marine sediment** *noun* OCEANOG solid particles that fall to the seabed

**maritime** *adjective* referring to the sea

**maritime climate** *noun* METEOROL a climate that is modified by the influence of the sea, giving mild winters and warm summers, but with high rainfall

**mark** COMPUT *noun* **1.** a sign put on a page to show something **2.** a transmitted signal that represents a logical one or true condition ■ *verb* to put a mark on something

**marked** *adjective* **1.** very noticeable **2.** clear and definite

**marked increase** *noun* a noticeable, therefore possibly large, increase

**marker** *noun* **1.** something that acts as an indicator of something such as distance or position **2.** GENETICS same as **genetic marker**

**market garden** *noun* AGRIC a place for the commercial growing of plants, usually vegetables, soft fruit, salad crops and flowers, found near a large urban centre which provides a steady outlet for the sale of its produce

**market gardener** *noun* AGRIC a person who runs a market garden

**market gardening** *noun* AGRIC the business of growing vegetables, salad crops and fruit for sale

**marl** *noun* EARTH SCI a fine soil formed of a mixture of clay and lime, used for making bricks

**marram grass** *noun* PLANTS a type of grass which is planted on sand dunes to stabilise them and prevent them being extended by the wind. Latin name: *Ammophila arenaria*.

**marrow** *noun* ANAT same as **bone marrow**

**Mars** *noun* ASTRON the fourth planet of the solar system, orbiting the Sun at an average distance of 228 million km in an orbit taking 687 days

COMMENT: Mars is accompanied by two small satellites, Phobos and Deimos. It rotates on its axis in about half an hour longer than the Earth, and has white polar caps reminiscent of the Earth's. But Mars is unlike Earth in several key ways. It is far colder, with about 15° C the warmest summer surface temperature at the equator. It also has far less atmosphere, with a surface pressure of 0.7% that of the Earth, and its atmosphere consists mostly of carbon dioxide, with only small amounts of oxygen, nitrogen, water vapour, argon and other constituents. The planet surface exhibits large extinct volcanoes and erosional features showing that there was once a lot of liquid water on Mars. Mars has about 10% the mass of the Earth and an equatorial radius half that of the Earth. Over the years, much effort has been expended on searching for life on Mars.

**marsh** *noun* EARTH SCI an area of permanently wet land and the plants that grow on it

COMMENT: A marsh usually has a soil base, as opposed to a bog or fen, which is composed of peat.

**marsh gas** *noun* CHEM same as **methane**

**marshland** *noun* EARTH SCI an area of land covered with marsh

**marshy** *adjective* EARTH SCI referring to land that is permanently wet

**marsupial** *noun* ZOOL a mammal with a pouch in which the young are carried

COMMENT: Marsupials give birth to young at a much earlier stage of development than other mammals so that the young need to be protected in the mother's pouch for some months until they become able to look after themselves. Familiar marsupials include Australian kangaroos and wallabies and South American opossums.

**Martian** *adjective* ASTRON referring to Mars

**mascon** *noun* ASTRON an area on the surface of the Moon in which the gravity is unusually high

**maser** *noun* ASTRON the microwave version of a laser (NOTE: Celestial masers of great power are observed by radio astronomers and are the result of microwaves being trapped and amplified in gas clouds.)

**mask** *noun* **1.** a device to cover the face **2.** COMPUT an integrated circuit layout that is used to define the pattern to be etched or doped onto a slice of semiconductor ○ *a mask or stencil is used to transfer the transistor design onto silicon* **3.** COMPUT a pattern of binary digits used to select various bits from a binary word (NOTE: A one in the mask retains that bit in the word.) ■ *verb* COMPUT to cover an area with something

**maskable** *adjective* COMPUT able to be masked

**maskable interrupt** *noun* COMPUT an interrupt line that can be disabled and ignored by using an interrupt mask

**mask bit** *noun* COMPUT (*in a mask*) one bit used to select the required bit from a word or string

**masked ROM** *noun* COMPUT a read-only memory device that is programmed during manufacture by depositing metal onto selected regions dictated by the shape of a mask

**masking** *noun* COMPUT an operation used to select various bits in a word

**mask register** *noun* COMPUT a storage location in a computer that contains the pattern of bits used as a mask

**mass** *noun* **1.** PHYS a body of matter **2.** a large quantity or large number

**mass action** *noun* CHEM a law that describes that the rate of a chemical reaction at a constant temperature is proportional to the active mass of the reactants, so that as the reaction continues, the rate slows down

**mass decrement, mass defect** *noun* PHYS the amount by which the mass of an isotope is less than the element's mass number

**mass driver** *noun* ASTRON a device using electromagnetic fields to propel mass to high speeds

COMMENT: Mass drivers have been built on a small scale and fairly detailed engineering proposals have been drawn up for mass drivers that could shift lunar material to space colony sites by means of magnetic levitation. A mass driver would consist essentially of electric coils through which a phased current would pass, accelerating material in metal buckets.

**mass extinction** *noun* ECOL the disappearance of numerous species over a relatively short time ○ *The mass extinction of the dinosaurs 65 million years ago may have been caused by the impact of a comet.*

**mass flow** *noun* GEOL a slide of sediment down a slope

**massive** *adjective* very large ○ *In the accident some of the personnel received massive doses of radiation.*

**mass number** *noun* PHYS the sum total of all the protons and neutrons in the nucleus of an atom

**mass production** *noun* INDUST the process of manufacturing large quantities of identical products

**mass radiography** *noun* MED the taking of X-ray photographs of large numbers of people to check for tuberculosis

**mass screening** *noun* MED the testing of large numbers of people for the presence of a disease

**mass spectrometer** *noun* CHEM a device used in chemical analysis which separates particles according to their masses

**mass spectrum** *noun* PHYS a graph of the relative amounts of the chemical constituents of a substance plotted against their mass

**mass storage** *noun* COMPUT the storage and retrieval of large amounts of data

**mass storage system** *noun* COMPUT a data storage system that can hold more than one million million bits of data

**mass wasting** *noun* GEOL a downhill movement of weathered rock, e.g. a landslide

**mast** *noun* **1.** a vertical pole for a flag or antenna ○ *Ice accretes on the leading edge of the detector mast.* **2.** BOT the seeds of the beech tree

**mast cell** *noun* BIOL a large cell in connective tissue, which carries histamine and reacts to allergens

**master** *adjective* **1.** main or principal **2.** COMPUT referring to the most important device or person in a system ○ *The master computer controls everything else.* **3.** COMPUT most up-to-date and correct ■ *verb* **1.** to overcome the difficulty of something ○ *It takes practice to master crosswind landings in light aircraft.* **2.** to learn and understand a language or process

**master clock** *noun* COMPUT a timing signal to which all components in a system are synchronised

**master computer** *noun* COMPUT a computer in a multiprocessor system that controls the other processors and allocates jobs to them

**master control program** *noun* COMPUT a piece of software that controls the operations in a system. Abbreviation **MCP**

**master cylinder** *noun* MECH ENG a hydraulic cylinder from which pressure is transmitted to smaller slave cylinders

**master data** *noun* COMPUT reference data which is stored in a master file

**master file** *noun* COMPUT a set of all the reference data required for an application, which is updated periodically

**mastering** *noun* COMPUT the process of converting finished data to a master disc

**master/master computer system** *noun* COMPUT a system in which each processor is a master, dedicated to one task

**master/slave computer system** *noun* COMPUT a system with a master controlling computer and a slave that takes commands from the master

**master switch** *noun* the most important of a number of switches operating a system

**mastoid antrum** *noun* ANAT a cavity linking the air cells of the mastoid process with the middle ear

**mastoid process** *noun* ANAT a part of the vertebrate skull that forms a bony lump behind the ear

**mat** *noun* COMPUT a plain coloured border that is displayed around an image that is smaller than the window in which it is displayed

**match** *verb* COMPUT **1.** to search through a database for a similar piece of information **2.** to set a register equal to another

**material** *noun* **1.** matter that can be used to make something **2.** cloth

**maternity** *noun* BIOL **1.** the state of being a mother **2.** the identity of a mother ○ *The court had first to establish the child's maternity.* Compare **paternity**

**math** *noun* US same as **mathematics** (*informal*)

**mathematical** *adjective* referring to mathematics

**mathematical model** *noun* MATHS a representation of a system using mathematical ideas and formulae

**mathematical subroutine** *noun* COMPUT a library routine that carries out standard mathematical functions such as square root, logarithm, cosine or sine

**mathematics** *noun* the science of the relationship between numbers and their manipulation and organisation to prove facts and theories. Also called **maths**

**maths** *noun* same as **mathematics** (*informal*) (NOTE: American English is math)

**maths chip, maths coprocessor** *noun* COMPUT a dedicated circuit that can be added to a system to carry out mathematical functions far more rapidly than a standard central processing unit

**matrix** *noun* **1.** a grid-like arrangement of circuit elements ○ *Oil coolers consist of a matrix, divided into sections by baffle plates.* **2.** MATHS a grid of numbers, often used to represent the dimensions of an object or its properties arranged in rows and columns ○ *We used a 3 x 3 matrix for the calculations.* **3.** COMPUT an array of connections between logic gates providing a number of possible logical functions **4.** COMPUT the pattern of dots that make up a character on a computer screen or dot-matrix or laser printer

**matrix printer** *noun* COMPUT same as **dot-matrix printer**

**matrix rotation** *noun* MATHS the exchanging of rows and columns in an array, equal to rotating by 90°

**matrix transform** *noun* MATHS a mathematical process used to rotate a line in any direction, which involves multiplying a 4 x 4 transform matrix with the matrix of the line's coordinates

**matter** *noun* **1.** PHYS a physical substance ○ *Mass is a basic property of matter.* **2.** trouble or difficulty

**maturation** *noun* BIOL the process of becoming mature or fully developed

**maturation lagoon, maturation pond** *noun* INDUST a pond used in the final stages of sewage treatment

**mature** BIOL *adjective* fully developed
■ *verb* to become fully developed

**maturing** *adjective* BIOL in the process of becoming mature

**maturity** *noun* BIOL the state of being fully developed

**Mauna Loa** *noun* EARTH SCI a volcano on the island of Hawaii where scientists have maintained the longest continuous collection of reliable daily atmospheric records

**maxilla** *noun* ZOOL one of a pair of extra jaws in insects and other arthropods

**maxillary antrum** *noun* ANAT one of two sinuses behind the cheekbones in the upper jaw of vertebrates

**maximise** *verb* **1.** to make something as large as possible **2.** COMPUT to expand an application icon back to its original display window. Compare **minimise**

**maximum** *adjective* the greatest possible ○ *maximum effect* ○ *The maximum capacity of the vehicle is 12.* ■ *noun* the greatest possible quantity, amount, degree or value ○ *There is a net gain of heat by the Earth until terrestrial radiation balances solar radiation when the daily temperature is at its maximum.* (NOTE: The plural is **maximums** or **maxima**.)

**maximum allowable concentration** *noun* ENVIRON the largest amount of a pollutant with which workers are allowed to be in contact in their work environment. Abbreviation **MAC**

**maximum capacity** *noun* COMPUT the greatest amount of data that can be stored

**maximum–minimum thermometer** *noun* a thermometer that shows the highest and lowest temperatures reached since it was last checked, as well as the current temperature

**maximum permissible dose** *noun* ENVIRON the highest amount of radiation to which a person may safely be exposed during a certain period

**maximum permissible level** *noun* ENVIRON the highest level of radiation

that is allowed to be present in a certain environment

**maximum transmission rate** *noun* COMPUT the greatest amount of data that can be transmitted every second

**maximum users** *noun* COMPUT the greatest number of users that a system can support at any one time

**maxwell** *noun* PHYS the centimetre-gram-second unit of magnetic flux, equal to the flux over one square centimetre perpendicular to a magnetic field of one gauss

**mb** *abbreviation* MEASURE, PHYS millibar

**Mb** *abbreviation* MEASURE, COMPUT megabit

**MB** *abbreviation* MEASURE, COMPUT megabyte

**Mbps** *abbreviation* MEASURE, COMPUT megabits per second

**MBR** *abbreviation* COMPUT memory buffer register

**Mbyte** *abbreviation* MEASURE, COMPUT megabyte

**MCP** *abbreviation* COMPUT master control program

**MCPA** *noun* AGRIC 2-methyl-4chloro-phenoxy-acetic acid, used as a herbicide

COMMENT: MCPA kills the most persistent broad-leaved weeds: nettle, buttercups, charlock, dock seedlings, plantains and thistles.

**MCPP** *abbreviation* AGRIC mecoprop

**MDR** *abbreviation* COMPUT memory data register

**meadow** *noun* AGRIC a field of grass and other wild plants, grown for fodder

**mean** *adjective* **1.** referring to something midway between two extremes **2.** MATHS referring to an arithmetic mean ■ *noun* **1.** something having a position midway between two extremes **2.** MATHS same as **arithmetic mean** ■ *verb* **1.** to signify something ○ *Airspeed means the speed of the aircraft in relation to the air around it.* **2.** to intend to do something ○ *I meant to telephone the reservations desk this morning but I forgot.* **3.** to result in something ○ *Installing a new computer network means a lot of problems for everybody.* (NOTE: **meaning – meant**)

**mean daily temperature** *noun* METEOROL the average daily temperature

**meander** *noun* EARTH SCI a bend in the course of a river

**meander belt** *noun* EARTH SCI the total width of the area covered by a river which meanders

**mean free path** *noun* PHYS the average distance travelled by a gas molecule before it hits another molecule or the side of the container

**mean free time** *noun* PHYS the average time between collisions of gas molecules

**means** *noun* a way of doing something which brings a result ○ *A clear window fitted in the reservoir provides a means of checking hydraulic fluid level during servicing.* ○ *The means of restarting the engine were unorthodox, but successful.* □ **a means of transport** a way of getting someone or something from one place to another ○ *Walking is my only means of transport.*

**mean sea level** *noun* OCEANOG the average level of the sea taking tidal variations into account ○ *Altitude is the vertical distance between a specific point and mean sea level.*

**mean solar day** *noun* TIME the time between two successive transits of the mean sun across the meridian at noon (NOTE: It is the standard measurement of the 24 hour day.)

**mean temperature** *noun* an average temperature ○ *The mean temperature for July is 25 ° C.*

**mean time between failures** *noun* COMPUT the average period of time for which a piece of equipment will operate between breakdowns. Abbreviation **MTBF**

**mean time to failure** *noun* COMPUT the average period of time for which a device will operate, usually continuously, before failing. Abbreviation **MTF**

**mean time to repair** *noun* COMPUT the average period of time required to repair a faulty piece of equipment

**measure** *noun* 1. a reference for discovering the dimensions or amount of something ○ *The litre is a measure of capacity.* 2. a device used for measuring 3. an amount of something 4. an action taken to get a result ○ *Stricter safety measures were introduced.* ■ *verb* 1. to

find the dimensions or amount of something ○ *to measure a distance* 2. to be of a particular size, length or quantity ○ *How much does the pipe measure?*

**measurement** *noun* 1. the act of measuring something ○ *Measurement of relative humidity is done using an instrument called a hygrometer.* 2. a result of measuring, expressed in standard units ○ *The measurements of the room are: height = 4 metres, length = 10 metres, width = 4 metres.*

**meat** *noun* FOOD animal flesh that is eaten as food

**meat-eating animal** *noun* ZOOL same as **carnivore**

**mechanical** *adjective* referring to machines ○ *Activation may be electrical or mechanical.*

**mechanical actuation** *noun* MECH ENG a movement caused by a mechanism such as a rod, arm or lever

**mechanical advantage** *noun* MECH ENG 1. the ratio of the output force produced by a machine to the input force 2. an increase in force gained by using mechanisms such as levers or gears

**mechanical engineering** *noun* MECH ENG the study of the design, construction and use of machinery or mechanical structures

**mechanical pump** *noun* MECH ENG a pump operated by an engine rather than by electrical power

**mechanical treatment** *noun* ENVIRON the processing of sewage by mechanical means such as agitating or stirring

**mechanics** *noun* PHYS the study of the action of forces on matter or material systems ■ *plural noun* the way something works ○ *The mechanics of the föhn wind provide a good illustration of the adiabatic process.*

**mechanism** *noun* 1. MECH ENG an arrangement of connected parts in a machine or system ○ *the landing gear mechanism* 2. a physical process ○ *the mechanism by which thunderstorms develop* 3. a method of achieving something ○ *a mechanism for receiving feedback from students*

**mecoprop** *noun* AGRIC a herbicide used to control weeds such as chickweed and cleavers, as well as the weeds controlled by MCPA. Abbreviation **MCPP**

**media** *noun* plural of **medium**

**media access control** *noun* COMPUT a sublayer within the data-link layer of the OSI network model that provides access to the transmission media. Abbreviation **MAC**

**medial** *adjective* BIOL situated near to the central midline of the body or to the centre of an organ. Compare **lateral**

**median** *noun* STATS the value in a frequency distribution that has equal total frequencies above and below it

**median lethal dose** *noun* BIOL the dose of a substance that will kill half of a sample of experimental animals within a specified time

**medical** *adjective* MED **1.** referring to the diagnosis and treatment of disease and injury in humans **2.** referring the treatment of disease in humans that does not involve surgery

**medical entomologist** *noun* a scientist who studies insects that may carry diseases that affect humans

**medical supplies** *plural noun* MED consumables used in medical treatment, e.g. drugs, bandages and syringes

**medical waste** *noun* MED waste from hospitals, clinics or other health care facilities that contains or has come into contact with diseased tissues or infectious microorganisms

**medication** *noun* MED **1.** a method of treatment by giving drugs to a patient **2.** a drug or preparation taken to treat a disease or condition

**medicinal** *adjective* MED **1.** referring to medicine ○ *medicinal properties* **2.** referring to a substance or plant that has healing properties

**medicinal herb** *noun* MED, BOT a plant that can be used to treat a disease

**medicinally** *adverb* MED in the treatment of disease ○ *The herb can be used medicinally.*

**medicinal spring** *noun* MED, EARTH SCI water coming naturally out of the ground which is thought to be beneficial in the treatment of disease

**medicine** *noun* MED **1.** a drug or preparation taken to treat a disease or condition ○ *Take some cough medicine if your cough is bad.* **2.** the study of diseases and how to cure or prevent them ○ *He is studying medicine because he wants to be a doctor.* **3.** the study and

treatment of diseases that does not involve surgery

**medium** *adjective* middle or average ○ *a medium-sized computer system* ■ *noun* **1.** PHYS a substance through which something else is transmitted or carried ○ *Tubes convey the cooling medium.* **2.** COMPUT a physical material that can be used to store data ○ *Computers can store data on a variety of media, including disk, punched card and CD-ROM.* (NOTE: [all noun senses] The plural is **mediums** or **media**.)

**medium frequency band** *noun* PHYS a radio frequency range between 300 kHz and 3000 kHz. Abbreviation **MF**. Also called **medium wave**

**medium model** *noun* COMPUT a memory model of the Intel 80x86 processor family that allows 64 Kb of data and up to 1 MB of code

**medium-range weather forecast** *noun* METEOROL a forecast covering two to five days

**medium scale integration** *noun* ELEC an integrated circuit with 10 − 500 components. Abbreviation **MSI**

**medulla** *noun* ANAT **1.** the soft inner part of an organ surrounded by the cortex **2.** same as **bone marrow**

**medulla oblongata** *noun* ANAT the lowermost part of the vertebrate brain (NOTE: It controls involuntary vital functions such as heartbeat and breathing.)

**medullary ray** *noun* BOT a band or sheet of connective tissue between the pith and the bark in the stems of some woody plants

**meet** *noun* COMPUT a logical function whose output is true if both inputs are true

**mega-** *prefix* **1.** large. Opposite **micro-** **2.** MEASURE one million, $10^6$ ○ *megahertz* ○ *megawatt* Symbol **M 3.** COMPUT (*in computing and electronic applications*) 1 048 576, equal to $2^{20}$

**megabit** *noun* MEASURE, COMPUT 1 048 576 bits or 131 072 bytes of storage. Abbreviation **Mb**

**megabits per second** *noun* MEASURE, COMPUT the number of megabits transmitted every second. Abbreviation **Mbps**

**megabyte** *noun* MEASURE, COMPUT 1 048 576 bytes of storage. Abbreviation **MB, Mbyte**

**megadose** MEASURE a large dose ○ *received a megadose of radiation*

**megaflops** *noun* MEASURE, COMPUT a measure of computing power and speed equal to one million floating point instructions per second

**megahertz** *noun* MEASURE, PHYS a measure of frequency equal to one million cycles per second. Abbreviation **MHz**

**megalo-** *prefix* abnormally large. Opposite **micro-**

**megapixel display** *noun* COMPUT a display adapter and monitor that are capable of displaying over one million pixels (NOTE: This means a resolution of at least 1024 x 1024 pixels.)

**meiosis** *noun* BIOL the process of cell division that results in four cells (**gametes**) each with only one set of chromosomes from each parent. Compare **mitosis** (NOTE: At meiosis each cell divides into four to produce sperm or ova, each with half the usual number of chromosomes.)

**meitnerium** *noun* CHEM ELEM an artificially produced radioactive chemical element (NOTE: The chemical symbol is **Mt**; the atomic number is **109** and the atomic weight is **268**.)

**melamine** *noun* CHEM a white crystalline solid, used for making synthetic resins and tanning leather. Formula: $C_3H_6N_6$.

**melanic** *adjective* ZOOL being unusually dark in appearance

**melanin** *noun* ZOOL a dark pigment which gives colour to skin and hair

**melanism** *noun* **1.** MED abnormal deposits of dark pigment on the skin **2.** ZOOL the condition of being black or very dark in appearance in contrast to the normal coloration of the animal

**melanoma** *noun* MED ◊ **malignant melanoma**

**melatonin** *noun* BIOCHEM a hormone secreted by the pineal gland that produces changes in the skin colour of vertebrates and is involved in regulating biorhythms

**melt** *verb* **1.** PHYS to heat a solid so that it becomes liquid ○ *The gradual rise in air temperature melted the glaciers.* **2.** (*of solid*) to become liquid after being heated ○ *The gradual rise in air temperature made the glaciers melt.* ◆ **molten**

**meltdown** *noun* INDUST a point in an accident in a nuclear reactor at which the fuel overheats and the core melts while the nuclear reaction is still in progress

**melting point** *noun* PHYS the temperature at which a solid turns to liquid ○ *The melting point of ice is 0 ° C.*

**meltwater** *noun* EARTH SCI water from melting ice, especially from a glacier or from winter snow

**member** *noun* **1.** ENG a main structural unit ○ *A beam is a member that is designed to withstand loading applied at an angle to it, often perpendicular.* **2.** an individual that belongs to a group ○ *Black bryony is the only British member of the yam family.* **3.** COMPUT one object on a page of a multimedia book **4.** COMPUT an individual record or item in a field

**membrane** *noun* BIOL a thin layer of tissue that lines or covers an organ

**membrane bone** *noun* BIOL bone that develops from tissue and not from cartilage

**membranous labyrinth** *noun* ANAT a system of fluid-filled structures in the inner ear that are necessary for hearing and balance

**memo field** *noun* COMPUT a field in a database or text window in an application that allows a user to add comments or a memo about the entry

**memorise** *verb* **1.** to remember something deliberately **2.** COMPUT to retain data or instructions in the memory

**memory** *noun* **1.** PHYSIOL the means by which the brain stores information and experiences **2.** COMPUT storage space in a computer system or medium that is capable of retaining data or instructions **3.** a problem with some batteries, e.g. nickel-cadmium batteries, which gradually reduces their ability to retain charge

**memory address register** *noun* COMPUT a register within the computer that contains the address of the next location to be accessed. Abbreviation **MAR**

**memory bank** *noun* COMPUT a number of smaller storage devices connected together to form one large area of memory

**memory buffer register** *noun* COMPUT a register in a computer that temporarily buffers all inputs and outputs. Abbreviation **MBR**

**memory bus** *noun* COMPUT a bus carrying address data between a central processing unit and memory devices

**memory chip** *noun* COMPUT an electronic component that is able to store binary data

**memory cycle** *noun* COMPUT a period of time from when the central processing unit reads or writes to a location and the action being performed

**memory data register** *noun* COMPUT a register in a computer which holds data before it is processed or moved to a memory location. Abbreviation **MDR**

**memory management unit** *noun* COMPUT the electronic logic circuits that generate the memory refresh signals and manage the mapping of virtual memory addresses to physical memory locations. Abbreviation **MMU** (NOTE: The memory management unit is usually integrated into the processor chip.)

**memory map** *noun* COMPUT a diagram indicating the allocation of address ranges to various memory devices such as RAM, ROM and memory-mapped input/output devices

**memory model** *noun* COMPUT a method used in a program to address the code and data that is used within that program (NOTE: The memory model defines how much memory is available for code and data. Processors with a segmented address space can support multiple memory models.)

**memory-resident software** *noun* COMPUT same as **resident software** ○ *The system can bomb if you set up too many memory-resident programs at the same time.*

**mendelevium** *noun* CHEM ELEM a synthetic radioactive element obtained by bombardment of einsteinium atoms with helium particles (NOTE: The chemical symbol is **Md**; the atomic number is **101** and the atomic weight is **258**.)

**Mendelism** *noun* GENETICS the theory of heredity which states that characteristics are transferred from one generation to the next as individual units (**genes**) rather than being mixed together in the offspring

**Mendel's laws** *plural noun* GENETICS the laws governing heredity

COMMENT: The two laws set out by Gregor Mendel following his experiments growing peas, were (in modern terms): that genes for separate genetic characters assort independently of each other and that the genes for a pair of genetic characters are carried by different gametes.

**meninges** *plural noun* ANAT the set of three protective membranes around the brain and spinal cord of vertebrates (NOTE: Their names are dura mater, arachnoid and pia mater.)

**meniscus** *noun* **1.** OPTICS a lens that is concave on one side and convex on the other **2.** PHYS the curved surface of a narrow column of water **3.** ANAT a small plate of cartilage between vertebrae

**menopause** *noun* BIOL the time when a woman's periods stop and she is no longer fertile (NOTE: It usually occurs between the ages of 45 and 50.)

**menstrual** *adjective* BIOL referring to menstruation

**menstrual cycle** *noun* BIOL the period, usually about 28 days, during which a woman ovulates, when the walls of the uterus swell and bleeding takes place if the egg cell has not been fertilised

**menstruation** *noun* BIOL the bleeding from the uterus which occurs in a woman each month if the egg cell has not been fertilised

**menu** *noun* COMPUT a list of options or programs available to the user

**menu bar** *noun* COMPUT a menu displayed on a horizontal line along the top of the screen or window

**menu item** *noun* COMPUT one of the choices in a menu

**menu shortcut** *noun* COMPUT a key combination of two or more keys that is the same as selecting a menu option

**Mercalli** EARTH SCI ▷ **Modified Mercalli Scale**

**Mercator's projection** *noun* a map projection of the Earth onto a cylinder so that all the parallels of latitude are the same length as the equator ○ *It is therefore impossible to represent the poles on Mercator's projection.*

**Mercurian** *adjective* ASTRON referring to Mercury

**mercuric chloride** *noun* CHEM same as **mercury (II) chloride**

**mercuric oxide** noun CHEM same as **mercury (II) oxide**

**mercuric sulfide, mercuric sulphide** noun CHEM same as **mercury (II) sulfide**

**mercurous chloride** noun CHEM same as **mercury (I) chloride**

**mercury** noun CHEM ELEM a poisonous metal that is liquid at room temperature, used in thermometers and electric batteries. Also called **quicksilver** (NOTE: The chemical symbol is **Hg**; the atomic number is **80** and the atomic weight is **200.59**.)

**Mercury** noun ASTRON the innermost planet of the solar system, orbiting the Sun in 88 days at an average distance of 58 million km

COMMENT: Mercury has the least circular orbit of the major planets, with an eccentricity of 0.2. Mercury is a cratered planet like the Moon without the maria. Mercury has a magnetic field about 1% as strong as the Earth's, indicating a possible metal core, although this seems not to be hot enough to be liquid. Mercury also rotates very slowly, in a special version of captured rotation. Its day of 57 Earth days means that it makes three turns on its axis for every two orbits of the Sun. Mercury has an exceptionally thin atmosphere, dominated by hydrogen and helium. Surface temperatures on Mercury can reach over 400 ° C and fall to perhaps −200 ° C during the Mercurian night.

**mercury barometer** noun METEOROL a barometer made of a glass tube containing mercury (NOTE: One end of the tube is sealed, the other is open, resting in a bowl of mercury. As the atmospheric pressure changes, so the column of mercury in the tube rises or falls.)

**mercury cell** noun PHYS an electrolytic or dry cell that has an electrode made of mercury

**mercury (I) chloride** noun CHEM a poisonous white compound of mercury and chlorine, used as a moss killer and laxative. Formula: $Hg_2Cl_2$. Also called **mercurous chloride**

**mercury (II) chloride** noun CHEM a poisonous compound of mercury and chlorine, used as an antiseptic and wood preservative. Formula: $HgCl_2$. Also called **mercuric chloride**

**mercury (II) oxide** noun CHEM a red or yellow toxic compound of mercury and oxygen, used as pigment. Formula: $Hg_2O$. Also called **mercuric oxide** (NOTE: Mercury (I) or mercurous oxide, $Hg_2O$, has never been conclusively proven to exist.)

**mercury poisoning** noun MED poisoning by eating or drinking mercury or mercury compounds, or by inhaling mercury vapour

**mercury (II) sulfide, mercury (II) sulphide** noun CHEM a black or red compound of mercury and sulfur used in pigments such as vermilion. Formula: HgS. Also called **mercuric sulfide**

**mercury-vapour lamp** noun PHYS a lamp that produces ultraviolet radiation by applying an electric current through mercury vapour within a sealed quartz glass bulb

**merge** verb COMPUT to combine two data files while retaining the overall order ○ *The system automatically merges text and illustrations into the document.*

**meridian** noun EARTH SCI an imaginary great circle on the Earth's surface passing through the north and south geographic poles

**meridional** adjective EARTH SCI going from the North Pole to the South Pole or from the South Pole to the North Pole

**meridional airstream** noun METEOROL an airstream blowing from north to south or from south to north

**meridionality** noun METEOROL a phenomenon of air blowing from north to south or from south to north

**meristem** noun BOT a plant tissue at the tips of stems and roots in which cells are actively dividing

**mes-, meso-** prefix same as **meso-** (NOTE: used before vowels)

**mesa** noun EARTH SCI a high plateau in the southwest of the USA, with steep sides and a flat top

**mesencephalon** noun ANAT same as **midbrain**

**mesenteric artery** noun ANAT one of two arteries that supply the small intestine or the transverse colon and rectum

**mesenteric ganglion** noun ANAT a plexus of sympathetic nerve fibres and ganglion cells around the superior mesenteric artery

**mesentery** *noun, noun* ANAT a membrane in the body cavity that supports the weight of the small intestine

**mesh** *noun* 1. a net-like structure 2. COMPUT a system with two or more possible paths at each interconnection

**mesh model** *noun* COMPUT a graphical object that is displayed as a mesh created from polygons, which can then be used to shade the object

**mesh network** *noun* COMPUT a method of connecting several machines together in which each device is directly connected to every other device in the network

**meso-** *prefix* middle

**mesobenthos** *noun* MARINE BIOL the animals or plants living on the seabed, between 250 and 1000 metres below the surface

**mesoclimate** *noun* ECOL a variant of climate only found in a specific locality, extending no more than several kilometres in radius

**mesoderm** *noun* BIOL the middle layer of cells in an embryo (NOTE: It develops into blood, connective tissue, muscle, skin and bone.)

**mesoglea, mesogloea** *noun* MARINE BIOL a gelatinous layer between the inner and outer tissue layers of coelenterates such as jellyfish

**mesohaline** *adjective* CHEM (*of water*) partly salt

**mesomerism** *noun* CHEM the property of a chemical compound having different structures by alteration of the covalent bonds

**meson** *noun* PHYS an elementary particle with a rest mass between that of an electron and a proton, involved in the strong interaction (NOTE: A meson consists of a quark and an antiquark.)

**mesopause** *noun* EARTH SCI a thin layer of cold atmosphere between the mesosphere and the thermosphere

**mesophyll** *noun* BOT the tissue inside a leaf where photosynthesis takes place

**mesophyte** *noun* BOT a plant that needs a normal amount of water to survive

**mesoplankton** *plural noun* MARINE BIOL organisms that take the form of plankton for part of their life cycle

**mesosaprobic** *adjective* BIOL referring to an organism that can survive in moderately polluted water

**mesosphere** *noun* METEOROL the zone of Earth's atmosphere between the stratosphere and the thermosphere (NOTE: It lies between 50 and 80 kilometres above the surface, with the stratopause at the bottom and the mesopause at the top. The air temperature falls steadily as one rises through the mesosphere.)

**mesothelium** *noun* ANAT a layer of cells lining a membrane. Compare **endothelium, epithelium**

**mesotherm** *noun* BOT a plant that grows in warm conditions

**mesotrophic** *adjective* BIOCHEM referring to water that contains a moderate amount of nutrients

**mesotrophic lake** *noun* EARTH SCI a lake that has a moderate amount of nutrients in its water

**message** *noun* 1. a piece of information sent from one person to another 2. COMPUT a defined amount of information

**message authentication code** *noun* COMPUT full form of **MAC**

**message box** *noun* COMPUT a small window that is displayed on screen to warn of an event, condition or error

**messenger RNA** *noun* GENETICS a type of RNA that transmits information from DNA to the ribosomes where protein synthesis occurs. Abbreviation **mRNA**

**meta-** *prefix* 1. which changes 2. which follows

**metabit** *noun* COMPUT an extra identifying bit for each data word

**metabolic** *adjective* PHYSIOL referring to metabolism

**metabolic cycle** *noun* BOT a cycle by which plants absorb sunlight, transform it into energy by photosynthesis and create carbon compounds

**metabolic pathway** *noun* BIOCHEM a series of chemical reactions in the body, controlled by enzymes

**metabolic rate** *noun* BIOCHEM a measure of how fast the chemical reactions in living cells happen

**metabolic waste** *noun* BIOCHEM a substance produced by metabolism, e.g.

carbon dioxide, which is not needed by the organism which produces it

**metabolise** *verb* PHYSIOL to change the nature of something by metabolism ○ *The liver metabolises proteins and carbohydrates.*

**metabolism** *noun* PHYSIOL the chemical processes which are continually taking place in the human body and which are essential to life

COMMENT: Metabolism covers all changes which take place in the body: the building of tissue (anabolism), the breaking down of tissue (catabolism), the conversion of nutrients into tissue, the elimination of waste matter and the action of hormones.

**metabolite** *noun* BIOCHEM a chemical produced as a result of metabolism

**metacarpus** *noun* ANAT the part of a hand, or a front foot of an animal, between the wrist and the fingers or toes

**metacentric** *adjective* GENETICS referring to a chromosome whose centromere is at or near the middle

**metacompiler** *noun* COMPUT a compiler that is used to create another compiler

**metafemale** *noun* GENETICS a female organism that has an extra female chromosome

**metafile** *noun* COMPUT **1.** a file that contains other files ○ *The operating system uses a metafile to hold data that defines where each file is stored on disk.* **2.** a file that defines or contains data about other files

**metal** *noun* METALL an element or a compound that can carry heat and electricity

**metalanguage** *noun* COMPUT a language that describes a programming language

**metaldehyde** *noun* CHEM a substance, sold in small blocks, used to light fires or to kill slugs and snails

**metal fatigue** *noun* METALL the appearance of cracks and weaknesses in metal that has been exposed to a long period of stress

**metalimnion** *noun* EARTH SCI the middle layer of water in a lake. Compare **epilimnion, hypolimnion**

**metallic** *adjective* **1.** CHEM referring to metal ○ *metallic materials* **2.** like metal, especially in appearance

**metallic bond** *noun* CHEM a chemical bond in which electrons are shared between atoms and are able to move within the structure (NOTE: Such bonds are characteristic of metals.)

**metallic crystal** *noun* CHEM a crystal formed by metal atoms in their solid state that can conduct electricity

**metallic element** *noun* CHEM a chemical element that is a metal

**metalloid** *adjective* CHEM **1.** an element such as silicon that has some properties of a metal and some of a non-metal **2.** like a metal

**metal oxide semiconductor** *noun* ELEC a production and design method for a certain family of integrated circuits using patterns of metal conductors and oxide deposited onto a semiconductor. Abbreviation **MOS**

**metamale** *noun* GENETICS a male organism that has an extra male chromosome

**metameric segmentation** *noun* ZOOL the repetition of identical segments along the length of an organism's body, e.g. in an earthworm. Also called **metamerism**

**metamerism** *noun* ZOOL same as **metameric segmentation**

**metamorphic** *adjective* EARTH SCI referring to rock that has changed because of external influences such as pressure from other rocks or temperature changes

**metamorphism** *noun* EARTH SCI the creation of metamorphic rock

**metamorphose** *verb* **1.** ZOOL (*of an animal*) to change into another form **2.** EARTH SCI (*of rock*) to undergo metamorphism

**metamorphosis** *noun* ZOOL a change into a different form, especially the change of a larva into an adult insect

**metaphase** *noun* BIOL the stage of cell division at which chromosomes line up before the daughter cells separate

**metaplasia** *noun* BIOL the process that changes healthy tissue into a diseased form such as a cancerous tumour

**metapopulation** *noun* ECOL a set of populations that exchange individuals through migration

**metastasis** *noun* MED the spreading of a malignant disease from one part of the body to another through the bloodstream or the lymph system (NOTE: The plural is **metastases**.)

**metatarsal** *noun* ANAT a bone of the set found between the toes and ankle

**metatarsus** *noun* ZOOL the part of animal's hind foot between the ankle and toes

**metatherian** *adjective* ZOOL referring to marsupials

**metazoan** *noun* ZOOL an animal whose body consists of cells that are separated into specialised tissues and organs. Group: *Metazoa*. (NOTE: All animals except for sponges and protozoans are classified as metazoans.)

**meteor** *noun* ASTRON a solid body that enters Earth's atmosphere from outer space, usually burning up as it does so

**meteoric** *adjective* ASTRON referring to meteors

**meteorite** *noun* ASTRON a solid body that falls from outer space onto Earth's surface

COMMENT: Outer space contains many millions of small solid bodies which sometimes come into contact with Earth. Large meteorites can create craters and form dust clouds when they hit Earth and it is believed that the impact of very large meteorites may have been responsible for major climatic changes in the past.

**meteoroid** *noun* ASTRON a piece of material in interplanetary space that is too small to be viewed as an asteroid (NOTE: Meteoroids range from dust grain size up to several hundred tonnes.)

**meteorological** *adjective* METEOROL referring to meteorology or to the climate

**meteorologist** *noun* METEOROL a person who studies, reports and forecasts the weather

**meteorology** *noun* METEOROL the scientific study of weather and weather conditions ○ *Terrestrial radiation plays an important part in meteorology.*

**meter** *noun* **1.** a device to measure a physical property such as current, rate of flow or air speed **2.** MEASURE US spelling of **metre**

**methaemoglobin** *noun* MED a dark brown substance formed from haemoglobin which develops during illness or following treatment with some drugs

(NOTE: Methaemoglobin cannot transport oxygen round the body and so causes cyanosis.)

**methaemoglobinaemia** *noun* MED the presence of methaemoglobin in the blood

**methanation** *noun* CHEM the process of converting a mixture into methane. Also called **methanisation**

**methane** *noun* CHEM a colourless flammable gas. Formula: $CH_4$. Also called **marsh gas**

COMMENT: Methane is produced naturally from rotting vegetation in marshes, where it can sometimes catch fire, creating the phenomenon called will o' the wisp, a light flickering over a marsh. It is also found in coal mines, where it is called firedamp. It occurs as a product of animal excreta in farming. Methane is an important greenhouse gas.

**methane converter** *noun* ENVIRON a process that takes the gas produced by rotting waste in a landfill site and processes it into a usable form

**methane fermentation** *noun* BIOCHEM the breaking down of food in the gut of ruminant animals, especially cattle, producing methane which is eliminated from the animal's body

**methanisation** *noun* CHEM same as **methanation**

**methanogenesis** *noun* CHEM the generation of methane

**methanoic acid** *noun* CHEM same as **formic acid**

**methanol** *noun* CHEM an alcohol manufactured from coal, natural gas or waste wood, which is used as a fuel or solvent. Formula: $CH_3OH$. Also called **methyl alcohol, wood alcohol**

COMMENT: Methanol can be used as a fuel in any type of burner. Its main disadvantage is that it is less efficient than petrol and can cause pollution if it escapes into the environment, as it mixes easily with water. Production of methanol from coal or natural gas does not help fuel conservation, since it depletes Earth's fossil fuel resources.

**methionine** *noun* BIOCHEM an essential amino acid

**method** *noun* a particular way of doing something, especially if it is well thought out and systematic ○ *The most common method of displaying radar information is on a cathode ray tube.*

**methyl alcohol** *noun* CHEM same as **methanol**

**methylamine** *noun* CHEM a transparent flammable gas derived from ammonia used in medicines, dyes and weedkillers. Formula: $CH_5N$.

**methylate** *verb* CHEM to add a methyl group in place of one of the hydrogen atoms in a molecule

**methylated spirit** *noun* CHEM ethanol with added methanol and violet dye, used as a solvent or fuel (NOTE: The methanol makes it unsuitable for people to drink and the dye serves as a warning.)

**methylbenzene** *noun* CHEM same as **toluene**

**methylene blue** *noun* CHEM a blue dye

**methylene blue test** *noun* CHEM a test to see whether a sample of effluent has the ability to remain in an oxidised condition (NOTE: The effluent is considered stable if it retains the blue colour of the dye throughout the testing period.)

**methyl isocyanate** *noun* CHEM a compound used in the production of insecticides. Abbreviation **MIC**

COMMENT: Methyl isocyanate is very toxic and was the gas which leaked at Bhopal in India in 1984.

**metre** *noun* MEASURE the SI unit of length ○ *The room is four metres by three.* Symbol **m**

**metres per second** *noun* MEASURE a system of measuring speed ○ *One metre per second is equal to 2.2 miles per hour.* Abbreviation **m/s** (NOTE: It is often used to measure wind speed.)

**metric system** *noun* MEASURE a decimal measuring system, calculated in units of ten, e.g. the SI system

**metric ton** *noun* MEASURE same as **tonne**

**metropolitan area network** *noun* COMPUT a network extending over a limited area such as a city

**MF band** *abbreviation* MEDIA medium frequency band

**MFM** *abbreviation* ELEC modified frequency modulation

**mg** *abbreviation* MEASURE milligram

**Mg** *symbol* CHEM ELEM magnesium

**MHC** *noun* GENETICS (*in mammals*) a group of genes located next or near to one another that make cells separate and distinguishable from those of other organisms

**MHD** *abbreviation* EARTH SCI magnetohydrodynamics

**MHz** *abbreviation* MEASURE, PHYS megahertz

**MIC** *abbreviation* CHEM methyl isocyanate

**mica** *noun* MINERALS, INDUST a silicate mineral which splits into thin transparent flakes, used as an insulator in electrical appliances

**micro** *noun* COMPUT same as **microcomputer**

**micro-** *prefix* **1.** very small. Opposite **macro-, mega-, megalo- 2.** MEASURE one millionth, $10^{-6}$. Symbol **µ**

**microarray** *noun* BIOTECH same as **gene chip**

**microbalance** *noun* MEASURE a device that can weigh very small quantities accurately

**microbe** *noun* MICROBIOL a microorganism (NOTE: Viruses, bacteria, protozoa and microscopic fungi are informally referred to as microbes.)

**microbial** *adjective* MICROBIOL referring to microbes

**microbial disease** *noun* MED a disease caused by a microbe

**microbial ecology** *noun* MICROBIOL the study of the way in which microbes develop in nature

**microbial fermentation** *noun* MICROBIOL, BIOCHEM the breaking down of a substance by the action of microbes

**microbiological** *adjective* MICROBIOL referring to microbiology

**microbiologist** *noun* MICROBIOL a scientist who specialises in the study of microorganisms

**microbiology** *noun* BIOL the scientific study of microorganisms

**microcarrier** *noun* BIOTECH (*in cell cultures and drug delivery systems*) a microscopic particle to which something is attached

**microchip** *noun* ELECTRONICS a circuit in which all the active and passive components are formed on one small piece of semiconductor, by means of etching and chemical processes

**microcircuit** *noun* ELECTRONICS a complex integrated circuit

**microclimate** *noun* METEOROL, ECOL a climate covering a restricted area such as a pond, a tree or a field. Compare **macroclimate**

**microcode** *noun* COMPUT control instructions for an arithmetic logic unit implemented as hardwired software

**microcomputer** *noun* COMPUT a complete small-scale, cheap and low-powered computer system based around a microprocessor chip with limited memory capacity. Also called **micro**

**microcomputer architecture** *noun* COMPUT the layout and interconnection of a microcomputer's internal hardware

**microcycle** *noun* COMPUT a unit of time usually a multiple of the system clock period, used to give the execution time of instructions

**microdevice** *noun* ELECTRONICS a very small device such as a microprocessor

**microelectronics** *noun* ELECTRONICS the design and manufacture of electronic circuits with integrated circuits and chips

**microenvironment** *noun* ECOL same as **microhabitat**

**microfauna** *noun* 1. MICROBIOL very small animals which can only be seen with a microscope 2. ECOL the animals living in a microhabitat

**microgram** *noun* MEASURE a unit of measurement of weight, equal to one millionth of a gram. Symbol **µm**

**microhabitat** *noun* ECOL a single small area, e.g. the bark of a tree, where fauna and/or flora live. Also called **microenvironment**

**micro-hydro system** *noun* INDUST a small system that uses water to produce electricity

**microinstruction** *noun* COMPUT a hardwired instruction in a microcode that controls the actions of the arithmetic logic unit in a processor

**micrometer** *noun* MEASURE 1. an instrument for taking very small measurements such as of the width or

thickness of very thin pieces of tissue 2. US spelling of **micrometre**

**micrometre** *noun* MEASURE one thousandth of a millimetre. Symbol **µm**

**micromole** *noun* MEASURE, CHEM a unit of measurement of the amount of substance equal to one millionth of a mole

**micron** *noun* MEASURE symbol **µ**. Former name for **micrometre**

**micronutrient** *noun* BIOL a nutrient which an organism uses in very small quantities, e.g. iron, zinc or copper

**microorganism** *noun* MICROBIOL an organism which can only be seen with a microscope. Compare **microbe** (NOTE: Viruses, bacteria, protozoa and fungi are all forms of microorganism.)

**microphone** *noun* ELEC a device that converts sound waves into electrical signals

**microplankton** *plural noun* MICROBIOL plankton in the size range 20 to 200 µm

**micropollutant** *noun* ENVIRON a pollutant which occurs in very small quantities

**microprocessor** *noun* COMPUT the central processing unit of a computer, often contained on a single integrated circuit chip

**microprocessor architecture** *noun* COMPUT the layout of the basic parts of a CPU

**microprocessor chip** *noun* COMPUT an integrated circuit which contains all the elements of the central processing unit of a computer

**microprocessor unit** *noun* COMPUT a unit containing the main elements of a microprocessor. Abbreviation **MPU**

**micropyle** *noun* BOT a tiny hole through which a pollen tube enters in order to fertilise a plant ovule and which later allows water uptake when the seed germinates

**microscope** *noun* BIOL a scientific instrument which makes very small objects appear larger ○ *The tissue was examined under the microscope.* ○ *Under the microscope it was possible to see the cancer cells.*

COMMENT: In an ordinary or light microscope the image is magnified by lenses. In an electron microscope the lenses are electromagnets and a beam of electrons is used instead of light, thereby achieving much greater magnifications.

**microscopic** noun SCI so small that it can only be seen through a microscope

**microscopy** noun SCI the science of the use of microscopes

**microsecond** noun MEASURE a unit of measurement of time, equal to one millionth of a second. Symbol **μs**

**microtherm** noun BOT a plant which grows in cool regions

**microtome** noun BIOL a device for cutting very thin slices of tissue or other material so they can be examined under a microscope

**microtubule** noun BIOL a tiny tube of protein within a living cell, occurring singly or in groups (NOTE: Microtubules enable the cell to move, maintain its shape and move materials around inside itself.)

**microwave background radiation** noun PHYS microwave radiation that occurs naturally

**mid-** prefix middle

**midbrain** noun ANAT the middle of the three main divisions of the vertebrate brain. Compare **forebrain, hindbrain**

**middle ear** noun ANAT the part of the ear between the eardrum and the inner ear, containing the ossicles

**middle lamella** noun BOT a thin membrane that makes the walls of plant cells stick together, composed of pectin and other polysaccharides

**middleware** noun COMPUT system software that has been customised by a dealer for a particular user

**MIDI** abbreviation COMPUT musical instrument digital interface

**mid-latitude desert** noun EARTH SCI a desert situated between the tropics, e.g. the Gobi Desert or the Turkestan Desert. Also called **warm desert**

**mid-latitudes** plural noun EARTH SCI areas halfway between the poles and the equator ○ In the mid-latitudes, global warming would produce dry hot summers and mild winters.

**mid-ocean ridge** noun OCEANOG a ridge running down the middle of an ocean such as the Atlantic, caused by the upward movement of magma

**mid-user** noun COMPUT an operator who retrieves relevant information from a database for a customer or end user

**migrant** noun ZOOL an animal or bird that moves from one place to another according to the season

**migrate** verb **1.** ZOOL (of a bird or other animal) to move from one place to another according to the season ○ As winter approaches, the herds of deer migrate south. **2.** to move to another place ○ Waste materials are allowed to migrate from landfill sites into the surrounding soil.

**migration** noun **1.** ZOOL the process of a bird or other animal moving from one place to another according to the season ○ The islands lie along one of the main migration routes from Siberia to Australia. **2.** COMPUT the movement of users from one hardware platform to another **3.** movement from one place to another

COMMENT: Some examples of animal migration: birds such as swallows breed in Northern Europe but fly south for the winter; fish such as salmon and eels spawn in one place, often a river, and then migrate to the sea after spawning.

**migratory** adjective ZOOL moving from one place to another according to the season ○ Estuaries are important feeding grounds for migratory birds, and are also important for the passage of migratory fish like salmon.

**mildew** noun FUNGI a fungus which produces a fine powdery film on the surface of an organism

**mile** noun MEASURE an imperial measurement of distance, equal to 1.609 km

**mileage** noun MEASURE a distance measured in miles

**milk sugar** noun BIOCHEM same as **lactose**

**milk teeth** plural noun ANAT the first teeth of a human, which are gradually replaced by permanent teeth (NOTE: In other mammals they are called deciduous teeth.)

**Milky Way** noun ASTRON a band of light stretching across the sky and caused by the high concentration of stars in the plane of our galaxy

COMMENT: The Milky Way can be resolved into its constituent stars and other objects by telescope. The name is also applied to the galaxy itself – the only visible galaxy not present in even the most reliable catalogues of nebulae. The Milky Way galaxy seems to be about 20,000 parsecs across, making it a large but not giant galaxy, of about 100 billion stars. The solar system is about 8,500 parsecs from its centre.

**mill** *noun* INDUST a factory where a substance is crushed to make a powder, especially one for making flour from the dried seeds of wheat ■ *verb* to crush a substance to make a powder

**millet** *noun* PLANTS a common cereal crop grown in many of the hot, dry regions of Africa and Asia, where it is a staple food. Latin name: *Panicum miliaceum*.

COMMENT: The two most important species are finger millet and bulrush millet. Millet grains are used in various types of food. They can be boiled and eaten like rice, made into flour for porridge, pasta or chapatis, and mixed with wheat flour to make bread. Millets can be malted to make beer. Millets are also grown as forage crops, and the seed is used as a poultry feed.

**milli-** *prefix* MEASURE one thousandth or $10^{-3}$. Symbol **m**

**milliampere** *noun* MEASURE, ELEC an electrical measure of current, equal to one thousandth of an ampere. Abbreviation **mA**

**millibar** *noun* MEASURE, PHYS a unit of pressure equal to one thousandth of a bar or 100 Pa. Symbol **mbar** (NOTE: This unit is often used in meteorology to express atmospheric pressure since standard atmospheric pressure at sea level being 1013.25 millibars.)

**milligauss** *noun* MEASURE, PHYS the cgs unit of magnetic flux density ○ *A person living under a low-voltage power line is exposed to 20 milligauss of radiation.*

**milligram** *noun* MEASURE a unit of measurement of weight, equal to one thousandth of a gram. Abbreviation **mg**

**millilitre** *noun* MEASURE a unit of measurement of liquid equal to one thousandth of a litre. Abbreviation **ml**. US spelling **milliliter**

**millimeter** *noun* US spelling of **millimetre**

**millimetre** *noun* a unit of measurement of length, equal to one thousandth of a metre. Abbreviation **mm**. US spelling **millimeter**

**millimole** *noun* MEASURE, CHEM a unit of measurement of the amount of substance equal to one thousandth of a mole. Abbreviation **mmol**

**milling** *noun* INDUST the process of crushing and grinding mineral ores to separate the useful materials from the non-useful ones

**million instructions per second** *noun* MEASURE, COMPUT a measure of processor speed that defines the number of instructions it can carry out per second. Abbreviation **MIPS**. Compare **megaflops**

**million tonnes of coal equivalent** *noun* MEASURE, INDUST a measure of energy from a source that is not coal. Abbreviation **MTCE**

**millisecond** *noun* MEASURE a unit of time equal to one thousandth of a second. Abbreviation **ms**

**millisievert** *noun* MEASURE a unit of measurement of radiation. Abbreviation **mSv**

**mill race** *noun* ENG a channel of water which turns the wheel of a water mill

**millwheel** *noun* ENG a large wheel with wooden bars which is turned by the force of water

**MIMD** *noun* COMPUT architecture of a parallel processor that uses a number of arithmetic logic units and memory devices in parallel to provide high speed processing. Full form **multiple instruction stream – multiple data stream**

**MIME** *noun* COMPUT a standard that defines a way of sending files using electronic mail software. Full form **multipurpose Internet mail extensions**

COMMENT: MIME allows a user to send files over the Internet to another user without having to carry out any other encoding or conversion actions. MIME was developed to get around a problem of many electronic mail systems that could only transmit text stored in a 7-bit data format. Programs, multimedia, graphics and other files are stored using an 8-bit data format.

**mimic** ZOOL *noun* an animal which imitates another ○ *Starlings are excellent mimics.* ■ *verb* to imitate another animal ○ *The starling mimicked the call of the thrush.*

**mimicry** *noun* ZOOL a situation where an animal imitates another, to prevent itself from being attacked

COMMENT: Some animals mimic others which are unpleasant or poisonous so that predators will not try to eat them (Batesian mimicry). Other animals mimic animals which have an unpleasant taste (Mullerian mimicry). In some animals, mimicry is a form of camouflage: insects mimic sticks or leaves so that predators cannot see them clearly.

**Minamata disease** noun MED a form of mercury poisoning from eating polluted fish, first identified in Japan

**mine** INDUST noun a hole dug in the ground to extract a mineral ■ verb to dig into the ground to extract a mineral

**mineral** noun CHEM an inorganic solid substance which is found in nature

COMMENT: The most important minerals required by the body are: calcium (found in cheese, milk and green vegetables) which helps the growth of bones and encourages blood clotting; iron (found in bread and liver) which helps produce red blood cells; phosphorus (found in bread and fish) which helps in the growth of bones and the metabolism of fats; and iodine (found in fish) which is essential to the functioning of the thyroid gland.

**mineral acid** noun CHEM an inorganic acid

**mineral deposit** noun EARTH SCI a deposit of rocks containing useful minerals

**mineralisation** noun CHEM the breaking down of organic waste into its non-organic chemical components

**mineral kingdom** noun GEOL a category of all non-living substances such as minerals and rocks

**mineral matter** noun EARTH SCI the solid part of the soil composed of stones, sand, silt and clay as opposed to the vegetable matter, formed from dead or decaying plants

**mineral nutrient** noun BIOL an inorganic element other than carbon, hydrogen and oxygen that is absorbed by plants from the soil

**mineralogy** noun GEOL the study of minerals and how to find, name and classify them

**mineral oil** noun US 1. CHEM oil which derives from petroleum and is made up of hydrocarbons 2. EARTH SCI same as **liquid paraffin** (NOTE: [all senses] The UK term is **liquid paraffin**.)

**mineral pitch** noun MINERALS same as **asphalt**

**mineral resources** plural noun MINERALS the supply of minerals and metals which are available in an area

**mineral water** noun FOOD INDUST water taken from a natural spring for human consumption

**mini** noun COMPUT same as **minicomputer**

**mini-** prefix COMPUT small

**miniaturisation** noun the process of making something very small

**minicomputer** noun COMPUT a small computer with a greater range of instructions and processing power than a microcomputer, but not able to compete with the speed or data handling capacity of a mainframe computer. Also called **mini**

**minidisk** noun COMPUT a magnetic disk smaller than the 5.25 in. standard, usually 3.5 in.

**minifloppy** noun COMPUT a magnetic disk usually measuring 5.25 in

**minimal** adjective small in amount or importance ○ Any attempt to increase range by applying power is of minimal benefit.

**minimal area** noun ECOL the smallest area for sampling in which specimens of all species can be found

**minimal tree** noun COMPUT a tree whose nodes are organised in the optimum way, providing maximum efficiency

**minimise** verb 1. to make something as small as possible ○ We minimised costs by cutting down the number of components. 2. COMPUT to shrink an application window to an icon 3. INDUST to reduce the amount of waste generated during industrial production processes. Compare **maximise**

**minimum** adjective smallest possible ○ the minimum amount required ○ minimum requirements ■ noun the smallest or least possible quantity or amount ○ Fires should be tackled with the minimum of delay. ○ Keep the weight to a minimum. (NOTE: The plural is **minima** or **minimums**.)

**minimum access code** noun COMPUT a coding system that provides the fastest access and retrieval time for stored data items

**mining subsidence area** *noun* ENVIRON a region in which the ground has subsided because of mine workings

**minmax** *noun* COMPUT a method used in artificial intelligence to solve problems

**minor axis** *noun* MATHS, ASTRON the smallest diameter of an ellipse

**minority** *noun* the lower quantity or smaller part. Opposite **majority**

**minuend** *noun* MATHS a number from which another is subtracted

**minus** *preposition* **1.** reduced by ○ *6 minus 2 equals 4 (6 – 2 = 4).* **2.** less than ○ *minus forty degrees Celsius (-40° Celsius)*

**minus sign** *noun* MATHS a sign (-) used to show that a following number is subtracted or is negative. Also called **minus**

**minute** *noun* **1.** MEASURE, TIME a time period of 60 seconds ○ *There are 60 minutes in one hour.* **2.** a unit of angular measurement equal to one sixtieth of a degree ○ *20 degrees and 20 minutes east (20° 20'E).* Symbol ' (NOTE: One degree equals 60 minutes.) ■ *adjective* very small indeed ○ *Metal fatigue begins as minute cracks, too small to be seen, at the point of maximum stress.*

**MIPS** *abbreviation* COMPUT million instructions per second. Compare **megaflops**

**mirage** *noun* OPTICS the apparent presence of a pool of water on a hot surface such as that of a desert or a road (NOTE: It is caused by light being bent and reflected by layers of cooler and warmer air.)

**mire** *noun* EARTH SCI an area of land saturated with water

**mirror** *noun* PHYS a device for reflecting light or other radiation ■ *verb* COMPUT **1.** to create an identical copy **2.** to duplicate all disk operations onto a second disk drive that can be used if the first breaks down ○ *There's less chance of losing our data now that we have mirrored the server's disk drive.*

**MIS** *abbreviation* COMPUT management information system

**miscarry** *verb* BIOL same as **abort** (*technical*)

**miscible** *adjective* CHEM able to be completely mixed together (NOTE: This term is usually applied to liquids.)

**MISD** *noun* COMPUT architecture of a parallel computer that has a single ALU and data bus with a number of control units. Full form **multiple instruction stream – single data stream**

**missense** *noun* GENETICS a mutation in which a gene coding sequence or codon for one amino acid is changed to one that codes for another

**mission-critical application** *noun* COMPUT a software program without which a company or project cannot function

**mist** *noun* **1.** METEOROL visible water vapour, in the form of very fine droplets, in the atmosphere ○ *Mist is thinner than fog.* **2.** water vapour that has condensed on a cool surface **3.** a liquid in spray form ○ *an air/oil mist*

**mistral** *noun* METEOROL a strong, cold wind from the north which blows down the Rhone valley into the Mediterranean

**mist up** *verb* to become covered in tiny water droplets of condensation and therefore prevent clear vision through a surface ○ *The windscreen misted up.*

**misty** *adjective* METEOROL referring to mist ○ *a misty autumn morning* ○ *a misty window*

**misuse** *verb* to use something wrongly or inappropriately

**mite** *noun* ZOOL a tiny animal of the spider family which may be free-living in the soil or parasitic on animals or plants

**miticide** *noun* AGRIC a substance that kills mites

**mitochondria** *plural noun* BIOL plural of **mitoohondrion**

**mitochondrial DNA** *noun* GENETICS a small circular molecule of DNA found in the mitochondria of a cell (NOTE: Mitochondrial DNA is inherited only from a mother.)

**mitochondrion** *noun* BIOL a tiny rod-shaped structure found in the cytoplasm of a cell that is responsible for cell respiration (NOTE: The plural is **mitochondria**.)

**mitosis** *noun* BIOL the process of cell division that results in two identical cells being formed. Compare **meiosis**

**mix** *verb* to come together or put things together in order to form one mass ○ *Air is mixed with fuel which then flows into the cylinder through the inlet valve.*

**mixed** *adjective* made up of different elements or categories

**mixed cropping**, **mixed culture** *noun* AGRIC the practice of growing more than one species of plant on the same piece of land at the same time. Opposite **monocropping**

**mixed farming** *noun* AGRIC the practice of combining arable and dairy farming

**mixed fertiliser** *noun* AGRIC same as **compound fertiliser**

**mixed forest** *noun* FORESTRY a forest containing more than one species of tree

**mixed race** *adjective* (*of people*) having parents who differ in the physical features usually attributed to ethnic origin

**mixed woodland** *noun* FORESTRY woodland containing conifers and deciduous trees

**mixture** *noun* something which is the result of mixing a number of things together

**mixture control** *noun* AUTOMOT a device for controlling the ratio of fuel to air entering an engine's carburettor or fuel injection system ○ *In order to stop the engine, the mixture control should be moved to the left.*

**ml** *abbreviation* MEASURE millilitre

**mm** *abbreviation* MEASURE millimetre

**MMI** *abbreviation* COMPUT man machine interface

**mmol** *abbreviation* MEASURE, CHEM millimole

**MMU** *abbreviation* COMPUT memory management unit (NOTE: The MMU is normally integrated into the processor chip.)

**Mn** *symbol* CHEM ELEM manganese

**mnemonic** *noun* COMPUT the shortened form of a word or function that is helpful as a reminder, e.g. INCA for increment register A

**Mo** *symbol* CHEM ELEM molybdenum

**mock-up** *noun* INDUST a model of a new product for testing or to show to possible customers

**mod** *abbreviation* MATHS modulus ○ *7 mod 3 = 1*

**modal** *adjective* COMPUT **1.** referring to modes ○ *Dialog boxes are normally modal windows.* **2.** (*in a graphical user interface*) referring to a window that is displayed and does not allow a user to do anything outside it. Compare **nonmodal**

**mode** *noun* **1.** a particular way of doing something ○ *Texting is a popular mode of communication.* **2.** a particular selected setting for the operation or functioning of equipment ○ *automatic mode* ○ *manual mode* **3.** ENG a letter or number given to various pulse spacing of airborne transponders and ground interrogators ○ *Mode A and mode C for altitude reporting are used in air traffic control.*

**model** *noun* **1.** a small copy of something to show what it will look like when finished ○ *He showed us a model of the new building.* **2.** a version of a product ○ *The new model B has taken the place of model A.* ○ *This is the latest model.* **3.** a simplified description of a system, often a mathematical one, to make calculation simpler ○ *The description of the weather patterns is a model only which, in reality, is modified greatly by a number of factors.* ■ *adjective* which is a perfect example to be copied ○ *a model agreement* ■ *verb* to make a computerised model of a new product or a system

**modem** *noun* COMPUT a device that allows data to be sent over telephone lines by converting binary signals from a computer into analog sound signals which can be transmitted over a telephone line. Full form **modulator/demodulator**

COMMENT: The process of converting binary signals to analog by a modem is called modulation. When the signal is received, another modem reverses the process, called DEMODULATION. Both modems must be working according to the same standards.

**moder** *noun* EARTH SCI humus which is partly acid mor and partly neutral mull

**moderate** *adjective* **1.** referring to something well within specific limits **2.** referring to the middle of three descriptions of intensity or amount, i.e. light, moderate and severe ○ *moderate humidity* ○ *moderate to severe turbulence* ■ *verb* to become or make something less extreme ○ *The south west wind moderates the climate of the UK* ○ *As the wind moderated, the aircraft was allowed to take off.*

**moderate climate** *noun* a climate which is not too hot or too cold

**moderated newsgroup** *noun* COMPUT a newsgroup in which a moderator reads all the material that has been submitted before it is published in the newsgroup (NOTE: Moderated newsgroups usually have a '-d' after their name.)

**moderator** *noun* **1.** COMPUT a person responsible for reading messages sent to a mailing list and editing any messages that do not conform to the rules of the list, e.g. by deleting commercial messages **2.** CHEM a substance such as graphite or heavy water which is used to slow down the speed of the neutrons in a nuclear reactor (NOTE: Using a moderator allows fuel enriched with uranium-235 to be used in a reactor.)

**modification** *noun* an alteration in character or form which is usually an improvement ○ *As a result of the crash, modifications were made to the rudder linkage.*

**modified frequency modulation** *noun* COMPUT a method of storing data on magnetic media such as a magnetic disk that encodes the data bit according to the state of the previous bit. Abbreviation **MFM** (NOTE: MFM is more efficient than FM, but less efficient than RLL encoding.)

**Modified Mercalli Scale** *noun* MEASURE, GEOL a scale rising from 1 to 12 used for measuring the damage caused by an earthquake

**modifier** *noun* COMPUT a programming instruction that alters the normal action of a command

**modify** *verb* to change or alter something in order to improve it (NOTE: **modifying** – **modified**)

**Modula-2** *noun* COMPUT a high-level programming language derived from Pascal that supports modular programming techniques and data abstraction

**modular** *adjective* formed by connecting several smaller parts together to produce a customised product

**modularity** *noun* COMPUT the state of being made up from modules ○ *The modularity of the software* or *hardware allows the system to be changed.*

**modular programming** *noun* COMPUT the programming of small individually written sections of computer code that can be made to fit into a structured program and can be called up from a main program

**modulate** *verb* ELEC to change the frequency, amplitude, phase, or other characteristic of an electromagnetic wave

**modulated signal** *noun* ELEC a constant frequency and amplitude carrier signal that is used in a modulated form to transmit data

**modulating signal** *noun* ELEC a signal to be transmitted that is used to modulate a carrier

**modulation** *noun* ELEC a change in a property such as amplitude, frequency or phase of an electromagnetic wave or signal ○ *Pulse modulation is a series of quick, short bursts of energy which are radiated from an antenna which serves both the transmitter and the receiver.*

**modulator** *noun* ELEC an electronic circuit that varies a carrier signal according to an applied signal

**module** *noun* **1.** a part that together with other parts makes up another structure or system **2.** COMPUT a small section of a large program that can, if required, function independently as a program in its own right **3.** COMPUT a self-contained piece of hardware that can be connected with other modules to form a new system ○ *A multifunction analog interface module includes analog to digital and digital to analog converters.*

**modulo arithmetic** *noun* MATHS a branch of arithmetic that uses the remainder of one number when divided by another

**modulo-N** *noun* MATHS modulo arithmetic using base N

**modulus** *noun* MATHS a number by which two other numbers can be divided to give the same remainder. Abbreviation **mod**

**Mohorovicic discontinuity, Moho** *noun* EARTH SCI a boundary layer in the interior of the Earth between the crust and the mantle, below which seismic shocks move more rapidly

**moiré effect** *noun* PHYS a pattern of interference caused by printing with the wrong screen angle

**moist** *adjective* damp or humid

**moist tropical forest** *noun* ECOL a forest which receives less rain than other types of tropical forest

**moisture** *noun* water or other liquid

**moisture meter** *noun* MEASURE a device for measuring the amount of water or other liquid which a substance contains

**mol** *symbol* MEASURE, CHEM mole

**molality** *noun* CHEM the concentration of a solution, expressed as the number of moles of a dissolved substance (**solute**) in one thousand grams of solvent

**molar** *adjective* **1.** PHYS (*of physical properties*) measured per mole of a substance **2.** CHEM (*of solutions*) containing one mole of solute per litre of solution

**molar concentration** *noun* CHEM the concentration of a substance measured as the physical quantity divided by the amount in moles

**molar conductivity** *noun* CHEM the electrical conductivity of an electrolyte that has one mole of a solute dissolved in one litre of solution

**molar heat capacity** *noun* CHEM the heat required to increase the temperature of one mole of a substance by one kelvin

**mold** *noun, verb* US spelling of **mould**

**mole** *noun* **1.** ANAT a dark raised spot on the skin ○ *She has a large mole on her chin.* **2.** MEASURE an SI unit of measurement of the amount of substance. Symbol **mol** (NOTE: It is the amount of a substance containing Avogadro's number of atoms or molecules.) **3.** ZOOL a small dark grey mammal which lives underground and eats worms and insects

**molecular** *adjective* CHEM referring to molecules

**molecular biology** *noun* BIOL the study of the molecules which form the structure of living matter

**molecular distillation** *noun* CHEM distillation carried out in a vacuum, in which the condenser is very close to the substance being distilled so that no molecules hit each other before reaching the condenser surface

**molecular ecology** *noun* ECOL the study of ecological problems using molecular biology

**molecular formula** *noun* CHEM a chemical formula that specifies the numbers of specific atoms in a molecule (NOTE: For example, a molecule of water contains two atoms of hydrogen and one of oxygen and its molecular formula is written $H_2O$.)

**molecular genetics** *noun* GENETICS the branch of genetics that studies genes, chromosomes and the transmission of hereditary characteristics at the biochemical level

**molecular weight** *noun* CHEM the sum of all the atomic weights of the atoms in a molecule

**molecular weight unit** *noun* PHYS a ratio of the average mass of one molecule of a substance to one twelfth of the mass of an atom of carbon-12

**molecule** *noun* PHYS the smallest particle into which a substance can be divided without changing its chemical and physical properties ○ *The molecules of a gas move more quickly than the molecules of a liquid.*

**mollusc** *noun* ZOOL an invertebrate animal with a soft body, a muscular foot on the underside used for movement and, in many species, a protective shell ○ *Slugs and snails are molluscs, as are oysters and other shellfish.* (NOTE: Molluscs are found on land as well as in fresh and salt water. The US spelling is **mollusk**.)

**molluscicide** *noun* ZOOL a substance used to kill molluscs such as snails

**molt** *noun, verb* ZOOL US spelling of **moult**

**molten** *adjective* CHEM, PHYS which has become liquid with heat. ♦ **melt**

**molten lava** *noun* EARTH SCI a liquid rock which flows out of an erupting volcano

**molybdenum** *noun* CHEM ELEM a metallic trace element, essential to biological life and also used in electric wiring (NOTE: The chemical symbol is **Mo**; the atomic number is **42** and the atomic weight is **95.94**.)

**moment** *noun* **1.** a short period of time ○ *It only takes a moment to fill in the log book.* **2.** a point in time □ **at the moment** at this particular time ○ *He's not in the office at the moment.* **3.** PHYS a product of a quantity and its perpendicular distance from a reference point, giving it a tendency to cause rotation about a point or an axis ○ *A load on the end of a beam creates a bending moment.* ○ *The tailplane provides a pitching moment to keep the aircraft level.*

**momentary switch** *noun* ELEC a switch that only conducts while it is being pressed

**moment of inertia** *noun* PHYS the resistance to changes in speed of rotation (NOTE: It is calculated as the sum of the products of the component masses of an object multiplied by the square of their distance from the axis.)

**momentum** *noun* PHYS a measure of the motion of a body equal to the product of its mass and velocity. Also called **linear momentum**

**monadic Boolean operation** *noun* COMPUT same as **monadic operation**

**monadic Boolean operator** *noun* COMPUT same as **monadic operator**

**monadic operation** *noun* COMPUT an operation that uses one operand to produce one result. Also called **monadic Boolean operation**

**monadic operator** *noun* COMPUT a logical operator with only one operand ○ *The monadic operator NOT can be used here.* Also called **monadic Boolean operator**

**monatomic** *adjective* CHEM same as **monovalent**

**monazite** *noun* CHEM a phosphate containing cerium and some thorium

**monitor** *noun* COMPUT **1.** a screen for a computer display **2.** a system that watches for faults or failures in a circuit ■ *verb* **1.** to check or to examine how something is working **2.** to look after and supervise a process or experiment to make sure it is operating correctly ○ *The machine monitors each signal as it is sent out.* ○ *He is monitoring the progress of the trainee programmers.*

**monitoring** *noun* a process of regular checking on the progress of something ○ *health monitoring* ○ *Scientists have set up a monitoring programme to check the changes in the Sun's radiation.*

**monitoring well** *noun* ENVIRON a well used to take water quality samples or to measure ground water levels

**mono** *adjective* ACOUSTICS same as **monophonic**

**mono-** *prefix* single or one

**monoaural, mono** *adjective* COMPUT referring to one source of sound or one sound signal. Compare **stereo**

**monobasic acid** *noun* CHEM an acid with a single replaceable hydrogen atom in each molecule

**monochrome** *adjective* in one colour, usually shades of grey and black and white

**monochrome monitor** *noun* COMPUT a computer monitor that displays text and graphics in black, white and shades of grey rather than colours

**monocline** *noun* EARTH SCI a rock formation where sedimentary rock slopes sharply on one side of a fold

**monoclonal antibody** *noun* IMMUNOL an antibody produced from a single line or clone of cells

**monocoque** *noun* MECH ENG a three-dimensional body such as a car or aircraft that has all the strength in the skin and immediately underlying framework (NOTE: There is no internal stiffening as the thickness of the skin gives the strength and stability.)

**monocot** *noun* BOT same as **monocotyledon** (*informal*)

**monocotyledenous** *adjective* BOT referring to monocotyledons

**monocotyledon** *noun* BOT a plant such as a grass or lily that has a single cotyledon or seed leaf. Compare **dicotyledon**

**monocropping, monocrop system** *noun* AGRIC a system of cultivation in which a single crop plant such as wheat is grown over a large area of land often for several years. Opposite **mixed cropping**. Also called **monoculture**

**monocular vision** *noun* OPHTHALMOL the ability to see with one eye only, so that the sense of distance is impaired

**monoculture** *noun* AGRIC same as **monocropping**

**monocyte** *noun* BIOL a large circulating white blood cell with a single well-defined nucleus (NOTE: Monocytes are made in the bone marrow and spleen and clear the blood of dead cells and foreign particles by ingesting them.)

**monoecious** *adjective* BOT with male and female flowers on separate plants

**monogamy** *noun* ZOOL a breeding arrangement where a male and female mate for life. Compare **polygamy**

**monogenic** *adjective* GENETICS **1.** referring to a characteristic that is controlled by a single gene or a pair of genes **2.** producing offspring that all belong to the same sex

**monohybrid** *noun* GENETICS a hybrid from parents that differ only in a single pair of genes

**monohydrate** *noun* CHEM a hydrate that contains one molecule of water per molecule of the salt

**monolayer** *noun* BIOL a layer of cultured cells that is one cell thick

**monolithic driver** *noun* COMPUT a driver that has a range of different functions or applications within one program

**monomer** *noun* CHEM a small organic molecule that can join to others like itself to form a long chain (**polymer**)

**monophagous** *adjective* BIOL referring to an organism that feeds on only one kind of food

**monophonic** *adjective* ACOUSTICS recorded or played back through a single channel. Compare **stereophonic**

**monophyodont** *noun* ZOOL an animal that has only one set of teeth in its lifetime

**monopodium** *noun* BOT the main axis of a tree or plant that produces side branches and continues to grow at the top

**monoprogramming system** *noun* COMPUT a computer batch processing system that executes one program at a time

**monosaccharide** *noun* CHEM a sugar such as glucose or fructose that cannot be broken down into simpler units

**monosodium glutamate** *noun* FOOD INDUST a substance, labelled E621, added to processed food to enhance the flavour. Abbreviation **MSG** (NOTE: It can cause a reaction in hypersensitive people.)

**monosome** *noun* GENETICS an isolated chromosome, especially an unpaired X-chromosome

**monosomic** *adjective* GENETICS referring to an unpaired chromosome, or an organism containing such a feature ○ *a monosomic line*

**monospaced font** *noun* COMPUT a font in which each character has the same width, making it easy to align tables and columns ○ *In Windows, the monospaced font is called Courier.*

**monovalent** *adjective* **1.** CHEM with a valency of one **2.** IMMUNOL containing only a single type of antibody

**monoxide** *noun* CHEM a chemical compound made up of atoms of an element combined with a single oxygen atom

**monozygotic twins** *plural noun* BIOL two offspring born at the same time and from the same ovum, so exactly the same in appearance and sex. Also called **identical twins**. Compare **dizygotic twins**

**monsoon** *noun* METEOROL **1.** a season of wind and rain in tropical countries **2.** a wind which blows in opposite directions according to the season, especially the wind blowing north from the Indian Ocean in the summer

**monsoon forest** *noun* ECOL a tropical rainforest in an area where rain falls during the monsoon season

**Monte Carlo method** *noun* STATS a statistical analysis technique based on random sampling

**month** *noun* MEASURE, TIME the time taken for the Moon to orbit Earth

COMMENT: Several types of month are defined for different purposes, including the draconitic month, the time the Moon takes to reappear at the same node of its orbit on the celestial equator, which is the most realistic measure and totals 27.21 days, and the sidereal month of 27.32 days, the time the Moon takes to reappear at the same point in the sky relative to the fixed stars. It differs from the draconitic month because of the motion of the Earth and Moon around the Sun. The anomalistic month of 27.55 days is the total time needed for the Moon's cycle of slowing and speeding up in its orbit as it is carried nearer and farther from the Earth.

**Moon** *noun* ASTRON a natural satellite of earth, which orbits Earth every 27 days

COMMENT: The moon always shows the same face to Earth as it rotates on its axis once per lunar month and shines with light reflected from the Sun. As it moves round the Earth, the face of the Moon gradually becomes completely lit by the Sun and is then said to be full. See also lunar phases. The Moon exerts a gravitational pull on Earth and influences the tides. The Moon has a diameter of 3500 km and a surface area about equal to that of Africa. Six US space missions have taken people to the Moon, and three unmanned Soviet missions have returned moon rock to the Earth.

**moor** *noun* EARTH SCI high land that is not cultivated, formed of acid soil covered with grass and low shrubs such as heather

**moorland** *noun* EARTH SCI a large area of moor

**mor** *noun* EARTH SCI a type of humus found under coniferous forests, which is acid and contains few nutrients. Compare **mull**

**moraine** *noun* EARTH SCI a deposit of gravel and sand left by a glacier

COMMENT: There are various types of moraine: ground moraine, which is a deposit left under a glacier; terminal moraine, which is the heap of soil and sand pushed by a glacier and left behind when it melts; and lateral moraines, which are deposits left at the sides of a glacier as it moves forward.

**moral justification** *noun* ENVIRON a rationale for nature conservation based on the idea that elements of the environment have a right to exist, independent of what may be beneficial to human beings or what human beings would like to happen

**moratorium** *noun* ENVIRON a period when everyone agrees to stop a certain activity ○ *They voted to impose a ten-year moratorium on whale catching.* ○ *The conference rejected a motion calling for a moratorium on nuclear reprocessing.*

**morbidity rate** *noun* MED the number of cases of a disease per 100 000 of population

**mordant** *noun* CHEM a chemical that fixes the dyes in textiles, so that the colours do not run or fade (NOTE: Some dyes turn different colours in conjunction with different mordants.)

**morgan** *noun* MEASURE, GENETICS a unit in which chromosome length is measured

**morph** *noun* BIOL an organism and its particular shape

**morphine** *noun* PHARM an alkaloid drug derived from opium, used as a sed-ative and painkiller, which can become addictive

**morphing** *noun* COMPUT a special effect used in multimedia and video and computer games in which one image gradually turns into another

**morphogenesis** *noun* BIOL the changes in shape and form of an organism over its lifetime or its evolutionary history

**morphology** *noun* BIOL the study of the structure and shape of living organisms. ♦ **geomorphology**

**mortality** *noun* BIOL the occurrence of death ○ *The population count in spring is always lower than that in the autumn because of winter mortality.*

**mortality rate** *noun* BIOL same as **death rate**

**mortar** *noun* INDUST a mixture of sand, cement and water, used to bind bricks together when building a wall

**MOS** *abbreviation* COMPUT metal oxide semiconductor. ♦ **MOSFET**

**mosaic** *noun* 1. BOT a disease of plants that makes yellowing patterns on the leaves and can seriously affect some crops 2. COMPUT a display character used in videotext systems that is made up of small dots

**mosaicism** *noun* GENETICS the occurrence, within tissue or an individual organism, of genetically distinct cells

**Moseley's law** *noun* PHYS a law that relates the frequencies of the lines within an X-ray spectrum of an element to the proton number of the element

**MOSFET** *noun* ELEC a high power and high speed field effect transistor manufactured using MOS techniques. Full form **metal oxide semiconductor field effect transistor**

**mosquito** *noun* INSECTS an insect which sucks blood and passes viruses or parasites into the bloodstream (NOTE: The plural is **mosquitoes** or **mosquitos**.)

COMMENT: In tropical countries dengue, filariasis, malaria and yellow fever are transmitted by mosquitoes. They breed in water and spread rapidly around lakes or canals created by dams and other irrigation schemes. As irrigation is more widely practised in tropical countries, mosquitoes are increasing and diseases such as malaria are spreading.

**mosquitocide** *noun* AGRIC a substance which kills mosquitoes

**moss** *noun* BOT a very small plant without roots, which grows in damp places and forms mats of vegetation

**Mössbauer effect** *noun* PHYS the emission or absorption of a gamma ray by a nucleus within a rigid crystal in which the recoil energy is shared between atoms in the crystal (NOTE: It is used in the study of quantum states of nuclei.)

**moss peat** *noun* AGRIC dried and sterilised peat formed from the remains of mosses, sold in bags for horticultural purposes

**most** *pronoun* **1.** the biggest amount or number ○ *Of the three choices, this course offers me most.* **2.** almost all ○ *Most of the plants grew well.* ■ *adjective* biggest in amount or number ○ *This tree produced most apples.* ■ *adverb* to the greatest degree ○ *These plants grew most.* □ **the most advantageous** the best ○ *The minimum time path is the most advantageous for economy.*

**most significant bit** *noun* COMPUT a bit in a computer word that represents the greatest power of two. Abbreviation **msb, MSB** (NOTE: In an 8-bit word the MSB is in bit position 8 and represents a decimal number of 2 to the power 8, or 128.)

**moth** *noun* INSECTS an insect that generally flies at night. Order: Lepidoptera.

COMMENT: Moths are similar to butterflies, but are dull in colour and fold their wings over their bodies when at rest.

**motherboard** *noun* COMPUT the main printed circuit board of a system, containing most of the components and connections for expansion boards

**mother cell** *noun* BIOL a cell that splits into daughter cells during mitosis

**mother-of-pearl** *noun* ZOOL a hard substance, mostly made up of calcium carbonate, which forms the inner layer of some shells such as oyster shells

**mother rock** *noun* EARTH SCI a main layer of rock. Also called **parent rock**

**motile** *adjective* BIOL able to move independently

**motion** *noun* **1.** a movement **2.** the act of changing position or place

**motor** *noun* MECH ENG a machine which provides power for moving a vehicle or device with moving parts ○ *an electric motor* ○ *a hydraulic motor* (NOTE: Piston or jet power plants for aircraft are referred to as **engines** not motors.)

**motor generator** *noun* PHYS an electric motor powered by one voltage, linked to an electric generator to generate a different voltage

**motor nerve** *noun* ANAT a nerve which carries impulses from the brain and spinal cord to muscles and causes movements. Also called **efferent nerve**

**motor neuron** *noun* ANAT a neuron that is part of a nerve pathway transmitting impulses from the brain to a muscle or gland

**mould** *noun* **1.** BIOL a fungus, especially one that produces a fine powdery layer on the surface of an organism **2.** a hollow shape into which liquid or molten material is poured to harden ○ *Moulds are used in the manufacture of plastic components.* ■ *verb* to shape something, often using a mould ○ *Thermo-plastic material become soft when heated and can be moulded again and again.* (NOTE: [all verb senses] The US spelling is **mold**.)

**moult** ZOOL *noun* an occasion of losing feathers or hair at a specific period of the year ■ *verb* to lose feathers or hair at a specific period of the year ○ *Most animals moult at the beginning of summer.* (NOTE: The US spelling is **molt**.)

**moulting** *noun* ZOOL the process by which fur or feathers are lost at a specific period of the year

**moulting season** *noun* ZOOL the time of year when feathers or hair are lost

**moult plumage** *noun* ZOOL the small feathers which remain on a bird when it is moulting

**mount** *verb* **1.** MECH ENG to fix something to a support ○ *A propeller consists of a number of separate blades mounted in a hub.* **2.** COMPUT to insert a disk in a disk drive or inform an operating system that a disk drive is ready to be used

**mountain** *noun* EARTH SCI a mass of rock rising higher than a hill

**mountainous** *adjective* EARTH SCI referring to an area of land where there are high mountains

**mountain plant** *noun* BOT a plant which grows in or comes originally from a mountain region

**mountain range** *noun* EARTH SCI a series of mountains running in a line for many miles

**mountain sheep** *noun* AGRIC a sheep belonging to a breed which lives in or comes originally from a mountain region

**mountainside** *noun* EARTH SCI the slopes of a mountain

**mounted** *adjective* fixed to a support

**mounting** *noun* a supporting component or attachment point

**mouse** *noun* COMPUT a small hand-held input device moved on a flat surface to control the position of a cursor on a computer screen

**mouse pointer** *noun* COMPUT a small arrow displayed on screen that moves around as the mouse is moved

**mouth** *noun* **1.** ANAT an opening in the head through which a person or animal takes in food **2.** EARTH SCI an opening where a river joins the sea

**mouthpart** *noun* ZOOL a structure close to the mouth of an insect or other arthropod used to gather or chew food

**M out of N code** *noun* COMPUT a coding system providing error detection by which each valid character which is N bits long must contain M binary 'one' bits

**move** *verb* to change position, or change the place of something

**movement** *noun* a change in place or position ○ *The upward movement of the piston compresses the fuel/air mixture.* □ **movement of the crankshaft** the rotation of the crankshaft □ **the downward movement of cool air** the downward flow of cool air

**movement file** *noun* COMPUT a file which contains recent changes to records, which is then used to update a master file

**moving pictures expert group** *noun* COMPUT full form of **MPEG**

**MP3** *noun* COMPUT a way of encoding digital audio data into a compressed data format that is approximately one twelfth the size of the original without perceptible loss of quality. Full form **MPEG audio level 3**

**MPEG** *noun* COMPUT a group of developers that have defined a series of standards to improve audio and video quality but at the same time increase data compression so that the audio or video information takes less space but retains its quality. Full form **moving pictures expert group**

COMMENT: MPEG is often used to compress video clips and its derivative standard MPEG audio level 3 (MP3) provides one of the most popular ways of compressing and storing audio information, while JPEG provides a popular way to store compressed still images.

**MPPP** *noun* COMPUT a communications protocol used with ISDN to link the two B-channels in a standard ISDN adapter to create a transmission channel that can transfer data at a higher speed. Full form **multi-link point to point protocol**

**MPU** *abbreviation* COMPUT microprocessor unit

**MRI** *abbreviation* MED magnetic resonance imaging

**mRNA** *abbreviation* GENETICS messenger RNA

**ms** *abbreviation* COMPUT, MEASURE millisecond

**m/s** *abbreviation* MEASURE metres per second

**msb, MSB** *abbreviation* COMPUT most significant bit

**MSB** *abbreviation* COMPUT most significant bit

**MS disk operating system** *noun* COMPUT a popular operating system for microcomputers. Abbreviation **MS-DOS**

**MSF time format** *noun* COMPUT a time format that counts frames per second used by MCI, normally used by CD audio devices in which there are 75 frames per second

**MSG** *abbreviation* FOOD INDUST monosodium glutamate

**MSI** *abbreviation* COMPUT medium scale integration

**mSv** *symbol* millisievert

**Mt** *symbol* CHEM ELEM meitnerium

**MTA** *abbreviation* COMPUT mail transfer agent

**MTBF** *abbreviation* COMPUT mean time between failures

**MTCE** *abbreviation* MEASURE million tonnes of coal equivalent

**MTF** *abbreviation* COMPUT mean time to failure

**MUA** *abbreviation* COMPUT mail user agent

**mucilage** *noun* BIOL slime secreted by some organisms such as seaweeds

**mucin** *noun* BIOCHEM a glycoprotein that is a constituent of mucus

**mucous cell** *noun* BIOL a cell that secretes mucin

**mucous membrane** *noun* ANAT a membrane that lines internal passages in the body such as the nose or mouth

**mucus** *noun* BIOL a slimy substance secreted onto a mucous membrane to provide lubrication

**mud** *noun* EARTH SCI a mixture of soil and water

**muddy** *adjective* EARTH SCI containing mud, or covered with mud

**mud flat** *noun* EARTH SCI an area of flat mud, usually in a river estuary

**mudslide** *noun* EARTH SCI a fall of a large amount of mud down a slope

**mud volcano** *noun* EARTH SCI a heap of hot mud thrown up round a hot spring

**mulch** AGRIC *noun* organic material such as dead leaves or straw, used to spread over the surface of the soil to prevent evaporation or erosion ■ *verb* to spread organic material over the surface of the soil to prevent evaporation or erosion

COMMENT: Black plastic sheeting is often used by commercial horticulturists, but the commonest mulches are organic. Apart from preventing evaporation, mulches reduce weed growth and encourage worms.

**mull** *noun* EARTH SCI a type of humus found under deciduous forests. Compare **mor** (NOTE: It is pH neutral, formed of rotted leaves and contains many nutrients.)

**Mullerian mimicry** *noun* ZOOL a form of mimicry where an animal mimics another animal which has an unpleasant taste

**multi-** *prefix* many or more than one

**multicast** *verb* TELECOM, COMPUT to transmit one message to a group of recipients (NOTE: This could be as simple as sending an email message to a list of addresses or posting a message to a mailing list. It can also refer to more complex transfers such as a teleconference or videoconference in which several users link together by telephone or video link.)

**multicellular** *adjective* BIOL composed of several or many cells

**multichannel** *adjective* ELEC with more than one channel

**multicolour** *adjective* with several colours

**multi-crop** *verb* AGRIC to grow more than one crop of something on the same piece of land in one year ○ *Wet rice is often multi-cropped.*

**multidimensional array** *noun* COMPUT a number of arrays arranged in parallel, providing depth

**multidimensional language** *noun* COMPUT a programming language that can be represented in a number of ways

**multidrop circuit** *noun* COMPUT a network allowing communications between a number of terminals and a central computer, but not directly between terminals

**multifactorial** *adjective* GENETICS referring to inheritance that depends on more than one gene

**multifactorial inheritance** *noun* GENETICS the control of an inherited characteristic by several genes

**multifrequency monitor** *noun* COMPUT same as **multisync monitor**

**multifunctional** *adjective* COMPUT having several functions ○ *a multifunctional scanner*

**multifunction card** *noun* COMPUT an add-on circuit board that provides many features to upgrade a computer

**multilayer** *noun* COMPUT a printed circuit board that has several layers or interconnecting conduction tracks

**multilevel** *adjective* COMPUT referring to a signal with a number of possible values (NOTE: Quaternary signals have four levels.)

**multilink point to point protocol** *noun* COMPUT full form of **MPPP**

**multilink system** *noun* COMPUT a system where there is more than one connection between two points

**multimedia** *adjective* COMPUT referring to the combination of sound, graphics, animation, video and text within an application

**multimeter** noun ELEC ENG a piece of equipment that measures several electrical parameters such as current, voltage and resistance

**multimode fibre** noun COMPUT a commonly used type of optic fibre (NOTE: It comprises a glass fibre with a diameter of 50–125 μm and can carry several different frequencies of light with a maximum bandwidth of 2.5 Gbps. The disadvantage is that, because the fibre is wide, the light disperses quickly and so repeaters need to be installed to boost the signal.)

**multipass overlap** noun COMPUT a system of producing higher quality print from a dot-matrix printer by repeating the line of characters but shifted slightly, so making the dots less noticeable

**multiphase program** noun COMPUT a program that requires more than one fetch operation before execution is complete

**multiple** adjective having many parts or acting in many ways

**multiple alleles** plural noun GENETICS three or more different forms of a gene, of which any two can be present in a normal diploid cell

**multiple factor** noun GENETICS same as **polygene**

**multiple precision** noun COMPUT the use of more than one byte of data for number storage to increase possible precision

**multiple star** noun ASTRON a group of three or more stars, usually with the same gravitational centre, that appears as one star to the unaided eye

**multiplex** verb to combine several messages in the same transmission medium

**multiplexed bus** noun COMPUT a single bus used to carry address, data and control signals at different times

**multiplexing** noun BIOTECH a technique of rapid gene sequencing that uses several pooled samples simultaneously

**multiplexor** noun ELEC ENG a circuit that combines a number of inputs into a smaller number of outputs ○ A 4 to 1 multiplexor combines four inputs into a single output. Abbreviation **MUX**

**multiplicand** noun MATHS a number which is multiplied by another number. Compare **multiplier**

**multiplication** noun MATHS a mathematical operation that adds one number to itself a number of times ○ The multiplication of 5 by 3 gives 15.

**multiplication sign** noun MATHS a sign (x) used to show that numbers are multiplied (NOTE: It is spoken as 'times'.)

**multiplier** noun MATHS a number which multiplies another number. Compare **multiplicand**

**multiply** verb MATHS to calculate a specified number of times the value of a number ○ 4 multiplied by 2 is 8 (4 x 2 = 8). ○ To multiply 20 by 6 is to calculate what is 6 times 20 (6 x 20). ○ To calculate fuel required, multiply the duration of the flight by the consumption of the engine at the required power.

**multipoint** adjective COMPUT referring to a connection with several lines, attaching several terminals to a single line to a single computer

**multipolar neuron** noun BIOL a neuron with several processes

**multiprecision** noun COMPUT the use of more than one data word to represent numbers, increasing the range or precision possible

**multiprocessing system** noun COMPUT a system in which several processing units work together sharing the same memory

**multiprocessor** noun COMPUT a number of processing units acting together or separately but sharing the same area of memory

**multiprocessor interleaving** noun COMPUT an operation where each processor in a multiprocessor system deals with a section of one or more processes

**multipurpose** adjective suitable for many different uses

**multipurpose tool** noun a tool which can be used in many different ways

**multiscan monitor** noun COMPUT same as **multisync monitor**

**multi statement line** noun COMPUT a line from a computer program that contains more than one instruction or statement

**multisync monitor** noun COMPUT a monitor which contains circuitry to lock onto the required scanning frequency of any type of graphics card ○ *If you want to plug a monitor into PCs with VGA, EGA and MDA adapters, you'll need a multisync monitor.* Also called **multifrequency monitor, multiscan monitor**

**multitasking, multi-tasking** *noun* COMPUT the ability of a computer system to run two or more programs at the same time

COMMENT: Few small systems are capable of simultaneous multitasking, since each program would require its own processor. This is overcome by allocating to each program an amount of processing time, executing each a little at a time so that they will appear to run simultaneously due to the speed of the processor and the relatively short gaps between programs.

**multithread** *noun* COMPUT a program design using more than one logical path through it, each path being concurrently executed

**multi-user system** *noun* COMPUT a computer system that can support more than one user at a time ○ *The program runs on a standalone machine or a multi-user system.*

**multivibrator** *noun* ELECTRONICS same as **bistable circuit**

**muon** *noun* PHYS an elementary particle whose mass is about 200 times that of an electron

**muscle** *noun* ANAT an organ that contracts to make part of the body move

COMMENT: There are three types of muscle: voluntary (striated) muscles, which are attached to bones and move parts of the body when made to do so by the brain; involuntary (smooth) muscles, which move essential organs such as the intestines and bladder; and cardiac muscle, which occurs only in the heart.

**muscle fatigue** *noun* MED tiredness in the muscles after strenuous exercise

**muscle fibre** *noun* ANAT a component of muscles

**muscle relaxant** *noun* PHARM a drug that reduces contractions in the muscles

**muscle spasm** *noun* BIOL a sudden sharp contraction of a muscle

**muscle spindle** *noun* BIOL a sensory receptor found along the length of striated muscle fibres

**muscle tissue** *noun* ANAT the tissue which forms the muscles and which is able to expand and contract

**muscle wasting** *noun* MED a condition where the muscles lose weight and become thin

**mushroom** *noun* FUNGI, AGRIC a common edible fungus, often grown commercially

**mushroom compost** *noun* AGRIC a special growing medium for the commercial production of mushrooms

**mushroom spawn** *noun* AGRIC a mass of spores of edible mushrooms, used in propagation

**musical instrument digital interface** *noun* COMPUT a serial interface that connects electronic musical instruments. Abbreviation **MIDI**

COMMENT: The MIDI interface carries signals from a controller or computer that instructs the different instruments to play notes.

**mustard gas** *noun* CHEM, MIL an oily liquid that gives off a toxic gas. Formula: $(CH_2ClCH_2)_2S$. (NOTE: It causes severe damage to the lungs and is used in chemical warfare.)

**mutable** *adjective* GENETICS referring to a gene or organism that has a tendency to mutate

**mutagen** *noun* GENETICS an agent such as a chemical or radiation that causes mutation

**mutagenicity** *noun* GENETICS the ability of an agent to make genes mutate

**mutant** *adjective* referring to a gene in which a mutation has occurred, or an organism carrying such a gene ○ *mutant mice* ■ *noun* GENETICS an organism carrying a gene in which mutation has occurred

**mutate** *verb* GENETICS (*of a gene or organism*) to undergo a genetic change ○ *Bacteria can mutate suddenly and become increasingly able to infect.*

**mutation** *noun* GENETICS **1.** the process of change occurring in a gene **2.** a gene or organism affected by mutation

**muton** *noun* GENETICS the smallest unit of DNA in which mutation can take place

**mutual** *adjective* directed and received in equal amount

**mutual inductance** *noun* ELEC an electro-magnetic field in one circuit caused by a quickly changing magnetic field in another circuit

**mutualism** *noun* BIOL a relationship between two different organisms that benefits both of them. Also called **symbiosis**

**mutual symbiosis** *noun* BIOL a condition where two organisms rely on each other for survival

**MUX** *abbreviation* COMPUT multiplexor

**MX record** *abbreviation* COMPUT mail exchange record (NOTE: Mail sent to 'smith&bloomsbury.com' will be sent to the 'bloomsbury.com' server by the MX record, the local server then has to send the message to the user 'smith'.)

**myc-** *prefix* same as **myco-** (NOTE: used before vowels)

**mycelium** *noun* FUNGI a mass of hyphae which forms the main part of a fungus

**myco-** *prefix* BIOL fungus or fungal

**Mycobacterium** *noun* MICROBIOL one of a group of bacteria that includes those which cause leprosy and tuberculosis

**mycology** *noun* FUNGI the study of fungi

**mycoplasm, mycoplasma** *noun* MICROBIOL a microorganism that lacks rigid cell walls. Genus: *Mycoplasma*. (NOTE: Some species cause respiratory diseases.)

**mycorrhiza** *noun* BIOL a mutual association of a fungus with the roots of a plant in which the fungus brings the plant water and minerals in exchange for plant sugars (NOTE: Many different fungi form mycorrhizas, especially with trees, and many plants such as orchids cannot grow without them.)

**myeloid tissue** *noun* ANAT tissue in bone marrow that produces red blood cells

**myiasis** *noun* ZOOL an infestation of animals by the larvae of flies

**myo-** *prefix* BIOL muscle

**myogenic** *adjective* ANAT originating in muscle cells without the need for stimulation by nerves (NOTE: The contractions of the heart muscles are myogenic.)

**myriapod** *noun* ZOOL an arthropod that lives on land, and has a head, a long segmented body and many legs, e.g. a centipede or millipede. Class: Myriapoda.

**Myrtaceae** *noun* BOT a family of Australian plants, including eucalyptus

**Mysticeti** *noun* MARINE BIOL baleen whales, including blue whales and humpbacks

**myxomatosis** *noun* ZOOL a usually fatal virus disease affecting rabbits, transmitted by fleas

# N

**n** *prefix* MATHS nano- or x $10^{-9}$

**N** *symbol* **1.** CHEM ELEM nitrogen **2.** MEASURE newton

**Na** *symbol* CHEM ELEM sodium

**nacelle** *noun* ENG a part of a wind generator that contains the generator and gearbox at the top of the tower

**nacreous clouds** *plural noun* METEOROL thin clouds, possibly made of ice crystals, which form a layer about 25 km above the Earth and look like mother-of-pearl

**nadir** *noun* ASTRON the point on the celestial sphere opposite the zenith and directly below the observer

**NAK** *abbreviation* COMPUT negative acknowledgement

**name** *noun* **1.** a word used to address or refer to a thing or a person **2.** COMPUT a word used to identify an address in machine language

**namespace** *noun* COMPUT a group of unique names (NOTE: In a small office network the namespace might include 20 users, but on the Internet the namespace runs into hundreds of millions.)

**naming services** *noun* COMPUT a method of assigning to each user, node or computer on a network a unique name that allows other users to access shared resources over a wide area network

**nand circuit** *noun* COMPUT an electronic component that performs the NAND function on two inputs

**NAND function** *noun* MATHS a logical function whose output is false if all inputs are true, and true if any input is false

COMMENT: The NAND function is equivalent to an AND function with a NOT function at the output. The output is 0 only if both inputs are 1; if one input is 1 and the

other 0, or if both inputs are 0, then the output is 1.

**NAND gate** *noun* ELECTRONICS an electronic circuit that provides a NAND function

**nano-** *prefix* MEASURE $10^{-9}$. Symbol **n**

**nanocircuit** *noun* ELECTRONICS an electronic and logic circuit that can respond to impulses within nanoseconds. Also called **nanosecond circuit**

**nanometer** *noun* MEASURE US spelling of **nanometre**

**nanometre** *noun* ACOUSTICS a unit of measurement of length, equal to one thousand millionth of a metre or $10^{-9}$ metre. Abbreviation **nm**

**nanomole** *noun* MEASURE a unit of measurement of the amount of substance, equal to one thousand millionth or $10^{-9}$ of a mole. Abbreviation **nmol**

**nanoplankton** *plural noun* MARINE BIOL plankton in the size range 10 to 50 µm

**nanosecond** *noun* MEASURE a unit of measurement of time, equal to one thousand millionth or $10^{-9}$ of a second. Abbreviation **ns**

**nanosecond circuit** *noun* ELECTRONICS same as **nanocircuit**

**nanotechnology** *noun* ENG the manipulation of very small components to build microscopic machinery

**naphthalene** *noun* CHEM a strong-smelling, volatile white solid used in the manufacture of explosives, dyes, resins and polyesters. Formula: $C_{10}H_8$. (NOTE: It is derived from coal tar, and gives the familiar smell to moth balls.)

**narcotic** *noun* PHARM a typically addictive drug, especially one derived from opium (NOTE: Narcotics may reduce pain, induce sleep or stupor and alter mood or behaviour.) ■ *adjective*

**1.** inducing sleep or stupor **2.** PHARM referring to narcotics

**narrative** *noun* COMPUT a set of explanatory notes or comments to help a user operate a program

**narrative statement** *noun* COMPUT a statement which sets variables and allocates storage at the start of a program

**narrow** *adjective* small in width ○ *a narrow beam of electrons*

**NASA** *abbreviation US* AEROSP National Aeronautics and Space Administration

**nastic response** *noun* BOT a response of plants and flowers to a stimulus which is not connected with the direction from which the stimulus comes, e.g. the closing of flowers at night

**-nasty** *suffix* BOT nastic response

**natality** *noun* ZOOL birth

**natality rate** *noun* ZOOL the number of births per year, expressed per thousand of the population

**national** *adjective* GEOG referring to a particular country

**National Aeronautics and Space Administration** *noun* AEROSP US government agency which carries out aviation and space research projects. Abbreviation **NASA**

**National Center for Supercomputing Applications** *noun* COMPUT a US organisation that helped define and create the World Wide Web with its Mosaic Web browser. Abbreviation **NCSA**

**national grid** *noun* ELEC same as **electricity grid**

**National Nature Reserve** *noun* ENVIRON (*in the UK*) a nature reserve designated by the Nature Conservancy Council for the protection of plants and animals living in it

**national park** *noun* ENVIRON a large area of unspoilt land, owned and managed by the government for recreational use by the public

**National Radiological Protection Board** *noun* HEALTH an agency that monitors radiation risks to the UK population. Abbreviation **NRPB**

**National Rivers Authority** *noun* ENVIRON a UK statutory body responsible for water management, flood defence and the regulation of water quality. Abbreviation **NRA**

**National Trust** *noun* ENVIRON a UK organisation that preserves historic buildings, parks and special areas of natural beauty

**native** *adjective* ECOL belonging to a place ○ *Tigers are native to Asia.*

**native compiler** *noun* COMPUT a compiler that produces code which will run on the same hardware system as the compiler

**native element** *noun* CHEM an element such as gold or carbon which exists in a pure state in nature

**native file format** *noun* COMPUT a default file format that is used by an application to store its data on disk

**native species** *noun* ECOL a species which exists naturally in an area

**natron** *noun* MINERALS a white, yellow, or grey mineral consisting of hydrated sodium carbonate, obtained from salt deposits and formerly used in embalming

**natural** *adjective* **1.** usual or expected ○ *The animal's behaviour was quite natural.* ○ *It's natural for wild animals to be frightened of people.* **2.** not made by people

**natural abundance** *noun* PHYS the relative amount of a nuclide occurring naturally

**natural amenities** *plural noun* ENVIRON features of the landscape such as rivers, lakes or moorland that are not made by humans and are regarded as contributing to a pleasant environment

**natural background** *noun* PHYS the surrounding level of radiation in a particular location

**natural binary coded decimal** *noun* COMPUT a representation of single decimal digits as a pattern of 4 bits. Abbreviation **NBCD**

**natural childbirth** *noun* MED childbirth during which mothers are not given pain-killing drugs but are encouraged to give birth with as little medical assistance as possible

**natural disaster** *noun* EARTH SCI a phenomenon such as a storm, earthquake or flood that destroys property and kills people and livestock

**natural environment** *noun* **1.** ECOL same as **natural habitat 2.** ENVIRON the part of the Earth that has not been built or formed by humans

**natural evaporation** *noun* METEOROL the evaporation of moisture from lakes and rivers caused by the wind or the sun

**natural gas** *noun* INDUST a gas found underground and not manufactured, used as a domestic fuel

COMMENT: Natural gas is often found near petroleum deposits, although it can occur without petroleum. It is mainly formed of methane but also contains small amounts of butane and propane. It contains no sulphur, unlike coal gas, and since it mixes with air it burns completely, creating very little carbon monoxide.

**natural habitat** *noun* ECOL the usual surroundings in which an organism lives in the wild

**natural historian** *noun* BIOL, GEOL a scientist who specialises in the study of natural history

**natural history** *noun* BIOL, GEOL the study of living organisms in their natural environments and of the features of the Earth not formed by humans

**natural immunity** *noun* IMMUNOL immunity from disease inherited by newborn offspring from birth, acquired in the womb or from the mother's milk

**natural increase** *noun* ZOOL an increase in a population when births exceed deaths

**natural insecticide** *noun* AGRIC an insecticide produced from plant extracts

**naturalise** *verb* ENVIRON to introduce a species into an area where it has not lived before so that it becomes established as part of the ecosystem

**naturalist** *noun* BIOL a person who is interested in and studies nature

**natural language** *noun* COMPUT a language that is used or understood by humans ○ *The expert system can be programmed in a natural language.*

**natural logarithm** *noun* MATHS a logarithm that has the constant *e* or 2.718 as a base

**natural pollutant** *noun* ENVIRON a polluting substance such as ash from a volcano which occurs naturally

**natural resources** *plural noun* ENVIRON parts of the environment which can be used commercially, e.g. oil deposits

**natural science** *noun* SCI a science such as biology, chemistry, geology or physics that studies the physical world

**natural scientist** *noun* SCI a person who specialises in natural science

**natural selection** *noun* BIOL the process of evolution of a species, whereby characteristics which help individual organisms to survive and reproduce are passed on to their offspring and those characteristics which do not help are not passed on

**natural vegetation** *noun* BOT the range of plants that exist in the wild, not planted or managed by people

**nature** *noun* **1.** an intrinsic quality of something **2.** ECOL all living organisms and the environment in which they live

**Nature Conservancy Council** *noun* ENVIRON an official UK organisation, established in 1973, that takes responsibility for the conservation of fauna and flora. Abbreviation **NCC** (NOTE: Since April 1991 the branch of the Council dealing with England has also been called English Nature.)

**nature conservation** *noun* ENVIRON the active management of the Earth's natural resources and environment to ensure their quality is maintained and that they are wisely used

**nature management** *noun* ENVIRON the action of managing a natural environment to encourage plant and animal life. Also called **habitat management**

**nature study** *noun* BIOL the study of natural history, especially at primary school

**nature trail** *noun* ENVIRON a path through the countryside with signs to draw attention to important and interesting features

**nauplius** *noun* MARINE BIOL a swimming larva of a crustacean (NOTE: The plural is **nauplii**.)

**nautical** *adjective* NAUT referring to ships and the sea

**nautical mile** *noun* MEASURE a unit of measurement of distance, equal to 1.852 km, used at sea and in the air. Abbreviation **nm**

COMMENT: A nautical mile is the length of an arc on the Earth's surface subtended by an angle of one minute at the centre of the Earth. One knot is equal to one nautical mile per hour.

**Nb** *symbol* CHEM ELEM niobium

**NBCD** *abbreviation* COMPUT natural binary coded decimal

**NC** *abbreviation* COMPUT network computer

**NCC** *abbreviation* ENVIRON Nature Conservancy Council

**NCSA** *abbreviation* COMPUT National Center for Supercomputing Applications

**Nd** *symbol* CHEM ELEM neodymium

**Ne** *symbol* CHEM ELEM neon

**Neandertal man** *noun* ANTHROP an extinct subspecies of human being, which populated Europe, North Africa, and western Asia in the early Stone Age

**neap tide** *noun* EARTH SCI a tide which occurs at the first and last quarters of the Moon, when the difference between high and low water is less than normal. Compare **spring tide**

**Nearctic Region** *noun* EARTH SCI a biogeographical region, part of Arctogea, comprising North America and Greenland

**near-earth object** *noun* ASTRON an asteroid or comet that may approach within 28 million miles of Earth's orbit. Abbreviation **NEO**

**nebula** *noun* ASTRON a region or cloud of interstellar dust and gas (NOTE: The term originally applied to any non-point source of light from outside the solar system, but is now no longer used to describe galaxies. A wide range of types of nebulae is recognised, including dark and bright types, some dominated by gas and others in which dust is a major component. The plural is **nebulae**)

**nebuliser** *noun* INDUST same as **atomiser**

**nectar** *noun* BOT a sweet sugary liquid that flowering plants produce to attract animals, usually insect pollinators

**nectary** *noun* BOT a plant part that produces nectar (NOTE: Nectaries are usually in the flowers but may also develop on other plant parts such as the traps of pitcher plants.)

**need** *noun* something that is necessary or required ○ *the need for clean water* □ **in need** requiring something, especially financial aid or food aid ■ *verb* to require something ○ *We need more resources.*

**needle** *noun* **1.** BOT a thin hard leaf of a conifer **2.** a thin metal pointer in an instrument ○ *The needle indicated zero.*

**needle valve** *noun* MECH ENG a valve formed of a tapered needle projecting into a small opening in a tube, usually connected to a float, which provides fine adjustment of fluid flow ○ *Atmospheric pressure will allow the capsule to expand, causing the needle valve to move into the opening, thus reducing the flow of fuel.*

**NEF** *abbreviation* ENVIRON noise exposure forecast

**negate** *verb* MATHS to reverse the sign of a number ○ *If you negate 23.4, the result is −23.4.*

**negation** *noun* **1.** MATHS the reversal of the sign of a number, e.g. from 5 to −5 **2.** ELEC a single input gate whose output is equal to the logical inverse of the input

**negative** *adjective* **1.** having a value of less than 0 ○ *The mechanism enables the propeller to be set to a negative pitch.* Symbol **-** **2.** ELEC referring to an electric charge of the same sign as that of an electron. Symbol **-** **3.** showing refusal ○ *a negative response* ○ *a negative answer* **4.** PHOTOGRAPHY (*of an image*) showing the light and dark areas of objects the opposite of how they are seen

**negative acknowledgement** *noun* COMPUT a signal sent by a receiver to indicate that data has been incorrectly or incompletely received. Abbreviation **NAK**

**negative feedback** *noun* a situation where the result of a process inhibits the action which caused the process

**negative ion generator** *noun* INDUST same as **ioniser**

**negative number** *noun* MATHS a number which represents the number subtracted from zero, indicated by a minus sign (-) in front of the number

**negative pressure** *noun* PHYS the condition that exists when less air is supplied to a space than is used up, so the air pressure in that space is less than that in surrounding areas ○ *Under negative pressure, if an opening exists, air will flow from surrounding areas.*

**negative terminal** *noun* ELEC the terminal of a battery marked with the symbol − and normally coloured black

**negative-true logic** *noun* COMPUT the use of a lower voltage level to represent binary 1 than for binary 0

**negligible** *adjective* small or unimportant to the extent that it is not worth considering ○ *negligible risk* ○ *Atmospheric attenuation is negligible until the upper end of the UHF (ultra high frequency) band when it increases rapidly.*

**neighbourhood noise** *noun* ENVIRON the general noise from a local source such as the noise of a factory which is disturbing to people living in the area

**neither-nor function** *noun* MATHS a logical function whose output is false if any input is true

**nekton** *noun* MARINE BIOL swimming marine animals such as fish, as opposed to floating or drifting animals like plankton

**nematicide** *noun* AGRIC a substance which kills nematode worms

**nematode** *noun* ZOOL a type of roundworm, some of which, e.g. hookworms, are parasites of animals while others live in the roots of plants

**NEO** *abbreviation* ASTRON near-earth object

**neo-** *prefix* new

**neo-Darwinism** *noun* BIOL a revised form of Darwin's theory of evolution which accounts for Mendel's laws of genetics and other more recent discoveries

**neodymium** *noun* CHEM ELEM a poisonous silvery-white or yellowish metallic element used in lasers and glass manufacture (NOTE: The chemical symbol is **Nd**; the atomic number is **60** and the atomic weight is **144.24**.)

**Neogea** *noun* EARTH SCI one of the main biogeographical regions of the Earth, comprising Central and South America together with the islands in the Caribbean. Also called **Neotropical Region**

**neo-Lamarckism** *noun* BIOL the modification of Lamarckism by a theory of the evolution of genetic variation influenced by environmental factors

**neon** *noun* CHEM ELEM an inert gas found in very small quantities in the atmosphere and used in illuminated signs (NOTE: The chemical symbol is **Ne**; the atomic number is **10** and the atomic weight is **20.18**.)

**neonatal** *adjective* MED referring to the first few weeks after birth

**neonatal death rate** *noun* MED a number of newborn babies who die, shown per thousand babies born

**neoplasm** *noun* MED an abnormal growth of tissue

**neoprene** *noun* INDUST a synthetic rubbery material, used in waterproof equipment such as wetsuits

**neoteny** *noun* ZOOL the continuing presence of larval features in an adult animal

**Neotropical Region** *noun* EARTH SCI same as **Neogea**

**Neptune** *noun* ASTRON the eighth planet of the solar system and the last of significant size, being the outermost of the gas giants (NOTE: Neptune has a diameter of 48 600 km and a mean distance from the Sun of 30 AU, and takes 165 years to make one orbit of the Sun.)

**neptunium** *noun* CHEM ELEM a naturally radioactive element (NOTE: The chemical symbol is **Np**; the atomic number is **93** and the atomic weight is **237.05**.)

**NEQ function** *noun* MATHS a logical function where the output is true if the inputs are not the same, otherwise the output is false

**neritic** *adjective* MARINE BIOL referring to an animal or plant which lives in the shallow sea over the continental shelf

**neritic facies** *noun* EARTH SCI the visual appearance of sedimentary rocks laid down in shallow water, where the ripple marks made by waves are clearly visible

**neritic zone** *noun* EARTH SCI an area of warm shallow water at the edge of a lake or sea, which is the habitat of plants and other organisms

**Nernst heat theorem** *noun* PHYS the theory stating that if a chemical change occurs between two crystalline solids at a temperature of zero, the entropy of the resulting substances is the same as that of the initial substances

**nerve** *noun* ANAT a bundle of fibres in a body which take impulses from one part of the body to another, each fibre being the axon of a nerve cell (NOTE: For other terms referring to nerves, see words beginning with **neur-**.)

COMMENT: Nerves are the fibres along which impulses are carried. Motor nerves or efferent nerves take messages between the central nervous system and muscles, making the muscles move. Sensory nerves or afferent nerves transmit impulses such as sight or pain from the sense organs to the brain.

**nerve block** *noun* PHARM an act of stopping the function of a nerve by injecting an anaesthetic

**nerve cell** *noun* BIOL same as **neuron**

**nerve centre** *noun* ANAT a point at which nerves come together

**nerve cord** *noun* ANAT a long bundle of nerve tissue that forms a major part of a central nervous system, e.g. the spinal cord in vertebrates

**nerve ending** *noun* ANAT a terminal at the end of a nerve fibre, where a nerve cell connects with another nerve or with a muscle

**nerve fibre** *noun* BIOL same as **axon**

**nerve gas** *noun* MIL a gas which attacks the nervous system

**nerve impulse** *noun* BIOCHEM an electrochemical impulse which is transmitted by nerve cells

**nerve root** *noun* ANAT the first part of a nerve as it leaves or joins the spinal column (NOTE: The dorsal nerve root is the entry for a sensory nerve and the ventral nerve root is the exit for a motor nerve.)

**nerve tissue** *noun* ANAT the tissue that forms nerves, and which is able to transmit the nerve impulses

**nervous system** *noun* ANAT the network of specialised cells that transmit nerve impulses in most animals

**nest** *noun* ZOOL a construction built by birds and some fish for their eggs on a construction made by some social insects such as ants and bees for the colony to live in ■ *verb* **1.** ZOOL to build a nest **2.** COMPUT to insert a subroutine within a program or another routine **3.** COMPUT to use a routine that calls itself recursively

**nest builder** *noun* ZOOL an animal which builds a nest

**nested loop** *noun* COMPUT a loop inside another loop in the same program

**nest epiphyte** *noun* BOT a plant whose aerial roots and stems collect rotting organic matter from which the plant takes nutrients

**nesting bird** *noun* ZOOL a bird which is sitting on its eggs to incubate them

**nesting level** *noun* COMPUT a number of subroutines within a subroutine

**nesting site** *noun* ZOOL a place where a bird builds or is likely to build a nest

**nestling** *noun* ZOOL a very small bird still in the nest

**net** *adjective* referring to the amount remaining after all deductions have been made ■ *noun* COMPUT same as **Internet** (*informal*)

**NetBIOS** *noun* COMPUT a set of basic operations such as a file sharing and the transfer of data between nodes within a network carried out by a widely used set of commands within application programs, using a system created by IBM ○ *This software uses NetBIOS calls to manage file sharing.* Full form **Network Basic Input Output System**

**net primary productivity** *noun* BOT the rate at which organic matter is incorporated into plants to produce growth

**net productivity** *noun* BOT the difference between the amount of organic matter produced by photosynthesis and the amount of organic matter used by plants in their growth

**net useful energy** *noun* PHYS a usable amount of energy available from an energy source over its lifetime

**network** *noun* **1.** a complex interconnected group or system of things ○ *A network of meteorological stations around the world exchange information.* **2.** a system of lines or channels which cross each other ○ *On a map, meridians of longitude and parallels of latitude form a network of lines called a graticule.* **3.** COMPUT a system made up of a number of points or circuits that are interconnected ■ *verb* to link points together in a network ○ *They run a system of networked micros.* ○ *The workstations have been networked together rather than used as standalone systems.*

**network adapter** *noun* COMPUT an add-in board that connects a computer to a network (NOTE: The board converts the computer's data into electrical signals that are then transmitted along the network cable.)

**network address** *noun* COMPUT the part of an IP address that defines the main network on which the domain is located (NOTE: For class A networks this is the first byte of the address, for class B networks it is the first two bytes and for class C networks it is the first three bytes. The rest of the IP address forms the host address.)

**network administrator** *noun* COMPUT a person who is responsible for looking after a network, with responsibilities that include installing, configuring and maintaining the network

**network alert** *noun* COMPUT a message sent from the network operating system to the user warning that the network hardware is not working properly

**network analysis** *noun* COMPUT the study of messages, destinations and routes in a network to provide a better operation

**network architecture** *noun* COMPUT the way in which a network is constructed, e.g. layers in an OSI system

**network computer** *noun* COMPUT a computer that is designed to run Java programs and access information using a web browser. Abbreviation **NC**

COMMENT: A network computer has a small desktop box that does not have a floppy disk drive. Instead it downloads any software it requires from a central server. Network computers are simpler and cheaper than current PCs and Macintosh computers, and are designed to be easier to manage in a large company.

**network drive** *noun* COMPUT a disk drive that is part of another computer on a network, but it can be used by anyone using the network

**networking** *noun* COMPUT **1.** the working or organisation of a network **2.** the interconnection of two or more computers either in the same room or different buildings, in the same town or different towns, allowing them to exchange information

COMMENT: Networking allows a machine with a floppy disk drive to use another PC's hard disk when both machines are linked by a cable and are using networking software.

**network interface card** *noun* COMPUT an add-in board that connects a computer to a network. Abbreviation **NIC** (NOTE: The board converts the computer's data into electrical signals that are then transmitted along the network cable.)

**network layer** *noun* COMPUT the third ISO/OSI layer that decides on the route to be used to send a packet of data

**network management** *noun* COMPUT the organisation, planning, running and upkeep of a network

**network news transfer protocol** *noun* COMPUT a set of commands used to interact with and control a news server on the Internet or an intranet to allow a newsreader to access news articles. Abbreviation **NNTP**

**network operating system** *noun* COMPUT an operating system running on a dedicated server computer that controls access to the network resources, and manages network links, printing and users. Abbreviation **NOS**

**network protocol** *noun* COMPUT a set of handshaking signals that defines how a workstation sends data over a network without clashing with other data transmissions

**network server** *noun* COMPUT a computer that runs a network operating system and controls the basic network operations (NOTE: All the workstations in a LAN are connected to the central network server and users log onto a network server.)

**network time protocol** *noun* COMPUT a protocol that provides an accurate time signal to computers on the Internet based on an atomic clock, which allows local computers to synchronise their clocks. Abbreviation **NTP**

**network topology** *noun* COMPUT a layout of machines in a network such as a star network, ring network or bus network that will determine what cabling and interfaces are needed and what possibilities the network can offer

**neural** *adjective* ANAT referring to a nerve or the nervous system

**neural arch** *noun* ANAT the curved part of a vertebra, which forms the space through which the spinal cord passes

**neural crest** *noun* BIOL a ridge of cells in an embryo which forms the nerve cells of the sensory and autonomic ganglia

**neural groove** *noun* BIOL a groove on the back of an embryo, formed as the neural plate closes to form the neural tube

**neural network** *noun* COMPUT a system running an artificial intelligence program which attempts to simulate the way the brain works

**neural plate** *noun* BIOL the thickening of an embryonic disc which folds over to form the neural tube

**neural tube** *noun* BIOL a tube lined with ectodermal cells running the length of an embryo, which develops into the brain and spinal cord

**neural tube defect** *noun* MED a congenital defect such as spina bifida which occurs when the edges of the neural tube do not close up properly during development

**neuron, neurone** *noun* ANAT a cell that transmits nerve impulses. Also called **nerve cell** (NOTE: It usually consists of a cell body, an axon and dendrites.)

**neurotoxin** *noun* BIOCHEM a natural substance such as the poison of a snake or insect which prevents the victim's nerve impulses from working

**neurotransmitter** *noun* BIOCHEM a chemical substance which transmits nerve impulses from one neuron to another

COMMENT: The main neurotransmitters are the catecholamines, adrenaline, noradrenaline, 5-hydroxytryptamine and acetylcholine. Other neurotransmitters such as gamma aminobutyric acid, glutamine and substance P are less common.

**neuston** *noun* MARINE BIOL organisms like plankton which float or swim in the surface film of a body of water

**neuter** *adjective* BIOL neither male nor female

**neutral** *adjective* CHEM referring to the state of being neither acid nor alkali ○ *A pH factor of 7 is neutral.* ■ *adjective, noun* **1.** ELEC referring to an electrical charge which is neither positive nor negative **2.** referring to the position of a switch or lever which leaves a system active but not engaged, e.g. an engine gear lever position in which the engine is disconnected from the driven parts **3.** AVIAT referring to the middle position of a control surface providing no aerodynamic effect other than that as part of the wing ○ *After a turn, the auto-control will return the ailerons to neutral as the aircraft returns to straight flight.*

**neutralisation, neutralization** *noun* CHEM a chemical process in which an acid reacts with a base to form a salt and water

**neutralise[1], neutralize** *verb* CHEM (*of an acid*) to react with a base to form a salt and a water

**neutralise[2]** *verb* **1.** CHEM to make an acid neutral ○ *Acid in drainage water can be neutralised by limestone.* ○ *Ammonia is produced in the nose to neutralise the effects of acid in the air.* **2.** MED (*in bacteriology*) to make a toxin harmless by combining it with the correct amount of antitoxin **3.** BIOCHEM to counteract the effect of something

**neutral soil** *noun* EARTH SCI soil which is neither acid nor alkaline, i.e. where the pH value is neutral

**neutrino** *noun* PHYS an elementary particle without mass or electric charge whose main property is spin (NOTE: Neutrinos are given off in immense numbers in nuclear reactions and billions of them pour off the Sun.)

**neutron** *noun* PHYS a particle with no electric charge in the nucleus of an atom. Compare **ion**

**neutron excess** *noun* PHYS ◊ **isotopic number**

**neutron star** *noun* ASTRON an object produced by the death of a star weighing 1.4 –2.3 solar masses

COMMENT: As soon as there is too little radiation emerging from stars of this mass to prevent their collapse, they shrink until the pressure between neutrons in the star's atomic nuclei will not allow them to become any smaller. Neutron stars are still able to emit energy, as observations of pulsars confirm.

**neutrophil** *noun* IMMUNOL the commonest type of white blood cell in vertebrates (NOTE: It is responsible for protecting against infections.)

**névé** *noun* EARTH SCI the spring snow on high mountains which becomes harder and more like ice during the summer

**new moon** *noun* ASTRON the beginning of a lunar phase, when the Moon's face is not lit by the Sun

**newsgroup** *noun* COMPUT a feature of the Internet that provides free-for-all discussion forums

**new technology** *noun* INDUST the range of electronic instruments and devices which have recently been developed and are being introduced into industry

**newton** *noun* MEASURE, PHYS an SI unit of measurement of force. Abbreviation **N** (NOTE: 1 newton is the force required to move 1 kilogram at the speed of 1 metre per second.)

**Newton, Isaac (1642–1727)** an English scientist and philosopher whose influence on astronomy ranged from the highly practical invention of the reflecting telescope to the theoretical insight of the universal theory of gravitation

**Newtonian fluid** *noun* PHYS a liquid that conforms to Newton's equation in which the amount of strain is proportional to the stress and to time, where the constant of proportionality is called the coefficient of viscosity

**Newtonian telescope** *noun* ASTRON a reflecting telescope in which mirrors form an image that is viewed through a hole in the side of the telescope

**Newton's law of cooling** *noun* PHYS a law that describes the rate of transfer of heat from a hot body cooling in air, which is proportional to the temperature difference between the body and the surrounding air

**Newton's rings** *plural noun* OPTICS a series of alternating bright and dark rings created by the contact of a convex lens with a glass plate

**next instruction register** *noun* COMPUT a register in a central processing unit that contains the location where the next instruction to be executed is stored. ♦ **register**

**nexus** *noun* COMPUT a connection point between units in a network

**NGO** CHEM symbol **nickel**

**Ni** *symbol* CHEM ELEM nickel

**niacin** *noun* CHEM a vitamin of the vitamin B complex found in milk, meat, liver, kidney, yeast, beans, peas and bread. Formula: $C_6H_5NO_2$. Also called **nicotinic acid** (NOTE: Lack of niacin can cause mental disorders and pellagra.)

**nibble, nybble** *noun* COMPUT half the length of a standard byte (*informal*) (NOTE: A nibble is usually 4 bits, but can vary according to different micros or people.)

**NIC** *abbreviation* COMPUT network interface card

**NiCad battery** *abbreviation* ELEC nickel–cadmium battery

**niche** *noun* ECOL a place in an ecosystem which a species is specially adapted to fit

**nickel** *noun* CHEM ELEM a metallic element, used in computer wiring (NOTE: The chemical symbol is **Ni**; the atomic number is **28** and the atomic weight is **58.71**.)

**nickel–cadmium battery, nickel–cadmium cell** *noun* ELECTRONICS, ELEC a type of rechargeable battery which has a higher storage density than a lead-acid battery. Abbreviation **NiCad battery**

COMMENT: NiCad batteries unfortunately have one problem called 'memory' which gradually reduces their ability to retain charge. To remove the memory the battery should be conditioned by running it right down so that it has no charge, before re-charging it.

**nickel carbonyl** *noun* CHEM a colourless liquid formed from nickel, carbon and oxygen, used as a catalyst and in the Mond process to prepare nickel. Formula: $Ni(CO)_4$.

**nickel metal hydride battery** *noun* ELEC a type of rechargeable battery which has better charge-carrying ability than a nickel–cadmium battery, is quicker to charge and does not suffer from 'memory'. Abbreviation **NiMH**

**nicotine** *noun* CHEM a toxic substance in tobacco, also used as an insecticide

**nicotinic acid** *noun* BIOCHEM same as **niacin**

**nictitating membrane** *noun* ZOOL a layer of skin underneath the eyelid that birds, reptiles, and some mammals can pull over the eye. Also called **third eyelid**

**nid-** *prefix* ZOOL nest

**nidicolous** *adjective* ZOOL referring to a baby bird which is helpless and remains in the nest for some time

**nidifugous** *adjective* ZOOL referring to a baby bird which is so well developed when hatched that it can leave the nest immediately

**night soil** *noun* AGRIC human excreta, collected and used for fertiliser in some parts of the world

**nil** *noun* zero

**nimbostratus** *noun* METEOROL a grey mass of cloud with precipitation in the form of rain or snow about 1000 m above the ground

**NiMH** *abbreviation* ELEC nickel metal hydride battery

**nine's complement** *noun* MATHS a decimal complement, equivalent to the complement of binary one, formed by subtracting each digit in the number from nine. ⧫ **ten's complement**

**niobium** *noun* CHEM ELEM a shiny pale grey superconducting metallic element used in steel alloys (NOTE: The chemical symbol is **Nb**; the atomic number is **41** and the atomic weight is **92.91**.)

**nipple** *noun* ZOOL the teat through which a baby or young mammal sucks milk

**nitrate** *noun* CHEM **1.** an ion with the formula $NO_3$ **2.** a chemical compound containing the nitrate ion, e.g. sodium nitrate

COMMENT: Nitrates are a source of nitrogen for plants. They are used as fertilisers but can poison babies if they get into drinking water.

**nitrate-sensitive area** *noun* ENVIRON a region of the country where nitrate pollution is likely and where the use of nitrate fertilisers is strictly controlled. Abbreviation **NSA**

**nitrate-vulnerable zone** *noun* ENVIRON same as **nitrate-sensitive area**. abbreviation **NVZ**

**nitric** *adjective* CHEM containing nitrogen

**nitric acid** *noun* CHEM a corrosive liquid and very reactive oxidising agent, used in making explosives, fertilisers and rocket fuels. Formula: $HNO_3$.

**nitric oxide** *noun* CHEM a colourless gas which forms red fumes of nitrogen dioxide in air. Formula: NO. Also called **nitrogen monoxide**

**nitrification** *noun* BIOL a process by which bacteria found in the soil break down nitrogen compounds and form nitrates which plants can absorb

**nitrify** *verb* CHEM to convert nitrogen or nitrogen compounds into nitrates

**nitrifying bacteria** *plural noun* CHEM bacteria which convert nitrogen into nitrates

**nitrite** *noun* CHEM **1.** an ion with the formula $NO_2$ **2.** a chemical compound containing the nitrite ion, e.g. sodium nitrite

COMMENT: Nitrites are formed by bacteria from nitrogen as an intermediate stage in the formation of nitrates.

**nitro compound** *noun* CHEM an organic compound formed of a nitro group ($-NO_2$) attached to an aromatic ring

**nitrogen** *noun* CHEM ELEM a chemical element that is a gas which is essential to biological life and which is the main component of air and an essential part of protein (NOTE: The chemical symbol is **N**; the atomic number is **7** and the atomic weight is **14.01**.)

COMMENT: Nitrogen is taken into the body by digesting protein-rich foods. Excess nitrogen is excreted in urine. When the intake of nitrogen and the excretion rate are equal, the body is in nitrogen balance or protein balance.

**nitrogen compound** *noun* CHEM a substance such as a fertiliser containing mostly nitrogen with other elements

**nitrogen cycle** *noun* BIOL the process by which nitrogen enters living organisms (NOTE: The nitrogen is absorbed into green plants in the form of nitrates, the plants are then eaten by animals and the nitrates are returned to the ecosystem through the animal's excreta or when an animal or a plant dies.)

**nitrogen deficiency** *noun* AGRIC a lack of nitrogen in soil, found where organic matter is low and resulting in thin, weak growth of plants

**nitrogen dioxide** *noun* CHEM a brown toxic irritant gas, used in the manufacture of nitric acid and in rocket fuels. Formula: $NO_2$. (NOTE: It is one of the pollutants produced by vehicle exhausts.)

**nitrogen fertiliser** *noun* AGRIC a fertiliser containing mainly nitrogen

**nitrogen fixation** *noun* CHEM the process by which nitrogen in the air is converted by bacteria on some plant roots into nitrogen compounds (NOTE: When the plants die the nitrogen is released into the soil and acts as a fertiliser.)

**nitrogen-fixing bacteria** *plural noun* CHEM bacteria in the soil which convert nitrogen in the air into nitrogen compounds by means of the process of nitrogen fixation in plants

**nitrogen-fixing plant** *noun* BOT a leguminous plant such as a bean which forms an association with bacteria that convert nitrogen from the air into nitrogen compounds in the soil

**nitrogen monoxide** *noun* CHEM same as **nitric oxide**

**nitrogenous** *adjective* CHEM containing nitrogen

**nitrogen oxide** *noun* CHEM an oxide such as nitric oxide or nitrogen dioxide formed when nitrogen is oxidised. Formula: $NO_x$.

COMMENT: In general nitrogen oxides form the major part of air pollution, though nitric oxide produced by burning fossil fuel is not directly dangerous to humans. Nitrogen dioxide is produced by car engines and is toxic. Nitrogen oxides are also produced when farmland is sprayed with fertilisers, as the bacteria in the soil feed on the fertiliser and produce the gas.

**nitroglycerine** *noun* INDUST a colourless thick oily liquid that is flammable and explosive, used in explosives manufacture and angina treatment. Formula: $C_3H_5(NO_3)_3$.

**nitrous acid** *noun* CHEM a weak acid that can exist only in solution or as salts. Formula: $HNO_2$.

**nitrous oxide** *noun* CHEM a colourless gas with a sweet smell, used as an anaesthetic in dentistry and surgery and as an aerosol propellant. Formula: $N_2O$.

**nm[1]** *abbreviation* MEASURE nautical mile

**nm[2]** *abbreviation* MEASURE nanometre

**NMI** *abbreviation* COMPUT non-maskable interrupt

**nmol** *abbreviation* MEASURE nanomole

**NMR** *abbreviation* PHYS nuclear magnetic resonance

**NNI** *abbreviation* ENVIRON noise and number index

**NNTP** *abbreviation* COMPUT network news transfer protocol

**no-address operation** *noun* COMPUT an instruction which does not require an address within it

**nobelium** *noun* CHEM ELEM a radioactive metallic element produced artificially from curium (NOTE: The chemical symbol is **No**; the atomic number is **102** and the atomic weight is **255**.)

**noble gas** *noun* CHEM a gas that does not react chemically with other substances. Also called **rare gas** (NOTE: The noble gases include helium, neon, argon, krypton, xenon and radon.)

**noble metal** *noun* METALL a metal such as gold or silver that resists corrosion and does not form compounds with nonmetals

**node** *noun* **1.** COMPUT an interconnection point in a structure or network ○ *This network has fibre optic connection with nodes up to one kilometre apart.* **2.** BOT a point on the stem of a plant where a leaf is attached

**nodule** *noun* BOT a small lump found on the roots of leguminous crops such as beans which contains bacteria can convert nitrogen from the air into nitrogen compounds

**noise** *noun* ENVIRON an unpleasant sound

**noise and number index** *noun* MEASURE a way of measuring noise from aircraft. Abbreviation **NNI**

**noise criteria** *plural noun* ENVIRON the levels of noise which are acceptable to people who hear them

**noise exposure forecast** *noun* ENVIRON a forecast of the effect which industrial or aircraft noise will have on people. Abbreviation **NEF**

**noise immunity** *noun* ENG the ability of a circuit to ignore or filter out or be protected from noise

**noise level** *noun* MEASURE the loudness of a noise which can be measured ○ *The factory has announced plans to keep noise levels down to a minimum.*

**noise nuisance** *noun* ENVIRON a noise which is annoying, disturbing or unpleasant

**noise pollution** *noun* ENVIRON unpleasant sounds which cause discomfort

**noise pollution level** *noun* MEASURE the loudness of unpleasant noise which can be measured. Abbreviation **NPL**

**noise zone** *noun* ENVIRON an area which is classified according to the amount of noise that exists in it

**noisy** *adjective* ENVIRON **1.** making a loud noise **2.** where there is a lot of noise

**noisy mode** *noun* COMPUT a floating point arithmetic system, in which a digit other than a zero is deliberately added in the least significant position during the normalisation of a floating point number

**nomadism** *noun* ZOOL a habit of some animals which move around from place to place without having a fixed habitat

**nomenclature** *noun* a predefined system for assigning words and symbols to represent numbers or terms

**nominal** *adjective* not significant or not important ○ *a nominal increase in the numbers of sparrows*

**non-** *prefix* not or no

**nonbiodegradable** *adjective* ENVIRON not able to be decomposed into environmentally safe waste materials by the action of soil bacteria

**noncoding** *adjective* GENETICS referring to the strand of a double-stranded DNA molecule that acts as a template for the synthesis of messenger RNA

**noncompatibility** *noun* COMPUT the state of two or more pieces of hardware or software that cannot exchange data or use the same peripherals

**non-conductor** *noun* PHYS a substance that is not a conductor of heat, electricity or sound

**non-contact cooling water** *noun* INDUST water used for cooling which does not come into contact with any raw material, product, by-product or waste

**nondegradable** *adjective* ENVIRON same as **nonbiodegradable**

**nondegradation** *noun* ENVIRON the prevention of the pollution of clean air

**nondisposable** *adjective* ENVIRON not thrown away after use, but able to be returned for recycling

**non-equivalence function** *noun* COMPUT a logical function where the output is true if the inputs are not the same, otherwise the output is false. Abbreviation **NEQ**

**non-ferrous** *adjective* CHEM not containing iron

**nonflammable** *adjective* difficult to set on fire

**non-genetically modified** *adjective* BIOTECH with a genetic composition that has not been altered by genetic manipulation

**non-governmental organisation** *noun* ENVIRON an organisation such as a pressure group, charity or voluntary

agency which is not funded by a government and which works on a local, national or international level. Abbreviation **NGO**

**nonhereditary** *adjective* GENETICS not transferred or not capable of being transferred genetically from one generation to the next

**non-indigenous** *adjective* ECOL not native to a place

**noninheritable** *adjective* GENETICS not able to be transferred genetically from one generation to the next

**non-interlaced** *adjective* COMPUT referring to a display system in which the picture electron beam scans each line of the display once during each refresh cycle (NOTE: The beam in an interlaced display scans every alternate line.)

**non-maskable interrupt** *noun* COMPUT a high priority interrupt signal that cannot be blocked by software and overrides other commands. Abbreviation **NMI**

**nonmetal** *noun* CHEM a chemical element that lacks the physical and chemical properties of a metal, e.g. carbon or oxygen

**nonmetallic material** *noun* a substance such as wood, plastic or fabric that is not made of metal

**nonmodal** *adjective* COMPUT (*in a graphical user interface*) displaying a window but still allowing a user to access other windows that are on-screen

**non-Newtonian fluid** *noun* PHYS a fluid that is made up of two different phases and does not conform to the rules of proportionality of a Newtonian fluid

**non-nucleated** *adjective* BIOL referring to a cell with no nucleus

**non-organic** *adjective* **1.** CHEM not containing carbon **2.** AGRIC not produced according to guidelines restricting the use of fertilisers and other practices

**non-persistent** *adjective* ENVIRON referring to a chemical, especially a pesticide, that decomposes quickly so does not enter the food chain

**nonpoint source** *noun* ENVIRON a source of pollution not associated with a distinct discharge point (NOTE: Nonpoint sources include rainwater and runoff from agricultural land and industrial sites, as well as escaping gases from pipes and fittings.)

**nonrenewable** *adjective* ENVIRON not able to be renewed indefinitely, because the supply is limited or regrowth is impossible

**nonrenewable energy** *noun* INDUST power generated from nonrenewable resources such as coal

**nonrenewable resource** *noun* ENVIRON a natural resource such as coal or oil which cannot be replaced once it is consumed

**non-resistant** *adjective* BIOL not having resistance to a disease, antibiotic, pesticide, herbicide or other agent

**non-return valve** *noun* ENG a valve which allows a fluid to pass in one direction only ○ *As the piston moves upwards in the cylinder, fluid is drawn in through a non-return valve.*

**non-selective weedkiller** *noun* AGRIC a weedkiller which kills all plants

**nonsense** *noun* GENETICS a set of three nucleotides (**codon**) in a DNA molecule that does not carry the genetic code for an amino acid but may signal the beginning and end of the synthesis of some protein molecules

**non-toxic** *adjective* BIOL not poisonous or harmful to humans, animals or the environment

**non-volatile memory** *noun* COMPUT a storage medium or memory that retains data even when the power has been switched off ○ *Using magnetic tape provides non-volatile memory.* ○ *Bubble memory is a non-volatile storage.* Also called **non-volatile store**, **non-volatile storage**. Compare **permanent memory**

**non-volatile random access memory (NVRAM)** *noun* COMPUT full form **NVRAM**

**non-volatile store, non-volatile storage** *noun* COMPUT same as **non-volatile memory**

**no parity** *noun* COMPUT data transmission which does not use a parity bit

**NOR function** *noun* MATHS a logical function whose output is false if either input is true

COMMENT: The output is 1 only if both inputs are 0. If the two inputs are different or if both are 1, the output is 0.

**NOR gate** *noun* ELECTRONICS a electronic circuit or chip which performs a NOR function

**normal** *adjective* referring to something which is usual and expected

**normal environmental lapse rate** *noun* EARTH SCI the rate at which the temperature of the air falls with height above the Earth (NOTE: This is about 6.4° C per thousand metres, under conditions where there are no upward air currents or wind.)

**normal form** *noun* COMPUT a method of structuring information in a database to avoid redundancy and improve storage efficiency

**normal format** *noun* COMPUT a standardised format for data storage

**normalisation, normalization** *noun* COMPUT the process of normalising data

**normalise** *verb* COMPUT **1.** to convert data into a form which can be read by a particular computer system **2.** to convert characters into only capitals or only lower case **3.** to store and represent numbers in a pre-agreed form, usually to provide maximum precision ○ *All the new data has been normalised to 10 decimal places.*

**normalised form** *noun* COMPUT a floating point number that has been normalised so that its mantissa is within a particular range

**normal range** *noun* the expected range for a result or number, any items outside this range being errors

**normal room temperature** *noun* ENVIRON the temperature regarded as comfortable for usual daily activity

**north** *noun* NAVIG **1.** the compass point at 360° towards which the magnetic needle points ○ *flying towards the north* ○ *The wind is blowing from the north.* **2.** same as **magnetic north** ■ *adjective* **1.** NAVIG referring to the compass point 360° **2.** GEOG situated in the north ○ *the north coast of France* ■ *adverb* NAVIG towards the north ○ *The aircraft was heading north.*

**North Atlantic Drift** *noun* EARTH SCI a current of warm water in the Atlantic Ocean, which flows north along the east coast of the USA, then crosses the Atlantic to reach Northern Europe

**north-east** *noun* NAVIG the direction between north and east ■ *adjective* **1.** GEOG situated in the north-east ○ *the north-east coast of England* **2.** METEOROL blowing from the north-east ○ *a north-east wind* ■ *adverb* NAVIG towards the north-east ○ *We are heading north-east.*

**northerly** *adjective* NAVIG to or from the north ○ *The cyclone moved in a northerly direction towards the coast.* ■ *noun* METEOROL a wind which blows from the north

**northern** *adjective* GEOG, NAVIG situated in the north or towards the north

**northern hemisphere** *noun* EARTH SCI the top half of the Earth

**Northern Lights** *plural noun* EARTH SCI a spectacular illumination of the sky in the northern hemisphere caused by ionised particles striking the atmosphere. Also called **Aurora Borealis**

**north-facing** *adjective* directed towards the north ○ *a north-facing slope*

**North Pole** *noun* GEOG the point which is furthest north on the Earth

**North Sea** *noun* GEOG a sea to the north of the Netherlands and Germany, east of the UK and west of Scandinavia

**North Sea oil** *noun* INDUST oil or gas extracted from the rocks under the North Sea

**north-west** *noun* NAVIG the direction between north and west ■ *adjective* **1.** GEOG situated in the north-west ○ *the north-west coast of England* **2.** METEOROL blowing from the north-west ○ *a north-west wind* ■ *adverb* NAVIG towards the north-west ○ *We are heading north-west.*

**north wind** *noun* METEOROL a wind blowing from or coming from the north (NOTE: A wind is named after the direction it comes from.)

**NOS** *abbreviation* COMPUT network operating system

**nose** *noun* ANAT the sense organ by which smells are detected

**NOT-AND** *noun* MATHS equivalent to the NAND function

**notation** *noun* a method of writing or representing numbers

**notebook computer** *noun* COMPUT a very small portable computer, usually smaller than a laptop computer, that but has a small keyboard and display and can be carried easily

**NOT function** *noun* MATHS a logical inverse function where the output is true if the input is false

COMMENT: If the input is 1, the output is 0. If the input is 0, the output is 1.

**NOT gate** *noun* ELECTRONICS an electronic circuit or chip which performs a NOT function

**notifiable disease** *noun* **1.** MED a serious infectious disease that has to be officially reported so that steps can be taken to stop it spreading **2.** VET a serious infectious disease of animals and poultry that has to be officially reported when an outbreak is confirmed on a farm **3.** AGRIC a disease of plants which must be officially reported if it occurs

**notification** *noun* the act or an instance of informing someone officially

**notify** *verb* to inform someone officially

**notocord** *noun* ZOOL a long flexible column of cells found in vertebrate embryos and in chordates which is a type of backbone

**Notogea** *noun* EARTH SCI one of the main biogeographical regions of the Earth, comprising Australia, New Zealand and the Pacific Islands

**nova** *noun* ASTRON a star which exhibits a sudden rapid increase of brightness, short of the massive brightening associated with a supernova (NOTE: The plural is **novae**.)

COMMENT: Novae are old stars prone to sudden brightening and most are seen to erupt only once. A nova can become 5–15 or more magnitudes brighter during an eruption.

**noxious** *adjective* harmful to people or animals

**noy** *noun* MEASURE a unit of measurement of perceived noise

**nozzle** *noun* a projecting part with an opening at the end of a pipe, for regulating and directing a flow of fluid

**Np** *symbol* CHEM ELEM neptunium

**NPK** *noun* AGRIC nitrogen, phosphorus and potassium, used in different combinations as a fertiliser

**NPL** *abbreviation* MEASURE noise pollution level

**npn transistor** *noun* ELECTRONICS a bipolar junction transistor that uses a p-type semiconductor for the base and an n-type for the collector and emitter

**NRA** *abbreviation* ENVIRON National Rivers Authority

**NRPB** *abbreviation* MED National Radiological Protection Board

**ns** *abbreviation* MEASURE nanosecond

**NSA** *abbreviation* ENVIRON nitrate-sensitive area

**NSFnet** *noun* COMPUT a wide area network developed by the National Science Foundation to replace ARPANET as the main government-funded network linking together universities and research laboratories (NOTE: NSFnet was a crucial stepping-stone in the development history of the Internet. It was closed down in 1995 and replaced by a commercial high-speed network backbone that formed one of the foundations for the current commercial Internet.)

**NTP** *abbreviation* COMPUT network time protocol

**n-type semiconductor** *noun* PHYS a semiconductor material such as silicon which has a substance added to increase the number of negatively charged electrons and thus increase electrical conduction

**nucellus** *noun* BOT the part in the middle of a plant ovule in which the embryo forms

**nuclear** *adjective* **1.** PHYS referring to an atomic nucleus, especially to the production of energy by fission or fusion of nuclei **2.** BIOL referring to a cell nucleus

**nuclear bomb** *noun* MIL a bomb whose destructive power is produced by nuclear fission or fusion

**nuclear contamination** *noun* ENVIRON damage done to an object, person or substance because of contact with nuclear radiation

**nuclear energy** *noun* **1.** PHYS the energy released during a nuclear reaction, either fission or fusion **2.** INDUST the power created in a nuclear power station by a nuclear reaction which produces heat that warms water, forming steam that runs a turbine to generate electricity

**nuclear family** *noun* EARTH SCI a family group composed of two parents and their offspring

**nuclear fission** *noun* PHYS same as **atomic fission**

**nuclear-free** *adjective* ENVIRON with no nuclear reactors or nuclear weapons ○ *While some countries remain nuclear-free, nuclear reactors supply about 15% of all electricity generated in the world.*

**nuclear-free zone** *noun* ENVIRON an area which will not allow the use of nuclear reactors or the use of nuclear weapons

**nuclear fuel** *noun* INDUST a substance such as uranium-238 which is fissile and can be used to create a controlled reaction in a nuclear reactor

**nuclear fuel cycle** *noun* INDUST a series of processes by which uranium ore is extracted, processed to make uranium oxide, then enriched until it is ready for use in a reactor

**nuclear fusion** *noun* PHYS the joining together of several atomic nuclei to form a single large nucleus, creating energy, as in a hydrogen bomb

**nuclear magnetic resonance** *noun* PHYS the energy pulse released by an atomic nucleus exposed to high-frequency radiation in a magnetic field. Abbreviation **NMR**

**nuclear physics** *noun* PHYS the study of the structure, forces and behaviour of atomic nuclei

**nuclear power** *noun* INDUST **1.** the power generated by a nuclear reactor **2.** electricity generated by a nuclear power station

**nuclear-powered** *adjective* INDUST operated by nuclear power

**nuclear power plant, nuclear power station** *noun* INDUST a power station in which nuclear reactions are used to provide energy to run turbines which generate electricity

**nuclear reaction** *noun* PHYS a physical reaction of the nucleus of an atom, which when bombarded by radiation particles creates an isotope

**nuclear reactor** *noun* INDUST a device which creates heat and energy by starting and controlling atomic fission

**nuclear reprocessing plant** *noun* INDUST a place where spent nuclear fuel is subjected to chemical processes which produce further useful materials such as plutonium

**nuclear waste** *noun* ENVIRON radioactive waste from a nuclear reactor including spent fuel rods and coolant

**nuclear weapon** *noun* MIL a bomb or missile whose destructive power is produced by nuclear fission or fusion

**nuclear winter** *noun* ENVIRON a period expected to follow a nuclear war, when there would be no warmth and light because dust particles would obscure the Sun and most life would be affected by radiation

**nuclease** *noun* BIOCHEM an enzyme that breaks down nucleic acids

**nucleating agent** *noun* METEOROL a substance, solid carbon dioxide, that is scattered on clouds to make them release rain

**nucleic acid** *noun* BIOCHEM a complex organic acid, either DNA or RNA, that exists in the nucleus and protoplasm of all cells

**nucleoid** *noun* MICROBIOL a compact structure seen in bacterial cells and made of DNA

**nucleolus** *noun* BIOL a small round body inside a cell nucleus (NOTE: It is made of protein and RNA and is involved in making ribosomes and ribosomal RNA.)

**nucleon** *noun* PHYS a proton or neutron, especially one in an atomic nucleus

**nucleonics** *noun* PHYS the branch of physics dealing with the study of nucleons and atomic nuclei

**nucleophile** *noun* CHEM an atom, ion or molecule that acts as an electron donor when forming chemical bonds

**nucleophilic addition** *noun* CHEM a chemical reaction in which a small molecule is added to an unsaturated organic compound

**nucleophilic substitution** *noun* CHEM a chemical reaction in which an atom or group of atoms in an organic compound are substituted with a nucleophile

**nucleoprotein** *noun* BIOCHEM a combination of a protein and a nucleic acid, as in a chromosome

**nucleoside** *noun* BIOCHEM a purine or pyrimidine base linked to a sugar, especially ribose or deoxyribose

**nucleotide** *noun* BIOCHEM a nucleoside linked to a phosphate group (NOTE: Nucleosides join together to form the polymers RNA and DNA.)

**nucleus** *noun* **1.** PHYS the central core of an atom, formed of neutrons and protons **2.** BIOL the central body in a cell, containing DNA and RNA, and controlling the function and characteristics of the cell **3.** a central part or focus round which something gathers

**nuclide** *noun* PHYS one or more atomic nuclei of the same element, defined by having the same number of protons and neutrons and the same energy content

**nué ardente** *noun* EARTH SCI a cloud of burning gas which flows downhill during a volcanic eruption

**NUL character** *noun* COMPUT same as **null character**

**null** *noun* an instrument reading of zero

**null character** *noun* a character which means nothing, usually code 0. Also called **NUL character**

**null instruction** *noun* COMPUT a program instruction that produces no result

**null list** *noun* a list which contains nothing

**null modem** *noun* COMPUT a circuit or cable that allows two computers to communicate via their serial ports ○ *This cable is configured as a null modem, allowing me to connect these two computers together easily.*

**null position** *noun* COMPUT the zero position

**null set** *noun* COMPUT same as **empty set**

**null string** *noun* COMPUT a string that contains no characters

**null terminated string** *noun* COMPUT a string of characters that has a null character to indicate the end of the string

**number** *noun* MATHS **1.** a representation of a quantity **2.** a written figure ○ *Each piece of hardware has a production number.* ○ *Please note the reference number of your order.* ■ *verb* **1.** to put a figure on a document ○ *The pages of the manual are numbered 1 to 196.* **2.** to assign digits to a list of items in an ordered manner

**number range** *noun* COMPUT a set of allowable values

**numeral** *noun* MATHS a character or symbol which represents a number

**numeric, numerical** *adjective* **1.** MATHS referring to numbers **2.** COMPUT containing only numbers ○ *a numeric code*

**numerical analysis** *noun* MATHS the study of ways of solving mathematical problems

**numerical keypad** *noun* COMPUT a set of ten keys with figures (0–9), included on most computer keyboards as a separate group, used for entering large amounts of data in numeric form

**numerical order** *noun* an arrangement with the lowest numbers (1, 2, 3 etc.) coming first and higher numbers (25, 26, 27 etc.) coming last

**numerical value** *noun* the number represented by a character or symbol

**numeric array** *noun* COMPUT an array containing numbers

**numeric operand** *noun* COMPUT an operand that only uses numerals

**numeric pad** *noun* COMPUT same as **numerical keypad**

**numerous** *adjective* very many ○ *Numerous refinements to the simple actuator will be found in use.*

**nursery** *noun* AGRIC a place where plants are grown until they are large enough to be planted in their final positions

**nut** *noun* **1.** MECH ENG a metal ring which screws on a bolt to hold it tight ○ *Turn the nut anticlockwise to loosen it.* **2.** BOT a hard seed case produced by some trees

**nutation** *noun* ASTRON an uneven rotation of a spinning object, especially a planet, caused by a temporary change in the position of its axis

**nutrient** *noun* **1.** BIOL a constituent of food which is necessary to provide energy or to help the body grow, repair and maintain itself, e.g. a protein, fat or vitamins **2.** EARTH SCI a substance which a plant needs to allow it to grow and produce seed, e.g. carbon, hydrogen, oxygen, nitrogen, phosphorus, potassium, calcium, magnesium or sulfur

**nutrient cycle** *noun* BIOL the process in which nutrients from living organisms are transferred into the physical environment and back to the organisms (NOTE: This process is essential for organic life to continue.)

**nutrient requirement** *noun* BIOL the type and amount of nutrients needed by an organism

**nutrient stripping** *noun* INDUST the removal of nutrients from sewage to prevent eutrophication of water in reservoirs

**nutrition** *noun* BIOL **1.** the process of taking in the necessary food components to grow and remain healthy **2.** food

**nutritional** *adjective* BIOL referring to nutrition ○ *the nutritional quality of meat*

**nutritional disorder** *noun* MED a disorder related to food intake or requirements

**nutritional requirement** *noun* BIOL the type and amount of food needed by an organism

**nutritionist** *noun* MED a person who specialises in the study of nutrition and advises on diets

**nutritious** *adjective* providing nutrition, especially for children

**nutritive** *adjective* BIOL providing some of the necessary components for growth and health

**nutritive value** *noun* BIOL the degree to which a food is valuable in promoting health ○ *The nutritive value of white flour is lower than wholemeal flour.*

**NVRAM** *noun* COMPUT memory that can permanently retain information. Full form **non-volatile random access memory**

**NVZ** *abbreviation* ENVIRON nitrate-vulnerable zone

**nybble, nibble** *noun* COMPUT half the length of a standard byte (*informal*)

COMMENT: A nybble is normally 4 bits, but can vary according to different micros.

**nyct-** *prefix* night

**nyctinasty** *noun* BOT a response of flowers to darkness at night, e.g. the closing of petals

**nylon** *noun* INDUST a tough, elastic synthetic polymer with molecules containing recurring amide groups

**nymph** *noun* ZOOL an insect at the stage in its development between the larval stage and adulthood

**nymphal** *adjective* ZOOL referring to the stage in the development of some insects between the larval stage and adulthood

# O

**O** *symbol* CHEM ELEM oxygen

**oak** *noun* TREES a common hardwood tree found in temperate regions. Genus: *Quercus*.

**oak apple, oak gall** *noun* BOT a small hard round growth found on oak trees, caused by a parasitic wasp

**oasis** *noun* EARTH SCI a place in an arid desert where the water table is near the surface and where vegetation can grow (NOTE: The plural is **oases**. In the oases of the hot desert regions, date palms form an important food supply.)

**oasis effect** *noun* AGRIC the loss of water from an irrigated area due to hot dry air coming from an unirrigated area nearby

**oat** *noun* PLANTS a hardy cereal crop grown in most types of soil in cool wet northern temperate regions. Latin name: *Avena sativa*.

**obey** *verb* **1.** to do what someone tells you to do **2.** to behave in the way expected or predicted by a physical law **3.** ○ *Winds obey Buys Ballot's Law.*

**object** *noun* **1.** a thing which you can experience physically by touch, sight, or another sense and which has a particular form and dimensions ○ *Any given object will collect more ice when travelling at high speed than at low speed.* **2.** an intention or aim ○ *The object of the briefing is to inform all aircrew of the new procedures.* **3.** COMPUT the data that makes up a particular image or sound **4.** COMPUT a variable used in an expert system within a reasoning operation **5.** COMPUT a piece of data in a statement which is to be operated on by the operator

**object code** *noun* COMPUT **1.** a binary code which directly operates a central processing unit **2.** program code after it has been translated, compiled or assembled into machine code

**object hierarchy** *noun* COMPUT an order in which messages are passed from one object to another

**objective** *noun* **1.** something that it is hoped to achieve **2.** ASTRON the light-gathering lens of a refracting telescope ■ *adjective* based on facts rather than personal feelings ○ *an objective assessment*

**object language** *noun* COMPUT the language of a program after it has been translated. Compare **source language**

**object-oriented** *adjective* COMPUT referring to a system or language that uses objects

**object-oriented graphics** *plural noun* COMPUT graphics which use vector definitions such as lines and curves to describe the shapes of an image rather than pixels in a bit-map image ○ *This object-oriented graphics program lets you move shapes around very easily.*

**object-oriented programming** *noun* COMPUT a method of programming such as C++ in which each element of the program is treated as an object that can interact with other objects within the program. Abbreviation **OOP**

**object program** *noun* COMPUT a computer program in object code form, produced by a compiler or assembler

**Object Request Broker** *noun* COMPUT the software that links objects together using the CORBA standard. Abbreviation **ORB**

**obligate** *adjective* BIOL existing or developing only in a particular set of circumstances ○ *an obligate parasite* ○ *an obligate anaerobe*

**obliquity** *noun* ASTRON the angle between the plane of Earth's equator and the plane of Earth's orbit around the Sun, approximately 23.5°

**obliterative shading, obliterative countershading** *noun* ZOOL the grading of the colour of an animal which minimises relief and gives a flat appearance as when the back of the animal is dark shading towards a light belly

**oblong** *adjective* MATHS rectangular ○ *an oblong piece of aluminium* ■ *noun* a rectangle

**obscure** *verb* **1.** to make something difficult to see or seeing difficult ○ *The ice forming on the window obscured vision.* ○ *The Moon obscured the Sun during the eclipse.* **2.** to make something difficult to realise or understand ○ *The low temperatures in the years after the volcanic eruption obscured the general trend of gradual global warming.* ■ *adjective* not clearly expressed and therefore difficult to understand ○ *an obscure explanation*

**observation** *noun* careful study by watching ○ *The type of cloud is established by observation and comparison with cloud photographs.*

**observations** *plural noun* SCI the pieces of scientific information gathered from use of any of the five human senses, but especially sight

**observe** *verb* **1.** to watch or study something carefully ○ *They observed the birds' behaviour for several weeks.* **2.** to obey something such as an agreement or a guideline ○ *We expect everyone to observe the safety guidelines.*

**obstruction** *noun* something which blocks a path or prevents progress ○ *Ensure the air intakes are free from any debris or obstruction.*

**obtain** *verb* to acquire something ○ *The probes are positioned in the gas stream in order to obtain an accurate temperature reading.*

**obvious** *adjective* clear and easily seen or understood ○ *an obvious error* ○ *It is obvious that high ground will disturb the smooth horizontal flow of air.*

**OC** *abbreviation* BIOCHEM organic carbon

**OCCAM** *noun* COMPUT a computer programming language used in large multiprocessor or multi-user systems (NOTE: OCCAM is the development language for transputer systems.)

**occidental** *adjective* EARTH SCI referring to the west

**occluded front** *noun* METEOROL a front where warm and cold air masses meet and mix together, with the warm air rising away from the surface of the ground

**occlusion** *noun* METEOROL the forcing of air upwards from the Earth's surface, as when a cold front overtakes and undercuts a warm front

**occupation** *noun* a job or type of work

**occupational** *adjective* referring to work

**occupational disease** *noun* MED a disease which is caused by the type of work someone does or the conditions in which someone works, e.g. disease caused by dust or chemicals in a factory

**occur** *verb* to happen or take place ○ *Data loss can occur because of power supply variations.*

**OCE** COMPUT same as **open collaboration environment**

**ocean** *noun* OCEANOG any of the major areas of sea of the world (NOTE: The five oceans are: the Atlantic, the Pacific, the Indian, the Arctic and the Antarctic or Southern.)

**oceanarium** *noun* MARINE BIOL a large saltwater aquarium where marine animals are kept

**ocean circulation** *noun* OCEANOG a system of movement of surface water between oceans, caused by wind, temperature or salinity

**ocean current** *noun* OCEANOG a movement of the surface water of an ocean, caused by wind, temperature or salinity

**ocean dumping** *noun* ENVIRON the discharging of waste, solid, liquid or radioactive, into the ocean

**oceanic** *adjective* **1.** OCEANOG referring to an ocean, especially to deep water beyond the continental shelf **2.** MARINE BIOL living in the ocean

**oceanic crust** *noun* EARTH SCI the part of the Earth's crust beneath the ocean

**oceanic trench** *noun* EARTH SCI a long deep valley in the floor of the ocean, where two tectonic plates meet, usually associated with volcanic activity

**ocean incineration** *noun* ENVIRON the burning of toxic waste in special ships at sea, at present only permitted in the North Sea

**oceanography** *noun* EARTH SCI the study of all the physical aspects of the ocean, including the fauna and flora living there

**oceanology** *noun* EARTH SCI the study of the geographical distribution of the ocean's economic resources

**Ocean Thermal Energy Conversion** *noun* INDUST the process whereby the difference in temperature between the upper and lower layers of water in tropical seas is used to generate electricity and fresh water. Abbreviation **OTEC** (NOTE: Warmer water from the upper layer is converted to steam to drive turbines and then condensed to provide fresh water.)

**ocellus** *noun* ZOOL a simple eye that can detect light but cannot focus clearly (NOTE: Eyes of this type are found in some insects and other invertebrates.)

**ocher** *noun* GEOL US spelling of **ochre**

**ochre** *noun* GEOL a reddish or yellowish oxide of iron used as pigment for paint

**OCP** *noun* COMPUT (*in a multiprocessor system*) a processor which decides and performs the arithmetic and logic operations according to the program code. Full form **order code processor**

**OCR** COMPUT same as **optical character reader** ■ *abbreviation* optical character recognition

**octa** *noun* MEASURE, METEOROL another spelling of **okta**

**octadecanoic acid** *noun* CHEM a naturally occurring carboxylic acid, present in fats and oils

**octahydrate** *noun* CHEM a crystalline compound with eight molecules of water of crystallisation for each molecule of the compound

**octal** MATHS *adjective* referring to a number system based on eight ■ *noun* same as **octal notation**

**octal digit** *noun* MATHS a digit between 0 and 7 used in octal notation

**octal notation** *noun* MATHS a number notation using base 8, with digits 0 to 7. Also called **octal**

COMMENT: In octal notation, the digits used are 0 to 7, so decimal 9 is octal 11.

**octal scale** *noun* MATHS the power of eight associated with each digit position in a number

**octane** *noun* CHEM a liquid hydrocarbon that exists in 18 structurally different forms. Formula: $C_8H_{18}$.

COMMENT: Petrol without the addition of hydrocarbons will make the engine knock. Hydrocarbons, such as octane or aromatic hydrocarbons, or lead tetraethyl can be added to the petrol to give better performance, while increasing the octane rating. Unleaded petrol has a relatively low octane rating and leaded petrol, which contains an antiknock additive, has a high rating. Leaded petrol produces more atmospheric pollution than unleaded.

**octane rating, octane number** *noun* CHEM a classification of the quality and performance of petrol, according to the amount of hydrocarbon in it

**octanoic acid** *noun* CHEM a straight-chain fatty acid. Formula: $CH_3(CH_2)_6COOH$. Also called **caprylic acid**

**octet** *noun* COMPUT same as **8-bit byte**

**octoploid** *noun* GENETICS referring to a cell nucleus or a plant that has eight haploid sets of chromosomes

**ocular** *adjective* OPTICS referring to the eye

**oculomotor nerve** *noun* ANAT the third cranial nerve which controls the eyeballs and eyelids

**odd** *adjective* referring to a number a little greater or smaller than the approximate number given ○ *There are 100 odd chemical elements.*

**odd-even check** *noun* COMPUT a method of checking that transmitted binary data has not been corrupted

**odd-even nucleus** *noun* PHYS a nucleus with an odd number of protons and an even number of neutrons

**odd number** *noun* MATHS a number which cannot be exactly divided by two, e.g. 1, 3, 5 or 7. Compare **even number**

**odd-odd nucleus** *noun* PHYS a nucleus with an odd number of protons and an odd number of neutrons

**odd parity check** *noun* an error checking system in which any series of bits transmitted must have an odd number of binary ones

**odd tenth** *noun* an odd decimal, e.g. 0.1 or 0.3 ○ *Frequency allocation of localisers in the VHF band is 108–112 MHz at odd tenths e.g. 108.1* and 109.3, the even decimals being allocated to VOR facilities.

**odonate** *noun* INSECTS an insect with biting mouth parts, large eyes and two pairs of wings, e.g. a dragonfly. Order: Odonata.

**Odontoceti** *plural noun* MARINE BIOL toothed whales

**odor** *noun* US spelling of **odour**

**odour** *noun* a smell, especially an unpleasant smell (NOTE: The US spelling is **odor**.)

**ODP** *abbreviation* ENVIRON ozone-depleting potential

**oersted** *noun* MEASURE the cgs unit of magnetic field strength, equal to the field strength that would cause a unit magnetic pole to experience a force of one dyne in a vacuum

**oesophagus** *noun* ANAT the tube down which food passes from the mouth to the stomach

**oestrogen** *noun* BIOCHEM a steroid hormone belonging to a group that controls the reproductive cycle and the development of secondary sexual characteristics in females (NOTE: The US spelling is **estrogen**.)

**oestrous cycle** *noun* ZOOL the pattern of reproductive activity shown by most female animals, except most primates

**oestrus** *noun* ZOOL one of the periods of the oestrous cycle that occurs in mature female mammals who are not pregnant; in this period ovulation normally occurs and the female is ready to mate. Also called **heat**

**offer** *verb* **1.** to indicate that something will be given or done if it is wanted **2.** to provide something ○ *The battery offers a short term power capability.*

**office** *noun* **1.** a room or building where a company works or where business is done **2.** a room, usually with a desk, where people can work

**offline** *adverb, adjective* COMPUT **1.** (*of a processor, printer or terminal*) not connected to a network or central computer, usually temporarily ○ *Before changing the paper in the printer, switch it off-line.* **2.** (*of a peripheral*) connected to a network, but not available for use. Opposite **online**

**off-line printing** *noun* COMPUT a printout operation that is not supervised by a computer

**off-line processing** *noun* COMPUT processing by devices not under the control of a central computer

**off-line storage** *noun* COMPUT a storage facility that is not currently available for access, e.g. a magnetic tape that must first be loaded into the tape machine

**offpeak** *adjective* INDUST referring to a period during which the consumption of something is low ○ *Offpeak electricity costs less.* ○ *By using thermal storage we can move 50% of electricity demand into offpeak hours.*

**offset** *noun* COMPUT a quantity added to a number or address to give a final number

**offshore** *adjective, adverb* EARTH SCI **1.** in sea water near the coast **2.** away from the coast

**offshore island** *noun* EARTH SCI an island or platform situated up to 12.5 kilometres or 20 miles from the coast

**offshore wind** *noun* METEOROL a wind which blows from the coast towards the sea

**offspring** *noun* BIOL a child, the young of an animal, or a descendant of a plant

**ohm** *noun* ELEC, MEASURE the SI unit of measurement of electrical resistance. Symbol

**Ohm's law** *noun* ELEC the physical principle that an electric current is directly proportional to the voltage and inversely proportional to the resistance

**oil** *noun* **1.** CHEM a liquid which cannot be mixed with water, occurring as three types, vegetable or animal oils, essential volatile oils and mineral oils **2.** INDUST mineral oil extracted from underground deposits, used to make petrol and other petroleum products

COMMENT: Oil is made up of different types of hydrocarbon together with sulphur compounds, and usually occurs in combination with natural gas or water. When these are removed it is called crude oil or crude petroleum. Refined crude oil gives products such as petrol, LPG, diesel oil, paraffin wax and tar. Crude oil is found in geological deposits, mainly in the Middle East, in the North Sea, Central America and Asia.

**oil-bearing** *adjective* EARTH SCI referring to rock, sand or shale that contains oil

**oil coke** *noun* INDUST coke resulting from the processing of oil

**oil-eating bacteria** *plural noun* MICROBIOL bacteria which can consume and destroy oil

**oil-exporting country** *noun* INDUST a country which produces enough oil for its own use and to sell to other countries

**oilfield** *noun* EARTH SCI an area of rock under which lie one or more pools of oil that can be exploited ○ *The search is on for new oilfields to replace fields which have been exhausted.*

**oil-fired** *adjective* INDUST using oil as fuel

**oil-importing country** *noun* INDUST a country which buys oil from other countries for home consumption

**oil industry** *noun* INDUST an industry which extracts and processes oil

**oil installation** *noun* INDUST a plant for processing and handling oil

**oil platform** *noun* INDUST a large construction which is positioned over an oil well in the sea, containing living quarters for workers and pumping and drilling equipment

**oil pollution** *noun* ENVIRON damage to an area caused by oil, e.g. pollution of the sea by oil from a damaged oil tanker

**oil pool** *noun* EARTH SCI a reservoir of oil found under rock

**oil regeneration plant** *noun* INDUST a place where waste oil is reprocessed into high-grade oil

**oil rig** *noun* INDUST a large metal construction containing the drilling and pumping equipment for an oil well

**oil sand** *noun* EARTH SCI a geological formation of sand or sandstone containing bitumen, which can be extracted and processed to give oil

**oilseed rape** *noun* PLANTS a plant of the cabbage family with distinctive yellow flowers, extensively grown to provide oil and also used as green manure. Latin name: *Brassica napus*. Also called **rape**

**oil shale** *noun* EARTH SCI a geological formation of sedimentary rocks containing oil or bitumen which can be extracted by crushing and heating the rock

**oil slick** *noun* ENVIRON oil which has escaped into water and floats on the surface

**oil spill** *noun* ENVIRON an escape of oil into the environment, e.g. from a tanker which hits rocks, or from a ruptured pipeline

**oil tanker** *noun* INDUST a large ship specially constructed for carrying oil

**oil well** INDUST a shaft drilled into the ground through which oil is extracted

**oily** *adjective* containing oil or covered with oil

**okta, octa** *noun* MEASURE, METEOROL a unit of visible sky equal to one eighth of total area visible to the horizon

COMMENT: To measure cloud cover, the sky is divided into imaginary sections, each covering one eighth of the total. A cloudless sky is 'zero oktas' and a sky which is completely covered with clouds is 'eight oktas'.

**olefin, olefine** *noun* CHEM an aliphatic hydrocarbon

**oleic acid** *noun* CHEM a colourless oily liquid obtained from animal and vegetable fats, used in the manufacture of soap, ointments, cosmetics and lubricating oils. Formula: $C_{18}H_{34}O_2$.

**oleo** *noun* AEROSP the telescopic strut in undercarriage which absorbs impact loads on landing ○ *A safety switch is fitted in such a way to the oleo, that when the oleo is compressed on the ground, the 'undercarriage up' selection cannot be operated.* (NOTE: short for **oleo-pneumatic**)

**oleum** *noun* CHEM sulfur trioxide dissolved in sulfuric acid

**olfaction** *noun* PHYSIOL the act of smelling

**olfactory** *adjective* PHYSIOL referring to the sense of smell

**olfactory nerve** *noun* ANAT the first cranial nerve which controls the sense of smell

**oligo-** *prefix* few or little

**oligochaete** *noun* ZOOL a worm such as an earthworm without a specialised head and with tiny bristles occurring singly along the length of its body. Class: Oligochaeta.

**oligohaline** *adjective* CHEM (*of water*) having traces of salt. Compare **polyhaline**

**oligosaprobic** *adjective* BIOL unable to survive in polluted water

**oligotrophic** *adjective* CHEM (*of water*) containing few nutrients. Compare **dystrophic, eutrophic, mesotrophic**

**oligotrophic lake** *noun* EARTH SCI a lake which has a balance between decaying vegetation and living organisms, where the lowest layer of water never loses its oxygen and where the water contains few nutrients but sustains a fish population (NOTE: This situation is typical of a young lake. Over a period of time the lake will eutrophy and become richer in nutrients and also in algae.)

**olive** *noun* TREES a Mediterranean tree with small edible fruit from which an edible oil can be produced. Latin name: *Olea europaea.*

**olivine** *noun* MINERALS an olive-green mineral belonging to a group consisting of crystalline magnesium iron silicate

**ombrogenous** *adjective* **1.** EARTH SCI (*of a bog*) receiving water only from rain and therefore being low in nutrients **2.** BOT (*of a plant*) obtaining nutrients only from rainwater

**omit** *verb* to leave something out (NOTE: **omitting – omitted**)

**omnivore** *noun* ZOOL an animal that will eat a wide range of both plant and animal foods (NOTE: Humans and pigs are examples of omnivores.)

**omnivorous** *noun* ZOOL referring to an animal which a wide range of both plant and animal foods

**OMR** *abbreviation* COMPUT **1.** optical mark reader **2.** optical mark recognition

**on-board** *adjective* COMPUT contained on a motherboard or main printed circuit board

**on-chip** *adjective* COMPUT constructed on a chip ○ *The processor uses on-chip bootstrap software to allow programs to be loaded rapidly.*

**on-chip cache** *noun* COMPUT a cache memory and controller circuitry built into a processor chip

**oncogene** *noun* GENETICS a gene that can cause a cell to become cancerous

**oncogenic** *adjective* MED referring to or causing the formation of a cancerous tumour

**oncology** *noun* MED the scientific study of tumours

**one address computer** *noun* COMPUT a computer structure whose machine code only uses one address at a time

**one element** *noun* MATHS a logical function that produces a true output if any input is true

**one for one** *noun* COMPUT a programming language, usually an assembler, that produces one machine code instruction for each instruction or command word in the language

COMMENT: Compilers and interpreters are usually used for translating high-level languages which use more than one machine code instruction for each high-level instruction.

**one-level address** *noun* COMPUT a storage address that directly, without any modification, accesses a location or device

**one-level code** *noun* COMPUT a binary code which directly operates the CPU, using only absolute addresses and values (NOTE: This is the final form of a program after a compiler or assembler pass.)

**one-level store** *noun* COMPUT an organisation of storage in which each different type of storage device is treated as if it were the same

**1-metre measure** *noun* a ruler that is 1 metre long

**10Base2** *noun* COMPUT the IEEE standard specification for running Ethernet over thin coaxial cable

**10Base5** *noun* COMPUT the IEEE standard specification for running Ethernet over thick coaxial cable

**10BaseT** *noun* COMPUT the IEEE standard specification for running Ethernet over unshielded twisted pair cable

**one-pass assembler** *noun* COMPUT an assembler program that translates the source code in one action

**one's complement** *noun* COMPUT the inverse of a binary number ○ *The one's complement of 10011 is 01100.*

**16:9** *noun* COMPUT the aspect ratio of a widescreen TV or HDTV or widescreen computer display. Compare **4:3**

**16-bit** *adjective* COMPUT referring to data that is transferred 16 bits at a time along 16 parallel conductors

**16-bit sample** *noun* COMPUT a single sample of an analog signal which is stored as a 16-bit digital number, meaning that there are 65 536 possible levels. A '16-bit sound card' can sometimes mean that the card generates 16-bit samples, but it can also mean that it generates 8-bit samples, but fits into a 16-bit expansion slot. ♦ **8-bit sample**

**one to zero ratio** *noun* COMPUT a ratio between the amplitude of a binary one and zero output

**onion skin architecture** *noun* COMPUT the design of a computer system in layers, according to function or priority ○ *The onion skin architecture of this computer is made up of a kernel at the centre, an operating system, a low-level language and then the user's program.*

**onium ion** *noun* CHEM a positively charged ion (**cation**) such as the ammonium ion, formed by attaching a proton to a neutral compound

**online** *adverb, adjective* COMPUT connected to and under the control of a central processing unit ○ *The terminal is on-line to the mainframe.*

**on local** *adjective* COMPUT (*of a terminal*) not working with a central processing unit, but being used as a stand-alone terminal

**onshore** *adjective, adverb* EARTH SCI **1.** situated on land **2.** towards the coast

**onshore oil installation** *noun* INDUST a plant for processing and handling oil, built on land

**onshore wind** *noun* METEOROL a wind which blows from the sea towards the coast

**ontogeny** *noun* BIOL the development of a living organism from its earliest stage to maturity

**oocyte** *noun* BIOL a cell that develops into a female reproductive cell or egg

**oogenesis** *noun* BIOL the formation and development of female reproductive cells or eggs

**OOP** *abbreviation* COMPUT object-oriented programming

**oospore** *noun* BIOL a fertilised female reproductive cell in fungi and algae

**ooze** *noun* EARTH SCI soft mud, especially at the bottom of a lake or the sea. Also called **ooze mud** ■ *verb* (*of liquid*) to flow slowly

**ooze mud** *noun* EARTH SCI same as **ooze**

**op** *noun* same as **operation** (*informal*)

**opacity** *noun* the characteristic of not allowing light or other rays to pass through ○ *Sometimes it is possible to estimate the depth and opacity of the layer of mist or fog from the ground observations.*

**opaque** *adjective* not allowing light or other rays to pass through it

**op code** *noun* COMPUT same as **operating code** (*informal*)

**open** *verb* **1.** to take a cover off something or to make a door open ○ *Open the disk drive door.* ○ *Open the top of the computer by lifting here.* **2.** COMPUT to prepare a file before accessing, editing or carrying out other transactions on stored records ○ *You cannot access the data unless the file has been opened.*

**open-air** *adjective* ENVIRON referring to the environment outside buildings

**open architecture** *noun* COMPUT a computer with a published expansion interface that has been designed to allow add-on hardware to be plugged in

**open burner** *noun* ENVIRON an outdoor site where waste such as automobile tyres or rags is destroyed by fire, thereby causing atmospheric pollution

**open burning** *noun* ENVIRON the burning of waste matter in the open air, creating pollution with smoke

**open-cast mining** *noun* INDUST a form of mining in which the mineral is dug from the surface instead of digging it from underground. Also called **open-cut mining, strip mining**

COMMENT: In open-cast mining the top layer of soil and rock is pushed away from the surface of the ground to expose the mineral without digging underground, destroying the natural vegetation of the mined area and its surroundings. Unless the site is filled in and replanted when mining is completed the whole area remains devastated.

**open chain** *noun* CHEM a string of atoms in a molecule that is open-ended and not joined in a ring

**open collaboration environment** *noun* COMPUT a set of standards that allow networked Macintosh users to share objects and files. Abbreviation **OCE**

**open-cut mining** *noun* INDUST same as **open-cast mining**

**open dump** *noun* ENVIRON a place where waste is left on the ground and not buried in a hole

**opening** *noun* a space which acts as a passage through which something or somebody can go ○ *an inlet valve opening*

**open shortest path first** *noun* COMPUT a protocol used with a TCP/IP network that will send packets of data on a route that has the least amount of traffic. Abbreviation **OSPF**

**open system** *noun* COMPUT **1.** a non-proprietary system that is not under the control of one company **2.** a system that is constructed in such a way that different operating systems can work together

**Open System Interconnection** *noun* COMPUT a standardised ISO network that is constructed in layered form, with each layer having a specific task, allowing different systems to communicate if they conform to the standard. Abbreviation **OSI** (NOTE: The seven layers are Physical, Data Link, Network, Transport, Session, Presentation, and Application.)

**operand** *noun* COMPUT data in a computer instruction that is to be operated on by an operator ○ *In the instruction ADD 74, the operator ADD will add the operand 74 to the accumulator.*

**operate** *verb* **1.** to control the working of something ○ *The control column operates the ailerons and elevators.* ○ *The flaps are operated by a switch.* **2.** MED to perform a surgical procedure, by cutting into the body ○ *The surgeon operated on the patient.* **3.** COMPUT to work or to make a machine work ○ *Do you know how to operate this equipment?* ○ *It operates like this.*

**operating code** *noun* COMPUT the part of the machine code instruction that defines the action to be performed. Also called **op code**

**operating costs** *plural noun* INDUST the amount of money required to keep a machine, factory or business working

**operating jack** *noun* ENG a device which converts rotary motion into linear or reciprocating motion in order to move heavy control surfaces

**operating system** *noun* COMPUT a set of basic software that controls the running of the hardware and the management of data files, without the user having to operate it. Also called **op sys**

**operation** *noun* **1.** an action or set of actions taken to make something work ○ *The operation of the ignition system is quite simple.* **2.** an organised activity designed to achieve something ○ *The cleanup operation after the oil spill lasted for months.* **3.** MATHS a procedure such as addition or subtraction **4.** MED a surgical intervention ○ *He underwent a brain operation last year.*

**operational** *adjective* **1.** working ○ *The system is not yet fully operational.* **2.** referring to the way a machine works

**operational definition** *noun* a term or concept that is defined in a precise, measurable way for a specific investigation

**operational information** *noun* information about the normal operations of a system

**operation cycle** *noun* COMPUT a section of a machine cycle during which an instruction is executed

**operation decoder** *noun* COMPUT a hardware device that converts a machine-code instruction in binary form into actions

**operation field** *noun* COMPUT a part of an assembly language statement that contains the mnemonic or symbol for the operating code

**operation register** *noun* COMPUT a register that contains the operating code during its execution

**operator** *noun* **1.** a person who makes a machine or process work ○ *The operator was sitting at his console.* **2.** COMPUT, MATHS a character, symbol or word that defines a function or operation ○ *x is the multiplication operator.*

**operator overloading** *noun* COMPUT the assigning of more than one function to a particular operator (NOTE: The function often depends on the type of data being operated on and is used in the C++ and ADA programming languages.)

**operator precedence** *noun* MATHS an order in which a number of mathematical operations will be carried out

**operator procedure** *noun* COMPUT a set of actions that an operator has to carry out to work a machine or process

**operon** *noun* GENETICS a segment of a chromosome containing genes that specify the structure of a specific protein together with genes that regulate its manufacture (NOTE: Operons are relatively simple units of genetic control and are found only in bacteria.)

**ophthalmic** *adjective* OPHTHALMOL referring to the eye

**ophthalmic nerve** *noun* ANAT a branch of the trigeminal nerve, supplying the eyeball, the upper eyelid, the brow and one side of the scalp

**ophthalmic optician, ophthalmic practitioner** *noun* OPHTHALMOL a qualified person who specialises in testing eyes and prescribing lenses

**ophthalmic surgeon** *noun* OPHTHALMOL a surgeon who specialises in surgery to treat eye disorders

**opportunist, opportunistic** *adjective* BIOL referring to an organism which quickly colonises an available habitat

**opportunity** *noun* a chance or situation where something can be done successfully

**opposite** *adjective* **1.** situated or placed directly across from something **2.** completely different or reverse ○ *For every action there is an equal and opposite reaction.* ■ *noun* something completely different from something else ◇ **going in opposite directions 1.** (*of two things*) moving away from each other **2.** (*of two things*) moving towards each other

**opposition** *noun* ASTRON the position of two astronomical objects that are directly opposite each other on the celestial sphere

**op register** *noun* COMPUT a register that contains the operating code for the instruction that is being executed

**op sys** *noun* same as **operating system** (*informal*)

**optic** *adjective* ANAT referring to the eye or to sight

**optical** *adjective* **1.** OPTICS referring to or making use of light ○ *An optical reader uses a light beam to scan characters, patterns or lines.* **2.** ANAT referring to the eye or to sight

**optical activity** *noun* CHEM the ability of a substance to rotate the plane of polarised light passing through it

**optical axis** *noun* ASTRON the centre line of a telescope or other optical instrument, joining the main mirror or lens to its focal point

**optical character reader** *noun* COMPUT a device for inputting text into a computer, which recognises written or printed characters and converts them to machine-readable code. Abbreviation **OCR**

**optical character recognition** *noun* COMPUT a process that allows characters to be recognised optically and converted into machine-readable code that can be input into a computer, using an optical character reader. Abbreviation **OCR**

COMMENT: There are two OCR fonts in common use: OCR-A, which is easy for scanners to read, and OCR-B, which is easier for people to read than the OCR-A font.

**optical data link** *noun* COMPUT a connection between two devices to allow the transmission of data using light, either via line-of-sight or using fibre optics

**optical disk** *noun* COMPUT a disk that contains binary data in the form of small holes in a metal layer under the surface which are read with a laser beam (NOTE: Examples are a WORM (write once, read many times memory) disk which can be programmed once, or a compact disc (CD) which is programmed at manufacture.)

**optical double star** *noun* ASTRON a pair of stars that appear close together when observed from Earth but are a long way apart on the same line of sight

**optical fibre** *noun* COMPUT a fine strand of glass or plastic protected by a surrounding material, which is used for the convenient transmission of light signals

**optical glass** *noun* OPTICS glass of high refractive quality suitable for use in lenses

**optical illusion** *noun* OPTICS something which is seen wrongly so that it appears to be something else

**optical mark reader** *noun* COMPUT a device that can recognise marks or lines on a special forms, e.g. an order form or a reply to a questionnaire, and convert them into a form a computer can process. Abbreviation **OMR**

**optical mark recognition** *noun* COMPUT a process that allows marks or lines on forms such as an order form or a questionnaire to be recognised by an optical mark reader and input into a computer. Abbreviation **OMR**

**optical microscope** noun OPTICS a device that uses optical lenses to magnify a tiny object

**optical mouse** noun COMPUT a pointing device that is operated by moving it across a mat on which is printed a grid of lines (NOTE: As the mouse is moved, two light sensors count the number of lines that have been passed to produce a measure of the distance and direction of travel.)

**optical scanner** noun COMPUT same as **bar-code reader**

**optical telescope** noun OPTICS a device that uses optical lenses and mirrors to magnify distant objects

**optic chiasma** noun ANAT a structure formed where some of the optic nerves from each eye partially cross each other in the hypothalamus

**optic disc** noun ANAT a point on the retina where the optic nerve starts. Also called **optic papilla**

**optician** noun OPHTHALMOL a person who is trained to examine people's eyes and prescribe lenses to correct poor sight

**optic nerve** noun ANAT the second cranial nerve which transmits the sensation of sight from the eye to the brain

**optic neuritis** noun MED an inflammation of the optic nerve, which makes objects appear blurred

**optic papilla** noun ANAT same as **optic disc**

**optic radiation** noun ANAT a nerve tract which takes an optic impulse from the optic tract to the visual cortex

**optics** noun PHYS the study of light rays and sight

**optic tract** noun ANAT a nerve tract which takes an optic nerve from the optic chiasma to the optic radiation

**optimisation, optimization** noun the process of making something as efficient as possible

**optimise** verb to make something as efficient as possible

**optimised code** noun COMPUT a program that has been passed through an optimiser to remove any inefficient code or statements

**optimiser, optimizer** noun COMPUT a program which adapts another program to run more efficiently

**optimising compiler** noun COMPUT a compiler that analyses the machine code it produces in order to improve the speed or efficiency of the code

**optimum** adjective referring to the point at which the condition or amount of something is the best ○ *The optimum altitude for jet aircraft is higher than that for piston engine aircraft.* ■ noun the point at which the condition or amount of something is most advantageous ○ *Generally speaking, engine output is at its optimum at cruising speed.*

**optimum code** noun COMPUT a coding system that provides the fastest access and retrieval time for stored data items

**oral** adjective ANAT referring to the mouth

**orally** adverb BIOL by the mouth ○ *The medication cannot be taken orally.*

**ORB** abbreviation COMPUT Object Request Broker

**orbit** ASTRON noun the curved path of a planet or satellite round another astronomical object ■ verb to go round a astronomical object in a curved path

**orbital** adjective ASTRON moving in an orbit

**orbital velocity** noun ASTRON the velocity of a body at a particular point in its orbit (NOTE: The Earth moves about the Sun at an average 30 km per second, while the Moon moves at only about 1 km per second around the Earth.)

**order** noun 1. a sequence of occurrence ○ *The firing order of sparking plugs in a piston engine is 1,3, 4, 2.* □ **in the order of** approximately □ **in order to** for the purpose of 2. a command or instruction 3. BIOL a classification of animals or plants, formed of several families (NOTE: Orders of animals have names ending in **-a**; orders of plants have names ending in **-ales**.) ■ verb 1. to direct or instruct someone to do something or that something be done or brought 2. to sort things into a particular sequence

**ordered list** noun COMPUT a list of data items which has been sorted into an order

**order of reaction** *noun* CHEM a way of classifying chemical reactions according to the concentration of a part of the reaction

**ore** *noun* EARTH SCI a mineral found in the ground containing a metal which can be extracted from it ○ *Iron ore deposits were found in the mountains.* ○ *The ore is heated to a high temperature to extract the metal.*

**ore-bearing** *adjective* EARTH SCI referring to rock that contains ore

**ore body** *noun* EARTH SCI a mass of ore that can be dug and processed

**OR function** *noun* MATHS a logical function that produces a true output if any input is true

COMMENT: The result of the OR function will be 1 if either or both inputs are 1; if both inputs are 0, then the result is 0.

**organ** *noun* BIOL a part of an organism that is distinct from other parts and has a particular function, e.g. an eye or a flower

**organ culture** *noun* MED the storing of an organ removed from someone's body in an artificial environment

**organelle** *noun* BIOL a specialised structure within a cell, e.g. a mitochondrion or nucleus

**organic** *adjective* **1.** ANAT referring to organs in the body **2.** CHEM containing carbon **3.** AGRIC referring to food produced naturally, without the use of any artificial fertilisers or pesticides, or to the production of such food

**organic acids** *plural noun* CHEM acids that come from plants, taken to stimulate the production of urine

**organic carbon** *noun* BIOCHEM carbon that comes from an animal or plant. Abbreviation **OC**

**organic chemistry** *noun* CHEM a branch of chemistry dealing with compounds that contain carbon

**organic compound** *noun* CHEM a compound that contains carbon

**organic disorder** *noun* MED a disorder caused by changes in body tissue or in an organ

**organic farming** *noun* AGRIC a method of farming which does not involve the use of artificial fertilisers or pesticides ○ *Organic farming may become more economic than conventional farming.*

**organic fertiliser** *noun* AGRIC a fertiliser made from dead or decaying plant matter or animal wastes, e.g. farmyard manure or bone meal

**organic matter** *noun* BIOL, CHEM a substance which comes from living organism and contains carbon

**organise, organize** *verb* **1.** to arrange something into a system ○ *Organise your notes so that you can find things easily.* **2.** to plan something ○ *organised a conference*

**organism** *noun* BIOL any individual life form that is able to reproduce and grow, e.g. a plant, animal or microorganism

**organochlorine** *noun* **1.** CHEM a chlorinated hydrocarbon **2.** CHEM, AGRIC a chemical compound containing chlorine, used as an insecticide

COMMENT: Organochlorine insecticides are very persistent, with a long half-life of up to 15 years. Chlorinated hydrocarbon insecticides can enter the food chain and kill small animals and birds which feed on insects.

**organ of reproduction** *noun* ANAT same as **reproductive organ**

**organometallic compound** *noun* CHEM organic compound that includes a carbon–metal bond

**organophosphate, organophosphorous insecticide** *noun* **1.** CHEM an organic compound that contains phosphate groups **2.** AGRIC a synthetic insecticide such as malathion that is based on organophosphate and attacks the nervous system. Also called **organophosphorous insecticide**

COMMENT: Organophosphates are not as persistent as organochlorines and do not enter the food chain. They are, however, very toxic and need to be handled carefully, as breathing in their vapour may be fatal.

**organophosphorous** *adjective* CHEM (*of an organic compound*) containing phosphorus

**organophosphorous insecticide** *noun* AGRIC same as **organophosphate**

**organotherapy** *noun* MED the treatment of a disease by using an extract from the organ of an animal, e.g. using liver extract to treat anaemia

**organo-tin paint** *noun* INDUST an antifouling paint which is based on tin

(NOTE: It is extremely toxic to organisms in the sea.)

**organ transplant** *noun* MED the removal of an organ from one person and insertion of it into another

**orgasm** *noun* PHYSIOL the climax of sexual excitement, characterised by contraction of the muscles of the genitals and pleasurable sensations, usually accompanied by ejaculation in males

**OR gate** *noun* ELECTRONICS an electronic circuit that provides the OR function

**oriental** *adjective* EARTH SCI referring to the east

**Oriental Region** *noun* EARTH SCI a biogeographical region, part of Arctogea, comprising South and Southeast Asia, Indonesia and the Philippines

**orientate** *verb* NAVIG to locate something in relation to a compass direction ○ *The first step in map reading is to orientate the chart by relating the direction of land features to their representation on the chart.*

**orientation** *noun* NAVIG **1.** a position in relation to a compass direction **2.** the process of locating something in relation to a compass direction

**orifice** *noun* an opening, mouth or vent ○ *The liquid expands and builds up a pressure differential across an orifice which leads to the expansion chamber.*

**origin** *noun* **1.** a point where something starts or comes from ○ *the origin of life* ○ *An air mass takes on the characteristics of its place of origin.* **2.** ANAT the end of muscle that is attached to a part of the skeleton that does not move as a result of a contraction. Compare **insertion 3.** ANAT the point where a nerve or blood vessel begins **4.** GEOG a base from which a map projection is drawn ○ *The value of convergence used is correct at the parallel of origin.* **5.** COMPUT a position on a display screen to which all coordinates are referenced, usually the top left hand corner of the screen **6.** COMPUT the location in memory at which the first instruction of a program is stored

**original** *adjective* used first or made first ■ *noun* COMPUT a master data disk, from which a copy can be made

**originate** *verb* to come or bring something into being ○ *Tropical revolving storms originate within 5–15° of the*

equator. ○ *Aircraft fires after an emergency landing often originate in the wing area.*

**origination** *noun* the work involved in creating something

**ornithine** *noun* BIOCHEM an amino acid made in the liver during the formation of urea

**ornithological** *adjective* ZOOL referring to ornithology

**ornithologist** *noun* ZOOL a scientist who studies birds

**ornithology** *noun* ZOOL the study of birds

**orographic effect** *noun* METEOROL an atmospheric disturbance that is caused by, or relates to, the existence of mountains or other high land

**orphan** *noun* PRINTING the first line of a paragraph of text printed alone at the bottom of a column, with the rest of the paragraph at the top of the next column

**orphan site** *noun* ENVIRON an area of contaminated land for which both polluter and owner reject responsibility

**orthophosphoric acid** *noun* CHEM same as **phosphoric acid**

**orthopteran** *noun* INSECTS a member of the group of generally large, winged insects that includes cockroaches, mantises, locusts and crickets. Order: Orthoptera. (NOTE: They are often good runners and jumpers, but many are flightless.)

**orthotropism** *noun* BOT growth directly towards or away from a stimulus

**Os** *symbol* CHEM ELEM osmium

**OS** *abbreviation* COMPUT operating system

**oscillate** *verb* **1.** to move regularly between extremes **2.** ELEC (*of electrical current*) to increase or decrease regularly, producing oscillations

**oscillation** *noun* ELEC a regular movement from side to side

**oscillator** *noun* ELECTRONICS an electronic circuit that produces a pulse or a signal at a particular frequency ○ *The local oscillator replicates the radio frequency of the frequency generator at the transmitter.*

**OSI** *abbreviation* COMPUT Open System Interconnection

**-osis** *suffix* MED referring to disease

**osmiridium** *noun* METALL a very hard natural alloy of osmium and iridium, often also containing platinum and other metals

**osmium** *noun* CHEM ELEM a hard white metallic element with a very strong smell, used as a catalyst (NOTE: It is the densest known element. The chemical symbol is **Os**; the atomic number is **76** and the atomic weight is **190.2.**)

**osmoreceptor** *noun* ANAT a cell in the hypothalamus which checks the level of osmotic pressure in the blood and regulates the amount of water in the blood

**osmoregulation** *noun* PHYSIOL the process by which cells and simple organisms maintain a balance with the fluid in their surroundings. Also called **osmotic regulation**

**osmosis** *noun* CHEM a movement of a solution from one region through a semi-permeable membrane to another region, in which enough of the molecules in solution pass through the membrane to make the two solutions balance in concentration

**osmotic pressure** *noun* PHYS the pressure required to stop the flow of a solvent through a membrane

**osmotic regulation** *noun* PHYSIOL same as **osmoregulation**

**OSPF** *abbreviation* COMPUT open shortest path first

**osteo-** *prefix* ANAT bone

**osteomalacia** *noun* MED a condition where the bones become soft because of lack of calcium or phosphate

**osteopathy** *noun* MED **1.** a way of treating diseases and disorders by massage and manipulation of bones and joints **2.** any disease of bone

**osteophony** *noun* BIOL conduction of sound waves to the inner ear through the bones of the skull

**osteoporosis** *noun* MED a condition in which the bones become thin, porous and brittle, owing to low levels of oestrogen, lack of calcium and lack of physical exercise

**OTEC** *abbreviation* METEOROL Ocean Thermal Energy Conversion

**otic ganglion** *noun* ANAT a ganglion associated with the mandibular nerve where it leaves the skull

**Otto cycle** *noun* PHYS a repeating sequence of processes that convert heat into work, e.g. the four-stroke engine cycle of suction, compression, ignition, and expulsion

**outage** *noun* ELEC the time during which a system is not operational

**outbreak** *noun* **1.** a sudden start ○ *Showers are local outbreaks of precipitation from detached cumulus or cumulonimbus.* **2.** MED a series of cases of a disease which start suddenly ○ *a typhoid outbreak*

**outbreeding** *noun* BIOL breeding between individuals who are not related. Compare **inbreeding**

**outcrop** EARTH SCI *noun* an area of rock which stands out above the surface of the soil ■ *verb* (*of rock*) to stand out above the surface of the soil

**outer** *adjective* furthest away from the centre ○ *The outer coating of the seed is very hard.*

**outer ear** *noun* ANAT the ear on the outside of the head together with the passage leading to the eardrum

**outer space** *noun* ASTRON an area outside Earth's atmosphere in which the Sun, stars and planets move

**outfall, outfall sewer** *noun* ENVIRON a pipe which takes sewage, either raw or treated, and discharges it into a river, lake or the sea ○ *27% of outfalls discharge totally untreated sewage.* ○ *Sewage should be discharged through outfall pipes which are situated far enough from the shore.*

**outflow** *noun* a flow in an outward direction ○ *The outflow valve is controlled by the cabin pressure controller.*

**outlet** *noun* **1.** a passage for exit or escape **2.** ELEC a connection or point in a circuit or network where a signal or data can be accessed

**outlier** *noun* **1.** ECOL an organism that occurs naturally some distance away from the principal area in which its species is found **2.** EARTH SCI an area in which younger rocks are completely surrounded by older rocks

**outline** *noun* **1.** a line around the shape of something ○ *Warning labels have a solid red outline.* **2.** a shape ○ *At low level, features are most easily recognised from their outline in elevation.* ○ *Cumulus cloud has detached domes or towers which are generally dense and* *have sharp outlines.* **3.** a summary ■ *verb* **1.** to form or draw round the shape of something ○ *The additional material is outlined in red.* **2.** to explain something simply and briefly ○ *The changes in conditions are outlined in the next paragraph.*

**outline flowchart** *noun* COMPUT a flowchart of the main features, steps and decisions in a program or system

**outline font** *noun* COMPUT a printer or display font stored as a set of outlines that mathematically describe the shape of each character

**output** *noun* **1.** the product of a process ○ *Air density will affect the output of the engine.* ○ *The function of the supercharger is to increase the power output.* **2.** COMPUT information or data that is transferred from a central processing unit or the main memory to another device such as a monitor, printer or secondary storage device **3.** COMPUT the action of transferring information or data from a store to a user ■ *verb* COMPUT to transfer data from a computer to a monitor or printer ○ *Finished documents can be output to the laser printer.*

**output area, output block** *noun* COMPUT a section of memory that contains data to be transferred to an output device

**output-bound** *adjective* COMPUT unable to function at normal speed because of a slower peripheral

**output buffer register** *noun* COMPUT a temporary store for data that is waiting to be output

**output device** *noun* COMPUT a device such as a monitor or printer that allows information to be displayed

**output file** *noun* COMPUT a set of records that have been completely processed according to various parameters

**output formatter** *noun* COMPUT **1.** a piece of software used to format data or programs and output them so that they are compatible with another sort of storage medium **2.** a part of a word processor program that formats text according to embedded commands

**output-limited** *adjective* COMPUT same as **output-bound**

**output mode** *noun* COMPUT a computer mode in which data is moved from internal storage or the central processing unit to external devices

**output port** *noun* COMPUT a circuit or connector that allows a computer to output or transmit data to another machine or device

**output register** *noun* COMPUT a register that stores data to be output until the receiver is ready or the channel is free

**output stream** *noun* COMPUT a communications channel carrying data output to a peripheral

**outward** *adjective* moving away from the centre or starting point ○ *The piston draws fluid into the cylinders on the outward stroke and expels fluid into the system on the inward stroke.* Opposite **inward** ■ *adverb* US same as **outwards**

**outwards** *adverb* away from the centre or starting point ○ *The door opens outwards.* (NOTE: The US term is **outward**)

**outwash** *noun* EARTH SCI water which flows from a melting glacier and creates deposits of silt

**outwash deposit, outwash fan** *noun* EARTH SCI a silt deposit formed by a melting glacier

**OV** *abbreviation* COMPUT overflow

**ova** *noun* ZOOL plural of **ovum**

**oval** *adjective* shaped like an egg

**oval window** *noun* ANAT a membrane-covered opening between the middle ear and the inner ear that transmits sound vibrations

**ovary** *noun* ANAT one of two organs in a woman that produce ova or egg cells and secrete the female hormone oestrogen

**over-** *prefix* too much

**overall** *adjective* including everything ○ *The total aerodynamic losses result in an overall turbine efficiency of 92%.* ■ *adverb* generally ○ *Overall, the test was a success.* ■ *noun* a one-piece item of protective clothing

**overalls** *plural noun* protective trousers with a bib and straps over the shoulders ○ *Wear overalls to protect your clothes.*

**overburden** *noun* EARTH SCI soil and rock lying on top of a coal seam or a mineral vein which is dug away from the surface of the land in strip mining to expose the coal or mineral below

**overburden pressure** *noun* EARTH SCI the force of the soil or rock pressing down onto a coal seam or mineral vein

**overcome** *verb* **1.** to fight something and win ○ *They failed to overcome public opposition to the construction of a nuclear power station.* **2.** MED to make someone lose consciousness ○ *Two people were overcome by smoke in the fire.*

**overcropping** *noun* AGRIC the practice of growing too many crops on poor soil, which has the effect of impoverishing the soil still further

**overcultivated** *adjective* AGRIC too intensively cultivated and so impoverished

**overexploit** *verb* ENVIRON to cultivate soil to the extent of impoverishing it or to work mineral deposits or use up other resources to the extent that they become exhausted

**overexploitation** *noun* ENVIRON the use of natural resources to the extent that they become exhausted ○ *Overexploitation has reduced herring stocks by half.*

**overfish** *verb* FISHERY to catch too many fish so that the fish become rare

**overfishing** *noun* FISHERY the catching of too many fish so that the fish become rare ○ *Herring stocks have been reduced by overfishing.*

**overflow** *noun* **1.** excess liquid that flows over the edge of a container **2.** COMPUT a mathematical result that is greater than the limits of the computer's number storage system **3.** a situation in a network when the number of transmissions is greater than the line capacity and they are transferred by another route. Abbreviation **OV** ■ *verb* to flow over the edge of a container ○ *The floods made the reservoir overflow.* ○ *The river overflowed its banks and flooded hundred of hectares of farmland.*

**overflow bit, overflow flag, overflow indicator** *noun* COMPUT a single

bit in a word that is set to 1 if a mathematical overflow has occurred

**overflow pipe** *noun* a pipe attached to the top of a container to channel away excess liquid

**overgraze** *verb* AGRIC to graze a pasture so much that it loses nutrients and is no longer rich enough to provide food for livestock

**overgrazing** *noun* AGRIC the grazing of a pasture so intensively that it loses nutrients and is no longer rich enough to provide food for livestock ○ *Overgrazing has led to soil erosion and desertification.*

**overhaul** *verb* to take apart and examine something carefully in order to repair, clean or adjust it ○ *To overhaul the whole system will take a couple of days.* ■ *noun* the act of taking something apart as a machine or engine apart in order to repair, clean or adjust it ○ *The moving parts require periodic overhaul.*

**overheat** *verb* to get too hot ○ *An acceleration/deceleration control is fitted to prevent the turbine assembly from overheating during acceleration.*

**overland flow** *noun* EARTH SCI a movement of rainwater or meltwater over the surface of the ground in a broad thin layer

**overlap** *noun* a part of one thing covering something else ■ *verb* **1.** to have an area or range in common with something else **2.** to cover part of something else ○ *The maps overlap each other at the edges by three centimetres.* (NOTE: **overlapping – overlapped**)

**overlay** *noun* COMPUT a small section of a program loaded into memory only when required (NOTE: This is done when the entire program is bigger than the main memory capacity of a computer.)

**overload** *noun* an excessive amount of work or electricity ○ *Resettable circuit protective devices should be designed so that when an overload or circuit fault exists, they will open the circuit.* ■ *verb* **1.** to load a device or system such as an electrical circuit with too much work ○ *Prevent overloading of the pumps.* **2.** to load something too heavily ○ *The aircraft failed to gain* *height after take-off because it was overloaded.*

**overproduction** *noun* INDUST the production of too much of a commodity

**override** *verb* to take over control of the operation of an automatic device or system ○ *A circuit-protective device must not be of a type which can be overridden manually.* (NOTE: **overriding – overrode – overridden**)

**overscan** *noun* COMPUT **1.** a faulty or badly adjusted monitor in which the displayed image runs off the edge of the screen **2.** display equipment in which the picture beam scans past the screen boundaries to ensure that the image fills the screen

**overstorey** *noun* FORESTRY the topmost vegetation layer in a forest formed by the highest trees. Also called **overwood**

**overtone** *noun* ACOUSTICS a higher musical note produced at the same time as the basic note, affecting the overall sound quality

**overuse** *noun* the excessive use of something ○ *The overuse of pesticides is contaminating the rivers.* ■ *verb* to use something too much ○ *Farmers are warned against overusing chemical fertilisers.*

**over-voltage protection** *noun* ELEC a safety device that prevents a power supply voltage exceeding certain specified limits

**overwinter** *verb* **1.** ZOOL to spend winter in a particular place ○ *The herds overwinter on the southern plains.* **2.** BIOL to remain alive though the winter ○ *Geraniums will not overwinter in areas that have frost.*

**overwood** *noun* FORESTRY same as **overstorey**

**overwrite** *verb* COMPUT to write data to a location and, in doing so, to destroy any data already contained in that location ○ *The latest data input has overwritten the old information.*

**ovicide** *noun* AGRIC a substance, especially an insecticide, which kills eggs

**oviduct** *noun* ANAT a tube that transports eggs from the ovary to the uterus in mammals or in birds and reptiles secretes the eggshell and conveys the egg to the outside (NOTE: In mammals it is also called fallopian tube.)

**oviparity** *noun* ZOOL animal reproduction in which a female lays eggs before or after fertilisation, as occurs in some fish and birds

**oviparous** *adjective* ZOOL referring to an animal that carries and lays eggs. Compare **viviparous**

**ovipositor** *noun* ZOOL a tube used for egg-laying (NOTE: It is present in turtles, some fish and many female insects.)

**ovoviviparity** *noun* ZOOL animal reproduction in which a female carries eggs within her body, where they hatch and the embryo stays protected (NOTE: It occurs in some reptiles and fish.)

**ovulate** *verb* PHYSIOL to release an ovum from the mature ovarian follicle into the fallopian tube

**ovulation** *noun* PHYSIOL the release of an ovum from the mature ovarian follicle into the fallopian tube

**ovule** *noun* BIOL an immature egg or an unfertilised seed

**ovum** *noun* BIOL a female egg cell which, when fertilised by a spermatazoon, begins to develop into an embryo (NOTE: The plural is **ova**. For other terms referring to ova, see words beginning with **oo-**.)

COMMENT: At regular intervals (in the human female, once a month) ova, or unfertilised eggs, leave the ovaries and move down the fallopian tubes to the uterus. At the point where the fallopian tubes join the uterus an ovum may be fertilised by a sperm cell.

**oxalic acid** *noun* CHEM a colourless poisonous acid. Formula: $H_2C_2O_4$.

**ox-bow lake** *noun* EARTH SCI a curved lake, formed when a large curve of a river becomes cut off from the main body of a river by silt

**oxidant** *noun* CHEM same as **oxidising agent**

**oxidase** *noun* CHEM an enzyme which encourages oxidation by removing hydrogen

**oxidation** *noun* CHEM a chemical reaction in which a substance combines with oxygen with loss of electrons ○ *When aluminium surfaces are exposed* *to the atmosphere, a thin invisible oxide skin forms immediately that protects the metal from further oxidation.*

**oxidation–reduction** *noun* CHEM a reversible chemical reaction between two substances where one is oxidised and the other is reduced

**oxide** *noun* CHEM a chemical compound of oxygen

COMMENT: Carbon compounds form oxides when metabolised with oxygen in the body, ultimately producing carbon dioxide.

**oxidisability, oxidizability** *noun* CHEM the ability of a substance to oxidise

**oxidisable matter** *noun* CHEM a substance that can oxidise

**oxidise, oxidize** *verb* to form an oxide by the reaction of oxygen with another chemical substance ○ *Over a period of time, the metal is oxidised by contact with air.*

**oxidising agent** *noun* CHEM a substance that forms an oxide with another substance. Also called **oxidant**

**oxidising atmosphere** *noun* CHEM a mixture of gases that contains oxygen and converts elements into oxides through chemical reactions

**oxo process** *noun* CHEM a method of manufacturing aldehydes in which a mixture of carbon monoxide, hydrogen and alkenes are passed over a catalyst at high pressure and temperature

**oxychlorination** *noun* INDUST the process of neutralising bacteria in water intended for drinking

**oxygen** *noun* CHEM ELEM a colourless, odourless gas, essential to human life, constituting 21% by volume of the Earth's atmosphere ○ *Our bodies can get oxygen through the lungs.* (NOTE: The chemical symbol is **O**; the atomic number is **8** and the atomic weight is **16.00**.)

COMMENT: Oxygen is an important constituent of living matter, as well as water and air. It is formed by plants from carbon dioxide in the atmosphere during photosynthesis and released back into the air. Oxygen is absorbed from the air into the bloodstream through the lungs and is carried to the tissues along the arteries. It is essential to normal metabolism.

**oxygen absorbent** *adjective* CHEM able to take up oxygen

**oxygenate** *verb* **1.** MED to treat blood with oxygen **2.** CHEM to become filled with oxygen

**oxygenation** *noun* CHEM the process of becoming filled with oxygen

**oxygen debt** *noun* PHYSIOL the amount of oxygen needed to replenish the body's oxygen stores after they become depleted by exercise such as running

**oxygen sink** *noun* BOT a part of a plant which stores oxygen

**oxyhaemoglobin** *noun* BIOCHEM a compound of haemoglobin and oxygen, which carries oxygen in arterial blood from the lungs to the tissues

**oxyntic cell** *noun* BIOL a cell in the gastric gland which secretes hydrochloric acid. Also called **parietal cell**

**oxyphobe** *noun* BOT a plant which cannot survive in acid soil

**oxyphyte** *noun* BOT a plant which lives on acid soil

**oxytocin** *noun* BIOCHEM a hormone produced by the pituitary gland, which controls the contractions of the uterus and encourages the flow of milk

COMMENT: An extract of oxytocin is sometimes used as an injection to start contractions of the uterus in childbirth.

**ozone** *noun* EARTH SCI poisonous form of oxygen found naturally in the atmosphere, which is toxic to humans at concentrations above 0.1 parts per million. Formula: $O_3$.

COMMENT: Ozone is created in the stratosphere by the effect of ultraviolet radiation from the Sun on oxygen. Ozone then splits and becomes oxygen again as part of a continuous cycle of chemical change. It is destroyed by reaction with nitric oxide (created by burning fossil fuel) or water or chlorine compounds (from chlorofluorocarbons used in aerosols and packaging). The reduction of ozone in the stratosphere by any of these reactions creates a thin area or 'hole' in the ozone layer.

**ozone-depleting potential** *noun* ENVIRON a measurement of the effect of a substance on the amount of ozone in the atmosphere. Abbreviation **ODP**

**ozone depletion** *noun* ENVIRON the loss of ozone from the atmosphere

**ozone-friendly** *adjective* ENVIRON not harmful to the ozone layer

**ozone hole** *noun* ENVIRON a thinning or gap in the ozone layer, which forms over Antarctica each year at the end of winter

**ozone layer** *noun* METEOROL the layer of ozone in the atmosphere between 20 and 50 km above the surface of the Earth. Also called **ozonosphere**

COMMENT: The ozone layer in the stratosphere acts as a protection against the harmful effects of the Sun's radiation, and the destruction or reduction of the layer has the effect of allowing more radiation to pass through the atmosphere with harmful effects such as skin cancer on humans. The first ozone hole was detected over Antarctica.

**ozonise, ozonize** *verb* CHEM **1.** to convert oxygen into ozone **2.** to treat a substance with ozone

**ozonosphere** *noun* METEOROL same as **ozone layer**

# P

**p** *abbreviation* MEASURE pico-

**P** *abbreviation* MEASURE peta- ■ *symbol* **1.** pecta- **2.** CHEM phosphorus

**Pa** *symbol* MEASURE, PHYS pascal

**pachytene** *noun* BIOL the third stage of meiosis, during which the paired chromosomes become shorter and thicker and divide into four chromatids

**pack** *noun* **1.** ZOOL a group of predatory animals which live and hunt together, especially of animals of the dog family such as wolves but also of other animals such as killer whales **2.** INDUST a detachable system ○ *Circuit packs consist of basic decision-making elements, referred to as logic gates, each performing combinational operations.* ○ *A power pack system is one in which most of the major components, with the exception of the actuators and, in some systems, the pumps, are included in a self-contained unit.* ■ *verb* **1.** to put things into a container for selling or sending ○ *to pack goods into cartons* ○ *The diskettes are packed in plastic wrappers.* ○ *The computer is packed in expanded polystyrene before being shipped.* **2.** COMPUT to store a quantity of data in a reduced form, often by representing several characters of data with one stored character

**packaged** *adjective* wrapped in paper, plastic, cardboard or other covering

**packaging** *noun* INDUST paper, plastic, cardboard or other covering used to wrap an object ○ *Many of the packaging materials we used to throw away may now be re-used to save energy and raw materials.*

**packed decimal** *noun* COMPUT a decimal digit stored in a small space, by using only four bits for each digit

**packed format** *noun* COMPUT a format in which two binary coded decimal digits are stored within one computer word or a byte, usually achieved by removing the check or a parity bit

**packet** *noun* COMPUT a group of data bits which can be transmitted as a group from one node to another over a network

**packet assembler/disassembler** *noun* COMPUT a dedicated computer which converts serial data from asynchronous terminals to a form that can be transmitted along a synchronous packet switched network. Abbreviation **PAD**

**packet Internet groper** COMPUT full form of **PING**

**packet switching** *noun* COMPUT a method of sending data across a wide area network in small packets, which are then reassembled in correct order at the receiving end

**packet switching service** *noun* COMPUT a commercial data transmission service that sends data over its wide area network using packet switching. Abbreviation **PSS**

**pack ice** *noun* EARTH SCI a large area of ice floating at sea consisting of a mixture of ice of various sizes and ages crushed together so that there is little or no open water

**packing** *noun* **1.** INDUST the action of putting goods into boxes and wrapping them for shipping ○ *What is the cost of the packing?* ○ *Packing is included in the price.* **2.** INDUST material used to protect goods ○ *sealed in airtight packing* **3.** COMPUT the inclusion of large amounts of data in a small area of storage. Opposite **padding 4.** COMPUT a number of bits that can be stored in a unit area on a magnetic disk or tape

**pad** *noun* COMPUT same as **keypad** ■ *verb* **1.** COMPUT to fill something out **2.** to cushion something

**PAD** *abbreviation* COMPUT packet assembler/disassembler

**pad character** *noun* COMPUT an extra character added to a string, packet or file until it is a required size

**padding** *noun* COMPUT the addition of characters or digits to fill out a string or packet until it is the right length. Opposite **packing**

**paddy, padi** *noun* AGRIC a growing rice crop

**page** *noun* **1.** a sheet of paper **2.** COMPUT an amount of text, displayed on a computer monitor or screen **3.** COMPUT a section of main store, which contains data or programs **4.** COMPUT one section of a main program which can be loaded into main memory when required ■ *verb* **1.** to make up a text into pages **2.** COMPUT to divide a computer backing store into sections to allow long programs to be executed in a small main memory

**paged address** *noun* COMPUT an actual physical memory address that is calculated from a logical address and its page address

**page description programming language** *noun* COMPUT a programming language that accepts commands to define the size, position and type style for text or graphics on a page

**paged-memory management unit** *noun* COMPUT an electronic logic circuit that manages the translation between logical addresses that refer to a particular page and the actual physical address that is being referenced

**paged-memory scheme** *noun* COMPUT a way of dividing memory into small blocks called pages which are then allocated a page number

**page printer** *noun* COMPUT a printer, usually a laser printer, which composes one page of text within memory and then prints it in one pass

**pagination** *noun* **1.** the numbering of pages in a book **2.** COMPUT the process of dividing text into pages

**paging** *noun* COMPUT a virtual memory technique of splitting main memory into small blocks called **pages** which are allocated an address and which can be called up when required

COMMENT: A virtual memory management system stores data as pages in memory to provide an apparently larger capacity main memory by storing unused pages in backing store, copying them into main memory only when required.

**paging algorithm** *noun* COMPUT a formula by which the memory management allocates memory to pages, also covering the transfer from backing storage to main memory in the most efficient way

**PAH** *abbreviation* CHEM polycyclic aromatic hydrocarbon

**paint** *noun* **1.** a liquid substance put on a surface to give it colour or to protect it **2.** COMPUT colour and pattern used to fill an area ■ *verb* COMPUT (*in a graphics program*) to fill an enclosed graphics shape with a colour

**pain threshold** *noun* PHYSIOL the point at which a person cannot bear pain without a significant reaction □ **to have a low** *or* **a high pain threshold** to be unable to bear much pain *or* considerable pain

**pair** *noun* a set of two matched items, similar in appearance and function ○ *A brake control valve usually contains four elements, one pair for the brakes on each side, to provide duplicated control.*

**paired register** *noun* COMPUT a basic word size register used with another as one large word size register, often for storing address words ○ *The 8-bit CPU uses a paired register to provide a 16-bit address register.*

**PAL** *abbreviation* COMPUT phase alternation line

**Palaearctic Region** *noun* EARTH SCI a biogeographical region, part of Arctogea covering Europe, North Asia and North Africa

**palaeo-** *prefix* ancient or prehistoric (NOTE: The US spelling is **paleo-**.)

**palaeobotany** *noun* BOT the study of fossil plants

**palaeoclimatology** *noun* METEOROL the scientific study of the climate of the geological past

**palaeoecology** *noun* ECOL the study of the ecology of fossils

**palaeomagnetism** *noun* EARTH SCI the study of the magnetism of ancient rocks

COMMENT: Rocks indicate the direction and therefore the position of the magnetic pole, which slowly changes its position over thousands of years, at the time the rocks were formed.

**palaeontology** *noun* BIOL the study of fossil organisms

**palaeozoology** *noun* ZOOL the study of fossil animals

**paleo-** *prefix* US spelling of **palaeo-**

**palette** *noun* COMPUT a range of colours which can be used on a printer or computer display

**palindrome** *noun* GENETICS a segment of DNA in which nucleotide sequences in complementary strands are the same when read from opposite ends of the segment, e.g. the sequences GGTACC and CCATGG

**palladium** *noun* CHEM ELEM a shiny metallic element that resembles platinum used as a catalyst and in electrical contacts, jewellery, dental fillings and medical instruments (NOTE: The chemical symbol is **Pd**; the atomic number is **46** and the atomic weight is **106.40**.)

**palm** *noun* **1.** TREES a large tropical plant like a tree with branching fern-like leaves, producing fruits which give oil and other foodstuffs **2.** ANAT the inner surface of the hand or the underside of a mammal's forefoot that is often in contact with the ground

**palmitic acid** *noun* CHEM a waxy solid derived from plant and animal fats and oils and used in making soap and candles and as a food additive. Formula: $C_{15}H_{31}COOH$.

**palm kernel oil** *noun* FOOD INDUST a vegetable oil produced from the kernels of the oil palm nut

**palmtop** *noun* COMPUT a personal computer that is small enough to be held in one hand and operated with the other ○ *This palmtop has a tiny keyboard and twenty-line LCD screen.*

**palp** *noun* ZOOL a sensory appendage near the mouth of many invertebrate animals

**paludism** *noun* MED same as **malaria**

**palynology** *noun* BOT the scientific study of pollen, especially of pollen found in peat and coal deposits. Also called **pollen analysis**

**pampas** *noun* EARTH SCI a wide area of grassy plains found in South America

**pampas grass** *noun* PLANTS a type of tall feathery grass found on the plains of South America and grown elsewhere for ornament. Latin name: *Cortaderia Selloana.*

**pan** *verb* **1.** COMPUT (*in computer graphics*) to move a viewing window smoothly across an image that is too wide to display all at once **2.** COMPUT (*in MIDI or sound*) to adjust the balance of a sound between the two stereo channels **3.** INDUST to search for precious minerals such as gold by passing sandy deposits through a sieve in running water, allowing the smaller particles to be washed away

**PAN** *abbreviation* CHEM peroxyacetyl nitrate

**pan-** *prefix* affecting everything or everywhere

**pancreas** *noun* ANAT a large gland next to the stomach that secretes digestive enzymes and also the hormones involved in regulating sugars in the blood

**pancreatic juice** *noun* PHYSIOL a watery alkaline secretion from the pancreas that contains digestive enzymes that break down food in the small intestine

**pandemic** *adjective, noun* MED (an epidemic disease) which affects many parts of the world. Compare **endemic, epidemic**

**panel** *noun* **1.** a flat, often rectangular piece of a construction ○ *Access to the engine compartment is normally via hinged cowling panels.* **2.** a board with switches, dials, control knobs or similar features for indicating performance ○ *an instrument panel*

**panemone** *noun* ENG a type of windmill in which flat surfaces spin round a vertical axis

**Pangaea** *noun* EARTH SCI an ancient continent thought to have contained all Earth's land mass before it gradually broke up into pieces that drifted apart

**panicle** *noun* BOT an inflorescence in which several small flowers branch from the same stem

**pantothenic acid** *noun* BIOCHEM a vitamin of the vitamin B complex, found in liver, yeast and eggs

**papain** *noun* BIOCHEM an enzyme found in the juice of the papaya, used as a meat tenderiser and in medicine to help wounds to heal

**paper** *noun* INDUST a substance made from the pulp of wood, rags or fibre rolled into sheets, used for writing on, wrapping and other purposes

**paper chromatography** *noun* CHEM chromatography that uses a strip of paper as the porous medium

**paper feed** *noun* COMPUT a mechanism that moves paper through a printer

**paper pulp** *noun* INDUST a wet mixture of pulverized of wood, rags or fibre from which paper is made

**para-** *prefix* **1.** similar to **2.** changed or beyond

**parabola** *noun* MATHS one of the conic sections, a curve formed by the intersection of a cone with a plave parallel to its side (NOTE: Parabolic sections have the property of being able to bring light to a focus at a single point, so that telescope makers aspire to create parabolic optical surfaces.)

**parabolic** *adjective* MATHS referring to a parabola

**paraffin** *noun* **1.** CHEM a saturated aliphatic hydrocarbon **2.** INDUST same as **paraffin oil**

**paraffin oil** *noun* INDUST oil produced from petroleum, used as a fuel in aircraft engines, for domestic heating and lighting and as a solvent. Also called **paraffin**

**paraffin wax** *noun* INDUST a white insoluble solid which melts at between 50 and 60° C, used to make candles, as a waterproofing and as the base of some ointments

**paragraph** *noun* COMPUT **1.** a section of text between two return characters **2.** a 16-byte section of memory which starts at a hexadecimal address that can be evenly divided by 16

**parallax** *noun* PHYS, ASTRON the change in apparent position of an object caused by movement on the part of the observer

**parallel** *adjective* **1.** (*of lines, planes or curved surfaces, routes or roads*) side by side and having the same distance between them at every point □ **in parallel** (*of electrical circuits*) arranged so as to join at common points at each end rather than to each other in sequence ○ *When batteries are connected in parallel, voltage remains constant but capacity increase.* **2.** COMPUT (*of a computer system*) in which two or more processors operate simultaneously on one or more items of data **3.** COMPUT transmitting two or more bits of a word over separate lines at the same time ■

*noun* **1.** a line which is parallel to another **2.** EARTH SCI an imaginary line running round the Earth, linking points at an equal distance from the equator. Also called **parallel of latitude 3.** GEOG a line representing a parallel on a map or chart

COMMENT: The parallels are numbered upwards from the equator and some of them act as national boundaries: the 49th parallel marks most of the border between the USA and Canada.

**parallel adder** *noun* COMPUT a number of adders joined together, allowing several digits to be added at once

**parallel circuit** *noun* ELEC an electric circuit in which all the components are connected directly to the voltage supply, so each component receives a fraction of the current

**parallel computer** *noun* COMPUT a computer with one or more logic or arithmetic units, allowing parallel processing

**parallel connection** *noun* COMPUT a connector on a computer allowing parallel data to be transferred ○ *Their transmission rate is 60 000 bps through parallel connection.*

**parallel data transmission** *noun* COMPUT the transmission of bits of data simultaneously along a number of data lines

**parallel input/output** *noun* COMPUT data input or output from a computer in a parallel form. Abbreviation **PIO**

**parallel input/parallel output** *noun* COMPUT a device that can accept and transmit parallel data. Abbreviation **PIPO**

**parallel input/serial output** *noun* COMPUT a device that can accept parallel data and transmit serial data. Abbreviation **PISO**

**parallel of latitude** *noun* EARTH SCI **1.** an angular distance north or south of the Earth's equator, measured in degrees, minutes and seconds, along a meridian **2.** an imaginary line running round the Earth, linking points at an equal distance from the equator. Also called **parallel**

**parallelogram** *noun* MATHS a four-sided figure in which both pairs of opposite sides are parallel to each other and of equal length and the opposite angles are equal

**parallelogram of forces** *noun* MATHS a graphical method of finding the resultant force from two separate forces by drawing the two forces as two sides of a parallelogram, with the diagonal equal to the resultant force

**parallelogram of vectors** *noun* MATHS a graphical method of finding the resultant vector from two separate vectors by drawing the two vectors as two sides of a parallelogram, with the diagonal equal to the resultant vector

**parallel printer** *noun* COMPUT a printer that is connected to a computer via a parallel interface and accepts character data in parallel form

**parallel running** *noun* COMPUT the process of running old and new computer systems together to allow the new system to be checked before it becomes the only system used

**paramagnetism** *noun* PHYS the phenomenon of small changes in the magnetic behaviour of a substance varying with temperature

**parameter** *noun* **1.** COMPUT a piece of information which defines the limits or actions of something such as a variable, routine or program ○ *The X parameter defines the number of characters displayed across a screen.* ○ *The size of the array is set with this parameter.* **2.** a variable quantity or value

**parameterisation,** **parameterization** *noun* COMPUT the action of setting parameters for software

**parameter passing** *noun* COMPUT a value passed to a routine or program when it is called

**parametric equation** *noun* MATHS a mathematical equation in which the co-ordinates of points are expressed in terms of independent parameters

**parametric subroutine** *noun* COMPUT a subroutine that uses parameters to define its limits or actions

**paraquat** *noun* AGRIC a non-selective contact herbicide that becomes inert on contact with the soil

**parasexual** *adjective* FUNGI referring to reproduction in some fungi in which the recombination of parental chromosomes takes place without the usual formation of sex cells (**meiosis**)

**parasite** *noun* BIOL a plant or animal which lives on or inside another organism, the host, and derives its nourishment and other needs from it

COMMENT: The commonest parasites affecting animals are lice on the skin and various types of worms in the intestines. Many diseases of humans such as malaria and amoebic dysentery are caused by infestation with parasites. Viruses are parasites on animals, plants and even on bacteria.

**parasitic** *adjective* BIOL referring to parasites ○ *a parasitic plant*

**parasitic disease** *noun* MED a disease caused by a parasite

**parasiticide** *noun* BIOL a substance that kills parasites

**parasitise, parasitize** *verb* BIOL to live as a parasite on another organism ○ *Sheep are parasitised by flukes.*

**parasitism** *noun* BIOL a state in which one organism, the parasite, lives on or inside another organism, the host, and derives its nourishment and other needs from it

**parasitoid** *noun* BIOL an organism that is a parasite only at one stage in its development

**parasitology** *noun* BIOL the scientific study of parasites

**parasympathetic nervous system** *noun* ANAT the parts of the autonomic nervous system that affects involuntary functions such as pupil diameter in response to light and muscle constriction in the alimentary canal

**parathion** *noun* AGRIC an organophosphorous insecticide

**parathyroid gland** *noun* ANAT one of four small glands, found in or near the thyroid gland, that secrete parathyroid hormone, which controls the laying down of minerals in bone

**parcel** *noun* FORESTRY a quantity of wood, either growing in a forest or felled, which is sold

**parcel of air** *noun* METEOROL a large mass of air

**parenchyma** *noun* BIOL a soft unspecialised tissue in between the essential organs of plants and some lower animals

**parent** *noun* BIOL a mother or father

**parental** *adjective* BIOL referring to a parent

**parent cell** *noun* BIOL an original cell which splits into daughter cells by mitosis. Also called **mother cell**

**parent directory** *noun* COMPUT the directory above a sub-directory

**parenteral** *adjective* MED referring to a drug which is not swallowed but is given in the form of injections or suppositories

**parenteral nutrition, parenteral feeding** *noun* MED the feeding of a patient by means other than by mouth, e.g. by giving injections of glucose

**parent plant** *noun* BOT a plant from which others are produced

**parent rock** *noun* EARTH SCI same as **mother rock**

**parhelic circle** *noun* ASTRON a luminous horizontal band passing through the Sun that is caused by the Sun's rays reflecting off ice crystals in the atmosphere

**parhelion** *noun* ASTRON a bright coloured spot near the Sun caused by ice crystals in the atmosphere diffracting light (NOTE: Parhelions are often observed in pairs.)

**parietal cell** *noun* BIOL same as **oxyntic cell**

**parity bit** *noun* COMPUT an extra bit added to a data word as a parity check

**parity check** *noun* COMPUT a method of checking for errors or corruption of transmitted binary data

**park** *noun* ENVIRON an area of open land used as a place of recreation ■ *verb* COMPUT to move the read/write head of a hard disk drive over a point on the disk where no data is stored ○ *When parked, the disk head will not damage any data if it touches the disk surface.*

**parse** *verb* COMPUT to break down high-level language code into its constituent parts when translating into machine code

**parsec** *noun* ASTRON, MEASURE the distance at which a star would have a parallax of one second, equal to 3.26 light years, 31 trillion km or 206 000 AU (NOTE: A parsec is the standard measure of distances in the universe beyond the solar system.)

**part** *noun* one of the sections which make up a whole

**parthenocarpy** *noun* BOT the production of seedless fruits without fertilisation having taken place

**parthenogenesis** *noun* BIOL a form of reproduction involving unfertilised ova

**partial** *adjective* 1. affecting only part of something 2. completing or constituting only part of something

**partial carry** *noun* COMPUT the temporary storage of all carries generated by parallel adders rather than a direct transfer

**partial cut** *noun* FORESTRY a method of foresting where only some trees are felled, leaving others standing to seed the area which has been left clear

**partial eclipse** *noun* ASTRON an eclipse where only part of the Sun or Moon is hidden

**partial pressure** *noun* PHYS the pressure that one gas in a mixture of gases would exert if the other gases were removed

**partial RAM** *noun* COMPUT a RAM chip in which only one area of the chip functions correctly

**partial vision** *noun* OPHTHALMOL the condition of being able to see only part of the total field of vision

**particle** *noun* 1. a very small piece of a substance ○ *Particles of volcanic ash were carried into the upper atmosphere.* 2. PHYS ◊ **elementary particle**

**particle accelerator** *noun* PHYS in particle physics note a device used to increase the velocity of elementary particles

**particle bombardment** *noun* BIOTECH a technique for inserting DNA from one organism into another by bombarding cell cultures with metal particles coated with DNA

**particle physics** *noun* PHYS the study of elementary particles (NOTE: It often involves the use of large high-energy apparatus such as particle accelerators to produce particles that can be studied.)

**particulate** *adjective* referring to particles ○ *Particulate matter in the atmosphere forms the nuclei around which raindrops form.* ■ *noun* ENVIRON a tiny solid particle of pollutant

COMMENT: The finest particulates are the most dangerous pollutants as they are easily inhaled into the bronchioles in the lungs. Fine particulates from volcanic eruptions can enter the stratosphere and have a cooling effect by preventing the heat from the Sun reaching the Earth's surface, i.e. the opposite of the greenhouse effect.

**particulate inheritance** *noun* GENETICS a theory stated by Mendel that parental genes do not mix together in offspring but retain their characteristics from generation to generation

**partition** COMPUT *noun* **1.** an area of a hard disk that is treated as a logical drive and can be accessed as a separate drive ○ *I defined two partitions on this hard disk called drive C: and D:.* **2.** a section of computer memory set aside as foreground or background memory ■ *verb* **1.** to divide a hard disk into two or more logical drives that can be accessed as separate drives **2.** to divide a large file or block into several smaller units which can be accessed and handled more easily

**parts per billion** *noun* CHEM a measure of the concentration of a substance in a gas, liquid or solid. Abbreviation **ppb**

**pascal** *noun* MEASURE, PHYS an SI unit of pressure. Symbol **Pa**

**PASCAL** COMPUT a high-level structured programming language used both on micros and for teaching programming

**pass** *noun* COMPUT **1.** the execution of a loop, once **2.** a single operation **3.** the action of moving the whole length of a magnetic tape over the read/write heads

**passage** *noun* **1.** EARTH SCI a long narrow channel **2.** a movement from one place to another

**passerine** *noun, adjective* ZOOL (a bird) belonging to an order which perch in branches. Order: Passeriformes.

**passive** *adjective* **1.** not actively participating. Opposite **active 2.** receiving an action but taking no action ○ *In primary radar systems, the target is passive.*

**passive margin** *noun* EARTH SCI an area at the edge of a continental mass where there is no volcanic activity

**passive state** *noun* the state of a system or device when it is switched on or 'live' but is not reacting to any input

**password** *noun* COMPUT a word or series of characters which identifies a user who can then access a system ○ *The user has to key in the password before being able to access the database.*

**paste** *verb* COMPUT to insert into a file text or graphics that has been copied or cut

**pasteurisation,** **pasteurization** *noun* FOOD INDUST the heating of food or food products for a specific period to destroy bacteria

COMMENT: Pasteurisation is carried out by heating food for a short time at a lower temperature than that used for sterilisation. The two methods used are heating to 72° C for fifteen seconds (the high-temperature-short-time method) or to 65° C for half an hour, and then cooling rapidly. This has the effect of killing tuberculosis bacteria.

**pasteurise,** **pasteurize** *verb* FOOD INDUST to kill bacteria in food by heating it

**pasture** AGRIC *noun* land covered with grass or other small plants, used by farmers as a feeding place for animals ■ *verb* to put animals onto land covered with grass or other small plants ○ *Their cows are pastured in fields high in the mountains.*

**pastureland** *noun* AGRIC land covered with grass or other small plants, used by farmers as a feeding place for animals

**pasture management** *noun* AGRIC the control of pasture by grazing, cutting, reseeding and similar techniques

**patch** *noun* COMPUT a small correction made to software by the user, on the instructions of the software publisher

**patch cord** *noun* TELECOM a short cable with a connector at each end, used to make an electrical connection on a patch panel

**patch dynamics** *noun* ECOL a process in which the disturbance of a community creates gaps which are then colonised by the same or another species

**patch panel** *noun* TELECOM a set of electrical terminals that can be interconnected using short patch cords, allowing quick and simple re-configuration of a network

**patent** *noun* an official confirmation that you have the sole right to make or sell a new invention. ◊ **copyright**

**paternity** *noun* BIOL **1.** the state of being a father **2.** the identity of a father ○ *The court had first to establish the child's paternity.* Compare **maternity**

**path** *noun* **1.** a route, or a way to reach or achieve something **2.** COMPUT a possible route or sequence of events or instructions within the execution of a program **3.** COMPUT the route from one point in a communications network to another

**patho-** *prefix* BIOL disease

**pathogen** *noun* BIOL an agent, usually a microorganism, that causes a disease

**pathogenesis** *noun* BIOL the origin, production or development of a disease

**pathogenetic** *adjective* BIOL referring to pathogenesis

**pathogenic** *adjective* BIOL able to cause or produce a disease

**pathogenic bacterium** *noun* MICROBIOL a bacterium responsible for causing a disease

**pathogenicity** *noun* MED the ability of a pathogen to cause a disease

**pathogenic organism** *noun* BIOL an organism responsible for causing a disease

**pathological** *adjective* BIOL **1.** referring to a disease **2.** caused by a disease **3.** indicating a disease

**pathological report** *noun* MED a report on tests carried out to find the cause of a disease that someone has

**pathological waste** *noun* MED waste, e.g. from a hospital, which may contain pathogens and which could cause disease

**pathologist** *noun* MED **1.** a scientist who specialises in the study of diseases **2.** a person who checks tissue and other samples for evidence of disease **3.** a doctor who examines dead bodies to find out the cause of death

**pathology** *noun* MED the study of diseases and the changes in structure and function which diseases can cause

**pathology report** *noun* MED a report on tests carried out to find the cause of a disease that someone has

**pattern** *noun* **1.** a series of regular lines or shapes which are repeated again and again **2.** a form or method which shows particular, consistent characteristics

**pattern palette** *noun* COMPUT a range of predefined patterns that can be used to fill an area of an image

**pattern recognition** *noun* COMPUT an algorithm or program function that can identify a shape from something such as a video camera

**Pauli exclusion principle** *noun* PHYS same as **exclusion principle**

**Pb** *symbol* CHEM ELEM lead

**PB** *abbreviation* COMPUT petabyte

**PBB** *abbreviation* CHEM polybrominated biphenyl

**p-block element** *noun* CHEM an element that has an electron configuration with occupied p levels

**PC** *noun* COMPUT same as **personal computer**

**PCB** *abbreviation* **1.** CHEM polychlorinated biphenyl **2.** COMPUT printed circuit board

**PC card** *noun* COMPUT an electronic device, about the same size as a thick credit card, that can be plugged into a PCMCIA adapter to provide a particular function such as extra memory

**PC-compatible** *noun* COMPUT a computer that is compatible with an IBM PC

**p-channel metal oxide semiconductor** *noun* ELECTRONICS full form of **PMOS**

**PCI** *noun* COMPUT a specification produced by Intel defining a type of fast local bus that allows high-speed data transfer between the processor and the PCI-compatible expansion cards. Full form **peripheral component interconnect**

**PCL** *abbreviation* COMPUT printer control language

**PCM** *abbreviation* COMPUT pulse-code modulation

**PCMCIA** *noun* COMPUT a specification for add-in expansion cards that are the size of a credit card with a connector at one end. Full form **Personal Computer Memory Card International Association**

**P-code** *noun* COMPUT an intermediate code produced by a compiler that is ready for an interpreter to process, usually for PASCAL programs

**PCR** *abbreviation* BIOTECH polymerase chain reaction

**PCS** *abbreviation* COMPUT personal communications services

**PCU** *noun* COMPUT same as **peripheral control unit**

**Pd** *symbol* CHEM ELEM palladium

**PD** *abbreviation* COMPUT public domain

**PDA** *abbreviation* COMPUT personal digital assistant

**PDN** *abbreviation* COMPUT public data network

**peak** *noun* **1.** EARTH SCI the top of a mountain **2.** the highest point ○ *The intensity of solar radiation reaches a peak around noon.* □ **time of peak demand** one of the times when something is being used most ■ *verb* to reach the highest point

**peak output** *noun* the highest output

**peak period** *noun* INDUST the time of the day when most electricity or other power is being used

**peak value** *noun* a maximum value

**peat** *noun* EARTH SCI wet, partly-decayed mosses and other plants which form the soil of a bog

COMMENT: Peat can be cut and dried in blocks, which can then be used as fuel. In some countries there are peat-fired power stations. It is in fact an early form of coal, as coal is peat which has been compressed by layers of sediment until it becomes rock.

**peat bog** *noun* EARTH SCI a soft wet area of land where peat has formed

**peatland** *noun* EARTH SCI an area of land covered with peat bog

**peaty** *adjective* EARTH SCI containing peat

**pebble** *noun* EARTH SCI a small piece of rock, less than 64 mm in diameter

**pebble beach** *noun* EARTH SCI a beach covered with small stones

**pectin** *noun* BIOCHEM a sticky mixture of various polysaccharides found in plant cell walls

**pectoral girdle** *noun* ZOOL the part of the skeleton of a vertebrate animal to which the forelimbs are attached and which provides support for the forelimbs

**pedal** *noun* MECH ENG a foot-operated lever

**pedicel** *noun* BOT a stalk that carries a single flower within an inflorescence

**pedigree** GENETICS *noun* **1.** the line of ancestors of an individual animal or person **2.** a document that records the line of ancestors of a person or animal ■ *adjective* descended from a line of animals whose pedigree has been recorded over several generations ○ *a pedigree dog*

**peduncle** *noun* ZOOL a stalk-like structure such as that attaching a polyp to the rock on which it lives

**peer** *noun* COMPUT either of two similar devices operating on the same network protocol level

**peer-to-peer network** *noun* COMPUT a local area network in which there is no central dedicated server but each computer in the network shares the jobs ○ *We have linked the four PCs in our small office using a peer-to-peer network.*

**pel** *abbreviation* COMPUT picture element. ◊ **pixel**

**pelagic** *adjective* OCEANOG referring to the top and middle layers of sea water

**pelagic deposits** *plural noun* OCEANOG material that has fallen to the floor of the pelagic zone. Also called **pelagic sediment**

**pelagic organism** *noun* MARINE BIOL an organism that lives in open water in the sea away from the seabed or the shore

**pelagic sediment** *noun* OCEANOG same as **pelagic deposits**

**pelagic zone** *noun* OCEANOG the part of the sea that is not near the shore and not immediately above the seabed

**Pelton wheel** *noun* ENG a type of water turbine that has specially shaped buckets attached to the edge of a wheel which are struck by a jet of water

**pelvic** *adjective* ANAT referring to the pelvis

**pelvis** *noun* ANAT **1.** (*in vertebrates*) the cavity formed by the hip bones and the base of the backbone **2.** a cup-shaped anatomical cavity such as the region of the kidney that collects urine before it is passed into the ureter

**pen computer** *noun* COMPUT a type of computer that uses a pen instead of a keyboard for input (NOTE: The computer has a touch-sensitive screen and uses handwriting recognition software to interpret the commands written on the screen with the pen.)

**peneplain** noun EARTH SCI a plain formed after mountains have been completely eroded

**penetrance** noun GENETICS the frequency with which an inherited characteristic such as a genetic disease occurs among individuals that carry the gene or genes for it

**penetrant** adjective forcing or obtaining entry into an area or substance ○ Penetrant dye inspection is a non-destructive test used mainly for the detection of defects open to the surface.

**penetrate** verb to enter something by making a way through it

**penetration** noun the act of making a way into or through something ○ Long-range radars suffer little weather interference and have good cloud penetration characteristics.

**penicillin** noun PHARM an antibiotic, originally produced from a fungus, that controls bacterial and fungal infections (NOTE: Penicillin and the related family of drugs have names ending in -cillin: amoxycillin.)

**Penicillium** noun PHARM the genus of fungus from which penicillin is derived

**peninsula** noun EARTH SCI a long narrow piece of land, surrounded on three sides by sea

**peninsular** adjective EARTH SCI referring to a peninsula

**penis** noun ANAT the male genital organ through which sperm enters the female during copulation (NOTE: It is also the means by which humans and many other mammals pass urine.)

**pentad** noun METEOROL a five-day period (NOTE: This term is used especially in meteorological forecasting and recording.)

**pentahydrate** noun CHEM a crystalline compound with five molecules of water of crystallisation for each molecule of the compound

**pentane** noun CHEM an organic hydrocarbon with five carbon atoms in each molecule, used as a solvent. Formula: $C_5H_{12}$.

**pentanoic acid** noun CHEM an isomer of valeric acid. Formula: $CH_3(CH_2)_3COOH$.

**pentavalent** adjective CHEM with a valency of five

**pentyl group** noun CHEM a group of compounds with the basic structure $CH_3CH_2CH_2CH_2CH_2$-

**pepsin** noun BIOCHEM an enzyme in the stomach which breaks down the proteins in food

**peptide** noun BIOCHEM a molecule made up of two or more amino acids

**per** preposition **1.** for each or every ○ a speed of a hundred feet per second **2.** out of each or every ○ The rate of imperfect items is about twenty-five per thousand.

**per annum** adverb for or in every year ○ 245 000 sq km of land per annum is cleared of trees.

**per capita** adverb, adjective of or for each person

**perceived noise level** noun ACOUSTICS a measurement of the loudness of a sound as heard by the human ear. Abbreviation **PNL**

**perceived noise level in decibels** noun ACOUSTICS a measurement of sound pressure in decibels. Abbreviation **PNdB**

**per cent** adverb, adjective MATHS out of each hundred ○ Only one per cent (1%) of all prosecutions for water pollution were successful. Symbol **%**

**percentage** noun **1.** MATHS the proportion or rate equivalent to a total divided by a hundred ○ Some 20% of those who caught the virus died, a much higher percentage than expected. **2.** an inexact proportion or amount ○ Developing countries possess the largest percentage of the world's rainforest.

**percentage point** noun MATHS one per cent

**percentile** noun MATHS, MEASURE one of a series of ninety-nine figures below which a particular percentage of the total falls

**percolate** verb PHYS to trickle slowly through a quantity of solid particles

**percolating filter** noun INDUST a filter bed through which liquid sewage is passed to purify it. Also called **trickling filter**

**percutaneous absorption** noun PHYSIOL the absorption of a substance through the skin

**perennial** *adjective* lasting for many years ■ *noun* BOT a plant that lives for a long time, flowering each year without dying

**perennial agriculture** *noun* AGRIC a system of agriculture in regions where there is no winter and several crops can be grown on the same land each year

**perfect** *adjective* completely correct, with no mistakes ○ *We check each batch to make sure it is perfect.* ■ *verb* to make something that is completely free from errors or problems as possible ○ *He perfected the process for making high grade steel.*

**perfect gas** *noun* PHYS same as **ideal gas**

**perfectly** *adverb* COMPUT in the best way possible ○ *perfectly aligned*

**perfluorocarbons** *plural noun* CHEM a group of synthetic chemicals composed of carbon and fluorine only. Abbreviation **PFCs**

**perforation** *noun* a small hole usually forming a line on a sheet of paper or continuous stationery, to help when tearing

**perform** *verb* **1.** to carry out an action or role ○ *to perform a biological experiment* ○ *The kidneys perform the function of eliminating nitrogenous waste.* **2.** COMPUT to operate in a particular way ○ *The machine is now performing satisfactorily.*

**performance** *noun* the way in which someone or something works □ **as a measure of the system's performance** as a way of judging if the system is working well

**per head** *adverb* for each person ○ *Average annual consumption has increased to 29 litres per head.* Also called **per capita**

**per hour** *adverb* in each hour ○ *We can complete five batches per hour.*

**perianth** *noun* BOT the outer parts of a flower, made up of the calyx, the corolla or both

**pericarp** *noun* BOT the part of a fruit that encloses the seed or seeds

**perigee** *noun* ASTRON the point in the orbit of a planet, satellite or other body orbiting Earth where it is closest to Earth

**perihelion** *noun* ASTRON the point in the orbit of a planet or other body orbiting the Sun where it is closest to the Sun

**perilune** *noun* ASTRON the point in the orbit of a planet or other body orbiting the Moon where it is the closest to the Moon

**perilymph** *noun* ANAT a liquid occurring between the bony labyrinth and membranous labyrinth of the inner ear

**period** *noun* **1.** a length of time ○ *for a period of time* ○ *for a period of months* ○ *for a six-year period* **2.** GEOL an interval of geological time, the subdivision of an era and itself divided into epochs

**periodic** *adjective* **1.** happening from time to time ○ *a periodic review of the company's performance* **2.** occurring regularly ○ *The clock signal is periodic.*

**periodically** *adverb* from time to time

**periodic table** *noun* CHEM a table of elements listed according to their atomic mass

**peripheral** *adjective* **1.** occurring at the edge **2.** which is not essential or which is attached to something else ■ *noun* COMPUT an item of hardware such as a terminal, printer or monitor that allows communication with a main computer system but is not directly operated by the system ○ *Peripherals such as disk drives or printers allow data transfer and are controlled by a system, but contain independent circuits for their operation.*

**peripheral component interconnect** *noun* COMPUT a high-speed local bus that runs at 33 MHz and is most often used in personal computers for network or graphics adapters. Abbreviation **PCI**

**peripheral control unit** *noun* COMPUT a device that converts the input/output signals and instructions from a computer to a form and protocol that a peripheral will understand. Abbreviation **PCU**

**peripheral interface adapter** *noun* COMPUT a circuit that allows a computer to communicate with a peripheral by providing serial and parallel ports and other handshaking signals required to interface the peripheral. Abbreviation **PIA**

**peripheral nerve** *noun* ANAT a motor or sensory nerve that branches from the brain and spinal cord

**peripheral nervous system** *noun* ANAT all the nerves in different parts of the body that are linked and governed by the central nervous system. Abbreviation **PNS**

**peripheral processing unit** *noun* COMPUT a device used for input, output or storage which is controlled by the central processing unit. Abbreviation **PPU**

**periphyton** *noun* BIOL a dense mass of strands of algal growth that covers the water surface between emerging aquatic plants

**periscope** *noun* OPTICS a long tubular optical instrument through which someone can see objects that are out of the direct line of sight (NOTE: It is often used on a submarine to look above the water surface.)

**perissodactyl** *noun* ZOOL any of the large hoofed mammals that walk on their toes of which there is an odd number. Order: Perissodactyla. (NOTE: Horses, rhinoceroses, and tapirs are perissodactyls.)

**Perl** *noun* COMPUT an interpreted programming language used to create CGI scripts that can process forms or carry out functions on a web server to enhance a website ○ *If you want to add a search engine to your website, you will need to write a Perl program.* Full form **practical extraction and report language** (NOTE: It is usually used under Unix.)

**permaculture** *noun* AGRIC a system of permanent agriculture, which involves designing human habitats and food production systems

**permafrost** *noun* GEOL ground that is permanently frozen, as in the Arctic regions (NOTE: Although the top layer of soil melts and softens in the summer the soil beneath remains frozen.)

**permanent** *adjective* lasting or remaining without change

**permanent deformation** *noun* ENG damage to a structure which must be repaired by replacing the damaged part

**permanent dynamic memory** *noun* COMPUT a storage medium that retains data even when power is removed

**permanent file** *noun* COMPUT a data file that is stored in a backing storage device such as a disk drive

**permanent grassland** *noun* AGRIC land that remains solely as grassland over a long period of time and is not ploughed. Also called **permanent pasture**

**permanent hardness** *noun* the hardness of water, caused by calcium and magnesium, which remains even after the water has been boiled

**permanently** *adverb* in a way which will last for a long time ○ *The production number is permanently engraved on the back of the computer casing.*

**permanent magnet** *noun* PHYS a metal component that always has a magnetic influence

**permanent memory** *noun* COMPUT a computer memory that retains data even when power is removed. Compare **non-volatile memory**

**permanent pasture** *noun* AGRIC same as **permanent grassland**

**permanent teeth** *plural noun* DENT (*in mammals*) the second set of teeth, which are used during the adult lifetime. Compare **milk teeth**

**permanent wilting point** *noun* BOT the soil water content below which plants wilt and are unable to recover

**permeability** *noun* **1.** EARTH SCI the ability of a rock to allow water to pass through it **2.** PHYS the ability of a membrane to allow fluid or chemical substances to pass through it

**permeable** *adjective* EARTH SCI, PHYS with a degree of permeability (NOTE: The US term is **pervious**.)

**permission** *noun* COMPUT authorisation given to a particular user to access a shared resource or area of disk

**permittivity** *noun* ELEC a measure of how well a non-conducting material retains electrical energy when placed in an electric field

**permutation** *noun* **1.** one of a number of different ways in which something can be arranged ○ *The cipher system is very secure since there are so many possible permutations for the key.* **2.** MATHS an ordered arrangement of elements from a set

**peroxide** *noun* CHEM a chemical compound that contains two oxygen atoms bound together (NOTE: Hydrogen peroxide is commonly used as a bleach.)

**peroxyacetyl nitrate** *noun* ENVIRON a substance contained in photochemical smog, which is extremely harmful to plants. Abbreviation **PAN**

**perpendicular** *adjective* MATHS at right angles or 90° to a base or a line ○ *The vertical grid lines are perpendicular to the horizontal ones.*

**persist** *verb* **1.** to continue to exist ○ *Snow cover tends to persist on north-facing slopes of mountains.* **2.** to remain active for a period of time ○ *Some substances persist in toxic forms in the air for weeks.* **3.** to continue doing something ○ *He persisted with his request until it was granted.*

**persistence** *noun* **1.** the ability to persist ○ *The persistence and movement of cols is governed by the movement of the adjacent pressure systems.* **2.** the action or quality of continuing without giving up ○ *He managed to overcome his difficulties through persistence and hard work.* **3.** COMPUT the length of time that a screen will continue to display an image after the picture beam has stopped tracing it on the screen ○ *Slow scan rate monitors need long persistence phosphor to prevent the image flickering.*

**persistent** *adjective* **1.** continuing for some time ○ *persistent flickering of the screen* **2.** remaining active for some time ○ *persistent chemicals*

**persistent insecticide, persistent pesticide** *noun* ENVIRON a chemical compound, especially one used to kill insect pests, that remains toxic either in the soil or in the body of an animal and is passed from animal to animal through the food chain

**person** *noun* a human being

**personal** *adjective* **1.** referring to one person ○ *a personal opinion* **2.** referring to direct relationships between people ○ *The information came through a personal contact.*

**personal communication** *noun* information given by one person directly to another

**personal communications services** *plural noun* COMPUT a range of wireless communication systems that allow computers to exchange data with other devices. Abbreviation **PCS**

**personal computer** *noun* COMPUT a low-cost microcomputer intended mainly for home and light business use. Abbreviation **PC**

**personal digital assistant** *noun* COMPUT a lightweight palmtop computer that provides the basic functions of a diary, notepad, address-book and to-do list together with fax or modem communications. Abbreviation **PDA**

**personal identification device** *noun* COMPUT full form of **PID**

**personal identification number** *noun* COMPUT full form of **PIN**

**personalise, personalize** *verb* COMPUT to customise or adapt a product specially for a certain user

**perspective** *noun* OPTICS an appearance of depth in an image in which objects that are further away from the viewer appear smaller

**perspective correction** *noun* COMPUT a method that is used to change the size and shape of an object to give the impression of depth and distance

**Perspex** *trademark* INDUST a robust transparent plastic that can be used as a substitute for glass

**PERT** *noun* COMPUT the definition of tasks or jobs and the time each requires, arranged in order to achieve a goal. Full form **program evaluation and review technique**

**pervious** *adjective* US EARTH SCI, PHYS same as **permeable**

**pest** *noun* BIOL an organism that carries disease or harms plants or animals ○ *a spray to remove insect pests*

**pest control** *noun* AGRIC the process of keeping down the number of pests by various methods

**pesticide** *noun* AGRIC a chemical compound used to kill pests such as insects, fungi, animals or weeds

**pesticide residue** *noun* ENVIRON the amount of a pesticide that remains in the environment after application

**PET** *abbreviation* CHEM polyethylene terephthalate

**peta-** *prefix* MEASURE one quadrillion, $10^{15}$. Symbol **P**

**petabyte** *noun* COMPUT one quadrillion bytes. Abbreviation **PB**

**petal** *noun* BOT the outer coloured part of the corolla of a flower

**petiole** *noun* BOT the stalk of a leaf

**petri dish** *noun* BIOL a small glass or plastic dish with a lid, in which a culture is grown

**petrifaction** *noun* EARTH SCI the process of turning into stone

**petrified forest** *noun* EARTH SCI remains of trees that have been petrified and are found in rocks

**petrify** *verb* EARTH SCI to turn something into stone

**petrochemical** *noun* CHEM a chemical derived from petroleum or natural gas

**petrochemical industry** *noun* INDUST an industry that processes petroleum or natural gas and produces petrochemicals

**petrochemistry** *noun* **1.** CHEM the scientific study of the chemical composition of petroleum and substances derived from it **2.** EARTH SCI the scientific study of the chemical composition of rocks

**petrol** *noun* CHEM, INDUST a liquid made from petroleum, used as a fuel in internal combustion engines ○ *We are looking for a car with a low petrol consumption.* (NOTE: The US term is **gasoline**.)

COMMENT: In a petrol engine the petrol is mixed with air making it more combustible. It is then sprayed or injected into the cylinders, where it is ignited by an electric spark. Petrol is made of a mixture of several hydrocarbons such as butane and benzene. It also contains additives, in particular tetraethyl lead, which prevent an engine from knocking. The use of petrol in vehicle engines is responsible for a high level of pollutants in the atmosphere, as the engines emit carbon monoxide and various lead compounds.

**petrol engine** *noun* AUTOMOT an engine which uses petrol as a fuel

**petrol-engined** *adjective* AUTOMOT referring to a motor vehicle which uses petrol as a fuel

**petroleum** *noun* EARTH SCI a mineral oil found in the ground

COMMENT: Petroleum is made up of varying types of hydrocarbon together with sulphur compounds. It usually occurs in combination with natural gas or water, and when these are removed it is called crude oil or crude petroleum. Refined crude petroleum gives various products such as petrol, diesel oil, paraffin wax and tar. Crude petroleum is found in geological deposits, mainly in the Middle East, the North Sea, Central America and Asia.

**petroleum derivative** *noun* INDUST a substance or product made from petroleum

**petroleum-exporting country** *noun* INDUST a country that produces enough petroleum for its own use and to sell to other countries

**petroleum gas** *noun* INDUST a natural gas occurring in combination with petroleum

**petroleum industry** *noun* INDUST an industry which makes products such as petrol, soap or paint from crude petroleum

**petroleum products** *plural noun* INDUST products such as petrol, soap or paint which are made from crude petroleum

**petrology** *noun* EARTH SCI the study of rocks and minerals (NOTE: Petrology has no connection with **petrol**.)

**PFBC** *abbreviation* INDUST pressurised fluidised-bed combustion

**PFCs** *abbreviation* CHEM perfluorocarbons

**PGP** *abbreviation* COMPUT pretty good privacy

**pH** *noun* CHEM a measure of the acidity of a solution, determined as the negative logarithm of the hydrogen ion concentration

COMMENT: A pH value of 7 is neutral, the same as that of pure water. Lower values indicate increasing acidity and higher values indicate increasing alkalinity: 0 is most acid and 14 is most alkaline. Acid rain has been known to have a pH of 2 or less, making it as acid as lemon juice. Most freshwater fish cannot survive even slightly acid conditions. Salmon and trout cannot stand a pH value of 6 and only pike can survive in water at less than pH 4.

**Phaeophyta** *plural noun* MARINE BIOL brown algae such as brown seaweed

**-phage** *suffix* BIOL eating

**phago-** *prefix* BIOL eating

**phagocyte** *noun* BIOL a cell such as a white blood cell that can surround and destroy other cells such as bacteria

**phagocytic** *adjective* BIOL referring to phagocytes

**phagocytosis** *noun* PHYSIOL the engulfing of foreign particles or other cells by phagocytes such as white blood cells

**phalanx** *noun* ANAT a finger or toe bone of a vertebrate (NOTE: The plural is **phalanges.**)

**pharm** *verb* BIOTECH to produce proteins that have medicinal value in the milk of genetically modified cows and sheep

**pharmaceutical** *adjective* PHARM referring to pharmacy or drugs

**pharmacist** *noun* PHARM a trained person who is qualified to prepare medicines according to the instructions on a doctor's prescription

**pharmacogenomics** *noun* GENETICS the study of the effect an individual's genetic makeup has on his or her response to drug treatments

**pharmacology** *noun* MED the study of drugs or medicines and their actions, properties and characteristics

**pharmacy** *noun* PHARM **1.** the study of the making and dispensing of drugs **2.** a shop or department in a hospital where drugs are prepared

**pharynx** *noun* ANAT the part of the throat between the mouth and the oesophagus

**phase** *noun* **1.** a stage or part of a larger process ○ *An emergency situation may occur during any phase of the flight.* **2.** ELEC a relationship between the voltage and current waveforms

**phase alternation line** *noun* TELECOM a standard for television transmission and reception that uses a 625-line picture transmitted at 25 frames per second. Abbreviation **PAL** (NOTE: PAL provides a clearer image than NTSC and is used in most of Europe, except for France.)

**phase angle** *noun* the difference between two periodic phenomena expressed as an angle

**phased change-over** *noun* COMPUT the gradual introduction of a new device as the old one is used less and less

**phase in** *verb* to introduce something gradually

**phase of the Moon** *noun* ASTRON one of various stages which the Moon's face appears to pass through every 29 days (NOTE: They are first quarter, full moon, last quarter and new moon.)

**phellem** *noun* BOT same as **cork**

**phellogen** *noun* BOT same as **cork cambium**

**phenol** *noun* CHEM a strong disinfectant for external use

**phenology** *noun* ECOL the effect of climate on annually recurring phenomena such as animal migration or plant budding

**phenomenon** *noun* an event that exists and is experienced ○ *Chemical reactions in the atmosphere generate phenomena such as acid rain.* (NOTE: The plural is **phenomena.**)

**phenotype** *noun* GENETICS the physical characteristics of an organism, produced by its genes. Compare **genotype**

**phenotypic** *adjective* relating to a phenotype

**phenotypic plasticity** *noun* GENETICS the ability of a phenotype to vary as a result of environmental influences on its genetic makeup

**phenylalanine** *noun* BIOCHEM an essential amino acid

**phenyl group** *noun* CHEM a hydrocarbon group with the basic structure $C_6H_5$ (NOTE: Phenyl groups are derived from benzene.)

**pheromone** *noun* BIOCHEM a chemical substance produced and released into the environment by an animal, influencing the behaviour of another individual of the same species

**pH factor** *noun* CHEM ◊ **pH**

**phial** *noun* PHARM a small medicine bottle

**PHIGS** *noun* COMPUT a standard application interface between software and a graphics adapter that uses a set of standard commands to draw and manipulate 2D and 3D images. Full form **programmer's hierarchical interactive graphics standard**

**-philia** *suffix* attraction towards or liking for something

**philoprogenitive** *adjective* BIOL producing many offspring

**phloem** *noun* BOT the tissue in a plant that carries organic substances from the leaves to the rest of the plant, and is formed of living cells. ♦ **xylem**

**pH meter** *noun* CHEM a device for measuring pH

**phone** *noun* TELECOM same as **telephone**

**phoneme** *noun* COMPUT one small sound, several of which may make up a spoken word (NOTE: Phonemes can be used to analyse voice input to recognise words or to produce speech by playing back a sequence of them.)

**Phong shading** *noun* COMPUT the most complex method of applying shading to a three-dimensional scene create the smoothest shading effects

**phono connector** *noun* COMPUT a plug and socket standard used to connect audio and video devices. Also called **RCA connector**

**phosgene** *noun* CHEM a very poisonous gas, used in the manufacture of pesticides, plastics and dyes, and as a chemical weapon in World War I. Formula: $COCl_2$.

**phosphate** *noun* CHEM a salt of phosphoric acid which is formed naturally by weathering of rocks (NOTE: It is an essential plant nutrient.)

COMMENT: Natural organic phosphates are provided by guano and fishmeal, otherwise phosphates are mined. Artificially produced phosphates are used in agriculture and are known as superphosphates because they are highly concentrated. Phosphates escape into water from sewage, especially waste water containing detergents, and encourage the growth of algae by eutrophication.

**phosphine** *noun* CHEM a flammable gas that smells of fish, used as a pesticide. Formula: $PH_3$.

**phospholipid** *noun* BIOCHEM a phosphorus-containing fat molecule that is an important component of double cell membranes

**phosphor** *noun* CHEM a substance that produces light when excited by some form of energy, usually an electron beam, and is used for coating the inside of a cathode ray tube

COMMENT: A thin layer of phosphor is arranged in a pattern of small dots on the inside of a television screen. These dots produce an image when scanned by the picture beam.

**phosphor coating** *noun* ELEC a thin layer of phosphor on the inside of a cathode ray tube

**phosphor dot** *noun* ELEC a dot of red, green or blue phosphor arranged with others in a pattern on a colour television screen

**phosphor efficiency** *noun* PHYS a measure of the amount of light produced in proportion to the energy received from an electron beam

**phosphorescence** *noun* CHEM the production of light with no heat (NOTE: It is either caused by oxidation of phosphorus as in sea water or generated by some animals such as glow-worms.)

**phosphorescent** *adjective* CHEM producing light without producing heat

**phosphoric acid** *noun* CHEM an acid that forms phosphates. Also called **orthophosphoric acid**

**phosphor triad** *noun* ELEC a group of three phosphor dots (representing red, green and blue) that together form a single pixel on a colour screen

**phosphorus** *noun* CHEM ELEM a toxic chemical element that is essential to biological life (NOTE: The chemical symbol is **P**; the atomic number is **15** and the atomic weight is **30.97**.)

COMMENT: Phosphorus is an essential part of bones, nerve tissue, DNA and RNA and is important in many biochemical processes, although in its pure form it is highly toxic. When an organism dies the phosphorus contained in its tissues returns to the soil and is taken up by plants in the phosphorus cycle.

**phosphorus (III) bromide** *noun* CHEM a colourless liquid. Formula: $PBr_3$.

**phosphorus (V) bromide** *noun* CHEM a yellow crystalline solid that sublimes easily. Formula: $PBr_5$.

**phosphorus (III) chloride** *noun* CHEM a colourless liquid. Formula: $PCl_3$.

**phosphorus (V) chloride** *noun* CHEM a white solid that sublimes easily. Formula: $PCl_5$.

**phosphorus cycle** *noun* BIOL a cycle by which phosphorus atoms are circulated through living organisms

**phosphorus (III) oxide** *noun* CHEM a white, waxy solid that dissolves in cold water and reacts with hot water and oxidises in air to phosphorus (V) oxide. Formula: $P_2O_3$.

**phosphorus (V) oxide** *noun* CHEM a white powder that is soluble in organic solvents and is used as a drying agent for gases, combining with water to form phosphoric acid. Formula: $P_2O_5$.

**phot-** *prefix* PHYS same as **photo-** (NOTE: used before vowels)

**photic zone** *noun* EARTH SCI the top layer of water in the sea or a lake, which sunlight can penetrate and in which photosynthesis takes place. Also called **euphotic zone**

**photo-** *prefix* PHYS light

**photoautotrophic** *adjective* BIOL using light energy to create a source of food

**photocell** *noun* PHYS same as **photoelectric cell**

**photochemical** *adjective* CHEM referring to a chemical reaction that is caused by light ○ *Gases rise into the upper atmosphere and undergo photochemical change.*

**photochemical oxidant** *noun* CHEM a substance such as ozone which is produced by a chemical reaction with light

**photochemical pollution** *noun* ENVIRON pollution caused by the action of light on chemicals in the lower atmosphere. Also called **photochemical smog**

COMMENT: When the atmosphere near ground level is polluted with nitrogen oxides from burning fossil fuels together with hydrocarbons, ultraviolet light from the Sun sets off a series of reactions that result in photochemical pollution, containing, among other substances, ozone.

**photochemical reaction** *noun* PHYS a chemical reaction started by the absorption of light (NOTE: Photosynthesis is an example of such a reaction.)

**photochemical smog** *noun* ENVIRON same as **photochemical pollution**

**photochemistry** *noun* CHEM the study of chemical changes brought about by light and other forms of radiation

**photochromism** *noun* PHYS a change in the colour of something caused by light

**photoconverter** *noun* ELEC a device that converts energy from light into electric energy

**photodecomposition** *noun* CHEM the breaking down of a substance by the action of light

**photoelectric cell** *noun* ELEC a cell in which light falling on the cell is converted to electricity. Also called **photocell**

**photoelectric effect** *noun* PHYS the production of electrons from a substance, caused by light or other electromagnetic radiation. Also called **photoemission**

**photoelectron** *noun* PHYS an electron emitted from a substance that has been struck by a photon of electromagnetic radiation

**photoemission** *noun* PHYS same as **photoelectric effect**

**photogenic** *adjective* 1. PHYS produced by the action of light 2. BIOL referring to an organism producing light

**photograph** *noun* a picture taken with a camera, using the chemical action of light on sensitive film

**photography** *noun* the process of taking pictures with a camera

**photoionisation** *noun* PHYS the removal of one or more electrons from an atom or molecule when it absorbs a photon of electromagnetic radiation, especially visible or ultraviolet light

**photoluminescence** *noun* PHYS the emission of light from a substance that has absorbed electromagnetic radiation

**photolysis** *noun* CHEM the breakdown of a chemical by light or other electromagnetic radiation

**photometry** *noun* PHYS the measurement of the luminous intensity of a source of visible light

**photomultiplier** *noun* PHYS a device that uses electronics to increase the intensity of incoming light (NOTE: Photomultipliers use materials that emit electrons when light falls on them (the photoelectric effect) and an electronic 'cascade' to increase the number of electrons before they are counted by a sensor.)

**photon** *noun* PHYS the elementary particle of electromagnetic radiation (NOTE: Radiation can be thought of as a particle or as a wave, and the shorter the wavelength of the radiation the more energetic the equivalent photon.)

**photonastic** *adjective* BOT referring to photonasty

**photonasty** *noun* BOT a response of plants to light without movement towards the light source

**photo-oxidant** *noun* CHEM a chemical compound produced by the action of sunlight on nitrogen oxides and hydrocarbons

**photo-oxidation** *noun* CHEM a change in the chemical constitution of a compound by the action of sunlight ○ *Photo-oxidation breaks down polluted air and converts the gases to sulfur dioxide.*

**photoperiod** *noun* BIOL the period in every 24 hours when an organism is exposed to daylight

**photoperiodicity** *noun* BIOL the way in which plants and animals react to changes in the length of the period of daylight from summer to winter

**photoperiodism** *noun* BIOL the response of an organism in its growth and behaviour to the amount of daylight it receives in every 24 hours

**photophilic, photophilous** *adjective* BIOL growing best in strong light

**photophosphorylation** *noun* BIOCHEM a key process in photosynthesis in which energy from light is stored in the form of chemical bonds

**photoreceptor** *noun* ZOOL a structure that can detect light

**photoresist** *noun* ELECTRONICS a chemical or material that hardens into an etch-resistant material when light is shone on it

**photorespiration** *noun* BOT a reaction that occurs in plants alongside photosynthesis, in which the plant fixes oxygen from the air and loses carbon dioxide (NOTE: It slows down the production of sugars by photosynthesis. Some crop plants have been bred to reduce their photorespiration rate.)

**photosensitive** *adjective* **1.** PHYS which is sensitive to light **2.** BIOL stimulated by light

**photosensitivity** *noun* PHYS, BIOL the state of being sensitive to or stimulated by light

**photosynthesis** *noun* BOT the process by which green plants convert carbon dioxide and water into sugar and oxygen using sunlight as energy

**photosynthesise, photosynthesize** *verb* BOT to carry out photosynthesis ○ *Acid rain falling on trees reduces their ability to photosynthesise.*

**photosynthetic pigment** *noun* BOT a pigment that traps light energy during photosynthesis (NOTE: The main photosynthetic pigments in green plants are chlorophylls.)

**phototaxis** *noun* BIOL a movement of all or part of an organism in response to light either towards or away from it

**phototrophic** *adjective* BIOL obtaining energy from sunlight (NOTE: Plants are phototrophic.)

**phototropic** *adjective* BIOL (*of a plant or cell*) turning or growing towards or away from light

**phototropism** *noun* BOT response to light by turning or growing towards or away from it (NOTE: Most plant shoots show positive phototropism, i.e. they grow towards the light.)

**phototypesetter** *noun* PRINTING a device that can produce very high-resolution text on photo-sensitive paper or film

**photovoltaic** *adjective* ELEC converting the energy from electromagnetic radiation such as light into electricity

**photovoltaic effect** *noun* ELEC an effect that causes a voltage to develop where two different materials meet when they are exposed to light

**phreatic** *adjective* EARTH SCI referring to the water table

**phreatic gas** *noun* EARTH SCI a gas produced when water comes into contact with magma

**phreatic water** *noun* EARTH SCI the water in the layers of soil beneath the water table

**phreatophyte** *noun* BOT a plant whose roots go down into the water table

**phrenic nerve** *noun* ANAT a nerve that controls the muscles in the diaphragm

**pH test** *noun* CHEM a test to see how acid or alkaline a solution is

**phthalic acid** *noun* CHEM a colourless soluble crystalline acid used in dyes, perfumes, medicines and synthetic textiles. Formula: $C_6H_4(CO_2H)_2$.

**phycology** *noun* BIOL the scientific study of algae

**phylogenesis, phylogeny** *noun* BIOL the evolution of a taxon of organisms

**phylum** *noun* BIOL a major subdivision in the classification of organisms, below kingdom (NOTE: The plural is **phyla**.)

**physical** *adjective* 1. PHYS referring to matter and energy or the sciences dealing with them, especially physics 2. BIOL referring to the human body ○ *physical discomfort*

**physical address** *noun* COMPUT a memory address that corresponds to a hardware memory location in a memory device

**physical change** *noun* PHYS a process that alters one or more physical properties of an element or compound without altering its chemical composition

**physical chemistry** *noun* CHEM the study of how the physical attributes of substances are related to their chemical properties and reactions

**physical fitness** *noun* HEALTH the state of health of the body, especially as related to exercise

**physical geography** *noun* EARTH SCI the study of the physical features of the Earth's surface, and of their development and how they are related to the core beneath

**physical layer** *noun* COMPUT the lowest ISO/OSI standard network layer that defines rules for bit rate, power and medium for signal transmission

**physically** *adverb* BIOL by means of or with respect to the body ○ *An organism adapts physically to changes in temperature.*

**physical medicine** *noun* MED a branch of medicine which deals with physical disabilities or with the treatment of disorders after they have been diagnosed

**physical memory** *noun* COMPUT the memory fitted in a computer. Compare **virtual memory**

**physics** *noun* PHYS the scientific study of matter, including electricity, radiation, magnetism and other phenomena that do not change the chemical composition of matter

**physio-** *prefix* 1. PHYSIOL physiology 2. BIOL, PHYS physical

**physiological** *adjective* PHYSIOL referring to physiology

**physiological ecology** *noun* ECOL the study of the physiology of an individual and the effects on function and behaviour

**physiological specialisation** *noun* BIOL a phenomenon whereby some members of a population are identical in appearance but differ biochemically from each other

**physiologist** *noun* PHYSIOL a scientist who specialises in the study of the functions of living organisms

**physiology** *noun* BIOL the scientific study of the functions of living organisms

**phyto-** *prefix* BOT coming from plants

**phytoaccumulation** *noun* ENVIRON same as **phytoextraction**

**phytobenthos** *noun* BOT the plants that live on the bottom of a stream or lake

**phytochemistry** *noun* BOT, CHEM the study of the chemistry of plants

**phytochrome** *noun* BIOCHEM a pigment molecule in a plant which is sensitive to slight changes in day length and controls the plant's growth timetable

**phytoextraction** *noun* ENVIRON the absorption by plants of metal contaminants through their roots and subsequent storage in their upper parts, allowing the decontamination of land. Also called **phytoaccumulation**

**phytogeography** *noun* BOT the study of plants and their geographical distribution

**phytome** *noun* BOT a plant community

**phytophagous** *adjective* ZOOL referring to an animal that eats plants

**phytoplankter** *noun* BOT a single microscopic plant that floats in the sea or in a lake

**phytoplankton** *plural noun* BOT microscopic plants that float in the sea or in a lake. Also called **plant plankton**

COMMENT: Phytoplankton are formed mainly of diatoms and use the sunlight in the surface layers of the water to photosynthesise. Phytoplankton are the basis of the food chain of almost all aquatic animals.

**phytoplankton bloom** *noun* BOT a large mass of plankton that develops regularly at different periods of the year and floats on the surface of the sea or of a lake

**phytoplanktonic** *adjective* BOT referring to phytoplankton

**phytoremediation** *noun* ENVIRON the decontamination of land by growing plants to absorb heavy metals or other soil contaminants

**phytostabilisation** *noun* ENVIRON the use of plants to immobilise soil contaminants in their roots and prevent them from polluting ground water

**phytotoxic** *adjective* BOT, CHEM poisonous to plants

**phytotoxicant** *noun* BOT, CHEM a substance that is phytotoxic

**phytotoxin** *noun* BOT, CHEM a poisonous substance produced by a plant

**pi** *noun* MATHS the ratio of the circumference of a circle to its diameter. Symbol (NOTE: Its approximate value is 3.14159.)

**PIA** *abbreviation* COMPUT peripheral interface adapter

**PIC** *abbreviation* CHEM product of incomplete combustion

**pica** *noun* PRINTING a size of typeface equal to 0.422 cm or ten characters to the inch

**PICK** *noun* COMPUT a multiuser, multitasking operating system that runs on mainframe, mini or PC computers

**pico-** *prefix* MEASURE one million millionth, $10^{-12}$. Symbol **p**

**picomole** *noun* MEASURE a unit of measurement of the amount of a substance, equal to one million millionth of a mole. Symbol **pmol**

**picosecond** *noun* MEASURE one million millionth of a second. Abbreviation **pS**

**picric acid** *noun* CHEM a poisonous yellow crystalline acid used in disinfectants, dyes and high explosives. Formula: $C_6H_3N_3O_7$.

**picture** *noun* a printed or drawn image of an object or scene ○ *This picture shows the new design.* ■ *verb* to visualise an object or scene ○ *Try to picture the layout before starting to draw it in.*

**picture beam** *noun* COMPUT a moving electron beam that produces an image on a cathode ray tube screen by illuminating the phosphor coating and by varying its intensity according to the received signal

**picture element** *noun* COMPUT same as **pixel**

**picture object** *noun* COMPUT an image created with a vector drawing package and stored as vectors rather than as a bitmap

**PID** *noun* COMPUT a device such as a bank card connected with or inserted into a system to identify or provide authorisation for a user. Full form **personal identification device**

**pie chart** *noun* MATHS a diagram in which ratios are shown as slices of a circle ○ *The memory allocation is shown on this pie chart.*

**piezometer** *noun* PHYS an instrument for measuring the pressure of a liquid

COMMENT: To measure the pressure of water in the ground, a tube is inserted into the soil and readings are taken from it.

**piezometric, piezometrical** *adjective* PHYS referring to the level reached by water under its own pressure in a borehole or in a piezometer

**piggyback** *verb* ELEC to connect two integrated circuits in parallel, one on top of the other to save space ○ *Piggyback those two memory chips to boost the memory capacity.*

**piggyback entry** *noun* COMPUT an unauthorised access to a computer system gained by using an authorised user's password or terminal

**piggybacking** *noun* COMPUT the use of transmitted messages to carry acknowledgements from a message that has been received earlier

**pig iron** *noun* INDUST an impure form of iron produced in a blast furnace and used to make purer forms of iron or steel

**pigment** *noun* BIOCHEM a substance that gives colour to a part of an organism

COMMENT: The human body contains many substances that control colour: melanin gives dark colour to the skin and hair, bilirubin gives a yellow colour to bile and urine, haemoglobin gives blood a red colour. In plants, chlorophyll gives leaves their green colour and anthocyanin produces blue to purple coloration.

**pigmentary** *adjective* BIOL referring to or producing pigment

**pigmentation** *noun* BIOL the colouring of a body, especially that produced by deposits of pigment

**pigment cell** *noun* ANAT a cell in an organism that contains pigment

**pileus** *noun* **1.** MARINE BIOL the domed or bell-shaped part of the body of a jellyfish **2.** FUNGI the cap of a mushroom or toadstool

**piliferous layer** *noun* BOT the part of the epidermis of a plant's root that produces root hair cells

**pilot** *adjective* used as a test, which if successful will then be expanded into a full operation ○ *The pilot factory has been built to test the new production process.* ■ *verb* to test something with a view to expansion ○ *They are piloting the new system in the south-east.*

**PILOT** *noun* COMPUT a computer programming language that uses a text based format and is mainly used in computer-aided learning

**pilot project** *noun* a small-scale project carried out to see whether a large-scale project will work ○ *They are running a pilot project in the area for three months before deciding on the next stage.*

**pin** *noun* **1.** a short, usually cylindrical metal rod **2.** ELEC one of several short pieces of wire attached to an integrated circuit package that allows the circuit to be connected to a circuit board **3.** ELEC a projecting part of a plug which fits into a hole in a socket ○ *Use a three-pin plug to connect the printer to the mains.*

**PIN** *noun* COMPUT a unique sequence of digits that identifies the user. Full form **personal identification number**

COMMENT: A PIN is commonly used in automatic cash machines in banks, along with a card that allows the user to be identified.

**pin-compatible** *adjective* ELECTRONICS referring to an electronic chip that can directly replace another because the arrangement of the pins is the same and they carry the same signals ○ *It's easy to upgrade the processor because the new one is pin-compatible.*

**pincushion distortion** *noun* OPTICS a fault in a monitor that causes a distortion of an image in which the edges curve in towards the centre

**pine** *noun* TREES an evergreen coniferous tree growing in temperate latitudes.

Genus: *Pinus*. ○ *The north of the country is covered with pine forests.*

**pineal gland** *noun* ANAT a tiny gland within the brain that secretes the hormone melatonin into the bloodstream

**pine cone** *noun* BOT a hard reproductive structure containing the seeds of a pine

**pine oil** *noun* INDUST an essential oil obtained from pines

**pine tar** *noun* INDUST a brown or black sticky substance derived from the wood of pines and used in medicines, soap and paint

**pinewood** *noun* BOT a forest of pines

**PING** *noun* COMPUT a software utility that will test all the nodes on a network or Internet to ensure that they are working correctly. Full form **packet Internet groper**

**pinna** *noun* ZOOL a thin, flat, tapering body part such as a feather or fin

**pinout** *noun* ELECTRONICS a description of the position of all the pins on an integrated circuit together with their function and signal

**pinpoint** AEROSP *noun* a visual observation of the precise position of an aircraft ■ *verb* **1.** to find the precise position of something **2.** to identify something accurately ○ *to pinpoint a problem*

**PIO** *abbreviation* COMPUT parallel input/output

**pipe** *noun* **1.** ENG a hollow cylinder or tube down which a fluid or gas can flow ○ *a delivery pipe* ○ *an exhaust pipe* **2.** COMPUT a symbol, usually ( | ), that tells the operating system to send the output of one command to another command instead of displaying it

**pipe drain** *noun* ENG an underground drain made of lengths of tiles linked together (NOTE: Pipe drains may be made of clay, concrete or plastic pipes.)

**pipeline** *noun* **1.** ENG a long hollow cylinder or tube that conveys a fluid or gas ○ *The incompressibility of liquids enables force to be transmitted long distances through pipelines.* **2.** COMPUT a central processing unit or arithmetic logic unit that is constructed in blocks and executes instructions in steps, each block dealing with one part of the instruction, so speeding up program execution. Also called **pipeline computer**

■ *verb* COMPUT **1.** to schedule inputs to arrive at the microprocessor when nothing else is happening, so increasing apparent speed **2.** to execute several instructions in parallel to increase performance

**pipeline computer** *noun* COMPUT same as **pipeline**

**pipette** *noun* SCI a thin glass tube used in the laboratory for taking or measuring samples of liquid

**PIPO** *abbreviation* COMPUT parallel input/parallel output

**piracy** *noun* the unauthorised copying of patented inventions or copyright works

**pirate** *noun* COMPUT a person who copies a patented invention or a copyright work and sells it ○ *The company is trying to take the software pirates to court.* ■ *verb* to manufacture copies of an original copyrighted work illegally

**pisciculture** *noun* FISHERY the breeding of edible fish in special pools for sale as food

**PISO** *abbreviation* COMPUT parallel input/serial output

**pistil** *noun* BOT the female reproductive part of a flower, made up of the ovary, the style and the stigma

**piston** *noun* ENG a solid cylinder that fits into a larger cylinder and moves under fluid pressure, as in petrol and diesel engines, or compresses fluids, as in pumps and compressors

**piston engine** *noun* ENG a petrol or diesel engine in which pistons are moved by combustion of fuel, this reciprocating movement producing rotating movement

**piston ring** *noun* ENG one of the metal rings that seal the space between the piston and the cylinder wall ○ *There should be a loose fit between the cylinder and the piston, the difference being taken up by the piston rings.*

**pit** *noun* **1.** INDUST a large hole in the ground, e.g. for burying something or for the extraction of minerals, especially coal **2.** a small indentation in a surface **3.** COMPUT a bump or impression on the surface of an optical disk that represents a bit of data

**pitch** *noun* **1.** ACOUSTICS the frequency of a sound (NOTE: A low-pitched sound has a low frequency and a high-pitched sound has a high fre-

quency.) **2.** AEROSP a nose up/down movement of an aircraft about its lateral axis ○ *If the control column is moved forward or aft, the pitch attitude of the aircraft changes.* **3.** CHEM a dark sticky substance obtained from tar, used to make objects watertight **4.** ENG the angle of the blades of a wind or water turbine in relation to the flow of wind or water ■ *verb* AEROSP (*of aircraft*) to move about the lateral axis ○ *Move the yoke fore and aft to pitch down and up.*

**pitchblende** *noun* MINERALS a form of the mineral uraninite, which is a source of uranium and radium

**pitot, Pitot tube** *noun* PHYS an open-ended tube used to measure the speed of flow of a fluid

**pitted** *adjective* with small indentations

**pituitary gland** *noun* ANAT a gland at the base of the brain that produces hormones that control other glands and influence many body functions

COMMENT: The pituitary gland is about the size of a pea and hangs down from the base of the brain. The front lobe of the gland secretes several hormones that stimulate the adrenal and thyroid glands, and stimulate the production of sex hormones, melanin and milk. The posterior lobe of the gland secretes oxytocin. The pituitary gland is the most important gland in the body because the hormones it secretes control the functioning of the other glands.

**pivot** *noun* ENG a short rod on which another part rotates ■ *verb* to turn on a point ○ *The rocker arm pivots on a bearing and opens the valve.*

**pixel** *noun* COMPUT the smallest single unit or point of a display whose colour or brightness can be controlled. Also called **picture element**

COMMENT: In high-resolution display systems the colour or brightness of a single pixel can be controlled. In low-resolution systems a group of pixels are controlled at the same time.

**pK** *noun* CHEM a measure of how readily an acid dissociates, calculated as the negative logarithm of its dissociation constant K

**PLA** *noun* COMPUT same as **programmable logic array**

**place** *noun* **1.** a space or area ○ *Greenwich is a place on the 0° meridian.* **2.** a position ○ *a decimal place* **3.** □ **in place of** instead of ■ *verb* to put something in position ○ *Place the symbols at the bottom of the chart.*

**placebo** *noun* MED a liquid or tablet that appears to be a drug but has no medicinal substance in it

COMMENT: Placebos may be given to patients who have imagined illnesses. Placebos can also help in treating real disorders by stimulating the patient's psychological will to be cured. Placebos are also used on control groups in tests of new drugs (placebo-controlled studies).

**placebo effect** *noun* MED the apparently beneficial effect of telling patients that they are having treatment, even if this is not true, that arises from a desire for the treatment to be effective

**placenta** *noun* ANAT the tissue which grows inside the uterus in mammals during pregnancy and links the baby to the mother

COMMENT: The vascular system of the foetus is not directly connected to that of the mother. The placenta allows an exchange of oxygen and nutrients between the mother to the foetus, to which she is linked by the umbilical cord. It stops functioning when the baby breathes for the first time and then passes out of the uterus as the afterbirth.

**placental** *adjective* ANAT referring to the placenta

**placental mammal** *noun* ZOOL a mammal that has a placenta. Also called **eutherian** (NOTE: All mammals are placental except for the monotremes and marsupials.)

**plagioclimax** *noun* ECOL a stage in the development of a plant ecosystem where the system is kept stable by outside interference, as in managed woodlands

**plague** *noun* **1.** MED an infectious disease that occurs in epidemics which kill many organisms **2.** AGRIC a widespread infestation by a pest ○ *A plague of locusts has invaded the region and is destroying crops.*

**plain** *noun* EARTH SCI a level area with few trees

**plain old telephone service** *noun* TELECOM full form of **POTS**

**plaintext** *noun* COMPUT text or information that has not been encrypted or coded ○ *The messages were sent as plaintext by telephone.*

**plan** *noun* **1.** an organised way of doing something **2.** a drawing that shows how something is arranged or how something will be built ■ *verb* to organise carefully how something should be done

**PLAN** *noun* COMPUT a low-level programming language

**planar** *noun* **1.** ELECTRONICS a method of producing integrated circuits by diffusing chemicals into a slice of silicon to create the different components **2.** COMPUT a set of graphical objects or images arranged on the same plane

**Planck, Max (1858–1947)** PHYS a German physicist who set out quantum theory in work first published in 1900. He also set out the formula for the energy distribution in the spectrum of a black body.

**Planck's constant** *noun* PHYS a basic physical constant equal to the energy of a photon divided by its frequency (NOTE: Its approximate value is 6.6261 x $10^{-34}$ joule seconds.)

**Planck's radiation law** *noun* PHYS a physical law that describes the energy radiated from a black body per unit area per unit time per unit wavelength at a particular temperature

**plane** *noun*, *noun* MATHS an imaginary surface containing all the straight lines that connect any two points on it ○ *The planes of parallels of latitude are parallel to the plane of the equator.* ■ *noun* **1.** same as **aeroplane 2.** COMPUT one layer of an image that can be manipulated independently within a graphics program **3.** TREES a common temperate deciduous hardwood tree, frequently grown in towns because of its resistance to air pollution. Genus: *Platanus.*

**planet** *noun* ASTRON a large body in the solar system, e.g. Earth, Mars or Mercury

COMMENT: Planets are aggregations of material formed in the early days of the solar system. There is direct knowledge of only the nine planets of the solar system. It seems from close observation of their proper motions that other nearby stars may have large planets much bigger than Jupiter, the largest planet in the solar system, although this method does not allow smaller planets to be detected. But it is not known how often planets might form near other stars.

**planetary** *adjective* ASTRON referring to a planet

**planisphere** *noun* ASTRON a representation on a flat surface of a map of the night sky as seen from one location at a point in time

**plankter** *noun* BIOL a single microscopic animal or plant that lives and drifts in water

**planktivorous** *adjective* ZOOL referring to an animal that eats plankton

**plankton** *plural noun* BIOL the microscopic animals and plants that live and drift in water (NOTE: A single organism is a **plankter**.)

COMMENT: Plankton are divided into two groups: zooplankton, which are microscopic animals, and phytoplankton, which are microscopic plants capable of photosynthesis. Plankton float near the surface of the water and provide food for many fish and other marine animals.

**planktonic** *adjective* BIOL referring to plankton ○ *Blooms are population explosions of planktonic plants.*

**planogamete** *noun* GENETICS a gamete that is capable of moving, e.g. a spermatozoon

**plant** *noun* **1.** BOT an organism containing chlorophyll with which it carries out photosynthesis **2.** INDUST a very large factory or installation ○ *A nuclear power plant is to be built near the town.* ■ *verb* **1.** AGRIC to put plants in the ground ○ *to plant a crop of winter wheat* **2.** COMPUT to store a result in memory for later use

**plantation** *noun* **1.** AGRIC an estate, especially in the tropics, on which large-scale production of cash crops takes place (NOTE: Plantations specialise in the production of a single crop such as cocoa, coffee, cotton, tea or rubber.) **2.** FORESTRY an area of land planted with trees for commercial purposes (NOTE: Plantations of conifers are sometimes popularly called **forests**.)

**plant biology** *noun* BOT the study of the structure and functions of plants

**plant breeder** *noun* AGRIC a person who produces new forms of ornamental or crop plants

**plant breeding** *noun* AGRIC the practice of producing new forms of ornamental and crop plants by artificial selection

**plant community** *noun* ECOL a group of plants living together in an area

**plant cover** *noun* ECOL the number of plants growing on a specific area of land ○ *Plant cover at these altitudes is sparse.*

**plant-eater** *noun* ZOOL same as **herbivore**

**plant ecology** *noun* ECOL the study of the relationship between plants and their environment

**plant-feeder** *noun* ZOOL same as **herbivore**

**plant hormone** *noun* BOT a hormone that affects plant growth

**plant kingdom** *noun* BOT the category of all organisms classified as plants

**plant nutrient** *noun* BIOCHEM a mineral whose presence in the soil is essential for the healthy growth of plants

**plant physiology** *noun* BOT the study of the functions of plants

**plant plankton** *plural noun* BOT same as **phytoplankton**

**plant population** *noun* ECOL the number of plants found in a particular area

**plant sociology** *noun* ECOL the study of communities of plants

**plaque** *noun* **1.** MICROBIOL a clear area in a bacterial or cell culture that has been caused by a virus destroying the cells **2.** DENT a deposit of saliva, mucus, bacteria and food on the teeth

**plasma** *noun* **1.** ANAT the yellow watery liquid in which the blood or lymphatic cells float ○ *The accident victim was given plasma.* **2.** PHYS a form of ionised atomic material that is common where large amounts of energy are available, as in the atmospheres of stars or in Earth's outer atmosphere

COMMENT: If blood does not clot it separates into blood cells and plasma, which is formed of water and proteins, including the clotting agent fibrinogen. If blood clots, the blood cells separate from serum, which is a watery liquid similar to plasma, but not containing fibrinogen. Dried plasma can be kept for a long time, and is used, after water has been added, for transfusions.

**plasma cell** *noun* ANAT a white blood cell (**lymphocyte**) that produces a specific type of antibody

**plasma display** *noun* COMPUT a thin display screen using the electroluminescent properties of some gases to display text, usually used in small portable computers

**plasmagene** *noun* GENETICS a particle found in cytoplasm that can replicate itself and is thought to be able to pass on hereditary characteristics in the same way as a chromosomal gene

**plasma membrane** *noun* BIOL same as **cell membrane**

**plasma protein** *noun* BIOCHEM protein in plasma such as albumin, gamma globulin or fibrinogen

**plasmid** *noun* GENETICS a small circle of DNA that replicates itself (NOTE: Plasmids are mainly found in bacterial cells and are used in genetic modification, as they can be transmitted between bacteria of the same and different species.)

**Plasmodium** *noun* MED a genus of parasite that infests red blood cells and causes malaria

**plasmolysis** *noun* BIOL the shrinking of the cell contents away from the cell wall when a plant or bacterial cell loses water

**plasmon** *noun* GENETICS all the genetic material in the cytoplasm of a cell

**plaster of Paris** *noun* INDUST a white powder, calcium sulfate, that forms a rapidly hardening paste when mixed with water and is used in sculpture, plaster casts for broken limbs, and in the collection of delicate fossils

**plastic** *noun* INDUST an artificial, usually organic, material made from petroleum and used to make many objects ■ *adjective* **1.** PHYS able to take on different shapes when under stress and not returning to its original shape when the stress is removed **2.** INDUST made of plastic

COMMENT: Plastics are moulded by heating a substance under pressure and they retain their shape after being formed. Thermoplastics are heated while being shaped and can be heated and shaped again for re-use. Thermosetting plastics are heated while being shaped but cannot be reheated for recycling. Waste plastics containing chlorine can produce hydrogen

chloride when incinerated. Plastics formed from ethylene or propylene (i.e. polyethylene and polypropylene) are not degradable and must be recycled or destroyed by incineration.

**plastic foam** *noun* same as **foam plastic**

**plasticiser, plasticizer** *noun* INDUST a compound that makes other substances more plastic

**plastid** *noun* BIOL a structure (**organelle**) found in green plant cells that contains pigment, ribosomes and DNA and is important in food synthesis and storage

**plate** *noun* **1.** a smooth, flat rigid object with the same thickness all over **2.** EARTH SCI a large area of solid rock in the Earth's crust, which floats on the mantle and moves very slowly **3.** ELEC an electrode in a battery

**plateau** *noun* EARTH SCI an area of high flat land (NOTE: The plural is **plateaux**.)

**platelet** *noun* ANAT a tiny colourless circular structure in the blood (NOTE: Platelets are present in large numbers and are essential for blood clotting.)

**plate tectonics** *noun* EARTH SCI the mechanism that drives continental drift on the Earth, whereby large sections of the Earth's crust move relative to each other

**platform** *noun* COMPUT a standard type of hardware that makes up a particular range of computers ○ *This software will only work on the IBM PC platform.*

**platform-independent** *adjective* COMPUT (*of software or a network*) able to work with or connect to different types of incompatible hardware

**platinic chloride** *noun* CHEM same as **chloroplatinic acid**

**platinum** *noun* CHEM ELEM a rare metallic element that does not corrode (NOTE: The chemical symbol is **Pt**; atomic number is **78** and the atomic weight is **195.09**.)

**platinum black** *noun* CHEM a fine black powdery form of platinum used as a catalyst

**platinum metal** *noun* CHEM ELEM platinum or any of the metals chemically related to it (NOTE: The other platinum metals are iridium, osmium, palladium, rhodium and ruthenium.)

**platter** noun COMPUT one disk within a hard disk drive

COMMENT: The disks are made of metal or glass and coated with a magnetic compound. Each platter has a read/write head that moves across its surface to access stored data.

**platyhelminth** noun ZOOL same as **flatworm**

**playback head** noun ELEC a transducer that reads signals recorded on a storage medium and usually converts them to an electrical signal

**playback rate scale factor** noun COMPUT **1.** a sound played back at a different rate, directed by another application, to create a special effect **2.** the point at which video playback is no longer smooth and appears jerky owing to missed frames

**pleiotropic** adjective GENETICS referring to a gene that affects two or more apparently unrelated characteristics of an organism

**pleiotropism** noun GENETICS the control of two or more apparently unrelated characteristics of an organism by a single gene

**pleura** noun ANAT a thin transparent membrane that covers the lungs and folds back to form a lining for the chest cavity (NOTE: It secretes a fluid that acts as a lubricant as the lungs expand and contract during breathing. The plural is **pleurae**.)

**plexus** noun ANAT a network of nerves, blood vessels or lymph vessels

**ploidy** noun GENETICS the number of chromosome sets in a cell

**plot** MATHS, NAVIG noun a graph or chart that shows a relation between two sets of numbers as a series of points joined by a line ○ a plot of applied stress and resulting strain ■ verb to calculate and mark a line on a graph or chart □ **to plot a course** to calculate and draw the desired route of an aircraft or ship on a chart

**plotter** noun COMPUT a device peripheral that draws straight lines between two coordinates (NOTE: Plotters plot curved lines as a number of short straight lines.)

**plug** noun **1.** a device that fits into a hole to prevent liquid flowing out of a container ○ the oil drain plug **2.** ELEC a device for making an electrical connection ○ The printer is supplied with a plug. ♦ **spark plug 3.** EARTH SCI a round block of igneous rock forming the central vent of an old volcanic opening ■ verb to fill a hole with something so that fluid cannot escape

**plug-compatible** adjective COMPUT (of equipment) able to work with several different types of computer, so long as they have the correct type of connector

**plumbism** noun MED lead poisoning caused by taking in lead salts

**plume** noun **1.** INDUST a tall cloud of smoke or gas escaping from a factory chimney ○ a gas plume **2.** EARTH SCI a tall cloud of smoke or gas escaping from a volcano **3.** EARTH SCI a cloud of powdered snow blowing from a mountain crest **4.** ZOOL a large feather

**plumule** noun BOT the tiny structure in a plant embryo from which a shoot will develop

**plunger** noun ENG a machine part such as a piston that operates with a thrusting or plunging movement ○ A flow indicator valve comprises a body, a spring-loaded plunger connected to an actuator arm, and a micro-switch.

**plus** preposition with the addition of ○ At the selected decision height plus 50 feet, an aural alert chime sounds. ○ Four plus four equals eight (4 + 4 = 8).

**plus sign** noun MATHS same as **addition sign**

**Pluto** noun ASTRON the smallest and most distant planet of the solar system

COMMENT: From Pluto's density, it appears to be made of a mix of rock and ice. Pluto's mean distance from the Sun is 39AU. It takes 248 years to orbit the Sun.

**plutonium** noun CHEM ELEM a toxic and carcinogenic radioactive element extracted from uranium ore (NOTE: The chemical symbol is **Pu**; the atomic number is **94** and the atomic weight is **244**.)

**plutonium-239** noun CHEM an isotope of plutonium which is formed from uranium-238 and is used as a fuel in nuclear reactors (NOTE: It has a half-life of 24 360 years.)

**pmol** symbol CHEM picomole

**PMOS** noun ELECTRONICS a metal oxide semiconductor transistor that conducts via a small region of p-type semiconductor. Full form **p-channel metal oxide semiconductor**

**PNdB** *abbreviation* ACOUSTICS perceived noise level in decibels

**pneum-** *prefix* same as **pneumo-** (NOTE: used before vowels)

**pneumatic** *adjective* PHYS, ENG referring to air under pressure ○ *High-pressure pneumatic systems are generally fitted on the older types of piston-engine aircraft to operate the landing gear, wing flaps and wheel brakes.*

**pneumatically** *adverb* PHYS, ENG by using air under pressure ○ *The doors are hydraulically or pneumatically opened.*

**pneumo-** *prefix* air, the lungs or breathing

**pneumoconiosis** *noun* MED a lung disease in which fibrous tissue forms in the lungs because the patient has inhaled particles of stone or dust over a long period of time

**pneumogastric nerve** *noun* ANAT the tenth cranial nerve, which controls swallowing and nerve fibres in the heart and chest. Also called **vagus**

**PNL** *abbreviation* ACOUSTICS perceived noise level

**pnp transistor** *noun* ELECTRONICS a layout of a bipolar transistor whose collector and emitter are of p-type semiconductor and whose base is n-type semiconductor

**PNS** *abbreviation* ANAT peripheral nervous system

**Po** *symbol* CHEM ELEM polonium

**pod** *noun* **1.** BOT a casing for several seeds as in peas or beans **2.** ZOOL a small group of whales, dolphins, or seals **3.** AEROSP a detachable compartment on a spacecraft

**podsol, podzol** *noun* EARTH SCI a type of acid soil where oxides have been leached from the light-coloured top layer into a darker lower layer which is impermeable and contains little organic matter

COMMENT: On the whole podsols make poor agricultural soils, owing to their low nutrient status and the frequent presence of an iron pan. Large areas of the coniferous forest regions of Canada and Russia are covered with podsols.

**podsolic, podzolic** *adjective* EARTH SCI referring to podsol

**podsolic soil** *noun* EARTH SCI a soil that has formed a podsol. Also called **podsolised soil**

**podsolisation, podzolisation** *noun* EARTH SCI the process by which a podsol forms

**podsolised soil, podzolized soil** *noun* EARTH SCI same as **podsolic soil**

**podzol, etc** *noun* EARTH SCI another spelling of **podsol, etc**

**poikilo-** *prefix* irregular or varied

**poikilosmotic** *adjective* MARINE BIOL referring to an aquatic animal whose body fluids change by osmosis depending on the composition of the surrounding water

**poikilotherm** *noun* ZOOL same as **ectotherm**

**point** *noun* **1.** a particular figure on a scale ○ *The melting point of ice is 0 ° C (Celsius).* **2.** COMPUT a place or position **3.** the sharp end of something **4.** an object or aim in doing something

**pointer** *noun* **1.** a piece of helpful advice ○ *some useful pointers on writing up experiments* **2.** an indication of how something will develop ○ *a pointer to future research priorities* **3.** COMPUT a graphical symbol used to indicate the position of a cursor on a computer display ○ *Desktop publishing on a PC is greatly helped by the use of a pointer and mouse.* **4.** COMPUT a variable in a computer program that contains the address to a data item or instruction ○ *Increment the contents of the pointer to the address of the next instruction.*

**pointer file** *noun* COMPUT a file of pointers referring to large amounts of stored data

**pointing device** *noun* COMPUT an input device that controls the position of a cursor on screen as it is moved by the user. ♦ **mouse**

**point mutation** *noun* GENETICS a mutation that involves a change in a single base or base pair of the nucleotides in a gene sequence

**point of presence** *noun* COMPUT a telephone access number for a service provider that can be used to connect to the Internet via a modem. Abbreviation **POP**

**point out** *verb* **1.** to show someone something **2.** to make someone aware of a piece of information

**point quadrat** *noun* BOT a device for measuring the leaf cover of ground, comprising a piece of wood with many holes in it which is placed over a quadrat and rods are passed through the holes (NOTE: The number of leaves which they touch are then counted.)

**point size** *noun* PRINTING a unit of measure equal to 1/72 inch, used to measure type or text

**point source** *noun* ENVIRON a discharge from a single point, e.g. a pipe or a ship

**point to point protocol** *noun* COMPUT a protocol that supports a network link over an asynchronous, modem connection. Abbreviation **PPP** (NOTE: It is normally used to provide data transfer between a user's computer and a remote server on the Internet using the TCP/IP network protocol.)

**point-to-point tunneling protocol** *noun* COMPUT full form of **PPTP**

**poison** MED *noun* a substance which can kill or harm when eaten, drunk, breathed in or touched ■ *verb* to give someone or something a poison ○ *The workers were poisoned by toxic fumes.*

**poisoning** *noun* MED the act of killing or harming an organism with a poison

**poisonous** *adjective* MED toxic or full of poison ○ *a poisonous gas* ○ *Some fungi are good to eat and some are poisonous.*

**POL** *abbreviation* COMPUT problem-orientated language

**polar** *adjective* **1.** EARTH SCI referring to the North Pole or South Pole ○ *polar air* ○ *a polar region* **2.** PHYS referring to the poles of an electrical device or of a magnet ○ *Bar magnets attract each other because of polar differences.*

**polar body** *noun* GENETICS a cell with a nucleus but little cytoplasm that is produced along with an oocyte in meiosis and later discarded

**polar diameter** *noun* EARTH SCI the distance from one pole, passing through the centre of the earth, to the other pole ○ *The Earth's polar diameter is shorter than its average equatorial diameter.*

**polar ice cap** *noun* EARTH SCI a large area of thick ice covering the regions around the North or South Pole

**polarimeter** *noun* OPTICS a device for measuring the rotation of the plane of polarised light as it passes through a substance, usually a liquid or solution

**polarisation, polarization** *noun* **1.** PHYS a characteristic of light or radio or other electromagnetic waves in which the waves are aligned in one direction and show different properties in different directions ○ *The antenna must have the same effective length and the same polarisation as the transmitter.* **2.** ELEC a partial or complete polar separation of positive and negative electric charge

**polarise, polarize** *verb* **1.** (*of broadcast signal waveforms*) to align in one plane **2.** ELEC to separate positive and negative electric charges

**polarised plug** *noun* ELEC a plug which has a feature, usually a peg or a special shape, allowing it to be inserted into a socket only in one way

**polarity** *noun* ELEC the direction of flow of flux or current in an object ○ *During discharge, when the polarity of the supply changes, the stored energy is returned to the supply.*

**polarity test** *noun* ELEC a check to see which electrical terminal is positive and which negative

**polarography** *noun* CHEM a technique for studying ions in solution by comparing the strength of electric currents passing through the solution during electrolysis and the electric potential needed to produce them

**Polaroid** *trademark* a specially treated transparent plastic film that produces polarised light on transmission and is used for the reduction of glare in sunglasses and other applications

**polar vortex** *noun* METEOROL same as **circumpolar vortex**

**pole** *noun* **1.** a long, rounded piece of wood or metal **2.** one of two opposite points on an axis **3.** PHYS one of the two ends of a magnet that show magnetic attraction **4.** EARTH SCI the extreme north or south point of the Earth's axis ○ *A meridian is a line joining pole to pole.* **5.** ELEC a terminal of a battery ○ *a negative pole* ○ *a positive pole*

**Polish notation** *noun* MATHS ◊ **reverse Polish notation**

**poll** *noun* a survey that asks people's opinions about something ■ *verb* COMPUT (*of a computer*) to determine the state of a peripheral in a network

**pollard** FORESTRY *noun* a tree of which the branches have been cut back to a height of about two metres above the ground ■ *verb* to cut back the branches on a tree every year or every few years to a height of about two metres above the ground

COMMENT: Pollarding allows new shoots to grow, but high enough above the ground to prevent them from being eaten by animals. Willow trees are often pollarded.

**polled interrupt** *noun* COMPUT an interrupt signal determined by polling devices

**pollen** *noun* BOT the mass of cells in flowers which contain the male gametes

**pollen analysis** *noun* BOT same as **palynology**

**pollen count** *noun* ENVIRON a measurement of the amount of pollen in a sample of air

**pollen sac** *noun* BOT a hollow structure in which pollen is produced in a flower

**pollen tube** *noun* BOT a hollow tube that grows out of a pollen grain and carries the pollen nucleus to the egg cell through the micropyle

**pollinate** *verb* BOT to transfer pollen from male to female reproductive organs in a flower

**pollination** *noun* BOT the action of pollinating a flower

**pollinator** *noun* BOT an organism such as a bee, bird or other plant which helps pollinate a plant ○ *Some apple trees need to be planted with pollinators as they are not self-fertile.* ○ *Birds are pollinators for many types of tropical plant.*

**polling** *noun* COMPUT a system of communication between a controlling computer and a number of networked terminals in which the computer checks each terminal in turn to see if it is ready to receive or transmit data, and takes the required action (NOTE: The polling system differs from other communications systems in that the computer asks the terminals to transmit or receive, not the other way round.)

**pollinosis** *noun* MED inflammation of the nose and eyes caused by an allergic reaction to pollen, fungus spores or dust in the atmosphere. Also called **hay fever**

**pollutant** *noun* ENVIRON **1.** a substance that causes pollution ○ *Discharge pipes take pollutants away from the coastal area into the sea.* **2.** noise, smell or another unwanted occurrence that affects someone's surroundings unfavourably

**pollute** *verb* ENVIRON to discharge harmful substances in unusually high concentrations into the environment ○ *Polluting gases react with the Sun's rays.* ○ *Polluted soil must be removed and buried.*

**polluter** *noun* ENVIRON a person or company that causes pollution

**polluter pays principle** *noun* ENVIRON the principle that if pollution occurs, the person or company responsible should be required to pay for the consequences of the pollution and for avoiding it in future. Abbreviation **PPP**

**polluting agent** *noun* ENVIRON a substance that causes pollution

**pollution** *noun* ENVIRON the presence of unusually high concentrations of harmful substances in the environment ○ *In terms of pollution, gas is by far the cleanest fuel.* ○ *Pollution of the atmosphere has increased over the last 50 years.* ○ *Soil pollution round mines poses a problem for land reclamation.* (NOTE: Pollution is caused by natural events such as a volcanic eruption or by human action.)

**polonium** *noun* CHEM ELEM a natural radioactive element (NOTE: The chemical symbol is **Po**; the atomic number is 84 and the atomic weight is **209**.)

**poly-** *prefix* many

**polyamide** *noun* CHEM a synthetic polymer with recurring amide groups, e.g. nylon

**polyatomic ion** *noun* CHEM an ion containing two or more elements chemically combined

**polybrominated biphenyl** *noun* CHEM a highly toxic aromatic compound containing benzene and bromine, used in plastics and fire-retardant materials and thought to be carcinogenic. Abbreviation **PBB**

**polychaete** *noun* MARINE BIOL a marine worm with a segmented body on each of which is a pair of bristly extensions used in swimming. Class: Polychaeta.

**polychlorinated biphenyl, polychlorobiphenyl** *noun* CHEM one of a group of compounds produced by chlorination of biphenyl. Abbreviation **PCB**

COMMENT: PCBs are stable compounds and formerly were extensively used in electrical fittings and paints. Although they are no longer manufactured they are extremely persistent and remain in large quantities in the atmosphere and in landfill sites. They are not water-soluble and float on the surface of water where they are eaten by aquatic animals and so enter the food chain. PCBs are fat-soluble, and are therefore easy to take into the system, but difficult to excrete.

**polyclone** *noun* GENETICS a clone derived from groups of cells of different ancestry or genetic makeup

**polycondensed plastic** *noun* INDUST a type of plastic such as nylon which can be recycled

**polycrystalline silicon** *noun* INDUST silicon used to manufacture photovoltaic panels

**polyculture** *noun* AGRIC the rearing or growing of more than one species of plant or animal on the same area of land at the same time

**polycyclic** *adjective* ZOOL (*of snail shells*) making two or more complete whorls

**polycyclic aromatic hydrocarbon** *noun* CHEM one of a group of chemical compounds which are carcinogenic. Abbreviation **PAH**

**polyester** *noun* INDUST a synthetic polymer in which monomers are linked by the chemical group -COO⁻ (NOTE: It is used in resins, plastics, textiles and fibres.)

**polyethylene** *noun* CHEM same as **polythene**

**polyethylene terephthalate** *noun* INDUST a type of plastic that can be recycled, used to make artificial fibres and plastic bottles. Abbreviation **PET**

**polygamy** *noun* ZOOL a breeding arrangement where a male has several mates. Compare **monogamy**

**polygene** *noun* GENETICS one of a set of genes of which the whole set collectively determines a characteristic such as height

**polygon** *noun* MATHS a shape with three or more sides

**polygon mesh model** *noun* COMPUT same as **wire frame model**

**polyhaline** *adjective* CHEM (*of water*) containing almost as much salt as sea water. Compare **oligohaline**

**polyhydric alcohol** *noun* CHEM alcohol that includes more than one -OH group within its molecules

**polymer** *noun* CHEM a natural or artificial chemical compound whose large molecules are made up of smaller molecules combined in repeated groups

**polymerase chain reaction** *noun* BIOTECH a technique used to produce a large number of copies of a sequence of DNA. Abbreviation **PCR**

**polymerisation, polymerization** *noun* CHEM a chemical reaction or process in which a polymer is formed

**polymorphic** *adjective* BIOL existing in different forms

**polymorphism** *noun* BIOL **1.** the existence of different forms during the life cycle of an organism, as in the case of a butterfly which exists as a caterpillar, then a pupa, before becoming a butterfly **2.** the existence of different forms of an organism in a social system, as in the case of bees, which exist as workers, queens and drones

**polymorphous** *adjective* BIOL same as **polymorphic**

**polynomial code** *noun* COMPUT an error detection system that uses a set of mathematical rules applied to the message before it is transmitted and again when it is received to reproduce the original message

**polynucleotide** *noun* BIOCHEM a chain of nucleotides, as found in DNA and RNA

**polynyas** *noun* EARTH SCI an area of unfrozen sea water, created by local water currents in the northern oceans

**polyp** *noun* MARINE BIOL a sedentary form of aquatic animal, e.g. a sea anemone

**polypeptide** *noun* BIOCHEM a long chain of amino acids found in protein molecules

**polyphagous** *adjective* ZOOL eating more than one type of food ○ *a polyphagous animal*

**polyphony** *noun* COMPUT a device that can play more than one musical note at a time

**polyploid** *adjective* BIOL referring to an organism with more than two identical sets of chromosomes in each cell nucleus

**polypropylene** *noun* INDUST a thermoplastic used to make artificial fibres, bottles, pipes, and other articles, which is not degradable and must be recycled or destroyed by incineration

**polysaccharide** *noun* CHEM a complex sugar composed of simple sugar molecules linked into a branched or chain structure (NOTE: Cellulose and starch are polysaccharides.)

**polysaprobe** *noun* BIOL an organism which can survive in heavily polluted water

**polysaprobic** *adjective* BIOL able to survive in heavily polluted water

**polysomic** *adjective* GENETICS referring to a diploid cell in which some chromosomes occur more than twice

**polystyrene** *noun* INDUST a thermoplastic which can be made into hard lightweight foam by blowing air or gas into it, used as an insulating and packaging material

**polytene** GENETICS *adjective* referring to a giant chromosome formed from multiple strands of DNA ■ *noun* a polytene chromosome (NOTE: Polytenes found in drosophila fruit flies are useful in genetic research.)

**polytetrafluoroethene** *noun* INDUST a durable, nonflammable thermoplastic substance with good chemical resistance, used for coating metals for nonstick cookware

**polythene** *noun* INDUST a thermoplastic used to make artificial fibres, packaging, boxes and other articles. Also called **polyethylene**

**polyunsaturated fat** *noun* BIOCHEM a fatty acid capable of absorbing more hydrogen, typically found in vegetable and fish oils

**polyurethane** *noun* CHEM a tough flexible synthetic polymer, used in resins, varnish, glue, foams and fibres

**polyvinyl chloride** *noun* INDUST full form of **PVC**

**pome** *noun* BOT a type of fruit which develops from the axis of the flower in which the fleshy part develops from the receptacle of a flower and not from the ovary (NOTE: Apples and pears produce pomes.)

**pomology** *noun* BOT the study of growing fruit

**pond** *noun* EARTH SCI a small area of still water formed artificially or naturally

**ponding** *noun* EARTH SCI the formation of a small pool of liquid

**pond life** *noun* ECOL the community of organisms that live in a pond

**pondweed** *noun* BOT a plant that grows in a pond

**pons** *noun* ANAT a pale zone of nerve fibres on the surface of the brain stem, connecting the two hemispheres of the cerebellum

**pool** *noun* **1.** EARTH SCI a small area of still water, especially one formed naturally **2.** EARTH SCI an area of oil or gas which collects in porous sedimentary rock **3.** a group or combination of things or people. ◊ **gene pool**

**pop** *verb* COMPUT (*in an instruction to a computer*) to read and remove the last piece of data from a stack

**POP** *abbreviation* COMPUT point of presence

**POP 2** *noun* COMPUT a high level programming language used for list processing applications

**POP 3** *noun* COMPUT a system used to transfer electronic mail messages between a user's computer and a server such as one at an ISP. Full form **post office protocol 3**

**pop-down menu, pop-up menu** *noun* COMPUT a menu that can be displayed on the screen at any time by pressing the appropriate key, usually displayed over material already on the screen

**popliteal artery** *noun* ANAT an artery which branches from the femoral artery behind the knee and leads into the tibial arteries

**poppet valve** *noun* ENG an intake or exhaust valve of a piston engine, operated by springs and cams

**populate** *verb* **1.** ECOL to fill an area with organisms ○ *Starlings soon populated the whole eastern seaboard of the USA.* **2.** COMPUT to fill the sockets on a printed circuit board with components

**population** *noun* **1.** a number of people living in a country or town ○ *The government has decided to screen the whole population of the area.* ○ *Popula-*

tion growth is a major threat to conservation efforts. **2.** ECOL a number of organisms of the same species living and breeding in a specific area ○ *The fish population has been severely reduced.*

**population age structure** *noun* ENVIRON the distribution of the population by age, used when analysing demographic trends

**population control** *noun* ENVIRON the process of limiting the number of organisms living in a specific area

**population cycle** *noun* ECOL a series of regular changes in the population of a species, usually a cycle in which the population gradually increases and then falls away again

**population decrease** *noun* ECOL a reduction in the number of organisms living in a specific area

**population density** *noun* ECOL the number of organisms living in a specific area

**population dispersion** *noun* ECOL a pattern of organisms found over a wide area

**population dynamics** *noun* ECOL the study of the changes in the number of organisms living in a specific area

**population ecology** *noun* ECOL the study of the factors determining abundance and fluctuations in the population of a species

**population equilibrium** *noun* ECOL a situation in which the population stays at the same level, because the number of deaths is the same as the number of births

**population explosion** *noun* ECOL a rapid increase in the number of specific organisms living in an area

**population genetics** *noun* GENETICS the study of how genes behave in the organisms of a community during evolution

**population growth** *noun* ECOL an increase in the size of a population

**population inversion** *noun* PHYS the condition in which a higher energy state has more electrons than a lower energy state

**population momentum** *noun* ECOL a continuation of population growth for several generations after the population has achieved replacement fertility

**population pyramid** *noun* ECOL a graphical representation showing the distribution of a population according to age, sex or other characteristic

**population transfer** *noun* ECOL a movement of people or organisms from one place to another

**pore** *noun* **1.** ANAT a tiny hole in the skin through which sweat passes **2.** EARTH SCI a tiny space in a rock formation **3.** BOT same as **stoma**

**porosity** *noun* PHYS the degree to which a substance is porous ○ *Clay has a lower porosity than lighter soils.*

**porous** *adjective* **1.** with many holes or spaces **2.** ○ *Porous rock is not necessarily permeable.*

**porphyrin** *noun* BIOCHEM a metal-containing pigment with a ring-like molecular structure (NOTE: Haemoglobin is an important porphyrin in many animals.)

**port** *noun* COMPUT a socket or physical connection allowing data transfer between a computer's internal communications channel and another external device

**portable** *adjective* **1.** capable of being carried in the hands ○ *a portable fire extinguisher* ○ *An aneroid barometer is a more portable device than a mercury barometer.* **2.** COMPUT (*of hardware, software or data files*) able to be used on a range of different computers ■ *noun* COMPUT a compact self-contained computer that can be carried around and used either with a battery pack or mains power supply

**portable operating system interface** *noun* COMPUT full form of **POSIX**

**portal vein** *noun* ANAT a vein that takes blood from the stomach, pancreas, intestines and spleen to the liver

**portrait** *adjective* PRINTING the orientation of a page or piece of paper so that the longest edge is vertical. Compare **landscape**

**port replicator** *noun* COMPUT a version of a docking station that allows a laptop computer to be connected to duplicate the connection ports on the back of the laptop (NOTE: This allows a user to keep a mouse, power cable and printer connected to the port replicator and easily insert the laptop to use these ports without having to plug in cables each time the machine is used.)

**position** *noun* **1.** a place or location ○ *The prime meridian and the equator are the axes of the system of latitude and longitude which is used for expressing position on the globe.* **2.** a setting of a control ○ *the neutral position* ■ *verb* to place something somewhere ○ *The magnetic compass is positioned away from magnetic sources.*

**position effect** *noun* GENETICS a change in the expression of a gene that occurs if its location on the chromosome changes

**positive** *adjective* **1.** definite and without any doubt ○ *a positive identification* **2.** MATHS having a value of more than 0. Opposite **negative**. Symbol **+ 3.** meaning 'yes' **4.** PHOTOGRAPHY (*of an image*) showing the light and dark areas of objects as they are seen **5.** ELEC referring to an electrical voltage greater than zero

**positive display** *noun* COMPUT a display of text and graphics as black on a white background to imitate a printed page

**positive feedback** *noun* a situation where the result of a process stimulates the process which caused it

**positive logic** *noun* ELECTRONICS a logic system in which a logical one is represented by a positive voltage level, and a logical zero represented by a zero or negative voltage level

**positively** *adverb* **1.** in a positive way **2.** extremely ○ *The results of the eating habits survey were positively alarming.*

**positive presentation** *noun* COMPUT a screen image that is coloured on a white background

**positive pressure** *noun* PHYS the condition that exists when more air is supplied to a space than is used up, so the air pressure in that space is greater than that in the surrounding area ○ *Under positive pressure, if an opening exists, air will flow from the positively pressurised space into surrounding areas.*

**positive response** *noun* a communication signal that indicates correct reception of a message

**positive terminal** *noun* ELEC a terminal of a battery marked with the symbol +

**positron** *noun* PHYS a particle identical to an electron but bearing a positive rather than a negative electric charge

**POSIX** *noun* COMPUT an IEEE standard that defines a set of services provided by an operating system. Full form **portable operating system interface** (NOTE: Software that works to the POSIX standard can be easily ported between hardware platforms.)

**possibility** *noun* **1.** a chance occurrence ○ *The guidelines are designed to prevent the possibility of laboratory accidents.* ○ *We cannot rule out the possibility of error.* **2.** an available choice ○ *Several possibilities are open to us.*

**possible** *adjective* **1.** capable of happening ○ *There will be a possible delay.* **2.** to the greatest degree ○ *We received the best possible support from our colleagues.* ○ *They were the worst possible results we could have expected.*

**post** *verb* COMPUT **1.** to enter data into a record in a file **2.** to publish text online or in an Internet location

**POST** *abbreviation* COMPUT power-on self test

**post-** *prefix* after or later

**postbyte** *noun* COMPUT (*in a program instruction*) the data byte following the op code that defines the register to be used

**postclimax** *noun* ECOL a climax community still existing in a place where the environmental conditions are no longer suitable for it

**posterior aspect** *noun* BIOL a view of the back of the body, or of the back of part of the body

**postfix** *noun* COMPUT a word or letter written after another

**postfix notation** *noun* MATHS a logical way of writing mathematical operations, so that the operator appears after the operands, thus removing the need for brackets ○ *Normal notation is: (x-y) + z, but postfix notation is: xy – z +.*

**post office** *noun* COMPUT a central store for the messages for users on a local area network

**post office protocol 3** *noun* COMPUT full form of **POP 3**

**postsynaptic axon** *noun* ANAT a nerve that receives messages at a synapse. Compare **presynaptic axon**

**posttranscriptional** *adjective* GENETICS referring to processes or components that carry out genetic instructions only after the stage of transcription of a gene or genes

**posttranslational** *adjective* GENETICS referring to processes or components that carry out genetic instructions only after translation of RNA to protein

**potamology** *noun* EARTH SCI the scientific study of rivers

**potamoplankton** *plural noun* BIOL plankton that live in rivers

**potamous** *adjective* ZOOL referring to animals that live in rivers

**potash** *noun* CHEM any potassium salt (NOTE: Potash salts are crude minerals and contain much sodium chloride.)

**potash fertiliser** *noun* AGRIC a fertiliser based on potassium

**potassium** *noun* CHEM ELEM a soft metallic element, essential to biological life (NOTE: The chemical symbol is **K**; the atomic number is **19** and the atomic weight is **39.10**.)

> COMMENT: Potassium is one of the three major soil nutrients needed by growing plants. The others are nitrogen and phosphorus.

**potassium bicarbonate** *noun* CHEM same as **potassium hydrogen carbonate**

**potassium bitartrate** *noun* CHEM a white powder or crystalline compound used as a rising agent in baking. Formula: $KHC_4H_4O_6$.

**potassium bromide** *noun* CHEM a white crystalline compound, used in lithography, medicine, photography and the manufacture of soap. Formula: KBr.

**potassium carbonate** *noun* CHEM a white salt used in brewing and in the manufacture of ceramics, explosives, fertilisers, glass and soap. Formula: $K_2CO_3$.

**potassium chloride** *noun* CHEM a colourless crystalline salt used as a fertiliser and in photography and medicine. Formula: KCl.

**potassium cyanide** *noun* CHEM a very poisonous white crystalline salt used in the extraction of gold and silver from ore, in photography and as an insecticide. Formula: KCN.

**potassium hydrogen carbonate** *noun* CHEM a white powder or granular compound used in baking powder and as an antacid. Formula: $KHCO_3$.

**potassium hydroxide** *noun* CHEM a caustic and poisonous white solid, used in making soap, detergents, liquid shampoos and matches. Formula: KOH.

**potassium iodide** *noun* CHEM a white crystalline compound with a salty taste, used in medicine and photography and added to table salt. Formula: KI.

**potassium manganate (VII)** *noun* CHEM same as **potassium permanganate**

**potassium nitrate** *noun* CHEM a white crystalline salt, used as a fertiliser and meat preservative and in fireworks, explosives and matches. Formula: $KNO_3$.

**potassium permanganate** *noun* CHEM a purple-coloured salt that is soluble in water, used as a disinfectant. Formula: $KMnO_4$. Also called **potassium manganate (VII)**, **primary alcohol**

**potassium sulfate**, **potassium sulphate** *noun* CHEM a white crystalline powder that is soluble in water. Formula: $K_2SO_4$. Also called **sulfate of potash**

**potential** *adjective* capable of being, but not yet in existence ○ *A designated fire zone is a region where a potential fire risk may exist.* ■ *noun* **1.** ELEC voltage ○ *charged to a high potential* **2.** ELEC the ability of energy to carry out work, by transformation **3.** PHYS ◊ **electric potential**

**potential difference** *noun* ELEC the voltage difference between two points in a circuit

**potential divider** *noun* ELEC same as **voltage divider**

**potential energy** *noun* PHYS the energy of an object because of its position or due to its being stretched or compressed (NOTE: The energy is equal to mgh where m=mass of the object, g=acceleration of gravity and h=height.)

**potential evapotranspiration rate** *noun* EARTH SCI the amount of water transpired from a site assuming no soil water limitation and complete vegetation cover

**potentiate** *verb* BIOCHEM (*of two substances*) to increase each other's toxic effects

**potentiation** *noun* BIOCHEM the degree of probable increased damage caused by the combined action of toxic substances compared with their individual effects

**potentiometer** *noun* ELEC ENG a device for measuring an unknown potential difference or electromotive force without drawing current by comparing it against a known standard

**POTS** *noun* TELECOM a standard telephone line without any special features such as call waiting or forwarding and without high-speed digital access. Full form **plain old telephone service**

**pound** *noun* MEASURE a measure of weight, equal to 16 ounces or 453.592 grams. Symbol **lb**

**powder** *noun* a substance made of ground or otherwise finely dispersed solid particles ○ *Dry chemical fire-extinguishers contain a non-toxic powder.*

**powdered** *adjective* crushed to a fine dry dust

**powder metallurgy** *noun* METALL the technique of producing solid objects from powdered metals or carbides by compressing or heating them without melting them

**powdery** *adjective* having the texture or appearance of powder ○ *The fungus forms as a powdery layer on leaves.*

**power** *noun* **1.** ENG the energy, especially electricity, which makes something operate **2.** ELEC a unit of energy equal to the product of voltage and current, measured in watts **3.** MATHS the number of times a number is to be multiplied by itself ○ *5 to the power 2 is equal to 25.* (NOTE: It is written as a small figure in superscript: $10^5$: say 'ten to the power five') ■ *verb* ENG to provide electrical or mechanical energy to a device ○ *The monitor is powered from a supply in the main PC.*

**power cable** *noun* INDUST a wire which takes high-tension electric current from a power station, carried across the countryside on pylons. Also called **power line**

**power down** *noun* ELEC to turn off the electricity supply to a device

**-powered** *suffix* INDUST operated by a particular type of energy ○ *a wind-powered pump* ○ *a nuclear-powered submarine*

**power failure** *noun* **1.** ENG a loss of engine power **2.** INDUST a loss of electrical power supply

**power line** *noun* INDUST same as **power cable**

**power loss** *noun* ELEC the amount of power lost in transmission or due to connection equipment

**power management** *noun* COMPUT software built into laptop computers and some desktop PCs and monitors that will automatically turn off components that are not being used in order to save energy

**power monitor** *noun* ELEC a circuit that shuts off the electricity supply if it is faulty or likely to damage equipment

**power off** *noun* ELEC the switching off or disconnecting of an electrical device from its power supply

**power on** *noun* ELEC an indication that a voltage is being supplied to a piece of electrical equipment

**power-on reset** *noun* COMPUT the automatic reset of a computer to a known initial state immediately after power is applied

**power-on self test** *noun* COMPUT a series of hardware tests that a computer carries out when it is first switched on. Abbreviation **POST**

**power pack** *noun* ELEC a self-contained box that will provide a voltage and current supply for a circuit

**power plant** *noun* INDUST a building with machines which make electricity. Also called **power station**

COMMENT: A power plant makes electricity by using steam to turn turbines which themselves drive generators. High-pressure steam is heated by burning coal or oil, or by energy from a nuclear reactor. The steam passes over the turbines as a high-pressure jet, making the turbines rotate. The steam is produced from fresh water which is heated in a boiler, then passed through the furnace again to be superheated. Superheated steam drives the first turbine and then is returned to the boiler again for reheating and then passing over the second and third turbines. The steam is then condensed into water which then passes back through the system again. Although the steam used in power plants is heated several times and is condensed into reusable water at the end of the cycle, much of the energy generated to heat the water and create steam is not translated into electric power and is therefore wasted.

**power raising** *noun* INDUST the action of starting up a power station

**power station** *noun* INDUST same as **power plant**

**power supply** *noun* ELEC **1.** an electrical circuit that provides certain direct current voltage and current levels from an alternating current source for use in other electrical circuits ○ *If the power supply from the amplifier to the gauge fails, the needle slowly falls to zero.* **2.** same as **power supply unit**

**power supply unit, power supply** *noun* ELEC a device that regulates, smooths and reduces the mains voltage level for use in low power electronic circuits. Abbreviation **PSU**. Also called **power supply**

**power surge** *noun* ELEC same as **surge**

**power transient** *noun* ELEC a very short duration voltage pulse or spike

**power up** *verb* ELEC to switch on or apply a voltage to a electrical device

**ppb** *abbreviation* MEASURE parts per billion

**PPP** *abbreviation* COMPUT point to point protocol ■ ENVIRON same as **polluter pays principle**

**PPTP** *noun* COMPUT a protocol that allows a standard local area network protocol to be sent over the Internet in a transparent manner without the user or operating system noticing. Full form **point-to-point tunneling protocol**

**PPU** *abbreviation* COMPUT peripheral processing unit

**practical extraction and report language** *noun* COMPUT full form of **Perl** ○ *If you want to add a search engine to your website, you will need to write a Perl program.* (NOTE: It is usually used under Unix.)

**prairie** *noun* EARTH SCI an area of grass-covered plain in North America, mainly without trees (NOTE: The prairie lands of the United States and Canada are responsible for most of the North America's wheat production. In Europe and Asia, the equivalent term is **steppe**.)

**praseodymium** *noun* CHEM ELEM a soft silvery metallic element, used in al-

loys, arc lights and colouring for glass (NOTE: The chemical symbol is **Pr**; the atomic number is **59** and the atomic weight is **140.91**.)

**pre-** *prefix* COMPUT before or in front of

**pre-amplifier** *noun* ELECTRONICS an electronic circuit which amplifies a signal to a particular level before it is fed to an amplifier for output

**precautionary principle** *noun* ENVIRON the view within the Framework Convention on Climate Change that action should be taken to prevent large-scale, irreversible damage from climate change even though the effects of climate change are not yet fully understood

**precede** *verb* to come before something ○ *This instruction cancels the instruction which precedes it.*

**precedence** *noun* COMPUT a set of computational rules defining the order in which mathematical operations are calculated (NOTE: Usually multiplications are done first, followed by divisions, additions and finally subtractions.)

**precession** *noun* ASTRON the tendency of Earth's axis to wobble in space over a period of 23 000 years (NOTE: The Earth's precession is one of the factors that results in the planet's receiving different amounts of solar energy over long periods of time.)

**precipitant** *noun* CHEM a substance added to a solution to make solid dissolved particles separate from it

**precipitate** CHEM *noun* the mass of solid particles that separate from a solution during a chemical reaction ■ *verb* to make solid dissolved particles separate from a solution

**precipitation** *noun* **1.** CHEM the action of forming solid particles in a solution **2.** METEOROL water which falls from clouds as rain, snow or hail ○ *Annual precipitation is high in the mountain areas.*

**precipitation interference** *noun* interference to signals caused by rain, snow or hail

**precipitation scavenging** *noun* ENVIRON the removal of particles of polluting substances from the air in the form of acid rain

**precipitation tank** *noun* INDUST a sewage tank in which a chemical is added to the sewage before it passes to the sedimentation tanks

**precise** *adjective* exact or accurate ○ *A precise interval is essential to obtain correct ignition timing on all cylinders during engine running.* ○ *The atomic clock will give the precise time of starting the process.*

**precompiled code** *noun* COMPUT a code that is output from a compiler, ready to be executed

**precondition** *verb* COMPUT to condition data before it is processed

**precursor** *noun* CHEM, BIOL a substance or cell from which another substance or cell is developed ○ *The biggest share of ozone precursors comes from emissions from vehicles.*

**predation** *noun* ZOOL the killing and eating of other animals

**predator** *noun* ZOOL an animal that kills and eats other animals ○ *The larvae are predators of aphids.* Opposite **prey**

**predatory** *adjective* ZOOL referring to a predator ○ *predatory animals such as lions and tigers*

**predefined** *adjective* defined in advance

**predicate** *noun* COMPUT a function or statement used in rule-based programs such as expert systems

**predominance** *noun* the condition of being more powerful than others

**predominant** *adjective* **1.** more powerful than others ○ *The predominant airstream is from the west.* **2.** most common ○ *The predominant hair colour in this population is black.*

**predominate** *verb* **1.** to be more powerful than others ○ *A cold northerly airstream predominates during the winter.* **2.** to be more common than others

**preemptive multitasking** *noun* COMPUT a form of multitasking in which the operating system executes a program for a period of time then passes control to the next program, so preventing any one program using all the processor time

**preferendum** *noun* ECOL the area where a species flourishes best

**pre-fetch** *noun* COMPUT a short temporary queue where instructions for a central processing unit are stored before

being processed, increasing the speed of execution

**prefix** *noun* **1.** a part of word added at the beginning of a word to alter the meaning ○ *Pre- is a prefix meaning 'before'.* **2.** COMPUT a code, instruction or character at the beginning of a message or instruction

**prefix notation** *noun* MATHS a logical way of writing mathematical operations, so that the operator appears before the operands, removing the need for brackets ○ *Normal notation is (x-y) + z, but prefix notation is − xy + z.*

**pregnancy** *noun* BIOL the time between fertilisation and birth when the developing offspring grows inside the mother's body

**pre-ignition** *noun* AUTOMOT the ignition of the fuel/air mixture in the combustion chamber, occurring before the spark ○ *Pre-ignition is often caused by a hot spot in the combustion chamber which ignites the mixture.*

**pre-imaging** *noun* COMPUT the generation of one frame of an animation or video in a memory buffer before it is transferred on-screen for display

**premolar** *noun* DENT a chewing tooth between the canines and the molars in each jaw

**preparation** *noun* the act or a process of getting something ready

**prepotent** *adjective* GENETICS effective in conferring genetic characteristics or in fertilisation

**preprocess** *verb* COMPUT to carry out initial organisation and simple processing of data

**preprocessor** *noun* COMPUT **1.** a piece of software that partly processes or prepares data before it is compiled or translated **2.** a small computer that carries out some initial processing of raw data before passing it to the main computer

**preprogrammed** *adjective* COMPUT referring to a chip that has been programmed during manufacture to perform one function

**presbyopia** *noun* OPHTHALMOL a reduction in the eye's ability to focus with age

**prescan** *noun* COMPUT a quick, low-resolution scan to allow re-positioning of the original or delimitation of an area that is to be scanned at a higher resolution

**prescribe** *verb* to set something down as a rule or a guide

**prescribed procedure** *noun* an agreed or accepted pattern of doing something

**presentation layer** *noun* COMPUT the sixth ISO/OSI standard network layer that agrees on formats, codes and requests for start and end of a connection

**preservation** *noun* the process of protecting something from damage or decay ○ *Food preservation allows some types of perishable food to be eaten during the winter months when fresh food is not available.*

**preservative** *noun* FOOD INDUST a substance added to food to preserve it by slowing natural decay caused by microorganisms (NOTE: In the EU, preservatives are given E numbers E200 – E297.)

**preserve** *verb* ENVIRON, FOOD INDUST to protect something from damage or decay

**preset** *verb* COMPUT to set something in advance ○ *The printer was preset with new page parameters.*

**press** *verb* to push something with the fingers ○ *To end the program press ESCAPE.*

**pressure** *noun* **1.** the physical action of squeezing or forcing **2.** PHYS the force of something on its surroundings **3.** strong influence to make someone take or change an action

**pressure altimeter** *noun* AVIAT an altimeter which operates using atmospheric pressure (NOTE: The altitude indicated by a pressure altimeter is the height of the altimeter above the level of the pressure set on the sub-scale.)

**pressure gauge** *noun* PHYS a device used for measuring the pressure of a gas or liquid

**pressure gradient** *noun* METEOROL a change in atmospheric pressure from one place to another on the ground (NOTE: It is shown on a map by isobars.)

**pressure pattern** *noun* METEOROL a series of changes in pressure areas which take place regularly, e.g. every year

**pressure vessel** *noun* INDUST a container that houses the core, coolant and moderator in a nuclear reactor

**pressurise, pressurize** *verb* PHYS to increase the atmospheric pressure in a container

**pressurised fluidised-bed combustion** *noun* INDUST an economic method of burning low-grade coal in a furnace in which air is blown upwards through the burning fuel. Abbreviation **PFBC**

**pressurised water reactor** *noun* INDUST a type of nuclear reactor in which water is heated to steam under high pressure to turn turbines to generate electricity. Abbreviation **PWR**

**prestore** *verb* COMPUT to store data in memory before it is processed

**presumptive address** *noun* COMPUT an initial address in a program, used as a reference for others

**presumptive instruction** *noun* COMPUT an unmodified program instruction which is processed to obtain the instruction to be executed

**presynaptic axon** *noun* ANAT a nerve that transmits messages across a synapse. Compare **postsynaptic axon**

**pretty good privacy** *noun* COMPUT an encryption system developed to allow anyone to protect the contents of his or her e-mail messages from unauthorised readers. Abbreviation **PGP** (NOTE: This system is often used when sending credit card or payment details over the Internet.)

**prevailing wind** *noun* METEOROL the wind that is most frequent in a specific place ○ *The prevailing wind is from the south.*

**prevalence** *noun* frequency of occurrence ○ *the prevalence of malaria in some tropical countries* ○ *the prevalence of cases of malnutrition in large towns*

**prevalent** *adjective* occurring frequently ○ *a fungus which is more prevalent in deciduous forests* ○ *The disease is prevalent in some African countries.*

**prevent** *verb* to stop something happening

**prevention** *noun* an act or process of stopping something happening

**preventive maintenance** *noun* ENG regular inspection and cleaning of a system to prevent faults occurring

**preventive medicine** *noun* MED the practice of taking measures to prevent the occurrence of diseases

**prey** *noun* ZOOL an animal which is killed and eaten by another ○ *Small mammals are the prey of owls.* Opposite **predator**

**prey on** *verb* ZOOL to kill and eat another animal ○ *Water snakes prey on frogs and small fish.*

**primary** *adjective* first, basic or most important. Compare **secondary**

**primary alcohol** *noun* CHEM same as **potassium permanganate**

**primary cell** *noun* ELEC an apparatus that generates electricity by means of an irreversible chemical reaction (NOTE: A primary cell is not rechargeable.)

**primary channel** *noun* COMPUT a channel that carries the data transmission between two devices

**primary colour** *noun* one of the three main colours in the spectrum, red, green and blue, from which other colours are formed

**primary commodity** *noun* a basic raw material or food

**primary consumer** *noun* ECOL an animal that eats plants, which are producers in the food chain

**primary coolant** *noun* INDUST a substance used to cool a nuclear reactor, which then passes to a heat exchanger to transfer its heat to another coolant which is used to turn the turbines

**primary energy** *noun* INDUST the power required to produce other forms of energy such as heat or electricity

**primary forest** *noun* ENVIRON a forest which originally covered a region before changes in the environment brought about by human activity

**primary industry** *noun* INDUST an industry dealing with raw materials such as coal, food, farm produce or wood

**primary key** *noun* COMPUT a unique identifying word that selects one entry from a database

**primary mineral** *noun* EARTH SCI a mineral formed initially from cooling magma, which has remained unchanged

**primary particulates** *plural noun* ENVIRON particles of matter sent into the air from fires, industrial processes, volcanic eruptions, sandstorms and similar phenomena

**primary product** *noun* a product such as wood, milk or fish which is a basic raw material

**primary production** *noun* ECOL the amount of organic matter formed by photosynthesis

**primary productivity** *noun* 1. BOT the rate at which plants produce organic matter through photosynthesis 2. ECOL the amount of organic matter produced in a specific area over a specific period of time, e.g. by a crop during a growing season

**primary sere** *noun* ECOL the first plant community that develops on ground such as cooled lava from a volcano where no plants have grown before

**primary storage** *noun* COMPUT 1. a small fast-access internal memory of a system that contains the program currently being executed 2. the main internal memory of a system

**primary succession** *noun* ECOL an ecological community that develops in a place where nothing has lived before

**primary treatment** *noun* INDUST the first stage in the treatment of sewage in which suspended solids are removed

**primate** *noun* VERTEB a mammal with a relatively large brain, well developed eyesight, diminished sense of smell and complex hands and feet, including humans, apes and monkeys. Order: Primates.

**prime** *adjective* first □ **of prime importance** very important ■ *verb* MECH ENG to pump fuel spray into a piston engine inlet manifold to make starting a cold engine easier

**prime meridian** *noun* GEOG same as **Greenwich meridian**

**prime number** *noun* MATHS a number, which, if there is to be no remainder, is only divisible by itself and 1, e.g. 13, 17, 19, 23, 29

**primer** *noun* 1. INDUST a protective substance which is applied to a metal or wood surface before painting ○ *Interior metal finishing is done with dust shedding gloss paint over a primer.* 2. MECH ENG a small hand-operated pump used to spray fuel into the piston engine inlet manifold to make starting a cold engine easier

**prime vertical** *noun* ASTRON the imaginary circle around the Earth that goes through the highest point of the celestial sphere directly above an observer and crosses the horizon at east and west

**primitive** *adjective* **1.** referring to very early or prehistoric times **2.** BIOL referring to an early stage in an organism's development **3.** COMPUT (*in programming*) referring to a basic routine that can be used to create more complex routines **4.** COMPUT (*in graphics*) referring to a simple shape such as circle, square, line or curve that is used to create more complex shapes

**primitive area** *noun* ENVIRON an area of undeveloped land, e.g. a forest, which is set aside and protected as a national park or reserve

**primitive rock** *noun* EARTH SCI a rock formed in or before the Palaeozoic era

**primordial** *adjective* in a very early stage of development

**primordium** *noun* BIOL a tissue or organ at its earliest stage of development

**principal** *adjective* most important

**principle** *noun* a theory, rule or natural or scientific law

**print** *noun* characters made in ink on a surface ■ *verb* COMPUT to put letters characters in ink on a surface ○ *a printed agreement* ○ *printed regulations* ○ *The printer prints at 60 characters per second.*

**printed circuit board** *noun* COMPUT a flat insulating material that has conducting tracks of metal printed or etched onto its surface, which complete a circuit when components are mounted on it. Abbreviation **PCB**

**printer** *noun* COMPUT a device that converts input data in an electrical form into a printed readable form

**printer buffer** *noun* COMPUT a temporary store for character data waiting to be printed, used to free the computer before the printing is completed, making the operation faster

**printer control language** *noun* COMPUT a standard set of commands, defined by Hewlett Packard, that allow a computer to control a printer. Abbreviation **PCL**

**printer emulation** *noun* COMPUT a printer that is able to interpret the standard set of commands used to control another brand of printer

**printer port** *noun* COMPUT an output port of a computer with a standard connector to which a printer is connected to receive character data, either serial or parallel

**printing** *noun* **1.** COMPUT the action of printing out text stored in a computer **2.** PRINTING the process of making books, newspapers and other printed products

**print job** *noun* COMPUT a file in a print queue that contains all the characters and printer control codes needed to print one document or page

**print out** *verb* COMPUT to print information stored in a computer with a printer

**print preview** *noun* COMPUT a function of a software product that lets the user see how a page will appear when printed

**print queue** *noun* COMPUT an area of memory that stores print jobs ready to send to the printer when it has finished its current work

**print server** *noun* COMPUT a computer in a network that is dedicated to managing print queues and printers

**print style** *noun* COMPUT a typeface used on a printer or for a specific document

**prion** *noun* BIOL a variant form of a protein found in the brains of mammals and causing diseases such as scrapie in sheep, BSE in cattle and variant CJD in humans

**priority** *noun* COMPUT the importance of a device or software routine in a computer system ○ *The operating system has priority over the application when disk space is allocated.*

**priority interrupt** *noun* COMPUT a signal to a computer that takes precedence over any other task

**priority scheduler** *noun* COMPUT a system that organises tasks into correct processing priority to improve performance

**prism** *noun* OPTICS triangular-sectioned glass cylinder that can be used to split light into its spectral components or to recombine it once divided, because of the differential rate at which glass refracts light of different wavelengths (NOTE: In astronomical equipment diffraction gratings have largely replaced prisms.)

**privileged account** *noun* COMPUT a computer account that allows special programs or access to sensitive system data ○ *The system manager can access anyone else's account from his privileged account.*

**privileged instruction** *noun* COMPUT a command that can only be executed via a privileged account, e.g. delete another account, set up a new user or examine passwords

**privileged mode** *noun* COMPUT a mode of an Intel 80286 processor that is in protected mode and allows a program to modify vital parts of the operating environment

**probability** *noun* a chance of occurrence ○ *The probability of aquaplaning increases as the depth of tyre tread decreases.*

**probe** *noun* a device inserted into something to investigate the inside or to obtain information ■ *verb* to investigate the inside of something

**problem** *noun* **1.** a difficulty **2.** COMPUT a malfunction or fault **3.** MATHS a mathematical question

**problem definition** *noun* COMPUT the clear explanation, in logical steps, of a problem that is to be solved

**problem-orientated language** *noun* COMPUT a high-level programming language that allows some problems to be expressed easily. Abbreviation **POL**

**proboscis** *noun* ZOOL **1.** a long tube that forms the mouthparts in butterflies and some other insects **2.** an elephant's trunk

**procedural** *adjective* referring to procedure

**procedural language** *noun* COMPUT a high-level programming language in which the programmer enters the actions required to achieve the result wanted

**procedure** *noun* **1.** a method or way of doing something, especially the usual or expected way ○ *You should use this procedure to retrieve lost files.* ○ *The procedure is given in the manual.* **2.** COMPUT a small section of computer instruction code that provides a frequently used function and can be called upon from a main program ○ *This procedure*

sorts all the files into alphabetical order, you can call it from the main program by the instruction SORT.*

**procedure-orientated language** *noun* COMPUT a high-level programming language that allows procedures to be programmed easily

**process** *noun* a series of actions or changes that achieve a particular result ○ *the combustion process* ○ *the cooling process* ■ *verb* **1.** to deal with something in a particular way ○ *The applications for permits have still to be processed.* ○ *The core samples are being processed by the laboratory.* **2.** INDUST to produce something by treating a raw material in a factory **3.** CHEM to make a substance undergo a chemical reaction **4.** COMPUT to carry out a number of tasks to produce a result such as sorting data or finding the solution to a problem ○ *We processed the new data.* ○ *Processing all the information will take a long time.*

**process bound** *adjective* COMPUT referring to a program that spends more time executing instructions and using the central processing unit than in input/output operations

**process chemical** *noun* INDUST a chemical that is manufactured by an industrial process

**process control system** *noun* COMPUT a system with complete input and output modules, a central processing unit with memory and a program, usually stored in ROM, and control and feedback devices such as A/D and D/A converters that completely monitors, manages and regulates a process

**processing** *noun* **1.** the activity of dealing with something **2.** COMPUT the use of a computer to solve a problem or organise data ○ *Page processing time depends on the complexity of a given page.*

**processor** *noun* COMPUT a hardware or software device that is able to manipulate or modify data according to instructions

**produce** *verb* to make something ○ *a factory producing agricultural machinery* ○ *a drug which increases the amount of milk produced by cows*

**producer** *noun* **1.** a person or company that produces something **2.** BIOL an organism such as a green plant that takes energy from outside an ecosystem and channels it into the system (NOTE: Producers are the first level in the food chain.)

**producer gas** *noun* INDUST same as **air gas**

**product** *noun* **1.** MATHS the result after multiplication **2.** CHEM something that is produced in a chemical reaction **3.** the result or effect of a process

**production** *noun* **1.** the act of manufacturing or producing something **2.** BIOL the amount of heat or energy produced by the biomass in an area

**production ecology** *noun* ECOL the study of groups of organisms from the point of view of the food which they produce

**production line** *noun* INDUST a system of manufacturing a product in which the item moves slowly through a factory with new pieces being added to it as it goes along

**production platform** *noun* INDUST an oil rig in the sea where oil from several wells is collected

**production ration** *noun* AGRIC the quantity of food needed to make a farm animal produce meat, milk or eggs, which is always more than the basic maintenance ration

**production residue** *noun* the waste left after a production process

**productive** *adjective* **1.** producing a lot of something that can be used or sold ○ *highly efficient and productive forms* ○ *making productive use of waste ground* **2.** giving a good outcome ○ *a productive collaboration*

**productive soil** *noun* AGRIC soil which is very fertile and produces large crops

**productivity** *noun* the rate at which something is produced ○ *With new strains of rice, productivity per hectare can be increased.*

**product of incomplete combustion** *noun* CHEM a compound formed when combustion does not destroy all the waste being incinerated. Abbreviation **PIC**

**proenzyme** *noun* MICROBIOL a biologically inactive substance that is the precursor of an enzyme. Also called **zymogen**

**profession** *noun* ECOL all the chemical, physical and biological characters that determine the position of an organism or species in an ecosystem (NOTE: Examples would be aquatic predator or terrestrial herbivore.)

**profundal zone** *noun* EARTH SCI an area of water in a lake below the limnetic zone

**progeny** *noun* BIOL the offspring of any living thing

**progesterone** *noun* BIOCHEM a female sex hormone produced by the corpus luteum of the ovary to prepare the lining of the womb for a fertilised ovum. Formula: $C_{21}H_{30}O_2$.

**program** *noun* **1.** COMPUT a complete set of instructions which direct a computer to carry out a particular task **2.** US spelling of **programme** ■ *verb* **1.** COMPUT to write or prepare a set of instructions which direct a computer to perform a particular task **2.** US spelling of **programme**

**program branch** *noun* COMPUT one or more paths that can be followed after a conditional statement

**program compatibility** *noun* COMPUT the ability of two pieces of software to function correctly together

**program compilation** *noun* COMPUT the translation of an encoded source program into machine code

**program crash** *noun* COMPUT the unexpected failure of a program due to a programming error or a hardware fault

**program development** *noun* COMPUT all the operations involved in creating a computer program from first ideas, initial writing and debugging to the final product

**program execution** *noun* COMPUT the process of instructing a processor to execute in sequence the instructions in a program

**program file** *noun* COMPUT a file containing a program rather than data

**program flowchart** *noun* COMPUT a diagram that graphically describes the various steps in a program

**program instruction** *noun* COMPUT a single word or expression that represents one operation (NOTE: In a high level program each program instruction can consist of a number of low level machine code instructions.)

**programmable** *adjective* COMPUT able to accept and store instructions then execute them

**programmable interrupt controller** *noun* COMPUT a circuit or chip that can be programmed to ignore specific interrupts, accept only high priority interrupts and select the priority of interrupts

**programmable logic array, programmable logic device** *noun* COMPUT an integrated circuit that can be permanently programmed to perform logic operations on data using a matrix of links between input and output pins. Abbreviation **PLA, PLD**

COMMENT: A programmable logic array consists of a large matrix of paths between input and output pins, with logic gates and a fusible link at each connection point which can be broken or left to conduct when programming to define a function from input to output.

**programmable memory** *noun* COMPUT an electronic device in which data can be stored. Abbreviation **PROM**

**programmable read-only memory** *noun* COMPUT a memory integrated circuit that can be programmed with data by a user. Abbreviation **PROM** (NOTE: Some PROMs provide permanent storage, others such as EPROMs are erasable.)

**programme** *noun* a planned course of action ○ *a research programme* ■ *verb* **1.** to make something or someone behave in a particular way ○ *Some plants are naturally programmed to respond to day length.* **2.** to analyse or plan something ○ *The review is programmed to take place next month.*

**programmer** *noun* COMPUT **1.** a person who is capable of designing and writing a working program ○ *The programmer is still working on the new software.* **2.** a device that allows data to be written into a programmable read only memory

**programmer's hierachical interactive graphics standard** *noun* COMPUT full form of **PHIGS**

**programming** *noun* COMPUT **1.** the writing of programs for computers **2.** the writing of data into a PROM device

**programming language** *noun* COMPUT a set of rules and vocabulary that allows users to write a series of instructions to define a particular task, which will then be translated to a form that is understood by the computer

COMMENT: Programming languages are grouped into different levels. The high-level languages such as BASIC and PASCAL are easy to understand and use, but offer slow execution time since each instruction is made up of a number of machine code instructions. Low-level languages such as assembler are more complex to read and program in but offer faster execution time.

**program register** *noun* COMPUT a register in a central processing unit that contains an instruction during decoding and execution operations

**program report generator** *noun* COMPUT a piece of software that allows users to create reports from files, databases and other stored data

**program run** *noun* COMPUT the execution of the instructions in a program in the correct order

**program segment** *noun* COMPUT a section of a main program that can be executed in its own right, without the rest of the main program being required

**program stack** *noun* COMPUT a section of memory reserved for storing temporary system or program data

**program status word** *noun* COMPUT a word which contains a number of status bits such as carry flag, zero flag or overflow bit. Abbreviation **PSW**

**program testing** *noun* COMPUT the testing of a new program with test data to ensure that it functions correctly

**progression** *noun* a continuous series or sequence ○ *The instruments are checked in logical progression from left to right.*

**progressive** *adjective* (*of movement*) gradual ○ *progressive deterioration of muscle function* ○ *Throttle movements should be kept to a minimum and be smooth and progressive.*

**prohibit** *verb* **1.** to say that something should not be done ○ *prohibit the use of CFCs in aerosols* ○ *Smoking is prohibited in this area.* **2.** to prevent something from happening ○ *The persistence of the DDT prohibits its general use for malaria control.*

**project** *noun* a plan or scheme of work ○ *a land reclamation project* ■ *verb* **1.** to stick out **2.** to estimate something in the future from current information ○ *Reserach costs are projected to rise by more than the rate of inflation.* **3.** to make an image appear on a surface

**projectile** *adjective* **1.** moving forwards with force **2.** ZOOL able to push suddenly forward, as the jaws of some fish or the mask of a dragonfly larva ■ *noun* an object that is thrown or moves with force

**projection** *noun* **1.** a part that sticks out **2.** an estimate or assessment of something that will happen in the future **3.** the production of an image on a surface **4.** GEOG a technique for making a map

**prokaryote** *noun* BIOL a simple organism such as a bacterium whose DNA is not contained within a nucleus

**prokaryotic** *adjective* BIOL referring to prokaryotes

**prolactin** *noun* BIOCHEM a hormone produced by the pituitary gland that stimulates milk production after childbirth

**proline** *noun* BIOCHEM an amino acid found in many proteins, especially collagen. Formula: $C_5H_9NO_2$.

**PROLOG** *noun* COMPUT a high-level programming language using logical operations for artificial intelligence and data retrieval applications. Full form **programming in logic**

**prolong** *verb* to increase the duration or time of something, sometimes unnecessarily ○ *to prolong the life of an engine*

**prolonged** *adjective* lasting for a long time ○ *Avoid prolonged exposure to the sun.*

**PROM** COMPUT **1.** same as **programmable memory 2.** same as **programmable read-only memory**

**promethium** *noun* CHEM ELEM a radioactive metallic element used in phosphorescent paints and as an X-ray source (NOTE: The chemical symbol is **Pm**; the atomic number is **61** and the atomic weight is **145**.)

**prominence** *noun* ASTRON a visible stream of glowing gas that shoots out from the Sun, seen in the upper chromosphere and lower corona (NOTE: Prominences are visible at the rim of the Sun during an eclipse.)

**promontory** *noun* EARTH SCI an area of high land which sticks out into the sea

**promote** *verb* to encourage or enable something to take place ○ *Growth-promoting hormones are used to increase the weight of beef cattle.*

**promoter** *noun* **1.** CHEM a substance that increases the activity of a catalyst **2.** GENETICS a gene that controls the expression of structural genes. Also called **promoter gene**

**promoter gene** *noun* GENETICS same as **promoter**

**promotion** *noun* the activity of encouraging or enabling something to take place

**prompt** *noun* COMPUT a message or character displayed to remind the user that an input is expected ○ *The prompt READY indicates that the system is available to receive instructions.*

**proof** *noun* MATHS the series of logical stages used to establish whether a mathematical or philosophical proposition is valid

**propagate** *verb* **1.** BIOL to reproduce **2.** AGRIC to produce new plants by a technique such as taking cuttings, grafting, budding or layering **3.** COMPUT to travel or spread

**propagated error** *noun* COMPUT one error in a process that has affected later operations

**propagation** *noun* **1.** AGRIC the production of new plants **2.** ELEC the transmission of radio waves ○ *The speed of propagation of radio waves is slower over land than sea.*

**propagation delay** *noun* COMPUT **1.** the time taken for an output to appear in a logic gate after the input is applied **2.** the time taken for a data bit to travel over a network from the source to the destination

**propagator** *noun* BOT a closed but transparent container in which seed can be sown or cuttings grown in a moist, warm atmosphere

**propanal** *noun* CHEM a colourless liquid aldehyde. Formula: $C_2H_5CHO$.

**propane** *noun* INDUST a gas found in petroleum, which is sold commercially in liquid form under pressure as LPG

**propel** *verb* to cause something to move, especially at speed ○ *Fronts are propelled by the wind behind them.*

**propellant** *noun* INDUST **1.** a gas used in an aerosol can to make the spray come out **2.** a substance used to make something move forwards, e.g. rocket fuel

**propeller** *noun* AEROSP a rotating shaft with blades which, together with the engine, moves an aircraft through the air

**propeller blade** *noun* AEROSP one of the elements of a propeller which generate lift when the unit is turning

**propelling nozzle** *noun* the extreme rear part of a jet engine where the jet exhaust enters the atmosphere

**propene** *noun* CHEM same as **propylene**

**propenoic acid** *noun* CHEM same as **acrylic acid**

**propenonitrile** *noun* CHEM same as **acrylonitrile**

**property** *noun* **1.** a distinctive characteristic of something ○ *We use the energy-producing properties of uranium isotopes in nuclear reactors.* **2.** something which belongs to someone ○ *The institute is the property of a large corporation.* ○ *Inventions are regarded as intellectual property.* **3.** land and buildings

**prophage** *noun* GENETICS a dormant form of a virus that infects bacteria (**bacteriophage**) that has integrated its genetic material into its host or replicates without harm to the host

**prophase** *noun* BIOL the first stage of cell division, when the nuclear membrane vanishes and the chromosomes can be seen

**prophylactic** *adjective* MED helping to prevent the development of disease or infection

**prophylaxis** *noun* MED the taking of measures to prevent disease or infection

**proportion** *noun* **1.** a part of the whole compared with another part ○ *a small proportion* **2.** □ **in proportion to** directly related to ○ *The force required to move the control column is in proportion to the force being exerted by the control surface.*

**proportional** *adjective* **1.** comparable **2.** related to something by a constant ratio ○ *The wind blows along contours with low values on the left, and the speed is directly proportional to the contour gradient.*

**proportional spacing** *noun* COMPUT a printing system where each letter takes a space proportional to the character width 'i' taking less space than 'm'

**proprietary file format** *noun* COMPUT a method of storing data devised by a company for its products and incompatible with other products

**propulsion** *noun* the act or an instance of pushing or driving forwards

**propulsive** *adjective* pushing or driving ○ *The propeller is a means of converting engine power into a propulsive force called thrust.*

**propylene** *noun* INDUST a substance obtained from petroleum, used in the manufacture of plastics and chemicals. Formula: $C_3H_6$. Also called **propene**

**prosthetic group** *noun* BIOCHEM the nonprotein part of a conjugated protein, e.g. the lipid group in a lipoprotein

**protactinium** *noun* CHEM ELEM a poisonous radioactive metallic element derived from uranium ores (NOTE: The chemical symbol is **Pa**; the atomic number is **91** and the atomic weight is **231.04**.)

**protease** *noun* BIOCHEM a digestive enzyme which breaks down proteins in food

**protect** *verb* to stop something being damaged or harmed

**protected** *adjective* ENVIRON legally identified as a species in danger of extinction

**protected field** *noun* COMPUT storage or a display area that cannot be altered by the user

**protected location** *noun* COMPUT a memory location that cannot be altered or accessed without authorisation

**protected storage** *noun* COMPUT a section of memory that cannot be altered

**protection** *noun* the act or an instance of keeping something from harm, injury or damage

**protection master** *noun* a spare copy of a master film or tape

**protective** *adjective* intended or able to keep something else from harm, injury or damage ○ *Busbars are insulated from the main structure and are normally provided with some form of protective covering.*

**protective coloration** *noun* ZOOL a pattern of colouring that protects an animal from attack

**protein** *noun* BIOCHEM a nitrogen compound formed by the condensation of amino acids that is present in and is an essential part of all living cells in the body

COMMENT: Proteins are necessary for the growth and repair of the body's tissue. They are mainly formed of carbon, nitrogen and oxygen in various combinations as amino acids. Foods such as beans, meat, eggs, fish and milk are rich in protein.

**protein balance** *noun* PHYSIOL a situation when the nitrogen intake in protein is equal to the excretion rate in urine

**protein deficiency** *noun* HEALTH a lack of enough proteins in the diet

**protein engineering** *noun* BIOTECH the process of changing the sequence of a gene coding for a protein in order to bring about desirable changes in function

**proteolysis** *noun* PHYSIOL the breaking down of proteins in food by digestive enzymes

**proteolytic** *adjective* PHYSIOL referring to proteolysis ○ *a proteolytic enzyme*

**prothallus** *noun* BOT a tiny green structure that produces the sex cells of ferns and related plants

**prothrombin** *noun* BIOCHEM a protein in blood which helps it to coagulate and which needs vitamin K to be effective

**protist** *noun* BIOL an organism belonging to an older system of classification that includes protozoans, bacteria, and single-celled algae and fungi. Kingdom: *Protista.*

**protium** *noun* CHEM the commonest light isotope of hydrogen

**proto-** *prefix* first

**protocol** *noun* COMPUT a set of pre-agreed signals, codes and rules to be used for data exchange between systems

**protocol stack** *noun* COMPUT the separate parts of a protocol, each with a different function, that work together to provide a complete set of network functions

**proton** *noun* PHYS a particle with a positive charge and with mass almost identical to that of a neutron, found in the nucleus of an atom

**protonic acid** *noun* CHEM a compound that frees solvated hydrogen ions from a polar solvent

**proton number** *noun* PHYS same as **atomic number**

**proto-oncogene** *noun* GENETICS a gene that may mutate or be activated by a cancer-causing virus to become a cancer-causing gene

**protoplasm** *noun* BIOL a substance like a jelly which makes up the largest part of each cell

**protoplasmic** *adjective* BIOL referring to protoplasm

**protoplast** *noun* BIOL a basic cell unit in a plant formed of a nucleus and protoplasm

**prototype** *noun* COMPUT the first working model of a device or program, which is then tested and adapted to improve it

**prototyping** *noun* COMPUT the construction of a prototype

**protozoan** *noun* MICROBIOL a single-celled organism that is able to move and feeds on organic nitrogen and carbon compounds, e.g. an amoeba (NOTE: Protozoans are now regarded as part of the kingdom *Protoctista.*)

**prove** *verb* **1.** to show that something is true ○ *The pilot proved that he was not at fault.* **2.** to be discovered to have a particular quality ○ *Dry chemical extinguishers are used primarily for electrical fires and have also proved effective on liquid fires.*

**proventriculus** *noun* ZOOL the gizzard of birds, or the thick-walled stomach of insects and crustaceans

**provirus** *noun* MICROBIOL a form of a virus that integrates into the genetic material of the host and is passed on from one generation to the next

**proximity** *noun* nearness in space or time ○ *The two aircraft were in close proximity.*

**prussic acid** *noun* CHEM same as **hydrocyanic acid**

**pry-** same as **pyro-** (NOTE: used before vowels)

**pS** *abbreviation* MEASURE, COMPUT picosecond

**pseudo-** *prefix* similar to something, but not the same

**pseudocarp** *noun* BOT a fruit such as a strawberry formed by fusion of the ripened ovary with another structure, usually the receptacle

**pseudogene** *noun* GENETICS a non-functional DNA sequence that resembles the sequence of a functional gene

**pseudohalogen** *noun* CHEM a group of simple inorganic compounds that resemble halogens

**pseudo-instruction** *noun* COMPUT (*in an assembly language program*) a label that represents a number of instructions

**pseudo-operation** *noun* COMPUT (*in an assembler program*) a command that controls the assembler rather than producing machine code

**pseudoparenchyma** *noun* FUNGI a mass of interwoven hyphae

**pseudopodium** *noun* ZOOL a temporary bulge in part of the cell wall of a protozoan that helps it to move around and capture its food

**pseudo-random** *adjective* COMPUT referring to a generated sequence that appears random but is repeated over a long period

**PSS** *abbreviation* COMPUT packet switching service

**PSU** *abbreviation* ELEC power supply unit

COMMENT: A PSU will regulate, smooth and step down a higher voltage supply for use in small pieces of electronic equipment.

**psych-** *prefix* PSYCHIAT same as **psycho-** (NOTE: used before vowels)

**psychiatric** *adjective* PSYCHIAT referring to psychiatry ○ *psychiatric treatment*

**psychiatrist** *noun* PSYCHIAT a doctor who specialises in the diagnosis and treatment of patients with mental disorders

**psychiatry** *noun* PSYCHIAT a branch of medicine concerned with the diagnosis and treatment of mental disorders

**psycho-** *prefix* PSYCHIAT the mind

**psychoanalysis** *noun* PSYCHIAT treatment of mental disorder in which a specialist talks to the patient about the past events which might have caused it

**psychoanalyst** *noun* PSYCHIAT a specialist in psychoanalysis

**psychoanalytic, psychoanalytical** *adjective* PSYCHIAT referring to psychoanalysis

**psychogenic, psychogenetic, psychogenous** *adjective* PSYCHIAT (*of an illness*) starting in the mind, rather than in a physical state

**psychological** *adjective* 1. referring to psychology 2. caused by a mental state

**psychological dependence** *noun* HEALTH a state where a person is addicted to a drug such as cannabis but does not suffer physical effects if they stop taking it

**psychology** *noun* the study of human behaviour and mental processes

**psychometrics** *noun* a way of measuring intelligence and personality where the result is shown as a number on a scale

**Pt** *symbol* CHEM ELEM platinum

**pteridophyte** *noun* BOT a plant that does not produce flowers or seeds and reproduces by means of spores, e.g. ferns and some mosses. Division: *Pteridophyta*.

**p-type conductivity** *noun* PHYS conduction within a p-type semiconductor provided by positively charged holes where there were once electrons

**p-type semiconductor** *noun* PHYS a semiconductor material such as silicon which has an impurity added to remove some electrons, creating positively charged holes which can carry electrical charge

**Pu** *symbol* CHEM ELEM plutonium

**puberty** *noun* PHYSIOL the human process of becoming sexually mature, marked by the development of secondary sex characteristics and, in girls, by the start of menstruation

**pubes** ANAT plural of **pubis**

**pubic** *adjective* ANAT referring to or located near the pubes

**pubis** *noun* ANAT one of a pair of bones that form the lower front section of each hipbone and are joined at the front of the pelvis

**public** *adjective* **1.** concerning or available to all people in general **2.** COMPUT open to anyone to use

**public data network** *noun* COMPUT, TELECOM a data transmission service for the public, e.g. the main telephone system in a country. Abbreviation **PDN**

**public domain** *adjective* **1.** (*of documents or programs*) not protected by copyright **2.** generally known

**public key encryption** *noun* COMPUT a method of encrypting data that uses one key to encrypt the data and another different key to decrypt the data

**puddingstone** *noun* EARTH SCI a type of stone which is formed from other stones fused together

**puff** *noun* GENETICS an enlarged region on a chromosome where RNA synthesis is taking place

**pull** *verb* COMPUT to remove data from a stack. Compare **push**

**pull-down menu** *noun* COMPUT a set of options that are displayed below the relevant entry on a menu bar ○ *The pull-down menu is viewed by clicking on the menu bar at the top of the screen.* Compare **pop-down menu**

**pulmonary** *adjective* ANAT referring to the lungs

**pulmonary artery** *noun* ANAT either of the two arteries that take blood from the right side of the heart to the lungs to collect oxygen

**pulmonary circulation** *noun* PHYSIOL the circulation of blood from the heart through the pulmonary arteries to the lungs for oxygenation and back to the heart through the pulmonary veins. Also called **lesser circulation**

**pulmonary valve** *noun* ANAT a valve at the opening of the pulmonary artery

**pulmonary vein** *noun* ANAT one of the four veins that carry oxygenated blood from the lungs back to the left atrium of the heart (NOTE: The pulmonary veins are the only veins that carry oxygenated blood.)

**pulp** *noun* any soft wet matter, usually inside a harder exterior

**pulpwood** *noun* INDUST a softwood used for making paper

**pulsar** *noun* ASTRON a small dense star that emits brief intense bursts of visible radiation, radio waves and X-rays (NOTE: Pulsars are believed to be rapidly rotating neutron stars.)

**pulse** *noun* **1.** ELEC a short burst of current or voltage **2.** PHYSIOL a pressure wave that can be felt in an artery each time the heart beats to pump blood ○ *Her pulse is very irregular.* (NOTE: The normal adult pulse is about 72 beats per minute.) □ **to take** *or* **feel someone's pulse** to place fingers on an artery to feel the pulse and count the number of beats per minute **3.** any regular recurring variation in quantity **4.** PLANTS a leguminous plant that produces seeds eaten as food, e.g. a bean or pea ○ *Pulses provide a large amount of protein.* ■ *verb* ELEC to apply a short-duration voltage level to a circuit ○ *We pulsed the input but it still would not work.*

COMMENT: Electric pulses can be used to transmit information, as the binary digits 0 and 1 correspond to 'no pulse' and 'pulse'. The voltage level used to distinguish the binary digits is often zero, for the digit 0, and 5 or 12 volts, for the digit 1, with the pulse width depending on transmission rate.

**pulse-code modulation** *noun* COMPUT a way of storing sounds in an accurate, compact format that is used by high-end sound cards. Abbreviation **PCM**

**pulse-dialling** *noun* TELECOM telephone dialling that dials a telephone number by sending a series of pulses along the line (NOTE: Pulse-dialling takes longer to dial than the tone-dialling system.)

**pulse oximetry** *noun* MED a method of measuring the oxygen content of arterial blood

**pulse point** *noun* MED a place on the body where the pulse can be easily taken

**pulse pressure** *noun* MED the difference between the diastolic and systolic pressure

**pulse stream, pulse train** *noun* ELEC a continuous series of similar pulses

**pulverisation, pulverization** *noun* INDUST a process by which something is reduced to small particles (NOTE: Waste may be treated by this method.)

**pulverize** *verb* INDUST to reduce something to small particles

**pumice, pumice stone** *noun* EARTH SCI a light glass-like substance formed from foam at the edge of a lava flow

**pump** *noun* MECH ENG a machine which forces liquid or air into or out of something ■ *verb* to force liquid or air into or out of something

**pumped-storage system** *noun* INDUST a hydroelectric system in which electricity is generated at times of peak demand and water is pumped up to a high reservoir during offpeak periods

COMMENT: A pumped-storage turbine acts as an electricity generator when water pressure is high and becomes a water pump when water pressure is low, pumping water back up to the reservoir.

**pumping station** *noun* INDUST an installation where water, sewage or gas is pumped along a pipe or out of the ground, up to a storage tank

**pupa** *noun* INSECTS a stage in the development of some insects such as butterflies when the larva becomes encased in a hard shell (NOTE: The plural is **pupae**.)

**pupal** *adjective* INSECTS referring to a pupa

**pupate** *verb* INSECTS (*of an insect*) to move from the larval to the pupal stage

**pupil** *noun* ANAT the circular opening at the centre of the iris through which light enters the eye (NOTE: It becomes larger in dim light and smaller in bright light.)

**pure** *adjective* uncontaminated or unmixed ○ *Magnesium does not possess sufficient strength in its pure state for structural uses.*

**pure alcohol** *noun* CHEM **1.** a colourless liquid which is the basis of alcohols that are drunk, e.g. whisky, gin or vodka, and which is also used in medicines and as a disinfectant **2.** alcohol with 5% water. Also called **ethyl alcohol, ethanol**

**pure aluminium** *noun* METALL aluminium which has not been combined with any other metal to create an aluminium alloy

**purebred** *adjective* ZOOL referring to an animal which is the offspring of parents which are themselves the offspring of parents of the same breed

**pure strain** *noun* BOT a group of plants bred by self-fertilisation whose characteristics remain always the same

**pure tone** *noun* ACOUSTICS a sound formed of a single frequency containing no harmonics

**purge** *verb* **1.** to flush a system with a liquid or gas to clean it **2.** COMPUT to remove unnecessary or out-of-date data from a file or disk ○ *Each month, I purge the disk of all the old email messages.*

**purification** *noun* the action of making something pure or of removing impurities ○ *Activated sludge speeds up the process of purification.*

**purification plant** *noun* INDUST an installation where impurities are removed from water

**purify** *verb* to make something pure or to remove impurities from something

**purine** *noun* BIOCHEM a chemical belonging to a group derived from uric acid that includes the bases adenine and guanine found in DNA and RNA

**purity** *noun* the state of being pure

**purpose** *noun* a function or use ○ *The purpose of the engine is to convert heat energy to mechanical energy.*

**pus** *noun* PHYSIOL the thick, yellowish-white fluid that forms in infected tissue and consists of white blood cells, tissue debris and bacteria

**push** *verb* to press something or to move something by pressing on it

**pushbutton** *adjective* activated by pressing on a button

**push-down stack, push-down list** *noun* COMPUT a method of storing data in which the last item stored is always at the same location, the rest of the list being pushed down by one address

**push instruction, push operation** *noun* COMPUT a computer instruction that stores data on a LIFO list or stack

**pushrod** *noun* MECH ENG a steel or aluminium rod that moves a rocker arm (*in a valve mechanism*) ○ *The camshaft operates the pushrod.*

**push-up list, push-up stack** *noun* COMPUT a temporary storage queue system where the last item added is at the bottom of the list

**putrefaction** *noun* BIOL the decomposition of dead organic substances by bacteria

**putrefy** *verb* BIOL to decompose or rot

**putrescibility** *noun* ENVIRON the ability of waste matter to decompose or rot

**putrescible** *adjective* ENVIRON (*of waste matter*) able to decompose or rot

**PV** *abbreviation* ELEC photovoltaic

**PVC** *noun* CHEM a thermoplastic that is not biodegradable, used for floor coverings, clothes, shoes, pipes, etc. Full form **polyvinylchloride**

**PWR** *abbreviation* INDUST pressurised water reactor

**pylon** *noun* **1.** ELEC a tall metal structure that supports electricity cables **2.** AEROSP the structure on the wing of an aircraft that supports an engine

**pyloric antrum** *noun* ANAT a space at the bottom of the stomach, before the pyloric sphincter

**pyramid** *noun* **1.** MATHS a solid of which each side is a triangle, with either a square or triangular base **2.** ECOL same as **pyramid of biomass**

**pyramid of biomass** *noun* ECOL a graphical representation of the different amounts of biomass at each trophic level, with the highest biomass at producer level and the lowest at secondary consumer level. Also called **pyramid** (NOTE: The biomass at each level is about ten per cent of that of the level beneath.)

**pyramid of energy** *noun* ECOL a graphical representation of the amounts of energy consumed at each trophic level

**pyramid of numbers** *noun* ECOL a graphical representation of the structure of an ecosystem in terms of what eats what (NOTE: The base is composed of producer organisms, usually plants, then herbivores, then carnivores.)

**pyrenocarp** *noun* BOT same as **drupe**

**pyrethrum** *noun* AGRIC an organic pesticide, developed from a form of chrysanthemum, which is not very toxic and is non-persistent

**pyridine** *noun* CHEM a poisonous flammable liquid with an unpleasant smell used in the manufacture of chemicals, drugs and paints, and in textile dyeing. Formula: $C_5H_5N$. (NOTE: It occurs naturally in bone oil and coal tar.)

**pyridoxine** *noun* BIOCHEM vitamin $B_6$
COMMENT: Pyridoxine is present in meat, cereals and treacle. Lack of pyridoxine causes vomiting and convulsions in babies.

**pyrimidine** *noun* BIOCHEM a chemical belonging to a group derived from pyrimidine that includes the bases cytosine, thymine, and uracil found in RNA and DNA

**pyrite, pyrites** *noun* EARTH SCI gold-coloured form of iron sulfide. Formula: $Fe_2S$.

**pyro-** *prefix* burning

**pyrolysis** *noun* CHEM the decomposition or conversion of one substance into another by heat

**pyrometry** *noun* PHYS the measurement of high temperatures using a pyrometer

**pyrophoric** *adjective* CHEM **1.** igniting spontaneously in air **2.** giving off sparks when struck

**pyrotechnic** *adjective* CHEM relating to fireworks

**pyrrole** *noun* CHEM a colourless toxic liquid with a ring-like molecular structure found in biological substances such as chlorophyll, haemoglobin and bile pigments. Formula: $C_4H_5N$.

**pyruvic acid** *noun* CHEM a chemical formed in living cells when carbohydrates and proteins are metabolised. Formula: $C_3H_4O_3$.

**Pythagoras** ASTRON a Greek philosopher (6thC BC) remembered mainly for his theorem about the properties of right-angled triangles. He was an adherent of the idea that the Earth is round. His religious and mathematical school produced ideas about the relative distance of objects from the Earth, based on their relative velocities across the sky.

# Q

**Q** *noun* MEASURE, PHYS unit of energy equal to $10^{18}$ Btu

**QAM** *abbreviation* COMPUT quadrature amplitude modulation

**QBE** *abbreviation* COMPUT query by example ○ *In most QBE databases, the query form looks like the record format in the database and retrieving data is as easy as filling in a form.*

**QISAM** *abbreviation* COMPUT queued indexed sequential access method

**QSAM** *abbreviation* COMPUT queued sequential access method

**QSO** *abbreviation* ASTRON quasi-stellar object

**quad** *noun* MEASURE, PHYS a unit of energy equal to $10^{15}$ Btu

**quadbit** *noun* COMPUT four bits that are used by modems to increase transmission rates when using quadrature amplitude modulation

**quad density** *noun* COMPUT four bits of data stored in the usual place of one

**quadr-** *prefix* four

**quadrant** *noun* **1.** MATHS a quarter of a circle **2.** NAVIG a device for measuring the height of stars, formerly used in calculating direction at sea

**quadrantal** *adjective* **1.** MATHS referring to a quarter of a circle **2.** NAVIG referring to a quadrant

**quadrantal error** *noun* TELECOM a radio signal error caused by the metal structure of the receiving aircraft

**quadrantal height** *noun* NAVIG a flight level in each of the compass quadrants designed to provide safe separation for aircraft heading towards each other

**quadrat** *noun* MEASURE, ECOL an area of land measuring one square metre, chosen as a sample for research into plant populations ○ *The vegetation of the area was sampled using the quadrats.*

**quadratic equation** *noun* MATHS an equation in which one or more terms are raised to the power of two but no higher

**quadrature amplitude modulation** *noun* COMPUT a data encoding method used by high-speed modems, transmitting at rates above 2400 bps. Abbreviation **QAM** (NOTE: QAM combines amplitude modulation and phase modulation to increase the data transmission rate.)

**quadruplex** *noun* ELEC a set of four signals combined into a single signal

**quake** EARTH SCI same as **earthquake** (*informal*)

**qualitative** *adjective* referring to quality

**qualitative analysis** *noun* CHEM an analysis of what is present in a sample without reference to its quantities

**qualitative data** *plural noun* non-numerical records of variables kept during experiments

**qualitative inheritance** *noun* GENETICS the inheritance of a major characteristic that distinguishes individual specimens of a species

**quality** *noun* how good or bad something is ■ *adjective* of a high standard ○ *a quality product*

**quality assurance** *noun* INDUST the system of procedures used in checking that the quality of a product is good

**quality control** *noun* INDUST the process of checking that the quality of a product is good

**quantifiable** *adjective* able to be quantified ○ *The effect of the change in the waste disposal systems is not quantifiable.*

**quantifier** *noun* MATHS a sign or symbol that indicates the quantity or range of a predicate

**quantify** *verb* to state something as a quantity or in figures ○ *to quantify the* *effect of the new legislation on pollution levels* ○ *The environmental benefits are difficult to quantify.*

**quantisation, quantization** *noun* **1.** PHYS the division of the energy of a system into separate small amounts (**quanta**) **2.** ELEC the conversion of an analog signal to a numerical representation

**quantisation error** *noun* ELEC an error in converting an analog signal into a numerical form due to limited accuracy or a rapidly changing signal

**quantise, quantize** *verb* **1.** PHYS to divide the energy of a system into separate small amounts (**quanta**) **2.** ELEC to convert an analog signal into a numerical representation ○ *The input signal is quantised by an analog to digital converter.*

**quantiser, quantizer** *noun* ELEC a device used to convert an analog input signal to a numerical form that can be processed by a computer

**quantising noise** *noun* ELEC a noise on a signal due to inaccuracies in the quantising process

**quantitative** *adjective* referring to quantity

**quantitative analysis** *noun* CHEM an analysis of the quantity of a substance present in a sample

**quantitative data** *plural noun* numerical records of variables kept during experiments

**quantitative inheritance** *noun* GENETICS the inheritance of a characteristic that can vary slightly from specimen to specimen in a species

**quantity** *noun* **1.** an amount or number of items ○ *He bought a large quantity of spare parts.* **2.** a large amount ○ *The company offers a discount for quantity.* ○ *He bought a large quantity of spare parts.*

**quantum** *noun* **1.** PHYS the smallest amount of a property of a system that can change (NOTE: The plural is **quanta**.) **2.** COMPUT a packet of data that is the result of a signal being quantised

**quantum electrodynamics** *noun* PHYS a quantum field theory that describes the properties of electromagnetic radiation and how it interacts with electrically charged particles

**quantum field theory** *noun* PHYS a quantum theory that assumes that elementary particles interact through the influence of fields around them

**quantum Hall effect** PHYS same as **Hall effect**

**quantum mechanics** *noun* PHYS the study of how atoms and elementary particles such as electrons interact, based on quantum theory

**quantum number** *noun* PHYS one of the set of whole or half numbers that describe the properties and energy states of an elementary particle such as an electron or system

**quantum theory, quantum theory of radiation** *noun* PHYS a theory developed by a Danish physicist Neils Bohr (1885–1962) which states that at the smallest scale, energy exists in discontinuous 'lumps' or quanta rather than being infinitely divisible (NOTE: Thus lines in the spectra of stars mark the quantum of energy separating two different energy levels of a particular electron in an atom, the energy of the transition being given by Planck's constant, h, multiplied by the frequency of the spectral line.)

**quarantine** MED, VET *noun* the period when an animal, person or ship just arrived in a country is kept separate in case it carries a serious disease, to allow the disease time to develop and so be detected ■ *verb* to put a person, animal or ship in quarantine

**quark** *noun* PHYS an elementary particle that forms part of a hadron or a meson (NOTE: There are six 'flavours' or types of quark, each of which occurs in three 'colours'.)

**quarry** INDUST *noun* a place where rock is removed from the ground for commercial purposes ■ *verb* to remove rock from the ground for commercial purposes

**quarter** *noun* MATHS one fourth of something (1/4 or 25%) ○ *The fuel tank is only a quarter full.*

**quartile** *noun* STATS one of three figures below which 25%, 50% and 75% of a total falls

**quartz** *noun* EARTH SCI a mineral form of silica, often found as crystals in igneous rocks (NOTE: Pure quartz is known as rock crystal.)

**quartz clock, quartz crystal clock** *noun* TECH a small slice of a quartz crystal which vibrates at a specific frequency when an electrical voltage is supplied, used as a very accurate clock signal for computers and other high precision timing applications

**quasar** *noun* ASTRON a compact object in space that emits huge amounts of energy, sometimes equal to the energy output of an entire galaxy. Also called **quasi-stellar object** (NOTE: Quasars usually have a large red shift which indicates extreme remoteness.)

**quasi-** *prefix* almost ○ *a quasi-official body*

**quasi-instruction** *noun* COMPUT (*in an assembly program*) a label which represents a number of instructions

**quasi-stellar object** *noun* ASTRON same as **quasar**

**quaternary** *adjective* 1. consisting of four parts 2. COMPUT referring to four bits, levels or objects

**quaternary ammonium compound** *noun* CHEM a chemical whose structure is similar to that of an ammonium compound but in which organic groups replace the four hydrogen atoms

**quench** *verb* 1. to extinguish a flame or a light 2. CHEM to cool a metal rapidly by placing it in liquid, in order to make it harder or softer depending on the metal

**quench layer** *noun* AUTOMOT a deposit of unburnt hydrocarbons on the walls of cylinders in an internal combustion engine

**query** *noun* 1. COMPUT a request for information 2. a question arising from doubt or uncertainty about something ○ *a query on the validity of the experimental method* ■ *verb* 1. COMPUT to ask a question about something 2. to suggest that something may be wrong

**query by example** *noun* COMPUT a simple language used to retrieve information from a database management system by, usually, entering a query with known values, which is then matched with the database and used to retrieve the correct data. Abbreviation **QBE**

**queue** *noun* 1. a line of people or vehicles waiting one behind the other ○ *to form a queue* or *to join a queue* 2. a series of documents such as orders or application forms which are dealt with in order 3. COMPUT a list of data or tasks that are waiting to be processed ■ *verb* COMPUT to add more data or tasks to the end of a queue

**queued access method** *noun* COMPUT a programming method that minimises input/output delays by ensuring that data transferred between software and an input/output device is synchronised with that device

**queued indexed sequential access method** *noun* COMPUT an indexed sequential file that is read item by item into a buffer. Abbreviation **QISAM**

**queued sequential access method** *noun* COMPUT a queue of blocks waiting to be processed, which are retrieved using a sequential access method. Abbreviation **QSAM**

**quick-freeze** *verb* FOOD INDUST to preserve food products by freezing them rapidly

**quicklime** *noun* AGRIC, INDUST a calcium compound made from burnt limestone, used to spread on soil to reduce acidity and add calcium. Also called **calcium oxide** (NOTE: It is used in the composition of cement and in many industrial processes.)

**quicksilver** *noun* CHEM same as **mercury**

**quicksort** *noun* COMPUT a very rapid file sorting and ordering method

**quiescent** *adjective* 1. EARTH SCI (*of a volcano*) inactive 2. BOT (*of a seed*) not germinating because the conditions for germination are unsatisfactory 3. COMPUT (*of a process, circuit or device*) not receiving an input signal

**quinine** *noun* PHARM an alkaloid drug made from the bark of a South American tree, the cinchona, formerly used to treat the fever symptoms of malaria

**quintet** *noun* 1. a group of five things 2. COMPUT a byte made up of five bits

**quit** *verb* COMPUT to leave a system or a program ○ *Do not forget to save your text before you quit the system.*

**quota** *noun* a fixed amount of something which is allowed ○ *A quota has been imposed on the fishing of herring.*

**quota system** *noun* a system where imports or supplies are regulated by fixing maximum or minimum amounts

**quotidian** *adjective* recurring daily

**quotient** *noun* MATHS the result when one number is divided by another

COMMENT: When one number is divided by another, the answer is made up of a quotient and a remainder, the fractional part. So 16 divided by 4 is equal to a quotient of 4 and zero remainder, and 16 divided by 5 is equal to a quotient of 3 and a remainder of 1.

**QWERTY keyboard** *noun* COMPUT a keyboard with the standard English language key layout, where the first six letters on the top left row of keys are QWERTY

# R

**R** *symbol* MEASURE, PHYS roentgen

**Ra** *symbol* CHEM ELEM radium

**race** *noun* **1.** BIOL a group of people who are similar in general physical features and distinct from others **2.** BIOL a group of individuals within a species that are distinct, especially physiologically or ecologically, from other members of the species **3.** COMPUT an error condition in a digital circuit, in which the state or output of the circuit is very dependent on the exact timing between the input signals (NOTE: Faulty output is due to unequal propagation delays on the separate input signals at a gate.)

**raceme** *noun* BOT an inflorescence in which flowers are borne on individual stalks on a main flower stem with the youngest flowers at the top of the main stalk

**racemic mixture** *noun* CHEM a chemical compound that neither deflects nor absorbs light passing through it because it consists of a mixture of dextrorotatory and laevorotatory isomers

**racemisation** *noun* CHEM the process of turning an optically active compound or mixture into a racemic one that has no optical properties

**racemose inflorescence** *noun* BOT a pyramidal or flat-topped flower head with the youngest flowers developing nearest the tip of the main stem or main side branches

**rachis** *noun* BOT the main stem that supports an inflorescence or a compound leaf

**rack** *noun* **1.** a storage unit consisting of shelves, compartments or bars for hanging things **2.** COMPUT a metal supporting frame for electronic circuit boards and peripheral devices such as disk drives

**rack-mounted** *adjective* COMPUT referring to a system consisting of removable circuit boards in a supporting frame

**rad** *noun* MEASURE, PHYS a former unit of measurement of absorbed radiation dose (NOTE: The gray is now used for one hundred rads.)

**radar** *noun* PHYS a method of detecting distant objects and establishing their position, velocity or other characteristics by analysis of very high frequency radio waves reflected from their surfaces. Full form **radio detection and ranging**

COMMENT: Radar can detect storm clouds and is used in meteorology as well as by aircraft to avoid flying through storm clouds.

**radar beam** *noun* PHYS a shaft of radar waves directed towards a distant point

**radial** *adjective* referring to lines of radius having a common centre

**radial artery** *noun* ANAT an artery which branches from the brachial artery, running near the radius, from the elbow to the palm of the hand

**radial engine** *noun* MECH ENG an engine in which the pistons are arranged like the spokes of a wheel

**radial nerve** *noun* ANAT the main motor nerve of the arm

**radial pulse** *noun* MED the main pulse in the wrist, taken near the outer edge of the forearm, just above the wrist

**radial transfer** *noun* COMPUT data transfer between two peripherals or programs that are on different layers of a structured system such as an ISO/OSI system

**radian** *noun* MATHS a unit of measure of angles

**radiant** *adjective* PHYS sent out in the form of rays

**radiant flux** *noun* PHYS the flow rate of radiant energy

**radiant heat** *noun* PHYS heat which is transmitted by infrared rays from hot bodies (NOTE: An electric fire sends out radiant heat from a hot wire coil.)

**radiant heat transfer** *noun* PHYS the transfer of heat that occurs when there is a large difference between the temperatures of two surfaces that are exposed to each other but are not touching

**radiate** *verb* 1. to spread out in all directions from a central point 2. PHYS to send out rays ○ *Heat radiates from the body.* ○ *Beta rays are radiated from a radioactive isotope.*

**radiation** *noun* 1. the process or state of spreading out in all directions from a central point 2. PHYS waves of energy which are given off when heat is transferred 3. PHYS waves of energy which are given off by a radioactive substance

COMMENT: Prolonged exposure to ionising radiation from various sources can be harmful. Nuclear radiation from fallout from nuclear weapons or from power stations, background radiation from substances naturally present in the soil or exposure to X-rays, either as a patient being treated or as a radiographer, can cause radiation sickness. First symptoms of the sickness are diarrhoea and vomiting, but radiation can also be followed by skin burns and loss of hair. Massive exposure to radiation can kill quickly and any person exposed to radiation is more likely to develop some types of cancer than other members of the population. The main radioactive pollutants are strontium-90, caesium-137, iodine-131 and plutonium-239.

**radiation burn** *noun* MED a burn on the skin caused by exposure to a radioactive substance

**radiation carcinogenesis** *noun* MED the formation of cancer in tissue caused by exposure to a radioactive agent

**radiation enteritis** *noun* MED enteritis caused by exposure to X-rays

**radiation fog** *noun* METEOROL a fog that forms when the air just above ground level is cooled as the land surface immediately beneath it cools at night due to radiation of heat

**radiation injury** *noun* MED an injury caused by exposure to a radioactive agent

**radiation ionisation** *noun* PHYS same as **ionising radiation**

**radiation pollution** *noun* ENVIRON contamination of the environment by radiation from a radioactive agent

**radiation sickness** *noun* MED illness caused by exposure to a radioactive agent

**radiation unit** *noun* PHYS a measure of the radiation activity of a radio-isotope, given in disintegrations per second. Former name **curie**

**radiation zone** *noun* ENVIRON an area that is contaminated by radiation and which people are not allowed to enter

**radiative forcing** *noun* EARTH SCI a change in balance between incoming solar radiation and outgoing infrared radiation

**radiator** *noun* ENG a liquid-to-air heat exchanger that transfers engine heat to the outside air ○ *Anti-icing additives are used in radiator coolants.*

**radical** *adjective* MATHS referring to a mathematical root of another number or quantity ■ *noun* 1. MATHS a mathematical root of another number or quantity 2. CHEM same as **free radical**

**radicle** *noun* BOT the tiny structure in a plant embryo from which the root will develop

**radii** *noun* MATHS plural of **radius**

**radio** *noun* PHYS wireless transmission through space of electromagnetic waves in the approximate frequency range 10 kHz to 300 000 MHz

**radio-** *prefix* PHYS 1. radiation 2. radioactive substances

**radioactive** *adjective* PHYS referring to a substance whose nucleus disintegrates and gives off energy in the form of radiation that can pass through other substances

COMMENT: The most common naturally radioactive substances are radium and uranium. Other substances can be made radioactive for industrial or medical purposes by making their nuclei unstable, so forming radioactive isotopes. Radioactive wastes are classified as low-level, i.e. not considered to be very dangerous, intermediate and high-level, i.e. emitting dangerous levels of radiation and causing disposal problems.

**radioactive decay** *noun* PHYS a gradual disintegration of the nucleus of radioactive matter

**radioactive isotope** *noun* PHYS a natural or artificial isotope which gives off radiation

**radioactive series** *noun* PHYS a series of related radioactive nuclides, each of which decays into the next by emitting an elementary particle until a stable nuclide results

**radioactive waste** *noun* INDUST used radioactive materials produced by nuclear power stations, industrial plants, hospitals and other installations

**radioactive waste conditioning** *noun* INDUST the processing of radioactive waste to use it again or to make it safe for disposal

**radioactivity** *noun* PHYS energy in the form of radiation emitted by a radioactive substance

**radio altimeter** *noun* AVIAT an altimeter that operates using a radio signal directed vertically downwards, giving height above ground level

**radio astronomy** *noun* ASTRON a branch of astronomy that deals with the detection and analysis of radio waves emitted from objects in space

**radiobiologist** *noun* BIOL a scientist who specialises in radiobiology

**radiobiology** *noun* BIOL the scientific study of radiation and its effects on living things

**radio button** *noun* COMPUT a circle displayed beside an option on screen that, when selected, has a dark centre (NOTE: Only one radio button can be selected at one time.)

**radiocarbon** *noun* PHYS a radioactive isotope of carbon with an atomic number of 14

**radiocarbon dating** *noun* PHYS the process of determining the age of an object by assessing the amount of radiocarbon that has decayed

**radiodermatitis** *noun* MED an inflammation of the skin caused by exposure to a radioactive agent

**radio frequency** *noun* PHYS the electromagnetic spectrum that lies in the frequency range 10 KHz–3000 GHz. Abbreviation **RF, R/F**

**radio galaxy** *noun* ASTRON a galaxy that emits waves in the radio frequency

**radiogenic heat** *noun* PHYS the heat generated by the decay of a radioactive substance

**radiograph** *noun* MED a X-ray photograph

**radiographer** *noun* MED a person specially trained to operate a machine to take X-ray photographs

**radiography** *noun* MED the examination of the internal parts of a patient by taking X-ray photographs

**radio horizon** *noun* PHYS a line along which direct rays from a radio frequency transmitter become tangential to the Earth's surface

**radioisotope** *noun* CHEM a radioactive isotope of a chemical element

COMMENT: Radioisotopes are used in medicine to provide radiation for radiation treatment. They are also used to check how organs function or if they are diseased, e.g. radioisotopes of iodine are used to investigate thyroid activity.

**radiologist** *noun* MED a doctor who specialises in radiology

**radiology** *noun* MED the use of radiation to diagnose disorders, as in the use of X-rays or radioactive tracers, or to treat diseases such as cancer

**radio-opaque dye** *noun* MED a liquid which is introduced into soft organs such as kidneys so that they show up clearly on an X-ray photograph

**radiopaque** *adjective* PHYS opaque to or blocking the passage of X-rays and other forms of electromagnetic radiation

**radio scintillation** *noun* ASTRON the series of fluctuations in the strength of star signals caused by fluctuations in solar wind

**radioscopy** *noun* MED the examination of an X-ray photograph on a fluorescent screen

**radiosensitive** *adjective* MED (*of a cancer cell*) sensitive to radiation and able to be treated by radiotherapy

**radiosensitivity** *noun* MED the sensitivity of a cancer cell to treatment by radiation

**radiosonde** *noun* METEOROL a radio transmitter sent into the atmosphere attached to a balloon to take readings such as altitude, pressure and temperature

**radiotelephony** *noun* TELECOM the transmission of speech by radio. Abbreviation **R/T**

**radio telescope** *noun* ASTRON a telescope used to receive incoming radiation from the sky

**radiotherapy** *noun* MED the treatment of a disease such as cancer by exposing the affected part to radioactive rays such as X-rays or gamma rays

**radio wave** *noun* PHYS a type of electromagnetic radiation of relatively low frequency

**radium** *noun* CHEM ELEM a naturally radioactive metallic element (NOTE: The chemical symbol is **Ra**; atomic number is **88** and the atomic weight is **226.**)

**radius** *noun* **1.** MATHS a line drawn from a point on the circumference of a circle to the centre point, or the length of this **2.** ANAT the smaller of the two bones in an arm or foreleg

**radius of curvature** *noun* MATHS the radius of a circle whose curvature matches that of a curve at some given point

**radius of gyration** *noun* PHYS the distance from the axis of rotation in a rotating object where the mass of the object could be located without changing its moment of inertia

**radius vector** *noun* ASTRON a line connecting the centre of one astronomical object and that of another in orbit around it

**radix** *noun* MATHS the value of the base of the number system being used ○ *The hexadecimal system has a radix of 16.*

**radix complement** *noun* MATHS ◊ **ten's complement, two's complement**

**radix notation** *noun* MATHS a system of numbers based on a particular radix

**radix point** *noun* MATHS a dot which indicates the division between a whole unit and its fractional parts

**radon** *noun* CHEM ELEM an inert naturally radioactive gas formed by the radioactive decay of radium (NOTE: The chemical symbol is **Rn**; the atomic number is **86** and the atomic weight is **222.**)

COMMENT: Radon occurs naturally in soil, in construction materials and even in ground water. It can seep into houses and cause radiation sickness.

**radon decay products** *plural noun* CHEM substances that can be breathed into the lungs where they continue to release radiation as they decay further

**radula** *noun* ZOOL the feeding structure of slugs and snails, consisting of a ribbon-shaped tongue covered in tiny teeth which rasp off small particles of food

**raffinate** *noun* CHEM the part of a liquid mixture that remains after the extraction of other substances dissolved in it

**ragged left** *noun* PRINTING a printed text with a flush right-hand margin and uneven left-hand margin

**ragged right** *noun* PRINTING a printed text with a flush left-hand margin and uneven right-hand margin

**RAID** *abbreviation* COMPUT redundant array of inexpensive disks

**rain** *noun* METEOROL water that falls from clouds as small drops

COMMENT: Rain is normally slightly acid, about pH 5.6, but becomes more acid when pollutants from burning fossil fuels are released into the atmosphere.

**rain-bearing cloud** *noun* METEOROL a cloud that carries moisture in droplet form which can fall as rain

**rainbow** *noun* METEOROL a natural phenomenon that occurs when light strikes water droplets, especially when sunlight hits rain or spray from a waterfall, creating a semicircle of rings of each of the colours of the spectrum

**raindrop** *noun* METEOROL a drop of water that falls from a cloud

**rainfall** *noun* METEOROL the amount of water that falls as rain on an area over a period of time ○ *an area of high rainfall*

**rainforest** *noun* EARTH SCI a thick tropical forest which grows in regions where the rainfall is very high

**rainmaking** *noun* METEOROL the attempt to create rain by releasing crystals of salt, carbon dioxide and other substances into clouds

**rainout** *noun* METEOROL a process whereby particles in the atmosphere act as centres round which water can form drops which then fall as rain. Compare **washout**

**rains** *plural noun* METEOROL **1.** heavy repeated falls of rain **2.** the season when heavy rain falls

**rain shadow** *noun* METEOROL a reduction in rainfall on the lee side of a mountain

**rainstorm** *noun* METEOROL a period of heavy rain accompanied by wind

**rainwash** *noun* EARTH SCI the erosion of soil by rain

**rainwater** *noun* METEOROL water which falls as rain from clouds

**rainy** *adjective* METEOROL characterised by a lot of rain

**rainy season** *noun* METEOROL the period in some countries when a lot of rain falls. Also called **wet season**

**raise** *verb* **1.** to increase something **2.** to make something higher **3.** AGRIC to make plants germinate and nurture them as seedlings ○ *The plants are raised from seed.* **4.** AGRIC to breed and keep livestock

**raised beach** *noun* EARTH SCI a beach of sand left higher than sea level because the level of the sea has fallen

**raised bog** *noun* EARTH SCI a bog where the dead moss has accumulated without decomposing, so raising the level of the bog above the surrounding land

**ram** *noun* **1.** AEROSP an increase in air pressure caused by the forward speed of an aircraft **2.** ZOOL a male sheep

**RAM** *noun* COMPUT memory that allows access to any location in any order, without having to access the rest first. Full form **random access memory**. Compare **SAM**

COMMENT: Dynamic RAM which uses a capacitor to store a bit of data as a charge needs to have each location refreshed from time to time to retain the data. However it is very fast and can contain more data per unit area than static RAM, which uses a latch to store the state of a bit. It has the advantage of not requiring to be refreshed to retain its data, and will keep data for as long as power is supplied.

**ram air** *noun* AEROSP an airflow created by the movement of an aircraft, which is used to cool, ventilate or drive turbines ○ *Oil cooling may be achieved by using ram air or fuel.*

**Raman effect** *noun* PHYS the change in wavelength and phase of monochromatic light as it travels through a transparent substance (NOTE: It is used in Raman spectroscopy to study molecular structures.)

**RAM cache** *noun* COMPUT a section of high-speed RAM that is used to buffer data transfers between the faster processor and a slower disk drive

**RAM chip** *noun* COMPUT a chip that stores data, allowing random access

**RAM disk** *noun* COMPUT a section of RAM that is made to look like and behave as a high-speed disk drive, using special software

**ramet** *noun* BIOL a single cloned organism

**ram pump** *noun* ENG a water pumping device that is powered by falling water

**RAM refresh rate** *noun* COMPUT the number of times every second that the data in a dynamic RAM chip has to be read and rewritten

**R & D** *abbreviation* INDUST research and development

**R & D department** *noun* a department in a company that investigates new products, discoveries and techniques

**random** *adjective* not specially selected □ **at random** not using a particular method or pattern

**random access** *noun* COMPUT the ability to access immediately memory locations in any order ○ *Disk drives are random access, magnetic tape is sequential access memory.*

**random access memory** *noun* COMPUT full form of **RAM**

**random number** *noun* MATHS a number which cannot be predicted

**random number generator** *noun* COMPUT a program which generates random numbers, used in lotteries, games and sampling

**random process** *noun* COMPUT a system whose output cannot be related to its input or internal structure. Also called **direct access**

**random sample** *noun* a sample for testing taken without any special selection

**random segregation** *noun* GENETICS a principle stating that during meiosis the two separated partners of a chromosome pair are distributed randomly to the reproductive cells **gametes**, so that each gamete has the same chance of receiving either chromosome

**Raney nickel** *noun* METALL a form of the metal nickel, used as a catalyst

**range** *noun* **1.** a series of different but similar things **2.** the difference between the lowest and highest values in a series of data ○ *The temperature range is over 50° C.* **3.** a set of allowed values between a maximum and minimum **4.** an area within two or more points ○ *The geographical range of the plant is from the Arctic Circle to Southern Europe.* **5.** AGRIC a large area of grass-covered farmland used for raising cattle or sheep **6.** EARTH SCI a group of mountains ■ *verb* **1.** to be included within limits ○ *The temperature ranges from 13° C to 18° C in that month.* **2.** PRINTING to put text in order to one side □ **range left** *or* **right** to move text to align it to the left or right margin, or to move the contents of a word to the left or right edge **3.** to include many things ○ *The lecture ranged over the whole area of genetic modification.* ○ *The company's products range from a cheap lapheld micro to a multistation mainframe.* **4.** to move over a wide area

**ranger** *noun* FORESTRY a person in charge of the management and protection of a forest, park or reserve

**rank** *verb* COMPUT to sort data into an order, usually according to size or importance

**Rankine scale** *noun* PHYS an absolute temperature scale in which each degree is equal to 1° F, with zero at –459.67° F and the boiling point of water at 671.67° F

**Raoult's law** *noun* CHEM a law that states that the partial vapour pressure of a solvent is proportional to its mole fraction (NOTE: If a solution follows this law, it is usually described as an ideal solution.)

**rape** *noun* PLANTS same as **oilseed rape**

**rapid** *adjective* acting, moving or changing quickly

**rapid access** *noun* COMPUT a device or memory whose access time is very short

**rapid access memory** *noun* a storage location that can be read from or written to very quickly

**rapids** *plural noun* EARTH SCI a part of a river where water flows rapidly over large rocks

**raptor** *noun* ZOOL a bird of prey

**raptorial** *adjective* ZOOL referring to raptors

**rare** *adjective* **1.** not common **2.** ENVIRON (*of a species*) existing only in small local populations **3.** EARTH SCI (*of air*) not containing much oxygen, especially at high altitudes

**rare earth, rare-earth element** *noun* CHEM ELEM a member of the lanthanide series of the periodic table, which contains fifteen chemically similar elements with atomic numbers between 57 and 71

**rare gas** *noun* CHEM same as **noble gas**

**rarity** *noun* the state of being rare

COMMENT: Species of animals and plants are classified internationally into several degrees of rarity. Rare means that a species is not numerous and is confined to small local populations, but is not necessarily likely to become extinct. Vulnerable means that a species has a small population and that population is declining. Endangered means that a species has such a small population that it is likely to become extinct.

**raster graphics** *plural noun* COMPUT graphics in which the picture is built up in lines across the screen or page

**raster image processor** *noun* COMPUT a raster that translates software instructions into an image or complete page which is then printed by the printer ○ *An electronic page can be converted to a printer-readable video image by an on-board raster image processor.* Abbreviation **RIP**

**raster scan** *noun* COMPUT one sweep of the picture beam horizontally across the front of a screen

**rate** *noun* **1.** an amount or proportion of something compared to something else □ **the rate of population growth** the increase in population in an area divided by the initial population **2.** the speed at which something moves or changes compared with another measurable quantity such as time ○ *the rate of descent of the aircraft* **3.** the number of times something happens **4.** COMPUT a quantity of data or tasks that can be processed in a set time ○ *The processor's instruction execution rate is better than the older version.* ■ *verb* to evaluate how good something is or how large something is

**rate constant** *noun* CHEM the proportionality constant in the equation that relates the rate of a chemical reaction to the concentrations of its reactants

**rate-determining step** *noun* CHEM the slowest part of a chemical reaction that determines the overall rate of the reaction

**rated throughput** *noun* the maximum throughput of a device that will still meet original specifications

**rating** *noun* a classification according to a scale

**ratio** *noun* MATHS a relationship between two quantities expressed as the quotient of one divided by the other ○ *The air/fuel ratio is 15:1.* ○ *Chart scale is the ratio of the chart distance to earth distance.* (NOTE: The ratio of 7 to 4 is written 7:4 or 7/4.)

**rational number** *noun* MATHS a number that can be written as the ratio of two whole numbers ○ *24 over 7 is a rational number.* ○ *0.333 can be written as the rational number 1/3.*

**raw** *adjective* **1.** FOOD INDUST (*of food*) uncooked **2.** INDUST (*of sewage, water or waste*) untreated

**raw data** *noun* COMPUT **1.** data which have to be processed to provide useful information to the user **2.** pieces of information which have not been input into a computer system for analysis

**raw material** *noun* INDUST a substance which is used to manufacture something, e.g. ore for making metals or wood for making furniture

**raw sewage** *noun* INDUST sewage which has not been treated in a sewage farm ○ *The regulations prevent the discharge of raw sewage.*

**raw sludge** *noun* INDUST the solid part of sewage before it is treated, which falls to the bottom of a sedimentation tank

**ray** *noun* **1.** PHYS a line of light, radiation or heat **2.** ZOOL an arm of a starfish **3.** BOT a distinct radial band of tissue in the stem of a plant

**rayon** *noun* TEXTILES a synthetic textile fibre made from cellulose, often regarded as artificial silk

**ray tracing** *noun* COMPUT a method of creating life-like computer-generated graphics which correctly show shadows and highlights on an object as if coming from a light source

**Rb** *symbol* CHEM ELEM rubidium

**RBE** *abbreviation* BIOL relative biological effectiveness

**RDBMS** *abbreviation* COMPUT relational database management system

**RDF** *abbreviation* INDUST refuse-derived fuel

**Re** *symbol* CHEM ELEM rhenium

**react** *verb* **1.** to act in response to an action ○ *Because the rotors and stators of a compressor are of aerofoil shape, the airflow reacts in a similar way to the airflow over a wing.* **2.** CHEM to change chemical composition on contact with a substance ○ *The electrolyte in the cells of a lead-acid battery reacts chemically with the plates.* ○ *Ozone is produced as a result of oxides reacting with sunlight.*

**reactance** *noun* ELEC a component of impedance in an alternating current circuit

**reactant** *noun* CHEM a substance that reacts chemically with another

**reaction** *noun* **1.** the action that takes place because of something which has happened earlier **2.** an effect produced by a stimulus **3.** CHEM a chemical change that occurs when two substances come into contact and cause each other to change

**reaction turbine** *noun* ENG a turbine where the blades on the turbine adjust to the angle at which the jets of water hit them

**reactive** *adjective* CHEM referring to a chemical that reacts easily with other substances

**reactive dye** *noun* CHEM a coloured dye that forms a chemical bond with a fabric, providing very good colour fastness

**reactive mode** *noun* COMPUT a computer operating mode in which each entry by the user causes something to happen but does not provide an immediate response

**reactivity** *noun* CHEM the ability of a substance to react

**read** *verb* **1.** to look at printed words and understand them ○ *Conditions of sale are printed in such small characters that they are difficult to read.* **2.** COMPUT (*of an electronic device*) to scan printed text ○ *Can the OCR read typeset characters?* **3.** COMPUT to retrieve data from a storage medium ○

*This instruction reads the first record of a file.* ○ *Access time can be the time taken to read from a record.*

**reader level** *noun* COMPUT one of two modes that allows a user to run and interact with a multimedia application, but not modify it in any way

**read error** *noun* COMPUT an error that occurs during a read operation, often because the stored data has been corrupted

**read head** *noun* ELEC ENG a transducer that reads signals stored on a magnetic medium such as a floppy disk and converts them back to their original electrical form

**reading** *noun* a piece of information indicated by an instrument or gauge

**reading frame** *noun* GENETICS a sequence of three nucleotides on DNA or messenger RNA that indicates the starting point for the instruction controlling the production of a polypeptide

**read only** *adjective* COMPUT referring to a device or circuit whose stored data cannot be changed

**read only memory** *noun* COMPUT full form of **ROM**

**readout** *noun* a display or presentation of data from calculations or storage ○ *The rotating beam cloud base recorder/indicator operates continuously, day and night, and produces an automatic readout of cloud base height.*

**readout device** *noun* a device that allows data to be displayed as numbers or characters

**ready-state** *adjective* TELECOM (*of a communication line or device*) waiting to accept data

**reafforest** *verb* FORESTRY to plant trees again in an area which was formerly covered by forest

**reafforestation** *noun* FORESTRY the planting of trees in an area which was formerly covered by forest

**reagent** *noun* CHEM a chemical substance which reacts with another substance, especially referring to a laboratory chemical

**real address** *noun* COMPUT an absolute address that directly accesses a memory location

**real gas** *noun* CHEM a gas that does not behave as an ideal gas

**realised niche** *noun* ECOL a portion of a fundamental niche actually occu-

pied by a species, which results from the sharing of resources in an ecosystem

**real memory** *noun* COMPUT the actual physical memory that can be addressed by a central processing unit. Compare **virtual memory**

**real number** *noun* MATHS a number that is represented with a fractional part (NOTE: It sometimes refers to a number represented in a floating-point form.)

**real time** *noun* 1. □ **in real time** happening at the same time as something else, without a time delay ○ *The scan allowed us to watch the baby moving in real time.* 2. COMPUT the processing of data as soon as it is received

**real-time** *adjective* COMPUT processing data as soon as it is received

**real-time animation** *noun* COMPUT animation in which objects appear to move at the same speed as they would in real life (NOTE: Real-time animation requires display hardware capable of displaying a sequence with tens of different images every second.)

**real-time operating system** *noun* COMPUT an operating system designed to control a real-time system or process-control system

**real-time processing** *noun* COMPUT the processing of data as they are received, without a time delay

**real-time system** *noun* COMPUT a system whose processing time is within the time span of the event being dealt with, so that it can influence the source of the data ○ *In a real-time system, as you move the joystick left, the image on the screen moves left.*

**real-time transport protocol** *noun* COMPUT a data transport protocol developed by the IETF that provides a guaranteed data delivery over a network that does not usually provide this type of quality of service. Abbreviation **RTP** (NOTE: It is usually used to transfer video or multimedia data over a packet network such as the Internet.)

**rear** *noun* the part farthest from the front ○ *the rear of the aircraft* ■ *adjective* at or referring to the back ○ *The rear part of the aircraft is called the aft section.* ■ *verb* AGRIC to look after young animals until they are old enough to look after themselves

**reboot** *verb* COMPUT to reload an operating system during a computing session ○ *We rebooted and the files reappeared.*

**recall** COMPUT *noun* the bringing back of text or files from store ■ *verb* to bring back text or files from store

**receive only** *noun* COMPUT a computer terminal that can accept and display data but not transmit

**receiver** *noun* PHYS a device that receives incoming radio signals and converts them to sound or light ○ *The transponder in the aircraft consists of a transmitter and a receiver.*

**receiver register** *noun* COMPUT a temporary storage register for data inputs, before processing

**receiving waters** *plural noun* ENVIRON rivers, lakes, oceans, streams or other bodies of water into which waste water or treated effluent is discharged

**receptacle** *noun* BOT **1.** the top part of a flower stalk that supports the flower (NOTE: In some plants such as strawberry it forms part of the fruit.) **2.** the plant part that carries the reproductive organs in lower plants such as mosses and liverworts

**reception** *noun* TELECOM an act or instance of receiving radio signals ○ *The antenna is highly directive in transmission and reception.*

**receptor** *noun* ANAT a nerve ending which senses a change such as cold or heat in the surrounding environment or in the body and reacts to it by sending an impulse to the central nervous system

**receptor cell** *noun* ANAT a cell in a nerve ending which senses a change such as cold or heat in the surrounding environment or in the body and reacts to it by sending an impulse to the central nervous system

**recessive** *adjective* GENETICS (*of a gene or genetic trait*) suppressed by the presence of a corresponding dominant gene

COMMENT: Since each physical characteristic is governed by two genes, if one gene is dominant and the other recessive, the resulting trait will be that of the dominant gene. Traits governed by recessive genes will appear if genes from both parents are recessive.

**recessiveness** *noun* GENETICS the characteristic of a gene that leads to its not being expressed in the individual carrying it when a corresponding dominant gene is present. Compare **dominance**

**recharge** *verb* ELEC to charge a battery again

**rechargeable battery** *noun* ELEC a type of battery that uses a reversible chemical reaction to produce electricity, allowing it to be recharged and used again ○ *A rechargeable battery is used for RAM backup when the system is switched off.*

**recharge area** *noun* EARTH SCI an area of land where there is a net annual transfer of water from the surface to ground water

**recipient** *noun* MED somebody who receives blood, tissue or an organ from a donor

**reciprocal** *adjective* **1.** referring to an action that each of two does to the other **2.** MATHS referring to a number or quantity related to another in that they give one when multiplied by each other ■ *noun* **1.** NAVIG an exactly opposite direction ○ *A wave transmitted vertically returns to Earth on its reciprocal.* **2.** MATHS a number or quantity related to another in that they give one when multiplied by each other

**reciprocal heading** *noun* NAVIG the direction 180° from a given direction ○ *The reciprocal heading of 090° is 270°.*

**reciprocating** *adjective* MECH ENG (*of a machine*) moving backwards and forwards or up and down ○ *A cam is an oval-shaped wheel which, when rotating, converts circular motion into reciprocating motion.*

**reclaim** *verb* ENVIRON **1.** to take virgin land, marshland, a waste site or land which has already been developed and make it available for agricultural or commercial purposes **2.** to recover useful materials from waste

**reclamation** *noun* ENVIRON **1.** the act of reclaiming land ○ *land reclamation scheme in urban centres* **2.** the recovery of useful materials from waste

**recode** *verb* COMPUT to code a program which has been coded for one system so that it will work on another

**recognition** *noun* **1.** the ability to recognise someone or something **2.** COMPUT a process that allows something such as letters on a printed text or bars on bar codes to be recognised **3.** respect or official acceptance □ **in recognition of** or **for** as a mark of respect for ○ *He was awarded the Nobel prize in recognition of his work on the human genome.*

**recombinant** GENETICS *noun* a cell or organism that results from the joining together of DNA fragments ■ *adjective* **1.** referring to genetic recombination **2.** referring to recombinant DNA or produced by recombinant DNA technology

**recombinant DNA** *noun* GENETICS DNA produced by joining together DNA extracted from two or more different sources such as cells or different organisms

**recombination** *noun* GENETICS any process that results in offspring that have combinations of genes different from those of either parent, e.g. the crossing-over and independent assortment of chromosomes during gamete formation

**recombine** *verb* GENETICS to undergo or cause an organism to undergo recombination

**recommend** *verb* to suggest that something should be done ○ *The report recommended choosing a different site for the disposal of radioactive waste.*

**recommendation** *noun* a strong suggestion that something should be done ○ *The council accepted the committee's recommendations about disposal of waste.*

**recompile** *verb* COMPUT to compile a source program again, usually after changes or debugging

**reconfiguration** *noun* COMPUT the alteration of the structure of data in a system

**reconfigure** *verb* COMPUT to alter the structure of data in a system ○ *I reconfigured the field structure in the file.* ○ *This program allows us to reconfigure the system to our own requirements.*

**reconstitute** *verb* to put something back into its original state ○ *The mining company should reconstitute the site after the open-cast mining operation has closed down.*

**record** *noun* **1.** a written account of facts and information for future reference **2.** COMPUT a set of electronically stored data ○ *Your record contains several fields that have been grouped together under the one heading.* ○ *This*

*record contains all their personal details.* ■ *verb* **1.** to write down information or data ○ *Record the results in this column.* ○ *Measure track angles and distances and record them in a log.* **2.** COMPUT to store data or signals on tape, on disk or in a computer ○ *This device records signals onto magnetic tape.* ○ *Digitally recorded data are used to generate images.*

**recordable CD, recordable compact disc** *noun* COMPUT full form of **CD-R**

**recorder** *noun* COMPUT a piece of equipment able to transfer input signals onto a storage medium

COMMENT: The signal recorded is not always in the same form as the input signal: many recorders record a modulated carrier signal for better quality. A recorder is usually combined with a suitable playback circuit since the read and write heads are often the same physical device.

**record gap** *noun* COMPUT a blank section of magnetic tape between two consecutive records

**record head** *noun* COMPUT a transducer that converts an electrical signal into a magnetic field to write the data onto a magnetic medium. Also called **write head**

**recording** *noun* the action of storing signals or data on tape or in a computer

**recording level** *noun* ACOUSTICS an amplification of an input signal before it is recorded (NOTE: If a voice is very quiet, the recording level can be increased to ensure that the sound signal is not degraded by noise.)

**record length** *noun* COMPUT the total number of characters contained in the various fields within a stored record

**record locking** *noun* COMPUT software that prevents more than one user writing data to a record at the same time

**recordset** *noun* COMPUT a group of records selected from a main database by a filter, search or query

**record structure** *noun* COMPUT a list of the fields which make up a record, together with their length and data type

**recover** *verb* **1.** to return to a better condition ○ *The fish populations may never recover from overfishing.* **2.** INDUST to obtain metals or other useful materials from waste by separating and purifying it

**recoverable error** *noun* COMPUT an error type that allows program execution to be continued after it has occurred

**recovery** *noun* **1.** the action of getting back something which has been lost ○ *The recovery of lost files can be carried out using the recovery procedure.* **2.** a return to a better condition ○ *The area has been overfished to such an extent that the recovery of the fish population is impossible.* **3.** INDUST the process of obtaining metals or other useful materials from waste

**recrystallisation** *noun* CHEM **1.** a change in the structure of something from one crystal structure to another, usually as the object changes temperature **2.** the purification of a substance by repeatedly crystallising a solution

**rectangle** *noun* MATHS a four-sided plane figure with four right angles, and with opposite sides of equal length

**rectangular** *adjective* referring to something with the shape of a rectangle ○ *a rectangular wing panel*

**rectification** *noun* **1.** ELEC the change from an alternating current to a direct current using a rectifier **2.** CHEM the purification of a liquid by distillation

**rectified airspeed** *noun* AEROSP same as **calibrated airspeed**

**rectifier** *noun* ELECTRONICS an electronic circuit that converts an alternating current supply into a direct current supply ○ *The ignition unit receives an alternating current which is passed through a transformer and rectifier.*

**rectify** *verb* **1.** ELECTRONICS to change alternating current into direct current **2.** CHEM to purify a liquid by a repeated process **3.** to correct something ○ *to rectify a mistake*

**rectum** *noun* ANAT the last part of the large intestine, where waste material accumulates before leaving the body through the anus

**recursion** *noun* **1.** the repetition of steps to give a result **2.** COMPUT a subroutine in a program that calls itself during execution. Also called **recursive routine**

**recursive** *adjective* repeating itself

**recursive call** *noun* COMPUT a subroutine that calls itself when it is run

**recursive routine** *noun* COMPUT same as **recursion**

**recyclable** *adjective* ENVIRON referring to waste that can be processed so that it can be used again

**recycle** *verb* ENVIRON to process waste so that it can be used again ○ *The glass industry recycles tonnes of waste glass each year.*

COMMENT: Many waste items can be recycled. In particular, precious metals such as lead, copper and silver can be recovered from old batteries or computers, paper can be recycled from old newspapers and packaging materials after ink removal. Glass can be manufactured from old bottles.

**recycled** *adjective* ENVIRON made from waste ○ *recycled paper*

**recycling** *noun* ENVIRON the processing of waste so that it can be used again

**red** *adjective*, *noun* (of) a colour like the colour of blood

**red, green, blue** *noun* COMPUT a high-definition monitor system that uses three separate input signals controlling red, green and blue colour picture beams. Abbreviation **RGB** (NOTE: There are three colour guns producing red, green and blue beams acting on groups of three phosphor dots at each pixel location.)

**red algae** *plural noun* MARINE BIOL phytoplankton mainly found on the seabed which cause the phenomenon called red tide. Phylum: Rhodophyta.

**red blood cell** *noun* BIOL a blood cell which contains haemoglobin and carries oxygen

**Red Data Book** *noun* ENVIRON a catalogue published by the IUCN, listing species which are rare or in danger of becoming extinct

**redefinable** *adjective* COMPUT able to be redefined

**redefine** *verb* COMPUT to change the function or value assigned to a variable or object ○ *We redefined the initial parameters.*

**red giant** *noun* ASTRON a star with a relatively low surface temperature and a diameter much greater than that of the Sun, that appears red

**redirect** *verb* COMPUT **1.** to send a message to its destination by another route **2.** (*in the DOS and UNIX operating systems*) to treat the output of one program as input for another program ○ *You can sort the results from a DIR* *command by redirecting to the SORT command.*

**redirection** *noun* COMPUT the sending of a message to its destination by another route ○ *Call forwarding is the automatic redirection of calls to another number.*

**red lead** *noun* CHEM a poisonous red oxide of lead, used as a colouring in paints. Formula: $Pb_3O_4$.

**red mud** *noun* OCEANOG a deposit found on the seabed in the China Sea and elsewhere, containing dust and iron oxide, the latter giving it its red colour

**redness** *noun* the condition or degree of being red

**redox** CHEM same as oxidation–reduction

**redox potential** *noun* CHEM the cell potential required relative to a standard hydrogen electrode to cause oxidation at an anode and reduction at a cathode. Abbreviation **rH**

**red sea** *noun* MARINE BIOL same as **red tide**

**redshift** *noun* ASTRON a movement of the spectral lines of an astronomical object towards red, caused by the object moving away from the Earth

**red snow** *noun* EARTH SCI snow coloured red by the presence of algae

**red tide** *noun* MARINE BIOL a phenomenon where the sea becomes red, caused by phytoplankton of the phylum Rhodophyta. Also called **red sea**

**reduce** *verb* **1.** to make something less, smaller or lower or to become less, smaller or lower **2.** CHEM to add electrons or hydrogen to a substance

**reduced instruction set computer** *noun* COMPUT a design for a central processing unit whose instruction set contains a small number of simple fast-executing instructions, which makes program writing more complex but increases speed. Abbreviation **RISC**

**reducer** *noun* BIOL an organism such as an earthworm, fungus or bacterium that breaks down dead organic matter

**reducing agent** *noun* CHEM a chemical that reduces another substance and is itself oxidised as a result

**reducing atmosphere** *noun* CHEM an atmosphere that does not contain free oxygen gas and in which compounds combine chemically with hydrogen

**reducing sugar** *noun* BIOCHEM a sugar that can act as a reducing agent

**reduction** *noun* **1.** the process of making something less, smaller or lower or of becoming less, smaller or lower ○ *The key to controlling acid rain must be the reduction of emissions from fossil-fuelled power stations.* **2.** CHEM the addition of electrons or hydrogen to a substance

**reduction division** *noun* BIOL same as **meiosis**

**redundancy** *noun* **1.** the situation of not being needed because other similar things exist **2.** ENG a duplication of component parts of a system to enable the system to function even if one component fails ○ *With system redundancy, a single failure within a system will have little effect on the aircraft's performance during the approach and landing operation.*

**redundancy checking** *noun* COMPUT the checking of received data for correct redundant codes to detect any errors

**redundant** *adjective* **1.** no longer useful **2.** COMPUT (*of data*) able to be removed without losing any information ○ *The parity bits on the received data are redundant and can be removed.* **3.** ELECTRONICS (*of an extra piece of equipment*) kept ready for a task in case of faults

**redundant array of inexpensive disks** *noun* COMPUT a fast, fault tolerant disk drive system that uses multiple drives which would, typically, each store one byte of a word of data, so allowing the data to be saved faster. Abbreviation **RAID** (NOTE: One drive in the array would also store a check byte for error detection.)

**redundant code** *noun* COMPUT a check bit or data that added to a block of data for error detection purposes and carries no information

**reed** *noun* PLANTS an aquatic plant, growing near the shores of lakes, used to make thatched roofs

**reef** *noun* EARTH SCI a series of low rocks or coral near the surface of the sea

**re-entrant program, re-entrant code, re-entrant routine** *noun* COMPUT one program or code shared by many users in a multi-user system (NOTE: It can be interrupted or called again by another user before it has finished its previous run, and returns to the point at which it was interrupted when it has finished that run.)

**re-entry** *noun* COMPUT the calling of a routine or program from within a routine or program

**reference** *noun* **1.** something used as a basis for further calculation or investigation ○ *Use 2001 as a reference point.* □ **by reference to** by looking at and comparing a value used as a starting point with other values, often zero **2.** a comment about something ○ *The paper made a reference to our work.* **3.** a piece of work mentioned in a publication by someone else, usually listed at the end with details of the author, source and date ○ *The paper had a list of about 20 references.* ■ *verb* COMPUT to access a location in memory ○ *The access time taken to reference an item in memory is short.*

**reference address** *noun* COMPUT an initial address in a program used as an origin or base for others

**reference book** *noun* a book such as a dictionary or encyclopaedia, where you can look for information

**reference file** *noun* COMPUT a file of data which is kept so that it can be referred to

**reference program table** *noun* COMPUT a list produced by a compiler or system of the location, size and type of the variables, routines and macros within a program

**reference retrieval system** *noun* COMPUT an index which provides a reference to a document

**reference signal** *noun* PHYS a signal against which telemetry data signals are compared

**reference table** *noun* a list of ordered items

**refine** *verb* **1.** INDUST to process something to remove impurities ○ *a by-product of refining oil* **2.** to make changes in order to improve something ○ *We've refined the procedures.*

**refined** *adjective* INDUST purified ○ *refined oil*

**refinement** *noun* **1.** a small change that is an improvement ○ *An internal locking device is one of the numerous refinements to the simple actuator.* **2.**

INDUST the process of purifying something

**refinery** *noun* INDUST a plant where raw materials such as ore, oil or sugar are processed to remove impurities

**reflect** *verb* PHYS to send back light, heat or sound towards its source or in a different direction ○ *Some solar radiation is reflected back by clouds or by the Earth's surface.*

**reflectance** *noun* PHYS the ratio of the energy of a wave reflected by a surface to the total wave striking the surface. Symbol

**reflected code** *noun* COMPUT a code in which the binary representation of decimal numbers changes by only one bit at a time from one number to the next

**reflecting telescope** *noun* ASTRON a telescope in which a concave mirror initially focuses the light from an object

**reflection** *noun* PHYS **1.** the process of sending light, sound or heat back towards its source **2.** a reflected image or sound ○ *Bats find their way by sending out high-frequency sounds and listening to the reflection of the sound from objects in their way.*

**reflection seismology** *noun* EARTH SCI the study of the way pressure waves from seismic movements are reflected by rock structures

**reflective** *adjective* PHYS referring to the sending back of something such as radio waves or light towards its source ○ *Reflective power means that at low angles of elevation of the Sun, water reflects a great amount of solar radiation thus slowing down the rise in sea surface temperatures.*

**reflector** *noun* a device that sends back something such as light towards its source ○ *The shape of a water droplet makes it a good reflector, so water in the atmosphere absorbs and scatters radio waves.*

**reflector telescope** *noun* ASTRON a telescope that uses a mirror rather than a lens as the main optical component to collect light. Compare **refractor telescope**

**reflex** *noun* PHYSIOL a rapid automatic reaction to a stimulus

**reflex action** *noun* PHYSIOL an automatic movement in response to a stimulus

**reflux** *noun* **1.** INDUST a backwards flow of a liquid from a boiler in the opposite direction to normal flow, collecting vapour and condensing it so that it can return to the boiler again **2.** CHEM a backwards flow in distillation **3.** MED a bringing up of stomach acid ■ *verb* CHEM to cause a liquid to flow backwards

**reflux condenser** *noun* CHEM a tall condenser that is placed above the vessel used to reflux a liquid (NOTE: The condenser ensures that the vapour produced by the boiling liquid is not lost but runs back into the vessel.)

**reforest** *verb* FORESTRY same as **reafforest**

**reforestation** *noun* FORESTRY same as **reafforestation**

**reformat** *verb* COMPUT to format a disk that already contains data, erasing the data by doing so ○ *Do not reformat your hard disk unless you can't do anything else.*

**reformatting** *noun* COMPUT the act of formatting a disk which already contains data (NOTE: Reformatting destroys all the data on a disk.)

**reforming** *noun* CHEM the process of converting straight-chain alkanes into branched-chain alkanes by heating or the use of catalysts (NOTE: The technique is used in refining petroleum.)

**refract** *verb* PHYS to cause a wave such as light or sound to change direction or turn as it passes from one medium into another of different density ○ *On reaching the ionosphere, a direct wave is refracted and returns to the Earth's surface.*

**refracting telescope** *noun* ASTRON a telescope in which a lens initially focuses light from an object, which then passes through a second magnifying lens in the eyepiece

**refraction** *noun* PHYS a change in direction of a wave such as light or sound as it passes from one medium into another of different density

**refractive index** *noun* PHYS the ratio of the speed of refracted light in a vacuum to its speed in the medium being studied

**refractometer** *noun* PHYS a device for measuring the refractive index of a medium

**refractor telescope** *noun* ASTRON a telescope that uses a lens, rather than a mirror, as the main optical component to collect light (NOTE: Refractor telescopes have been surpassed by reflector telescopes.)

**refractory** *adjective* PHYS having a high melting point

**refresh** *verb* COMPUT to update regularly the contents of dynamic RAM by reading and rewriting stored data to ensure data is retained

**refresh rate** *noun* COMPUT the number of times every second that the image on a screen is redrawn

**refrigerant** INDUST *noun* a substance used to provide cooling or freezing either as the working substance of a refrigerator or by direct absorption of heat ○ *Heated air from the main air supply system passes through the evaporator matrix and by induction releases heat into the liquid refrigerant.* ■ *adjective* used for cooling or freezing purposes

**refrigerate** *verb* PHYS, INDUST to make something cold to prevent deterioration

**refrigeration** *noun* PHYS, INDUST the process of making something cold to prevent deterioration

**refrigerator** *noun* INDUST a machine which keeps things cold

**refuel, re-fuel** *verb* MECH ENG to fill an engine or vehicle with fuel again

**refuge** *noun* ENVIRON a safe place where a species can escape environmental change and continue to exist as before. Also called **refugium**

**refugium** *noun* ENVIRON same as **refuge** (NOTE: The plural is **refugia**.)

**refuse** *noun* ENVIRON rubbish or waste matter

**refuse-derived fuel** *noun* INDUST a fuel which is made or processed from refuse. Abbreviation **RDF**

**regenerate** *verb* **1.** BIOL to grow, or grow something, again ○ *A forest takes about ten years to regenerate after a fire.* ○ *Salamanders can regenerate limbs.* **2.** COMPUT to redraw an image on a screen many times a second so that it remains visible **3.** COMPUT to receive distorted signals, process and error check them, then retransmit the same data

**regeneration** *noun* ENVIRON the process of vegetation growing back on land which has been cleared ○ *Grazing by herbivores prevents forest regeneration.*

**regenerative** *adjective* BIOL allowing new growth to replace damaged tissue

**regenerative memory** *noun* COMPUT a storage medium whose contents need to be regularly refreshed to retain its contents ○ *Dynamic RAM is regenerative memory which needs to be refreshed every 250 ns.*

**regime** *noun* a general pattern or system ○ *a strict dietary regime* ○ *The two rivers have very different flow regimes: one has very rapid flow down from high mountains, while the other is slower and mainly crosses fertile plains.*

**region** *noun* 1. EARTH SCI an area of a surface, especially the Earth's surface ○ *The troposphere is deepest over equatorial regions and shallowest near the Poles.* 2. □ **in the region of** approximately ○ *The burning temperature of the fuel is in the region of 2000° C.* 3. COMPUT a special or reserved area of memory, program or screen

**regional breakpoint** *noun* COMPUT a breakpoint that can be inserted anywhere within a program that is being debugged

**region fill** *noun* COMPUT the filling of an area of a screen or a graphics shape with a particular colour

**register** *noun* COMPUT a reserved memory location within a central processing unit, usually one or two words wide, that is used to hold data and addresses to be processed in a machine code operation ■ *verb* to make something known, or to display something ○ *The indicator registered zero.* ○ *We registered our concern about the procedure.*

**regolith** *noun* EARTH SCI a layer of weathered rock fragments which covers most of the Earth's land area

**regress** *verb* ENVIRON, BIOL to return to a more primitive earlier state

**regression** *noun* ENVIRON, BIOL the process of returning to a more primitive earlier state, as when cultivated land returns to a wild state

**regressive** *adjective* EARTH SCI (*of a water level*) getting lower

**regulate** *verb* to control a process or activity

**regulated power supply** *noun* ELEC a constant controlled voltage source of current whose output will not vary with input supply variation

COMMENT: A regulated power supply is required for all computers where components cannot withstand voltage variations.

**regulation** *noun* 1. the control of a process or activity 2. a rule ○ *The safety regulations have not been complied with.* ○ *The pamphlet lists the regulations concerning visits to nature reserves.*

**regulator** *noun* 1. something that controls a process or activity 2. ELEC a device used to limit the current and voltage in a circuit ○ *Regulators allow the correct charging of batteries from solar panels and wind generators.*

**regulator gene** *noun* GENETICS a gene that modifies the action of one or more structural genes, thus controlling the synthesis of their corresponding proteins

**regulatory** *adjective* controlling a process or activity according to specific rules ○ *a regulatory body*

**reheat** *verb* PHYS to heat something again ○ *Water that has been cooled and condensed after passing through the boilers is sent back to the boilers for reheating.*

**reheater** *noun* INDUST a section of a power station where steam which has been used to turn the first turbine is heated again to create enough pressure to turn the second turbine

**rehydration** *noun* MED the giving of water or liquid to a patient suffering from dehydration

**Reid vapour pressure test** *noun* PHYS a test to determine the pressure required above a liquid to hold the vapours in the liquid at a given temperature

**reinforce** *verb* to strengthen something ○ *Typical skin materials used in aircraft are made from epoxy resins which are reinforced with glass, carbon or Kevlar fibres.*

**reinforced** *adjective* strengthened

**reinforced concrete** *noun* CONSTR concrete with steel rods embedded in it for extra strength, used in the construction of large buildings

**reinforced plastic** *noun* INDUST, AVIAT plastic used with glass fibres to repair some types of aircraft structure

**reinforcement** *noun* **1.** the act of strengthening something **2.** a strengthened structure ○ *There is reinforcement around each opening.*

**reintroduce** *verb* ENVIRON to help a species to return to an area it had formerly inhabited

**reintroduction** *noun* ENVIRON the process of reintroducing a species

**reject** *verb* **1.** to refuse to accept something or someone **2.** PHYSIOL to vomit up food **3.** MED to fail to accept a transplanted organ or foreign tissue, because of immunological incompatibility

**rejection** *noun* the process or an instance of rejecting something or someone

**rejection error** *noun* COMPUT an error by a scanner which cannot read a character and so leaves a blank

**relate** *verb* **1.** to make a connection or link between two things ○ *Orientating the chart relates the direction of land features to their representation on the chart and aids recognition.* **2.** to be connected to or concerned with something ○ *The results relate to experiments over the last decade.*

**-related** *suffix* connected to ○ *a heat-related change*

**relation** *noun* **1.** a connection or link between two things **2.** a member of the same family as someone else

**relational database** *noun* COMPUT a database in which all the items of data can be interconnected ○ *If you search the relational database for the surname, you can pull out the relevant salary from the related accounts database.* (NOTE: Data is retrieved by using one item of data to search for a related field.)

**relational database management system** *noun* COMPUT a system in which data are retrieved by using one item of data to search for a related field. Abbreviation **RDBMS**

**relationship** *noun* the way in which someone or something is connected to another

**relative** *adjective* compared to something else

**relative abundance** *noun* ECOL the number of individual specimens of an animal or plant seen over a period of time in a specific place

**relative address** *noun* COMPUT a location specified in relation to a reference address. Also called **indirect address**

**relative atomic mass** *noun* PHYS the mean mass of one atom of an element relative to one twelfth of the mass of one atom of carbon-12

**relative biological effectiveness** *noun* PHYS a measure of radiation used as a protection. Abbreviation **RBE**

**relative coordinate** *noun* positional information given in relation to a reference point

**relative density** *noun* PHYS the ratio of the density of a liquid with reference to water, or of a gas with reference to air

**relative humidity** *noun* METEOROL a ratio between the amount of water vapour in air and the amount which would be present if the air was saturated, shown as a percentage

**relative permittivity** *noun* PHYS a measure of the resistance of a substance to an electric field

**relative transpiration** *noun* BOT the rate at which water transpires from the surface of a plant

**relativity** *noun* PHYS a theoretical explanation of the nature of gravitation and of motion (NOTE: Einstein proposed two theories: the **General Theory of Relativity** was confirmed by astronomical observations of the effect of the mass of the Sun on passing starlight. The **Special Theory of Relativity** remains controversial, although evidence for some of its predictions, such as the increase in mass of particles approaching the velocity of light, has been obtained in particle accelerators.)

**relaxation** *noun* PHYS the process of losing energy between excited states or between an excited state and the ground state

**relay** *noun* ELEC an electromagnetically controlled switch ○ *There is a relay in the circuit.* ○ *It is relay-rated at 5 amps.* ■ *verb* COMPUT, TELECOM to receive data from one source and then retransmit it to another point ○ *All* *messages are relayed through this small micro.*

**release** *noun* **1.** COMPUT a version of a product ○ *The latest software is release 5.* **2.** ACOUSTICS the shape of a sound signal that shows the speed at which a sound signal decreases in strength after a note has stopped playing ■ *verb* **1.** to let something go that has been contained ○ *Acid rain leaches out nutrients from the soil and releases harmful substances such as lead into the soil.* ○ *Using an aerosol spray releases CFCs into the atmosphere.* **2.** MECH ENG to take the tension off something such as a catch and allow something to move or operate **3.** COMPUT (*of software*) to relinquish control of a block of memory or file

**releaser** *noun* ZOOL a stimulus that provokes a reaction in an animal, e.g. the sight of a hawk or the sound of a gun

**relev** *noun* BOT a list of plant species growing in a specific area

**reliability** *noun* the degree to which someone or something can be trusted ○ *Check the reliability of the data.*

**reliable** *adjective* able to be trusted ○ *It is not a very reliable method of measuring the depth.*

**relict** *noun* ECOL a species that is still in existence, even though the environment in which it originally developed is no longer present

**relief** *noun* **1.** EARTH SCI a difference in height between points on the Earth's surface **2.** a reduction in stress

**relief map** *noun* EARTH SCI a map with contour lines that show differences in height between points on the Earth's surface

**relief valve** *noun* MECH ENG a valve that opens at maximum safe pressure and closes again upon return to normal operating conditions

**reload** *verb* COMPUT to load something again ○ *We reloaded the program after the crash.*

**relocatable program** *noun* COMPUT a computer program that can be loaded into and executed from any area of memory ○ *The operating system can load and run a relocatable program from any area of memory.*

**relocate** *verb* COMPUT to move data from one area of storage to another ○ *The data is relocated during execution.*

**relocation** *noun* COMPUT the moving of data from one area of storage to another

**reluctance** *noun* PHYS the resistance of a closed magnetic circuit to a magnetic flux

**rely on** *verb* to trust someone or something

**rem** *abbreviation* MEASURE, PHYS roentgen equivalent man

**REM** *abbreviation* COMPUT remark

**remain** *verb* to be left behind after others have been removed or excluded

**remainder** *noun* **1.** something left after excluding other parts ○ *The auxiliary power unit is usually found in the tail section, separated from the remainder of the fuselage by a firewall.* **2.** MATHS a number left over when one number is divided by another ○ *7 divided by 3 is equal to 2 remainder 1.* Compare **quotient**

**remark** *noun* COMPUT a statement in a BASIC program that is ignored by the interpreter, allowing the programmer to write explanatory notes. Abbreviation **REM**

**remedial maintenance** *noun* COMPUT maintenance to repair faults which have developed in a system

**remediation** *noun* ENVIRON a course of action intended to reverse environmental damage

**remedy** MED *noun* a treatment for a disease or disorder ■ *verb* to relieve or cure a disease or disorder

**remote** *adjective* TELECOM, COMPUT capable of being operated from a distance by electronic technology, or able to operate a device from a distance ○ *a remote user* ○ *Users can print reports on remote printers.*

**remote access** *noun* COMPUT a link that allows a user to access a computer from a distance, usually via a modem

**remote client** *noun* COMPUT a user who accesses mail without being connected to the mail server's local network

**remote control** *noun* TELECOM, COMPUT a system that allows a user to operate a computer or other device from a distance

**remote job entry** *noun* COMPUT full form of **RJE**

**remote procedure call** *noun* COMPUT a method of communication between two programs running on two separate, but connected, computers. Abbreviation **RPC** (NOTE: A software routine asks another computer on the network to process a problem and then displays the results.)

**remote sensing** *noun* EARTH SCI the collection of information via satellite observation and aerial photography about physical aspects of the Earth such as the location of mineral deposits, the movement of water or pests

**removable** *adjective* able to be removed ○ *a removable hard disk*

**removal** *noun* **1.** the process of removing something **2.** INDUST the extraction of minerals from the ground

**remove** *verb* **1.** to take something out **2.** INDUST to extract a mineral from the ground

**renal** *adjective* ANAT referring to the kidneys

**renal artery** *noun* ANAT one of two arteries running from the abdominal aorta to the kidneys

**rename** *verb* to give a new name to something ○ *Save the file and rename it CUSTOM.* ○ *Species are renamed if their taxonomic classification changes.*

**render** *verb* **1.** to cause someone or something to become a particular thing ○ *The failure of any component in the fire detection system will render the system inoperative.* ○ *Tropical air moving northwards is subjected to surface cooling and rendered increasingly stable in its lower layers.* **2.** to give something (*formal*) □ **to render assistance** to provide help **3.** to express or show something in a particular way (*formal*) **4.** COMPUT to colour and shade a graphic object so that it looks solid and real ○ *We rendered the wire-frame model.*

**renew** *verb* to replace or replenish something

**renewable** *adjective* ENVIRON able to be replaced or able to replenish itself ○ *Herring stocks are a renewable resource if they are not overfished.*

**renewable energy** *noun* INDUST energy from the Sun, wind, waves, tides, from geothermal deposits or from burning waste

**renewable resources** *plural noun* ENVIRON resources such as forests that can be replaced by natural environmen-

tal processes in a reasonably short period of time

**renin** *noun* BIOCHEM an enzyme produced by the kidneys, involved in protein breakdown and the regulation of blood pressure

**renumber** COMPUT *noun* a feature of some computer languages which allows the programmer to allocate new values to all or some of a program's line numbers ■ *verb* to allocate new numbers or values to something

**repeat** *verb* COMPUT to do something again ■ *noun* a thing done for a second or subsequent time

**repeat counter** *noun* COMPUT a register that holds the number of times a routine or task has been repeated

**repeater** *noun* TELECOM a device used in communications that amplifies or regenerates a received signal and transmits it on (NOTE: Regenerators are often used to extend the range of a network, while repeaters work at the physical layer of the OSI network model.)

**repeating group** *noun* COMPUT a pattern of data that is duplicated in a bit stream

**repel** *verb* to push something away by force ○ *Like poles (i.e. north and north or south and south) of a magnet repel each other.* (NOTE: **repelling – repelled**)

**repellent** *adjective, noun* (referring to) a substance that repels ○ *The coating of wax on leaves acts as a repellent to pollutants.*

**repetitive strain injury, repetitive stress injury** *noun* MED a pain in the arm felt by someone who performs the same movement many times over a period of time. Abbreviation **RSI**

**replace** *verb* **1.** to put something back where it was before **2.** to put something in the place of something else ■ *noun* COMPUT an instruction to a computer to find an item of data and put another in its place. ♦ **search and replace**

**replacement fertility** *noun* ECOL the fertility rate needed to ensure that a population remains constant as each set of parents is replaced by its offspring

**replant** *verb* AGRIC, FORESTRY **1.** to plant an area again ○ *After the trees were felled the land was cleared and replanted with mixed conifers and* *broad-leaved species.* **2.** to put a plant in the ground again

**replay** *noun* COMPUT the playback or reading back of data or a signal from a recording ■ *verb* to play back something that has been recorded

**replenish** *verb* **1.** to replace something that has been used **2.** ELEC to charge a battery with electricity again

**replicase** *noun* GENETICS a polymerase enzyme, especially one that uses RNA molecules as a template to make new RNA molecules when RNA viruses are replicating

**replicate** *verb* **1.** to do something again in the same way ○ *The routine will replicate your results with very little effort.* **2.** BIOL (*of a cell or microorganism*) to reproduce

**replication** *noun* **1.** COMPUT the provision of extra components in a system in case there is a breakdown or fault in one of them **2.** COMPUT the copying of a record or data to another location **3.** BIOL the process in the division of a cell during which DNA makes copies of itself **4.** BIOL the process of reproduction of a cell or microorganism ○ *virus replication* **5.** SCI the repetition of an experiment several times in order to achieve a reliably consistent result

**replicon** *noun* GENETICS a segment of DNA or RNA that forms a unit that replicates and is distinct from adjacent segments

**report** *noun* an official document giving an account of something, stating what action has been taken, what the current state is or what the results of a test or experiment are ■ *verb* to give an account of something

**reportable disease** *noun* MED a disease such as asbestosis, hepatitis or anthrax that may be caused by working conditions or may infect other people and must be officially reported

**report generator** *noun* COMPUT a piece of software that allows data in the form of graphs or tables from database files to be merged with a document to provide a complete report

**report program generator** *noun* COMPUT a programming language used mainly on personal computers for the preparation of business reports, allowing data in files or databases to be included. Abbreviation **RPG**

**repower** *verb* INDUST to rebuild an old power station, converting it to a more modern combustion system such as a pressurised fluidised-bed combustion

**represent** *verb* **1.** to act as a symbol for something ○ *The hash sign is used to represent a number in a series.* **2.** to speak or act on behalf of others

**representation** *noun* a way of showing something using signs or symbols

**representative** *adjective* being an example of what all others are like ■ *noun* **1.** a thing that acts as a symbol for something else **2.** a person who speaks or acts on behalf of others

**reprocess** *verb* INDUST to process something again

**reprocessing** *noun* INDUST the processing of something again, e.g. taking spent nuclear fuel and subjecting it to chemical processes which produce further useful materials such as plutonium

COMMENT: Reprocessing plants are the cause of much controversy. Some countries do not have facilities for reprocessing spent nuclear fuel and therefore export it to those countries with suitable installations. Reprocessing plants are just as likely to cause radioactive waste as nuclear power stations and the transport of the spent material from the power station to the processing plant is also a potential radiation hazard.

**reprocessing plant** *noun* INDUST an installation that reprocesses nuclear fuel

**reproduce** *verb* **1.** BIOL to produce offspring **2.** SCI to do a test again in exactly the same way **3.** COMPUT to copy data or text from one material or medium to another similar one

**reproduction** *noun* **1.** BIOL the production of offspring **2.** SCI the performance of a test again in exactly the same way **3.** COMPUT the copying of data or text from one material or medium to another similar one

**reproductive** *adjective* BIOL referring to the production of offspring

**reproductive organ** *noun* ANAT an organ such as a womb in mammals or a stamen in a flowering plant involved in reproduction

**reproductive system** *noun* ANAT the arrangement of organs and ducts which produce spermatozoa and ova

**reproductive tract** *noun* ANAT the series of tubes and ducts which carry spermatozoa and ova from one part of the body to another

**reprogram** *verb* COMPUT to alter a program so that it can be run on another type of computer

**reptile** *noun* ZOOL a cold-blooded animal such as a crocodile, tortoise or snake that lays eggs and has a scaly skin. Class: Reptilia.

**request** *noun* an act of requesting something or a thing requested ■ *verb* to ask for something

**request for comment** *noun* COMPUT a document that contains information about a proposed new standard and asks users to look at the document and make any comments. Abbreviation **RFC**

**request to send signal** *noun* COMPUT a signal sent by a transmitter to a receiver asking if the receiver is ready to accept data. Abbreviation **RTS** (NOTE: It is used in the RS-232C serial connection.)

**require** *verb* to need something ○ *Delicate computer systems require careful handling.*

**requirement** *noun* something that is needed

**re-route** *verb* to send something by a different route

**rerun** *verb* COMPUT to run a program or a printing job again

**rerun point** *noun* COMPUT the place in the program from where to start running it again after a crash or halt

**resample** *verb* COMPUT to change the number of pixels used to make up an image

**resave** *verb* COMPUT to save something again ○ *The program automatically resaves the text.*

**research** SCI *noun* a scientific study which investigates something new ○ *recent research into diet* ○ *medical research* ○ *a research programme* ■ *verb* to carry out a scientific study of something ○ *He is researching the changes in the ozone hole.*

**research and development** *noun* INDUST the investigation of new products, discoveries and techniques. Abbreviation **R & D**

**research centre** *noun* SCI a place where scientific research is carried out

**reseau** *noun* ASTRON a grid of lines photographed onto or cut into a glass plate that is used as a reference for astronomical observations

**reservation** *noun* **1.** ENVIRON an area of land set aside for a special purpose **2.** a doubt about something ○ *The journal had reservations about the thoroughness of the investigation and so rejected the paper.*

**reserve** *noun* **1.** an amount stored or kept back for future use **2.** ENVIRON an area of unspoilt land where no commercial exploitation is allowed ■ *verb* to store or keep back something for future use

**reservoir** *noun* **1.** INDUST an artificial or natural area of water, used for storing water for domestic or industrial use ○ *The town's water supply comes from reservoirs in the mountains.* ○ *After two months of drought the reservoirs were beginning to run dry.* **2.** EARTH SCI a natural hole in rock which contains water, oil or gas **3.** INDUST a container for holding a store of fluid ○ *A reservoir provides both storage space for the system fluid, and sufficient air space to allow for any variations in the volume of the fluid in the system.*

**reservoir rock** *noun* ENVIRON a source of energy that cannot be completely used up, e.g. sunlight, wind or waves

**reset** *verb* **1.** to set a register or counter to its initial state or to return to an initial state ○ *When it reaches 999 this counter resets to zero.* ○ *Reset the gauge and try the experiment again.* **2.** COMPUT to return a system to its initial state, to allow a program or process to be started again ■ *noun* the process or an act of returning something to its original state

COMMENT: In computers, hard reset is similar to soft reset but with a few important differences: it is a switch that directly signals the central processing unit, while soft reset signals the operating system. A hard reset clears all memory contents, a soft reset does not affect memory contents. A hard reset should always reset the system, a soft reset does not always work.

**reset button, reset key** *noun* COMPUT a switch that allows a program to be terminated and reset manually

**reshape handle** *noun* COMPUT a small square displayed on a frame around an object or image that a user can select and drag to change the shape of the frame or graphical object

**residence time** *noun* the amount of time during which something remains in the same place or in the same state until it is lost or transformed into something else

**resident** *adjective* **1.** living in a place, especially for a long time ○ *The introduced species wiped out the resident population of flightless birds.* **2.** COMPUT (*of data or a program*) always present in a computer ■ *noun* **1.** a person who lives in a place, especially for a long time **2.** ZOOL a bird, insect or other animal that does not migrate **3.** COMPUT a program or item of data that is always present in a computer

**resident font** *noun* COMPUT same as **internal font**

**resident software** *noun* COMPUT a program that is held permanently in memory whilst the machine is on. Also called **memory-resident software**

**residual** *adjective* referring to the amount of something that is left behind ○ *After de-icing operations, external surfaces should be examined for signs of residual ice or snow.* ■ *noun* same as **residue**

**residual error rate** *noun* COMPUT a ratio between incorrect and undetected received data and total data transmitted

**residual herbicide** *noun* AGRIC a herbicide applied to the surface of the soil which acts through the roots of existing plants and also new plants as they germinate

**residual oil** *noun* INDUST oil that is left after crude oil has been through various refining processes

**residue** *noun* material left after a process has taken place or after a material has been used

**resilience** *noun* **1.** BIOL the ability of an organism to resist or recover from adverse conditions **2.** ECOL the ability of an ecosystem to return to its usual state after being disturbed **3.** PHYS the ability of something to return to its original shape

**resin** *noun* **1.** BOT a sticky oil which comes from some types of conifer **2.** CHEM a solid or liquid organic compound used in the making of plastic

**resinous** *adjective* BOT referring to resin

**resist** *verb* to fight off or not be subject to the effects of something ○ *A tube resists bending in any direction but beams are designed usually to resist bending in one or two directions only.* ○ *In order for an aeroplane to fly, lift and thrust must resist and overcome the forces of gravity and drag.* ■ *noun* ELECTRONICS a substance used to protect a pattern of tracks on a printed circuit board, which is not affected by etching chemicals

**resistance** *noun* **1.** BIOL the ability of an organism not to be affected by something such as a disease ○ *The bacteria have developed a resistance to some antibiotics.* ○ *Increasing insect resistance to chemical pesticides is a major problem.* **2.** ELEC the opposition of a body or substance to current passing through it ○ *The shunt coil is made of fine wire which gives a high resistance and small current flow.* **3.** PHYS the ability of a material to restrict the flow of electrical current through itself

**resistant** *adjective* referring to something which is unaffected by a force, process, substance, materials or disease ○ *Some alloys are less resistant to corrosion than others.*

**-resistant** *suffix* not adversely affected by something ○ *heat-resistant* ○ *a DDT-resistant strain of insects* ○ *disease-resistant genetic material* ○ *a new strain of virus-resistant rice*

**resistive** *adjective* **1.** ELEC referring to electrical resistance ○ *Windscreen heating and electrical de-icing systems are resistive load circuits.* **2.** same as **resistant** (*force*) ○ *the resistive force of drag*

**resistivity** *noun* ELEC a measure of the electrical resistance of a material of a standard length and cross-section. Symbol

**resistor** *noun* ELEC a device used to control current in an electric circuit by providing a known resistance ○ *Components such as resistors, rectifiers and internal switches are all embedded in micro-size sections of semiconductor material.*

**resolution** *noun* **1.** CHEM the separation of a racemic mixture into its constituent isomers **2.** COMPUT the number of pixels that a screen or printer can display per unit area ○ *The resolution of* *most personal computer screens is not much more than 70 dots per inch.*

**resolve** *verb* **1.** to cause something to divide into its constituents **2.** to become determined to do something

**resolving power** *noun* OPTICS a measurement of the ability of an optical system to detect fine black lines on a white background, given as the number of lines per millimetre

**resonance** *noun* **1.** PHYS a situation where a frequency applied to a body which is the same as its natural frequency causes it to oscillate with a very large amplitude **2.** CHEM the property of a chemical compound having several possible structural arrangements of electrons in a molecule. ♦ **mesomerism**

**resonate** *verb* PHYS to produce or cause something to produce resonance

**resorption** *noun* BIOL the absorption of a substance already produced back into the organism that produced it

**resource** *noun* **1.** a useful source of something ○ *reference resources such as encyclopaedias* **2.** ECOL anything in the environment which can be used **3.** COMPUT a device, product, program or graphics object which is useful or used

**resource allocation** *noun* the division of available resources between people or activities

**resource interchange file format** *noun* COMPUT a multimedia data format jointly introduced by IBM and Microsoft that uses tags to identify parts of a multimedia file structure and allows the file to be exchanged between platforms. Abbreviation **RIFF**

**resource management** *noun* a system of controlling the use of resources in such a way as to avoid waste and to use them in the most effective way

**respiration** *noun* PHYSIOL the action of breathing

COMMENT: Respiration includes two stages: breathing in (inhalation) and breathing out (exhalation). Air is taken into the respiratory system through the nose or mouth and goes down into the lungs through the pharynx, larynx and windpipe. In the lungs, the bronchi take the air to the alveoli (air sacs) where oxygen in the air is passed to the bloodstream in exchange for waste carbon dioxide which is then breathed out.

**respiratory** *adjective* PHYSIOL referring to respiration

**respiratory allergy** *noun* MED an allergy caused by a substance which is inhaled

**respiratory disorder** *noun* MED an illness which affects the patient's breathing

**respiratory movement** *noun* PHYSIOL a movement or change in shape of an animal, that is required for respiration, e.g. a chest movement in a mammal

**respiratory organ** *noun* ANAT an organ in which respiration takes place, e.g. a lung in mammals

**respiratory pigment** *noun* BIOCHEM a blood pigment that carries oxygen collected in the lungs and releases it in tissues, e.g. haemoglobin

**respiratory quotient** *noun* PHYSIOL the ratio of the amount of carbon dioxide passed from the blood into the lungs to the amount of oxygen absorbed into the blood from the air. Abbreviation **RQ**

**respiratory system** *noun* ANAT a series of organs and passages that take air into the lungs and exchange oxygen for carbon dioxide

**respond** *verb* to react (to something) □ *the aircraft responds to the controls* the aircraft attitude changes as a result of the pilot's movements of the flying controls

**response** *noun* a reaction

**response frame** *noun* COMPUT a page in a videotext system that allows a user to enter data

**response time** *noun* COMPUT the speed with which a system responds to a stimulus

**responsibility** *noun* the state of being answerable for something, or in charge of something

**responsible** *adjective* **1.** answerable for something or in charge of something ○ *responsible for safety checks* **2.** causing something ○ *The action of sunlight on gases is responsible for the formation of ozone.*

**rest** *noun* **1.** the state of not moving **2.** a period of not moving or using energy ■ *verb* **1.** to be still and not moving or using energy **2.** to keep something still and not moving or using energy

**resting potential** *noun* PHYSIOL the potential difference, in millivolts, between the inner and outer parts of a nerve

**restitution coefficient** *noun* PHYS the difference in velocity of two objects before they impact compared to their velocity after they impact

**restock** *verb* to provide something with another supply of something that has been used up ○ *So many animals died that they had to restock the farm in the spring.*

**restoration** *noun* the act or process of giving something back or of getting back

**restore** *verb* to give something back or put something back to a previous state or position

**restrict** *verb* to keep something within a certain limit ○ *The document is restricted, and cannot be placed on open access.*

**restriction** *noun* something which restricts

**restriction fragment** *noun* GENETICS a section of DNA cut out by a specific restriction enzyme

**restriction fragment length polymorphism** *noun* GENETICS a variation observed between individuals in the length of the DNA fragments produced by a specific restriction enzyme. Abbreviation **RFLP** (NOTE: They are caused by mutations and can be used to detect genetic anomalies.)

**restrictor valve, restrictor** *noun* ENG a valve designed to permit limited flow in one direction and full flow in the other direction ○ *The extent to which the oil pressure will fall depends on the size of the restrictor valve.*

**result** *noun* a consequence or outcome ○ *Engine oil and cylinder temperature will also increase as a result of higher combustion temperatures.*

**resultant** *adjective* happening as a result or consequence ○ *The temperature of the land rises, causing the layer of air in contact with it to warm up and expand with a resultant decrease in density.* ○ *When two or more velocities act simultaneously on a body, the aircraft movement is called the resultant velocity due to the two or more component velocities.* ■ *noun* MATHS one vector that is the equivalent of a set of vectors

**result code** *noun* COMPUT a message sent from a modem to a local computer indicating the state of the modem

**result from** *verb* to happen as a consequence of something ○ *The structural weakness resulted from a minor collision while taxiing two years previously.*

**result in** *verb* to produce something as an effect ○ *Failure to secure seat belts could result in serious injury.*

**resume** *verb* to restart something from the point where it was left

**retard** *verb* to make something slower ○ *The injections retard the effect of the anaesthetic.*

**retentivity** *noun* METALL the ability to remain magnetised after the magnetising force has gone ○ *Steel has high retentivity, but soft iron has low retentivity.*

**reticulum** *noun* ZOOL the second stomach compartment of ruminants such as cows and sheep

**retina** *noun* ANAT the inside layer of the eye which is sensitive to light

**retinal artery** *noun* ANAT the artery that supplies the retina, which accompanies the optic nerve

**retinol** *noun* BIOCHEM a vitamin that is soluble in fat and can be formed in the body but is mainly found in food such as liver, vegetables, eggs and cod liver oil. Also called **vitamin A**

**retort** *noun* CHEM a glass container with a long downwards-pointing spout, used in distillation

**retractable** *adjective* able to be pulled back or raised

**retractable undercarriage** *noun* AEROSP an undercarriage which can be raised into the fuselage or wings after use (NOTE: Early aircraft had non-retractable undercarriages.)

**retrain** *verb* TELECOM to re-establish a better quality connection when the quality of a line is very bad

**retrieval** *noun* COMPUT the process of searching, locating and recovering information from a file or storage device

**retrieve** *verb* COMPUT to extract information from a file or storage device ○ *These are the records retrieved in that search.* ○ *This command will retrieve all names beginning with S.*

**retrofit** *noun* COMPUT a device or accessory added to a system to upgrade it

**retrospective parallel running** *noun* COMPUT the running of a new computer system with old data to check if it is accurate

**retrovirus** *noun* MICROBIOL a virus whose genetic information is contained in RNA rather than DNA (NOTE: A retrovirus is the cause of AIDS and some can also cause cancer.)

**return** *noun* COMPUT **1.** an instruction that causes program execution to go back to the main program from a subroutine ○ *The program is not working because you missed out the return instruction at the end of the subroutine.* **2.** a key on a keyboard used to indicate that all the required data has been entered ○ *You type in your name and code number then press return.* **3.** an indication of an end of line in printing ■ *verb* to come back or to go back to an earlier position or place, or cause something to do so

**return address** *noun* COMPUT the address to be returned to after a called routine finishes

**return valve** *noun* ENG a valve which allows a flow of fluid in both directions

**reuse** ENVIRON *noun* the use of a product or a material for an additional time or a different purpose, usually as an alternative to throwing it away ■ *verb* to use a product or a material for an additional time or a different purpose, usually as an alternative to throwing it away

**reveal** *verb* to bring something to view ○ *A closer inspection revealed small cracks in the surface.*

**reverberatory furnace** *noun* INDUST a furnace in which heat reflected from above heats the material inside

**reversal** *noun* a change to the opposite position, direction or order

**reverse** *noun* the opposite ○ *One would expect a unit of humid air to be heavier than a similar unit of dry air but, in fact, the reverse is true.* ■ *adjective* going backwards or in the opposite direction ■ *verb* **1.** to go or travel in the opposite direction **2.** TELECOM to send control data from a receiver to a transmitter

**reverse channel** *noun* TELECOM a low-speed control data channel between a receiver and transmitter

**reverse characters** *plural noun* PRINTING characters which are displayed in the opposite way to other characters for emphasis, as black on white or white on black, when other characters are the opposite

**reversed fault** *noun* EARTH SCI a fault in which the upper layers of rock have been pushed forwards over the lower layers. Also called **thrust fault**

**reverse engineering** *noun* INDUST a method of product design in which the finished item is analysed to determine how it should be constructed

**reverse flow** *noun* PHYS the flow of a fluid in the opposite direction to normal

**reverse index** *noun* COMPUT a movement of a printer head up half a line to print superscripts

**reverse interrupt** *noun* TELECOM a signal sent by a receiver to request the termination of transmissions

**reverse polarity** *noun* ELEC a situation where positive and negative terminals have been confused, resulting in the equipment not functioning

**reverse Polish notation** *noun* MATHS a set of mathematical operations written in a logical way, so that the operator appears after the numbers to be acted upon, thus removing the need for brackets ○ *Three plus four, minus two is written in reverse Polish notation as 3 4 + 2 − = 5.* ○ *Normal notation is (x-y) + z, but using RPN it is xy − z +.* Also called **postfix notation**. Abbreviation **RPN**

**reverse thrust** *noun* AEROSP a thrust in the opposite direction to the usual one in order to decelerate an aircraft after landing

**reverse video** *noun* COMPUT a screen display mode where white and black are reversed

**reversible** *adjective* which can be made to go backwards or to change direction ○ *a reversible electric motor*

**reversible pitch propeller** *noun* AEROSP a propeller that allows an aircraft to be propelled backwards when taxiing

**reversion** *noun* a return to an earlier condition or state ○ *In smaller aircraft, reversion to manual control is possible if complete loss of hydraulic power occurs.*

**revert** *verb* to return to an earlier condition or state ○ *The elevator system has the ability to revert to manual control after a hydraulic failure.*

**revertant** BIOL *adjective* referring to an organism or part of an organism that has redeveloped characteristics that had been lost ■ *noun* an organism or part of an organism that has redeveloped characteristics that had been lost

**revert command** *noun* COMPUT a command in text that returns a formatted page to its original state

**revise** *verb* COMPUT to update or correct a version of a document or file ○ *The revised version has no mistakes.*

**revolution** *noun* a rotation or 360° turn about an axis ○ *a revolution of the Earth* ○ *revolutions of a crankshaft*

**revolutions per minute** *noun* the speed of an engine or the number of rotations of a crankshaft per minute. Abbreviation **r.p.m., rpm**

**revolve** *verb* to turn about an axis ○ *The Earth revolves around the Sun.*

**Reynolds number** *noun* PHYS a number that indicates the density and velocity of flow of a fluid through a pipe or around an obstruction

**Rf** *symbol* CHEM ELEM rutherfordium

**RF, R/F** *abbreviation* PHYS radio frequency

**RFC** *abbreviation* COMPUT request for comment

**RFLP** *abbreviation* BIOTECH restriction fragment length polymorphism

**RF shielding** *noun* ELEC a thin metal foil wrapped around a cable that prevents the transmission of radio frequency interference signals ○ *Without RF shielding, the transmitted signal would be distorted by the interference.*

**RGB** *abbreviation* COMPUT red, green, blue

**RGB display, RGB monitor** *noun* COMPUT a high-definition monitor system that uses three separate input signals controlling red, green and blue colour picture beams

COMMENT: There are three colour guns producing red, green and blue beams acting on groups of three phosphor dots at each pixel location.

**rH** *abbreviation* redox potential

**Rh** *symbol* CHEM ELEM rhodium

**rhenium** *noun* CHEM ELEM a rare heavy metallic element with a high melting point, used as a catalyst with tungsten in thermocouples (NOTE: The chemical symbol is **Re**; the atomic

number is **75** and the atomic weight is **186.2**.)

**rhesus factor** *noun* BIOCHEM an antigen in red blood cells which is an element in blood grouping. Also called **Rh factor**

COMMENT: The rhesus factor is important in blood grouping. Most people are Rh-positive and an Rh-negative patient should not receive an Rh-positive blood transfusion as this will cause the formation of permanent antibodies. If an Rh-negative mother has a child by an Rh-positive father, the baby will inherit Rh-positive blood, which may then pass into the mother's circulation at childbirth and cause antibodies to form. This can be prevented by an injection of anti D immunoglobulin immediately after the birth of the first Rh-positive child and any subsequent Rh-positive children. If an Rh-negative mother has formed antibodies to Rh-positive blood in the past, these antibodies will affect the blood of the foetus and may cause erythroblastosis fetalis.

**rhesus factor disease** *noun* MED a disease which occurs when the blood of a foetus is incompatible with that of the mother

**Rh factor** *noun* BIOCHEM same as **rhesus factor**

**rhizofiltration** *noun* ENVIRON the use of plants to absorb or precipitate ground-water contaminants in their roots

**rhizoid** *noun* BOT a thin rootlike structure in lower plants such as mosses and liverworts

**rhizome** *noun* BOT a plant stem which lies under the ground and contains leaf buds

**rhizosphere** *noun* BOT the soil surrounding the roots of a plant

**Rh-negative** *adjective* MED not having the rhesus factor

**rhodium** *noun* CHEM ELEM a silvery-white metallic element that occurs with platinum and is used for plating jewellery and in alloys (NOTE: The chemical symbol is **Rh**; the atomic number is **45** and the atomic weight is **102.91**.)

**Rhodophyta** *plural noun* MARINE BIOL red algae, mainly found on the seabed

**rhodopsin** *noun* BIOCHEM a reddish light-sensitive pigment in the rod cells of the retina

**Rh-positive** *adjective* MED having the rhesus factor

**rhumb** *noun* NAVIG one of the points of a compass

**rhumb line** *noun* NAVIG a regularly curved imaginary line on the surface of the Earth which cuts all meridians at the same angle

**rhumb line direction** *noun* NAVIG the average of all the great circle directions between the two points (NOTE: Because the great circle direction between two points on the surface of the Earth is not constant, it is often more convenient to consider the rhumb line direction.)

**ria** *noun* EARTH SCI a valley which has been filled by the sea

**rib** *noun* **1.** ANAT a curved bone in the chest, one of a set of pairs that form the rib cage **2.** AEROSP one of many cross pieces of an airframe that provide an aircraft wing with shape and strength

**ribbon** *noun* a long thin flat piece of material

**ribbon cable** *noun* ELEC a number of insulated conductors arranged next to each other forming a flat cable

**ribbon development** *noun* ENVIRON the building of houses in an uninterrupted row along a main road

**rib cage** *noun* ANAT the structure formed by the ribs that protects the heart and lungs

**riboflavin, riboflavine** *noun* BIOCHEM a vitamin found in eggs, liver, green vegetables, milk and yeast and also used as an additive (E101) in processed food. Also called **vitamin B$_2$** (NOTE: Lack of riboflavine will affect a child's growth and can cause anaemia and inflammation of the mouth and tongue.)

**ribonuclease** *noun* BIOCHEM an enzyme which breaks down RNA

**ribonucleic acid** *noun* BIOCHEM full form of **RNA**

**ribose** *noun* BIOCHEM a type of sugar found in RNA

**ribosomal** *adjective* BIOL referring to ribosomes

**ribosome** *noun* BIOL a structure in a cell, containing RNA and protein, where protein is synthesised

**rice** *noun* PLANTS a cereal plant that is the most important cereal crop and the staple food of half the population of the world. Latin name: *Oryza sativa*.

**rich** *adjective* **1.** EARTH SCI (*of soil*) having many useful nutrients for plant growth **2.** (*of food*) having a high calorific value **3.** ENG (*of a mixture of fuel and air*) having a relatively high ratio of fuel to air **4.** □ **rich in** having a lot of something ○ *Green vegetables are rich in minerals.* ○ *The doctor has prescribed a diet which is rich in protein.* ○ *The forests are rich in mosses and other forms of moisture-loving plants.*

**-rich** *suffix* having a lot of something ○ *a nutrient-rich detergent* ○ *a protein-rich diet* ○ *Many wild plants have oil-rich seeds which can help in the manufacture of detergents.*

**Richter scale** *noun* MEASURE, EARTH SCI a scale of measurement of the force of an earthquake from zero to ten, with the strongest earthquake ever recorded being 8.9 ○ *There were no reports of injuries after the quake which hit 5.2 on the Richter scale.*

COMMENT: Earthquakes of 5 or more on the Richter scale cause damage. The Richter scale measures the force of an earthquake: the damage caused is measured on the Modified Mercalli scale.

**rich text format** *noun* COMPUT a way of storing a document that includes all the commands that describe the page, type, font and formatting. Abbreviation **RTF**

**ridge** *noun* **1.** EARTH SCI a long raised section of ground, occurring as part of a mountain range or on the ocean floor **2.** METEOROL a long narrow band of high pressure leading away from the centre of an anticyclone ○ *A ridge of high pressure is lying across the country.*

**ridge waves** *plural noun* METEOROL oscillations about the stable state of an undisturbed air flow with a range of hills providing the disturbance

**RIFF** *abbreviation* COMPUT resource interchange file format

**RIFF file** *noun* COMPUT a file that contains multimedia data stored in the resource interchange file format

**rift valley** noun EARTH SCI a long valley with steep walls, formed when land between two fault lines sinks or possibly when a fault widens as plates forming the Earth's crust move apart

**right justify** verb COMPUT to adjust the right-hand margin so that the text finishes at the same place on every line with no lines indented

**right shift** verb COMPUT to move a section of data one bit to the right

**rightsizing** noun COMPUT the process of moving a company's information technology structure to the most cost-effective hardware, especially moving from a mainframe-based network to a PC-based network

**rigid** adjective inflexible, hard or stiff ○ *rigid pipes* ○ *a rigid structure* Opposite **flexible**

**rigid disk** noun COMPUT a rigid magnetic disk that is able to store many times more data than a floppy disk and usually cannot be removed from the disk drive

**rigidity** noun **1.** inflexibility, hardness or stiffness ○ *Extra strength and rigidity must be provided in the tail section for aircraft with a tail wheel unit.* **2.** strictness of control or adherence to a way of doing something ○ *the rigidity of the guidelines* Opposite **flexibility**

**rigidity modulus** noun PHYS same as **elastic modulus**

**rill** noun EARTH SCI a very narrow stream

**rim** noun the outer edge of a circular object such as a wheel ○ *Creep marks are painted on the tyre and the wheel rim.* ○ *The rim of the air intake is prone to icing.*

**rime** noun METEOROL feathery ice formed when freezing fog settles on surfaces

**ring** noun **1.** a circle which goes round something **2.** COMPUT a data list whose last entry points back to the first entry **3.** COMPUT the topology of a network in which the wiring sequentially connects one workstation to another **4.** CHEM a closed loop of atoms in a molecule **5.** a metallic sound like the sound of a bell ■ verb **1.** TELECOM to telephone someone **2.** to make a metallic sound like the sound of a bell **3.** ZOOL to attach a numbered ring to the leg of a bird so that its movements can be recorded

COMMENT: Ringing is a very common method of tracing bird movements and providing information about birds' ages. It can also cause stress to the birds.

**ring back system** noun COMPUT (*usually in a bulletin board system*) a remote computer system in which a user attempting to access it phones once, allows it to ring a number of times, disconnects, waits a moment then redials

**Ringer's solution** noun CHEM a solution of various salts, used to keep cells or organs alive for study after they are removed from the body

**ring shift** noun COMPUT the movement of data to the left or right in a word where the bits falling outside the word boundary are discarded and the free positions are filled with zeros

**ring topology** noun COMPUT a network structure in which each node, computer or printer, is connected one after the other in a loop

**ring topology network** noun COMPUT a network where each node, computer or printer is connected one after the other in a loop

**Rio Declaration** noun ENVIRON the statement laying down the broad principles of environmentally sound development adopted at the Earth Summit in Rio de Janeiro in 1992

**RIP** abbreviation COMPUT **1.** raster image processor **2.** routing information protocol

**riparian** noun EARTH SCI referring to the bank of a river ○ *riparian fauna*

**rip current** noun EARTH SCI same as **riptide**

**ripple** noun EARTH SCI a little wave on the surface of water ○ *Ripple marks can be seen in some sedimentary rocks showing where the sand was marked by water.*

**ripple-through carry** noun COMPUT an operation producing a carry out from a sum and a carry in

**riptide** noun EARTH SCI **1.** an area of rough water in the sea where currents meet **2.** a current that flows against the flow of the incoming waves ▶ also called **rip current**

**RISC** abbreviation COMPUT reduced instruction set computer

**risk** *noun* the possibility that injury, damage or loss can be caused by some substance, technology or activity

**risk assessment** *noun* ENVIRON a process used to determine the increased risk from a substance, technology or activity

**river** *noun* EARTH SCI a large flow of water, running from a natural source under mountains or hills down to the sea

**river authority** *noun* ENVIRON an official body which manages the rivers in an area

**river basin** *noun* EARTH SCI a large low-lying area of land, drained by a river

**river capture** *noun* EARTH SCI the incorporation of smaller streams into a large river by a process of erosion

**riverine** *adjective* EARTH SCI referring to a river ○ *The dam has destroyed the riverine fauna and flora for hundreds of kilometres.*

**river profile** *noun* EARTH SCI a slope along the bed of a river, expressed as a graph of distance-from-source against height

**river system** *noun* EARTH SCI a series of small streams and rivers which connect with each other

**river terrace** *noun* EARTH SCI same as **alluvial terrace**

**rivet** ENG *noun* a metal bolt or pin with a head on one end, inserted through one of the aligned holes in parts to be joined and then compressed on the plain end to form a second head ■ *verb* to join metal parts with rivets ○ *The panel is riveted to the frame.*

**RJE** *noun* COMPUT a batch processing system where instructions are transmitted to the computer from a remote terminal. Full form **remote job entry**

**RLE** *noun* COMPUT a data compression technique that stores any sequence of bits of data with the same value to a single value. Full form **run-length encoding**

**RLL encoding** *noun* COMPUT a fast and efficient method of storing data onto a disk in which the changes in a run of data bits are stored. Full form **run-length limited encoding**

**Rn** *symbol* CHEM ELEM radon

**RNA** *noun* GENETICS a nucleic acid chain that takes coded information from DNA and translates it into specific proteins. Full form **ribonucleic acid**. ◆ **DNA**

**RNA polymerase** *noun* GENETICS a polymerase that aids RNA synthesis

**roam** *verb* TELECOM to move around freely and still be in contact with a wireless communications transmitter

**robot** *noun* INDUST a device which can be programmed to carry out certain manufacturing tasks which are similar to tasks carried out by people

**robotics** *noun* COMPUT the study of artificial intelligence, programming and building involved in robot construction

**robust** *adjective* **1.** (*of people*) strong and healthy **2.** (*of objects or organisations*) effective and unlikely to fail **3.** COMPUT (*of a computer system*) able to resume working after a fault has occurred

**rock** *noun* **1.** EARTH SCI a solid mineral substance which forms the outside crust of the Earth **2.** a mass of rock, especially an isolated or projecting one

**rock crystal** *noun* EARTH SCI a pure form of quartz

**rock desert** *noun* EARTH SCI a desert where underlying rock has been exposed by the wind blowing away topsoil

**rocker arm** *noun* AUTOMOT a part of the valve mechanism in an internal combustion engine, which transmits the movement of the pushrod to the valve

**rock pool** *noun* EARTH SCI a pool of salt water left in rocks by the sea

**rock salt** *noun* MINERALS same as **halite**

**rod** *noun* **1.** a thin straight piece of metal ○ *Aluminium rods and bars can readily be employed in the high-speed manufacture of parts.* **2.** ANAT a light-sensitive cell in the retina of the eye, especially sensitive to poor light. ◆ **cone**

**rodent** *noun* ZOOL a mammal such as a rat or mouse that has sharp teeth for gnawing

**roentgen, röntgen** *noun* MEASURE, PHYS a unit of measurement of the amount of exposure to X-rays or gamma rays. Symbol **R**

**roentgen equivalent man** *noun* MEASURE, PHYS a unit of measurement of ionising radiation equivalent to the effect of absorbing one roentgen. Abbreviation **rem** (NOTE: It has been replaced by the sievert.)

**roentgenology, röntgenology** *noun* MED same as **radiology**

**roentgen ray** *noun* MED same as **X-ray, gamma ray**

**rogue value, rogue terminator** *noun* COMPUT an item in a list of data that shows that the list is terminated

**role** *noun* **1.** a function that something or someone performs ○ *Movement of air plays a major role in the development of weather patterns.* **2.** ECOL the set of characters, chemical, physical and biological, that determine the position of an organism or species in an ecosystem, e.g. aquatic predator or terrestrial herbivore

**role indicator** *noun* COMPUT a symbol used to show the role of a index entry in its particular context

**roll** AEROSP *noun* a rotation about the longitudinal axis of an aircraft, created by movement of the ailerons ○ *Roll is produced by moving the stick to the left or right.* ■ *verb* to rotate an aircraft around its longitudinal axis ○ *Move the control column to the left to roll the aircraft to the left.*

COMMENT: The difference between roll and bank is that roll is movement whereas bank suggests a fixed attitude of the aircraft. Consequently, a turn might be expressed in angles of bank: 'turn at a bank angle of 30°', and the movement to obtain the bank might be expressed as roll: 'roll the aircraft to the left'.

**roll back** *noun* COMPUT a function of a database application to stop a transaction and return the database to its previous state

**roll forward** *noun* COMPUT a function of a database application that allows the user to recover from a disaster such as a power cut by reading the transaction log and re-executing all the instructions to return the database to the state just before the disaster

**ROM** *abbreviation* COMPUT read only memory

**Roman numeral** *noun* MATHS one of the numbers written as I, II, III, IV, V etc.

**ROM BIOS** *noun* COMPUT a code which makes up the BIOS routines stored in a ROM chip, usually executed automatically when the computer is switched on

**röntgen** *noun* MEASURE, PHYS another spelling of **roentgen**

**röntgenology** *noun* MED another spelling of **roentgenology**

**root** *noun* **1.** BOT a part of a plant which is usually under the ground and absorbs water and nutrients from the surrounding soil **2.** COMPUT a starting node from which all paths branch in a data tree structure ■ *verb* BOT (*of a plant*) to produce roots ○ *The cuttings root easily in moist sand.*

**root crop** *noun* AGRIC a plant that stores edible material in a root, corm or tuber and is grown as food (NOTE: Root crops include carrots, parsnips, swedes and turnips. Starchy root crops include potatoes, cassavas and yams.)

**root cutting** *noun* BOT a piece of root cut from a living plant and put in soil, where it will sprout and grow into a new plant

**root directory** *noun* COMPUT the topmost directory from which all other directories branch ○ *In DOS, the root directory on drive C: is called C:.*

**root hair** *noun* BOT a hollow elongated epidermal cell that grows like a fine hair from the outer cells of a root to take in water and nutrients from the soil

**rooting compound** *noun* AGRIC a powder containing plant hormones (**auxins**) into which cuttings can be dipped to encourage the formation of roots

**root nodule** *noun* BOT a lump on a plant root that contains nitrogen-fixing bacteria (NOTE: Root nodules are found in peas, beans and other leguminous plants.)

**root pressure** *noun* BOT the pressure that pushes water from the roots up through the vascular tissues of a plant

**rootstock** *noun* **1.** BOT same as **rhizome 2.** AGRIC a plant with roots onto which a piece of another plant is grafted

**root system** *noun* BOT all the roots of a plant

**Rossby wave** *noun* EARTH SCI a huge side-to-side swing in air and ocean currents caused by the Coriolis force

**rot** *verb* BIOL (*of organic tissue*) to decay or become putrefied because of bacterial or fungal action

**rotary** *adjective* ENG moving around an axis or fixed point

**rotary actuator** *noun* ENG an actuator which rotates and operates a screw jack, e.g. to extend flaps

**rotary converter** *noun* ELEC ENG an electric motor powered by an alternating current, linked to a dynamo and used to generate direct current

**rotary inverter** *noun* ELEC ENG a direct current motor driving an alternating current generator, the output of which must be regulated to give constant voltage and frequency

**rotary motion** *noun* ENG a circular movement around an axis or fixed point

**rotary wing aircraft** *noun* AEROSP an aircraft with a rotor which provides lift, e.g. a helicopter

**rotate** *verb* **1.** to turn around on an axis or fixed point ○ *Counter-rotating propellers rotate in opposite directions.* **2.** AGRIC to grow different crops from year to year in a field

COMMENT: The advantages of rotating crops are, firstly, that different crops utilise soil nutrients differently, secondly that pests particular to one crop are discouraged from spreading and, thirdly, that some crops actually benefit the soil. Legumes such as peas and beans increase the nitrogen content of the soil if their roots are left in the soil after harvesting.

**rotation** *noun* **1.** ENG the process of turning around an axis or fixed point ○ *the rotation of the Earth* ○ *crankshaft rotation* ○ *The speed of rotation determines the frequency of the generator output.* **2.** MATHS the amount by which an object has been rotated **3.** the act of moving in a circle

**rotation of crops** *noun* AGRIC same as **crop rotation**

**rotenone** *noun* AGRIC an insecticide derived from derris

**rotor** *noun* **1.** ENG the central shaft of a generator, which turns inside the stator **2.** METEOROL a rapidly turning mass of air, surrounded by clouds

**rotor blade** *noun* AEROSP a long thin aerofoil on a helicopter rotor

**rough** *adjective* **1.** having an irregular surface or action **2.** not fully detailed

**roughage** *noun* BIOL fibrous matter in food, which cannot be digested. Also called **dietary fibre**

**rough air** *noun* AEROSP turbulent air

**rough calculation** *noun* an operation giving an approximate answer ○ *I made some rough calculations on the back of an envelope.* ○ *According to my calculations, we have six months' stock left.*

**rough drawing** *noun* a quick drawing usually used to illustrate or explain something

**rough estimate** *noun* an approximate calculation, good enough for a given purpose

**roughness** *noun* unevenness of a surface ○ *The strength of turbulence near the Earth's surface depends largely on the surface temperature, the surface wind and the roughness of the surface.*

**rough running** *noun* ENG the incorrect operation of a piston engine

**round** *adjective* MATHS **1.** shaped like a circle or a globe **2.** not exact, but given to the nearest whole number ○ *a round figure of 300*

**round bracket** *noun* a type of bracket with round sides, (( )), used in pairs

**round down** *verb* MATHS to approximate a number to a slightly lower one of less precision ○ *We can round down 2.651 to 2.65.*

**rounding** *noun* **1.** MATHS an approximation of a number to a slightly larger or smaller one of lower precision **2.** COMPUT the process of giving graphics a smoother look

**rounding error** *noun* MATHS an error in a result caused by rounding off the number

**round off** *verb* MATHS to approximate a number to a slightly larger or smaller one of less precision ○ *round off 23.456 to 23.46*

**round off errors** *plural noun* MATHS inaccuracies in numbers due to rounding off

**round up** *verb* MATHS to approximate a number to a slightly larger one of lower precision ○ *We can round up 2.647 to 2.65.*

**roundworm** *noun* ZOOL a type of worm with a round body, some of which are parasites of animals, others of roots of plants

**route** *noun* COMPUT the path taken by a message between a transmitter and receiver in a network ○ *The route taken was not the most direct since a lot of nodes were busy.*

**router** *noun* COMPUT **1.** a communications device that receives data packets in a particular protocol and forwards them to their correct location via the most efficient route **2.** a device that connects two or more LANs that use the same protocol, and allows data to be transmitted between each network (NOTE: The router works at the network-layer level of the OSI model.)

**routine** *noun* **1.** a regular pattern of activity **2.** COMPUT a number of instructions included in a program that perform a particular task, but are not a complete program ○ *The routine copies the screen display onto a printer.* ○ *The RETURN instruction at the end of the routine sends control back to the main program.* ■ *adjective* usual and expected ○ *a routine check*

COMMENT: Routines are usually called from a main program to perform a task, control is then returned to the part of the main program from which the routine was called once that task is complete.

**routing** *noun* COMPUT the determination of a suitable route for a message through a network

**routing information protocol** *noun* COMPUT a protocol used on the Internet to calculate the best route by which to transfer information over the Internet, based on the distance that each route takes. Abbreviation **RIP**

**routing table** *noun* COMPUT a list of preferred choices for a route for a message stored within a router

**row** *noun* COMPUT a horizontal set of data elements in an array or matrix

**RPC** *abbreviation* COMPUT remote procedure call

**RPG** *abbreviation* COMPUT report program generator

**r.p.m., rpm** *abbreviation* MEASURE revolutions per minute

**RPN** *abbreviation* MATHS reverse Polish notation

**RQ** *abbreviation* MEASURE, PHYSIOL respiratory quotient

**RS-232C** ELECTRONICS approved by the Electronics Industry Association standard used in serial data transmission, covering voltage and control signals

**RSA** *noun* COMPUT a public-key cryptography system used to provide high-level security

**RSI** *abbreviation* MED repetitive strain injury

**R/T** *abbreviation* TELECOM radiotelephony

**RTF** *abbreviation* COMPUT rich text format

**RTP** *abbreviation* COMPUT real-time transport protocol

**RTS** *abbreviation* COMPUT request to send signal

**Ru** *symbol* CHEM ELEM ruthenium

**rubber** *noun* INDUST a material which can be stretched and compressed, made from a thick white fluid (**latex**) from a tropical tree

**rubidium** *noun* CHEM ELEM a soft silvery radioactive element that reacts strongly with water and ignites in air, used in photocells and glass manufacture (NOTE: The chemical symbol is **Rb**; the atomic number is **37** and the atomic weight is **85.47**.)

**ruby** *noun* MINERALS a deep red form of corundum that is a precious stone

**rudder** *noun* AVIAT a control surface on the fin which rotates an aircraft about its vertical axis to produce yaw

COMMENT: The rudder does not turn the aircraft. It is used, together with aileron deflection, to initiate turns, to balance forces in turns and to counteract yawing motions created by the propeller during flight.

**ruderal** *adjective* BOT growing in rubbish or on wasteland

**rule** *noun* **1.** a standard and authoritative instruction or guideline ○ *I'd like to give a few safety rules before we start.* ○ *According to the rules, your ticket must be paid for two weeks in advance.* ○ *A useful rule for the application of variation is – variation east magnetic least, variation west magnetic best.* **2.** a principle that has been established by observation **3.** COMPUT a set of conditions that describe a function ○ *The rule states that you wait for the clear signal before transmitting.*

**rule-based system** *noun* COMPUT a software system that applies the rules and knowledge defined by experts in a particular field to a user's data to solve a problem

**rule of thumb** *noun* an easily remembered, useful guide to a more complex principle

**ruler** *noun* **1.** MEASURE a short flat piece of rigid material, marked with units for measuring lengths of up to about 100 cm **2.** COMPUT a bar displayed on screen that indicates a unit of measurement

**ruminant** *noun* ZOOL an animal such as a cow or sheep that chews the cud

**rumination** *noun* ZOOL the process by which food taken to the stomach of a ruminant is returned to the mouth, chewed again and then swallowed

COMMENT: Ruminants have stomachs with four sections. They take foodstuffs into the upper chamber where it is acted upon by bacteria. The food is then regurgitated into their mouths where they chew it again before passing it to the last two sections where normal digestion takes place.

**run** *noun* **1.** a length of something ○ *a long unbroken run of tubing* **2.** INDUST a period of operation of a machine, or the amount produced in one period of operation ○ *three runs a day* ○ *a production run of 5000 units* **3.** COMPUT an execution by a computer of a set of instructions, programs or procedures ○ *The next invoice run will be on Friday.* ■ *verb* **1.** (of a machine or device) to work or operate ○ *The computer has been running ten hours a day.* ○ *The new package runs on our PC.* **2.** to extend ○ *Magnetic lines of force run from the north magnetic pole to the south magnetic pole.* **3.** to operate an engine or other device ○ *An engine should be run at low r.p.m. after flight to allow engine components to cool to a more uniform temperature.* **4.** ZOOL to move rapidly with both feet sometimes off the ground

**run around** *verb* COMPUT to fit text around an image on a printed page

**run-duration** *noun* COMPUT same as **run-time**

**run in** *verb* to operate a system at a lower capacity for a time in case of any faults

**run-length encoding** *noun* COMPUT full form of **RLE**

**run-length limited encoding** *noun* COMPUT full form of **RLL encoding**

**runoff** *noun* **1.** ENG the removal of water from a water system by opening sluices **2.** EARTH SCI the flow of rainwater or melted snow from the surface of land into streams and rivers **3.** ENVIRON the flow of excess fertiliser or pesticide from farmland into rivers ○ *Nitrate runoff causes pollution of lakes and rivers.* ○ *Fish are extremely susceptible to runoff of organophosphates.*

**runoff rate** *noun* ENVIRON the amount of excess fertiliser or pesticide from farmland that flows into rivers

**runoff water** *noun* EARTH SCI rainwater or melted snow that flows into rivers and streams

**run phase** *noun* COMPUT a period of time during which a program is run

**run-time** COMPUT *noun* **1.** the period of time a program takes to run. Also called **run-duration 2.** the time during which a computer is executing a program ■ *adjective* referring to an operation carried out only when a program is running

**run-time error** *noun* COMPUT a fault only detected when a program is run or an error made while a program is running

**run-time library** *noun* COMPUT a library of routines that are only accessed by an application when it is running

**run-time system** *noun* COMPUT a system of software that is required in main storage while a program is running, e.g. to execute instructions to peripherals

**rupture** *noun* **1.** the process of breaking open or bursting ○ *Pressure in the fuel tanks must be controlled to prevent rupture or collapse.* **2.** MED a tear in bodily tissue ■ *verb* to break open or burst, or to cause something to do this ○ *The impact ruptured the fuel tank.* ○ *The fuel tank ruptured.*

**rural** *adjective* ENVIRON referring to the country, as opposed to the town ○ *Many rural areas have been cut off by floods.*

**rural environment** *noun* ENVIRON the countryside

**rust** *noun* **1.** CHEM a reddish powder that forms on the surface of iron and iron compounds on contact with damp air **2.** FUNGI a fungal disease that gives plants a reddish powdery covering ■ *verb* CHEM to become covered with reddish powder through contact with damp air

**ruthenium** *noun* CHEM ELEM a brittle white metallic element used in hardening of platinum and palladium alloys (NOTE: The chemical symbol is **Ru**; the atomic number is **44** and the atomic weight is **101.07**.)

**rutherfordium** *noun* CHEM ELEM a radioactive element produced artificially in high-energy atomic collisions (NOTE: The chemical symbol is **Rf**; the atomic number is **104** and the atomic weight is **261**.)

**rutile** *noun* MINERALS a dark brown or shiny black mineral that forms needle-shaped crystals and is a source of titanium

**R-value** *noun* MEASURE, PHYS a unit of measurement of resistance to the flow of heat (NOTE: An insulated outside wall has an R-value of R-11, while an internal ceiling has a value of R-19.)

**Rydberg constant** *noun* PHYS a constant that relates to the wave number of spectral lines for a particular element

**rye** *noun* PLANTS a hardy cereal crop grown in temperate areas

# S

**S** *symbol* **1.** CHEM sulfur **2.** MEASURE, PHYS siemens

**SAA** *abbreviation* COMPUT Systems Application Architecture

**saccharide** *noun* CHEM a sugar, particularly a simple one

**saccharin** *noun* FOOD INDUST a substance used as a substitute for sugar. Formula: $C_7H_5NO_3S$.

**saccharose** *noun* CHEM same as **sucrose**

**sacral nerves** *plural noun* ANAT the nerves which branch from the spinal cord in the sacrum and govern the legs, arms and genital area

**safe** *adjective* not likely to hurt or cause damage ○ *Technicians are trying to make the damaged reactor safe.* ○ *It is not safe to drink the water here.*

**safe dose** *noun* MED the amount of radiation which can be absorbed without causing harm to someone

**safe format** *noun* COMPUT a format operation that does not destroy the existing data and allows the data to be recovered in case the wrong disk was formatted

**safely** *adverb* without danger or damage ○ *Low-level waste can be safely disposed of by burying.*

**safety** *noun* the condition of being safe or without danger

**safety factor** *noun* something which plays an important part in safety

**safety precaution** *noun* an action taken in order to make subsequent actions or a situation safe

**safety rod** *noun* INDUST a tube inserted into a nuclear reactor in order to alter the speed of the reaction

**safety zone** *noun* ENVIRON an area in which people are not at risk from radiation

**sag** *noun* ELEC a short drop in the voltage level from a power supply

**sagittal** *adjective* BIOL going from the front of the body to the back, dividing it into right and left parts

**sagittal plane** *noun* BIOL the division of the body along the midline, at right angles to the coronal plane, dividing the body into right and left parts

**sagittal section** *noun* BIOL a section or cut through the body going from the front to the back along the length of the body

**sagittal suture** *noun* ANAT a joint along the top of the head where the two parietal bones are fused

**Sahara** *noun* EARTH SCI a large desert region running across North Africa

**Saharan** *adjective* EARTH SCI referring to the Sahara

**Sahel** *noun* EARTH SCI a semi-desert region south of the Sahara in the process of being desertified

**Sahelian** *adjective* EARTH SCI referring to the Sahel

**sal ammoniac** *noun* CHEM same as **ammonium chloride**

**salicylic acid** *noun* CHEM a white crystalline acid used in making aspirin and dyes and as a preservative. Formula: $C_7H_6O_3$.

**salination** *noun* EARTH SCI a process by which soil or water becomes more salty, especially as a result of irrigation in hot climates. Also called **salination**

**saline** *adjective* CHEM referring to salt ■ *noun* CHEM, MED a saline solution

**saline drip** *noun* MED a drip containing a saline solution

**saline solution** *noun* CHEM, MED a salt solution, made of distilled water and sodium chloride, which is introduced into the body intravenously through a drip

**salinisation** *noun* EARTH SCI same as **salination**

**salinised, salinized** *adjective* EARTH SCI referring to soil where evaporation leaves salts as a crust on the dry surface

**salinity** *noun* CHEM the proportion of salt present in a given amount of water or soil

**salinometer** *noun* CHEM an instrument for measuring the amount of salt in a saline solution or in sea water

**saliva** *noun* PHYSIOL a clear fluid secreted by the salivary glands into the mouth, and containing water, mucus and enzymes to lubricate food and break down starch into sugars

**salmon** *noun* ZOOL a large fish that spawns in fresh water and swims down to the ocean to develop into an adult

**Salmonella** *noun* MICROBIOL a genus of bacteria found in the intestines, which are acquired by eating contaminated food (NOTE: Different species cause food poisoning and typhoid fever.)

**salmonella poisoning** *noun* MED an illness caused by eating food which is contaminated with *Salmonella* bacteria which develop in the intestines

**salmonid** *noun* ZOOL a fish such as the trout belonging to a family that is very susceptible to pollution in water and whose presence in water indicates that it is pure

**salt** *noun* CHEM **1.** a chemical compound formed from an acid and a metal **2.** sodium chloride as part of the diet ○ *A patient with heart failure is put on a salt-restricted diet.* ○ *He should reduce his intake of salt.* ■ *adjective* BIOL tasting of salt ○ *sea water is salt* ○ *sweat tastes salt* ■ *verb* FOOD INDUST to preserve food by keeping it in salt or in salt water

COMMENT: Salt forms a necessary part of diet, as it replaces salt lost in sweating and helps to control the water balance in the body. It also improves the working of the muscles and nerves. Most diets contain more salt than each person actually needs.

**salt bridge** *noun* PHYS a tube containing a solution of potassium chloride, used to connect two half-cells

**salt depletion** *noun* PHYSIOL the loss of salt from the body by sweating or vomiting, which causes cramp and other problems

**salt-free diet** *noun* HEALTH a diet which does not contain salt

**salting out** *noun* CHEM the precipitation of a colloid as a result of the addition of a large quantity of a salt

**salt lake** *noun* EARTH SCI a low-lying saltwater lake which is not connected with the sea but where the water contains a lot of salt because of evaporation and lack of incoming fresh water

**salt marsh** *noun* EARTH SCI a marsh over which the sea flows ○ *Salt marshes are covered by salt water at high tide.*

**saltpan** *noun* EARTH SCI an area where salt from beneath the soil surface rises to form crystals on the surface

**saltpetre** *noun* CHEM potassium nitrate, when used commercially

**salt water** *noun* EARTH SCI water which contains salt, e.g. sea water. Compare **fresh water**

**saltwater** *adjective* **1.** EARTH SCI containing salt water **2.** MARINE BIOL living in salt water

**salty** *adjective* **1.** full of salt ○ *Excess minerals in fertilisers combined with naturally saline ground to make the land so salty that it can no longer produce crops.* **2.** tasting of salt

**SAM** *noun* COMPUT storage where a particular data item can only be accessed by reading through all the previous items in the list. Full form **serial access memory**. Compare **RAM**

COMMENT: Magnetic tape is a form of SAM; you have to go through the whole tape to access one item, while disks provide random access to stored data.

**samara** *noun* BOT a dry winged one-seed fruit such as one produced by a sycamore

**samarium** *noun* CHEM ELEM a shiny metallic element used in strong magnets, carbon-arc lighting and laser materials (NOTE: The chemical symbol is **Sm**; the atomic number is **62** and the atomic weight is **150.40**.)

**sample** *noun* a small amount which is representative of the whole ○ *If fuel contamination by water is suspected, a sample of fuel should be drained from the tank for inspection.* ○ *Blood samples were taken from all the staff in the hospital.* ○ *The doctor asked her to provide a urine sample.* ■ *verb* to take a small quantity of something to test

**sample and hold circuit** *noun* ELECTRONICS a circuit that freezes an analog input signal for long enough for an A/D converter to produce a stable output

**sampler** *noun* ELECTRONICS an electronic circuit that takes many samples of a signal and stores them for future analysis

**San Andreas Fault** *noun* EARTH SCI a crack in the Earth's crust in California, running parallel to the coast and passing close to San Francisco

**sanctuary** *noun* ENVIRON a special area where the wildlife is protected ○ *A bird sanctuary has been created on the island.*

**sand** *noun* EARTH SCI fine grains of weathered rock, usually round grains of quartz, found especially on beaches and in the desert

**sand bar** *noun* EARTH SCI a long bank of sand in shallow water either in a river or the sea

**sand dune** *noun* EARTH SCI an area of sand blown by the wind into a small hill or ridge, often crescent-shaped in the desert and sometimes covered with sparse grass when near the sea

**sandstone** *noun* EARTH SCI a sedimentary rock formed of round particles of quartz

**sandstorm** *noun* METEOROL a high wind in the desert, which carries large amounts of sand with it

**sandwich** *noun* ENG a construction of three layers, the material of the one in the middle being different from the two on each side ○ *Standard connectors consist of a metal coupling with a rubber sandwich joint.*

**sandy soil** *noun* EARTH SCI soil containing a high proportion of sand particles

**sanitary** *adjective* **1.** clean ○ *They did not have the sanitary conditions necessary to perform the operation.* **2.** referring to hygiene or to health

**sanitary landfill, sanitary landfilling** *noun* ENVIRON the disposal of waste in specially dug holes in the ground, as opposed to throwing it away anywhere

**sanitation** *noun* MED the systems of waste disposal and water provision that are the basis of public hygiene ○ *Poor sanitation in crowded conditions can result in the spread of disease.*

**sanitation control** *noun* MED the measures taken to protect public hygiene, e.g. spraying oil onto the surface of water to prevent insects such as mosquitoes from breeding

**sap** *noun* BOT a liquid carrying nutrients which flows inside a plant

**sapling** *noun* BOT a young tree

**saponification** *noun* CHEM the hydrolysis of an ester, generally by an alkali, to form a salt that is a soap in the case of higher fatty acids, and a free alcohol

**sapphire** *noun* MINERALS a clear blue precious stone that is a variety of the mineral corundum

**sappy** *adjective* BOT referring to tree trunks or branches, or wood that is full of sap

**sapro-** *prefix* BIOL decay or rotting

**saprobe** *noun* MICROBIOL a bacterium that lives in rotting matter

**saprobic** *adjective* BIOL referring to the classification of organisms according to the way in which they tolerate pollution. ♦ **mesosaprobic, oligosaprobic, polysaprobic**

**saprogenic, saprogenous** *adjective* BIOL referring to organisms that grow on decaying organic matter

**saprophagous** *adjective* BIOL referring to organisms that feed on decaying organic matter

**saprophyte** *noun* BIOL an organism such as a fungus that lives and feeds on dead or decaying organic matter

**saprophytic** *adjective* BIOL referring to organisms that live and feed on dead or decaying organic matter

**saproplankton** *plural noun* BIOL plankton that live and feed on dead or decaying organic matter

**sapwood** *noun* BOT an outer layer of wood on the trunk of a tree, which is younger than the heartwood inside and carries the sap

**SAR** *abbreviation* COMPUT store address register

**sarcoma** *noun* MED a cancer of connective tissue such as bone, muscle or cartilage

**Sargasso Sea** *noun* EARTH SCI an area of still water in the North Atlantic

Ocean, which is surrounded by currents and contains drifting weed

**SARS** *noun* MED a serious infection affecting the respiration system, that is caused by a virus and has a high fatality rate. Full form **severe acute respiratory syndrome** (NOTE: It first appeared in Hong Kong in 2003 and spread rapidly in China.)

**satellite** *noun* **1.** AEROSP an object launched to orbit the Earth, usually receiving and transmitting signals, pictures and data ○ *a weather satellite* **2.** ASTRON an astronomical object that orbits a larger body in space ○ *The Moon is the Earth's only satellite.* **3.** something that is controlled by but separate from a computer **4.** TECH same as **satellite television**

COMMENT: In a network the floppy disk units are called 'satellites' and the hard disk unit the 'server'. In a star network each satellite is linked individually to a central server.

**satellite computer** *noun* COMPUT a computer doing various tasks under the control of another computer

**satellite DNA** *noun* GENETICS a component of DNA in animals that differs in density from surrounding DNA, consists of short repeating sequences of nucleotide pairs, and does not undergo transcription

**satellite remote sensing** *noun* TECH a collection of data on land use, industrial activity, weather, climate, geology and other processes based on observations of the Earth taken from satellites in outer space

**satellite television**, **satellite TV** *noun* TECH television that is provided by satellite communications rather than cables or land-based transmitters

**saturate** *verb* CHEM to fill something with the maximum amount of a liquid that can be absorbed ○ *Nitrates leached from forest soils, showing that the soils are saturated with nitrogen.*

**saturated colour** *noun* COMPUT a bright colour such as red or orange that does not reproduce well on video and can cause distortion or can spread over the screen

**saturated compound** *noun* CHEM a chemical compound that consists of molecules having only single bonds

**saturated fat** *noun* BIOCHEM a fat that contains the maximum equilibrium amount of hydrogen

COMMENT: Animal fats such as butter and fat meat are saturated fats and contain large amounts of hydrogen. It is known that increasing the amount of unsaturated and polyunsaturated fats (mainly vegetable oils and fish oil) and reducing saturated fats in the food intake help reduce the level of cholesterol in the blood.

**saturation** *noun* CHEM, PHYS the state of being filled with the maximum amount of something which can be absorbed ○ *The various types of fog are classified by the manner in which saturation is reached.*

COMMENT: Air has different saturation levels at different temperatures. The hotter the air temperature, the more moisture the air can absorb.

**saturation noise** *noun* PHYS error due to saturation of a magnetic storage medium

**saturation point** *noun* CHEM, PHYS a level at which no more of a substance can be absorbed

**saturation testing** *noun* TELECOM the testing of a communications network by transmitting large quantities of data and messages over it

**Saturn** *noun* ASTRON the sixth planet of the solar system, 95 times as massive as Earth

COMMENT: Saturn has an equatorial diameter of 120,000 km, but its polar diameter is 10 per cent less, giving it much the greatest polar flattening of any planet of the solar system. It is accompanied by a ring system and by a large family of satellites.

**saturnism** *noun* MED lead poisoning

**savanna**, **savannah** *noun* EARTH SCI a dry grass-covered plain with few trees, especially in South America or Africa, where growth is abundant during the rainy season but vegetation dies back during the dry season

**save** *verb* COMPUT to store data or a program on an auxiliary storage device ○ *Don't forget to save the file before switching off.*

**sawtooth waveform** *noun* PHYS the shape of a changing electrical voltage that repeatedly rises steadily, then drops steadily, giving a triangular-shaped waveform

**Sb** *symbol* CHEM ELEM antimony

**s-block element** *noun* CHEM an element in groups IA and IIA of the periodic table, including alkali metals

**SBM** *abbreviation* COMPUT super bit mapping

**Sc** *symbol* CHEM ELEM scandium

**scalable font** *noun* COMPUT a method of describing a font so that it can produce characters of different sizes

**scalar** *noun* MATHS a variable that has a single value denoting magnitude assigned to it (NOTE: A scalar has a single magnitude value, while a vector has two or more positional values.)

**scalar data** *plural noun* COMPUT data containing single values that are predictable and follow a sequence

**scalar processor** *noun* COMPUT a processor designed to operate at high speed on scalar values

**scalar value** *noun* MATHS a single value rather than a matrix or record (NOTE: Scalar values are not normally floating-point numbers.)

**scalar variable** *noun* COMPUT a variable which can contain a single value rather than a complex data type such as an array or record

**scale** *noun* **1.** a series of marks at fixed intervals used as a reference standard in measurement ○ *This rule has scales in inches and centimetres.* **2.** a graded system of classification **3.** a ratio of two values **4.** ZOOL a flake or plate of tissue as found on the skins of reptiles and fish **5.** CHEM a calcium deposit that forms in pipes and kettles, caused by the hardness of the water

**scale down** *verb* to lower or decrease something in proportion

**scale insect** *noun* INSECTS a parasitic insect that secretes a protective scale around itself and lives on plants

**scale up** *verb* to raise or increase something in proportion

**scaly** *adjective* ZOOL covered in flakes of tissue, like a reptile or fish

**scan** *noun* **1.** MED the examination of an internal part of the body using computer-interpreted X-rays to create a picture ○ *a whole-body scan* **2.** MED a picture of an internal part of the body produced by computer-interpreted

X-rays ○ *They examined the brain scan.* **3.** COMPUT an examination of an image, object or list of items to obtain data describing it ○ *The heat scan of the computer quickly showed which component was overheating.* ○ *The scan revealed which records were now out of date.* ■ *verb* **1.** MED to examine an internal part of the body using computer-interpreted X-rays to create a picture **2.** COMPUT to examine and produce data from the shape or state of an object, or drawing, file or list of items ○ *The fax machine scans the picture and converts this to digital form before transmission.* ○ *The machine scans at up to 300 dpi resolution.*

**scandium** *noun* CHEM ELEM a rare shiny transition metal used as a tracer, found in wolframite and other minerals (NOTE: The chemical symbol is **Sc**; the atomic number is **21** and the atomic weight is **44.96**.)

**scan head** *noun* COMPUT a device used in scanners, photocopiers and fax machines which uses photoelectric cells to turn an image into a pattern of pixels ○ *This model uses a scan head that can distinguish 256 different colours.*

**scan line** *noun* COMPUT one of the horizontal lines of phosphor or phosphor dots on the inside of a cathode ray tube or monitor (NOTE: The monitor's picture beam sweeps along each scan line to create the image on the screen.)

**scanner** *noun* COMPUT a device which converts an image, drawing, photograph or document into graphical data which can be manipulated by a computer

COMMENT: A scanner is connected and controlled by a computer which can then display or process the image data. A scanner can be a device using photoelectric cells, as in an image digitiser, or a device that samples data from a process. Flat-bed scanners are more accurate than hand-held scanners.

**scanning** *noun* COMPUT the action of examining and producing data from the shape of an object or drawing

COMMENT: A modem with auto-baud scanning can automatically sense which baud rate to operate on and switches automatically to that baud rate.

**scanning electron microscope** *noun* PHYS a microscope that uses an electron beam instead of light to produce highly magnified images

**scanning error** *noun* COMPUT an error introduced while scanning an image

**scanning line** *noun* COMPUT a path traced on a cathode ray tube screen by the picture beam

**scanning rate** *noun* COMPUT the time taken to scan one line of an image on a cathode ray tube screen

**scanning resolution** *noun* COMPUT the ability of a scanner to distinguish between small points (NOTE: The usual resolution is 300 dpi.)

**scan rate** *noun* COMPUT the number of times every second that the image on a cathode ray tube screen is redrawn

**scapula** *noun* ANAT a broad flattened bone at the rear of the shoulder in vertebrates. Also called **shoulderblade**

**scar** *noun* 1. MED a mark left on the skin surface after a wound has healed 2. a mark or blemish ■ *verb* to leave a mark on the surface of something ○ *The landscape was scarred by open-cast mines.*

**scarce** *adjective* uncommon, rare or in short supply

**scarcity** *noun* rareness, shortage or lack

**scar tissue** *noun* ANAT fibrous tissue which forms a scar

**scatter** PHYS *noun* the deflection of radiation or a signal ○ *High frequencies are freer of ionospheric scatter.* ■ *verb* to deflect radiation or a signal

**scattering** *noun* PHYS the diversion of light by matter, as seen in the effect Earth's upper atmosphere has on incoming sunlight, causing the sky to look blue, or the effect of dust or gas nebulae on starlight

**scatter load** *verb* COMPUT to load sequential data into various non-continuous locations in memory

**scavenge** *verb* 1. BIOL (*of organisms*) to feed on dead and decaying matter 2. CHEM to remove impurities or pollutants from a substance

**scavenger** *noun* ZOOL 1. an organism such as a bacterium, fungus or worm which feeds on dead matter like leaf litter or refuse. Also called **detritivore 2.** a mammal or bird which feeds on animals which have been killed by lions or other predators

**scavenging** *noun* 1. ZOOL the activity of eating organic matter or dead animals

○ *Vultures and hyenas sometimes feed by scavenging.* **2.** CHEM the removal of impurities or pollutants from a gas

**scent** *noun* 1. CHEM a smell given off by a substance that stimulates the sense of smell **2.** ENVIRON a pleasant smell ○ *the scent of flowers*

**schedule** *noun* 1. a plan of future activities **2.** an order in which tasks are to be done **3.** COMPUT the order in which CPU time will be allocated to processes in a multi-user system ■ *verb* 1. to make a plan of future activities **2.** to arrange an order in which tasks are to be done

**scheduler** *noun* COMPUT a program which organises the use of a central processing unit or of peripherals which are shared by several users

**schema** *noun* COMPUT a graphical description of a process or database structure

**schematic** *adjective* (*of diagram*) showing the function of a device or system without trying to create a realistic image ○ *Figure 3 shows a schematic diagram of the autopilot.*

**Schiff's base** *noun* CHEM an organic compound formed in a condensation reaction between an aromatic amine and a ketone or aldehyde

**Schiff's reagent** *noun* CHEM an acid solution of fuchsine, used as a standard test for the presence of aldehydes

**schist** *noun* EARTH SCI a type of metamorphic rock that splits easily into flakes

**Schistosoma** *noun* ZOOL a fluke which enters the patient's bloodstream and causes schistosomiasis

**schistosomiasis** *noun* MED a tropical disease caused by flukes in the intestine or bladder. Also called **bilharziasis**

COMMENT: The larvae of the fluke enter through the skin of the feet and lodge in the walls of the intestine or bladder. They are passed out of the body in stools or urine and return to water, where they enter and develop in water snails, the secondary host, before returning to humans. Patients suffer from fever and anaemia.

**schizogony** *noun* GENETICS a form of asexual reproduction in some single-celled organisms (**protozoans**), in which a cell nucleus divides many times before the cytoplasm divides to form the daughter cells (NOTE: This process enables some parasites such as the malaria parasite to undergo rapid proliferation in the tissues of an infected organism.)

**schizont** *noun* ANAT a cell in some single-celled organisms (**protozoans**) that is formed during the asexual phase of the life cycle

**school** *noun* MARINE BIOL a group of aquatic animals such as fish or porpoises which all move together and keep an equal distance apart

**Schwann cell** *noun* ANAT a cell that forms part of the myelin sheath around a nerve fibre

**scientific method** *noun* SCI the systematic method used in investigations of the natural world, which include designing controlled experiments, collecting data and developing and testing hypotheses

**scintillation** *noun* ASTRON the series of fluctuations in brightness of stars caused by atmospheric instability

**scintillation counter** *noun* PHYS a machine that detects and counts the flashes of light produced when high-energy ionising radiation strikes a phosphorescent substance

**scion** *noun* AGRIC a piece of a plant which is grafted onto a rootstock

**scissor** *verb* COMPUT 1. to define an area of an image and then cut it out so it can be pasted into another image 2. to define an area of an image and delete any information that is outside this area

**sclera** *noun* ANAT the outer coating of an eyeball, which forms the white of the eye. Also called **sclerotic**

**sclerenchyma** *noun* BOT a strengthening or supporting plant tissue made up of dead cells with thickened walls

**sclerophyll** *noun* BOT a woody plant that grows in hot dry regions, with thick leathery evergreen leaves that lose very little moisture

**scleroprotein** *noun* BIOCHEM a tough insoluble protein produced by humans and other animals (NOTE: Examples of scleroproteins are keratin in hair and nails and collagen in the skin.)

**sclerosis** *noun* 1. MED the hardening and thickening of body tissue 2. BOT the hardening and thickening of plant cell walls as lignin is deposited, making stems woody

**sclerotic** *adjective* 1. MED referring to the hardening and thickening of body tissue 2. BOT referring to the hardening and thickening process in plant cell walls that makes stems woody ■ *noun* ANAT same as **sclera**

**-scope** *suffix* an instrument for examining by sight

**scorbutic** *adjective* MED referring to scurvy

**scorbutus** *noun* MED same as **scurvy** (*technical*)

**Scots pine** *noun* TREES a common commercially grown European conifer. Latin name: *Pinus sylvestris*.

**SCR** *abbreviation* COMPUT sequence control register

**scrambler** *noun* COMPUT a device that codes a data stream into a pseudorandom form before transmission to eliminate any combination of ones, zeros or alternate ones and zeros that would cause synchronisation problems at the receiver

**scrap** INDUST *noun* waste material, especially metal ○ *scrap paper* ○ *scrap metal* ○ *Some 50% of steel is made from recycled scrap.* (NOTE: no plural) ■ *verb* to demolish or destroy something because it is no longer useful

**scrapie** *noun* VET a brain disease of sheep and goats

**scratch** COMPUT *noun* an area of memory or a file used for temporary storage of data ■ *verb* to delete or move an area of memory to provide room for other data

**scratch file¹** *noun* COMPUT same as **work file**

**scratch file²** *noun* COMPUT an area which is being used for current work. Also called **work file**

**scratchpad memory** *noun* COMPUT a cache memory used to buffer data being transferred between a fast processor and a slow input/output device such as a disk drive

**scree** *noun* EARTH SCI loose rocks and stones covering the side of a mountain

**screen** *noun* 1. something which protects 2. COMPUT a display device capable of showing a quantity of information, e.g. a VDU 3. ENVIRON a hedge or row of trees grown to shelter other plants, to protect something from the wind or to prevent something from being seen ■ *verb* **1.** to protect something with a screen ○ *The power supply unit is screened against interference.* **2.** SCI to examine people, animals or plants to test for the presence of a disease ○ *The population of the village was screened for meningitis.* **3.** to examine material for the presence of something ○ *screened the samples for high protein content*

**screen buffer** *noun* COMPUT a temporary storage area for characters or graphics before they are displayed

**screen capture** *noun* COMPUT the act of storing an image displayed on screen in a file

**screen dump** *noun* COMPUT the act of outputting the text or graphics displayed on a screen to a printer

**screening** *noun* SCI the process of testing for the presence of something

**screen refresh** *verb* COMPUT to update regularly the images on a screen by scanning each pixel with a picture beam to make sure the image is still visible

**screen saver** *noun* COMPUT a piece of software that, after a pre-determined period of user inactivity, replaces the existing image on screen and displays moving objects to protect against screen burn

**screw** *noun* ENG a type of threaded connector used to fix things together by rotating it

**screw jack, screwjack** *noun* ENG a lifting device working with rotary input

**script** *noun* COMPUT a set of instructions which carry out a function, normally used with a macro language or batch language

**scroll** *verb* COMPUT to move displayed text vertically up or down the screen, one line or pixel at a time

**scroll arrow** *noun* COMPUT an arrow belonging to a set that, when clicked, move the contents of the window up or down or sideways

**scroll bar** *noun* COMPUT a bar displayed along the side of a window with a marker which indicates how far you have scrolled

**scrotum** *noun* ANAT a bag of muscle and skin that contains the testes of a mammal (NOTE: Its position is outside the body to keep the testes cool.)

**scrub** *noun* **1.** BOT small trees and bushes **2.** EARTH SCI an area of land covered with small trees and bushes ■ *verb* **1.** COMPUT to wipe information off a disk or remove data from store ○ *Scrub all the files with a date before 2000.* **2.** INDUST to remove sulfur and other pollutants from waste gases produced by power stations

**scrubber** *noun* INDUST a device for removing sulfur and other pollutants from waste gases

**scrubland** *noun* EARTH SCI land covered with small trees and bushes

**SCSI** COMPUT same as **small computer systems interface**

**scurvy** *noun* MED a disease caused by lack of vitamin C. Also called **scorbutus**

COMMENT: Scurvy causes general weakness and anaemia, with bleeding from the gums, joints and under the skin. In severe cases the teeth drop out. Treatment consists of vitamin C tablets and a change of diet to include more fruit and vegetables.

**SDLC** *abbreviation* COMPUT synchronous data link control

**SDR** *abbreviation* COMPUT store data register

**SDRAM** *abbreviation* COMPUT synchronised dynamic RAM

**Se** *symbol* CHEM ELEM selenium

**sea** *noun* EARTH SCI a body of salt water between land masses

**seabed** *noun* OCEANOG the bottom of the sea ○ *These fish feed on minute debris on the seabed.*

**seabird** *noun* ZOOL a bird such as a gull which lives near the sea and eats fish

**seaborgium** *noun* CHEM ELEM an unstable, artificially produced chemical element (NOTE: The chemical symbol is **Sg**; the atomic number is **106** and the atomic weight is **266**.)

**sea breeze** *noun* METEOROL a light wind which blows from the sea towards the land, e.g. in the evening when the land cools

**sea current** *noun* OCEANOG a flow of water in the sea

**sea fog** *noun* METEOROL a coastal fog arising from a difference in sea and land temperatures

**seagull** *noun* ZOOL a bird, belonging to several species, that lives near the sea and has a stout build, a rather hooked bill and webbed feet

**seal** *noun* **1.** ENG a device that joins two parts and prevents leakage ○ *an oil seal* **2.** ENG a means of preventing a liquid or a gas from escaping ○ *Gaskets effect a seal by being squeezed between two surfaces.* **3.** MARINE BIOL a mammal with a sleek body and flippers that swims in cold seas ■ *verb* ENG to join two parts in such a way as to prevent leakage

**sealant** *noun* INDUST a substance painted or sprayed onto a surface to prevent the escape of a liquid or gas ○ *The integral fuel tank may be completely coated on the inside with a layer of sealant.* Also called **sealing compound**

**sea level** *noun* EARTH SCI the average level of the surface of the sea

COMMENT: Sea level is taken as the base for references to altitude: a mountain 300 m high is three hundred metres above sea level. The Dead Sea is 395 m below sea level. Sea levels in general have risen over the past hundred years and much more rapid rises are forecast if the greenhouse effect results in the melting of the polar ice caps. Sea level is also used as a basis for measuring barometric pressure.

**sealing compound** *noun* INDUST same as **sealant**

**seam** *noun* EARTH SCI a layer of mineral in rock beneath the Earth's surface ○ *The coal seams are two metres thick.* ○ *The gold seam was worked out some years ago.*

**search** COMPUT *noun* a process of looking for and identifying a character, word or section of data in a document or file ■ *verb* to look for something

**search and replace** *noun* COMPUT a feature on word-processors that allows the user to find specified words or phrases, then replace them with another word or phrase

**search engine** *noun* COMPUT **1.** a piece of software that searches a database **2.** a website that compiles a list of websites and allows a visitor to find a website by searching for words

**search key** *noun* COMPUT **1.** a word or phrase that is to be found in a text **2.** a field and other data used to select various records in a database

**search memory** *noun* COMPUT a method of data retrieval that uses part of the data rather than an address to locate the data

**sea salt** *noun* FOOD crystals of sodium chloride, extracted from sea water

**season** *noun* TIME **1.** one of the four parts into which a year is divided, i.e. spring, summer, autumn and winter **2.** the time of year when something happens ○ *the mating season* ■ *verb* INDUST to allow the sap in timber to dry so that the wood can be used for making things ○ *The construction industry needs large quantities of properly seasoned wood.*

**seasonal** *adjective* referring to or occurring at a season ○ *seasonal changes in temperature* ○ *Plants grow according to a seasonal pattern.*

**sea water** *noun* EARTH SCI the salty water in the sea

**seaweed** *noun* MARINE BIOL any of the large algae that grow in the sea and are usually rooted to a surface

**sebaceous gland** *noun* ANAT a gland that secretes sebum into hair follicles (NOTE: Sebaceous glands are found all over the human body except for the palms of the hands and the soles of the feet.)

**sebum** *noun* PHYSIOL a greasy substance secreted by the sebaceous glands that lubricates the hair and skin

**second** *noun* **1.** MEASURE a base SI unit of measurement of time, equal to one sixtieth of a minute **2.** MEASURE a unit of measurement of the circumference of a circle, equal to one sixtieth of a degree **3.** the one that comes after the first ○ *We have two computers, the second one being used if the first is being repaired.* ■ *adjective* coming after the first

**secondary** *adjective* **1.** coming after something else **2.** less important than something else ○ *a secondary reason* **3.** developing from another condition **4.** indirectly related to something. Compare **primary**

**secondary cell** *noun* ELEC an apparatus that generates electricity by means of a reversible chemical reaction (NOTE: A secondary cell is rechargeable and can be used to store electrical energy.)

**secondary channel** *noun* COMPUT a second channel containing control information transmitted at the same time as data

**secondary consumer** *noun* ZOOL an animal such as a carnivore that eats other consumers in the food chain

**secondary growth** *noun* BOT growth that occurs in a plant's stem and root, increasing the diameter of the stem or root. Also called **secondary thickening**

**secondary industry** *noun* INDUST an industry that uses basic raw materials to make manufactured goods

**secondary memory** *noun* COMPUT a permanent storage device in a computer that is used for storing files and data

**secondary mineral** *noun* EARTH SCI a mineral formed after chemical reactions or weathering have taken place in magma

**secondary particulates** *plural noun* ENVIRON particles of matter formed in the air by chemical reactions such as smog

**secondary sexual characteristic** *noun* ZOOL a characteristic controlled by sex hormones that distinguishes sexually mature males and females but is not directly involved in reproduction, e.g. facial hair in men

**secondary substance** *noun* BOT a chemical substance found in plant leaves, believed to be a form of defence against herbivores

**secondary succession** *noun* ECOL an ecological community which develops in a place where a previous community has been removed as a result of fire, flooding, cutting down of trees or some other event

**secondary thickening** *noun* BOT same as **secondary growth**

**second generation computer** *noun* COMPUT a computer that used transistors instead of valves

**second law of thermodynamics** *noun* PHYS ◊ **thermodynamics**

**second-level addressing** *noun* COMPUT an instruction that contains an address at which the operand is stored

**second quartile** *noun* STATS a number below which fifty per cent of numbers in a sample fall ○ *This group falls within the second quartile.*

**secrete** *verb* PHYSIOL (*of a gland*) to produce a substance such as a hormone, oil or enzyme

**secretion** *noun* BIOL a substance produced by a gland

**section** *noun* **1.** BIOL a piece cut from a plant or animal for examination **2.** COMPUT a part of a main program which can be executed in its own right, without the rest of the main program being required

**sectional** *adjective* **1.** referring to a section **2.** composed of sections

**sector** *noun* **1.** MATHS a portion of a circle inside two radii and the included arc **2.** COMPUT the smallest area on a magnetic disk which can be addressed by a computer. Also called **disk sector** (NOTE: The disk is divided into concentric tracks and each track is divided into sectors which, typically, can store 512 bytes of data.)

**sector formatting** *noun* COMPUT the division of a disk into a series of addressable sectors (NOTE: A table of their addresses is also formed, allowing each sector to be accessed.)

**sector map** *noun* COMPUT a table which contains the addresses of unusable sectors on a hard disk

**secure encryption payment protocol** *noun* COMPUT a system developed to provide a secure link between a user's browser and a vendor's website in order to allow the user to pay for goods over the Internet. Abbreviation **SEPP**

**secure hypertext transfer protocol** *noun* COMPUT an extension of the HTTP protocol that allows an encrypted and authenticated session between a user's web browser and a secure web server. Abbreviation **S-HTTP**

**secure/multipurpose Internet mail extension** *noun* COMPUT a method of providing secure electronic mail messages by which the system encrypts the main message using a standard cipher then sends the key in encrypted form using a second, public-key encryption system. Abbreviation **S/MIME**

**secure site** *noun* COMPUT a website that includes features to ensure that any information transferred between the user and the website is encrypted and cannot be read by a hacker. Also called **secure website**

COMMENT: A secure site is typically used in a shopping site to allow customers to type in their personal details such as their credit-card numbers without risk. Secure sites almost always use a system called SSL (secure sockets layer) that creates a secure channel. A small padlock icon in the status bar shows as locked when the site is secure.

**secure sockets layer** *noun* COMPUT an encrypted transmission protocol designed by Netscape that provides secure communications between a browser and a web server over the Internet. Abbreviation **SSL**

**secure website** *noun* COMPUT same as **secure site**

**security** *noun* the condition of being protected or being secret ○ *The system has been designed to assure the security of the stored data.*

**security backup** *noun* COMPUT a copy of a disk, tape or file kept in a safe place in case the working copy is lost or damaged

**sedentary** *adjective* BIOL not moving

**sediment** *noun* CHEM a mass of solid particles, usually insoluble, that fall to the bottom of a liquid

**sedimentary** *adjective* **1.** CHEM falling to the bottom of a liquid **2.** EARTH SCI referring to rock formed from silt

**sedimentary cycle** *noun* EARTH SCI the process by which sediment falls to the bottom of water, becomes rock, then is weathered to form sediment again

**sedimentary deposit** *noun* CHEM a mass of solid particles that have fallen to the bottom of a liquid

**sedimentary rock** *noun* EARTH SCI a rock which has been formed from silt, broken down from older rocks, deposited as sediment at the bottom of lakes or the sea, and then subjected to pressure

**sedimentation** *noun* **1.** EARTH SCI the process of formation of sedimentary rock **2.** CHEM, INDUST the process of solid particles falling to the bottom of a liquid, as in the treatment of sewage

**sedimentation basin** *noun* EARTH SCI an area of land where the rocks have been formed from matter carried there by wind and water

**sedimentation rate** *noun* CHEM the speed with which solid particles fall to the bottom of a liquid

**sedimentation tank** *noun* INDUST a tank in which sewage is allowed to stand so that solid particles can sink to the bottom

**seed** *noun* **1.** BOT a fertilized ovule that forms a new plant on germination **2.** COMPUT a starting value used when generating random or pseudorandom numbers ■ *verb* **1.** BOT (*of a plant*) to produce offspring by dropping seed which germinates and grows into plants in following seasons ○ *The poppies seeded all over the garden.* **2.** AGRIC to sow seeds in an area ○ *The area of woodland was cut and then seeded with pines.* **3.** CHEM to add crystals to a supersaturated solution to encourage crystallisation **4.** METEOROL to drop crystals of salt, carbon dioxide and other substances onto clouds from an aeroplane in order to encourage rain to fall

**seed bank** *noun* **1.** ECOL all the seeds existing in the soil **2.** BOT a collection of seeds from plants, kept for research purposes

**seedcase** *noun* BOT a hard outside cover that protects the seeds of some plants

**seed leaf** *noun* BOT the first leaf of a plant forming as the seed sprouts. Also called **cotyledon**

**seedling** *noun* BOT a small plant which has just sprouted from a seed

**seek area** *noun* COMPUT a section of memory to be searched for a particular item of data or a word

**seek time** *noun* COMPUT the time taken by a read/write head to find the right track on a disk ○ *The new hard disk drive has a seek time of just 35 mS.*

**seep** *verb* PHYS (*of a liquid*) to flow slowly through a substance ○ *Water seeped through the rock.* ○ *Chemicals seeped out of the container.*

**seepage** *noun* PHYS the action of flowing slowly·

**seepage tank** *noun* INDUST a tank attached to a septic tank, into which the liquids from the septic tank are drained

**segment** COMPUT *noun* a section of a main program which can be executed in its own right, without the rest of the main program being required ■ *verb* to divide a long program into shorter sections which can then be called up when required

**segregant** GENETICS *adjective* referring to an organism that is genetically different from either parent because of the process of segregation ■ *noun* an organism that is genetically different from either parent because of the process of segregation. Also called **segregate**

**segregate** GENETICS *verb* to undergo or to cause genes to undergo segregation ■ *noun* same as **segregant**

**segregation** *noun* GENETICS (*in organisms with paired chromosomes*) the separation of the two variant forms (**alleles**) of each gene and their distribution to separate reproductive cells (**gametes**) during meiosis

**seiche** *noun* EARTH SCI a tide in a lake, usually caused by the wind or by movements in water level

**seism** *noun* EARTH SCI an earthquake

**seismic** *adjective* EARTH SCI referring to earthquakes

**seismic shock, seismic wave** *noun* EARTH SCI a shock wave which spreads out from the centre or focus of an earthquake travelling through the Earth's crust

**seismograph** *noun* EARTH SCI, MEASURE an instrument for measuring earthquakes

**seismological** *adjective* EARTH SCI referring to the study of earthquakes

**seismologist** *noun* EARTH SCI a scientist who studies earthquakes

**seismology** *noun* EARTH SCI the scientific study of earthquakes

**seismonasty** *noun* BOT a response of plants to a physical stimulus such as touch

**select** *verb* **1.** to choose one thing but not others **2.** COMPUT to find and retrieve specific information from a database **3.** AGRIC to identify plants or animals with desirable characteristics such as high yield or disease resistance as part of the activity of breeding new varieties

**selectable attributes** *plural noun* COMPUT the functions or attributes of a device which can be chosen by the user

**selection** *noun* **1.** the act of choosing one thing but not others **2.** COMPUT the finding and retrieval of specific information from a database ○ *By manual selection of the heating switch, the formed ice can be dispersed.* **3.** AGRIC the process of identifying plants or animals with desirable characteristics such as high yield or disease resistance as part

of the activity of breeding new varieties **4.** something chosen **5.** a collection of carefully chosen things ○ *a selection of photographs*

**selection handle** *noun* COMPUT a small square displayed on a frame around a selected area that allows the user to change the shape of the area

**selective herbicide** *noun* AGRIC a weedkiller which is designed to kill only some plants and not others. Also called **selective weedkiller**

**selective resistance** *noun* BIOL the ability of an organism to be unaffected by specific poisons, pollutants, pesticides or herbicides

**selective sort** *noun* COMPUT the process of sorting a section of data items into order

**selective weedkiller** *noun* AGRIC same as **selective herbicide**

**selector** *noun* a manually operated device such as a switch, which offers a choice of settings ○ *Turn the selector control.* ○ *The purpose of this selector is to direct fluid to the appropriate side of an actuator.*

**selenium** *noun* CHEM ELEM a non-metallic trace element (NOTE: The chemical symbol is **Se**; the atomic number is **34** and thr atomic weight is **78.96**.)

**self-** *prefix* a person's own self or a thing itself

**self-checking code** *noun* COMPUT a character coding system which is able to detect an error or bad character but not correct it

**self-contained** *adjective* independent and complete in itself ○ *The auxiliary power unit is a self-contained unit.*

**self-correcting code** *noun* COMPUT a character coding system which is able to detect and correct an error or bad character

**self-diagnostic** *adjective* COMPUT referring to a computer that runs a series of diagnostic programs, usually when the computer is switched on, to ensure that all circuits, memory and peripherals are working correctly

**self-evident** *adjective* clear in itself, without further explanation

**self-explanatory** *adjective* not needing any further explanation

**self-extracting archive** *noun* COMPUT a compressed file that includes the program to de-compress the contents

**self-fertile** *noun* BOT referring to a plant that fertilises itself with pollen from its own flowers

**self-fertilisation, self-fertilization** *noun* BIOL the fertilisation of a plant or invertebrate animal with its own pollen or sperm

**self-fertility** *noun* BIOL the ability of a plant or animal to fertilise itself

**selfish gene** *noun* GENETICS a gene that uses the organism in which it occurs to reproduce itself (NOTE: The concept, proposed by the biologist Richard Dawkins in 1976, contrasts with the traditional concept of the gene acting as a means of inheritance for the organism.)

**self-pollination** *noun* BOT the pollination of a plant by pollen from its own flowers. Compare **cross-pollination**

**self-refreshing RAM** *noun* COMPUT a dynamic RAM chip that has built-in circuitry to generate refresh signals, allowing data to be retained when the power is off by using a battery

**self-regulating** *adjective* ECOL controlling itself without outside intervention ○ *Most tropical rainforests are self-regulating environments.*

**self-replicating** *adjective* GENETICS referring to a molecule or bacterium that reproduces by making copies of itself

**self-sterile** *adjective* BOT referring to a plant that cannot fertilise itself from its own flowers

**self-sterility** *noun* BOT the inability of a plant to fertilise itself

**self-thinning** *noun* ECOL a process by which only a few individuals of a larger size survive in a group of plants of the same age, since plants cannot escape competition by moving away to a different place

**sell-by date** *noun* FOOD INDUST a date on the label of a food product which is the last date on which the product should be sold and be guaranteed as of good quality

**selva** *noun* ECOL a tropical rain forest in the Amazon basin

**semantics** *noun* 1. the meanings of words, parts of words or combinations of words 2. COMPUT the meanings of words or symbols used in programs

**semaphore** *noun* COMPUT the coordination of two jobs and appropriate hand-shaking to prevent lock-outs or other problems when both require a peripheral or function

**semen** *noun* PHYSIOL a thick pale fluid containing spermatozoa, produced by the testes and ejaculated from the penis

**semi-** *prefix* half

**semi-arid** *noun* EARTH SCI receiving very little rain

**semicircle** *noun* MATHS a half circle

**semicircular** *adjective* MATHS in the shape of a half circle ○ *Most mathematical protractors are semicircular in shape.*

**semicircular canal** *noun* ANAT one of a set of three tubes in the inner ear that provide the sense of balance

**semi-compiled** *adjective* COMPUT referring to an object code program converted from a source code program but not containing the code for functions from libraries and other elements that were used in the source code

**semiconductor** *noun* ELECTRONICS a material with conductive properties between those of a conductor such as a metal and an insulator

COMMENT: Semiconductor material such as silicon is used as a base for manufacturing integrated circuits and other solid-state components, usually by depositing various types of doping substances on or into its surface.

**semi-deciduous forest** *noun* EARTH SCI a forest in which some trees lose their leaves or needles at some point during the year

**semi-desert** *noun* EARTH SCI an area of land which has very little rain

**semilunar valve** *noun* ANAT one of two valves in the heart, either the aortic valve or pulmonary valve

**seminal vesicle** *noun* ANAT one of a pair of glands that produce some of the liquid components of semen

**semiparasitic** *adjective* BIOL 1. living as a parasite but also undergoing photosynthesis 2. living as a parasite but also capable of living on dead or decaying organic matter

**semipermeable** *adjective* CHEM allowing a liquid to pass through but not substances dissolved in the liquid

**semipermeable membrane** *noun* CHEM a membrane that allows some substances to pass through it, but not others

**semi-processed data** *noun* COMPUT raw data which has had some processing carried out, such as sorting, recording or error detection

**sense** *noun* BIOL one of the five faculties by which a person or animal notices things in the outside world (NOTE: They are sight, hearing, smell, taste and touch.) ■ *verb* **1.** BIOL to be aware of something without being directly told **2.** TECH to examine or detect the state of a device or electronic component ○ *The condition of the switch was sensed by the program.*

**sense of balance** *noun* PHYSIOL the mechanism that keeps someone upright, governed by the fluid in the inner ear balance mechanism

**sense organ** *noun* ANAT a part of the body that detects some particular aspect of the outside world such as light or sound (NOTE: Sense organs include eyes, ears, insect antennae and the lateral lines of fish.)

**sense recovery time** *noun* COMPUT the time that a RAM device takes to switch from read to write mode

**sensible horizon** *noun* ASTRON same as **horizon**

**sensitive** *adjective* **1.** BIOL able to respond to stimuli ○ *The leaves of the plant are sensitive to frost.* **2.** TECH able to record very small changes ○ *The earthquake was a small one and only registered on the most sensitive equipment.*

**sensitive plant** *noun* BOT a tropical shrub with leaves which fold up when touched. Latin name: *Mimosa pudica*.

**sensitivity** *noun* **1.** BIOL the ability or tendency to respond to stimuli ○ *the scanner's sensitivity to small objects* Also called **irritability 2.** TECH the ability to record very small changes **3.** TELECOM a minimum power of a received signal that is necessary for a receiver to distinguish the signal

**sensitise, sensitize** *verb* MED to make someone sensitive to a drug or allergen

**sensor** *noun* a device which receives and responds to a signal or stimulus ○ *a pressure sensor* ○ *a temperature sensor* ○ *The inlet pressure is sensed by a single pitot-type sensor.*

**sensor glove** *noun* COMPUT (*in virtual reality applications*) a glove that fits over a user's hand and has sensors that detect when the user moves his or her fingers or arm and so control an image on screen

**sensory** *adjective* BIOL referring to the senses

**sensory adaptation** *noun* BIOL an alteration in a receptor because of increased, decreased or prolonged stimulation

**sensory nerve** *noun* ANAT a nerve that registers a sensation such as heat, taste or smell and carries impulses to the brain and spinal cord. Also called **afferent nerve**

**sensory neuron** *noun* ANAT a neuron which receives its stimulus directly from a receptor, and passes the impulse to the sensory cortex

**sensory organ** *noun* ANAT a part of an organism such as a nerve which receives stimuli

**sentinel** *noun* COMPUT **1.** a pointer to a special section of data **2.** a flag which reports the status of a register after a mathematical or logical operation

**sepal** *noun* BOT a part of the calyx surrounding a flower, usually green and sometimes hairy

**separate** *adjective* **1.** distinct and not related **2.** not joined or together ■ *verb* **1.** to move or keep something apart **2.** to distinguish one thing from another **3.** to divide or split something into its parts

**separate channel signalling** *noun* COMPUT the use of an independent communications channel or bands in a multichannel system to send control data and messages

**separation** *noun* **1.** the condition of being spaced apart ○ *Airways and advisory routes provide a high degree of safety by maintaining separation between aircraft.* **2.** TECH the removal of a component from a mixture or combination ○ *The oil and air mixture flows over the de-aerator tray in the oil tank, where partial separation takes place.*

**separator** *noun* **1.** TECH a device which removes a component from a mixture or combination ○ *The water separator will extract a percentage of free moisture from the air.* **2.** COMPUT a symbol used in an instruction line in a program, to distinguish parts such as command and argument

**SEPP** *abbreviation* COMPUT secure encryption payment protocol

**sepsis** *noun* MED the condition caused by microorganisms or their toxins in the tissues or blood

**septet** *noun* COMPUT a word made up of seven bits

**septic** *adjective* **1.** BIOL referring to the process of decomposition of organic matter **2.** MED referring to sepsis

**septic sludge** *noun* INDUST a solid part of sewage undergoing the process of purification by decomposition

**septic tank** *noun* INDUST **1.** a tank at a sewage treatment works in which sewage is collected to begin its treatment by anaerobic bacteria **2.** an underground tank for household sewage

COMMENT: The sewage collects in the septic tank, the solids settle and are decomposed and the liquid, purified by bacterial action, drains off into the soil or into a seepage tank.

**septum** *noun* BIOL a thin partition or dividing membrane such as the tissue separating the nostrils or the internal dividing walls in the spores of some fungi

**sequence** *noun* **1.** a series of things or events that follow one another ○ *The ignition system provides a rapid series of sparks timed to fire in each cylinder in the correct sequence.* □ **in sequence** sequentially **2.** COMPUT a number of items or data arranged as a logical, ordered list ○ *The sequence of names is arranged alphabetically.* ○ *The program instructions are arranged in sequence according to line numbers.*

**sequence check** *noun* COMPUT a check to ensure that sorted data is in the correct order

**sequence control register** *noun* COMPUT a CPU register that contains the address of the next instruction to be processed. Abbreviation **SCR**

**sequencer** *noun* COMPUT a section within a bit-slice microprocessor which contains the next microprogram address

**sequence tagged site** *noun* GENETICS a short sequence of DNA, usually 200 to 500 base pairs, that occurs only once in the human genome and is useful in genetic mapping

**sequence valve** *noun* ENG a fluid flow controller which performs a number of actions in a specific order ○ *Sequence valves are often fitted in a landing gear circuit to ensure correct operation of the landing gear doors and actuators.*

**sequential** *adjective* having a fixed order or happening one after the other

**sequential access** *noun* COMPUT a method of retrieving data from a storage device by starting at the beginning of the medium such as tape and reading each record until the required data is found. Also called **serial access**

**sequential access storage** *noun* COMPUT a storage medium such as a tape in which the data is accessed sequentially

**sequential batch processing** *noun* COMPUT the completion of one job in a batch before the next can be started

**sequential computer** *noun* COMPUT a computer for which each instruction must be completed before the next is started and so which cannot handle parallel processing

**sequential logic** *noun* ELECTRONICS a logic circuit whose output depends on the logic state of the previous inputs

**sequentially** *adverb* in a fixed order or one after the other

**sequential search** *noun* COMPUT a search where each item in a list starting at the beginning is checked until the required one is found

**sequestration** *noun* CHEM the process of forming a complex with an ion, thus making it chemically ineffective

**sere** *noun* ECOL a series of plant communities which succeed one another in an area

**serial** *adjective* COMPUT referring to data or instructions ordered one after the other rather than in parallel

**serial access** *noun* COMPUT same as **sequential access**

**serial-access memory** *noun* COMPUT full form of **SAM**

**serial computer** *noun* COMPUT a computer system which has a single arithmetic logic unit and carries out instructions one at a time

**serial input/output** *adjective* COMPUT ◊ **serial transmission**. Abbreviation **SIO**

**serial input/parallel output** *noun* COMPUT a device which can accept serial data and transmit parallel data. Abbreviation **SIPO**

**serial input/serial output** *adjective* COMPUT ◊ **serial transmission**. Abbreviation **SISO**

**serial printer** *noun* COMPUT a printer which prints characters one at a time

**serial transmission, serial input/output** *noun* COMPUT data transmission one bit at a time (this is the normal method of transmission over longer distances, since although slower, it uses fewer lines and so is cheaper than parallel)

**series** *noun* a number of things or events which come one after the other in a particular order ○ *a series of photographs* ○ *a series of switches*

**series circuit** *noun* ELEC an electric circuit connected so that current passes through each component of the circuit in turn without branching

COMMENT: In a series circuit the same current flows through each component; in a parallel circuit the current flow is dependent upon the component impedance.

**serine** *noun* BIOCHEM an amino acid that is involved in making some important proteins in the body

**serological** *adjective* IMMUNOL referring to serology

**serological type** *noun* BIOCHEM, MICROBIOL same as **serotype**

**serology** *noun* IMMUNOL the study of blood serum and its components and how they protect against disease

**serotonin** *noun* BIOCHEM a compound that exists mainly in blood platelets and is released after tissue injury (NOTE: It is a neurotransmitter important in sleep, mood and blood vessel constriction.)

**serotype** *noun* BIOCHEM, MICROBIOL a group of microorganisms that have some antigens in common. Also called **serological type** ■ *verb* BIOCHEM to group microorganisms according to their antigens

**serous membrane** *noun* ANAT a membrane that lines an internal cavity which does not come into contact with

air (NOTE: The peritoneum and pericardium are serous membranes.)

**serum albumin** *noun* BIOCHEM a major protein in blood serum

**serum globulin** *noun* BIOCHEM a major protein in blood serum which is an antibody

**server** *noun* COMPUT a dedicated computer which provides a function to a network

COMMENT: In a network the hard disk machine is called the 'server' and the floppy disk units the 'satellites'. In a star network each satellite is linked individually to a central server.

**server message block** *noun* COMPUT a system that allows a user to access another computer's files and peripherals over a network as if they were local resources. Abbreviation **SMB**

**service bit** *noun* COMPUT a transmitted bit used for control rather than data

**service provider** *noun* COMPUT same as **Internet service provider**

**services** *plural noun* COMPUT **1.** the functions provided by a device **2.** the functions provided by one OSI layer for use by a higher layer

**servo** *noun* MECH ENG same as **servomechanism**

**servo-assisted** *adjective* MECH ENG partially operated by a servomechanism ○ *servo-assisted brakes* ○ *servo-assisted steering*

**servo-control unit** *noun* MECH ENG a combined selector valve and actuator that moves a control surface ○ *A servo-control unit is part of the system which relieves the effects of aerodynamic forces on the flight controls.*

**servomechanism** *noun* MECH ENG a device to convert input forces into much larger output forces ○ *Two phase motors are normally used for very small or miniature motors in servomechanisms.* Also called **servo**

**sessile** *adjective* **1.** BOT attached directly to a branch or stem without a stalk **2.** EARTH SCI permanently attached to a surface

**session** *noun* **1.** a period of time during which something is done **2.** COMPUT the time during which a program or process is running or active

**session layer** *noun* COMPUT the fifth layer in the ISO/OSI standard model which connects and disconnects the transmitter and receiver

**set** *noun* **1.** a group of things which belong together ○ *a set of instruments* ○ *a set of figures* **2.** MATHS, COMPUT a number of related data items ■ *adjective* fixed or established ○ *a set procedure* ■ *verb* **1.** to make one variable equal to a value ○ *We set the right-hand margin at 80 characters.* **2.** COMPUT to define a parameter value □ **to set breakpoints** to define the position of breakpoints within a program being debugged **3.** COMPUT to give a binary data bit the value of one **4.** to put something in a particular position ○ *set the throttle fully closed* **5.** CHEM to harden ○ *The resin sets in a couple of hours.*

**SET** *noun* COMPUT a set of standards created by a group of banks and Internet companies that allow users to buy goods over the Internet without risk from hackers. Full form **secure electronic transactions**

**set aside** *verb* ENVIRON to use a piece of formerly arable land for something other than growing crops, e.g. allowing it to lie fallow or using it as woodland or for recreation

**set-aside** *noun* ENVIRON a piece of formerly arable land used for growing crops

**set theory** *noun* MATHS the mathematics of numerical sets

**setting** *noun* **1.** a particular figure or position to which a device is adjusted ○ *Turn the thermostat to a low setting.* **2.** the action of adjusting a device to a particular position ○ *The setting of the altimeter is done prior to take-off.*

**settle** *verb* **1.** to stop moving and stay in one place **2.** (*of sediment*) to fall to the bottom of a liquid

**settlement** *noun* **1.** the process of coming to stay in one place **2.** (*of sediment*) the process of falling to the bottom of a liquid **3.** ENVIRON a place where people have settled

**settling basin, settling pond** *noun* INDUST a tank in which a liquid is allowed to stand so that solid particles can sink to the bottom

**set up** *verb* COMPUT to configure, initialize, define or start an application or system ○ *The new computer worked well as soon as the engineer had set it up.*

**set-up** *noun* COMPUT the way in which an application or system is initialised, defined or started

**severe acute respiratory syndrome** *noun* MED full form of **SARS**

**sewage** *noun* ENVIRON, INDUST waste water and other refuse such as faeces, carried away in sewers. Also called **sewage waste**

**sewage disposal** *noun* ENVIRON, INDUST the removal of sewage from buildings for processing

**sewage effluent** *noun* ENVIRON liquid or solid waste carried away in sewers

**sewage farm** *noun* INDUST same as **sewage treatment plant**

**sewage gas** *noun* CHEM methane mixed with carbon dioxide which is given off by sewage

**sewage sludge** *noun* ENVIRON the solid part of sewage

**sewage treatment plant** *noun* INDUST a place where sewage from houses and other buildings is brought for processing. Also called **sewage farm, sewage works**

COMMENT: A modern sewage treatment plant works by passing the sewage through a series of processes. It is first screened to remove large particles, then passed into sedimentation tanks where part of the solids remaining in the sewage settle. The sewage then continues into an aerator which adds air to activate the bacteria. The sewage then settles in a second sedimentation tank before being discharged into a river or the sea. Sludge which settles at the bottom of the sedimentation tanks is treated in digestion tanks where it is digested anaerobically by bacteria.

**sewage waste** *noun* ENVIRON, INDUST same as **sewage**

**sewage works** *noun* INDUST same as **sewage treatment plant**

**sex** *noun* BIOL one of the two groups, male and female, into which animals and plants can be divided ○ *The relative numbers of the two sexes in the human population are not equal, more males being born than females.*

COMMENT: In mammals, females have a pair of identical XX chromosomes and males or have one X and one Y chromosome. Out of the twenty-three pairs of chromosomes in each human cell, only two are sex chromosomes. The sex of a baby is determined by the father's sperm. While the mother's ovum only carries X chromosomes, the father's sperm can carry either an X or a Y chromosome. If the ovum is fertilized by a sperm carrying an X chromosome, the embryo will contain the XX pair and so be female.

**sexadecimal notation** *noun* COMPUT same as **hexadecimal notation**

**sex cell** *noun* GENETICS same as **gamete**

**sex chromatin** *noun* BIOCHEM chromatin that is only found in female cells and which can be used to identify the sex of a baby before birth

**sex chromosome** *noun* BIOL one of two chromosomes, the X chromosome and the Y chromosome, which determine if an organism is male or female (NOTE: Individuals carrying a Y chromosome are male.)

**sex determination** *noun* BIOL the way in which the sex of an individual organism is fixed, usually genetically controlled

**sex hormone** *noun* BIOCHEM one of a group of hormones involved in the development and control of the reproductive organs and sexual characteristics

**sex-limited** *adjective* GENETICS referring to inherited characteristics that appear in one sex only although the genes controlling the characteristics may be found in either sex

**sex linkage** *noun* BIOL the appearance of some genetically inherited characteristics in only one sex

**sex-linked** *adjective* BIOL referring to a genetically inherited characteristic that appears in only one sex

**sexology** *noun* BIOL the study of sex and sexual behaviour

**sex organ** *noun* ANAT an organ that is associated with reproduction and sexual intercourse

**sextet** *noun* COMPUT a byte made up of six bits

**sexual** *adjective* BIOL referring to sex ○ *A study of the sexual behaviour of moths.*

**sexual attractant** *noun* CHEM a chemical produced by an insect which attracts other insects of the same species

**sexual reproduction** *noun* BIOL reproduction in which gametes from two individuals fuse together

**Sg** *symbol* CHEM ELEM seaborgium

**SGML** *noun* COMPUT a hardware-independent standard that defines how documents should be marked up to indicate bold, italics, margins and so on. Full form **Standard Generalized Markup Language**

**shade** *noun* 1. a place sheltered from direct sunlight 2. shelter from direct sunlight 3. the relative darkness of a colour ○ *The new leaves are a light shade of green.*

**shade-intolerant tree** *noun* BOT a tree such as Douglas fir which will not grow in the shade of other trees

**shade plant** *noun* BOT a plant which prefers to grow in the shade

**shade-tolerant tree** *noun* BOT a tree such as beech which will grow in the shade of a larger tree

**shading** *noun* 1. the action of cutting off the light of the sun ○ *Parts of the field near tall trees suffer from shading.* 2. variation in the strength of colours 3. COMPUT the action of changing the strength of colours 4. COMPUT a simple method of applying shading to a three-dimensional scene using a single point of light and calculating the shade and highlights on each object (NOTE: This type of shading is calculated for each polygon that makes up an object and can sometimes cause unwanted effects as shading may differ on each polygon.)

**shadow** *noun* 1. an area which is not affected by sunlight 2. PHYS an area which is not affected by full radiation because of partial or full blocking of rays by something between the area and the source of the radiation ○ *Line-of-sight transmission path means that obstacles and terrain can create shadow zones.*

**shadowmask** *noun* COMPUT a sheet with holes placed just behind the front of a colour monitor screen to separate the three-colour picture beams

**shadow memory, shadow page** *noun* COMPUT duplicate memory location accessed by a special code

**shadow RAM** *noun* COMPUT a method of improving the performance of a PC by copying the contents of a slow ROM chip to a faster RAM chip when the computer is first switched on

**shaft** *noun* ENG a long, generally cylindrical bar, especially one that rotates and transmits power ○ *engine drive shaft* ○ *propeller shaft*

**shaft-driven** *adjective* ENG using a rotating shaft as a means of transmitting power from one part of a machine to another such as from a turbine engine to a helicopter rotor

**shale** *noun* EARTH SCI sedimentary rock formed from clay, which cracks along horizontal straight lines

**Shannon's Law** *noun* COMPUT a law defining the maximum information carrying capacity of a transmission line

COMMENT: Shannon's Law is defined as B lg(1 + S/N) where B = Bandwidth, lg is logarithm to the base two and S/N is Signal to Noise ratio

**shared file** *noun* COMPUT a stored file which can be accessed by more than one user or system

**shared logic system** *noun* COMPUT a computer and a backing storage device used by a number of people in a network for an application

**shared memory** *noun* COMPUT a memory accessed by more than one central processing unit

**share-level access** *noun* COMPUT a method used to set up network security to protect local resources

**shareware** *noun* COMPUT software that is available to try free, but if kept the user is expected to pay a fee to the writer

**sharp** *adjective* **1.** thin and capable of cutting or piercing ○ *If a piece of thermosetting plastic is hit hard enough, it breaks into pieces with straight sharp edges.* **2.** PHYS (*of a signal*) clear to the hearing ○ *The sharp setting means the bandwidth is reduced to 1 kHz to minimise noise or interference.* **3.** (*of an image or shape*) clear and distinct to the sight ○ *Cumulus clouds have sharp outlines.* **4.** sudden and acute □ **a sharp increase** a sudden large increase

**shatter** *verb* to break, or break something, into a number of pieces when hit ○ *Clear ice is hard to shatter and break off.*

**shear** *verb* to move laterally, often causing a break

**shearing load** *noun* PHYS a load caused by sliding apart the layers of a structure

**shear modulus** *noun* PHYS the ratio of shear stress to shear strain (NOTE: It is a measure of the strength of a material under shearing forces.)

**shear stress** *noun* PHYS stress that resists the force tending to cause one layer of a material to slide over an adjacent layer as in riveted and bolted joints

**shear wave** *noun* EARTH SCI a type of slow seismic wave that alters direction as it passes through different types of rock

**sheep** *noun* ZOOL a mammal of a group related to goats and cattle, farmed for their wool and meat

**sheet** *noun* a large, thin, flat piece of something ○ *a sheet of aluminium*

**sheet feed** *noun* COMPUT a device which puts in one sheet at a time into a printer

**sheet lightning** *noun* METEOROL lightning where the flash cannot be seen, but where the clouds are lit by it

**shelf** *noun* EARTH SCI a layer of rock or ice which juts out

**shelf-life** *noun* FOOD INDUST a number of days or weeks which a product can stay on the shelf of a shop and still be good to use

**shell** *noun* **1.** BIOL a hard outer covering of an animal, egg or seed **2.** COMPUT a piece of software which operates between the user and the operating system, often to try and make the operating system more friendly or easier to use ○ *MS-DOS's COMMAND.COM is a basic shell that interprets commands typed in at the prompt.* ○ *The Macintosh Finder is a sophisticated shell with a GUI front-end.*

**shellfish** *noun* MARINE BIOL a sea animal that has a hard shell and is used as food

**shell out** *verb* COMPUT to exit temporarily to the operating system, while the original application is still in memory before returning to the application ○ *I shelled out from the word-processor to check which files were on the floppy, then went back to the program.*

**shell script** *noun* COMPUT a scripting language such as Perl that is used to create programs that can enhance a website

**shell sort** *noun* COMPUT an algorithm for sorting data items, in which items can be moved more than one position per action

**shell star** *noun* ASTRON a star that is regarded as having a surrounding shell of gas

**shelter** *noun* protection from wind, sun, rain or other weather conditions ■ *verb* to protect something from weather conditions

**shelter belt** *noun* FORESTRY, AGRIC a row of trees planted to give protection from wind

**shelterwood** *noun* FORESTRY a large area of trees left standing when others are cut, to act as shelter for seedling trees

**shield** *noun* 1. ELECTRONICS a metal screen connected to earth, used to prevent harmful voltages or interference reaching sensitive electronic equipment 2. EARTH SCI a large area of very old rocks ○ *the Canadian shield* ■ *verb* ELECTRONICS to protect a signal or device from external interference or harmful voltages

**shielded cable** *noun* ELEC a cable made up of a conductive core surrounded by an insulator, then a conductive layer to protect the transmitted signal against interference

**shielded twisted pair cable** *noun* ELEC a cable consisting of two insulated copper wires twisted around each other to reduce induction and so interference and then themselves wrapped in an insulated shielding layer to further reduce interference. Abbreviation **STP cable**

**shift** *verb* COMPUT 1. to move a bit or word of data left or right by, usually, one bit 2. to change from one character set to another, allowing other characters such as capitals to be used

**shifting cultivation** *noun* AGRIC 1. an agricultural practice using the rotation of fields rather than crops, short cropping periods followed by long fallows and the maintenance of fertility by the regeneration of vegetation 2. a form of cultivation practised in some tropical countries, where land is cultivated until it is exhausted and then left as the farmers move on to another area

**shingle** *noun* EARTH SCI pebbles found on beaches, between about 1 and 7 cm in diameter

**shingle beach** *noun* EARTH SCI a beach covered with pebbles

**shock** *noun* a sudden violent impact

**shock absorber** *noun* MECH ENG, AUTOMOT a device to minimise the shock to a main structure, e.g. of an aircraft when it lands or a car when it goes over an uneven road surface

**shock wave** *noun* PHYS a compression wave caused by supersonic motion

**shore** *noun* EARTH SCI land at the edge of the sea or a lake

COMMENT: The shore is divided into different zones. The upper shore is the area which is only occasionally covered by sea water at the very highest tides. The middle shore is the main area of shore which is covered and uncovered by the sea at each tide. The lower shore is the area which is very rarely uncovered and only at the lowest tides.

**shorebird** *noun* ZOOL a bird which lives and nests on the shore

**shoreline** *noun* EARTH SCI a line of land at the edge of the sea or a lake

**shore terrace** *noun* EARTH SCI a flat strip of land on a sloping shore

**short** *adjective* not long

**shortage** *noun* a lack ○ *There is a shortage of qualified geologists for the project.*

**short card** *noun* COMPUT an add-on expansion board which is shorter than a standard size

**short circuit** *noun* ELEC ENG an electrical failure caused by an accidental flow of current between two points in a circuit (NOTE: The fuses in household electrical plugs are there to protect appliances from damage caused by excessive current if a short circuit happens.)

**short-circuit** *verb* ELEC ENG to fail because of a short circuit (NOTE: The fuses in household electrical plugs are there to protect appliances from damage caused by excessive current if a short circuit happens.)

**short-day plant** *noun* BOT a plant such as a chrysanthemum that flowers as the days get shorter in the autumn

**shorten** *verb* to become short or shorter or to make something short or shorter ○ *We had to shorten the file to be able to save it on one floppy.* Opposite **lengthen**

**short haul modem** *noun* COMPUT a modem used to transmit data over short distances, often within a building, usually without using a carrier

**short-sighted** *adjective* OPHTHALMOL able only to see close objects clearly, while distant objects appear indistinct

**short-sightedness** *noun* OPHTHALMOL the state of being short-sighted

**short ton** *noun US* MEASURE a unit of measurement of weight, equal to 2000 lbs or 0.907 tonnes (907 kg)

**shotgun cloning** *noun* BIOTECH a technique used for cloning a gene segment that involves dividing the original into many random fragments and then mapping and sequencing the fragments to reconstruct the segment or genome

**shoulderblade** *noun* ANAT same as **scapula**

**shower** *noun* METEOROL a brief fall of rain

**shrivel** *verb* to become dry and wrinkled

**shrub** *noun* BOT a plant with several woody stems that lives over many years

**shrubby** *adjective* BOT growing like a shrub

**S-HTTP** *abbreviation* COMPUT secure hypertext transfer protocol

**shunt** *noun* ELEC a low-resistance connection between two points in an electric circuit that forms an alternative path for a portion of the current. Also called **bypass**

**shut down** *verb* to stop working

**shutter** *noun* a hinged door which controls flow of air ○ *oil cooler shutters* ○ *radiator shutters*

**Si** *symbol* CHEM ELEM silicon

**SI** *noun* MEASURE the international system of metric measurements. Full form **Système International**

**sib, sibling** *noun* BIOL one of the offspring of the same parents ○ *Brothers and sisters are all siblings.*

**sibling species** *plural noun* BIOL species which look alike but which cannot interbreed

**sick** *adjective* MED not in good health

**sick building syndrome** *noun* ENVIRON a set of symptoms that affect people when they are in a building and go away when they leave the building, but that cannot be traced to specific pollutants or sources within the building

COMMENT: Symptoms of sick building syndrome include headaches, sore throats, dry skin, general tired feeling and depression. Some features which seem to be common to the buildings affected are artificial ventilation systems with windows that do not open and energy-efficient heating, bright lighting and the use of carpeting on floors.

**-side** *suffix* side or edge ○ *eroded hillsides* ○ *Waterside plants.*

**side chain** *noun* CHEM a group of atoms attached to an atom in a principal chain or ring of a bigger molecule (NOTE: Side chains occur most commonly in carbon compounds.)

**side effect** *noun* a secondary and undesirable effect ○ *Draining the marsh has had several unexpected side effects.* ○ *The antibiotics produced the unpleasant side effects of an itchy rash and a stomach upset.*

**side reaction** *noun* CHEM a chemical reaction that occurs after or alongside the primary one

**sidereal** *adjective* ASTRON referring to the stars or determined with reference to their apparent motion

**sidereal time** *noun* TIME time based on Earth's rotation with respect to a particular star

**sidereal year** *noun* TIME the time taken for the Sun to make one apparent evolution with reference to fixed stars

**siemens** *noun* MEASURE, PHYS the SI unit of electrical conductance, equal to one ampere per volt. Symbol **S**

**sievert** *noun* MEASURE, PHYS a unit of measurement of the absorbed dose of radiation, calculated as the amount of radiation from one milligram of radium at a distance of one centimetre for one hour. Symbol **Sv**

**sign** *noun* **1.** a small quantity or amount of something which may suggest the existence of a much larger quantity ○ *Any sign of smoke or fire outside a wing exit makes it unusable.* **2.** MATHS a symbol such as -, +, x or ÷ that represents an operation **3.** MATHS the polarity of a number or signal, i.e. whether it is positive or negative

**signal** *noun* **1.** COMPUT, TELECOM a generated analog or digital waveform used to carry information ○ *The signal received from the computer contained the answer.* **2.** COMPUT a short message used to carry control codes ■ *verb* COMPUT to send a message to a computer ○ *Signal to the network that we are busy.*

**signal conditioning** *noun* COMPUT the conversion or translation of a signal into a form that is accepted by a device

**signal conversion** *noun* COMPUT the processing, changing or modulation of a signal

**signal distance** *noun* COMPUT a number of bit positions with different contents in two data words

**signalling** *noun* COMPUT **1.** a method used by a transmitter to warn a receiver that a message is to be sent **2.** a communication to the transmitter about the state of the receiver

**signal processing** *noun* COMPUT the processing of signals to extract the information contained ○ *The system is used by students doing research on signal processing techniques.* ○ *The message was recovered by carrier signal processing.*

**signal to noise ratio** *noun* PHYS the difference between the power of the transmitted signal and the noise on the line. Abbreviation **S/N**

**sign and magnitude** *noun* MATHS a number representation in which the most significant part indicates the sign of the number the remainder its value

**sign and modulus** *noun* MATHS a way of representing numbers in which one part shows whether the number is positive or negative (NOTE: Usually 0 = positive, 1 = negative.)

**signature** *noun* COMPUT a special authentication code such as a password that a user gives prior to access to a system or prior to the execution of a task to prove identity

**sign bit** *noun* COMPUT a single bit that indicates if a binary number is positive or negative. Also called **sign indicator** (NOTE: Usually 0 = positive, 1 = negative.)

**sign digit** *noun* MATHS one digit that indicates if a number is positive or negative

**signed field** *noun* COMPUT a storage field that can contain a number and a sign bit

**significance** *noun* special meaning or importance

**significant** *adjective* important, considerable or notable ○ *There has been no significant reduction in the amount of raw sewage being released into the sea.*

**significant digit code** *noun* COMPUT a code that indicate various details of an item, by assigning each one a value

**significant figures** *plural noun* MATHS the figures in a decimal number that express accuracy, beginning with the first non-zero figure on the left and ending with the figure on the right ○ *shown to three significant figures*

**significantly** *adverb* to any considerable or notable degree ○ *The amount has not been significantly reduced.*

**sign indicator** *noun* COMPUT same as **sign bit**

**silage** *noun* AGRIC food for cattle formed of grass and other green plants, cut and stored in silos

COMMENT: Silage is made by fermenting a crop with a high moisture content under anaerobic conditions.

**silage additive** *noun* AGRIC a substance containing bacteria and/or chemicals, used to speed up or improve the fermentation process in silage or to increase the amount of nutrients in it

**silage effluent** *noun* AGRIC an acidic liquid produced by the silage process which can be a serious pollutant, especially if it drains into a watercourse

**silence** *noun* the complete absence of noise

**silencer** *noun* ENG a device to reduce noise fitted to a machine ○ *In order to reduce the level of noise from the blower, silencers are incorporated in the main supply ducting.*

**silica** *noun* MINERALS a mineral which forms quartz and sand, and is used to make glass. Also called **silicon dioxide**

**silica gel** *noun* INDUST silica in a form that absorbs water from the air, used as a drying agent and anticaking agent

**silicate** noun 1. CHEM a chemical compound of silicon and oxygen, the most widespread form of mineral being found in most rocks and soils 2. EARTH SCI particles of silica found in clay

**silicon** noun CHEM ELEM an element with semiconductor properties, used in crystal form as a base for integrated circuit manufacture (NOTE: The chemical symbol is **Si**; the atomic number is **14** and the atomic weight is **28.09**.)

COMMENT: Silicon is used in the electronics industry as a base material for integrated circuits. It is grown as a long crystal which is then sliced into wafers before being etched or treated, producing several hundred chips per wafer. Other materials, for example germanium or gallium arsenide, are also used as a base for integrated circuits.

**silicon carbide** noun CHEM a very hard bluish-black crystalline solid, used as an abrasive and refractory, and in pure form as a semiconductor. Formula: SiC.

**silicon chip** noun ELEC a small piece of silicon in and on the surface of which a complete circuit or logic function has been produced, by depositing other substances or by doping

**silicon dioxide** noun CHEM same as **silica**

**silicon wafer** noun ELECTRONICS a thin slice of a pure silicon crystal, usually around 10 cm or 4 in. in diameter, on which integrated circuits are produced. (NOTE: These are then cut out of the wafer to produce individual chips.)

**silicosis** noun MED a type of pneumoconiosis caused by inhaling silica dust from mining or stone-crushing operations, which makes breathing difficult and can lead to emphysema and bronchitis

**silk** noun INSECTS, INDUST a thread produced by the larvae of a moth to make its cocoon (NOTE: It is used to make a smooth light fabric.)

**silkworm** noun INSECTS a moth larva which produces silk thread

**silo** noun AGRIC a large container for storing grain or silage

**silt** noun EARTH SCI 1. soft mud which settles at the bottom of water 2. particles of fine quartz with a diameter of between 0.002 and 0.06 mm

**siltation, silting** noun EARTH SCI the action of depositing silt at the bottom of water, or the state of having a silt deposit ○ *Increased sedimentation and siltation in backwaters.*

**silt up** verb EARTH SCI (*of a harbour or river*) to become full of silt, so that boats can no longer sail

**silver** noun CHEM ELEM a white metallic element which is not corroded by exposure to air (NOTE: The chemical symbol is **Ag**; the atomic number is **47** and the atomic weight is **107.87**.)

**silver bromide** noun CHEM a yellowish insoluble salt that darkens on exposure to light, used in photography. Formula: AgBr.

**silver chloride** noun CHEM a white insoluble salt that darkens on exposure to light, used in photography. Formula: AgCl.

**silver iodide** noun CHEM a yellow insoluble salt that darkens on exposure to light, used in photography, antiseptics and to seed clouds to make rain. Formula: AgI.

**silver nitrate** noun CHEM a white soluble salt that is toxic and turns black on exposure to light while in contact with organic matter. Used in photography, and as an analytical reagent, antiseptic and astringent. Formula: $AgNO_3$.

**silver oxide** noun CHEM 1. a brown, strongly basic powder. Formula: $Ag_2O$. 2. a black solid. Formula: AgO.

**silvi-** prefix BOT, FORESTRY trees

**silvicide** noun BOT a substance which kills trees

**silvicolous** adjective BIOL living or growing in woodland

**silvicultural** adjective FORESTRY referring to the cultivation of trees

**silviculture** noun FORESTRY the cultivation of trees

**SIMD** abbreviation COMPUT single instruction stream multiple data stream

**similar** adjective sharing some qualities but not exactly the same

**similarity** noun the state of being alike

**similarity coefficient** noun ECOL the degree to which two areas of vegetation are alike

**SIMM** abbreviation COMPUT single in-line memory module

**simple mail transfer protocol**
*noun* COMPUT a standard protocol that
allows electronic mail messages to be
transferred from one system to another.
Abbreviation **SMTP** (NOTE: It is usually
used as the method of transferring mail
from one Internet server to another or
to send mail from a personal computer
to a server.)

**simple network management
protocol** *noun* COMPUT a network
management system that defines how
status data is sent from monitored nodes
back to a control station. Abbreviation
**SNMP** (NOTE: It is able to work with vir-
tually any type of network hardware
and software.)

**simplex** *noun* COMPUT data transmission in only one direction. Opposite **duplex**. Abbreviation **SPX**

**simulate** *verb* to imitate the conditions or behaviour of something ○ *The
computer program simulates the action
of an aircraft.*

**simulation** *noun* the imitation of a
real situation, often created for training
purposes ○ *a simulation of an engine
fire* ○ *The computer animation showed
a simulation of the events which followed the explosion on board the
aircraft.*

**simulator** *noun* COMPUT a device that
simulates another system

**simultaneous** *adjective* happening at
the same time

**simultaneous processing** *noun*
COMPUT the execution of two or more
processes at the same time

**simultaneous transmission** *noun*
COMPUT the transmission of data or control codes in two directions at the same
time. Also called **duplex**

**sine wave** *noun* PHYS a waveform
with a simple shape like a sine curve,
produced by a single frequency

**single address code, single ad-
dress instruction** *noun* COMPUT a machine code instruction that contains one
operator and one address

**single address message** *noun*
COMPUT a message with a single
destination

**single bond** *noun* CHEM a covalent
bond between two atoms, formed by
sharing a pair of electrons

**single chip computer** *noun*
COMPUT a complete simple computer including central processing unit, memory
and input/output ports on one chip

**single cross** *noun* GENETICS the production of a hybrid by crossing two inbred lines, or the hybrid produced

**single frequency signalling** *noun*
COMPUT the use of various frequency
signals to represent different control
codes

**single in-line memory module**
*noun* COMPUT a small, compact circuit
board with an edge connector along one
edge that carries densely-packed memory chips. Abbreviation **SIMM**

**single in-line package** *noun*
COMPUT an electronic component that
has all its leads on one side of its package. Abbreviation **SIP**

**single instruction stream multi-
ple data stream** *noun* COMPUT the
architecture of a parallel computer,
which has a number of arithmetic logic
units and data buses with one control
unit. Abbreviation **SIMD**

**single instruction stream single
data stream** *noun* COMPUT the architecture of a serial computer, which has
one arithmetic logic unit and data bus
with one control unit. Abbreviation
**SISD**

**single mode** *noun* TELECOM an optic
fibre with a very narrow diameter, 10
microns or less, designed to transmit a
single light signal over a long distance
(NOTE: This type of fibre has a bandwidth of 5 Gbits/second and is normally used for long distance telephone
networks.)

**single nucleotide polymor-
phism** *noun* BIOTECH a commonly
found change in a single nucleotide base
of a DNA sequence, occurring about every 1000 bases. Abbreviation **SNP**
(NOTE: It is of significance in biomedi-
cal research.)

**single precision** *noun* COMPUT the
use of one data word to store a number

**singularity** *noun* ASTRON the point
where the curvature of spacetime is infinite and all the usual rules of physics
cease to have effect

**sink** *verb* to fall to the bottom of water
■ *noun* **1.** CHEM a place into which a
substance passes to be stored or to be
absorbed **2.** CHEM, PHYS a chemical or
physical process which removes or absorbs a substance ○ *The commonest*

*ozone sink is the reaction with nitric oxide to form nitrogen dioxide and oxygen.* **3.** TELECOM the receiving end of a communications line **4.** EARTH SCI a low-lying piece of land where water collects to form a pond

**sinter** *noun* EARTH SCI a whitish chemical sediment or rock consisting of porous silica or calcium carbonate deposited by a mineral spring

**sintering** *noun* INDUST the process of fusing particles together to form a mass by heating below melting point

**sinus** *noun* **1.** ANAT an air-filled cavity in the bones of the face and skull, especially one that opens into the nasal passages **2.** BOT an indentation between petals or the lobes of a leaf

**sinusoidal wave** *noun* PHYS the shape of a signal or voltage that is described by the sin formula, giving a rounded wave that repeatedly rises and falls with time

**SIO** *abbreviation* COMPUT serial input/output

**SIP** *abbreviation* COMPUT single in-line package

**SIPO** *abbreviation* COMPUT serial input/parallel output

**sirenian** *noun* MARINE BIOL a large marine animal such as a manatee or sea cow, living in warm estuaries. Order: Sirenia.

**sirocco** *noun* METEOROL a dry wind blowing from the desert northwards in North Africa

**SISD** *abbreviation* COMPUT single instruction stream single data stream

**SISO** *abbreviation* COMPUT serial input/serial output

**site** *noun* a place or position of something ○ *The area around the nuclear test site is closed to the public.* ○ *Hazardous chemicals found on the site include arsenic, lead mercury and cyanide.* ■ *verb* to be in or put something in a particular place ○ *The nesting area is sited on the west side of the cliff.*

**Site of Special Scientific Interest** *noun* ENVIRON a small area of land which is officially preserved for its fauna, flora or geology. Abbreviation **SSSI**

**Sitka spruce** *noun* TREES a fast-growing temperate softwood tree,

used for making paper. Latin name: *Picea sitchensis.*

**SI unit** *noun* MEASURE a standard international unit of measurement adopted under the Système International d'Unités (NOTE: The seven fundamental units are the metre, kilogram, second, ampere, kelvin, candela, and mole, and there are two supplementary units, the radian and steradian.)

**6 degrees of freedom** *plural noun* COMPUT the limits of movement and vision that a user can interpret, normally three visual dimensions together with movement

**sixth decile** *noun* STATS a number below which sixty per cent of numbers fall ○ *This group falls within the sixth decile of consumers.*

**size** *noun* how big something is, or how many there are of something ■ *verb* **1.** to establish the size of something **2.** COMPUT to calculate the resources available, and those required to carry out a particular job

**skeletal** *adjective* ANAT referring to a skeleton

**skeletal code** *noun* COMPUT a program which is not complete, with the basic structure coded

**skeletal muscle** *noun* ANAT a muscle attached to a bone, which makes a limb move. Also called **voluntary muscle**

**skeleton** *noun* ANAT the framework of bones which make up a body

**skew** *verb* to make something inaccurate or unbalanced ■ *noun* the amount by which something is not correctly aligned

**skewed** *adjective* unbalanced or biased

**skin** *noun* **1.** ANAT the tissue, the epidermis and dermis, that forms the outside surface of the body **2.** AEROSP the outer layer of an aircraft ○ *The aircraft skin is riveted to stringers and frames.*

COMMENT: The skin is the largest organ in the human body. It is formed of two layers: the epidermis is the outer layer, and includes the top layer of particles of dead skin which are continuously flaking off. Beneath the epidermis is the dermis, which is the main layer of living skin. Hairs and nails are produced by the skin, and pores in the skin secrete sweat from the sweat glands underneath the dermis. The skin is sensitive to touch and heat and cold, which are sensed by the nerve endings in the skin. The skin is a major source of vitamin D which it produces when exposed to sunlight.

**skin graft** *noun* MED **1.** a layer of skin transplanted from one part of the body to cover an area where the skin has been destroyed **2.** a surgical operation to transplant skin ○ *After the operation she had to have a skin graft.*

**skip distance** *noun* TELECOM the shortest distance at which a sky wave can be received ○ *The higher the layer in which a direct wave signal is totally refracted and returns as a sky wave, the greater the skip distance.*

**skull** *noun* ANAT the bony part of the head in humans and other vertebrates (NOTE: It consists of the cranium, which encloses and protects the brain, and the bones of the face.)

**sky** *noun* the atmosphere and outer space as seen from the Earth ○ *The higher the Sun is in the sky, the more intense is the radiation per unit area.*

COMMENT: The sunlight that strikes the atmosphere is scattered by the particles which it hits. The scattering affects short light waves most, hence the short blue light waves colour the sky.

**sky wave** *noun* TELECOM that part of a radiated wave which is returned to Earth by refraction from the ionosphere

**slack** *adjective* **1.** not tight or taut ○ *a slack cable* **2.** (*of isobars*) widely spaced ○ *Throughout the tropics and sub-tropics, where pressure gradients are normally slack, the sea breeze is a regular feature.*

**slack water** *noun* OCEANOG the part of the tidal cycle occurring between the ebb and flood tides at the point when the flows are reversing direction

**slag** *noun* INDUST waste matter which floats on top of the molten metal during smelting, used to lighten heavy soils, e.g. clay, and also for making cement

**slag heap** *noun* INDUST a large pile of waste material from an industrial process such as smelting or from coal mining

**slaked lime** *noun* AGRIC calcium hydroxide, used to spread on soil to reduce acidity and add calcium

**slant** *noun* a slope or inclination ■ *verb* to slope

**slash** *verb* to make a long cut with a knife

**slash and burn agriculture** *noun* AGRIC a form of agriculture in which forest is cut down and burnt to create open space for growing crops. Also called **swidden farming** (NOTE: The space is abandoned after several crops have been grown and further forest is cut down.)

**slate** *noun* EARTH SCI a hard metamorphic rock which splits easily along cleavage lines, used especially for making roofs

**slaughter** *noun* the killing of a large number of animals ■ *verb* **1.** to kill large numbers of animals **2.** AGRIC to kill animals for food

**slaughterhouse** *noun* FOOD INDUST a building where animals are slaughtered and the carcasses prepared for sale for human consumption

**slave processor** *noun* COMPUT a dedicated processor controlled by a master processor

**sleep** *noun* **1.** BIOL a state of unconsciousness during which the body rests **2.** COMPUT the state of a system that is waiting for a log-on signal before doing anything ■ *verb* to be asleep or fall asleep

**sleeping sickness** *noun* MED an African disease caused by trypanosomes spread by the tsetse fly infesting the blood

**sleet** METEOROL *noun* ice and rain mixed together ■ *verb* to fall as ice and rain mixed together

**slice** *noun* a section or piece of something

**slick** *noun* a patch of something thin or slippery on a surface, especially of oil floating on water

**slide** *noun* a device which allows continuous movement over a smooth surface ■ *verb* to move continuously over a smooth surface ○ *Shear stress is the stress that resists the force tending to cause one layer of a material to slide over an adjacent layer.* (NOTE: **sliding – slid**)

**slide rule** *noun* MATHS a graduated device with sliding parts marked with scales for performing complex mathematical operations

**slime** *noun* **1.** any thick liquid substance regarded as unpleasant **2.** BIOL a mucous substance secreted by an organism such as a snail or fungus

**slip-off slope** *noun* EARTH SCI a gently sloping bank on the inside of a meandering river

**slit** *noun* a long thin gap in something ■ *verb* to cut a slit in something

**slope** *noun* a slanting surface or slanting piece of ground ■ *verb* to be inclined at an angle

**slot** *noun* a long thin hole that can hold something ○ *The system disk should be inserted into the left-hand slot on the front of the computer.* ■ *verb* to fit into or insert an object into a hole ○ *The disk slots into one of the floppy drive apertures.*

**slough** BIOL *noun* dead tissue, especially dead skin, which has separated from healthy tissue ■ *verb* (*of a snake*) to lose dead skin which falls off

**slow neutron** *noun* PHYS a relatively slow-moving neutron with low kinetic energy. Also called **thermal neutron** (NOTE: Slow neutrons can cause nuclear fission.)

**SLSI** *abbreviation* ELECTRONICS super large scale integration

**sludge** *noun* INDUST the solid part of sewage

**sludge composting** *noun* AGRIC the decomposition of sewage for use as a fertiliser or mulch

**sludge digestion** *noun* INDUST a final treatment of sewage when it is digested anaerobically by bacteria

**sludge gas** *noun* CHEM methane mixed with carbon dioxide which is given off by sewage

**sludge processing** *noun* INDUST the treating of the solid part of sewage so that it may safely be dumped or used as a fertiliser

**slurry** *noun* **1.** CHEM a liquid containing a suspended solid **2.** AGRIC liquid or semiliquid waste from animals, stored in tanks or lagoons and treated to be used as fertiliser

**small computer systems interface** *noun* COMPUT a standard high-speed parallel interface used to connect computers to peripheral devices such as disk drives and scanners. Abbreviation **SCSI**

**small intestine** *noun* ANAT the narrow section of the gut after the stomach, where most of the food is digested and absorbed (NOTE: Its three sections are called the duodenum, jejunum and ileum.)

**small-scale** *adjective* small in size or limited in scope. Compare **large-scale**

**small-scale integration** *noun* ELECTRONICS an integrated circuit with 1 to 10 components. Abbreviation **SSI**

**Smalltalk** *noun* COMPUT an object-oriented programming language developed by Xerox

**smart card** *noun* ELECTRONICS a plastic card with a memory and microprocessor device embedded in it, so that it can be used for electronic funds transfer or for identification of the user

**smart wiring hub** *noun* COMPUT a network hub or concentrator that can transmit status information back to a managing station and allows management software to configure each port remotely ○ *Using this management software, I can shut down Tom's port on the remote smart wiring hub.*

**SMB** *abbreviation* COMPUT server message block

**smear** *noun* BIOTECH a sample of soft tissue such as blood or mucus taken from a patient and spread over a glass slide to be examined under a microscope

**smelt** *verb* INDUST to extract metal from ore by heating it

**smelter** *noun* INDUST a plant where ore is heated and metal extracted from it

**smelting** *noun* INDUST the process of extracting metal from ore by heating

**smiley** *noun* COMPUT a face created with text characters, used to provide the real meaning to an email message. Also called **emoticon** (NOTE: For example, :-) means laughter or a joke and :-( means sad.)

**S/MIME** *abbreviation* COMPUT secure/multipurpose Internet mail extension

**smog** *noun* ENVIRON a form of air pollution in towns, caused by warm damp air combined with exhaust fumes from cars

COMMENT: Smog originally meant smoke and fog, and it was caused by coal smoke in foggy weather in winter. Today's smog is usually caused by car exhaust fumes and can occur in sunny weather. When the atmosphere near ground level is polluted with nitrogen oxides from burning fossil fuels together with hydrocarbons, ultraviolet light from the Sun sets off a series of reactions that result in photochemical smog, containing, among other substances, ozone. Temperature inversion (where the air temperature at ground level is colder than the air above) helps to form smog by making it impossible for the pollutants in the air to rise.

**smoke** *noun* CHEM a white, grey or black product formed of small particles, given off by something which is burning ○ *The room was full of cigarette smoke.* ○ *Several people died from inhaling toxic smoke.* ■ *verb* **1.** to emit smoke ○ *The volcano is still smoking.* **2.** FOOD INDUST to preserve food by hanging it in the smoke from a fire (NOTE: Smoking is used mainly for fish, but also for some bacon and cheese.)

COMMENT: By banning the use of fuels which create smoke, the air above towns has become much cleaner than it was. This has the disadvantage of allowing the sunlight to penetrate and cause photochemical reactions to take place, increasing the acidity of the atmosphere, with the result that apparently clean air can be as dangerous as smog.

**smokestack** *noun* INDUST a very tall chimney usually containing several flues, as found in a factory

**smoky** *adjective* ENVIRON full of smoke or producing a lot of smoke

**smooth** *adjective* **1.** even and without lumps or dents ○ *a smooth surface* **2.** not rough or turbulent ○ *High ground will disturb the smooth, horizontal flow of air.* □ **a smooth running engine** an engine which is operating well

**smooth muscle** *noun* ANAT a type of muscle found in involuntary muscles. Also called **unstriated muscle**

**SMT** *abbreviation* COMPUT surface-mount technology ○ *SMT is faster and more space-efficient than soldering.*

**SMTP** *abbreviation* COMPUT simple mail transfer protocol. Compare **POP 3**

**smut** *noun* **1.** CHEM a black flake of oily carbon emitted from a fire ○ *Smuts from the oil depot fire covered the town.* **2.** BIOL a disease of cereal plants, caused by a fungus, which covers the plant with black spots

**Sn** *symbol* CHEM ELEM tin

**SNA** *abbreviation* COMPUT Systems Network Architecture

**SNMP** *abbreviation* COMPUT simple network management protocol

**SNOBOL** *noun* COMPUT a high-level programming language that uses string processing methods. Full form **string orientated symbolic language**

**snow** *noun* **1.** METEOROL water which falls as white flakes of ice crystals in cold weather **2.** PHYS interference displayed as flickering white flecks on a monitor ■ *verb* to fall as snow ○ *It snowed heavily during the night.*

**snow blindness** *noun* MED a temporary painful blindness caused by bright sunlight shining on snow

**snowfall** *noun* METEOROL a quantity of snow that comes down at any one time ○ *A heavy snowfall blocked the main roads.*

**snowflake** *noun* METEOROL a small piece of snow formed from a number of ice crystals

**snow line** *noun* EARTH SCI a line on a high mountain above which there is permanent snow

**snow-melt** *noun* EARTH SCI the melting of snow in spring, often the cause of floods

**snowstorm** *noun* METEOROL a heavy fall of snow accompanied by wind

**snowy** *adjective* **1.** METEOROL characterised by a lot of snow falls ○ *a period of snowy weather* **2.** covered with snow

**SNP** *abbreviation* BIOTECH single nucleotide polymorphism

**soak** *verb* **1.** PHYS to put something in liquid, so that it absorbs some of it ○ *The newspaper is soaked in water, then formed into bricks and dried.* **2.** COMPUT to run a program or device continuously for a period of time to make sure it functions correctly

**soak-test** *verb* COMPUT same as **soak** ○ *The device was soak-tested prior to delivery.*

**soak up** *verb* PHYS to absorb a liquid

**soap** *noun* CHEM a metallic salt of a fatty acid such as stearic acid, used as a cleansing agent

**soar** *verb* ZOOL (*of a bird*) to fly higher or stay airborne without any movement of the wings using updraughts of warm air

**social** *adjective* ECOL referring to a group of animals or people

**social animal** *noun* ZOOL an animal such as an ant or bee that lives in an organised society

**social carnivore** *noun* ZOOL a meat-eating animal such as a lion or wolf that lives and hunts in a group

**social group** *noun* 1. ZOOL a group of people or animals living together in an organised way 2. a group of people with a similar position in society

**social parasite** *noun* BIOL a parasite that benefits from the host's usual behaviour, e.g. a cuckoo, which lays its eggs in the nest of another bird who then brings up the cuckoo's young as if it were its own

**society** *noun* 1. ZOOL a group of animals that live together in an organised way 2. BOT a group of plants within a larger community 3. a group of people who live together and have the same laws and customs

**socket** *noun* ELEC a device with a set of holes, into which a plug fits

**soda** *noun* CHEM same as **sodium hydroxide**

**soda ash** *noun* CHEM same as **sodium carbonate**

**soda lake** *noun* EARTH SCI a salt lake with a high proportion of sodium in the water

**soda lime** *noun* CHEM a mixture of sodium hydroxide and calcium hydroxide, used to absorb moisture and carbon dioxide

**sodium** *noun* CHEM ELEM a chemical element which is the basic substance in salt (NOTE: The chemical symbol is **Na**; the atomic number of **11** and the atomic weight is **22.99**.)

**sodium aluminate** *noun* CHEM a solid, white-coloured substance, normally used in water-purification. Formula: $NaAlO_2$.

**sodium balance** *noun* PHYSIOL a balance maintained in the body between salt lost in sweat and urine, and salt taken in from food (NOTE: The balance is regulated by aldosterone.)

**sodium bicarbonate** *noun* CHEM a white crystalline alkaline salt, used as a raising agent, antacid and in fizzy drinks and fire extinguishers. Formula: $NaHCO_3$.

**sodium bisulfate** *noun* CHEM same as **sodium hydrogensulfate**

**sodium bisulfite** *noun* CHEM same as **sodium hydrogensulfite**

**sodium bromide** *noun* CHEM a white crystalline solid. Formula: NaBr.

**sodium carbonate** *noun* CHEM a white crystalline salt of carbonic acid. Formula: $Na_2CO_3$.

**sodium chlorate** *noun* AGRIC a herbicide which is taken up into the plant through the roots

**sodium chloride** *noun* CHEM common salt, important in the diet. Formula: NaCl.

**sodium hydrogensulfate, sodium hydrogensulphate** *noun* CHEM a white solid used in making sulfuric acid. Formula: $NaHSO_4H_2O$. Also called **sodium bisulfate**

**sodium hydrogensulfite, sodium hydrogensulphite** *noun* CHEM a white powder, used as an antiseptic. Formula: $NaHSO_3$. Also called **sodium bisulfite**

**sodium hydroxide** *noun* CHEM a compound of sodium and water which is used to make soap and to clear blocked drains. Formula: NaOH. Also called **caustic soda, soda**

**sodium monoxide** *noun* CHEM a white solid that is a strong base. Formula: $Na_2O$.

**sodium nitrate** *noun* CHEM a white crystalline salt, used as a fertiliser and in curing meat. Formula: $NaNO_3$.

**sodium peroxide** *noun* CHEM an odourless yellowish powder, used as a bleaching agent, antiseptic and disinfectant. Formula: $Na_2O_2$.

**sodium pump** *noun* BIOCHEM the active process that exchanges sodium ions for potassium ions across a cell membrane

**sodium sulfate, sodium sulphate** *noun* CHEM a bitter-tasting white solid, used in making glass, rayon, dyes, detergents and purgatives. Formula: $Na_2SO_4$.

**sodium sulfide, sodium sulphide** *noun* CHEM an amorphous solid that dissolves in moist air. Formula: $NaS_2$.

**sodium sulfite, sodium sulphite** *noun* CHEM a white soluble crystalline solid, used in photography and as a bleach. Formula: $Na_2SO_3$.

**soft** *adjective* 1. not hard 2. PHYS referring to material that loses its magnetic effects when removed from a magnetic field **3.** COMPUT referring to data that is not permanently stored in hardware (NOTE: It usually refers to data stored on a magnetic medium.)

**soft coal** *noun* INDUST coal which is not as efficient a fuel as anthracite and produces more smoke when it burns

**soft copy** *noun* COMPUT text displayed on a computer screen. Compare **hard copy**

**soft detergent** *noun* INDUST a detergent that is broken down in water but which can cause eutrophication and algal bloom

**soften** *verb* to make something soft or become soft

**softener** *noun* CHEM a substance which makes something become soft

**soft error** *noun* COMPUT a random error caused by software or data errors (NOTE: This type of error is very difficult to trace and identify since it only appears in some conditions.)

**soft goods** *plural noun* COMPUT software that is purchased and paid for in an online shop, but is then downloaded directly onto the computer

**soft hyphen** *noun* PRINTING a hyphen that is inserted only when a word is split at the end of a line

**soft reset** *noun* COMPUT an instruction that terminates any program execution and returns the user to the monitor program or BIOS

**soft return** *noun* COMPUT a code that moves the cursor down to the start of the next line

**software** *noun* COMPUT any program or group of programs that instructs the hardware on how it should perform, including operating systems, word processors and applications programs (NOTE: no plural)

**software-compatible** *adjective* COMPUT referring to a computer that will load and run programs written for another computer

**software developer** *noun* COMPUT a person or company that writes software

**software engineering** *noun* COMPUT a field of study covering all software-related subjects

**software system** *noun* COMPUT an assembly of all the programs required for one or more tasks

**soft water** *noun* CHEM water that does not contain calcium and other minerals that are found in hard water and is easily able to make soap lather

**softwood** *noun* **1.** INDUST the open-grained wood produced by pine trees and other conifers **2.** TREES a pine tree or other conifer that produces such wood. Compare **hardwood**

**soil** *noun* EARTH SCI the earth in which plants grow

COMMENT: Soil is a mixture of mineral particles, decayed organic matter and water. Topsoil contains chemical substances which are leached through into the subsoil where they are retained. Soils are classified according to the areas of the world in which they are found, according to the types of minerals they contain or according to the stage of development they have reached.

**soil conservation** *noun* AGRIC the use of a range of methods to prevent soil from being eroded or overcultivated

**soil creep** *noun* EARTH SCI a slow movement of soil downhill

**soil depletion** *noun* EARTH SCI a reduction of the soil layer by erosion

**soil drainage** *noun* EARTH SCI the flow of water from soil, either naturally or through pipes and drainage channels inserted into the ground

**soil erosion** *noun* EARTH SCI the removal of soil by the effects of rain, wind, sea or cultivation practices

**soil fauna** *plural noun* ZOOL fauna that live in soil

**soil fertility** *noun* EARTH SCI the potential capacity of soil to support plant growth based on its content of nitrogen and other nutrients

**soil flora** *plural noun* BOT microorganisms such as fungi and algae that live in the soil

**soil horizon** *noun* EARTH SCI a layer of soil that is of a different colour or texture from the rest

COMMENT: There are four soil horizons: the A horizon or topsoil containing humus; the B horizon or subsoil containing minerals leached from the topsoil and little organic matter; the C horizon or weathered rock; and the D horizon or bedrock.

**soil improvement** *noun* AGRIC the practice of making the soil more fertile by methods such as draining and manuring

**soilless gardening** *noun* AGRIC same as **hydroponics**

**soil map** *noun* EARTH SCI a map showing the different types of soil found in an area

**soil profile** *noun* EARTH SCI a vertical section through the soil showing the different layers

**soil salinity** *noun* EARTH SCI the quantity of mineral salts found in a soil (NOTE: High soil salinity is detrimental to most agricultural crops, although some plants are adapted to such conditions.)

**soil sample** *noun* EARTH SCI a small quantity of soil used for testing

**soil science** *noun* EARTH SCI the scientific study of all aspects of soil, including its formation, distribution and structure

**soil structure** *noun* EARTH SCI the arrangement of soil particles in groups or individually, giving a loose or firm texture

**soil texture** *noun* EARTH SCI the relative proportion of sand, silt and clay particles in soil

COMMENT: There are four main classes of soil texture, based on the relative amounts of soil particles of different sizes a soil contains: clay, silt, sand and loam. Loam, which contains a mixture of soil particles, is the most suitable for growing crops.

**solar** *adjective* **1.** ASTRON referring to the Sun **2.** INDUST using the energy of the Sun or driven by power from the Sun

**solar cell** *noun* ELEC a photoelectric device that converts solar energy into electricity

**solar collector** *noun* INDUST same as **solar panel**

**solar constant** *noun* PHYS the rate at which solar energy arrives at the Earth, equal to about 13.5 watts per square metre in space just above Earth's atmosphere (NOTE: The solar constant is not constant, and it is unclear whether its day-to-day and year-to-year variations are accompanied by long-term variations which could have important effects on the evolution of life on Earth, modern-day climate change and the incidence of Ice Ages.)

**solar cycle** *noun* ASTRON the 22-year period over which the pattern of sunspots on the Sun's surface repeats itself (NOTE: Analysis of sunspot records shows that the full cycle appears to incorporate two 11-year periods.)

**solar day** *noun* TIME the day measured in terms of the time taken for the Sun to return to the same point in the sky, equal to about 24 hours 4 minutes

**solar dryer** *noun* AGRIC a device for drying crops using the heat of the sun

**solar eclipse** *noun* ASTRON a situation when the Moon passes between the Sun and the Earth during the daytime and the shadow of the Moon falls across the Earth, so cutting off the Sun's light

**solar energy** *noun* INDUST electricity produced from the radiation of the Sun. Also called **solar power, solar-generated energy, solar-generated power**

COMMENT: The sun emits radiation in the form of ultraviolet rays, visible light and infrared heating rays. Solar energy can be collected by various methods, most often by heating water which is then passed into storage tanks. Although solar power is easy to collect, the problem is in storing it in order to make sure that the power is available for use during the night or when the Sun does not shine.

**solar flare** *noun* ASTRON a sudden flash of bright radiation from the Sun which affects radio waves and is associated with sunspot activity

**solar gain** *noun* ENVIRON the amount of heat in a building derived from solar radiation through windows or transparent walls

**solar-generated energy, solar-generated power** *noun* INDUST same as **solar energy**

**solar heating** *noun* ENG the use of the Sun's energy to heat water as it passes through heat-absorbing panels

**solar irradiation** *noun* PHYS rays which are emitted by the Sun

**solarisation, solarization** *noun* AGRIC exposure to the rays of the Sun, especially for the purpose of killing pests in the soil by covering the soil with plastic sheets and letting it warm up in the sunshine

**solar panel** *noun* ENG a device with a dark surface which absorbs the sun's radiation and uses it to heat water. Also called **solar collector, collector panel**

**solar power** *noun* INDUST same as **solar energy**

**solar-powered** *adjective* INDUST powered by energy derived from the Sun's rays ○ *a solar-powered steam pump*

**solar radiation** *noun* PHYS rays which are emitted by the Sun

**solar system** *noun* ASTRON the Sun and all the objects under its gravitational influence

**solar thermal** *noun* INDUST a form of power generation that uses concentrated sunlight to heat a fluid that is then used to drive a motor or turbine

**solar wind** *noun* ASTRON the stream of particles being driven constantly off the surface of the Sun into interplanetary space, moving at several hundred kilometres per second, and consisting largely of protons and electrons plus a few per cent of alpha particles (NOTE: The Earth is protected from the solar wind by its own atmosphere and its magnetic field.)

**solar year** *noun* TIME the year measured from equinox to equinox, equal to 365.24 days. Also called **tropical year**

**solder** *noun* METALL an alloy with a low melting point, typically a mixture of tin and lead, used to join metallic parts ■ *verb* INDUST to join parts using solder

**solenoid** *noun* ELEC a cylindrical coil of wire acting as a magnet when carrying electric current ○ *Fuel is metered from the fuel system by a solenoid-operated control valve.*

**solid** *adjective* **1.** CHEM not liquid or gaseous ○ *a lump of solid matter* ○ *a solid object* ○ *Visibility is reduced by the presence of solid particles such as dust or sand in the atmosphere.* **2.** continuous, unbroken or overall ○ *a solid line* ○ *a solid block of colour* ■ *noun* CHEM a substance which is not a liquid or a gas ○ *Ice is a solid, water is a liquid and vapour is a gas.*

**solid colour** *noun* COMPUT a colour that can be displayed on a screen or printed on a colour printer without dithering

**solid error** *noun* COMPUT an error that is always present when certain equipment is used

**solid fuel** *noun* INDUST coal, coke or wood

**solidification** *noun* the process of becoming solid

**solidify** *verb* to become solid ○ *Carbon dioxide solidifies at low temperatures.*

**solid modelling** *noun* COMPUT a function in a graphics program that creates three-dimensional solid-looking objects by shading

**solids** *plural noun* FOOD food that has to be chewed

**solid-state** *adjective* ELECTRONICS referring to semiconductor devices

**solid-state ballast lamp** *noun* ELEC a fluorescent light bulb containing a ballast that reduces the amount of current needed to keep the lamp bright

**solid-state device** *noun* ELECTRONICS an electronic device that operates by using the effects of electrical or magnetic signals in a solid semiconductor material

**solid-state technology** *noun* ELECTRONICS the technology using the electronic properties of solids to replace those of valves

**solid waste** *noun* ENVIRON waste matter that is hard and not liquid

**solifluction** *noun* EARTH SCI a gradual downhill movement of wet soil

**solstice** *noun* ASTRON one of the two times of year when the Sun is at its furthest point, either north or south, from the equator

**solubility** *noun* CHEM the ability of a substance to dissolve in another substance or solvent at a given temperature and pressure

**solubility product** *noun* CHEM a concentration of ions in a solution saturated with an electrolyte

**soluble** *adjective* CHEM able to dissolve ○ *a tablet of soluble aspirin* ○ *fat-soluble* ○ *water-soluble*

**soluble fibre** *noun* FOOD fibre found in vegetables, fruit, pulses and porridge oats, which is partly digested in the intestine and reduces the absorption of fats and sugar into the body, so lowering the level of cholesterol

**solum** *noun* EARTH SCI soil, including both topsoil and subsoil (*technical*)

**solute** *noun* CHEM a solid substance which is dissolved in a solvent to make a solution

**solution** *noun* **1.** the act or means of solving a problem or difficulty ○ *struggling with the solution of a mathematical problem* **2.** the answer to or a way of removing a problem or difficulty ○ *found a solution* **3.** CHEM a change of a solid or gas into a liquid by dissolving in water or some other liquid **4.** CHEM a mixture of a solid substance dissolved in a liquid ○ *a dilute solution of sodium bicarbonate*

**Solvay process** *noun* INDUST the industrial process that produces sodium carbonate or washing soda from common salt

**solve** *verb* to find the answer to, or a way of removing, a difficulty or problem ○ *The triangle of velocities is used to solve navigation problems.*

**solvent** *noun* CHEM a liquid in which a solid substance can be dissolved

**solvolysis** *noun* CHEM a chemical reaction between a solute and its solvent

**somatic** *adjective* BIOL referring to cells not involved in sexual reproduction

**sonar** *noun* PHYS a method of finding objects under water by sending out sound waves and detecting returning sound waves reflected by the object

**sonde** *noun* METEOROL a device attached to a balloon or rocket, for measuring and taking samples of the atmosphere

**son file** *noun* COMPUT the latest working version of a file

**sonic** *adjective* PHYS referring to sound waves

**sonic boom** *noun* ACOUSTICS a loud noise made by the shock waves produced by an object such as an aircraft or a bullet travelling through the air at or faster than the speed of sound

COMMENT: The shock waves of a sonic boom can cause objects to resonate so violently that they are damaged. Supersonic aircraft generally fly at speeds greater than the speed of sound only over the sea, to avoid noise nuisance and damage to property.

**soot** *noun* ENVIRON a black deposit of fine particles of carbon which rise in the smoke produced by the burning of material such as coal, wood or oil

**sorghum** *noun* PLANTS a drought-resistant cereal plant grown in semi-arid tropical regions such as Mexico, Nigeria and Sudan. Latin name: *Sorghum vulgare.*

**sort** *verb* to put data into order, according to a system ○ *Sort the addresses into alphabetical order.* ○ *Sort orders according to account numbers.*

**sorting pass** *noun* COMPUT a single run through a list of items to put them into order

**sortkey, sort field** *noun* COMPUT a field in a stored file which is used to sort the file ○ *The orders were sorted according to dates by assigning the date field as the sortkey.*

**sort/merge** *noun* COMPUT a program which allows new files to be sorted and then merged in correct order into existing files

**sound** *adjective* strong ○ *a sound structure* ■ *noun* ACOUSTICS something that can be heard and is caused by vibration of the surrounding air ■ *verb* **1.** to make a noise ○ *A warning horn will sound if the door opens.* **2.** to seem on the basis of an account ○ *It sounds as if there is a problem.*

**sound absorption factor** *noun* PHYS a number indicating the amount of sound energy absorbed by a surface

**sound bandwidth** *noun* ACOUSTICS the range of frequencies that a human ear can register, normally from 20 Hz to 20 KHz

**sound barrier** *noun* PHYS the air resistance encountered by objects moving at speeds near the speed of sound

**sound capture** *noun* COMPUT the conversion of an analog sound into a digital form that can be used by a computer

**sound card** *noun* COMPUT expansion card which produces analog sound signals under the control of a computer ○ *This software lets you create almost any sound – but you can only hear them if you have a sound card fitted.*

**sound pressure level** *noun* MEASURE, ACOUSTICS a measure of loudness, in decibels. Abbreviation **SPL**

**sound wave** *noun* ACOUSTICS a pressure wave produced by vibrations, which is transmitted through air or a solid and detected by a human ear or a microphone (NOTE: In a microphone sound waves are converted to electrical signals.)

**source** *noun* **1.** a substance or object which produces something ○ *Hot rocks are a potential energy source.* ○ *Plants tend to turn towards the light source.* **2.** EARTH SCI the place where a river starts to flow ○ *The source of the Nile is in the mountains of Ethiopia.* **3.** TELECOM a point where a transmitted signal enters a network **4.** an original or initial point

**source address filtering** *noun* COMPUT a feature of some bridges which detects a particular address in the received packet and either rejects or forwards the data

**source book** *noun* COMPUT a library file from which elements or objects are copied and used

**source code** *noun* COMPUT a set of codes written by a programmer that cannot be directly executed by a computer but has to be translated into an object code program by a compiler or interpreter

**source language** *noun* COMPUT the language of a program prior to translation

**source program** *noun* a program, prior to translation, written in a programming language by a programmer

**south** *noun* NAVIG the compass point 180° clockwise from due north and directly opposite north ○ *fly towards the south* ■ *adjective* **1.** NAVIG referring to the compass point 180° from north ○ *the south side of the river* **2.** GEOG situated in the south ■ *adverb* NAVIG towards the south ○ *The aircraft is flying south.*

**south-east** *noun* NAVIG the direction between south and east ○ *a region in the south-east of Canada* ■ *adjective* **1.** GEOG situated in the south-east ○ *the south-east coast of England* **2.** METEOROL blowing from the south-east ○ *a south-east wind* ■ *adverb* NAVIG towards the south-east ○ *We were heading south-east.*

**southerly** *adjective* NAVIG to or from the south ○ *The typhoon is moving in a southerly direction at 25 knots.* ■ *noun* METEOROL a wind which blows from the south

**southern** *adjective* GEOG, NAVIG situated in the south or towards the south

**Southern blot** *noun* BIOTECH a technique for transferring DNA restriction fragments onto a membrane filter for identification with a gene probe

**southern hemisphere** *noun* EARTH SCI the bottom half of the Earth

**Southern Lights** *plural noun* METEOROL a spectacular illumination of the sky in the southern hemisphere caused by ionised particles striking the atmosphere. Also called **Aurora Australis**

**Southern Oscillation** *noun* METEOROL a regular cycle by which air is exchanged between the Pacific basin and the Indian Ocean, occurring every two to five years and linked to changes in the sea temperature and to the El Niño effect

**South Pole** *noun* EARTH SCI the point which is furthest south on the earth

**south-west** *noun* NAVIG the direction between south and west ○ *a region in the south-west of Canada* ■ *adjective* **1.** GEOG situated in the south-west ○ *the south-west coast of England* **2.** METEOROL blowing from the south-west ○ *a south-west wind* ■ *adverb* NAVIG towards the south-west ○ *We were heading south-west.*

**south wind** *noun* METEOROL a wind blowing from or coming from the south (NOTE: A wind is named after the direction it comes from.)

**sow** *verb* AGRIC to put seeds into soil so that they will germinate and grow ■ *noun* ZOOL a female pig

**soya** *noun* PLANTS a plant that produces edible beans which have a high protein and fat content and very little starch. Also called **soya bean, soybean**

**soya bean, soybean** *noun* **1.** BOT a bean from a soya plant **2.** PLANTS same as **soya**

COMMENT: Soya beans are very rich in protein and apart from direct human consumption are used for their oil and as livestock feed.

**SP** *abbreviation* COMPUT stack pointer

**sp.** *abbreviation* BIOL one species (*singular*) (NOTE: The plural is **ssp.**)

**space** *noun* **1.** a gap between things **2.** PHYS the physical universe outside Earth's atmosphere ○ *VHF waves tend to pass through the layers of the ionosphere into space.*

**space bar** *noun* COMPUT a long bar at the bottom of a keyboard, which inserts a space into the text when pressed

**space character** *noun* COMPUT a character code which prints a space

**space probe** *noun* AEROSP a device sent into space to obtain information about conditions in space

**Space Shuttle** *noun* AEROSP a reusable space launcher developed in the US by NASA and first used in 1981

**spacing** *noun* PRINTING the insertion of spaces between characters or lines of printed text, or the way in which spaces were inserted ○ *The spacing on some lines is very uneven.*

**span** *noun* 1. the distance between two points 2. COMPUT a set of allowed values between a maximum and minimum ■ *verb* to bridge a distance between two points

**spanning tree** *noun* COMPUT a method of creating a network topology that does not contain any loops and provides redundancy in case of a network fault or problem

**spar** *noun* AEROSP the main longitudinal beam of an aircraft wing

**SPARC** *noun* COMPUT a RISC processor designed by Sun Microsystems which is used in its range of workstations. Full form **scalar processor architecture**

**spare part** *noun* ENG a small piece of a machine that is needed to replace a piece which is broken or missing

**spark** *noun* ELEC a light produced by a sudden electrical discharge ○ *An electric spark from an igniter plug starts combustion and the flame is then continuous.*

**spark plug** *noun* MECH ENG a device screwed into each cylinder head of a spark ignition engine, which initiates fuel combustion by an electric spark

**sparse array** *noun* MATHS a data matrix structure that contains mainly zero or null entries

**spathe** *noun* BOT a large funnel-shaped bract, often coloured, around a flower of the lily family

**spawn** ZOOL *noun* a mass of eggs produced by a fish or reptile ■ *verb* (*of a fish or reptile*) to produce a mass of eggs

**spawning ground** *noun* ZOOL an area of water where fish come each year to produce their eggs

**speaker** *noun* ACOUSTICS same as **loudspeaker**

**special** *adjective* 1. not usual 2. for one particular purpose 3. highly valued ○ *The doctor has put him on a special diet.*

**specialisation, specialization** *noun* 1. the act of studying one particular branch of science in detail 2. a particular branch of science that a person studies in detail

**specialise, specialize** *verb* to study one particular branch of science in detail ○ *He specialises in the study of conifers.*

**specialist** *noun* 1. a person who specialises in a particular branch of study ○ *They have called in a contamination specialist.* 2. BIOL an organism which only lives on one type of food or in a very restricted area

**speciality** *noun* a particular branch of science that a person studies in detail

**Special Theory of Relativity** *noun* PHYS ◊ **relativity**

**speciation** *noun* BIOL the process of developing new species

**species** *noun* BIOL a group of living things that can interbreed. A species is a division of a genus. Abbreviation **sp.** (NOTE: The plural is **species**.)

**species barrier** *noun* GENETICS the inability of members of different species to produce healthy offspring if they mate or cross

**species diversity** *noun* ECOL the richness of the number of species

**specific** *adjective* 1. clearly defined and definite ○ *The airframe has to be built to very specific requirements.* 2. characteristic of something 3. BIOL referring to species 4. PHYS referring to a physical quantity expressed per unit mass

**specific activity** *noun* PHYS the number of disintegrations of a radio-isotope in a period of time

**specific address** *noun* COMPUT a storage address which directly, without any modification, accesses a location or device

**specification** *noun* a detailed description of the composition of something, of what is needed, or of what is involved in doing something ○ *The specification requires gaps of 5 mm.* ○ *Fluids are coloured for recognition purposes and fluids of different specifications must never be mixed.* ○ *The work was rejected as not up to specification.* ○ *The product meets the customer's specifications.*

**specific charge** *noun* PHYS the electric charge of an elementary particle divided by its mass

**specific coding** *noun* COMPUT a program code which has been written so that it only uses absolute addresses and values

**specific gravity** *noun* PHYS a measure of the density of a substance

**specific heat capacity** *noun* PHYS the amount of energy needed to raise the temperature of unit mass of a substance by unit temperature interval under constant conditions (NOTE: It is usually measured in joules per kelvin per kilogram.)

**specific humidity** *noun* PHYS a ratio between the amount of water vapour in air and the total mass of the mixture of air and water vapour

**specificity** *noun* the characteristic of having a specific range or use ○ *Parasites show specificity in that they live on only a limited number of hosts.*

**specific name** *noun* BIOL a name by which a species is differentiated from other members of the genus (NOTE: It is the second name in the binomial classification system, the first being the generic name which identifies the genus.)

**specific surface** *noun* CHEM the surface area of a solid substance per unit mass

**specify** *verb* to state clearly what is needed

**specimen** *noun* 1. a representative of a group, especially an animal or plant ○ *a rare double-flowered specimen* 2. SCI, MED a small quantity of something given for testing ○ *Scientists have taken away soil specimens for analysis.*

**spectra** *noun* PHYS plural of **spectrum**

**spectral type** *noun* ASTRON a classification system of stars based on an analysis of the light they emit which also gives information on a star's temperature and chemical composition

**spectrography** *noun* PHYS the recording of a spectrum on photographic film

**spectrometer** *noun* PHYS an instrument for measuring and sometimes recording a spectrum

**spectrometry** *noun* ASTRON the measurement and analysis of spectra for the determination of characteristics such as the composition and motion of astronomical objects

**spectrophotometer** *noun* PHYS an apparatus for measuring the relative intensities of wavelengths in a spectrum

**spectroscope** *noun* PHYS an instrument used to analyse a spectrum

**spectroscopy** *noun* PHYS the science of producing and analysing spectra

**spectrum** *noun* 1. a range of different but related things or stages 2. PHYS the distribution of energy from a body in terms of its frequency, in any part of the electromagnetic spectrum or the whole of it

**speech chip** *noun* COMPUT an integrated circuit which generates sounds, usually phonemes, which when played together sound similar to human speech

**speech quality** *noun* COMPUT a sound recorded at a low bandwidth with a small sample size (NOTE: For example, in CD-i it is Level C with 4-bit samples and a rate of 18.9 KHz.)

**speech recognition** *noun* COMPUT the analysis of spoken words in such a way that a computer can recognise spoken words and commands

**speech synthesis** *noun* COMPUT the production of spoken words by a speech synthesiser

**speed** *noun* PHYS the rate of motion over a distance in time

**speed brake** *noun* AEROSP same as **spoiler**

**speed of light** *noun* PHYS the constant speed at which light and all electromagnetic radiation travels through a vacuum, equal to $2.998 \times 10^8$ metres per second

**speed of loop** *noun* COMPUT a method of benchmarking a computer by measuring the number of loops executed in a particular amount of time

**speed of sound** *noun* PHYS the speed at which sound waves travel through a medium (NOTE: It is slower than the speed of light, so the rumble of thunder is heard after the flash of lightning from a distant storm has been seen.)

**spell** *noun* **1.** a short period ○ *take a spell at the wheel* **2.** METEOROL a short period when the weather does not change ○ *There will be some fine spells over the east of the country.* ○ *The south has experienced the longest spell of rainy weather since records were first taken.*

**spellcheck** *verb* COMPUT to check the spelling in a text by comparing it with a dictionary held in the computer

**spellchecker, spelling checker** *noun* COMPUT a program that checks the spelling in a text by comparing it with a dictionary held in the computer ○ *The program will be upgraded with a word-processor and a spelling checker.*

**spent fuel** *noun* INDUST fuel which has been used in a nuclear reactor but which is still fissile and can be reprocessed ○ *Tonnes of spent fuel are sent for reprocessing.*

**sperm** *noun* BIOL same as **spermatozoon** (NOTE: The plural is **sperm.**)

**spermat-** *prefix* BIOL same as **spermato-** (NOTE: used before vowels)

**spermatic** *adjective* BIOL referring to spermatozoa

**spermatic artery** *noun* ANAT an artery which leads into the testes. Also called **testicular artery**

**spermatid** *noun* BIOL an immature cell, formed from a spermatocyte, which becomes a spermatozoon

**spermato-** *prefix* BIOL spermatozoa

**spermatocyte** *noun* BIOL an early stage in the development of a spermatozoon

**spermatogenesis** *noun* BIOL the formation and development of spermatozoa

**spermatogonium** *noun* BIOL a cell which forms a spermatocyte

**spermatophyte** *noun* BOT a seed-producing plant such as an angiosperm or a gymnosperm

**spermatozoon** *noun* BIOL a mature male sex cell, which is capable of fertilising an ovum (NOTE: The plural is **spermatozoa.**)

COMMENT: A spermatozoon is very small and comprises a head, neck and very

long tail. It can swim by moving its tail from side to side.

**sperm bank** *noun* MED a collection of spermatozoa from donors, kept until needed for artificial insemination

**sperm count** *noun* MED a calculation of the number of spermatozoa in a quantity of semen

**spermicide** *noun* MED a substance which kills spermatozoa

**sperm whale** *noun* MARINE BIOL a large toothed whale, hunted for various substances which can be extracted from it

**sphagnum** *noun* PLANTS a type of moss which grows in bogs

**sphagnum peat** *noun* EARTH SCI a peaty soil made up of dead sphagnum moss

**sphere** *noun* an object in the shape of a ball ○ *The Earth is not a perfect sphere.*

**spherical** *adjective* shaped like a sphere ○ *The Earth is almost spherical in shape.* ○ *Drain cocks are generally simple, manually operated spherical valves.*

**spherical aberration** *noun* OPTICS distortion caused by the use of spherical surfaces in mirrors or lenses in optical equipment (NOTE: Spherical shapes do not bring light to a precise focus, and it is necessary to use a more complex parabola shape to produce precise images.)

**spherometer** *noun* MECH ENG a device for measuring the curvature of a surface

**sphincter** *noun* ANAT a ring of muscles that surrounds an opening in the body and controls what passes through it (NOTE: Sphincters are found at the exits of the stomach, bladder and anus.)

**spicule** *noun* ASTRON a slender column of relatively cool high-density gas that rises rapidly from the Sun's atmosphere and then falls back (NOTE: There can be as many as 250 000 spicules rising above the solar surface at any time.)

**spider** *noun* ZOOL one of a large group of animals, with two parts to their bodies and eight legs. Order: Araneae.

**spike** *noun* **1.** BOT a tall pointed flower head in which small flowers without stalks grow from a central flower stem **2.** ELEC a very short duration voltage pulse

**spill** PHYS *noun* a quantity of liquid which has escaped from a container or confined area ■ *verb* to escape from a container or confined area ○ *About 200 000 barrels of oil spilled into the sea.*

**spillage** *noun* **1.** PHYS the act of escaping from a container or confined area ○ *spillage of the river onto the adjacent land* **2.** a quantity of liquid which has escaped from a container or confined area

**spin** *noun* fast rotation, or an instance of this ■ *verb* to rotate rapidly or cause something to rotate rapidly ○ *spun the car off the road* ○ *The Earth spins on its axis.*

**spinal** *adjective* ANAT referring to the spine

**spinal anaesthesia** *noun* MED local anaesthesia in which an anaesthetic is injected into the cerebrospinal fluid

**spinal anaesthetic** *noun* MED an anaesthetic given by injection into the spine, which results in large parts of the body losing the sense of feeling

**spinal canal** *noun* ANAT the hollow interior of the bones (**vertebrae**) of the spine that contains the spinal cord

**spinal column** *noun* ANAT a row of connected bones (**vertebrae**) that surround the spinal cord along the back of vertebrates, including humans, and support the skeleton

**spinal cord** *noun* ANAT a cord of nerve tissue that runs down from the brain through the spinal column and gives rise to pairs of spinal nerves that connect to different parts of the body (NOTE: The central nervous system consists of the spinal cord plus the brain.)

**spinal ganglion** *noun* ANAT a cone-shaped mass of cells, the main axons of which form the posterior root of the spinal nerve

**spinal nerve** *noun* ANAT a nerve of the thirty-one pairs that lead from the spinal cord and govern mainly the trunk and limbs

**spindle** *noun* a pin or bar which rotates or on which something rotates ○ *A cup anemometer has three cups*

mounted on a spindle that are driven by the wind, causing the spindle to rotate.

**spine** *noun* **1.** ANAT the series of bones (**vertebrae**) linked together to form a flexible supporting column running from the pelvis to the skull (NOTE: The spine is made up of twenty-four ring-shaped vertebrae, with the sacrum and coccyx, separated by discs of cartilage.) **2.** BIOL a sharp projecting part of a bone **3.** BOT a pointed structure that is either a modified leaf, as in cacti, or part of a leaf or leaf base

**spiracle** *noun* **1.** INSECTS one of several small holes through which an insect breathes **2.** MARINE BIOL the breathing hole of a whale or dolphin

**spiral** *adjective* circling around a central point and constantly increasing or decreasing in size

**spiral galaxy** *noun* ASTRON a galaxy consisting of an older set of stars in the centre from which two spiral arms of gas, dust, and newer stars extend

**spirochaete** *noun* MICROBIOL a bacterium with a spiral shape

**spit** *noun* EARTH SCI a long, narrow accumulation of sand or gravel that projects from the shore into the sea

**SPL** *abbreviation* MEASURE, ACOUSTICS sound pressure level

**spleen** *noun* ANAT an organ in the left upper abdomen that stores blood, destroys old red blood cells, forms lymphocytes and filters foreign substances

**spline** *noun* ENG a groove in a shaft for meshing, or engaging with another component ○ *For satisfactory operation, an engine requires an adequate supply of oil at all bearings, gears and driving splines.*

**split baud rate** *noun* COMPUT a feature of a modem which receives data at one baud rate but transmits data at another ○ *The viewdata modem uses a 1200/75 split baud rate.*

**spoil** *noun* INDUST rubbish and waste minerals dug out of a mine ■ *verb* **1.** (*of food*) to rot or decay **2.** to destroy the quality or usefulness of something

**spoilage** *noun* FOOD INDUST the process of food becoming inedible, especially because of poor storage conditions

**spoil bank, spoil heap** *noun* INDUST a heap of waste soil produced in surface mining and deposited at the side of the worked coal seam

**spoiler** *noun* **1.** AVIAT a hinged surface on an upper wing which, when opened, decreases lift and increases drag **2.** AUTOMOT a fixed extension on the rear of a car designed to deflect air and keep the wheels on the ground at high speed

COMMENT: Aircraft spoilers are sometimes called 'speed brakes'. They are used during the descent prior to landing and immediately after landing to decrease lift and increase braking effect.

**sponge** *noun* MARINE BIOL an invertebrate animal with a porous flexible skeleton (NOTE: Most sponges live in colonies in the sea.)

**spongy** *adjective* having the open porous texture of a sponge

**spongy mesophyll** *noun* BOT a loosely packed layer of irregularly shaped green cells that forms the middle layer of a leaf

**spontaneous** *adjective* happening without an external stimulus

**spontaneous combustion** *noun* PHYS the starting of a fire by heat generated inside a material by oxidation or decay processes

**spontaneous generation** *noun* BIOL same as **abiogenesis**

**sporangium** *noun* BOT, FUNGI the organ that produces spores in some fungi, ferns and some other non-flowering plants (NOTE: The plural is **sporangia**.)

**spore** *noun* BIOL the microscopic reproductive body of fungi, bacteria and some non-flowering plants such as ferns which can survive in extremely hot or cold conditions for a long time

**sporicidal** *adjective* AGRIC able to kill spores

**sporicide** *noun* AGRIC a substance that kills spores

**sporocyte** *noun* BIOL a cell that divides to form spores

**sporophyll** *noun* BOT a leaf with spore-producing organs, e.g. the fertile frond of a fern

**sporophyte** *noun* BOT the spore-producing non-sexual phase in the life cycle of some plants such as ferns

**spp.** *abbreviation* BIOL species (*plural*) (NOTE: The singular is **sp.**)

**spreadsheet** *noun* COMPUT **1.** a program which allows calculations to be carried out on several columns of numbers **2.** a printout of calculations on wide computer stationary

**spring** *noun* **1.** EARTH SCI a place where water comes naturally out of the ground **2.** the first season of the year, following winter and before summer, when days become longer and the weather progressively warmer **3.** a metal device which, when under tension, tries to resume its previous position **4.** a rapid upwards or forwards movement ■ *verb* to make a rapid upwards or forwards movement

**spring equinox** *noun* EARTH SCI one of the two occasions in the year when the Sun crosses the celestial equator and night and day are each twelve hours long, taking place about 21 March

**spring tide** *noun* EARTH SCI a tide which occurs at the new and full moon when the influence of the Sun and Moon act together and the difference between high and low water is more than normal. Compare **neap tide**

**spring wheat** *noun* AGRIC wheat which is sown in spring and harvested towards the end of the summer

**springwood** *noun* BOT wood that develops just below the bark of trees in spring. Compare **summerwood**

**sprite** *noun* COMPUT an object which moves round the screen in computer graphics

**sprocket, sprocket wheel** *noun* ENG a wheel with teeth round it which fit into holes in a continuous strip of something

**sprout** BOT *noun* a little shoot from a plant, with a stem and small leaves ■ *verb* (*of plant*) to send out new growth

**spruce** *noun* TREES a temperate softwood tree. Genus: *Picea*.

**SPS** *abbreviation* PHYS standard pressure setting

**spur** *noun* EARTH SCI a ridge of land that descends towards a valley floor from higher land above

**spurious data** *noun* COMPUT unexpected or unwanted data or an error in a signal, often due to noise

**SPX** *abbreviation* COMPUT simplex. Opposite **duplex**

**SQL** *abbreviation* COMPUT structured query language

**squall** *noun* METEOROL a sharp gust of wind

**squally** *adjective* METEOROL (*of weather*) characterised by sharp gusts of wind

**square** *noun* MATHS **1.** a shape with four equal sides and four right angles **2.** the product of multiplying a number by itself ○ *The square of 4 is 16.* ■ *adjective* **1.** shaped like a square ○ *a square panel* **2.** MATHS referring to a unit of measurement of area representing the length of each side of a square ○ *ten square centimetres* **3.** MATHS referring to the length of the sides that an area has ○ *ten metres square*

**square bracket** *noun* a type of bracket with straight sides ( [ ] ), used in pairs

**square foot** *noun* MEASURE a measurement of area in feet

**square metre** *noun* a measurement of area in metres

**square root** *noun* MATHS a divider of a quantity that when multiplied by itself gives the quantity ○ *3 is the square root of 9.*

**square wave** *noun* ELEC a pulse that rises vertically, levels off, then drops vertically (NOTE: It is the ideal shape for a digital signal.)

**Sr** *symbol* CHEM ELEM strontium

**SSI** *abbreviation* ELECTRONICS small-scale integration

**SSL** *abbreviation* COMPUT secure sockets layer

**SSSI** *abbreviation* ENVIRON Site of Special Scientific Interest

**stabilisation lagoon** *noun* INDUST a pond used to purify sewage by allowing sunlight to fall on the mixture of sewage and water

**stabilise, stabilize** *verb* to become steady and unchanging or to make something steady and unchanging ○ *After the engine has been started, engine speed is increased to 1000 r.p.m. until cylinder head and oil temperatures have stabilised at normal operating temperatures.* ○ *Drugs stabilised her temperature.*

**stabiliser, stabilizer** *noun* AEROSP a device to improve the tendency of an aircraft to return to its original attitude after being deflected ■ *interjection* CHEM a substance that prevents a chemi-

cal change taking place ■ *noun* **1.** FOOD INDUST an artificial substance added to processed food such as sauces containing water and fat to stop the mixture from changing. Also called **stabilising agent** (NOTE: In the EU, emulsifiers and stabilisers have E numbers E322 to E495.) **2.** INDUST an artificial substance added to plastics to prevent degradation

**stabilising agent** *noun* FOOD INDUST same as **stabiliser**

**stability** *noun* **1.** the state of being stable or steady **2.** METEOROL a state of the atmosphere in which air will resist vertical displacement ○ *When air moves away from its source region, the stability of the lower atmosphere changes.*

COMMENT: Stability can be classified as three types. Positive stability is the tendency of a body to return to its original state after being displaced. Neutral stability is the tendency of a body to remain in the new position after displacement. Negative stability is the tendency of a body to continue moving away from its original position after displacement.

**stable** *adjective* **1.** steady and not easily moved ○ *a stable surface* **2.** not changing ○ *In parts of Southeast Asia, temperatures remain stable for most of the year.* **3.** CHEM referring to a chemical compound that does not react readily with other chemicals **4.** PHYS not radioactive

**stable climax** *noun* ECOL a more or less stable community of plants and animals in equilibrium with its environment, the final stage of an ecological succession

**stable population** *noun* ECOL a population which remains at the same level because births and deaths are equal

**stable state** *noun* PHYS the state of a system when no external signals are applied

**stack** *noun* **1.** COMPUT an area of temporary storage for data, registers or tasks where items are added and retrieved from the same end of the list **2.** INDUST a very tall chimney, as in a factory, usually containing several flues ○ *The use of high stacks in power stations means that pollution is now more widely spread.* Also called **chimney stack 3.** EARTH SCI a steep-sided pillar of rock which stands in the sea near a cliff

**stack gases** *plural noun* INDUST gases that are emitted from chimney stacks

**stack overflow** *noun* COMPUT an error message that is sometimes displayed when there is not enough free memory on a computer for a program's needs

**stack pointer** *noun* COMPUT an address register containing the location of the most recently stored item of data or the location of the next item of data to be retrieved. Abbreviation **SP**

**stage** *noun* one of several points in a process ○ *The text is ready for the printing stage.* ○ *We are in the first stage of running in the new computer system.*

**stain** *noun* **1.** a coloured mark on a surface **2.** BIOL a substance used to increase contrast in the colour of something such as a piece of tissue or a bacterial sample before examining it under a microscope ■ *verb* **1.** to make a coloured mark on a surface ○ *Peaty water stains the rocks brown.* **2.** BIOL to treat something such as a piece of tissue or a bacterial sample with a dye so as to increase contrast in the colour before examining it under a microscope

**staining** *noun* BIOL the treating of a piece of something such as tissue or a bacterial sample with a dye so as to increase contrast in the colour before examining it under a microscope

**stainless steel** *noun* METALL steel that includes chromium and nickel ○ *Tubing in parts of the system containing fluid at high pressure are usually made from stainless steel.*

**stalactite** *noun* EARTH SCI a long pointed growth of mineral from the ceiling of a cave, formed by the constant dripping of water which is rich in minerals

**stalagmite** *noun* EARTH SCI a long pointed growth of mineral upwards from the floor of a cave, formed by the constant dripping of water which is rich in minerals from the tip of a stalactite

**stalk** *noun* BOT **1.** the main stem of a plant which holds the plant upright **2.** a subsidiary stem of a plant, branching out from the main stem or attaching a leaf, flower or fruit

**stall** *noun* **1.** AVIAT a loss of lift caused by the breakdown of airflow over the wing when the angle of attack passes a critical point ○ *In certain configurations*

*it is possible for the buffet speed to be less than the required 7% margin ahead of the stall.* **2.** ENG the point at which opposing force overcomes that of the driving part ○ *Compressor stall can be caused by ice formation in the air intake.* ■ *verb* **1.** AVIAT to lose lift by the breakdown of airflow over the wing when the angle of attack passes a critical point ○ *Many light aircraft stall when the angle of attack exceeds 15°.* **2.** AUTOMOT to stop operating suddenly or to cause an engine to do this ○ *The car keeps stalling.*

COMMENT: An aircraft stall has nothing to do with the engine stopping. An aircraft can stall at any airspeed and in any attitude.

**stalling speed** *noun* AVIAT the speed at which the angle of attack is such that lift over the wing surface breaks down

**stamen** *noun* BOT a male part of a flower consisting of a stalk (**filament**) bearing a container (**anther**) in which pollen is produced

**stand** *noun* BOT a group of plants or trees growing together ○ *a stand of conifers*

**standalone, stand-alone** COMPUT *adjective* referring to a device or system that can operate without the need of any other devices ○ *The workstations have been networked together rather than used as standalone systems.* ■ *noun* a computer operating independently from other devices

**standard** *noun* something which has been agreed on and is used to measure other things by ○ *Water is the standard for determining relative density.* ■ *adjective* usual or officially accepted ○ *standard procedures*

**standard atmosphere** *noun* METEOROL a model atmosphere defined by pressure, temperature, density and similar factors, used in instrument calibration

**standard deviation** *noun* STATS a measure of the amount by which a set of values differs from the arithmetic mean (NOTE: It is equal to the square root of the mean of the differences' squares.)

**standard electrode** *noun* PHYS a hydrogen electrode, with a potential of zero, used to measure the potential of other electrodes

**standard electrode potential** *noun* PHYS the voltage developed by an electrode of an element placed in a solution of that element's ions, relative to that of hydrogen under standard conditions

**Standard Generalized Markup Language** noun COMPUT full form of SGML

**standard parallels** plural noun EARTH SCI (*in a conical projection*) the parallels of latitude where the cone cuts the surface

**standard pressure setting** noun PHYS 1013.25 millibars. Abbreviation SPS

**standard state** noun CHEM the pure form of a chemical that is stable under given conditions of pressure and temperature

**standard temperature and pressure** noun PHYS the standard conditions used as the basis for comparing thwe proeties of gases. Abbreviation **s.t.p., STP** (NOTE: Standard temperature is taken as 298.15 K and standard pressure as $10^5$ Pa.)

**Standard Time** noun TIME a universally adopted time for all countries within a given time zone on the Earth's surface

**standby** adjective ready for use in case of failure

**standby equipment** noun a secondary system identical to the main system, to be used if the main system breaks down

**standing wave** noun PHYS a wave motion in which the high and low points of the wave do not move. Also called **stationary wave**

**stannane** noun CHEM same as **tin (IV) hydride**

**stapes** noun ANAT a tiny stirrup-shaped bone in the middle ear, one of a set of three that help sound to pass from the eardrum to the inner ear

**staphylococcal** adjective MED caused by staphylococci

COMMENT: Staphylococcal infections are treated with antibiotics such as penicillin, or broad-spectrum antibiotics such as tetracycline.

**staphylococcal poisoning** noun MED poisoning by staphylococci which have spread in food

**staphylococcus** noun BIOL a bacterium that causes boils and food poisoning. Genus: *Staphylococcus*. (NOTE: The plural is **staphylococci**.)

**staple commodity** noun INDUST a basic food or raw material

**star** noun ASTRON an astronomical object whose temperature and density is high enough to allow energy to be generated by nuclear fusion (NOTE: Stars range in size from less than 0.1 solar masses to about 100 and most have a simple relationship linking their mass to their light output or luminosity.)

**starboard** noun, adjective (referring to) the right-hand side of an aircraft when facing forwards

**starburst galaxy** noun ASTRON a galaxy that is in a phase of intense star production

**starch** noun CHEM, FOOD a substance composed of chains of glucose units, found in green plants (NOTE: It is the usual form in which carbohydrates exist in food, especially in bread, rice and potatoes, and is broken down by the digestive process into forms of sugar.)

**starchy** adjective CHEM, FOOD containing a lot of starch ○ *starchy food*

**star classification** noun ASTRON a system of identifying stars

COMMENT: Numerous overlapping systems are used to identify stars. The oldest is simply to give conspicuous stars a name, in many cases handed down via Arab countries in the Middle Ages. The first systematic approach was pioneered in the 17th century by **Bayer** who gave the stars designations consisting of a letter of the Greek alphabet, usually starting with Alpha for the brightest, and the genitive of the name of its constellation: so Alpha Canis Minoris is the brightest star in Canis Minor. Many other systems were developed in the 20th century.

**starfish** noun MARINE BIOL one of a group of flat sea animals characterised by five arms branching from a central body

**star network** noun COMPUT a network of several machines where each node is linked individually to a central hub

**star system** noun ASTRON a group of astronomical objects such as a star and its planets or a cluster of stars that forms a distinct unit

**starter motor, starter** noun AUTOMOT in a piston engine, a small electrically operated device to turn the engine until ignition starts

**startup disk** *noun* COMPUT a floppy disk that holds the operating system and system configuration files which can, in case of hard disk failure, be used to boot the computer

**startup screen** *noun* COMPUT text or graphics displayed when an application or multimedia book is run

**starvation** *noun* MED the state of having very little or no food

**starvation diet** *noun* MED a diet that contains little nourishment and is not enough to keep a person healthy

**starve** *verb* MED to have little or no food or nourishment

**stasis** *noun* a state when there is no change, growth or movement

**statement** *noun* COMPUT **1.** an expression used to convey an instruction or define a process **2.** an instruction in a source language which is translated into several machine code instructions

**static** *adjective* **1.** not changing, moving or growing **2.** COMPUT referring to data that do not change with time **3.** COMPUT referring to a system that is not dynamic

COMMENT: Static RAM uses bistable devices such as flip-flops to store data. These take up more space on a chip than the capacitative storage method of dynamic RAM but do not require refreshing.

**static electricity** *noun* PHYS electricity that is in a static state and not flowing in a current

**static memory** *noun* COMPUT a non-volatile memory that does not require refreshing

**static object** *noun* COMPUT an object in an animation or video that does not move within the frame

**statics** *noun* MECH ENG the mechanics of forces and systems in equilibrium

**static seal** *noun* ENG a seal which is part of a non-moving component ○ *Static seals, gaskets and packing are used in many locations.*

**station** *noun* a building used for some specific purpose, a research station

**stationary** *adjective* not moving, especially after having previously been in motion

**stationary state** *noun* PHYS an energy level of a system, defined by the quantum theory

**stationary wave** *noun* PHYS same as **standing wave**

**statistical mechanics** *noun* PHYS the analysis of macroscopic systems by applying statistical principles to their microscopic constituents

**statistics** STATS *plural noun* figures relating to measurements taken from samples ○ *Population statistics show that the birth rate is slowing down.* ■ *noun* the study of measurements taken from samples

**statocyst** *noun* ZOOL an organ that maintains balance in some invertebrates such as crabs and lobsters

**stator** *noun* ENG a fixed part of a rotary machine ○ *The low pressure compressor has large rotor blades and stator blades.*

**status** *noun* **1.** the relative position of somebody or something in a group **2.** a condition that is likely to change ○ *the current status of the research programme*

**status bar** *noun* COMPUT a line at the top or bottom of a screen that gives information about the task currently being worked on. Also called **status line**

**status bit** *noun* COMPUT a single bit in a word used to provide information about the state or result of an operation

**status line** *noun* COMPUT same as **status bar**

**status poll** *noun* COMPUT a signal from a computer requesting information on the current status of a terminal

**statute mile** *noun* MEASURE same as **mile** (*technical*)

**steady** *adjective* constant and unchanging ○ *The manual test will give a steady red light.*

**steady state** *noun* **1.** a situation where the input, output and properties of a system remain constant over time **2.** COMPUT a circuit, device or program state in which no action is occurring but the system can accept an input

**steady-state theory** *noun* ASTRON a theory that the universe has always existed at a uniform density that is maintained because new matter is created continuously as the universe expands

**steady wind** *noun* METEOROL a wind of constant speed and direction

**steam** *noun* PHYS vapour that comes off boiling water and condenses in the atmosphere

**steam coal** *noun* INDUST coal with a lot of sulfur in it, which is suitable for generating steam but not for turning into coke

**steam distillation** *noun* CHEM the distillation of a liquid by passing steam through it

**steam fog**, **steam mist** *noun* METEOROL fog that forms when a cold air mass moves over a warmer body of water, giving the appearance of steam or smoke

**steam turbine** *noun* INDUST a turbine driven by steam

**stearic acid** *noun* CHEM a colourless insoluble fatty acid, used for making candles and soap. Formula: $C_{18}H_{36}O_3$.

**steel** *noun* METALL an alloy of iron, carbon and other compounds

**steelworks** *noun* INDUST a factory where steel is produced from iron ore

**steep** *adjective* **1.** sloping very sharply ○ *a steep curve* **2.** METEOROL referring to isobars that are closely spaced **3.** PHYS referring to marked changes in pressure or temperature in a relatively short horizontal distance ○ *Cooling of the air in contact with the ground at night can cause a very steep inversion of temperature at the surface.*

**steering** *noun* MECH ENG a system for guiding or directing a vehicle ○ *Steering is controlled by rudder pedals.* ○ *Most modern light aircraft have nose-wheel steering.*

**stele** *noun* BOT the core of roots and stems, consisting of vascular tissue arranged in different patterns in different types of plant

**stellar wind** *noun* ASTRON a stream of ionised particles coming from the surface of a star

**stellate ganglion** *noun* ANAT a group of nerve cells in the neck, shaped like a star

**stem** *noun* BOT **1.** the main stalk of a plant that holds it upright **2.** a subsidiary plant stalk, branching out from the main stalk or attaching a leaf, flower or fruit

**stem cell** *noun* ANAT an unspecialised cell that can either give rise to other cells of the same type indefinitely or develop into specialised cells in different parts of the organism

**steno-** *prefix* narrow or constricted

**stenohaline** *adjective* BIOL referring to an organism that cannot tolerate variations in salt concentration in its environment. Compare **euryhaline**

**stenothermous** *adjective* BIOL referring to an organism that cannot tolerate changes of temperature. Compare **eurythermous**

**steppe** *noun* EARTH SCI a wide grassy plain with no trees, especially in Eurasia (NOTE: The North American equivalent of a steppe is a **prairie**.)

**step through** *noun* COMPUT the function of a debugger that allows a developer to execute a program one instruction at a time to see where the fault lies

**steradian** *noun* MEASURE, MATHS the supplementary SI unit of measurement for solid angle. Symbol **sr**

**stereo** *adjective* ACOUSTICS same as **stereophonic**

**stereochemistry** *noun* CHEM the study of the spatial distribution of atoms in molecules and of how this affects chemical properties

**stereoisomerism** *noun* CHEM isomerism in which the atoms in molecules are present in the same order but in different spatial arrangements

**stereophonic** *adjective* ACOUSTICS recorded onto two separate channels from two separate microphone elements and played back through a pair of headphones or two speakers. Compare **monophonic**

**stereoregular** *adjective* CHEM referring to a compound in which the atoms of each molecule are arranged in a regular pattern

**stereoscopic** *adjective* PHYS referring to the effects of seeing something as three-dimensional

**stereoscopic vision** *noun* BIOL the ability of being able to judge how far away something is, because of seeing it with both eyes at the same time

**stereospecific** *adjective* CHEM referring to a chemical reaction that produces a fixed spatial arrangement of atoms

**steric effect** *noun* CHEM an effect in which the shape of a molecule changes its chemical properties

**sterile** *adjective* 1. MICROBIOL free from microorganisms 2. BIOL infertile or not able to produce offspring

**sterilise, sterilize** *verb* 1. to make something sterile by killing the microorganisms in it or on it ○ *The soil needs to be sterilised before being used for intensive greenhouse cultivation.* 2. BIOL to make an organism unable to have offspring (NOTE: This may be done by various means including drugs, surgery or irradiation.)

**sterilised milk** *noun* FOOD INDUST milk prepared for human consumption by heating in sealed airtight containers to kill all bacteria

**sterility** *noun* 1. MED the state of being free from infectious organisms 2. BIOL the inability to produce offspring

**sternum** *noun* 1. ANAT a long bone running down the front of the upper body. Also called **breastbone** 2. ZOOL the hard covering underneath a body segment of an insect or other arthropod

**steroid** *noun* BIOCHEM a fatty compound belonging to a large group that includes the human sex hormones

**sterol** *noun* BIOCHEM a steroid alcohol such as cholesterol

**Stevenson screen** *noun* METEOROL a shelter that contains meteorological instruments, arranged to give standard readings

**stiff** *adjective* 1. rigid or inflexible 2. not easily bent or turned

**stiffen** *verb* to make something rigid or inflexible ○ *Beams can be additionally stiffened in a downward direction by vertical and diagonal members.*

**stigma** *noun* BOT the part of a flower's female reproductive organ that receives the pollen grains (NOTE: It is generally located at the tip of the **style**)

**stimulate** *verb* BIOL to make an organism or organ react or respond

**stimulus** *noun* BIOL something such as light, heat or noise that makes an organism or organ react or respond (NOTE: The plural is **stimuli**.)

**sting** *noun* 1. ZOOL an organ with a sharp point, used by an insect or scorpion to pierce the skin of its victim and inject a toxic substance into the victim's bloodstream 2. ZOOL the action of using a sting 3. MED a swelling or mark produced by stinging ○ *He had several bee stings on his face.* ■ *verb* ZOOL to use a sting to pierce a victim ○ *Do not touch the scorpion or it will sting you.*

COMMENT: Stings by some insects such as tsetse flies can transmit a bacterial infection. Other insects such as bees have toxic substances which they pass into the bloodstream of the victim, causing irritating swellings.

**stochastic model** *noun* MATHS a mathematical representation of a system that includes the effects of random actions

**stock** *noun* 1. BIOL animals or plants that are derived from a common ancestor 2. AGRIC a plant with roots onto which a piece of another plant (the **scion**) is grafted 3. a supply of something held for future use ○ *Stocks of herring are being decimated by overfishing.* ■ *verb* to provide a supply of something for future use ○ *a well-stocked garden* ○ *He stocked the ponds with a rare breed of fish.*

**stock culture** *noun* BIOL a basic culture from which other cultures can be taken

**stock farming** *noun* AGRIC the rearing of livestock for sale

**stoichiometric mixture** *noun* CHEM a mix of reactants that produces a compound with no excess reactant

**stoichiometry** *noun* CHEM the branch of chemistry concerned with measuring the composition of chemical compounds or reaction mixtures in terms of the relative proportions or equivalents of different elements within them

**Stokes' law** *noun* PHYS a formula used to define the viscosity of a fluid

**stolon** *noun* 1. BOT a stem that grows along the ground and gives rise to a new plant when it roots 2. ZOOL a structure found in some simple animals, sometimes used to anchor an organism to a surface

**stoma** *noun* BOT a pore in a plant, especially in the leaves, through which carbon dioxide is taken in and oxygen is sent out (NOTE: The plural is **stomata**. Each stoma in a leaf is surrounded by a pair of guard cells, which the plant can use to close the stomata if it needs to conserve water.)

**stomach** *noun* ZOOL a bag-like organ that processes and partly digests food before passing it into the intestines

**stomata** *noun* BIOL plural of **stoma**

**stone** *noun* EARTH SCI **1.** a single small piece of rock **2.** a mineral formation

**stony** *adjective* **1.** EARTH SCI covered with stones **2.** resembling stone

**stop** *noun* **1.** the end of a movement □ **to come to a stop** to stop moving **2.** MECH ENG a component which limits the movement of a part ○ *An adjustable stop on the throttle control ensures a positive idling speed.*

**stop bit** *noun* COMPUT a transmitted bit used in asynchronous communications to indicate the end of a character. Also called **stop element**

**stop codon** *noun* GENETICS a sequence of three base pairs linking complementary strands of DNA or RNA that indicates the end of a genetic instruction for protein synthesis (NOTE: The three stop codons are thymine-adenine-guanine, thymine-adenine-adenine, and thymine-guanine-adenine.)

**stop element** *noun* COMPUT same as **stop bit**

**storage** *noun* **1.** the act of keeping something until it is needed **2.** a space or especially the amount of space for keeping something until it is needed **3.** COMPUT the memory or part of the computer system in which data or programs are kept for further use

**storage capacity** *noun* the amount of space available for storage

**storage device** *noun* COMPUT a device that can store data and then allow it to be retrieved when required

**storage media** *plural noun* COMPUT the various materials that are able to store data

**storage weight density** *noun* MEASURE, ELEC the capacity of a lithium ion battery, compared to its weight, calculated in watt-hours per kilogram

**store** *noun* **1.** a supply of something kept for future use **2.** a place where something is kept until needed **3.** COMPUT the memory or part of the computer system in which data or programs are kept for further use ■ *verb* **1.** to keep something until it is needed ○ *Whales store energy in the blubber under the skin.* **2.** COMPUT to save data, which can

then be used again as necessary ○ *Storing a page of high resolution graphics can require 3 Mb.*

**store address register** *noun* COMPUT a register in a central processing unit that contains the address of the next location to be accessed. Abbreviation **SAR**

**store and forward** *noun* COMPUT an electronic mail communications system which stores a number of messages before retransmitting them

**store data register** *noun* COMPUT a register in a central processing unit that holds data before it is processed or moved to a memory location. Abbreviation **SDR**

**stored program** *noun* COMPUT a computer program that is stored in memory

**storm** *noun* METEOROL a period of violent weather, with wind and rain or snow ○ *There was a storm during the night.* ○ *Storms swept the northern region.*

**storm beach** *noun* EARTH SCI an accumulation of coarse beach sediments built up above the high-water mark during storms

**storm centre** *noun* METEOROL a low pressure point in the centre of a cyclone

**storm cloud** *noun* METEOROL a dark-coloured cloud in which vigorous activity produces heavy rain or snow and sometimes other pronounced meteorological effects such as squalls of wind

**storm surge** *noun* METEOROL a rush of water in a tide, pushed by the strong winds in a storm

**storm swell** *noun* METEOROL a long, often massive and crestless wave or succession of waves caused by a hurricane

**STP, s.t.p.** *abbreviation* PHYS standard temperature and pressure

**STP cable** *abbreviation* COMPUT shielded twisted pair cable

**straight chain** *noun* CHEM a molecular structure, usually of a carbon compound, that has no side chains or branches

**straight fertiliser** *noun* AGRIC a fertiliser that supplies only one nutrient, as opposed to a compound fertiliser or mixed fertiliser

**straight-line coding** *noun* COMPUT a program written to avoid the use of loops and branches, providing a faster execution time

**strain** *noun* **1.** PHYS deformation caused by stress ○ *At low value of stress the plot of stress and strain is basically a straight line.* **2.** BIOL a subgroup of a species with distinct characteristics ○ *They have developed a new strain of virus-resistant rice.*

**strait** *noun* EARTH SCI a narrow passage of sea between two larger areas of sea

**strangeness** *noun* PHYS a quantum characteristic of some elementary particles

**strata** *noun* EARTH SCI plural of **stratum**

**stratification** *noun* EARTH SCI the formation of several layers in substances such as sedimentary rocks, or water in a lake or air in the atmosphere

**stratified** *adjective* PHYS formed of several layers

**stratigraphy** *noun* EARTH SCI the science of studying rock strata

**stratocumulus** *noun* METEOROL a layer of small cumulus clouds below 3000 m

**stratopause** *noun* METEOROL a thin layer of the Earth's atmosphere between the stratosphere and the mesosphere

**stratosphere** *noun* METEOROL a layer of the Earth's atmosphere, above the troposphere and the tropopause and separated from the mesosphere by the stratopause

COMMENT: The stratosphere rises from about 18 km to 50 km above the surface of the Earth. It is formed of nitrogen (80%), oxygen (18%), ozone, argon and trace gases. The ozone in it forms the ozone layer.

**stratospheric** *adjective* METEOROL referring to the stratosphere ○ *CFCs are responsible for damage to the ozone in the Earth's stratospheric zone.*

**stratum** *noun* **1.** PHYS a layer **2.** EARTH SCI a layer of rock (NOTE: The plural is **strata**.)

**stratus** *noun* METEOROL a type of grey cloud, often producing light rain

**straw** *noun* AGRIC the dry stems and leaves of cereal crops left after the grains have been removed

COMMENT: Straw can be ploughed back into the soil or is sometimes burned as stubble. It can be cut, compressed into bundles and burned as fuel for heating.

**stream** *noun* **1.** PHYS a steady current of a fluid ○ *Probes are positioned in the gas stream, so as to obtain a good average temperature reading.* **2.** EARTH SCI a narrow and shallow river

**stream erosion** *noun* ENVIRON the wearing away of soil or rock by the effect of a stream of water

**streamflow** *noun* EARTH SCI the amount and speed of water flowing in a stream

**streaming audio** *noun* COMPUT digital audio data that are continuously transmitted using a streaming protocol to provide stereo sound

**streaming protocol** *noun* COMPUT a method of sending a continuous stream of data over the Internet to provide live video or sound transmission

COMMENT: Older methods of sending continuous live data used a standard web server to transmit the data. To provide a good multimedia server, the data delivery must be regulated and ideally synchronised. There are many different standards used to deliver sound and video over the Internet, each of which allows the user or publisher to limit the delivery of data to a maximum data rate.

**streaming video** *noun* COMPUT video image data that are continuously transmitted over the Internet by using a streaming protocol to provide smooth moving images

**strength** *noun* **1.** the physical quality of being strong **2.** the ability of a material to support a load ○ *Aircraft wheels require great strength and are constructed in two halves which are bolted together after the tyre is fitted.* **3.** PHYS the degree of clarity and volume of a signal ○ *A radio wave loses strength as range increases.* **4.** CHEM the degree of dilution of a substance in solution ○ *Incorrect mixture strength may cause detonation.* **5.** PHYS the intensity of radiation ○ *The strength of the Sun's radiation varies with latitude.* **6.** the force of something such as wind ○ *The degree of air disturbance depends upon the strength of the wind and the roughness of the terrain.*

**strengthen** *verb* to make something strong or stronger, or to become strong or stronger ○ *Some alloys are hardened and strengthened by heat treatment.* □ **the wind is strengthening** the wind is increasing in speed

**strengthening** *noun* **1.** something such as a structure that helps to make something else stronger ○ *Aircraft which require large apertures in the fuselage for freight doors need increased strengthening around these areas.* **2.** the process of becoming stronger ○ *a strengthening of the wind*

**streptococcal** *adjective* MED referring to an infection caused by streptococci

**streptococcus** *noun* BIOL a bacterium belonging to a genus that grows in long chains and causes diseases such as scarlet fever, tonsillitis and rheumatic fever (NOTE: The plural is **streptococci.**)

**streptomycin** *noun* PHARM an antibiotic used against many types of infection, especially streptococcal ones

**stress** *noun* **1.** the internal force, or load per unit area of a body that resists distortion or change of shape of the body ○ *Turbine blades in the average jet engine vibrate at frequencies of 1 million per minute, and in each cycle experience stress.* **2.** a condition where an outside influence changes the composition or functioning of something ○ *Plants in dry environments experience stress due to lack of water.* ■ *verb* **1.** to subject something to stress **2.** to emphasise something ○ *It must be stressed that the description is a model and departures from it often occur.*

**striated muscle** *noun* ANAT a type of muscle tissue found in skeletal muscles whose movements are controlled by the central nervous system. Also called **striped muscle**

**striation** *noun* **1.** a pattern of parallel lines or grooves **2.** EARTH SCI a narrow groove or scratch on rock, caused by the action of a glacier

**stridulate** *verb* INSECTS to rub parts of the body together to make the chirping or grating sound typical of male crickets and grasshoppers

**string** *noun* COMPUT a series of consecutive alphanumeric characters or words that is manipulated and treated as a single unit by the computer

**string array** *noun* COMPUT an array whose elements can be strings of alphanumeric characters

**string concatenation** *noun* COMPUT the process of linking a series of strings together

**string function** *noun* COMPUT a program operation that can act on strings

**string length** *noun* COMPUT the number of characters in a string

**string name** *noun* COMPUT the identification label assigned to a string

**string variable** *noun* COMPUT a variable used in a computer language that can contain alphanumeric characters as well as numbers

**strip** *noun* a long narrow piece, usually of the same width from end to end ○ *a strip of paper* ○ *a strip of land* ■ *verb* **1.** COMPUT to remove the control data from a received message, leaving only the relevant information **2.** ENG to dismantle an engine or other device ○ *After the collision, the engine was stripped down to its component parts.* **3.** to remove a covering from something ○ *Spraying with defoliant strips the leaves off all plants.*

**strip cropping** *noun* AGRIC a method of farming in which long thin pieces of land across the contours are planted with different crops in order to reduce soil erosion

**strip cultivation** *noun* AGRIC a method of communal farming in which each family has a long thin piece or several long thin pieces of land to cultivate

**striped muscle** *noun* ANAT same as **striated muscle**

**strip mining** *noun* INDUST a form of mining where the mineral is dug from the surface instead of digging underground. ♦ **open-cast mining**

**strobe** *verb* ELECTRONICS to send a pulse, usually on the selection line of an electronic circuit ■ *noun* **1.** ELECTRONICS the pulse of an electronic circuit **2.** PHYS a high-intensity flashing beam of light that makes objects in rapidly repeating motion appear to slow down or stop

**strobilus** *noun* BOT same as **cone** (*technical*)

**stroboscope** *noun* PHYS a light that can be flashed very fast so as to make objects in rapidly repeating motion appear to slow down or stop (NOTE: It is often used to observe or photograph moving machinery or insects in flight.)

**stroke** noun **1.** ENG a movement of a piston from one end of the limit of its movement to another ○ *The connecting rod links the piston to the crankshaft and transmits the force of the power stroke from the piston to the crankshaft.* **2.** COMPUT the width in pixels of a pen or brush used to draw on-screen **3.** COMPUT the thickness of a printed character

**stroma** noun BOT the inner part of a chloroplast that contains the pigments and enzymes needed for photosynthesis

**strong** adjective **1.** physically powerful **2.** not easily damaged or broken **3.** easily perceived and distinctive **4.** having a high degree, level, intensity or concentration

**strong acid** noun CHEM an acid that is totally dissociated into its component ions in solution

**strong interaction** noun PHYS a short-range force that holds protons and neutrons together in an atomic nucleus

**strontium** noun CHEM ELEM a radioactive metallic element (NOTE: The chemical symbol is **Sr**; the atomic number is **38** and the atomic weight is **87.62**.)

**strontium-90** noun CHEM an isotope of strontium that is formed in nuclear reactions and, because it is part of the fallout of nuclear explosions, can enter the food chain, affecting in particular animals' bones

**strontium hydroxide** noun CHEM a strong base formed when strontium monoxide dissolves in water. Formula: $Sr(OH)_2$.

**strontium monoxide** noun CHEM an amorphous solid that dissolves in water to form strontium hydroxide. Formula: SrO.

**structural** adjective referring to the structure of something ○ *The structural limitations must never be exceeded.*

**structural failure** noun the breaking of part of the structure of something

**structural formula** noun CHEM an expanded chemical formula that gives information about the arrangement of atoms and bonds in a molecule

**structural gene** noun GENETICS a gene that controls the synthesis of a protein required for the cell's own use

**structural geology** noun EARTH SCI the scientific study of the structure and distribution of the rocks forming the Earth's crust

**structural isomer** noun CHEM one of two or more related chemical compounds that have the same molecular formula but different structural formulae

**structure** noun **1.** a whole or a system that is made of different parts **2.** something that has been constructed ○ *a glass and steel structure* **3.** the different parts that make up a whole, or the arrangement of parts ○ *the structure of DNA* ○ *Aircraft structure serves the same purpose for an aircraft as the skeleton for a human body.* ■ *verb* to organise or arrange something in a systematic way ○ *You first structure a document to meet your requirements and then fill in the blanks.*

**structured cabling** noun COMPUT the use of UTP cable feeding into hubs designed in such a way that it is easy to trace and repair cable faults and also to add new stations or more cable

**structured programming** noun COMPUT a well-ordered and logical technique of assembling programs

**structured query language** noun COMPUT a simple, commonly used, standard database programming language which is only used to create queries to retrieve data from a database. Abbreviation **SQL**

**structured wiring** noun ELEC ENG a planned installation of all the cables that will be required in an office or building for computer networks and telephone

**strut** noun ENG a bar or rod used to strengthen a structure against forces from the side ○ *A strut is designed to withstand compressive loads.*

**strychnine** noun CHEM a very poisonous alkaloid substance made from the seeds of a tropical tree

**STS** abbreviation GENETICS sequence tagged site

**stub** noun COMPUT a short program routine that contains comments to describe the executable code that will eventually be inserted into the routine

**stubble** noun AGRIC the short stems left in the ground after a crop of wheat or other cereal has been cut

**stuck beacon** *noun* COMPUT an error condition in which a station continuously transmits beacon frames

**stunt** *verb* to reduce the growth of something ○ *The poor soil stunts the growth of the trees.*

**style** *noun* **1.** COMPUT the specification of the font, point size, colour, spacing and margins of text in a formatted document **2.** BOT the elongated structure that carries the stigma at its tip in many flowers

**style sheet** *noun* COMPUT a template that can be formatted in advance to generate automatically the style or layout of a document such as a manual or a newsletter

**styrene** *noun* CHEM a flammable liquid hydrocarbon that polymerises easily, used in the manufacture of synthetic rubber, plastic and polystyrene. Formula: $C_8H_8$.

**sub-** *prefix* **1.** less important than **2.** lower than

**subacute** *adjective* MED referring to a disease or condition that is between acute and chronic

**subaddress** *noun* COMPUT a peripheral identification code, used to access one peripheral, followed by address data to access a location within the peripheral's memory

**subarctic region** *noun* GEOG a region near to, but south of, the Arctic

**subatomic particle** *noun* PHYS same as **elementary particle**

**sub-beam** *noun* PHYS (*of directional radar*) a less important or minor beam ○ *A lobe is one of two, four or more sub-beams that form a directional radar beam.*

**subclass** *noun* **1.** BIOL a subgroup of a class in the scientific classification of organisms **2.** COMPUT a number of data items related to one item in a master class

**subclavian artery** *noun* ANAT one of two arteries branching from the aorta on the left and from the innominate artery on the right, continuing into the brachial arteries and supplying blood to each arm

**subclimax** *noun* ECOL a stage in the development of a plant community where development stops before reaching its final stable state or **climax**

**subcloud layer** *noun* METEOROL the air immediately underneath a cloud layer

**subcontinent** *noun* EARTH SCI a very large land mass, that is a distinct part of a continent ○ *the Indian subcontinent*

**subcritical** *adjective* PHYS referring to a chain reaction that cannot sustain itself

**subculture** *noun* BIOL a culture of microorganisms or cells that is grown from another culture

**subcutaneous injection** *noun* MED same as **hypodermic injection**

**subcutaneous tissue** *noun* ANAT the layer of tissue below the dermis in the skin

**subdirectory** *noun* COMPUT a directory of disk contents contained within the main directory

**subdivision** *noun* BIOL a subgroup of a division in the scientific classification of organisms

**subdomain** *noun* COMPUT a second level of addressing on the Internet that usually refers to a department name within a larger organisation

**subdominant** *adjective* ECOL referring to a species that is not as important as the dominant species

**subduct** *verb* to pull something underneath ○ *The oceanic crust is being subducted under the continents which surround it.*

**subduction** *noun* EARTH SCI the process by which a tectonic plate such as the oceanic crust is slowly being pulled under another plate

**sublimate** *noun* CHEM the deposit left when a vapour condenses ■ *verb* **1.** PHYS to change from solid to vapour without passing through a liquid state **2.** PSYCHIAT to convert violent emotion into an action which is not antisocial

**sublime** *verb* CHEM same as **sublimate**

**subliminal** *adjective* BIOL referring to a stimulus that is too slight to be noticed by the senses

**sublingual** *adjective* ANAT situated under the tongue

**sublittoral** *adjective* EARTH SCI further inland from a shore than the littoral zone

**sublittoral plant** *noun* BOT a plant that grows near the sea but not on the shore

**submandibular** *adjective* ANAT situated under the lower jaw

**submandibular ganglion** *noun* ANAT a ganglion associated with the lingual nerve, relaying impulses to the submandibular and sublingual salivary glands

**submarine** *adjective* MARINE BIOL situated or existing beneath the sea ○ *Shellfish collect round warm submarine vents.*

**submenu** *noun* COMPUT a secondary menu displayed as a choice from a menu

**submerge** *verb* to cover something with water or to become covered with water ○ *The coast is dangerous, with rocks submerged at intervals along it.*

**submicroscopic** *adjective* too small to be seen with an ordinary microscope

**submit button** *noun* COMPUT a button displayed on a webpage that sends information entered by a user on a web form to a program running on a web server for processing

**subnet** *noun* COMPUT a self-contained part of a large network, usually an independently managed part of the Internet

**subnet address** *noun* COMPUT part of an IP address that identifies a subnet that is connected to a larger network. Also called **subnet number** (NOTE: The first part of the IP address identifies the network, the next part identifies the subnet and the last part identifies a single host server.)

**subnet mask** *noun* COMPUT a filter that is used to select the portion of an IP address that contains the subnet address

**subnet number** *noun* COMPUT same as **subnet address**

**subnotebook** *noun* COMPUT a very small portable computer that is smaller and lighter than a standard full-size notebook or laptop computer

**subprogram** *noun* COMPUT **1.** same as **subroutine 2.** a program called up by a main program

**subroutine** *noun* COMPUT a section of a program that performs a required function and can be called upon at any time from inside the main program. Also called **subprogram**

COMMENT: A subroutine is executed by a call instruction that directs the processor to its address. When finished it returns to the instruction after the call instruction in the main program.

**subroutine call** *noun* COMPUT a computer programming instruction that directs control to a subroutine

**sub-Saharan** *noun* GEOG referring to the area south of the Sahara ○ *Rural woodfuel supplies are falling in many countries of sub-Saharan Africa.*

**subscale** *noun* the secondary scale on an instrument ○ *The barometric pressure is set on the subscale and the altimeter main scale displays height or altitude.*

**subscript** *noun* PRINTING a small character that is printed lower than the other characters. ▶ **superscript** (NOTE: Subscripts are used in chemical formulae: $CO_2$)

**subscripted variable** *noun* COMPUT an element in an array that is identified by a subscript

**subset** *noun* MATHS a small set of data items that forms part of another larger set

**subside** *verb* **1.** to go down or to become less violent ○ *After the rainstorms passed, the flood waters gradually subsided.* **2.** to sink or fall to a lower level ○ *The office block is subsiding owing to the shrinkage of the clay it is built on.*

**subsidence** *noun* **1.** (*of a piece of ground or a building*) the process of sinking or falling to a lower level ○ *Subsidence caused by the old mine shaft closed the main road.* **2.** METEOROL a gradual downward movement of a mass of air

**subsidence inversion** *noun* METEOROL a phenomenon produced when a mass of air gradually sinks and becomes warmer

**subsistence** *noun* BIOL the smallest amount of food needed to stay alive

**subsistence farming** *noun* AGRIC the activity of growing just enough crops to feed the farmer's family and having none left to sell

**subsoil** *noun* EARTH SCI a layer of soil under the topsoil (NOTE: The subsoil contains little organic matter but chemical substances from the topsoil leach into it.)

**subsoil water** noun EARTH SCI water held in the subsoil

**subspecies** noun BIOL a group of organisms that is part of a species but which shows slight differences from the main group, with which it can still interbreed

**substance** noun 1. CHEM material of a particular type ○ *a sticky substance* ○ *a harmful substance* ○ *toxic substances* 2. MED a drug, especially an illegal drug ○ *an addictive substance*

**substance P** noun BIOCHEM a neurotransmitter involved in pain pathways

**substitute** noun a thing used in place of another ■ verb to replace one thing with another ○ *Farmers have been told to plough up pastureland and substitute woodlots.*

**substitution** noun the replacement of one thing by another ○ *the substitution of natural fibres by synthetic materials*

**substitution error** noun COMPUT an error made by a scanner which mistakes one character or letter for another

**substitution reaction** noun CHEM a chemical reaction that replaces an atom in a molecule with another atom. Also called **displacement reaction**

**substitution table** noun COMPUT a list of characters or codes that are to be inserted instead of received codes

**substitution therapy** noun MED the treatment of a condition by using a different drug from the one used before

**substrata** noun EARTH SCI plural of **substratum**

**substrate** noun 1. ELECTRONICS the base material on which an integrated circuit is constructed 2. CHEM a substance that is acted on by a catalyst such as an enzyme 3. BIOL the matter or surface on which an organism lives

**substratum** noun EARTH SCI a layer of rock beneath the topsoil and subsoil (NOTE: The plural is **substrata**.)

**subtend** verb to be opposite to and delimit something ○ *The angle subtended by an arc equal to one 360th part of the circumference of a circle is called 1 degree.*

**subtract** verb 1. to deduct or take away something from a larger unit 2. MATHS to deduct or take away one number or quantity from another to calculate

a remainder ○ *6 subtracted from 10 equals 4 (10 − 6 = 4).*

**subtraction** noun MATHS the operation of taking away or deducting one number or quantity from another to calculate a remainder ○ *The major arithmetic operations are addition, subtraction, multiplication and division.*

**subtrahend** noun MATHS in a subtraction operation, the number to be subtracted from the minuend

**subtropical** adjective EARTH SCI referring to the subtropics ○ *The islands enjoy a subtropical climate.* ○ *Subtropical plants grow in the sheltered parts of the coast.*

**subtropical high** noun METEOROL an area of high pressure normally found in the subtropics

**subtropics** plural noun EARTH SCI an area between the tropics and the temperate zone

**sub-zero** adjective PHYS, METEOROL below zero degrees ○ *a week of sub-zero temperatures* ○ *In sub-zero conditions sublimation will occur when air is cooled below the frost point, producing a deposit of ice crystals.*

**succession** noun ECOL a series of stages, one after the other, by which a group of organisms living in a community reaches its final stable state or **climax**

**successional cropping** noun AGRIC the growing of several crops one after the other during the same growing season

**successive** adjective following on one after another

**succinic acid** noun CHEM a colourless water-soluble acid used in the manufacture of lacquers, perfumes and pharmaceuticals. Formula: $C_4H_6O_4$. (NOTE: It is derived from amber and from plant and animal tissues or is artificially synthesised.)

**succulent** noun BOT a plant such as a cactus that has fleshy leaves or stems in which it stores water

**sucrose** noun BIOCHEM a sugar that is abundant in many plants, which consists of one molecule of glucose joined to one of fructose

**suction** noun PHYS the force that causes a fluid or solid to be drawn into a space because of the difference between the external and internal pressures ○ *In* *a fuel injection system, fuel is induced into the inlet port or combustion chamber by a pump rather than the suction caused by the venturi of a carburettor.*

**sudden warming** *noun* METEOROL a rapid rise in the temperature of the stratosphere, which occurs at the beginning of spring

**sufficiency** *noun* a large enough amount of something

**sufficient** *adjective* large enough as an amount of something

**suffix** *noun* an addition to the end of a word to create a new word ○ *Apart from cirrus and stratus, which are complete names, all layer cloud names consist of a prefix according to height of base, and a suffix according to shape.*

**suffix notation** *noun* MATHS the system of writing mathematical operations in a logical way, so that the symbol appears after the numbers to be acted upon

**suffrutescent, suffruticose** *adjective* BOT referring to a perennial plant that has a woody base to its stem and does not die down to ground level in winter

**sugar** *noun* 1. FOOD INDUST same as **sucrose** 2. CHEM any chemical of the saccharide group

**sugar-free** *noun* FOOD INDUST not containing sugar

**sugar substitute** *noun* FOOD INDUST a sweetener such as saccharin, used in place of sugar

**sulfate, sulphate** *verb* ELEC to cause a layer of lead sulfate to form on the plates of an accumulator

**sulfate aerosol, sulphate aerosol** *noun* CHEM particulate matter consisting of sulfur compounds formed by the interaction of sulfur dioxide and sulfur trioxide with other compounds in the atmosphere ○ *Sulfate aerosols are injected into the atmosphere from the combustion of fossil fuels and the eruption of volcanoes.*

**sulfate of ammonia, sulphate of ammonia** *noun* AGRIC same as **ammonium sulfate**

**sulfate of potash, sulphate of potash** *noun* AGRIC same as **potassium sulfate**

**sulfide, sulphide** *noun* CHEM an ion of sulfur present in chemical compounds and mineral ores

**sulfite, sulphite** *noun* CHEM a salt of sulfuric acid that forms part of several chemical compounds which are used in processing paper

**sulfonation, sulphonation** *noun* CHEM the incorporation of sulfonic acid into an organic substance

**sulfonator, sulphonator** *noun* CHEM an apparatus for adding sulfur dioxide to water to remove excess chlorine

**sulfonic acid, sulphonic acid** *noun* CHEM any strong organic acid containing the group $SO_2OH$, used in the manufacture of dyes and pharmaceuticals

**sulfonium compound, sulphonium compound** *noun* CHEM any organic compound with the general formula $R_3SX$, where R is an organic group and X is an electronegative element

**sulfur, sulphur** *noun* CHEM ELEM a yellow non-metallic chemical element that is essential to biological life, used in the manufacture of sulfuric acid and in the vulcanisation of rubber (NOTE: The chemical symbol is **S**; the atomic number is **16** and the atomic weight is **32.06**. The usual and recommended scientific spelling of sulphur and derivatives such as sulphate, sulphide and sulphonate is with an -f-, though the spelling with -ph- is still common in general usage.)

**sulfur cycle, sulphur cycle** *noun* ECOL the process by which sulfur flows from the environment, through organisms and back to the environment again

**sulfur dioxide, sulphur dioxide** *noun* CHEM an unpleasant-smelling gas formed when sulfur is burnt with oxygen, used in disinfectants and as a food preservative. Formula: $SO_2$.

COMMENT: Sulfur dioxide produced from burning coal or oil is an important cause of smog. Today the atmospheric concentration of sulfur dioxide has fallen with the reduction in the use of coal and this type of pollution has been replaced by nitrogen dioxide produced by car exhausts.

**sulfur hexafluoride, sulphur hexafluoride** *noun* CHEM a very powerful greenhouse gas, used mostly in electrical transmission and distribution systems. Formula: $SF_6$.

**sulfuric acid, sulphuric acid** *noun* CHEM a strong acid that exists as a colourless oily corrosive liquid and is made by reacting sulfur trioxide with water. It is used in batteries and in the manufacture of fertilisers, explosives, detergents, dyes and many other chemicals. Formula: $H_2SO_4$.

**sulfurous acid, sulphurous acid** noun CHEM a weak unstable acid made by dissolving sulphur dioxide in water, used as a disinfectant, food preservative and bleaching agent. Formula: $H_2SO_3$.

**sulfur oxide, sulphur oxide** noun CHEM sulfur dioxide or sulfur trioxide, both of which are present in sulfur pollution

**sulfur trioxide, sulphur trioxide** noun CHEM a corrosive white solid that readily forms sulfuric acid when dissolved in water. Formula: SO3. (NOTE: It is formed when fossil fuels burn, and dissolves in water droplets in the air forming sulfuric acid.)

**sullage** noun **1.** EARTH SCI mud brought down by mountain streams **2.** ENVIRON the liquid waste from a building

**sum** noun MATHS the result of two or more numbers added together ○ *When the component velocities act in the same direction, the resultant velocity is equal to the sum of their speeds in that direction.*

**summation check** noun COMPUT an error detection check performed by adding together the characters received and comparing with the required total

**summer** noun the season following spring and before autumn, when the weather is warmest, the Sun is highest in the sky and most plants flower and set seed ■ verb to spend the summer in a place ○ *The birds summer on the shores of the lake.*

**summer solstice** noun ASTRON 21 June, the longest day in the northern hemisphere, when the Sun is as its furthest point south of the equator

**summerwood** noun BOT dense wood formed by trees during the later part of the growing season. Compare **springwood**

**summit** noun EARTH SCI the highest point of a hill or mountain ○ *The climber reached the summit of the mountain.*

**sump** noun AUTOMOT the oil reservoir of a piston engine, situated at its base ○ *The oil level in the sump or tank is normally checked after the engine has been stopped for a time.*

**sun** noun ASTRON **1.** sunlight or the rays of the sun ○ *sitting in the sun* **2.** another spelling of **Sun**

**Sun** noun ASTRON a very hot star round which the Earth and other planets orbit and which gives energy in the form of light and heat

COMMENT: The Sun dominates the solar system and contains most of its matter. It has a surface temperature of some 6000 K and is about 329 ,000 times as massive as the Earth. The Sun is notable among other stars for being solitary rather than part of a multiple system. The energy source that powers the Sun is now known to be nuclear fusion. It is a variable star with regular cycles of sunspot activity over 22 years. The variation in its energy output is closely linked to its intense magnetism, which is also involved in other surface and atmosphere effects.

**sunlight** noun ASTRON the light from the sun

COMMENT: Sunlight is essential to give the body vitamin D. However, excessive exposure to the ultraviolet radiation in sunlight will not simply turn white skin brown, but may also burn the surface of the skin so badly that the skin dies and pus forms beneath. There is evidence that constant exposure to the sun can cause cancer (**melanoma**) of white skin. Depletion of the ozone layer in the atmosphere may increase the incidence of skin cancer.

**sunquake** noun ASTRON a violent seismic event on the Sun associated with solar flares

**sunrise** noun ASTRON the time when the Sun appears above the eastern horizon

**sunset** noun ASTRON the time when the Sun disappears below the western horizon

**sunspot** noun ASTRON a darker patch on the surface of the Sun, caused by a stream of gas shooting outwards

**sunstroke** noun MED a serious condition caused by excessive exposure to strong sunlight or to hot conditions, in which the patient becomes dizzy and has a high body temperature but does not perspire

**super-** prefix **1.** above **2.** extremely

**super bit mapping** noun COMPUT an extension to the Red Book CD-Audio specification in which studio-quality 20-bit sound samples are stored in the 16-bit data format used by CD-Audio. Abbreviation **SBM**

**supercharge** verb MECH ENG to increase the power of an engine by using a supercharger ○ *A supercharged engine delivers greater power than a non-supercharged engine of the same size.*

**supercharger** noun MECH ENG a blower or compressor, usually driven by the engine, for supplying air under high pressure to the cylinders of an internal combustion engine ○ *The function of the supercharger is to increase the power output and maintain sea-level conditions at altitude.*

**supercluster** noun ASTRON a grouping of clusters of galaxies. Also called **supergalaxy**

**supercomputer** noun COMPUT a very powerful mainframe computer used for high-speed mathematical tasks

**superconductivity** noun PHYS the ability of some solids to conduct electric current with almost no internal resistance at very low temperatures

**supercool** verb PHYS to reduce the temperature of a substance below its usual freezing point without freezing actually occurring

**supercooled** adjective cooled below freezing point without solidification ○ *Nimbo-stratus cloud is composed of liquid water droplets some of which are supercooled.*

**supercooled fog** noun METEOROL fog that has cooled below freezing point, but still remains liquid

COMMENT: Supercooled fog contributes to the phenomenon known as freezing fog, where droplets of fog remain liquid in the air even though the temperature is below 0 °C, but freeze into hoar frost as soon as they touch a surface.

**supercritical** adjective PHYS referring to a nuclear chain reaction that has become explosively self-sustaining

**superficial** adjective **1.** on or near the surface ○ *superficial scratches* **2.** not thorough ○ *a superficial study of the results* ○ *superficial knowledge* **3.** apparent but not real ○ *a superficial resemblance*

**superficial vein** noun ANAT a vein that is near the surface of the skin

**supergalaxy** noun ASTRON same as **supercluster**

**supergene** noun GENETICS a set of genes that are close together on a chromosome, function as a unit and are rarely inherited separately

**supergiant** noun ASTRON an extremely large brilliant star that has a luminosity thousands of times greater than that of the Sun (NOTE: The stars Rigel and Betelgeuse are supergiants.)

**superheat** verb PHYS to heat a liquid to a temperature above its boiling point without causing it to vaporise

**superheated** adjective INDUST referring to steam that is heated to a high temperature in a power station

COMMENT: Steam made by heating water in a boiler is passed through the furnace a second time to heat it again. This superheated steam is produced under very high pressure to turn the first, or high-pressure, turbine in a power generating plant.

**superheater** noun INDUST a section of a power station boiler where steam is heated to a higher temperature

**superheterodyne receiver** noun PHYS a radio receiver that operates using the method by which the frequency of the carrier wave is changed in the receiver to an intermediate frequency

**superior conjunction** noun ASTRON the position of an astronomical object when it is opposite Earth on the far side of the Sun

**superior planet** noun ASTRON a planet that is further from the Sun than the Earth (NOTE: The superior planets are Mars, Jupiter, Saturn, Uranus, Neptune and Pluto.)

**super large scale integration** noun ELECTRONICS an integrated circuit with more than 100 000 components. Abbreviation **SLSI**

**supermassive black hole** noun ASTRON an extremely large black hole with a mass ranging from a few million to more than several billion solar masses (NOTE: Supermassive black holes are believed to be at the centre of many large galaxies, driving quasar formation.)

**supernatant liquid** noun CHEM the liquid above a precipitate or sediment

**supernova** *noun* ASTRON the catastrophic and explosive disruption of a heavy star late in its evolution

COMMENT: Some supernovae are bright enough to outshine the galaxy in which they erupt. Supernovae are now known to be major sources of material erupted into interstellar space. They are the origin of all the universe's heavy elements, those beyond iron in atomic weight, as well as producers of intense cosmic rays and severe shock waves.

**superorder** *noun* BIOL one of the groups in the scientific classification of organisms, ranking next above order

**superorganism** *noun* ECOL a group or community of individual organisms that functions as a single unit (NOTE: A forest, a termite colony and even human society can all be viewed as superorganisms.)

**superphosphate** *noun* AGRIC a chemical compound formed from calcium phosphate and sulfuric acid, used as a fertiliser

**supersaturated** *adjective* **1.** PHYS referring to air which contains more moisture than the amount required to saturate it **2.** CHEM referring to a solution that contains more solute than the amount required to saturate it

**superscript** *noun* PRINTING a small character that is printed higher than the other characters. ♦ **subscript** (NOTE: Superscripts are used in mathematics: $10^5$)

**supersonic** *adjective* PHYS faster than the speed of sound ○ *For sustained supersonic flight, tank insulation is necessary to reduce the effect of kinetic heating.*

**superstring theory** *noun* PHYS a development of the **general theory of relativity** that postulates the existence of multi-dimensional defects in spacetime, left over from the early universe

**super VGA** *noun* COMPUT an enhancement to the standard VGA graphics display system that allows resolutions of up to 800 x 600 pixels with 16 million colours. Abbreviation **SVGA**

**supervisory program** *noun* COMPUT a master program in a computer system that controls the execution of other programs. Also called **executive control program**

**superweed** *noun* BIOTECH a weed that might evolve as a hybrid of ordinary weeds and genetically modified plants and be hard to eradicate

**supplement** *noun* **1.** MATHS an angle or arc that when added to a given angle or arc makes 180° or a semicircle **2.** HEALTH a substance taken to make up for a real or supposed deficiency in the diet **3.** something added in order to make something more complete ■ *verb* to add to something in order to make it more complete ○ *The main power plant fire detection system should contain an audible warning device to supplement the visual indication.*

**supplementary** *adjective* extra or additional ○ *supplementary information*

**supplementary angle** *noun* MATHS an angle that when added to a given angle makes 180° or a semicircle

**supply** *noun* **1.** the provision of something that is needed ○ *The reservoir ensures a good supply of water.* **2.** a stock of something that is needed ○ *a year's supply of chemicals* **3.** the act or process of providing something that is needed ○ *the supply of power to the building* ■ *verb* to provide something that is needed ○ *The computer was supplied by a recognised dealer.*

**support** *verb* **1.** to hold the weight of something ○ *to support the saplings with stakes* **2.** BIOL to provide what is necessary for organisms to live ○ *These wetlands support a natural community of plants, animals and birds.*

**support chip** *noun* COMPUT a dedicated circuit that carries out an additional function or a standard function very rapidly, so speeding up the processing time ○ *The maths support chip can be plugged in here.*

**suppressor** *noun* ELEC, ELECTRONICS a device, e.g. a resistor or grid, used in an electrical or electronic system to reduce unwanted currents ○ *A suppressor improves the quality of the signal.*

**supra-** *prefix* above or over

**suprarenal gland** *noun* ANAT same as **adrenal gland**

**surf** *verb* COMPUT to explore a website looking at the webpages in no particular order, but simply moving between pages by using the links

**surface** *noun* **1.** the outer covering or layer of something **2.** the top part of something ○ *the surface of the liquid* **3.** EARTH SCI the Earth's surface or ground level

**surface-active agent** *noun* CHEM same as **surfactant**

**surface air temperature** *noun* the temperature recorded in the shade at a height just above ground level

**surface area** *noun* the total of all the outer surfaces of an object ○ *a surface area of 10 square metres*

**surface drainage** *noun* EARTH SCI the removal of surplus water from an area of land by means of ditches and channels

**surface evaporation** *noun* PHYS evaporation of water from the surface of a body of water

**surface front** *noun* METEOROL a front at the surface of the Earth ○ *The cirrus cloud can be 900 miles ahead of the surface front with a rain belt as wide as 200 miles.*

**surface heating** *noun* EARTH SCI the heating of the ground by the Sun

**surface-mount technology** *noun* ELEC a method of manufacturing circuit boards in which the electronic components are bonded directly onto the surface of the board rather than being inserted into holes and soldered into place ○ *Surface-mount technology is faster and more space-efficient than soldering.* Abbreviation **SMT**

**surface runoff** *noun* EARTH SCI a flow of rainwater, melted snow or excess fertiliser from the surface of land into streams and rivers

**surface soil** *noun* EARTH SCI same as **topsoil**

**surface tension** *noun* PHYS the appearance of a film on the surface of a liquid caused by the attraction between its molecules

**surface water** *noun* EARTH SCI water after rain that flows across the surface of the soil as a stream and drains into rivers rather than seeping into the soil itself

**surface wind** *noun* METEOROL a wind that blows across the land surface, rather than higher in the atmosphere

**surfactant** *noun* CHEM a substance that reduces surface tension. Also called **surface-active agent**

**surge** *noun* ELEC a sudden increase in electrical power. Also called **power**

**surge** ■ *verb* PHYS to move with force like a wave ○ *If combustion pressure increases above compressor outlet pressure, the airflow will reverse in direction and surge forward through the compressor.*

COMMENT: Power surges can burn out circuits before you have time to pull the plug. A surge protector between the computer and the wall outlet helps prevent damage.

**surge arrester** *noun* ELEC a device to prevent surges of current in an electric system

**surge protector** *noun* ELEC an electronic device that cuts off the power supply to sensitive equipment if it detects a power surge that could cause damage

**surplus** *adjective* excess ○ *Surplus water will flow away in storm drains.* ■ *noun* something that is more than is needed ○ *produced a surplus of wheat*

**survey** *noun* **1.** an investigation or inspection **2.** EARTH SCI the taking of measurements of the height of buildings or mountains and the length of roads, rivers and other features in order to make a detailed plan or map **3.** EARTH SCI a document, plan or map showing the results of an investigation or of the measurements taken ■ *verb* to carry out a survey of something

**survival** *noun* BIOL the situation of continuing to live, especially if conditions are difficult

**survival of the fittest** *noun* BIOL same as **natural selection**

**survival rate** *noun* BIOL the number of organisms that continue to live ○ *The survival rate of newborn babies has begun to fall.*

**survive** *verb* BIOL **1.** to continue to live after an event ○ *The plants survive even the hottest desert temperatures.* ○ *After the fire, only a few trees survived.* **2.** to overcome a difficult situation

**survivor** *noun* BIOL an organism that continues to live when others have died

**survivorship** *noun* BIOL the number of individuals of a population surviving at a specific time

**survivorship curve** *noun* BIOL a graph showing the number of individuals of a population that survive to a particular age

**suspend** *verb* **1.** to hang something from above **2.** CHEM to hold particles in a liquid or in air ○ *an aerosol of suspended particles*

**suspension** *noun* **1.** the state of being suspended **2.** CHEM a liquid with solid particles in it, not settling to the bottom nor floating on the surface

**suspensory ligament** *noun* ANAT a ligament that keeps an organ or body part in place (NOTE: It most commonly refers to the ligament that supports the lens of the eye.)

**sustain** *verb* **1.** to provide the necessary conditions for something ○ *The land is fertile enough to sustain a wide variety of fauna and flora.* **2.** to support something from below **3.** to continue doing something in spite of adverse circumstances or events

**sustainability** *noun* ENVIRON the ability of a process to maintain natural resources and leave the environment in good order for future generations

COMMENT: Sustainability has been described as 'meeting the needs of the present without compromising the ability of future generations to meet their own needs', but there is no internationally agreed definition of sustainability.

**sustainable** *adjective* ENVIRON not depleting or damaging natural resources ○ *hardwood from a sustainable source*

**sustainable agriculture** *noun* AGRIC environmentally friendly methods of farming that allow the production of crops or livestock without damage to the farm ecosystem

**sustainable development** *noun* ENVIRON development that balances the satisfaction of people's immediate interests and the protection of future generations' interests

**sustainable yield** *noun* ENVIRON the greatest productivity that can be derived from a renewable resource without depleting the supply in a given area

**Sv** *symbol* MEASURE, PHYS sievert

**SVGA** *abbreviation* COMPUT super VGA

**swallow** *verb* PHYSIOL to take food into the stomach through the mouth and throat

**swallow hole** *noun* EARTH SCI a hole that forms in limestone rock as rainwater drains through it, dissolving minerals in the rock and sometimes forming underground caverns

**swamp** *noun* EARTH SCI an area of permanently wet land and the plants that grow on it

**swampland** *noun* EARTH SCI an area of land covered with swamp

**swampy** *adjective* EARTH SCI referring to land that is permanently wet

**swap** *verb* COMPUT to stop using one program, put it into store temporarily, run another program, and when that is finished, return to the first one

**swap file** *noun* COMPUT a file stored on the hard disk used as a temporary storage area for data held in RAM, to provide virtual memory

**swarm** ZOOL *noun* a large number of insects such as bees or locusts flying as a group ■ *verb* (*of insects*) to fly in a large group

**swash** *noun* EARTH SCI a rush of water up a beach from a breaking wave

**sweat** *noun* **1.** PHYSIOL a salty liquid secreted by glands onto the skin's surface as a means of reducing body heat **2.** PHYS drops of liquid generated on a surface, usually by condensation of water vapour from the air

**sweet chestnut** *noun* TREES a European hardwood tree grown for its nuts and timber. Latin name: *Castanea sativa.*

**sweetener** *noun* FOOD INDUST an artificial substance such as saccharin added to food to make it sweet

**swidden farming** *noun* AGRIC same as **slash and burn agriculture**

**swim** *verb* COMPUT (*of computer graphics*) to move slightly owing to a faulty display unit

**swim bladder** *noun* ZOOL same as **air bladder**

**swirl** *noun* **1.** a movement with a twisting motion **2.** an eddy ○ *Swirls of smoke came out of the engine.*

**swirl chamber** *noun* AUTOMOT a small chamber in the cylinder head to promote swirl ○ *The usual method of atomising the fuel is to pass it through a swirl chamber, so converting its pressure energy to kinetic energy.*

**switch** *noun* **1.** ELEC a mechanical or solid state device that can electrically connect or isolate two or more lines ○ *There is an on/off switch on the front* *panel*. **2.** COMPUT an additional character entered on the same line as the program command, which affects how the program runs ○ *Add the switch '/W' to the DOS command DIR and the directory listing will be displayed across the screen.* **3.** COMPUT a point in a computer program where control can be passed to one of a number of choices ■ *verb* ELEC to connect or disconnect two lines by activating a switch

**switching** *noun* COMPUT a constant update of connections between changing sinks and sources in a network

**switching centre** *noun* ELECTRONICS a point in a communications network where messages can be switched to and from the various lines and circuits that end there

**switching circuit** *noun* ELECTRONICS an electronic circuit that can direct messages from one line or circuit to another in a switching centre

**switchmode** *noun* ELEC a way of converting one form of electricity to another by rapidly switching it on and off and feeding it through a transformer to produce a voltage change

**switch off** *verb* ELEC to disconnect the power supply to a device

**switch on** *verb* ELEC to start to provide power to a system by using a switch to connect the power supply lines to the circuit

**switch over** *verb* to start using an alternative device when the primary one becomes faulty

**sycamore** *noun* TREES a large hardwood tree of the maple family. Latin name: *Acer pseudoplatanus*.

**symbiont** *noun* ECOL one of the organisms living in symbiosis. Compare **commensal**

**symbiosis** *noun* ECOL a condition where two or more organisms exist together and help each other to survive. Also called **symbiotic relationship**

**symbiotic** *adjective* ECOL referring to symbiosis ○ *The rainforest has evolved symbiotic mechanisms to recycle minerals.*

**symbiotically** *adverb* ECOL in symbiosis ○ *Colonies of shellfish have parasites that live symbiotically with them.*

**symbiotic relationship** *noun* ECOL same as **symbiosis**

**symbol** *noun* a printed or written sign used to represent something

**symbolic** *adjective* referring to symbols ○ *A symbolic code is used for synoptic charts.*

**symbolic address** *noun* COMPUT an address represented by a symbol or name

**symbolic code, symbolic instruction** *noun* COMPUT an instruction that is in mnemonic form rather than a binary number

**symbolic language** *noun* COMPUT **1.** a computer language in which locations are represented by names **2.** any language used to write source code

**symbolic logic** *noun* LOGIC the study of reasoning and thought

**symbolic name** *noun* COMPUT a name used as a label for a variable or location

**symmetrical, symmetric** *adjective* with an exact likeness of form on opposite sides of a central dividing line ○ *The area covered by the forecast is divided into a series of grid or reference points at approximately 300 km symmetrical spacing.*

**symmetrical compression** *noun* COMPUT a compression system that requires the same processing power and time scale to compress and decompress an image

**symmetric difference** *noun* MATHS a logical function whose output is true if either of two inputs is true, and false if both inputs are the same

**symmetry** *noun* an exact matching in position or form of points on an object that are equally positioned about a given point, line or plane bisecting the object

**sympathetic nervous system** *noun* ANAT one of two complementary parts of the nervous system that affects involuntary functions. Compare **autonomic nervous system** (NOTE: It is activated by danger or stress and causes responses such as dilated pupils and a rapid heart rate.)

**symphile** *noun* ECOL an insect or other organism that lives in the nests of social insects such as ants or termites and is fed by them

**symptom** *noun* **1.** an indication of something **2.** MED a change in the functioning or appearance of an organism, which shows that a disease or disorder is present

**symptomatic** *adjective* 1. characteristic or typical of something 2. MED referring to a medical symptom ○ *The rash is symptomatic of measles.*

**syn-** *prefix* joint or fused

**synapse** *noun* ANAT a point in the nervous system where the axons of neurons are in contact with the dendrites of other neurons ■ *verb* BIOL to link with a neuron

**synchronisation** *noun* the action of synchronising two or more devices

**synchronisation pulse** *noun* ELEC a transmitted pulse used to make sure that the receiver is synchronised with the transmitter

**synchronise** *verb* to cause things to occur or operate at the same time or rate

**synchronised dynamic RAM** *noun* COMPUT an enhanced memory component in which the memory access cycle is synchronised with the main processor clock, eliminating wait time between memory operations. Abbreviation **SDRAM**

**synchronous** *adjective* COMPUT being synchronised with something else such as a main clock

**synchronous cache** *noun* COMPUT a high-speed secondary cache system used in many computers that use the Pentium processor chip

**synchronous computer** *noun* COMPUT a computer in which each action can only take place when a timing pulse arrives

**synchronous data link control** *noun* COMPUT a data transmission protocol, most often used in IBM's Systems Network Architecture, that defines how synchronous data is transmitted. Abbreviation **SDLC**

**synchronous network** *noun* COMPUT a network in which all the links are synchronised with a single timing signal

**synchronous transmission** *noun* COMPUT the transmission of data from one device to another, where both devices are controlled by the same clock and the transmitted data is synchronised with the clock signal

**syncline** *noun* EARTH SCI a concave downwards fold of rock, with the youngest rock on the inside. Compare **anticline**

**sync pulse** *noun* ELEC a transmitted pulse used to make sure that the receiver is synchronised with the transmitter

**syndrome** *noun* MED a group of symptoms and other changes in the body's functions which, when taken together, show that a particular disease or disorder is present

**synecology** *noun* ECOL the study of communities of organisms in their environments. Compare **autecology**

**synergism** *noun* CHEM a phenomenon where two substances act more strongly together than they would independently

**synergist** *noun* CHEM a substance that increases the effect of another

**synfuel** *noun* INDUST a fuel similar to those produced from crude oil but produced from more plentiful resources, e.g. coal, shale or tar

**synodic** *adjective* ASTRON 1. referring to the alignment of astronomical objects 2. referring to the interval between the occasions when the same astronomical objects are aligned

**synovial membrane** *noun* ANAT a smooth membrane that forms the inner lining of the capsule covering a joint, and secretes the fluid which lubricates the joint

**synroc** *noun* INDUST an artificial mineral compound formed of nuclear waste fused into minerals which will never deteriorate

**syntactic error** *noun* COMPUT a programming error in which the program statement does not follow the syntax of the language. Also called **syntax error**

**syntax** *noun* COMPUT the grammatical rules which apply to a programming language

**syntax error** *noun* COMPUT same as **syntactic error**

**syntenic** *adjective* GENETICS referring to genes that occur on the same chromosome

**synteny** *noun* GENETICS the occurrence of genes on the same chromosome, whether or not they are linked

**synthesis** *noun* 1. the process of combining things to form a whole 2. CHEM the process of producing a compound by a chemical reaction

**synthesise, synthesize** *verb* **1.** to combine things to form a whole **2.** CHEM to produce a compound by a chemical reaction ○ *The body cannot synthesise essential fatty acids and has to absorb them from food.*

**synthetic** *adjective* INDUST made in an industrial process and not occurring naturally ○ *synthetic rubber*

**synthetically** *adverb* INDUST by an industrial process ○ *Synthetically produced hormones are used in hormone therapy.*

**synthetic insecticide** *noun* AGRIC an insecticide that is made artificially from chemicals that do not occur naturally in plants

**synusia** *noun* ECOL a group of plants living in the same habitat

**syringe** *noun* MED **1.** a device consisting of a needle attached to a tube, used for injecting fluids into the body or for taking blood **2.** to clean, spray or inject something by using a syringe

**syrinx** *noun* ZOOL the vocal organ of a bird

**sysop** *noun* COMPUT a person who maintains a bulletin board system or network

**system** *noun* **1.** a group of interdependent parts forming and operating as a whole ○ *a braking system* ○ *an electrical system* **2.** an arrangement of things or phenomena that act together ○ *a weather system* **3.** COMPUT a group of hardware or software components that work together **4.** BIOL an arrangement of parts of the body that work together ○ *the nervous system* **5.** a way of classifying something scientifically ○ *the Linnaean system*

**systematic** *adjective* **1.** organised in a planned way **2.** being part of a system

**systematics** *noun* BIOL the scientific study of systems, especially of the system of classifying organisms

**system clock** *noun* COMPUT an electronic component that generates a regular signal that is used to synchronise all the components in the computer

**system colours** *noun* COMPUT same as **default palette**

**system console** *noun* COMPUT the main terminal or control centre for a computer which includes status lights and control switches

**system crash** *noun* COMPUT a situation in which the operating system stops working and has to be restarted

**system disk** *noun* COMPUT a disk that holds the system software

**Système International** *noun* MEASURE full form of **SI**

**systemic** *adjective* BIOL affecting the whole organism

**systemic circulation** *noun* PHYSIOL the circulation of blood around the whole body, except the lungs, starting with the aorta and returning through the venae cavae

**systemic fungicide** *noun* AGRIC a fungicide that is absorbed into a plant's sap system through its leaves and makes the plant lethal to fungi without killing the plant itself

**systemic herbicide** *noun* AGRIC a herbicide that is absorbed into a plant's sap system through its leaves and travels through the plant to kill the roots. Also called **systemic weedkiller**

**systemic pesticide** *noun* AGRIC a pesticide that is absorbed into a plant's sap system through its leaves and makes the plant lethal to pests without killing the plant itself

**systemic weedkiller** *noun* AGRIC same as **systemic herbicide**

**systems analysis** *noun* COMPUT **1.** the analysis of a process or system to see if it could be more efficiently carried out by a computer **2.** the examination of an existing system with the aim of improving or replacing it

**Systems Application Architecture** *noun* COMPUT a standard that defines the look and feel of an application regardless of the hardware platform. Abbreviation **SAA** (NOTE: SAA defines which keystrokes carry out standard functions (such as F1 to display help), the application's display and how the application interacts with the operating system.)

**Systems Network Architecture** *noun* COMPUT the design methods that define how communications in a network should occur and allow different hardware to communicate. Abbreviation **SNA**

**system software** *noun* COMPUT the set of programs that direct the basic functions of a computer

**systems    programmer**    *noun* COMPUT a person who writes system software

**systole** *noun* PHYSIOL the contraction of the heart that pumps blood into the arteries. Compare **diastole**

**syzygy** *noun* ASTRON the conjunction or opposition of three astronomical objects such as the Sun, Earth and Moon in a straight line

# T

**T** *symbol* **1.** MEASURE tera- **2.** MEASURE, PHYS tesla

**Ta** *symbol* CHEM ELEM tantalum

**tab** *noun* COMPUT a key that moves a printing head or cursor a preset distance along a line

**tab character** *noun* COMPUT an ASCII character that is used to align text at a preset tab stop

**table** *noun* **1.** COMPUT, PRINTING a list of data in columns and rows on a printed page or on the screen **2.** COMPUT a structure that shows how records and data items are linked by relations between the rows and columns of the table **3.** ENG a level structure

**tableland** *noun* EARTH SCI an area of high flat land

**table lookup** *noun* COMPUT the use of one known value to select one entry in a table, providing a secondary value

**table mountain** *noun* EARTH SCI a flat-topped mountain

**table of contents** *noun* COMPUT **1.** a set of data at the start of a disk that describes how many tracks are on the disk, their position and length **2.** a page with a list of the headings of all the other main pages in the title and links so that a user can move to them

**tab stop** *noun* COMPUT a preset point along a line at which a printing head or cursor will stop for each tabulation command. Also called **tabulation stop**

**tabular** *adjective* referring to a table of or for data □ **in tabular form** (*of facts and figures*) arranged in a table ○ *The most widely acceptable presentation of fuel data is in tabular form but graphical presentations may also be used.*

**tabulation** *noun* COMPUT **1.** the arrangement of a table of figures **2.** the movement of a printing head or cursor a preset distance along a line

**tabulation stop** *noun* COMPUT same as **tab stop**

**tachometer** *noun* MECH ENG an instrument for the measurement of the revolutions per minute of a rotating shaft ○ *The pilot checks the tachometer and notes the resulting drop in r.p.m. for each magneto.*

**tachyon** *noun* PHYS a hypothetical elementary particle whose speed is greater than that of light

**tag** *noun* COMPUT an identifying character attached to a file or item of data ○ *Each file has a three letter tag for rapid identification.*

**taiga** *noun* EARTH SCI a forested region between the Arctic tundra and the steppe

**tail** *noun* **1.** the rear part of a bird or aircraft **2.** COMPUT a control code used to signal the end of a message

**tailings** *plural noun* INDUST refuse or waste ore from mining operations

**talc** *noun* MINERALS a soft mineral consisting of hydrated magnesium silicate, found in igneous and metamorphic rocks and used to make talcum powder (NOTE: It is the softest mineral on a scale of hardness that runs from talc to diamond.)

**tall-grass prairie** *noun* EARTH SCI same as **long-grass prairie**

**tandem processors** *plural noun* COMPUT two processors connected so that if one fails, the second takes over

**tangent** *noun* MATHS a straight line, curve or surface that meets another curve or curved surface at a point, but which, if extended, does not cut through at that point ○ *The glide path is at a tangent to the runway.*

**tank** *noun* INDUST a large container for storing fluid ○ *An aluminium alloy fuel tank is housed in each wing.*

**tanker** *noun* INDUST **1.** a large ship used to carry petrol or oil **2.** a truck used to carry liquids such as petrol or milk

**tannin, tannic acid** *noun* BIOCHEM a brownish or yellowish compound formed in leaves and bark, used in the tanning of leather and in dyes and astringents (NOTE: Tannins help protect plants from being eaten.)

**tantalum** *noun* CHEM ELEM a rare metal that does not corrode, used to repair damaged bones (NOTE: The chemical symbol is **Ta**; the atomic number is **73** and the atomic weight is **180.95**.)

**tap** *noun* a pipe with a handle that can be turned to make a liquid or gas come out of a container ■ *verb* to remove or drain liquid from something □ **to tap oil resources** to bring up oil from the ground. ◆

**tape archive** *noun* COMPUT full form of **TAR**

**taper** *verb* to reduce in thickness towards one end

**tapered** *adjective* reducing in thickness towards one end ○ *Fuel flowing from the float chamber passes through a jet, in which is positioned a tapered needle valve.*

**tapered wing** *noun* AEROSP a wing which becomes narrower in width from root to tip

**tapeworm** *noun* ZOOL a parasitic worm with a long flattened segmented body that lives mainly in the guts of vertebrate animals, including humans. Class: Cestoda.

**taproot** *noun* BOT the thick main root of a plant which grows straight down into the soil (NOTE. A taproot system has a main root with smaller roots branching off it, as opposed to a fibrous root system which has no main root.)

**tap water** *noun* the mains water that comes out of the tap in a house

**tar** *noun* INDUST a thick black sticky substance derived from coal

**TAR** *noun* COMPUT a file compression system used on a computer running the Unix operating system. Full form **tape archive**

**target** *noun* **1.** a goal to be achieved **2.** something that is being aimed at

**target computer** *noun* COMPUT a computer on which software is to be run

**target program** *noun* COMPUT an object program or computer program in object code form, produced by a compiler

**tariff** *noun* COMPUT, TELECOM a charge incurred by a user of a communications or computer system ○ *There is a set tariff for logging on, then a rate for every minute of computer time used.*

**tarn** *noun* EARTH SCI a small lake in a depression high in the hills

**tar oil** *noun* AGRIC a winter wash used to control aphids and scale insects on fruit trees

**tar pit** *noun* EARTH SCI a natural hole in the ground containing bitumen

**tarsal** *noun* ANAT one of the bones in the ankle

**tar sand** *noun* EARTH SCI same as **oil sand**

**tarsus** *noun* ANAT the ankle or a similar joint in the hindlimb of an animal

**tartaric acid** *noun* CHEM a white crystalline organic acid found in fruit, used as baking powder and in photographic processes and tanning leather. Formula: $(CHOH)_2(COOH)_2$.

**tartrate** *noun* CHEM a salt or ester of tartaric acid

**tartrazine** *noun* FOOD INDUST a yellow substance added to food to give it an attractive colour (NOTE: It is coded E102. Although widely used, tartrazine provokes reactions in hypersensitive people and is banned in some countries.)

**task** *noun* **1.** a job that someone has to do **2.** COMPUT a job that is to be carried out by a computer

**taskbar** *noun* COMPUT a bar that usually runs along the bottom of the screen and displays the Start button and a list of other programs or windows that are currently active

**task-management** *adjective* COMPUT referring to system software which controls the use and allocation of resources to programs

**task queue** *noun* COMPUT the temporary storage of jobs waiting to be processed

**task swapping, task switching** *noun* the exchanging of one program in memory for another which is temporarily stored on disk

**taste bud** *noun* ANAT one of many small structures on the surface of the tongue or in the mouth that respond to various chemicals to give the sense of taste (NOTE: Each taste bud responds to one of four basic tastes: sweet, sour, bitter or salty.)

**tautomerism** *noun* CHEM the existence at equilibrium of a mixture of two isomers that readily convert from one to the other

**taxis** *noun* BIOL a movement of a cell or microorganism towards or away from a stimulus such as light

**-taxis** *suffix* BIOL the response of an organism which moves towards or away from a stimulus

**taxon** *noun* BIOL a grouping such as family, genus or species in a scientific classification of organisms (NOTE: The plural is **taxa**.)

**taxonomic, taxonomical** *adjective* BIOL referring to taxonomy

**taxonomic group** *noun* BIOL a group of organisms classified together according to a specific system

**taxonomy** *noun* BIOL the techniques and system of classifying organisms according to their characteristics

**Tc** *symbol* CHEM ELEM technetium

**TCDD** *noun* ENVIRON a highly toxic persistent by-product of the herbicide 2,4,5-T. Full form **tetrachlorodibenzoparadioxin**

**T cell** *noun* ANAT a white blood cell (**lymphocyte**) that matures in the thymus and is essential for immunity, especially in combating viral infections and cancers. Also called **T lymphocyte** (NOTE: T cells include cytotoxic T cells that directly attack virus-infected or cancerous body cells, helper T cells that stimulate other T cells, and suppressor T cells that play a restraining role.)

**TCP/IP** *noun* COMPUT a data transfer protocol often used in Unix-based networks and used for all communications over the Internet. Full form **transmission control protocol/interface program**

**TDM** *abbreviation* COMPUT time division multiplexing

**TDR** *abbreviation* COMPUT time domain reflectometry

**TDS** *abbreviation* COMPUT transaction-driven system

**Te** *symbol* CHEM ELEM tellurium

**teak** *noun* TREES a tropical tree that produces a hardwood which is resistant to water. Latin name: *Tectona grandis*.

**tear duct** *noun* ANAT a tube through which tears flow, especially the one that drains tears from the inner corner of the eye into the nasal cavity

**tears** *plural noun* PHYSIOL the salty fluid secreted in the eye by the lacrimal glands

**technetium** *noun* CHEM ELEM a radioactive metallic element used as a tracer and in corrosion-resistant materials (NOTE: The chemical symbol is **Tc**; the atomic number is **43** and the atomic weight is **98.91**.)

**technical** *adjective* referring to practical or scientific work

**technician** *noun* a person who does practical work in a laboratory or scientific institution ○ *a laboratory technician*

**technique** *noun* a way of doing scientific or medical work ○ *a new technique for dating fossils*

**technological** *adjective* referring to technology

**technological fix** *noun* the solution to a problem based on technology, generally not a really satisfactory solution

**technological revolution** *noun* INDUST the changing of industrial methods by introducing new technology

**technology** *noun* the application of scientific knowledge to industrial processes ○ *The technology has to be related to user requirements.*

**technology transfer** *noun* **1.** the practical application of research results **2.** the passing of technological information from a developed country to a developing one or from one company to another

**technosphere** *noun* an environment built or modified by humans

**tectonic** *adjective* EARTH SCI referring to faults or movements in the Earth's crust

**tectonic plate** *noun* EARTH SCI a large area of solid rock in the Earth's crust, which floats on the mantle and moves very slowly

**tectorial membrane** *noun* ANAT a spiral membrane in the inner ear above the organ of Corti, containing the hair cells which transmit impulses to the auditory nerve

**teeth** *noun* ANAT plural of tooth

**Teflon** *trademark* INDUST polytetrafluoroethylene, a plastic used as a non-stick coating on articles such as saucepans

**tele-** *prefix* COMPUT long distance

**telecommunications** *plural noun* TELECOM the network for passing and receiving messages over a distance by systems such as telephone, satellite and radio

**telematics** *noun* COMPUT the study of the processes involved in interaction of all data processing and communications devices such as computers and networks

**telephone** *noun* TELECOM a machine used for speaking to someone or communicating with another computer using modems over a long distance

**telephone line** *noun* TELECOM a cable used to connect a telephone handset with a central exchange

**telephony** *noun* TELECOM a series of standards that define the way in which computers can work with a telephone system to provide voice-mail, telephone answering and fax services

**teleprocessing** *noun* COMPUT the processing of data at a distance, e.g. using outside terminals to access a central computer. Abbreviation **TP**

**telescope** *noun* ASTRON a device for concentrating electromagnetic radiation for human study

**telesoftware** *noun* COMPUT software which is received from a viewdata or teletext service ○ *The telesoftware was downloaded yesterday.* Abbreviation **TSW**

**teletext** *noun* TELECOM a method of transmitting text and information with a normal television signal, usually as a serial bit stream which can be displayed using a special decoder

**television** *noun* a device which can receive modulated video signals via a cable or broadcast signals via an aerial and display images on a cathode ray tube screen together with sound. Abbreviation **TV**

**telluric** *adjective* ASTRON coming from Earth or its atmosphere

**tellurium** *noun* CHEM ELEM a shiny brittle semimetallic element, used in alloys and manufacturing processes and as a semiconductor (NOTE: The chemical symbol is **Te**; the atomic number is **52** and the atomic weight is **127.60**.)

**telnet** *noun* COMPUT the TCP/IP protocol that allows a user to connect to and control a remote computer via the Internet and type in commands as if they were sitting in front of the computer

**telocentric** *adjective* GENETICS referring to a chromosome with a centromere that is located at or near one end

**telomere** *noun* GENETICS a piece of noncoding DNA at the end of a chromosome (NOTE: It protects the genetically important parts of the DNA against damage when the chromosome divides.)

**telophase** *noun* BIOL the fourth and last stage of cell division, in which new nuclei form around chromosomes at opposite ends of the dividing cell

**temper** *verb* METALL to heat and rapidly cool a metal to increase its hardness

**temperate** *adjective* METEOROL neither very hot nor very cold

**temperate climate** *noun* EARTH SCI a climate which is neither very hot in summer nor very cold in winter

**temperate forest** *noun* EARTH SCI a forest in a temperate region

**temperate region** *noun* EARTH SCI a region which is neither very hot in summer nor very cold in winter

**temperature** *noun* **1.** PHYS a measurement of heat **2.** how hot something is **3.** MED a body temperature that is higher than usual, as a sign of illness ○ *She has a temperature.* ○ *He is running a temperature.*

COMMENT: The normal average body temperature is about 37° C (98° F). This temperature may vary during the day, and can rise if a person has taken a hot bath or had a hot drink. If the environmental temperature is high, the body has to sweat to reduce the heat gained from the air around it. If the outside temperature is low, the body shivers, because rapid movement of the muscles generates heat. A fever will cause the body temperature to rise sharply, to 40° C (103°F) or more.

Hypothermia exists when the body temperature falls below about 35° C (95°F).

**temperature coefficient** *noun* PHYS a ratio of the speed at which a process develops compared to the speed of the same process at a 10° C cooler temperature

**temperature gradient** *noun* **1.** METEOROL a gradual increase in temperature travelling from the North or South Pole towards the equator **2.** PHYS a change in temperature with distance from a hot or cold object

**temperature graph** *noun* PHYS, METEOROL a graph showing how the temperature of something rises and falls

**temperature inversion** *noun* METEOROL an atmospheric phenomenon in which cold air is nearer the ground than warm air, making the temperature of the air rise as it gets further from the ground, trapping pollutants between the layers of air

**temperature lapse rate** *noun* EARTH SCI same as **lapse rate**

**template** *noun* **1.** a plastic or metal object used as a pattern for drawing or cutting shapes **2.** COMPUT a file containing a standard text such as a standard letter or invoice into which specific details can be added

**temporarily** *adverb* for a time or not permanently

**temporary** *adjective* lasting for a short time and not permanent

**temporary hardness** *noun* CHEM the hardness of water caused by carbonates of calcium, which can be removed by boiling the water

**temporary parasite** *noun* BIOL a parasite which does not live permanently on the host

**temporary register** *noun* COMPUT a register used for temporary storage for the results of an arithmetic logic unit operation

**tender** *adjective* **1.** soft or susceptible to damage **2.** MED painful to touch **3.** BOT referring to a plant which cannot tolerate frost

**tendon** *noun* ANAT a strip of connective tissue that attaches a muscle to a bone

**tendon sheath** *noun* ANAT a tube of membrane that covers and protects a membrane

**tendril** *noun* BOT a stem, leaf or petiole of a climbing plant modified into a thin strip that clings to a surface, so allowing the plant to climb

**ten's complement** *noun* MATHS a decimal complement, formed by adding one to the nine's complement of a decimal number

**tensile** *adjective* referring to stretching or pulling out

**tensile load** *noun* PHYS a load caused by forces acting in opposite directions away from each other

**tensile strength** *noun* PHYS the strength of a structure to resist forces pulling it apart from opposite directions

**tensile stress** *noun* PHYS the forces that try to pull a structure apart from opposite directions

**tension** *noun* PHYS a strained condition resulting from forces acting in opposition to each other ○ *A rod which is bent is shortened or in compression on the inside of the bend and is stretched or in tension on the outside of the bend.*

**tera-** *prefix* MEASURE one trillion, $10^{12}$. Symbol **T**

**terabyte** *noun* COMPUT one thousand gigabytes

**teragram** *noun* MEASURE one trillionth of a gram

**teratogen** *noun* MED a substance or agent that causes birth defects

**teratogenesis** *noun* MED the production of birth defects

**teratogenic** *adjective* MED causing birth defects

**terawatt** *noun* MEASURE, ELEC a unit of measurement of electric energy, equal to one billion watts. Abbreviation **TW**

**terbium** *noun* CHEM ELEM a shiny metallic element used in lasers, X-rays and television tubes (NOTE: The chemical symbol is **Tb**; the atomic number is **65** and the atomic weight is **158.93**.)

**terminal** *noun* **1.** COMPUT a device usually made up of a display unit and a keyboard which allows entry and display of information when on-line to a central computer system **2.** ELEC an electrical connection point **3.** COMPUT a point in a network where a message can be transmitted or received ■ *adjective* **1.** coming at the end **2.** MED causing death ○ *a terminal illness* **3.** COMPUT fatal or unable to be repaired ○ *The computer has a terminal fault.*

**terminal adapter** *noun* COMPUT a device that transfers digital signals from a computer to a digital communications line such as an ISDN line

**terminal emulation** *noun* COMPUT the ability of a terminal to emulate the functions of another type of terminal so that display codes can be correctly decoded and displayed and keystrokes correctly coded and transmitted

**terminal moraine** *noun* EARTH SCI a heap of soil and sand pushed by a glacier and left behind when the glacier melts

**terminal strip** *noun* ELEC a row of electrical connectors that allow pairs of wires to be electrically connected using a screw-down metal plate

**terminal velocity** *noun* PHYS the constant maximum velocity reached by a falling object

**terminator** *noun* COMPUT **1.** a resistor that fits onto each end of a coaxial cable in a bus network to create an electrical circuit **2.** a resistor that fits onto the last SCSI device in the daisy chain, creating an electrical circuit

**terminator gene** *noun* GENETICS a gene that can be inserted into genetically modified plants to make them unable to produce seed after one season

**terminology** *noun* the set of words or expressions used for a particular subject ○ *scientific terminology*

**termitarium** *noun* ZOOL a nest made by termites formed in the shape of a hill of hard earth

**termite** *noun* ZOOL an insect resembling a large ant, which lives in colonies and eats cellulose

**tern** *noun* ZOOL a species of small gull

**ternary** *adjective* **1.** MATHS referring to a number system with three possible states **2.** CHEM referring to a compound containing three different elements

**terrace** *noun* EARTH SCI a flat strip of land across a sloping hillside, lying level along the contours ■ *verb* AGRIC to build terraces on a mountainside ○ *The hills are covered with terraced rice fields.*

COMMENT: Terracing is widely used to create small flat fields on steeply sloping

land, so as to bring more land into productive use, and also to prevent soil erosion.

**terrace cultivation** *noun* AGRIC hill slopes cut to form terraced fields which rise in steps one above the other and are cultivated, often with the aid of irrigation

**terrain** *noun* EARTH SCI the ground or an area of land in terms of its physical surface features ○ *mountainous terrain*

**terrestrial** *adjective* **1.** EARTH SCI referring to the Earth **2.** TELECOM referring to land-based communications ○ *a terrestrial link*

**terrestrial animal** *noun* ZOOL an animal which lives on dry land

**terrestrial equator** *noun* EARTH SCI an imaginary line running round the surface of the Earth, at an equal distance from the North and South Poles

**terrestrial magnetism** *noun* EARTH SCI the magnetic properties of the Earth

**terrestrial planet** *noun* ASTRON one of the four planets nearest the Sun that are similar in density and composition (NOTE: The terrestrial planets are Mars, Venus, Mercury and Earth.)

**terrestrial radiation** *noun* EARTH SCI loss of heat from the Earth ○ *Clear skies allow terrestrial radiation to escape.*

**terricolous** *adjective* ZOOL referring to an animal that lives in or on soil

**territorial** *adjective* referring to territory

**territorialism, territoriality** *noun* ZOOL a pattern of behaviour involving the establishment and defence of a territory

**territorial species** *noun* ZOOL a species which occupies and defends a territory

**territory** *noun* ZOOL an area of land occupied and defended by an animal, which may be all or part of the animal's home range ○ *A robin defends its territory by attacking other robins that enter it.*

**tertiary** *adjective* coming after two other things

**tertiary consumer** *noun* ZOOL a carnivore which only eats other carnivores

**tertiary treatment** *noun* ENVIRON an advanced stage in the processing of waste

**tesla** *noun* MEASURE, PHYS the derived SI unit of magnetic flux density, equal to a flux of one weber per square metre. Symbol **T**

**tessellate** *verb* **1.** (*of shapes*) to fit together without leaving spaces **2.** COMPUT to reduce a complex shape to a collection of simple shapes, often triangles

**test** *noun* an examination to see if a sample of something matches criteria or if a device is working well ○ *Laboratory tests showed that the sample was positive.* ○ *Government officials have carried out tests on samples of drinking water.* ■ *verb* to examine a sample or device to see if it is working well ○ *They tested the water sample for microorganisms.*

**testa** *noun* BOT the tough protective skin around a seed

**test bed** *noun* COMPUT an environment used to test programs

**test data** *plural noun* COMPUT data with known results prepared to allow a new program to be tested

**test equipment** *noun* COMPUT special equipment used to test hardware or software ○ *The engineer has special test equipment for this model.*

**testicle** *noun* ANAT same as **testis**

**testicular artery** *noun* ANAT same as **spermatic artery**

**testis** *noun* ANAT a male gland that produces sperm (NOTE: In mammals, including humans, the paired testes also secrete sex hormones and lie within the scrotum. The plural of **testis** is **testes**.)

**testosterone** *noun* BIOCHEM a male steroid hormone produced by the testes, that controls the development of secondary sexual characteristics at puberty

**test run** *noun* COMPUT a program run with test data to ensure that the software is working correctly ○ *A test run will soon show up any errors.*

**test tube** *noun* CHEM a small glass tube with a rounded bottom, used in laboratories to hold samples of liquids

**tetanus** *noun* MED an infection caused by *Clostridium tetani* in the soil, which affects the spinal cord and causes spasms which occur first in the jaw

**tetrachlorodibenzoparadioxin** *noun* CHEM full form **TCDD**

**tetrad** *noun* **1.** BIOL a group of four cells produced by meiosis of a single parent cell into sex cells **2.** GENETICS a group of four chromosomes in a diploid cell that is about to undergo meiosis

**tetraethyl lead** *noun* INDUST an additive added to petrol to prevent knocking

**tetrahedral compound** *noun* CHEM a compound in which the main atom joins other atoms at four corners around the atom

**tetrahedron** *noun* MATHS a solid object with four identical triangular faces

**tetrahydrate** *noun* CHEM a chemical with four molecules of water of crystallisation

**tetraploid** *adjective* GENETICS referring to an organism that has four sets of chromosomes in a cell nucleus

**tetravalent** *adjective* CHEM with a valency of four

**tex** *noun* MEASURE, TEXTILES a measure of mass per unit length of fibres. Symbol **tex**

**texel** *noun* COMPUT a collection of pixels that are treated as a single unit when texture mapping is being applied over an object

**text** *noun* COMPUT information consisting of alphanumeric characters

**text file** *noun* COMPUT a stored file on a computer containing text rather than digits or data

**text processing** *noun* COMPUT the use of a computer to keyboard, edit and output text

**texture** *noun* the roughness or smoothness of a surface or substance

**textured vegetable protein** *noun* FOOD INDUST a substance made from processed soya beans or other vegetables, used as a substitute for meat. Abbreviation **TVP**

**texture mapping** *noun* COMPUT **1.** a computer graphics effect using algorithms to produce an image that looks like the surface of something such as marble, brick, stone or water **2.** the covering of one image with another to give the first a texture

**TFT screen** *noun* COMPUT a method of creating a high-quality LCD display often used in laptop computers. Full form **thin film transistor screen**

**Th** *symbol* CHEM ELEM thorium

**thalamus** *noun* BOT same as **receptacle 2**

**thallium** *noun* CHEM ELEM a metallic element which is poisonous and used in pesticides (NOTE: The chemical symbol is **Tl**; the atomic number is **81** and the atomic weight is **204.37**.)

**thallophyte** *noun* BOT a plant without stem, roots, or leaves, e.g. an alga, lichen or fungus

**thallus** *noun* BOT the flat green body of a simple plant such as an alga or liverwort (NOTE: It is not differentiated into leaves, stems and roots.)

**thaw** *noun* METEOROL a period when the weather becomes warmer after a heavy frost, and ice and snow melt ■ *verb* to melt or make something melt ○ *As the polar ice thaws, the sea level rises.* ○ *It is possible that rising atmospheric temperatures will thaw the polar ice caps and raise the level of the sea.*

**thaw water** *noun* EARTH SCI water from melted snow and ice

**theodolite** *noun* ENG an instrument formed of a telescope mounted in such a way that it can rotate, used by surveyors for measuring angles

**theory** *noun* an explanation of something which has not been proved but which is believed to be correct

**therm** *noun* MEASURE, PHYS a unit of heat equal to 100 000 British thermal units or $1.055 \times 10^8$ joules

**thermal** *adjective* PHYS referring to heat ○ *Intense surface heating causes thermal currents to develop and create convection.* ■ *noun* METEOROL a rising current of relatively warm air in the lower atmosphere ○ *Glider pilots circle in thermals in order to gain height.*

**thermal accumulator** *noun* PHYS same as **heat accumulator**

**thermal analysis** *noun* PHYS the analysis of the properties of a compound or metal at different temperatures

**thermal diffusion** *noun* PHYS a concentration gradient within a fluid created by a temperature gradient

**thermal discharge** *noun* INDUST same as **heat discharge**

**thermal dissociation** *noun* PHYS the reversible decomposition of a chemical compound into its components when heat is applied

**thermal efficiency** *noun* PHYS the efficiency of conversion of fuel energy to kinetic energy

**thermal energy** *noun* INDUST energy in the form of heat

**thermal inkjet printer** *noun* COMPUT a computer printer which produces characters by sending a stream of tiny drops of electrically charged ink onto paper

**thermalisation,** **thermalization** *verb* PHYS the reduction of the speed and energy of neutrons in a nuclear reactor to a point at which they have thermal energy so that they can be captured and produce fission

**thermal neutron** PHYS **1.** a neutron produced in the process of thermalisation **2.** same as **slow neutron**

**thermal pollution** *noun* ENVIRON a change in the quality of an environment by increasing its temperature, e.g. by the release of heat from the cooling towers of a power station or from discharge of a coolant

**thermal radiation** *noun* PHYS the emission of radiant heat

**thermal reactor** *noun* INDUST a nuclear reactor that heats using a moderator, as opposed to a breeder reactor

**thermal spring** *noun* EARTH SCI a stream of hot water running out of the ground continuously

**thermal storage** *noun* INDUST same as **heat storage**

**thermal stratification** *noun* EARTH SCI the different layers of heat in a body of water

**thermionic emission** *noun* PHYS the emission of ions or electrons from very hot solids or liquids (NOTE: It is used to produce electrons in electron microscopes and X-ray tubes.)

**thermionics** *noun* PHYS the study of the emission of electrons from hot substances

**thermionic valve** *noun* ELECTRONICS an electronic component in which electrons are emitted from a heated cathode in a glass tube containing a vacuum

**thermistor** *noun* ELECTRONICS a semiconductor device whose resistance decreases as the temperature increases

**thermite** *noun* CHEM a mixture of powdered aluminium and iron (III) oxide that produces very high temperatures when ignited

**thermo-** *prefix* heat or temperature

**thermochemistry** *noun* CHEM the study of the heat produced by chemical reactions

**thermocline** *noun* EARTH SCI the middle layer of water in a lake in which heat decreases rapidly as the depth increases. Also called **metalimnion**

**thermocouple** *noun* PHYS a device for measuring temperature

**thermodynamics** *noun* PHYS the study of the processes involving heat changes and conservation of energy □ **first law of thermodynamics** a general scientific rule that during a physical or chemical change, energy is neither created nor destroyed □ **second law of thermodynamics** a general scientific rule that heat cannot pass from a colder to a warmer body and that with each change in form, some energy is degraded to a less useful form and given off into the surroundings, usually as heat

**thermodynamic temperature** *noun* PHYS temperature measured on a scale that is independent of the substance being used, expressed in a unit called kelvin

**thermoelectricity** *noun* ELEC electricity produced by maintaining a temperature difference at the point where two materials meet

**thermograph** *noun* PHYS an instrument that records changes in temperature on a roll of paper

**thermolysis** *noun* BIOL a reduction in body temperature, e.g. by sweating

**thermometer** *noun* PHYS an instrument for measuring temperature

**thermometry** *noun* PHYS the science of measuring temperature

**thermonasty** *noun* BOT a response of plants to heat

**thermoneutral zone** *noun* BIOL a range of environmental temperatures in which an endotherm has to exert only a minimum effort to maintain a constant body temperature

**thermonuclear energy** *noun* PHYS energy produced by fusion of nuclei

**thermonuclear reaction** *noun* PHYS a nuclear reaction in which atomic nuclei are fused together to make heavier types

COMMENT: Thermonuclear reactions occur in stars as well as hydrogen bombs and potential fusion power reactors, because the creation of nuclei up to iron releases energy. Nuclei beyond iron can only be produced by absorbing energy, which is why they are rare by comparison with lighter species.

**thermoperiodic** *adjective* BIOL referring to an organism that reacts to regular changes in temperature

**thermophilic** *adjective* BIOL referring to an organism that needs a high temperature to grow, e.g. one living in the hot water of thermal springs

**thermopile** *noun* ELEC a device that is used for measuring radiant energy or converting it into electricity, consisting of a set of thermocouples joined either in series or in parallel

**thermoplastic** INDUST *noun* a type of plastic which can be repeatedly softened by heating and formed into shapes ■ *adjective* able to be recycled by heating and cooling ○ *thermoplastic materials*

**thermoregulation** *noun* BIOL the control of body temperature by processes such as sweating and shivering

**thermosetting** *adjective* INDUST able to be heated to be shaped but unable to be reheated for recycling

**thermosetting plastic** *noun* INDUST a type of plastic that can be heated to be shaped but which cannot be softened by reheating

**thermosphere** *noun* EARTH SCI the zone of the Earth's atmosphere above 80 km from the surface of the Earth, where the temperature increases with altitude

**thermostat** *noun* PHYS a device that responds to temperature change by activating a mechanism, used for controlling the temperature of a space or process

**therophyte** *noun* BOT an annual that completes its life cycle rapidly in favourable conditions, growing from a seed and dying within one season (NOTE: Desert plants and plants growing on cultivated land are often therophytes.)

**thiamine, thiamin** *noun* BIOCHEM vitamin $B_1$, found in yeast, cereals, liver and pork

**thick** *adjective* **1.** deep or broad ○ *This sheet of aluminium is not very thick.* **2.**

of a particular extent between two surfaces ○ *a 1 cm thick steel bar* **3.** with a large diameter ○ *thick wire* **4.** METEOROL dense ○ *thick fog* ○ *thick cloud* **5.** PHYS of a consistency which does not flow easily ○ *thick oil*

**thicken** *verb* to make something thicker or to become thicker

**thickening agent** *noun* CHEM a substance that causes a liquid to become thicker

**thick-Ethernet** *noun* COMPUT a network that can extend long distances, implemented using thick coaxial cable and transceivers to connect branch cables

**thick film** *noun* ELECTRONICS a miniature electronic circuit design in which miniature electronic components are mounted on an insulating base, then connected as required

**thickness** *noun* **1.** the extent between two surfaces ○ *In monocoque construction, there is no internal stiffening because the thickness of the skin gives strength and stability.* **2.** the extent of the diameter of a wire **3.** METEOROL (*of fog or cloud*) the state of being dense **4.** PHYS (*of a liquid*) the state of not flowing easily

**thigmotropism** *noun* BOT a directional growth movement (**tropism**) of a plant part in response to touch (NOTE: It is often seen in plant tendrils such as those of peas.)

**thin** *adjective* **1.** of small extent between two surfaces ○ *a thin layer of paint* **2.** with a small diameter ○ *thin wire* **3.** METEOROL not dense ○ *thin mist* ○ *Altostratus cloud is thin enough for the Sun to be dimly visible.* **4.** PHYS of a consistency which flows easily ○ *thin oil* Opposite **thick**

**thin-Ethernet** *noun* COMPUT a network that is limited to distances of around 1000 m, implemented using thin coaxial cable and BNC connectors

**thin film** *noun* ELECTRONICS a method of constructing integrated circuits by depositing in a vacuum very thin patterns of various materials onto a substrate to form the required interconnected components

**thin film memory** *noun* COMPUT a high-speed access RAM device using a matrix of magnetic cells and a matrix of read/write heads to access them

**thin film transistor screen** *noun* COMPUT full form of **TFT screen**

**thin-layer chromatography** *noun* CHEM a method of separating substances in a solution using a solid adsorbent material on which the different substances move up at different speeds, allowing them to be separated. Abbreviation **TLC**

**thinness** *noun* **1.** the smallness of extent between two surfaces ○ *The thinness of the material makes it unsuitable.* **2.** the smallness of extent of the diameter of a wire **3.** METEOROL (*of fog or cloud*) the state or condition of being thin enough to see through ■ PHYS (*of a liquid*) the state or condition of flowing easily

**thionyl chloride** *noun* CHEM a colourless liquid used in organic synthesis. Formula: $SOCl_2$.

**thiosulfate,** **thiosulphate** *noun* CHEM a salt or ester of thiosulfuric acid

**thiosulfuric acid** *noun* CHEM an unstable acid that exists only as salts or esters or in solution. Formula: $H_2S_2O_3$.

**thiourea** *noun* CHEM a soluble crystalline solid used in the manufacture of resins and in photography. Formula: $CS(NH_2)_2$.

**third eyelid** *noun* ZOOL same as **nictitating membrane**

**third generation** *noun* TELECOM the latest specification for mobile communication systems including mobile telephones, permitting very fast data transfer rates of between 128 Kbps and 2 Mbps. Abbreviation **3G**

**third generation computer** *noun* COMPUT a computer which uses integrated circuits instead of transistors

**thixotropy** *noun* CHEM the property of becoming thinner or more fluid when shaken or stirred and returning to a gel state when allowed to stand, as in many paints

**Thomson effect** *noun* PHYS the phenomenon whereby a temperature gradient along a conductor or semiconductor causes an electric potential gradient

**thoracic** *adjective* ANAT referring to the thorax

**thoracic aorta** *noun* ANAT the part of the aorta which crosses the thorax

**thorax** *noun* **1.** ANAT a cavity in the top part of the body of an animal above the abdomen, containing the diaphragm, heart and lungs, all surrounded by the rib cage **2.** ZOOL the middle section of the body of an insect, between the head and the abdomen

**thorium** noun CHEM ELEM a natural radioactive element which decomposes to radioactive radon gas (NOTE: The chemical symbol is **Th**; the atomic number is **90** and the atomic weight is **232.04**.)

**thorn** noun **1.** BOT a sharp woody point on the stem of a plant **2.** PLANTS a plant or tree which has sharp woody points on its stems or branches

**thornbush** noun PLANTS a shrub or bush which has sharp woody points on its stems

**thorn scrub** noun ECOL an area of land covered with bushes and small trees which have sharp woody points on their stems and branches

**thorn woodland** noun ECOL an area of land covered with trees which have sharp woody points on their stems and branches

**thrashing** noun COMPUT **1.** excessive disk activity **2.** a configuration or program fault in a virtual memory system that results in a central processing unit wasting time moving pages of data between main memory and disk or backing store

**thread** noun **1.** COMPUT a program which consists of many independent smaller sections or **beads 2.** MECH ENG a continuous ridge on a screw or pipe ■ verb to pass a thread or strand of something through a hole or gap

**threaded file** noun COMPUT same as **chained file**

**threaded language** noun COMPUT a programming language which allows many small sections of code to be written then used by a main program

**threaded tree** noun COMPUT a structure in which each node contains a pointer to other nodes

**threadworm** noun ZOOL a thin parasitic worm which infests the large intestine. Genus: *Enterobius*.

**threat** noun something dangerous which may cause harm ○ *Lead pollution is a threat to small babies.*

**threaten** verb **1.** to be a danger or harmful to something ○ *Plant species growing in arid or semi-arid lands are threatened by the expansion of livestock herding.* **2.** to be likely to do something

harmful ○ *The plan for the new road threatens to damage the ecology of the wood.*

**threatened** adjective ENVIRON in danger of becoming an extinct organism or species

**threatened species** noun ECOL a species which is not in as much danger of extinction as an endangered species, but which needs protection

**three-address instruction** noun COMPUT an instruction which contains the addresses of two operands and the location where the result is to be stored

**three-dimensional** adjective COMPUT having three dimensions, width, breadth and depth, and therefore giving the impression of being solid. Abbreviation **3D**

**three-dimensional array** noun COMPUT an array made up of a number of two dimensional arrays, arranged in parallel, giving rows, columns and depth

**three-pin plug** noun ELEC a standard plug with three connections, one neutral, one live and one earthed, to connect an electric device to the mains electricity supply

**three state logic** noun COMPUT a logic gate or integrated circuit that has three possible output states rather than the usual two (NOTE: These are logic high, logic low and high impedance.)

**32-bit system** noun COMPUT a microcomputer system or central processing unit that handles data in 32-bit words

**threonine** noun BIOCHEM an essential amino acid

**threshold** noun **1.** a point or limit at which something changes **2.** ENVIRON a point below which the environment is not harmed by something **3.** PHYSIOL the point below which a drug has no effect **4.** a point at which something is strong enough to be sensed by an instrument or by a sensory nerve

**thrive** verb BIOL (*of an animal or plant*) to develop and grow strongly ○ *These plants thrive in very cold environments.*

**thrombin** noun BIOCHEM a substance that coagulates blood

**thromboplastin** noun BIOCHEM a lipoprotein that converts prothrombin into thrombin

**throttle** *noun* MECH ENG **1.** same as **throttle lever 2.** same as **throttle valve**

**throttle back** *verb* MECH ENG to reduce engine power ○ *Throttle back to increase the rate of descent.*

**throttle lever** *noun* MECH ENG a device operating the throttle valve ○ *When starting an engine, it is inadvisable to pump the throttle lever because of the risk of fire.* Also called **throttle**

**throttle setting** *noun* a particular position of the throttle which gives the required revolutions per minute power

**throttle valve** *noun* MECH ENG a device controlling the flow of fuel in an engine

**throughput** *noun* COMPUT the rate of production by a machine or system, measured as total useful information processed in a set period of time ○ *For this machine, throughput is 1.3 inches per second scanning speed.*

**thrush** *noun* MED an infection of the mouth or vagina caused by the fungus *Candida albicans*

**thrust** *noun* **1.** AEROSP the force produced by a propeller, jet or rocket ○ *A propeller converts engine power into thrust.* ○ *In order for the aircraft to increase speed, thrust must overcome drag.* ○ *In constant unaccelerated flight, thrust equals drag.* **2.** EARTH SCI a force in the crust of the Earth that squeezes and so produces folds ■ *verb* to push something suddenly with force ○ *A nozzle is an opening at the rear of a jet engine through which exhaust gases are thrust.*

**thrust fault** *noun* EARTH SCI a fault in which the upper layers of rock have been pushed forward over the lower layers

**thrust reverser** *noun* ENG a device to change the direction of thrust so that it operates in the opposite direction to the usual direction

**thulium** *noun* CHEM ELEM a very rare soft shiny metallic element used as an X-ray source (NOTE: The chemical symbol is **Tm**; the atomic number is **69** and the atomic weight is **168.93**.)

**thumb** *noun* ANAT a short thick finger, with only two phalanges, which is separated from the other four fingers on a hand

**thumbnail** *noun* **1.** ANAT the nail on a thumb **2.** COMPUT a miniature graphical

representation of an image, used as a quick and convenient method of viewing the contents of graphics or DTP files before they are retrieved

**thunder** *noun* METEOROL a loud sound generated by lightning in the atmosphere ○ *The storm was accompanied by thunder and lightning.*

**thunderstorm** *noun* METEOROL a storm with rain, thunder and lightning

COMMENT: The distance of a storm from the person hearing the thunder can be calculated by counting the number of seconds between the lightning flash and the sound of the thunder. Dividing this figure by three gives the distance in kilometres to the centre of the storm.

**thymine** *noun* BIOCHEM one of the four basic components of DNA

**thymus** *noun* ANAT an organ at the base of the neck that is involved in the development of the immune system, particularly T-cells (NOTE: It is relatively large in young children but shrinks after puberty.)

**thyratron** *noun* ELECTRONICS an electronic relay made up of a gas-filled tube in which a signal applied to the control grid initiates, but then cannot control, a transient anode current

**thyristor** *noun* ELECTRONICS a semiconductor device with three electrodes in which a signal to one electrode causes an independent current to flow between the other two

**thyroid** *adjective* ANAT referring to the thyroid gland

**thyroid gland** *noun* ANAT an endocrine gland in the neck of humans and other vertebrates that secretes the hormones that control metabolism and growth

COMMENT: The thyroid gland is activated by the pituitary gland and produces thyroxine, a hormone that regulates the body's metabolism. The thyroid gland needs a supply of iodine in order to produce thyroxine.

**thyroid hormone** *noun* BIOCHEM a hormone produced by the thyroid gland

**thyroid-releasing hormone** *noun* BIOCHEM a hormone secreted by the hypothalamus that controls the secretion of thyroid-stimulating hormone. Abbreviation **TRH**

**thyroid-stimulating hormone** *noun* BIOCHEM a hormone secreted by the pituitary gland that controls the secretion of thyroxine and triiodothyronine in the thyroid gland. Abbreviation **TSH**

**thyroxine** *noun* BIOCHEM the main hormone produced by the thyroid gland which regulates the body's metabolism and conversion of food into heat

**Ti** *symbol* CHEM ELEM titanium

**tibia** *noun* ZOOL a long straight bone below the knee in vertebrates (NOTE: In humans this is often called the shinbone.)

**tibial arteries** *plural noun* ANAT the two arteries which run down the front and back of the lower leg

**tick** *noun* ZOOL a tiny parasite that sucks blood from the skin. Order: Acarida.

**tidal** *adjective* EARTH SCI referring to the tide

**tidal current** *noun* EARTH SCI a flow of water into or out of a bay, harbour or estuary

**tidal energy** *noun* INDUST electricity produced by turbines driven by the force of the tides or waves. Also called **tidal power, wave power**

**tidal marsh** *noun* EARTH SCI a marsh in which the water level rises and falls twice daily

**tidal power** *noun* INDUST same as **tidal energy**

**tidal power plant** *noun* INDUST an installation where electricity is produced by turbines driven by the force of the tides

**tidal range** *noun* EARTH SCI the difference in height between high water and low water

**tidal river** *noun* EARTH SCI a river in which the water level rises and falls twice daily

**tidal wave** *noun* EARTH SCI a wave caused by an earthquake under the sea, which moves rapidly across the surface of the sea and becomes very large when it hits the shore. Also called **tsunami**

**tidal zone** *noun* EARTH SCI an area where the water level rises and falls twice daily

**tide** *noun* EARTH SCI a regular rising and falling of the sea, in a twice-daily rhythm

COMMENT: The tides are caused by the gravitational pull of the Moon, taken together with the centrifugal force of the Earth as it rotates, which make the water on the surface of the Earth move to high peaks at opposite sides of the globe with low troughs halfway between. Twice each month, at the new and full moon, the Sun, Moon and the Earth are directly aligned, giving the highest gravitational pull and causing the spring tides.

**tie** *noun* a basic structural member which is designed to withstand mainly tensile loads ○ *Diagonal ties can be used to relieve tension.*

**tilapia** *noun* ZOOL a tropical white fish, suitable for growing in fish farms

**tile** *verb* COMPUT to arrange a group of windows in a graphical user interface so that they are displayed side by side without overlapping

**till** *noun* EARTH SCI a boulder clay soil mixed with rocks of different sizes, found in glacial deposits ■ *verb* AGRIC to plough, dig or harrow soil to make it ready for the cultivation of crops

**tillage** *noun* AGRIC the activity of preparing the soil for cultivation

**tilt** *noun* a sloping position ○ *Land creates a drag effect on an electromagnetic wave-front, reducing the velocity of the wave and thereby causing a tilt.* ■ *verb* to be at an angle to the vertical or horizontal ○ *The Earth tilts on its axis.*

**tilt and swivel** *adjective* COMPUT referring to a monitor that is mounted on a pivot so that it can be moved to point in the most convenient direction for the operator

**tilth** *noun* AGRIC a good light crumbling soil prepared to be suitable for growing plants ○ *Work the soil into a fine tilth before sowing seeds.*

**timber** *noun* FORESTRY trees which have been or are to be felled and cut into logs

**timberline** *noun US* EARTH SCI same as **treeline** ○ *The slopes above the timberline were covered with boulders, rocks and pebbles.*

**timbre** *noun* ACOUSTICS the quality of a sound that can be identified by the human ear, e.g. that of a musical note which when played on two different musical instruments will not sound the same

**time** *noun* a dimension that relates the occurrence of events, expressed in intervals such as hours, minutes and seconds

■ *verb* to measure the time taken by an operation

**time base** *noun* PHYS **1.** a signal used as a basis for timing purposes **2.** a regular sawtooth waveform used in an oscilloscope to sweep the beam across the screen

**time code** *noun* COMPUT a record of timed information on an audio track in a video tape

**time dilation** *noun* PHYS variation in the apparent rate at which time passes as measured by clocks moving with relative velocities which are a significant fraction of the velocity of light (NOTE: Time dilation is a consequence of the Special Theory of Relativity.)

**time division multiplexing** *noun* COMPUT a method of combining several signals into one high-speed transmission carrier, each input signal being sampled in turn and the result transmitted to be reconstructed by the receiver. Abbreviation **TDM**

**time domain reflectometry** *noun* COMPUT a test which identifies where cable faults lie by sending a signal down the cable and measuring how long it takes for the reflection to come back. Abbreviation **TDR**

**time out** *verb* COMPUT to become no longer valid after a period of time ○ *If you do not answer this question within one minute, the program times out and moves onto the next question.*

**timer** *noun* a device which records the time taken for an operation to be completed

**time-sharing** *noun* COMPUT a computer system which allows several independent users to use it or be online at the same time

COMMENT: In time-sharing, each user appears to be using the computer all the time, when in fact each is using the central processing unit for a short time only, the central processing unit processing one user for a period then moving on to the next.

**tin** *noun* **1.** CHEM ELEM a metallic element, used especially to form alloys (NOTE: The chemical symbol is **Sn**; the atomic number is **50** and the atomic weight is **118.69**.) **2.** INDUST a metal container for food or drink, made of iron with a lining of tin or of aluminium. Also called **tin can** (NOTE: The US term is **can**.)

**tin can** *noun* INDUST same as **tin**

**tin (II) chloride** *noun* CHEM a white solid used as a reducing agent. Formula: $SnCl_2$.

**tincture** *noun* CHEM a solution of a plant extract or chemical in alcohol

**tincture of iodine** *noun* CHEM a weak solution of iodine in alcohol, used as an antiseptic

**tin (IV) hydride** *noun* CHEM a volatile gas used as a reducing agent. Formula: $SnH_4$.

**tin (IV) oxide** *noun* CHEM a crystalline solid. Formula: $SnO_2$.

**tin (IV) sulfide, tin (IV) sulphide** *noun* CHEM a solid used as a yellow-coloured pigment. Formula: $SnS_2$.

**tire** *noun* US AUTOMOT US spelling of **tyre**

**tissue** *noun* BIOL a group of cells that carries out a specific function, of which the organs of an animal's or plant's body are formed ○ *Most of an animal's body is made up of soft tissue, with the exception of the bones and cartilage.*

**tissue culture** *noun* **1.** BIOL plant or animal tissue grown in a culture medium **2.** BOT a method of plant propagation which reproduces clones of the original plant on media containing plant hormones

**tissue fluid** *noun* PHYSIOL the lymph that is found in the intercellular spaces

**titanium** *noun* CHEM ELEM a light metal used to make strong alloys (NOTE: The fatigue resistance of titanium is greater than that of aluminium or steel. The chemical symbol is **Ti**; the atomic number **22** and the atomic weight is **47.90**.)

**titanium dioxide** *noun* CHEM a white crystalline solid used as a white pigment for durable paints and plastics. Formula: $TiO_2$.

**titanium (IV) oxide** *noun* CHEM an inert solid that has three crystalline forms. Formula: $TiO_2$.

**titer** *noun* CHEM US spelling of **titre**

**titration** *noun* CHEM a process for measuring the concentration of a solution

**titre** *noun* CHEM a measurement of the concentration of a solution, as determined by titration (NOTE: The US spelling is **titer**.)

**Tl** *symbol* CHEM ELEM thallium

**TLC** *abbreviation* thin-layer chromatography

**T lymphocyte** *noun* ANAT same as **T cell**

**toadstool** *noun* FUNGI a poisonous fungus that has a cap resembling a mushroom's

**tocopherol** *noun* BIOCHEM one of a group of fat-soluble chemicals that make up vitamin E (NOTE: It is particularly abundant in vegetable oils and leafy green vegetables.)

**toe** *noun* ANAT one of the five separate parts at the end of a foot

**TOE** *abbreviation* MEASURE tonnes of oil equivalent

**toggle** *verb* COMPUT to switch between two states

**toggle switch** *noun* ELEC an electrical switch which has only two positions

**token** *noun* COMPUT **1.** an internal code which replaces a reserved word or program statement in a high-level language **2.** a control packet which is passed between workstations to control access to the network

**token bus network** *noun* COMPUT an IEEE 802.4 standard for a local area network formed with a bus-topology cable in which workstations transfer data by passing a token

**token ring network** *noun* COMPUT an IEEE 802.5 standard that uses a token passed from one workstation to the next in a ring network, so that a workstation can only transmit data if it captures the token (NOTE: Although logically a ring, token ring networks are often physically wired in a star topology.)

**tolerance** *noun* **1.** BIOL the ability of an organism to accept something, or not to react to something ○ *He has developed a tolerance to the drug.* **2.** MEASURE an allowable variation in something which can be measured ○ *a tolerance of 2°* ○ *a tolerance of 1 mm*

**tolerance dose** *noun* MED the amount of radiation which can be given without harm in radiotherapy

**tolerant** *adjective* not reacting adversely to something ○ *a salt-tolerant plant*

**tolerate** *verb* not to react adversely to something

**toleration** *noun* the act of tolerating something

**toleration level** *noun* BIOL a limit below which an organism will accept something or not react to something ○ *Waste hot water from power stations can kill freshwater fish if the water temperature rises above toleration levels.*

**Tollen's reagent** *noun* CHEM a mixed solution of silver nitrate, ammonia and sodium bicarbonate, used in testing for aldehydes

**toluene** *noun* CHEM a colourless liquid hydrocarbon similar to benzene, but less flammable, and lower in toxicity, used as a solvent and high-octane fuel. Formula: $C_7H_8$.

**ton** *noun* MEASURE **1.** a unit of measurement of weight, equal to 1016 kg. Also called **long ton 2.** *US* a unit of measurement of weight, equal to 907 kg. Also called **short ton 3.** same as **tonne**

**tone** *noun* ACOUSTICS the sound of one pitch ○ *The ground transmits a code in two short bursts each of which is modulated with two tones.*

**toner** *noun* COMPUT a finely powdered, usually black ink, used in laser printers. It is transferred onto paper by electrical charge and then fixed permanently to the paper by heating.

**tongue** *noun* **1.** ANAT a muscular organ in the mouth, used during eating to move food and, in humans, to produce speech sounds **2.** EARTH SCI a narrow strip of land that sticks out into water

**tonne** *noun* MEASURE a unit of measurement of weight, equal to 1000 kg. Also called **metric ton, ton**

**tonnes of oil equivalent** *noun* MEASURE a unit of measurement of the energy content of a fuel, calculated by comparing its heat energy with that of oil. Abbreviation **TOE**

**tonsil** *noun* ANAT either of two small oval masses of lymphoid tissue, one on either side of the throat

**tool** *noun* **1.** an object that is designed to help in carrying out particular task ○ *a cutting tool* **2.** COMPUT in a graphical user interface, a function accessed from an icon in a toolbar

**toolbar** *noun* COMPUT a window that contains a range of icons that access tools

**toolbox** *noun* **1.** ENG a box containing instruments needed to repair or maintain or install equipment **2.** COMPUT a set of predefined routines or functions that are used when writing a program

**toolkit** *noun* a set of tools consisting of spanners, screwdrivers, pliers and similar implements

**tools** *plural noun* COMPUT the utility programs such as backup or format found in a computer system

**tooth** *noun* **1.** ANAT a hard white object that is part of a set found in the jaws of vertebrates, used for biting and chewing **2.** ZOOL a hard, sharp projection on an invertebrate that functions like or resembles a vertebrate tooth (NOTE: The plural is **teeth**.)

**toothed** *adjective* ZOOL having teeth

**toothed whale** *noun* MARINE BIOL a whale such as a sperm whale, killer whale, porpoise or dolphin, which has teeth. Suborder: Odontoceti.

**top** *noun* the highest point or part ○ *the top of the cloud*

**topaz** *noun* MINERALS a yellow mineral, especially yellow sapphire or a yellow variety of quartz

**top-dead-centre** *noun* ENG the position of the piston at the extreme top of its stroke in a piston engine ○ *Ignition should occur just before top-dead-centre.*

**top down programming** *noun* COMPUT a method of writing programs in which a complete system is divided into simple blocks or tasks, each block unit being written and tested before proceeding with the next one

**topic** *noun* the subject of something heard, said, written or read ○ *The first section in the book deals with the topic of planning.*

**topical** *adjective* **1.** of particular interest at the moment **2.** MED referring to one particular part of the body

**topical drug** *noun* PHARM a drug which is applied to one part of the body only

**topically** *adverb* PHARM to one part of the body only ○ *The drug is applied topically.*

**top of stack** *noun* COMPUT the newest data item added to a stack

**topographic, topographical** *adjective* EARTH SCI referring to topography

**topography** *noun* EARTH SCI the study of the physical features of a geographical area

**topology** *noun* COMPUT the way in which the various elements in a network are interconnected

**topotype** *noun* ECOL a population which has become different from other populations of a species because of adaptation to local geographical features

**topset bed** *noun* EARTH SCI a layer of fine-grained sediment in a delta

**topsoil** *noun* EARTH SCI the top layer of soil, often containing organic material, from which chemical substances are leached into the subsoil below

**tor** *noun* EARTH SCI a pile of blocks or rounded granite rocks found on summits and hillsides

**tornado** *noun* METEOROL a violent storm with a column of rapidly turning air at the centre of an area of very low pressure, giving very high winds and causing damage to buildings

COMMENT: Tornadoes are formed by rising air currents associated with large cumulonimbus clouds. They rotate anticlockwise in the northern hemisphere and clockwise in the southern. Passing over the sea they pick up water and become waterspouts.

**torque** *noun* MECH ENG, PHYS a tangential of force causing rotation ○ *Torque forces try to bend the propeller against the direction of rotation.* ○ *High current flows through both the field and armature windings producing the high torque required for engine starting.*

**torquemeter** *noun* MECH ENG a device for measuring forces causing rotation ○ *Engine torque is used to indicate the power that is developed by a turboprop engine and the indicator is known as a torquemeter.*

**torr** *noun* MEASURE a unit of pressure equal to about 133.3 pascal or one conventional millimetre of mercury

**torrent** *noun* EARTH SCI a violent rapidly flowing stream of water or lava

**torrential** *adjective* METEOROL referring to very heavy rain ○ *The storm brought a torrential downpour of rain.*

**torsion** *noun* PHYS the action or force of twisting, especially of one end of a body while the other is fixed ○ *Rivets are subjected to torsion and may break.*

**torsion load** *noun* PHYS a load caused by the twisting of a structure

**torso** *noun* ANAT the main part of the body, not including the arms, legs and head

**total** *adjective* complete or entire ○ *The total world population of the animal is no more than four or five hundred pairs.*

**total body irradiation** *noun* MED the treatment of the whole body with radiation

**total eclipse** *noun* ASTRON an eclipse when the whole of the Sun or Moon is hidden

**total fertility rate** *noun* MED an average number of children expected to be born to a woman during her lifetime

**total internal reflection** *noun* PHYS the complete reflection of a light ray at the boundary of the medium through which it passes

**touch pad** *noun* COMPUT a flat device which can sense where on its surface and when it is touched, used to control a cursor position or switch a device on or off

**touch screen** *noun* COMPUT a computer display which allows the user to control the cursor position by touching the screen

**town gas** *noun* INDUST same as **coal gas**

**tox-, toxi-** *prefix* poison

**toxic** *adjective* CHEM poisonous or harmful to humans, animals or the environment

**toxic agent** *noun* CHEM a substance which is poisonous or harmful to humans, animals or the environment

**toxicant** *noun* CHEM a toxic substance

**toxic fumes** *plural noun* CHEM poisonous gases or smoke given off by a substance

**toxicity** *noun* CHEM **1.** the degree to which a substance is poisonous or harmful ○ *They were concerned about the high level of toxicity of the fumes.* **2.** the state of being poisonous or harmful ○ *The toxicity of the compound has limited its use.*

**toxicity threshold** same as **toxic threshold**

**toxico-** *prefix* poison

**toxicological** *adjective* MED referring to toxicology ○ *Irradiated food presents no toxicological hazard to humans.*

**toxicologist** *noun* MED a scientist who specialises in the study of poisons

**toxicology** *noun* MED the scientific study of poisons and their effects on the human body

**toxicosis** *noun* MED poisoning

**toxic substance** *noun* ENVIRON a substance that is poisonous or harmful to humans, animals or the environment

**toxic threshold** *noun* MED the point at which a poison starts to have a noticeably harmful effect. Also called **toxicity threshold**

**toxic waste** *noun* ENVIRON industrial or chemical waste that is poisonous or harmful

**toxigenomics** *noun* GENETICS the study of genetic effects on toxicology

**toxin** *noun* BIOCHEM a poisonous substance produced in the body by microorganisms, and which, if injected into an animal, stimulates the production of antitoxins

**toxoid** *noun* BIOCHEM a toxin which has been treated and is no longer poisonous but which can still provoke the formation of antibodies

COMMENT: Toxoids are used as vaccines, and are injected into a patient to give immunity against a disease.

**TP** *abbreviation* COMPUT **1.** teleprocessing **2.** transaction processing

**T piece adapter** *noun* COMPUT a device for connecting two inputs to one output or vice versa

**trace** *noun* **1.** a very small amount ○ *There are traces of radioactivity in the blood sample.* **2.** COMPUT a method of verifying that a program is functioning correctly, in which the current status and contents of the registers and variables used are displayed after each instruction step

**trace element** *noun* BIOCHEM a chemical element that is essential to organic growth but only in very small quantities

COMMENT: Plants require traces of copper, iron, manganese and zinc. Humans require the trace elements chromium, cobalt, copper, magnesium, manganese, molybdenum, selenium and zinc.

**trace gas** *noun* CHEM a gas such as xenon or helium that exists in the atmosphere in very small quantities

**trace metal** *noun* METALL a metal that is essential to organic growth but only in very small quantities

**tracer** *noun* BIOL a substance inserted into an organism so that its movements may be tracked from its colour, radioactivity, fluorescence or other traceable characteristic

**tracer element** *noun* MED a radioactive element used as a tracer

**traceroute** *noun* COMPUT a software utility that finds and displays the route taken for data travelling between a computer and a distant server on the Internet

COMMENT: The display shows the different servers that the data travels through, together with the time taken to travel between each server.

**trachea** *noun* **1.** ANAT the tube through which air travels from the throat to the lungs **2.** ZOOL a tube used for breathing air by insects and other invertebrates

**tracheid** *noun* BOT a thickened supporting cell found in conifers and their relatives

**tracing** *noun* COMPUT a function of a graphics program that takes a bit-map image, processes it to find the edges of the shapes and converts these into a vector line image that can be more easily manipulated

**track** COMPUT *noun* one of a series of thin concentric rings on a magnetic disk or of thin lines on a tape, which the read/write head accesses and along which the data is stored in separate sectors ■ *verb* to follow a path or track correctly ○ *The read head is not tracking the recorded track correctly.*

COMMENT: The first track on a tape is along the edge and the tape may have up to nine different tracks on it, while a disk has many concentric tracks around the central hub. The track and sector addresses are set-up during formatting.

**trackball** *noun* COMPUT a device used to move a cursor on-screen, which is controlled by turning a ball contained in a case

**tract** *noun* **1.** ANAT a system of internal organs ○ *the digestive tract* **2.** EARTH SCI a large area, especially of land ○

*Large tracts of forest have been destroyed by fire.*

**trade wind** *noun* METEOROL a wind that blows towards the equator, from the north-east in the northern hemisphere and from the south-east in the southern hemisphere

**trade-wind**    **cumulus**    *noun* METEOROL cumulus cloud usually associated with the trade winds

**tradition** *noun* a long-established way of doing something

**traditional** *adjective* having always been done in the same way ○ *Traditional technologies met basic subsistence needs.* ○ *The traditional system of agriculture has been revolutionised by the application of modern technology.*

**traffic** *noun* **1.** ENVIRON the vehicles coming and going on a road, the planes in the air or the ships at sea **2.** COMPUT, TELECOM all the messages and other signals processed by a system or carried by a communications link ○ *Our network begins to slow down if the traffic reaches 60 per cent of the bandwidth.*

**trail** *noun* **1.** ENVIRON a path or track **2.** ZOOL a mark or scent left by an animal

**trait** *noun* BIOL a genetically controlled characteristic

**trajectory** *noun* MATHS a curve that intersects all of a family of curves or surfaces at a constant angle

**trans-** *prefix* through or across

**transaction** *noun* COMPUT one single action which affects a database, e.g. a sale, a change of address or a new customer

**transaction-driven system** *noun* COMPUT a computer system that will usually run batch processing tasks until interrupted by a new transaction, at which point it allocates resources to that transaction. Abbreviation **TDS**

**transaction file** *noun* COMPUT same as **update file**

**transaction processing** *noun* COMPUT interactive processing in which a user enters commands and data on a terminal which is linked to a central computer, with results being displayed on-screen. Abbreviation **TP**

**transactivation** *noun* GENETICS the activation by an infecting virus of the genes of another virus that is already integrated into the chromosomes of a host bacterium, inducing the host to replicate the infecting virus

**transalpine** *adjective* EARTH SCI on or to the other side of the Alps ○ *All transalpine roads are closed.*

**transamination** *noun* BIOCHEM the changing of one amino acid into another

**transboundary pollution** *noun* ENVIRON airborne or waterborne pollution produced in one country which crosses to another. Also called **transfrontier pollution**

**transceiver** *noun* COMPUT a device that can both transmit and receive signals, e.g. a terminal or modem

**transcribe** *verb* COMPUT to copy data from one backing storage unit or medium to another

**transcript** *noun* GENETICS **1.** a molecule of messenger RNA carrying coded genetic information derived from DNA during the process of transcription in living cells **2.** the DNA carrying the genetic information of a retrovirus derived from the virus's RNA during transcription following the infection of a living cell

**transcription** *noun* GENETICS **1.** the transfer of genetic information from DNA to molecules of messenger RNA, which subsequently control protein synthesis **2.** the first step in the replication of a retrovirus in a host cell, in which its genetic code is transferred from RNA to a molecule of DNA

**transcriptome** *noun* GENETICS the full complement of unique sequenced RNA transcripts that an individual produces

**transcriptomics** *noun* GENETICS the scientific classification and analysis of RNA transcripts and their formation, structure and function in an individual

**transduce** *verb* **1.** GENETICS to transfer genetic material from one bacterium to another using a bacteriophage **2.** ELEC ENG to convert a non-electrical signal into an electrical one

**transducer** *noun* ELEC a device which converts a non-electrical signal into an electrical one

**transduction** *noun* **1.** GENETICS the transfer of genetic material between bacteria using a bacteriophage **2.** ELEC the conversion of a non-electrical signal into an electrical one

**transect** *noun* ECOL a line used in ecological surveys to provide a way of measuring and showing the distribution of organisms

**transfer** *verb* **1.** to move, or move someone or something, from one place to another **2.** COMPUT to change command or control from one location to another ○ *All processing activities have been transferred to the mainframe.* **3.** COMPUT to copy a section of memory to another location ■ *noun* **1.** the moving of someone or something from one place to another **2.** COMPUT the changing of command or control from one location to another

**transfer rate** *noun* COMPUT the speed at which data is transferred from a backing store to main memory or from one device to another ○ *With a good telephone line, this pair of modems can achieve a transfer rate of 14.4 Kbps.*

**transfer RNA** *noun* GENETICS a type of RNA that binds amino acids to protein chains in the ribosomes

**transform** *verb* to change the structure or appearance of something

**transformation** *noun* a change in structure or appearance

**transformational rules** *plural noun* COMPUT a set of rules applied to data which is to be transformed into coded form

**transformer** *noun* ELEC a device for changing the voltage or current amplitude of an alternating current signal (NOTE: Current transformers differ from voltage transformers in that the primary circuit consists of a supply feeder cable rather than a coil connected across a supply.)

**transfrontier pollution** *noun* ENVIRON same as **transboundary pollution**

**transgene** *noun* BIOTECH a gene from one organism that is transferred to another

**transgenic** *adjective* BIOTECH **1.** referring to an animal or plant into which genetic material from a different species has been transferred using the techniques of genetic modification **2.** referring to the techniques of transferring genetic material from one organism to another

**transhumance** *noun* AGRIC the practice of moving flocks and herds up to high summer pastures and bringing them down to a valley again in winter

**transient** COMPUT *adjective* referring to a state or signal that is present for a short period of time ■ *noun* something that is present for a short period

**transient area** *noun* COMPUT a section of memory for user programs and data

**transient error** *noun* COMPUT a temporary error which occurs for a short period of time

**transient suppressor** *noun* ELEC a device which suppresses voltage transients

**transistor** *noun* ELECTRONICS an electronic semiconductor device that can control the current flow in a circuit (NOTE: There are two main types of transistors: bipolar and unipolar.)

**transistor-transistor logic** *noun* ELECTRONICS the most common family of logic gates and high-speed transistor circuit design, in which the bipolar transistors are directly connected, usually collector to base, to provide the logic function. Abbreviation **TTL**

**transit** *noun* ASTRON the apparent movement of a star or planet across the meridian from which it is being observed, caused by Earth's rotation

**transition** *noun* a change from one state to another

**transition element** *noun* CHEM a metallic element such as copper or gold that has variable valencies (NOTE: Such elements often form brightly coloured compounds.)

**transition phase** *noun* a period when something is changing from one state to another

**transition temperature** *noun* CHEM, PHYS a temperature at which a substance changes from one form or phase to another, or at which some other initial change takes place

**translation** *noun* 1. PHYS the movement of a body in a straight line without rotation 2. GENETICS the process by which information in messenger RNA controls the sequence of amino acids that a ribosome assembles during protein synthesis 3. COMPUT the conversion of data from one form into another

**translocate** *verb* BOT to move substances through the tissues of a plant

**translocated herbicide** *noun* AGRIC a herbicide which kills a plant after being absorbed through its leaves

**translocation** *noun* BOT a movement of substances through the tissues of a plant

**transmission control protocol/interface program** *noun* COMPUT full form of **TCP/IP**

**transmit** *verb* 1. to send something somewhere else ○ *As the camshaft rotates, the cam will transmit a lifting force through rods and pivots to open the valve.* ○ *The charts are transmitted from one station to another by fax.* 2. TELECOM to send out a radio signal ○ *Survival beacons transmit a signal which enables search aircraft to rapidly locate survivors in the water.* 3. BIOL to pass on a disease to another animal or plant ○ *Some diseases are transmitted by insects.* (NOTE: **transmitting – transmitted**)

**transmittance** *noun* PHYS a measure of how well a material allows radiation to pass through it, measured as the ratio of incident radiation to transmitted radiation

**transmitter** *noun* 1. TELECOM a device for sending out radio signals ○ *Although continuous wave radars operate continuously, separate transmitter and receiver antennae must be used.* ○ *Signal strength is inversely proportional to the distance from the transmitter.* 2. COMPUT a device which will take an input signal, process it by modulation or conversion to sound, then transmit it by a medium such as radio or light

**transparency** *noun* 1. PHYS the condition of being transparent ○ *Meteorological visibility gives information on the transparency of the atmosphere to a stationary ground observer.* 2. COMPUT a computer program which is not obvious to the user or which cannot be seen by the user when it is running 3. PHOTOGRAPHY a positive image on a film or slide that can be viewed when light is passed through it

**transparent** *adjective* PHYS allowing electromagnetic radiation of specific wavelengths to pass through (NOTE: It is often used to describe materials such as glass that allow light to pass and hence can be seen through.)

**transparent interrupt** *noun* COMPUT a mode in which, if an interrupt occurs, all machine and program states are saved (NOTE: When the interrupt is serviced the system restores all previous states and continues as usual.)

**transphasor** *noun* ELEC an optical transistor, constructed from a crystal, that is able to switch a main beam of light according to a smaller input signal (NOTE: Transphasors are used in optical computers which could run at very high speeds, i.e. the speed of light.)

**transpiration** *noun* BOT the loss of water from a plant through its stomata

COMMENT: Transpiration accounts for a large amount of water vapour in the atmosphere. A tropical rainforest will transpire more water per square kilometre than is evaporated from the same area of sea. Clearance of forest has the effect of reducing transpiration, with an accompanying change in climate: less rain, leading to eventual desertification.

**transpire** *verb* BOT (*of a plant*) to lose water through stomata ○ *In tropical rainforests, up to 75% of rainfall will evaporate and transpire into the atmosphere.*

**transplant** *noun* **1.** MED the transfer of an organ or tissue from one person into or onto another ○ *a kidney transplant* **2.** MED a transplanted organ or tissue **3.** AGRIC a plant taken from one place and planted in the soil in another place ■ *verb* **1.** AGRIC to take a growing plant from one place and plant it in the soil in another place **2.** MED to take an organ or tissue from one person and put it into or onto another

**transponder** *noun* AVIAT a device in an aircraft for receiving and automatically transmitting radio signals so that an air traffic control station can identify the aircraft ○ *The transponder in the aircraft comprises a transmitter and a receiver.* (NOTE: The pilot sets an identification code, or 'squawk', assigned by air traffic control, on the transponder in the aircraft.)

**transport** *noun* a system of moving things from one place to another. Also called **transportation** ■ *verb* to move something from one place to another ○ *Xylem and phloem transport nutrients around a plant.*

**transportation** *noun* same as **transport**

**transport layer** *noun* COMPUT the fourth layer in the ISO/OSI network model that provides a reliable connection and checks and controls the quality of the connection

**transport number** *noun* PHYS (*in electrolysis*) the fraction of the total current carried by an ion in the electrolyte

**transpose** *verb* **1.** to reverse the usual order of things **2.** to move something to a different position in a sequence

**transposition** *noun* GENETICS a movement of a DNA segment to a new position on the same or another chromosome

**transposon** *noun* GENETICS a segment of DNA that can move to a new position on the same or another chromosome, often modifying the effect of neighbouring genes. Also called **jumping gene** (NOTE: These elements occur in bacteria, plants and animals.)

**transputer** *noun* COMPUT a single large very powerful chip containing a 32-bit microprocessor running at around 10 MIPS, that can be connected together to form a parallel processing system running OCCAM

**transuranic element** *noun* CHEM an artificial radioactive element which is beyond uranium in the periodic table

COMMENT: The transuranic elements have higher atomic numbers than uranium, which has an atomic number of 92. Apart from neptunium and plutonium they do not occur naturally but are formed from uranium in nuclear reactions.

**transverse wave** *noun* PHYS a wave that causes vibrations in a medium at right angles to the direction of its travel

**trap** *noun* COMPUT a device or piece of software or hardware that will catch something, e.g. a variable, fault or value

**trapdoor** *noun* COMPUT a way of getting into a system to change data, browse or hack

**trap handler** *noun* COMPUT a piece of software that accepts interrupt signals and acts on them, e.g. by running a special routine or sending data to a peripheral

**travelling wave** *noun* PHYS a wave that carries energy away from its source

**tread** *noun* a series of patterns moulded into the surface of a tyre to provide grip ○ *The risk of aquaplaning* *increases as the depth of tyre tread is reduced.*

**treat** *verb* **1.** INDUST to apply a process to something in order to get a specific result ○ *The fabric has been treated to make it waterproof.* **2.** MED to give medical aid to someone or to apply medical techniques to a disease or condition

**treatment** *noun* **1.** the application of a chemical or physical process ○ *anti-corrosion treatment* ○ *heat treatment* ○ *the treatment of sewage* **2.** MED the application of medical techniques to a patient, disease or condition **3.** MED a particular medical course of action to treat a disease or condition

**tree** *noun* **1.** BOT a plant typically with one main woody stem that may grow to a great height **2.** COMPUT same as **tree structure**

**tree and branch network system** *noun* COMPUT a system of networking in which data is transmitted along a single output line, from which other lines branch out, forming a tree structure that feeds individual stations

**tree cover** *noun* BOT the number of trees growing on a specific area of land

**tree fern** *noun* PLANTS a very large fern found in Australasia, which grows like a tree with a single thick stem

**treeline** *noun* EARTH SCI **1.** a line at a specific altitude, above which trees will not grow ○ *The slopes above the treeline were covered with boulders, rocks and pebbles.* **2.** a line in the northern or southern hemisphere, north or south of which trees will not grow

**tree ring** *noun* BOT same as **annual ring**

**tree savanna** *noun* EARTH SCI a dry grass-covered plain with some trees

**tree selection sort** *noun* COMPUT a rapid form of selection in which the information from the first sort pass is used in the second pass to speed up selection

**tree structure** *noun* COMPUT a data structure system in which each item of data is linked to several others by branches. Also called **tree**

**trellis coding** *noun* COMPUT a method of modulating a signal that uses both amplitude and phase modulation to give a greater throughput and lower error rates for data transmission speeds of over 9600 bits per second

**trembler** *noun* ELEC an automatic vibrator for making and breaking an electrical circuit ○ *An ignition unit may be supplied with direct current and operated by a trembler mechanism.*

**tremor** *noun* **1.** a slight shaking movement **2.** EARTH SCI a minor earthquake

**trend** *noun* a gradual or prevailing development ○ *a trend towards organic farming*

**TRH** *abbreviation* BIOCHEM thyroid-releasing hormone

**triad** *noun* COMPUT **1.** a group of three elements, characters or bits **2.** a triangular shaped grouping of the red, green and blue phosphor spots at each pixel location on the screen of a colour monitor

**triangle** *noun* MATHS a plane figure with three sides and three angles

**triangle of vectors** *noun* MATHS same as **parallelogram of vectors**

**triatomic molecule** *noun* CHEM an element with three atoms in a molecule

**triazine** *noun* CHEM an organic compound containing a ring of three carbon and three nitrogen atoms per molecule, or a derivative of such a compound (NOTE: Triazines are used in weedkillers, pesticides and dyes.)

**tribe** *noun* BIOL a category between subfamily and genus in the scientific classification of living things

**tribromomethane** *noun* CHEM a colourless liquid with a sweet smell, formed as a by-product when chlorine is added to drinking water. Formula: $CHBr_3$. (NOTE: It is used as a laboratory reagent.)

**tributary** *noun* EARTH SCI a stream or river flowing into a larger river

**tricarboxylic acid cycle** *noun* BIOCHEM same as **Krebs cycle**

**trichloroethanal,** **trichloroacetaldehyde** *noun* CHEM a colourless liquid aldehyde, used in making DDT. Formula: $CCl_3CHO$.

**trichlorophenoxyacetic acid** *noun* CHEM a herbicide which forms dioxin as a by-product during the manufacturing process. Also called **2,4,5-T**

**trickle** *verb* (*of liquid*) to flow gently ■ *noun* a gentle flow

**trickle system** *noun* AGRIC an irrigation system in which water is brought to the base of each plant and drips slowly into the soil

**trickling filter** *noun* INDUST a filter bed through which liquid sewage is passed to purify it

**tricuspid valve** *noun* ANAT an inlet valve with three cusps between the right atrium and the right ventricle in the heart

**trigeminal ganglion** *noun* ANAT a sensory ganglion containing the cells of origin of the sensory fibres in the fifth cranial nerve. Also called **Gasserian ganglion**

**trigeminal nerve** *noun* ANAT the fifth cranial nerve which controls the sensory nerves in the forehead and face as well as the muscles in the jaw

**trigger** *verb* to cause something to operate or come into effect ○ *The indicator triggers an aural warning if specific limits are exceeded.* ○ *It is not known what triggered the avalanche.*

**triglyceride** *noun* CHEM an ester formed from one glycerol molecule and three fatty acid molecules (NOTE: Large amounts of triglycerides in the diet are harmful to human health. They are found in animal and plant fats and oils.)

**triiodothyronine** *noun* BIOCHEM a hormone that is secreted by the thyroid gland

**trilobite** *noun* PALAEONT an extinct Palaeozoic marine arthropod with a flat oval segmented body and compound eyes. Class: Trilobita.

**trioxide** *noun* CHEM an oxide containing three oxygen atoms per molecule

**triple** *adjective* consisting of three parts ○ *Probes may be of single, double or triple element construction.*

**triple bond** *noun* CHEM a chemical bond composed of three covalent bonds

**triple point** *noun* CHEM the temperature and pressure at which the solid, liquid and gaseous phases of a substance exist in equilibrium

**triplet** *noun* GENETICS same as **codon**

**triploblastic** *adjective* ZOOL having a body that develops from all three layers of cells: ectoderm, endoderm and mesoderm (NOTE: All many-celled animals are triploblastic except for the coelenterates, the group to which jellyfish and sea anemones belong.)

**triploid** *adjective* GENETICS referring to an organism that has three representatives of each chromosome in a cell nucleus

**trisomy** *noun* GENETICS the occurrence of one or more sets of three chromosomes instead of chromosome pairs

**tritium** *noun* CHEM a rare isotope of hydrogen

**triton** *noun* MARINE BIOL a large tropical marine snail with a thick brightly coloured shell. Family: Cymatiidae.

**trivalent** *adjective* **1.** GENETICS referring to three structurally identical chromosomes that associate during the initial stage of meiosis **2.** CHEM having a valency of three

**trochlear nerve** *noun* ANAT the fourth cranial nerve which controls the muscles of the eyeball

**trophic** *adjective* BIOL referring to nutrition

**trophic cascade** *noun* ENVIRON the effect that a change in the size of one population in a food web has on the populations below it

**trophic chain** *noun* ECOL same as **food chain**

**trophic level** *noun* ECOL one of the levels in a food chain

COMMENT: There are three trophic levels. Producers, organisms such as plants, take energy from the Sun or the environment and convert it into matter. Primary consumers, organisms such as herbivores, eat producers. Secondary consumers, organisms such as carnivores, eat other consumers.

**trophic structure** *noun* ECOL the structure of an ecosystem, shown by food chains and food webs

**-trophy** *suffix* BIOL **1.** nourishment **2.** development of an organ

**-tropic** *suffix* **1.** turning towards **2.** having an influence

**tropical** *adjective* EARTH SCI referring to the tropics ○ *The disease is carried by a tropical insect.*

**tropical air** *noun* METEOROL a mass of air that originates in the tropics

**tropical climate** *noun* METEOROL the type of climate found in the tropics and characterised by very high temperatures and often high humidity

**tropical cyclone** *noun* METEOROL a tropical storm in the Indian Ocean, with masses of air turning rapidly round a low pressure area

**tropical desert** *noun* EARTH SCI same as **hot desert**

**tropical disease** *noun* MED a disease such as malaria, dengue or Lassa fever that occurs in tropical countries

**tropical disturbance** *noun* METEOROL a powerful storm that forms over water in the tropics or subtropics and lasts for 24 hours or more ○ *As it gains power, a tropical disturbance may become a tropical wave, tropical depression, tropical storm or hurricane.*

**tropical hygiene** *noun* MED health concerns relating to tropical regions

**tropical medicine** *noun* MED a branch of medicine which deals with tropical diseases

**tropical month** *noun* TIME a period of 27.32 days, the time taken for the Moon to return to the celestial equator

**tropical rainforest** *noun* EARTH SCI a biome where almost constant rain and high temperature permit plants to grow throughout the year

**tropical revolving storm** *noun* METEOROL an intense depression that develops over a tropical ocean (NOTE: Tropical revolving storms originate within 5–15° of the equator and generally occur from June to October.)

**tropical seasonal forest** *noun* EARTH SCI a biome where plants only grow at a specific time of year

**tropical storm** *noun* METEOROL a violent storm occurring in the tropics

**tropical year** *noun* TIME same as **solar year**

**tropical zone** *noun* EARTH SCI the region between the Tropic of Cancer and the Tropic of Capricorn

**Tropic of Cancer** *noun* EARTH SCI a parallel running round the Earth at latitude 23°28N

**Tropic of Capricorn** *noun* EARTH SCI a parallel running round the Earth at latitude 23°28S

**tropics** *plural noun* EARTH SCI the region between the Tropic of Cancer and the Tropic of Capricorn, where the climate is hot and often humid ○ *a disease which is endemic in the tropics* ○ *He lives in the tropics.*

**tropism** *noun* BOT the action of a plant organ turning towards a stimulus

**tropopause** *noun* METEOROL a layer of the atmosphere between the troposphere and the stratosphere

**troposphere** *noun* METEOROL the lowest region of the atmosphere, extending to about 12 km above sea level

COMMENT: The troposphere is at its deepest near the equator and shallowest near the poles. It is formed largely of nitrogen (78%) and oxygen (21%), plus argon and some trace gases. The temperature in the troposphere falls about 6.5° C per thousand metres of altitude, the temperature at 16 km being about −55° C.

**tropospheric** *adjective* METEOROL referring to the troposphere

**tropospheric ozone** *noun* METEOROL the ozone that is located in the troposphere and plays a significant role in the greenhouse gas effect and urban smog

**troubleshoot** *verb* **1.** to look for the causes of problems and resolve them **2.** COMPUT to debug computer software **3.** COMPUT to locate and repair faults in hardware

**trough** *noun* **1.** a low point in a cycle ○ *The graph shows the peaks and troughs of pollution over the seasons.* **2.** METEOROL a long narrow area of low pressure with cold air in it, leading away from the centre of a depression

**true** *adjective* **1.** correct **2.** COMPUT having the logical condition representing binary one. Compare **false**

**true bearing** *noun* NAVIG a bearing with reference to true north, rather than magnetic north

**true north** *noun* NAVIG the direction along any line of longitude towards the North Pole. Compare **magnetic north**

**true vocal cords** *plural noun* ANAT the cords in the larynx which can be brought together to make sounds as air passes between them

**truncate** *verb* MATHS to give an approximate value to a number by reducing it to a specific number of digits

**truncation** *noun* MATHS the removal of digits from a number so that it is a specific length ○ *3.5678 truncated to 3.56*

**truncation error** *noun* MATHS an error caused when a number is truncated

**trunk** *noun* **1.** BOT the main stem of a tree **2.** COMPUT a bus or communication link consisting of wires or leads which connect different parts of a hardware system

**truth table** *noun* COMPUT a method of defining a logic function as the output state for all possible inputs

**truth value** *noun* MATHS one of two values true or false, T or F, 1 or 0, used in Boolean algebra

**trypanosome** *noun* ZOOL a parasite which causes sleeping sickness, transmitted by the tsetse fly

**trypanosomiasis** *noun* MED same as **sleeping sickness**

**trypsin** *noun* BIOCHEM a protein-digesting enzyme secreted by the pancreas

**tryptophan** *noun* BIOCHEM an essential amino acid

**tsetse fly** *noun* ZOOL an African insect which passes trypanosomes into the bloodstream of humans and livestock, causing sleeping sickness

**TSH** *abbreviation* BIOCHEM thyroid-stimulating hormone

**tsunami** *noun* METEOROL a wave caused by an earthquake under the sea, which moves rapidly across the surface of the sea and becomes very large when it hits the shore. Also called **tidal wave**

**TSW** *abbreviation* COMPUT telesoftware

**TTL** *abbreviation* ELEC transistor-transistor logic

**TTL compatible** *noun* ELEC a MOS or other electronic circuit or component that can directly connect to and drive TTL circuits

**TTL logic** *noun* ELEC the use of TTL design and components to implement logic circuits and gates

**TTL monitor** *noun* ELEC a design of monitor which can only accept digital signals, so can only display monochrome images or a limited range of colours

**tube** *noun* **1.** a long, hollow cylindrical device for holding or carrying fluids ○ *A liquid-type fire detector consists of a tube and expansion chamber filled with liquid.* **2.** ANAT a long, hollow cylindrical organ that carries fluids around the body

**tuber** *noun* BOT the fat part of an underground stem or root, which holds nutrients and which has buds from which shoots develop ○ *A potato is the tuber of a potato plant.*

**tuberous** *adjective* **1.** like a tuber **2.** BOT referring to a plant that grows from a tuber

**tubing** *noun* a system of tubes ○ *hydraulic tubing*

**tubular** *adjective* shaped like a tube ○ *Diagonal members can be of angle section, box spar or tubular in shape.*

**tufa** *noun* EARTH SCI a form of calcareous deposit found near hot springs

**tundra** *noun* EARTH SCI a cold treeless Arctic region which may be covered with low shrubs, grasses, mosses and lichens

**tune** *verb* **1.** ENG to set a system at its optimum point by careful adjustment ○ *The engine has not been properly tuned.* **2.** PHYS to adjust a radio receiver to the particular frequency of the required signal ○ *The RBI shows the bearing of the tuned radio beacon with reference to the aircraft's heading.*

**tuner** *noun* a part of a radio receiver which allows the operator to select the particular frequency of the required signal ○ *The tuner reduces interference.*

**tungsten** *noun* CHEM ELEM a hard shiny grey metallic element with a very high melting point, used in high-temperature alloys, lamp filaments and high-speed cutting tools (NOTE: The chemical symbol is **W**; the atomic number is **74** and the atomic weight is **183.85**.)

**tungsten carbide** *noun* CHEM a fine, very hard, grey powder made by heating tungsten with carbon and used in the manufacture of cutting and grinding tools and durable machine parts

**tunnel effect** *noun* PHYS a quantum mechanical effect in which fundamental particles pass through an energy barrier even if they do not have enough energy to do so

**tunnelling** *noun* **1.** COMPUT a method of enclosing a packet of data from one type of network within another packet so that it can be sent over a different, incompatible, network **2.** ASTRON an effect of relativity whereby electrons might travel through rather than over the gravitational wall around a black hole, especially one of low mass

**tunnel vision** *noun* BIOL a field of vision which is restricted to the area immediately in front of the eye

**turbid** *adjective* PHYS referring to a liquid which is cloudy because of particles suspended in it

**turbidity** *noun* PHYS cloudiness of a liquid, because of particles suspended in it

**turbine** *noun* ENG a mechanical device which converts moving liquid, steam or air into energy by turning a generator

COMMENT: Water turbines create electricity from water power. Water is channelled from a reservoir through pipes which turn the vanes of the turbine, which then turn the rotor of the generator. Axial-flow turbines have blades like those on a ship's propeller, rotating horizontally. The impulse turbine has jets of water directed at bucket-shaped blades which catch the water. Reaction turbines have blades on the turbine which adjust to the angle at which the jets of water hit them. Pumped storage turbines act as generators when water pressure is high, but become water pumps when pressure is low, pumping water back into the reservoir.

**turbine blade** *noun* ENG a part of a turbine which has an aerodynamic effect on the air

**turbo-** *prefix* ENG turbine

**turbocharger** *noun* ENG a supercharger driven by a turbine powered by exhaust gases ○ *The turbocharger significantly increases engine power.*

**turbofan** *noun* AEROSP a jet engine in which most of the thrust is produced by air, accelerated by a large fan, which does not pass through the combustion chamber of the engine

COMMENT: Turbofan engines are much quieter than older turbojets and make a characteristic sound when in operation. The fan can be clearly seen in the front part of the engine.

**turbojet** *noun* AEROSP a jet engine which includes a turbine-driven compressor for the air taken into the engine ○ *The de Havilland Comet was the world's first turbojet commercial transport aircraft.*

COMMENT: Frank Whittle (1907–96) was an English engineer and RAF officer who invented the turbojet aircraft engine. Whit-

tle developed a jet aircraft by 1941 and the first military jet aircraft, the Gloster Meteor, became operational in 1944. Turbofan engines have now taken over from turbojet engines.

**turbopropeller, turboprop** *noun* AEROSP a turbojet engine in which the turbine also drives a propeller

COMMENT: Turboprop aircraft are efficient at lower speeds than turbojet aircraft and are often used for short haul operations.

**turbulence** *noun* 1. METEOROL an irregular motion of the atmosphere 2. PHYS secondary motion within a moving fluid

**turbulent** *adjective* METEOROL referring to the irregular motion of the atmosphere ○ *When flying in turbulent air conditions, an aircraft is subjected to upward and downward gust loads.*

**turf moor** *noun* EARTH SCI an area of land where peat is found

**turgid** *adjective* BOT referring to plant tissue that is swollen with liquid and therefore firm. Opposite **flaccid**

**turgidity** *noun* BOT the condition of being turgid

**turgor** *noun* BOT the normal state of a plant cell when the vacuole is full of water

**Turing machine** *noun* COMPUT a mathematical model of a device which could read and write data to a controllable tape storage while altering its internal states

**Turing test** *noun* COMPUT a test to decide if a computer is intelligent

**turnkey system** *noun* COMPUT a complete system which is designed to a customer's needs and is ready to use (NOTE: To operate it, the user only has to switch it on or turn a key.)

**turquoise** *noun* MINERALS a bright greenish-blue form of aluminium copper phosphate, used in jewellery

**TV** *abbreviation* COMPUT television

**TVP** *abbreviation* FOOD INDUST textured vegetable protein

**TW** *abbreviation* MEASURE terawatt

**tweak** *verb* COMPUT to make small adjustments to a program or hardware to improve performance

**tweening** *noun* COMPUT the process of calculating the intermediate images that lead from a starting image to a different finished image ○ *Using tweening, we can show how a frog turns into a princess in five steps.*

**twenty-twenty vision, 20/20 vision** *noun* BIOL perfect normal vision

**twin** *noun* BIOL one of two babies or animals born at the same time from two ova fertilised at the same time or from one ovum that splits in two

**twinkling** *noun* ASTRON same as **scintillation**

**twist** *verb* **1.** to change the shape of something by bending or turning it, or to bend or turn into another shape ○ *He twisted the wire into the shape of an S.* ○ *The rods twist easily when heated.* **2.** to wind something around something else ○ *She twisted the wire around the post.* **3.** to turn against resistance ○ *Centrifugal, bending and twisting forces act on a propeller during flight.*

**twisted-pair cable** *noun* ELEC a cable which consists of two insulated copper wires twisted around each other, to reduce induction and so interference

COMMENT: The EIA specifies five levels of cable for different purposes. The Category 1 standard defines an older-style unshielded twisted-pair cable that is formed by loosely twisting two insulated wires together to reduce noise and interference. This type of cable is not suitable for data transmission. The Category 2 (part of the EIA/TIA 568 specification) standard defines a type of unshielded twisted-pair cable that can be used to transmit data at rates up to 4 MHz. The Category 3, part of the EIA/TIA 568 specification, standard defines a type of unshielded twisted-pair cable that can be used to transmit data at rates up to 10 MHz. This type of cable is the minimum standard of cable required for a 10BaseT network (the standard suggests that the cable should have three twists per foot of cable). The Category 4, part of the EIA/TIA 568 specification, standard defines a type of unshielded twisted-pair cable that is the minimum standard of cable required for data transmission rates up to 16 Mbit/second on a Token Ring network. The Category 5, part of the EIA/TIA 568 specification, standard defines a type of cable that can carry data transmitted at up to 100 MHz and is suit-

able for FDDI over copper wire, 100BaseT or other high-speed networks.

**twisted-pair Ethernet** *noun* COMPUT a star-topology network that uses twisted-pair cable and transmits data at 10 Mbps, normally called 10BaseT

**twister** *noun US* METEOROL a tornado (*informal*)

**two-address instruction** *noun* COMPUT an instruction format containing the location of two operands, the result being stored in one of the operand locations

**two-dimensional** *adjective* having only two dimensions, so being flat with no depth

**two-figure code** *noun* COMPUT a code with two numbers between 0 and 9

**two input adder** *noun* MATHS ◊ **half adder**

**two-pin mains plug** *noun* ELEC a plug with two pins, one neutral, one live

**two's complement** *noun* COMPUT a decimal complement, formed by adding one to the one's complement of a binary number, often used to represent negative binary numbers

**tympanic membrane** *noun* ANAT same as **eardrum**

**tympanum** *noun* ACOUSTICS a membrane or diaphragm that vibrates to produce sound

**Tyndall effect** *noun* PHYS the scattering of light by particles in its path (NOTE: An example is the way in which a sunbeam becomes visible as it passes through dust in the air.)

**type** *noun* **1.** a category with members sharing some properties **2.** COMPUT a definition of the processes or sorts of data which a variable in a computer can contain, e.g. numbers or text only **3.** PRINTING printed words, letters or symbols

**typeface** *noun* PRINTING a set of characters in a particular design and particular weight ○ *Most of this book is set in the Times typeface.*

**type size** *noun* PRINTING the size of a font, measured in points

**type style** *noun* PRINTING the weight and angle of a font, e.g. bold or italic

**typhoid, typhoid fever** *noun* MED an infection of the intestine caused by *Salmonella* in food or water, which causes fever and diarrhoea and may be fatal

**typhoon** *noun* METEOROL a tropical cyclone in the Far East

**typhus** *noun* MED one of several fevers caused by the Rickettsia bacterium, making the patient very weak

**tyramine** *noun* BIOCHEM an enzyme found in cheese, beans, tinned fish, red wine and yeast extract, which can cause high blood pressure if found in excessive quantities in the brain

**tyre** *noun* ENG a rubber covering for a wheel (NOTE: The US spelling is **tire**.)

**tyre creep** *noun* AEROSP a gradual rotation of the tyre in relation to the wheel, caused by landing ○ *Aligned white marks on the wheel and tyre indicate that there is no tyre creep.*

COMMENT: Tyre creep can lead to damage to the tyre valve and subsequent unwanted and possibly dangerous deflation of the tyre.

**tyre pressure** *noun* ENG the air pressure in a tyre

**tyrosine** *noun* BIOCHEM an amino acid which is a component of thyroxine

# U

**U** *symbol* CHEM ELEM uranium

**UART** *abbreviation* COMPUT universal asynchronous receiver/transmitter

**UDP** *noun* COMPUT a protocol that is part of TCP/IP that is often used in network management and SNMP applications. Full form **user datagram protocol**

**UHF** *abbreviation* PHYS ultra high frequency

**ULA** *abbreviation* COMPUT uncommitted logic array

**ulna** *noun* ANAT one of two parallel long bones in the lower forelimb of vertebrates or the forearm of humans

**ulnar artery** *noun* ANAT an artery which branches from the brachial artery at the elbow and runs down the inside of the forearm to join the radial artery in the palm of the hand

**ulnar nerve** *noun* ANAT a nerve running from the neck to the elbow, which controls the muscles in the forearm and fingers

**ulnar pulse** *noun* BIOL a secondary pulse in the wrist, taken near the inner edge of the forearm

**ultra-** *prefix* beyond

**ultrabasic** *adjective* EARTH SCI referring to rock which has even less silica and more magnesium than basic rock

**ultra high frequency** *noun* PHYS a range of frequencies usually used to transmit television signals. Abbreviation **UHF**

**ultra high frequency band** *noun* ELEC a radio frequency range between 300 MHz and 3000 MHz

**ultramicroscope** *noun* BIOL a microscope that uses scattered light to form images of submicroscopic objects

**ultramicroscopic** *adjective* BIOL too small to be seen with an ordinary microscope

**ultrananoplankton** *plural noun* MARINE BIOL plankton less than 2 μm in size

**ultraplankton** *plural noun* MARINE BIOL plankton in the size range 0.5–10 μm

**ultrasonic** *adjective* ACOUSTICS referring to the frequencies in the range of 20 000 Hz which cannot be heard by the human ear

**ultrasonic detection** *adjective* INDUST a method using high frequency sound to check metal components for internal weaknesses

**ultrasonic inspection** *noun* INDUST a non-destructive inspection of materials using extremely high frequency vibrations

**ultrasonic waves** *plural noun* ACOUSTICS sound waves in the range of ultrasound

**ultrasound** *noun* ACOUSTICS, MED sound in the range of 20 000 Hz which cannot be heard by the human ear ○ *The nature of the tissue may be made clear on ultrasound examination.* ○ *Ultrasound scanning provides a picture of the ovary and the eggs inside it.*

COMMENT: The very high frequency waves of ultrasound can be used to detect and record organs or growths inside the body, in a similar way to the use of X-rays, by recording the differences in echoes sent back from different tissues. Ultrasound is used routinely to monitor growth of the fetus in the uterus, and to treat some conditions such as internal bruising. It can also destroy bacteria and calculi.

**ultrasound scan** *noun* MED the examination of an internal part of the body using very high frequency sound waves to create a picture

**ultrasound treatment** *noun* MED the treatment of soft tissue inflammation using ultrasound waves

**ultraviolet** *adjective* PHYS referring to electromagnetic radiation with a wavelength just greater than the visible spectrum, from 200 to 4000 angstrom. Abbreviation **UV**

**ultraviolet erasable PROM** *noun* COMPUT an EPROM whose contents are erased by exposing to UV light

**ultraviolet radiation** *noun* PHYS an invisible light which has a very short wavelength beyond the violet end of the spectrum and causes tanning and burning. Abbreviation **UVR**

**ultraviolet rays** *plural noun* the short invisible rays, beyond the violet end of the colour spectrum, which form the tanning and burning element in sunlight

COMMENT: UV rays form part of the high-energy radiation which the Earth receives from the Sun. UV rays are classified as UVA and UVB rays. UVB rays form only a small part of radiation from the Sun but they are dangerous and can cause skin cancer if a person is exposed to them for long periods. The effect of UVB rays is reduced by the ozone layer in the stratosphere

**umbilical cord** *noun* ANAT the flexible cord that connects the fetus to the mother's placenta during pregnancy, and through which nutrients are delivered and waste expelled

**UMTS** *noun* COMPUT a third generation mobile communication system that supports voice, data, and video signals to the handset. Full form **universal mobile telecommunications system**

**un-** *prefix* **1.** not **2.** reversing an action or state

**unary operation** *noun* COMPUT a computing operation on only one operand, e.g. the logical NOT operation

**unblock** *verb* to remove a blockage from something

**unboiled** *adjective* FOOD SCI which has not been boiled ○ *In some areas, it is dangerous to drink unboiled water.*

**unclocked** *adjective* COMPUT referring to an electronic circuit or flip-flop which changes state as soon as an input changes, not with a clock signal

**uncommitted logic array** *noun* COMPUT a chip containing a number of unconnected logic circuits and gates which can then be connected by a customer to provide a required function. Abbreviation **ULA**

**unconditional** *adjective* which does not depend on any condition being met

**unconditional branch, unconditional jump, unconditional transfer** *noun* COMPUT an instruction which transfers control from one point in the program to another, without depending on any condition being met

**unconfined** *adjective* EARTH SCI referring to ground water or an aquifer of which the upper surface is at ground level

**uncontaminated** *adjective* ENVIRON not having been contaminated

**uncontrollable** *adjective* unable to be controlled

**uncontrolled** *adjective* not controlled

**uncontrolled dumping** *noun* ENVIRON the throwing away of waste anywhere

**uncontrolled dumpsite** *noun* ENVIRON a place where waste is left on the ground and not buried in a hole

**uncontrolled fire** *noun* ENVIRON a fire which has ignited accidentally and burns out of control

**uncoordinated** *adjective* not joined together or working together

**uncultivated** *adjective* AGRIC not cultivated

**undelete** *verb* COMPUT to restore deleted information or a deleted file ○ *This function will undelete your cuts to the letter.*

**under-** *prefix* **1.** below or underneath **2.** less than or not as strong

**underflow** *noun* COMPUT the result of a numerical operation that is too small to be represented with the given accuracy of a computer

**underground** *adjective, adverb* EARTH SCI beneath the surface of the ground ○ *Foxes live in underground holes.* ○ *An underground nuclear test was carried out at the desert test site.* ○ *Worms live all their life underground.* ○ *If power cables were placed underground they would be less of an eyesore.*

**underground water** *noun* EARTH SCI water in porous rocks underground

**undergrowth** *noun* BOT shrubs and other plants growing under large trees

**underline** *noun* COMPUT, PRINTING a line drawn or printed under a piece of text. Also called **underscore**

**under normal conditions** *adverb* when everything is as it usually is

**undernourished** *noun* BIOL having too little food

**underproduction** *noun* INDUST the production of less than usual

**underscore** *noun* COMPUT, PRINTING same as **underline**

**understorey** *noun* BOT the lowest layer of small trees and shrubs in a wood, below the canopy

**underwood** *noun* BOT small trees in a wood, below the canopy

**undo** *verb* COMPUT to reverse the previous action ○ *You've just deleted the paragraph, but you can undo it from the option in the Edit menu.* (NOTE: It is often an option in a program and an editing command.)

**undulating** *adjective* rising and falling in gentle slopes ○ *Flight over undulating terrain will result in changing indications of aircraft height on the indicator of the radio altimeter.*

**unedited** *adjective* having not been edited

**unexpressed** *adjective* GENETICS referring to a gene that does not produce an observable effect on the organism that carries it

**unformatted** *adjective* COMPUT **1.** referring to a text file which contains no formatting commands, margins or typographical commands ○ *It is impossible to copy to an unformatted disk.* **2.** referring to a disk which has not been formatted ○ *The cartridge drive provides 12.7 Mbyte of unformatted storage.*

**ungroup** *verb* COMPUT to convert a single complex object back into a series of separate objects

**ungulate** *noun, adjective* ZOOL (*a mammal*) that has hoofs (NOTE: Ungulates are divided into two groups, odd-toed such as horses or even-toed such as cows.)

**uni-** *prefix* one

**unicellular** *adjective* BIOL referring to an organism formed of one cell

**unified atomic mass unit** *noun* PHYS same as **atomic mass unit**

**unified field theory** *noun* PHYS a single theory that defines the interrelationships between the theories of nuclear, electromagnetic and gravitational forces

**uniform** *adjective* consistent and not varying in characteristics ○ *An engine should be run at low revolutions per minute after flight to allow engine components to cool to a uniform temperature.*

**uniform resource locator** *noun* COMPUT same as **universal resource locator**. abbreviation **URL**

**unimolecular reaction** *noun* CHEM a chemical reaction with just one type of molecule working as the reactant

**uninterruptable power supply** *noun* COMPUT a power supply that can continue to provide a regulated supply to equipment even after mains power failure. Abbreviation **UPS**

**union** *noun* MATHS a logical function which produces a true output if any input is true

**unipolar** *adjective* ELEC referring to a transmission system in which a positive voltage pulse and zero volts represent the binary bits 1 and 0

**unipolar neuron** *noun* ANAT a neuron with a single process

**unipolar signal** *noun* ELEC a signal that uses only positive voltage levels

**unipolar transistor** *noun* ELECTRONICS same as **field-effect transistor**

**unique** *adjective* being the one and only of its sort ○ *The pulse coded message contains a unique 4-number identification.*

**unique identifier** *noun* COMPUT a set of characters used to distinguish between different resources in a multimedia book

**unisexual** *adjective* BIOL having either male or female sex organs, but not both, in one individual

**unit** *noun* **1.** a component of something larger **2.** MEASURE a quantity or amount used as a standard, accepted measurement ○ *The internationally agreed unit of pressure is the millibar.* ○ *The higher the Sun is in the sky, the more intense is the radiation per unit area.* **3.** a person, group or device that is complete in itself ○ *The operation of flying controls is by means of self-contained power flying control units (PFCUs).* **4.** MECH ENG a single machine, possibly with many different parts

**unit cell** *noun* CRYSTALS the smallest structural unit of a crystal that can be repeated in three dimensions to make its full lattice

**univalent** *adjective* **1.** GENETICS referring to a chromosome that does not pair with another structurally identical chromosome during the initial stage of meiosis **2.** CHEM having a valency of one

**universal asynchronous receiver/transmitter** *noun* COMPUT a chip which converts an asynchronous serial bit stream to a parallel form or parallel data to a serial bit stream. Abbreviation **UART**

**universal indicator** *noun* CHEM a solution that turns different colours according to a range of pH values

**universal law of gravitation** *noun* PHYS the law of gravitation stating that every body in the universe exerts an attraction on every other, proportional to their masses multiplied together divided by the square of the distance between them (NOTE: The gravitational constant G gives the force between any pair of objects whose masses and separation are known, and equals 6.672 x 10 11 kg −1 m 3 s −2.)

**universal mobile telecommunications system** *noun* COMPUT full form of **UMTS**

**universal product code** *noun* COMPUT a standard printed bar coding system used to identify products. Abbreviation **UPC**

**universal programming** *noun* COMPUT the writing of a programs which are not specific to one machine, so that they can run on several machines

**universal resource locator** *noun* COMPUT an Internet system used to standardise the way in which World Wide Web addresses are written. Also called **uniform resource locator**. Abbreviation **URL** (NOTE: It is made up of three parts: the first is the protocol such as HTTP or FTP, then the domain name of the service and finally the directory or file name.)

**universal serial bus** *noun* COMPUT full form of **USB**

**universal synchronous asynchronous receiver-transmitter** *noun* COMPUT a chip that can be instructed by a central processing unit to communicate with asynchronous or synchronous bit streams or parallel data lines. Abbreviation **USART**

**universal synchronous receiver/transmitter** *noun* COMPUT a single integrated circuit that can carry out all the serial to parallel and interfacing operations required between a computer and transmission line. Abbreviation **USRT**

**universe** *noun* ASTRON the total existing amount of mass, space and radiation

**UNIX** *trademark* COMPUT a popular multiuser, multitasking operating system developed by AT&T Bell Laboratories to run on almost any computer, from a PC, to minicomputers and large mainframes

**unjustified** *adjective* COMPUT, PRINTING referring to text which has not been justified

**unleaded petrol** *noun* INDUST petrol with a low octane rating, which has no lead additives such as tetraethyl lead and therefore creates less lead pollution in the atmosphere

**unlined** *adjective* ENVIRON referring to a landfill site with no lining, so that waste liquids can leak out into the surrounding soil

**unmapped** *adjective* **1.** GENETICS not identified as a gene on a particular chromosome **2.** BIOTECH not identified as a DNA sequence coding for a specific gene

**unmoderated list** *noun* COMPUT a mailing list which sends any material submitted to the listserv on to all the subscribers without a person reading or checking the content

**unmodified instruction** *noun* COMPUT a program instruction which is directly processed without modification to obtain the operation to be performed

**unmodulated** *adjective* COMPUT referring to a signal which has not been modulated

**unnatural** *adjective* not found in nature

**unneutralised, unneutralized** *adjective* having not been made neutral

**unpaired** *adjective* GENETICS referring to a chromosome which is not associated with another chromosome of the same type ○ *an unpaired X chromosome in males*

**unpasteurised, unpasteurized** *adjective* FOOD INDUST which has not been pasteurised ○ *Unpasteurised milk can carry bacilli.*

**unpolluted** *adjective* ENVIRON not affected by pollution ○ *unpolluted atmosphere in the mountain areas*

**unpopulated** *adjective* COMPUT referring to a printed circuit board which does not yet contain any components or whose sockets are empty ○ *You can buy an unpopulated RAM card and fit your own RAM chips.*

**unrecoverable error** *noun* COMPUT a computer hardware or software error which causes a program to crash

**unsaturated compound** *noun* CHEM a chemical compound that consists of molecules having double or triple bonds

**unsaturated fat** *noun* FOOD INDUST, BIOCHEM a fat which does not have a large amount of hydrogen and so can be broken down more easily

**unsettled** *adjective* METEOROL referring to weather which changes frequently from rainy to fine and back again

**unshielded twisted pair cable** *noun* ELEC a cable made of two insulated copper wires twisted around each other to reduce induction and therefore interference but not wrapped in any other outer layer, unlike STP cable. Abbreviation **UTP cable**

**unsightly** *adjective* ENVIRON not pleasant to look at ○ *The company is proposing to run a line of unsightly pylons across the moors.*

**unsigned** *adjective* MATHS referring to a number system which does not represent negative numbers

**unspoilt** *adjective* ENVIRON referring to a landscape which has not been ruined by development ○ *The highland region is still unspoilt.* ○ *The conservancy council is hoping to preserve the area of unspoilt woodland.*

**unstable** *adjective* not stable and liable to change easily

**unstable air mass** *noun* METEOROL a mass of air in which a sample of wet air, in rising, cools less rapidly than the surrounding air and thus continues to rise until ultimately condensation and precipitation of the water content occur

**unsterilised, unsterilized** *adjective* HEALTH not sterilised ○ *The milk was sold in unsterilised bottles.*

**unstriated muscle** *noun* ANAT same as **smooth muscle**

**unsustainable** *adjective* ENVIRON referring to a development or process which depletes or damages natural resources irreparably and which does not leave the environment in good order for future generations

**untapped** *adjective* not yet utilised ○ *untapped mineral resources*

**untreated** *adjective* not subjected to a treatment process ○ *Untreated sewage leaked into the river.*

**ununbium** *noun* CHEM ELEM an artificially produced radioactive metallic chemical element (NOTE: The chemical symbol is **Uub**; the atomic number is **112** and the atomic weight is **277**.)

**ununquadium** *noun* CHEM ELEM a chemical element produced by bombarding plutonium with calcium ions (NOTE: The chemical symbol is **Uuq**; the atomic number is **114** and the atomic weight is **285**.)

**unununium** *noun* CHEM ELEM a chemical element produced by bombarding bismuth-209 with nickel-60 (NOTE: The chemical symbol is **Uuu**; the atomic number is **111** and the atomic weight is **272**.)

**UPC** *abbreviation* COMPUT universal product code

**update file** *noun* COMPUT a file containing recent changes or transactions to records which is used to update the master file. Also called **transaction file**

**updraught** *noun* METEOROL a rising air current, usually of warm air

**upgrade** *verb* COMPUT to make a system more powerful or more up-to-date by adding new equipment ○ *They can upgrade the printer.* ○ *The single processor with 2 Mbytes of memory can be upgraded to 4 Mbytes.* ○ *All three models have an on-site upgrade facility.*

**upland** EARTH SCI *noun* an area of high land ○ *The uplands have different ecosystems from the lowlands.* ■ *adjective* referring to an upland ○ *upland farming*

**uplink** *noun* TELECOM the transmission link from an Earth station to a satellite

**upload** *verb* COMPUT **1.** to transfer data files or programs from a small computer to a main CPU ○ *The user can upload PC data to update mainframe applications.* **2.** to transfer a file from one computer to a BBS or host computer ○ *The image can be manipulated* *before uploading to the host computer.* Opposite **download**

**upper** *adjective* **1.** referring to something that is at a high level or towards the top **2.** referring to something which is above something ▶ opposite **lower**

**upper case** *noun* capital letters ○ *He corrected the word 'coMputer', replacing the upper case M with a lower case letter.*

**upper limb** *noun* ANAT an arm

**upper motor neuron** *noun* ANAT a neuron which takes impulses from the cerebral cortex

**UPS** *abbreviation* COMPUT uninterruptable power supply

**upstream** *adverb, adjective* EARTH SCI towards the source of a river ○ *The river is contaminated for several miles upstream from the estuary.* ○ *Pollution has spread into the lake upstream of the waterfall.* ○ *Upstream communities have not yet been affected.*

**upthrust** *noun* EARTH SCI a piece of rock that has moved upwards in a low-angle fault

**uptime** *noun* COMPUT the time when a computer is operational and functioning correctly. Compare **downtime**

**upward compatible, upwards compatible** *adjective* COMPUT referring to hardware or software designed to be compatible either with earlier models or with future models which have not yet been invented

**upwelling** *noun* EARTH SCI the process by which warmer surface water in the sea is drawn away from the shore and replaced by colder water from beneath the surface

**uraninite** *noun* MINERALS a black uranium oxide mineral that also contains thorium, radium and lead

**uranium** *noun* CHEM ELEM a natural radioactive metallic element which is an essential fuel for nuclear power (NOTE: The chemical symbol is $U$; the atomic number is **92** and the atomic weight is **283.04**.)

COMMENT: Three uranium isotopes are found in ores: uranium-234, uranium-235 and uranium-238. Of these, U-235 is the only fissionable isotope occurring in nature and so is an essential fuel for reactors.

**uranium-lead dating** *noun* EARTH SCI the process of finding out the age of uranium-containing mineral by measuring the amount of lead isotope produced by the radioactive decay of uranium, which occurs at a known rate

**uranium (IV) oxide, uranium dioxide** *noun* CHEM a toxic radioactive crystalline solid, used in photography. Formula: $UO_2$.

**Uranus** *noun* ASTRON the seventh planet of the solar system

COMMENT: Uranus takes 84 years to orbit the Sun at an average distance of 19 AU from it. Uranus is one of the giant gas planets, 15 times as massive as the Earth and 52,000 km in diameter.

**urea** *noun* PHYSIOL a crystalline solid produced in the liver from excess amino acids and excreted by the kidneys into the urine (NOTE: It is made commercially from carbon dioxide and ammonia and is used as a fertiliser and in other products.)

**urea-formaldehyde resin** *noun* INDUST a resin made by the polymerisation of urea and formaldehyde with good oil resistant properties, used in electrical fittings and in cavity insulation

**ureter** *noun* ANAT one of a pair of ducts through which urine flows from the kidneys to the bladder in mammals or to the cloaca in lower vertebrates

**urethane resin** *noun* CHEM same as **polyurethane**

**urethra** *noun* ANAT the tube in humans and other mammals through which urine passes from the bladder out of the body (NOTE: In the male, semen also passes through it at ejaculation.)

**uric acid** *noun* CHEM a chemical compound which is formed from nitrogen in waste products from the body and which also forms crystals in the joints of patients suffering from gout

**urinary bladder** *noun* ANAT a sac where the urine collects from the kidneys through the ureters, before being passed out of the body through the urethra

**urine** *noun* BIOL a liquid containing uric acid, secreted as waste from an animal's body

**URL** *abbreviation* COMPUT **1.** uniform resource locator **2.** universal resource locator ○ *The URL of the Blooms-*

*bury Publishing home page is 'http://www.bloomsburymagazine.com'.*

**usability** *noun* COMPUT the ease with which hardware or software can be used ○ *We have studied usability tests and found that a GUI is easier for new users than a command line.*

**USART** *abbreviation* COMPUT universal synchronous asynchronous receiver/transmitter

**USB** *noun* COMPUT a standard that defines a high-speed serial interface that transfers data at up to 12 Mbps and allows up to 127 compatible peripherals to be connected to a computer. Full form **universal serial bus**

**Usenet** *noun* COMPUT a section of the Internet that provides forums called newsgroups in which any user can add a message or comment on any other message

**user** *noun* COMPUT **1.** a person who uses a computer, machine or software **2.** a keyboard operator

**user datagram protocol** *noun* COMPUT full form of **UDP**

**user-definable** *adjective* COMPUT referring to a feature or section of a program that a user can customise as required ○ *The style sheet contains 125 user-definable symbols.*

**user-friendly** *adjective* COMPUT referring to a language, system or program that is easy to use and interact with ○ *It's such a user-friendly machine.* ○ *Compared with the previous version this one is very user-friendly.*

**user's manual** *noun* COMPUT a booklet showing how a device or system should be used

**USRT** *abbreviation* COMPUT universal synchronous receiver/transmitter

**UTC** *abbreviation* TIME Coordinated Universal Time

**uterus** *noun* ANAT an organ inside which the eggs or young of animals develop (NOTE: In humans and other mammals it is often called the womb and has strong muscles to push the baby out at birth.)

**utilitarian justification** *noun* ENVIRON an argument for conservation based on the idea that the environment should provide direct economic benefits to the population

**utility** *noun* **1.** ENVIRON a company that organises an essential public service, e.g. providing electricity, gas or public transport **2.** COMPUT same as **utility program** ○ *A lost file cannot be found without a file-recovery utility.* ○ *On the disk is a utility for backing up a hard disk.* **3.** the state of being useful

**utility program** *noun* COMPUT a program concerned with routine activities such as file searching, copying files, file directories, sorting and debugging and various mathematical functions. Also called **utility**

**UTP cable** *abbreviation* COMPUT unshielded twisted pair cable

**Uub** *symbol* CHEM ELEM ununbium

**Uuencoding** *noun* COMPUT a method of converting documents and files to a pseudo-text format that allows them to be transmitted as an electronic mail message

COMMENT: This gets around the Internet's inability to transfer messages that are not text. It has now been largely replaced by MIME.

**Uuq** *symbol* CHEM ELEM ununquadium

**Uuu** *symbol* CHEM ELEM unununium

**UV** *abbreviation* PHYS ultraviolet

**UVA** *noun* **UV-A** PHYS ultraviolet radiation in the wavelengths 320–400 nm, not harmful to human skin under normal exposure

**UV-absorbing lens** *noun* OPHTHALMOL a lens specially devised to absorb ultraviolet radiation in order to protect the eyes against the sun

**UVB, UV-B** *noun* PHYS ultraviolet radiation in the wavelengths 290–320 nm, causing first reddening and then browning of skin

**UVC, UV-C** *noun* PHYS ultraviolet radiation in the wavelengths 230–290 nm, causing blistering to skin and possibly giving rise to skin cancer

**UVR** *abbreviation* PHYS ultraviolet radiation

# V

**V** *symbol* MEASURE, ELEC volt

**vaccinate** *verb* MED to use a vaccine to give a person immunisation against a specific disease ○ *She was vaccinated against smallpox as a child.*

**vaccination** *noun* MED the action of vaccinating someone against a disease. ♦ **immunisation** (NOTE: Originally the words **vaccination** and **vaccine** applied only to smallpox immunisation, but they are now used for immunisation against any disease)

**vaccine** *noun* IMMUNOL a substance which contains the germs of a disease, used to inoculate or vaccinate someone against it ○ *The hospital is waiting for a new batch of vaccine to come from the laboratory.* ○ *New vaccines are being developed all the time.* ○ *MMR vaccine is given to control measles, mumps and rubella.* ○ *There is, as yet, no vaccine for meningococcal meningitis.*

> COMMENT: A vaccine contains the germs of the disease, sometimes alive and sometimes dead, and this is injected into the patient so that his or her body will develop immunity to the disease. The vaccine contains antigens, and these provoke the body to produce antibodies, some of which remain in the bloodstream for a very long time and react against the same antigens if they enter the body naturally at a later date when the patient is exposed to the disease. Vaccination is mainly given against cholera, diphtheria, rabies, smallpox, tuberculosis and typhoid.

**vacuole** *noun* BIOL a fluid-filled compartment in the cytoplasm of a cell

**vacuum** *noun* PHYS a space completely empty of everything, even air ○ *If the fuel tank vent pipe is blocked, a vacuum will form in the tank and fuel flow to the engine will be restricted.*

**vacuum distillation** *noun* CHEM the distillation of liquid at low pressure so that it boils at a lower temperature

**vacuum pump** *noun* PHYS a pump used to reduce the gas pressure of a container

**vadose** *adjective* EARTH SCI referring to an area which lies between the surface of the ground and the water table

**vagina** *noun* ANAT any part of an animal or plant that forms a sheath, in particular the lowest part of the birth canal in humans and other mammals

**vagrant** *noun* ZOOL a bird which only visits a country occasionally

**vagus** *noun* ANAT one of the tenth pair of cranial nerves carrying the sensory and motor neurons that serve the heart, lungs, stomach, intestines and various other organs

**vale** *noun* EARTH SCI same as **valley**

**valence** *noun* IMMUNOL, CHEM same as **valency**

**valence electron** *noun* CHEM an electron in an outer shell of an atom that can take part in a bond with another atom to form a molecule

**valency** *noun* **1.** CHEM the ability of atoms or groups to combine, measured by the number of hydrogen atoms received, lost or shared in forming a compound **2.** IMMUNOL the number of sites on an antibody at which an antigen can bind ▶ also called **valence**

**valeric acid** *noun* CHEM a fatty acid with four isomers

**validate** *verb* COMPUT to check that an input is or data are correct according to a set of rules

**validation** *noun* COMPUT a check performed to validate data

**valine** *noun* BIOCHEM an essential amino acid

**valley** *noun* EARTH SCI a long low area, usually with a river at the bottom, between hills or mountains ○ *Fog forms in the valleys at night.* Also called **vale**

**valley bog** *noun* EARTH SCI a peat bog which forms in the damp bottom of a valley

**valley glacier** *noun* EARTH SCI a large mass of ice which moves down a valley from above the snowline towards the sea

**value** *noun* MATHS a quantity shown as a number

**value-added network** *noun* COMPUT a commercial network which offers information services such as stock prices, weather, e-mail or advice as well as basic file transfer. Abbreviation **VAN**

**value-added reseller** *noun* COMPUT a company which buys hardware or software and adds another feature, customises it or offers an extra service to attract customers. Abbreviation **VAR**

**valve** *noun* **1.** MECH ENG a mechanical device for controlling the flow of a fluid **2.** ANAT a flap in the heart, blood vessels or lymphatic vessels or other organs, which opens and closes to allow liquid to pass in one direction only

**valve gear** *noun* MECH ENG a mechanism for opening and closing valves

**valve overlap** *noun* MECH ENG the period when both the exhaust and inlet valves are open together, with the exhaust valve closing and the inlet valve opening

**valve seat** *noun* MECH ENG an angled ring in a cylinder head on which the poppet valve sits when closed. ◆ **sequence**

**VAN** *abbreviation* COMPUT value-added network

**vanadium** *noun* CHEM ELEM a toxic silvery white metallic element, used in the manufacture of tough steel alloys and as a catalyst (NOTE: The chemical symbol is **V**; the atomic number is **23** and the atomic weight is **50.94**.)

**Van Allen belt** *noun* EARTH SCI either of two regions of high-energy, ionised particles surrounding the Earth (NOTE: The inner belt is formed mainly of protons, and lies at an altitude of 3000–6000 km above the Earth's surface, while the outer belt is formed mainly of electrons, and lies at an altitude of 20 000–30 000 km.)

**van de Graaff generator** *noun* PHYS an electrostatic generator that produces electrical discharges at extremely high voltages, used in particle accelerators and for testing electrical insulators (NOTE: The electric charge from a source of direct current accumulates on a high-speed belt inside an insulated metal sphere filled with Freon or nitrogen gas under high pressure.)

**van der Waals' equation** *noun* PHYS a modified equation of state that describes the physical properties of gases allowing for the volumes of molecules and the interactions between them

**van der Waals' force** *noun* PHYS a weak force of attraction between atoms or molecules

**vanishing point perspective** *noun* COMPUT graphics displayed in two-dimensions that have the appearance of depth as all lines converge at a vanishing point and objects appear smaller as they are further from the user

**vapor** *noun* US spelling of **vapour**

**vaporisation, vaporization** *noun* CHEM the process by which a liquid or solid is converted to gas or vapour by heat, with the rate of vaporisation increasing with a higher temperature

**vaporise, vaporize** *verb* to turn into vapour or to turn something into a vapour ○ *Water vaporises when heated.*

**vaporiser, vaporizer** *noun* MED **1.** an instrument which sprays liquid in the form of very small drops like mist **2.** a device which warms a liquid to which medicinal oil has been added so that it provides a vapour which a patient can inhale

**vapour** *noun* PHYS a gaseous form of a liquid (NOTE: The US spelling is **vapor**.)

**vapour concentration** *noun* PHYS a ratio of the mass of a vaporised substance in a given quantity of air to the amount of air

**vapour density** *noun* PHYS the density of a gas relative to that of hydrogen

**vapour lock** *noun* ENG a blockage of fuel flow from a tank caused by a bubble of vapour at a high point in the pipeline

**vapour pressure** *noun* PHYS the pressure exerted by a gas, in particular one that is in contact with its liquid state

**vapour trail** *noun* AEROSP a white streak in the sky left by an aircraft flying at high altitude and caused by condensation and freezing of components of its exhaust gases, mainly water. Also called **condensation trail**

**VAR** *abbreviation* COMPUT value-added reseller

**variable** *adjective* changing or changeable ○ *Winds are more variable in the northern hemisphere than in the southern hemisphere.* ■ *noun* **1.** COMPUT a computer program identifier for a register or storage location which can contain any number or character and which may vary during the program run **2.** a quantity or quality which changes

**variable data** *plural noun* COMPUT data which can be modified, and are not write protected

**variable geometry** *noun* AEROSP the technology which allows the angle between an aircraft's wing and fuselage to be altered to give a more or less swept wing for better high-speed and low-speed flight characteristics

**variable name** *noun* COMPUT a word used to identify a variable in a program

**variable pitch propeller** *noun* AEROSP a propeller with a mechanism that changes the blade angle to suit flight conditions

**variable star** *noun* ASTRON a star that changes in brightness at regular or irregular intervals

**variant** *noun* BIOL a specimen of a plant or animal which is different from the usual type

**variation** *noun* **1.** a change or amount of change **2.** NAVIG an angular difference between magnetic north and true north, which is measured in degrees and is named east or west according to whether the north-seeking end of a freely suspended magnet lies to the east or to the west of the true meridian at that point

**variety** *noun* BIOL a type of organism, especially a named cultivated plant

**vascular bundle** *noun* BOT a strand of plant tissue containing the xylem and phloem tubes that transport water and food to and from different parts of the plant

**vascular plant** *noun* BOT a plant that has specialised tubes within it for transporting sap (NOTE: All flowering plants, conifers, ferns, clubmosses and horsetails, but not mosses and liverworts, are vascular plants.)

**vascular system** *noun* **1.** ANAT (*in animals*) a system of tubes that carry liquid, e.g. blood **2.** BOT (*in plants*) a system of conducting tissues that carry nutrients from the roots to the upper parts of the plant

**vascular tissue** *noun* BOT a specialised plant tissue consisting of phloem and xylem, which transports dissolved sugar, water and dissolved minerals throughout the plant

**vas deferens** *noun* ANAT one of a pair of ducts through which sperm passes from the testes to the urethra during ejaculation

**vasoconstriction** *noun* PHYSIOL the narrowing of the blood vessels (NOTE: It decreases blood flow and increases blood pressure.)

**vasodilation** *noun* PHYSIOL the widening of the blood vessels, especially the arteries (NOTE: It increases blood flow and reduces blood pressure.)

**vasomotor nerve** *noun* ANAT a nerve whose impulses make the arterioles become narrower

**vasopressin** *noun* BIOCHEM a hormone secreted from the pituitary gland (NOTE: It raises blood pressure and causes the kidneys to excrete less urine.)

**VDT** *abbreviation* COMPUT visual display terminal

**VDU** *abbreviation* COMPUT visual display unit

**vector** *noun* **1.** MATHS a quantity with magnitude and direction indicated by a line of a given length, representing magnitude and specific direction ○ *The triangle of velocities is a vector solution of what happens to an aircraft when wind causes drift.* **2.** NAVIG a heading given to a pilot to provide navigational guidance by radar ○ *Wind velocity is indicated by a vector, identified by a single arrow, pointing in the direction the wind is blowing towards.* **3.** COMPUT an address which directs a computer to a new memory location **4.** MATHS a shape described using coordinates of magnitude and direction **5.** BIOL an insect or animal which carries a disease or parasite and can pass it to other organisms ○ *The tsetse fly is a vector of sleeping sickness.* **6.** an agent such as a plasmid or bacteriophage that is used to transfer a segment of DNA from one organism to another

**vectored interrupt** *noun* COMPUT an interrupt which directs the central processing unit to transfer to a particular location

**vector font** *noun* COMPUT a shape of characters within a font that are drawn using vector graphics, allowing the characters to be scaled to almost any size without changing the quality

**vector graphics** *noun* COMPUT a computer drawing system which uses line length and direction from an origin to plot lines

**vector processor** *noun* COMPUT a coprocessor which operates on one row or column of an array at a time

**veer** *noun* METEOROL a shifting of the wind, in a clockwise direction in the northern hemisphere ○ *The passing of a weather trough is marked by a sharp veer in the direction of the wind.* ■ *verb* **1.** METEOROL (*of wind*) to change in a clockwise direction, in the northern hemisphere ○ *Winds veer and increase with height ahead of a warm front.* Opposite **back 2.** to change direction, especially as in an uncontrolled movement ○ *The aircraft veered off the runway into the grass.*

**vegan** *noun* a strict vegetarian who eats only vegetables and fruit and no animal products like milk, fish, eggs or meat ■ *adjective* referring to vegans or their diet

**vegetable** *noun* AGRIC a plant grown for food ○ *Green vegetables are a source of dietary fibre.*

**vegetable oil** *noun* FOOD INDUST an oil obtained from a plant and its seeds, low in saturated fat

**vegetarian** *noun, adjective* MED a person who does not eat meat ■ *adjective* referring to vegetarians or their diet ○ *He is on a vegetarian diet.*

**vegetation** *noun* BOT growing plants ○ *The vegetation was destroyed by fire.* ○ *Very little vegetation is found in the Arctic regions.* ○ *He is studying the vegetation of the island.*

**vegetation loss** *noun* ENVIRON the loss of plants from an area by processes such as pollution or clearing

**vegetation map** *noun* BOT a simple map showing the pattern of vegetation on the ground

**vegetative** *adjective* **1.** BOT referring to plants ○ *The loss of vegetative cover increases the accumulation of carbon dioxide in the atmosphere.* **2.** BIOL referring to the process of growth and development **3.** BIOL referring to reproduction that does not involve sex cells

**vegetative propagation, vegetative reproduction** *noun* BOT the reproduction of plants by taking cuttings or by grafting, not by seed

**vehicle** *noun* a machine for moving people or goods, e.g. a car, truck, train or boat

**vehicular** *adjective* referring to a vehicle

**vein** *noun* **1.** ANAT a blood vessel which takes deoxygenated blood containing waste carbon dioxide from the tissues back to the heart **2.** BOT a thin tube which forms part of the structure of a leaf

**Veitch diagram** *noun* COMPUT a graphical representation of a truth table

**velamen** *noun* BOT a spongy layer covering the aerial roots of plants such as tree-dwelling orchids (NOTE: It protects the roots and helps them absorb water.)

**velocity** *noun* PHYS the rate of change of position in a given direction which is composed of both speed and direction ○ *The anemograph gives a continuous recording of wind velocity which is displayed on a chart and reveals gusts, squalls and lulls.*

**velocity of light** *noun* the speed of light, which is almost 300 000 km a second in a vacuum (NOTE: The velocity of light in a vacuum is the same as that of all other electromagnetic radiation. This is much more than a mere measure of distance covered in a given amount of time, because c, the velocity of light, appears in the fundamental equations of relativity as the factor linking mass with the amount of energy to which it is equivalent, and as a basic speed limit for all objects in the universe.)

**velocity of sound** *noun* the speed of sound, which is equal to 331 metres per second through air (NOTE: The speed of sound varies in different materials.)

**vena cava** *noun* ANAT one of two major veins that carry blood from the body back to the heart (NOTE: The inferior vena cava brings blood from the lower half of the body and the superior vena cava brings it from the head and upper body.)

**venation** *noun* BIOL the pattern of veins in a leaf or an insect's wing

**Venn diagram** *noun* MATHS a graphical representation of the relationships between the states in a system or circuit

**venom** *noun* BIOL a liquid poison secreted by an animal (NOTE: Venoms are produced in many different animals, including snakes, scorpions, spiders and fish.)

**vent** *noun* **1.** MECH ENG a hole serving as an inlet or outlet for a fluid, usually a gas such as air ○ *During the inspection, check that the fuel tank vent pipe is not blocked.* **2.** EARTH SCI a hole through which gases or lava escape from a volcano

**ventilate** *verb* to cause air to pass in and out of a place freely ○ *The water separator is installed downstream of the cold air unit to extract a percentage of free moisture from the air, which subsequently ventilates and pressurises the cabin.*

**ventilation** *noun* the passing of air in and out of a place freely ○ *A constant supply of air for ventilation purposes is always available from the air conditioning system.*

**ventilator** *noun* ENG a device which circulates fresh air into a room or building

**ventral** *adjective* ANAT **1.** referring to the abdomen or the front of the human body **2.** referring to the surface on the underside of a plant or animal's body ○ *The fish has two ventral fins.*

**ventral root** *noun* ANAT the spinal nerve root that arises from the surface of the spinal cord that is facing the stomach

**ventricle** *noun* ANAT **1.** one of a number of chambers or cavities in the body or an organ **2.** a chamber of the heart that receives blood from the atria and pumps it to the arteries **3.** one of the cavities of the vertebrate brain that connects with the others and contains cerebrospinal fluid

**venturi effect** *noun* PHYS the rapid flow of a liquid or a gas as it passes through a narrower channel

**venturi tube** *noun* PHYS a tube with a constriction in the middle that measures fluid flow rate based on the pressure

drop in the fluid as it travels from one end of the tube to the other

**venule** *noun* BIOL a small offshoot from a vein in a leaf or insect wing

**Venus** *noun* ASTRON the second planet of the solar system, and the closest in size to the Earth, being 82 per cent as massive (NOTE: Venus orbits the Sun in 225 days, at an average distance of 0.72 AU (108 million km), and has no satellites. Venus is swathed in clouds and has a high albedo, so is brighter than anything in the sky apart from the Sun and Moon.)

**Venusian** *adjective* ASTRON referring to Venus

**verdigris** *noun* CHEM a green or greenish-blue poisonous powder formed by the reaction of acetic acid with a copper surface, used as a paint pigment and fungicide

**verification** *noun* COMPUT the process of checking that data has been keyboarded correctly or that data transferred from one medium to another has been transferred correctly

**vermicide** *noun* MED, VET a substance which kills worms

**vermiculite** *noun* AGRIC a substance that is a form of silica processed into small pieces and used instead of soil in horticulture because it retains moisture

**vermiform** *adjective* BIOL shaped like a worm

**vermin** *noun* AGRIC an organism that is looked upon as a pest by some people (NOTE: Usually treated as plural.)

**vermis** *noun* ANAT the central part of the cerebellum

**vernal** *adjective* referring to the spring

**vernal equinox** *noun* ASTRON same as **spring equinox**

**vernalisation, vernalization** *noun* BOT the technique of making a seed germinate early by refrigerating it for a time

**vernier** *noun* MEASURE a small movable scale parallel to the main scale of some measuring instruments such as calipers (NOTE: It enables the user to obtain more precise measurements from the larger scale.)

**version** *noun* a copy of something which is slightly different from others ○ *The latest version of the software includes an improved graphics routine.*

**version control** *noun* COMPUT utility software which allows several programmers to work on a source file and monitors the changes that have been made by each programmer

**vertebra** *noun* ANAT one of the ring-shaped bones which link together to form the backbone (NOTE: The plural is **vertebrae**.)

**vertebral** *adjective* ANAT referring to the vertebrae

**vertebral artery** *noun* ANAT one of the two arteries which go up the back of the neck into the brain

**vertebral column** *noun* ANAT same as **spinal column**

**vertebral ganglion** *noun* ANAT a ganglion in front of the origin of a vertebral artery

**vertebrate** ZOOL *noun* an animal that has a backbone. Compare **invertebrate** ■ *adjective* referring to animals that have a backbone

**vertex** *noun* MATHS a point in space defined by three coordinates: x, y and z

**vertical** *adjective* at right angles to a horizontal line

**vertical application** *noun* COMPUT application software that has been designed for a specific use, rather than for general use

**vertical axis** *noun* **1.** AEROSP an imaginary line running through the fuselage of an aircraft at the centre of gravity from top to bottom, around which the aircraft rotates when it yaws ○ *The rudder is a control surface on the fin which rotates the aircraft about its vertical axis to produce yaw.* **2.** MATHS a vertical reference line of a graph ○ *The vertical axis shows engine power available.* Also called **Y-axis**

**vertical-axis wind turbine** *noun* ENG a type of wind turbine with a vertical main shaft

**vertically** *adverb* in a vertical position ○ *The aircraft pitched up vertically.*

**vertical motion** *noun* an up and down movement

**vertical redundancy check** *noun* COMPUT a parity check on each character of a block received, to detect any errors. Abbreviation **VRC**

**vertical scan frequency** *noun* COMPUT the number of times a picture beam in a monitor moves from the last line back up to the first

**vertical scrolling** *noun* COMPUT the movement of a displayed text up or down the computer screen one line at a time

**vertical stabiliser** *noun* AEROSP a fin at the rear of an aircraft

**very high frequency** *noun* PHYS the radio frequency band between 30 and 300 MHz. Abbreviation **VHF** (NOTE: This frequency band is used to transmit television and FM radio signals.)

**very large scale integration** *noun* ELECTRONICS an integrated circuit with 10 000 to 100 000 components. Abbreviation **VLSI**

**very low frequency** *noun* PHYS the radio frequency band between 3 and 3 kHz

**vesicle** *noun* **1.** BOT a rounded air-filled structure that helps seaweeds and aquatic plants to float **2.** ZOOL, MED any small rounded structure filled with fluid or gas

**vessel** *noun* **1.** a container for liquids **2.** INDUST a container for nuclear fuel or radioactive waste **3.** BIOL a tubular structure which carries fluid around the body of an animal or plant

**vestibulocochlear nerve** *noun* ANAT the eighth cranial nerve, which controls hearing and balance

**vestigial** *adjective* existing in a simple and reduced form ○ *Some snakes have vestigial legs.*

**vestigial organ** *noun* ANAT an organ which has lost its original function and, through evolution, is fully developed but non-functioning

**vestigial side band** *noun* COMPUT full form of **VSB**

**VHD** *noun* COMPUT a capacitance type video disk able to store very large quantities of data. Full form **very high density**

**VHF** *abbreviation* PHYS very high frequency

**vibrate** *verb* to move rapidly and continuously backwards and forwards or to cause something to do this ○ *Turbine blades in the average jet engine vibrate at frequencies of 1 million per minute.* ○ *The passing traffic makes the foundations of the bridge vibrate.*

**vibration** *noun* a rapid and continuous movement ○ *Engine vibration was detected in engine number one.* ○ *Vibrations caused by aircraft can shatter windows.*

**vibrio** *noun* MICROBIOL a bacterium with a wavy or curved shape. Genus: *Vibrio*. (NOTE: Cholera is a disease caused by a vibrio.)

**video** *noun* text, images or graphics viewed on television or a monitor

**video bandwidth** *noun* COMPUT the maximum display resolution, measured in MHz, and calculated by horizontal x vertical resolution x refreshes/sec (NOTE: TV studio recording is limited to 5 MHz. TV broadcasting is limited to 3.58 Mhz.)

**video codec** *noun* TELECOM an electronic device to convert a video signal to or from a digital form

**video display** *noun* COMPUT a device that can display text or graphical information, e.g. a cathode ray tube

**video graphics card** *noun* COMPUT an expansion card that fits into an expansion slot inside a PC and allows a computer to display generated text and graphics as well as moving video images from an external camera or video recorder

**video memory, video RAM** *noun* COMPUT a high speed random access memory used to store computer-generated or digitised images. Abbreviation **VRAM**

**video signal** *noun* COMPUT a signal that provides line picture information and synchronisation pulses

**viewdata** *noun* COMPUT an interactive system for transmitting text or graphics from a database to a user's terminal by telephone lines, providing facilities for information retrieval, transactions, education, games and recreation

COMMENT: The user of viewdata calls up the page of information required, using a telephone and modem. With teletext, the pages of information are repeated one after the other automatically.

**vigor** *noun* US spelling of **vigour**

**vigorous** *adjective* BIOL growing strongly ○ *Plants put out vigorous shoots in a warm damp atmosphere.*

**vigour** *noun* strength and energy (NOTE: The US spelling is **vigor**.)

**villus** *noun* BIOL a small finger-shaped structure sticking out from a tissue or organ surface (NOTE: The lining of the gut is covered with villi to increase its surface area for food absorption.)

**vinyl** *noun* INDUST a plastic that is not biodegradable

**vinyl chloride** *noun* INDUST a chemical compound of chlorine and ethylene, used as a refrigerant and in the making of PVC

**vinyl group** *noun* CHEM a group of organic compounds with one double bond, $CH_2$=CH-

**viral** *adjective* MICROBIOL referring to or caused by a virus ○ *a viral disease*

**viral infection** *noun* MED an infection caused by a virus

**viral pneumonia** *noun* MED an inflammation of the lungs caused by a virus

**virgin** *adjective* ENVIRON in its natural state, untouched by humans ○ *Virgin rainforest was being cleared at the rate of 1000 hectares per month.*

**virgin land** *noun* AGRIC land which has never been cultivated

**virgin ore** *noun* INDUST ore as it is extracted from the ground, before it has been processed

**virtual** *adjective* COMPUT referring to a feature or device which does not actually exist but which is simulated by a computer and can be used by a user as if it did exist

**virtual circuit** *noun* COMPUT the link established between a source and sink in a packet-switching network for the duration of the call

**virtual disk** *noun* COMPUT a section of RAM used with a short controlling program as if it were a fast disk storage system

**virtual machine** *noun* COMPUT a simulated machine and its operations

**virtual memory** *noun* COMPUT a system of providing extra main memory by using a disk drive as if it were RAM. Also called **virtual storage**

**virtual reality** *noun* COMPUT a simulation of a real-life scene or environment by a computer ○ *This new virtual reality software can create a three-dimensional room that you can navigate around.*

**virtual storage** COMPUT same as **virtual memory**. Abbreviation **VS**

**virus** *noun* **1.** MICROBIOL a microorganism consisting of a nucleic acid surounded by a protein coat which can only develop in other cells, and often destroys them (NOTE: Many common diseases such as measles or the common cold are caused by viruses. Viral diseases cannot be treated with antibiotics.) **2.** COMPUT a program which adds itself to an executable file and copies or spreads itself to other executable files each time an infected file is run (NOTE: A virus can corrupt data, display a message or do nothing. If your PC is infected with a virus, your data is at risk. Computer viruses are spread by downloading unchecked files from a bulletin board system or via unregulated networks or by inserting an unchecked floppy disk into your PC. Always use a virus detector.)

**virus detector** *noun* COMPUT utility software which checks executable files to see if they contain a known virus

**viscera** *plural noun* ANAT the internal organs, in particular the intestines and other contents of the abdomen

**visceral** *noun* ANAT referring to the viscera

**visceral muscle** *noun* ANAT a muscle in the walls of the intestines which makes the intestine contract

**viscid** *adjective* PHYS same as **viscous**

**viscometer** *noun* PHYS a piece of equipment for measuring the viscosity of a substance

**viscosity** *noun* PHYS a liquid's internal resistance to flowing ○ *Excessive oil temperatures are dangerous, as the oil viscosity is reduced and inadequate bearing lubrication results.*

**viscous** *adjective* PHYS referring to a liquid which is thick, sticky and slow-moving. Also called **viscid**

**visibility** *noun* PHYS the degree to which unlit objects can be seen by day and lighted objects can be seen by night ○ *Measurement of visibility by day is made by direct observation of objects at known distances and is therefore an estimated value.*

**visibility-by-day values** *plural noun* PHYS the values which indicate how easily seen an object is in a horizontal line from an observer in daylight conditions

**visible** *adjective* PHYS referring to something that can be seen ○ *If the Sun is seen through cumulus cloud it will be clearly visible.*

**visible spectrum** *noun* PHYS the range of wavelengths of light visible to a human

**vision** *noun* **1.** BIOL the ability to see ○ *After the age of 50, many people's vision begins to fail.* Also called **eyesight 2.** the picture on a television screen ○ *You need to adjust the vision on the set.* **3.** an image seen in the imagination or in a dream

**visitant, visitor** *noun* ZOOL a migrant bird which comes to a region regularly ○ *The flycatcher is a summer visitor to Britain.*

**visual** *adjective* PHYS referring to seeing

**visual acuity** *noun* BIOL the state or degree of being able to see objects clearly

**visual display unit** *noun* COMPUT a terminal with a screen and a keyboard, on which text or graphics can be viewed and information entered. Abbreviation **VDU** (NOTE: The US term is **visual display terminal**.)

**visual examination** *noun* an examination of something using the eyes only. Also called **visual inspection**

**visual horizon** *noun* EARTH SCI the horizon which can be seen (NOTE: Because of the curvature of the Earth, the visual horizon looks curved when seen from a ship.)

**visual indication** *noun* something which is seen and which serves as a warning of a more serious condition

**visual inspection** *noun* same as **visual examination**

**visualisation, visualization** *noun* COMPUT the conversion of numbers or data into a graphical format that can be more easily understood

**visual programming** *noun* COMPUT a method of programming a computer by dragging icons into a flowchart that describes the program's actions rather than writing a series of instructions

**visual purple** *noun* BIOCHEM same as **rhodopsin**

**visual reference** *noun* something seen and used as a guide to something else

**vital** *adjective* BIOL essential for life ○ *Vital nutrients are leached from the topsoil.* ○ *Oxygen is vital to the human system.*

**vital organs** *plural noun* ANAT the organs in the body without which a human being cannot live, e.g. the heart, lungs and brain

**vital statistics** *plural noun* STATS official statistics relating to the population of a place, e.g. the percentage of live births per thousand, the incidence of a specific disease or the numbers of births and deaths

**vitamin** *noun* BIOCHEM an essential substance not synthesised in the body, but found in most foods, and needed for good health

**vitamin A** *noun* BIOCHEM a vitamin which is soluble in fat and can be synthesised in the body from precursors, but is mainly found in food such as liver, vegetables, eggs and cod liver oil. Also called **retinol** (NOTE: Lack of vitamin A affects the body's growth and resistance to disease.)

**vitamin B₁** *noun* BIOCHEM a vitamin found in yeast, liver, cereals and pork. Also called **thiamine**

**vitamin B₁₂** *noun* BIOCHEM a water-soluble vitamin found especially in liver, milk, and eggs but not in vegetables and important for blood formation, nerve function, and growth. Also called **cyanocobalamin** (NOTE: A deficiency of B₁₂ causes pernicious anaemia.)

**vitamin B₂** *noun* BIOCHEM a vitamin found in eggs, liver, green vegetables, milk and yeast. Also called **riboflavin**

**vitamin B₆** *noun* BIOCHEM a vitamin found in meat, cereals and molasses. Also called **pyridoxine**

**vitamin B complex** *noun* BIOCHEM a group of vitamins which are soluble in water, including folic acid, pyridoxine and riboflavine

**vitamin C** *noun* BIOCHEM a vitamin which is soluble in water and is found in fresh fruit, especially oranges and lemons, raw vegetables and liver. Also called **ascorbic acid** (NOTE: Lack of vitamin C can cause anaemia and scurvy.)

**vitamin D** *noun* BIOCHEM a vitamin which is soluble in fat, and is found in butter, eggs and fish (NOTE: It is also produced by the skin when exposed to sunlight. Vitamin D helps in the formation of bones, and lack of it causes rickets in children.)

**vitamin deficiency** *noun* MED a lack of necessary vitamins

**vitamin E** *noun* BIOCHEM a vitamin found in vegetables, vegetable oils, eggs and wholemeal bread

**vitamin K** *noun* BIOCHEM a vitamin found in green vegetables such as spinach and cabbage, which helps the clotting of blood and is needed to activate prothrombin

**vitreous** *adjective* CHEM being like glass in appearance or characteristics

**vitreous humour** *noun* ANAT the colourless gel that lies between the lens and the retina of the eye

**viviparous** *adjective* ZOOL referring to an animal such as a mammal which bears live young. Compare **oviparous** (NOTE: In contrast to mammals, birds and reptiles lay eggs and are oviparous.)

**vivisection** *noun* ZOOL, MED the dissection of a living animal under experimental conditions

**VLSI** *abbreviation* ELECTRONICS very large scale integration

**vocal** *adjective* BIOL referring to the voice

**vocal cords** *plural noun* ANAT a pair of fibrous structures that run across the voice box and produce sounds by vibrating

**vocal fremitus** *noun* MED a vibration of the chest as a patient speaks or coughs

**vocal ligament** *noun* ANAT a ligament in the centre of the vocal cords

**voice** *noun* the sound made when a person speaks or sings ○ *The doctor has a quiet and comforting voice.* ○ *I didn't recognise your voice over the phone.*

**voice box** *noun* ANAT the hollow organ at the back of the throat containing the vocal cords. Also called **larynx**

**voice coil** *noun* ACOUSTICS **1.** an element in a dynamic microphone which vibrates when sound waves strike it causing variations in an electrical signal **2.** an element in a loudspeaker that vibrates according to a signal and so produces sound waves

**voice data entry, voice data input** *noun* COMPUT an input of information into a computer using a speech recognition system and the user's voice

**voice recognition** *noun* COMPUT the ability of a computer to recognise specific words produced by a human voice and to provide a suitable response

**voice synthesis** *noun* COMPUT the reproduction of sounds similar to those produced by a human voice

**volatile** *adjective* CHEM referring to a liquid which easily changes into a gas or vapour

**volatile memory** *noun* COMPUT a memory or storage medium which loses data stored in it when its power supply is switched off

**volatile oil** *noun* PHARM same as **essential oil**

**volatile organic compound** *noun* CHEM an organic compound which evaporates at a relatively low temperature (NOTE: Volatile organic compounds such as ethylene, propylene, benzene and styrene contribute to air pollution.)

**volatility** *noun* CHEM, PHYS the ease with which a liquid changes into a gas or vapour ○ *With kerosene-type fuels, volatility is controlled by distillation and flash point.*

**volcanic** *adjective* EARTH SCI referring to volcanoes

**volcanic activity** *noun* EARTH SCI something such as an earthquake, eruption, lava flow or smoke emission that shows that a volcano is not extinct

**volcanic ash** *noun* EARTH SCI ash and small pieces of lava and rock which are thrown up by an erupting volcano

**volcanic dust** *noun* EARTH SCI fine ash thrown up by an erupting volcano

**volcanic rock** *noun* EARTH SCI rock formed from lava

**volcano** *noun* EARTH SCI a mountain surrounding a hole in the Earth's crust, formed of solidified molten rock sent up from the interior of the Earth

COMMENT: Volcanoes occur along faults in the Earth's surface and exist in well-known chains. Some are extinct, but others erupt relatively frequently. Some are always active, in that they emit sulphurous gases and smoke, without actually erupting. Volcanic eruptions are a major source of atmospheric pollution, in particular of sulphur dioxide. Very large eruptions cause a mass of dust to enter the atmosphere, which has a noticeable effect on the world's climate.

**volt** *noun* MEASURE, ELEC the SI unit of electrical potential ○ *The system requires a power supply of either 115 volts AC (alternating current), 28 volts DC (direct current), or both.* Symbol **V**

**voltage** *noun* MEASURE, ELEC an electrical force measured in volts ○ *As an installed battery becomes fully charged by the aircraft generator, the battery voltage nears its nominal level and the charging current decreases.*

COMMENT: Electricity supplies can have peaks and troughs of current, depending on the users in the area. Fluctuations in voltage can affect computers and a voltage regulator will provide a steady supply of electricity.

**voltage divider** *noun* ELEC a resistor or series of resistors that can produce voltages that are fractions of the source voltage. Also called **potential divider**

**voltage regulator** *noun* ELEC a device to control the level of voltage

**voltage transient** *noun* ELEC a spike of voltage which is caused by a time delay in two devices switching or by noise on the line

**voltaic cell** *noun* ELEC same as **primary cell**

**voltmeter** *noun* ELEC an instrument for measuring the potential difference between two points in an electrical circuit

**volume** *noun* **1.** PHYS the amount of space occupied by a solid, a liquid or a gas ○ *If the pressure of a given mass of gas is maintained constant, the volume of gas increases as its temperature is increased.* **2.** ACOUSTICS the loudness of a transmission □ **to turn down the volume** to make the sound less loud by adjusting the volume control □ **to turn up the volume** to make the sound louder by adjusting the volume control **3.** COMPUT the total disk space occupied by data in a storage system

**volume control** *noun* a knob used to adjust the sound on a device by making it louder or less loud

**volumetric analysis** *noun* CHEM the analysis of gas by volume

**voluntary muscle** *noun* ANAT a muscle that is under conscious control (NOTE: It is usually a striated muscle.)

**von Neumann machine** *noun* PHYS a machine whose abilities include the skills needed to reproduce itself from commonly available materials

**von Willebrand's factor** *noun* BIOCHEM a protein substance in plasma involved in platelet aggregation

**-vore** *suffix* BIOL an organism that eats a particular diet

**-vorous** *suffix* BIOL eating a particular diet

**vortex** *noun* PHYS a flow of a liquid in a whirlpool or of a gas in a whirlwind ○ *The most destructive winds are in the vortex, where the rotation of the whirlwind produces very high wind speeds.*

**VRAM** *noun* COMPUT high speed random access memory used to store computer-generated or digitised images. Full form **video random access memory**

**VRC** *abbreviation* COMPUT vertical redundancy check

**VS** *abbreviation* COMPUT virtual storage

**VSB** *noun* COMPUT a method of transferring data over coaxial cable, used to modulate and transmit digital television signals. Full form **vestigial side band**

**VU** *abbreviation* ENVIRON vulnerable

**vulcanisation, vulcanization** *verb* INDUST to strengthen a material such as rubber in a reaction with sulfur and other additives at increased temperature and pressure

**vulcanism** *noun* EARTH SCI a movement of magma or molten rock onto or towards the Earth's surface

**vulnerable** *adjective* ENVIRON referring to a species that is likely to become endangered unless protective measures are taken. See Comment at **endangered species**. Abbreviation **VU**

**vulture** *noun* ZOOL a large bird of prey which feeds on carrion

**vulva** *noun* ANAT the external fleshy structures around the opening of the vagina

# W

**W** *symbol* **1.** CHEM ELEM tungsten **2.** ELEC, MEASURE watt

**W3C** *noun* COMPUT a group of international industry members that work together to develop common standards for the World Wide Web. Full form **World Wide Web Consortium** (NOTE: Visit the www.w3.org website for new standards and developments.)

**wader** *noun* BIRDS a bird that feeds on organisms or plants found in shallow water

**wadi** *noun* EARTH SCI a gully with a stream at the bottom, found in the desert regions of North Africa. Compare **arroyo**

**wafer** *noun* ELECTRONICS a thin round slice of a large single crystal of silicon onto which hundreds of individual integrated circuits are constructed (NOTE: The wafer is then cut into individual chips.)

**wafer scale integration** *noun* ELECTRONICS one large chip, the size of a wafer, made up of smaller integrated circuits connected together (NOTE: These are still in the research stage.)

**WAIS** *noun* COMPUT a system that allows a user to search for information stored on the Internet. Full form **wide area information server**

**wait condition** *noun* COMPUT **1.** a state in which a processor is not active, but waiting for input from peripherals **2.** a null instruction which is used to slow down a processor so that slower memory or a peripheral can keep up. Also called **wait state**

**wait loop** *noun* COMPUT a processor that repeats one loop of program until some action occurs

**wait state** *noun* COMPUT same as **wait condition**

**wake-on-LAN** *noun* COMPUT technology that allows a personal computer or workstation to be switched on automatically by sending it a signal over a local area network connection (NOTE: The system is built into the network interface card fitted to the computer and allows a network manager or network server software to manage the computers linked to the network.)

**Waldsterben** *noun* BOT same as **forest dieback** (NOTE: From a German word meaning 'the dying of trees'.)

**Wallace's line** *noun* EARTH SCI a line dividing the Australasian biogeographical region from the Southeast Asian region

**wallpaper** *noun* COMPUT an image or pattern used as a background in a window

**WAN** *abbreviation* COMPUT wide area network

**wand** *noun* COMPUT an optical device which is held in the hand to read bar codes on products. Also called **bar code reader**

**WAP** *abbreviation* COMPUT **1.** wireless application protocol **2.** wireless access point ○ *The WAP has an aerial and a built-in hub.*

COMMENT: WAP can be used over almost all of the current wireless networks, including the popular GSM mobile telephone standard, and can run on almost any operating system or hardware device. A device that supports WAP provides a very simple browser that can display basic graphics and text-based pages of information on a small, monochrome, 6–10 line display, similar to a tiny, simple webpage. The user can navigate between pages using two or three buttons on the handheld device or mobile telephone. The arrival of WAP allows users to access e-mail and news-based websites from a mobile telephone, but users have been put off by the very slow speed (no more than 9,600 bps) at which data can be transferred over current wireless telephone systems.

**WAP browser** *noun* COMPUT a simple web browser that works on a handheld WAP device

COMMENT: A WAP browser supports the HTML and XML web page markup standards, but also supports its own markup system, WML (WAP markup language) allowing designers to create simple pages that can be transferred efficiently over the often slow wireless link (usually at a maximum of 9,600bps) and navigated using two or three buttons on a handheld device or mobile telephone.

**WAP markup language** *noun* COMPUT a webpage formatting language that is similar to a very simple version of the standard HTML webpage coding system, but does not include many of the extra features that cannot be displayed on the small screen of a WAP handheld device or navigated with two or three buttons. Abbreviation **WML**

**WAP markup language script** *noun* COMPUT a scripting language similar to a very simple version of JavaScript that allows WML webpages to include scripting functions

**warble fly** *noun* ZOOL, INSECTS a parasitic fly whose larvae infest cattle

**warfarin** *noun* AGRIC, PHARM a substance used to poison rats and as a blood-thinning agent in humans

**warm** *adjective* quite or pleasantly hot ○ *These plants grow fast in the warm season.* ■ *verb* to make something hotter ○ *The greenhouse effect has the result of warming the general atmospheric temperature.*

**warm-blooded** *adjective* ZOOL referring to an animal, such as a mammal which has warm blood, as opposed to a reptile or fish

**warm boot** *noun* COMPUT a system restart which usually reloads the operating system but does not reset or check the hardware

**warm desert** *noun* EARTH SCI same as **mid-latitude desert**

**warm front** *noun* METEOROL a movement of a mass of warm air which displaces a mass of cold air and gives rain

**warming** *noun* the action of making something hotter ○ *At the poles, warming would be two or three times the*

global average if the greenhouse effect makes the Earth's temperature rise.

**warm start** *noun* COMPUT an act of restarting a programme which has stopped, without losing any data. Compare **cold start**

**warm up** *verb* to allow a machine to stand idle for a time after switching on, to reach the optimum operating conditions

**warning lamp** *noun* a small light, often red, which indicates a possible danger by lighting up ○ *The switch is connected to a warning lamp on the instrument panel which will illuminate if the oil pressure falls below an acceptable minimum.*

**washland** *noun* EARTH SCI an area of land which is regularly flooded

**wash out** *verb* EARTH SCI, INDUST to remove a mineral by the action of running water ○ *Most minerals are washed out of the soil during heavy rains.*

**washout** *noun* METEOROL, ENVIRON a process in which raindrops form in the atmosphere and then collect pollutant particles as they fall. Compare **rainout**

**wash PROM** *verb* COMPUT to erase the data from a PROM

**wastage** *noun* INDUST **1.** the act of wasting something ○ *There is an enormous wastage of mineral resources.* **2.** the amount wasted

**waste** *adjective* without a specific use and unwanted ○ *Waste products are dumped in the sea.* ○ *Waste matter is excreted by the body in the faeces or urine.* ■ *noun* material which is not needed by people or which is an unwanted by-product of a process ■ *verb* to use more of something than is needed

**waste disposal** *noun* ENVIRON the process of getting rid of household or industrial waste

**waste dump** *noun* ENVIRON a place where household or industrial waste is left. Also called **waste site**

**waste ground** *noun* ENVIRON an area of land which is not used for any purpose

**waste instruction** *noun* COMPUT an instruction which does not carry out any action except increasing the program counter to the location of next instruction

**wasteland** *noun* ENVIRON an area of land which is no longer usable for agriculture or for any other purpose ○ *Overgrazing has produced wastelands in Central Africa.*

**waste management** *noun* ENVIRON the action of controlling and processing household or industrial waste

**wastepaper** *noun* ENVIRON paper which has been thrown away after use

**waste processing plant** *noun* ENVIRON a place where waste material is treated to make it reusable or so that it may be disposed of safely

**waste product** *noun* a substance which is produced in a process but is not needed

**waste site** *noun* ENVIRON same as **waste dump**

**waste sorting** *noun* ENVIRON the process of separating waste into different materials, e.g. glass, metal, paper and plastic

**wastewater** *noun* INDUST, ENVIRON water that is part of effluent or sewage, especially from industrial processes ○ *There is considerable interest in the anaerobic treatment of industrial wastewaters.* ○ *Wastewater will add small but significant quantities of heavy metals to the aquatic environment.*

**wastewater treatment** *noun* ENVIRON the processing of wastewater to make it reusable or so that it may be disposed of safely

**water** *noun* CHEM a liquid which forms rain, rivers, lakes and the sea and which makes up a large part of the bodies of organisms. Formula: $H_2O$. ■ *verb* **1.** AGRIC to give water to a plant **2.** BIOL to fill with tears or saliva ○ *Onions made his eyes water.* ○ *Her mouth watered when she saw the ice cream.*

COMMENT: Water is essential to plant and animal life. Since the human body is formed of more than 50% water, an adult needs to drink about 2.5 litres of fluid each day. Water pollution can take many forms: the most common are discharges from industrial processes, household sewage and the runoff of chemicals used in agriculture.

**water balance** *noun* **1.** EARTH SCI a state in which the water lost in an area by evaporation or by runoff is replaced by water received in the form of rain **2.** PHYSIOL a state in which the water lost

by the body in urine and perspiration or by other physiological processes is balanced by water absorbed from food and drink

**waterborne** *adjective* MED referring to a disease carried in water

**watercourse** *noun* EARTH SCI a stream, river, canal or other flow of water

**water cycle** *noun* EARTH SCI the circulation of water between atmosphere, land, and sea

**water dispersal** *noun* BOT the spreading of plant seeds by water

**waterfall** *noun* EARTH SCI a place where water falls over a steep vertical drop

**waterfowl** *plural noun* BIRDS birds such as ducks which live on water

**water glass** *noun* CHEM a very concentrated and viscous solution of sodium silicate in water, used in cement and as a waterproofing and fireproofing agent

**waterhole** *noun* EARTH SCI **1.** a place where water rises naturally to the surface ○ *In the evening, the animals gather round the waterholes to drink.* **2.** a pool of water created by boring holes in the ground

**watering eye** *noun* MED an eye which fills with tears because of an irritation

**waterlogged** *adjective* EARTH SCI referring to soil that is saturated with water and so cannot keep oxygen between its particles (NOTE: Most plants cannot grow in waterlogged soil.)

**water meadow** *noun* EARTH SCI a grassy field near a river, which is often flooded

**water mill** *noun* INDUST a mill driven by water

**water of crystallisation** *noun* CHEM water molecules that form part of the structure of a crystal

**water plant** *noun* BOT a plant that grows in water

**water pollution** *noun* ENVIRON the introduction of pollutants into watercourses or the sea, rivers, lakes or canals

**water pollution abatement** *noun* ENVIRON a reduction of pollution in watercourses or the sea

**water power** *noun* INDUST power derived from a descending water supply that is converted to electricity by hydraulic turbines

**waterproof** *adjective* not allowing water to pass through

**water purification** *noun* INDUST the removal of impurities from water

**water quality** *noun* ENVIRON how good water is to drink or to swim in

**water resources** *plural noun* ENVIRON rivers, lakes and other surface waters that supply water for human use

**water-salt balance** *noun* EARTH SCI a state where the water in the soil balances the amount of salts in the soil

**watershed** *noun* EARTH SCI a natural dividing line between the headstreams of river systems, dividing one catchment area from another

**waterside** *adjective* BOT referring to a plant which grows next to a river, lake or other body of water

**water softener** *noun* **1.** INDUST a device attached to the water supply to remove nitrates or calcium from the water **2.** a chemical added to water to remove calcium

**water-soluble** *adjective* CHEM able to dissolve in water

**waterspout** *noun* METEOROL a phenomenon caused when a rapidly turning column of air forms over water, sucking the water up into the column

COMMENT: Waterspouts form in summer weather as air rises rapidly from the warm surface of the sea. Waterspouts turn cyclonically, i.e. anticlockwise in the northern hemisphere. When the waterspout moves onto dry land, it loses momentum and falls as saltwater rain. The rain sometimes contains fish which have been sucked up into the spout.

**water table** *noun* EARTH SCI the top level of water in the ground that occupies spaces in rock or soil and is above a layer of impermeable rock

**watertight** *adjective* not leaking water or other fluid

**water turbine** *noun* INDUST a device that converts the motion of the flow of water into the turning movement of a wheel ○ *Water turbines are often used to drive generators or pumps.*

**water vapour** *noun* METEOROL air containing suspended particles of water

**waterwheel** *noun* INDUST a wheel with wooden steps or buckets, which is turned by the flow of water against it and itself turns machinery such as a mill or an electric generator

**waterworks** *noun* INDUST a plant for treating and purifying water before it is pumped into pipes for distribution to houses, factories, schools and other places for use

**watt** *noun* MEASURE, ELEC an SI unit of measurement of electrical power ○ *The work done by an electrical circuit or the power consumed is measured in watts.* Symbol **W**

**watt-hour** *noun* MEASURE, ELEC a measurement of power with respect to time ○ *One watt-hour is equal to one watt being used for a period of one hour.*

**wattmeter** *noun* ELEC ENG an instrument for measuring electrical power

**wave** *noun* **1.** EARTH SCI a mass of water moving across the surface of a lake or the sea, rising higher than the surrounding water as it moves **2.** PHYS a motion by which heat, light, sound or electric current is spread

**waveform** *noun* PHYS the shape of a wave, especially the graphic representation of its characteristics such as frequency or amplitude relative to time

**waveform audio** *noun* ELEC a method of storing analog audio signals as digital data

**waveform digitisation** *noun* ELEC the conversion and storage of a waveform in numerical form using an A/D converter

**waveform editor** *noun* COMPUT a software program that displays a graphical representation of a sound wave and allows a user to edit, adjust levels and frequencies or add special effects

**waveform synthesiser** *noun* COMPUT a musical device that creates the sounds of an instrument by using recorded samples of the original waveform produced by the instrument

**waveform table** *noun* COMPUT data that describe a sound clip

**wave function** *noun* PHYS a quantum equation that shows how a wave's amplitude varies in space and time

**wavelength** *noun* PHYS the distance from the highest point of one wave to the highest point of the next ○ *Short wavelength permits sharper beams for* *direction finding and more efficient reflections.*

**wavelength division multiplexing** *noun* ELEC ENG a method of increasing the data capacity of an optic fibre by transmitting several light signals at different wavelengths along the same fibre. Abbreviation **WDM**

**wave number** *noun* PHYS the number of electromagnetic waves per unit distance (NOTE: It is inversely related to the wavelength, so radiation with a short wavelength will have a high wave number.)

**wave–particle duality** *noun* PHYS the quantum concept that energy can behave as either a particle or a wave

**wave power** *noun* same as **tidal energy**

COMMENT: In harnessing wave power, the movement of waves on the surface of the sea is used to make large floats move up and down. These act as pumps which pump a continuous flow of water to turn a turbine.

**wave refraction** *noun* OCEANOG the tendency of wave crests to turn from their original direction and become more parallel to the shore as they move into shallower water

**wavetable** *noun* COMPUT a memory in a sound card that contains a recording of a real musical instrument that is played back

**wave theory** *noun* PHYS the theory that the behaviour of electromagnetic radiation such as light can be explained by assuming that it travels in waves

**wax** *noun* CHEM a semisolid or solid substance of animal, plant or mineral origin ■ *verb* ASTRON (*of the Moon or a planet*) to appear to grow bigger as more of the illuminated face becomes visible (NOTE: The Moon waxes between its new and full phases.)

**Wb** *symbol* MEASURE, PHYS weber

**WDM** *abbreviation* COMPUT wavelength division multiplexing

**weak** *adjective* **1.** not strong ○ *a weak radio signal* **2.** CHEM overdiluted with water or air

**weak acid** *noun* CHEM an acid that does not ionise or dissociate in a solution

**weak interaction** *noun* PHYS the short-range interaction between elementary particles that is involved in radioactive decay

**weak mixture** *noun* AUTOMOT a fuel/air mixture in which there is more air than usual ○ *Excessive cylinder head temperatures could be caused by prolonged use of a weak mixture, especially at high altitude.* Also called **lean mixture**

**weak solution** *noun* CHEM a mixture of water and some other substance in which the amount of water is more than usual

**wear** *noun* damage or loss of quality by use ○ *Poor handling of aero-engines during operation can cause considerable damage and wear which can shorten the life of the engine.* ■ *verb* to become damaged or to lose quality because of use ○ *The more the brakes are used, the more they wear.*

**weather** *noun* METEOROL daily atmospheric conditions such as sunshine, wind and precipitation in an area ■ *verb* EARTH SCI to change the state of soil or rock through the action of rain, sun, frost, wind, etc. or by chemical pollutants

**weather chart** *noun* METEOROL a chart showing the state of the weather at a particular moment or changes which are expected to happen in the weather in the near future. Also called **weather map**

**weather forecast** *noun* METEOROL a description of what the weather will be for a period in the future

**weather forecasting** *noun* METEOROL the scientific study of weather conditions and patterns, which allows the description of what the weather will be for a period in the future

**weather map** *noun* METEOROL same as **weather chart**

**weather station** *noun* METEOROL a place where weather is recorded

**web, Web** *noun* **1.** ZOOL a structure of threads secreted by a spider in the form of a net **2.** COMPUT a collection of the millions of websites and webpages that together form the part of the Internet that is most often seen by users. Also called **www, World Wide Web**

COMMENT: The Internet includes electronic mail, Usenet and newsgroups as well as the web. Each website is a collection of webpages; each web page contains text, graphics and links to other websites. Each page is created using the HTML language and is viewed by a user with a web browser. Navigation between webpages and websites is called surfing. This requires a computer with a link to the Internet (usually using a modem) and a web browser to view the webpages stored on the remote web servers.

**webbed** *adjective* ZOOL with skin between the toes ○ *Ducks and other aquatic birds have webbed feet.*

**web browser** *noun* COMPUT same as **browser**

**weber** *noun* MEASURE, PHYS the SI unit of magnetic flux. Symbol **Wb** (NOTE: It is equal to 1 joule per ampere or 1 volt second.)

**webpage** *noun* COMPUT a single file stored on a web server that contains formatted text, graphics and hypertext links to other pages on the Internet or within a website

**web server** *noun* COMPUT a computer that stores the collection of webpages that make up a website

**website** *noun* COMPUT a collection of webpages that are linked and related and can be accessed by a user with a web browser

**weed** *noun* AGRIC a wild plant which grows in cultivated land

**weedkiller** *noun* AGRIC a substance used to kill weeds

**weigh** *verb* **1.** to measure how heavy something is ○ *He weighed the sample carefully.* **2.** to have a particular degree of heaviness ○ *A given quantity of lead weighs more than the same quantity of aluminium.*

**weight** *noun* **1.** the force with which a body is drawn towards the centre of the Earth **2.** a measure of how heavy something is

**weighted average** *noun* STATS an average which is calculated by taking several factors into account, giving some more value than others

**weighted bit** *noun* COMPUT a bit that has a different value depending on its position in a word

**weighting** *noun* COMPUT the process of sorting users, programs or data by their importance or priority

**weightlessness** *adjective* PHYS, AEROSP the state of having no weight,

generally as a result of being outside the gravitational pull of the Earth, the Moon or other planet

**Weismannism** *noun* GENETICS the principle that the inherited characteristics of any organism are determined only by the components of the male and female gametes from which the organism develops (NOTE: This theory rules out the inheritance of characteristics acquired during an organism's lifetime and is the basis of modern genetics.)

**well** *noun* INDUST, AGRIC a hole dug in the ground to the level of the water table, from which water can be removed by a pump or bucket

**well-behaved** *adjective* COMPUT referring to a program which does not make any non-standard system calls, using only the standard BIOS input/output calls rather than directly addressing peripherals or memory

**wellhead** *noun* INDUST, AGRIC the top of a well

**Wentworth-Udden scale** *noun* MEASURE, GEOL a scale for measuring and describing the size of grains of minerals

COMMENT: The scale runs from the largest size, the boulder, down to the finest grain, clay. The approximate diameters of each grain are: boulder, up to 256 mm; cobble, above 64 mm; pebble, between 4 and 64 mm; gravel, between 2 and 4 mm; sand, between 0.06 and 2 mm; silt and clay are the finest sizes.

**west** *noun* **1.** NAVIG the compass point 270° clockwise from due north and directly opposite east **2.** the direction of the setting sun ■ *adjective* GEOG **1.** referring to areas or regions lying in the west **2.** referring to western part of a country ■ *adverb* NAVIG towards the west ○ *The aircraft was flying west.*

**westerly** *adjective* NAVIG to or from the west ○ *The ship was proceeding in a westerly direction.* ○ *A westerly airstream covers the country.* ■ *noun* METEOROL a wind that blows from the west

**western** *adjective* NAVIG in the west or towards the west ○ *the western plains*

**west wind** *noun* METEOROL a wind which blows from the west

**wet** *adjective* with a lot of moisture ■ *verb* to add moisture to something

**wetland** *noun* EARTH SCI an area of land where the soil surface is almost level with the water table and where specially adapted vegetation has developed

**wetland hydrology** *noun* EARTH SCI the study of periodic flooding or soil saturation which creates anaerobic conditions in the soil of wetlands

**wet season** *noun* METEOROL the time of year in some countries when a lot of rain falls

**whale** *noun* MARINE BIOL a very large mammal living in the sea. Order: Cetacea.

COMMENT: Whales are the largest mammals still in existence. There are two groups of whales: the toothed whales and the baleen whales. Baleen whales have no teeth and feed by sucking in large quantities of water which they then force out again through their baleen, which is a series of fine plates like a comb hanging down from the upper jaw. The baleen acts like a sieve and traps any plankton and krill which are in the water. The toothed whales have teeth and eat fish. They include the sperm whale, the killer whale and porpoises and dolphins. Whales are caught mainly for their oils, though also in some cases for food. Some species of whale have become extinct because of overexploitation and the population of many of the existing species is dangerously low. Commercial whaling is severely restricted.

**what you see is what you get** *noun* COMPUT full form of **WYSIWYG**

**wheat** *noun* PLANTS a cereal crop grown in temperate regions. Genus: *Triticum*.

**wheatgerm** *noun* FOOD INDUST the central part of the wheat seed, which contains valuable nutrients

**wheatmeal** *noun* FOOD INDUST brown flour with a large amount of bran, but not as much as is in wholemeal

**Wheatstone bridge** *noun* ELEC a piece of equipment for measuring an unknown electrical resistance

**wheel** *noun* MECH ENG **1.** a circular, rotating, load-carrying part between the tyre and axle of a vehicle **2.** the whole wheel and tyre assembly on which a vehicle rolls

**wheel bearing** *noun* MECH ENG a device which allows a wheel to rotate freely around an axle

**while-loop** *noun* COMPUT a set of conditional program instructions that carries out a loop while a condition is true

**whirlpool** *noun* EARTH SCI a rapidly turning eddy of water

**whirlwind** *noun* METEOROL a column of rapidly turning air at the centre of an area of very low pressure (NOTE: Over water a whirlwind becomes a waterspout and over desert a dust devil.)

**white arsenic** *noun* CHEM same as **arsenic oxide**

**white blood cell** *noun* BIOL a blood cell containing a nucleus, that is formed in bone marrow and creates antibodies

**white dwarf** *noun* ASTRON one of the possible remnants which can be formed from stars after they cease producing energy by fusion

COMMENT: If less than 1.4 solar masses of material remain after the star leaves the main sequence and loses mass, it will collapse into a white dwarf when the outward radiation pressure which holds active stars up is removed. White dwarfs are held up instead by the mutual repulsion between the electrons in their atoms. They emit small amounts of residual heat and when this is gone reach the black dwarf stage – or will do so, since the process takes so long that no star in the universe has completed it yet.

**white hole** *noun* ASTRON the exact opposite of a black hole, a singularity from which matter emerges instead of being sucked in (NOTE: White holes are speculative constructs, unlike black holes which have a solid theoretical backing. They open up the possibility of allowing matter to be sent to alternative universes.)

**white light** *noun* PHYS light containing a perfect or near-perfect mix of the colours of the visible spectrum and appearing white to the eye

**white matter** *noun* ANAT the pale-coloured nerve tissue in the brain and spinal cord

**white spirit** *noun* INDUST a colourless flammable liquid derived from petroleum and used for cleaning paintbrushes and as paint thinner

**wholefood** *noun* FOOD INDUST a naturally or organically grown food which has not been processed ○ *A wholefood diet is regarded as healthier than eating processed foods.*

**wholegrain** *noun* FOOD INDUST food such as rice of which the whole of the seed is eaten

**wholemeal** *noun* FOOD INDUST flour which has had nothing removed or added to it and contains a large proportion of the original wheat seed, including the bran

**wholemeal bread, wholewheat bread** *noun* FOOD INDUST bread made from wholemeal flour

**wide** *adjective* large from side to side

**wide area information server** COMPUT full form of **WAIS**

**wide area network** *noun* COMPUT a network in which the various terminals are far apart and linked by radio, satellite and cable. Abbreviation **WAN**

COMMENT: Wide area networks use modems, radio and other long distance transmission methods. Local area networks use cables or optical fibre links

**wideband** *noun* TELECOM a transmission method that combines several channels of data onto a carrier signal and can carry the data over long distances

**widely adopted** *adjective* now in standard use with many companies, institutions and organisations

**width** *noun* the size of something from side to side

**wild** *adjective* BIOL not domesticated

**wilderness** *noun* ENVIRON an area of wild uncultivated land, usually far from human habitation

**wilderness area** *noun* ENVIRON an area of undeveloped land which is set aside and protected, e.g. as a national park

**wildlife** *noun* ZOOL wild animals and birds ○ *Plantations of conifers are poorer for wildlife than mixed or deciduous woodlands.* ○ *The effects of the open-cast mining scheme would be disastrous on wildlife, particularly on moorland birds.*

**wild rice** *noun* PLANTS a species of grass found naturally in North America which is similar to rice. Latin name: *Zizania aquatica.*

**Williamson's synthesis** *noun* CHEM a method of synthesising ethers

from alkyl iodides and sodium alcoholates

**willow** *noun* TREES a temperate hardwood tree often coppiced or pollarded. Genus: *Salix.*

**wilt** *noun* BOT **1.** the drooping of plants particularly young stems, leaves and flowers, as a result of a lack of water, too much heat or disease **2.** one of a group of plant diseases that cause drooping and shrivelling of leaves (NOTE: It is caused by fungi, bacteria, or viruses that block the plant's water-carrying vessels.)

**WIMP** *abbreviation* COMPUT window, icon, mouse, pointer

COMMENT: WIMPs usually use a combination of windows, icons and a mouse to control the operating system. In many graphical user interfaces all the functions of the operating system can be controlled just using the mouse. Icons represent programs and files, so instead of entering the file name, the file is selected by moving a pointer with a mouse.

**winch** *noun* MECH ENG a handle used to turn a machine manually

**wind** *noun* **1.** METEOROL air which moves in the lower atmosphere, or a stream of air ○ *The weather station has instruments to measure the speed of the wind.* **2.** PHYSIOL gas which builds up in the stomach and intestines during the digestion of food

**wind chill factor** *noun* METEOROL a way of calculating the risk of exposure in cold weather by adding the speed of the wind to the number of degrees of temperature below zero

**wind dispersal** *noun* BOT the spreading of plant seeds by being blown by the wind

**wind-driven** *noun* INDUST powered by the wind

**wind erosion** *noun* EARTH SCI erosion of soil or rock by wind

**wind farm** *noun* INDUST a group of large windmills or wind turbines, built to harness the wind to produce electricity. Also called **wind park**

**wind generator** *noun* INDUST a machine used to produce electricity from the wind

**wind gradient** *noun* METEOROL, AEROSP the rate of increase of wind strength with unit increase in height above ground level ○ *After take-off, as* *the aircraft gains altitude, the ground speed may be affected by the wind gradient.*

**windmill** *noun* INDUST a construction with sails which are turned by the wind, so driving a machine

COMMENT: Windmills were originally built to grind corn or to pump water from marshes. Large modern windmills are used to harness the wind to produce electricity.

**window** COMPUT *noun* **1.** a reserved section of screen used to display special information, which can be selected and looked at at any time and which overwrites information already on the screen ○ *Several remote stations are connected to the network and each has its own window onto the hard disk.* **2.** a part of a document currently displayed on a screen ○ *The operating system will allow other programs to be displayed on-screen at the same time in different windows.* **3.** an area of memory or access to a storage device ■ *verb* to set up a section of screen by defining the coordinates of its corners, allowing information to be temporarily displayed, overwriting previous information but without altering information in the workspace

**window, icon, mouse, pointer** *noun* COMPUT a program display which uses graphics or icons to control the software and make it easier to use as system commands do not have to be typed in. Abbreviation **WIMP**

**windowing** *noun* COMPUT **1.** the action of setting up a window to show information on the screen ○ *The network system uses the latest windowing techniques.* **2.** the displaying or accessing of information via a window

**wind park** *noun* INDUST same as **wind farm**

**windpipe** *noun* ANAT the tube through which air travels from the throat to the lungs. Also called **trachea**

**wind pollination** *noun* BOT pollination of flowers by pollen which is blown by the wind

**wind power** *noun* INDUST the power generated by using wind to drive a machine or turbine which creates electricity

**wind pump** *noun* INDUST, AGRIC a pump driven by the wind, which raises water out of the ground

**wind rose** *noun* METEOROL a chart showing the direction of the prevalent winds in an area

**windrow** *noun* AGRIC the cut stalks of a crop, gathered into a row to be dried by the wind

**wind shear** *noun* METEOROL a change in wind direction and speed between slightly different altitudes, which can be dangerous ○ *Wind shear, if strong enough, can produce clear air turbulence.* ○ *Fly-by-wire technology can be very useful in wind shear situations.*

**windspeed** *noun* METEOROL the speed of the wind, usually measured in knots (NOTE: If combined with a direction, windspeed is called velocity.)

**wind turbine** *noun* INDUST a turbine driven by wind

**windward** *adjective* EARTH SCI referring to a position exposed to the wind ○ *The trees provide shelter on the windward side of the house.*

**wing** *noun* **1.** ZOOL one of the feather-covered limbs of a bird or membrane-covered limbs of a bat that are used for flying **2.** AVIAT the main horizontal aerofoil of an aircraft ○ *The wing supports the weight of the aircraft in flight.*

**wing loading** *noun* AVIAT the weight of an aircraft per unit of wing area

**wing root** *noun* AVIAT the part of the wing of an aircraft where it meets the fuselage

**wing span** *noun* ZOOL, AVIAT the distance between the tip of one wing to the tip of the other wing

**wing tip** *noun* ZOOL, AVIAT the outermost part of a wing

**winter** *noun* the last season of the year, following autumn and before spring, when the weather is coldest, the days are short, most plants do not flower or produce new shoots and some animals hibernate ■ *verb* ZOOL to spend the winter in a place

**winterbourne** *noun* EARTH SCI a stream which flows only in the wetter part of the year, usually in winter

**wintering ground** *noun* ECOL an area where birds come each year to spend the winter

**winter solstice** *noun* ASTRON 21 December, the shortest day in the northern hemisphere, when the Sun is at its furthest point north of the equator

**winter wheat** *noun* AGRIC wheat of a variety sown in the autumn or early winter months and harvested early the following summer

**wipe** *verb* COMPUT to clean data from a disk ○ *By reformatting you will wipe the disk clean.*

**wire** *noun* a thin metal filament, often one carrying electric current ■ *verb* ELEC to install wiring in a place

**wired** *adjective* COMPUT referring to a computer with a program built into the hardware which cannot be changed

**wire frame model** *noun* COMPUT a method of displaying objects using lines and arcs rather than filled areas or with the appearance of being solid. Also called **wire mesh model, polygon mesh model**

**wireless access point** *noun* COMPUT a device that connects to a LAN and allows a computer to access the network using wireless data transmission. Abbreviation **WAP**

**wireless application protocol** *noun* COMPUT a system that allows a user to access information on an Internet server using a wireless handheld device such as a mobile telephone. Abbreviation **WAP**. See Comment at **WAP**

**wireless modem** *noun* TELECOM a modem that can be used with a wireless mobile telephone system (NOTE: A wireless modem usually includes the telephone hardware and an aerial, so does not need to be plugged into a separate mobile telephone.)

**wireless network** *noun* TELECOM a network that does not use cable to transmit the data between computers, but instead uses radio signals to transmit signals, normally using the 802.11b or 802.11a transmission protocol

**wire mesh** *noun* ENG metal sheeting made of criss-crossed wiring

**wire mesh model** *noun* COMPUT same as **wire frame model**

**wire printer** *noun* COMPUT a dot-matrix printer

**wiring** *noun* a series of wires ○ *The wiring in the system had to be replaced.*

**wiring closet** *noun* COMPUT a box in which the cabling for a network or part

of network is terminated and interconnected

**wiring frame** *noun* COMPUT a metal structure used to support incoming cables and to provide connectors to allow cables to be interconnected

**WISC** *abbreviation* COMPUT writable instruction set computer

**wither** *verb* BOT (*of plants, leaves, flowers*) to shrivel and die

**wizard** *noun* COMPUT a software utility that helps someone create something

**WML** *abbreviation* COMPUT WAP markup language

**Wohler's synthesis** *noun* CHEM a way of producing urea from inorganic ammonium isocyanate by heating

**wolds** *plural noun* EARTH SCI an area of upland country, on chalk or limestone

**wolfram** *noun* CHEM ELEM same as **tungsten**

**woman** *noun* BIOL a female adult person (NOTE: The plural is **women**. For other terms referring to women, see words beginning with **gyn-**.)

**womb** *noun* ANAT a hollow organ in a woman's pelvic cavity in which a fertilised ovum develops into a fetus. Also called **uterus**

**wood** *noun* **1.** BOT a hard tissue which forms the main body of a tree **2.** INDUST a construction material that comes from trees **3.** FORESTRY a large number of trees growing together

**wood alcohol** *noun* CHEM an alcohol manufactured from waste wood, which is used as a fuel or solvent. Also called **methanol**

**woodfuel** *noun* INDUST wood which is used as fuel

**woodland** *noun* FORESTRY land covered with trees with clear spaces between them

**woodland management** *noun* FORESTRY the controlling of an area of woodland so that it is productive, e.g. by regular felling, coppicing and planting

**woodlot** *noun* FORESTRY a small area of land planted with trees

**wood pulp** *noun* INDUST a softwood which has been pulverised into small fibres and mixed with water, used to make paper

**word** *noun* **1.** a separate item of language, which is used with others to form speech or writing **2.** COMPUT a separate item of data on a computer, formed of a group of bits, stored in a single location in a memory

**word-processing** *noun* COMPUT the use of a computer to produce, edit and output text. Also called **text processing**

**word-processor** *noun* COMPUT a word-processing package or program for a computer which allows the editing and manipulation and output of text, e.g. as letters, labels or address lists

**word wrap** *noun* COMPUT a system in word processing in which the operator does not have to indicate the line endings, but can keyboard continuously, leaving the program to insert word breaks and to continue the text on the next line. Also called **wraparound**

**work** *noun* **1.** PHYS energy used when something is forced to move **2.** paid employment, or the duties of a job

**work area** *noun* COMPUT a memory space which is being used by an operator

**work disk** *noun* COMPUT a disk on which current work is stored

**worker** *noun* **1.** a person who works, especially as an employee **2.** INSECTS (*in a colony of insects*) a sterile female that forages for food

**work file** *noun* COMPUT a temporary work area which is being used for current work. Also called **scratch file**

**workflow** *noun* COMPUT software designed to improve the flow of electronic documents around an office network, from user to user

**workgroup** *noun* COMPUT a small group of users who are working on a project or connected with a local area network

**work hardening** *verb* METALL the increasing of the hardness and strength of a metal by subjecting it to cold work such as compression or tension

**workings** *plural noun* INDUST underground tunnels in a mine

**workload** *noun* **1.** an amount of work which a person or computer has to do ○ *He has difficulty in dealing with his heavy workload.* **2.** the share of work done by a person, system or device

**work out** *verb* INDUST to use up something such as a mineral resource completely ○ *The coal mine was worked out years ago.*

**worksheet** *noun* COMPUT a two-dimensional matrix of rows and columns that contains cells which can, themselves, contain equations

**workspace** *noun* COMPUT a space on memory which is available for use or is being used currently by an operator

**workstation** *noun* COMPUT a place where a computer user works, with a terminal, VDU, printer, modem and other facilities ○ *The system includes five workstations linked together in a ring network.* ○ *The archive storage has a total capacity of 1200 Mb between seven workstations.*

**world** *noun* **1.** EARTH SCI the planet Earth ○ *a map of the world* ○ *to sail round the world* **2.** all the people who live on the Earth

**worldwide** *adjective, adverb* referring to or covering the whole world ○ *the worldwide energy crisis* ○ *We sell our products worldwide.*

**World Wide Web** *noun* COMPUT the millions of websites and webpages that together form the part of the Internet that is most often seen by users. Abbreviation **www**. Also called **web**. See Comment at **web**

**World Wide Web consortium** *noun* COMPUT full form of **W3C**

**worm** *noun* ZOOL **1.** an invertebrate animal with a soft body and no limbs, e.g., a nematode or a flatworm **2.** an invertebrate animal with a long thin body living in large numbers in the soil. Also called **earthworm**

COMMENT: Earthworms provide a useful service by aerating the soil as they tunnel. They also eat organic matter and help increase the soil's fertility. It is believed that they also secrete a hormone which encourages rooting by plants.

**WORM** *abbreviation* COMPUT write once, read many times memory

**wormhole** *noun* ASTRON a temporary path which might in theory exist to connect black holes in different universes

**wraparound** *noun* COMPUT same as **word wrap**

**writable instruction set computer** *noun* COMPUT a design for a central processing unit that allows a programmer to add extra machine code instructions using microcode, to customise the instruction set. Abbreviation **WISC**

**write head** *noun* ELECTRONICS a transducer that can write data onto a magnetic medium

**write once, read many times memory** *noun* COMPUT an optical disk storage system that allows one writing action but many reading actions in its life. Abbreviation **WORM**

**write protect** *verb* COMPUT to make it impossible to write to a floppy disk by moving a special write-protect tab

**Wurtz reaction** *noun* CHEM a method of synthesising hydrocarbons using iodides and sodium

**www** *abbreviation* COMPUT World Wide Web

**WYSIWYG** *noun* COMPUT a program where the output on the screen is exactly the same as the output on printout, including graphics and special fonts. Full form **what you see is what you get**

# X

**X.25** *noun* COMPUT a CCITT standard that defines the connection between a terminal and a packet-switching network

**X.400** *noun* COMPUT a CCITT standard that defines an electronic mail transfer method

**X.500** *noun* COMPUT a CCITT standard that defines a method of global naming which allows every individual user to have a unique identity and allows any user to address an electronic mail message to any other user

**X-axis** *noun* MATHS the horizontal axis of a graph. ♦ **Y-axis**

**X chromosome** *noun* GENETICS a chromosome that determines sex. ♦ **Y chromosome**

COMMENT: Mammals have a pair of chromosomes determining sex, one of which is always an X chromosome. A female usually has one pair of XX chromosomes, while a male usually has one XY pair. Haemophilia is a disorder linked to the part of the X chromosome that is unpaired with the shorter Y chromosome and so appears only in males.

**X-coordinate** *noun* MATHS a horizontal axis position coordinate. ♦ **Y-coordinate**

**X-direction** *noun* MATHS a movement horizontally. ♦ **Y-direction**

**X-distance** *noun* MATHS the distance along an X-axis from the origin. ♦ **Y-distance**

**Xe** *symbol* CHEM ELEM xenon

**xeno-** *prefix* different

**xenobiotics** *plural noun* BIOCHEM chemical compounds that are foreign to an organism

**xenon** *noun* CHEM ELEM an inert gas, traces of which are found in the atmosphere (NOTE: The chemical symbol is **Xe**; the atomic number is **54** and the atomic weight is **131.30**.)

**xeric** *adjective* ECOL referring to a dry environment

**xero-** *prefix* dry

**xeromorphic** *adjective* BOT referring to a plant which can prevent water loss from its stems during hot weather

**xerophilous** *adjective* BOT referring to a plant which lives in very dry conditions

**xerophyte** *noun* BOT a plant which is adapted to living in very dry conditions

**xerosere** *noun* ECOL a succession of communities growing in very dry conditions

**xerothermic** *adjective* BIOL referring to an organism which is adapted to living in very dry conditions

**XML** *noun* COMPUT a webpage markup language that is a simplifed version of the SGML system and allows designers to create their own customised markup tags to improve flexibility. Full form **extensible markup language**

**XNS** *noun* COMPUT a network protocol developed by Xerox that has provided the basis for the Novell IPX network protocols

**XON/XOFF** *noun* COMPUT an asynchronous transmission protocol in which each end can regulate the data flow by transmitting special codes

**X-ray** *noun* **1.** PHYS a ray with a very short wavelength, which is invisible, but can go through soft tissue and register as a photograph on a film **2.** MED an examination using X-rays **3.** MED, PHYS a photograph taken using X-rays ○ *The dentist took some X-rays of the patient's teeth.* ○ *He pinned the X-rays to the light screen.* ○ *All the staff had to have chest X-rays.* ■ *verb* MED to take an X-ray photograph of a patient ○ *There are six patients waiting to be X-rayed.*

COMMENT: Because X-rays go through soft tissue, it is sometimes necessary to make internal organs opaque so that they will show up on the film. In the case of stomach X-rays, patients take a barium meal before being photographed; in other cases, for example kidney X-rays, radioactive substances are injected into the bloodstream or into the organ itself. X-rays are used not only in radiography for diagnosis but as a treatment in radiotherapy because rapidly dividing cells such as cancer cells are most affected. Excessive exposure to X-rays, either as a patient being treated, or as a radiographer, can cause radiation sickness.

**X-ray crystallography** *noun* CRYSTALS the study of crystal structures by means of the diffraction patterns produced when X-rays are scattered by the crystal

**X-ray diffraction** *noun* CRYSTALS the diffraction of X-rays arising due to the position and size of the atoms within a crystal, used to obtain structured information about a crystal

**X-ray tube** *noun* PHYS an evacuated tube in which a stream of high-energy electrons hits a metal target to produce X-rays

**X-series** *noun* COMPUT a set of recommendations for data communications over public data networks

**X-Y** *noun* MATHS coordinates for drawing a graph, where X is the horizontal and Y the vertical value

**xylem** *noun* BOT the tissue in a plant which takes water and dissolved minerals from the roots to the rest of the plant. Compare **phloem**

**xylene** *noun* CHEM a flammable volatile colourless liquid hydrocarbon, used as a solvent and in aviation fuel. Formula: $C_8H_{10}$.

**xylophagous** *adjective* ZOOL wood-eating

**xylophilous** *adjective* BOT preferring to grow on wood

# Y

**y** *symbol* MEASURE yocto-

**Y** *symbol* **1.** MEASURE yotta- **2.** CHEM ELEM yttrium

**YAC** *abbreviation* GENETICS yeast artificial chromosome

**yard** *noun* MEASURE a unit of length in the US and British Imperial Systems equal to 3 ft or 0.9144 m. Abbreviation **yd**

**yaw** AEROSP *noun* a rotation of an aircraft around its vertical axis ○ *Three-axis control of roll, pitch and yaw is effected by ailerons, elevators and rudder.* ■ *verb* (*of an aircraft*) to rotate around the vertical axis ○ *Single engine, propeller driven aircraft tend to yaw on take-off.*

**Y-axis** *noun* MATHS the vertical axis of a graph. ♦ **X-axis**

**Y chromosome** *noun* GENETICS a chromosome that determines sex, carried by males and shorter than an X chromosome. ♦ **X chromosome** (NOTE: A male usually has an XY pair of chromosomes.)

**Y-coordinate** *noun* MATHS a vertical axis position coordinate. ♦ **X-coordinate**

**yd** *abbreviation* MEASURE yard

**Y-direction** *noun* MATHS a vertical movement. ♦ **X-direction**

**Y-distance** *noun* MATHS the distance along the Y-axis from the origin. ♦ **X-distance**

**year** *noun* TIME a period of just over 365 days, or 366 days in every fourth year, in which the Earth makes an orbit of the Sun

**yeast** *noun* FUNGI, FOOD INDUST a unicellular fungus which is used in the fermentation of alcohol and in making bread (NOTE: Yeast is a good source of vitamin B.)

**yeast artificial chromosome** *noun* BIOTECH a sequence of DNA taken from an organism and inserted in a yeast to reveal its function. Abbreviation **YAC**

**yellowing** *noun* BOT **1.** a condition where the leaves of plants turn yellow, caused by lack of light **2.** a sign of disease or of nutrient deficiency

**yellow spot** *noun* ANAT same as **macula 2**

**yield** AGRIC *noun* the quantity of a crop or a product produced from a plant or from an area of land ○ *The usual yield is 8 tonnes per hectare.* ○ *The green revolution increased rice yields in parts of Asia.* ■ *verb* to produce a quantity of a crop or a product ○ *The rice can yield up to 2 tonnes per hectare.* ○ *The oil deposits may yield 100 000 barrels a month.*

**yocto-** *prefix* MEASURE $10^{-24}$. Symbol **y**

**yolk** *noun* ZOOL the yellow central part of an egg

**yolk sac** *noun* ZOOL a membrane which encloses the yolk in embryo fish, reptiles and birds

**yotta-** *prefix* MEASURE $10^{24}$. Symbol **Y**

**Young modulus of elasticity** *noun* PHYS same as **elastic modulus**

**ytterbium** *noun* CHEM ELEM a soft silvery metallic element, used in strengthening steel, in laser devices and in portable X-ray units (NOTE: The chemical symbol is **Yb**; the atomic number is **70** and the atomic weight is **173.04**.)

**yttrium** *noun* CHEM ELEM a silvery-grey metallic element used in superconducting alloys and permanent magnets (NOTE: The chemical symbol is **Y**; the atomic number is **39** and the atomic weight is **88.91**.)

# Z

**z** *symbol* MEASURE zepto-

**Z** *symbol* MEASURE zetta- ■ *abbreviation* TIME Zulu time

**zap** *verb* COMPUT to wipe off all data currently in the workspace ○ *He pressed CONTROL Z and zapped all the text.*

**z-axis** *noun* MATHS an axis for depth in a three-dimensional graph or plot

**z buffer** *noun* COMPUT an area of memory used to store the z-axis information for a graphics object displayed on screen

**Zeeman effect** *noun* OPTICS the splitting of single spectrum lines into two or more polarised ones when the spectrum's source is put in a magnetic field

**zener diode** *noun* ELECTRONICS a semiconductor-based device used as a voltage regulator because the voltage across it is independent of the current through it

**zenith** *noun* ASTRON the point of the celestial sphere that is 90 degrees from all points on the horizon and directly over the observer

**zeolite** *noun* MINERALS one of a large group of minerals based on aluminium silicates, used in water purification and ion exchange

**zepto-** *prefix* MEASURE $10^{-21}$. Symbol **z**

**zero** *noun* **1.** MATHS the digit 0 ○ *The code for international calls is zero one zero (010).* **2.** COMPUT the equivalent of logical off or false state

**zero compression** *noun* COMPUT the shortening of a file by the removal of unnecessary zeros. Also called **zero suppression**

**zero flag** *noun* COMPUT an indicator that the contents of a register or result is zero ○ *The jump on zero instruction tests the zero flag.*

**zero gravity experiments** *plural noun* AEROSP experiments in biology, materials science, physics, medicine and other sciences carried out in orbit at a velocity high enough to cancel the influence of the Earth's gravitation (NOTE: More generally called microgravity experiments because in practice the gravitation obtainable in orbit not quite zero, typically amounting to $10^{-3}$–$10^{-6}$ of that at the Earth's surface.)

**zero insertion force socket** *noun* ELECTRONICS a chip socket that has movable connection terminals, allowing the chip to be inserted without using any force, then a small lever is turned to grip the legs of the chip. Abbreviation **ZIF socket**

**zero-level address** *noun* COMPUT an instruction in which the address is the operand. Also called **immediate address**

**zero population growth** *noun* ZOOL a state when the numbers of births and deaths in a population are equal and so the size of the population remains the same

**zero slot LAN** *noun* COMPUT a local area network that does not use internal expansion adapters, but instead uses the serial port or sometimes an external pocket network adapter connected to the printer port

**zero suppression** *noun* COMPUT same as **zero compression**

**zero wait state** *noun* COMPUT the state of a device, usually a processor or memory chip, that is fast enough to run at the same speed as the other components in a computer, so does not have to be artificially slowed down by inserting wait states

**zetta-** *prefix* MEASURE $10^{21}$. Symbol **Z**

**Ziegler process** *noun* INDUST a method of producing polyethylene or polypropylene using a catalyst

**ZIF socket** *abbreviation* COMPUT zero insertion force socket

**zinc** *noun* CHEM ELEM a white metallic trace element, essential to biological life, used in alloys and as a protective coating for steel (NOTE: The chemical symbol is **Zn**; the atomic number is **30** and the atomic weight is **65.38**.)

**zinc chloride** *noun* CHEM a toxic soluble salt, used as a wood preservative, antiseptic and catalyst. Formula: $ZnCl_2$.

**zinc oxide** *noun* CHEM a compound of zinc and oxygen, which forms a soft white soothing powder that is used in creams and lotions. Formula: $ZnO$.

**zinc sulfate, zinc sulphate** *noun* CHEM a colourless crystalline powder used as emetic, wood preservative, crop spray and mordant for dyeing. Formula: $ZnSO_4$.

**zinc sulfide, zinc sulphide** *noun* CHEM a white or yellowish crystalline powder used as a pigment or phosphor on cathode ray tubes. Formula: $ZnS$.

**zirconium** *noun* CHEM ELEM a greyish-white metal with good corrosion resistance, used in alloys, abrasives, flame proofing compounds and fuel rod cooling in nuclear reactors (NOTE: The chemical symbol is **Zr**; the atomic number is **40** and the atomic weight is **91.22**.)

**Zn** *symbol* CHEM ELEM zinc

**zonal** *adjective* EARTH SCI referring to a zone

**zonal airstream** *noun* METEOROL a stream of air blowing from west to east in the upper atmosphere of the northern hemisphere

**zone** *noun* EARTH SCI an area of land, sea or of the atmosphere

**zone of saturation** *noun* EARTH SCI a layer beneath the surface of the land in which all openings are filled with water

**zoo-** *prefix* ZOOL animal

**zooecology** *noun* ECOL the scientific study of the relationship between animals and their environment

**zoogeographical** *adjective* ECOL referring to animals and geography

**zoogeographical region** *noun* ZOOL a large area of the world where the fauna is different from that in other areas. ◊ **biogeographical region**

**zoological** *adjective* ZOOL referring to zoology

**zoologist** *noun* ZOOL a scientist who specialises in zoology

**zoology** *noun* ZOOL the scientific study of animals

**zoophyte** *noun* ZOOL an animal such as a sea anemone which looks like a plant

**zooplankton** *plural noun* ZOOL microscopic animals which live and drift in water

**zooxanthellae** *plural noun* MARINE BIOL microscopic algae living inside cells of marine animals, especially corals, where each profits from the relationship

**Zr** *symbol* CHEM ELEM zirconium

**Zulu time** *noun* same as **Greenwich Mean Time**. abbreviation **Z**

**zygote** *noun* BIOL a fertilised ovum, the first stage of development of an embryo

**zymogen** *noun* BIOCHEM same as **proenzyme**

# SUPPLEMENT

# THE PLANETS OF THE SOLAR SYSTEM

| | Mean distance from Sun (AU*) | Time taken to orbit Sun | Time taken to rotate on axis | Mass relative to Earth | Radius relative to Earth | Number of known satellites |
|---|---|---|---|---|---|---|
| MERCURY | 0.39 | 88 days | 58.6 days | 0.06 | 0.38 | 0 |
| VENUS | 0.72 | 226 days | 243 days | 0.82 | 0.95 | 0 |
| EARTH | 1 | 1 year | 24 hrs | 1 | 1 | 1 |
| MARS | 1.52 | 1.88 yrs | 24.6 hrs | 0.11 | 0.53 | 2 |
| JUPITER | 5.2 | 11.86 yrs | 9.9 hrs | 317.8 | 11.2 | 16 |
| SATURN | 9.54 | 29.46 yrs | 10.7 hrs | 95.1 | 9.42 | 18 |
| URANUS | 19.18 | 84 yrs | 17.2 hrs | 14.5 | 4.01 | 18 |
| NEPTUNE | 30.06 | 164.79 yrs | 16 hrs | 17.2 | 3.88 | 8 |
| PLUTO | 39.33 | 247.7 yrs | 6.4 days | 0.004 | 0.18 | 1 |

*1 AU is equivalent to approximately 150 million km (93 million miles)

# MATHEMATICAL SYMBOLS

| | | | |
|---|---|---|---|
| + | plus; positive | — | minus; negative |
| ± | plus or minus; positive or negative; approximate | = | equals |
| × | multiplied by | ÷ | divided by |
| < | is less than | > | is greater than |
| ≠ | is not equal to | ≡ | is identical with |
| ~ | is equivalent to; is similar to | ≈ | is approximately equal to |
| : | shows a ratio | :: | shows the equality of a ratio |
| # | number | % | per cent |
| / | indicates a fraction or division | √ | square root of |
| ∝ | is directly proportional to | ∞ | infinity |
| ∪ | union | ∩ | intersection |
| ⊂⊆ | is a subset of | ⊃⊇ | contains a subset |
| ∈ | is a member of | ∉ | is not a member of |
| ∠ | angle | ≅≡ | is congruent to |
| \ | therefore | π | pi |
| ( ), [ ] | brackets, square brackets | { } | braces |

# MEASUREMENTS

## SI METRIC SYSTEM
The SI (Système International d'Unités) system is founded on seven base units that can be multiplied or divided by each other to yield derived units. Values of the base and derived units can be increased or decreased by using SI prefixes indicating decimal multiplication factors. Units and prefixes are assigned internationally accepted symbols.

### BASE UNITS

| Name | Physical Quantity | Symbol |
|---|---|---|
| metre | length | m |
| kilogram | mass | kg |
| second | time | s |
| ampere | electric current | A |
| kelvin | thermodynamic temperature | K |
| mole | amount of substance | mol |
| candela | luminous intensity | cd |

### DERIVED UNITS WITH SPECIAL NAMES AND SYMBOLS

| Name | Physical Quantity | Symbol |
|---|---|---|
| becquerel | radioactivity | Bq |
| coulomb | electric charge | C |
| degree Celsius | temperature | °C |
| farad | electric capacitance | F |
| gray | absorbed dose of radiation | Gy |
| henry | inductance | H |
| hertz | frequency | Hz |
| joule | energy | J |
| lumen | luminous flux | lm |
| lux | illumination | lx |
| newton | force | N |
| ohm | electrical resistance | Ω |
| pascal | pressure, stress | Pa |
| radian | plane angle | rad |
| siemens | electrical conductance | S |
| sievert | radiation dose equivalent | Sv |
| steradian | solid angle | sr |
| tesla | magnetic flux density | T |
| volt | electric potential difference | V |
| watt | power | W |
| weber | magnetic flux | Wb |

# MEASUREMENTS

## SOME DERIVED UNITS WITHOUT SPECIAL NAMES AND SYMBOLS

| Name | Physical Quantity | Symbol |
|---|---|---|
| ampere per metre | magnetic field strength | A/m |
| cubic metre | volume | $m^3$ |
| henry per metre | permeability | H/m |
| joule per kelvin | heat capacity, entropy | J/K |
| kilogram per cubic metre | mass density | $kg/m^3$ |
| metre per second | linear speed | m/s |
| metre per second squared | linear acceleration | $m/s^2$ |
| mole per cubic metre | concentration of substance | $mol/m^3$ |
| newton metre | moment of force, torque | N•m |
| radian per second | angular speed | rad/s |
| square metre | area | $m^2$ |
| volt per metre | electric field strength | V/m |
| watt per metre kelvin | thermal conductivity | W/(m•K) |
| watt per steradian | radian intensity | W/sr |

## PREFIXES

| Multiplication Factor | Name | Symbol |
|---|---|---|
| $10^{24}$ | yotta- | Y |
| $10^{21}$ | zetta- | Z |
| $10^{18}$ | exa- | E |
| $10^{15}$ | peta- | P |
| $10^{12}$ | tera- | T |
| $10^9$ | giga- | G |
| $10^6$ | mega- | M |
| $10^3$ | kilo- | K |
| $10^2$ | hecto- | H |
| $10^1$ | deca- or deka- | da |
| $10^{-1}$ | deci- | d |
| $10^{-2}$ | centi- | c |
| $10^{-3}$ | milli- | m |
| $10^{-6}$ | micro- | μ |
| $10^{-9}$ | nano- | n |
| $10^{-12}$ | pico- | p |
| $10^{-15}$ | femto- | f |
| $10^{-18}$ | atto- | a |
| $10^{-21}$ | zepto- | z |
| $10^{-24}$ | yocto- | y |

# MEASUREMENTS

## CONVERSION OF COMMON SI UNITS

Conversions for some common SI units or those used with the SI to imperial or US customary units are given below.

| SI unit | Conversion |
|---|---|
| *length* | |
| micrometre | = 0.00003937 inches |
| millimetre | = 0.03937 inches |
| centimetre | = 0.3937 inches |
| metre | = 39.37 inches |
| metre | = 1.094 yards |
| kilometre | ≈ 0.621 miles |
| *area* | |
| square millimetre | ≈ 0.00155 square inches |
| square centimetre | ≈ 0.155 square inches |
| square metre | ≈ 1.196 square yards |
| square metre | ≈ 10.76 square feet |
| hectare | ≈ 2.471 acres |
| square kilometre | ≈ 0.386 square miles |
| *volume or capacity* | |
| cubic millimetre | ≈ 0.000061 cubic inches |
| cubic centimetre | ≈ 0.0610 cubic inches |
| cubic centimetre | ≈ 0.0352 imperial fluid ounces |
| cubic centimetre | ≈ 0.0338 US fluid. ounces |
| millilitre | ≈ 0.0610 cubic inches |
| millilitre | ≈ 0.0352 imperial fluid ounces |
| millilitre | ≈ 0.0338 US fluid ounces |
| cubic decilitre | ≈ 61.0 cubic inches |
| cubic decilitre | ≈ 0.880 imperial quarts |
| cubic decilitre | ≈ 1.057 US liquid quarts |
| cubic decilitre | ≈ 0.908 US dry quarts |
| litre | ≈ 61.0 cubic inches |
| litre | ≈ 0.880 imperial quarts |
| litre | ≈ 1.057 US liquid quarts |
| litre | ≈ 0.908 US dry quarts |
| *mass* | |
| gram | ≈ 0.0353 ounces avoirdupois |
| gram | ≈ 0.0322 ounces troy |
| kilogram | ≈ 2.205 pounds avoirdupois |
| tonne | ≈ 2205 pounds avoirdupois |
| *temperature* | |
| degree Celsius | (°C×1.8)+32 = degrees Fahrenheit |

# THE PERIODIC TABLE

Each chemical element is represented by its symbol. Atomic numbers are shown above each symbol and atomic weights below. Atomic weights shown in brackets are for longest-lived isotopes. Elements 113, 115 and 117 are unknown; the report of 118 has been retracted, throwing doubt on 116.

| Group / Period | 1 | 2 | 3 | 4 | 5 | 6 | 7 | 8 | 9 | 10 | 11 | 12 | 13 | 14 | 15 | 16 | 17 | 18 |
|---|---|---|---|---|---|---|---|---|---|---|---|---|---|---|---|---|---|---|
| 1 | 1<br>H<br>1.01 | | | | | | | | | | | | | | | | | 2<br>He<br>4.00 |
| 2 | 3<br>Li<br>6.94 | 4<br>Be<br>9.01 | | | | | | | | | | | 5<br>B<br>10.81 | 6<br>C<br>12.01 | 7<br>N<br>14.01 | 8<br>O<br>16.00 | 9<br>F<br>19.00 | 10<br>Ne<br>20.18 |
| 3 | 11<br>Na<br>22.99 | 12<br>Mg<br>24.31 | | | | | | | | | | | 13<br>Al<br>26.98 | 14<br>Si<br>28.09 | 15<br>P<br>30.97 | 16<br>S<br>32.06 | 17<br>Cl<br>35.45 | 18<br>Ar<br>39.95 |
| 4 | 19<br>K<br>39.10 | 20<br>Ca<br>40.08 | 21<br>Sc<br>44.96 | 22<br>Ti<br>47.90 | 23<br>V<br>50.94 | 24<br>Cr<br>52.00 | 25<br>Mn<br>54.94 | 26<br>Fe<br>55.85 | 27<br>Co<br>58.93 | 28<br>Ni<br>58.71 | 29<br>Cu<br>63.55 | 30<br>Zn<br>65.38 | 31<br>Ga<br>69.72 | 32<br>Ge<br>72.59 | 33<br>As<br>74.92 | 34<br>Se<br>78.96 | 35<br>Br<br>79.90 | 36<br>Kr<br>83.80 |
| 5 | 37<br>Rb<br>85.47 | 38<br>Sr<br>87.62 | 39<br>Y<br>88.91 | 40<br>Zr<br>91.22 | 41<br>Nb<br>92.91 | 42<br>Mo<br>95.94 | 43<br>Tc<br>98.91 | 44<br>Ru<br>101.07 | 45<br>Rh<br>102.91 | 46<br>Pd<br>106.40 | 47<br>Ag<br>107.87 | 48<br>Cd<br>112.40 | 49<br>In<br>114.82 | 50<br>Sn<br>118.69 | 51<br>Sb<br>121.75 | 52<br>Te<br>127.60 | 53<br>I<br>126.90 | 54<br>Xe<br>131.30 |
| 6 | 55<br>Cs<br>132.91 | 56<br>Ba<br>137.34 | 57 *<br>La<br>138.91 | 72<br>Hf<br>178.49 | 73<br>Ta<br>180.95 | 74<br>W<br>183.85 | 75<br>Re<br>186.2 | 76<br>Os<br>190.2 | 77<br>Ir<br>192.22 | 78<br>Pt<br>195.09 | 79<br>Au<br>196.97 | 80<br>Hg<br>200.59 | 81<br>Tl<br>204.37 | 82<br>Pb<br>207.20 | 83<br>Bi<br>208.98 | 84<br>Po<br>209 | 85<br>At<br>(210) | 86<br>Rn<br>(222) |
| 7 | 87<br>Fr<br>(223) | 88<br>Ra<br>(226) | 89 ‡<br>Ac<br>(226) | 104<br>Rf<br>(261) | 105<br>Db<br>(262) | 106<br>Sg<br>(266) | 107<br>Bh<br>(264) | 108<br>Hs<br>(269) | 109<br>Mt<br>(268) | 110<br>Ds<br>(269) | 111<br>Uuu<br>(272) | 112<br>Uub<br>(277) | 113<br>Uut<br>- | 114<br>Uuq<br>(285) | 115<br>Uup<br>- | 116<br>Uuh<br>- | 117<br>Uus<br>- | 118<br>Uuo<br>- |

| Lanthanides * | 57<br>La<br>138.91 | 58<br>Ce<br>140.12 | 59<br>Pr<br>140.91 | 60<br>Nd<br>144.24 | 61<br>Pm<br>(145) | 62<br>Sm<br>150.40 | 63<br>Eu<br>151.96 | 64<br>Gd<br>157.93 | 65<br>Tb<br>153.93 | 66<br>Dy<br>162.50 | 67<br>Ho<br>164.26 | 68<br>Er<br>167.26 | 69<br>Tm<br>168.93 | 70<br>Yb<br>173.04 | 71<br>Lu<br>174.97 |
|---|---|---|---|---|---|---|---|---|---|---|---|---|---|---|---|
| Actinides ‡ | 89<br>Ac<br>(226) | 90<br>Th<br>232.04 | 91<br>Pa<br>231.04 | 92<br>U<br>283.04 | 93<br>Np<br>237.05 | 94<br>Pu<br>(244) | 95<br>Am<br>(243) | 96<br>Cm<br>(247) | 97<br>Bk<br>(247) | 98<br>Cf<br>(251) | 99<br>Es<br>(254) | 100<br>Fm<br>(257) | 101<br>Md<br>(258) | 102<br>No<br>(255) | 103<br>Lr<br>(256) |